# COMMERCIAL LAW

SEVENTH EDITION

*by*

WILLIAM D. WARREN
Connell Professor of Law Emeritus
University of California, Los Angeles

STEVEN D. WALT
Professor of Law
University of Virginia School of Law

FOUNDATION PRESS

2007

THOMSON

WEST

© 1983, 1987, 1992, 1997, 2000, 2004 FOUNDATION PRESS
© 2007 By FOUNDATION PRESS
        395 Hudson Street
        New York, NY 10014
        Phone Toll Free 1–877–888–1330
        Fax (212) 367–6799
        foundation-press.com
Printed in the United States of America

**ISBN:** 978–1–59941–185–9

 TEXT IS PRINTED ON 10% POST CONSUMER RECYCLED PAPER

# PREFACE

The Seventh Edition is a substantial updating of the Sixth Edition. Important Commercial Law cases continue to come down in volume and we have included 20 new opinions in this edition, some of which promise to take their place in the canon. New Notes and text passages discuss other new cases and emerging issues. We gather from the reaction of teachers to our books that most prefer to teach from a mix of cases and problems, and the Seventh Edition takes this approach throughout. Since Revised Article 9 did not become effective until 2001, the case law on the new statute is at an early stage of development, but several important decisions interpreting the new law have been decided since our last edition and we have included these. For the many significant issues raised by Revised Article 9 that have not been before the courts, we use problems that force close consideration of relevant statutory provisions and allow for tightly structured class sessions. Throughout, the Seventh Edition discusses policies underlying Revised Article 9's important provisions and explores the interface of Article 9 with Article 5 (Letters of Credit), Article 8 (Investment Securities), the burgeoning law of Intellectual Property, and the Bankruptcy Code with its 2005 amendments.

Now that Revised Articles 3 (Negotiable Instruments) and 4 (Bank Deposits and Collections) and new Article 4A (Funds Transfers), promulgated more than a decade ago, have substantially become the law of the land, authoritative appellate decisions are appearing. Part II (Payments and Credits) of the Seventh Edition features a selection of these recent decisions that promise to become leading cases. The 2002 amendments to Articles 3 and 4 are considered, as are the 2003 federal "Check 21" Act and important new federal banking regulations. Materials on technological advances in payment systems have been updated, and emerging consumer issues have been highlighted throughout. The increasing federalization of bank-customer relations is treated in detail.

We are particularly grateful to Arthur G. Spence, Esq., Associate General Counsel of City National Bank of Beverly Hills, California, and to the Bank for allowing us to use several of the Bank's forms. The cooperation of Mr. Spence and others at the Bank in sharing their experience with law students through the use of their forms has been outstanding.

Robert Jordan, whose name this book bore for the first five editions, has not participated in recent editions. However, evidence of his keen analytical mind and precise draftsmanship is still seen throughout this volume, as well as in Revised Articles 3, 4, and new Article 4A, for which he served as a Reporter.

We are deeply grateful to Tal Grietzer for his skill and dedication in formatting and preparing the manuscript for publication. We also thank David Chen, UCLA School of Law, Class of 2008, for his editorial assistance and research.

WILLIAM D. WARREN
STEVEN D. WALT

January 2007

# ACKNOWLEDGMENTS

We gratefully acknowledge the permission extended to reprint excerpts from the following works:

The American Law Institute has given permission to reprint the following materials:

Restatement (Third) of Property (Mortgages) § 5.5 (1996). Copyright © 1997 by the American Law Institute.

Uniform Commercial Code Article 9. Official Text. Copyright © 2003 by The American Law Institute and the National Conference of Commissioners on Uniform State Laws. Selected Sections and Official Comments.

Uniform Commercial Code Revised Article 8 Prefatory Note 1.A-1. D (1994). Copyright © 1994 by The American Law Institute and the National Conference of Commissioners on Uniform State Laws.

John D. Ayer, On the Vacuity of the Sale/Lease Distinction, 68 Iowa L. Rev. 667 (1983) (reprinted with permission).

James W. Bowers, Of Bureaucrats' Brothers-in-Law and Bankruptcy Taxes: Article 9 Filing Systems and the Market for Information, 79 Minnesota Law Review 721, 724 (1995). Reprinted with permission.

City National Bank. All forms in this book are reprinted with permission of City National Bank, a national banking association, of Beverly Hills, California.

Corinne Cooper, Identifying a Personal Property Lease under the UCC, 49 Ohio State Law Journal 195, 245-246 (1988). Originally published in 49 Ohio St. L.J. 195 (1988). Reprinted with permission.

Grant Gilmore, Formalism and the Law of Negotiable Instruments, 13 Creighton Law Review 441, 446-450 (1979). Copyright © 1979 Creighton University School of Law. Reprinted from the Creighton Law Review by permission.

Grant Gilmore, Security Interests in Personal Property (1965), Volume 1, portions of pages 24, 73, 327 and 1227. © 1965, Little, Brown and Company, assigned to The Law Book Exchange, Ltd. Reprinted with permission.

Thomas H. Jackson & Anthony Kronman, Secured Financing Priorities Among Creditors, 88 Yale Law Journal 1143, 1147-1148 (1979). Reprinted by permission of the Yale Law Journal Company and Fred B. Rothman & Company from The Yale Law Journal, Vol. 88, pages 1143-1182.

Lynn M. LoPucki, The Unsecured Creditor's Bargain, 80 Virginia Law Review 1887, 1893 (1994). Reprinted with permission.

James Steven Rogers, Policy Perspectives on Revised UCC Article 8, 43 UCLA Law Review 1431, 1480-1481 (1996). Originally published in 43 UCLA L.Rev. 1431. Copyright 1996, The Regents of the University of California. All rights reserved.

Albert J. Rosenthal, Negotiability – Who Needs It?, 71 Colum. L. Rev. 375, 378-381, 283-385 (1971). Copyright © 1971 by the Directors of the Columbia Law Review Association, Inc. All Rights Reserved. This article originally appeared at 71 Colum. L. Rev. 375 (1971). Reprinted with permission.

Harold R. Weinberg & William J. Woodard, Jr., Legislative Process and Commercial Law: Lessons from the Copyright Act of 1976 and the Uniform Commercial Code, 48 Bus.Law 437, 475 (1993). Copyright © 1993 American Bar Association. Reprinted with permission.

Mark B. Wessman, Purchase Money Inventory Financing: The Case for Limiting Cross-Collateralization, 51 Ohio State Law Journal 1283, 1309 (1990). Originally published in 51 Ohio St. L.J. 1283 (1990). Reprinted with permission.

# SUMMARY OF CONTENTS

# TABLE OF CONTENTS

\*

# TABLE OF CASES

Principal cases are in bold type. Non-principal cases are in roman type. References are to Pages.

# TABLE OF STATUTES

# COMMERCIAL LAW

\*

# PART I

# SECURED TRANSACTIONS IN PERSONAL PROPERTY

# CHAPTER 1

# CREATING A SECURITY INTEREST

## A. WHY SECURED CREDIT?

In discussing secured credit transactions, our first inquiry should be why we have secured credit. The usual assumptions are that credit is a good thing: businesses use it to leverage their capital and consumers enjoy goods and services as they pay for them; the economy grows. Permitting lenders to take security interests in debtors' property reduces their risk of not being repaid and expands the volume of credit. It is the secured creditor's advantage over unsecured creditors in cases of the debtor's insolvency that both strongly motivates creditors to use secured credit and most often calls into question its fairness. See Claire A. Hill, Is Secured Debt Efficient?, 80 Tex. L. Rev. 1117 (2002); Allen N. Berger & Gregory F. Udell, Collateral, Loan Quality and Bank Risk, 25 J. Mon. Econ. 21 (1990).

Business lending takes many forms. At the top level are unsecured loans based on the borrower's projected cash flow and creditworthiness. Established companies, usually large publicly traded companies with good credit ratings, avail themselves of this form of lending. Unsecured creditors face risks that the financial position of their borrowers may deteriorate or their borrowers may incur debt from other lenders, perhaps even secured debt. They reduce these risks by carefully monitoring their borrower's activities against a background of covenants in the loan agreement.

> Covenants may be able to achieve the same effects as a security interest by requiring that the borrower not encumber or transfer certain assets. In addition, covenants can be used to restrict, directly or indirectly, the borrower's investment activities, to bar the creation of certain security interests, to limit dividend and other payments to shareholders, or even to require the borrower to remain in the same line of business.

Lucian A. Bebchuk & Jesse M. Fried, The Uneasy Case for the Priority of Secured Claims in Bankruptcy, 105 Yale L.J. 857, 879 (1996). On covenants as a substitute or complement to security interests, see Carl S. Bjerre, Secured Transactions Inside Out: Negative Pledge Covenants, Property and Perfection, 84 Cornell L. Rev. 305 (1999); George G. Triantis, Secured Debt Under Conditions of Imperfect Information, 21 J. Legal Stud. 225, 235–36 (1992). See also 1 Sandra Schnitzer Stern, Structuring Commercial Loan Agreements ¶ 5 (2d ed. 1990); Clifford W. Smith & Jerold B. Warner, On Financial Contracting: An Analysis of Bond Covenants, 7 J. Fin. Econ. 117 (1979).

If the borrower doesn't qualify for unsecured credit, it may be able to obtain credit through asset-based loans. Here the lender takes a first security interest in the borrower's assets, such as equipment, inventory or real estate, as well as intangibles such as rights to payment or intellectual property. The amount of the loan may be based on the value of the borrower's assets. These loans may be used for a wide variety of needs including seasonal cash requirements, business expansion and acquisitions. A major area of asset-based lending is inventory financing in which lenders finance the seller's acquisition of inventory and take security interests in the acquired inventory and its proceeds. Sellers may also finance the acquisition of inventory by securitization, that is by pooling the proceeds of inventory sales (accounts receivables and other rights to payment) and selling these pools to institutional investors, thus obtaining financing at lower than bank rates.

Consumer lending has evolved from the tradition forms of (i) personal loans, secured by all the borrower's household goods, (ii) purchase money credit sales in which the seller takes a security interest in the goods sold to secure the unpaid indebtedness to be repaid in monthly installments, and (iii) unsecured retail charge account credit (open-end credit), in which buyers make monthly payments on balances owed. As we will see, credit and debit card credit has swallowed up old-fashioned charge accounts, has limited purchase money secured credit to only big-ticket items like motor vehicles, and has lessened the need for personal loans. Most credit and debit card credit is unsecured. We are left with the paradox that in business lending only the best credit risks receive unsecured credit, while in consumer financing, owing to competition by card issuers for market share, some of the worst credit risks are accorded unsecured credit with generous balance limits.

The following elementary cases illustrate the advantages of secured credit and its harshness in insolvencies. We compare the rights of unsecured and secured creditors.

## 1.    RIGHTS OF UNSECURED CREDITOR

Case #1. *Seller vs. Debtor*. Debtor operates a winery and buys wine barrels from Seller on credit. When Seller delivered a shipment of barrels, Debtor made a cash down payment and gave Seller its note, promising to pay Seller the balance of the price of the barrels with interest in twelve monthly installments. After Debtor failed to make the third and fourth payments on the note, Seller notified Debtor that it was in default on the note and exercised the right of Seller under the terms of the note to declare the entire unpaid balance due. If Debtor is unable or unwilling to pay the balance owing on the note, how can Seller collect from Debtor?

Seller would probably like to reclaim the barrels that Debtor failed to pay for, but they now belong to Debtor, and the historic principle is "that before judgment (or its equivalent) an unsecured creditor has no rights at law or in equity in the property of his debtor." Grupo Mexicano de

Desarrollo, S.A. v. Alliance Bond Fund, Inc., 527 U.S. 308, 330 (1999). Thus, for Seller to collect, it must incur the expense and suffer the delay of hiring a lawyer and litigating the case. Seller first must sue Debtor on the promissory note and obtain a money judgment against Debtor. Then it must do whatever is required under state law to authorize the sheriff to seize (levy on) Debtor's assets and sell them in payment of the judgment debt, subject to certain exemptions that allow debtors to protect some of their property from the reach of involuntary creditors. Traditionally the seizure was a physical taking of the property, but in more recent years, in some cases the seizure can be symbolic and occurs by the public filing of a document. In either case the seizure results in the transfer from the debtor to the creditor of an interest in the seized property, and that interest is called a judicial lien. Under 9–102(a)(52)(A), Seller is now a "lien creditor," and has rights akin to those of a creditor holding a security interest.

If Debtor chooses to oppose Seller's action, one can scarcely imagine a less efficient, more cumbersome procedure for Seller to collect its debt than that described in the previous paragraph. Unless the sum sought by Seller is large, the cost of collection makes this procedure too expensive to pursue. And if Debtor has no unencumbered, nonexempt assets left that Seller can reach, the judgment may be worthless. Doubtless, the *in terrorem* effect of arming Seller with the power to dismember Debtor's business is substantial and gives Debtor an incentive to pay its debt to Seller. A judgment against Debtor may include not only the balance of the unpaid purchase price of the barrels but also collection costs such as attorney's fees, if the note so provides. But, as we see in the following paragraph, even if Debtor wishes to pay Seller to stave off disaster, Debtor's other creditors can deprive it of the means to do so.

> Case #2. *Seller vs. Other Unsecured Creditors and Trustee in Bankruptcy.* If Debtor is unable to pay Seller for assets as central to the function of a winery as wine barrels, it may be in financial trouble. If so, there are probably other unpaid creditors pursuing Seller. Suppose C1 sold grapes to Debtor in September, Seller sold barrels to Debtor in October, and C2 sold equipment to Debtor in November. All the sales were made on unsecured credit and by the end of the year Debtor had defaulted on each debt. In March of the following year, C2 followed the procedures outlined in Case #1, and the sheriff, acting under C2's judgment, seized not only the equipment that it had sold Debtor but also the barrels that Seller had sold Debtor. By the time Seller had obtained a judgment against Debtor in May, the sheriff had already sold both the equipment and the barrels in payment of C2's claim, and Debtor had no unencumbered assets left for Seller to reach. Assume that under the law of the state, priority among judgment creditors is based on the time the sheriff seizes the assets; thus, C2 has won the "race to the courthouse," and even though Seller advanced credit to Debtor before C2, it is subordinate to C2's rights as a lien creditor.

Assume that Debtor filed in bankruptcy four months after C2 became a lien creditor but before Seller did so. Seller has only an unsecured claim and will share in the distribution of the assets of Debtor's estate pro rata with other unsecured creditors. But, unless C2's lien creditor status runs afoul of preference law (which it would only if Debtor filed within 90 days after C2 acquired its judicial lien), C2 will be treated as a secured creditor in bankruptcy and prior to the unsecured claims of C1 and Seller.

## 2. RIGHTS OF SECURED CREDITOR

Case #1. *Seller vs. Debtor.* How would Seller improve its position against Debtor by taking a security interest in the wine barrels that it sold to Debtor to secure the obligation evidenced by the promissory note? By acquiring a property right in the barrels. This property right is called a "lien," and a typical sort of consensual lien is a "security interest." As we will see, creating the security interest is quite simple under Article 9. Seller could enter into a written security agreement with Debtor providing for a security interest in the barrels. If the parties are at a distance from each other and desire an immediate security agreement, the agreement may be evidenced by an electronic record, like an e-mail document, sent by Seller to Debtor and authenticated by Debtor's reply e-mail. When this is done, Seller's security interest in the barrels has "attached," that is become enforceable against Debtor with respect to the collateral. 9–203(a). Upon Debtor's default in its payment schedule, Seller could retake the barrels from Debtor, usually without going to court, and resell them at an auction sale conducted by Seller at which Seller can bid. Usually, no court proceedings are necessary unless the proceeds of the resale are inadequate to discharge the debt and Seller wishes to collect the amount of the deficiency. If so, she must bring suit against Debtor and obtain a judgment for the deficiency.

Case #2. *Seller vs. Other Creditors and Trustee in Bankruptcy.* How would Seller improve her position against C1 and C2 as described in Case #2 above and Debtor's trustee in bankruptcy by taking a security interest in the wine barrels? So long as C1 and C2 remain unsecured creditors without judicial liens in the barrels, Seller is prior to them under one of the golden rules of secured transactions law, 9–201(a): "Except as otherwise provided [in the UCC], a security agreement is effective according to its terms between the parties, against purchasers of the collateral, and against creditors." Secured claims trump unsecured claims, unless specific provisions of Article 9 provide "otherwise."

And, in several important instances, Article 9 does provide otherwise. Under 9–317(a)(2)(A), until Seller "perfects" her security interest, she is at risk of having her security interest primed by C1, C2 and Debtor's trustee in bankruptcy, for Article 9 makes an unperfected security interest subordinate to lien creditors. Thus, if either C1 or C2 goes through the process described above to acquire lien creditor status before Seller perfects, Seller's unperfected security interest is subordinate. And since a trustee in bankruptcy acquires lien creditor status from the date Debtor files in bankruptcy (9–102(a)(52)(C)), Seller's unperfected security interest may be avoided by the trustee under BC 544(a). Given the high volume of bankruptcy filings, the major reason creditors seek perfected security interests is to provide protection against the possibility of their debtors' subsequent bankruptcy filings. Bankruptcy proceedings generally leave unaffected property rights covered by perfected security interests.

In the usual commercial case like that described above, perfection is easily achieved by Seller's filing a simple financing statement, giving only minimal information about the secured transaction, in the state's filing office for a minimal fee. The filing may be hastened by use of electronic transmission.

## 3.  IS SECURED CREDIT EFFICIENT OR FAIR?

PROBLEM

Seller sold wine barrels to Debtor on February 1 on unsecured credit. By July, Debtor needed an immediate loan in order to stay in business. After examining Debtor's financial situation, Bank agreed to make the loan only if Debtor granted it a security interest in all its assets, now owned or thereafter acquired, to secure all present and future advances Bank made to Debtor. With no other sources of credit available, Debtor had no choice but to accept Bank's terms and signed a security agreement granting Bank the security interest that it requested. The security agreement described the collateral as including all wine barrels. Bank immediately filed an appropriate financing statement. Although Bank knew about Seller's transaction with Debtor, neither Bank nor Debtor notified Seller of the secured transaction. Based on what you have learned from the Cases above, what is Bank's priority with respect to Seller's rights, inside and outside bankruptcy?

---

Why do we allow a debtor to contract with a creditor to award that creditor a priority over the debtor's other creditors, however meritorious their claims and whenever they extended credit, by taking a security interest in the debtor's assets? We will learn that Article 9 allows a secured creditor to take a security interest in all of a debtor's personal property then owned or acquired in the future; moreover the security interest may not only extend to the debtor's tangible assets, such as inventory or equipment, but also to the debtor's stream of earnings or cash flow, that is, the proceeds of sales of inventory or services. It is from this stream of earnings that unsecured creditors like trade creditors and employees expect to be paid. Thus, Article 9, in sweeping away all the historic judicial constraints on the creation of secured credit, has made it simple for secured creditors to take a priority in all of a debtor's assets, present and future, to the exclusion of all other creditors. Upon the insolvency of a debtor its secured creditor may take all the debtor's assets, leaving the very deserving unsecured claims of the debtor's trade creditors and employees, as well as tort creditors, worthless. Has Article 9 been too successful in making the secured creditor's status impregnable?

Secured credit is justified by Thomas Jackson and Anthony Kronman in Secured Financing and Priorities Among Creditors, 88 Yale L.J. 1143, 1147–1148 (1979):

> At first blush, it may seem unfair that a debtor should be allowed to make a private contract with one creditor that demotes the claims of other creditors from an initial position of parity to one of subordination. This thought may in turn suggest that debtors should be denied the power to prefer some creditors over others, and that all creditors should instead be required to share equally in the event of their common debtor's insolvency, each receiving a pro rata portion of his claim. * * * When a debtor grants a security interest to one of his creditors, he increases the riskiness of other creditor's claims by reducing their expected value in bankruptcy. It is a fair assumption, however, that these other creditors will be aware of this risk and will insist on a premium for lending on an unsecured basis, will demand collateral (or some other form of protection) to secure their own claims, or will search for another borrower whose enterprise is less risky. In general, whatever level of risk he faces, if his transaction with the debtor is a voluntary one, a creditor may be expected to adjust his interest rate accordingly and to take whatever risk-reducing precautions he deems appropriate. Since creditors remain free to select their own debtors and to set the terms on which they will lend, there is no compelling argument based upon considerations of fairness for adopting one legal rule (debtors can rank creditor claims in whatever way they see fit) rather than another (all creditors must share equally in the event of bankruptcy).

Lynn LoPucki in The Unsecured Creditor's Bargain, 80 Va. L. Rev. 1887, 1893 (1994), challenges the Jackson and Kronman view:

> Jackson and Kronman's reasoning was based on two false assumptions. First, they assumed that unsecured creditors agree to subordinate status when in fact a substantial number of unsecured creditors are creditors such as tort victims whose unsecured status is imposed on them against their will. Second, Jackson and Kronman assumed that voluntary creditors contract for unsecured status with a full awareness of the consequences when in fact they contract under varying levels of coercion with varying levels of awareness.

LoPucki would subordinate security interests to tort claims and claims of other involuntary creditors. Debtors could no longer render themselves effectively judgment proof by granting security interests in all their assets. Under a regime of secured credit subordination, secured creditors would either charge more for their credit extensions or insure against loss from subordination with the cost of the insurance borne by debtors. In either case secured creditors would suffer no loss and debtors would bear the costs of their wrongs. With respect to voluntary unsecured creditors, LoPucki would require that the Article 9 filing system be revised to give better notice, and he would award priority to secured creditors only in instances in which a jury would find that a reasonable person in the position of the unsecured creditor would expect to be subordinated. Which viewpoint is more persuasive, that of Jackson and Kronman or that of LoPucki? Replies to LoPucki are found in Steve Knippenberg, The Unsecured Creditor's Bargain: An Essay in Reply, Reprisal or Support?, 80 Va. L. Rev. 1967 (1994); Susan Block–Lieb, The Unsecured Creditor's Bargain: A Reply, 80 Va. L. Rev. 1989 (1994). In addition to the Bebchuk & Fried, Jackson & Kronman, and LoPucki articles, other relevant articles are Ronald J. Mann, Explaining the Pattern of Secured Credit, 110 Harv. L. Rev. 625 (1997); Steven L. Schwarcz, The Easy Case for the Priority of Secured Claims in Bankruptcy, 47 Duke L.J. 425 (1997); Alan Schwartz, Priority Contracts and Priority in Bankruptcy, 82 Cornell L. Rev. 1396 (1997); Alan Schwartz, Security Interests and Bankruptcy Priorities: A Review of Current Theories, 10 J. Legal Stud. 1 (1981); and Paul M. Shupack, Solving the Puzzle of Secured Transactions, 41 Rutgers L. Rev. 1067 (1989).

It is worth asking why borrowers issue secured debt. A lender who is granted a security interest will reduce the interest rate on its loan to reflect the reduced risk of nonrepayment. However, the risk of nonrepayment for the borrower's unsecured lenders is correspondingly increased. These lenders will increase the interest rate on their loans accordingly. Thus, the gain to the borrower in the form of reduced interest rate associated with secured debt is offset by the loss to it in the form of increased interest charges associated with unsecured debt. The size of the borrower's total debt bill is unchanged. Because secured debt is costly to issue, the prevalence of secured debt therefore is puzzling. The problem is not that some lenders will demand security interests. The puzzle is to explain why borrowers will issue secured debt when doing so is costly.

One explanation is efficiency: secured debt reduces the size of the debtor's debt bill. There are basically three sorts of efficiency explanations: monitoring cost, bonding, and signaling. Security interests in particular assets allow a creditor to monitor a limited range of assets to protect against the debtor taking actions that effect its repayment prospects from these assets. Alternatively, security interests can align the debtor and the creditors' interests by giving the creditor the right to foreclose on particular assets upon default. Such bonding arrangements enable a debtor to credibly commit not to take actions that affect a creditor's repayment prospects, when credible commitment is otherwise costly. Finally, secured debt allows a debtor to signal to a creditor that its prospects of repaying a loan are good. This is because the power of foreclosure imposes a cost on a debtor which the debtor will bear only if it debtor believes that it will not experience financial difficulties over the term of the loan. The issuance of secured debt reliably conveys this information to creditors. A nonefficiency explanation of secured debt is redistributional. Security interests reduce repayment risk to secured creditors and therefore the effective interest charge on their loans. However, the repayment risk is shifted to unsecured creditors who do not adjust the effective interest rate on their debts accordingly. LoPucki calls such a redistribution of risk "theft" in the excerpt above, and describes its apparent operation. See also Lucian A. Bebchuk & Jesse M. Fried, The Uneasy Case for the Priority of Secured Claims in Bankruptcy: Further Thoughts and a Reply to Critics, 82 Cornell L. Rev. 1279, 1293–1314 (1997).

Revised Article 9 does not explicitly take a position in this debate. However, by increasing the range of collateral and transactions subject to Article 9, as well as reducing the cost of creating and enforcing security interests, Revised Article 9's drafters implicitly assume that security interests are wealth-enhancing transactions. This assumption was endorsed by Professors Steven L. Harris and Charles W. Mooney, Jr., the Reporters for Revised Article 9, in their article, A Property–Based Theory of Security Interests: Taking Debtor's Choices Seriously, 80 Va. L. Rev. 2021 (1994). Their view: "The law should not impair the ability of debtors to secure as much or as little of their debts with as much or as little of their existing and future property as they deem appropriate." Supra, at 2021–2022. Harris and Mooney assert that although secured creditors undeniably enjoy an advantage over unsecured creditors in insolvency situations, most debtors do not become insolvent, and much credit would never be granted unless the grantor could obtain collateral. They note that for years secured creditors battled with courts and legislators to allow them to acquire reliable security interests; Revised Article 9 finally gives secured creditors what they want. Harris and Mooney conclude that until someone can demonstrate empirically that, overall, this is a bad thing, freedom of contract should govern.

## 4.   SECURED CREDIT AND EQUITABLE REMEDIES

In the following case an unsecured creditor attacks the priority given a secured creditor by Article 9 on equitable grounds.

## Knox v. Phoenix Leasing Incorporated

Court of Appeal, First District, Division 4, 1994.
35 Cal.Rptr.2d 141.

■ POCHE, ASSOCIATE JUSTICE.

The issue presented is whether a secured creditor who obtains a defaulted debtor's property can be subject to restitution for the amount of the value of goods furnished the debtor by a third party. The answer is no: unless there are unusual circumstances the equitable remedy of restitution must defer to the rights given a secured creditor by the California Uniform Commercial Code (UCC).

In March of 1990 as part of a concerted effort to expand the capacity of its plant in Sonoma County, Domaine Laurier Winery (Domaine) contracted with Mel Knox to purchase 200 seasoned oak wine barrels made in France. Four months later Domaine executed an agreement with Phoenix Leasing Incorporated (Phoenix) whereby Phoenix undertook to provide financing for the expansion. Phoenix was protected by (among other things) a security agreement covering all personal property, including "all equipment . . . whether now owned or hereafter acquired" by Domaine.

The wine barrels came in two shipments. Upon arrival of the first lot, Knox sent an invoice to Domaine; Domaine forwarded the invoice to Phoenix, which paid it in August of 1990. With the second lot, Knox sent the invoice for $33,011.37 directly to Phoenix. Domaine also requested Phoenix to pay Knox. Approximately two months after the second shipment was delivered, but before any payment for it, Phoenix declared Domaine in default of their agreement. The barrels were included in Phoenix's subsequent liquidation of Domaine's assets.[2]

By the time Knox's complaint came on for trial it had been reduced to a single cause of action for "Restitution–Unjust Enrichment" against Phoenix. The case was tried on the short cause calendar following denial of Phoenix's motion that, because it was a secured creditor while Knox was not, it was entitled to judgment on the pleadings. The trial did not produce a statement of decision, simply the court's announcement that Knox was entitled to judgment for $21,350 (70 percent of the original cost of the barrels, which was essentially their undisputed resale value).

Phoenix perfected this timely appeal from the ensuing judgment.

According to the UCC, Domaine's execution of a security agreement describing the property covered gave Phoenix a security interest in that collateral (§§ 9–203(1), 9–402(1)). Phoenix perfected that security interest when it filed a financing statement with the Secretary of State (§§ 9–302(1), 9–401(c)). Phoenix thus acquired priority over other Domaine creditors (§§ 9–201, 9–301, 9–312(3)–(5)), including the right to take possession and sell the collateral if Domaine defaulted (§§ 9–503, 9–504(1)). It being undisputed that Phoenix complied with all of these steps, Phoenix maintains that it is immune to Knox's restitution claim.

The opposing argument, which springs from the UCC's general directive that its provisions are to be supplemented by "principles of law and equity" (§ 1–103), has divided courts considering whether restitution can be had from a code-protected secured creditor. On the one hand, a decided majority of jurisdictions have disallowed the equitable remedy of restitution (whether termed unjust enrichment, quantum meruit, contract implied in law, etc.). They are willing to accept occasionally harsh results as the price to be paid for preserving the integrity of the UCC's scheme for secured transactions, encouraging compliance with the UCC, and thereby ensuring a predictable system of creditor priorities. * * * On the other hand, California and more recently Colorado, while conceding considerable soundness to the majority position, have permitted restitution from a secured creditor. (Producers Cotton Oil Co. v. Amstar Corp. (1988) 197 Cal.App.3d 638, 242 Cal.Rptr. 914; Ninth Dist. Prod. Credit v. Ed Duggan (Colo.1991)

---

**2.** Phoenix advanced Domaine approximately $1.1 million, but recovered only about $400,000 from the liquidation. * * *

821 P.2d 788 * * *.) An examination of these decisions demonstrates that their disagreement with the majority position is one of degree and is not nearly so profound as appears at first glance.[5] Recovery is clearly the exception, not the norm, and is subject to stern limitations.

The first member of the minority camp—and the sole reported California decision in this area—is Producers Cotton Oil Co. v. Amstar Corp., supra, 197 Cal.App.3d 638, 242 Cal.Rptr. 914 (*Producers Cotton*). The Producers Cotton firm held a security interest in the farm crops of its debtor. Amstar bought the crops and paid to have them harvested. Amstar knew of Producers' security interest, but neglected to obtain Producers' agreement to subordinate that interest. Amstar deducted the harvesting costs before remitting the sale proceeds of the crops to Producers. Producers sued Amstar and obtained a judgment on the theory that the deduction constituted conversion of its secured collateral.

Amstar appealed, arguing that the UCC's article 9 governing secured transactions left room for the equitable principle of restitution. It relied on § 1–103, which provides: "Unless displaced by the particular provisions of this code, the principles of law and equity, including the law merchant and the law relative to capacity to contract, principal and agent, estoppel, fraud, misrepresentation, duress, coercion, mistake, bankruptcy, or other validating or invalidating cause shall supplement its provisions." Producers responded that "in order to give stability and predictability to commercial transactions, the priorities dictated by article 9 must prevail over equitable principles that might otherwise apply." Concluding that "the facts present a classic case for establishing an implied in law contract, or quasi-contract," the Court of Appeal tersely concurred with Amstar: "We agree with the position of Amstar and hold that when a party possessing a security interest in a crop and its proceeds has knowledge of and acquiesces in expenditures made which are *necessary* to the development of the crop, and ultimately benefits from the expenditure, a party who, through mistake, pays such costs without first obtaining subordination, is entitled to recover." (*Producers Cotton*, supra, 197 Cal.App.3d 638 at pp. 658, 660, 242 Cal.Rptr. 914, original emphasis.)

A considerably more detailed discussion of the problem was developed in Ninth Dist. Prod. Credit v. Ed Duggan, supra, 821 P.2d 788 (*Duggan*). Like *Producers Cotton*, the context was agricultural. Duggan furnished feedgrain to a livestock company whose accounts receivable and personal property were the subject of a perfected security interest held by a credit association. In accordance with its standard practice, the association financed the livestock company's operations by paying sight drafts given creditors by the livestock company. Duggan continued deliveries while an

---

**5.** A process which works both ways. Even courts in the majority camp acknowledge that a secured creditor should not expect to escape liability after committing either actual or virtual fraud (Peerless Packing Co. v. Malone & Hyde, supra, 376 S.E.2d 161 at pp. 161–165, fn. 4 (W.Va.1988)), especially if the issue can be presented as involving priorities among creditors. (See authorities cited in Ninth Dist. Prod. Credit v. Ed Duggan, supra, 821 P.2d 788 at pp. 797–798.)

unsuccessful effort to sell the livestock company was overseen by the credit association. Cattle fed with Duggan's grain were sold and the proceeds paid to the credit association, which also received payment for feedlot services given cattle awaiting slaughter. When the livestock company became financially unable to pay Duggan, suit was brought against the association.

The Colorado Supreme Court upheld the lower courts' determination that Duggan could obtain restitution from the credit association notwithstanding the latter's superior statutory priority as a secured creditor. It opened its analysis by noting that the central issue "whether a creditor that holds a perfected security interest in collateral can be held liable to an unsecured creditor based on a theory of unjust enrichment for benefits that enhance the value of the collateral . . . cannot be answered categorically." (*Duggan*, supra, 821 P.2d 788 at p. 793.) Recognizing that this problem presented "obvious tension between the doctrine of unjust enrichment and the priority system established by Article 9," the Court reviewed the relevant decisions and discerned that the "central point of distinction . . . is the extent to which the secured creditor was involved in the transaction by which the unsecured creditor supplied goods or services that enhanced the value of the secured collateral." (*Id.* at pp. 795–797.) Acknowledging that the UCC's priority system "reflects the legislative judgment that the value of a predictable system of priorities ordinarily outweighs the disadvantage of the system's occasional inequities," the Court formulated this rule: "In a situation where a secured creditor initiates or encourages transactions between the debtor and suppliers of goods or services, and benefits from the goods or services supplied to produce such debts, equitable principles require that the secured creditor compensate even an unsecured creditor to avoid being unjustly enriched. The equitable claim is at its strongest when the goods or services are necessary to preserve the security, as in *Producers Cotton Oil*."[6] (*Id.* at pp. 797–798.)

*Producers Cotton* and *Duggan* have been subjected to critical comment, some of which is unusually hostile.[7] Were we the first California court to consider the issue, we might well agree with the strict position that

---

**6.** Stated negatively, the Court's rule is that "Where a secured creditor does not itself initiate or encourage the transaction that creates the unsecured obligation giving rise to the unjust enrichment claim, retention of any benefit realized by the secured creditor without compensating the supplier is not unjust and thus an unjust enrichment claim cannot be supported." (*Duggan*, supra, 821 P.2d 788 at p. 797 [fn. omitted].)

**7.** The authors of the leading treatise on the UCC—who disagree between themselves as to the proper scope for equitable considerations—list *Producers Cotton* and *Duggan* in a section entitled "Weird Cases: The Creeping Infestation of Article Nine Priority Rules by 'Principles of Law and Equi-

ty.'" (2 White & Summers, Uniform Commercial Code (3d pract.ed.1988) § 26–20, pp. 554–555; id. (1993 supp.) pp. 160–164; see also Summers, General Equitable Principles Under Section 1–103 of the Uniform Commercial Code (1978) 72 Nw.U.L.Rev. 906 [favoring broad application of equity].) The author of a treatise on secured transactions excoriates *Duggan* in particular as an "aberration" that is not only "flat wrong" but "makes the mind spin," "turns the world upside down," and "should send chills down the backs of secured lenders everywhere." (Clark, The Law of Secured Transactions Under the Uniform Commercial Code (1993 supp.) § 3.14, pp. S3–35–S3–39.)

allowing restitution claims would be incompatible with the UCC's priority system. The primary purpose and chief benefit of article 9 is the stability and certainty provided by those rules. (E.g., *Duggan*, supra, 821 P.2d 788 at p. 797; 2 White & Summers, op. cit. supra, § 26–20, p. 555.) These are significant policy considerations which should not be disregarded lightly. So weighty is their value that most courts and commentators agree that it is better to accept the occasional "harsh application of the law than to disrupt thousands of other transactions by injecting uncertainty and by encouraging swarms of potential litigants and their lawyers to challenge what would otherwise be clear and fair rules." (2 White & Summers, supra, at pp. 554–555 * * *.) Any other approach threatens to "render the secured creditor status useless" (SMP Sales Management, Inc. v. Fleet Credit Corp., supra, 960 F.2d 557 at p. 560) and thus badly impair the utility of the article 9 framework.

But we do not come to this subject with a blank screen. As evidenced by *Producers Cotton*, California has opted to allow restitution claims against a secured creditor. When properly restricted to a very limited class of cases, this principle is sound.

The reasons supporting the primacy of the article 9 scheme are unquestionably weighty. Article 9 has been in place for more than three decades. Its requirements are by now familiar and integrated into commercial practice. The corresponding benefit is the stability that is essential to a healthy business climate. Compliance with the obligations of article 9 should have a positive consequence.

A secured creditor which has complied with all relevant UCC requirements to perfect its security interest, should therefore start with something like a presumption in its favor. The whole point of article 9 is to establish a comprehensive scheme affording maximum protection to the secured creditor who has followed its provisions. * * * This does not, of course, guarantee payment in full. Even a secured creditor which has perfected its security interest may be subordinated to another of like status which is chronologically senior, or to other specified classes of creditors, the most prominent of which are those having a purchase money security interest[8] (see § 9–312). But, having taken the trouble to satisfy all statutory requirements for protecting its interest, a secured creditor is entitled to a rebuttable preference for payment as against a creditor who has not demonstrated a similar compliance.

This preference would be reinforced by the failure of the unsecured creditor to use various nonstatutory protections. As courts and commentators have noted, the unsecured creditor could have (1) demanded cash payment on delivery, (2) perfected a purchase money security interest (see fn. 8, ante), (3) checked with the appropriate governmental office to determine if the debtor had already granted a security interest posing a

---

**8.** * * * We have discussed the purchase money security interest because it is what Knox could have obtained to protect his sale to Domaine.

possible threat to repayment, or (4) obtained a secured creditor's agreement to subordinate its priority (§ 9–312). * * *

But victory for a secured creditor is not an immutable law of nature. Fraud, for example, is expressly put beyond the pale. * * * A code may strive for comprehensiveness, but exceptional situations will arise. Equity is ordinarily meant to operate in these situations * * *, but its operation is subject to the principle that "equity follows the law." * * * This deference requires that equitable exceptions to statutory law be carefully limited to reduce any possible conflict with an express statutory command. * * * *Producers Cotton* and *Duggan* show how this may be accomplished.

Those decisions begin with the premise that simply pointing to benefit realized by the secured creditor will not suffice. As *Duggan* notes, gain to the creditor is almost universally present. * * * Something more is required to displace the creditor's favored position. That something is either conduct by the secured creditor or the nature of the unsecured creditor's contribution to the collateral.

What the *Duggan* court termed "the extent to which the secured creditor was involved in the transaction by which the unsecured creditor supplied goods or services" (*Duggan*, supra, 821 P.2d 788 at p. 797) can take many forms. At one end of the scale is fraud, which in its myriad forms is "the very essence of wrong; conduct that has always been and always will be wrong, according to the common judgment of mankind; conduct that cannot be dressed up or manipulated or associated so as to invest it with any element of right." (Morton v. Petitt (1931) 124 Ohio St. 241, 177 N.E. 591, 593.) The UCC gives it no sanction (§ 1–103) and courts applying the UCC are equally stern. * * *

Harder to resolve are the less egregious situations "where a secured creditor initiates or encourages transactions between the debtor and suppliers of goods or services, and benefits from the goods or services supplied to produce such debts." (*Duggan*, supra, 821 P.2d 788 at p. 798.) These situations present a fertile opportunity for trapping the unwary. If what the secured creditor did or failed to do can be reached by the doctrines of estoppel, misrepresentation not amounting to fraud, or mistake, the UCC allows redress to an innocent supplier (§ 1–103). Just as contribution among tortfeasors is proportioned by fault (Tech–Bilt, Inc. v. Woodward–Clyde & Associates (1985) 38 Cal.3d 488, 495, 213 Cal.Rptr. 256, 698 P.2d 159), commercial loss allocation responds to the same impulse. If it had an active hand in promoting a transaction that goes bad, a secured creditor should not escape with a victimized supplier left behind holding an empty bag alone. In simple terms, the creditor should not be allowed to profit from the wrong of its own bad faith. (Cf. § 1–203; Civ.Code, § 3517.)

The most difficult factor is the secured creditor's acquiescence when an unsecured creditor provides goods or services to their common debtor. First raised in *Producers Cotton*, it was given a restrictive gloss by *Duggan*: "In *Producers Cotton Oil* the court held that the secured creditor's act of acquiescing in the harvesting of the secured collateral (crops) was a sufficient basis for holding the secured creditor liable on the theory of unjust enrichment. However, in that case, the harvesting was necessary to the actual *preservation* of the secured collateral. Here, the delivery of corn was not essential to preserve the secured collateral, but instead served to augment or enhance its value. In such a case, more than mere acquiescence is required to hold a secured creditor liable on the basis of unjust enrichment." (*Duggan*, supra, 821 P.2d 788 at p. 797, fn. 17 [original emphasis; citation omitted].) Subject to two reservations, we agree with this reasoning, which is sound and reflective of commercial realities.

When an unsecured creditor provides goods or services that are necessary to preserve the collateral, this is an expense the secured creditor would ordinarily incur as part of the duty to use "reasonable care in the custody and preservation of collateral in his possession" (§ 9–207(1)). This would be especially true in situations like *Producers Cotton* and *Duggan*, where the collateral is perishable. In such a case the unsecured status of the creditor appears less important than the fact that the secured creditor directly benefits from expenditures the creditor is spared having to make on its own behalf. Matters become less clear when the unsecured creditor's expenditures are not essential but merely useful, in the sense that the collateral available for liquidation is being increased.

One of the notable features of article 9 is its approval of the concept of the so-called "floating lien" generated by security interests extending to after-acquired debtor property. This measure of creditor protection is vital to the feasibility of long-term procedures such as inventory, accounts receivable, or agriculture crop financing. * * * Risk to other creditors is inherent in the operation of this mechanism (see Jackson & Kronman, Secured Financing and Priorities Among Creditors (1978) 88 Yale L.J. 1143, 1166), whose utility would be severely impaired if unsecured additions to the protected collateral could be excluded from its reach. Virtually every addition will augment or enhance the value of the pool of collateral already pledged to the secured creditor. Unless the unsecured creditor uses one of the means the UCC permits to ensure payment, the risk of loss must be deemed a cost of doing business (cf. § 9–207(2)(c)). This is the defining characteristic of a perfected security interest—"the degree to which it insulates the secured party from the claims of the debtor's other creditors." (Jackson & Kronman, supra, at p. 1143.) The mere fact of augmenting or enhancing the collateral's value is by itself insufficiently notable to justify special equitable protection from article 9's priority structure. If allowed, this exception would swallow the rule.

The same is true concerning a secured creditor's acquiescence to such collateral pool augmentations. If acquiescence is to carry the risk of restitution liability, the secured creditor cannot afford silence. The creditor would be compelled to advise those who might deal with the debtor of the security arrangement and to disclaim responsibility for any obligation incurred by the debtor.[9] In order to know to whom these warnings must be

---

**9.** The *Duggan* court appears to have endorsed a creditor's need to "inform[ ] . . . the proper parties of its intent not to pay for debts incurred in maintaining, enhancing, or

given, the creditor would have to keep close tabs on the debtor's business dealings. Regardless of whether such a monitoring regime could overcome objections of cost, intrusiveness, and ineffectiveness, its conclusive flaw is that it would negate the utility of article 9's notice-filing system. One of the primary benefits of that system is that filing a financing statement relieves the now-secured creditor from the necessity of taking further action to protect its security interest; thereafter prospective creditors must watch out for themselves by checking the filings. Basing unjust enrichment liability on acquiescence would turn the filing system on its head, destroying existing creditors' reliance on that system and substituting a prospective creditor's duty to check with a new duty to warn and disclaim imposed on existing creditors. It would in plain effect reward ignorance and establish an incentive for ignoring the filing system. Acquiescence liability, because it would upend article 9's interlocking notice-filing and priority provisions, cannot be accepted.

How does the evidence in this case measure up according to this legal template? Nothing in Phoenix's conduct amounted to fraud, actual or virtual, and Knox does not contend otherwise.

The transaction between Knox and Domaine owed nothing to Phoenix in its inception. The contract for the barrels makes no reference to Phoenix, and was executed prior to Domaine's agreement with Phoenix. The barrels were ordered by Domaine, they were shipped to Domaine, and Knox initially looked to Domaine for payment. In light of Knox's testimony that he had no knowledge of Phoenix at the time he made the contract with Domaine, he could not have had any expectation of payment from Phoenix. The transaction between Knox and Domaine being in place and under way before Phoenix made any appearance, it is impossible to say that Phoenix initiated it. Similarly, the sole circumstance that Knox was paid for the first shipment with a check from Phoenix does not establish that Phoenix encouraged the deal; the course of performance under the Knox–Domaine contract owed nothing to anything said or done by Phoenix, or to the fact that Phoenix would be the true source of Domaine's payment to Knox. Phoenix never asked Knox to provide anything. * * *

We have already determined that any acquiescence by Phoenix will not support restitution liability. Phoenix had no duty to overcome the failure of Knox, a merchant knowledgeable about article 9 procedures,[10] to acquaint himself with public information concerning the Phoenix–Domaine relationship.

The barrels provided by Knox were not necessary to preserve the collateral covered by Phoenix's security interest in Domaine's "after ac-

---

making additions to secured collateral" in order to "protect itself from unjust enrichment claims." (*Duggan,* supra, 821 P.2d 788 at p. 798.) For the reasons stated in the text, we do not agree with this part of *Duggan.*

**10.** Although Knox testified at trial that he knew he could have filed a financing statement to protect his purchase money security interest, as he had done in the past, Phoenix showed that he did not do so for this transaction until February of 1991 the month Domaine became involved in bankruptcy proceedings.

quired" property. The mere fact that the secured collateral was enhanced by the addition of the barrels does not support liability in these circumstances.

The trial court's conclusion has an undeniable common sense allure—Knox provided barrels; Phoenix ended up with the barrels; Phoenix should therefore pay Knox for their value. Ordinarily this would be sound reasoning supporting an equitable result. Article 9, however, compels a different conclusion. Phoenix complied with statutory provisions intended to immunize secured creditors from such claims in all but the rarest of cases. As this is not that sort of case, the equitable impulse for restitution must yield to the Legislature's command. * * *

The judgment is reversed.


NOTES

**1.** The court explains that one reason creditors seek security interests is to relieve themselves of having to monitor the activities of their debtors. This view is espoused by Jackson and Kronman in their article quoted in the text before *Knox*, 88 Yale L.J. at 1149–1161. An unsecured creditor should know that if another creditor subsequently extends credit to the debtor, the effect may be to dilute the first creditor's claim to the debtor's asset pool and impair the prospect of repayment. Thus, prudent unsecured creditors will monitor the activities of their debtors. A trade creditor who constantly supplies inventory to a debtor may be so knowledgeable about the debtor's business that the monitoring function is a light one, but a bank may be more remote from the debtor and find monitoring more costly. Sophisticated unsecured creditors may demand covenants from their debtors limiting the debtor's right to incur further debt and to grant security interests in its assets. But observance of these covenants must be monitored as well. The court in *Knox* believes that allowing unsecured creditors restitution rights would impose monitoring costs on secured creditors that would defeat one of the major reasons for taking a security interest.

**2.** See Professor LoPucki's comment on *Ed Duggan*, discussed in *Knox*, in The Unsecured Creditor's Bargain, 80 Va. L. Rev. 1887, 1959–60 (1994). He would allow an unsecured supplier of corn to a debtor operating a feedlot to recover against a lender who authorized the debtor to continue buying corn from the supplier if the supplier could make out a case of implied contract. In *Ed Duggan* the debtor disclosed the lender's authorization to the supplier who, on the strength of the authorization, continued to sell corn on an unsecured basis to the debtor for several months before lender called the loan, sold the cattle, and refused to pay the supplier for the corn. If the supplier had supplied the corn with the reasonable expectation, based on all the circumstances, that the lender would pay it for the corn, LoPucki believes that the lender should be liable. A secured creditor's authorization to the debtor to buy corn for the benefit of the secured creditor's collateral implies that the secured creditor will pay for the benefit that it receives from the corn.

---

## B. INTRODUCTION TO ARTICLE 9

### 1. HISTORICAL NOTE

We introduce you to secured credit transactions law through the study of Article 9, the most innovative part of the Uniform Commercial Code. Article 9 is best understood against a brief historical background. Professor Grant Gilmore observes: "Until early in the nineteenth century the only security devices which were known in our legal system were the mortgage of real property and the pledge of chattels. Security interests in personal property which remained in the borrower's possession during the loan period were unknown. A transfer of an interest in personal property without delivery of possession was looked on as being in essence a fraudulent conveyance, invalid against creditors and purchasers."[1]

Not until a way could be found to allow the debtor to retain the possession and enjoyment of personal property collateral while paying off the debt would secured financing in personal property become economically significant. Two nineteenth century developments, one statutory and the other common law, legitimized nonpossessory personal property financing. Statutes allowed the creation of a mortgage in chattels in the possession of the mortgagor which was valid against creditors and purchasers so long as the chattel mortgagee spread the mortgage document on the public records. Meanwhile the courts were using the complex law of conditions to hold that a seller could sell a chattel to a buyer on condition that the buyer pay the price, and retake the property on the buyer's default. In contrast to the statutory chattel mortgage, the common law conditional sale was valid against third parties even though no public filing occurred.

Though the advent of the chattel mortgage and the conditional sale removed the traditional requirement that possession was required for the validity of secured transactions involving personal property, both these security devices were effective only when the collateral was static and the transaction was terminal. Neither device was sufficient when the collateral, as in the case of inventory or accounts receivable, would in the ordinary course of business be converted into cash or other proceeds in the hands of the debtor. In these cases the creditor needed a security device that would attach automatically to the proceeds resulting from the sale of inventory or the collection of accounts, or would attach to the inventory or accounts acquired by the debtor as replacements for the original collateral.

The first half of the twentieth century saw the invention of a series of security devices—trust receipts, factors' liens, and assignments of accounts

---

**1.** Gilmore, Security Interests in Personal Property § 2.1, at 24 (1965). This introductory statement is largely based on Gilmore's extensive treatment of the history of chattel security devices in volume 1 of his treatise.

receivable—that gave secured creditors more or less effective security interests in shifting stocks of collateral like inventory and accounts. By the time drafting began on Article 9 in the late 1940s, the leading commercial states had separate and wholly disparate laws on chattel mortgages, conditional sales, trust receipts, factors' liens, and assignments of accounts receivable. The law of chattel security was as provincial and nonuniform then as the law of real estate mortgages is today. Gilmore describes this body of law as one of "extraordinary complexity."[2]

## 2. 1962 ARTICLE 9

The primary drafters of Article 9, Professors Grant Gilmore and Allison Dunham, began the project resolved to junk the historical and conceptual categories that had characterized chattel security law and to strive for a functional approach to the area. Accordingly, instead of drafting revised and updated chattel mortgage or conditional sales acts, they set out to produce a series of separate statutes on each major type of financing: business equipment, consumer goods, agricultural products, inventory and accounts, and intangibles. As their work progressed they found that there were more similarities than differences among the various kinds of financing transactions. Hence, they decided to draft a unified statute, covering all secured transactions in personal property, that contained within it different rules for what were functionally different transactions.[3]

Article 9 does not abolish the pre-Code security devices, but it renders the formal distinctions among them irrelevant. Comment 2 to 9–109 states: "When a security interest is created, this Article applies regardless of the form of the transaction or the name that parties have given to it." Lawyers and judges may continue to talk about chattel mortgages or floor-planning, but the old categories have no meaning except as a shorthand way of describing familiar transactions. The overriding statement is found in 9–109(a)(1): "[T]his article applies to a transaction, regardless of its form, that creates a security interest in personal property or fixtures by contract."

## 3. ARTICLE 9 REVISION

Over the past two decades, the Uniform Commercial Code has undergone a thorough revision: Articles 1, 2, 3, 4, 5, 6, 7, 8 and 9 have been revised, and Articles 2A (leases) and 4A (funds transfers) have been added. In 1990 the Permanent Editorial Board of the Uniform Commercial Code (PEB), with support of its sponsors, the American Law Institute (ALI) and the National Conference of Commissioners on Uniform State Laws, formed a Study Group to consider whether Article 9 should be revised. To no one's surprise, it concluded that revision was needed and set out 249 pages of recommendations for change. The report is referred to in this book as PEB Study Group Report. The Drafting Committee began work in 1993. It was

**2.** Id. § 9.1, at 288.    **3.** Id. § 9.2.

chaired by William M. Burke, Esq., a commercial lawyer of broad experience, and its Co–Reporters were Professors Steven Harris and Charles W. Mooney, experienced commercial law scholars and teachers. After an enormous amount of work by the Reporters, the Drafting Committee, ad hoc consultative committees and a host of other interested groups, the draft of Revised Article 9 was promulgated in 1999. Section 9–701 provided that the Act would take effect on July 1, 2001 in those states that had adopted it by that time. Considering the complexities of the revision, state legislatures enacted the new Act with surprising speed, and 48 of the 50 states were on board by that date. The Revised Act has now been adopted by all the states as well as Washington D.C. and the Virgin Islands. The Revised Act provisions cited in this book are usually identified only by section number, without reference to their status as Revised Act provisions. References in the text to pre-revision Article 9 are prefaced by the word "former," e.g., "former 9–201."

In only 52 substantive sections, the 1962 Article 9, with its unitary concept, revolutionized the American law of secured transactions in personal property, and its success has influenced the law of Canada and other nations. Mindful of the widespread view that former Article 9 was probably the best commercial law statute ever written, the Revised Article 9 Drafting Committee proceeded with due deference to the formulations of secured transaction law adopted by the former Act. But a code drafted in the 1950s could not possibly foresee the new patterns of personal property financing that arose during the huge economic expansion of the second half of the 20th century. In 1950, "health care insurance receivables," "commercial tort claims," and "software" were unknown and what to do about lottery winnings had not attracted legislative attention. Expansion of Article 9 was clearly called for. In the early stages of drafting, Professors Harris and Mooney, in setting out their goals for Revised Article 9, responded: "[T]he scope of Article 9 should be expanded. Many of the common-law rules governing the creation of security interests in personal property are uncertain and cumbersome. Insofar as the creation of security interests is easier, less costly, and more certain under Article 9 than under common-law rules, expansion of the statute is likely to serve the overarching goal of effectuating the will of the parties." A Property–Based Theory of Security Interests: Taking Debtors' Choices Seriously, 80 Va. L. Rev. 2021, 2053 (1994).

## 4.   WORKING DEFINITIONS

The number of definitions in 9–102 is formidable, and as we proceed we will discuss many of them in detail, but we need a few basic terms to begin to communicate with each other about Article 9. The following are offered as rough working definitions of some of the basic terms that we will use in this course. We will refine and elaborate on these terms throughout the course.

"Debtor," 9–102(a)(28) and "Obligor," 9–102(a)(59). Security interests usually secure the payment of a debt. An obligor is one who owes payment of the secured debt. A debtor is the person whose property is subject to the creditor's security interest. Usually, the same person is both the debtor and the obligor, and we will call this person a debtor.

"Secured Party." 9–102(a)(72). The creditor in whose favor the security interest is created.

"Security Agreement." 9–102(a)(73). The agreement that creates the security interest. The medium may be either tangible or electronic.

"Security Interest." 1–201(b)(35). The interest in property that secures payment of the debt. Note that this definition applies to all Articles of the UCC and is found in Article 1. The term "security interest" also applies to interests created by specific transactions, such as consignments and sales of accounts, that do not create security interests but are nonetheless covered by Article 9. In these cases the buyer or consignor is referred to as the "secured party," the seller or consignee the "debtor," and the assets sold or consigned the "collateral."

"Collateral." 9–102(a)(12). The property subject to the security interest. Collateral may be tangible property like "goods," 9–102(a)(44). Goods may include "inventory," 9–102(a)(48), goods held for sale or lease; "farm products," 9–102(a)(34), crops or livestock; "consumer goods," goods for primarily personal, family or household purposes; or "equipment," 9–102(a)(33), any other kind of goods, for instance, business machines. But increasingly collateral is intangible property like "accounts," rights to payment arising out of the sale, lease or licensing of property; and "general intangibles," other kinds of rights to payment as well as intangible property like copyrights, software and a myriad of other kinds of property. In 1978 the tangible assets of publicly traded corporations was more than 83% of the market value of those companies, but recent estimates are that this figure has fallen to 30% or 40%, with the remaining value coming from intangible assets such as patents, copyrights, brands, customer lists, unique designs, processes and the like. Alan Murray, Accounting Rules Still Should Adapt to New Economy, Wall St. J., July 23, 2002, at A4.

"Financing Statement." 9–102(a)(39). The record (tangible or electronic) that the secured party files in public records, usually the state's filing office.

"Attachment." 9–203(a). A security interest attaches to collateral when it becomes enforceable against the debtor. This usually occurs when the debtor and secured party have entered into a security agreement and the secured party has given value to the debtor, either by making a loan or selling property on credit to the debtor.

"Perfection." 9–308(a). Usually, a security interest is perfected when it has attached and the secured party has either filed a financing statement or taken possession of the collateral. But in some cases it is perfected automatically at the time it attaches. Perfection establishes the secured party's priority in the collateral with respect to third parties.

"Proceeds." 9–102(a)(64). The property acquired by the debtor upon the sale, lease, license or other disposition of the collateral. If a retail merchant sells an item of inventory that is subject to a security interest, it may receive in payment money or a check from the buyer. These are "cash proceeds," 9–102(a)(9). Or it may sell on credit and take the buyer's unsecured obligation to pay for the purchase, which may be an "account," 9–102(a)(2), a "promissory note," 9–102(a)(65) in which the buyer promises to pay, or a credit or charge card, which obligates the card issuer to pay. The capacious definition of proceeds covers the money, checks, obligations to pay, and credit card receivables. The security interest in the inventory carries over into the proceeds. 9–315(a)(2).

"Record." 9–102(a)(69). Information either inscribed in a tangible medium, e.g., a writing, or stored in an electronic or other medium and retrievable in perceivable form, e.g., an e-mail.

## C. ATTACHMENT

### 1. THE SECURITY AGREEMENT

Article 9 makes creating a security interest easy. Under 9–203(b), a security interest attaches, that is, becomes enforceable against the debtor, when the secured party gives value, the debtor has rights in the collateral, and one of the conditions of 9–203(b)(3) is met. The first of these, which applies in the great majority of cases, is that the debtor has authenticated a security agreement that provides a description of the collateral. 9–203(b)(3)(A). "Security agreement" means an agreement that creates or provides for a security interest. 9–102(a)(73). These are simple, common sense requirements. In the usual case, the secured party gives value either by making a loan or a credit sale to the debtor. The debtor meets the rights-in-collateral test because it owns the collateral. And the debtor has signed a written security agreement that grants to the secured party a security interest in designated collateral. By signing the agreement, the debtor has authenticated it. 9–102(a)(7).

Article 9 recognizes that business transactions have become national or even international and that persons can do business with each other at a distance swiftly only by electronic communications. Hence, Article 9 is medium-neutral, and the term "record" replaces the terms "writing" and "written" in the former Act. "Record" includes information in a tangible form such as on paper as well as information in an intangible form that is stored in an electronic or other medium and is "retrievable in perceivable form." 9–102(a)(69). Comment 9a to 9–102 explains that "record" may include "magnetic media, optical discs, digital voice messaging systems, electronic mail, audio tapes, and photographic media, as well as paper." The requirement that a security agreement be signed by the debtor is replaced by the requirement that the debtor must "authenticate" a "record" evidencing the security agreement. "Authenticate" is defined in 9–102(a)(7) to include either signing a record or adopting a symbol or encrypt "with the present intent of the authenticating person to identify that person and to adopt or accept the record." Thus, in an agreement written on paper, the debtor authenticates by signing; if the agreement is stored in an electronic medium, the debtor authenticates by identifying itself and manifesting acceptance of the terms of the agreement.

PROBLEMS

**1.** Patrick, a Chicago businessman, finds himself in negotiations in New York to purchase goods at a favorable price. He can close the deal only by wiring $100,000 to Seller's deposit account in New York Bank (NYB) by the end of the business day. Patrick does not have enough money in his account in Chicago Bank (CB) to make the funds transfer. Although he has borrowed money in the past from that bank, he has no present line of credit outstanding. However, in the course of an extended telephone conversation, Patrick and CB agree that CB will wire the requested funds and, in order to secure the debt, Patrick grants CB a security interest in certain described personal property that he owns. The terms of the loan and security agreement are discussed in detail. CB sends the funds by Fedwire and they are received by NYB and deposited in the seller's account by the end of the day.

a. Does CB have an enforceable security interest in Patrick's personal property? See Comment 9a to 9–102.

b. Would CB have an enforceable security interest if it had tape recorded the telephone call in its entirety with Patrick's consent? CB retains such recorded tapes for six months.

**2.** Assume the facts in Problem 1. At the end of their negotiations when agreement had been reached, CB sent a confirmatory e-mail to Patrick's New York hotel room that accurately recited the terms that the parties had orally agreed to. This communication concluded by stating that if Patrick agreed to these terms he should indicate his consent by return e-mail. Patrick immediately replied by e-mail: "I agree to the terms set out in your message. Patrick." Does CB have an enforceable security interest?

**3.** Anabel has fallen on hard times and needs money quickly. She has an engagement ring valued at $5,000, all that is left from her disastrous, now-dissolved marriage. Uncle is rich but not generous, and when he reluctantly advanced her $3,000, he required that she give him possession of the ring until her debt to him, evidenced by a written promissory note signed by Anabel and due a year later, is paid, at which time Uncle will return the ring to her. Except for the promissory note, which said nothing about a secured interest in the ring, the agreement was entirely oral. Does Uncle have an enforceable security interest in the ring under 9–203(b)(3)(B)? See Comment 4 to 9–203.

## 2.   THE COMPOSITE DOCUMENT RULE

However easy it is to create a security interest, the parties continue to make mistakes of the kind discussed by the case below. Their mistakes can be fatal to the security interest in bankruptcy. In reading this case, be sure you understand why the bankruptcy court concluded that the note and financing statement, taken together, were not intended to be the security agreement. This opinion is generally believed to be the classic statement of the composite document rule. Most jurisdictions accept some version of the rule, and Revised Article 9 makes no changes that would affect it.

# In re Bollinger Corp.

United States Court of Appeals, Third Circuit, 1980.
614 F.2d 924.

■ ROSENN, CIRCUIT JUDGE.

This appeal from a district court review of an order in bankruptcy presents a question that has troubled courts since the enactment of Article Nine of the Uniform Commercial Code (U.C.C.) governing secured transactions. Can a creditor assert a secured claim against the debtor when no formal security agreement was ever signed, but where various documents executed in connection with a loan evince an intent to create a security interest? The district court answered this question in the affirmative and permitted the creditor, Zimmerman & Jansen, to assert a secured claim against the debtor, bankrupt Bollinger Corporation in the amount of $150,000. We affirm.

I.

The facts of this case are not in dispute. Industrial Credit Company (ICC) made a loan to Bollinger Corporation (Bollinger) on January 13, 1972, in the amount of $150,000. As evidence of the loan, Bollinger executed a promissory note in the sum of $150,000 and signed a security agreement with ICC giving it a security interest in certain machinery and equipment. ICC in due course perfected its security interest in the collateral by filing a financing statement in accordance with Pennsylvania's enactment of Article Nine of the U.C.C.

Bollinger faithfully met its obligations under the note and by December 4, 1974, had repaid $85,000 of the loan leaving $65,000 in unpaid principal. Bollinger, however, required additional capital and on December 5, 1974, entered into a loan agreement with Zimmerman & Jansen, Inc. (Z & J), by which Z & J agreed to lend Bollinger $150,000. Z & J undertook as part of this transaction to pay off the $65,000 still owed to ICC in return for an assignment by ICC to Z & J of the original note and security agreement between Bollinger and ICC. Bollinger executed a promissory note to Z & J, evidencing the agreement containing the following provision:

> Security. This Promissory Note is secured by security interests in a certain Security Agreement between Bollinger and Industrial Credit Company * * * and in a Financing Statement filed by [ICC] * * *, and is further secured by security interests in a certain security agreement to be delivered by Bollinger to Z and J with this Promissory Note covering the identical machinery and equipment as identified in the ICC Agreement and with identical schedule attached in the principal amount of Eighty–Five Thousand Dollars. ($85,000).

No formal security agreement was ever executed between Bollinger and Z & J. Z & J did, however, in connection with the promissory note, record a new financing statement signed by Bollinger containing a detailed list of the machinery and equipment originally taken as collateral by ICC for its loan to Bollinger.

Bollinger filed a petition for an arrangement under Chapter XI of the Bankruptcy Act in March, 1975 and was adjudicated bankrupt one year later. In administrating the bankrupt's estate, the receiver sold some of Bollinger's equipment but agreed that Z & J would receive a $10,000 credit on its secured claim.

Z & J asserted a secured claim against the bankrupt in the amount of $150,000, arguing that although it never signed a security agreement with Bollinger, the parties had intended that a security interest in the sum of $150,000 be created to protect the loan. The trustee in bankruptcy conceded that the assignment to Z & J of ICC's original security agreement with Bollinger gave Z & J a secured claim in the amount of $65,000, the balance owed by Bollinger to ICC at the time of the assignment. The trustee, however, refused to recognize Z & J's asserted claim of an additional secured claim of $85,000 because of the absence of a security agreement between Bollinger and Z & J. The bankruptcy court agreed and entered judgment for Z & J in the amount of $55,000, representing a secured claim in the amount of $65,000 less $10,000 credit received by Z & J.

Z & J appealed to the United States District Court for the Western District of Pennsylvania, which reversed the bankruptcy court and entered judgment for Z & J in the full amount of the asserted $150,000 secured claim. The trustee in bankruptcy appeals.

## II.

Under Article Nine of the U.C.C., two documents are generally required to create a perfected security interest in a debtor's collateral. First, there must be a "security agreement" giving the creditor an interest in the collateral. Section 9–203(1)(b) contains minimal requirements for the creation of a security agreement. In order to create a security agreement, there must be: (1) a writing (2) signed by the debtor (3) containing a description of the collateral or the types of collateral. Section 9–203, Comment 1. The requirements of section 9–203(1)(b) further two basic policies. First, an evidentiary function is served by requiring a signed security agreement and second, a written agreement also obviates any Statute of Frauds problems with the debtor-creditor relationship. *Id.* Comments 3, 5. The second document generally required is a "financing statement," which is a document signed by both parties and filed for public record. The financing statement serves the purpose of giving public notice to other creditors that a security interest is claimed in the debtor's collateral.

Despite the minimal formal requirements set forth in section 9–203 for the creation of a security agreement, the commercial world has frequently neglected to comply with this simple Code provision. Soon after Article

Nine's enactment, creditors who had failed to obtain formal security agreements, but who nevertheless had obtained and filed financing statements, sought to enforce secured claims. Under section 9–402, a security agreement may serve as a financing statement if it is signed by both parties. The question arises whether the converse is true: Can a signed financing statement operate as a security agreement? The earliest case to consider this question was American Card Co. v. H.M.H. Co., 97 R.I. 59, 196 A.2d 150, 152 (1963) which held that a financing statement could *not* operate as a security agreement because there was no language *granting* a security interest to a creditor. Although section 9–203(1)(b) makes no mention of such a grant language requirement, the court in *American Card* thought that implicit in the definition of "security agreement" under section 9–105(1)(h) was such a requirement; some grant language was necessary to "create or provide security." This view also was adopted by the Tenth Circuit in Shelton v. Erwin, 472 F.2d 1118, 1120 (8th Cir.1973). Thus, under the holdings of these cases, the creditor's assertion of a secured claim must fall in the absence of language connoting a grant of a security interest.

The Ninth Circuit in In re Amex–Protein Development Corp., 504 F.2d 1056 (9th Cir.1974), echoed criticism by commentators of the *American Card* rule. The court wrote: "There is no support in legislative history or grammatical logic for the substitution of the word 'grant' for the phrase 'creates or provides for'." *Id.* at 1059–60. It concluded that as long as the financing statement contains a description of the collateral signed by the debtor, the financing statement may serve as the security agreement and the formal requirements of section 9–203(1)(b) are met. The tack pursued by the Ninth Circuit is supported by legal commentary on the issue. See G. Gilmore, Security Interests in Personal Property, § 11.4 at 347–48 (1965).

Some courts have declined to follow the Ninth Circuit's liberal rule allowing the financing statement alone to stand as the security agreement, but have permitted the financing statement, when read in conjunction with other documents executed by the parties, to satisfy the requirements of section 9–203(1)(b). The court in In re Numeric Corp., 485 F.2d 1328 (1st Cir.1973) held that a financing statement coupled with a board of directors' resolution revealing an intent to create a security interest were sufficient to act as a security agreement. The court concluded from its reading of the Code that there appears no need to insist upon a separate document entitled "security agreement" as a prerequisite for an otherwise valid security interest.

> A writing or writings, regardless of label, which adequately describes the collateral, carries the signature of the debtor, and establishes that in fact a security interest was agreed upon, would satisfy both the formal requirements of the statute and the policies behind it.

*Id.* at 1331. The court went on to hold that "although a standard form financing statement by itself cannot be considered a security agreement, an adequate agreement can be found when a financing statement is considered together with other documents." *Id.* at 1332. * * *

More recently, the Supreme Court of Maine in Casco Bank & Trust Co. v. Cloutier, 398 A.2d 1224, 1231–32 (Me.1979) considered the question of whether composite documents were sufficient to create a security interest within the terms of the Code. Writing for the court, Justice Wernick allowed a financing statement to be joined with a promissory note for purposes of determining whether the note contained an adequate description of the collateral to create a security agreement. The court indicated that the evidentiary and Statute of Frauds policies behind section 9–203(1)(b) were satisfied by reading the note and financing statement together as the security agreement.

In the case before us, the district court went a step further and held that the promissory note executed by Bollinger in favor of Z & J, standing alone, was sufficient to act as the security agreement between the parties. In so doing, the court implicitly rejected the *American Card* rule requiring grant language before a security agreement arises under section 9–203(1)(b). The parties have not referred to any Pennsylvania state cases on the question and our independent research has failed to uncover any. But although we agree that no formal grant of a security interest need exist before a security agreement arises, we do not think that the promissory note standing alone would be sufficient under Pennsylvania law to act as the security agreement. We believe, however, that the promissory note, read in conjunction with the financing statement duly filed and supported, as it is here, by correspondence during the course of the transaction between the parties, would be sufficient under Pennsylvania law to establish a valid security agreement.[3]

## III.

We think Pennsylvania courts would accept the logic behind the First and Ninth Circuit rule and reject the *American Card* rule imposing the requirement of a formal grant of a security interest before a security agreement may exist. When the parties have neglected to sign a separate security agreement, it would appear that the better and more practical view is to look at the transaction as a whole in order to determine if there is a writing, or writings, signed by the debtor describing the collateral which demonstrates an intent to create a security interest in the collateral. In connection with Z & J's loan of $150,000 to Bollinger, the relevant writings to be considered are: (1) the promissory note; (2) the financing statement; (3) a group of letters constituting the course of dealing between the parties. The district court focused solely on the promissory note finding it sufficient

**3.** The district court held alternatively that the assignment of the 1972 security agreement between Bollinger and ICC to Z & J was sufficient to give Z & J a secured claim in the amount of $150,000. The 1972 security agreement contained a "future advances" clause, allowing ICC to use the collateral for its original loan to Bollinger as security for any future sums advanced by it to Bollinger, as permitted by 9–204(3).... Although we have serious reservations whether the "future advances" clause was broad enough to encompass a loan made by a third party, we need not consider this alternative theory offered by the district court because we are convinced that the documents executed between Bollinger and Z & J were sufficient to secure Z & J.

to constitute the security agreement. Reference, however, to the language in the note reveals that the note standing alone cannot serve as the security agreement. The note recites that along with the assigned 1972 security agreement between Bollinger and ICC, the Z & J loan is "further secured by security interests in a certain Security Agreement *to be delivered* by Bollinger to Z & J with this Promissory Note \* \* \*." (Emphasis added.) The bankruptcy judge correctly reasoned that "[t]he intention to create a separate security agreement negates any inference that the debtor intended that the promissory note constitute the security agreement." At best, the note is some evidence that a security agreement was contemplated by the parties, but by its own terms, plainly indicates that it is not the security agreement.

Looking beyond the promissory note, Z & J did file a financing statement signed by Bollinger containing a detailed list of all the collateral intended to secure the $150,000 loan to Bollinger. The financing statement alone meets the basic section 9–203(1)(b) requirements of a writing, signed by the debtor, describing the collateral. However, the financing statement provides only an inferential basis for concluding that the parties intended a security agreement. There would be little reason to file such a detailed financing statement unless the parties intended to create a security interest.[5] The intention of the parties to create a security interest may be gleaned from the expression of future intent to create one in the promissory note and the intention of the parties as expressed in letters constituting their course of dealing.

The promissory note was executed by Bollinger in favor of Z & J in December 1974. Prior to the consummation of the loan, Z & J sent a letter to Bollinger on May 30, 1974, indicating that the loan would be made "provided" Bollinger secured the loan by a mortgage on its machinery and equipment. Bollinger sent a letter to Z & J on September 19, 1974, indicating:

> With your [Z & J's] stated desire to obtain security for material and funds advanced, it would appear that the use of the note would answer both our problems. Since the draft forwarded to you offers full collateralization for the funds to be advanced under it and bears normal interest during its term, it should offer you maximum security.

Subsequent to the execution of the promissory note, Bollinger sent to Z & J a list of the equipment and machinery intended as collateral under the security agreement which was to be, but never was, delivered to Z & J. In November 1975, the parties exchanged letters clarifying whether Bollinger could substitute or replace equipment in the ordinary course of business without Z & J's consent. Such a clarification would not have been necessary had a security interest not been intended by the parties. Finally, a letter of

---

**5.**  Z & J would not have had to file a financing statement for the $65,000 covered by the 1972 security agreement between ICC and Bollinger, inasmuch as the assignee of a security interest is protected by the assignor's filing. Section 9–302(2).

November 18, 1975, from Bollinger to Z & J indicated that "any attempted impairment of the collateral would constitute an event of default."

From the course of dealing between Z & J and Bollinger, we conclude there is sufficient evidence that the parties intended a security agreement to be created separate from the assigned ICC agreement with Bollinger. All the evidence points towards the intended creation of such an agreement and since the financing statement contains a detailed list of the collateral, signed by Bollinger, we hold that a valid Article Nine security agreement existed under Pennsylvania law between the parties which secured Z & J in the full amount of the loan to Bollinger.

IV.

The minimal formal requirements of section 9–203(1)(b) were met by the financing statement and the promissory note, and the course of dealing between the parties indicated the intent to create a security interest. The judgment of the district court recognizing Z & J's secured claim in the amount of $150,000 will be affirmed.

NOTE

A gross characterization of the conflict in the decisions regarding the existence of a valid security agreement follows:

The pro-secured-creditor view: The requirement of a written security agreement is merely evidentiary. If the creditor advances money to a debtor, the debtor signs a promissory note and the financing statement describes the collateral, this is enough to show intent to create a security interest; no additional formal security agreement is needed. Why else would the parties have done this unless they were entering into a secured transaction? *American Card* and its ilk are throwbacks to rigid, formalistic pre-Code thinking. *Bollinger* recognizes the clear intent of the parties even though the creditor was a little careless.

The pro-trustee-in-bankruptcy view: The secured creditor has a very strong position against other creditors in bankruptcy. Recognition of the security interest may clean out the bankrupt's estate, leaving nothing for others. Since the Article 9 requirements for creating an enforceable security agreement are so minimal and the benefits conferred by secured creditor status are so great, we should demand that the creditor who seeks these benefits must comply fully with these simple requirements. *American Card* merely requires that the writing contain some words unequivocally granting a security interest to the creditor. *Bollinger* is wrong in protecting the negligent creditor by finding a security agreement when the promissory note stated that a security agreement would subsequently be delivered to the debtor and none was. Why protect a negligent creditor at the expense of others?

Most courts have adopted the pro-secured-creditor view, as indicated in the authorities cited in *Bollinger* See White & Summers, Uniform Commercial Code § 22–3a (5th ed. 2000); Expeditors Int. of Washington, Inc. v.

Citicorp North America, Inc., 218 B.R. 507 (9th Cir.BAP 1997); In re Tracy's Flowers and Gifts, 264 B.R. 1 (Bankr.W.D. Ark. 2001); Oginz v. Craftsman Electrical Mfg., Inc., 35 UCC Rep. Serv. 2d 309, 1998 WL 564367 (Cir. Ct. Richmond, Va. 1998). For the pro-trustee view, see In re Sabol, 337 B.R. 195 (Bankr. C.D. Ill. 2006).

## PROBLEMS

**1.** Debtor's security agreement granted Bank a security interest in machinery, equipment, and furniture and fixtures. The financing statement included these items of collateral and added inventory and accounts. When Debtor filed in bankruptcy, Bank claimed a security interest in the inventory and accounts. Bank contended that the composite document rule allowed it to use the financing statement to add inventory and accounts to the collateral covered by the security agreement; no one doubted that the intent of the parties was to include inventory and accounts. Debtor argued that if the parties have executed a document that is clearly intended to contain the security agreement, under the parol evidence rule the security interest is limited to the collateral described in that document. Bank replied that under Debtor's view, a secured party is better off under the composite document rule not having any document designated as the security agreement. Which side is correct? The facts are based on Matter of Martin Grinding & Machine Works, Inc., 793 F.2d 592 (7th Cir.1986). Can you reconcile this case with *Bollinger*?

**2.** Store wishes to take security interests in goods purchased by customers using its charge card. When Store issues a charge card to a customer, it includes a copy of a detailed security agreement that purports to grant Store a security interest in goods purchased by customers using Store's charge card. Upon making a purchase by use of the charge card, the customer signs a sales slip which recites: "Purchased under my Store account and security agreement, incorporated by reference. I grant Store a security interest in this merchandise until paid." The sales slip describes the merchandise and is signed by the customer. In litigation about the effect of this transaction, customers have contended that since they never signed the detailed security agreement sent out by Store, there is no enforceable security interest in the goods they have purchased. Does Store have an enforceable security interest in goods purchased pursuant to their charge cards? Do the terms of its security agreement include those in the master agreement? See Sears, Roebuck & Co. v. Conry, 321 Ill.App.3d 997, 748 N.E.2d 1248 (2001).

## 3.   Description of Collateral

## In re Grabowski

United States Bankruptcy Court, S.D. Illinois, 2002.
277 B.R. 388.

■ Kenneth J. Meyers, Bankruptcy Judge.

This case involves a priority dispute between defendants Bank of America and South Pointe Bank ("South Pointe") regarding their security interests in three items of farm equipment owned by the debtors. Both lenders filed financing statements perfecting their interests. Bank of America, the first to file, described its collateral in general terms and listed the debtors' business address, rather than their home address where the collateral was located. South Pointe, by contrast, described the collateral more specifically and included the debtors' home address. South Pointe contends that Bank of America's description was ineffective to perfect the Bank's security interest in the equipment and that South Pointe has a superior interest by reason of its subsequently filed financing statement.

The facts are undisputed. In April 2001, debtors Ronald and Trenna Grabowski of Dubois, Illinois, filed this Chapter 11 proceeding to reorganize their farming operation in Washington and Perry counties, Illinois. The debtors have been engaged in farming at this location for the past 30 years. Beginning in 1993, the debtors also owned and operated a John Deere farm equipment business, Grabowski Tractor–Benton, Inc., at 12047 Highway 37, Benton, Illinois. During this time, debtor Trenna Grabowski, a certified public accountant, moved her accounting practice to the Benton dealership. Although the dealership was sold in 1999, Trenna Grabowski continues to conduct her accounting practice from the Benton location.

The debtors' schedules include a list of items of equipment used in their farming operation. The debtors filed the present proceeding to determine the validity, priority, and extent of liens held by various lenders in this equipment. Subsequently, the lenders reached an agreement concerning their respective interests in the farm equipment with the exception of three items. (*See* Stip., Doc. No. 20, filed February 1, 2002.) These items, as to which a dispute remains between Bank of America and South Pointe, consist of a John Deere 925 flex platform, a John Deere 4630 tractor, and a John Deere 630 disk. (*See* Stip. at 3–4.)

Bank of America claims a prior security interest in this equipment by virtue of a security agreement signed by the debtors in December 1998. The Bank's financing statement, filed on December 31, 1998, identifies the debtors as "Ronald and Trenna Grabowski" and lists their address as "12047 State Highway #37, Benton, Illinois 62812." The financing statement describes the Bank's collateral as:

All Inventory, Chattel Paper, Accounts, *Equipment* and General Intangibles[.][2]

South Pointe subsequently obtained a lien on the debtors' equipment in January 2000. South Pointe's financing statement, filed January 18, 2000, identifies the debtors as "Ronald and Trenna Grabowski" at "P.O. Box 38, Dubois, Illinois 62831" and describes South Pointe's collateral as:

**2.** The description of collateral in the Bank's security agreement is virtually identical.

JD 1995 9600 combine ..., JD 925 FLEX PLATFORM ..., JD 4630 TRACTOR ..., JD 630 DISK 28' 1998....[4]

South Pointe asserts that Bank of America's financing statement, although prior in time, was insufficient to perfect the Bank's interest because it failed to place other lenders on notice of Bank of America's interest in the subject equipment. Specifically, South Pointe notes that the Bank's financing statement contained the address of the debtors' farm equipment business rather than that of the debtors' home where their farming operation is located and, further, that it failed to mention any specific items of equipment or even make reference to "farm equipment" or "farm machinery." South Pointe argues that, based on this description, a subsequent lender would reasonably conclude that Bank of America's intended security was the personal property of the debtors' business rather than equipment used in the debtors' farming operation. South Pointe maintains, therefore, that the Bank's financing statement did not reasonably identify the Bank's collateral as required to fulfill the notice function of a financing statement under Illinois' Uniform Commercial Code. * * *

The UCC sets forth the requirements for a creditor to obtain and perfect a security interest in personal property of the debtor. Section 9–203 governs the attachment and enforcement of security interests through the parties' execution of a security agreement, while § 9–502 relates to the requisites of a financing statement filed to perfect the creditor's interest against the interests of third parties. Both sections call for a description of the debtor's property.[5] However, the degree of specificity required of such description depends on the nature of the document involved—whether it is a security agreement or financing statement—and the purpose to be fulfilled by such document. *See* 9A Hawkland, *Uniform Commercial Code Series*, [Rev] § 9–108:2, at 291–92; [Rev] § 9–108:2, at 294–96 (2001). While a security agreement defines and limits the collateral subject to the creditor's security interest, a financing statement puts third parties on notice that the creditor may have a lien on the property described and that further inquiry into the extent of the security interest is prudent.

Section 9–108 sets forth the test for sufficiency of a description under the UCC, stating:

**4.** South Pointe's security agreement describes the property subject to its lien as: Equipment: All equipment including ... *farm machinery and equipment....*

The secured property includes ... the following: JD 1995 9600 COMBINE ..., JD 925 FLEX PLATFORM ..., JD 4630 TRACTOR ..., JD 630 DISK 28' 1998....

**5.** Section 9–203 provides in pertinent part:

(b) ... [A] security interest is enforceable against the debtor and third parties with respect to the collateral only if:

.... (A) the debtor has authenticated a security agreement *that provides a description of the collateral....*

....

Section 9–502 states:

(a) ... [A] financing statement is sufficient only if it:

(3) *indicates the collateral covered by the financing statement*

9–502(a)(3) (2001) (emphasis added)

(a) ... a description of personal ... property is sufficient, whether or not it is specific, *if it reasonably identifies what is described.*

9–108(a) (emphasis added) (2001). Examples of descriptions that meet this "reasonable identification" test include identification by "category" or by "type of collateral defined in the UCC." *See* § 9–108(b)(2), (3). In addition, identification "by any other method" is sufficient, "if the identity of the collateral is objectively determinable." *See* § 9–108(b)(6). Only a supergeneric such as "all the debtor's assets" or "all the debtor's personal property" is insufficient under the "reasonable identification" standard of § 9–108. *See* 9–108(c).

While § 9–108 provides a flexible standard for determining the sufficiency of a description in a security agreement, § 9–504 provides an even broader standard with regard to a financing statement. This section states:

A financing statement sufficiently indicates the collateral that it covers if the financing statement provides:

(1) a description of the collateral pursuant to Section 9–108; or

(2) *an indication that the financing statement covers all assets or all personal property*

9–504 (2001) (emphasis added). Thus, in the case of a financing statement, a creditor may either describe its collateral by "type" or "category" as set forth in § 9–108 or may simply indicate its lien on "all assets" of the debtor.

This exceedingly general standard for describing collateral in a financing statement, which is new to the UCC under revised Article 9, is consistent with the "inquiry notice" function of a financing statement under previous law. A financing statement need not specify the property encumbered by a secured party's lien, but need merely notify subsequent creditors that a lien may exist and that further inquiry is necessary "to disclose the complete state of affairs." Uniform Commercial Code Comment 2, 9–502. In the present case, Bank of America filed a financing statement indicating it had a lien on the debtors' property consisting of "all inventory, chattel paper, accounts, equipment, and general intangibles." Despite the generality of the Bank's description, it was sufficient to notify subsequent creditors, including South Pointe, that a lien existed on the debtors' property and that further inquiry was necessary to determine the extent of the Bank's lien. For this reason, the Court finds no merit in South Pointe's argument that the description of the Bank's collateral was too general to fulfill the notice function of a financing statement under the UCC.

South Pointe asserts, however, that it was misled by the incorrect address contained in Bank of America's financing statement and "reasonably concluded" that the only equipment subject to the Bank's lien was that located at the debtors' farm equipment dealership. The Court disagrees that such conclusion was "reasonable." The debtors' business address was not part of the Bank's description of its collateral and, thus, did not serve to limit the collateral subject to the Bank's lien as South Pointe argues. In fact, Bank of America's financing statement indicated the Bank had a lien on the debtors' "equipment," with no indication that its interest was confined to equipment located in a particular place. Rather than serving to describe the Bank's collateral, therefore, the debtors' address merely provided a means by which subsequent lenders could contact the debtors to inquire concerning the Bank's lien.[6] *See* 9 Hawkland, *supra*, § 9–402:11, at 724–25.

While a subsequent creditor should not be imposed upon to be a "super-detective" in investigating prior secured transactions, the debtors' address in this case was an accurate and ready means of contacting the debtors. The Court notes, moreover, that even though the mailing address on the Bank's financing statement was that of the debtors' business, the debtors' names were listed as "Ronald and Trenna Grabowski," not "Grabowski Tractor–Benton, Inc.," the name of the debtors' business. Accordingly, the Court finds that a reasonably prudent lender would not be misled into believing that the collateral listed was property of the debtors' business, rather than that of the debtors individually.

For the reasons stated, the Court concludes that Bank of America's financing statement was sufficient to perfect its security interest in the subject farm equipment and that the Bank's interest, being prior in time, is superior to that of South Pointe. Accordingly, the Court finds in favor of Bank of America and against South Pointe on the debtors' complaint to determine validity, priority, and extent of liens in the debtors' farm equipment.

---

Article 9's rules for describing collateral are very forgiving; they offer secured parties a great deal of latitude. For a security interest to be enforceable under 9–203(b)(3)(A), the security agreement must describe the collateral, but, under 9–108(a), a description is sufficient if it merely "reasonably identifies what is described." 9–108(b) supplements this by providing that a description of collateral reasonably identifies the collateral if it does so either specifically, or by category, type (with certain exceptions), or "any other method if the identity of the collateral is objectively determinable." 9–108(b)(6). Comment 2 to 9–108 states that the test of sufficiency for a description is whether it "make[s] possible the identification of the collateral described." Taking this Comment and the "objectively determinable" test of 9–108(b)(6) together, they state a pliant rule that a description is sufficient if the secured party can show that a reasonable person could identify the collateral from the description given.

---

**6.**  Bank of America points out that although former § 9–402 specified that "a mailing address of the debtor" be included as one of the requisites of a financing statement, 9–402(1) (2000), § 9–502 of revised Article 9 does not contain such a requirement. *See* 9–502(a) (2001). The Court notes, however, that § 9–516(b)(5)(A) specifies that a financing statement that is refused by the filing officer for failure to include "a mailing address of the debtor" is ineffective. 9–516(b)(5)(A). Accordingly, it is at least questionable whether the "mailing address" requirement has been eliminated. *See* 9–Hawkland, *supra*, [Rev] § 9:502:3, at 742, [Rev] § 9–516:3, at 841.

Section 9–108(b)(2) and (3) approves generic descriptions of collateral by "category" and "a type of collateral defined in" the UCC. There is no indication of what is intended by the term "category," but "type" of collateral presumably means types set out in 9–102(a), such as accounts, inventory, equipment, chattel paper, deposit accounts, farm products, general intangibles, and the like. The use of types of collateral for collateral description is very common in security agreements covering a broad spectrum of a debtor's property. However, 9–108(e) provides that the use of a description only by type is insufficient with respect to commercial tort claims and, in consumer transactions, consumer goods, security entitlements, securities accounts and commodity accounts. The concern is that without a more specific definition debtors might encumber this property inadvertently. Consumers can't be expected to know what these generic terms include, and the scope of commercial tort claims is probably pretty uncertain to most people.

### PROBLEM

Dealer sold Farmer a John Deere tractor on credit. Farmer signed a security agreement that described the tractor as "farm equipment." In what, if any, property of Farmer does Dealer have a security interest if:

a. Farmer owned no other items of farm equipment?

b. Farmer owned several other items of farm equipment?

---

Descriptions that are generic in nature, such as the types of collateral defined in the UCC (e.g., inventory, accounts, equipment), can be acceptable descriptions under 9–108(b) if they reasonably describe the collateral. "All equipment" might suffice, even though "equipment" alone might not. A familiar belt-and-suspender's approach is: "all equipment of Debtor, including but not limited to the following: [specific enumeration follows]." Even broader than the use of "types" is the acceptance of "categories," with no indication of what is intended. But 9–108(c) rules out the use of "supergeneric" descriptions, like "all the debtor's personal property." In contrast, we will see that 9–504(2) approves a description of collateral in a financing statement if it "covers all assets or all personal property."

Why does Article 9 allow supergeneric descriptions in the financing statement but not in the security agreement? As *Grabowski* points out, security agreements and financing statements perform different functions. The security agreement is an agreement between debtor and creditor. Comment 3 to 9–203 states that this agreement must meet evidentiary requirements "in the nature of a Statute of Frauds." A description of the collateral in the agreement reduces proof costs associated with establishing the terms of the parties' agreement. But supergeneric descriptions such as "all assets of the debtor" do so at least as well as descriptions by type, such as "all equipment of the debtor," or by category, such as "all crops." Section 9–108(c) disagrees with this view. Why? The function of the financing statement is to put third parties on notice about the possibility of a security interest granted by the debtor to a creditor and to establish priority. The description of collateral serves part of the notice and priority function in ways discussed below. Supergeneric descriptions provide adequate notice, as in 9–504(2). Why, if at all, would a supergeneric description be adequate for notice or priority purposes but inadequate to reduce the proof costs associated with proving a contract? See Comment 5 to 9–203.

The requirement of more specific description of collateral in the security agreement serves functions other than reducing proof costs. One additional function might be to induce creditors to disclose information to their debtors about the precise nature of the assets the security agreement is to cover, where debtors otherwise would remain ignorant. Section 9–108(e) acknowledges this "disclosure" function, by not recognizing supergeneric descriptions in the case of commercial tort claims and consumer transactions. Aside from this exception, however, is there a good reason for not allowing supergeneric descriptions of collateral in security agreement? Are there benefits realized that offset the increased costs the rule imposes on the parties? Where such regulation yield net benefits, perhaps Article 9 should simply have enumerated the transactions in which they are present, adding them to 9–108(e). If regulation almost always produces a net cost, perhaps 9–108(c) should not have been adopted.

### PROBLEMS

The following fact situations are based on two cases that were decided by the same court with opinions by the same judge. He upheld the validity of the collateral description in one case and rejected it in the other. In your view which is the more vulnerable description? Can you distinguish the cases?

**1.** The security agreement granted a security interest in certain specifically described items, including an International truck, and contained the following omnibus clause:

In addition to all the above enumerated items, it is the intention that this mortgage shall cover all chattels, machinery, equipment, tables, chairs, work benches, factory chairs, stools, shelving, cabinets, power lines, switch boxes, control panels, machine parts, motors, pumps, electrical equipment, measuring and calibrating instruments, office supplies, sundries, office furniture, fixtures, and all other items of equipment and fixtures belonging to the mortgagor, whether herein enumerated or not, now at the plant of [Debtor] located at 115–02 15th Ave. College Point, New York, and all chattels, machinery, fixtures, or equipment that may hereafter be brought in or installed in said premises or any new premises of the mortgagor, to replace, substitute for, or in addition to the above mentioned chattels and equipment with the exception of stock in trade.

The issue was whether the omnibus clause covered two Oldsmobile automobiles used in Debtor's business. The clause covered "equipment," defined in 9–102(a)(33). The two automobiles clearly are within the UCC definition. See In re Laminated Veneers Co., Inc., 471 F.2d 1124, 1125 (2d Cir.1973).

**2.** The security agreement described the collateral as the following:

**Items**

> Machinery, equipment and fixtures; Molds, tools, dies, component parts including specifically the 1 x 1 two cavity cassette cover and base mold, 2 x 2 four cavity cassette cover and base mold, One twenty-four cavity roller mold, One sixteen cavity hub mold

**Location, etc.**

> To be located either at the Debtor's plant in North Bergen, New Jersey; and in the case of the molds also at the plants of contractors who may be using said molds in the manufacture of products for the Debtor

The issue was whether the security agreement covered only the specifically described molds or whether it also covered other machinery and tools of the Debtor. If it were held to apply to other machinery and tools, could one identify which articles of machinery and tools were covered? See In re Sarex Corp., 509 F.2d 689 (2d Cir.1975).

## 4. AFTER-ACQUIRED COLLATERAL

Under Article 9 a security interest may not only apply to the collateral the debtor owns at the time the security interest is granted but also to later-acquired collateral. Under 9–204(a) no new security agreement is necessary when the collateral is acquired later if the security agreement provides that it applies to after-acquired collateral. In transactions like inventory financing in which goods are sold and replaced, or accounts financing in which accounts are collected and replaced, it is important that the security agreement cover later-acquired inventory or accounts, lest the collateral liquidate over time leaving the secured creditor with a claim only to proceeds. In the usual inventory or accounts financing transactions the description of the collateral will include a phrase like "now owned or hereafter acquired." When the parties have left out after-acquired property clauses in situations like inventory or accounts financing transactions in which it is likely that they intended to include them, the courts have been divided on whether to imply them. The drafters of Revised Article 9 decided to take no position on this issue: "This question is one of contract interpretation and is not susceptible to a statutory rule (other than a rule to the effect that it is a question of contract interpretation). Accordingly, this section contains no reference to descriptions of after-acquired collateral." Comment 3 to 9–108. Hence, pre-revision case law is still guiding precedent. The following case inventories the authorities and takes the majority view of the case law on the issue.

# In re Filtercorp, Inc.

United States Court of Appeals, Ninth Circuit, 1998.
163 F.3d 570.

■ Schwarzer, Senior District Judge:

We must decide whether under Washington law a security agreement that grants an interest in "inventory" or "accounts receivable," without more, presumptively includes after-acquired inventory or accounts receivable. The bankruptcy court and Bankruptcy Appellate Panel (BAP) held that to secure after-acquired property, an express after-acquired property clause is required. We reverse, holding that Washington law would presume security interests in "inventory" and "accounts receivable" to include after-acquired property, absent evidence of intent to the contrary. Applying this rule to the security agreement at issue between Henry Paulman and Filtercorp, Inc., we hold that Paulman had a security interest in after-acquired accounts receivable, but not in after-acquired inventory because the security agreement demonstrated an intent to limit the inventory collateral by referencing an attached inventory listing.

\* \* \*

## I.  PAULMAN'S LOANS TO FILTERCORP, INC.

Filtercorp, Inc. was a Washington corporation which developed and distributed carbonated pads used in the food service industry to filter cooking oils. Beginning in November 1991, the company took out a series of loans from Paulman, an individual salesman, to help fund further development and meet large orders. The loans were short term, ranging from two to three months, and memorialized by promissory notes drafted by Paulman's attorney. The final note—the subject of this litigation—was a three-month note, executed on June 30, 1992, and due September 30, 1992.

The June 1992 note provided for the following security:

> This note is secured by 75,000 shares of Filter Corp. [sic] stock owned by Robin Bernard, the accounts receivable and inventory of Filter Corp. [sic] (See UCC–1 filing and attached inventory listing.) and John Gardner personally.

The parties never executed a separate security agreement. However, Paulman perfected his security interest by filing a UCC–1 financing statement on October 5, 1992. The UCC–1 statement identified the collateral as (1) accounts receivable and (2) materials inventory. Despite the note's reference to an inventory listing, none was ever attached to the note or the financing statement.

There is no contemporaneous evidence shedding light on whether the parties intended to secure after-acquired inventory or accounts receivable with the June 1992 note. In the course of this litigation, the parties presented conflicting versions of their intent. Paulman claimed that he and Filtercorp, Inc. understood the security interest to attach to future rather than presently-held inventory and accounts receivable so as not to interfere with the company's ability to raise additional capital. Hence, he did not attach the inventory listing. In contrast, Robin Bernard, President of Filtercorp, Inc., stated that in light of the short, three-month term of the loan he did not contemplate an ongoing security interest.

\* \* \*

## III. SUMMARY JUDGMENT RULING ON PAULMAN'S SECURITY INTEREST

\* \* \*

### A. Principles Governing Security Interests in Inventory and Accounts Receivable

Whether a security agreement creates a lien on particular assets is a question of state law. See Butner v. United States, 440 U.S. 48, 55, 99 S.Ct. 914, 59 L.Ed.2d 136 (1979). Because no reported decisions of Washington courts or federal courts interpreting Washington law have answered the question whether a security agreement that grants an interest in "inventory" or "accounts receivable," without more, extends to after-acquired property, we must determine how Washington's highest court would resolve the issue. \* \* \*

Whether security interests in "inventory" presumptively include after-acquired property under Washington law came before us in Stoumbos v. Kilimnik, 988 F.2d 949, 954–56 (9th Cir.1993). We acknowledged the existence of a split of authority on whether a security interest in inventory or receivables automatically extended to after-acquired inventory or receivables despite the absence of an after-acquired property clause, but, on the facts of the case, did not have to decide the issue. See *id.* at 955–56. We now hold that if the issue came before the Washington Supreme Court, it would hold that security interests in "inventory" and "accounts receivable" presumptively include after-acquired inventory and receivables, subject to rebuttal by evidence that the parties intended otherwise.

Courts disagree over what terms are required in a security agreement to cover after-acquired inventory and accounts receivable. A minority of jurisdictions require express language evidencing the parties' intent to cover after-acquired inventory or accounts receivable. See, e.g., In re Middle Atl. Stud Welding Co., 503 F.2d 1133, 1135–36 (3d Cir.1974) (applying Delaware law) \* \* \*. These courts view the Uniform Commercial Code provision concerning after-acquired property, U.C.C. § 9–204, as contemplating express after-acquired property clauses. \* \* \* They reason that it is "neither onerous nor unreasonable to require a security agreement to make clear its intended collateral." Middle Atlantic, 503 F.2d at 1136. To do so simplifies the interpretation of security agreements and provides more precise notice to third parties of the extent of a perfected security interest in the debtor's property. See *id.* (noting that a "subsequent lender might expect the parties to make explicit an intention to include this kind of property, both for precision and because of the [pre-U.C.C.] law's historic hostility" to floating liens). In these jurisdictions, a grant of a security interest in "inventory" or "accounts receivable," without more, is insufficient to include after-acquired property.

However, we find more persuasive the contrary position, adopted by the majority of jurisdictions, that a security interest in inventory or accounts receivables presumptively includes an interest in after-acquired inventory or accounts receivables, respectively. * * * The rationale for this position rests on the unique nature of inventory and accounts receivable as "cyclically depleted and replenished assets." Stoumbos, 988 F.2d at 956; * * * Because inventory and accounts receivable are constantly turning over, "no creditor could reasonably agree to be secured by an asset that would vanish in a short time in the normal course of business." Stoumbos, 988 F.2d at 955. * * * Essentially, a floating lien on inventory and accounts receivable is presumed because the collateral is viewed in aggregate as a shifting body of assets. * * *

Commentators support the majority position. See, e.g., * * * Barkley Clark, The Law of Secured Transactions Under the Uniform Commercial Code & 2.09 [5][b] at 2–98 n. 338 (1993) ("The best rule for the courts is to excuse any reference to after-acquired property in the financing statement, but to draw the line in the security agreement according to real expectations in the commercial world; inventory, accounts, and farm products should not require inclusion of after-acquired property clauses in the security agreement, while equipment or general intangibles should."). * * *

* * *

[T]he majority of courts and commentators reason that the presumption of a floating lien on inventory and accounts receivable is not created by particular language but rather springs from an appreciation of the cyclical nature of the collateral itself. * * *

* * *

The presumption that a grant of a security interest in inventory or accounts receivable includes after-acquired property is of course rebuttable. For example, the presumption would be overcome where the security agreement language itself manifests an intent to limit the collateral to specific identified property, where a party presents clear evidence of contemporaneous intent to limit the collateral, or where the debtor can demonstrate that it was engaged in a type of business where the named collateral, whether inventory or receivables, does not regularly turn over so that the rationale for the presumption does not apply. * * *

We conclude that were the issue to come before the Washington Supreme Court, it would hold that after-acquired collateral is presumptively covered by a security agreement referencing "inventory" or "accounts receivable." Because Washington has recognized that "the Uniform Commercial Code was promulgated in order to develop uniformity in commercial transactions," Schroeder v. Fageol Motors, Inc., 86 Wash.2d 256, 544

P.2d 20, 24 (Wash.1975) (en banc), it can be expected to follow the rule adopted by a majority of the jurisdictions that have addressed the issue and that conforms to commercial practice and common sense.

### B.   Security Agreement Between Paulman and Filtercorp

Applying the foregoing analysis to the security agreement between Paulman and Filtercorp, we reach different results with respect to accounts receivable and inventory. The note (which serves as the security agreement) states that it was secured by "the accounts receivable and inventory of Filter Corp. [sic] (see UCC–1 filing and attached inventory listing.)." While the presumption that after-acquired property is included stands unrebutted as to accounts receivable, it is rebutted for inventory by the reference to the attached inventory listing.

Under the approach we adopt, the reference to "accounts receivable" presumptively includes after-acquired accounts receivable. The bankruptcy court found the opposing declarations of Paulman and Filtercorp, Inc.'s President as to their contemporaneous intent to be inconclusive. That finding of fact is not clearly erroneous. There is no other evidence of intent in the record. Therefore, we hold that Paulman has a security interest in after-acquired accounts receivable of Filtercorp. That security interest was perfected when Paulman filed a UCC–1 financing statement before other creditors and before Filtercorp filed for bankruptcy.

With respect to the security interest in inventory, the note referenced an "attached inventory listing" which, however, was never attached to either the note or the financing statement. Paulman claims that he did not attach the listing because he agreed with Filtercorp, Inc.'s President Bernard to create a security interest in inventory in general, including after-acquired inventory. Bernard, in contrast, claims that after-acquired inventory was never discussed by the parties prior to entering into the loan agreement and that he did not intend to attach after-acquired property given the short term nature of the loans. The bankruptcy court's finding that this conflicting evidence is inconclusive is not clearly erroneous. Thus, we are left with the language of the note itself.

When, as in this case, a security interest in inventory is described by reference to a list, it suggests an intent to limit the collateral rather than cover inventory as a floating mass including after-acquired inventory. * * * Yet, reference to an attached list does not preclude securing after-acquired collateral when the agreement or the listing demonstrate an intent to do so. * * *

Here, the Paulman–Filtercorp note referenced an inventory listing, which rebuts the presumption that after-acquired inventory is attached, and failed to demonstrate any particular intent to cover after-acquired inventory. The note's ambiguity regarding the security interest in inventory must be construed against Paulman, the drafter of the note. * * * We conclude that Paulman does not have a security interest in after-acquired inventory of Filtercorp.

Accordingly, we reverse the summary judgment with respect to Paulman's lien on accounts receivable, including after-acquired accounts receivable, of Filtercorp, and affirm with respect to his lien on inventory.

\* \* \*

## 5.   Proceeds

We will have much to say about proceeds elsewhere in this book. For the purpose of our discussion of the security agreement, it is sufficient to make two points: (1) Article 9 continues the rule that the description of collateral in the security agreement automatically covers proceeds; and (2) the definition of "proceeds" in 9–102(a)(64) significantly expands the scope of the definition.

Revised Article 9 continues the assumption of former Article 9 that the parties intend that the security agreement cover proceeds unless otherwise agreed. Taken together, 9–203(f) and 9–315(a)(2) provide that a security interest that has attached to collateral automatically attaches to any identifiable proceeds of the collateral. Thus, the description of collateral in a security agreement need say nothing about proceeds. Although this is entirely clear under Article 9, in many descriptions of collateral that will cross your desk, there will be a specific reference to proceeds. It's easy to do and drafters are always concerned about independent minded federal courts that may be somewhat selective in their application of state law to bankruptcy.

The definition of proceeds has always been a work in progress: as new issues have arisen the definition has been amended to resolve them. In the 1972 version of Article 9, the term "proceeds" was limited to whatever was received when collateral was "sold, exchanged, collected or otherwise disposed of." "Collected" refers to payments received by the debtor from obligors on accounts or other rights to payment. In other cases, the emphasis on disposition of collateral left many unanswered questions. For example, are insurance proceeds from loss or damage to collateral covered? What about dividends from investment securities? At the time of the original draft of Article 9, equipment and consumer goods leasing were far less popular than they now are, and disputes arose over whether leasing of the collateral was a disposition that gave the secured creditor rights in the rental payments. Similar problems arose with respect to the royalties arising from licensing of intellectual property. A 1994 amendment to Article 9 answered some of these questions, by providing that "proceeds" includes payment or distributions made with respect to investment property collateral (see former 9–306(2)). Dividend distributions therefore clearly are proceeds. However, former Article 9's definition still left uncertain the status of insurance, lease and royalty payments.

Revised 9–102(a)(64) is the latest expansion of the definition of "proceeds." It broadens the scope of the term in two ways. First, Revised Article 9's definition eliminates the former restriction that the debtor receive what is yielded from the disposition of the collateral. Second, it broadens the scope of the term. As under former Article 9, "proceeds" includes what is "acquired upon the sale, lease, license, exchange, or other disposition of collateral." 9–102(a)(64)(A). It also includes cash or stock dividends are covered by whatever is "distributed on account of, collateral." 9–102(a)(64)(B). Claims arising from loss or damage to the collateral are covered by 9–102(a)(64)(D). Insurance payments arising from such loss or damage also are "proceeds" to the extent of the value of the collateral. 9–102(a)(64)(E); see Steven Walt, When Are Insurance Payments Recoverable Proceeds Under Revised Article 9?, 38 U.C.C. L. J. 159 (2005). The expanded scope of "proceeds" means that dispositions of collateral whose status previously was uncertain now are covered by the term.

The definition of proceeds in former versions of Article 9 included whatever is received from the disposition, etc., of "collateral or proceeds." Perhaps it was a little confusing to see a definition of proceeds that included the word "proceeds," the very term being defined. But all the reference to proceeds in the definition was intended do was to make sure that the term covered not only first generation proceeds, e.g., the cash the debtor received when it sold inventory, but also later generation proceeds, e.g., new inventory the debtor received that was purchased by the cash. The new inventory was the proceeds of proceeds. Revised Article 9 takes a different approach by defining "collateral" to include proceeds. 9–102(a)(12)(A). Hence, in the above case, the cash realized from the sale of the original inventory is "proceeds." When the new inventory is purchased with the cash, both the original collateral and the cash are considered "collateral," and the new inventory "proceeds." So, as under former Article 9, the final-generation proceeds are considered "proceeds" under Revised Article 9. Earlier generations of proceeds are considered "collateral" under 9–102(a)(12)(A). Comment 13c. to 9–102 recognizes this and states: "No change in meaning is intended." Note, however, an important qualification: security interests in collateral attach only to "identifiable proceeds," 9–315(a)(2), and, as we will see later, identifying second generation proceeds, much less succeeding generations, is problematic.

Some assets are backed or "supported" by other assets. Their value is enhanced by the assets supporting them. For instance, guarantees frequently are issued to back account receivables. The guarantees increase the accounts' value because the obligee of the account can obtain payment on the accounts from the guarantor if the account debtors refuse to pay. Accordingly, when the supported assets are used as collateral, assets which back or support them increase the value of the supported assets. Supporting assets are credit-enhancement devices: they reduce loss to the creditor when the debtor defaults and the supported collateral is insufficient to satisfy the outstanding debt. Guarantees are common types of credit-enhancement devices. Participants in the markets for particular types of assets typically understand that these assets are often backed by various sorts of credit-enhancements. Section 9–102(a)(77) defines a "supporting obligation" to include letter-of-credit rights or secondary obligations, such as guarantees, which support the payment or perfection of specified rights to payment, such as accounts. And 9–203(f) provides that a security interest that attaches to collateral automatically attaches to obligations supporting the collateral. Thus, Revised Article 9 treats supporting obligations in the same way it treats proceeds. Comment 9 to 9–203 states that the same treatment of supporting obligations was "implicit" under former Article 9.

## PROBLEMS

**1.** Debtor pledged stock with Creditor. When Debtor's stock became worthless, Debtor sued the promoters of the stock for security fraud and recovered a sum of money almost equaling the market value of the stock at the time the stock was pledged. Creditor claimed the money as proceeds as a substitute for the stock, but Debtor objected on the ground that there was no disposition of the stock. Under the definition of proceeds under former 9–306(1), courts were divided on this issue. Compare McGonigle v. Combs, 968 F.2d 810 (9th Cir.1992) (amount recovered was proceeds), with McDannold v. Star Bank, N.A., 261 F.3d 478 (6th Cir.2001) (not proceeds). How would this be decided under 9–102(a)(64)?

**2.** Debtor is the named beneficiary on a letter of credit ("LC1") that undertakes to pay it a fixed sum of money. The issuance of LC1 was unrelated to Debtor's sales activities. Debtor also is owed payment from a number of customers for goods it sold them. Guarantor has agreed to pay Debtor amounts owed it by these customers if they fail to pay Debtor. In order to maintain Debtor's high credit rating, Bank issues a letter of credit ("LC2") undertaking to pay Debtor in the event neither Guarantor nor Debtor's customers pay it. Debtor grants Creditor a security interest in its right in "all account receivables, existing or hereafter acquired, arising from its sales of goods." Does Creditor's security interest attach to Guarantor's obligation? To Debtor's rights to payment under LC1 and LC2? See 9–102(a)(51), (77), 9–203(f).

## 6.   VALUE AND RIGHTS IN COLLATERAL

### a.   VALUE

Under 9–203(b), a security interest does not attach in collateral until value has been given and the debtor has rights in the collateral. In the simple case, the secured party gives value in a loan transaction when it makes the loan and in credit sales when it makes the sale. This is value under 1–204(4): "any consideration sufficient to support a simple contract." It is also "new value" under 9–102(a)(57) as money, property or new credit given up front. We will see later that new value plays a role in Article 9, e.g., 9–330, but, for the purpose of attachment of a security interest, all that we are interested in is the general definition of value in 1–204. Under 1–204(2), a creditor gives value by taking a security interest "for, or in total or partial satisfaction of, a preexisting claim." The importance of this provision to the operation of the "floating lien" in inventory and accounts financing is seen in the elementary Problem below.

PROBLEM

Debtor, a wholesale furniture dealer, entered into a revolving credit agreement with Bank, under which Bank made advances to Debtor from time to time, which Debtor used to purchase new inventory. Debtor and Bank entered into a written security agreement, signed by Debtor, in which Debtor granted Bank a security interest in all its inventory and accounts, now owned or thereafter acquired (9–204(a)), to secure all present indebtedness and future advances (9–204(c)). On January 1, Debtor owed Bank $1 million; Bank made no further advances to Debtor. On February 1, Debtor received a shipment of inventory from Manufacturer for which Debtor paid cash. Does Bank have a security interest in the February shipment of furniture that is enforceable against Debtor under 9–203? If so, when did it attach?

### b. RIGHTS IN COLLATERAL

Under 9–203(b)(2), a security interest does not attach unless the debtor has "rights in the collateral or the power to transfer rights in the collateral." As far as the phrase "rights in the collateral" goes, 9–203(b)(2) may be stating only the obvious. The phrase is not defined, and it is doubtful if any precise definition is possible. In the usual case, due diligence will show that the debtor owns the collateral outright and there is no issue of rights in collateral. In the fraud case in which the debtor is a thief who stole the collateral, the secured party whose diligence failed to discover the debtor's deception takes the loss.

However, the rights-in-collateral concept goes far beyond the simple full title/no title cases in at least two respects. First, under 9–203(b)(2), a debtor may have rights in collateral in cases in which it has less than the full bundle of ownership rights in the collateral. Comment 6 to 9–203 explains that: "A debtor's limited rights in collateral, short of full ownership, are sufficient for a security interest to attach * * * to whatever rights a debtor may have, broad or limited as those rights may be." For instance, a lessee of personal property doesn't "own" the leased property but may create a security interest in its valuable rights under the lease. Second, 9–203(b)(2) goes beyond this by allowing a security interest to attach when the debtor has the "power to transfer rights in collateral to a secured party." As the subsection recognizes, the debtor need not actually have rights in the collateral; it need only have the power to transfer rights. Comment 6 says that this language enables a "debtor to transfer, and a security interest to attach to, greater rights than the debtor has."

What body of law tells us when persons have "power" to transfer rights in collateral? What body of law tells us when persons can transfer greater rights than they have? If you were to go through the many decisions, you would probably conclude that debtors can exercise this power through any of the traditional bodies of law mentioned in 1–103(b), which states that "the principles of law and equity, including the law merchant and the law relative to the capacity to contract, principal and agent, estoppel, fraud, misrepresentation, duress, coercion, mistake, bankruptcy, and other validating or invalidating cause" may supplement the provisions of the UCC. Another source of this power may be found in specific provisions of the Code, as in *Swets* that follows. One bit of guidance we find in the Code is that under 1–201(b)(29) and (30) a secured party enjoys the status of a "purchaser;" hence, provisions like 2–403(1) that grant purchasers greater rights than their transferors apply to benefit secured parties.

The rights-in-collateral issue is significantly involved in the priority matters treated in a later chapter, and we will have more to say about it in that context.

## Swets Motor Sales, Inc. v. Pruisner

Supreme Court of Iowa, 1975.
236 N.W.2d 299.

■ REES, JUSTICE.

Plaintiff Swets Motor Sales, Inc., appeals from an order of trial court sustaining motion for summary judgment of defendant Chrysler Credit Corporation and therein adjudicating the latter's interest in certain automobiles to be superior to the interest of plaintiff. We affirm in part, reverse in part, and remand for appropriate proceedings in conformity with this opinion.

Plaintiff Swets Motor Sales, Inc., (hereinafter Swets), an Illinois automobile "wholesaler," sold used cars and trucks to defendant Pruisner, a retail automobile dealer at Waverly. Pursuant to an oral arrangement, plaintiff delivered vehicles to defendant Pruisner with unencumbered certificates of title and was paid by Pruisner at the time of delivery of the cars. Chrysler Credit Corporation, joined as a defendant in this action, financed defendant Pruisner's inventory under a floor planning arrangement which the parties have stipulated was a valid security agreement with filed financing statements covering new and used vehicles in Pruisner's possession.

From July 1973 until the end of September of the same year, Swets sold to Pruisner approximately 60 vehicles which were resold by Pruisner under the foregoing arrangement. In September 1973 four of Pruisner's checks written to plaintiff Swets, totaling approximately $31,000, were dishonored. Swets filed his petition at law and obtained a writ of attachment for the seizure of the vehicles then in Pruisner's possession, then amended his petition to an action sounding in equity, seeking a declaration that his interest in the automobiles was superior to that of Chrysler Credit Corporation. Chrysler Credit answered and counterclaimed against Swets, asserting therein that its interest in the vehicles was superior to that of plaintiff. It was stipulated that at the time of the issuance of the writ of attachment Chrysler Credit had in its possession the unencumbered titles to the vehicles in question.

Trial of the action commenced January 18, 1974, and on January 21, apparently after a substantial portion of the evidence had been presented, defendant Chrysler Credit moved for a summary judgment on the issue of priority of its security interest. Swets thereafter filed a resistance to such motion, alleging the existence of genuine issues of material fact regarding the possibility that, through fraud or mutual mistake, Swets' contract with Pruisner might be determined to be void. Swets also alleged the existence of genuine issues of material fact with respect to the proper valuation of the vehicles in question and Chrysler Credit's failure to minimize or mitigate damages.

On January 24 trial court sustained Chrysler Credit's motion for summary judgment and made various findings of fact and reached conclusions of law. In its findings of fact pertinent to this appeal was the trial court's determination the value of the attached vehicles was $9,300 at the date of the attachment and $5,100 on the date of the hearing. Trial court concluded as a matter of law that defendant Chrysler Credit Corporation had a right to assume defendant Pruisner's ownership of the vehicles in question from the latter's possession of unencumbered certificates of title. Trial court also concluded UCC § 2–403 precluded Swets from prevailing.

Accordingly, trial court decreed Chrysler Credit was entitled to possession of the vehicles under attachment and held valid title to them [with the exception of a certain Ford Torino automobile with which we are not concerned]. Trial court further found and adjudged the difference between the sum of $9,300 [which the court had determined to be the value of the vehicles at the time of attachment] and the subsequent sales price of the vehicles should be assessed against plaintiff Swets and paid out of its attachment bond.

\* \* \*

It was stipulated by the parties to this action that defendant Chrysler Credit Corporation had a valid outstanding security agreement with defendant Pruisner covering new and used vehicles in the latter's possession at all times pertinent to the action. The Uniform Commercial Code provides the resolution of the priority problem in this case. Section 2–403 provides in pertinent part:

> "1. A purchaser of goods acquires all title which his transferor had or had power to transfer except that a purchaser of a limited interest acquires rights only to the extent of the interest purchased. A person with voidable title has power to transfer a good title to a good faith purchaser for value. When goods have been delivered under a transaction of purchase the purchaser has such power even though
>
> " \* \* \*
>
> "b. the delivery was in exchange for a check which is later dishonored, \* \* \*."

The above section of the Uniform Commercial Code indicates that despite the fact Pruisner tendered, for the purchase of the vehicles, a check which was subsequently dishonored, he could, nonetheless, transfer good title to a "good faith purchaser for value."

"Good faith" is defined in the Uniform Commercial Code as "honesty in fact in the conduct or transaction concerned." Section 1–201(19). Plaintiff did not, and does not now, present any factual question as to the good faith of defendant Chrysler Credit, whose security interest under the floor planning scheme predated the execution and delivery to plaintiff of the dishonored checks.

A purchaser is defined by section 1–201(33) as "a person who takes by purchase." Section 1–201(32) defines "purchase" as including "taking by sale, discount, negotiation, mortgage, pledge, lien, issue or reissue, gift or any other voluntary transaction creating an interest in property."

Section 1–201(44)(b) provides that a person gives "value" for rights if he acquires them "as security for or in total or partial satisfaction of a pre-existing claim." From the above definitions it is abidingly clear that we must conclude defendant Chrysler Credit acted in good faith and "gave value." It is equally clear that a secured party under Article 9 of the Uniform Commercial Code (§ 9–105(1)(i)) is a "purchaser" within the meaning of § 1–201(33) above. The central contention of Swets, however, is that if his contract with Pruisner were affected by fraud or mutual mistake, defendant Chrysler Credit would not be a secured party with respect to the vehicles in question in this case.

In support of this contention Swets directs our attention to § 9–204(1) [§ 9–203(1)] which provides that a security interest cannot attach until there is agreement that it attach and value is given and the debtor has rights in the collateral. Swets argues that if the purchase by Pruisner was accomplished as a result of fraud or mutual mistake, Pruisner would have no "rights" in the collateral and, consequently, defendant Chrysler Corporation would be neither a secured party nor a purchaser. We find this contention to be without merit.

Particularly pertinent to our conclusion in this regard is our decision in Herington Livestock Auction Company v. Verschoor, 179 N.W.2d 491 (Iowa 1970). In *Herington* plaintiff had sold 84 head of cattle to a speculator, using an invoice which provided on its face: "The purchaser agrees that title of stock listed above shall be retained by us until check or draft in payment of same is paid." The speculator, in turn, delivered the cattle to defendant who, acting on the speculator's directions, sold them and tendered a check to the latter. Subsequently plaintiff was not paid for the cattle by the speculator, and brought an action against defendant for conversion. After a motion for judgment notwithstanding verdict had been resolved adversely to plaintiff, he appealed, claiming title to the cattle had not passed to the speculator, due to the reservation in the invoice.

We affirmed in *Herington*, holding that plaintiff seller could at most have reserved only a security interest in the cattle. Pertinent to our disposition of the appeal was Code section 2–401(2) which provides in material part:

"Unless otherwise explicitly agreed title passes to the buyer at the time and place at which the seller completes his performance with reference to the physical delivery of the goods, despite any reservation of a security interest * * *.''

In the matter before us here plaintiff did not even reserve a security interest in the vehicles in question. At the time of the delivery of the vehicles, Pruisner acquired sufficient rights in the same to permit Chrysler Credit Corporation's security interest to attach.

An almost identical analysis was employed by the Supreme Court of Nebraska under identical Uniform Commercial Code provisions in Jordan v. Butler, 182 Neb. 626, 156 N.W.2d 778, a case involving the respective rights of a defrauded initial seller and a subsequent good faith purchaser for value.

We also note that when goods have been delivered under a transaction of purchase the purchaser has power to transfer good title to a subsequent good faith purchaser for value even though the original delivery was procured through fraud punishable as larcenous under the criminal law. Section 2–403(1)(d).

\* \* \*

In summary, we conclude and hold:

(1) Trial court was correct in sustaining motion for summary judgment of defendant Chrysler Credit Corporation insofar as it sought an adjudication that its interest in the automobiles in question was senior and superior to plaintiff's claim of ownership thereto.

(2) Trial court erred in failing to find there was a genuine issue of material fact regarding the value of the automobiles at time of attachment of same, and accordingly erred in fixing the value of the cars at $9,300.

We therefore affirm trial court in its findings, conclusions and decree adjudicating the rights of plaintiff Swets in the automobiles in question to be junior and inferior to the claim of ownership of defendant Chrysler Credit Corporation. We reverse the judgment of trial court relative to the value of the vehicles and remand for further hearing and determination of the value of the same. * * *

Affirmed in part, reversed in part and remanded for further proceedings.

NOTE

In American Bank & Trust v. Shaull, 678 N.W.2d 779 (S.D. 2004), Shaull operated a livestock auction barn and bought and sold cattle. He obtained a substantial loan from American Bank (''Bank'') secured by a security interest in a herd of approximately 900 cattle maintained on land leased by Shaull. Bank filed a financing statement covering the livestock. Before making the loan, Bank investigated Shaull's finances (financial statement, tax return and the like), did a record search and spoke with Shaull's previous financer. Bank also inspected the herd and was led by

Shaull to believe that Shaull owned the cattle. When Shaull defaulted, Bank claimed a valid first security interest in the herd, only to learn that Feldman, who operated a cattle feeder business, owned the herd, which he had entrusted to Shaull under a feeding and care agreement. Since Feldman was the owner-bailor of the cattle, there is no requirement in Article 9 that a financing statement be filed to protect his interest, and he had not filed one. Feldman challenged Bank's security interest on the ground that Shaull lacked rights in the collateral under § 9–203(b)(2). The court held that Feldman was estopped from claiming that Shaull lacked sufficient rights in the cattle for a security interest to attach; under South Dakota precedents, control rather than ownership of collateral determines a debtor's rights to collateral. It quoted from a previous supreme court opinion: "If the owner of collateral allows another to appear as owner or to dispose of the collateral, such that a third party is led into dealing with the apparent owner as though he were the actual owner, then the owner will be estopped from asserting that the apparent owner did not have rights in the collateral." First National Bank of Omaha v. Pleasant Hollow Farm, Inc., 532 N.W.2d 60, 63 (S.D. 1995). Is there any basis in the UCC for such a holding? See 1–103(b). Is a bailor required to give public notice of bailment interest? What could Feldman have done to protect his interest in the cattle?

# CHAPTER 2

# PERFECTION

## A. INTRODUCTION

If a security interest has attached, it is enforceable against the debtor (9–203(b)) and unsecured creditors (9–201(a)). However, for a security interest to have the most favorable status with respect to third party claimants, such as other secured parties, buyers and lien creditors, it must be perfected. "Perfection" is a legal conclusion indicating that a security interest is enforceable against a third party. It is somewhat misleading to say that a security interest that has attached but has not been perfected is enforceable against unsecured creditors. The statement is true only outside of bankruptcy. In bankruptcy unperfected security interests can be avoided by the debtor's bankruptcy trustee, who represents the unsecured creditors. As we saw in the previous chapter, under BC 544(a) the trustee in bankruptcy has the rights of a hypothetical lien creditor, and under 9–317(a)(2) an unperfected security interest is generally subordinate to the rights of a lien creditor. If the security interest is avoided in bankruptcy, the former secured party is demoted to the status of an unsecured creditor and must share the assets of the estate pro rata with the other unsecured creditors.

In sections 9–308 through 9–316, Article 9 offers detailed guidelines for how security interests are perfected. A summary follows; we will discuss each of these methods in this chapter.

(1) Attachment. Section 9–309 sets out the cases in which security interests are automatically perfected when they attach. For instance, the traditional rule that purchase money security interests in consumer goods require no filing is continued in 9–309(1). If a retailer retains a security interest in goods sold to a consumer, its un-filed security interest is good as against other secured parties and trustees in bankruptcy, but not against a subsequent consumer who buys the property from the first consumer. 9–320(b). A garage or yard sale comes to mind.

(2) Possession. The oldest form of security interest in personal property is the "pledge," in which the secured party takes possession of the collateral. Section 9–313(a) states that possession of the collateral by the secured party constitutes perfection with respect to goods, instruments (promissory notes, checks) negotiable documents (bills of lading, warehouse receipts), chattel paper (leases of personal property, sales contracts reserving a security interest), money (currency) and certificated securities (stocks, bonds). What these types of collateral have in common is that they are capable of being possessed. Goods and money are tangible items of collater-

al. Instruments, chattel paper, and certificated securities are rights to payment that are represented by writings whose delivery operates to transfer the rights to payment to another. These writings represent the rights to payment. Negotiable documents represent rights to goods being shipped or stored. 9–312(c). Both instruments and negotiable documents are semi-intangible items of collateral, and they too can be possessed. Items of collateral such as general intangibles and accounts are not represented by essential writings. As pure intangibles, security interests in them cannot be perfected by possession.

(3) Control. Revised Article 9 expands the role of perfection by control present in former Article 9. In general, "control" is the ability to dispose of collateral unilaterally, without the cooperation of the debtor. See Comments 1 and 7 to 8–106. Where perfection by control is permitted for an item of collateral, the means of obtaining control are specifically defined. Control is a permissible method of perfection for letter-of-credit rights, investment property, electronic chattel paper, and deposit accounts. 9–314(a). For some items of collateral, control is the exclusive method of perfection. For example, under 9–312(b)(1), the only method of perfecting a security interest in a deposit account (checking or savings accounts maintained with a bank) as *original collateral* is by control. "As explained in Section 9–104, 'control' can arise as a result of an agreement among the secured party, debtor, and bank, whereby the bank agrees to comply with instructions of the secured party with respect to disposition of the funds on deposit, even though the debtor retains the right to direct disposition of the funds." Comment 5 to 9–312. But if the funds added to a deposit account are *proceeds*, a security interest perfected in those proceeds by other means follows into the account to the extent the proceeds are traceable. 9–315.

(4) Compliance with other law. Section 9–311 provides that security interests subject to other law can be perfected only in compliance with that law; filing under Article 9 is neither necessary nor effective. For instance, security interests in motor vehicles are perfected by notation of the lien on the certificate of title pursuant to the state vehicle code. 9–311(a)(2). Security interests in registered copyrights must be recorded in the Copyright Office in Washington D.C. 9–311(a)(1). Compliance with these laws is the equivalent to filing under Article 9. 9–311(b).

(5) Filing. Section 9–310(a) sets out the basic rule that perfection must be by filing a financing statement. Section 9–310(b) enumerates the cases discussed above in which filing is not necessary to perfect a security interest. In most of the cases in which a security interest can be perfected by possession, it can also be perfected by filing: goods, instruments, negotiable documents, chattel paper, and certificated securities. 9–312(a). But security interests in money can be perfected only by possession, owing to the negotiability of currency. 9–312(b)(3). Before Revised Article 9, the same was true of instruments, but, for the reasons set out in Comment 2 to 9–312, the drafters chose to allow perfection by filing even though instruments are highly negotiable: purchasers for value who take possession of an instrument without knowledge of a security interest in the instrument

usually take free of a security interest perfected by filing. Security interests in accounts and payment intangibles can be perfected only by filing.

In the course of this chapter, we will examine these methods of perfection in detail. The following illustrative Problem presents the sequence of events involved in perfecting a security interest.

## PROBLEM

On September 1, Debtor (D) requested a loan from Secured Party (SP). After examining D's financial condition, SP agreed to make the loan. D signed a security agreement on September 3 covering certain described collateral of D. On that date SP initiated a search of the records in the state filing office, and, when it discovered that no other financing statements were on record, it filed its financing statement on September 5 and advanced the requested funds to D on September 6. When did SP's security interest attach? When was SP's security interest perfected? See 9–308(a), 9–502(d). Assume that D purchased an asset on September 6 covered by the collateral description in SP's filed financing statement. When was SP's security interest in it perfected?

## B.   PERFECTION BY FILING

### 1.   NOTICE FILING

Reform of the filing system was one of the most important contributions of the 1962 version of Article 9 to personal property financing, and Revised Article 9 has gone even further in improving the filing system. Before the UCC, filing with respect to chattel mortgage and conditional sale transactions followed the archaic patterns set by real estate mortgage recordings: the chattel mortgage document or the conditional sale contract was recorded in the local county recorder's office. Under Revised Article 9, we now have a regime under which *notice filing* and *central filing* are fully operative. Notice filing means that the only record filed is a financing statement that merely gives notice that a security interest may exist in the debtor's collateral. Turn to 9–521(a) and examine the UCC Financing Statement Form (UCC 1), the written initial financing statement form. The 1962 version of Article 9 struggled for a system of central filing but fell short in a number of respects. In 9–501(a)(2), Revised Article 9 fully achieved the goal of central filing in most instances.

The Article 9 filing system has two purposes: to allow the filing party to establish a priority in the debtor's collateral and to provide information to the searching party about security interests in this property. It has been reasonably successful in serving the first of these purposes, but less so with respect to the second. The authoritative statement on notice filing is found in Comment 2 to 9–502:

This section adopts the system of "notice filing." What is required to be filed is not, as under pre-UCC chattel mortgage and conditional sales acts, the security agreement itself, but only a simple record providing a limited amount of information (financing statement). The financing statement may be filed before the security interest attaches or thereafter. See subsection (d). See also Section 9–308(a) (contemplating situations in which a financing statement is filed before a security interest attaches).

The notice itself indicates merely that a person may have a security interest in the collateral indicated. Further inquiry from the parties concerned will be necessary to disclose the complete state of affairs. Section 9–210 provides a statutory procedure under which the secured party, at the debtor's request, may be required to make disclosure. However, in many cases, information may be forthcoming without the need to resort to the formalities of that section.

Notice filing has proved to be of great use in financing transactions involving inventory, accounts and chattel paper, because it obviates the necessity of refiling on each of a series of transactions in a continuing arrangement under which the collateral changes from day to day. However, even in the case of filings that do not necessarily involve a series of transactions (e.g., a loan secured by a single item of equipment), a financing statement is effective to encompass transactions under a security agreement not in existence and not contemplated at the time the notice was filed, if the indication of collateral in the financing statement is sufficient to cover the collateral concerned. Similarly, a financing statement is effective to cover after-acquired property of the type indicated and to perfect with respect to future advances under security agreements, regardless of whether after-acquired property or future advances are mentioned in the financing statement and even if not in the contemplation of the parties at the time the financing statement was authorized to be filed.

What is remarkable about Article 9's notice filing system is how little information the filer's financing statement discloses to searchers. The only public document in an Article 9 secured transaction is the financing statement. The security agreement is not open to public scrutiny. Unless the debtor or secured creditor is willing to allow a searcher to see the security agreement or to reveal to the searcher the details of the secured transaction, only the fragmentary statements in the financing statement are available to the searcher. See 9–210.

What is the justification for allowing secured parties to perfect a security interest in collateral by filing a public statement that gives searching parties so little information? If you were interested in a debtor's financial position, wouldn't you be interested in the amount of the credit the collateral secured, where the collateral is located, whether the creditor intended to make further advances, and so forth? The law of real estate mortgages typically requires the filing of the mortgage document, a detailed description of the mortgaged real estate, and in a number of jurisdictions requires a description of the debt secured. Because Article 9's notice filing system requires secured parties to provide far less information, searchers have to invest in acquiring the information from sources other than the filed records. The expense and delay of this off-record search may be great. The obvious source of information is the debtor, and if the debtor is seeking credit from the searcher, it can be expected to cooperate by showing the searcher the security agreement and other documents. But the searcher may not feel safe until it confirms the information with the secured creditor of record, who may have no incentive beyond business comity to make any disclosure to the searcher. If the searcher is a judgment creditor of the debtor who is looking for assets to seize to satisfy the judgment, not even the debtor is likely to be a willing source of information.

Section 9–210 is the only provision of Article 9 that addresses the informational deficiency facing a person searching the filing office records. Read that section and the Comment following and apply it to the following Problems.

## PROBLEMS

**1.** Debtor, Medicorp, operates a health maintenance organization (HMO) and contracts with a partnership of physicians, Doctors LLP, to provide the required medical services to members of the HMO. Medicorp is having financial problems. It has fallen $500,000 behind in its payments to Doctors, which has consulted your firm about collecting the money by a lawsuit against Medicorp. You have searched the UCC records and discovered a financing statement filed by Lender against Medicorp covering "medical equipment, proceeds thereof and replacements thereof." Doctors' personnel have informed you that they believe Lender financed Medicorp's purchase of some of the expensive diagnostic equipment used for patients. The financing statement indicates to you that Lender probably took purchase-money security interests in this equipment to secure Medicorp's loan. Doctors has no information about which items of equipment are covered by Lender's security interest or how much Medicorp owes on the loan. You need to have this information in order to evaluate the desirability of your client's initiation of a lawsuit against Medicorp. What help does 9–210 give you? What help would it give Medicorp if it were trying to ascertain the extent of Lender's claims against it?

**2.** In January Lender took a perfected security interest in all Debtor's personal property to secure the present advance of $1 million and all future advances made by Lender. In July Bank took a perfected security interest in the same collateral to secure an advance of $500,000. In doing so Bank relied on a statement of account (9–210(a)(4)) approved by Lender in July that Debtor owed Lender only $1 million. But in August Lender advanced another $500,000 to Debtor, which, as we will see later, under Article 9 priority rules, primed Bank's intervening security interest. 9–322 and 9–323. Bank contended that Lender's approval of the statement of account in July implied that it would not be making further advances to Debtor, otherwise 9–210 statements of account are misleading and worthless in any case in which the prior security interest covers future advances. Does Bank have a case?

## 2.   SUFFICIENCY OF FINANCING STATEMENT

Section 9–502(a) provides that a financing statement is "sufficient" only if it provides the names of the debtor and secured party or its representative (9–503), and indicates the collateral covered (9–504) by the financing statement. Section 9–520(c) states that if the financing statement contains this information, it is "effective." What does this mean? Article 9's answer is complicated.

The three basic requirements in 9–502(a) do not include some information that is important to the operation of a filing system, such as the addresses of the debtor and secured party, whether the debtor is an individual or an organization and, if the debtor is an organization, the type of organization and the jurisdiction in which it is organized. The UCC Financing Statement Form in 9–521(a) has spaces for all this information. Section 9–516(b)(5) provides that filing doesn't occur if the filing office refuses to accept a record that lacks this information; and 9–520(a) states that filing doesn't occur with respect to a record that a filing office rejects because it lacks this information. Thus, a financing statement is effective even if it does not include some of the information set out in 9–516(b)(5) so long as it meets the basic requirements of 9–502(a). Sections 9–516 and 9–520, taken together, effectively compel this additional information to be included in a financing statement by directing the filing officer in 9–520 to reject financing statements that don't comply with 9–516(b). Section 9–516(b), in turn, provides that filing doesn't occur with respect to a financing statement rejected by a filing office because the financing statement fails to set out, among other things, the information mentioned in the previous sentence. It is clear that if the financing statement doesn't contain the information stated in 9–516(b), the financing office can reject it and it doesn't become effective. What happens if the financing office accepts it without such information? See 9–516(a).

## PROBLEMS

**1.**  Debtor, Inc. (D) granted a security interest to Secured Party (SP) in business machinery, properly described in the security agreement. SP filed a written financing statement using the form set out in 9–521(a). The filing office accepted the financing statement and duly indexed it. Later D defaulted on its obligation to SP and filed in bankruptcy. T, D's trustee in bankruptcy, combed through D's case file in the hope of finding some basis for avoiding SP's security interest and discovered that although all the other relevant blanks in the form were properly filled in, SP had not entered the type of organization or any organizational ID for D. Can T avoid SP's security interest on the ground that it was not perfected?

**2.** Harold Kim (D), an individual, granted Lender a security interest in identified personal property. Lender filed a written financing statement using the form set out in 9–521(a) but filled in the mailing address of another Harold Kim. The filing office accepted the financing statement and duly indexed it. Later, after D had fallen into default on his loan transaction with Lender, he applied for a loan from Bank to finance a real property purchase. Bank's loan department made the loan because it confused D with the Harold Kim whose address was on the filed financing statement and whose credit report showed him to be an excellent credit risk. Bank contends that it would never have made the loan to D had it not been misled by the incorrect address. Does Bank have rights against Lender under 9–338?

# In re Hergert

United States Bankruptcy Court for the District of Idaho, 2002.
275 B.R. 58.

■ TERRY L. MYERS

.  .  .

## II.   RELEVANT FACTS

The Debtors' farming business was originally financed through Pacific One Bank ("Pacific"). As part of a merger in 1998, all of the assets of Pacific were acquired by the Bank.

These assets included three secured loans of the Debtors: (i) a commercial loan with an outstanding amount of principal, interest and late fees as of trial on January 8, 2002 of $182,051.68; (ii) a commercial loan with an outstanding amount of principal, interest and late fees as of January 8, 2002 of $51,595.44; and (iii) a consumer loan with an outstanding balance of $45,395.12 as of the Petition Date, August 9, 2001.

The two commercial loans are secured under an Agricultural Security Agreement and two Commercial Security Agreements. By their terms, these security agreements cross-collateralize the commercial loan obligations. The consumer loan is secured by an interest in the Debtors' manufactured home.

In connection with the Agricultural Security Agreement, and to perfect the security interest granted thereunder, Pacific filed a UCC–1F (farm products) financing statement. See Exhibit H. In connection with the Commercial Security Agreements, and to perfect the security interests described therein, Pacific filed a UCC–1 financing statement, Exhibit G, and obtained notation of its lien on certificates of title to several vehicles. In regard to the consumer loan, Pacific is shown as a lienholder on the certificate of title ("Title") to the Debtors' manufactured home.

Both the UCC–1 and the Title identify the secured party as "Pacific One Bank" with a mailing address of P.O. Box 40108, Portland, Oregon, 97240 (the "Portland Address"). The UCC–1 lists an additional address of

P.O. Box 9344, Nampa, Idaho 83652–9344 (the "Nampa Address") as the address to which the Secretary of State should return its "acknowledgment" copy of the filing.

The UCC–1F also identifies "Pacific One Bank" as the secured party, with the Nampa Address shown as the address of the secured party. The Debtors do not dispute that the names and addresses on the UCC–1 and UCC–1F were accurate when the documents were created and filed. *See* Pre-trial Stipulation, at p.2, P 6.[1]

After origination of the Debtors' loans, and before the chapter 12 filing, Pacific was merged into the Bank. The Bank has never amended the secured party's name or address(es) in any of the above-described documents.

The Bank has maintained and continues to use the Portland Address. The Bank has been receiving mail there since the merger, and today still is, even if the mail is addressed to Pacific.

At some point subsequent to the merger, the Nampa Address expired and the Bank no longer received mail there. This was the situation at the time of Debtors' chapter 12 petition on August 9, 2001. *See* Pre–Trial Stipulation, at p.3, P 9.

Ann Ybarguen, a special credits representative of the Bank, testified regarding this situation. The Nampa Address was for a post office box within the main building of the Karcher Mall, a retail shopping facility in Nampa, Idaho. Mail sent there after the Nampa Address had expired would be marked as undeliverable. Pacific's old physical address inside the Karcher Mall was also an invalid address. However, at times the local postman would take mail improperly addressed to Pacific's old physical address to the Bank's new physical location, which happened to be on a retail pad in the parking lot of the Karcher Mall. This method of delivery was inconsistent and unpredictable.

\* \* \*

### III.

### B.   The Commercial Loans

Idaho has repealed Idaho Code Title 28, Chapter 9 ("Old Article 9") and enacted a revised Chapter 9 of that Title ("New Article 9"). New Article 9 became effective on July 1, 2001 (the "Effective Date"). See revised I.C. § 28–9–702, compiler's notes.

\* \* \*

---

**1.** For additional clarity, the Court notes that the Debtors do not dispute the creation of security interests as described in the documents. Pre–Trial Stipulation, at p.2, P 4. Rather, the Debtors dispute only that the Bank's perfection remained valid at the Petition Date. In turn, this dispute relates solely to the issue regarding the accuracy of the names and addresses shown for the secured party on that date. No other issues concerning the sufficiency of the financing statements on the Petition Date are alleged.

### 3.   The UCC–1F

\* \* \*

### b.   New Article 9

To evaluate the effectiveness of the UCC–1F on the Effective Date, reference is first made to revised I.C. § 28–9–502, which establishes the prerequisites for effective financing statements. In pertinent part, it provides:

(a) Subject to subsection (b) of this section, a financing statement is sufficient only if it:

  (1) Provides the name of the debtor;

  (2) Provides the name of the secured party or a representative of the secured party; and

  (3) Indicates the collateral covered by the financing statement.

(b) Except as otherwise provided in section 28–9–501(b), to be sufficient, a financing statement that covers as-extracted collateral or timber to be cut, or which is filed as a fixture filing and covers goods that are or are to become fixtures, must satisfy subsection (a) of this section and also:

  (1) Indicate that it covers this type of collateral;

  (2) Indicate that it is to be filed in the real property records;

  (3) Provide a description of the real property to which the collateral is related sufficient to give constructive notice of a mortgage under the law of this state if the description were contained in a record of the mortgage of the real property; and

  (4) If the debtor does not have an interest of record in the real property, provide the name of a record owner.

. . .

(e) A financing statement covering farm products is sufficient if it contains the following information:

  (1) The name and address of the debtor;

  (2) The debtor's signature;

  (3) The name, address and signature of the secured party;

  (4) The social security number of the debtor, or in the case of a debtor doing business other than as an individual, the debtor's internal revenue service taxpayer identification number;

  (5) A description by category of the farm products subject to the security interest and the amount of such products, where applicable;

  (6) A reasonable description of the real estate where the farm products are produced or located. This provision may be satis-

fied by a designation of the county or counties, and a legal description is not required.

Under revised I.C. § 28–9–520(a), a filing officer shall refuse to accept a financing statement if it is not in compliance with revised I.C. § 28–9–516(b). Revised I.C. § 28–9–516(b)(4) indicates that a filing officer is entitled to reject a financing statement if it lacks a name or mailing address for the secured party. Revised I.C. § 28–9–516(b)(8) indicates that the filing officer may reject a farm products financing statement if it does not contain all the information specified in revised I.C. § 28–9–502(e) or conform to the official form of the Idaho secretary of state.

However, revised I.C. § 28–9–520(c) protects improper statements so long as they are in fact filed and contain certain essential information. That section states:

> A filed financing statement satisfying section 28–9–502(a) and (b) is effective, even if the filing office is required to refuse to accept it for filing under subsection (a) of this section.

Id.; see also, revised I.C. § 28–9–516, Official Comment 9 (Effectiveness of Rejectable but Unrejected Record); revised I.C. § 28–9–520, Official Comment 3 (Consequences of Accepting Rejectable Record).

Note that under revised I.C. § 28–9–520(c), the filed statement need only meet the requirements of subsections (a) and (b) of revised I.C. § 28–9–502 in order to benefit from the protection which actual filing affords. Unlike revised I.C. § 28–9–502(e), those two subsections do not contain a requirement for the secured party's address or signature, only its name. See revised I.C. § 28–9–502(a)(2).

## I.  NAME

The name of the secured party shown on the UCC–1F on the Effective Date was Pacific, not the Bank. To determine whether this is sufficient identification of the secured party, the Court looks to several provisions of New Article 9.

First, revised I.C. § 28–9–506 provides in part:

> (a) A financing statement substantially satisfying the requirements of this part is effective, even if it has minor errors or omissions, unless the errors or omissions make the financing statement seriously misleading.
>
> (b) Except as otherwise provided in subsection (c) of this section, a financing statement that fails to sufficiently provide the name of the debtor in accordance with section 28–9–503(a) is seriously misleading.

Subsection (b) makes a failure to sufficiently provide the name of the debtor a seriously misleading error. Negative inference would indicate that an error in the name of the secured party is not of the same magnitude. At a minimum, it is not automatically or *per se* seriously misleading.

Second, Official Comment 2 to revised I.C. § 28–9–506 states, in part:

In addition to requiring the debtor's name and an indication of the collateral, Section 9–502(a) requires a financing statement to provide the name of the secured party or a representative of the secured party. Inasmuch as searches are not conducted under the secured party's name, and no filing is needed to continue the perfected status of a security interest after it is assigned, an error in the name of the secured party or its representative will not be seriously misleading. However, in an appropriate case, an error of this kind may give rise to an estoppel in favor of a particular holder of a conflicting claim to the collateral. See Section 1–103.

Id.[9]

Third, revised I.C. § 28–9–511 indicates that the secured party identified in the financing statement is the "secured party of record" and will remain such until the situation is altered by amendment. Official Comment 3 to revised I.C. § 28–9–511 recognizes:

> Application of other law may result in a person succeeding to the powers of a secured party of record. For example, if the secured party of record (A) merges into another corporation (B) and the other corporation (B) survives, other law may provide that B has all of A's powers. In that case, B is authorized to take all actions under this Part that A would have been authorized to take. Similarly, acts taken by a person who is authorized under generally applicable principles of agency to act on behalf of the secured party of record are effective under this Part.

While amendments of financing statements can be made, *see* revised I.C. §§ 28–9–511, 28–9–512, nothing in those sections appears to indicate that they must be made. It is particularly relevant here that revised I.C. § 28–9–511 does not require an amendment of the financing statement to reflect a succession in interest such as by merger, but instead addresses the question as one of the actor's authority.

## II.  ADDRESS

Closely related to questions under New Article 9 regarding the name of the secured party are questions of that party's address. New Article 9 recognizes that a limited function is served by the inclusion on the financing statement of the secured party's address; it only indicates a place to which others can send any required notifications. See revised I.C. § 28–9–516, Official Comment 5:

> 5.  Address for Secured Party of Record. Under subsection (b)(4) and Section 9–520(a), the lack of a mailing address for the secured

---

**9.** However, to give rise to such an estoppel, the name error would have to actually result "in prejudice to a particular searcher that reasonably relied to its detriment on the error and would be harmed unfairly if the filer who committed the error were allowed to assert its priority." Harry C. Sigman, Twenty Questions About Filing Under Revised Article 9: The Rules of the Game, 74 Chi.-Kent L.Rev. 861, 866 (1999) (addressing UCC § 9–506, Official Comment 2).

party of record requires the filing office to reject an initial financing statement. The failure to include an address for the secured party of record no longer renders a financing statement ineffective. See Section 502(a). The function of the address is not to identify the secured party of record but rather to provide an address to which others can send required notifications, e.g., of a purchase money security interest in inventory or of the disposition of collateral. Inasmuch as the address shown on a filed financing statement is "an address that is reasonable under the circumstances," a person required to send a notification to the secured party may satisfy the requirement by sending a notification to that address, even if the address is or becomes incorrect. See Section 9–102 (definition of "send"). Similarly, because the address is "held out by [the secured party] as the place for receipt of such communications [i.e., communications relating to security interests]," the secured party is deemed to have received a notification delivered to that address. See Section 1–201(26).

For all these reasons, the errors in name or address on the UCC–1F cannot be viewed as rendering the filing of that statement ineffective to perfect the security interest in farm products as of the Effective Date. The structure of New Article 9 makes the absence of a name or address grounds for the filing officer to reject the statement, but if accepted for filing it will be effective.[10] Errors in the secured party's name or address as shown are, by virtue of the structure of New Article 9, not seriously misleading, and do not vitiate the effectiveness of the filing.[11]

\* \* \*

## IV.  CONCLUSION

The Effective Date of New Article 9 was July 1, 2001. This preceded the filing of the Debtors' chapter 12 petition on August 9, 2001. On the date this bankruptcy case commenced, both the UCC–1 and UCC–1F financing statements of record were sufficient to perfect the security interests granted the Bank.

---

**10.** Additionally, revised I.C. § 28–9–507(b) states that:

(b) Except as otherwise provided in subsection (c) of this section and section 28–9–508, a financing statement is not rendered ineffective if, after the financing statement is filed, the information provided in the financing statement becomes seriously misleading under section 28–9–506.

As Official Comment 4 to revised I.C. § 28–9–507 makes clear, post-filing changes that render a financing statement inaccurate—and even seriously misleading—do not render that financing statement ineffective.

**11.** See also Sigman, supra, at 868: "The secured party's address is not an element of sufficiency under [revised] Section 9–502[(a)(2)]. Failure to provide an address for the secured party is a ground for rejection under [revised] Section 9–516(b)(4), but if the financing statement is nevertheless accepted by the filing office, it is effective. Since a filed financing statement that lacks a secured party address would be effective, a filed financing statement with an erroneous address or an address that was correct when filed but is no longer correct must surely remain effective."

Based upon the foregoing, the Court finds and concludes that the Bank has a valid, perfected security interest in the property described in the UCC–1 and in the UCC–1F, and in the manufactured home shown on the Title. These are the sole questions posed by the parties' pleadings and stipulations. Counsel for the Bank shall prepare a form of Judgment consistent with this Decision.

## 3.  FINANCING STATEMENT AUTHORIZED BY DEBTOR

In a major change in law, Article 9 no longer requires that a financing statement be signed by the debtor. It is hoped that eventually all filing will be done electronically, and, at the time the statute was drafted, there was unease about whether one could "sign" an electronic financing statement. Article 9 puts this issue to rest: 9–502(a) drops the signature requirement. But this doesn't mean that all filings are authorized, and 9–509(a) provides that a person (usually the secured party) may file an initial financing statement only if the "debtor authorizes the filing in an authenticated record." And 9–510(a) states that a "filed record is effective only to the extent that it was filed by a person that may file it under Section 9–509." Thus, although the debtor doesn't have to authenticate the financing statement, it must authorize the filing of the financing statement in an authenticated record. The convenience to the secured party is evident: at any point in the process of granting the credit, the secured party may have the debtor sign or otherwise authenticate an authorization empowering the secured party to file an initial financing statement. The secured party may then file the financing statement electronically or in writing at the appropriate time without further consent from the debtor. In most cases, no separate authorization need be sought because, under 9–509(b), by signing or otherwise authenticating the security agreement, the debtor authorizes the secured party to file a financing statement covering the collateral described in the security agreement.

If the secured party files a financing statement without the requisite authorization by the debtor, 9–625(b) allows the debtor to collect damages in the amount of the loss caused by the secured party's act, and 9–625(e)(3) provides for a $500 penalty recoverable by the debtor. Moreover, in such a case 9–513(c)(4) gives the debtor the right to demand a termination statement from the secured party that must be sent within 20 days after it receives the demand.

## PROBLEMS

**1.**  Debtor signed a security agreement granting Lender a security interest in all Debtor's inventory and accounts, now owned or thereafter acquired. Lender subsequently filed a financing statement identifying the collateral as "all Debtor's personal property." Did Debtor's authentication of the security agreement authorize Lender to file the financing statement under 9–509(b)?

**2.** Does Article 9 raise problems for creditors who use the common practice of "pre-filing" financing statements? Lender uses a detailed security agreement form that specifically authorizes Lender to file all financing statements relating to the security interest created by the security agreement. Lender's practice upon receiving a prospective debtor's application for a loan is to evaluate the debtor's financial position and request a search of the UCC filing office records to see if there are any financing statements against debtor. Section 9–523(c) requires the filing office to respond to a request for information on whether any financing statement designating a particular debtor is on file. If Lender likes the debtor's balance sheet and there are no financing statements on file, it immediately files a Form UCC1 naming the debtor and describing the collateral as "all personal property." Lender pre-files in order to assure a first priority against creditor claims arising between the time of the filing and the date Lender advances funds. If Lender and the debtor later reach agreement on a secured loan transaction, the debtor signs the security agreement and Lender advances the cash. Does Lender have a perfected security interest in the collateral described in the security agreement? Comment 3 (fourth paragraph) to 9–502 gives a hint. If the parties do not reach an agreement and no security interest attaches, is Lender liable for sanctions under 9–625 for unauthorized filing of the financing statement? Does the debtor have a remedy? See 9–518.

## 4.   INDICATION OF COLLATERAL

### a.   ORIGINAL COLLATERAL

The requirement of 9–502(a)(3) that the financing statement must indicate the collateral covered by the financing statement is met under 9–504(2) by either a description of the collateral pursuant to 9–108 or "an indication that the financing statement covers all assets or all personal property." Under a regime of notice filing, a financing statement indicates the collateral covered if it provides notice that the person identified as the secured party may have a security interest in the collateral claimed. Generic descriptions by types of collateral (e.g., inventory, accounts, equipment) suffice under 9–108(b)(3). In the previous chapter, we debated the issue of why a supergeneric description is satisfactory for the financing statement but not for the security agreement. Comment 2 to 9–504 justifies the supergeneric description:

> Debtors sometimes create a security interest in all, or substantially all, of their assets. To accommodate this practice, paragraph (2) expands the class of sufficient collateral references to embrace "an indication that the financing statement covers all assets or all personal property." If the property in question belongs to the debtor and is personal property, any searcher will know that the property is covered by the financing statement.

As 9–504(1) suggests, a sufficient description of collateral in the security agreement may be used to indicate the collateral in the financing statement, and often drafters use the same description in both records. But the secured party may wish to use a broader indication in the financing statement than in the security agreement.

Case #1. D's security agreement grants SP a security interest in all D's equipment, inventory and accounts. The financing statement covers inventory and accounts. Case #2. D's security agreement grants SP a security interest in inventory and accounts. The financing statement covers equipment, inventory and accounts. In what collateral does SP have a perfected security interest in Case #1? In Case #2?

A notice filing regime in which filers need only describe collateral in terms of broad generic types is a huge convenience to secured parties. By use of simple, easy-to-draft generic descriptions in their financing statements, they can establish reliable priority for many years in a wide spectrum of collateral, including after-acquired property, to secure a multitude of future credit extensions, some of which may have been unforeseen at the time the financing statement was filed. Thus, in "floating lien" cases involving shifting collateral like inventory or accounts, additional supplementary financing statements need be filed only in unusual cases in which the identities of the parties change or the nature of the collateral changes radically. For secured parties the system not only offers priority over unsecured creditors and subsequent secured creditors but is also effective insurance against the debtor's potential bankruptcy.

On the face of it, for a relatively small filing fee, a secured party can establish its priority against all claimants in a broad spectrum of a debtor's collateral for many years in the future. For the most part, filers are also searchers since a filer must determine who else has an interest in the debtor's property before it can safely claim a priority. The financing statement reveals so little that much of the information a searcher seeks is off record. Which items of a debtor's property are covered by a generic description like "inventory" or "equipment"? Where are they located? Are they in more than one jurisdiction? What is the amount of the debt the property secures? Does it secure future advances as well as present debts? Whether the searcher's costs would be significantly lessened by requiring more information in financing statements is the subject of endless debate. Compare Peter Alces, Abolish the Article 9 Filing System, 79 Minn. L. Rev. 679, 701 (1995) ("Do we know enough to say with any confidence that the benefits of relying on the system to provide broader credit information would exceed the costs of such a model?"), with Lynn LoPucki, Computerization of the Article 9 Filing System: Thoughts on Building the Electronic Highway, 55 Law & Contemp. Probs. 5, 37 (1992) ("The need for some additional types of data will be apparent."). It is ironic that the party who most frequently litigates the validity of the secured party's financing statement is the debtor's trustee in bankruptcy who, as a hypothetical creditor, never relies on the filing system.

Some commentators contend that since Article 9 does not require that the financing statement give enough information to searchers to determine whether specific items of property are encumbered, the requirement of a collateral description should be abolished. They believe that if this were done, in most instances the diligence required of searchers to determine the scope of the filer's security interest would not be appreciably greater and losses resulting from errors in describing collateral in the financing statement would be obviated. Carl Bjerre, Bankruptcy Taxes and Other Filing Facts: A Commentary on Professor Bowers, 79 Minn. L. Rev. 757, 762–765 (1995). The same arguments support the supergeneric or one-size-fits-all indications that Article 9 approves in 9–504(2).

Allowing supergeneric descriptions has proved to be one of the most controversial changes made by the revision in that it is seen as making it even easier for creditors to take a security interest in all the debtor's assets, to the disadvantage of meritorious creditors who have dealt with the debtor on an unsecured basis. We discussed this policy issue in the introductory material early in the preceding chapter. The Drafting Committee was unmoved by the proposals of academics and bankruptcy lawyers to carve out of assets of the debtor subject to a security interest a 20% share that would be free of the security interest and available for distribution to the holders of unsecured claims.

## PROBLEM

Debtor executed a security agreement granting Bank a security interest in a broad spectrum of Debtor's personal property, appropriately described in the security agreement. The financing statement described the collateral as "general business security agreement now owned or hereafter acquired." Neither the security agreement nor other documents were attached to the financing statement. Debtor's trustee in bankruptcy challenged the adequacy of the financing statement on the ground that it did not identify the collateral covered by it. It failed to put third parties on notice as to which property of Debtor is subject to Bank's security interest. Bank argued that all that is required of a financing statement is that third parties be put on notice of the existence of a security interest, and inquiry notice to third parties was given by the financing statement. Which side is correct? See In re Lynch, 313 B.R. 798 (Bankr. W.D. Wisc. 2004).

## b.   PROCEEDS

We discussed the creation of security interests in proceeds in the previous chapter and will treat priorities in proceeds in the next chapter. At this point we briefly examine how to perfect a security interest in proceeds. The basic rules are easily stated: (1) A perfected security interest in the original collateral automatically continues in the proceeds, whether or not the financing statement mentions proceeds. 9–315(c). (2) If a filed financing statement covers the original collateral, the security interest in the proceeds continues until the financing statement either lapses or is terminated, 9–315(e)(1), so long as (a) the proceeds are collateral in which a security interest may be perfected by filing in the office in which the financing statement is filed, and (b) the proceeds are not acquired with cash proceeds. 9–315(d)(1). (3) A security interest in cash proceeds continues indefinitely, so long as they can be identified. 9–315(d)(2). (4) If the debtor uses cash proceeds to buy new collateral, such as inventory or equipment, the security interest continues in the collateral for only 21 days unless the financing statement indicates the type of collateral purchased. For instance, if the financing statement covers only inventory but the cash proceeds are used to purchase equipment, the financing statement does not afford adequate public notice. See 9–315(d)(3) and Comment 5 to 9–315.

Two innovations in Article 9 tend to assure that in the ordinary commercial case a security interest perfected by filing will continue in the proceeds until the filing lapses or is terminated. The first is that filing for registered organizations must be made in the place of registration. This means that for most tangible collateral there need be no concerns about the movement of the collateral from one jurisdiction to another, or, with respect to intangible collateral, no worries about changes in the location of the debtor's chief executive office. Hence, a financing statement covering the original collateral belonging to a corporation is almost always filed in the correct place to cover the kinds of collateral represented by the proceeds. The second is Article 9's controversial embrace of the supergeneric identification of collateral discussed in the previous section. If the financing statement covers "all personal property of the debtor," it will be an appropriate indication of most kinds of collateral purchased by cash proceeds, and 9–315(d)(3) poses no problems. Of course, if none of 9–315(d)'s conditions are satisfied, the secured creditor must take action to continue its security interest in proceeds past 20 days after its security interest attached to them.

### PROBLEM

On February 1 Secured Party (SP) perfected a security interest in all of Debtor's existing and after-acquired inventory by properly filing a financing statement. SP's security agreement also covered Debtor's deposit accounts, and SP took control of them on February 1. On March 1 Debtor sold some of its inventory on an unsecured credit basis and other items of inventory for cash. Debtor kept the cash separate in marked envelopes in its safe. Also on March 1 Debtor had its depository bank issue a cashier's check in its favor and debit its account in the amount of the check. Debtor retained possession of the check.

By April 14 SP had not taken any action with respect to any of the items above. Does SP have a perfected security interest in (a) Debtor's rights arising from the March 1 credit sales of its inventory, (b) the cash Debtor received from the March 1 cash sales, and (c) the cashier's check in Debtor's possession? Suppose Debtor purchased accounts with the cash it received from the March 1 sales?

## 5.   NAME OF DEBTOR

### a.   BASIC RULES

Financing statements are indexed under the name of the debtor. If a financing statement contains an incorrect name for the debtor, searchers will be misled and may not find the financing statement. Such a financing statement doesn't provide notice. The basic rules are set out in 9–503(a). A financing statement "sufficiently provides the name of the debtor":

(1) If the debtor is an individual, by giving the name of the individual, not the trade name or d/b/a of the debtor. If George Jenkins operates under the trade name of Best Buy Used Autos, the correct name is George Jenkins. 9–503(a)(4)(A).

(2) If the debtor is a general partnership, by giving the name of the partnership, not that of the partners. This is explained by the use of the term "organizational name of the debtor" in 9–503(a)(4)(A). Under the broad definition of "organization" in 1–201(b)(25), all partnerships are organizations, and if the partnership has a name it must be used. Of course, the enterprise may not have a name. If Thomas Jones and Robert Wagner, without any formal agreement, operate a restaurant that has a sign out in front saying "Tom & Rob's Cafe," their business has no name and a financing statement would have to provide the names of the two individuals. 9–503(a)(4)(B).

(3) If the debtor is a "registered organization," defined in 9–102(a)(70) as an organization that is organized under the law of a state or federal government that requires the maintenance of a public record showing the organization to have been organized, by giving the name of the organization indicated in the public records of the debtor's organizing jurisdiction. 9–503(a)(1). Among the registered organizations are corporations, limited liability companies, and limited partnerships. General partnerships are not registered organizations. Comment 2 to 9–503. This provision is a major and welcome clarification of the law. No matter what the corporation's letterhead or checks say, the person responsible for drafting the financing statement must check the records of the domestic jurisdiction where the corporation was organized to find the correct name. This is available by computer search. We will speak more about the jurisdictional problems later.

### b.  MINOR ERRORS RULE

Mistakes occur in entering the debtor's name in financing statements and, despite the simple rules stated above, they probably always will. Names are misspelled, parts of organizational names such as "Incorporated" or "Corporation" are omitted or abbreviated, last names are transposed with first names, and so on. Section 9–506 sets out a series of rules to assist courts in resolving disputes regarding these errors. The general rule of 9–506(a) is a tolerant one: a financing statement that has minor errors is effective unless the errors "make the financing statement seriously misleading." But the importance of having the correct name of the debtor is demonstrated by the special rule set out in 9–506(b), which says that, except otherwise provided in subsection (c), a financing statement "that fails sufficiently to provide the name of the debtor in accordance with Section 9–503 is seriously misleading." This means that such a financing statement is ineffective as a matter or law.

(1) TRADE NAMES

PROBLEM

Suppose that Debtor's legal name is Beacon Realty Investment Co., a general partnership, but everyone in the business community calls it "Hilton Inn." We can enhance this by supposing that nobody in that community has ever heard it called anything but "Hilton Inn" because that is the name Debtor itself uses on all it correspondence, contracts and checks, and this is the name that Secured Party (SP) used in its financing statement. Now Debtor is in bankruptcy and its trustee in bankruptcy, examining the documentation of SP's security interest, contends that SP used the wrong name under 9–503(a)(4) for a general partnership. But SP comes back with the common sense argument that everyone in the financial community interested in Debtor's credit record would search under the name "Hilton Inn" and they would find the financing statement. If it were filed under Debtor's correct name, they wouldn't have found the financing statement. Shouldn't an exception be made for cases in which the debtor is known to its creditors and to the public at large only by its trade name? The facts in this Problem are based on those in Pearson v. Salina Coffee House, Inc., 831 F.2d 1531 (10th Cir.1987). Before Revised Article 9, a number of cases held that the use of a trade name in the financing statement in a case like this was appropriate. How would this case be decided under 9–503(c)? Is there a sound policy basis for this resolution? Which party should have the burden of discovering the debtor's correct name, the secured party or the searchers? Why?

(2) SEARCH LOGIC ISSUES

Different filing offices may use different search logic procedures. A search using the correct name of the debtor may turn up a financing statement filed under an erroneously stated name under one search logic but not under another. Before Revised Article 9, courts had difficulties with cases in which the secured party asserted that even though the debtor's name was not correctly stated, diligent searchers using the debtor's correct name should, nonetheless, have found the defective financing statement. This is called the "reasonably diligent searcher rule." Some examples follow:

Case #1. Debtor's correct name was "Voyageur Corporation." The name on the financing statement was "Voyager Corporation." The court, without reference to the nature of the state's filing system, held the description adequate under the doctrine of *idem sonans*, under which absolute accuracy in spelling names is not required in a legal document if the misspelled name and the correct name sound alike. Corporate Financers, Inc. v. Voyageur Trading Co., 519 N.W.2d 238 (Minn. App. 1994). Apparently the filing system was manual: the original copy of the financing statement is placed in a file drawer in alphabetical order and the filing officer is supposed to search for the correct name by leafing through the files. The filing office determines the extent to which name variations are sought.

Case #2. Debtor's correct name was "Mines Tire Company, Inc.," but the financing statement gave the name as "Mines Company, Inc." The trustee in bankruptcy challenged the financing statement as seriously misleading and stated to the court that it had conducted a computer search using the correct name of the debtor and had failed to turn up the financing statement. To counter this evidence, the creditor then had a manual search done that located the financing statement. Exasperated by these contradictions, the court made its own inquiry through Westlaw; its search request was for any debtor's name that included the root name, "Mines." It found the financing statement among 109 responses and held that it was not seriously misleading. The court proclaimed that computers are just machines and: "no person should ever become a servant of a machine." "To the extent that a human searcher would inevitably examine all corporate names having certain basic components, a computer searcher should act similarly. It will not suffice to perform a word search for the precise corporate name. Rather, the interested party should expand its investigation to include all related entries through which a manual searcher might have stumbled." 194 B.R. 23, 26. Thus, the burden is on the searcher to come up with all the variations that a manual searcher would have used.

One of the most important policy decisions made by the drafters of Revised Article 9 was to shift the burden from the searching creditor to the filing creditor with respect to the name of the debtor on the financing statement. The following opinion treats in detail two of the most important issues that have arisen under the new filing provisions: The first is the meaning of the "safe harbor" provision of 9–506(c). The second is the use of a name other than the legal name of a debtor on financing statements.

## Pankratz Implement Company v. Citizens National Bank

Supreme Court of Kansas, 2006.
130 P.3d 57.

■ The opinion of the court was delivered by DAVIS, J.:

Pankratz Implement Co. (Pankratz) attempted to perfect its security interest in equipment sold to Rodger House. In filing with the Secretary of State, Pankratz spelled the debtor's name as *Roger* House. Citizens National Bank (CNB) later attempted to secure the same property using the debtor's correct name, Rodger House. Rodger House filed for bankruptcy; Pankratz obtained relief from the bankruptcy stay order and filed suit against CNB in order to realize its security interest. The district court determined in accordance with recently enacted amendments to Article 9 of the Kansas Uniform Commercial Code (UCC) effective July 1, 2001, K.S.A. 2003 Supp. 84–9–101 *et seq.*, that Pankratz was entitled to summary judgment because use of the debtor's incorrect name was a minor error and not seriously misleading. The Court of Appeals reversed, concluding that the use of the debtor's incorrect name was seriously misleading. *Pankratz Implement Co. v. Citizens Nat'l Bank*, 33 Kan.App.2d 279, 102 P.3d 1165 (2004). We granted Pankratz' petition for review and affirm the Court of Appeals.

## FACTS

The facts in this case are uncontroverted. On March 18, 1998, Rodger House purchased a Steiger Bearcat tractor from Pankratz. House signed a note and security agreement in favor of Pankratz using his correct name, Rodger House. Pankratz listed the debtor's name in the agreement as "Roger House" instead of "Rodger House." Pankratz, in turn, assigned its interest in the note and the collateral to Deere and Company (Deere). Deere then filed a financing statement with the Kansas Secretary of State on March 23, 1998, using the same misspelled name, Roger House.

On April 8, 1999, House executed a note and security agreement in favor of Citizens National Bank (CNB), from which House obtained a loan. House pledged as collateral, among other things, all equipment "that I now own and that I may own in the future." On March 4, 1999, CNB filed a financing statement with the Kansas Secretary of State using the correct name of the debtor, Rodger House.

On June 10, 2002, House filed a petition for bankruptcy under Chapter 7 in the United States Bankruptcy Court for the District of Kansas. On July 1, 2002, Deere reassigned the House note and security interest to Pankratz. Pankratz obtained relief from the automatic stay pursuant to 11 U.S.C. § 362 (2000) and filed suit in the district court against CNB seeking a declaratory judgment concerning its purchase money security interest.

## District Court

Both parties moved for summary judgment. The district court identified the issue for resolution: "The sole issue in this case is whether the filing of a financing statement which misspells the debtor's name is insufficient to render a filed financing statement seriously misleading under the UCC and therefore ineffective as to other creditors ... claiming a security interest in the same collateral."

The district court adopted the reasoning and legal principles set forth in the trial court's decisions in *In re Erwin*, 2003 WL 21513158 (Bankr. D.Kan.2003) (unpublished opinion), and *In re Kinderknecht*, 300 B.R. 47 (Bankr.D.Kan.2003). Summary judgment was granted to Pankratz based upon the court's conclusion that the misspelled first name of the debtor was a minor error, not seriously misleading under K.S.A.2003 Supp. 84–9–506.

## Court of Appeals

The Court of Appeals first noted that "[o]n its face, to hold that a missing 'd' in a debtor's first name renders a financing statement 'seriously misleading' seems harsh," and that the misspelling would seem to fall under 84–9–506(a) as a minor error or omission that would not have an impact on the effectiveness of the financing statement. The court, however, determined that the ultimate inquiry was "one of whether a reasonably diligent searcher would find the prior security interest." 33 Kan.App.2d at 281, 102 P.3d 1165.

K.S.A.2003 Supp. 84–9–506 states that a misspelling will not be considered seriously misleading if a search using the standard search logic, under the correct name, would turn up the financing statement. The Court of Appeals found that the "standard search logic" for a financing statement search found in K.A.R. 7–17–22 was not synonymous with the "temporary internet search logic" accessible at www.accesskansas.org. 33 Kan.App.2d at 281, 102 P.3d 1165. The Court of Appeals agreed with CNB that "the only searches that would have produced the Pankratz prior security interest for 'Roger House' would have been completed on the temporary internet search logic." 33 Kan.App.2d at 282, 102 P.3d 1165. Using the "standard search logic" provided by the Secretary of State under the name Rodger House did not disclose the prior security interest of Pankratz. Thus, the Court of Appeals concluded that the filing under the misspelled name of Roger House was seriously misleading. 33 Kan.App.2d at 282, 102 P.3d 1165.

The Court of Appeals relied upon the 10th Circuit Bankruptcy Appellate Panel's reversal of the bankruptcy court in *In re Kinderknecht*, 308 B.R. 71 (B.A.P. 10th Cir.2004), holding that the use of the debtor's nickname under the facts of the case was seriously misleading. The court adopted the reasoning in *Kinderknecht*, which was based largely on the Revised Article 9's stated goals of simplicity and avoiding needless litigation. See 308 B.R. at 75–76.

The Court of Appeals further discussed the minor error rule, citing *Millennium Financial Services, LLC v. Thole*, 31 Kan.App.2d 798, 74 P.3d 57 (2003), and determined that a search using the standard search logic under the debtor's correct name, Rodger House, would not disclose the prior security interest of Pankratz. K.S.A.2003 Supp. 84–9–506 places the burden on the filing creditor to list the debtor correctly. The searching creditor is under no obligation to conduct searches under variants of the debtor's name. Thus, the error could not be considered a minor error. The district court's summary judgment in favor of Pankratz was reversed, and the case was remanded with directions to enter judgment for CNB. 33 Kan.App.2d at 283, 102 P.3d 1165.

### DISCUSSION AND ANALYSIS

\* \* \*

Pankratz argues that at the heart of the Court of Appeals decision lies a fundamental misunderstanding of the Revised Article 9 standard of the legal name requirement for financing statements regarding individual debtors set forth in K.S.A.2003 Supp. 84–9–503(a)(5)(A). Pankratz also claims that the Court of Appeals misapplied the provisions of K.S.A.2003 Supp. 84–9–506(c) regarding its safe harbor provisions. Before addressing these contentions it is helpful to set forth the complete text of the two statutory amendments involved in this case:

K.S.A.2003 Supp. 84–9–503 provides:

"(a) **Sufficiency of debtor's name.** A financing statement sufficiently provides the name of the debtor:

(1) If the debtor is a registered organization, only if the financing statement provides the name of the debtor indicated on the public record of the debtor's jurisdiction of organization which shows the debtor to have been organized; * * *

(5) in other cases:

(A) *If the debtor has a name, only if it provides the individual or organizational name of the debtor; and*

(B) if the debtor does not have a name, only if it provides the names of the partners, members, associates, or other persons comprising the debtor." (Emphasis added.) * * *

K.S.A.2003 Supp. 84–9–506 provides:

"(a) **Minor errors and omissions.** A financing statement substantially satisfying the requirements of this part is effective, even if it has minor errors or omissions, unless the errors or omissions make the financing statement seriously misleading.

"(b) **Financing statement seriously misleading.** Except as otherwise provided in subsection (c), a financing statement that fails sufficiently to provide the name of the debtor in accordance with K.S.A. 2003 Supp. 84–9–503(a) and amendments thereto, is seriously misleading.

"(c) **Financing statement not seriously misleading.** If a search of the records of the filing office under the debtor's correct name, using the filing office's standard search logic, if any, would disclose a financing statement that fails sufficiently to provide the name of the debtor in accordance with K.S.A.2003 Supp. 84–9–503(a) and amendments thereto, the name provided does not make the financing statement seriously misleading. * * *"

Since our answer in this case depends upon the interpretation of the two above quoted statutes, it is also helpful to consider in our interpretation a cardinal principle of statutory interpretation:

"In construing statutes and determining legislative intent, several provisions of an act or acts, *in pari materia*, must be construed together with a view of reconciling and bringing them into workable harmony if possible. Effect must be given, if possible, to the entire act and every part thereof. To this end, it is the duty of the court, as far as practicable, to reconcile the different provisions so as to make them consistent, harmonious, and sensible. The court must give effect to the legislature's intent even though words, phrases, or clauses at some place in the statute must be omitted or inserted." *State ex rel. Morrison v. Oshman Sporting Goods Co. Kansas*, 275 Kan. 763, Syl. ¶ 2, 69 P.3d 1087 (2003).

Our construction of the above statutes provides the following analysis under the facts of this case. K.S.A.2003 Supp. 84–9–503(a)(5)(A) provides that a financing statement sufficiently provides the debtor's name only if the financial statement provides the individual name of the debtor. In this case, Pankratz used an incorrect name by misspelling the debtor's name in the financing statement. Pankratz argues that the misspelled name was only a minor error under K.S.A.2003 Supp. 84–9–506(a) and was not seriously misleading.

K.S.A.2003 Supp. 84–9–506(a) provides that a financing statement "is effective, even if it has minor errors or omissions, unless the errors or omissions make the financing statement seriously misleading." Except as otherwise provided in subsection (c) a financing statement that fails sufficiently to provide the name of the debtor in accordance with K.S.A.2003 Supp. 84–9–503(a) is seriously misleading. Pankratz' use of the debtor's misspelled name failed to provide the individual name of the debtor in accord with K.S.A.2003 Supp. 84–9–503(a); however, according to the safe harbor provisions of subsection 84–9–503(c), the error may not be seriously misleading.

K.S.A.2003 Supp. 84–9–506(c) provides that

"[i]f a search of the records of the filing office under the debtor's correct name, *using the filing office's standard search logic*, if any, would disclose a financing statement that fails sufficiently to provide the name of the debtor in accordance with K.S.A.2003 Supp. 84–9–503(a) and amendments thereto, the name provided does not make the financing statement seriously misleading." (Emphasis added.)

Under such circumstances a search using the debtor's correct name would reveal the prior security interest of Pankratz with the misspelled debtor's name and its financing statement would not be seriously misleading.

However, the undisputed facts in this case establish that a search under the debtor's correct name *using the filing office's standard search logic* did not disclose Pankratz' financing statement with the debtor's misspelled name. The express provisions of K.S.A.2003 Supp. 84–9–506(b) provide that "[e]xcept as otherwise provided in subsection (c), a financing statement that fails sufficiently to provide the name of the debtor in accordance with K.S.A.2003 Supp. 84–9–503(a) and amendments thereto, is seriously misleading." Thus, Pankratz' financing statement using the misspelled name of the debtor, while prior in time, was seriously misleading, causing the Court of Appeals to direct that judgment be entered for CNB.

Our analysis involves a construction of the provisions of both statutes, *in pari materia*, and leads us to the conclusion that Pankratz' filed financing statement was seriously misleading, confirming the Court of

Appeals decision. We could end our discussion and conclude that the expressed provisions of the law support the decision of the Court of Appeals. However, Pankratz advances several arguments in support of its position that the misspelled name of the debtor is only a minor error not seriously misleading. Pankratz asserts that the name requirements are not sufficiently defined especially for individuals under the new amendments and that a careful reading of subsection (c) does not support the bright-line rule adopted by the Court of Appeals, *viz.*, that failing to meet the requirements of subsection (c) makes the financing statement seriously misleading. The object of Pankratz' arguments is to place upon the party claiming a superior lien the responsibility to conduct a diligent search of past records filed with the Secretary of State to determine whether a prior lien exists. If the name requirements of the debtor are not fixed and certain, the use of a nickname or a misspelled name on the financing statement filed with the Secretary of State may require just such a search on the part of the party claiming a superior lien.

On the other hand, if the legislature intended by its amended version of the UCC set forth above to fix and make certain the name of the debtor requirement, such a change shifts the responsibility of the one filing with the Secretary of State to follow the name requirement with the effect being that the party searching for prior liens on the same property may rely on the name used on the financing statement eliminating the need to conduct diligent searches. We believe that the language used by the legislature and the intent behind the adoption of the most recent amendments had the effect of shifting the responsibility of getting the name on the financing statement right to the filing party, thereby enabling the searching party to rely upon that name and eliminating the need for multiple searches using variations of the debtor's name. This would have the effect of providing more certainty in the commercial world and reducing litigation as was required prior to the amendments to determine whether an adequate search was made.

The facts in this case establish that two types of searches for prior liens were available to a creditor hoping to perfect his or her lien upon specific property. The first is the temporary internet search logic found at www.accesskansas.org. The facts establish that a search using the debtor's name in this case would have disclosed Pankratz' financing statement with the misspelled name of the debtor. However, the provisions of K.A.R. 7–17–24, as set forth below, make it clear that such a search shall not constitute an official search by the Secretary of State.

> "During the transition period of July 1, 2001 through June 30, 2006, public access to a database that produces search results beyond exact name matches may be provided by the secretary of state. The supplemental database [www.accesskansas.org.] shall not be considered part of the standard search logic and shall not constitute an official search by the secretary of state." K.A.R. 7–17–24.

The database provided a further disclaimer:

"Searches conducted on the internet are not official searches under Revised Article Nine of the Uniform Commercial Code. This search engine is intended to provide a more flexible search logic so as to identify UCC filings under the old law, which employed different name requirements. Therefore searches conducted on this page will not determine whether a name is seriously misleading under K.S.A. 84–9–506. If you want an official search using the correct and current search logic given in KAR 7–17–22, contact the Kansas Secretary of State's Office at (785) 296–4564."

The "standard search logic" noted in K.S.A.2003 Supp. 84–9–506(c) and provided by the Secretary of State is the official and only search that determines whether a name is seriously misleading under K.S.A.2003 Supp. 84–9–506. See K.A.R. 7–17–21 and 7–17–22.

Pankratz, in support of its first argument, acknowledges that under K.S.A.2003 Supp. 84–9–506(c), a search of the records of the Secretary of State, using the debtor's correct name and the filing office's standard search logic, would not disclose his financing statement using the misspelled name of the debtor, Roger House. However, Pankratz argues that the Court of Appeals erred in concluding under these circumstances that the financing statement is seriously misleading. Pankratz believes that the correct interpretation of K.S.A.2003 Supp. 84–9–506(c) is that of Professors Barkley and Barbara Clark in volume one of their treatise, The Law of Secured Transactions Under the Uniform Commercial Code ¶ 2.09(1)(e), P.2–164 (2003):

> " '[R]ead carefully, ... § 9–506(c) provides only that a financing statement is not seriously misleading if, using standard search logic, a search under the debtor's correct name would reveal the statement containing the debtor's incorrect name. It does not provide that a financing statement is not seriously misleading *only* if a search using the debtor's correct name would reveal the statement containing the debtor's incorrect name in the circumstances.... [§ 9–506(c)] does not say that financing statements that do not satisfy subsection (c)'s "safe harbor" are seriously misleading and therefore ineffective. Thus ... § 9–506(c) leaves open the possibility that an error in the debtor's name does not render the financing statement seriously misleading, even if a search using the debtor's correct name and standard search logic would not turn up the statement.' " (Quoting Jordan, Warren, and Walt, Secured Transactions in Personal Property, p. 59).

The above observation quoted by Professors Clarks is correct in that the provisions of subsection (c) are positive in recognizing that if a search under the debtor's correct name discloses the financing statement filed with a minor error, then the minor error does not make the filed statement seriously misleading. It does not say that such a filed statement that is not disclosed using standard logic search is seriously misleading. If all we were dealing with was subsection (c), then there would be the possibility that an error in the filed financing statement not meeting the safe harbor provisions of subsection (c) would not render the financing statement seriously misleading. However, as more fully discussed below, consideration of both amendments *in para materia* rather than focusing exclusively on subsection (c) supports the opposite conclusion.

Pankratz relies heavily upon Professors Clarks' interpretation as it relates to the crux of its argument. Pankratz argues that there is then no bright-line standard and the ultimate determination regarding the effectiveness a filed financing statement with an incorrect name that is not disclosed under the provisions of subsection (c) must be resolved on a case-by-case basis. Thus, depending again upon the diligence of the search by the creditor claiming a superior interest by reason of his or her later filed statement, the case must be resolved through a judicial determination of whether a particular financing statement is "seriously misleading."

The answer to this argument lies in the consideration of the two amendments together and interpreted as a whole scheme adopted by the Kansas Legislature rather than to focus exclusively upon one section alone. The answer also depends upon the express language used in both amendments, as well as the intent of the legislature in the adoption of the changes enacted.

A reading of the provisions of K.S.A.2003 Supp. 84–9–503 with the provisions of K.S.A.2003 Supp. 84–9–506 makes clear that the safe harbor provision of K.S.A.2003 Supp. 84–9–506(c) applies to both 84–9–506 and 84–9–503. "A financing statement sufficiently provides the name of the debtor . . . [i]f the debtor has a name, *only if it provides the individual or organizational name of the debtor.*" (Emphasis added.) K.S.A.2003 Supp. 84–9–503(a)(5)(A). Referring to the case before us, the error in Pankratz' filed financing statement was the misspelling of the debtor's first name. Thus, Pankratz' financing statement failed to use the "name of the debtor" and therefore does not satisfy the provisions of 84–9–503(a). However, the provisions of K.S.A.2003 Supp. 84–9–506(a) provide that "[a] financing statement substantially satisfying the requirements of this part is effective, even if it has minor errors or omissions, unless the errors or omissions make the financing statement seriously misleading." Pankratz' financial statement has a minor error; under K.S.A.2003 Supp. 84–9–506(b), if the financing statement "*[e]xcept as otherwise provided in subsection (c)* [safe harbor provision], . . . fails sufficiently to provide the name of the debtor in accordance with K.S.A.2003 Supp. 84–9–503(a) and amendments thereto [only if the financing statement provides the name of the debtor], [it] is seriously misleading." The undisputed evidence establishes that Pankratz' financing statement did not satisfy the provisions of subsection (c), the safe harbor provisions, in that a search using debtor's correct name did not disclose Pankratz' statement.

Pankratz failed to satisfy the requirement of using the correct name of the debtor and thus did not satisfy the name requirements of 84–9–503(a)(5)(A). Nevertheless, minor errors will not destroy the effectiveness of that statement unless the errors make the statement seriously misleading. Pankratz' failing to meet the naming requirements is seriously misleading except in the case where a search using the debtor's correct name discloses the defective financing statement. In this case it did not and therefore remains seriously misleading. K.S.A.2003 Supp. 84–9–506(b).

Pankratz' second argument focuses on the naming requirements set forth in K.S.A.2003 Supp. 84–9–503. Pankratz asks what constitutes a sufficient name, a term not defined in the statute. Pankratz argues there is no requirement that a legal name must be used and bolsters this argument by pointing out the differences in the statute's loose requirements for an individual name and the exactness of the requirements for an organizational name. Pankratz' attack is aimed at the conclusion that if there is no exactness required for the name placed upon the financing statement, a nickname or even a slight variation in the name used would satisfy K.S.A.2003 Supp. 84–9–503. If this is the case, then it follows that the law would therefore require a case-by-case determination regarding the sufficiency of the name with the result that the creditor claiming a superior lien on the property would be required to conduct a diligent search using variations of the debtor's name before it could be said that the prior filed statement is ineffective.

Pankratz is correct that K.S.A.2003 Supp. 84–9–503 provides no specific rule or guidance concerning what constitutes a sufficient debtor "name." The term "name," name of debtor, debtor's name, or "correct name" is not defined in Article 9. At the same time, the statute sets forth exact requirements for the name of registered organizations. According to Pankratz, the difference in language indicates a legislative "loud silence," which means that there is no specific mandate to use the individual debtor's legal name in all circumstances. If there are no requirements as to the individual name, errors in the debtor's name in a financing statement must be judged on a case-by-case basis and the very minor error in this case, misspelling the debtor's first name by leaving out a "d" in Rodger, is only a minor error under K.S.A.2003 Supp. 84–9–506(a).

Pankratz, as well as the district court, in this case relied upon the recent United States Bankruptcy Court decision *In re Kinderknecht*, 300 B.R. 47 (Bankr.D.Kan.2003), and cases cited therein. In that case, Terry J. Kinderknecht granted defendants a security interest in two farm implements, and they promptly filed financing statements on the collateral in the name "Terry J. Kinderknecht." Kinderknecht later filed a petition for Chapter 7 bankruptcy relief in his legal name "Terrance J. Kinderknecht," listing defendants as secured creditors. The trustee brought a strong-arm proceeding to set aside the security interests as not having been properly perfected in accordance with Kansas law.

The focal issue in the case involved the same amendments to the UCC that we deal with in this opinion; more specifically, the primary issue in *Kinderknecht* is the provision of K.S.A.2003 Supp. 84–9–503 relating to the name of the debtor. The trustee argued that the name of the debtor means the debtor's legal name while the defendants' claimed that the debtor's name requirements are not defined and would include "Terry" instead of "Terrance." Neither a search using the standard search logic provided by the secretary of state's office nor a search using the more broad search method under Access Kansas with the name Terrance J. Kinderknecht disclosed the financing statement of defendants filed under the name of Terry J. Kinderknecht. Thus, much like in the present case, the trustee argued that the financing statement used by the defendants was seriously misleading.

The bankruptcy court noted:

"If the drafters of the Model Code and the Kansas Legislature intended to require that financing statements include debtors' legal names, they should have said so clearly in the test of Article 9.

. . .

"... Nothing in Revised Article 9 mandates a debtor's legal name ... [and] [n]othing in Revised Article 9 requires that a legal name must be used in a financing statement. Therefore, a commonly used nickname may be a debtor's correct name and under § 9–506(c), if a search using a nickname and the filing office's standard search logic produces a financing statement, it is not misleading. This is the case here." *Kinderknecht*, 300 B.R. at 51.

The court therefore denied the claim of the trustee and held that use of the individual name "Terry J. Kinderknecht" in the financing statements did not make the financing statements insufficient or seriously misleading.

The trustee in the *Kinderknecht* case filed a timely appeal and the parties consented to jurisdiction of the United States 10th Circuit Bankruptcy Appellate Panel without a hearing before the United States District Court for the District of Kansas. *In re Kinderknecht*, 308 B.R. 71 (B.A.P. 10th Cir.2004), interpreting Kansas law, reversed the bankruptcy judge, holding *inter alia* that for a financing statement to be effective under Kansas law, the secured creditor must list "an individual debtor ... by his or her legal name, not by a nickname." 308 B.R. at 75 (citing 84–9–502[a], 84–9–503[a] [A], 84–9–506[b]). Its decision and reasoning are particularly helpful in resolving this case:

"This could be construed, as it was by the bankruptcy court, as allowing a debtor to be listed in a financing statement by his or her commonly-used nickname. But, we do not agree with that interpretation *because the purpose of § 89–4–503, as well as a reading of that section as a whole, leads us to conclude that an individual debtor's legal name must be used in the financing statement to make it sufficient under § 84–9–502(a)(1)* [which is simply the requirement of 'the name of the debtor' on a financing statement]." (Emphasis added.) 308 B.R. at 75.

The 10th Circuit reasoned that K.S.A.2003 Supp. 84–9–503

"was enacted to clarify the sufficiency of a debtor's name in financing statements. The intent to clarify when a debtor's name is sufficient shows a desire to foreclose fact-intensive tests, such as those that existed under the former Article 9 of the UCC, inquiring into whether a person conducting a search would discover a filing under any given name. Requiring a financing statement to provide a debtor's legal name is a clear cut test that is in accord with that intent.

"Furthermore, § 84–9–503, read as a whole, indicates that a legal name should be used for an individual debtor. In the case of debtor-entities, § 84–9–503(a) states that legal names must be used to render them sufficient under § 84–9–502(a). Trade names or other names may be listed, but it is insufficient to list a debtor by such names alone. A different standard should not apply to individual debtors. The more specific provisions applicable to entities, together with the importance of naming the debtor in the financing statement to facilitate the notice filing system and increase commercial certainty, indicates that an individual debtor must be listed on a financing statement by his or her legal name, not by a nickname.

"Our conclusion that a legal name is necessary to sufficiently provide the name of an individual debtor within the meaning of § 84–9–503(a) is also supported by four practical considerations. First, mandating the debtor's legal name sets a clear test so as [to] simplify the drafting of financing statements. Second, setting a clear test simplifies the parameters of UCC searches. Persons searching UCC filings will know that they need the debtor's legal name to conduct a search, they will not be penalized if they do not know that a debtor has a nickname, and they will not have to guess any number of nicknames that could exist to conduct a search. Third, requiring the debtor's legal name will avoid litigation as to the commonality or appropriateness of a debtor's nickname, and as to whether a reasonable searcher would have or should have known to use the name. Finally, obtaining a debtor's legal name is not difficult or burdensome for the creditor taking a secured interest in a debtor's property. Indeed, knowing the individual's legal name will assure the accuracy of any search that creditor conducts prior to taking its secured interest in property." 308 B.R. at 75–76.

We believe the decision and reasoning of the 10th Circuit is sound and accurately reflects the legislative intent behind the adoption of new amendments to the UCC. Pankratz fails to harmonize what it calls a legislative silence in 84–9–503(a) with the specific provisions of 84–9–506. It is illogical to assert that the legislature would intend a rigorous requirement for business entity names and a vague, less rigorous standard for individual names, which would operate, by implication, as a kind of safe harbor, and then, in K.S.A.2003 Supp. 84–9–506(c), expressly provide another safe harbor provision for the use of incorrect names on a filed financing statement. * * *

The purpose of the Revised Article 9 as a whole is the simplification of formal requirements, and the purpose of 84–9–506 in particular is to lessen the need for judicial hairsplitting (and, by implication, to move toward a bright-line rule). Harmonizing 84–9–506 with these purposes thus becomes the goal of any interpretation, despite the fact that other interpretations may be implied through omission in the statutory language. Pankratz argues that the legislature intended a case-by-case determination of "seriously misleading," based upon the absence of definitive language regarding the naming requirements for individuals in K.S.A.2003 Supp. 84–9–503(a). Such an interpretation is contrary to the Comment's policy statement that the Revised Article 9 seeks to simplify filing requirements and to move away from judicial interpretation. Rather than judicial determinations, the Official UCC Comment 2 to K.S.A.2003 Supp. 84–9–506 makes clear that

> "subsection (a) is in line with the policy of this Article to simplify formal requisites and filing requirements. It is designed to discourage the fanatical and impossibly refined reading of statutory requirements in which courts occasionally have indulged themselves.... Subsection (b) contains the general rule: a financing statement that fails sufficiently to provide the debtor's name in accordance with Section 9–503(a) is seriously misleading as a matter of law. Subsection (c) provides an exception...." * * *

Finally, in determining legislative intent, the *amicus* brief filed by the Secretary of State proves instructive. The brief reinforces the notion, implied very strongly by the above discussion, that the intent of the filing requirements of Revised Article 9 is to shift the burden of filing correctly onto the filers and to allow searchers to rely on one search under the correct legal name of the debtor. Several experts who played a role in drafting and implementing the Revised Article 9 share this interpretation of the filing requirements of Revised Article 9. * * *

Harry Sigman sat on the Revised Article 9 Drafting Committee, and wrote that Article 9

> "does not provide an absolute requirement of perfection. At the same time, it does not burden searchers with the obligation to dream up every potential error and name variation and perform searches under all possibilities. Revised Article 9 allows a searcher to rely on a single search conducted under the correct name of the debtor and penalizes filers only for errors that result in the nondisclosure of the financing statement in a search under the correct name." Sigman, *The Filing System Under Revised Article 9*, 73 Am. Bankr.L.J. 61, 73 (1999). * * *

The Kansas Court of Appeals in its decision, the express provisions of the revised amendments read *in para materia*, and the Official UCC Comments are all in accord that the primary purpose of the revision of the name requirement is to lessen the amount of fact-intensive, case-by-case determinations that plagued earlier versions of the UCC, and to simplify the filing system as a whole. The object of the revisions was to shift the responsibility to the filer by requiring the not too heavy burden of using the legal name of the debtor, thereby relieving the searcher from conducting numerous searches using every conceivable name variation of the debtor. The effect of the revision is to provide more certainty in the commercial world and reduce litigation to determine whether an adequate search was done. The cases cited by Pankratz in support of its position mostly were decided prior to the adoption of the revisions. The more recent cases decided after the revisions of UCC Article 9 are in accord with the Court of Appeals' decision in this case.

Finally, the practical public policy considerations outlined by the 10th Circuit Bankruptcy Appellate Panel in *Kinderknecht*, and the opinions of several of the drafters of the Revised Article 9, while merely persuasive authority, support the decision of the Court of Appeals in this case. We conclude that such authority, as well as the express provisions of K.S.A. 2003 Supp. 84–9–503 and K.S.A.2003 Supp. 84–9–506 construed *in pari materia*, demonstrate that Pankratz' filed financing statement was "seriously misleading." * * *

* * * The decision of the Court of Appeals reversing the district court is affirmed. The decision of the district court is reversed, and the case is remanded to enter summary judgment on behalf of Citizens National Bank.

Affirmed.

### NOTES

**1.** The plaintiff, Pankratz, relied on a quotation from Barkley and Barbara Clarks' treatise that referred to a previous edition of this Casebook in which we noted that 9–506(c), the safe harbor provision, states positively that an incorrect name on a financing statement is not seriously misleading if, using the filing office's standard search logic, a search under the debtor's correct name would have turned up the financing statement. In our book our concern was whether this provision was bullet-proof, and we suggested that it might have been better if 9–506(c) had said "using *only* the filing office's standard search logic." The justification for our critique is found in decades of cases in which courts have found ways to blatantly favor careless filers over searchers in harsh cases like *Pankratz*. The *Pankratz* decision is a persuasive holding that, viewed in light of the avowed policy of Revised Article 9 to shift the burden from searchers to filers in financing statement searches and, when read *in pari materia* with 9–506(a) and (b) and other provisions of the statute, 9–506(c) must be interpreted to mean "only the filing office's standard search logic."

**2.** The *Pankratz* court approves the holding in In re Kinderknecht, 308 B.R. 71 (B.A.P. 10th Cir.2004), that a financing statement bearing the nickname of the debtor ("Terry" rather than "Terrance" J. Kindernecht) is seriously misleading. The court's conclusion is that an individual debtor's "legal name" must be used on a financing statement to qualify as the debtor's name under 9–502(a)(1), 9–503(a) and 9–506(b). The difficulty is that none of these statutes uses the term "legal name" and the quotation from *Kindernecht* in *Pankratz* asserting that "9–503(a) states that legal names must be used to render them sufficient under 9–502(a)" is incorrect. Section 506(c) uses the term "debtor's correct name," and the other sections use no modifier for the debtor's name. The truth is that the drafters of Revised Article 9 simply could not agree on a definition an individual's name, and litigation like that in *Kindernechth* was sure to follow. In that case, the court narrowed the meaning of "the debtor's name" by requiring that the financing statement be filed under the debtor's "legal name," but there is no commonly accepted definition of "legal name" in the law. Is it the debtor's "full name," the name on a birth certificate, a driver's license, a Social Security card, or a passport? Given the policy of Revised Article 9 to shift the burden of filing errors from the searching creditor to the filing creditor, the *Kindernecht* court seems correct in stating that, under the facts of that case, a nickname was seriously misleading. Surely, a filing creditor can more easily discover a debtor's correct name than searching creditors can learn his nicknames.

**3.** Article 9 encourages the harmonization of filing office practices among jurisdictions through a set of provisions. In order to maintain uniformity, 9–526(b)(2) requires jurisdictions to consult current model rules of the International Association of Corporate Administrators (IACA) or any successor organization. The IACA is the trade group of state filing officers. Rule 503 of the IACA's Model Administrative Rules requires filing offices to adopt a strict search logic in its search procedures. The Rule also requires search procedures to ignore "the" at the beginning of a debtor's name, capital letters, spaces between names, and "noise" words enumerated in a list of corporate endings. See Rules 503.2–503.7.

## 6.  POST–FILING CHANGES

Events occurring after a financing statement has been filed can affect the accuracy of information contained in it. Examples include changes in the debtor's name, transfers of collateral, changes in the use of the collateral, and changes in the legal identity of the debtor. Former law never adequately dealt with all of the changes that take place after the filing of a financing statement, particularly changes in the name or business structure of the debtor. The drafters of Revised Article 9 have dealt extensively with post-filing changes and even coined a new term, "new debtor," to do so. Our inquiry describes how these new provisions fit together.

### a.  TRANSFER OF COLLATERAL

D granted a security interest to SP in all its equipment, and the security agreement contained a provision forbidding D to sell the equipment without SP's express written consent. SP filed a financing statement covering equipment with D named as the debtor. In violation of the security agreement prohibition, D sold some of the equipment to Buyer, who had no actual knowledge of SP's security interest or financing statement. Six months after the transfer of property Buyer filed a bankruptcy petition. (a) Does SP retain a perfected security interest in the equipment that Buyer obtained from D? (b) Would your answer change if it can be shown that SP learned of the unauthorized sale shortly after it was made but did nothing to assert its rights in the collateral until it learned of Buyer's bankruptcy?

Perfection of a nonpossessory security interest requires two things: filing of an effective financing statement and an attached security interest. Accordingly, D's transfer of equipment to Buyer could affect either the continued effectiveness of SP's financing statement or its attached security interest. The two possibilities are independent of each other. See Comment 3 to 9–507. If either eventuality occurred, SP's security interest would be unperfected. Section 9–507(a) deals with the effect of a transfer of collateral on the continued effectiveness of a financing statement. Section 9–315(a)(1) addresses the effect of a disposition of collateral on a security interest in it.

The issue present in the ongoing example is one that has long been debated. What is the duty of a secured party to monitor its debtor with respect to post-filing changes? Section 9–315(a)(1) states the general rule that a security interest continues in collateral after the debtor transfers it to another person unless the secured party "authorized the disposition free of the security interest." Section 9–315(a)(2) says that the security interest attaches to "any identifiable proceeds of the collateral." Thus, in this case SP has a security interest both in the equipment in the possession of Buyer as well as the proceeds of that collateral, i.e., consideration that Buyer gave D for the equipment. We will take up the proceeds issues later. Section 9–507(a) provides that SP's financing statement remains effective with respect to the collateral that D sold Buyer "even if the secured party knows of or consents to the disposition."

Section 9–507(a) and 9–315(a)(1)s' rules together work to save the secured creditor monitoring costs and impose search costs on third parties dealing with transferees of collateral. But this is true only within a range of transfers of collateral. For transfers outside this range, Revised Article 9 indirectly imposes monitoring costs on the secured creditor. This is true where the debtor transfers collateral to a transferee-debtor located in another jurisdiction. Section 9–316(a)(3) provides in this case that the security interest remains perfected for one year after the transfer. Thus, to remain perfected, the secured creditor must perfect its security interest in the transferee-debtor's jurisdiction within that time. Given this consequence of collateral transfers, prudent secured creditors must monitor their collateral to some extent. Notice that 9–102(a)(28)(A) defines a "debtor" to include "a person having an interest . . . in the collateral." In the ongoing example, Buyer therefore is a "debtor" because, as the transferee of collateral, it acquired such an interest. See Comment 2a. to 9–102. However, 9–316(a)(3)'s "one year" limitation doesn't apply in the ongoing example to render SP's security interest unperfected: Buyer filed a bankruptcy petition six months after Debtor transferred the collateral to it. Buyer's location therefore has no effect on the result.

Do you believe that the result in this example is fair? Don't these rules mislead searchers attempting to assess the extent of Buyer's financial resources? SP has what amounts to a secret lien in property in the possession of Buyer that searchers may believe is unencumbered. No search of filings in Buyer's name is likely to turn up SP's interest.

PROBLEM

If you are representing a creditor planning to make a secured loan to a person like Buyer in the previous discussion, what steps do you have to take in exercise of due diligence? See Comment 3 to 9–507.

### b.   NAME CHANGE

In the Problem below, there is what Comment 4 to 9–507 refers to as a "pure" name change. The business entity has not changed, only its name has.

### PROBLEM

Shannon and Patricia Scott own all of the stock of K.C. of Camden, Inc., which entered into a security agreement granting a security interest in all inventory, accounts, machinery, equipment, furniture, and fixtures, now owned or thereafter acquired, to Bank as security for a loan. Bank promptly filed a financing statement naming K.C. of Camden, Inc. as the debtor. A year later the Scotts decided to change the name of their company to "Camden Audio & Video, Inc." They did not inform Bank of the change. The newly renamed company applied for a loan from Lender, which advanced the funds after finding no financing statement on record in the name of Camden Audio & Video, Inc. Lender took a security interest in the same assets covered by Bank's security interest and filed a financing statement naming Camden Audio & Video, Inc. as the debtor. Which secured party is prior as to the described collateral acquired by the debtor before and after the name change? Would you get the same result if the new name were "K.C. of Camden Audio & Video, Inc."? See 9–507(b) and (c) and Comment 4 to 9–507.

### c.   CHANGE IN BUSINESS STRUCTURE

In this section we deal with changes in business structure: the original debtor is an individual proprietor who incorporates or is a corporate debtor that merges into another corporation. The issues we face are whether a security interest in the collateral of the original debtor continues in this collateral after it has passed to what Article 9 calls the "new debtor," which will have a different name than the original debtor, and whether the security interest also covers collateral of the new debtor acquired after the change in business structure. See Comment 2 to 9–508. We raise these issues in the following Problem. After the Problem, we set out the conflicting views of pre-Revision authorities on these issues. Then we lead you through the rather complex statutory edifice that Revised Article 9 has constructed to deal with these issues.

### PROBLEM

Shannon and Patricia Scott, as individuals, bought a business in May 2004. They granted a security interest to Bank in all inventory, accounts, machinery, equipment, furniture, and fixtures to secure a loan. Bank perfected its security interest by filing. The security agreement included an after-acquired property clause, and the financing statement described this collateral and identified the debtors as Shannon and Patricia Scott "d/b/a K/C Audio/Video Center of Camden." In July 2004 the Scotts incorporated the business as "KC of Camden, Inc." (Corporation) and transferred all their business assets to Corporation, which assumed all their business debts. In August 2004, Borg–Warner (BW) agreed to supply inventory to Corporation on credit. Corporation granted BW a security interest in all Corporation's inventory in a security agreement containing an after-acquired property clause. The financing statement identified the debtor as "KC of Camden, Inc." In 2005, Corporation defaulted on all its debts. Bank sued to foreclose on its collateral, and BW intervened claiming a security interest in the collateral purchased from it. Does BW or Bank have a first priority security interest in inventory acquired by Corporation from BW after the time of incorporation?

### (1) Pre-Revision Authorities

Before Revised Article 9, on facts resembling those in the Problem, judicial authority was divided. One view was represented by In re Scott, 113 B.R. 516 (Bankr. W.D. Ark. 1990), in which the court, applying former Article 9 law, held for BW on the ground that Bank had no security interest in the inventory purchased by debtor from BW because the new corporate entity, KC of Camden, Inc., had not entered into a security agreement with Bank. Bank retained its security interest only in the collateral transferred by the Scotts to Corporation and the proceeds of that collateral. Inventory acquired by Corporation from BW was not proceeds of any of Bank's collateral. Bank did not acquire a security interest in this collateral because Corporation did not sign a security agreement with Bank providing for a security interest in this collateral.

A second view, held by some courts, as well as some commentators, rejected the position of the *Scott* court as unrealistically strict. In cases in which the old debtor entity merely takes a new legal form, such as an individual or a partnership incorporating, the creditor community is dealing with the same people and the same business operations as before. If the financing statement after the transformation is not seriously misleading, searchers are not really misled by the change in form of the debtor. Nobody is hurt merely because the new entity didn't enter into a new security agreement with the secured party because the new entity usually takes a transfer of all the assets of the old entity and assumes liability on all its debts, including the security interest. It didn't stretch matters to say that the new entity adopted the security agreement of the old entity. This is the view taken by the drafters of the new law, but in order to reach this result they had to build an elaborate statutory structure, centering on the "new debtor" concept.

### (2) "New Debtor" under Article 9

Using the facts of the above Problem, KC of Camden, Inc. is a "new debtor" under 9–102(a)(56) if it "becomes bound as debtor under 9–203(d) by a security agreement previously entered into by another person." Section 9–203(d) in turn provides that a person may become bound as a debtor on a security agreement entered into by another person either by contract or by operation of law. A common manner for a successor entity to become bound as a debtor is for it to agree to become liable for all debts of its predecessor at the time when it receives transfer of its predecessor's assets. This general liability would include liability on the predecessor's security agreement. Another way of becoming bound as a debtor is by operation of law. In some cases, such as mergers, state corporate law renders successor entities liable for the debts of the old entities. State law generally does not make a corporation liable for the debts of its incorporator. However, if state law holds the corporation liable for the incorporator's debts, KC Camden, Inc. is a "new debtor." See Comment 7 to 9–203 and Comment 3 to 9–508. The Scotts in that case become the "original debtor" under 9–102(a)(60).

Section 9–203(e) provides that if KC Camden, Inc. is a new debtor, bound by the security agreement of the Scotts with Bank, there is no requirement that the new debtor enter into a new security agreement with Bank; Bank's security interest attaches to all the existing or after-acquired property of the new debtor (Corporation) that is described in the security agreement with the original debtor. Comment 7 to 9–203.

Now that the security agreement issue has been taken care of, what about the financing statement? Section 9–508(a) provides that a financing statement naming the original debtor is effective to perfect a security interest in collateral of the new debtor to the extent that the financing statement would have been effective had the original debtor acquired the collateral. This includes existing collateral held by the new debtor covered by the original debtor's security agreement, not just the collateral acquired from the original debtor. Section 9–508(b) states an exception to this rule in cases in which the difference between the names of the original debtor and the new debtor causes the financing statement to be "seriously misleading." If the financing statement has become seriously misleading, it is effective to perfect a security interest only in collateral acquired by the new debtor before, and within four months after, the new debtor becomes bound unless a financing statement naming the new debtor is filed before expiration of the four-month period. So, if the financing statement is not seriously misleading with respect to Corporation, Bank does not have to re-file against Corporation. If it has become seriously misleading, Bank does not have a perfected security interest in collateral acquired by Corporation more than four months after Corporation becomes bound unless it re-files before the expiration of that time.

So far, we see that in a new debtor case the effect of the elaborate statutory provisions we have considered above is to benefit the secured creditor of the original debtor. This is because the new debtor is bound by original debtor's security agreement, and its security interest remains perfected in old and newly acquired collateral without the filing of a new financing statement, at least for four months. Thus, the solution to the Problem above would seem to be that Bank's security interest is prior to that of BW even in collateral purchased by Corporation from BW after incorporation. So far, we have pulled the laboring oar in the new debtor analysis in the Problem above, but there is still another step to take, which we pose in the following Problem and leave for your solution.

## PROBLEM

In settlement negotiations regarding the case posed by the Problem stated above, Bank argued that the analysis described above establishes its priority with respect to the collateral acquired by Corporation from BW. But BW disagrees, contending that under 9–326(a) Bank's security interest is subordinated to that of BW in collateral acquired by Corporation from BW. Bank replies, with exasperation, if you are right why does Article 9 have all that stuff about new debtors? Which party is correct? See Comment 2 to 9–326.

------

We see in this section that Article 9 is very kind to filers and tough on searchers. In cases of transfer of assets, the burden is on prospective lenders or other searchers to ascertain whether a prospective debtor has acquired property that is subject to a prior security interest. Article 9 does not force a secured party that has perfected by filing to monitor its debtor to learn whether it has transferred collateral to another. In name-change cases, the secured party that has filed has four months to learn of the change and to file an amended financing statement containing the new name. Four months should be enough for a secured party to become aware of the fact that the debtor's payment checks and correspondence bear a different name. In the new debtor cases the secured party that has filed on the property of the original debtor need take no action to protect itself against creditors of the new debtor unless the name change has made the financing statement seriously misleading, and even then the four-month rule applies. But 9–326 poses an exception to this rule.

## C.   The Filing System

### 1.   Central Filing

Section 9–501(a)(2) adopts the state's central filing office, usually the office of the Secretary of State, as the place of filing a financing statement in all cases except those involving certain real property-related collateral. In the latter case filing must occur locally in the office where real property mortgages are recorded. This provision finally abolishes the wasteful practice of requiring dual filing that prevailed in several states. The belief that it is more convenient to have the files in the courthouse downtown than on an easily accessible central database is an illusion. Comment 2 to 9–501.

Before Revised Article 9, estimates are that the requirement of dual filing in a number of states produced a system of more than 4300 UCC filing offices. Lynn M. LoPucki, Why the Debtor's State of Incorporation Should be the Proper Place for Article 9 Filing: A Systems Analysis, 79

Minn. L. Rev. 577, 579 (1995). The increased costs of a system requiring dual filing are obvious: filing creditors have more records to file; filers have more chances for error; more fees are paid.

The professed reason for requiring local filing was stated in Comment 1 to former 9–401(a): "[I]t can be said that most credit inquiries about local businesses, farmers and consumers come from local sources; convenience is served by having the files locally available and there is not great advantage in centralized filing." This statement assumes a business world that no longer exists. It is difficult to believe that today it is more convenient for a filer or searcher to go to the county court house and hunt around in the records there than it is to deal with a central, computer-accessible database. In truth, it is likely that the statement quoted above is little more than a rationalization of the political reality that in many states the county recorders were a powerful force that demanded as much local filing as possible as a condition to removing their opposition to the Code. Central filing cost them the fees they had been accustomed to collecting for filing chattel mortgages and other types of security interests. Anecdotal evidence shows that the Code's enactment would have been blocked in some of the early adopting states if the recorders had not been placated.

If any evidence is necessary that local recording officials were still zealously looking out for their own interests on the eve of the Revised Article 9 project, read the chronicle of the belated enactment of Article 9 in Louisiana, effective 1990, in James W. Bowers, Of Bureaucrats' Brothers-in-Law and Bankruptcy Taxes: Article 9 Filing Systems and the Market for Information, 79 Minn. L. Rev. 721 (1995). Bowers describes the ultimate compromise:

> A deal was struck. Filing fees for a financing statement in Louisiana are fifteen dollars per form, and most of that money is paid to the local clerks of court. The balance goes to the secretary of state, who maintains a technologically whiz-bang, computerized, central filing system. All filing is done, however, with the local clerks, who simply fax copies of all the financing statements to Baton Rouge, collect the fees, live off the float, and eventually pay the secretary of state his or her share.

Id. at 724.

In adopting Revised Article 9, Louisiana has retained its system of local filing. Under its nonuniform version of 9–501, financing statements are filed with any local clerk of courts, wherever the debtor or collateral is located. There is no exception for fixtures or reality-related collateral. Central filing with the Secretary of State is not permitted. Instead, local filings are transmitted to the Secretary of State, which maintains a database. Searches of the database can be conducted at any local clerk of court.

## 2.   KINDS OF RECORDS FILED

### a.   FINANCING STATEMENT RECORDS

Section 9–102(a)(39) defines "financing statement" as meaning "a record or records composed of an initial financing statement and any filed record relating to the initial financing statement." This definition includes amendments, continuation statements and termination statements.

*Initial Financing Statement.* When we speak of a financing statement, we usually mean the initial financing statement. Such a financing statement is effective for five years, 9–515(a), and lapses at the end of this period unless before that time a continuation statement is filed, 9–515(c). The UCC Financing Statement (Form UCC1) found in 9–521(a) is the safe harbor written form for an initial financing statement that must be accepted by all filing offices. Comment 2 to 9–521. A person is entitled to file an initial financing statement only if the debtor has authorized the filing in an authenticated record. 9–509(a). But the debtor's authentication of a security agreement automatically authorizes the filing of a financing statement covering the collateral described in the security agreement and the proceeds of that collateral. 9–509(a). An unauthorized filing of a financing statement is ineffective (9–510(a)), and the filer is liable under 9–625 for actual and statutory damages. If more than two debtors or one secured party are involved in the transaction or more space is needed for the description of collateral, the Addendum form (Form UCC1Ad) may be used as a supplement to the financing statement.

## PROBLEMS

**1.** In a signed written security agreement, Debtor grants Secured Party a security interest in all its medical equipment now owned or thereafter acquired, and Secured Party advances funds. Subsequently, Secured Party files a financing statement naming Debtor and describing the collateral as "all personal property." Has Debtor authorized Secured Party to file the financing statement? 9–509(b).

**2.** On January 1 Secured Party files a financing statement naming Debtor and covering machine XYZ. On that date Debtor and Secured Party were negotiating the terms of a security agreement. On February 1 they came to terms and executed a written security agreement covering machine XYZ, which Debtor signed. Two weeks before, Debtor signed a security agreement with Bank covering machine XYZ, and Bank on the same day filed a proper financing statement. Both Secured Party and Bank made loans to Debtor as part of their respective security agreements. Is Secured Party's filing authorized? If so, on what date? See Comment 3 to 9–509. For the bearing of the question on Secured Party and Bank's respective rights in machine XYZ, see 9–322(a)(1).

---

*Amendment.* Under 9–512(a) "amendment" is a generic term that includes continuation or termination of an existing financing statement, adding or deleting collateral, or otherwise changing the information provided in a financing statement. The amendment must identify by its file number the initial financing statement to which it relates. UCC Financing

Statement Amendment (Form UCC3Ad) set out in 9–521(b) is the safe harbor written amendment form. If the amendment adds collateral or an additional debtor to a financing statement, the debtor must authorize the filing. 9–509(a). Otherwise, under 9–509(d), amendments usually may be authorized by the secured party of record, defined in 9–511.

*Continuation Statement.* The effectiveness of a financing statement may be extended for an additional five years by the filing of a continuation statement (line 3 of Form UCC3) before lapse of the financing statement. 9–515(e). The new five-year period runs from the time the financing statement would have become ineffective if no continuation statement had been filed. Additional continuation statements may be filed, but the filer cannot achieve ten years' protection by filing a continuation statement the day after filing the initial financing statement. Under 9–515(d) a continuation statement may be filed only within six months before expiration of the financing statement. A continuation statement that is not filed within the six-month period is ineffective. 9–510(c). The filing of an amendment other than a continuation statement does not extend the period of effectiveness of the financing statement. 9–512(b). The secured party of record (9–511) may authorize the filing of a continuation statement without further authorization by the debtor if some part of the obligation secured by the security interest is still owing. 9–509(d)(1).

*Termination Statement.* Line 2 of UCC3 applies to termination statements. In commercial cases, when the obligation secured by the collateral covered by the financing statement is paid in full, the debtor may demand that, within 20 days, the secured party either send debtor a termination statement that debtor may file or file the termination statement itself. 9–513(c). Since secured parties have no desire to pay additional filing fees, the common practice is to send the statement to the debtor for filing. The requirement of 9–513(c) means that the secured party has no duty to send debtor a termination statement until debtor demands one. Comment 2 to 9–513(c) assures us that even if debtors forget, the files won't be cluttered with financing statements covering defunct transactions because they automatically lose effectiveness after five years unless they are continued. Section 9–513(a) and (b) recognize that it would be unrealistic to expect consumer debtors to request termination statements and place the burden on the secured party to file a termination statement within one month after the obligation secured by the financing statement is paid. If the secured party fails to comply with 9–513(a) or (b), the debtor may authorize the filing of a termination statement. 9–509(d)(2).

*Assignment.* Security interests are frequently assigned. Section 9–514 prescribes the methods for reflecting assignments in the filing records. Line 4 of UCC3 applies to assignments. Case #1. A common transaction is for a dealer to take a security interest in goods sold and, almost immediately, assign the security interest to a financer. 9–514(a). In cases of this sort, the initial financing statement is commonly filed by the assignee with its name and address as the secured party. The assignee becomes the secured party of record and only it can authorize amendments. 9–511(a). It is not apparent to a searcher that the security interest has been assigned. Case #2. Another familiar transaction is for the original secured party to become the secured party of record by filing the original financing statement. Later the secured party may assign the security interest to an assignee and reflect this by filing an amendment to the initial financing statement that provides the name and address of the assignee. 9–514(b). The person named in the amendment is the secured party of record. 9–511(b).

PROBLEM

What are the consequences in Case #2 if no amendment reflecting the assignment to the assignee is ever filed? The security interest is now owned by the assignee with no public notice given that the secured party of record (the original secured party) no longer owns the security interest. If the debtor goes into bankruptcy, is the assignee left with an unperfected security interest? See 9–310(c) and Comment 4 to 9–310.

b. SAFE HARBOR FORM

*A National Form.* Throughout the drafting of Revised Article 9, the goal was to find a safe harbor financing statement form acceptable to filing offices all over the nation. American business is increasingly national in operation, and secured parties may file in a number of states. Uniformity in filing office requirements therefore is desirable. The acceptance by the Drafting Committee of the UCC Financing Statement Form (UCC 1), set out in 9–521(a), achieves that goal, and there is now a national financing statement that filing offices everywhere must accept. In fact, to date almost half of state filing offices will accept only the national form. For the background of the preparation of the national form, together with an analysis of its contents, see Harry C. Sigman, Putting Uniformity Into— and Improving the Operation of—the Uniform Commercial Code: The New National Financing Statement Form, 51 Bus. Law. 721 (1996) (the author, a member of the Drafting Committee, played a major role in the development of this form).

*Additional Debtor Information.* Box 1d. calls for stating either the debtor's social security number or a taxpayer identification number. This information is useful as a cross-check to the debtor's name but is not infallible; SSNs are not verifiable from public records and debtors may have more than one taxpayer ID. Of course, there are privacy objections to giving this information. Although the form does not disclose that giving this information is optional, the failure of 9–516(b) to include absence of this information as mandating rejection effectively makes it optional. This is not true with respect to Box 1e. "type of organization," Box 1f. "jurisdiction of organization," and Box 1g. "organizational ID, if any." Under 9–516(b)(5)(C), if this information is not given the filing office must refuse to accept the record for filing under 9–520(a). Organizational IDs apply only to registered organizations like corporations; states assign these numbers at the time the entity is organized. Availability of these numbers, coupled with disclosure of the jurisdiction or organization, will make identification of registered entities much easier.

*Financing Statement Addendum.* Form UCC1Ad. 9–521(a). Most filers will not need an addendum, but some will. An addendum should be filed when there are more than two debtors or more than one secured party of record. These are relatively rare occurrences. Box 16 provides space for additional collateral descriptions in cases in which the space on the financing statement is inadequate. Some of the need for lengthy collateral descriptions has been removed by the decision in 9–504(2) to allow as an adequate description a statement that the financing statement "covers all assets or all personal property." The addendum must be used if collateral is real property-related collateral such as timber to be cut or goods that are or are to become fixtures. Section 9–502(b) requires a financing statement covering such collateral to indicate that it is to be filed in the real property records and provide a description of the real property. See Boxes 13 and 14. The statement that the financing statement will be filed in real property records appears in Box 6 of the financing statement. An indication that the debtor is a transmitting utility has been taken from the financing statement, where it causes confusion, and placed in Box 18 where fewer people will have to deal with it.

*Financing Statement Amendment.* Form UCC3Ad. 9–521(b). This is the Swiss Army Knife of UCC forms. It allows the secured party to (1) terminate the effectiveness of the financing statement, (2) continue the effectiveness of the financing statement, (3) give the name of an assignee of the security interest, (4) change debtors or secured parties of record, and (5) add or delete collateral. It too has an addendum for additional information.

## 3.   When Filing Becomes Effective

### a.   FILING OFFICE INDEXING ERRORS

Section 9–516(a) continues the rule that filing occurs either when a financing statement is presented to the filing office, with tender of the filing fee, or the filing office accepts the record. But what if the filing office does not correctly index the record after it is received? Section 9–517 provides that the failure of the filing office to index a record correctly does not affect the effectiveness of the filing. A secured party that has presented an appropriate financing statement does not bear the risk that the filing office will not perform its duties even though no public notice is given. How far does this protection of the secured party extend?

### PROBLEM

Secured Party (SP) filed a written financing statement that meets all requirements of Article 9 with Filing Office (FO). SP availed itself of its right under 9–523(a) to furnish a copy of the financing statement to FO with a request that it note on the copy a file number and the date and time of the record and send the copy to SP. Under 9–519(h), FO is obliged to send the copy to SP not later than two business days after it received the record in question. SP's practice is to file another financing statement in any case in which it has not received the copy from FO within ten calendar days after it dispatched the financing statement to FO. Although SP can prove that FO received the financing statement, for unknown reasons FO never indexed it. Owing to staff error, SP failed to note that the copy had not been returned; hence, it did not refile with the FO. Has SP made an effective filing in this case? See 9–516(a).

### b.   DUTY OF FILING OFFICE TO ACCEPT OR REJECT

Pre–Revision law prescribed the requirements for a "sufficient" financing statement but was silent on what a filing office could or should do if presented with a document that did not meet these requirements. The assumption was that the filing office could reject such documents, but nothing in the statute said that it must do so. There was no uniformity among filing offices on the extent to which in deciding whether to accept a financing statement a filing office's duties were merely ministerial (e.g., no mailing address for debtor) or whether some discretion could be exercised in interpreting the statutory requirements (e.g., adequacy of description of collateral).

Revised Article 9 is decisive on these issues. Under 9–520(a), "[a] filing office shall refuse to accept a record for filing for a reason set forth in Section 9–516(b) and may refuse to accept a record for filing only for a reason set forth in Section 9–516(b)." Thus, a filing office's discretion is curbed; it must reject any financing statement that lacks the information prescribed in 9–516(b), and it may reject only if it lacks this information. Hence, a filing office is not permitted to impose conditions or requirements other than those stated in 9–516(b). But what if it wrongfully rejects a record on an extra–9–516(b) ground? Section 9–516(d) provides that such a record is effective as a filed record "except as against a purchaser of the collateral which gives value in reasonable reliance upon the absence of the record from the files." Earlier in this Chapter we examined the consequence of when a filing office wrongful accepts a record that does not contain the information set out in 9–516. See 9–520(c).

Revised Article 9 does not address the liability of a filing officer to those harmed by the officer's acts. State tort law normally applies to hold the filing officer liable for its negligence resulting in harm to filing or searching parties. Of course, wrongful rejection by the officer of a financing statement for reasons other than those stated in 9–516(b) does not cause harm to the filing party because 9–516(d) considers the statement effective as a filed record, except as against relying purchasers. There is no negligence liability. In other cases, such as the negligent issuance of a certification where no financing statement was filed, filing office acts might cause harm. Jurisdictions generally take one of three positions on the matter: (1) allow recovery against the filing officer, usually based on negligence, subject to standard tort defenses; (2) insulate the officer from personal liability through coverage by liability insurance; or (3) insulate the officer from personal liability through state sovereign immunity.

## D.   PERFECTION BY POSSESSION

### 1.   POSSESSION BY AGENT

The transaction in which perfection occurs by the secured party's possession is often called a pledge. Section 9–310(b)(6) follows traditional law in empowering secured parties to perfect security interests by taking possession of goods, certificated securities (stock and bond certificates), instruments (promissory notes), and documents of title (bills of lading, warehouse receipts). These items have in common the fact that they can be physically possessed. Although a promissory note is a promise to pay money, the promise is exclusively embodied in a piece of paper and can be enforced only by the holder of the note. This is not true of a contract to build a house; one gains no rights by being in possession of the written contract. Nor is it true of accounts, such as rights to payment arising from the credit sale of inventory, or general intangibles such as copyrights; intangibles cannot be possessed.

If the secured party physically possesses an article of collateral belonging to the debtor, the debtor's other creditors should be on notice and have reason to investigate. Thus, both attachment (9–203(b)(3)(B)) and perfection (9–313(a)) occur when a secured party takes possession of collateral pursuant to the agreement of the debtor. No authenticated security agreement is required. See the discussion on this point in Comment 4 to 9–203.

Modern commercial affairs are conducted by organizations that must operate through their agents, and possession by an agent of the secured party for the purpose of possessing on behalf of the secured party is perfection. See the important discussion of possession in Comment 3 to 9–313. The following case discusses the limits of perfection by possession of an agent.

## In re Rolain

United States Court of Appeals, Eighth Circuit, 1987.
823 F.2d 198.

■ EUGENE A. WRIGHT, CIRCUIT JUDGE.

We are asked to apply Minnesota law in this appeal arising from bankruptcy proceedings. The trustee in bankruptcy contends that the creditor bank has no perfected security interest in a negotiable instrument entrusted by the bank to an attorney agent. We find that there was a perfected security interest and affirm the judgment of the district court.

Norwest Bank loaned $163,000 to Rolain and a corporation of which he was president, United Wisconsin Properties. United Wisconsin executed a promissory note that was later partially guaranteed by United Corporations of Minnesota (UCM), its parent company. UCM's guarantee was secured by a note of one of its debtors, Owen. The Owen note was the collateral pledged by UCM to Norwest to secure the loan.

Norwest wished to perfect its security interest in the Owen note, which would require the bank or its agent to hold the document. Rolain was reluctant to let Norwest hold the note, however, because its terms were subject to a confidentiality agreement between himself and Owen. The parties agreed that the note would be held by Rolain's attorney, Mannikko, under a written agency agreement.

In November 1981, in consideration for Norwest extending the note's due date, UCM increased its guarantee of the note between Norwest and United Wisconsin. The agency agreement was amended accordingly. Rolain later filed for bankruptcy under Chapter VII and that proceeding was consolidated with those of the corporations owned by Rolain, including UCM and United Wisconsin.

Norwest moved in the bankruptcy court for a partial summary judgment that it had perfected its security interest in the Owen note. Bergquist, the trustee in bankruptcy, filed a cross-motion for summary judgment. The bankruptcy court granted the bank's motion and denied Bergquist's, and the district court affirmed.

\* \* \*

A trustee may avoid transfers or encumbrances on property of the bankrupt estate. 11 U.S.C. § 544(a) (1982). The [Bankruptcy] Code vests him with the rights of a bona fide purchaser of real property from the debtor or a creditor having a judicial lien or an unsatisfied execution. *Id.* The trustee's rights under section 544 are derivative. They are those of a creditor under state law. \* \* \*

Here, the applicable law is UCC § 9–305:

When Possession By Secured Party Perfects Security Interest Without Filing.

A security interest in letters of credit and advice of credit . . . goods, instruments (other than certificated securities), money, negotiable documents, or chattel paper may be perfected by the secured party's taking possession of the collateral. If such collateral other than goods covered by a negotiable document is held by a bailee, the secured party is deemed to have possession from the time the bailee receives notification of the secured party's interest.

Comment 2 to this provision states:

[p]ossession may be by the secured party himself or by an agent on his behalf: it is of course clear, however, that the debtor or a person controlled by him cannot qualify as such an agent for the secured party. . . .

The issue is whether Mannikko was under such control by Rolain that he could not serve as a bailee/agent under § 9–305.

The leading case on the issue of bailee/agent possession is In re Copeland, 531 F.2d 1195 (3d Cir.1976). The court held that an escrow agent, acting for the benefit of both parties, was a "bailee with notice" within the meaning of § 9–305 and that his possession perfected the creditor's security interest. *Id.* at 1203–04. *Copeland* and subsequent cases explained that the purpose of the perfection requirement is to give notice to all current and potential creditors that the property was being used as collateral and could not be repledged. * * *

*Copeland* noted that if the debtor or "an individual closely associated" with him holds the collateral, this would not sufficiently alert prospective creditors that the debtor's property is encumbered. *Copeland*, 531 F.2d at 1204. However, the holder of the document need not be under the sole control of the creditor. "[P]ossession by a third party bailee, who is not controlled by the debtor, which adequately informs potential lenders of the possible existence of a perfected security interest" satisfies the notice requirements of § 9–305. *Id.*

Once the parties have designated an agent with no interest in the collateral, * * * and the collateral is delivered to him, the debtor no longer has unfettered use of the collateral and the notice function of section 9–305 is served by the agent's possession. * * *

Mannikko is a third party who asserts no interest in the collateral. Because the Owen note was delivered to him under a written agency agreement, Rolain would not have unfettered use of it and could not repledge it. If he did so, his lack of possession would notify the third party creditor that the note was encumbered.

Bergquist argues that a debtor's attorney may never be a suitable bailee because the attorney-client relationship necessarily means that the attorney is under the control of the client. However, courts have held explicitly that attorneys may act as valid § 9–305 agents. In *O.P.M. Leasing*, the debtor deposited money with its firm of lawyers to be held in escrow as security for performance under a lease contract. 46 B.R. at 664. The court found that the law firm was a valid bailee. *Id.* at 670; see also Barney v. Rigby Loan & Investment Co., 344 F.Supp. 694, 697 (D.Idaho 1972) (citing Henry v. Hutchins, 146 Minn. 381, 178 N.W. 807, 809 (Minn.1920) for proposition that debtor's attorney may serve as bailee or pledge holder).

The lawyers' possession of the security served " 'to provide notice to prospective third party creditors that the debtor no longer has unfettered use of [his] collateral.' " *O.P.M. Leasing*, 46 B.R. at 670 (quoting *Ingersoll–Rand*, 671 F.2d at 844–45). Because the debtor's attorneys had their client's consent and were acting as a fiduciary to the secured creditor, they were bound by the terms of the escrow agreement. 41 Bus. Law. at 1478. Possession of the negotiable documents served notice to third parties that the documents were encumbered. *Id.*

The same may be said here. With Rolain's consent, Mannikko signed an agency agreement, promising to act as Norwest's agent in holding the note and perfecting Norwest's security interests. He acted as a fiduciary to Norwest, was bound to respect the agency, and did so.

Bergquist argues that, even if a debtor's attorney may serve as a creditor's § 9–305 agent, the personal relationship between Rolain and Mannikko was so close that there was debtor control of the agent. He says that the two engaged in business ventures, vacationed together, and confided in each other about personal matters. Therefore, says Bergquist, Rolain controlled Mannikko and that Norwest and others were aware of that control. The argument concludes that Mannikko's possession of the note did not put others on notice of the note's encumbrance.

This is unpersuasive. Except for Rolain's claims, the record indicates nothing unusual about selecting Mannikko as Norwest's agent. All parties agreed to the arrangement. Indeed, it was desirable because Mannikko was one of the few persons whom both parties could trust to hold the note without disclosing its confidential terms. There is no remaining question of material fact.

Norwest's security interest in the Owen note was perfected.

AFFIRMED.

### NOTES

**1.** Article 9 does not define "possession." See Comment 3 to 9–313. Thus, the term must be defined by the purpose of the requirement of perfection by possession. If the purpose of possession by a secured creditor is to put third parties on notice that the creditor might have an interest in the debtor's possessed asset, then a secured creditor or its agent has possession when the debtor lacks unrestricted control of the asset. When does that occur? When the debtor no longer has exclusive control over the asset? Or when the secured creditor or its agent has exclusive control?

**2.** Can possession by an agent of both the debtor and secured party perfect a security interest in the secured party? Should entrustment of possession of the collateral, a note, by the secured party, Bank, to Mannikko, *the debtor's lawyer*, be enough to perfect Bank's security interest under 9–313(a)? Isn't Mannikko the debtor's agent? How does this act give the debtor's other creditors notice of Bank's security interest in the note? Wouldn't creditors assume that Rolain still controls the note? See Comment 3 to 9–313. Would *Rolain* be decided under 9–313(a) or (c)?

**3.** The *Copeland* case, discussed in *Rolain*, involves the pledge of corporate stock. We will discuss perfection of security interests in investment securities in Chapter 7.

## 2.  Possession by Bailee

Under pre-Revision law, if the debtor's property was in possession of a non-agent bailee, the debtor and secured party could create a perfected security interest in the property. How perfection could be achieved depended on the nature of the bailment. If the bailee had issued a negotiable document of title covering the goods, perfection could occur either in the document or the goods. In all other bailments, perfection could occur if the secured creditor had the bailee issue a document of title in its name, notified the bailee of its security interest, or filed as to the goods. These "other" cases are bailments in which the bailee either issues a non-negotiable document of title or issues no document at all. Revised Article 9 retains these rules in the case of bailments in which negotiable and nonnegotiable documents of title covering the goods are issued. See 9–312(c) and (d). It alters the perfection requirements when the bailee has not issued a document of title.

Section 9–313(c) makes an abrupt change in law. Under pre-Revision law, the secured creditor could perfect in the bailed property simply by notifying the bailee that it holds the property for the secured creditor's benefit. The bailee's agreement was not required, and the question of its duties under such an arrangement was never clearly resolved by case law. Under 9–313(c), a secured party does not have a perfected security interest in property in possession of a third person unless the person acknowledges that it holds possession of the collateral for the secured party and does so in an authenticated record, either a signed writing or an authenticated electronic record. And if a third person is instructed by the debtor and secured party to acknowledge that it holds possession for the secured party, the person may decline; it is not required to acknowledge that it holds the property for the secured party. 9–313(f). Comment 8 notes that there are many reasons why a third person may possess debtor's goods, e.g., storage, repair, use by a lessee, that may be inconsistent with holding for the secured party.

If the third person does acknowledge that it holds possession for the secured party, the nature of its duties and responsibilities is left to the agreement of the parties or other applicable law. 9–313(g). Comment 8 states: "For example, by acknowledging, a third party does not become obliged to act on the secured party's direction or to remain in possession of the collateral unless it agrees to do so or other law so provides."

In summary, under 9–313, a secured party cannot perfect a security interest in property in possession of a non-agent third person unless the person agrees in an authenticated record to hold possession of the goods for the secured party and further agrees as to the nature of the duties and responsibilities under which it holds the property. One issue on which pre-Revision law was particularly unsettled was whether a junior secured party could take a security interest in collateral already in the possession of a senior secured party without the consent of that party. How would the following Problems be decided under 9–313?

PROBLEMS

Debtor, the payee of a negotiable promissory note for the amount of $100,000, borrowed $10,000 from Bank and pledged the note to Bank to secure the loan. Debtor indorsed the note and delivered it to Bank. The pledge agreement provided that upon payment by Debtor of its debt to Bank, the note would be returned to Debtor with Bank's indorsement. The agreement also provided that if Debtor defaulted Bank could either collect from the maker of the note if the note was due or sell the note to the highest bidder. If collection or sale of the note brought more than the amount of Debtor's debt, Bank was required to return the surplus to Debtor. Later, Lender agreed to lend Debtor $15,000, and to secure the loan Debtor executed a security agreement granting Lender a junior security interest in the note which was in Bank's possession. Debtor and Lender jointly sent a letter to Bank directing Bank to hold the note for the benefit of the Lender and, (1) deliver the note to Lender if the debt to Bank was paid and (2) pay any surplus over $10,000 to Lender, to the extent needed to pay Debtor's debt to Lender, with the remaining surplus going to Debtor, if the note was collected from the maker or sold.

**1.**   Bank did not reply to the letter from Debtor and Lender. Does Lender have a perfected security interest in the note?

**2.**   Bank promptly replied to the letter and stated that it declined to serve in any capacity on behalf of Lender. When Debtor repaid the $10,000 loan, Bank indorsed and returned the note to Debtor without notification to Lender. Did Lender have a perfected security interest before Bank returned the note to Debtor? Did it have a perfected security interest after Bank returned the note to Debtor? 9–313(d).

**3.**   When Bank failed to reply to the letter, Lender decided to file a financing statement describing the note as collateral. What are Lender's rights with respect to the collateral. Recall that 9–312(a) provides that security interests in instruments may be perfected by filing.

## E.   PERFECTION BY CONTROL

Control will be discussed more fully in the context of the materials on deposit accounts in chapter 3 and investment securities in chapter 7. At this point, we discuss briefly the part played in Revised Article 9 by the control concept. As is noted above, Revised Article 9 expands the role of perfection by control. Control is an alternative way of perfecting a security interest in the following types of collateral: deposit accounts (9–104), electronic chattel paper (9–105), investment property (9–106) and letter-of-credit rights (9–107). See 9–314(a). In the case of deposit accounts as original collateral and letter-of-credit rights other than as supporting obligations, control is the only means of perfection. 9–312(b). The notion of control at work closely follows its use in Article 8 with respect to investment property. Comment 7 to 8–106 identifies the characteristic feature of control: "The key to the control concept is that the purchaser has the ability to have the securities sold or transferred without further action by the transferor."

Article 9 defines the requirements for control for each type of collateral. The requirements differ. For instance, control of a letter-of-credit right requires the issuer of a letter of credit to "consent" to the assignment of proceeds of the letter of credit. 9–107. On the other hand, control of a certificated security—a type of investment property (9–102(a)(49))—requires control as provided by 8–106. See 9–106(a). According to 8–106(b), control of a certificated security occurs when the certificate is delivered and endorsed to the purchaser or in blank or registered by the issuer in the purchaser's name. Delivery and endorsement or registration are more onerous requirements than "consent."

As a method of perfection, control can be evaluated. The purpose of a requirement of perfection is to cure the ostensible ownership problem: the inference of unencumbered ownership third parties draw from the debtor's possession of collateral. A filed financing statement provides information that prevents third parties from (wrongly) drawing the inference. Obviously, a pledge does too, because the pledged collateral no longer remains in the debtor's possession. The control concept in Revised Article 9 does not always cure the ostensible ownership problem; it sometimes doesn't serve as a substitute for filing or possession.

For instance, control is the exclusive means of perfecting a security interest in deposit accounts as original collateral. 9–312(b)(1). Control in a deposit account can be obtained in three different ways: (i) when the secured party is the depository bank at which the account is held; (ii) when the debtor, secured party and bank agree in an authenticated record that the bank will comply with the secured party's instructions with respect to the deposit account; or (iii) when the secured party becomes the bank's customer with respect to the deposit account. 9–104(a)(1)–(3). On the other hand, control by a secured creditor other than the depository bank requires it to either obtain the depository bank's "authenticated agreement" or become the bank's customer with respect to the deposit account. 9–104(a)(2)–(3). Where there is a qualifying three-party authenticated agreement, third parties are on notice that a deposit account might be subject to a security interest. Record evidence provided by the authenticated agreement signals that further inquiry might be warranted. The same is true, of course, when the secured party is the bank's customer with respect to a deposit account, because the secured party is the owner of record of the deposit account. No notice at all is provided to third parties when the depository bank is the secured party. Although Comment 3 to 9–104 says that in this case "no other form of public notice is necessary," in fact no public notice is given. Perfection instead occurs automatically, by virtue of the depository bank's status as a secured creditor having a security interest in the debtor's deposit account. The ostensible ownership problem remains uncured. Earlier versions of Revised Article 9 allowed filing of a financing statement to perfect in deposit accounts. Filing would have given notice of the depository bank's possible security interest. The final version of the Revision eliminated filing as a permissible perfection method.

## F.  SECURITY INTERESTS IN CONSUMER GOODS

### 1.  CONSUMER TRANSACTIONS UNDER ARTICLE 9

Article 9 was drafted at the dawn of the movement for reform of consumer credit law. By the end of the 1940s a few states had retail installment sales acts and most had personal loan laws. Professor Gilmore recalls that at an early drafting stage it was contemplated that a number of the provisions found in retail installment sales acts would be incorporated into Article 9. Disclosure requirements and abolition of holding in due course with respect to consumer paper were examples of these provisions. It soon became apparent that no agreement could be reached on the desirability of these consumer protection provisions, and the final draft contained only a few remnants of the original grand scheme to protect the consumer debtor. The story is told in 1 Grant Gilmore, Security Interests in Personal Property § 9.2 (1965). The fall-back position taken was to provide in former 9–203(2) that Article 9 should be subordinate to those consumer protection laws passed in states that enacted the Code. A comparable provision is now found in 9–201(b). This handed back to state legislatures the bone of contention concerning consumer credit protection on which they were to gnaw for the next 30 years. Former 9–206 also relinquished to the enacting states the determination of the validity of waiver of defenses clauses in consumer credit transactions. This provision is now found in 9–403(e).

In former Article 9, special protection for defaulting consumer debtors was found in 9–505(1) on mandatory disposition of consumer goods (now found in 9–620(e)) and 9–507(1) on statutory damages for failure to comply with the provisions on default in consumer transactions (now found in 9–625(c)(2)). The most interesting vestige of the consumer protection phase of Article 9 was former 9–204(2), which greatly limited the effect of an after-acquired property clause in secured transactions involving consumer goods. This provision is now found in 9–204(b)(1). The purpose of this section was to prevent a seller from adding on new sales to the balances of old ones merely by use of an after-acquired property clause in the original security agreement. But all a seller had to do to avoid this provision was to require the buyer to sign new security agreements at the time of subsequent sales. Nothing in Article 9 then prevented the seller from consolidating the sales and subjecting all the goods sold to the buyer to a security interest securing the combined balances of all the sales. This left the unfortunate buyer in the position, described in Williams v. Walker–Thomas Furniture Co., 350 F.2d 445 (D.C.Cir.1965), of being subjected to a lien on all property purchased until the last dollar of the consolidated balance was paid off. The solution to this abuse is found in Uniform Consumer Credit Code 3.303 (1974) and other state statutes that allocate the debtor's payments entirely to discharging the debts first incurred, thus releasing from the seller's security interest each item sold as soon as the debtor's payments equal the debt arising from that sale.

So we see that in the drafting of the 1962 UCC most of the consumer protection provisions—finance charge disclosure, abolition of holding in due course, rate regulation, and the like—failed to make it into the final draft owing to the difficulty of finding consensus on these provisions. The same fate befell the Uniform Consumer Credit Code, drafted in the late 1960s, which included these provisions, and was enacted in only a few states. Not until the federal government intervened, beginning with the Truth in Lending Act of 1968, did uniformity come to consumer credit protection.

During the long drafting process for Revised Article 9, a number of pro-debtor provisions were proposed that were not included in the final draft for lack of consensus, e.g., limits on deficiency judgments, award of attorney's fees to debtor if successful, right to cure default, absolute bar rule. But as we go through chapter 4 on Default and Enforcement, we will see that some significant pro-consumer provisions were added. In some instances consumer transactions are excluded from provisions viewed as too pro-creditor, e.g., 9–626(b) excludes consumer transactions from the rebuttable presumption rule, allowing courts that embrace the absolute bar rule to apply it in consumer cases. Similarly, the transformation rule, which turns purchase money transactions into non-purchase money transactions, to the advantage of consumers in bankruptcy, is not abolished for consumer transactions as it is for commercial transactions. 9–103(f). Greatly improved disclosure for consumers is required by 9–614 for notification before disposition of collateral, and by 9–616(b) for calculation of the surplus or deficiency after disposition. Although consumer advocates didn't achieve as much as they might have wished, they apparently saw enough progress in Revised Article 9 to allow it to be enacted without their opposition, which in some states is powerful.

## 2.   PERFECTION OF SECURITY INTERESTS IN CONSUMER GOODS

Revised Article 9 continues the rule that a purchase money security interest in consumer goods is automatically perfected at the time of attachment, with no requirement of filing. 9–309(1). The reasons for this exception are: (1) consumer transactions are frequently small, so the expense of filing can significantly add to the price that the consumer will have to pay; (2) consumer transactions are very numerous and they would unduly burden the filing system; (3) the pre-Code rule in most states did not require filing in conditional sale transactions; and (4) parties to consumer transactions are less likely to search the records. See 2 Grant Gilmore, Security Interests in Personal Property § 19.4 (1965). However, filing is necessary to perfect a nonpurchase money security interest in consumer goods and, as we shall see, is required for priority in consumer-to-consumer sales under 9–320(b). Comment 5 to 9–320.

Two circumstances reduce the importance of 9–309(1) today. The first is that automatic perfection does not apply to some of the most valuable kinds of consumer goods: motor vehicles, boats and the like. Under certificate of title laws, perfection of security interests in these items must usually be accomplished by listing the security interest on the certificate of title. 9–311. Security interests in airplanes must be recorded in the federal registry. See In re Avcentral, Inc., 289 B.R. 170 (Bankr. D. Kan. 2003). The second is the advent of debit and credit cards, which has almost entirely taken over the credit purchase of "small ticket" consumer goods; most of these purchases are unsecured. However, some retailers who issue their own credit cards retain security interests in sales made pursuant to these cards. Except for the use of secured credit card transactions by a few retailers, the purchase money security interest in "small ticket" consumer goods sales is a thing of the past. Problem 1 below helps illustrate the operational problems with 9–309(1), but it is a bit dated because Music Center probably got rid of its credit department years ago and has been letting Visa and MasterCard worry about its customers' payment habits.

The following two elementary Problems show that the same article of goods can be defined differently in different transactions with very different legal consequences.

## PROBLEMS

**1.** Your client, Music Center, sells musical instruments of all kinds: strings (electric guitars are its best seller), pianos, brasses, and woodwinds. Music Center reserves a security interest in goods sold on credit. Some items run in excess of $5,000 in price, but most sales are between $250 and $1,000. Among its customers are amateur musicians: high school band and orchestra members, and adults who play instruments for their own pleasure. Perhaps a fourth of Music Center's credit sales are made to professional musicians: members of professional performing groups and teachers who use their instruments in giving lessons. Your client complains that some of his customers sell their instruments at swap meets to raise money before they have paid for them; others file in bankruptcy when they lose their jobs. Advise him how to set up workable operating procedures that will protect its security interest in goods sold. 9–309(1), and 9–320(b)(2). Assume that in the jurisdiction, filing fees are $20 for a written financing statement and $15 for an electronic filing. Would your advice change if some of Music Center's amateur musicians become so proficient at their purchased instruments that they later become professional musicians? What if a buyer signs a written representation in the contract that she intends to use the goods for a consumer purpose but, in fact, uses them for a business purpose? See In re Troupe, 340 B.R. 86 (Bankr. W.D. Okla. 2006).

**2.** Manufacturer sold furniture to Retailer on credit, reserving a security interest in the furniture and its proceeds after it had been sold. Retailer sold furniture to numerous consumers, reserving a security interest in the furniture. Neither Manufacturer nor Retailer filed financing statements covering the furniture they sold. Does Manufacturer have a perfected security interest in the furniture that it sold to Retailer which is still in Retailer's possession? Does Retailer have a perfected security interest in furniture sold to consumers? See the definitions of "consumer goods" in 9–102(a)(23) and "inventory" in 9–102(a)(48).

## G.   CHOICE OF LAW

### 1.   LOCATION OF DEBTOR GOVERNS TANGIBLE AND INTANGIBLE COLLATERAL

Article 9's provisions on choice-of-law radically simplify the law and make it much easier to apply. Moreover, choice-of-law issues will probably be somewhat less important under the new law. This is true because all 50 states enacted the revision in time for the effective date—July 1, 2001—to be the same for all states. From that date on, all jurisdictions have virtually identical provisions on perfection, priority and enforcement of secured transactions in personal property. So if we have the identical law in effect in every state, why are we concerned with deciding what state's law controls? One reason is different case law: jurisdictions develop nonuniform case law interpreting the same model rules. A second reason is that, although adoptions of the Revision have been mostly uniform, states have adopted some nonuniform amendments to Article 9. In order to decide whether a nonuniform amendment applies, we need to know which state's law controls. A third reason is that although the provisions of the statute are identical, there is no national filing office for UCC financing statements. Therefore, if perfection is by filing, the filing must be done in the filing office of some state. Our principal inquiry is, which state? Where would the debtor's prospective creditors be most likely to look for financing statements filed against the debtor: where the debtor resides, where the debtor does business, where the collateral is located, or where a corporate debtor is chartered?

A word about the prior law is helpful in appreciating the magnitude of the change wrought by Revised Article 9 in the choice-of-law area. Under the former law, for "ordinary" goods, a situs test applied: the financing statement had to be filed in the state where the goods were located. For intangibles, such as accounts and general intangibles, there could be no physical location of the collateral, thus, the location of the debtor was the place of filing. What happened when the proceeds of the sale of goods were intangibles? Then filing in both the location of the goods and the location of the debtor was required to cover both goods and proceeds. What if the goods were removed from one state to another? Follow the goods. What about goods that were "mobile" and moved about constantly? Here the debtor's location governed. These rules seem sensible but, in spite of a substantial revision in 1972, problems continued to arise and litigation on these issues flourished.

One of the major recommendations of the Article 9 study group was to abolish the dual choice-of-law rules: location of collateral and location of debtor. PEB Study Group, Recommendation 9.A recommended a single debtor-location rule to cover both goods and intangibles. This recommendation is implemented by 9–301(1), which states the general rule that the law of the location of the debtor governs issues of perfection, the effect of perfection, and priority with respect to both tangible and intangible collateral, whether perfected by filing or automatically. Comment 4. But this rule is subject to the exceptions set out in 9–301, as well as exceptions for particular sorts of collateral such as deposit accounts, investment property and letter-of-credit rights described in other sections. See 9–302–305.

Section 9–301(2) provides that with respect to *possessory* security interests the issues of perfection, the effect of perfection and priority are governed by a situs test: the location of the collateral controls, not debtor's location. A rather confusing exception is found in paragraph (3)(C), which provides that, with respect to nonpossessory perfection of security interests in tangible property, the law of the situs of the collateral governs the *effect* of perfection and the priority of the security interest. The subsection leaves the issue of perfection to be determined by the law of the location of the debtor. Comment 7 explains the reason for this bifurcation between perfection and the effect of perfection and priority:

> For example, assume a security interest in equipment located in Pennsylvania is perfected by filing in Illinois, where the debtor is located. If the law of the jurisdiction in which the debtor is located were to govern priority, then the priority of an execution lien on goods located in Pennsylvania would be governed by rules enacted by the Illinois legislature.

We will say no more about this bifurcation at this point because our mission in this chapter is to decide merely where and how to perfect and not such issues as the priority of a perfected security interest. Moreover, since all the states now have Revised Article 9, the laws governing priority and the effect of the perfection of security interests are usually going to be the same in the jurisdiction of the debtor's location as in that of the location of the collateral.

In summary, 9–301 retains the traditional rule that the location of the debtor governs the perfection, effect of perfection, and priority of security interests in intangible collateral, for intangible collateral has no location. For tangible collateral in which perfection is by possession, the law of the location of the collateral governs perfection, the effect of possession, and priority. But for tangible property in which perfection is by filing, the law of the location of the debtor governs perfection, but that of the location of the collateral governs the effect of possession and priority.

## 2.  LOCATION OF THE DEBTOR

As we have seen, 9–301(1)'s general rule is that with respect to nonpossessory security interests, the law of the debtor's location governs questions of perfection, the effect of perfection and priority. Under 9–307(b), a debtor who is an organization is located at its place of business if it has one, at its chief executive office if it has more than one place of business, and at the debtor's residence if the debtor is an individual. "Organization" is defined broadly to include every legal or commercial entity other than an individual. 1–201(b)(25). Subsection 9–307(b) is mildly misleading because it is subject to an exception that almost devours the rule in most business cases. The exception is contained in 9–307(e), which states that a "registered organization" organized under state law is located in the state of organization. "Registered organization" is defined in 9–102(a)(70) broadly enough to include limited partnerships and limited liability companies, in addition to corporations. For convenience we will refer to this as the place-of-incorporation test. The location of individual debtors and unregistered partnerships continues to be the debtor's chief executive office.

The seminal article recommending and justifying the place-of-incorporation test is the piece by Lynn M. LoPucki, Why the Debtor's State of Incorporation Should be the Proper Place for Article 9 Filing: A Systems Analysis, 79 Minn. L. Rev. 577, 595–597 (1995). The Drafting Committee was persuaded by his reasoning and adopted the test. Professor LoPucki's thesis is that the two principal bases for attacking the validity of financing statements, errors in the debtor's name and filing in the wrong office, can both be largely removed by adoption of the place-of-incorporation test. A corporation can have but a single state of incorporation, and that place is discoverable from public incorporation records with relatively little expense and effort, either by a telephone call or on the Internet. This is in contrast to a location-of-collateral test or a chief-executive-office test, neither of which is based on a matter of public record or verifiable by computer, and both of which will often require multiple filings. Since the place-of-incorporation test will drive filers and searchers to consult public incorporation records to verify where the debtor is incorporated, errors with respect to the debtor's name should be reduced because these records will show the correct name of the debtor. This development will allow the Code to require that the debtor's exact name and state of incorporation be used on financing statements.

The Drafting Committee has not followed LoPucki's reasoning completely. LoPucki's thesis would locate the debtor at its place of registration, wherever the place of registration. The thesis would direct prospective creditors to search records at that location, whether the location is domestic or foreign. Section 9–307, however, does not locate foreign registered organizations at the place of their registration. Section 9–102(a)(70) limits "registered organizations" to state or federally registered organizations. Hence 9–307(e)'s registration-locus rule doesn't apply to foreign registered organizations. Further, 9–307(c) contains an exception (a "limitation," according to the subsection's title) to 9–307(b)'s location-of-debtor test for debtors located in jurisdictions other than the United States. The exception makes 9–307(b)'s location test applicable to non-United States debtors only when the foreign jurisdiction's law generally requires public record notice of nonpossessory security interests as a condition of priority. If the foreign jurisdiction's law does not generally do so, 9–307(c) locates the foreign debtor in the District of Columbia. In this case creditors are to direct their searches to Washington D.C., not to the place of registration. The actual location of the foreign debtor (place of business or chief executive office) is irrelevant.

Section 9–307(c)'s exception to 9–307(b)'s location-of-debtor test is difficult to justify, for two reasons. First, as a comparative matter, a creditor can determine its debtor's location, wherever the location, at less cost than it can determine whether 9–307(c) deems the debtor to be located in the District of Columbia. Arguably it is also less costly to determine whether the debtor's chief executive office or its place of business is located. Second, and related, in order to know whether 9–307(b)'s location-of-debtor test is inapplicable to foreign debtors, a creditor must know a fair amount about applicable foreign substantive law. It must know whether foreign law "generally" subordinates nonpossessory security interests which have not been made public through record notice. The creditor needs to know this in order to know the proper place to file or search. The only safe (and costly) alternative is to file and search in two jurisdictions: the foreign location of the debtor and the District of Columbia. By requiring a fair amount of knowledge of foreign law, 9–307(c) requires creditors to make a significant initial investment in vetting their prospective debtors. It is worth asking whether 9–307(c)'s exception to 9–307(b)'s location-of-debtor test yields benefits that justify the additional costs imposed on creditors. It's also worth asking whether a simple place-of-registration test for registered debtors, domestic or foreign, wouldn't be less costly for filing and searching creditors. Section 9–316(a) continues perfection for different periods when the debtor or collateral moves to another jurisdiction. Section 9–316(a)(2) provides that when the debtor changes its location to another jurisdiction the secured party has four months after removal to file in the state of removal. Strictly speaking, a corporation doesn't change its place of incorporation; it must incorporate in the state of removal, or merge with or be acquired by a corporation in the other state. Because a corporation doesn't retain its legal status when it reincorporates or merges, reincorporation or merger can't constitute "a change of the debtor's location in another jurisdiction" for 9–316(a)(2)'s purposes. Instead, 9–316(a)(3) applies so that the secured creditor's security interest remains perfected for "one year after a transfer of collateral to a person that becomes a debtor and is located in another jurisdiction." See Example 4, Comment 2 to 9–316. Monitoring will always be required in these situations, but a corporation is probably less likely to change its place of incorporation than its chief place of business, and it is certainly less likely to do so than to move its goods around.

At first glance, a state-of-incorporation test might seem to direct a disproportionate number of filings to Delaware, but Professor LoPucki has found that there is a 93% chance that a corporation is incorporated in the state where it operates. 79 Minn. L. Rev. at 600. With respect to the large corporations that do incorporate in Delaware, many have no secured debt, and, for those that do, their creditors are likely to be sufficiently sophisticated to deal with the new system. The location of a company's chief place of business is only important for businesses that are not registered organizations, e.g., sole proprietorships and general partnerships.

## 3.   GOODS COVERED BY CERTIFICATE OF TITLE

### a.   THE BASIC RULES OF PERFECTION

Filing a financing statement is neither necessary nor effective to perfect a security interest in goods in which a certificate-of-title law provides for a security interest to be indicated on the certificate as a condition or result of perfection. 9–311(a)(2). Compliance with such a statute is the equivalent to filing a financing statement, and a security interest in such property may be perfected only by compliance. 9–311(b). "[A] security interest so perfected remains perfected notwithstanding a change in use or transfer of possession of the collateral." 9–311(b).

A special rule is made for goods held in inventory for sale or lease by a dealer who sells goods of that kind. Ordinarily no certificate of title for a motor vehicle is issued by the state until the vehicle is sold or leased by the dealer. The manufacturer sends a certificate of origin to the dealer, and when the vehicle is sold the dealer sends the certificate of origin along with the buyer's application for a certificate of title to the state's department of motor vehicles (DMV). If the sale is being financed, the certificate of title issued must indicate the security interest of the financer as a condition of perfection. Hence, during the time the dealer holds the vehicles for sale or lease, no certificate of title has yet been issued, and 9–311(d) provides that during this time 9–311 does not apply. A secured party financing the dealer's inventory may perfect its security under normal rules applying to inventory, that is by filing a financing statement. Section 9–311(d) does not apply to dealers who only lease goods; even though they eventually sell the goods, they should not be considered to be "in the business of selling goods of that kind." Comment 4 to 9–311. See Union Planters Bank, N.A. v. Peninsula Bank, 897 So.2d 499 (Fla. Dist. Ct. App. 2005) (debtor is car rental company).

### b.   WHAT LAW GOVERNS PERFECTION?

Section 9–303(c) states: "The local law of the jurisdiction under whose certificate of title the goods are covered governs perfection, the effect of perfection or nonperfection, and the priority of a security interest in the goods covered by a certificate of title from the time the goods become covered by the certificate of title until the goods cease to be covered by the certificate of title." Can the parties obtain a certificate of title from any jurisdiction or must it be issued by the jurisdiction where the debtor is located?

## Meeks v. Mercedes Benz Credit Corporation

United States Court of Appeals, Eighth Circuit, 2001.
257 F.3d 843.

■ PER CURIAM.

Bankruptcy trustee William S. Meeks (Trustee) appeals the district court's judgment affirming the bankruptcy court's judgment in favor of

Mercedes–Benz Credit Corporation (MBCC) in his adversary proceeding to avoid MBCC's lien on proceeds from the sale of a truck.

Billy Stinnett (Debtor) purchased a Freightliner truck (on credit) from Texarkana Truck Center, Inc. (TTC), in Texas. The parties' security agreement indicated that Debtor's home address was in Arkansas. TTC immediately assigned the contract and its interest in the truck to MBCC. On Debtor's behalf, Trux, Inc. registered and titled the truck in Oklahoma, using a business address it acquired for him. Oklahoma subsequently issued a title reflecting a lien in favor of MBCC. Upon purchasing the truck, Debtor immediately drove it to his Arkansas residence, and thereafter operated the truck from his residence, hauling loads primarily to Texas, Colorado, Oklahoma, and Kansas. Debtor never owned a business in Oklahoma.

The bankruptcy court concluded that under Ark.Code Ann. § 4–9–103(2)(b), Oklahoma law controlled the perfection of MBCC's security interest; and because Oklahoma law required indication of a security interest on the certificate of title for perfection, MBCC's interest was perfected for purposes of Arkansas law. The court thus entered judgment for MBCC. Trustee appealed to the district court. * * * [T]he district court affirmed the decision of the bankruptcy court. This appeal followed.

After de novo review, * * * we conclude the bankruptcy court correctly determined MBCC's interest was perfected for purposes of Arkansas law. *See* * * * Ark.Code Ann. § 4–9–103(2) (Supp.1999) (where goods are covered by certificate of title issued under statute of another jurisdiction—under law of which security interest must be indicated on certificate as condition of perfection—perfection of security interest is governed by law of jurisdiction issuing certificate of title; law continues to govern until goods are registered in another jurisdiction); Okla.Stat.Ann. tit. 47 § 1105(G) (2000) (statement of lien or encumbrance shall be included on Oklahoma certificate of title and shall be deemed continuously perfected).

The Trustee argues that Arkansas's statutes concerning motor vehicle registration, *see* Ark.Code Ann. §§ 27–14–801, 802 (1994), apply to determine the validity of MBCC's security interest, and that under these provisions, the security interest was not perfected because the truck was never registered in Arkansas. We agree with the bankruptcy court and the district court, however, that section 4–9–103(2)(a), (b) (Supp.1999)—Arkansas's codification of a section of the Uniform Commercial Code (UCC)—applies instead. The issue involved in this appeal is the perfection of MBCC's security interest, not compliance with Arkansas's vehicle registration laws, which serve a different purpose. *See In re Durette*, 228 B.R. 70, 72–74 (Bankr.D.Conn.1998) (considering virtually identical factual situation involving similar motor-vehicle-statute conflict with UCC provision; vehicle registrations and certificates of title are governed by separate statutes and serve distinct purposes: purpose of registration requirements is identification and revenue while purpose of requiring that lien be noted on title certificate for perfection is to provide notice of encumbrance to potential purchasers or creditors); *Commercial Nat'l Bank of Shreveport v. McWilliams*, 270 Ark. 826, 606 S.W.2d 363, 365 (1980) ("the general policy involved in certificate of title laws ... is that lien holders and third parties should be able to rely upon certificates of title").

As the district court noted, applying the UCC provision enables buyers and lenders readily to ascertain the existence of liens on vehicles and promotes the purpose of the UCC. *See In re Paige*, 679 F.2d 601, 602 (6th Cir.1982) (purpose of UCC is to promote uniform recognition of security interests which have been noted on certificate of title; where Michigan debtor purchased truck in Indiana and titled and registered truck in Illinois using Illinois address, creditor's lien was validly perfected under Michigan's codification of UCC § 9–103(2) because Illinois certificate of title indicated lien).

Finally, we have considered but reject Trustee's remaining arguments.

Accordingly, we affirm.


NOTES

**1.**   Section 9–303(a) agrees. See Comment 1 to 9–303. Grant Gilmore disagrees. See 1 Gilmore, Security Interests in Personal Property § 10.10, at 327 (1965), states: "[T]he certificate must have been issued, although the subsection does not say so, by a 'jurisdiction' which had power to do so; if the state of Saskatchewan or the principality of Lichtenstein issues a certificate of title covering a truck owned by a debtor whose chief place of business is in Massachusetts (a Code state) and if the truck has never been operated in Saskatchewan or Lichtenstein, then the purported 'certificate of title' is merely waste paper and nothing in [§ 9–103] gives it any 'jural significance'." Which is better: to allow the parties to shop for motor vehicle friendly states, as 9–303(a) does, or, to make the determination of the effectiveness of a certificate of title depend on a troublesome issue of fact regarding the quantum of contact that the owner has with the titling jurisdiction, as Gilmore would do?

**2.**   The bankruptcy court opinion in *Meeks*, In re Stinnett, 241 B.R. 599 (Bankr. WD Ark. 1999), has more information about the role of Trux. Debtor hired Trux to process the paperwork, including the titling and licensing of the vehicle. Although Debtor didn't direct Trux in any manner, he assumed that the title and licensing would be in Oklahoma, a "trucker friendly state." Trux acquired an Oklahoma business address for Debtor. Debtor's Arkansas address appeared on the paperwork including the title. The court commented on the evidence introduced by Mercedes–Benz Credit: "The testimony was undisputed that it is common for a truck driver to have operations in multiple states and that many truck owners will title their vehicles in a trucker friendly state, one of which is Oklahoma. In this manner, truck owners attempt to reduce their costs for sales tax and other regulatory fees. The testimony was uncontroverted that the transactions in this case were typical compared to those within the industry." 241 B.R. at 600.

### c. CHANGE IN DEBTOR'S LOCATION

Typically, state laws require that motor vehicles have certificates of title and that perfection of security interests in goods covered by certificates of title occurs either upon indication of a security interest on a certificate of title or upon receipt by a state's department of motor vehicles (DMV) of a properly tendered application for a certificate of title on which the security interest is to be indicated. See Legislative Note at end of 9–311. In the following case Baker bought a car in New Mexico and obtained a certificate of title in that state when she registered the car. The certificate of title listed Primus as the lienholder. She moved to Wisconsin and registered the car there but she did not obtain a Wisconsin certificate of title. Three years after her move to Wisconsin she filed in bankruptcy. Must Primus take action to perfect its security interest in Wisconsin? Since anyone buying the car from Baker or lending money on the security of the car would demand to see the certificate of title and would learn about Primus's security interest, why should Primus have to take any action in Wisconsin at all?

## In re Baker

United States Court of Appeals, Seventh Circuit, 2005.
430 F.3d 858.

■ TERRENCE T. EVANS, CIRCUIT JUDGE.

In 2001, Judith K. Baker purchased a 2000 Oldsmobile Alero. Financing was provided by Primus Financial Services, and the State of New Mexico issued a certificate of title listing Primus as the lienholder. Soon after the deal was made, Baker moved to Wisconsin. Although she registered her vehicle in Wisconsin after the move, Baker never obtained a Wisconsin certificate of title. The New Mexico certificate of title, however, remained in place.

In 2004, some 3 years after her move to Wisconsin, Baker filed a Chapter 7 petition in the bankruptcy court. Claire Ann Resop was appointed trustee of Baker's bankruptcy estate. As bankruptcy trustee, Resop enjoys "strongarm" powers and may seek to avoid unperfected liens, assert a superior interest in assets, and distribute the value of those assets to other creditors. *See* 11 U.S.C. § 103(a); 11 U.S.C. § 544(a). This means she could, for example, challenge the validity of the lien Primus holds on Baker's vehicle, seek to gain control over it, sell it, and use the funds it yields to pay off general creditors to whom Baker owes money. That is what the trustee wanted to do in this case, but her efforts were thwarted by both the bankruptcy court and the district court. Today we resolve her appeal from the final judgment of the district court.

This appeal requires that we interpret several Wisconsin statutes. Under her reading of these statutes, the trustee argues that within 4 months of Baker's move to Wisconsin, Primus was required to reperfect its security interest in her vehicle there. Since Primus did not do so, the trustee believes that Primus's lien may be avoided.

Primus counters that this argument misreads Wisconsin law and that it had no duty to reperfect its interest simply because Baker moved herself and her vehicle to a different state but neglected to apply for a new title when she got there. Under Wisconsin law, Primus argues, the lien recorded on the New Mexico title remained valid.

The bankruptcy court examined the relevant statutes and agreed with Primus, as did the district court on appeal. * * *

Our starting point is the Wisconsin motor vehicle code. Wis. Stat. § 342.19(6) provides: "If a vehicle is subject to a security interest when brought into this state, § 409.316 states the rules which apply to determine the validity and perfection of the security interest in this state."

In turn, § 409.316, which is part of the state's codification of the Uniform Commercial Code, tells us in relevant portion: "A security interest perfected pursuant to the law of the jurisdiction designated in § 409.301(1) or 409.305(3) remains perfected until the earliest of: . . . (b) The expiration of 4 months after a change of the debtor's location to another jurisdiction." § 409.316(1). Finally, we consult § 409.301(1), which instructs us that "while a debtor is located in a jurisdiction, the local law of that jurisdiction governs perfection, the effect of perfection or nonperfection, and the priority of a security interest in collateral."

The trustee urges us to stop here and conclude that Primus's security interest in the vehicle became unperfected when Baker moved to Wisconsin and 4 months passed without Primus doing anything to reperfect its interest. And that might be a reasonable reading were it not for the fact that, as the district court explained, § 409.301(1) cannot be read without reference to the limiting language in the introduction to § 409.301. That limiting language tells us that the subsections provide the rules governing perfection "*[e]xcept as otherwise provided* in §§ 409.303 to 409.306." (Emphasis added.)

And so, turning to § 409.303, as the statutory guideposts tell us we must, we find the reason why the trustee's attempt to avoid the lien must fail. Section 409.303 provides the relevant law on the perfection and priority of security interests for "goods covered by a certificate of title." Specifically, § 409.303(3) states: "The local law of the jurisdiction under whose certificate of title the goods are covered governs perfection, the effect of perfection or nonperfection, and the priority of a security interest in goods covered by a certificate of title from the time the goods become covered by the certificate of title until the goods cease to be covered by the certificate of title." In nonlawyer speak, the 4–month period for reperfection provided by § 409.316(1)(b) does not apply to titled goods. Under

Wisconsin law, as long as the New Mexico title continued in force, it was sufficient to protect Primus's interest. * * *

* * * The rule that a security interest must be reperfected within 4 months after a debtor moves to a new jurisdiction makes sense in the context of untitled goods. But it is unreasonable to suggest that a lienholder's interest can become undone simply because an owner neglects her duty to apply for a new title when she changes states. Finance companies do not title vehicles, owners do. Had Baker retitled her vehicle in Wisconsin, Primus would have had to reperfect when its interest became unperfected under New Mexico law. Wis. Stat. § 409.316(4). But we know of no authority for the notion, suggested by the trustee at oral argument, that a secured creditor is obligated to keep track of the domiciles of its debtors. An important function of a title is to record a secured creditor's interest, regardless of where the payments come from, or where the debtor and vehicle may roam. In this case, the New Mexico title is the only record available, and the Wisconsin statutes yield the sensible result that, under that valid title, the creditor's interest remains perfected. The judgment of the district court is AFFIRMED.

## NOTES

**1.** States usually require owners to register their vehicles in the state where the owner is located and pay regulatory fees in order to obtain license plates or tags. When a debtor moves from State A to State B, she usually has a limited period of time in which to register the auto in that state and obtain State B license plates or tags before traffic police start issuing citations. The purpose of the registration statutes is identification and revenue, and the sooner the owner registers the sooner the state gets its money. When the debtor registers the auto in State B, DMV will demand to see the certificate of title issued by State A as proof of her ownership. Typically, the law of State B will require the surrender of the State A title before State B will issue a new one. DMV is required to indicate SP's security interest on the new State B title. If this is done, SP's security interest continues perfected in the auto pursuant to the new certificate of title and the former certificate of title is no longer effective because the auto has become covered by a certificate of title issued by another jurisdiction. 9–303(b). As Comment 6 to 9–303 states: "Ideally, at any given time, only one certificate of title is outstanding with respect to particular goods." And in most cases this is true, but things can go wrong, as in *Baker*. We are not told why the Wisconsin DMV did not take up the New Mexico certificate of title and issue a Wisconsin certificate of title when Baker registered the car in Wisconsin.

**2.** (a) Assume that Baker had (i) obtained a Wisconsin certificate of title when she registered her car in Wisconsin, (ii) the Wisconsin DMV neglected to list Primus's lien on the certificate of title, and (iii) Ms. Baker sold the car to a consumer buyer who had no knowledge of Primus's security interest. Does the buyer take free of Primus's security interest?

See 9–316(e), 9–337(1). *See* Metzger v. Americredit Financial Services, Inc., 615 S.E.2d 120 (Ga. App. 2005).

(b) Same facts as in (a), except that instead of selling the car, Baker filed in bankruptcy two months after she moved to Wisconsin and obtained the certificate of title. Is Baker's trustee in bankruptcy prior to Primus? What if Baker filed six months after issuance of the new title? See 9–316(d) and Comment 5. Does 9–316(e) apply in this case? See the definition of "purchaser" in 1–201(b)(30).

## 4. REVIEW PROBLEMS ON CHOICE OF LAW

PROBLEMS

**1.** Ace Gaming Supplies, Inc. ("AGS") is a Delaware corporation that sells slot machines, gaming tables, billiard tables, and related products, to casinos and other end-users, as well as to some retail dealerships that resell these goods. The headquarters of AGS is in Century City in Los Angeles. All marketing, financial and accounting services are conducted in this office. AGS maintains warehouses in Reno and Las Vegas, Nevada, and in Phoenix, Arizona, where gaming products are stored pending sale. The founder, Ace Goodman, is the Chief Executive Officer of AGS, and his son, Gerald, is the Chief Operating Officer. Ace has an apartment in Century City but spends most of the year in Aspen, Colorado, where, as his son puts it, he still "calls the shots." Gerald lives in Beverly Hills the year around. The years 2007–2009 have not been kind either to the company or Ace personally. AGS's sales were off, and Ace's personal investment portfolio, heavy in hedge funds, suffered heavy losses. Bank had been financing the company from its inception entirely on the basis of unsecured loans that were personally guaranteed by Ace. In late 2009, the company needed a major cash infusion to meet some of the mounting bills that it owed its suppliers and other impatient creditors, but, when Bank examined Ace's personal financial situation to determine the value of his guarantee, it decided that any new loan to the company would have to be secured.

In what jurisdiction should Bank perfect security interests in the assets of the company listed below and how should perfection be accomplished? In answering these questions, see the definitions of some of the kinds of collateral involved in this case: "account" 9–102(a)(2); "chattel paper" 9–102(a)(11); "deposit account" 9–102(a)(29); "general intangible" 9–102(a)(42); "instrument" 9–102(a)(47); and "promissory note" 9–102(a)(65). We will revisit some of these definitions in more detail in the next chapter, but for now you need a general idea of their meaning. See also "registered organization" 9–102(a)(70) and Comment 4 to 9–307. The rules for how to perfect security interests in these types of collateral are found in 9–310 through 9–316.

    a. The goods located in the warehouses in Nevada and Arizona.

    b. The proceeds of the sale of these goods. These proceeds may consist of the following: (1) Checks received from cash buyers and buyers making payments on credit contracts. These checks are deposited daily in the AGS's deposit account in Bank in its Los Angeles office. We will discuss methods of perfecting security interests in deposit accounts (9–314) in more detail in the next chapter. (2) For those buyers who are better credit risks, the unsecured obligations, set out in written contracts, that arise upon the credit sale of the goods to casinos or dealers who agree to pay in cash the entire amount within 90 days of the sale. (3) For less creditworthy buyers, the secured obligations, set out in written contracts, that arise upon the credit sale of the goods to casinos or dealers who agree to pay the purchase price in monthly installments over a period of one or two years and to grant the company a security interest in the goods they buy to secure the unpaid portion of the purchase price. See 9–315.

c. The business machines: (1) computers, printers, scanners, copiers, etc., located at both the Century City office and at the warehouses; and (2) the heavy loading machines located at the three warehouses in Nevada and Arizona.

d. Several promissory notes, totaling over $250,000, which are made payable to the order of AGS "on demand" and held by the company in its safe in Century City. These notes result from AGS's practice of demanding that buyers delinquent more than 60 days on an unsecured debt give AGS a note as evidence of their indebtedness until they can come up with the money. See 9–312(a) and 9–313(a).

**2.** Change the facts in Problem 1 to these: AGS is a general partnership in which the only partners are Ace and Gerald Goodman. Ace has a 75% share and Gerald, the remaining 25%. The name of the partnership is "Ace Gaming Supplies." Under these changed facts, how would you answer the question asked in Problem 1? See Comment 2 to 9–307.

**3.** What action would Bank have to take to safeguard its security interests if: (1) the corporation in Problem 1 subsequently moved the company headquarters to Dallas, Texas, in order to take advantage of the more favorable tax climate in Texas? or (2) the partnership in Problem 2 made the same move? Assume in each case that Ace and Gerald moved their personal residences to Texas as well. See 9–316.

**4.** Change the facts in Problem 1 to these. AGS owns 20 trucks and cars. All of the trucks and most of the cars are located at the warehouses. A few cars are at the Century City office. How should Bank perfect its security interest in these motor vehicles? And in what jurisdiction? See 9–303, as well as Comment 3 to that section, 9–311(a)(2) and (3), and 9–316(d) and (e). You may assume that all the states involved have laws similar to that described in the italicized Legislative Note appended to 9–311.

# CHAPTER 3

# PRIORITY

## A. INTRODUCTION

Before former Article 9 there was no coherent law of priority with respect to competing interests in personal property. As Gilmore observed, "[m]ost of the pre-Code security statutes ignored priority problems, leaving them to be solved, as they arose, by the courts on whatever principles occurred to the judges." 2 Grant Gilmore, Security Interests in Personal Property 655 (1965). One of the most ambitious reforms brought about by former Article 9 was the attempt to establish a comprehensive structure for determining priorities between the interests of UCC secured parties and those of such competing claimants as other secured parties, buyers, lien creditors (including trustees in bankruptcy), real property mortgagees, statutory lien creditors, and others. After former Article 9 had become law, the leading drafter conceded that the goal had been unattainable: "Once embarked on the course of solving some priority problems, the draftsmen—afflicted, it may be, by some sort of hubris—seem to have set themselves the task of solving all priority problems, past, present and future. In this, needless to say, they did not succeed." Gilmore, supra, at 656. This is true, but the priority rules in former Article 9 were a vast improvement over pre-Code law and have yielded a degree of predictability never before experienced in the personal property security area. Revised Article 9 has addressed the earlier law's shortcomings by even more extensive priority provisions that we will discuss in this chapter.

Section 9–201(a) proclaims the primacy of security interests: "Except as otherwise provided in [the UCC], a security agreement is effective according to its terms between the parties, against purchasers of the collateral, and against creditors." As we have seen, this provision provides that even an unperfected security interest is prior to the rights of unsecured creditors and to any other purchaser or creditor unless the UCC provides otherwise. Hence, the study of priorities under Article 9 is the examination of the provisions in Subpart 3 of Part 3 that do provide otherwise. By and large Article 9 has worked well, but whether its priority rules operate fairly raises policy questions that will be addressed throughout this chapter. In greatly strengthening the position of the first party to file, has the Code been overly protective of banks and other institutional creditors at the expense of other meritorious claimants, or has the Code in fact succeeded in constructing an efficient system of priority allocation, the benefits of which outweigh the hardship that some of its rigid rules occasion? The classic tension between efficiency and fairness is evident in this area. There is also disagreement as to which priority rules are efficient.

## B.   THE FIRST-TO-FILE RULE

The key provisions in any study of UCC priority law are:

Section 9–317(a): A security interest or agricultural lien is subordinate to the rights of:

(1) a person entitled to priority under Section 9–322; and

(2) except as otherwise provided in subsection (e) [with respect to purchase-money security interests], a person that becomes a lien creditor before the earlier of the time:

    (A) the security interest or agricultural lien is perfected; or

    (B) one of the conditions specified in Section 9–203(b)(3) is met and a financing statement covering the collateral is filed.

Section 9–322(a): Except as otherwise provided in this section, priority among conflicting security interests and agricultural liens in the same collateral is determined according to the following rules:

(1) Conflicting perfected security interests and agricultural liens rank according to priority in time of filing or perfection. Priority dates from the earlier of the time a filing covering the collateral is first made or the security interest or agricultural lien is first perfected, if there is no period thereafter when there is neither filing nor perfection.

The first thing to notice is that the priority rules in both sections apply to agricultural liens as well as security interests. Agricultural liens essentially are statutorily created property rights in farm products that secure obligations incurred by the debtor in connection with its farming operations. 9–102(a)(5). They are not consensually created security interests, although Revised Article 9 considers the holder of an agricultural lien to be a "secured party." 9–102(a)(72)(B). Under 9–109(a)(2), Article 9 covers agricultural liens. Except for proceeds of farm products subject to an agricultural lien and the place of filing, the same rules that apply to security interests generally apply to agricultural liens. Although extra-Code law governs the creation of agricultural liens, Article 9 governs issues of their perfection and priority. See Dean v. Hall, 50 UCC Rep. Serv.2d 618 (E.D. Va. 2003). Sections 9–317 and 9–322's priority rules control unless the statute creating the agricultural lien gives the lien priority over a conflicting security interest. 9–322(g). The material below focuses only on security interests.

### 1.   CONFLICTING SECURITY INTERESTS

Section 9–317(a)(1) cedes to 9–322 the first issue that we will address: the priority with respect to conflicting Article 9 security interests in the same collateral. Under traditional law, the basic priority rule was "first in time, first in right," but we see in the following problems that this dictum is too imprecise to deal with a notice filing system in which filing and attachment of a security interest can happen at different times. In Problem 1, Bank is first to file but Lender is first to perfect. In Problem 2, Bank is first to perfect and Lender is first to file. See Comments 3 and 4 to 9–322. What is the justification for the results in these problems?

PROBLEMS

**1.** Debtor applied to Bank for a loan. Bank filed a financing statement authorized by Debtor covering all Debtor's equipment on February 2, along with a search request for information about any other financing statements on file under Debtor's name. Debtor also applied to Lender for a loan. On February 5, Debtor signed a written security agreement covering all its equipment, Lender advanced the proceeds of the loan to D, and electronically filed a financing statement covering the equipment. On February 9, the filing office notified Bank that there were no other financing statements on Debtor on file on February 2. Bank advanced the loan proceeds to Debtor on that date and Debtor signed the security agreement. Which creditor is prior under 9–322(a)(1) with respect to the collateral in which each party claims a perfected security interest?

**2.** Debtor applied to Bank for a loan. When Bank asked for collateral, Debtor entrusted a valuable jewel to Bank under a pledge agreement that allowed Bank to retain possession of the jewel until Debtor repaid the loan with interest. Bank advanced the funds. Later, Debtor borrowed money from Lender, and granted Lender a security interest in various items of its property in a security agreement, including the jewel. Lender perfected its security interest by filing a financing statement. Which creditor is prior under 9–322(a)(1)?

---

The guiding principle of Article 9 priority law is usually referred to as the "first-to-file rule." Now we see that this is a misnomer and, as Comment 3 to 9–323 suggests, the correct statement is "the first-to-file-or-to-perfect rule." However, the great preponderance of nonpossessory secured transactions over possessory secured transactions justifies the usual description of the rule. Perfection by possession is usually infeasible in cases of inventory or equipment financing, as well as in most cases of intangibles. We therefore sometimes follow predominant practice and refer to 9–322(a)(1)'s rule as the "first-to-file rule."

## 2. FUTURE ADVANCES

Any debt can be secured. Some security agreements cover all obligations owed by the debtor to the creditor, however they arise. Such agreements accomplish this through the use of what are called "all obligations" clauses. Frequently, security agreements cover a more limited type of obligation: "future advances." Article 9 doesn't define an "advance."

However, the term generally connotes value given by the creditor to the debtor or from which the debtor benefits. Among the first issues debated and litigated under former Article 9 were those involving its application to future advances.

In understanding Article 9's treatment of future advances, future advances clauses must be distinguished from after-acquired property clauses. Future advances clauses concern the type of debt (future advances) secured by the debtor's assets. After-acquired property clauses concern the collateral (after-acquired) that secures the debt. The two clauses deal with different things and have different effects. For instance, future advances could be secured only by existing collateral and, conversely, after-acquired collateral could secure only existing debt. Security agreements often cover both future advances and after-acquired property. Earlier, we established that if a security agreement includes an after-acquired property clause and future advances clause, the security interest automatically attaches to any after-acquired property at the time when the debtor acquires rights in this collateral, and the collateral secures all future advances made by the secured party to the debtor. See 9–203, 9–204. Thus, if the secured party has perfected its security interest in the original collateral, its security interest becomes perfected in the after-acquired collateral when it attaches. The issue we consider in this section is whether the priority of the secured party's future advances dates from the time the secured party first perfected or from the time it made the future advances.

A contractual device frequently used to secure future advances is a dragnet clause. A dragnet clause is a provision in a security agreement that secures both a specific loan as well as future loans made by the creditor to the debtor with the same collateral. To do so the clause provides for cross-collateralization: collateral securing the specific loan also secures future advances. For example, suppose a creditor makes a secured loan to a debtor as part of a security agreement listing particular items of the debtor's personal property as collateral. The agreement contains a dragnet clause securing "all loans" made by the creditor to the debtor, whenever made. Later, the creditor makes an unsecured loan to the debtor. With the dragnet clause, the later loan is secured by the same collateral securing the earlier secured loan. Although some courts finds dragnet clauses in an adhesion contract unenforceable when part of a secured loan to a consumer, most courts enforce them. Dragnet clauses generally are considered valid unless specific grounds for invalidating them exist. See In re Watson, 49 U.C.C. Rep. Serv.2d 674 (Bankr. D.N.J. 2002).

## PROBLEMS

**1.** Bank lent Debtor $100,000 and took a security interest in Debtor's equipment to secure the obligation. On October 1, Bank filed a financing statement covering the equipment. The security agreement stated that the collateral covered not only the original advance but any future advances that Bank made to Debtor. Later Lender advanced $75,000 to Debtor on the same equipment and filed a financing statement on November 1. On December 1, Bank made an additional advance of $100,000 to Debtor pursuant to the future advances clause. When Debtor defaulted on all debts, the collateral was found to be worth only $150,000. (a) How should this sum be divided between Bank and Lender? (b) Would your answer change if Lender had notified Bank of its loan before Bank made its subsequent advance? See 9–322(a) and Comment 4. (c) Would it matter if Bank's financing statement mentioned nothing about future advances? Why reward Bank, which is arguably in bad faith, with priority as to the subsequent advance? In some states the pre-UCC law was contrary, and, with respect to real estate transactions, notice to the senior mortgagee is still important. Restatement of the Law (Third) Property: Mortgages § 2.3 (1996). What interest was Article 9 furthering by omitting the notice rule?

**2.** On October 1, Bank lent Debtor $100,000 and took possession of a painting, known as "Red Square," pursuant to a pledge agreement, which provided that Bank could retain the painting until Debtor repaid its obligations. The agreement contained a future advances clause. On November 1, Debtor borrowed $75,000 from Lender pursuant to a security agreement that granted Lender a security interest in several works of art, including "Red Square." Lender perfected its security interest by filing. On December 1, Bank advanced an additional $100,000 to Debtor. When Debtor defaulted on all its debts, "Red Square" was found to be worth only $150,000 and Lender's remaining collateral was valueless. How should this sum be divided between Bank and Lender? See 9–322(a)(1) and Comment 4.

In Problems 1 and 2, in order to determine the priority of future advances, we looked only to 9–322(a) and Comment 4 to 9–322. Why didn't we look at 9–323, which is entitled "Future Advances"? Do you find any provisions in 9–323 that pertain to the above Problems? Comment 3 to 9–323 is helpful in explaining the relationship of 9–322 and 9–323:

> Under a proper reading of the first-to-file-or-perfect rule of Section 9–322(a)(1) * * *, it is abundantly clear that the time when an advance is made plays no role in determining priorities among conflicting security interests except when a financing statement was not filed and the advance is the giving of value as the last step for attachment and perfection. Thus, a secured party takes subject to all advances secured by a competing security interest having priority under Section 9–322(a)(1). This result generally obtains regardless of how the competing security interest is perfected and regardless of whether the advances are made "pursuant to commitment" (Section 9–102). * * * Thus, an advance has priority from the date it is made only in the rare case in which it is made without commitment and while the security interest is perfected only temporarily under 9–312.

------

## PROBLEM

In 2006 Dealer and Financer entered into a retail finance agreement containing the terms under which Financer would purchase the retail installment contracts entered into by buyers who bought cars from Dealer on credit. These contracts granted Dealer a security interest in the cars securing the unpaid portion of the obligations owed by buyers to Dealer for the purchase of the cars. Financer purchased these agreements from Dealer coincident with or shortly after the sale of the cars and thereafter buyers made their monthly installment payments to Financer, which now held security interests in the buyers' cars and a right to repossess upon default. The retail finance agreement between Dealer and Financer set up a "charge-back" account, common in the retail finance industry, in which Dealer agreed to maintain an account with Financer of 1.5% of the value of the outstanding installment contracts that Dealer had assigned to Financer. The agreement gave Financer the right to charge back against this account for any losses it suffered upon defaults by buyers on their retail installment contracts. The retail finance agreement did not grant Financer a security interest in Dealer's assets to secure Dealer's obligation to contribute to this account.

In 2007 Dealer and Financer entered into a wholesale finance agreement under which Financer would lend Dealer the funds to buy new cars from the manufacturer. This inventory financing transaction is sometimes described as "floor-planning." The agreement provided that Financer would maintain a security interest in all cars it financed under the wholesale finance agreement and this inventory lien would secure the full payment of all advances made, interest, all costs and expenses incurred by Financer in the collection or enforcement of the obligations under the agreement, and *"each and every other indebtedness or obligation now or hereafter owing by [Dealer] to [Financer] including any collection or enforcement costs and expenses or monies advanced on behalf of [Dealer] in connection with any such other indebtedness or obligations."*

When relations between Dealer and Financer became strained, the question arose whether under 9–204(c) the quoted provision in the 2007 wholesale finance agreement granted Financer a security interest in all Dealer's cars to secure Dealer's obligation established by the 2006 retail finance agreement to contribute to the charge-back account. Dealer argued that the retail and wholesale agreements were separate transactions and that the industry norm was that the terms of retail finance agreements do not provide for a security interest in a dealership's general assets. Financer contended that under 9–204(c) the quoted provision swept in any obligation that Dealer owed Financer under the retail finance agreement as well as under the wholesale agreement. Which party is correct? The facts are based on Pride Hyundai, Inc. v. Chrysler Financial Company, L.L.C., 369 F.3d 603 (1st Cir.2004). See Comment 5 to 9–204(c), 1–201(a)(20).

## 3.  FINANCING STATEMENT AS AN UMBRELLA

In the following Problem we examine how far the priority of the first party to file extends in a case in which there was no future advances clause in the original security agreement and the later advance was made pursuant to a subsequent security agreement, for which a new financing statement had been filed.

## PROBLEM

Transaction One. Bank lent Debtor $20,000 in January to buy First Combine. In order to secure the obligation, Bank took a security interest in the combine, which it perfected by filing a financing statement that described the collateral as "Allis–Chalmers Combine, Model G, Serial No. 77665533." The security agreement did not contain a future advances clause.

Transaction Two. Lender lent Debtor $15,000 in June and secured the obligation by taking a security interest in the First Combine, which it perfected by filing a financing statement describing the combine in the same manner as in Transaction One. The security agreement did not contain a future advances clause. Lender knew nothing about Transaction One.

Transaction Three. In December, Debtor bought Second Combine with money borrowed from Bank. Since Debtor had not fully paid its obligation to Bank for First Combine, in a new security agreement Bank took a security interest in both First and Second Combines as security for both the unpaid balance on the first transaction and the amount of the loan advanced to enable Debtor to buy Second Combine. Bank filed a new financing statement that described each combine by the same "serial number" description as used in the first transaction. Bank cancelled the contract used to finance the purchase of First Combine but forgot to terminate the financing statement filed in January.

When Debtor defaulted on all debts, Lender claimed a priority to the extent of $15,000 in First Combine under the first-to-file rule. Before entering into the second contract with Debtor, Bank had failed to check the filings and was chagrined to learn of Lender's claim of priority. However, its analysis of these transactions convinced Bank that its January financing statement, still on file, gave Bank a priority over Lender in First Combine even though the first security agreement had been cancelled. Lender replied that the absence of a future advances clause in the first security agreement precluded Bank from making such a claim; Bank should not enjoy a windfall from a prior financing statement, inadvertently left on file, arising from an earlier transaction that had been cancelled. How would this case be decided under 9–322(a)?

––––––––––

Since the controversy in the financial community on the issue raised in this Problem caused further amendments to former Article 9 on future advances and shaped somewhat the view taken by Revised Article 9 on that subject, a brief example of the differing judicial views on this threshold priority issue follows. The first decision on facts like those in the Problem,

Coin–O–Matic Service Co. v. Rhode Island Hospital Trust Co., 3 UCC Rptr. Serv. 1112 (R.I. Super. Ct. 1966), held that Lender was prior. For Bank to enjoy priority for future advances based on its January financing statement, the January security agreement must have contained a future advances clause and the advances must be made pursuant to that contract. Bank's January financing statement is not an "umbrella" giving Bank a priority with respect to advances made pursuant to subsequent security agreements covering the same collateral between the same parties. The court concluded that Bank's view:

> [p]laces a lender in an unusually strong position, vis-a-vis, the debtor and any subsequent lenders. In fact, it gives the lender a throttle hold on the debtor. For example, a debtor borrows $25,000 from a lender to be paid over a three-year period without any right of anticipation. The security is the equipment of the debtor. No provision is made for future advances. The financing statement is filed. The debtor reduces the obligation to $12,500.00 and now seeks to borrow an additional $5,000.00. The original lender is not interested in making a second loan. The debtor is in no position to pay off the loan without borrowing from another lender. The original lender does not desire to liquidate the obligation except in strict accordance with the agreement. Under the theory advanced by the defendant the original debtor cannot borrow from the second lender because no second lender can safely advance the money as long as there is a possibility that a future advance by the original lender would have priority in the collateral over the second lender . . . .

## 4.  COIN-O–MATIC REJECTED

Members of the financial bar were very upset by *Coin–O–Matic* and were pleased that most other courts disagreed. An example is Allis–Chalmers Credit Corp. v. Cheney Investment, Inc., 605 P.2d 525 (Kan. 1980), on which the facts in the Problem are roughly based. In that case, the court held that Bank was prior as to First Combine even though the security agreement did not contain a future advances clause. It stated:

> The holding in *Coin–O–Matic*, requiring a future advance clause in the original security instrument in order for future advances to have 9–312 priority, has been rejected by the vast majority of the jurisdictions in subsequent cases. In rejecting *Coin–O–Matic*, those courts generally stress the "notice" or "red flag" function of the code and hold that a financing statement on file is notice to the entire world of present or *future* security interests in the collateral. * * *

The rationale found in James Talcott, Inc. v. Franklin National Bank, 292 Minn. at 290–292, 194 N.W.2d at 784, well illustrates the approach taken by those courts which have rejected the rule adopted in *Coin–O–Matic:*

> "Even where the parties originally contemplate a single debt, secured by a single item of property or a single group of items, the secured

party and the debtor may enter into further transactions whereby the debtor obtains additional credit and the secured party is granted more security. The validity of such arrangements as against creditors, trustees in bankruptcy, and other secured parties has been widely recognized by many courts. * * *

"Using future-advance clauses and using after-acquired property clauses in the original security agreement are not the only means by which perfected security interests can be obtained in subsequently contracted obligations or in goods the debtor may later come to own. There is nothing exclusive about § 9–204(3, 5). Parties may use future-advance and after-acquired clauses, and they are a great convenience. But, if they are not used, there is nothing in the code which prevents the parties from accomplishing the same result by entering into one or more additional security agreements.

". . . The better view holds that, where originally a security agreement is executed, an indebtedness created, and a financing statement describing the collateral filed, followed at a later date by another advance made pursuant to a subsequent security agreement covering the same collateral, the lender has a perfected security interest in the collateral not only for the original debt but also for the later advance."

605 P.2d at 528–30.

In re Estate of Gruder's Will, 392 N.Y.S.2d 203, at 206 (N.Y. Sur. 1977), reached the same result, quoting White & Summers, U.C.C. HB, § 25–4 at p. 908, as follows:

"We reject the Coin–O–Matic holding for three reasons. First, it provides little protection against overreaching, for a creditor can avoid the holding simply by including a future advance clause in his security agreement. Second, we suspect that the Coin–O–Matic court misunderstands commercial practice. We suspect that it is a rare banker who will lend against the same collateral which secures a prior loan; in our experience the commercial practice is for the second lender to pay off the first and so take a first priority as to all of the collateral. Finally, Coin–O–Matic conflicts with the most obvious and we think intended meaning of 9–312(5)(a); if the draftsmen had wished to qualify the rule as the Coin–O–Matic court did, they could have done so."

605 P.2d at 528–530.

Revised Article 9 leaves unchanged former Article 9's treatment of future advance priority. However, the drafting of its provisions to reach this result is opaque. Section 9–322(a)(1)'s general first-to-file-or-perfect priority rule applies to "conflicting perfected security interests." Since a security interest can be perfected by a future advance, the general rule governs the priority of future advances too. Under 9–322(a)(1), the time at which value is given doesn't determine the priority of the security interest, unless a financing statement hasn't been filed and the giving of value is the final perfection event. When a financing statement has been filed, priority is determined by the date of its filing. This goes for secured future advances as well. When the advance was made therefore generally is irrelevant for purposes of priority. See Comment 3 to 9–323. Section 9–323(a) states a limited exception to this rule. Under this limited exception, for 9–322(a)(1)'s purposes, the priority of an advance dates from the time it was made. Here timing matters. The exception only applies when a security interest is perfected automatically or temporarily, and not made pursuant to a commitment while the security interest was perfected by some other method. See 9–323(a). These are somewhat unusual circumstances. When they don't apply, 9–323(a)'s exception is inapplicable, and 9–322(a)(1)'s general priority rule controls. Under 9–322(a)(1), where a financing statement has been filed, the timing of an advance is irrelevant for priority purposes.

## 5.   POSITION OF FIRST-TO-FILE SECURED PARTY

Now all the pieces are in place for an understanding of the position of the first party to file with respect to after-acquired property and future advances under Article 9. Notice filing allows a secured party to file a financing statement that will be effective for five years and may be continued so long as debt is still outstanding. The financing statement may indicate the collateral covered by a supergeneric indication: "all personal property." See 9–504(2).

Case #1. Assume that Debtor authorizes Bank to file a financing statement covering "all personal property," and the security agreement contains after-acquired property and future advances clauses. Now Bank takes a perfected security interest in all personal property acquired by Debtor pursuant to that security agreement and all subsequent advances made by the secured party pursuant to that agreement are secured by that collateral. Bank has priority over competing secured parties with respect to the after-acquired property to the full extent of the advances made.

Case #2. Assume that over a period of several years Debtor buys items of heavy equipment with money borrowed from Bank. Each time Bank finances a purchase, it enters into a new security agreement with Debtor granting Bank a security interest in the specifically described equipment purchased. The security agreement does not contain after-acquired property or future advances clauses. Before the first of these transactions, Debtor authorized Bank to file a financing statement covering "all personal property." No subsequent financing statement was filed by Bank. Bank has priority over competing secured parties with respect to the collateral covered by each of the discrete security agreements over the five-year life of the financing statement. Comment 3 to 9–323, in discussing a case similar to Case #1, says that in Case #2 Bank would have priority even if the subsequent advance "was not made under the original agreement with the debtor, but was under a new agreement."

Thus, a creditor can take a security interest in all the personal property a debtor now owns, or ever will own, to secure all extensions of credit for so long as a financing statement is effective, which can be forever, and, with certain exceptions, this security interest is prior as to competing secured parties. This allows a secured creditor to clean out a debtor's bankruptcy estate without a penny for either the unsecured creditors or junior secured creditors. Moreover, it allows the first-to-file creditor to monopolize the debtor's credit; subsequent creditors cannot afford to take junior security interests. The explanation for the primacy accorded first-to-file creditors given in Comment 4 to 9–322 is on efficiency grounds: "The justification for determining priority by order of filing lies in the necessity of protecting the filing system—that is, of allowing the first secured party who has filed to make subsequent advances without each time having to check for subsequent filings as a condition of protection."

## 6. OPERATING UNDER THE FIRST–TO–FILE RULE

In the preceding Problems, we have examined in detail the consequences of the first-to-file rule with respect to competing secured parties. Here we see characteristic Article 9 drafting: precise, sharp-edged and ruthless. The first-to-file provisions offer such an attractive pedagogical opportunity for introducing students to Article 9 analysis that we have probably over-emphasized their importance. The lesson to be learned from this analysis is that secured creditors should never allow themselves to become involved in a conflict with another secured creditor who has filed first unless they have taken the precautions discussed below. The presence of junior secured creditors in each of the hypothetical cases posed in these Problems is the result of classroom license to illustrate a point. In the real commercial world there would be no junior creditors involved in these cases unless they were terribly uninformed.

One reason that cases involving junior creditors are scarce is the custom of including covenants in loan agreements prohibiting the debtor from granting security interests in the collateral to other parties or incurring additional debt from other lenders without the consent of the secured party. The purpose of these covenants is to prevent the debtor from impairing its ability to repay its loan. Their breach constitutes an event of default that results in the debt becoming immediately due and payable. Hence, in practice a debtor may grant a security interest to a junior creditor only at the sufferance of the senior creditor.

Assuming that the senior creditor does not object to the creation of a junior security interest, the situations in which a creditor can safely deal with a debtor with respect to collateral in which another creditor has a senior security interest are: (i) the junior creditor has a purchase money security interest; (ii) the senior creditor has agreed to subordinate its security interest in part or in whole to that of the junior creditor; or (iii) the junior creditor has bought out the senior creditor. We will discuss the purchase money priority in the next section. In the last two situations, the junior creditor in effect becomes the senior creditor in part or whole.

There may be situations in which it is in the interest of the senior creditor to allow a junior creditor to make advances to the debtor. For example, the debtor needs further advances to keep afloat but the senior creditor does not wish to make them. In such a case the senior may be willing to agree to subordinate its security interest to that of the junior in some of the debtor's collateral. The law is very accommodating to subordination agreements. Section 9–339 states: "This article does not preclude subordination by agreement by a person entitled to priority." And BC 510 provides that subordination agreements are enforceable in bankruptcy to the same extent as under nonbankruptcy law.

If the prior secured creditor will not agree to subordination, a subsequent creditor who wishes to deal with a debtor has no choice but to pay off the prior creditor and have the financing statement on record terminated. There are different ways to do this and, as the following Problem shows, some are misguided.

## PROBLEM

Bank One and Lender have security interests perfected by filing in Debtor's collateral. Bank One, who was first to file, refused to extend further credit to Debtor and wished to terminate its credit relationship with Debtor. Bank Two agreed with Debtor to replace Bank One and, in time, to advance more funds to Debtor.

Case #1. Bank Two agreed to advance funds to Debtor to be used to pay off Debtor's remaining obligation to Bank One on condition that Bank One send Debtor a termination statement, which would then be filed. Debtor granted Bank Two a security interest in its collateral, and Bank Two advanced the funds. Debtor paid Bank One and Bank Two filed a financing statement on Debtor.

Case #2. Bank Two agreed to pay off Bank One and to take an assignment of Bank One's security interest in Debtor's collateral. Bank Two paid Bank One and received the requested assignment. What is Bank Two's priority with respect to Lender in these two cases? What if Bank Two neglected to file a financing statement in Case #2? See 9–310(c) and Comment 4.

What assistance does 9–210 offer to guide the decision of a junior creditor whether to make an advance to a debtor whose collateral is covered by a senior security interest?

## PROBLEM

On February 1, Bank advanced $50,000 on the security of Debtor's equipment and filed a financing statement covering the equipment. When Bank refused to grant more credit, Debtor induced Lender to advance $40,000 on the security of Debtor's equipment. Lender filed a financing statement on June 15. Before advancing the funds to Debtor, Lender had noted Bank's filed financing statement and had requested that Debtor submit to Bank under 9–210(a) a "request for an accounting" asking Bank's approval of the fact that only $50,000 was owed by Debtor to Bank.

When the request was made, Bank promptly approved the statement. Lender examined Debtor's security agreement with Bank and found that it did not contain a future advance clause. Lender assumed from the 9–210 statement and the fact that neither Bank's financing statement nor security agreement mentioned future advances that Bank would not be lending Debtor more money on the security of Debtor's equipment. Lender advanced the funds. But Lender's assumption was wrong, for in July Bank advanced another $60,000 to Debtor pursuant to a new security agreement granting Bank a security interest in Debtor's equipment. Debtor's equipment is worth $100,000. What is the priority of Lender in this case? Does Lender have rights against Bank based on 9–210?

## C.  PURCHASE MONEY PRIORITY

## 1.  COLLATERAL OTHER THAN INVENTORY

### a.  PURCHASE MONEY SECURITY INTERESTS

Section 9–324(a) restates the traditional rule that a purchase money security interest (PMSI) has priority over conflicting security interests in the same collateral. If the priority of the first party to file is justified by its effect in lowering monitoring costs or realizing economies of scale in secured lending, thereby encouraging the greater extension of credit at lower interest rates, how can the purchase money priority exception to the first-to-file rule be accounted for? Assume that a first-to-file lender has a security interest in all of a debtor's now owned or after-acquired equipment. Seller sells the debtor additional equipment and reserves a PMSI in the new equipment. The lender claims a priority in the new equipment under its after-acquired property clause by virtue of its status as the first party to file, but 9–324(a) accords Seller's PMSI priority as to the new equipment. The effect is to impose a burden on the lender of monitoring the records for subsequently filed financing statements and tracing the origin of the debtor's after-acquired equipment to be sure that it is not collateral in which a seller has a PMSI. Does not the purchase money priority undercut the very basis for the first-to-file rule? We will cite other justifications for the purchase money priority in Note 3 following *Brodie* below, but, for now, in the light of our discussion of the first-to-file rule in the previous section, we note that the purchase money priority is sometimes pointed to as a welcome means of allowing debtors to break the monopoly of the first party to file over the debtor's credit supply.

Section 9–103(a)(2) defines a purchase money obligation as one incurred (i) as all or part of the price of collateral (seller sells goods to buyer and takes a security interest in the goods to secure the unpaid price), or (ii) for value given to enable the debtor to acquire rights in or the use of the collateral if the value is in fact so used (lender lends money to debtor to enable it to buy goods). We will refer to these as seller purchase money and lender purchase money obligations, respectively. A purchase money obligation includes all expenses incurred in connection with the purchase of collateral, not just the purchase price. Comment 3 to 9–103. Unlike under former Article 9, a PMSI is limited to goods and software; see 9–103(a)(1). See First Bethany Bank & Trust, N.A. v. Arvest United Bank, 77 P.3d 595 (Okla. 2003) (no PMSI in accounts). Under 9–324(a), a PMSI in goods other than inventory or livestock has priority over a conflicting security interest in the same goods and their identifiable proceeds, if the PMSI is perfected when the debtor receives possession of the collateral or within 20 days thereafter. Section 9–324(b) grants PMSI priority in inventory under prescribed conditions having to do with notice.

Courts sometimes have difficulty deciding when the debtor has received possession of the collateral for the purpose of 9–324. See Note 2 following *Brodie*. An example is the following case, decided at a time when the period within which to perfect was ten days. Restaurants are among the leading candidates for bankruptcy, and, when the inevitable happens, unpaid suppliers of the restaurant equipment, like Brodie, would prefer having the new tenant of the restaurant, Lyon, buy the equipment in place rather than to rip it out and try to sell it on the used goods market. But Lyon takes awhile to make up his mind. Does this delay cost Brodie his purchase-money priority?

## Brodie Hotel Supply, Inc. v. United States

United States Court of Appeals, Ninth Circuit, 1970.
431 F.2d 1316.

■ HAMLEY, CIRCUIT JUDGE:

Brodie Hotel Supply, Inc. (Brodie), brought this action against the United States to determine which of the parties had priority, under their respective chattel mortgages, to the proceeds of the sale of certain restaurant equipment. The facts were stipulated and the property was sold and proceeds impounded by agreement. The district court granted summary judgment for Brodie and the United States appeals.

In 1959, Brodie sold the restaurant equipment to Standard Management Company, Inc., for use in a restaurant at Anchorage, Alaska. Standard Management went bankrupt. Brodie repossessed the equipment but left it in the restaurant. With the consent of Brodie, James Lyon took possession of the restaurant and began operating it on June 1, 1964. Throughout the summer of 1964, Brodie and Lyon negotiated over the price and terms under which Lyon was to purchase the equipment.

On November 2, 1964, Lyon borrowed seventeen thousand dollars from the National Bank of Alaska and, as security for the loan, which was evidenced by a promissory note, executed a chattel mortgage covering the restaurant equipment. This equipment consisted of 159 separate types of items, including a refrigerator, a dishwasher, an ice cream cabinet, spoons, forks, cups, ladles, pots, pans, and assorted glassware and chinaware. The bank assigned its mortgage to the Small Business Administration (SBA), represented in this action by the United States. On November 4, 1964, the bank filed a financing statement, showing the SBA as assignee.

On November 12, Brodie delivered to Lyon a bill of sale covering the equipment. On the same day Lyon executed a chattel mortgage on the equipment, naming Brodie as mortgagee. This mortgage was given to secure the unpaid purchase price of the equipment. Brodie filed a financing statement on November 23, 1964.

Alaska has adopted the Uniform Commercial Code (Code). Under § 9–312(5)(a), the general rule of priority, if both interests are perfected by filing, is that the secured party who first files a financing statement (in this case SBA as assignee of the bank) prevails, regardless of when his security interest attached. However, there is a special exception for purchase-money security interests in collateral other than inventory. Brodie had such an interest. Under this exception, the purchase-money security interest prevails over conflicting interests in non-inventory collateral if "the purchase money security interest is perfected [i.e., here it was perfected by filing a financing statement] at the time the debtor receives possession of the collateral or within 10 days after the debtor receives possession." § 9–312(4).

On the basis of these stipulated facts, Brodie moved for summary judgment. Brodie contended that although Lyon received possession of the restaurant equipment on June 1, 1964, over five months before Brodie's financing statement was filed, Lyon did not become a "debtor," and the equipment did not become "collateral" until November 12, 1964, when Lyon received the bill of sale and executed Brodie's chattel mortgage. Accordingly, Brodie contended, it was not until November 12, that "the debtor [Lyon] receive[d] possession of the collateral" within the meaning of the statute referred to above. As already indicated, Brodie's financing statement was filed within ten days of that date. The district court agreed with this analysis in granting summary judgment for Brodie.

If the term "debtor" is given the meaning ascribed to it in § 9–105(d), Brodie was entitled to priority.[1] It was not until November 12, 1964, that Lyon purchased the equipment and became obligated to pay the purchase price. Until that obligation came into being, Lyon was not Brodie's debtor with power to mortgage the restaurant equipment as collateral for the unpaid purchase price.

But the United States argues that in the context of this case the priority statute, § 9–312(4), is ambiguous as to whether "debtor" is used in the sense defined in § 9–105(d), or whether it is used merely to identify an individual in possession, who ultimately becomes indebted to the purchase-money mortgagee. In contending that this "ambiguity" should be resolved

---

1. " '[D]ebtor' means the person who owes payment or other performance of the obligation secured, whether or not he owns or has rights in the collateral, and includes the seller of accounts, contract rights, or chattel paper; where the debtor and the owner of the collateral are not the same person, the term 'debtor' means the owner of the collateral in any provision of the article dealing with the collateral, the obligor in any provision dealing with the obligation, and may include both where the context so requires." § 9–105(d).

in favor of the latter construction, the United States refers to the history and underlying purposes and policies of the Code, the assertedly different language of the prior Uniform Conditional Sales Act, and the fact that, under § 9–402(1) a financing statement may be filed before a security agreement is made or a security interest otherwise attaches, notwithstanding the fact that this section refers to "debtor," "secured party," and "security interest."

We are not persuaded that either recourse to the history or consideration of the underlying purposes of the Code supports the Government's position. In our view, the term "debtor" as it is used in this particular priority statute, § 9–312(4), means "the person who owes payment or other performance of the obligation secured." § 9–105(d). Although Lyon might have been liable for the reasonable rental of the equipment or for its return to Brodie, he did not owe performance of an "obligation secured" by the collateral in question until November 12, 1964, and therefore was not a "debtor" for purposes of § 9–312(4). Brodie's filing was therefore within the ten-day period and Brodie has priority over the conflicting security interest held by SBA.

The Government has urged us to look at the policy and the purposes of the Code to resolve what it considers to be the ambiguous meaning of "debtor." The Code has granted a specially favored position to the holder of a purchase-money security interest in non-inventory collateral. The holder of such an interest need not follow the notice procedures which are prescribed for the holders of purchase-money interests in inventory. § 9–312(3). Such a holder is also given a special priority position. His interest, perfected second, but within the ten-day grace period, will prevail over any previously perfected security interest. This priority exists even though the framers of the Code knew that the holder of the conflicting security interest would be relying on the possession of the collateral and upon the absence of a prior filing. Similarly, the holder of a purchase-money security interest in non-inventory collateral will have priority over a previously perfected security interest which includes the collateral by virtue of an after-acquired property clause. § 9–312(4), Official Comment 3. Such a holder therefore is not required to search the files to determine the existence of such a conflicting interest in order to be sure of his priority.

The protection which the Code confers upon a purchase-money interest in non-inventory collateral is not unduly extended by a decision giving priority to Brodie's interest. Although it is true that Brodie could have filed a financing statement as soon as Lyon went into possession and thus protected itself, it is also true that the bank, SBA's assignor, could have protected itself by inquiring into Lyon's interest in the equipment before accepting his chattel mortgage. Due to the favored status given by the Code to the holder of a purchase-money interest in non-inventory collateral, we are not convinced that the trial court erred in refusing to impose this burden on Brodie.

Affirmed.

NOTES

**1.** You might wonder how Brodie could come within former 9–312(3)'s ten-day period: Brodie seemingly would have to file by November 22, ten calendar days after November 12, and Brodie filed on November 23. The answer is contained in Alaska's general statute controlling the computation of time. Under that statute, in effect when *Brodie* was decided, "[t]he time in which an act provided by law is required to be done is computed by excluding the first day and including the last, unless the last day is a holiday, and then it is also excluded." Alaska § 01.10.080 (2002). In *Brodie* former 9–312(3)'s ten-day period therefore began to run on November 13, and Brodie filed within ten days of that date.

**2.** Section 9–324(a) awards a creditor a purchase money priority if the creditor perfects within 20 days after "the debtor receives possession of the collateral." Courts have had difficulty in applying this language to cases like *Brodie* in which the goods have been in possession of a person for more than 20 days without any indication on the record of the existence of a security interest in them. The possibility that third parties, like the bank in *Brodie*, could be misled by the ostensible ownership of a person like Lyon is obvious. Nonetheless, the court decided the case on the ground that the possession must be that of a debtor and the possessor did not become a debtor until it agreed to buy the goods. Not until then was an obligation incurred and a security interest created. Comment 3 to 9–324 approves the *Brodie* analysis. Brodie might have prevented the bank's loss by filing as soon as possession passed to Lyon; the bank might have avoided loss by inquiring of Lyon about its rights in the goods. The court places the burden on the bank. But if a seller sells and delivers goods to a buyer on unsecured credit and more than 20 days later converts the transaction into a secured transaction by taking a security interest in the goods sold, the buyer incurred an obligation to pay at the outset and the 20–day period commences then. See Comment 3 (second paragraph) to 9–103. For another aspect of the case in which unsecured credit is transformed into secured, see Problem 1 below.

*Brodie* imposes on prospective creditors the burden of inquiring into the nature of the obligations acquired by their debtors as well as the dates on which those obligations were acquired. It does so by closely parsing former 9–105(d)'s definition of "debtor." Statutory provisions aside, is the burden placed on prospective creditors justified? Would the same analysis be made under Revised Article 9?

Suppose 9–324(a) were read so that the 20–day period begins to run from the date at which a person obtains possession of the collateral, even if it becomes a debtor subsequently. What costs would this create for secured sellers who wanted to retain purchase money priority? Consider in this regard three things the creditor could do. (1) Require her debtor to buy prior to taking possession. Alternatively, if the person already is in possession and wants to purchase the asset on a secured basis, require her to relinquish it and redeliver the collateral later. (2) File a financing statement covering the goods delivered prior to delivery, even if a sale ultimately is not concluded. (3) Deliver the goods on a "sale on approval" basis. Goods delivered on this basis are not subject to the claims of the buyer's creditors until the goods are accepted. See 2–326(1) and (2). Significant transaction costs can be produced by each of these devices. As to (1), buyers might not agree to purchase prior to taking delivery and examining the goods. As to (2), a prospective buyer might not want a financing statement filed if it decides not to buy, given the possibly adverse affects a filing might have on its credit standing. As to (3), "sales on approval" allow a buyer to return even conforming goods prior to acceptance, and a seller might not want to continue to bear this risk.

**3.** Since the seller or lender granting credit in a purchase money transaction gives the debtor new value—goods, in seller credit, or loans, in lender credit—how has the security interest of the prior secured party been impaired by awarding the seller or lender a priority in the new collateral that it enabled the debtor to acquire? For different efficiency justifications of purchase money priority, see Hideki Kanda & Saul Levmore, Explaining Creditor Priorities, 80 Va. L. Rev. 2103 (1994); Alan Schwartz, A Theory of Loan Priorities, 18 J. Legal Stud. 209 (1989); Robert E. Scott, A Relational Theory of Secured Financing, 86 Colum. L. Rev. 901 (1986); Thomas H. Jackson & Anthony T. Kronman, Secured Financing and Priorities Among Creditors, 88 Yale L. J. 1143 (1979). James J. White questions the purchase money priority in his article, Reforming Article 9 Priorities in Light of Old Ignorance and New Filing Rules, 79 Minn. L. Rev. 529, 560–563 (1995), on both efficiency and fairness grounds. He believes the strongest case for the priority is with respect to vendors who take a security interest in goods sold for the amount of the price. Still, he concludes: "I would not shed a tear over the abolition of [former] sections 9–312(3) and (4)." Id. at 563.

## PROBLEMS

**1.** On July 1, Seller sold goods to Debtor on unsecured credit. On July 7, Debtor borrowed $50,000 from Bank to pay Seller. Bank wrote the check to Seller and Debtor as joint payees and Debtor indorsed the check to Seller. Does Bank have a purchase money security interest when Debtor granted Bank a security interest in the goods to secure the debt? 9–103(a)(2). Suppose Debtor has sufficient funds to purchase goods from Seller on a cash basis, but its financial position does not allow it to buy from Seller and continue operating unless it can subsequently borrow the amount of the price from Bank. Debtor pays Seller in cash on July 7 and later obtains a loan from Bank, granting Bank a security interest in the goods purchased earlier from Seller. Does Bank have a purchase money security interest in the goods purchased on July 7?

**2.** Debtor borrowed $10,000 from Bank on July 1 for the purpose of buying a machine. Bank advanced the money by immediately crediting Debtor's checking account. Debtor granted Bank a security interest in the machine on July 1 and Bank immediately filed a financing statement. Debtor purchased the machine on July 3 and paid Seller by a check for

$10,000 drawn on the checking account in Bank. The balance in Debtor's account just before Bank credited the account was $15,000. When Debtor's check to Seller was paid the balance was $22,000. Does Bank have a purchase money security interest in the machine? 9–103(a)(2).

**3.** At the beginning of the year Debtor granted Bank a security interest in all of Debtor's equipment then owned or after acquired. Bank filed a financing statement covering equipment. In March Seller agreed to sell Debtor equipment for a price of $100,000, on terms calling for 20% down. Bank agreed to advance $20,000 to enable Debtor to buy the equipment. Bank wrote a check for $20,000 to Debtor and Seller as joint payees and Debtor indorsed it to Seller. Seller retained a security interest in the equipment which it perfected by filing upon delivery of the equipment to Debtor. What are the priorities as to the equipment between Bank and Seller? See Thet Mah & Associates, Inc. v. First Bank of North Dakota, 336 N.W.2d 134 (N.D.1983); 2 Grant Gilmore, Security Interests in Personal Property § 29.2, at 784 (1965). Section 9–324(g), discussed below, resolves the matter.

--------

At issue in this Problem is priority among multiple purchase money security interests. There are three possible resolutions: (i) priority goes to the first purchase money security interest to file, (ii) priority goes to a favored type of purchase money security interest, or (iii) the purchase money security interests rank equally and priority is awarded on a pro rata basis. Although former 9–312(4) favored (iii), a pro rata distribution, and former 9–312(5) favored (i), the first PMSI to file, neither provision clearly has the stronger statutory case. Section 9–324(g) endorses possibility (ii) and awards priority to Seller. The policy reason for doing so, recited in Comment 13 to 9–324, relies on justifications given in the Restatement (Third) of the Law of Property, Mortgages § 7.2(c) (1997). One justification is that "equities favor the vendor" and that purchase money vendors would not agree to extend credit unless they were given a priority. As to the equities, they are at least as much with the enabling lender as with the purchase money seller. After all, the lender also has provided a valuable financial input into the debtor's acquisition of the collateral. The fact that cash rather than a specific asset purchased is provided is unimportant. Both are needed for the debtor's acquisition of the asset. As to the terms of the secured interest, the lender also might not make a loan unless it were given a purchase money security interest. Focusing on the terms of the credit agreement does not favor the credit seller over the lender. A second justification, which the Restatement finds decisive, is the law's "sympathy" for the vendor. The descriptive observation about existing law does not justify continuing to favor the purchase money seller over purchase money creditors. The question is whether the "sympathy" is appropriate or misplaced.

Revised Article 9 also is inconsistent in its commitment to awarding priority among multiple purchase money security interests. Sometimes it awards priority to the purchase money seller and sometimes not. Priority in investment property under 9–328(1) is given to the secured party who has control over the collateral. Cf. 9–327(4) (security interest in deposit account perfected by control enjoys priority over security interest held by bank). If two or more secured parties have control, 9–328(2) priority is determined by the order in time in which they obtained control. (This changes the priority rule under former 9–115(5)(b), which ranks them equally.) Section 9–328(6) awards priority on a pro rata basis among claimants when perfection occurs without control and the debtor is a broker, securities intermediary or commodities intermediary. None of these priority rules favors a particular type of purchase money security interest. In fact, none recognize purchase money priority at all. Cf. 9–324(a) (purchase money priority applies where the collateral is goods).

A more convincing way of settling priority among multiple purchase money creditors perhaps is the following. A creditor with a security interest in collateral has a property right in it, and multiple secured creditors in effect have joint property rights in collateral. Joint property rights generally create inefficiencies in use. For example, some of the benefits of monitoring an item of collateral by one creditor flow to other creditors who have security interests in the same item. Because the monitoring creditor does not capture the full benefit of its monitoring efforts, it will invest suboptimally in monitoring. The same is true for the other secured creditors. Allocating priority to one or another purchase money creditor creates an exclusive property right (up to the amount of the secured debt held by the creditor) and allows a creditor to capture the full benefits of its monitoring activities. This is a reason for not ranking purchase money security interests equally and distributing collateral on a pro rata basis between them. The next question is which among the remaining ways of assigning priority are preferred. Revised Article 9 prefers the purchase money seller over other purchasers. Doing so creates an exclusive property right and is defensible for that reason. However, the same would be true if the purchase money lender were preferred. The law's sympathy for the purchase money seller provides a certain salience to the Revision's preference. But the preference at bottom is arbitrary. Some means of creating an exclusive property right is needed. The particular means used is less important and might lack a compelling justification.

## b. THE TRANSFORMATION RULE

Seller sold goods to Debtor who granted Seller a security interest in the goods sold to secure the unpaid portion of the price. Does Seller's security interest remain, in whole or in part, a purchase money security interest in the following cases?

Case #1. Debtor found it difficult to make the required monthly payments. Seller accommodated Debtor's needs by reducing the amount of the monthly payments and extending the duration of the debt. The refinancing was done by canceling the old security agreement and entering into a new security agreement embodying the new terms. In re Matthews, 724 F.2d 798 (9th Cir.1984), treated this transaction as a new loan, the proceeds of which were not used to acquire rights in the collateral; hence, the security interest was no longer purchase money. The court believed that this result was supported by the last sentence of Comment 2 to former 9–107. In re Billings, 838 F.2d 405 (10th Cir.1988), disagreed, holding that the refinancing did not extinguish the old obligation and create a new one.

Case #2. Seller sold additional goods to Debtor. The parties entered into a new security agreement in which the old and new debts were consolidated and were secured by both the old and new collateral (cross-collateralization). In re Manuel, 507 F.2d 990 (5th Cir.1975), held that, as to the old collateral, Seller's security interest lost its purchase money character because, under former 9–107(a), the security interest in that property was not retained solely to secure "all or part of its price." The same principle would invalidate the purchase money nature of Seller's security interest in the new collateral as well. This view has come to be known as the "transformation" rule, in which a security interest in any item securing more than its own price is transformed into a nonpurchase money security interest. Pristas v. Landaus of Plymouth, Inc., 742 F.2d 797 (3d Cir.1984), rejected the transformation rule in favor of a "dual status" doctrine which holds that the presence of a nonpurchase money security interest does not destroy the purchase money aspect. A purchase money security interest can remain such "to the extent" (former 9–107) that it secures the price of the goods even though it secures the price of other items as well.

Section 9–103(f) adopts the "dual status" rule for nonconsumer-goods transactions: "A purchase-money security interest does not lose its status as such, even if: (1) the purchase money collateral also secures an obligation that is not a purchase-money obligation; (2) collateral that is not purchase money collateral also secures the purchase-money obligation; or (3) the purchase money obligation has been renewed, refinanced, consolidated, or restructured." See Comment 7a. to 9–103.

*Matthews, Manuel* and *Pristas* involve consumer transactions. Section 9–103(h) provides that the dual status rule of 9–103(f) does not apply to consumer-goods transactions and prevents courts in such transactions from relying on (f) to characterize them. It doesn't disturb relevant existing case law and leaves to courts the fashioning of the proper rules in consumer-goods transactions. Of course, 9–103(h)'s exclusion does not prevent a court from deciding, on independent grounds, to apply the "dual status" rule to consumer-goods transactions. Section 9–103(h) reflects a compromise between consumer and commercial interests to retain, for the most part, the status quo concerning consumer protection. Consumer advocates wished to preserve the transformation rule in consumer cases because some bankruptcy courts used it to broaden the scope of the kinds of nonpurchase money security interests subject to avoidance under BC 522(f)(1)(B). This issue is discussed in subsection b. of the section on Inventory immediately below. The compromise means that Revised Article 9's provisions either exclude consumer transactions from their scope or restrict particular rules to commercial transactions. See, e.g., 9–108(e)(2), 9–109(d)(12), (13), 9–620(g), 9–626(a). For a description of the consumer interests implicated in the drafting of Revised Article 9, see Jean Braucher, Deadlock: Consumer Transactions Under Revised Article 9, 73 Am. Bankr. L. J. 83 (1999); Gail Hillebrand, The Uniform Commercial Code Drafting Process: Will Articles 2, 2B and 9 be Fair to Consumers?, 75 Wash. U. L. Q. 69, 119–147 (1997).

For a thorough discussion of the meaning of purchase money under the UCC, see Mark B. Wessman, Purchase Money Inventory Financing: The Case for Limited Cross–Collateralization, 51 Ohio St. L. J. 1283 (1990). The matter is further discussed in Note 2 following *Southtrust Bank, infra.*

## 2.   INVENTORY

### a.   REQUIREMENTS FOR PURCHASE MONEY SECURITY INTEREST IN INVENTORY

Section 9–324(b) states requirements for establishing a purchase money priority in inventory quite different from those found in 9–324(a) for other types of collateral. The first major difference is the requirement that the purchase money secured party must notify any prior holders of security interests in the debtor's inventory who have filed financing statements that it intends to engage in purchase money financing of the debtor's inventory. The notice is good for a five-year period, and the PMSI does not begin to run for goods delivered until the purchase money secured party perfects. The notice requirement for inventory collateral contrasts with non-inventory financing under 9–324(a), which has no notice requirement; the purchase money secured party does not have to search for prior filings. The notice requirement is explained in Comment 4 to 9–324 as needed because inventory financing typically requires the secured party to make periodic advances against incoming inventory or periodic releases of old inventory as new inventory is received. The inventory financer is entitled to notice before it makes further advances that are secured by incoming inventory in which a creditor has taken a PSMI.

The second important difference is 9–324(b)'s treatment of proceeds. Under 9–324(a), the purchase money priority carries over to the proceeds of the original collateral, but under 9–324(b), with certain exceptions with respect to chattel paper and instruments, it is limited to identifiable cash proceeds received on or before delivery of the inventory to the buyer, i.e., cash down payments. This effectively deprives purchase money creditors of a priority in all of the usual proceeds from credit sales of inventory, e.g., goods traded-in, accounts, and cash payments on accounts received after delivery of the goods to a buyer. Comment 8 attempts to explain the line-drawing in this complex section as reflecting the expectations of the parties engaged in inventory financing. We are comforted to learn: "Many parties financing inventory are quite content to protect their first-priority security interest in the inventory 'itself.'' Comment 8. Thus, in bankruptcy, all the purchase money secured party receives is what is left of the inventory it financed but is shut out of the obligations of and collections from buyers of inventory previously sold.

PROBLEM

On January 1 Ace makes a loan to Debtor secured by Debtor's existing and after-acquired inventory. At the same time Ace files a proper financing statement. On March 1 Bank lends Debtor funds to purchase new inventory and Debtor grants it a security interest in the inventory purchased with Bank's funds. On the same date Bank sends Ace by letter notice of the interest in the new inventory it intends to obtain, which Ace receives on March 5. Bank files a proper financing statement covering the new inventory on March 1. Later, Debtor defaults on its obligations to both Ace and Bank.

(a) If Debtor receives the new inventory on March 2, who has priority in Debtor's inventory purchased with Bank's funds: Ace or Bank?

(b) What result if Debtor received the inventory on March 10?

(c) Suppose Debtor sold 5 items of the new inventory to buyers, who paid a total of $500 in cash and another 5 items to buyers, each of whom promises to pay $110 per item. The buyers later pay Debtor in full so that Debtor receives a total of $1050 for the 10 items of new inventory. The money is traceable to each item of inventory sold. Who has priority in the $500: Ace or Bank? In the $550 Debtor eventually receives?

(d) Would the result in (c) change if 5 buyers executed promissory notes and granted Debtor security interests in the items purchased? Would the result change if Debtor delivered the notes to Bank?

(e) Would the result in (c) change if Debtor had granted Bank a security interest in new machinery to be used in its factory, to be purchased with Bank's funds?

---

The following opinion challenges whether the purchase money financer has a priority in even the remaining inventory. Why has this case been so controversial?

# Southtrust Bank v. Borg–Warner Acceptance Corp.

United States Court of Appeals, Eleventh Circuit, 1985.
760 F.2d 1240.

■ TUTTLE, SENIOR CIRCUIT JUDGE:

Borg–Warner Acceptance Corporation (''BWAC'') appeals from a decision of the district court denying its motion for summary judgment and granting summary judgment to Southtrust Bank ("the Bank") in a diversity suit. The Bank filed a declaratory judgment action to ascertain which of the parties has priority in the inventory of four debtors, Molay Brothers Supply Company, Inc., Gulf City Distributors, Inc., Standard Wholesale Supply Company and Crest Refrigeration, Inc. These debtors, which are no longer in existence, defaulted on obligations they owed to one or the other party.

Both the Bank and BWAC have perfected security interests in the inventory of the debtors. In each case, the Bank filed its financing statement first. BWAC contends that as a purchase money lender it falls within the purchase money security interest exception to the first to file rule and therefore is entitled to possession of the inventory. The Uniform Commercial Code (UCC) as adopted in both Alabama and Georgia, provides in pertinent part:

A security interest is a "purchase money security interest" to the extent that it is:

(a) Taken or retained by the seller of the collateral to secure all or part of its price; or

(b) Taken by a person who by making advances or incurring an obligation gives value to enable the debtor to acquire rights in or the use of collateral if such value is in fact so used.

BWAC engages in purchase money financing. Here, BWAC purchased invoices from vendors who supplied inventory items to the debtors in question. The security agreements between BWAC and each of the debtors contained the following provision:

In order to secure repayment to Secured Party of all such extensions of credit made by Secured Party in accordance with this Agreement, and to secure payment of all other debts or liabilities and performance of all obligations of Debtor to Secured Party, whether now existing or hereafter arising, Debtor agrees that Secured Party shall have and hereby grants to Secured Party a security interest in all Inventory of Debtor, whether now owned or hereafter acquired, and all Proceeds and products thereof.

The term "Inventory" was defined as "all inventory, of whatever kind or nature, wherever located, now owned or hereafter acquired ... when such inventory has been financed by Borg–Warner Acceptance Corporation."

BWAC and the debtors employed a scheduled liquidation arrangement to reduce the debt owed BWAC. Under this arrangement a debtor was permitted to pay a percentage of the invoice each month, without regard to whether the item was actually sold. If an unpaid item was sold, then the remaining inventory served as collateral to secure the unpaid balance.

The key issue for decision by this Court is whether inclusion of an after-acquired property clause and a future advances clause in BWAC's security agreements converted its purchase money security interest (PMSI) into an ordinary security interest.

The district court held that inclusion of after-acquired property and future advances clauses ("the clauses") in the security agreement converted BWAC's PMSI into an ordinary security interest. The court relied on In re Manuel, 507 F.2d 990 (5th Cir.1975) (holding, in a consumer bankruptcy context, that PMSI must be limited to the item purchased at time of the agreement and cannot exceed the price of that item); In re Norrell, 426 F.Supp. 435 (M.D.Ga.1977) (same); and In re Simpson, 4 U.C.C.Rep.Serv. 243 (Bankr.W.D.Mich.1966) (inclusion of future advances clause in security agreement for farm equipment destroys PMSI).

BWAC argues that the cases relied on by the court are distinguishable. First, BWAC notes that almost all the cases following the "transformation" rule (i.e., inclusion of the clauses transforms a PMSI into an ordinary security interest) are consumer bankruptcy cases. It argues that the rationale of those cases, which is to protect the consumer, does not apply in commercial cases such as the case at bar. See In re Mid–Atlantic Flange, 26 U.C.C.Rep.Serv. 203, 208 (E.D.Pa.1979). BWAC argues that the policy considerations in a commercial setting, promoting commercial certainty and encouraging credit extension, do not support the application of the transformation rule. According to BWAC, applying the transformation rule to inventory financiers would require them to police inventory constantly and to see that inventory corresponds on an item-by-item basis with debt.

The Bank argues that the transformation rule is not a product of special bankruptcy considerations, and that if the drafters had intended to limit the rule to consumer transactions, they would have said so, as they did in other sections of the Code. The Bank contends that a holding that inclusion of the clauses destroys a PMSI would not have a serious negative effect on inventory financiers. It points out that such financiers could retain priority by obtaining a subordination agreement from the first-to-file creditor.

We see no reason to limit the holding of *In re Manuel* to consumer bankruptcy cases. In that case, the Fifth Circuit stated:

> A plain reading of the statutory requirements would indicate that they require the purchase money security interest to be in the item purchased, and that, as the judges below noted, the purchase money security interest cannot exceed the price of what is purchased in the transaction wherein the security interest is created. . . .

Id. at 993. Nothing in the language of U.C.C. § 9–312(3) or § 9–107 distinguishes between consumer and commercial transactions or between bankruptcy and nonbankruptcy contexts. We see no policy reasons for creating a distinction where the drafters have not done so.

Second, BWAC contends that the cases supporting the transformation rule involve situations in which the clauses were actually exercised, e.g., *Manuel* (agreement covered pre-existing debt); *Simpson* (future advances actually made). BWAC argues that mere inclusion of the clauses does not void a PMSI. In re Griffin, 9 B.R. 880 (Bankr.N.D.Ga.1981) (when creditor is seller, mere existence of unexercised future advances clause does not destroy PMSI); *Mid–Atlantic Flange* (same). We need not reach the issue of whether mere inclusion of unexercised future advances and after-acquired property clauses voids a PMSI because we find that BWAC exercised the clauses here. After entering the security agreements with the debtors, BWAC regularly purchased inventory for the debtors and now claims that the debtors' BWAC-financed inventory secures these purchases. This is an exercise of the future advances clause. Similarly, BWAC claims as collateral not only the inventory purchased at the time the security agreements were entered, but all BWAC-financed inventory. This is an exercise of the after-acquired property clause. We hold, therefore, that BWAC's exercise of the future advances and after-acquired property clauses in its security agreements with the debtors destroyed its PMSI.

We note, as did the district court, that BWAC retains a security interest in the goods. It merely loses its priority status as a purchase money secured lender. The concept of the floating lien under the U.C.C. remains intact. We hold, merely, that such a floating lien is inconsistent with a PMSI. A PMSI requires a one-to-one relationship between the debt and the collateral.

BWAC's final argument is that the court should adopt a "to the extent" rule, based on the literal language of UCC, § 9–107:

> A security interest is a "purchase money security interest" to the extent that it is ... (b) Taken by a person who by making advances or incurring an obligation gives value to enable the debtor to acquire rights in or the use of collateral if such value is in fact so used.

Some courts have held that the clauses, even if exercised, do not invalidate a PMSI if there is some method for determining the extent of the PMSI. For example, in In re Staley, 426 F.Supp. 437 (M.D.Ga.1977), the court held that the PMSI was valid because the security agreement specified that payments be allocated first to items bought first. Thus, it was easy for the court to ascertain which items had been fully paid for and hence no longer served as collateral. Here, however, nothing in the contract or in state law allocates payments to particular items of inventory. BWAC, in fact, claims all BWAC-financed inventory as its collateral without regard to payments made by the debtors. We agree with the court in In re Coomer, 8 B.R. 351, 355 (Bankr.E.D.Tenn.1980), that

> Without some guidelines, legislative or contractual, the court should not be required to distill from a mass of transactions the extent to which a security interest is purchase money.

Unless a lender contractually provides some method for determining the extent to which each item of collateral secures its purchase money, it effectively gives up its purchase money status.

Because we hold that BWAC's exercise of the after-acquired property and future advances clauses in its security agreements voided its PMSI, we need not reach the other issues raised by the Bank. We also do not reach the issue raised by BWAC concerning the district court's reference to proceeds from sales of the inventory being held "in trust." Whether the proceeds are held "in trust" is relevant only to the issue of damages. The district court entered final judgment only on the claim for declaratory relief and referred the damage claim to a magistrate. Because no final judgment has been entered as to damages, that issue is not properly before this Court.

AFFIRMED.

NOTES

**1.** Before *Southtrust*, we had thought that the incentive offered purchase money financers of inventory by 9–324(b) was rather meager. On the debtor's default, a secured party who had filed a financing statement with respect to the debtor's inventory before the purchase money financer filed would take precedence in the proceeds of the inventory supplied by the purchase money financer, leaving the purchase money financer with only the unsold inventory remaining at the time of the debtor's default. But *Southtrust* casts doubt on whether the purchase money financer will even have priority with respect to the unsold inventory. *Southtrust* is very controversial. Mark B. Wessman, Purchase Money Inventory Financing: The Case for Limited Cross–Collateralization, 51 Ohio St. L. J. 1283 (1990), describes the reaction of commentators on the case as quite critical. Wessman is also critical of the case.

**2.** Whether a security interest is purchase money under 9–103 is relevant in two other situations in addition to cases arising under 9–324. Under 9–309(1) a purchase money security interest in consumer goods is perfected without possession or filing, and BC 522(f)(1)(B) allows a trustee in bankruptcy to avoid a nonpossessory, nonpurchase money security interest in certain consumer goods. The great bulk of litigation on the meaning of purchase money has occurred in bankruptcy courts under BC 522(f)(1)(B). The distinction drawn in BC 522(f)(1)(B) between purchase money credit (e.g., retailer retains a security interest in household goods sold to the debtor) and nonpurchase money credit (e.g., a personal loan company takes a security interest in household goods the debtor had already purchased to secure a loan made to the debtor) is based on Congressional hostility toward the personal finance business, thought to be lenders of last resort, whose security interests are considered in terrorem collection devices used to coerce necessitous debtors into paying the loan company in preference to other creditors or reaffirming debts discharged in bankruptcy.

Although the consumer context of both BC 522(f)(1)(B) and 9–309(1) is wholly foreign to the issue raised by 9–324(b) of determining priorities between two sophisticated commercial financers, the court in *Southtrust* relies on these consumer cases for guidance and adopts the rigid rule that cross-collateralization destroys the purchase money nature of a transaction. As the court says, "[a] PMSI requires a one-to-one relationship between the debt and the collateral." Thus, *Southtrust* reduces former 9–312(3) [9–324(b)] to awarding a reliable purchase money priority only if each sale is treated as a separate transaction. This, of course, is totally infeasible in any but big-ticket items like motor vehicles, and, even in these cases, *Southtrust* seems to require compliance with the paper-shuffling pre-Code regime that 9–205 attempted to end.

**3.**   Section 9–103 alters the result in *Southtrust*. Subsection (f)(2)'s "dual status" rule preserves a PMSI even if purchase money collateral also secures nonpurchase money obligations. Thus, cross-collateralization does not destroy PMSI status. Section 9–103(f)(2) therefore statutorily overrules *Southtrust*'s requirement that there be a "one-to-one relationship between the debt and the collateral." Section 9–103(b)(2), in particular, changes the outcome in *Southtrust*. Subsection (b)(2) defines a security interest in goods as a PMSI "if the security interest is in inventory that is or was purchase money collateral, also to the extent that the security interest secures a purchase money obligation incurred with respect to other inventory in which the secured party holds or held a purchase money security interest." Each item of inventory covered by BWAC's security agreement is purchase money collateral for the purchase money obligation it secured, and the security agreement's cross-collateralization clause secures all of BWAC's other purchase money obligations with each item of inventory. Thus, 9–103(b)(2) considers all of BWAC's security interests in its debtors' inventory to be PMSIs.

Since under 9–103's rules a security interest may be purchase money to some extent and nonpurchase money to some extent (see 9–103(b)(1)), some method is required for allocating payments between purchase money and nonpurchase money obligations. Section 9–103(e) supplies a mechanism for allocating payments that the court in *Southtrust* found lacking. Under 9–103(e)'s mechanism, in nonconsumer-goods transactions payments are applied according to a "reasonable method" agreed upon by the parties. Absent such an agreement, in accordance with the debtor's manifested intent. If there is neither a reasonable method of allocation agreed upon nor the relevant intent manifested by the debtor, payments are allocated to unsecured obligations first. As between secured obligations, payments are allocated to purchase money obligations in the order in which they occurred. In *Southtrust* this final allocational method would apply to BWAC's purchase money and nonpurchase money obligations.

**4.**   In *Southtrust* the court suggests that a purchase money financer should protect its priority by an intercreditor subordination agreement with the first-to-file creditor. This is still good advice even though 9–103(f) statutorily overrules *Southtrust*; a subordination agreement avoids costly litigation over priority issues. Wessman, however, believes that there is usually little incentive on the part of the first-to-file creditor to subordinate its interest. Mark B. Wessman, Purchase Money Inventory Financing, 51 Ohio St. L. J. at 1338–39. There is still another barrier to recognition of an effective purchase money priority in inventory under 9–324(b). The following is a covenant of the debtor, generally known as a "negative pledge clause," taken from a standard loan and security agreement used in inventory financing by a leading financial institution:

> The Borrower is, and as to inventory to be acquired after the date hereof, shall be, the owner of all inventory and shall neither create nor suffer to exist any lien or encumbrance thereon or security interest therein * * * in favor of any person other than the Lender.

See Loan Agreement § 7 (Negative Covenants), Appendix I, which contains a negative pledge clause (§ 7.6) as well as a covenant on the borrower's part not to incur additional debt without Bank's consent (§ 7.1).

Since breach of these covenants constitutes an event of default which results in the debt secured by the inventory becoming immediately due and payable, the first-to-file creditor may call its loan if the debtor even attempts to enter into purchase money financing with another creditor. Query: does 9–324(b) have any commercial significance today? Would you counsel a client to rely on it for a priority without the consent of the prior secured party?

### b.   CONSUMER GOODS EXCEPTION IN SECTION 9–103(h)

As we saw in Note 2, supra, there are advantages to a secured party in having its security interest qualify as purchase money. A PMSI cannot be avoided under BC 522(f)(1)(B), and no financing statement need be filed to perfect a PMSI in consumer goods. Section 9–309(1). Hence, in consumer goods transactions trustees in bankruptcy for consumer debtors have attacked the purchase money status of secured interests reserved by sellers in add-on sales and revolving charge account transactions. They have enjoyed some success. In the add-on sale transaction described in Case #2 in the section on the Transformational Rule, supra, In re Manuel, 507 F.2d 990 (5th Cir.1975), held that a seller has a purchase money security interest in goods purchased only when the security interest is taken *solely* to secure all or part of its price. Since in that case the security agreement provided that the security interest in the goods purchased also secured debts arising from previous sales, the court held the security interest could not be purchase money.

Even more important to retailing than add-on sales is the revolving charge account in which the consumer opens an account with a retailer and is permitted to charge purchases, often pursuant to the retailer's credit card, to be paid for in monthly installments. If the doctrine of *Southtrust* is applied to such a transaction, an attempt by a seller to retain a purchase money security interest in goods sold to secure the running balance of the account would fail. Moreover, even if the seller attempted only to retain a security interest in each item sold to secure only the price of that item, the security interest could not be purchase money unless the agreement or, presumably the law of the state, prescribed an allocation formula for the consumer's payments. Such an allocation provision is set out in In re Cersey, 321 B.R. 352 (Bankr. M.D. Ga. 2004).

The provisions of 9–103(e) (allocation of payments) and (f) (dual status) would, if they were applied to the consumer goods transactions described above, overturn *Manuel*. And in earlier drafts of Revised Article 9 these provisions did apply to consumer goods as well as commercial transactions. However, in the final draft consumer goods transactions were excepted from subsections (e) and (f). Subsection (h) also was added which provides that in consumer goods transactions the courts are free to make their own rules about the desirability of the dual status and payment allocations rules; presumably they can embrace *Manuel*. Hostility of consumer groups toward security interests in low-priced goods manifested itself in a recommendation by the National Bankruptcy Review Commission to abolish in bankruptcy purchase money security interests in household goods worth less than $500. 1 The Report of the National Bankruptcy Review Commission 169 (1997). Doubtless the same pressure from consumer groups that resulted in this recommendation played a role in persuading the Article 9 Drafting Committee to leave retailers to the tender mercies of the bankruptcy courts without a statute establishing their rights in add-on and charge account sales transactions.

## D.   LIEN CREDITORS

### 1.   CONFLICT WITH AN UNPERFECTED SECURITY INTEREST

Section 9–317(a)(2) continues the rule that, with the exception set out in (2)(B), an unperfected security interest is subordinate to the rights of a lien creditor. Since a trustee in bankruptcy is a lien creditor under 9–102(a)(52)(C), this provision, together with BC 544(a) and BC 550(a), allows a trustee in bankruptcy to avoid an unperfected security interest. Thus, these provisions constitute the statutory anvil on which Article 9 security interests are pounded in bankruptcy.

PROBLEMS

**1.** On February 1, Debtor granted a nonpurchase money security interest in described collateral to SP in a signed security agreement; SP advanced value to Debtor on that date. On February 5, Creditor's judicial lien attached to the same collateral. On February 9, SP filed a financing statement covering the collateral. Who is prior under 9–317(a)(2)?

**2.** On February 1, Debtor granted a nonpurchase money security interest in described collateral to SP in a signed security agreement; SP filed a financing statement covering Debtor's collateral on that date. On February 5, Creditor's judicial lien attached to the same collateral. On February 9, SP advanced value to Debtor. Who is prior under 9–317(a)(2)? How can you reconcile the result in Problem 2 with that in Problem 1? See Comment 4 to 9–317. Are you persuaded by the explanation given in the Comment for the change in law in 9–317(a)(2)?

## 2.   CONFLICT WITH A FUTURE ADVANCE

The previous section discusses perhaps the most important conflict treated by Article 9; the conflict discussed in this section is much less significant. Earlier we saw that in a case of conflicting Article 9 security interests, 9–322(a)(1) protects the priority of the first party to file or perfect with respect to future advances even though the advances were made after that party had knowledge of a subsequent security interest in the same collateral. Comment 4 to 9–322 justified this rule on efficiency grounds as allowing the first secured party who has filed to make subsequent advances without each time having to check for subsequent filings as a condition of protection. But when the conflict is between an advance made pursuant to an Article 9 security interest and a subsequent lien creditor's rights, 9–323(b) states a rule that recognizes the priority of the future advance (i) if the advance is made or committed within 45 days after the lien arises even with knowledge of the lien, and (ii) if the advance is made or committed after the 45–day period, so long as the secured party is without knowledge of the lien at the time of the advance or commitment.

Thus, monitoring costs to the secured party are only slightly increased with respect to competing judicial liens: only if the secured party has actual knowledge of the lien must it hold up on future advances, and not even then if less than 45 days have gone by. It is highly improbable that any secured party will make an optional future advance, even within the 45–day window, if it knows that the collateral is subject to a judicial lien. In some instances a judicial lien may be obtained only by seizing the property, and property in the possession of a sheriff is not attractive collateral. So the question must be asked why the statute protects the priority of a secured party who makes a future advance with knowledge of the lien during the 45–day period after the lien arises—an advance no creditor will ever make. The provision is particularly difficult to justify given 9–323(d), which cuts off advance priority against a nonordinary course buyer when the advance is made with actual knowledge of the purchase, even within the 45–day period. Comment 4 to 9–323 reveals that it is important for purposes of the Federal Tax Lien Act to establish under state law an absolute priority for a future advance over a lien creditor for 45 days even if made with knowledge of the lien. No one expects any UCC cases to arise under it.

Notice a final implication of 9–323(b): because the subsection only deals with the subordination of future advances under prescribed conditions, it has no effect on the priority of *non*advance obligations incurred by the debtor after a lien attaches. In short, 9–323(b) doesn't address priority contests between a creditor whose nonadvance obligations are secured and the rights of a lien creditor. As Comment 4 to 9–323 reinforces, "[s]ubsection (b) of this section [9–323] provides that a security interest is subordinate to those rights to the extent that the specified circumstances occur." Priority contests pitting nonadvance secured obligations against a lien creditor's rights aren't among those "specified circumstances." Instead, 9–317(a)(2) controls them, and under 9–317(a)(2), aside from 9–317(a)(2)(B), the secured nonadvances are protected when made by a creditor perfected on or before the lien attaches. The date on which the nonadvance is made does not affect its priority. See Dick Warner Cargo Handling Corp. v. Aetna Business Credit, Inc., 746 F.2d 126 (2d Cir.1984). Nonadvances can include items ranging from collection and interest charges, as well as attorney's fees. Unlike advances, nonadvance obligations easily can be incurred by a debtor after a lien attaches.

## E.   BUYERS AND LESSEES

### 1.   BUYERS AND LESSEES OF NON-INVENTORY GOODS

Secured parties are in a very strong position with respect to persons who buy or lease goods from their debtors. Under 9–317(b), buyers and lessees take subject to perfected security interests, and 9–315(a) provides that the security interest continues in the goods sold or leased and in any identifiable proceeds. Section 9–317(e) grants purchase money secured parties who have not perfected at the time of the sale or lease a 20–day relation-back period after the buyer or lessee has received delivery in which to perfect. Even unperfected security interests are prior to the rights of buyers and lessees other than those who give value and receive delivery without knowledge of the security interest.

Case #1. Debtor, a manufacturer, granted Lender a security interest in its equipment to secure a loan of $100,000 on February 1. Debtor contracted to sell two pieces of equipment to Buyer on March 1, in violation of a provision in the security agreement forbidding sale of collateral without Lender's written permission. Buyer, who knew nothing of Lender's security interest, paid Debtor $10,000 at the time of the contract and agreed to pay the remaining $15,000 owing at the time of delivery. Lender discovered that it had failed to file before the sale and corrected its error by filing on March 15. Buyer paid the $15,000 balance on April 1 and Debtor delivered the equipment at that time. Is Lender's security interest prior to Buyer's rights in the equipment?

Case #2. Assume the facts are the same as those in Case #1 except that Debtor delivered the equipment to Buyer and paid the remaining balance of the price on March 10. Before Buyer made its final payment, it searched the record and found no financing statement on record under Debtor's name. (i) Is Lender's security interest prior to Buyer's rights in the equipment? (ii) What would the result be if Lender had lent money to Debtor that enabled Debtor to buy the equipment that it later sold to Buyer?

### 2.   BUYERS AND LESSEES OF INVENTORY GOODS

#### a.   BUYER IN THE ORDINARY COURSE OF BUSINESS

A major exception to the basic rule that buyers and lessees from a debtor take subject to perfected security interests is the traditional rule that buyers and lessees of inventory collateral take free of inventory security interests. Inventory is meant to be sold or leased (9–102(a)(48)(B)), with the secured party looking to the proceeds of the disposition for security rather than pursuing the goods in the hands of the buyer or lessee. This rule is stated in 9–320(a): "[A] buyer in the ordinary course of business * * * takes free of a security interest created by the buyer's seller, even if the security interest is perfected and the buyer knows of its existence." A comparable rule for lessees is found in 9–321(c). Section 1–201(b)(9) provides in part: " 'Buyer in the ordinary course of business' means a person that buys goods in good faith, without knowledge that the sale violates the rights of another person in the goods, and in the ordinary course from a person * * * in the business of selling goods of that kind." As Comment 3 to 9–320 notes, 9–320(a)'s rule is restricted primarily to inventory collateral. In the following Problems we pose some of the important issues that these statutes raise.

## PROBLEMS

**1.** Lender perfected a security interest in Debtor's equipment by filing. The equipment is business machines used in Debtor's accounting firm. In violation of a provision in the security agreement, Debtor sold some of the machines to Dealer without Lender's knowledge or consent. Dealer buys and sells used business machines and sold the machines in question to Buyer for cash. Buyer bought the machines for use in his business. Neither Dealer nor Buyer knew about Lender's security interest in the machines.

    a. Is Dealer a buyer in the ordinary course of business?

    b. Is Buyer a buyer in the ordinary course of business?

    c. What are Lender's rights with respect to the machines now in Buyer's possession? See Comment 3 to 9–320.

**2.** Lender has been financing Dealer's inventory for some time and it recently placed Dealer on "credit watch," with new restrictions on Dealer's operations. One of these limitations is that Dealer must obtain Lender's consent to the sale of any machine with a sale price exceeding $5,000. In violation of this limitation, Dealer sold and delivered to Buyer a machine for $10,000 cash. Buyer is a sophisticated person who was well aware that Debtor's inventory was very likely to be subject to a security interest in favor of a financial institution. Buyer also knew that Debtor was having financial problems and took this into consideration in negotiating for a low price for the machine. You may assume that Lender's security interest was perfected by filing. What are Lender's rights with respect to the machine now in Buyer's possession? See Comment 3 to 9–320.

## b. GOODS SUBJECT TO CERTIFICATE OF TITLE ACTS

One of the most valuable articles of goods is motor vehicles and these are covered by state motor vehicle acts which, given their anti-theft origin, usually provide that no one can acquire ownership without receiving a certificate of title or, in the case of new motor vehicles never sold at retail, the manufacturer's certificate of origin. But, as we have seen, 9–320(a) grants priority to a buyer in the ordinary course of business over a security interest created by the buyer's seller. Which party has priority when a secured party obtains a security interest in a car by having its lien indicated on a certificate of title covering the car and the owner sells the car to a buyer in the ordinary course of business without being able to deliver a clean certificate of title to the buyer? Given that the dollar volume of motor vehicle sales must exceed that of any other article of personal property sold at retail, one might expect that the conflict between Article 9 and the state's motor vehicle act would be resolved in the provisions of Article 9, but there is no explicit treatment of the issue in Article 9. These provisions tell us: (1) In 9–320(a), that a buyer in ordinary course of business takes free of a security interest created by the buyer's seller even if the security interest is perfected and the buyer knows of its existence. (2) In 9–311(a)(2), that, except as provided in 9–311(d), the exclusive method of perfecting a security interest in certain kinds of goods, which include motor vehicles, is by indicating the secured party's lien on the certificate of title. However, (d) excepts goods held in a dealer's inventory from certificate of title perfection. In such cases, the secured party can perfect by filing. And (3) in 1–201(b)(9), the definition of "buyer in ordinary course of business" requires that such a buyer buys in good faith, without knowledge that the sale violates the rights of another person in the goods, and in ordinary course from a person in the business of selling goods of that kind. How do these provisions deal with the following cases involving desperate dealers? Think the shifty-eyed William H. Macy character in the classic movie, Fargo.

> Case #1. Buyer purchased a new car from Dealer who was in financial trouble. Buyer paid cash. Among the numerous papers Buyer was required to sign at the time of sale was an application for issuance of title by the state department of motor vehicles (DMV). Dealer assured Buyer that the application and fee would be forwarded to DMV and Buyer would receive the certificate of title within a few weeks. Financer, who had perfected a security interest in Dealer's inventory of new cars by filing a financing statement under 9–311(d), had retained possession of the manufacturer's certificate of origin for all new vehicles. Financer obtained these certificates of origin by advancing to Manufacturer the price of each car sold to Dealer. By retaining possession of the certificates of origin, Financer expected to safeguard itself against Dealer's fraud because no one could obtain issuance of a certificate of title for a new car from DMV without presenting Manufacturer's certificate of origin. Financer's agreement with Dealer was that Financer would not surrender a certificate of origin to Dealer without receipt of the proceeds of Dealer's sale to a buyer. When Buyer did not receive the certificate of title within a reasonable time, inquiry disclosed that Dealer had not sent the proceeds of the sale to Financer, the application had not been sent to DMV, the certificate of origin was still in the possession of Financer, and Dealer had absconded with the

proceeds of the sale. Who is entitled to the car, Financer or Buyer? Is Buyer a buyer in the ordinary course of business when he bought a car without receiving the certificate of title. Some states amended their motor vehicle acts at the time of enactment of the UCC to provide that Article 9 governs the priority of security interests.

Case #2. Buyer purchased for cash a used car from Dealer who was in financial trouble. When Dealer took the car as a trade-in, the previous owner delivered the certificate of title to Dealer with the owner's name signed as transferor. The space for designating the name of the transferee was left blank. The practice was for a dealer to fill in as transferee the name of the buyer of the used car when sale occurred and to send the old title along with the buyer's application to DMV for issuance of a new title in the buyer's name. Dealer appeared to be following this practice when it asked Buyer to sign an application for a new title and assured Buyer that the new title would arrive in a few weeks. But Dealer had no intention of obtaining a new title for Buyer. Bank had an arrangement with Dealer that it would lend money on Dealer's used car inventory and would take from Dealer as security the certificate of title of each vehicle in the inventory when dealer obtained the car. When the used car was sold, Dealer could obtain the certificate of title only by paying Bank the proceeds of the sale. Bank had also filed a financing statement covering Dealer's used car inventory. Dealer absconded with the proceeds of the sale to Buyer who, consequently, never received a title. Who is entitled to the car, Bank or Buyer? Everyone knows that ownership of a used car is represented by an existing certificate of title. Can a buyer of a used car who doesn't receive a certificate of title qualify as a buyer in ordinary course of business within 1–201(b)(9)? See First National Bank of El Campo, Texas v. Buss, 143 S.W.3d 915 (Tex. App. 2004), which collects the authorities. What if the buyer is another dealer?

c. WAIVER

Section 9–315(a)(1) provides: "[A] security interest * * * continues in collateral notwithstanding sale, lease, license, exchange, or other disposition thereof unless the secured party authorized the disposition free of the security interest * * *." Since the purpose of inventory is to be sold, the inventory financer may expressly authorize the dealer to sell the inventory free of its security interest, while safeguarding its interest by imposing controls over the proceeds received by the dealer for the goods sold, such as requiring the dealer to deposit the proceeds in a lockbox account under the control of the secured party. In such cases, buyers take free of the financer's security interest without having to rely on 9–320.

A large body of conflicting case law grew up around the question of when courts would find the existence of a secured party's authorization to sell free of a security agreement, particularly in farm products financing in which there is no buyer-in-ordinary-course-of-business exception. See 9–320(a). For instance, the security agreement might give the debtor the right to sell without prior consent but only conditional on the proceeds of the sale being deposited in a designated account. Is this an authorization to sell even if the debtor violated the agreement and did not deposit the proceeds in that account? Section 9–315(a) requires that a secured party's waiver authorize disposition free of its security interest. Authorization to sell, without more, is insufficient. Other cases, with additional facts, will be more difficult. Comment 2 to 9–315 reports that Article 9 "leaves the determination of authorization to the courts, as under former Article 9."

### 3.   BUYERS OF CONSUMER GOODS

As we have seen, 9–309(1) provides for automatic perfection of security interests in consumer goods, defined as meaning goods that are used or bought for use primarily for "personal, family, or household purposes." Thus, a retailer who reserves security interests in the consumer goods it sells but does not file in such transactions has a perfected security interest in those goods and, therefore, is prior to the rights of the buyer's trustee in bankruptcy. But problems for a nonfiling retailer arise under 9–320(b) if its buyer sells the goods to other buyers. The following Problem examines Article 9's treatment of this issue.

#### PROBLEM

Wholesaler sells household appliances to Retailer who markets these goods to buyers who buy for their personal, family, or household purposes. Wholesaler reserves a security interest in the goods sold to Retailer and perfects its security interest by filing. Retailer reserves a security interest in the goods it sells to buyers but does not perfect by filing.

(a) If Retailer defaults on its secured obligation to Wholesaler, what rights does Wholesaler have against goods in the possession of consumer buyers who bought from Retailer? Since consumer goods are involved, which statute governs, 9–320(a) or (b)?

(b) If Buyer bought household goods from Retailer but sold them to Neighbor at a garage sale, what rights does Retailer have in the goods in Neighbor's possession if Buyer moved away and defaulted on its obligation to Retailer? See 9–320(b).

(c) How would your answer to question (b) change if Retailer had perfected by filing? Do you know any garage sale buyers who search the UCC records before buying?

### 4.   WHEN DOES A BUYER BUY?

Determining when someone becomes a buyer can be important for purposes of 9–320(a) and (b). It can make the difference between taking subject to and taking free of a security interest in goods purchased. Assume that Bank lends to Manufacturer on a secured basis, taking a security interest in all of Manufacturer's existing and after-acquired inventory, and files an effective financing statement. The security agreement defines a violation of the agreement to include default. Manufacturer both makes and sells custom desks, and Buyer orders a custom desk to be produced, paying the purchase price in advance. The sales contract calls for Buyer to take delivery of the desk at Manufacturer's place of business. Six months later, after the desk has been completed but before delivery, Manufacturer defaults on its payments to Bank and Bank seizes all of Manufacturer's inventory, including its desks. At the same time it informs Buyer of Manufacturer's violation of the security agreement. Is Buyer entitled to take delivery of the desk or must it satisfy Manufacturer's debt to Bank as a condition of doing so? The answer depends on whether Buyer became a buyer in the ordinary course. This in turn depends on when Buyer became a buyer.

Section 1–201(b)(9) defines a "buyer in ordinary course of business" to require that he buy "without knowledge that the sale violates the rights of another person in the goods." It does not specify the point in time at which someone buys and therefore the point at which the buyer's knowledge is relevant. Possible dates include (1) the execution of the sales contract (2–103(1)(a), 2–106), (2) identification of the goods under it (2–501), (3) passage of title in the goods (2–401(2)–(3)), (4) delivery of the goods, and (5) acceptance of them (2–606). The issue has arisen in contexts pitting consumer buyers against inventory financers of defaulting debtors. Most courts have sided with the consumer buyer, accelerating the date of purchase to the point at which the goods are identified to the contract. See, e.g., Daniel v. Bank of Hayward, 425 N.W.2d 416 (Wis. 1988); In re Darling's Homes, Inc., 46 B.R. 370 (Bankr. D.Del. 1985).

Former Article 9 did not answer the question, but the Revision makes dating the purchase more definite by requiring that a "buyer in ordinary course" take possession or have a possessory remedy available to it. Section 1–201(9) provides that "[o]nly a buyer that takes possession of the goods or has a right to recover the goods from the seller under Article 2 may be a buyer in ordinary course." The Revision also suggests a corresponding change in 2–716(3), giving a consumer buyer a right of replevin when it acquires a special property in the goods, which occurs upon their identification to the contract: "In the case of goods bought for personal, family or household purposes, the buyer's right of replevin vests upon acquisition of a special property * * * " Thus, a consumer buys when it has a right of replevin.

## 5.  DOUBLE DEBTORS

The following conundrum has long fascinated scholars and confounded law students, and has been a favorite on many secured transactions final exams: D1 granted SP1 a security interest in business equipment and SP1 filed a financing statement covering the equipment in 2004. D1 sold the equipment to D2, not a buyer in ordinary course of business, and D2 took the equipment subject to SP1's security interest. In 2003 D2 had granted a security interest in all its equipment, now owned or thereafter acquired, to SP2, who promptly filed a financing statement. Who is prior with respect to the equipment that D1 sold to D2? SP2 claims priority in the equipment as after-acquired property under the first-to-file rule of 9–322(a)(1). SP1 contends that SP2 took a security interest only to the extent that D2 had rights in the collateral, and the rights acquired from D1 were merely the equity that D1 may have had in the equipment over and above the amount of SP1's security interest.

For years litigants were quite uncooperative and failed to bring the problem before the appellate courts for resolution. *Bank of the West* finally resolved what Barkley Clark has called the "double debtor dilemma," also known as the "dual debtor problem." Clark, 1 The Law of Secured Transactions Under the Uniform Commercial Code § 3.08[4] (Rev. ed. 2005).

## Bank of the West v. Commercial Credit Financial Services, Inc.

United States Court of Appeals, Ninth Circuit, 1988.
852 F.2d 1162.

■ THOMPSON, CIRCUIT JUDGE.

\* \* \*

[Summarized by Eds. In 1982, Bank of the West made a loan to Allied and was granted a security interest in all of Allied's existing and after-acquired inventory and accounts as well as proceeds of that collateral. The bank promptly filed a financing statement that perfected that security interest. In 1984 CCFS entered into a factoring agreement with BCI, which owned a beverage business. Under the agreement CCFS made loans to BCI. To secure the loans, BCI granted to CCFS a security interest in all of its existing and after-acquired inventory and accounts as well as proceeds of that collateral. CCFS promptly filed a financing statement that perfected that security interest. Later in 1984, BCI sold its beverage business to Allied. As part of the sale, BCI transferred assets to Allied. Among the assets were inventory and accounts in which CCFS had a perfected security interest. Both Bank of the West and CCFS claim priority with respect to the inventory and accounts transferred by BCI to Allied and to proceeds of that collateral, including accounts that arose as the result of sales of inventory by Allied after its purchase of the beverage business from BCI.]

\* \* \*

### A.   THE POST–TRANSFER SECURITY INTERESTS

#### I.   The Bank's Security Interest

Bank of the West's security agreement with Allied granted the Bank a security interest in Allied's future-acquired inventory, accounts, and proceeds. \* \* \* Bank of the West's security interest became perfected at the moment of attachment as a result of the Bank's financing statement naming Allied as its debtor, which was filed with the California Secretary of

State on April 7, 1982. * * * In addition to its perfected security interest in assets actually transferred from BCI to Allied, because of the after-acquired property clause in its security agreement, Bank of the West had a perfected security interest in all inventory, accounts, and proceeds thereafter acquired by Allied.

## II.  CCFS's Security Interest

In its opinion, the district court concluded that it was unnecessary for it to determine whether CCFS's security interest remained perfected after the transfer. *Bank of the West*, 655 F.Supp. at 814. In light of our resolution of the priority dispute, we must address this question.

Two provisions of the commercial code are relevant to deciding whether CCFS's security interest continued after the transfer of the beverage business to Allied. We begin with section 9–306(2), which provides in pertinent part:

> Except where this division ... otherwise provides, a security interest continues in collateral notwithstanding sale, exchange or other disposition thereof unless the disposition was authorized by the secured party in the security agreement or otherwise, and also continues in any identifiable proceeds including collections received by the debtor.

Neither the factoring agreement nor the related security agreement expressly authorized BCI to transfer its assets to another corporation. There is no evidence to show that CCFS otherwise authorized this disposition of its collateral. California courts have made clear that implied authorizations of sales of the debtor's collateral will not be found absent clear evidence based on the prior conduct of the parties. * * * Because there is no evidence that CCFS authorized BCI's disposition of the collateral, CCFS's security interest in the collateral actually transferred (inventory and accounts) and its proceeds continued after the transfer. * * *

## B.  RESOLVING THE PRIORITY DISPUTE

Having concluded that both Bank of the West and CCFS had perfected security interests in the inventory and accounts actually transferred from BCI to Allied/BIBCO, as well as the inventory and accounts acquired by Allied/BIBCO after the July 1, 1984 transfer, we must decide which of these security interests is entitled to priority. The district court resolved this question by looking to section 9–312(5) * * *.

By applying section 9–312(5)(a) according to its literal language, the district court concluded that Bank of the West's security interest prevailed over that of CCFS. When BCI transferred the beverage business to Allied/BIBCO, Bank of the West's security interest attached under the after-acquired property clause in its security agreement. See § 9–203(1) and § 9–204(1). When Bank of the West's security interest attached, it automatically became perfected pursuant to the earlier filed financing statement naming Allied as its debtor. See § 9–303(1). Bank of the West's financing statement was filed on April 7, 1982. CCFS's financing statement was filed January 5, 1984, and its security interest became perfected on January 10,

1984 when BCI executed the factoring and related security agreements. Section 9–312(5) sets forth a "first to file or first to perfect" rule of priority. Because Bank of the West's financing statement was filed first, the district court concluded that the Bank's security interest prevailed over that of CCFS. *Bank of the West*, 655 F.Supp. at 817.

The situation we have described above has until this case been regarded by the commentators as only a hypothetical scenario. It is a scenario offered by the commentators, however, to illustrate a failure of the commercial code to resolve a priority dispute properly. See, e.g., B. Clark, The Law of Secured Transactions Under the Uniform Commercial Code & 3.8[4] (1980); Harris, The Interaction of Articles 6 and 9 of the Uniform Commercial Code: A Study in Conveyancing, Priorities, and Code Interpretation, 39 Vand. L. Rev. 179, 222–25, 225 n. 182 (1986); Oldfather, Floor Plan Financing Under Article 9 of the Uniform Commercial Code, 14 U.Kan. L. Rev. 571, 582–84 (1966); Skilton, Security Interests in After–Acquired Property Under the Uniform Commercial Code, 1974 Wis. L. Rev. 925, 948. The difficulty noted by these commentators is this: Before the transfer from BCI to Allied, CCFS (the transferor's creditor) had a perfected security interest in the collateral. After the transfer, CCFS's perfected security interest suddenly is subordinated to the perfected security interest of Bank of the West (the transferee's creditor). CCFS, which had taken all steps required of it by the commercial code to announce its interest in the collateral *to potential creditors of the transferor* (BCI), now finds its security interest subordinated to that of the *transferee*'s (Allied's) *creditor*, (Bank of the West), whose security interest came into play only because BCI made an unauthorized disposition of the collateral to which the Bank's security interest attached solely by operation of an after-acquired collateral clause. * * *

We agree with the commentators that applying section 9–312(5) to resolve this priority dispute produces an unsatisfactory result. The principal reason that section 9–312(5) fails to produce a proper result is that it does not appear the drafters contemplated what Professor Clark calls the "dual debtor dilemma." See B. Clark, supra, & 3.8[4]. Certainly the official comments to the Uniform Commercial Code, which offer several illustrations of the operation of section 9–312(5), do not address the situation in which the competing security interests are between creditors of *different* debtors. See § 9–312(5) Uniform Commercial Code Comments 4–8. In Mr. Coogan's seminal article, *The New UCC Article 9*, 86 Harv. L. Rev. 477 (1973), no mention of the dual debtor scenario is made in the thoughtful portion of the article addressing the drafters' reasons for adopting section 9–312(5). See id. at 507–11. Because section 9–312(5) does not contemplate the dual debtor scenario, we must resolve this priority dispute by returning to first principles.

As a general rule of construction, the commercial code "shall be liberally construed and applied to promote its underlying purposes and policies." § 1–102(1). The commercial code is intended to be flexible. "It is intended to make it possible for the law embodied in this Act to be developed by the courts in the light of unforeseen and new circumstances and practices. However, the proper construction of the Act requires that its interpretation and application be limited to its reason." Id. Uniform Commercial Code Comment 1. There are two reasons behind the rule of section 9–312(5)(a). First, the "first to file or first to perfect" rule serves to modify the common law notion of "first in time, first in right." Harris, supra, 39 Vand. L. Rev. at 222. Section 9–312(5) places a premium on prompt filing of financing statements as a means of protecting *future* creditors of the debtor. The financing statement alerts potential creditors that collateral against which they are contemplating making a loan already is encumbered. Thus, section 9–312(5)(a) penalizes a creditor who has a security interest but who does not promptly file a financing statement by awarding priority to a later creditor who acquires a security interest in the same collateral and who more promptly files a financing statement. The "first to file or first to perfect" rule of § 9–312(5)(a) thus addresses the problem of secret security interests that so concerned pre-Code courts. See id. But in the present case, the notice giving function of § 9–312(5)(a) does not apply. Bank of the West is a creditor of another debtor entity, and the Bank's interest in the collateral arises solely out of an after-acquired property clause. Bank of the West cannot claim that it has relied to its detriment on the absence of a filed financing statement by CCFS.

A second purpose behind section 9–312(5)(a) is an implied commitment to a secured creditor who has filed a financing statement that, absent special considerations such as a purchase money security interest, * * * no subsequent creditor will be able to defeat the complying creditor's security interest. This notion finds support in comment 5 to section 9–402(7), which reads in pertinent part: "The justification for this rule lies in the necessity of protecting the filing system—that is, of allowing the secured party who has first filed to make subsequent advances without each time having, as a precondition of protection, to check for filings later than his." * * * This has been described as the "claim staking" function of the financing statement. See Knippenberg, supra, 52 Mo. L. Rev. at 61 & n. 22. What this means is that by filing a proper financing statement in the proper place, a secured creditor has staked a claim to its collateral and knows that, absent special considerations, its claim will prevail against *subsequently arising* interests in the same property. By complying with the Code, the creditor is relieved of much of the responsibility of monitoring its debtor's collateral—the Code has allocated the burden of discovering prior filed financing statements to later lenders. Cf. § 9–402 Uniform Commercial Code Comment 8 ("[A]ny person searching the condition of ownership of a debtor must make inquiry as to the debtor's source of title, and must search in the name of a former owner if the circumstances seem to require it.").

Applying section 9–312(5)(a) to the present case serves neither of the rationales behind the "first to file or first to perfect" rule. The notice giving function is irrelevant because the creditor of a different debtor whose sole interest in disputed collateral arises from an after-acquired property clause has no incentive to check for financing statements against the property of another debtor. Certainly the burden is on a transferee's creditor to search the title to property, but this duty arises only when the transferee's creditor first appears on the scene after the transfer. Likewise, it makes no sense to use section 9–312(5)(a) to defeat CCFS's perfected security interest when CCFS has taken all steps required of it by the Code to proclaim its interest in the collateral. CCFS is entitled to rely on the Code's promise that a creditor who fully complies usually may expect its security interest to be given priority in a dispute with another secured creditor. To apply section 9–312(5)(a) to this case would produce an undesirable result that does not follow from the principles that the section is meant to promote.[8]

We think the correct result is reached in this case by applying the common sense notion that a creditor cannot convey to another more than it owns. Put another way, the transferee, Allied, cannot acquire any greater rights in the beverage business's assets than its transferor, BCI, had in them. Cf. § 2–403(1) ("A purchaser of goods acquires all title which his transferor had or had power to transfer except that a purchaser of a limited interest acquires rights only to the extent of the interest purchased."); see also B. Clark, supra, & 3.8[4] (suggesting principles of section 2–403(1) apply to this situation); Harris, supra, 39 Vand. L. Rev. at 223, 225 n. 182 (same). Our analysis also finds direct support in the California Commercial Code. Section 9–312(1) provides, "The rules of priority stated in other sections of this chapter . . . shall govern where applicable." And section 9–306(2) provides that a security interest follows collateral into the hands of a transferee when there is an unauthorized disposition by the transferor. * * * The drafters tell us that "[i]n most cases when a debtor makes an unauthorized disposition of the collateral, the security interest, under * * * this Article, continues in the original collateral in the hands of the purchaser or other transferee. That is to say, * * * the transferee *takes subject to the security interest . . . .* Subsection 9–306(2) codifies this rule."

---

**8.** It is possible to argue, of course, that our analysis does violence to the interest of the transferee's creditor, whose security interest has been perfected by filing just the same as the transferor's creditor. But it is important to remember that the situation we consider is one in which the transferee's creditor's security interest attaches to the transferred collateral solely by operation of an after-acquired property clause. Although the Uniform Commercial Code expressly validates after-acquired property clauses, § 9–204(1), these "floating liens" still have not been whole-heartedly accepted by the drafters.

Subsection 1 makes clear that a security interest arising by virtue of an after-acquired property clause has equal status with a security interest in collateral in which the debtor has rights at the time value is given under the security agreement. That is to say: secu-

rity interest in after-acquired property is not merely an "equitable" interest; no further action by the secured party * * * is required. This does *not* mean however *that the interest is proof against subordination or defeat* * * *.

§ 9–204 Uniform Commercial Code Comment 1 (emphasis added). To the extent our opinion results in holders of after-acquired property clauses not being able to prevail against the perfected security interest of a transferor's secured creditor, this is consistent with the drafters intention in validating after-acquired property clauses but not granting them an assurance of absolute priority in all cases.

For an excellent analysis of the monitoring burdens placed on creditors as they relate to the second sentence of section 9–402(7) and after-acquired property clauses, see Knippenberg, supra, 52 Mo. L. Rev. at 92–97.

§ 9–306 Uniform Commercial Code Comment 3. If the transferee (Allied) takes the transferred collateral subject to the transferor's creditor's (CCFS's) security interest, certainly the transferee's creditor (Bank of the West) can have no greater rights in the collateral than does its debtor (Allied). Because section 9–402(7) preserves CCFS's perfected security interest in the collateral actually transferred as well as in the property acquired in the four months after the transfer, CCFS's security interest continues to be superior to Bank of the West's interest during this period, even though Bank of the West's interest also is perfected. This result is consistent with the principles of the filing system that we have previously discussed. If the notice giving function does not apply because Bank of the West has no reason to check for filings against BCI, the claim-staking function that protects CCFS should be enforced. CCFS has done all that the Code asks of it to protect its interest. Absent some countervailing consideration, CCFS should be entitled to rely on its perfected security interest.

* * *

NOTE

Section 9–325 adopts the view of *Bank of the West*. See Comment 3 to 9–325. Comment 6 to 9–325 suggests that 9–325's resolution of the "double debtor" problem can be extended in appropriate circumstances, even if the section's conditions aren't satisfied. The following might be one such circumstance. Assume that Creditor 1 has a purchase money security interest in a piece of inventory acquired by Debtor on day 1. Creditor 1 files a financing statement covering the inventory on day 15. On day 10 Debtor sells the piece of inventory to Buyer out of the ordinary course. Buyer previously had granted Creditor 2 a security interest in all its existing and after-acquired inventory, and Creditor 2 had filed a proper financing statement a year before. Section 9–325(a) does not subordinate Creditor 2's security interest in the piece of inventory to Creditor 1's interest because (a)(2) isn't satisfied: Creditor 1's purchase money security interest was unperfected when Buyer acquired the inventory. Perfection occurred five days later when it filed. Still, the rationale underlying 9–325 (and *Bank of the West*) continues to apply. Creditor 2 has a comparative advantage at determining the value of the security interest it is obtaining in the piece of inventory. At the time Creditor 1 obtains its purchase money security interest, it has no reason to expect that Debtor will sell the purchase money collateral out of the ordinary course. Nor does it know to whom the sale will be made. Creditor 2, however, could adjust the terms of its loan ex ante to reflect the probability that its debtor, Buyer, will purchase collateral out of the ordinary course. Although Creditor 1 also could adjust its loan terms to reflect the corresponding risk of Debtor's behavior, 9–325 is premised on Creditor 2 being in a better position to do so in dealing with Buyer, its debtor.

## F.   RIGHTS TO PAYMENT

In the past century, the dollar volume in asset-based personal property financing has shifted from tangible to intangible collateral, and among the most important kinds of intangible collateral are rights to payment, such as accounts, payment intangibles, chattel paper and instruments. These are often referred to as "receivables." What commenced humbly as lending to distressed sellers on the security of their accounts has burgeoned into a trillion-dollar industry in which receivables of every conceivable kind are pooled and securitized, making up the collateral for the issuance of bonds and other investment securities. By financial alchemy, the obligation of a consumer to pay her credit card debt to a retailer is transformed into security for highly rated bonds. One of the challenges facing the drafters of Revised Article 9 was to come to grips with kinds of intangibles financing that were unimaginable when the 1962 UCC was promulgated.

Before dealing with priority rules for rights to payment, we discuss the categorization of rights to payment and its reordering under Revised Article 9. First we consider the coverage of rights to payment in Article 9.

### 1.   SCOPE OF ARTICLE 9

With respect to rights to payment, 9–109(a) provides that Article 9 applies to:

> (1) a transaction, regardless of its form, that creates a security interest in personal property or fixtures by contract; [and]

* * *

> (3) a sale of accounts, chattel paper, payment intangibles, or promissory notes;

---

It is a baseline principle that Article 9 applies to security interests in personal property and not to outright transfers. For instance, sales and leases of goods are treated in Articles 2 and 2A of the UCC, not in Article 9. Why did the drafters vary from this rule with respect to sales of the rights to payment enumerated in 9–109(a)(3)? Among the reasons is the difficulty in distinguishing between transactions creating security interests in rights to payment and those making outright transfers, often referred to as assignments. See Major's Furniture Mart, Inc. v. Castle Credit Corp., 602 F.2d 538, 542–43 (3d Cir.1979). Moreover, the Article 9 provisions for perfection by filing and priority under the first-to-file rule for security interests in rights to payment are equally appropriate for sales of these rights. In sum, with respect to rights to payment, it is convenient to cover two conceptually different transactions—secured loans and sales—in one statute: problems of distinguishing between the two transactions are lessened and the provisions for perfection and priority are appropriate for both.

## 2.   REORDERING OF RIGHTS TO PAYMENT IN ARTICLE 9

### a.   THE NEW DEFINITIONS

The extent to which Article 9 covers security interests in and outright transfers of rights to payment is determined by the definitions of the different kinds of rights to payment. Former Article 9 restricted its definition of accounts to rights to payment arising out of the sale or lease of goods or for services rendered. The definition of "account" in 9–102(a)(2) greatly expands the definition to include rights to payment arising either from the disposition of any kind of property, including real property and intellectual property, as well as the rendering of services. The term includes health-care receivables, lottery winnings, and credit card obligations. However, it does not include rights to payment evidenced by chattel paper or instruments or those for loan advances (the lender's right to repayment for money or funds advanced or sold) or commercial tort claims. In short, "account" includes most *unsecured* obligations arising from the disposition of property or the rendering of services that are not evidenced by negotiable instruments.

"Chattel paper" is succinctly described in Comment 5b. of 9–102 as consisting of a monetary obligation together with a security interest in or a lease of specific goods if the obligation and security interest or lease are evidenced by a record or records. Installment sale contracts and leases of goods are common examples. Chattel paper may be either tangible, 9–102(a)(78), or electronic, 9–102(a)(31).

"General intangible," defined in 9–102(a)(42), is a residual category, meaning any personal property other than "accounts, chattel paper, commercial tort claims, deposit accounts, documents, goods, instruments, investment property, letter-of-credit rights, letters of credit, money, and oil, gas, or other minerals before extraction. The term includes payment intangibles and software." The definition of general intangible covers important kinds of intangible property that are not rights to payment, such as rights in software, copyrights, trademarks, patents and characterization rights, but it also covers rights to payment that arise in transactions other than those expressly excluded from the definition of general intangibles. These rights to payment are described as "payment intangibles."

"Payment intangible," defined in 9–102(a)(61), is a subset of a general intangible under which the account debtor's principal obligation is a monetary obligation. Since the expanded definition of "account" broadly includes rights to payment arising from the disposition of almost any kind of property, what is left to fall within the payment intangibles category? An important example of a payment intangible is a bank loan. When the repayment obligation isn't evidenced by a instrument, it is a payment intangible. As we see below, obligations to repay bank loans form the basis for the loan participation industry and are important elements in asset securitization. The adjective "principal" should be noticed in the definition. There are some circumstances in almost any transaction under which the account debtor would owe a monetary obligation. For instance, a breach of contract giving rise to damages or a tort both would create an obligation to pay money. Cf. Comment 5d. to 9–102. This doesn't create a payment intangible. A payment intangible requires that the obligation to pay money be the main or primary obligation. Article 9 does not define when an obligation is "principal" and when ancillary, and the determination can turn on how the obligation arose. If the right to receive payment from the account debtor alone is assigned, the obligation to pay money is the main part of the transaction. If an entire contract is assigned, where the contract contains covenants and imposes duties of performance on the account debtor, the nature of the obligation to pay is less clear. A wrong guess can leave the creditor's security interest unperfected.

"Promissory note," as defined in 9–102(a)(65), is an instrument that evidences a promise to pay money. The definition excludes checks and certificates of deposit.

### b.   SALE OF RIGHTS TO PAYMENT

Although former Article 9 applied to both security interests in and sales of accounts and chattel paper, it applied only to security interests in general intangibles. Thus, sales of general intangibles fell outside the UCC, and were subject to the vagaries of the statutes and common law of each enacting state. Lending on the security of general intangibles has remained significant, but in the past half-century its importance has been dwarfed by the vast financial industries involving the outright sales of intangibles. These are the loan participation and asset securitization markets. Thus, the careful distinctions in Article 9 between accounts, general intangibles and payment intangibles were drawn for a very practical reason having to do with important patterns of financing and the preferences of financers. In fact the desire on the part of the financial community to redraw these boundaries was a major impetus for enactment of Revised Article 9.

Asset securitization is a technique for transforming financial assets into marketable securities. The process involves the transfer of assets to an entity usually created for that purpose and called a "special purpose vehicle." The assets transferred can be any money-generating item, from intellectual property to franchise fees, although often they are accounts, chattel paper and payment intangibles. The entity issues securities that are payable from the stream of revenues produced by the assets transferred to it, such as collections on the accounts or other money-generating item. The transferor of the assets is paid in cash raised from the sale of securities. Securitization offers the transferor access to financial markets that allows raising capital at a lower cost than that offered by bank loans or from alternative sources. See Steven L. Schwarcz, Structured Finance: A Guide to the Principles of Asset Securitization (2d ed. 1993). The lower cost of capital is due primarily to the elimination of financial intermediaries between investors and borrowers and the reduced business risk presented by the special purpose vehicle.

Under former Article 9, some rights to payment acquired for securitization purposes were covered by the UCC and some were not. A case in which a retail chain sells its accounts to a securitization entity would be covered as sales of accounts, but if the receivables sold were obligations on loans former Article 9 did not apply because this was a sale of general intangibles. The rapidly growing asset securitization industry wanted the certainty of knowing that all the receivables it dealt with were covered by the UCC. Revised Article 9 gave the industry what it wanted by broadening the definition of accounts and adding the new category of payment intangibles. Now 9–109(a)(3) covers virtually all the rights to payment, including promissory notes, that this industry deals with. But sales of other kinds of personal property falling within the definition of general intangibles that are not rights to payment, such as copyrights, trademarks and software are not covered by Article 9. See Paul M. Shupack, Preferred Capital Structures and the Question of Filing, 79 Minn. L. Rev. 787, 800–01 (1995).

The interest of parties in the loan participation market sharply diverged from those in the asset securitization business with respect to UCC coverage. The loan participation business, in which a bank sells participations in a debtor's obligation to repay a loan, had grown up outside former Article 9 because the transaction involved was the sale of a general intangibles. Hence, parties were unaccustomed to filing financing statements and dealing with the complexities of UCC filing system. As a flourishing mature industry, they could see no reason why they should have to incur the new transaction costs that the filing requirement would entail when the old system provided enough certainty at less cost.

Revised Article 9 settled on a compromise between the preferences of the two industries. Section 9–109(a)(3) extends Article 9 to cover the sale of payment intangibles. By implication, sales of other sorts of general intangibles are excluded. This satisfies the demand of parties operating in the market for asset securitization for legal certainty. (Neither industry thought that bringing all sales of general intangibles within Article 9 was desirable.) Section 9–309(3) provides that the sale of a payment intangible is perfected without filing. By eliminating the need to file and the attendant transaction costs, the provision satisfies the concerns of parties in the loan participation market. This sophisticated industry had operated without the requirement of public notice, and the Drafting Committee saw nothing to be gained by requiring filing. The statutory term "perfection" that the Revision uses in 9–309(3) with respect to sales of loan participation shares is mildly inartful. A creditor "perfects" a security interest; strictly, a buyer does not "perfect" the ownership interest it purchased. Still, the effect of automatically perfecting the buyer's interest in a payment intangible is clear: the buyer gets the benefit of Article 9's perfection and priority rules and is protected in its seller's bankruptcy proceeding. Section 9–309(4) provides that sales of promissory notes are also automatically perfected.

Thus has the long-simmering controversy over whether sales of general intangibles should be covered by Article 9 been resolved by the Solomonic decision to break the pre-Revision category of general intangibles into three parts. One part, the large volume of rights to payment arising from the disposition of real property and intellectual property, are brought within the definition of account, and the sale of these rights is treated accordingly. A second part, rights to payment that fall within the attenuated definition of general intangibles but are principally monetary obligations, are treated differently as payment intangibles, the sale of which is covered by Revised Article 9. The third part, other intangible property that is not rights to payment such as software, other intellectual property, and other personal property that is not goods, is retained in the definition of general intangibles, and its sale is not covered by 9–109(a)(3), which provides that Article 9 applies to "a sale of accounts, chattel paper, payment intangibles, or promissory notes."

Revised Article 9's handling of the sale of payment intangibles does not solve all problems. At least two difficulties remain. First, competing ownership claims among buyers of payment intangibles may not always be easily resolvable under the Revision. A buyer's interest in a payment intangible is perfected upon attachment, and the precise date or time at which attachment occurs sometimes can be difficult to determine or prove. Buyers therefore sometimes risk high litigation costs ex post in resolving priority contests. Second, because an interest in the sale of a payment intangible is automatically perfected while a security interest in a payment intangible is not, perfection of a security interest in a payment intangible still requires filing. Thus, a sale must be distinguished from a security interest. The Revision provides no help in characterizing a transaction, even on the order of a list of factors to consider. We anticipate that litigation interpreting 9–309(3) will focus on this unaddressed issue.

Still another issue in determining whether a right to payment is a payment intangible was identified in the following case, which has caused much concern in the securitization industry.

## In re Commercial Money Center, Inc.

United States Bankruptcy Appellate Panel, Ninth Circuit, 2006.
47 Bankr.Ct.Dec. 4.

■ Montali, Bankruptcy Judge.

The principal issue in this case appears to be one of first impression for us or any court of appeals. We are told that the multi-billion dollar securitization industry depends on being able to fractionalize financial assets, and specifically on stripping payment streams from underlying transactions such as the equipment leases in this case. The issue is whether those payment streams are chattel paper or payment intangibles. On cross-motions for partial summary judgment the bankruptcy court held that the payment streams are chattel paper. We disagree. The underlying equipment leases are chattel paper but the payment streams stripped from the leases are payment intangibles.

This means that the assignment of the payment streams could be automatically perfected under Revised Uniform Commercial Code ("UCC") Article 9, Section 9–309(3), but only if the assignment is a sale. We agree with the bankruptcy court that the transactions in this case are loans, not sales, so there is no automatic perfection. However, there are unresolved factual and legal issues as to whether perfection was accomplished by taking possession of the underlying leases through a third party agent.

Accordingly, we AFFIRM IN PART, REVERSE IN PART, AND RE-MAND.

## I.   FACTS

Commercial Money Center, Inc. ("Debtor") leased equipment to lessees with sub-prime credit. It packaged groups of leases together and assigned its contractual rights to future lease payments to entities such as NetBank, Inc., FSB ("NetBank"). To enhance the marketability of these payment streams Debtor obtained surety bonds guaranteeing the payments and it assigned its rights under the surety bonds to NetBank. As security for NetBank's receipt of the lease payments and any surety bond payments, Debtor granted NetBank a security interest in the underlying leases and other property. In other words, Debtor assigned NetBank both an interest in the payment streams and an interest in the underlying leases, but it separated the two interests.

### A.   *Transaction terms*

In 1999 and 2000 NetBank transferred over $47 million to Debtor in transactions involving 17 pools of leases. Seven lease pools remain at issue. Each transaction involved (1) a Sale and Servicing Agreement ("SSA") among NetBank, Debtor, and a surety company ("Surety"), (2) surety bonds issued by Surety to Debtor, which Debtor assigned to NetBank under the SSA and was supposed to deliver to NetBank, and (3) an indemnity agreement between Surety and Debtor. A typical lease involved 62 payments of which two had been paid at the inception, leaving 60 payments assigned by Debtor to NetBank. Debtor paid Surety a premium equal to approximately two percent of the total of all payments due under each lease.

A representative SSA in the excerpts of record states in one part (§ 2.1(c)) that Debtor and NetBank intend a sale, not a loan:

(c) The execution and delivery of this Agreement shall constitute an acknowledgment by each of [Debtor as] Seller and [NetBank as] Purchaser that they intend that each assignment and transfer herein contemplated *constitute a sale and assignment outright, and not for security*, of the [Transferred Assets, defined in Section 2.1(a) to include the payment streams due or on deposit, the surety bonds, and proceeds of those things], conveying good title thereto free and clear of any Liens, from [Debtor] to [NetBank], *and that all such property shall not be part of the estate of [Debtor] in the event of bankruptcy....* In the event that such conveyance is determined to be made as security for a loan made by [NetBank] to [Debtor], [Debtor] hereby grants to [Net-Bank] a first priority security interest in all of [Debtor's] right, title and interest in and to the [Transferred Assets].... [Emphasis added.]

\* On the other hand, Section 2.10 of the SSA characterizes the transaction as a loan, not a sale, for tax purposes:

SECTION 2.10 *Income Tax Characterization.* This Agreement has been structured with the intention that the [amounts payable to NetBank] will qualify under applicable federal, state, local and foreign tax law as *indebtedness* of [Debtor] secured by the Leases and other assets described in Section 2.1. The parties hereto agree to treat and to take no action inconsistent with the treatment of [such amounts] as such indebtedness for purposes of federal, state, local and foreign income or franchise taxes and any other tax imposed on or measured by income. [Emphasis added.]

Other provisions of the SSA also use both sale and loan terminology. The sample SSA provides for NetBank to wire an "Original Principal Amount" of $11,610,558.80 to Debtor "[a]s the purchase price," "being the Present Value of the payment stream discounted to effect Interest Rate yield" applying an "Interest Rate" of 12% per annum (later amended to 11.2287% per annum). SSA §§ 1.1, 2.7(d), Amendment I. In exchange Debtor assigns the Transferred Assets to NetBank "without recourse" and Debtor "shall have no interest in [the] Lease Assets which it may be permitted to sell, pledge, assign or transfer to any Person." SSA §§ 2.1(a), 6.4(c).

Debtor was required to perfect its own security interests in the leased equipment. SSA § 2.1(b). It was also supposed to list NetBank in financing statements and lease documents as the "assignee" of those security interests (SSA § 10.2(a)), stamp the original lease documents with an "appropriate legend ... indicating [NetBank's] ownership interest and security interest in the Lease and Transferred Assets" (SSA § 10.2(e)), and deliver to NetBank (A) evidence of the filing of financing statements, (B) a letter from Surety "acknowledging the valid issuance and delivery of the Surety Bonds," and (C) "the original of each executed Surety Bond with Power of Attorney and Notary attached...." SSA § 2.7(g). Debtor's Chapter 7 trustee, Richard M. Kipperman ("Trustee"), alleges that in fact Debtor did not fulfill all of these obligations and NetBank's interests were never perfected.

The SSA appoints Surety as "Servicer" of the leases and Debtor as "Sub–Servicer" to assume all responsibilities and perform all duties of the Servicer. SSA §§ 3.7, 7.4, Art. VIII. Despite the extensive financial and other obligations of the Servicer and Sub–Servicer, further described below, NetBank has "no obligation to pay any Servicing Fee." SSA Art. V.[4]

---

**4.** Under the SSA, Debtor theoretically could have been replaced as Sub–Servicer, if a new Sub–Servicer were willing to take on its obligations and if NetBank consented. Un-

Duties of the Servicer/Sub–Servicer include paying all taxes and insurance on the leased equipment (SSA § 3.4), collecting the payment streams from the lessees (SSA § 3.2), and holding the leases and associated files on NetBank's behalf. SSA § 2.7(a) (at closing Debtor must deliver the original "Lease Files" to Surety as Servicer "which shall then deliver the original Lease Files [back to Debtor] as Sub–Servicer"). Surety/Debtor have the option to commence legal proceedings to enforce the leases "at [their] own expense" (SSA § 3.1), but regardless of the amounts collected they must pay a fixed "Monthly Base Distribution Amount," which is $258,270.47 in the sample SSA, plus other sums including an initial payment of "Interest" and a final payment of any remaining "Principal Balance" and "Interest." SSA §§ 1.1, 3.7, 4.7(a). They are permitted to grant some extensions to lessees but "in no event shall such extension change the Monthly Base Distribution Amount [$258,270.47] to be received by [NetBank]." SSA § 1.1, 3.2(c)(iii). If a lessee falls behind then Surety/Debtor shall "as [their] first recourse . . . realize upon and collect the proceeds in respect of the Surety Bond" (SSA §§ 3.1, 3.3), but if Surety/Debtor wish to avoid whatever costs and consequences would flow from that choice, they can elect to make a "Servicer Advance" to NetBank to cover the shortfall. SSA § 4.6. When all "Principal" and "Interest" payments have been made Section 2.8 of the SSA provides for any residual Transferred Assets to be transferred back to Debtor:

> *\* Termination of this Agreement.* This agreement shall terminate upon the receipt by [NetBank] of the Original *Principal* Amount plus all *Interest* Distributable Amounts [i.e., any remaining unpaid monthly "interest" payments, equal to one-twelfth of the product of the Interest Rate and the Principal Balance of all outstanding Leases] and, if the Monthly Total Distribution Amount is not paid in full on the Stated Maturity Date, *interest* accrued at the Interest Rate on such unpaid portion from and after the Stated Maturity Date. Upon such termination, [Surety/Debtor] shall be entitled to any amounts payable to it as provided herein. *Any remaining Transferred Assets shall thence be conveyed to [Debtor] without recourse.* [Emphasis added.]

A sample indemnity agreement between Debtor and Surety, included in the excerpts of record, obligates Debtor and its principals to indemnify Surety and hold it harmless "against all demands, claims, loss, costs, damages, expenses and attorneys' fees whatever, and any and all liability therefore, sustained or incurred by the Surety" under any surety bonds. NetBank is not a party to the indemnity agreement or the bonds.

Section 10.3 of the SSA provides: "*Governing law.* This agreement shall be governed by and construed in accordance with the laws of the state of Nevada without regard to the principles of conflicts of laws thereof and

less and until that event, however, NetBank agrees to deal "directly" with Debtor as Sub–Servicer rather than dealing with Surety as Servicer. SSA § 3.7. Although Debtor eventu-ally resigned as Sub–Servicer, there is no evidence in the excerpts of record that a replacement was selected and served in that capacity.

the obligations, rights and remedies of the parties under this agreement shall be determined in accordance with such laws." (Original entirely in capital letters.)

B.   *Procedural background*

The initial Surety, Amwest Surety Insurance Company ("Amwest"), was replaced by Royal Indemnity Company ("Royal"). In early 2002 Royal commenced an action in federal district court to remove Debtor as Sub–Servicer under the SSA (*Royal Insurance Co. v. Commercial Money Ctr., Inc.*, 02–CV–0199–BTM (AJB, S.D.Cal.), transferred for pretrial purposes to Ohio, 02–CV–16002–KMO (N.D.Ohio)).

As stated above, SSA § 2.7(a) contemplated that at closing Debtor would retain the leases as Sub–Servicer. Pursuant to a stipulated order Debtor resigned as Sub–Servicer and Royal was authorized to take possession of the leases in March of 2002 (the "Royal Possession Order"). According to NetBank, it is not clear whether the leases were removed from Debtor's possession at an earlier date, perhaps pursuant to a temporary restraining order entered on February 1, 2002 (the "Royal TRO").

On May 30, 2002 (the "Petition Date") Debtor filed its voluntary Chapter 11 petition (Case No. 02–24068–BKC–RBR, Bankr.S.D. Fla., transferred Oct. 3, 2002, Case No. 02–09721–H7, Bankr.S.D. Cal.). After Debtor's case was converted to Chapter 7, Trustee was appointed and filed an adversary proceeding against NetBank (Adv. No. 03–90331–H7). Trustee initially negotiated a settlement with NetBank but Royal objected to the settlement and as an alternative offered its own settlement with Trustee which was ultimately approved by the bankruptcy court.

* Trustee's Complaint seeks declaratory relief and avoidance of Net-Bank's interests under a combination of the UCC and the Bankruptcy Code. Trustee claims that NetBank has not satisfied the requirements for perfection of its interests in the payment streams and therefore its interests are avoidable using his strong arm powers. *See* 11 U.S.C. §§ 544(a), 550 and 551. The Complaint also seeks a judgment avoiding as a preference any perfection of NetBank's interests in the Transferred Assets that might have occurred within 90 days of the Petition Date. *See* 11 U.S.C. § 547 (as enacted prior to any amendments by The Bankruptcy Abuse Prevention and Consumer Protection Act of 2005, Pub.L. 109–8, 119 Stat. 23, because this case was filed before its effective date). This preference claim anticipates NetBank's assertion that it obtained actual or constructive possession of the leases through the Royal Possession Order, which was issued within the 90 day preference period. *See* 11 U.S.C. § 547(b)(4)(A).

NetBank's Answer alleges (1) "that Royal had actual and constructive possession before and after the [Royal Possession Order]" which "led to [NetBank] being perfected with respect to [the Transferred Assets]," (2) more generally, that "agents and/or bailees always had possession of the items in which [NetBank] is secured," (3) that "while [NetBank] did not file a UCC–1 [financing statement] ... to the extent required, [Debtor and/or Surety] were legally responsible for such filings," and (4) that any transfers that might otherwise be avoidable as preferences were protected by the ordinary course of business defense of 11 U.S.C. § 547(c)(2). The Answer asserts numerous other affirmative defenses including equitable estoppel because Debtor and/or Surety "were responsible for, among other things, transferring the sold assets, and perfecting and protecting [Net-Bank's] secured rights and interests under the [SSAs] and under the surety bonds."

NetBank and Trustee filed cross-motions for partial summary judgment. After a hearing on December 20, 2004, the bankruptcy court issued a memorandum decision that Trustee is entitled to judgment on each of the claims described above. *In re Commercial Money Center, Inc.*, 2005 WL 1365055, 56 UCC Rep.Serv.2d 54 (Bankr.S.D.Cal.2005). It ruled that the payment streams constitute "chattel paper" and therefore NetBank was required to perfect its interests under the rules applicable to chattel paper. In the alternative, the bankruptcy court ruled that, even if the payment streams are not chattel paper, NetBank cannot benefit from the automatic perfection rule applicable to sales of payment intangibles (Rev. UCC § 9–309(3)) because the transactions at issue were loans rather than sales. The bankruptcy court's decision states, "It is undisputed" that NetBank did not perfect its interests in the payment streams either by filing financing statements or by taking possession of the underlying leases.

\* Pursuant to the parties' stipulation the bankruptcy court entered an amended partial judgment for Trustee (the "Judgment") under Fed. R.Civ.P. 54(b) (incorporated by Fed. R. Bankr.P. 7054). NetBank filed a timely notice of appeal. In response to questions from the panel at oral argument and in accordance with our orders, the parties have submitted supplemental post-argument letter briefs, and the submission of this appeal was deferred until the last of those letter briefs was received.

## II. ISSUES

A. Are the payment streams "chattel paper" within the meaning of Revised UCC Article 9?

B. Alternatively, were the transactions at issue loans, rather than sales?

C. If the answer to either question is affirmative, is there a genuine issue of material fact whether NetBank perfected its interests in the payment streams, or regarding NetBank's alleged equitable defenses?

\* \* \*

## IV. DISCUSSION

Trustee's strong arm powers generally enable him to avoid a prepetition unperfected transfer by Debtor of an interest in its property. 11 U.S.C. § 544. *See In re Jenson*, 980 F.2d 1254, 1258–59 and 1261 (9th Cir.1992) (majority and concurring opinions discussing avoidance of unperfected security interest under Nevada law and 11 U.S.C. §§ 544 and 547). Trustee argues that NetBank's interests were not perfected.

The parties agree that Nevada's version of Revised UCC Article 9 states the applicable law of perfection. There are no material differences between the Nevada version and the uniform versions of the relevant provisions.

Like other courts we recognize the usefulness of the Official Comments in interpreting the UCC. *See, e.g., In re Filtercorp., Inc.,* 163 F.3d 570, 580 (9th Cir.1998). We also recognize that some of the decisions cited below predate Revised UCC Article 9, but they are still useful on the issues discussed.

The perfection rules of Revised UCC Article 9 apply not just to security interests for *loans* but also to *sales* of chattel paper and payment intangibles. Nev.Rev.Stat. § 104.9109(1)(c) (with inapplicable exceptions, "this article applies to . . . (c) a *sale* of accounts, chattel paper, payment intangibles, or promissory notes") (emphasis added). Somewhat confusingly, the UCC uses lending terminology in provisions that are applicable to sales. *See* Nev.Rev.Stat. § 104.1201(2)(ii) (" 'Security interest' means an interest in personal property or fixtures which secures payment or performance of an obligation. 'Security interest' includes any interest of a consignor and a *buyer* of accounts, *chattel paper, a payment intangible* or a promissory note in a transaction that is subject to Article 9.") (emphasis added). *See also* Rev. UCC § 9–109, Official Comment 5 ("Use of terminology such as 'security interest,' 'debtor,' and 'collateral' is merely a drafting convention adopted to reach [the] end [of applying 'this Article's perfection and priority rules' to sales transactions], and its use has no relevance to distinguishing sales from other transactions. *See* PEB [Permanent Editorial Board] Commentary No. 14.").

* Most perfection is not automatic. One exception is a sale of payment intangibles (referred to as a security interest), which is perfected automatically: "The following *security interests* are perfected when they attach: . . . 3. a *sale* of a payment intangible[.]" Nev.Rev.Stat. § 104.9309(3) (emphasis added).

NetBank claims that its transactions with Debtor come within this exception and are automatically perfected. NetBank argues in the alternative that its interests were perfected by possession of the chattel paper or perhaps by filed financing statements. *See* Nev.Rev.Stat. §§ 104.9310(1) (filed financing statement generally required for perfection), 104.9312(1) (chattel paper, perfection by filing), 104.9313(1) (tangible chattel paper, perfection by possession).

A.   *The payment streams are payment intangibles, not chattel paper*

NetBank claims that the payment streams are payment intangibles, which is one of the requirements for automatic perfection under Nev.Rev. Stat. § 104.9309(3)—the other principal requirement is that the transactions be sales, which we address in the next section of this discussion. The bankruptcy court held that the payment streams are chattel paper.

The UCC distinguishes between the monetary obligation *evidenced* by chattel paper and the chattel paper itself:

1.  In this article:

\* \* \*

(k) "Chattel paper" means a *record or records* that *evidence* both a monetary obligation and a security interest in or a lease of specific goods.... As used in this paragraph, "monetary obligation" means a monetary obligation secured by the goods or owed under a lease of the goods.... [Emphasis added.]

Nev.Rev.Stat. § 104.9102(1)(k) (emphasis added).

This language on its face defines chattel paper to mean the "records" that "evidence" certain things, including monetary obligations. Payment streams stripped from the underlying leases are not records that evidence monetary obligations—they *are* monetary obligations. Therefore, we agree with NetBank that the payment streams are not chattel paper.

If they are not chattel paper, what are they? Most monetary obligations are "accounts" but the definition of account excludes "rights to payment evidenced by chattel paper." Therefore the monetary obligations in this case fall within the payment intangible subset of the catch-all definition of general intangibles. *See* Nev.Rev.Stat. §§ 104.9102(1)(b) ("Account" means "a right to payment of a monetary obligation . . . for property that has been or is to be . . . leased . . . [but the term] does not include rights to payment evidenced by chattel paper . . ."); 104.9102(1)(pp) ("General intangible" means any personal property other than accounts, chattel paper, and various other specified types of property, and specifically "includes payment intangibles");[7] 104.9102(1)(iii) (redesignated as (hhh) by S.B. 201) ("Payment intangible" means "a general intangible under which the account debtor's principal obligation is a monetary obligation"). *See generally In re Wiersma*, 324 B.R. 92, 106–07 (9th Cir. BAP2005) (discussing why definition of payment intangible includes assignment of payment right under settlement agreement).

\* As stated by one publication, the "carved-out payment streams seem to fit the definition of 'payment intangible' like a glove." Barkley Clark and Barbara Clark, *The Law of Secured Transactions Under the UCC*, ¶ 10.08 [D]. That publication specifically disagrees with the bankruptcy court's decision in this case that the payment streams are chattel paper. *See id.* (criticizing *Commercial Money Center*, 2005 WL 1365055, 56 UCC Rep. Serv.2d 54).

Our analysis might stop here. As the bankruptcy court noted, the plain language of the statute is usually conclusive. *See Roger Falcke and Herbig Props. Ltd. v. County of Douglas*, 116 Nev. 583, 588; 3 P.3d 661, 664 (2000) ("Where the language of a statute is plain and unambiguous . . . there is no room for construction, and the courts are not permitted to search for its meaning beyond the statute itself" and "words in a statute should be given

**7.** We recognize that the definition of general intangibles excludes chattel paper, but because the monetary obligations are not chattel paper they are not excluded from the definition of general intangibles.

their plain meaning unless this violates the spirit of the act") (citations omitted). *See also United States v. Ron Pair Enters., Inc.*, 489 U.S. 235, 240–42 (1989) (plain meaning legislation should be conclusive, "except in the 'rare cases [in which] the literal application of a statute will produce a result demonstrably at odds with the intentions of its drafters.'") (citation omitted). *Cf. In re Kane*, 336 B.R. 477, 487–88 and n. 19 (Bankr.D.Nev. 2006) (discussing plain meaning rule, while also noting that "the Supreme Court has not given unambiguous instructions on how to detect or treat legislative ambiguity").

Nevertheless, the bankruptcy court interpreted the plain words of the statute in a manner with which we do not agree:

> The definition [of chattel paper] states three requirements before collateral is characterized as chattel paper: 1) a record; 2) that evidences both a monetary obligation; and 3) a security in or a lease of specific goods. A monetary obligation is defined as a monetary obligation secured by the goods or owed under a lease of the goods. The parties do not dispute that all three elements for chattel paper are met with respect to the underlying equipment leases, but NetBank seeks to characterize the "monetary obligation" owed under the lease as a "payment intangible." This proposition does not follow from the plain language of the statutory definition of chattel paper and *such a reading would essentially delete the monetary obligation requirement from the definition. See* Singer, *Sutherland Statutes and Statutory Construction*, § 47.79 (6th ed. 2000) (A canon of statutory construction is that a definition which declares what a term "means" excludes any meaning that is not stated). The court finds that the monetary obligation (i.e., the payment streams) constitute chattel paper. [Emphasis added.]

We do not understand how NetBank's reading "would essentially delete the monetary obligation requirement from the definition" of chattel paper. That requirement simply describes the *type* of records involved— they must be records that "evidence" a monetary obligation, among other characteristics. Nev.Rev.Stat. § 104.9102(1)(k). The leases do that, so they are chattel paper, but the payment streams do not. As stated above, they are not "records" that "evidence" monetary obligations, they *are* the monetary obligations.

* The bankruptcy court's memorandum decision also comments, in a footnote, that "The Court views NetBank's argument that [Debtor] transferred only the payment streams, and not the underlying leases, immaterial to the legal issue involved." We disagree, for the reasons just stated.

As an alternative basis for its ruling, the bankruptcy court considered the policies behind the statute. We agree with the bankruptcy court that the UCC aims to provide certainty in financial transactions and some means for third parties to discover competing interests in property, at least when that property is collateral or some types of purchased property. We are not persuaded that the plain meaning of the statute conflicts with such policies, or alternatively that it is our role to rewrite the statute if there is any such conflict.

The principal decision cited by the bankruptcy court involved an assignee ("Jefferson") that had been assigned only the payment streams and not the underlying equipment leases. *In re Commercial Management Svc., Inc.*, 127 B.R. 296 (Bankr.D.Mass.1991). A critical difference is that Jefferson had also taken possession of the leases. *Id.* at 299. Here the possession of the leases is a disputed issue.

The Chapter 7 trustee in that case argued that the payment streams were general intangibles and that Jefferson had not perfected its interest in those payment streams because it had not filed any financing statements. The *Commercial Management* court rejected this argument, holding that "Jefferson perfected its security interest [in the payment streams] by possession" of the leases. *Id.* at 305. The *Commercial Management* court acknowledged that the UCC does not "specifically provide" for this result:

> The [UCC] does not specifically provide that the transfer of chattel paper transfers the obligation it represents; nor does it specifically provide that perfection of a security interest in the written paper, for example, by possession, perfects a security interest in those obligations. It merely provides in Section 9–305 that "[a] security interest in chattel paper may be perfected by the secured party's taking possession of the collateral."

*Commercial Management*, 127 B.R. at 302 (*quoting* Boss, "Lease Chattel Paper: Unitary Treatment of a 'Special Kind of Commercial Specialty,'" 1983 Duke L.J. 69, 92 (1983) (footnotes omitted)).

Nevertheless,

> [t]aking possession of the collateral, the chattel paper itself, would be meaningless unless the paper represented the underlying rights which were transferred by a transfer of the paper. Therefore, the necessary implication of [former UCC] Section 9–305 [permitting perfection by possession] is that delivery of chattel paper operates to transfer the claim that the paper represents....

*Commercial Management*, 127 B.R. at 302 (*quoting* Boss, 1983 Duke L.J. at 92–93 (footnotes omitted)).

*Commercial Management* is not binding precedent but we assume for purposes of this discussion that it is correct.[8] Nevertheless, it is distinguishable. As NetBank's attorney argued before the bankruptcy court:

> Certainly if you sell a piece of chattel paper, it does come with all the rights that are thereunder. But the flip side of that is not true. If you buy

---

**8.** *See generally* Rev. UCC § 9–109 Official Comment 5 (stating that a "'sale' of chattel paper" includes "a sale of a right in the receivable"); Rev. UCC § 9–313 Official Comment 2 (implying that delivery of a writing, such as tangible chattel paper, "operates to transfer the right to payment"); *Commercial Management*, 127 B.R. at 303–304 (quoting authority that the advantages of chattel paper would be lost if possession of the records does not perfect an interest in the payment streams, and such perfection prevents a dishonest pledgor from "misleading a potential subsequent lender into believing that [the pledgor] is free to pledge that same property again ...") (citations and footnotes omitted).

some of the pieces under the chattel paper [i.e. the payment streams], it doesn't mean that you're getting the chattel paper as well.

Transcript Dec. 20, 2004, p. 50:13–17.

In other words, delivery of the chattel paper may "operate[ ] to transfer" a perfected interest in the associated payment streams, as *Commercial Management* holds, but that does not mean that payment streams *are* chattel paper. When stripped from the chattel paper they are payment intangibles.

Trustee argues that the automatic perfection of payment intangibles in Revised UCC § 9–309(3) was only intended to address loan participations, not the payment streams in this case. We are not persuaded. Nothing in the statute limits its application to loan participations. *See* Nev.Rev.Stat. § 104.9309(3) (stating simply, "The following security interests are perfected when they attach: ... (3) a sale of a payment intangible," without mentioning loan participations). The official comments imply that a participation is just one type of interest that a party can assign in the monetary obligation. *See* Rev. UCC § 9–109, Official Comment 5 (a sale of chattel paper or certain other things, such as an account, "includes a sale of a right in the receivable, *such as* a sale of a participation interest") (emphasis added).

Trustee argues that our interpretation of the statute will lead to endless debates over whether particular assignments are actually sales or secured loans. Again, we are not persuaded. Many transactions fall clearly on one side or the other of the sale versus loan dichotomy. When the answer is not clear the UCC contemplates that courts will need to decide the issue. *See, e.g.,* Rev. UCC § 9–109, Official Comment 5 ("[N]either this Article nor the definition of 'security interest' in [Rev. UCC] Section 1–201 provides rules for distinguishing sales transactions from those that create a security interest...."). If such decisions are too burdensome on the commercial markets or on litigants then the remedy is with the legislature and not the courts. *See generally Roger Falcke*, 116 Nev. at 588; 3 P.3d at 664 ("Where the language of a statute is plain and unambiguous ... there is no room for construction, and the courts are not permitted to search for its meaning beyond the statute itself") (citation omitted).

Trustee also argues that if Revised UCC Article 9 permits purchases of payment streams to be automatically perfected, as we have held, then this permits secret interests and will wreak havoc on the financing markets. According to Trustee, there is no way for a hypothetical financier to protect itself against the possibility that an entity such as Debtor will transfer interests in the same payment streams more than once. NetBank responds that payment stripping is a bedrock principle of the securitization industry and that Trustee's concerns are misplaced.

NetBank argues persuasively that, if the hypothetical financier is the first to perfect, then generally it will be first in priority. *See* Nev.Rev.Stat.

§ 104.9322(1)(a).[9] For these purposes it does not matter if the transaction was a sale or a secured loan because the UCC covers both, as we have discussed. Nor does it matter if the financier's interest is in the payment streams alone or in the underlying chattel paper leases, because a perfected interest in chattel paper includes the associated payment streams, at least if the reasoning in *Commercial Management* applies. *Commercial Management*, 127 B.R. 296.

A more difficult example is if the financier purchased an interest in the chattel paper leases *after* Debtor had already sold the payment streams to someone else. The financier might have no way to know of that prior "security interest."[10] The holder of that secret interest might not have filed any financing statements, or taken possession of the leases, or given any other notice because, under our holding, its interest would be automatically perfected under Revised UCC § 9–309(3).

NetBank argues that the financier could protect itself by taking possession of the leases, which allegedly would give it priority over the secret interest under the special rule of Revised UCC § 9–330(b). That rule is codified in Nevada Revised Statutes § 104.9330(2):

> 104.9330. Priority of purchaser of chattel paper or instrument.
>
> * * *
>
> 2.  A purchaser [i.e., financier] has priority over a security interest [i.e. the secret interest] in the chattel paper which is claimed other than merely as proceeds of inventory subject to a security interest if the purchaser [financier] gives new value and takes possession of the chattel paper under NRS 104.9105 in good faith, in the ordinary course of [the financier's] business, and without knowledge that the purchase violates the rights of the secured party [i.e., the holder of the prior but secret interest].

Nev.Rev.Stat. § 104.9330(2).[11]

We note that this special priority rule only applies by its terms to an interest "in the chattel paper." We have just held that the payment streams stripped from the leases are not chattel paper, so arguably this special priority rule is inapplicable, although Trustee has not argued the point. On the other hand, from the financier's point of view the assignment of an interest in chattel paper includes the associated payment streams,

---

**9.** "1. Except as otherwise provided in this section, ... (a) Conflicting perfected security interests and agricultural liens rank according to priority in time of filing or perfection." Nev.Rev.Stat. § 104.9322(1)(a).

**10.** As noted at the start of this discussion, the term "security interest" includes sales, not just collateral for loans.

**11.** In the above hypothetical the chattel paper leases are sold to the financier, rather than assigned as security for a loan, but NetBank's argument is not limited to sales because the term "purchaser" includes not only a buyer but also a secured lender. *See* Nev.Rev.Stat. § 104.1201(2)(cc) (" 'Purchase' means taking by sale, lease, discount, negotiation, mortgage, pledge, *lien, security interest,* issue or reissue, gift or any other voluntary transaction creating an interest in property.") (emphasis added) and (dd) (" 'Purchaser' means a person that takes by purchase.").

under the reasoning in *Commercial Management*. Therefore, for purposes of competing priorities under Revised UCC Section 9–330(b), the secret interest may be an interest in the financier's "chattel paper." We explicitly decline to resolve this ambiguity in Revised UCC Section 9–330(b), because neither that statute nor the hypothetical situations posed by the parties are before us on this appeal. It is sufficient for our purposes that the plain meaning of the "chattel paper" definition in Nevada Revised Statutes § 104.9102(1)(k) does not lead to a result that is demonstrably counter to the legislative intent. *Roger Falcke*, 116 Nev. at 588; 3 P.3d at 664; *Ron Pair Enters.*, 489 U.S. at 240–42. If it turns out that the plain meaning of the "chattel paper" definition could cause problems under statutory provisions that are not at issue on this appeal, such as Revised UCC Section 9–330(b), then the answer lies either in the courts' interpretation of those provisions to harmonize the statute or in legislative amendment to the statute, not in disregarding the plain meaning of unambiguous provisions.

For all of these reasons we must apply the plain meaning of the statute: the payment streams separated from the underlying leases do not fall within the definition of chattel paper. Nev.Rev.Stat. § 104.9102(1)(k). Rather, these monetary obligations fall within the payment intangible subset of the catch-all definition of general intangibles. *See* Nev.Rev.Stat. § 104.9102(1)(b) ("Account") (UCC § 9–102(a)(2)); § 104.9102(1)(pp) ("General intangible") (UCC § 9–102(a)(42)); *and* § 104.9102(1)(iii) (redesignated as (hhh) by S.B. 201) ("Payment intangible") (UCC § 9–102(a)(61)).[12]

Because the payment streams are payment intangibles, NetBank's interest in them would be automatically perfected upon attachment under Nev.Rev.Stat. § 104.9309(3) if its transactions with Debtor were sales rather than loans. We now turn to that issue.

\* \* \*

We agree with the bankruptcy court that the transactions were loans, not sales. Therefore, NetBank does not satisfy one of the criteria under Nev.Rev.Stat. § 104.9309(3) ("The following security interests are perfect-

---

**12.** Both NetBank and Trustee submitted declarations of expert witnesses, which the bankruptcy court excluded. The declarants—Professor Steven L. Harris for Trustee and Professor Charles W. Mooney, Jr. for NetBank—were the two reporters for the Permanent Editorial Board who worked on the revisions that became Revised UCC Article 9. NetBank argues that the bankruptcy court improperly struck this evidence "to the extent it constituted factual testimony from a key participant in the drafting of Revised Article 9" to clarify any ambiguity in the statute, citing *In re Boogie Enter., Inc.*, 866 F.2d 1172, 1174 (9th Cir.1989) (citing treatise by "Professor Gilmore, who helped draft Article 9 of the UCC"); *Ritzau v. Warm Springs West*, 589 F.2d 1370, 1376 n.4 (9th Cir.1979) (citing article by "principal draftsman" of uniform code). Trustee argues, among other things, that "[m]aterial not available to the lawmakers is not considered, in the normal course, to be legislative history." *Gustafson v. Alloyd Co.*, 513 U.S. 561, 579 (1995). We need not decide this issue because if there was any error in excluding the Professors' declarations it was harmless: we have reviewed the declarations and they do not change our conclusions.

ed when they attach: . . . (3) a *sale* of a payment intangible[.]'') (emphasis added). NetBank's interest was not automatically perfected.

* * *

## V. CONCLUSION

NetBank entered into transactions with Debtor that were intentionally structured to have characteristics of both a loan and a sale. It relied on Debtor and others to file UCC–1 financing statements, or otherwise assure that its interests in the payment streams from Debtor's leases were perfected, if they were not automatically perfected.

We hold, contrary to the bankruptcy court, that the payment streams are payment intangibles under Revised UCC Article 9 and therefore could have been automatically perfected if the payment streams had been sold to NetBank. We agree with the bankruptcy court, however, that the transactions between NetBank and Debtor are not sales but are secured, non-recourse loans instead. Therefore, NetBank's interests were not automatically perfected. There remain genuine issues of fact and law as to whether NetBank's interests were perfected by possession through an agent such as Royal or Amwest. Trustee did not meet his burden on the factual issue by submitting uncontested evidence regarding who held the leases at the relevant times, nor did Trustee establish entitlement to a judgment as a matter of law by establishing that, contrary to *Commercial Management*, possession of the leases could not perfect an interest in the payment streams. These unresolved issues preclude summary judgment for Trustee.

Accordingly, we AFFIRM IN PART, REVERSE IN PART, AND REMAND.

## NOTE

Chattel paper is defined as a record that evidences both a monetary obligation and a security interest in or lease of specific goods. 9–102(a)(11). In this case, CMC leased equipment to users, whose payment under the leases was guaranteed by surety bonds. In a typical securitization transaction, CMC packaged these insured leases into a series of lease pools and assigned the payments owing on these leases to investors. Before assignment of the payments, CMC's property rights with respect to the leases are classified under Article 9 as chattel paper: it possessed written lease forms evidencing both an obligation of the lessees to make lease payments and a lease of specific goods. If CMC had sold these leases, the buyer could perfect its interest either by taking possession of the leases (9–313(a)) or by filing a financing statement (9–312(a)). But CMC sold only the monetary obligation of the lessees, the prospective payment stream, to the investors, who did not perfect by filing and, since CMC retained possession of the leases, could not perfect by taking possession.

*Commercial Money Center* finds that monetary obligations of lessees sold separately from leases are payment intangibles, not chattel paper. The court relies on a syllogism to determine the proper classification: 9–102(a)(11) defines chattel paper as a "record" or "records" that evidence inter alia a lease of specific goods and a monetary obligation; payment streams separated from a lease are monetary obligations, not "records" of any sort; therefore, the separated payment streams are not chattel paper. The syllogism's second step arguably is questionable. Once a lessee's monetary obligations under the lease are sold separately from the lease, the lease may no longer "record" or evidence the obligations. However, before their sale, at the inception of the lease transaction, a record evidences both the lease and the lessee's monetary obligations. At that time the lessee's monetary obligations therefore are part of chattel paper. Thus, the proper classification of the obligations turns on the relevant time to be used in characterizing the collateral. The *Commercial Money Center* court implicitly judges that the "plain meaning" of 9–102(a)(11)'s language compels classification of the lessee's monetary obligations after they have been separated from the lease. The court's opinion reads more into 9–102(a)(11) than its language supports. Section 9–102(a)(11) does not require the post-separation point in time in classifying monetary obligations. The subsection is completely silent on the matter of timing. However, pertinent case law and Comment suggest that the relevant time for classification purposes is when the asset first becomes collateral. Case law finds that the debtor's initial use of goods is determinative of their proper classification. See, e.g, In re Troupe, 340 B.R. 86 (Bankr. W.D. Okla 2006); In re Pettit, 18 B.R. 8 (E.D. Ark. 1981) (debtor's representations of use controlling when creditor had no reason to know about different use). The classification is not affected by the debtor's subsequent or different use of collateral. In the case of sold chattel paper, the debtor is the buyer and the chattel paper is collateral. 9–102(a)(12)(B), (28)(B). Thus, case law suggests that a monetary obligation arising from a lease is classified as of the time the lease was created, not when it is later separated from the lease. At the time a lease is created, the lease documents evidence the lessee's payment obligation. As such payment streams due under a lease are part of chattel paper, not a payment intangible. Where separated payments streams are sold, the buyer purchases a fragmented part of the chattel paper. Although the payment streams purchased are monetary obligations, not "records" that "evidence" a monetary obligation, they were evidenced by a record at the time the obligation was created, as part of the lease transaction. Their collateral classification therefore determined as of that time.

Several Comments to 9–102 suggest the same timing. Although not directly dealing with chattel paper, Comment 5d. to 9–102 classifies payment rights on the basis of the transaction from which they arose. The Comment states: "In classifying intangible collateral, a court should begin by identifying the particular rights that have been assigned. The account debtor (promissor) under a particular contract may owe several types of monetary obligations as well as other, nonmonetary obligations. If the promisee's right to payment of money is assigned separately, the right is an account or payment intangible, *depending on how the account debtor's obligation arose*" (emphasis added). A fair implication of the Comment is that if the lessee's payment obligations arose from a lease evidenced by a record, the payment obligation is part of chattel paper, not a payment intangible. The subsequent separate sale of the payment obligation does not affect the classification of the collateral as chattel paper.

Comment 5a to 9–102 can be read to reach the same result. Dealing with the classification of instruments, the Comment states in relevant part: "[e]xcept in the case of chattel paper, the fact that an instrument is secured by a security interest ... does not change the character of the instrument as such ..." Thus, in the case of chattel paper, the instrument is classified as part of the paper, not as an instrument. The Comment therefore suggests that classification is made at the time the instrument is issued or made part of the chattel paper. If the instrument later is sold apart from the security interest, the sale does not affect its character as part of chattel paper. The same is true with payment streams that initially are part of chattel paper and later separated from the security interest or lease.

*Commercial Money Center* is highly controversial, with experts divided on the correctness of the opinion. In fact, the Co–Reporters of Revised Article 9 testified as expert witnesses on opposite sides in the bankruptcy court, and the bankruptcy court and Bankruptcy Appellate Panel disagree about the classification of separated payment streams. *Commercial Money Center* creates a new sort of legal risk for securitization transactions. The risks usually considered focus on the true sale character of the transfer of income-generating assets from the originator to the special purpose entity. Bankruptcy related risks concerning fraudulent conveyance law and substantive consolidation of the special purpose vehicle's assets with the originator's assets if the originator goes bankrupt also are taken into account. *Commercial Money Center*'s result creates a somewhat new risk: a risk created by different judicial interpretations of Article 9's definitions of payment rights. Because most cases on the subject will be bankruptcy cases, the risk is that different judicial districts and circuits may adopt different interpretations of the same statutory language. In *Commercial Money Center* the bankruptcy court found that 9–102(a)(11) clearly deems separated payment streams chattel paper while the Bankruptcy Appellate Panel finds them to be payment intangibles under the subsection's plain language. On *Commercial Money Center*'s facts, the same pool of lease receivables might be treated as payment intangibles by some courts and as chattel paper by other courts. Whether investors retain or lose their interest in millions of dollars in receivables ultimately will depend on the judicial characterization of the property transferred. See Steven Walt, Article 9's New Threat to Securitization, 2 J. Payments Sys. L. 418 (2006).

## 3.   EFFECT OF SALES OF RECEIVABLES: THE *OCTAGON* HERESY

A goal in setting up a special purpose entity for asset securitization is to make it "bankruptcy proof." That is, the transaction is structured to make sure that in any possible bankruptcy of the transferor, the assets transferred to the special purpose vehicle cannot be considered part of the transferor's estate and subject to jurisdiction of the bankruptcy court. This requires that the securitization is structured so that the assets transferred are isolated from the transferor's creditors. Otherwise, investors in the special purpose vehicle will continue to bear some of the risk of the transferor's business activities. Isolation of assets typically involves the transferor selling outright the cash flow-generating assets to the special purpose vehicle. Risks associated with the transferred assets frequently are allocated by credit enhancements provided by the transferor or a third party (such as guarantees or letters of credit), repurchase options, and the prioritization of different classes of securities issued by the special purpose vehicle. Such allocations can affect the legal character of the transfer of assets. As part of a securitization transaction, law firms often are asked to give "true sale" opinion letters as well as opinion letters on the likely bankruptcy law treatment of the transfer.

In Octagon Gas Systems, Inc. v. Rimmer, 995 F.2d 948 (10th Cir.1993), the Tenth Circuit raised a major problem for the securitization industry by deciding that an outright sale of accounts leaves a residual interest in the transferor-debtor that can be used by the trustee to drag the accounts back into the debtor's bankruptcy estate and dealt with by the debtor's Chapter 11 plan in a manner that transferred the accounts free of the buyer's interest. The basis for the court's error was its belief that since under 1–201(b)(35), the buyer of accounts had a only a security interest, the seller must have some residual interest in the accounts. The court erred by failing to identify the limited purpose for which Article 9 covers outright sales of accounts. The purpose is filing: sales of accounts are assimilated to security interests to require accounts buyers to file. The assimilation requires accounts buyers to give public notice of their ownership interest in order to protect that interest from the claims of the seller's creditors. However, assimilation of sales of accounts and security interests is limited to filing; for other purposes the distinction is made: sales transfer all of the seller's interest to buyers; security interests taken by a secured creditor do not. Revised 9–318(a) makes this distinction. Comment 2 to 9–318 explains: "Subsection (a) makes explicit what was implicit, but perfectly obvious, under former Article 9: The fact that a sale of an account or chattel paper gives rise to a 'security interest' does not imply that the seller retains an interest in the property that has been sold. To the contrary, a seller of an account or chattel paper retains no interest whatsoever in the property to the extent that it has been sold." See Comment 5 to 9–109 for a helpful discussion of the issue.

## PROBLEM

Jones borrows $10,000 from Debtor, evidenced by a written obligation to Debtor's order. Later, Debtor sells outright to Bank 1 Jones' obligation. The sale is evidenced by an authenticated record. Still later, Debtor grants Bank 2 a security interest in its right to payment from Jones. Bank 2 immediately files a valid financing statement covering the obligation; Bank 1 files nothing. Throughout Debtor remains in possession of the writing evidencing Jones' obligation. Who has priority in Jones' obligation to Debtor, Bank 1 or Bank 2? See 9–109(a)(3), 9–309(4), 9–318(a).

## G.    ACCOUNTS AND GENERAL INTANGIBLES

### 1.    PRIORITY IN PROCEEDS

In this and the following sections, we examine the priority rules applicable to specific kinds of rights to payment: accounts and general intangibles, chattel paper, deposit accounts, and cash proceeds.

As a general rule, accounts and general intangibles can be perfected only by filing (9–310(a)): possession is not a means of possession for intangibles such as these. Priority between conflicting security interests in accounts and general intangibles is determined by the first-to-file rule of 9–322(a). Exceptions to this basic rule are found with respect to payment intangibles, discussed above, and security interests subject to other law, such as rights in registered copyrights (9–311(a)(1)), discussed in Chapter 6. Purchase money security interests can be created only in goods and software and not in accounts. See 9–103, Comment 2 to 9–324 and First Bethany Bank & Trust, N.A. v. Arvest United Bank, 77 P.3d 595 (Okla. 2003).

Since accounts are often the proceeds of collateral, such as inventory, an understanding of the provisions on proceeds in 9–315 is essential in determining priorities in accounts. How do these provisions apply in the following Problems?

PROBLEMS

**1.** Debtor sells goods to retailers who agree to pay Debtor for the goods within 90 days after delivery. Bank periodically advances funds to Debtor to allow it to buy new inventory while awaiting payment from the retailers.

(a) Debtor secured these advances by granting Bank a security interest in "all inventory now owned or hereafter acquired," which was perfected by filing. Later Lender made advances to Debtor, which Debtor secured by granting Lender a security interest in "all accounts now owned or hereafter acquired." Lender promptly filed a financing statement. No reference was made to proceeds in the security agreements and financing statements of either Bank or Lender. Who is prior with respect to the accounts arising from the sale of items from Debtor's inventory, Bank or Lender? See 9–203(f), 9–315(a), (c) and (d), and 9–322(b). See also Comment 6 to 9–322.

(b) Debtor secured these advances by granting Bank a security interest in "all inventory and accounts now owned or hereafter acquired," which was perfected by filing. The retailers were not told of Bank's security interest. Later Debtor made an outright sale of all its accounts to Factor, falsely assuring Factor that Bank's loan would be paid off with the funds received from Factor. Factor immediately filed a financing statement covering all Debtor's accounts, now owned or thereafter acquired, and notified the account debtors that it now owned the accounts and that all payments were to be made to it. Who is prior with respect to Debtor's accounts, Bank or Factor? See 9–109(a)(3) and 1–201(b)(35) (definition of security interest), in addition to the provisions mentioned in (a) above.

**2.** In a written security agreement, Debtor granted SPA a security interest in all its inventory, now owned or thereafter acquired, and all the proceeds thereof. SPA advanced value and filed a financing statement indicating the collateral as "inventory." Subsequently, in a written security agreement, Debtor granted SPB a security interest in all its equipment, and replacements, now owned or thereafter acquired, and the proceeds thereof. SPB filed a financing statement indicating the collateral as "equipment." Debtor sold items of its inventory on 30–day unsecured credit and deposited the checks received in payment in a special account in Bank, which held nothing but the proceeds of the sale of Debtor's inventory. Debtor drew checks on this account to purchase new equipment from Supplier.

(a) Is SPA's security interest prior to that of SPB in the newly acquired equipment? 9–315(d)(1)(C) and (3). See Comment 5.

(b) Would your answer change if SPA's financing statement indicated "all personal property of Debtor"?

## 2.   SECTION 9–309(2) EXCEPTION

A net cast as broadly as the definition of "account" in § 9–102(a)(2) may pull in some strange fish. Suppose your brother-in-law, a small-time painting contractor, borrows $10,000 from you to deal with what he describes as an emergency. You are skeptical both about the existence of an emergency and, in the light of his credit history with you, his likelihood of repaying the money within two months as he said he would. But, in the interest of family harmony, you give him the money. However, in order to impress upon him that you expect to get your money back fairly soon, you extract from him as security for the loan a written assignment of his right to be paid under the contract he has with the owner of the building that he is now working on. When he finishes his work he will be owed approximately $12,000 on that contract. Neither you nor he has ever been involved with the assignment of an account before and neither of you has ever heard about Article 9 or its filing requirements. Comment 4 to 9–309 explains: "The purpose of paragraph (2) is to save from *ex post facto* invalidation casual or isolated assignments—assignments which no one would think of filing. Any person who regularly takes assignments of any debtor's accounts or payment intangibles should file." Does § 9–309(2) exempt you from filing in this case?

# In re Tri–County Materials, Inc.

United States District Court, C.D. Illinois, 1990.
114 B.R. 160.

■ MIHM, DISTRICT JUDGE.

\* \* \*

## FACTS

Tri–County Materials, the Debtor below, operated a sand and gravel pit. Ladd Construction Company was a general contractor which had a contract with the State of Illinois to construct a portion of Interstate 39. Ladd and Tri–County entered into a contract according to which Tri–County would supply Ladd with 100,000 tons of sand and gravel at $2.50 per ton. In order to complete its contractual obligations, Tri–County needed certain equipment to process the sand and gravel from the land it leased. As a result, KMB, Inc. leased equipment to Tri–County for that purpose. The leased equipment was used only at the gravel pit. Once the material was processed, a trucking firm hired by Ladd transported the material to the construction site, some eight to ten miles from the gravel pit.

Although initially the agreement between Tri–County and KMB for the lease of the equipment was oral, that agreement was reduced to writing in June of 1988. In the agreement, Tri–County assigned part of its account with Ladd Construction Company to KMB for the purpose of securing the rental charges which Tri–County owed to KMB. Ladd was notified of the assignment and received bi-weekly notification of the amount due to KMB by Tri–County. KMB did not file a Uniform Commercial Code financing statement regarding the assignment.

Tri–County filed a voluntary petition for bankruptcy under Chapter 11 in October of 1988. At that time, Ladd owed Tri–County $43,413.71 for previously supplied material while Tri–County owed KMB $30,484.

The bankruptcy court found that KMB did not have a security interest in the funds due from Ladd because they had failed to perfect that interest as required under Article 9 of the Uniform Commercial Code. \* \* \*

## PERFECTION OF SECURITY INTEREST

Tri–County owed KMB $30,484 at the time of filing bankruptcy. KMB claims that, because Tri–County assigned its right to receive payments from Ladd to the extent that it owed money to KMB, it had a security interest in the money owed to Tri–County.

§ 9–302 provides as follows:

(1) a financing statement must be filed to perfect all security interests except the following: ... (e) an assignment of accounts which does not alone or in conjunction with other assignments to the same assignee transfer a significant part of the outstanding accounts of the assignor.

KMB takes the position that it is entitled to rely on § 9–302(1)(e) because it is not regularly engaged in accounts receivable financing, thus making this a casual and isolated transaction, and because the amount which Tri–County owed to KMB, when compared to the $250,000 which Tri–County was entitled to receive from Ladd was a mere 12%, thus making it an insignificant transfer. Appellant argues that because KMB fails to meet either test it did not have a perfected security interest in the Ladd account.

The burden of proving the applicability of § 9–302(1)(e) rests on the party asserting the exception. See, Consolidated Film Industries v. United States, 547 F.2d 533 (10th Cir.1977). Although the Code does not define "significant part," case law has developed two tests.

The first test is referred to as the percentage test. This test focuses on the size of the assignment in relation to the size of outstanding accounts. In re B. Hollis Knight Co., 605 F.2d 397 (8th Cir.1979); Standard Lumber Company v. Chamber Frames, Inc., 317 F.Supp. 837 (E.D.Ark.1970).

The second test is the "casual or isolated" test. This test is suggested by the language of Comment 5 to UCC § 9–302 which states that:

> The purpose of the subsection (e)(1) exemptions is to save from ex post facto invalidation casual or isolated assignments: some accounts receivable statutes have been so broadly drafted that all assignments, whatever their character or purpose, fall within their filing provisions. Under such statute many assignments which no one would think of filing may be subject to invalidation. The subsection (1)(e) exemptions go to that type of assignment. Any person who regularly takes assignments of any debtor's accounts should file.

The totality of circumstances surrounding the transaction determines whether an assignment was casual or isolated. If the transaction was not part of a regular course of commercial financing then under this test filing is not required. The rationale appears to be the reasonableness of requiring a secured creditor to file if assignment of debtor's accounts is a regular part of business and the corresponding unreasonableness of a filing requirement for casual or isolated transactions.

There is no authoritative determination of whether both tests must be met in order to claim the exemption or whether either by itself is sufficient. The bankruptcy court agreed with the *Hollis Knight* court which held that both tests must be met. This Court agrees with that assessment. The statutory language specifically requires that the assignment be an insignificant part of the outstanding account. Thus, at the very least, this test must be met in every instance. A showing of a casual or isolated assignment of a significant part of outstanding accounts would not be entitled to the exemption given this clear statutory requirement. On the other hand, given the comments to the UCC regarding the purpose of this exemption, in a case involving the transfer of an insignificant part of outstanding accounts to a creditor whose regular business is financing, such accounts should not fall within this exemption. Thus it is a logical result of the language and purpose of this section to require that both tests be met. * * *

The Debtor's bankruptcy schedules indicate that Tri–County had ten accounts at the time of the Chapter 11 filing, of which the largest by far was the Ladd contract for $250,000. The assignment to KMB permitted KMB to:

> request that the Ladd Construction Company ... make any and all payments to [Tri–County] by including on said check payment the name of [KMB] who shall have said check negotiated and endorsed by [Tri–County] and said check shall be deposited in [KMB's] account with [Tri–County's] endorsement, at which time [KMB] shall issue a check to [Tri–County] for the difference between the amount of the check issued and the rental payment owed to [KMB].

It is thus clear that the assignment was not of the entire Ladd account but only of that portion of the account necessary to cover the balance due to KMB. At the time the parties entered into the Agreement, the total rental amount was estimated at $30,000; the actual figure turned out to be $30,484. The ratio of the amount assigned to the total account, even assuming that the Ladd contract was the *only* account, is approximately 12%.

Although there is no bright line marking the division between significant and insignificant, the 12% figure is surely on the "insignificant" side. See, Standard Lumber Co. v. Chamber Frames, Inc., 317 F.Supp. 837 (D.C.Ark.1970) (16% insignificant). Thus, the first test, contrary to what the bankruptcy court found, has been satisfied. The bankruptcy court based its finding on the assumption that Tri–County had assigned the entire Ladd account to KMB, an assumption that is not supported by the record.

The record also shows without contradiction that KMB was not in the business of accepting contract assignments, nor had either party to the assignment engaged in such a transaction at other times. The bankruptcy court found that despite the "isolated" nature of this assignment, it was "a classic secured transaction," and thus failed to fall within the "casual and isolated" exception to the filing requirement.

This Court agrees with that assessment. This is not the type of "casual" transaction in which reasonable parties would fail to see the importance of filing. Rather, it was evidenced by a formal, written agreement between two corporations; notice of the agreement was sent to Ladd, and other conduct engaged in by KMB indicates the degree of formality attached to it. This is the type of transaction for which the UCC requires filing in order to perfect.

Because KMB failed to perfect its security interest, this Court affirms the bankruptcy court's ruling.

\* \* \*

## NOTES

**1.** How would the court in *Tri–County* apply the exception from filing in 9–309(2), as interpreted in Comment 4, to the following cases?

Case #1. The brother-in-law case in the text preceding *Tri–County* in which an assignment of all of the assignor's accounts, amounting to $12,000, was made to a noncommercial assignee who knew nothing about how to perfect a security interest in accounts.

Case #2. Large corporation assigns accounts amounting to $500,000 to a commercial bank. Both the assignor and assignee regularly engage in accounts financing. The accounts assigned amounted to less than 1% of the assignor's total accounts. Bank failed to file because of an oversight of a clerk.

**2.** Courts have had so much difficulty trying to make sense of former 9–302(1)(e) that the issue has generated more case law than almost any other aspect of accounts financing. The chaos in the cases is chronicled at length in Dan T. Coenen, Priorities in Accounts: The Crazy Quilt of Current Law and a Proposal for Reform, 45 Vand. L. Rev. 1061, 1080–1103 (1992). It is fair to say that 9–309(2), together with Comment 4, clears up none of the problems posed by their predecessors, former 9–302(1)(e) and Comment 5 to former 9–302.

## H.   CHATTEL PAPER AND INSTRUMENTS

### 1.   INTRODUCTION

Gilmore observes: " 'Chattel paper' is a novel term coined by the Code draftsmen to describe a species of property which had previously managed to exist without a name." 1 Grant Gilmore, Security Interests in Personal Property § 12.5, at 378 (1965). In general terms, chattel paper is a record or records that evidence both a monetary obligation and a security interest in specific goods or a lease of goods. Gilmore views some intangibles as non-pledgeable, e.g., accounts and general intangibles, and others as pledgeable, e.g., instruments, chattel paper and documents of title (bills of lading, warehouse receipts). 1 Gilmore, op. cit. supra, § 12.7, at 387 (1965). As we explained earlier, a security interest in accounts and general intangibles can be perfected only by filing; there is no physical embodiment of the right to payment that a creditor can be given possession of. However, with respect to instruments and chattel paper, the belief of the drafters was that the right to payment or performance is sufficiently embodied in written agreements so that possession of these writings gives the possessor control over the obligation. Hence, these writings are, in Gilmore's language, pledgeable. This is best seen with respect to instruments. The right to payment is merged into the instrument and the pledgee-holder of that instrument is the only person entitled to receive payment; any attempt by the original obligee (payee) to make a subsequent assignment of the right to payment represented by an instrument in possession of a pledgee-holder is futile. Although chattel paper is closely related to accounts, we find in the next case that former 9–308 prescribed a priority rule for chattel paper very different from that prevailing for accounts. Revised 9–330 substantially retains the priority rules of 9–308.

# Rex Financial Corp. v. Great Western Bank & Trust

Court of Appeals of Arizona, Division 1, Department A, 1975.
532 P.2d 558.

■ DONOFRIO, JUDGE.

This is an appeal from a judgment in favor of the appellee, Great Western Bank & Trust, on a motion to dismiss which was treated by the trial court as a motion for summary judgment under Rule 56 of the Arizona Rules of Civil Procedure, 16 A.R.S. The trial court considered all of the pleadings, affidavits, other matters of record, and the oral arguments of counsel and determined that there was no genuine issue of material fact, in reaching its judgment. For the reasons given below we affirm the judgment of the trial court.

The relevant facts are undisputed. In December of 1971 appellant entered into an agreement with Liberty Mobile Home Centers, Inc., a dealer in mobile homes, under which appellant agreed to finance this dealer's inventory of mobile homes. The dealer delivered to appellant certain manufacturer's certificates of origin on mobile homes to secure repayment of the loans, and gave appellant a security interest in the vehicles by way of a security agreement between the parties. This appeal concerns four of those mobile homes. The four mobile homes were sold by the dealer in the regular course of his business to certain individuals on security agreement contracts. These four security agreement contracts were then sold and assigned to the appellee, Great Western, in the ordinary course of its business for a certain sum which was paid to the dealer. Unfortunately, the dealer did not use these funds to pay off its outstanding loans owed to the appellant.

The basis for attacking a Rule 56 summary judgment ruling is that there were material factual issues disputed by the parties. All facts considered by the trial court appear in the pleadings, affidavits, depositions, and of course, oral arguments of the parties. On reviewing the record we are compelled to agree with the trial court that there were no material issues of fact, and that this was a question of law concerning the construction and application of U.C.C. § 9–308 concerning the priority between certain secured creditors and purchasers of chattel paper.

§ 9–308 states:

"A purchaser of chattel paper or a nonnegotiable instrument who gives new value and takes possession of it in the ordinary course of his business and without knowledge that the specific paper or instrument is subject to a security interest has priority over a security interest which is perfected under § 9–304 (permissive filing and temporary perfection). *A purchaser of chattel paper who gives new value and takes possession of it in the ordinary course of his business has priority over a security interest in chattel paper which is claimed merely as proceeds of inventory subject to a security interest (§ 9–306), even though he knows that the specific paper is subject to the security interest.*" (Emphasis added.)

Since it was established that Great Western Bank had knowledge of the security interest claimed by Rex Financial Corporation in the four mobile homes, the second sentence of the foregoing section is the critical one for our purposes.

Appellant's first argument concerns the definition of "chattel paper" used in the above-mentioned sentence of § 9–308. Appellant argues that the manufacturer's certificates of origin, which remained in its possession, were a part of the chattel paper and were necessary ingredients along with the security agreements purchased by Great Western to make up the "chattel paper" which must be possessed by the purchaser. We do not agree. § 9–105(1)(b) defines "chattel paper" as:

> " 'Chattel paper' means a writing or writings which evidence both a monetary obligation and a security interest in or a lease of specific goods. When a transaction is evidenced both by such a security agreement or a lease and by an instrument or a series of instruments, the group of writings taken together constitutes chattel paper."

Appellant asserts that * * * the Motor Vehicle Code contemplate[s] that a manufacturer's certificate of origin is a part of the "transaction" where chattel paper is purchased as in § 9–105(1)(b) above. We do not think that such comparison is relevant here. "Chattel paper" clearly must evidence "both a monetary obligation and a security interest in or a lease of specific goods." The manufacturer's certificates of origin do not meet this definition, and the trial court's construction of § 9–105(1)(b) was correct in the application to this factual situation. It was undisputed that Great Western gave "new value" for the four security agreements it purchased from the dealer, all in accordance with § 9–308.

The next requirement of § 9–308 which is attacked by appellant is the requirement that the purchase of the chattel paper be "in the ordinary course of *his* business." (emphasis added) Appellant maintains that this refers to a practice which "should have been followed" and not to the practice of this particular purchaser of chattel paper. Again we do not agree. The plain language of the statute refers to *"his business"* (meaning the purchaser of the chattel paper). It is undisputed that this purchase was the normal means used at Great Western to obtain this type of chattel paper. As was stated in the deposition of Mr. McFadden, a representative of Great Western, he expected the *dealer* to disburse funds to appellant to pay off the loans for the "floor plan" financing that the dealer had obtained from appellant. The term "buyer in the ordinary course of business" with its requirements of good faith, as used elsewhere in the Uniform Commercial Code, is to be distinguished from the use here of "[buyer] in the ordinary course of *his* business." In fact, § 9–308 (second sentence) allows the purchaser of the chattel paper to have priority even if he has knowledge of a prior security interest in the collateral. As noted by White and Summers in their Treatise on the Uniform Commercial Code, ". . . the later party is favored on the assumption that chattel paper is his main course but merely the frosting on the cake for the mere proceeds claimant." White and Summers, Uniform Commercial Code, Sec. 25–17, p. 951 (1972 Edition).

This brings us to the final issue raised by appellant: the fourth requirement of the second sentence of § 9–308, that the security interest claimed by appellant is claimed "merely as proceeds of inventory subject to a security interest." We find Comment 2 to this section of the U.C.C. (as found in the Final Report of the Permanent Editorial Board for the Uniform Commercial Code, Review Committee for Article 9, April 25, 1971) instructive on this issue. There it is stated:

> "Clause (b) of the section deals with the case where the security interest in the chattel paper is claimed merely as proceeds—i.e., on behalf of an inventory financer who has not by some new transaction with the debtor acquired a specific interest in the chattel paper. In that case a purchaser, even though he knows of the inventory financer's proceeds interest, takes priority provided he gives new value and takes possession of the paper in the ordinary course of his business."

We take this language to mean that the drafters of the Code contemplated a situation such as the instant one where the inventory financer, Rex Financial Corp., had a security interest in the collateral (mobile homes) and the proceeds upon sale. The record before us does *not* indicate that Rex entered into any new transaction with the debtor/dealer. The trial court had before it the security agreement between Rex and the dealer as well as the affidavit of Rex's president, and found that Rex's claim was merely to the proceeds of the inventory when sold. We do not find error in this construction and application of the term "mere proceeds of inventory" by the trial court. We think it is a reasonable interpretation of the record that the appellant, Rex, did *not* place a substantial reliance on the chattel paper in making the loan, but rather relied on the collateral (mobile homes) and the proceeds when the collateral was sold. The proceeds of the sale of these four mobile homes included the chattel paper sold by the dealer to Great Western. Rex could have protected itself by requiring all security agreements executed on sale of the mobile homes to be turned over immediately to Rex, or if sold, that all payments for the security agreements (chattel paper) be made to itself.

A case that aptly illustrates the operation of U.C.C. § 9–308 is Associates Discount Corporation v. Old Freeport Bank, 421 Pa. 609, 220 A.2d 621 (1966). In that case a finance company which purchased chattel paper from an auto dealer (in a factual situation somewhat similar to ours) prevailed over a bank which had "floor planned" the inventory of the dealer. The court found that the bank's claim was a mere proceeds claim to the chattel paper and that U.C.C. § 9–308 (second sentence) would operate to give priority to the purchaser of the chattel paper. The inventory financer's interest in the "proceeds" of the sale of the inventory had been shifted to the money paid by the purchaser of the chattel paper to the dealer. Another case in which the same result was obtained was Chrysler Credit Corporation v. Sharp, 56 Misc.2d 261, 288 N.Y.S.2d 525 (1968), a New York case, which again applied U.C.C. § 9–308 and held that the purchaser of an installment contract from an automobile dealer would prevail over a secured inventory financer.

The case of Price v. Universal C.I.T. Credit Corp., 427 P.2d 919 (1967), although decided before our state's adoption of the Uniform Commercial Code, is still instructive in the instant case. The court there held that an inventory financer who brought an action against, among others, the purchase money lender on the sale of an automobile should not have priority over the purchase money lender. The inventory financer sought to recover money loaned to the dealer on a "flooring loan" when the automobiles were sold out of trust. We realize that the Price case did not involve application of U.C.C. § 9–308, but it is indicative of the general feelings of our courts in the area of priorities between secured creditors and purchasers of chattel paper as proceeds of the sale of inventory collateral.

In any case, the construction and application of U.C.C. § 9–308 to undisputed facts is a question of law for the trial court which was reasonably determined in the instant case.

Affirmed.

## 2.   "MERELY AS PROCEEDS"

Whether subsection (a) or (b) of 9–330 applies depends on whether the chattel paper is claimed "merely as proceeds of inventory" or "other than merely as proceeds of inventory." Our experience is that students find this distinction difficult to understand, and well they might. The distinction simply isn't clear. There is no definition of these phrases in either the text of the statute or its Comments, nor is there a statement of any underlying principle on which the distinction is founded. For an "elaboration" of the term, we are referred by Comment 3 to 9–330 to PEB Commentary No. 8. We set out below three prototypic Illustrations that are based on the Commentary as an aid to understanding the distinction.

1.   Facts: In the following two Illustrations, General Motors Acceptance Corporation (GMAC) finances the new car inventory of a Chevrolet Dealer (Dealer). This is sometimes called "floor-planning," meaning that GMAC lends Dealer money to buy cars from the manufacturer, General Motors, and takes a security interest, perfected by filing, in the inventory and its proceeds. When Dealer sells a car, it must account to GMAC for the amount loaned against the car; if the car is not sold within 90 days, Dealer must account for it at the end of the period.

Illustration #1. Dealer sells a car to Buyer who pays 20% down and signs an installment sale contract in which she agrees to pay the balance of the price ($20,000) plus a finance charge in 36 monthly payments. The contract grants Dealer a security interest in the car to secure the unpaid balance. Dealer sells and delivers possession of the contract to Finance Company (Finance) for $20,000 in cash. Finance buys automobile paper in the ordinary course of its business and is well aware that GMAC is floor-planning Dealer's inventory. Dealer deposited the $20,000 check in its general operating deposit account and failed to account to GMAC for the proceeds of the sale to Finance. GMAC did not require Dealer to deposit cash proceeds in any form of restricted or blocked deposit account that would have given GMAC a measure of control over the account. Hence, it was easy for Dealer to use the funds for purposes other than accounting to GMAC. When GMAC discovered Dealer's failure to account, it asserted a priority interest in the chattel paper, as proceeds of its inventory collateral, in the possession of Finance. Finance is prior under 9–330(a).

Analysis of Illustration #1: This is the paradigm case under 9–330(a) in which GMAC is claiming its security interest in the contract *merely as proceeds*. Finance is giving new value in ordinary course of its business. Although Finance has not searched the filings, it knows that virtually every new car inventory is financed and that Chevrolet dealers are usually financed by GMAC. As Comment 5 to 9–330 points out with respect to 9–330(a), "[A] purchaser who meets the possession or control, ordinary course and new value requirements takes priority over a competing security interest unless the chattel paper itself indicates that it has been assigned to an identified assignee other than the purchaser. * * * This approach, under which the chattel paper purchaser who gives new value in ordinary course can rely on possession of unlegended, tangible chattel paper without any concern for other facts that it may know, comports with the expectations of both inventory and chattel paper financers."

A possible justification for this exception to the first-to-file-or-perfect rule of 9–322(a)(1) is that the position of GMAC has not worsened because of the sale of the paper to Finance. In place of the chattel paper, Dealer has the $20,000, and, if GMAC has maintained prudent controls over Dealer's handling of cash proceeds that allows it to trace the proceeds of the check, it has a secured claim in the cash proceeds. Common law cases typically awarded priority to purchasers of the chattel paper against the secured party who financed the inventory. 2 Grant Gilmore, Security Interests in Personal Property § 27.3 (1965). Former 9–308 and 9–330(a) continue this traditional priority. This rule is benign: it allows dealers to sell their paper to purchasers who offer better deals than the inventory financer, and, in doing so, encourages competition.

GMAC's problem in this case is its failure to impose controls over the cash proceeds in Dealer's possession. It shouldn't matter to GMAC whether the car was sold for $25,000 cash or for $5,000 down with the balance represented by chattel paper that was sold to Finance for $20,000. In both cases, Dealer ends up with $25,000 in cash, an agreed portion of which should have been paid over to GMAC. Prudent inventory financers shouldn't find the priority preference of 9–330(a) unsettling. In Illustration #1, carefully monitored cash management controls, such as blocked or lockbox accounts into which cash proceeds must go, imposed by GMAC on its dealers protects GMAC against any damage stemming from 9–330(a)'s awarding priority to Finance.

Illustration #2. Dealer sells a car to Buyer who pays $5,000 down and signs a contract agreeing to pay the balance of $20,000 plus interest in monthly installment payments over a three-year period. The contract granted a security interest in the car to Dealer to secure the unpaid balance. Dealer sold the contract to GMAC for $20,000. GMAC allowed Dealer to retain possession of the contract in order to serve as GMAC's agent in making collections under the contract. Dealer was in financial difficulties and wrongfully sold the contract to Finance for $20,000 in cash. Dealer did not account to GMAC for the cash. Finance is in the business of purchasing automobile paper from Dealers and is aware of the likelihood that GMAC may claim a security interest in the contract, but Finance has no knowledge that GMAC had bought the paper. When GMAC discovered Dealer's fraud, it asserted its priority over the chattel paper in Finance's possession. Finance is prior under 9–330(b).

Analysis of Illustration #2: Although the meaning of "merely as proceeds" is unclear, this is an easy case for finding that GMAC is claiming a security interest in the chattel paper "other than merely as proceeds of the inventory" because in a subsequent transaction it bought the paper from Dealer. Whatever else "merely as proceeds" means, GMAC clearly took the chattel paper out of the merely-as-proceeds category in this case by giving new value against it in a new transaction. It is claiming the paper as the purchaser of it, not as proceeds of Dealer's inventory in which GMAC had a security interest.

The possibility of this case occurring in modern automobile financing is remote in the extreme. First, GMAC can preclude any fraudulent double financing by a dealer merely by taking possession of the chattel paper, and this is the practice in the industry. Second, even though there is no pattern in automobile financing of purchasers of paper leaving possession of the paper with dealers, if GMAC were to do so it could establish its priority over Finance by stamping a legend on the paper indicating that it had been assigned to GMAC. In a 9–330(b) case Finance cannot prevail unless it is "without knowledge that the purchase violates the rights of the secured party." Under 9–330(f), an indication on the paper that it had already been assigned to GMAC would have given Finance the requisite knowledge of violation of GMAC's rights.

According to PEB Commentary No. 8, there was a practice in the 1950s when Article 9 was being drafted of chattel paper purchasers leaving possession of the paper with the dealers for collections. Department stores liked this practice because it often brought customers who bought goods on installment sale contracts back to the store to make their payments. The location of the credit department usually required the customer to walk past as much merchandise as possible, as a lure to impulse buyers, on the way to the credit department. Since the drafters of the original Article 9 did not want to disrupt these practices, they allowed such purchasers to perfect a security interest in chattel paper by filing and introduced the ungainly "other than merely as proceeds" distinction to protect such purchasers from subsequent buyers of the paper from the fraudulent dealer who knew about the purchaser's security interest. Legending the paper would be particularly useful to these chattel purchasers. In an age when most small goods purchases are done on credit cards on an unsecured basis rather than on installment sale contracts, the practices described by the Commentary seem hopelessly dated; nonetheless, the distinction based on the "merely as proceeds" test was carried over into 9–330, and remains there as a staple of law school exams and a trap for unwary lenders.

2.  Illustration #3. Dealer sells appliances and furniture. Smaller items are sold on an unsecured basis; larger items are sold on installment credit contracts in which security interests are taken. Bank finances Dealer's operations by taking a floating lien on all Dealer's inventory and receivables (accounts and chattel paper). Bank has filed a financing statement. Dealer is allowed to borrow as much as requested up to an agreed percentage of the value of Dealer's inventory and receivables. In violation of its agreement with Bank, Dealer sells chattel paper having a face value of $200,000 to Financer for $150,000 in cash. Financer takes possession of chattel paper in ordinary course of its business. If the issue of Financer's knowledge becomes an issue, is this case governed by subsection (a) or (b) of 9–330?

Analysis of Illustration #3: PEB Commentary No. 8 takes the view that Bank has more than a mere proceeds interest in the chattel paper in this case because it is part of the collateral on which the lending formula is based; therefore, the chattel paper is primary collateral. The Commentary observes: "The structure of the deal is such that the chattel paper is part of the primary collateral for the debt. That interest extends to any chattel paper subsequently generated by a sale of inventory whether or not at any particular time the existing inventory is adequate security for the debt actually outstanding." It is not clear how Financer is supposed to recognize whether Bank is relying on chattel paper as primary collateral in cases of this sort.

We question whether the "merely as proceeds" rule should have been continued in Article 9. Not only is it confusing, but a good argument can be made that it rests on a false distinction. No inventory financer claims chattel paper "merely as proceeds" of inventory. They always rely on chattel paper in setting loan terms, including the interest rate. This is because the inventory financer must consider a future contingency in which the debtor is insolvent or close to it. In these circumstances debtors have an incentive to take risks with collateral or proceeds in order to avoid default. The limit of debtor's risk-taking, of course, is to dissipate money received from the sale of chattel paper. Inventory financers, knowing of this possible contingency, must look primarily to the paper for repayment of their loans. They will adjust the interest charge of the loans if they cannot do so. Thus, the lenders are always looking substantially to the chattel paper at the time the loan is made. If the test is one of substantial reliance on the paper in making the loan, as followed by the court in *Rex Financial*, all inventory financers qualify. The financer who ignores the possibility of having to reach the paper does not exist. Chattel paper is always part of the cake and never the frosting for inventory financers. This conclusion might explain why a definition of a "mere proceeds" interest eludes the drafters of the Revision: none is consistent with the plausible pricing of loans by inventory financers.

Commentary No. 8 does not try to justify the distinction between "mere proceeds" and "other than mere proceeds" interests. It instead takes the distinction as given by former 9–308 and tries to describe it based on case law that relies on 9–308. The Commentary comforts us as we struggle with the meaning of the phrase "merely as proceeds" by noting that the problem is of only "limited importance since, even if the security interest is more than a mere proceeds interest, the chattel paper financer under 9–330 will take free of the interest unless it has knowledge that the purchase violates the rights of the secured party." So, why didn't they write it that way?

## 3.  Instruments

Suppose Bank takes a security interest in Debtor's inventory and all the proceeds thereof, including accounts, chattel paper and instruments. Bank perfected its security interest by filing a financing statement covering all Debtor's personal property. When Debtor sells some items of its inventory, it accepts promissory notes from buyers, in which they promise to pay to the order of Debtor a stated sum of money at a stated future time. Under 3–104(a), these notes are classified as "negotiable instruments," and under 3–104(b) are "instruments." But for Article 9 purposes "instruments" is broadened to include not only negotiable instruments but also other written promises to pay money that are, in effect, treated similarly in the market place. 9–102(a)(47). The question addressed by 9–330(d) is the priority between Bank and one who purchases an instrument from Debtor. This provision likens instruments to chattel paper for priority purposes. The purchaser of the instrument prevails if it gives value (not just new value), takes possession of the instrument in good faith and without knowledge that the purchase violates the rights of the secured party.

The question arises how to reconcile 9–330(d) with 9–331(a), which says that nothing in Article 9 limits the rights of a holder in due course of a negotiable instrument. If the purchaser of the instrument in the previous paragraph took delivery of the note for value in good faith and without notice of claims or defenses, it becomes a holder in due course who takes free of claims or defenses under 3–302. It is accepted negotiable instruments law that a holder in due course takes free of a prior security interest in the instrument (a claim of ownership) but a holder who knows of the security interest cannot qualify as a holder in due course. Thus, if the purchaser knew about the existence of Bank's security interest, it would be subject to Bank's security interest under Article 3. But under 9–330(d), the purchaser would be prior to Bank even though it knew of the security interest so long as it had no knowledge that the purchase violated Bank's rights. The Article 9 priority rule found in 9–330(d) would prevail. Section 9–330(d) provides that its rule applies "except as otherwise provided in Section 9–331(a)," and nothing in that section provides otherwise. Article 3 determines who is a holder in due course, but whether the purchaser is a holder in due course is irrelevant to the purchaser's rights under 9–330(d).

## 4.   REVIEW PROBLEMS

PROBLEMS

**1.**   ZBest is an appliance dealer. Bank advanced $250,000 operating capital to ZBest and took a security interest in all its inventory then owned or thereafter acquired including all proceeds from the disposition of that collateral. Bank filed a financing statement indicating the collateral as "all ZBest's personal property."

(a) ZBest sold a radio-CD player to A for $200. A used a ZBest credit card to pay for the merchandise.

(b) ZBest sold a refrigerator to B for $1,000 and in a written contract reserved a security interest in the refrigerator for the unpaid price plus the finance charge to be paid in 12 equal monthly installments.

(c) ZBest sold a washing machine and dryer unit to C for $1,000 and accepted C's negotiable promissory note, payable to the order of ZBest, for the balance of the price plus interest.

(d) ZBest leased a large-screen television set to D for one year at $100 per month rental. D has the right to renew the lease for an additional year at the same rental. At the expiration of the lease, D was obliged to return the set to ZBest at its own expense.

ZBest, desperate to survive the recession, sold all its receivables to Factor who paid $100,000 cash. Factor knew that Bank had a security interest in the inventory but knew nothing of its terms. In effectuating the sale, Factor took possession of all credit card slips, installment sale contracts, promissory notes (bearing ZBest's indorsement), and lease agreements.

a.   Which party has priority with respect to the receivables of ZBest arising out of the transactions with A, B, C and D?

b.   Which party has priority with respect to the ZBest's residual interest in the television set? See Comment 11 to 9–330.

**2.**   Debtor granted Bank a security interest in all its inventory and chattel paper, now owned or thereafter acquired, and the proceeds thereof. Bank perfected by filing. Later Debtor sold all its receivables, including its chattel paper, to Financer who paid cash, and took possession in good faith. After Debtor failed, both Bank and Financer claimed priority in the chattel paper sold to Financer. Assume that Bank can prove that Financer took the paper with knowledge that its purchase violated the rights of Bank. Financer asserted that this issue was irrelevant because 9–330(a) governed and knowledge is not a factor under that provision. Bank replied that 9–330(b) governed because the description of collateral in its security agreement mentioned chattel paper as primary collateral and not as proceeds, hence its claim to the chattel paper was not "merely as proceeds." Which subsection governs, (a) or (b)?

## I. Deposit Accounts

### 1. Introduction

Section 9–102(a)(29) defines a "deposit account" as a "demand, time, savings, passbook or similar account maintained with a bank." "Bank" includes "savings banks, savings and loan associations, credit unions, and trust companies." 9–102(a)(8). The definition of "deposit account" does not include accounts evidenced by negotiable certificates of deposit; these are covered in Article 3 as instruments. Section 3–104(j) defines a CD as an instrument issued to a depositor by a bank acknowledging that a sum of money has been deposited in the bank that the bank promises to repay. The depositor can pledge the CD, which amounts to a promissory note of the bank, as security for a loan in the same manner as any other instrument. Nor does the definition include "investment property," meaning money market funds or mutual fund accounts, even if redeemable by check.

The broad definition of deposit accounts sweeps in everything from simple checking accounts through savings and trust accounts. Customers of commercial and savings banks maintain deposit accounts in these institutions amounting to enormous sums of money. The question of how the holders of these accounts, which contain great wealth, can effectively use them as collateral for debt has long puzzled courts and legislatures. In this section we address the response to this question offered by Revised Article 9.

As Comment 16 to 9–109 explains, the pre-Revision state of the law with respect to the creation of security interests in deposit accounts "was nonuniform, often difficult to discover and comprehend, and frequently costly to implement. As a consequence, debtors who wished to use deposit accounts as collateral sometimes were precluded from doing so as a practical matter." Former Article 9 applied to security interests in deposit accounts only if the accounts were proceeds of other collateral, not if the security interest was taken in the deposit account as original collateral. A few states declined to adopt the exclusion of deposit accounts from Article 9, but their laws were rudimentary statutes usually prescribing perfection by notice to the depositary bank, with no attempt to deal with priority issues.

The major reform of Revised Article 9 with respect to security interests in deposit accounts is bringing them fully within the Act by covering security interests taken in deposit accounts as original collateral as well as proceeds. This step contributes greatly to the commendable goal of bringing uniformity and consistency into what had been a confusing area of law. However, attainment of this goal is somewhat frustrated by the exclusion in 9–109(d)(13) of security interests in deposit accounts as original collateral in consumer transactions, which leaves this area to the vagaries of pre-Revision law. This exclusion can be circumvented by turning the consumer's deposit account into either a certificate of deposit or investment property, such as a money market account. A few states have adopted nonuniform amendments to 9–109(d)(13) that bring within Article 9 security interests in deposit accounts in consumer transactions.

Section 9–109(d)(13)'s exclusion of security interests in deposit accounts as original collateral in consumer transactions apparently is a response to the concerns of consumer advocates. They took seriously the risk that consumers are prone to inadvertently grant security interests in their savings or retirement accounts. In their defense there exists some experimental evidence that decision makers in some settings systematically make erroneous probability judgments or inferences. See Eldar Shafir & Robyn A. LeBoeuf, Rationality, 53 Annual Rev. Psy. 491 (2002), Daniel Kahneman & Amos Tversky, eds., Choices, Values, and Frames (2000). These judgments or inferences can result in misestimates of the probability of events or overconfidence or underconfidence in predictions. A consumer's estimate of its prospects of default or repayment might be subject to such errors. However, even if consumers often are subject to such misjudgments or misestimates, 9–109(d)(13)'s exclusion isn't responsive to the problem. This is because 9–109(d)(13)'s exclusion doesn't prevent consumers from granting security interests in deposit accounts as original collateral. It only prevents the transaction from being governed by Article 9. Common law or extra-Article 9 statutory law instead controls. Further, as noted above, the exclusion in any case can be circumvented by having the consumer-debtor turn its deposit account into original collateral covered by Article 9, such as a certificate of deposit or investment property. In that case parties can "transact into" Article 9—with additional transaction costs. Thus, 9–109(d)(13)'s exclusion apparently only increases the costs of taking security interests in deposit accounts in consumer transactions.

Two factors, unique to deposit accounts, complicate the use of deposit accounts as collateral. When customers deposit money in banks, they enter into a debtor-creditor relationship with the banks in which the deposits are maintained. The depositor becomes a creditor of the bank and has a right to payment from the bank for the amount of the deposit. The customer may use this payment right as collateral, but the most common secured transaction in deposit accounts is one in which the security interest in the right to payment is created in favor of the depositary bank itself. Hence the bank finds itself as, in effect, both the account debtor and the secured party.

A second complication is the existence of the bank's traditional right of setoff. Under the common law a bank that has lent money to a customer has the right to offset the amount owing on a loan in default against a deposit account of the customer maintained in that bank. Since banks rarely loan money to debtors who do not have deposit accounts in the lender bank, the bank's right of setoff usually parallels any rights the bank may have under a security interest in the account. A common practice is for a lending bank to require the debtor to maintain a "compensating balance" in its deposit account equal to a fixed percentage of the amount of the loan, against which the bank may offset if the debtor defaults on the loan. Setoff may be accomplished informally by the bank's merely debiting the deposit account for the amount owed the bank. Thus, the bank's setoff rights are so similar to its rights under a security interest that Bankruptcy Code § 506(a) classifies the right of a creditor to offset as a "secured claim." Former Article 9 excluded setoff rights from coverage, and 9–109(d)(10) continues this exclusion with two exceptions. The first recognizes 9–340, which allows the depositary bank to exercise setoff against a secured party who holds a security interest in the deposit account. The second, 9–404, relates to defenses or claims of an account debtor.

## 2.   PRIORITY RULES

### a.   CONTROL

As we will see in Chapter 7, when Revised Article 8 was drafted a few years before Revised Article 9, the drafters adopted the concept of control as the method for both attachment and perfection of security interests in investment property. We explain in that chapter why it was thought necessary for the systemic safety of stock and bond markets that a single entity be in a position of full control over the transfer of securities without having to seek the consent of the debtor or other secured parties to liquidate the collateral expeditiously. The drafters of Revised Article 9 have taken the control concept out of its original context of securities markets, perhaps in the belief that security interests in deposit accounts could have an impact on the structural security of the banking system, and have applied it to deposit accounts so that attachment (9–203(b)(3)(D)), perfection (9–312(b)(1), 9–314(a)), and priority (9–327) depend on whether the secured party has "control" under 9–104. See Comment 2 to 9–341, which discusses the importance of not impeding the "free flow of funds" through the payment system.

Section 9–104 provides in part:

(a) A secured party has control of a deposit account if:

(1) the secured party is the bank with which the deposit account is maintained;

(2) the debtor, secured party, and bank have agreed in an authenticated record that the bank will comply with instructions originated by the secured party directing disposition of the funds in the account without further consent by the debtor; or

(3) the secured party becomes the bank's customer with respect to the deposit account.

Hence, we see that a third-party lender obtains control when, with the debtor's consent, it obtains the depositary bank's agreement to act on the lender's instructions, or when the account is placed in the name of the lender, making it the depositary bank's customer. On the other hand, a depositary bank gains control merely by obtaining a security interest in the deposit account. Simpler methods of establishing perfection and priority in a third-party lender, such as filing a finance statement or notification of the bank where the deposit is held, are rejected. Control is the sole method of perfection for security interests created in deposit accounts as original collateral. See 9–312(b)(1) and Comment 2 to 9–104.

Why perfection by control rather than by filing? The answer isn't clear. Security interests in deposit accounts resemble those in investment securities, and somewhat analogous laws apparently seemed appropriate to the drafters. However, the resemblance isn't telling: the drafters have allowed filing as an alternative method of perfection for investment property. Another factor favoring control over filing in the minds of the drafters was their concern about making it too easy to create security interests in deposit accounts. Under a filing regime, secured parties might sweep deposit accounts into the coverage of their security interests as a matter of course by boilerplate clauses without actually relying on them in extending credit. Secured parties might enjoy windfalls and debtors might suffer the unexpected loss of their bank balances. The view taken was that if creditors have to exercise control over the deposit accounts in order to effect perfection and to enjoy priority, they will do so only if they are in fact relying on the deposit account in granting the credit. Thus, the drafters treat deposit accounts very differently from other types of personal property. For other types of personal property, Article 9 makes it very easy to perfect security interests in property now owned or hereafter acquired, without caring much about what the secured party relied upon.

The drafter's justification for the special treatment of deposit accounts is weak, for three reasons. First, the justification applies equally to every type of collateral. Filing always carries the risk of a financing statement covering collateral that the secured party isn't relying upon and of which a debtor may be unaware. The risk isn't peculiar to deposit accounts. Thus, if the risk of "windfall" or "unexpected" coverage is enough to prevent filing as a perfection method for deposit accounts, it should also be enough to prevent filing as a perfection method for all types of collateral. Second, it's unclear whether the total costs associated with perfection are reduced by requiring control. When filing isn't a permissible perfection method, the generally increased cost of control over filing is borne only by relying secured creditors (and ultimately the debtor). Secured creditors who otherwise would rely on collateral described in a financing statement take control; creditors who would not rely remain unperfected with respect to deposit accounts. The increased cost of taking control per creditor, summed over the number of relying secured creditors, could increase the total costs of perfecting security interests in a deposit account. Whether total perfection costs are increased by requiring control depends on the size of the increased cost per relying secured creditor and the number of such creditors in the population of secured creditors. The drafters make no estimate of these numbers. Third, a better response to the risk of "windfall" or "unexpected" coverage is more disclosure, not preventing filing as a perfection method. Requiring more detailed collateral descriptions in financing statements, for instance, is a low-cost means of preventing unexpected loss by debtors. Section 9–108(e) already treats as insufficient collateral descriptions only by type with respect to certain items or in consumer transactions. This works to require increased disclosure in the areas covered by (e), and the same could be extended to deposit accounts.

### b. SECURITY INTERESTS IN DEPOSIT ACCOUNTS AS PROCEEDS OF OTHER COLLATERAL

The priority provisions of Article 9 with respect to deposit accounts are complex and we introduce them in two prototypic cases. Our first case is the common one in which third-party lenders have security interests in deposit accounts as proceeds of other collateral in which a lender has a security interest.

Illustration #1. Debtor, a retailer, granted SP a security interest in its inventory and proceeds, which SP perfected by filing a financing statement covering "all Debtor's personal property." Buyers of goods from Debtor's inventory usually paid either by check or by use of unsecured credit cards issued by Debtor. Debtor deposited the checks and payments received on the credit card accounts, usually checks, in the deposit account it maintained in Bank. At the time Debtor opened its account with Bank, it granted a security interest in the account to Bank to secure all its existing and future obligations to Bank. Bank subsequently granted credit to Debtor, but did not file a financing statement. At the time Debtor defaulted on its debt to SP, the deposit account held $100,000, all identifiable proceeds of the disposition of the inventory collateral. SP claimed the amount of the deposit account as cash proceeds (defined in 9–102(a)(9) as including deposit accounts) in which it had a perfected security interest under 9–315(d), the priority of which dated from the time it filed on the inventory. 9–322(b).

Comment on Illustration #1. Bank prevails in this priority dispute under 9–327(1), which provides that a security interest held by a secured party having control has priority over the security interest of a secured party that does not have control. SP's perfected security interest in the account does not give it control, but Bank has control under 9–104(a)(1), which provides that if the bank in which the deposit account is maintained has a security interest in the account it has control. Did Bank rely on its security interest in Debtor's deposit account in granting credit to Debtor? The most valuable lesson to be learned from Article 9's provisions on deposit accounts is that once proceeds are deposited in a deposit account in which the depositary bank has a security interest, the security interest in the proceeds is likely to be subordinated to the bank's security interest. The advice universally given to banks after enactment of Revised Article 9 is to take security interests as a matter of course upon opening a commercial deposit account to secure existing balances and future advances. Now you know why.

PROBLEM

Change the facts of Illustration #1 in one respect. Owing to the negligence of Bank's counsel, Bank failed to take a security interest in Debtor's deposit account before it learned of SP's claim. (i) Can Bank invoke its state-law right of setoff to gain priority over SP's security interest in the proceeds? See 9–340, 9–341, and Bank One, N.A. v. First National Bank of Baird, 2003 WL 22137171 (N.D. Tex. 2003). (ii) Can Bank gain priority by taking a security interest from Debtor in the deposit account after SP's claim arose, that is, is there any temporal requirement in 9–327?

c. SECURITY INTERESTS IN DEPOSIT ACCOUNTS AS ORIGINAL COLLATERAL

Illustration #2. Debtor, an entrepreneur, maintained a substantial savings account in Bank, which Debtor wished to use as collateral for a loan from Lender. Lender's due diligence inquiry uncovered the information that Bank had taken a security interest in Debtor's account at the time it was opened and subsequently advanced funds to Debtor, but Lender could find no financing statement on record. Ultimately, Lender refused to advance the funds to Debtor unless it could perfect its security interest in the account by control. Lender obtained control under 9–104(a)(2) by obtaining an agreement from Bank, with the consent of Debtor, that Bank would act on the Lender's instructions without further consent by Debtor. At the time Debtor defaulted on her obligation to Lender, Debtor was in default on a loan that Bank had previously made to Debtor. (i) Which creditor is prior with respect to the deposit account, Lender or Bank? (ii) Can Bank refuse to enter into such an agreement? (iii) Would the result in this Illustration differ if Debtor and Bank had agreed that the savings account be placed in Lender's name?

Comment on Illustration #2. (i) Even if Bank agrees to grant Lender control over the account under 9–104(a)(2), Bank is prior under 9–327(3). This result must seem extraordinary to Lender, given the consent on the part of Bank to Lender's assertion of control. The result is explained in Comment 4 to 9–327: "A rule of this kind enables banks to extend credit to their depositors without the need to examine either the public record or their own records to determine whether another party might have a security interest in the deposit account." One might ask why perfection under 9–104(a)(2) by agreement with a depositary bank is in the statute. It gives third-party lenders no reliable protection against depositary banks. True, it would allow third-party lenders to prevail against other secured creditors or trustees in bankruptcy, but depositary banks would presumably prevail over third-party lenders who have perfected by agreement under 9–104(a)(2) even though the depositary bank's security interest wasn't even created until after the lender had advanced funds. There are no temporal conditions to the application of 9–327(3). See Comment 4e. to 9–101.

(ii) Section 9–342 allows Bank to refuse to enter into a 9–104(a)(2) agreement like the one in this Illustration.

(iii) Lender is protected against Bank in only two instances. First, when Lender acquires control under 9–104(a)(3) by becoming the bank's "customer" with respect to the account. "Customer" is defined in 4–104(a)(5) as meaning "a person having an account with a bank." Thus, if the account is placed in the name of Lender, it becomes the customer of Bank, and, as such, would have the right to withdraw funds from or close the account. Under 9–327(4), Lender would be prior to Bank. The statute is not clear on whether this result would follow if Lender had merely become a joint holder of the account with Debtor. The second means Lender can use to protect itself is to enter into a subordination agreement with Bank under 9–339 in which the rights of Lender and Bank are spelled out in detail.

## PROBLEM

Change the facts in Illustration #2 to these: Debtor owed Bank a substantial sum on an unpaid loan. Lender entered into an agreement with Debtor in which Debtor agreed to place her account in Bank in Lender's name in order that Lender would have control under 9–104(a)(3), and Lender agreed that if this were done it would hold the account for Debtor's benefit, subject to Lender's rights to collect from the account if Debtor defaulted on its loan to Lender. Debtor requested Bank to place the account in Lender's name. You may assume that Banks have the discretion to decline to accept persons as customers and to close unwanted accounts. (i) If Bank made the name change, would it retain the right of setting off against the deposit account the amount of Debtor's debt to Bank? See 9–340(c) and Comment 3 to 9–341. (ii) Would you advise Bank to make the name change?

## d.   CRITIQUE

The principal accomplishment of Article 9's provisions on security interests in deposit accounts is to provide for the first time a coherent legal structure governing a subject area that had been uncertain and confused. Given the strongly held and contradictory views of the participants in the drafting process, this is no small achievement. The new provisions have been most successful in delineating and clarifying priority rules respecting conflicting security interests in cash proceeds. Now it is finally clear that if a third-party lender allows its debtor to deposit proceeds in a bank, the bank's interest will almost always take priority over the lender's interest, either because of the bank's inevitable security interest in the deposit account or its right to set off against that account. 9–327(1), 9–340. The lender can protect itself only by proceeding under 9–104(a)(3) and becoming the customer of the account, a step that presumably must be approved by the bank. 9–327(4). Non-bank lenders must value their rights in cash proceeds in the light of this severe limitation, which reverses most of the pre-revision law on the subject.

We believe that Article 9 is less successful in dealing with its major innovation, that is extending coverage to security interests in deposit accounts as original collateral. One might have hoped that in providing a legal framework for creating security interests in deposit accounts as original collateral, the drafters had taken some steps toward unlocking the great wealth in deposit accounts in a way that would enable debtors to use this value as security for needed credit extensions. But instead of making it easier for debtors to use their deposit accounts as security for needed credit, Article 9 makes it very difficult—sometimes impossible—for creditors to take reliable security interests in deposit accounts.

The indelible message of Article 9 is that debtors cannot create reliable security interests in deposit accounts as original collateral without the consent of the depositary bank. Only by obtaining control by becoming the bank's customer can a third-party lender enjoy priority over the bank's security interest or offset rights, 9–327(4), and, presumably, that can be done only with the bank's acquiescence. We anticipate that Article 9's provisions on security interests in deposit accounts as original collateral will languish as unused default provisions, ignored by informed participants, who will proceed under 9–339 to work out a subordination agreement with the bank that will clear up the details that Article 9's provisions omit. If a depositary bank is willing to give up its priority rights in a deposit account by agreeing to accept the lender as a customer under 9–104(a)(3), it should be even more willing to enter into an agreement that allows the parties rather than the sparse provisions of Article 9 to adjust the rights of the parties. We expect private ordering to preempt the field, leaving the Code provisions for the unwary.

Surprisingly, a risk of relying on a subordination agreement to work out the priorities between lenders and depository banks in deposit accounts is the possible bankruptcy of the debtor. If the third-party lender does not perfect its rights by taking control under 9–104, its security interest can be avoided in bankruptcy. This is true because control is the exclusive method for perfection of security interest in deposit accounts as original collateral; filing is of no effect. Thus, even though the parties enter into a subordination agreement, the lender must be sure that it also obtains control under 9–104 so that the lender's interest survives bankruptcy.

The draconian effect of these provisions is that if the bank withholds its consent to the lender's obtaining control, the lender's security interest is not only unperfected, it is *unperfectable*! This poses a unique situation under Article 9: a debtor and a creditor cannot perfect a security interest in a right to payment owed to the debtor by the bank without the consent of the account debtor, the bank. Even when the bank is not a creditor of the debtor, if it wishes to preserve debtor's deposit account as a source that it may setoff against for future claims, it has the arbitrary power to block secured parties from perfecting a security interest in the debtor's deposit account by withholding its consent to control.

It is not clear why Revised Article 9 does not allow lenders to perfect their security interest against lien creditors and trustees in bankruptcy by filing. The Article 8 control concept for investment property, 8–106(d), is accompanied by perfection by filing. A broker holding a securities account can prevent a secured party from gaining control by withholding its consent but the secured party can perfect by filing without the consent of the broker. 9–312(a). We assume that in part the drafters borrowed the control concept from Revised Article 8 because some investment property, like money market accounts, is so similar to deposit accounts. Why then should a lender be able to safeguard its security interest in a money market account against lien creditors and trustees in bankruptcy by filing a financing statement if it cannot do the same with respect to a bank account?

A depositary bank's complete power over perfection of a security interest by a lender in a deposit account is unnecessary to protect the bank. Under 9–341, without regard to perfection, depositary banks have no duties to secured parties with respect to deposit accounts that they don't agree to. The depositary bank's own priority is unaffected by a lender's perfection in the same account under 9–327 and 9–340. Thus, to the extent the control rule is intended to obviate the need for depositaries to search for filings, it is not needed. Since lenders can have a security interest that is perfected by filing in a deposit account as proceeds of other collateral, there seems little reason to deny perfection by filing for a security interest in a deposit account as original collateral.

Allowing perfection only by control is inefficient. It increases the cost of issuing secured credit without yielding a corresponding benefit. By requiring the depository bank's authenticated agreement, 9–104(a)(2) adds another party to the bargain between the debtor and secured creditor. Perfection of a security interest in favor of someone other than the depository bank requires concluding an agreement between the debtor, secured creditor and depository bank. The additional party creates an additional transaction cost. The cost of obtaining the bank's agreement may be substantial. (Some banks in Louisiana apparently include anti-pledge clauses in their standard deposit account contracts. See PEB Study Group, Uniform Commercial Code—Article 9: Appendices to Report 341 (1992). Altering a term in a standard contract requires negotiation.) Even if the depositor decides not to deal with its depository bank and instead transfers its deposit account to a compliant bank, an additional transaction cost is incurred. By comparison, perfection by filing only requires a bargain between debtor and secured creditor, and one fewer transaction. Because filing is a cheaper substitute than requiring the depository bank's agreement for control, 9–104(a)(2) increases the debtor's costs in using deposit accounts as collateral and reduces its net benefit from issuing debt secured by them. Before Revised Article 9, very few deposit accounts apparently were used as original collateral, so it is unclear whether most depositors would prefer to use their accounts as collateral with a change in law. See Eldon H. Reiley & Tom Stieber, Proposals to Expand the Scope of Article 9: Should Deposit Accounts, as Original Collateral, be Included?, 30 U.C.C. L. J. 82 (1997); PEB Study Group, Uniform Commercial Code—Article 9:

Appendices to Report 332 (1992). However, given uncertainty about depositors' preferences and the presence of higher transaction costs under the Revision than under a rule allowing for perfection by filing, the Revision arguably sets the rule for perfection incorrectly.

## J.    CASH PROCEEDS

### 1.    PRIORITY

#### a.    PRE–REVISION BACKGROUND

In this chapter we have traced the priority of the first-to-file secured party against conflicting interests in the original collateral and in the proceeds of its disposition. In the previous section we considered the priority of the secured party in proceeds deposited in a deposit account. In this section our inquiry is the priority of the secured party with respect to those to whom the debtor has made payments from the deposit account. What happens to the secured party's interest in the proceeds in the account if the debtor pays its bills by drawing on the account? It would be ridiculous to allow the secured party to snatch back the money paid by the debtor from the deposit account to its employees or trade creditors.

The text of former Article 9 was silent on the issue, and, as we see in the following case, courts looked for guidance to Comment 2(c) to former 9–306:

> Where cash proceeds are covered into the debtor's checking account and paid out in the operation of the debtor's business, recipients of the funds of course take free of any claim which the secured party may have in them as proceeds. What has been said relates to payments and transfers in ordinary course. The law of fraudulent conveyances would no doubt in appropriate cases support recovery of proceeds by a secured party from a transferee out of ordinary course or otherwise in collusion with the debtor to defraud the secured party.

Although Revised Article 9–332 offers a radical simplification of the solution to the problem, quite different from Comment 2(c), we include the following pre-Revision case to show the policy conflicts, as well as the case law background, facing the drafters when they addressed the issue. It is the most careful analysis of the policy considerations arising under Comment 2(c) that we have found. The court struggles with the issue of under what circumstances should a secured party bear the monitoring costs. Given that a debtor's payment to trade creditors from a deposit account containing proceeds is clearly in ordinary course, what about payments to a junior secured party?

## HCC Credit Corporation v. Springs Valley Bank & Trust

Supreme Court of Indiana, 1999.
712 N.E.2d 952.

■ SULLIVAN, JUSTICE.

Lindsey Tractor Sales, Inc., sold 14 tractors to a customer and used the $199,122 proceeds to pay off the debt it owed Springs Valley Bank & Trust.

Yet HCC Credit Corporation had financed Lindsey's purchase of the tractors and held a valid and perfected security interest in both the tractors and the proceeds from their sale. Because we hold that the payment to the bank was not in the ordinary course of the operation of Lindsey's business, HCC is entitled to recover the $199,122.

## BACKGROUND

Lindsey Tractor Sales, Inc., purchased wholesale farm equipment from Hesston Corporation for resale in Lindsey's French Lick farm machinery sales and service business. At the times relevant to this case, HCC Credit Corporation provided financing for the purchases.

Written contracts governed the relationship between Hesston and HCC and Lindsey, including a security agreement. In the security agreement, Lindsey granted HCC a security interest in all the equipment it purchased from Hesston and in the proceeds from the sale of the equipment. Lindsey also agreed to pay HCC immediately for equipment sold from the proceeds of the sale. However, at no time did Hesston or HCC require Lindsey to deposit or segregate proceeds from the sale of Hesston products in a separate account.

The parties agree and the trial court found that the security agreement was binding and enforceable against Lindsey, that Lindsey understood the purpose and effect of the security agreement (including the requirement of paying for equipment immediately when sold), and that HCC had a valid and perfected security interest in the equipment and proceeds from the sale thereof.

In 1991, the Indiana State Department of Transportation agreed to purchase from Lindsey 14 Hesston tractors. Lindsey acquired the tractors from Hesston on credit provided by, and subject to the security agreement in favor of, HCC. Lindsey received payment from the State on August 15, 1991, and deposited the proceeds of $199,122 in the company's checking account at Springs Valley Bank & Trust. At the time of the deposit, Lindsey had $22,870 in other monies on deposit in the account. On the next day, August 16, 1991, Lindsey wrote a check on this account payable to the bank for $212,104.75.

Lindsey's payment to the bank of the proceeds from the sale of the tractors was applied to pay debts owed by Lindsey to the bank. These debts were evidenced by four promissory notes dated January 23, 1987, November 19, 1990, February 7, 1991, and February 13, 1991. All four represented previously refinanced debts and three of them were not yet due when they were paid on August 16. The bank and Lindsey did not discuss paying off the four notes with Lindsey prior to their payment, nor did the bank seize the account to pay the notes. More specifically, Lindsey did not tell anyone associated with the bank that $199,122 of the $212,104.75 used to pay off the notes was from the sale of Hesston products. On the other hand, during the previous eight years Lindsey had borrowed funds or refinanced debts in excess of 100 times with the bank. The average debt balance outstanding during that period was between $100,000 and $200,000. After the notes were paid with the proceeds from the sale of the tractors, Lindsey owed the bank between $2,000 and $15,000.

Lindsey filed a bankruptcy liquidation proceeding in December of 1991, and dissolved shortly thereafter.

In the trial court, HCC sought to recover the $199,122 in proceeds from the sale of Hesston tractors that the bank received from Lindsey. Each party moved for summary judgment, agreeing that there were no genuine issues of material fact. The trial court granted summary judgment in favor of the bank and the Court of Appeals affirmed. HCC Credit Corp. v. Springs Valley Bank & Trust, 669 N.E.2d 1001 (Ind.Ct.App.1996).

## DISCUSSION

### I

Under both the terms of the security agreement between the parties and the provisions of Article 9 of the Uniform Commercial Code as adopted by our legislature, HCC had a valid and perfected security interest in the $199,122 proceeds from the sale of the tractors. See § 9–306(2) ("a security interest continues ... in any identifiable proceeds including collections received by the debtor"). If this were the end of the matter, there is no question but that HCC would be entitled to the money: U.C.C. Article 9 gives the "secured party, upon a debtor's default priority over 'anyone, anywhere, anyhow' except as otherwise provided by the remaining [U.C.C.] priority rules." Citizens Nat'l Bank of Whitley County v. Mid–States Dev. Co., 177 Ind.App. 548, 557, 380 N.E.2d 1243, 1248 (1978) (citing Ind.Code § 9–201; other citations omitted).

But in promulgating the 1972 version of Article 9 of the Uniform Commercial Code, the National Conference of Commissioners on Uniform State Laws (NCCUSL) appended the following "official comment":

> Where cash proceeds are covered into the debtor's checking account and paid out in the operation of the debtor's business, recipients of the funds of course take free of any claim which the secured party may have in them as proceeds. What has been said relates to payments and transfers in the ordinary course. The law of fraudulent conveyances would no doubt in appropriate cases support recovery of proceeds by a secured party from the transferee out of ordinary course or otherwise in collusion with the debtor to defraud the secured party.

U.C.C. § 9–306 cmt. 2(c) (1972), 3 U.L.A. 441 (1981) (emphasis supplied). We will refer to this official comment in this opinion as "Comment 2(c)."

Although our legislature has never adopted the NCCUSL comments as authoritative, there seems to be general agreement that, at least to some extent, Comment 2(c) is an exception to the Indiana U.C.C.'s general priority rules. The bank argues that in this case, the proceeds were paid out of Lindsey's checking account in the operation of Lindsey's business and that the payment was made in the ordinary course without any collusion with the debtor. As such, the bank contends, Comment 2(c) operates to provide that the bank received the $199,122 free of any claim which HCC had in it as proceeds.[3] The trial court and Court of Appeals adopted this rationale. HCC now seeks transfer, arguing that its perfected security interest entitles it to the proceeds.

## II

At a certain level of abstraction, this case requires us to assess the relative rights of a secured creditor to the proceeds of its collateral and of a third party to whom the debtor transfers those proceeds. Sound commercial policy considerations can be marshaled in support of both the rights of the secured party and the rights of the transferee.

\* \* \*

The court cites *Citizens National Bank* for its holding that a security interest in proceeds deposited in a deposit account is prior to the depositary bank's right of setoff because the secured party should not have to bear the burden of the monitoring costs.

\* \* \* *Citizens National Bank* helps us understand the policy interests that favor enforcing HCC's perfected security interest—that requiring secured parties to take steps beyond those specified in Article 9 to protect their interests "undercuts significant values of certainty, efficiency" and "tends to curtail commercial practice and business operation."

## B

Just as Judge Garrard gives sound policy reasons in *Citizens National Bank* for enforcing perfected security interests, there are sound policy reasons for allowing third party transferees to retain proceeds of another's collateral. When he was a judge of the United States Court of Appeals for the First Circuit, Justice Breyer had occasion to address this subject: "If ... courts too readily impose liability upon those who receive funds from the debtor's ordinary bank account—if, for example, they define 'ordinary course' of business too narrowly—then ordinary suppliers, sellers of gas, electricity, tables, chairs, etc., might find themselves called upon to return ordinary payments ... to a debtor's secured creditor, say a financier of inventory." Harley–Davidson Motor Co., Inc. v. Bank of New England–Old Colony, N.A., 897 F.2d 611, 622 (1st Cir.1990) (internal citation omitted).

Judge Breyer was also able to "imagine good commercial reasons for not imposing, even upon sophisticated suppliers or secondary lenders, who

---

**3.** As discussed under Background, supra, Lindsey deposited the proceeds from the tractors' sale into the business's checking account and then used those proceeds, along with other funds in the account, to pay the bank. The commingling of the proceeds with other funds does not cut off HCC's claim. It is well settled that in appropriate circumstances, "a secured party may trace 'identifiable proceeds' through a commingled bank account and into the hands of a recipient who lacks the right to keep them." Harley–Davidson Motor Co., Inc. v. Bank of New England–Old Colony, N.A., 897 F.2d 611, 620 (1st Cir.1990) (collecting cases).

are aware that inventory financiers often take senior secured interests in 'all inventory plus proceeds,' the complicated burden of contacting these financiers to secure permission to take payment from a dealer's ordinary commingled bank account. These considerations," he continued, "indicate that 'ordinary course' has a fairly broad meaning; and that a court should restrict the use of tracing rules to conduct that, in the commercial context, is rather clearly improper." Id.[6]

\* \* \*

### III

Judge Garrard's opinion in *Citizens National Bank* and Judge Breyer's in *Harley–Davidson* each illustrates the way the U.C.C. streamlines legal impediments to commerce: reducing the burden on perfected secured parties in the former and reducing the burden on ordinary course payees in the latter. But the drafters of the U.C.C. recognized that these two efforts could come into conflict as they do in this case. Comment 2(c) is meant to resolve that conflict.

Comment 2(c) is not a statute and is not written in the form of a statute; it does not set forth a tightly-worded rule, followed by equally tightly-worded elements necessary to establish its application. Rather, it is a narrative collection of three sentences from which we conclude that a recipient of a payment made "in the ordinary course" by a debtor takes that payment free and clear of any claim that a secured party may have in the payment as proceeds. The Comment also tells us that the payment (1) will be in the ordinary course if it was made "in the operation of the debtor's business" but (2) will not be in the ordinary course if there was "collusion with the debtor to defraud the secured party." We do not take these two factors to be the equivalent of statutory elements but rather descriptive of two parameters for determining "ordinary course." That is, whether a payment was made in the ordinary course will be a function of (1) the extent to which the payment was made in the routine operation of the debtor's business and (2) the extent to which the recipient was aware that it was acting to the prejudice of the secured party.

As to the routine operation of business parameter, payment of sales tax collections or F.I.C.A. withholdings would obviously be at the most routine

---

**6.** We note that in their most recent revision of Article 9, the American Law Institute and National Conference of Commissioners on Uniform State Laws have proposed that this liberal approach be codified. A new section would be added to Article 9 providing that "transferee of funds from a deposit account takes the funds free of a security interest in the deposit account unless the transferee acts in collusion with the debtor in violating the rights of the secured party." U.C.C. § 9–329 (1998). "Broad protection for transferees helps to ensure that security interests in deposit accounts do not impair the free flow of funds. It also minimizes the likelihood that a secured party will enjoy a claim to whatever the transferee purchases with the funds. Rules concerning recovery of payments traditionally have placed a high value on finality. The opportunity to upset a completed transaction, or even to place a completed transaction in jeopardy by bringing suit against the transferee of funds, should be severely limited." Revision of U.C.C. Article 9, § 9–329, cmt. 3 (Reporters' Interim Draft Aug. 7, 1997).

end and a one-shot payment of subordinated debt not yet due would be at the least. At various points between these extremes would fall payments ordered by how routine they were to both debtor and transferee—measured by such factors as their size, their frequency, whether the debtor received merchandise or services in return, whether the payment was on an obligation overdue, due or not yet due, etc. The cases have explored such payments as those for monthly marketing expenses, retainers to legal counsel by companies in financial difficulty, offsets against pre-existing debts, and periodic term loan payments in this or related bankruptcy contexts.

As to the awareness of prejudice parameter, it is hard to imagine the recipient of the monthly utility or rent payment having any knowledge that it was being paid with proceeds. At the other end of the spectrum is actual fraud in which debtor and recipient have colluded against the secured party. Between these poles will fall payments where the recipient knows that a security interest exists but does not know that the payment is being made in violation of that interest; payments where the recipient had sufficient notice to put a reasonable recipient, exercising prudent business practices, on notice that something was awry; and payments where the recipient has information causing it to suspect strongly that a payment violates a secured party's interest, yet takes deliberate steps to avoid discovering more.

The nature of the relationship between the debtor and the transferee can give rise to a presumption of the transferee's awareness of prejudice, especially where the transferee itself is a lender. Such a secondary lender whose debt is subordinated to the secured party's or who has explicitly excluded the debtor's obligations to the secured lender in computing the debtor's borrowing base will generally be presumed to have actual knowledge of prejudice to the secured party. This occurs because the secondary lender has extended credit to the debtor with the express understanding that the secured party stands in a superior position to be repaid, at least in certain circumstances.

We reaffirm that a security interest continues in any identifiable proceeds of collateral including collections received by the debtor. Ind.Code §§ 9–201 & 306(2). We also reaffirm that Comment 2(c) is the law of Indiana: a recipient of a payment made "in the ordinary course" by a debtor takes that payment free and clear of any claim that a secured party may have in the payment as proceeds. And we hold that whether a transfer of proceeds is "in the ordinary course" requires an assessment of both (1) the extent to which the payment was made in the routine operation of the debtor's business and (2) the extent to which the recipient was aware that it was acting to the prejudice of the secured party. Because we agree that "imposing liability too readily on payees ... could impede the free flow of goods and services essential to business," *J.I. Case Credit Corp. v. First National Bank of Madison County*, 991 F.2d 1272, 1277 (7th Cir.1993), we further hold that the transfer will be free of any claim that a secured party may have in it as proceeds unless the payment would constitute a windfall to the recipient. A windfall occurs in this context when the recipient has no reasonable expectation of being paid ahead of a secured creditor because of the extent to which the payment was made outside the routine operation of the debtor's business, because of the extent to which the recipient was aware that it was acting to the prejudice of the secured party, or because of both of these factors in combination.

While the determination of "ordinary course" is a question of law, sometimes an evaluation of the extent to which the payment was routine or the extent of the recipient's knowledge will require factual analysis. In such a situation, summary judgment would be inappropriate.

\* \* \*

V

We hold that Lindsey's payment of $199,122 to the bank here was not a payment in the ordinary course of the operation of Lindsey's business. There is no disagreement as to the following facts. The bank was aware that HCC had a valid and perfected security interest in Lindsey's tractor inventory. The bank took this into account in making its decision to extend credit to Lindsey and did not take a security interest in any of the collateral covered by HCC's security agreement. During the eight years prior to the payment at issue here, Lindsey had borrowed funds or refinanced debt in excess of 100 times with the bank and the average debt balance owed was between $100,000 and $200,000. Two of the notes Lindsey paid off represented a refinancing of approximately $225,000 in continuing debt carried by the bank. After the notes were paid off, Lindsey was in the unprecedented position of owing the bank only between $2,000 and $15,000. The bank's senior loan officer agreed with HCC's counsel that the $199,122 payment was "extraordinary" and constituted the largest ever made on any debt Lindsey owed the bank. The officer also said, "Anytime a significant loan balance is paid off you have to look at it as something that would not be a normal trade transaction, like paying interest or something like that."

The payment to the bank constituted the proceeds of collateral in which HCC had a valid and perfected security interest. The payment was used to liquidate a substantial secured debt which, for the most part, was not due. It was an extremely large payment, the likes of which Lindsey had never made before. And although the bank was not advised that the source of the payment it received constituted the proceeds of HCC's collateral, the bank knew of HCC's perfected security interest. As such, it had extended credit to Lindsey with the express understanding that HCC stood in a superior position to be repaid, at least in certain circumstances. We conclude that the payment was not in the ordinary course of Lindsey's business. For the bank to prevail would result in a windfall—a windfall because the bank had no reasonable expectation that Lindsey could or would liquidate its debt due the bank in advance of paying HCC for the tractors financed—at the expense of HCC which had taken all measures required by the U.C.C. to protect its interest. As a result, the exception to the Indiana U.C.C.'s priority rules provided by Comment 2(c) does not apply and HCC, not the bank, is entitled to the $199,122.

## CONCLUSION

Having previously granted transfer, thereby vacating the decision of the Court of Appeals, we now reverse the judgment of the trial court and remand this matter to the trial court with directions that summary judgment be entered for HCC and for any further proceedings that may be required.

## NOTES

**1.** The court's test places the issue of priority of security interests in cash proceeds back into the fact-intensive soup that the first-to-file rule endeavored to avoid in other contexts. In General Electric Capital Corp. v. Union Planters Bank, N.A., 409 F.3d 1049 (8th Cir.2005), GECC, a lender, financed Debtor's equipment inventory and took a security interest in the inventory that it financed. UPB, a bank, lent money to Debtor under a line of credit arrangement, secured by a blanket lien on all of Debtor's property. Debtor maintained its deposit account in UPB and deposited some of the proceeds of the sale of GECC collateral in that account where it was commingled with proceeds from UPB's loans. Since GECC and UPB were aware that they had conflicting security interests in the collateral financed by GECC and its proceeds, they entered into a subordination agreement in which UPB subordinated its security interest in the GECC financed inventory to the interest of GECC, as well as its interest in "all cash, rents and non-cash proceeds" arising from that property. Debtor and UPB set up a cash management system under which UPB was allowed to make automatic "sweeps" from Debtor's account when the balance of the account reached certain levels and apply the amounts swept to the payment of Debtor's $1,250,000 line of credit. When Debtor defaulted on its obligations, GECC sued UPB in conversion to recover the money that UPB had swept from the deposit account on the ground that this money could be identified as proceeds of inventory that GECC had financed. UPB contended that even if GECC could identify these funds as its proceeds, UPB was entitled to retain the funds as payments received in "ordinary course" under Comment 2(c) to former 9–306 because it had no knowledge that proceeds from the sale of GECC inventory had been commingled in the account. GECC argued that the subordination agreement precluded UPB from relying on Comment 2(c) even in the absence of UPB's knowledge. The district court held that the subordination agreement prevailed and that UPB could not avoid liability by claiming that it did not know that some of the funds taken under its sweeps were encumbered by GECC's security interest. The Eighth Circuit reversed, holding that the subordination agreement could not have been intended to prevent UPB from accepting payments from Debtor on its line of credit indebtedness in ordinary course, and the use of automatic sweeps was the ordinary-course method by which

Debtor paid its debt to UPB. How could GECC have reduced its monitoring burden in this case? See the following Note.

**2.**   Comment 2(c) adds a standard to Article 9's first-to-file or-perfect rule. Standards cost comparatively little to draft ex ante. "Good faith" and "ordinary course of business" are general terms that allow a drafter or court to avoid giving a precise or easily verifiable specification in advance. However, standards are comparatively costly to apply ex post in litigation. Comment 2(c) invites the secured party seeking to get the payment back to dispute the slippery issues of good faith, knowledge, reason to know, and recklessness—all factual issues that are anathema to bank lawyers. Conversely, rules are comparatively costly to draft ex ante. Their application ex post requires the expenditure of relatively few costs. See Louis Kaplow, Rules Versus Standards: An Economic Analysis, 42 Duke L. J. 557 (1992); Frederick Schauer, Playing by the Rules: A Philosophical Examination of Rule–Based Decision Making in Law and Life (1991). It is no wonder that financers often place tight controls on a debtor's cash proceeds through the use of lockbox accounts and the like which we will discuss later. See Appendix II for a lockbox agreement. Standards are preferable to rules when the sum of their ex ante drafting costs and ex post application costs are less than those associated with the relevant rule. Did Comment 2(c) accurately gauge these costs? Two factors bear on an informed estimate: the frequency of transactions likely to involve the behavior sought to be regulated (transference of cash proceeds), and the incentives a rule or standard gives to affected parties. Other things being equal, commonly encountered transactions justify regulation by rules because frequency of behavior justifies higher investment ex ante in precise drafting to regulate it. As an example of the latter factor, consider the effect of Comment 2(c)'s standard on secured creditors, who have an incentive to litigate the fact-intensive issues of good faith and the like.

b.   TRANSFEREES OF FUNDS UNDER SECTION 9–332

Section 9–332 is a bold clarification of the law on this subject. It provides:

(a) A transferee of money takes the money free of a security interest unless the transferee acts in collusion with the debtor in violating the rights of the secured party.

(b) A transferee of funds from a deposit account takes the funds free of a security interest in the deposit account unless the transferee acts in collusion with the debtor in violating the rights of the secured party.

Thus, if a depositor withdraws currency from a deposit account in which proceeds are deposited that are subject to a security interest and transfers it to another person, 9–332(a) protects the transferee against the claim of a secured party. If a depositor draws a check on such a deposit account in favor of another person, 9–332(b) protects the payee who receives the funds. Comment 3 to 9–332 states the policy basis for this major change in the law:

> Broad protection for transferees helps to ensure that security interests in deposit accounts do not impair the free flow of funds. It also minimizes the likelihood that a secured party will enjoy a claim to whatever the transferee purchases with the funds. Rules concerning recovery of payments traditionally have placed a high value on finality. The opportunity to upset a completed transaction, or even to place a completed transaction in jeopardy by bringing suit against the transferee of funds, should be severely limited. * * * [T]his section eliminates all reliance requirements whatsoever. Payments made by mistake are relatively rare, but payments of funds from encumbered deposit accounts (e.g., deposit accounts containing collections from accounts receivable) occur with great regularity. In most cases, unlike payment by mistake, no one would object to these payments. In the vast proportion of cases, the transferee probably would be able to show a change of position in reliance on the payment. This section does not put the transferee to the burden of having to make this proof.

PROBLEMS

You may assume that SPA and SPB both have security interests in Debtor's inventory collateral and its proceeds. Both perfected by filing; SPA filed first. Debtor deposited the cash proceeds of the sale of inventory and the collection of accounts in its deposit account in Bank, which held only proceeds from these sales and collections.

**1.** Debtor drew a check on Bank payable to SPB for $100,000 and delivered it to SPB, who deposited the check in its deposit account in another bank and eventually withdrew all of the funds from that account. SPB knew about SPA's senior security interest when it received the payment. Does SPB take free of SPA's prior security interest in the funds received?

**2.** Same facts as in the first sentence of Problem 1. Debtor was in financial trouble and both SPA and SPB knew it. SPB urged Debtor to pay him before SPA because of SPB's willingness to advance credit to Debtor earlier when SPA had refused to do so. Debtor agreed to do so even though both Debtor and SPB knew that they were violating SPA's rights and that payment to SPB would probably mean that SPA would not be paid from Debtor's diminishing assets. Can SPB keep the money when SPA claims priority?

NOTE

*General Electric Capital Corporation* has an epilogue that is relevant to the collusion limitation contained in 9–332. In the course of its bankruptcy proceeding, Debtor filed an amended plan of reorganization, which was confirmed in 2001. Between the date of confirmation and April 2003 Debtor continued to place proceeds from its sales of inventory in a deposit account held at UPB. UPB had by agreement with GECC subordinated its security interest in the proceeds to GECC's security interest in the proceeds of inventory GECC had financed. All of the cash proceeds Debtor placed in its deposit account at UPB were the product of sales of GECC-financed inventory. UPB and GECC both claimed priority in the post-confirmation cash proceeds Debtor placed in its deposit account. Applying Revised Article 9 to the transaction created by the amended reorganization plan, the court relied on 9–332 and its comments to determine UPB and GECC's priority in the cash proceeds deposited by Debtor with UPB between 2002 and April 2003. Comment 4 to 9–332 refers to the collusion standard described in the Restatement (Second) of Torts § 876. According to the Restatement, collusion occurs when a person either commits a tort in concert with another or knows that another's act is a breach of duty and gives substantial assistance or encourages another to commit the tort or gives substantial assistance to the other in committing the tort and in doing so breaches his own duty to the victim. The court found that UPB's protection and expansion of its rights in the cash proceeds under the amended reorganization plan wasn't wrongful as against GECC, notwithstanding the subordination agreement. UPB's conduct therefore didn't satisfy the Restatement's collusion standard. In re Machinery, Inc., 342 B.R. 790 (Bankr. E.D. Mo. 2006).

## c.   TRANSFEREES OF INSTRUMENTS UNDER SECTION 9–330(d)

Assume these facts: Debtor granted a security interest in its inventory and proceeds to SPA, who perfected by filing. Subsequently, Debtor granted a junior security interest in the same collateral to SPB, who also perfected by filing. When Debtor sells items of its inventory it receives checks payable to Debtor which, under its agreement with SPA, it is required to negotiate to SPA by indorsement and delivery without depositing them in a deposit account. Debtor violated the agreement by negotiating the checks to SPB who knew of SPA's prior security interest.

This is a familiar method of inventory control. By requiring a debtor who has received a check from an account debtor to indorse the check to the secured party, in specie, without running it through the debtor's bank account, the secured party can be sure that payments are actually being received from account debtors. Questions of priority in checks involve the law of negotiable instruments, found in Article 3, as well as Article 9.

Under 3–306, if a holder takes an instrument in which there is a security interest, it takes subject to that security interest (a claim of ownership) unless it is a holder in due course. Under 3–302(a), a holder is a holder in due course if it takes an instrument for value, in good faith and without notice of claims or defenses. Does SPB have notice of SPA's claim because of SPA's filed financing statement? Section 9–331(c) answers this question definitively by providing that filing under Article 9 does not constitute notice of a claim or defense to the holders or purchasers of instruments. But in this case SPB had actual knowledge of the earlier security interest of SPA and SPB therefore cannot be a holder in due course.

But there are two other Article 9 provisions that bear on this question. The first, 9–331(a), provides that Article 9 does not limit the rights of a holder in due course of a negotiable instrument and that such a holder takes priority over an earlier security interest, even if perfected, to the extent provided in Article 3. So, if SPB qualified as a holder in due course under Article 3, it would take free of SPA's security interest, but SPB does not qualify because of its knowledge of the claim of ownership. See Comment 5 to 9–331.

The second relevant provision, 9–330(d), is quoted:

> Except as otherwise provided in Section 9–331(a), a purchaser of an instrument has priority over a security interest in the instrument perfected by a method other than possession if the purchaser gives value and takes possession of the instrument in good faith and without knowledge that the purchase violates the rights of the secured party.

Since there are no facts showing that SPB knew that purchasing the checks violated the rights of SPA, SPB should prevail under this section. See Comment 7 to 9–330. SPB has given value by reason of its outstanding loans (1–204(2)); new value is not required. There is no reason to believe that SPB was other than in good faith: 1–201(b)(20) requires honesty in fact and observance of reasonable commercial standards. The good faith requirement does not impose on SPB a general duty of inquiry and not enough facts are given to evaluate its observance of reasonable commercial standards. Comment 5 to 9–331. Hence, the rights of a purchaser of instruments are roughly comparable to those of purchasers of chattel paper, except that the new value and ordinary course of business requirements are omitted.

## 2.   LOWEST INTERMEDIATE BALANCE RULE

A security interest in proceeds in a deposit account is a risky matter for the secured party. As we saw in the previous section, the debtor may drain the account by payments to transferees who take free of the security interest under 9–332. Or the debtor may commingle the proceeds in the account with nonproceeds, making it difficult for the secured party to identify the proceeds in compliance with 9–315(a)(2)'s requirement that for a security interest to continue in proceeds the proceeds must be identifiable. Gilmore's view was that a security interest in proceeds is lost when they are commingled with nonproceeds, 2 Grant Gilmore, Security Interests in Personal Property 736 (1965), but the courts have not agreed. Section 9–315(b)(2) clarifies the law by providing that proceeds that are commingled with nonproceeds are identifiable proceeds "to the extent that the secured party identifies the proceeds by a method of tracing, including application of equitable principles, that is permitted under law other than this article with respect to commingled property of the type involved." Most pre-Revision cases used the lowest intermediate balance rule (LIB), and Comment 3 to 9–315 approves the use of this rule. The following case shows the devastating consequences of LIB for a foolish lender.

# Chrysler Credit Corp. v. Superior Court

Court of Appeal, First District, Division 1, 1993.
22 Cal.Rptr.2d 37.

■ STEIN, ASSOCIATE JUSTICE.

East County Dodge was in the business, among other things, of selling vehicles supplied to it by Chrysler Credit Corporation (Chrysler) under a security agreement. For reasons which will be discussed, East County Dodge ostensibly deposited the proceeds from the sales of the vehicles in an account at Bank of the West to which both it and Chrysler were signatories. Chrysler ultimately obtained a writ of possession against the funds held in that account. The State Board of Equalization and the Employment Development Department filed third-party claims against the same funds. (Hereafter, except as indicated, these agencies will be referred to as third parties.) Chrysler here appeals the superior court's denial of its motion to dismiss the third-party claims.

\* \* \*

## FACTUAL/PROCEDURAL BACKGROUND

The essential facts are not in dispute.

On September 13, 1988, Chrysler entered into a master credit agreement with East County Dodge by which Chrysler agreed to provide financing to East County Dodge for the purpose of purchasing new vehicles from Chrysler and used vehicles from their sellers. The agreement gave Chrysler a "first and prior security interest" in every vehicle financed under the agreement and "all proceeds thereof." Chrysler perfected its security interest by filing its financing statement on October 6, 1988. \* \* \*

East County Dodge began having financial problems, and in April 1990, filed a Chapter 11 petition in the United States Bankruptcy Court. As part of those proceedings, the bankruptcy court authorized East County Dodge to sell vehicles financed by Chrysler under its master credit agreement, and ordered East County Dodge to "deposit into a special trust account ... in the name of East County Dodge and Chrysler the ... wholesale value upon the debtor completing a sale of any ... collateral vehicles (i.e., the vehicles secured under the security agreement.)" In purported compliance with this order, East County Dodge opened a trust account with the Bank of America for the deposit of funds received from the sales of collateral vehicles. East County Dodge later, with the agreement of Chrysler, moved those funds into an account at Bank of the West— the account at issue here. For purposes of clarity, we will adopt Chrysler's practice and refer to this account as the "cash collateral account."[1] There-

---

**1.** Third parties refer to this account as the "debtor-in-possession bank account." The superior court's judgment refers to it as the "so-called Cash Collateral Account." For

after, in connection with any sale of a financed vehicle, East County Dodge provided Chrysler with information referring to that sale, including the purchaser, the price, and a copy of the vehicle's invoice. East County Dodge also forwarded to Chrysler copies of bank deposits reflecting amounts deposited into the cash collateral account. East County Dodge, however, did not directly deposit the funds from the sales of collateral into the cash collateral account. Rather, it deposited these funds into its general operating account and, then, from time to time withdrew funds from the general account and deposited them into the cash collateral account. Thus, Armand Frumenti, the president of East County Dodge, declared, as relevant:

"The usual practice of East County Dodge, Inc. was to initially deposit all proceeds, including monies received from the sale of automobiles, automotive parts and remuneration for automotive repair services, into the general operating bank account.... Thereafter, monies were periodically transferred from the general operating bank account to the debtor-in-possession bank account by way of a check written against East County Dodge, Inc.'s general operating bank account to the East County Dodge, Inc.'s debtor-in-possession bank account."

Thus, it was East County Dodge's practice to deposit the full purchase price, including sales tax, of vehicles into the general operating account. Chrysler, of course, had no security interest in the sales tax. In addition, Chrysler had no security interest in the funds received by East County Dodge for labor, and these funds, too, were deposited into the general operating account. It follows that the funds in which Chrysler had a security interest—the proceeds of sales of collateral—were commingled with other funds.[2] The record contains no evidence tracing those funds to any account or entity other than to the cash collateral account. As Chrysler concedes, however, the general operating account regularly reflected a negative balance. Apparently, the Bank of the West would cover the checks drawn on the account and would then use the following day's deposits to recover the overdraft. As Chrysler asserts, "During this time, and without Chrysler's knowledge, Bank of the West allowed a $282,000 overdraft balance to build-up in the Operating Account. [East County Dodge] deposited funds to reduce the overdraft balance and the Bank continued to honor overdrafts, by advancing its own funds."

The bankruptcy proceedings were dismissed on May 1, 1991. On May 8, Chrysler filed a complaint, seeking as relevant here, to recover the funds held in the cash collateral account. In the meantime, third parties levied against East County Dodge's bank accounts, including the cash collateral account, claiming that East County Dodge owed the State Board of Equalization $211,165.07, plus interest, and the Employment Development De-

purposes of continuity, we will refer to it as the cash collateral account.

**2.** Indeed, from July 25, 1990, to December 18, 1990, East County Dodge deposited $1,782,883.85 into its operating account. For the same period Chrysler claimed proceeds from sales of collateral of only $353,131.82.

partment $23,600.54. Chrysler obtained a writ of possession as to the cash collateral account on June 24, 1991. Third parties subsequently filed third-party claims, claiming an interest in the funds held in that account.

## DISCUSSION

As all parties agree, the basic issue is whether the court erred in determining that Chrysler had no perfected security interest in the funds in the cash collateral account, a finding which means that the Board of Equalization and the Employment Development Department have the right to levy against those funds, and that their claims have priority over any claim Chrysler has to the funds as an unsecured creditor. There is no question but that Chrysler had a perfected security interest in the collateral—the financed automobiles—itself. The question, rather, is whether the funds deposited into the cash collateral account are the "identifiable proceeds" of the collateral such that Chrysler's security interest attached also to them. (§ 9–306(2).)

\* \* \*

\* \* \* Chrysler was entitled, if it could, to trace the proceeds through the operating account into the cash collateral account. As to each secured vehicle, Chrysler submitted evidence of (1) the date and amount of sale, (2) the amount of proceeds due to Chrysler for such sale, (3) the date the total proceeds from the sale were deposited into East County Dodge's general operating account, (4) the date funds, earmarked by East County Dodge as the amount due Chrysler, were deposited into the cash collateral account, and (5) the amount of these funds.

The California Uniform Commercial Code does not provide any aid in determining whether this information sufficiently traced the proceeds of the sales of collateral. We, as have other courts before us, will resort to principles developed in the common law. \* \* \*

The common law rule applicable here is the "lowest intermediate balance rule" used in tracing trust funds. Witkin describes it: "If the trustee withdraws money and dissipates it, the trust funds are only those which remain on deposit. Subsequent deposits ordinarily do not inure to the benefit of the trust. Hence, the beneficiary can have his prior lien only upon the *lowest intermediate balance* left in the account. And if at any time the trustee withdraws and dissipates the entire fund, the beneficiary loses all prior claim and is merely a general creditor of the trustee." (11 Witkin, Summary of Cal. Law (9th ed. 1990) Trusts, § 144(3), p. 1000; see also Rest.2d Trusts, § 202, coms. j and k; Rest., Restitution, § 212; 5 Scott on Trusts (4th ed. 1989) § 518; Bogert, Trusts & Trustees (Rev.2d ed. 1983) § 929; but cf. Church v. Bailey (1949) 90 Cal.App.2d 501, 203 P.2d 547.) The court in Ex Parte Alabama Mobile Homes, Inc. (1985) 468 So.2d 156, 160, elaborates: "When proceeds of a sale of collateral are placed in the debtor's bank account the proceeds remain identifiable and a security interest in the funds continues even if the funds are commingled with other funds. [Citation.] The rules employed to distinguish the identifiable proceeds from other funds are liberally construed in the creditor's favor by use of the 'intermediate balance rule.' [Citations.] This rule provides a presumption that proceeds of the sale of collateral remain in the account as long as the account balance equals or exceeds the amount of the proceeds. The funds are 'identified' based on the assumption that the debtor spends his own money out of the account before he spends the funds encumbered by the security interest. If the account balance drops below the amount of the proceeds, the security interest in the funds on deposit abates accordingly. This lower balance is not increased if funds are later deposited into the account. [Citation.] This rule is analogous to the presumption which arises when a trustee commingles trust funds with his own. [Citation.]"

In the present case East County Dodge deposited the proceeds of the sales of collateral into its general operating account. Assuming no further action was taken, Chrysler's security interest attached to those funds notwithstanding that they were commingled with other funds. But further action was taken. It appears that East County Dodge maintained a deficit balance in its general operating account and that the Bank of the West applied any funds deposited into that account to reduce the indebtedness. Under the intermediate balance rule, any nonproceeds would be applied first to reduce East County Dodge's debt to Bank of the West. Once those funds were exhausted, however, and proceeds were attached, Chrysler's security interest in the funds abated. When East County Dodge deposited funds into the cash collateral account, it wrote checks against the general operating account. If at the time such a check was written the general operating account had a positive balance, and if the funds might be deemed proceeds under the intermediate balance rule, the funds taken from the general operating account and deposited into the cash collateral account were in fact the identifiable proceeds of sales of collateral. The evidence, however, is that at the time East County Dodge wrote these checks there were no proceeds in the general operating account. Those funds, together with any other funds deposited, had been used to reduce the deficit in the account. Chrysler's security interest in the funds in the general operating account, accordingly, was reduced to zero. When Bank of the West honored the checks, it essentially advanced its own funds, increasing the deficit in the general operating account. Unless, as does not appear to be the case, Chrysler somehow obtained a security interest in these loan funds, it had no security interest in the funds deposited into the cash collateral account because they were not the proceeds of any sales of collateral; they were funds loaned by Bank of the West. * * *

Chrysler urges us to adopt an exception to the intermediate balance rule. It has been held that where a trustee commingles personal funds with trust funds, and dissipates the commingled funds such that the trust funds are affected, and then deposits additional personal funds into the account, it may be presumed that the trustee was intending to reimburse the trust funds. In such a situation, the trust funds will be replenished. * * * The case law does not recognize this exception in a situation such as exists here * * *; and in our view this exception, if broadly applied, would completely emasculate the rule. Rather, it is properly limited to contests between trustee and beneficiary, where the trustee essentially embezzles trust funds and subsequently intends to, and does, replace them. A different situation exists where, as here, third parties have competing interests in the funds at issue. Here, not only proceeds from the sales of collateral, but funds due other creditors, including third parties, were deposited into the general operating account. It would be inequitable to conclude that after that account was reduced to zero, any money deposited into it belonged only to Chrysler. In addition, were we to adopt the position urged by Chrysler we would, in effect, be giving the debtor, rather than the Commercial Code, the power to determine priorities among creditors.[9] We decline to adopt such a rule. It follows that, as the trial court concluded, the funds in the cash collateral account are not the identifiable proceeds of the sales of collateral.

The superior court correctly denied the motion to dismiss the third party claims. The petition for writ of mandate, as we have so construed Chrysler's appeal, is denied.

◼ STRANKMAN, P.J., and DOSSEE, J., concur.

## NOTES

**1.** Although 9–315(b)(2) clarifies the law by expressly allowing the use of tracing principles applicable under non-Article 9 law, the subsection still leaves some uncertainty. In particular, it appears to allow the use of any tracing rule to identify commingled non-goods as long as the rule is found in non-Article 9 law. The qualifying language in (b)(2), "permitted under law other than this article," places no restriction on the area of non-Article 9 law that recognizes a tracing rule. Thus, 9–315(b)(2)'s language appears to allow the secured party to choose the tracing rule that will benefit it from any area of non-Article 9 law that allows tracing. For example, clearly 9–315(b)(2) allows the use of the lowest intermediate balance rule in *Chrysler Credit Corp.*, applicable under the common law of trusts. See General Electric Capital Corp. v. Union Planters Bank, N.A., 409 F.3d 1049 (8th Cir.2005). However, the court rejects Chrysler's reliance on an exception to the lowest intermediate balance rule, recognized under the law of trusts, that allows the trustee's deposit of its funds in a commingled accounts to replenish the beneficiary's funds previously withdrawn by the trustee. The court said it would be "inappropriate" to adopt this exception. But under 9–315(b)(2), the exception is part of a tracing rule "permitted under law other than this article." Why can't Chrysler use the exception to trace proceeds in East County Dodge's commingled deposit account even after the account registered a zero balance?

**9.** It might be supposed, for example, that a particular debtor has several secured creditors, and has been ordered to maintain a cash collateral account for each. Instead, the debtor deposits all funds into a general operating account, reduces that account to zero, and then deposits any additional, nonproceeds into one of the cash collateral accounts. Under Chrysler's position, that creditor would be deemed reimbursed whether or not it otherwise had priority over the creditors.

**2.** As a policy matter, Gilmore's view that a security interest in proceeds is lost when they are commingled with nonproceeds has a strong position. Note first the extension that is involved in applying LIB to Article 9. As *Chrysler Credit Corp.* points out, the rule is borrowed from the law of trusts. There it is applied to a two-party dispute involving a misbehaving trustee and her victim, the trust beneficiary. The rule has the effect of imposing on the faithless trustee the cost of her own misbehavior. See GMAC v. Norstar Bank, N.A., 532 N.Y.S.2d 685 (Sup. Ct. 1988); Universal C.I.T. Credit Corp. v. Farmers Bank of Portageville, 358 F.Supp. 317 (E.D.Mo.1973). The rule's application in Article 9 involves a priority contest among two or more creditors, where the debtor has "misbehaved" and the loss is to allocated among two or more creditors, her "victims." Allowing tracing in this intra-creditor case imposes a cost on the other creditors: commingled proceeds that can be traced are unavailable to satisfy their claims. This result has none of the salience it has in the initial two-person case. Further, allowing a creditor to trace proceeds arguably produces suboptimal behavior. This is because tracing saves the creditor some of the cost of monitoring collateral. If the debtor misbehaves by commingling proceeds, tracing preserves the creditor's security interest in commingled funds. However, the secured creditor might be in a better position to monitor the debtor's assets than any of the other creditors. An optimal allocation of monitoring effort would assign it to the creditor. Tracing reduces the secured creditor's incentive to monitor her collateral. Its effect is to shift part or all of the responsibility to creditors who might be in an inferior position to undertake monitoring.

**3.** We have seen that the position of a secured party claiming proceeds in a deposit account is precarious, but sophisticated financers shed few tears for secured parties who allow their debtors to commingle proceeds in a deposit account. In some instances secured parties may write off any commingled proceeds because of the litigation costs of identification. The means by which these creditors could have protected themselves are well known and frequently used. They involve removing the debtor from control over the deposit account, usually by the use of some form of what is known as a "lockbox account." The device is described in Clark, 2 The Law of Secured Transactions Under the Uniform Commercial Code § 10.04[4] (Rev. ed. 2005). Under this device, account debtors are instructed to direct their payments to the debtor to a postal box directly controlled by the secured party who removes the checks daily, indorses them with the name of the debtor-payee, and deposits them in an account of the debtor in a bank. Restrictions can be imposed on such an account which preclude the debtor from either making deposits or withdrawals without the consent of the secured party. When the debtor needs advances, the secured party will move funds from the account into the debtor's operating account. Since the debtor cannot deposit nonproceeds in the account, there can be no commingling; since the debtor cannot draw on the account, no third parties can receive payments to the detriment of the secured party. The account is entirely proceeds, and if the debtor defaults messy problems of tracing proceeds through an active checking account are avoided. See Lockbox

Agreement, Appendix II, for a basic cash management arrangement showing the manner in which checks are processed.

## PROBLEM

On May 1 Bank loaned Debtor $10,000 and took a security interest in all of Debtor's existing and after-acquired accounts. The loan was effected by Bank crediting Debtor's general operating account held at Bank in the amount of the loan. At the time the account had a balance of $5000. Debtor deposited cash it received from its sales activities into that account. Debtor's activity in its account is as follows.

| Date | Transaction | Balance |
|------|-------------|---------|
| May 1 | $10,000 loan proceeds | $15,000 |
| May 20 | $1000 deposit from accounts paid | $16,000 |
| May 22 | $2000 withdrawn | $14,000 |
| June 1 | $13,500 withdrawn | $500 |
| June 4 | $100 withdrawn | $400 |
| June 10 | $500 deposit from inventory sold | $900 |
| June 15 | $3000 deposit from accounts paid | $3900 |

(a) On June 15 Debtor defaulted on all of its loan obligations without repaying Bank. Finance, one of Debtor's lenders, later garnished Debtor's deposit account. As between Bank and Finance, who has priority in the balance in Debtor's account?

(b) Would the result change if the June 10 deposit had not been made?

(c) Would the result change if Bank's security agreement granted it a security interest in "all of Debtor's existing accounts"?

## K. FEDERAL TAX LIENS

Debtors often owe tax obligations to the federal government: in the case of individual debtors, income or estate taxes; and in the case of employers, payroll taxes. Since a debtor in default on a secured loan sometimes also is in default on its obligations to other creditors, the government competes with other creditors for priority in the debtor's assets. Federal law, not Article 9 or other state law, determines the priority of the federal government against the debtor's other creditors. Two federal statutes potentially affect the priority of unpaid tax obligations to the United States government: the general federal priority statute (31 U.S.C. § 3713(a)) and the Federal Tax Lien Act (FTLA) contained in the Internal Revenue Code (26 U.S.C. § 6321 et seq. (2005)).

The general federal priority statute provides that the federal government "shall be paid first" when a bankruptcy case hasn't been filed and the debtor is insolvent. Section 3713(a) applies to any indebtedness owed to the federal government, not just to indebtedness arising from taxes. More important, the statute is absolute in its terms, making no exceptions in which the government "shall" not have priority. Section 3713(a) therefore seems to give the federal government unrestricted priority as against other claimants of the taxpayer. Prior to the FTLA's passage in 1966, courts created an exception which subordinated the federal government's claim to an earlier consensually or nonconsensually created property right (a lien) if the lien was "choate." A lien is choate when the identity of the lienor, the property subject to the lien and the amount of the lien are definite. United States v. City of New Britain, 347 U.S. 81, 85–86 (1954). Although courts have understood a lien to be choate when the lien is perfected, they have often used the choateness doctrine in unpredictable ways to disadvantage competing liens. The FTLA is much more restrictive than the general federal priority statute, subordinating federal tax liens under prescribed conditions described below. None of the FTLA's provisions say anything about "choateness."

Two questions therefore arise about the relation of the general federal priority statute and the FTLA: does the FTLA implicitly repeal § 3713(a) when the two conflict?; and does the choateness doctrine apply to competing liens under the FTLA? In United States v. City of Romani, 523 U.S. 517 (1998), the Supreme Court held that Congress intended the FTLA, a more recent, detailed and comprehensive statute, to apply when it conflicts with § 3713(a). *Romani*'s holding implicitly repeals the general federal priority statute by limiting its application to instances when it is compatible with the FTLA. The fate of the choateness doctrine under the FTLA is uncertain. Some courts have doubted that the doctrine survives the FTLA; e.g., Aetna Insurance Co. v. Texas Thermal Industries, 591 F.2d 1035, 1038 (5th Cir.1979); Pine Builders, Inc. v. United States, 413 F.Supp. 77 (E.D. Va. 1976). Other courts disagree, including the Supreme Court; e.g., United States v. McDermott, 507 U.S. 447 (1993); Trustees of Iron Workers v. Baldwin Steel Co., 2001 WL 1555539 (D. Mass. 2001). These courts apparently require that liens such as security interests both prime a tax lien under the FTLA *and* be choate at the time the tax lien attaches. The continued existence of the choateness doctrine under the FTLA is questionable. Congress enacted the FTLA "as an attempt to conform the lien provisions of the internal revenue laws to the concepts developed in this Uniform Commercial Code." S. Rep. No. 89–1708, at 1, reprinted in 1966 U.S.S. CAN. 3722. The FTLA, according to *Romani* (523 U.S. at 532), is a "specific" and "comprehensive" priority statute. If neither the UCC nor the FTLA mentions choateness, isn't the safer inference that the choateness doctrine doesn't apply under the FTLA?

## 1. CREATION AND ENFORCEABILITY OF FEDERAL TAX LIENS

The FTLA doesn't speak of a tax lien attaching or being perfected. It instead refers to a tax liability being "assessed" and the tax lien being "valid." Section 6321 provides that the United States government has a lien on all real and personal property of the taxpayer if the taxpayer neglects or refuses to pay after demand. The lien isn't restricted to property owned by the debtor at the time of the taxpayer's neglect or refusal; it reaches after-acquired property as well. Section 6322 in turn provides that the tax lien "arises" in favor of the government when the tax is assessed. Treasury Department regulations determine that assessment occurs when the tax liability is noted in the records by the appointed IRS assessment officer. 26 C.F.R. §§ 301.6201–1, 301.6203–1 (2003). Thus, the tax lien is enforceable against the debtor upon assessment. Because assessment doesn't require filing, the lien is secret. Although § 6334 exempts limited types of property or dollar amounts from a tax levy, the tax lien still attaches to all of the taxpayer's property.

Once the tax lien arises, it is enforceable against both the taxpayer and everyone else except "any purchaser, holder of security interest, mechanic's lienor, or judgment lien creditor." § 6323(a). To make its lien effective against these excepted classes, the IRS must file a notice of the lien. Thus, notice is the FTLA's counterpart of perfection. Under 6323(f) state law controls where notice must be given. The most recent uniform state law on the subject is the Uniform Federal Lien Registration Act, promulgated in 1978, which has widely been adopted. 7A Uniform Laws Annotated 336 (2002). In the case of real property, the IRS must file notice in the office designated by the state in which the property is located. For personal property, filing must be in the state of the taxpayer's residence. If the state hasn't designated an office for tax lien filings, filing is in the federal district court for the judicial district in which the real or personal property is located. Section 6323(g) makes a tax lien filing effective for ten years and 30 days after the date the tax is assessed. In a provision similar to 9–515(d)'s "refiling window," § 6323(g)(3)(A) allows refiling within one year of the end of the effectiveness period.

---

Professor Lynn LoPucki, who was largely responsible for Revised Article 9's reforms in the area of identifying debtors in filing systems, has written an article on the following case, "The *Spearing Tool* Filing System Disaster," to be published in 68 Ohio State Law Journal (forthcoming 2007), in the "Commercial Calamities Symposium." Since the court in *Spearing Tool* appears to have followed federal precedents faithfully in reaching its decision, what is the reason for Professor LoPucki's indictment?

## In re Spearing Tool and Manufacturing Co., Inc.

United States Court of Appeals, Sixth Circuit, 2005.
412 F.3d 653.

■ COOK, CIRCUIT JUDGE.

In this case arising out of bankruptcy proceedings, the government appeals the district court's reversal of the bankruptcy court's grant of summary judgment for the government. For the following reasons, we reverse the district court, and affirm the bankruptcy court.

## *I. Background and Procedural History*

In April 1998, Spearing Tool and Manufacturing Co. and appellee Crestmark entered into a lending agreement, which granted Crestmark a security interest in all of Spearing's assets. The bank perfected its security interest by filing a financing statement under the Uniform Commercial Code, identifying Spearing as "Spearing Tool and Manufacturing Co.," its precise name registered with the Michigan Secretary of State.

In April 2001, Spearing entered into a secured financing arrangement with Crestmark, under which Crestmark agreed to purchase accounts receivable from Spearing, and Spearing granted Crestmark a security interest in all its assets. Crestmark perfected its security interest by filing a UCC financing statement, again using Spearing's precise name registered with the Michigan Secretary of State.

Meanwhile, Spearing fell behind in its federal employment-tax payments. On October 15, 2001, the IRS filed two notices of federal tax lien against Spearing with the Michigan Secretary of State. Each lien identified Spearing as "SPEARING TOOL & MFG. COMPANY INC.," which varied from Spearing's precise Michigan-registered name, because it used an ampersand in place of "and," abbreviated "Manufacturing" as "Mfg.," and spelled out "Company" rather than use the abbreviation "Co." But the name on the IRS lien notices was the precise name Spearing gave on its quarterly federal tax return for the third quarter of 2001, as well as its return for fourth-quarter 1994, the first quarter for which it was delinquent. For most of the relevant tax periods, however, Spearing filed returns as "Spearing Tool & Manufacturing"—neither its precise Michigan-registered name, nor the name on the IRS tax liens.

Crestmark periodically submitted lien search requests to the Michigan Secretary of State, using Spearing's exact registered name. Because Michigan has limited electronic-search technology, searches disclose only liens matching the precise name searched—not liens such as the IRS's, filed under slightly different or abbreviated names.[2] Crestmark's February 2002 search results came back from the Secretary of State's office with a handwritten note stating: "You may wish to search using Spearing Tool & Mfg. Company Inc." But Crestmark did not search for that name at the time, and its exact-registered-name searches thus did not reveal the IRS liens. So Crestmark, unaware of the tax liens, advanced more funds to Spearing between October 2001 and April 2002.

On April 16, 2002, Spearing filed a Chapter–11 bankruptcy petition. Only afterward did Crestmark finally search for "Spearing Tool & Mfg. Company Inc." and discover the tax-lien notices. Crestmark then filed the complaint in this case to determine lien priority. The bankruptcy court determined the government had priority; the district court reversed. The questions now before us are whether state or federal law determines the

---

**2.** The search engine ignores various "noise words" and their abbreviations, including "Incorporated" and "Company," but not "Manufacturing" or "and."

sufficiency of the IRS's tax-lien notices, and whether the IRS notices sufficed to give the IRS liens priority.

## II.  *Federal law controls whether the IRS's lien notice sufficed.*

Crestmark argues Michigan law should control the form and content of the IRS's tax lien with respect to taxpayer identification. The district court, though it decided in favor of Crestmark on other grounds, rightly disagreed.

When the IRS files a lien against a taxpayer's property, it must do so "in one office within the State . . . as designated by the laws of such State, in which the property subject to the lien is situated." 26 U.S.C. § 6323(f)(1)(A). The Internal Revenue Code provides that the form and content "shall be prescribed by the [U.S. Treasury] Secretary" and "be valid *notwithstanding any other provision of law regarding the form or content of a notice of lien.*" 26 U.S.C. § 6323(f)(3) (emphasis added). Regulations provide that the IRS must file tax-lien notices using IRS Form 668, which must "identify the taxpayer, the tax liability giving rise to the lien, and the date the assessment arose." 26 C.F.R. § 301.6323(f)–1(d)(2). Form–668 notice "is valid notwithstanding any other provision of law regarding the form or content of a notice of lien. For example, omission from the notice of lien of a description of the property subject to the lien does not affect the validity thereof even though State law may require that the notice contain a description of property subject to the lien." § 301.6323(f)–1(d)(1); *see also United States v. Union Cent. Life Ins. Co.*, 368 U.S. 291 (1961) (Michigan's requirement that tax liens describe relevant property "placed obstacles to the enforcement of federal tax liens that Congress had not permitted.").

The plain text of the statute and regulations indicates Form–668 notice suffices, regardless of state law. We therefore need only consider how much specificity federal law requires for taxpayer identification on tax liens.

## III.  *The notice here sufficed.*

An IRS tax lien need not perfectly identify the taxpayer. * * * *See, e.g., Hudgins v. IRS (In re Hudgins)*, 967 F.2d 973, 976 (4th Cir.1992); *Tony Thornton Auction Serv., Inc. v. United States*, 791 F.2d 635, 639 (8th Cir.1986); *Reid v. IRS (In re Reid)*, 182 B.R. 443, 446 (Bankr.E.D.Va.1995). The question before us is whether the IRS's identification of Spearing was sufficient. We conclude it was.

The critical issue in determining whether an abbreviated or erroneous name sufficiently identifies a taxpayer is whether a "reasonable and diligent search would have revealed the existence of the notices of the federal tax liens under these names." *Tony Thornton*, 791 F.2d at 639. In *Tony Thornton*, for example, liens identifying the taxpayer as "Davis's Restaurant" and "Daviss (sic) Restaurant" sufficed to identify a business correctly known as "Davis Family Restaurant." *Id.* In *Hudgins*, the IRS lien identified the taxpayer as "Hudgins Masonry, Inc." instead of by the taxpayer's personal name, Michael Steven Hudgins. This notice nonetheless sufficed, given that both names would be listed on the same page of the state's lien index. 967 F.2d at 977.

Crestmark argues, and we agree, that those cases mean little here because in each, creditors could search a physical index and were likely to notice similar entries listed next to or near one another—an option which no longer exists under Michigan's electronic-search system. So the question for this case becomes whether Crestmark conducted a reasonable and diligent electronic search. It did not.

Crestmark should have searched here for "Spearing Tool & Mfg." as well as "Spearing Tool and Manufacturing." "Mfg." and the ampersand are, of course, most common abbreviations—so common that, for example, we use them as a rule in our case citations. Crestmark had notice that Spearing sometimes used these abbreviations, and the Michigan Secretary of State's office *recommended* a search using the abbreviations. Combined, these factors indicate that a reasonable, diligent search by Crestmark of the Michigan lien filings for this business would have disclosed Spearing's IRS tax liens.

Crestmark argues for the unreasonableness of requiring multiple searches by offering the extreme example of a name it claims could be abbreviated 288 different ways ("ABCD Christian Brothers Construction and Development Company of Michigan, Inc."). Here, however, only two relevant words could be, and commonly are, abbreviated: "Manufacturing" and "and"—and the Secretary of State specifically recommended searching for those abbreviations. We express no opinion about whether creditors have a general obligation to search name variations. Our holding is limited to these facts.

Finally, we note that policy considerations also support the IRS's position. A requirement that tax liens identify a taxpayer with absolute precision would be unduly burdensome to the government's tax-collection efforts. Indeed, such a requirement might burden the government at least as much as Crestmark claims it would be burdened by having to perform multiple lien searches. "The overriding purpose of the tax lien statute obviously is to ensure prompt revenue collection." *United States v. Kimbell Foods, Inc.*, 440 U.S. 715, 734–35 (1979). "[T]o attribute to Congress a purpose so to weaken the tax liens it has created would require very clear language," which we lack here. *Union Central*, 368 U.S. at 294. Further, to subject the federal government to different identification requirements— varying with each state's electronic-search technology—"would run counter to the principle of uniformity which has long been the accepted practice in the field of federal taxation." *Id.*

Crestmark urges us to require IRS liens to meet the same precise-identification requirement other lien notices now must meet under Uniform Commercial Code Article 9. *See* Mich. Comp. Laws § 440.9503(1) ("A financing statement sufficiently provides the name of [a] debtor [that is] a registered organization, only if the financing statement provides the name of the debtor indicated on the public record of the debtor's jurisdiction of organization which shows the debtor to have been organized."). We decline to do so. The UCC applies to transactions "that create[ ] a security interest in personal property or fixtures *by contract.*" Mich. Comp. Laws § 440.9109(1)(a) (emphasis added). Thus, the IRS would be exempt from UCC requirements even without the strong federal policy favoring unfettered tax collection.

More importantly, the Supreme Court has noted that the United States, as an involuntary creditor of delinquent taxpayers, is entitled to special priority over voluntary creditors. *See, e.g., Kimbell Foods*, 440 U.S. at 734–35, 737–38. Thus, while we understand that a requirement that the IRS comply with UCC Article 9 would spare banks considerable inconvenience, we conclude from Supreme–Court precedent that the federal government's interest in prompt, effective tax collection trumps the banks' convenience in loan collection.

## IV.   *Conclusion*

We reverse the district court and affirm the bankruptcy court's grant of summary judgment for the government.

## NOTE

As we saw in Chapter 2, Revised Article 9's break-through reforms with respect to debtor-name errors on financing statements provide that (i) financing statements for debtors that are "registered organizations"(corporations) must be filed in the organizing jurisdiction (the state of incorporation) of the debtor (9–301 and 9–307(e)), and (ii) the debtor must be identified on the financing statement by the name found in the public records of that jurisdiction (9–503(a)). Since technology has made it easy to discover the correct name of debtors from public records, these rules allow a searcher to conduct one search in the correct name of the debtor in the proper jurisdiction and be sure of finding every effective UCC filing. In many states federal tax liens and UCC financing statements are included in the same file. In such a case, if the IRS rules for the taxpayer's name were like those under Revised Article 9, a single search under the correct name would turn up all the liens, consensual and nonconsensual, state and federal, against a corporate debtor-taxpayer's property. After *Spearing Tool*, this is not possible. Federal court precedent adopts the reasonably diligent search rule, and the Sixth Circuit embraced the traditional interpretation of this rule as meaning that an incorrect version of the taxpayer's name on the notice is acceptable so long as a reasonably diligent search would have turned up the filing. This interpretation of the reasonably diligent searcher rule rejects 9–506(c)'s "standard search logic" standard. The indeterminate nature of this rule may require multiple searches under different versions of the debtor's name to look for a federal tax lien on the debtor's property, with no certainty that there is not another financing statement filed under another variation of the debtor's name yet undiscovered. *Spearing Tool* effectively undermines Congress' intent to make the FTLA consistent with Article 9.

The reasonably diligent searcher rule is a relic of the pre-digital past. A diligent searcher today can rather easily find the correct name of a corporation by calling up its incorporation records. If it finds nothing under this name, it is a waste of time and money to require the searcher to speculate on what erroneous name the IRS may have used. The teaching of this case is that the IRS can pretty well get away with filing under the name the taxpayer used on its tax returns without looking further for its correct name. Ironically, since tax returns are not public documents, the searcher, even one who has learned the taxpayer's correct name, has no sure way of finding this name, however diligent its search. The court had the opportunity to recognize how anachronistic the reasonably diligent search concept is after the Internet and to do something about it in this case, but it failed. Professor LoPucki observes that the IRS is so adroit in preventing cases that might overturn *Spearing Tool* from coming before other courts of appeal that the Sixth Circuit holding may prevail for many years. It is most likely that reform can come only through legislative or administrative intervention. One palliative sometimes discussed is the establishment by the IRS of a national filing system for tax liens in Washington. Another is to amend Treasury Department regulations to expressly require notice of a tax lien to supply the debtor's correct name.

Professor LoPucki's article contains an extensive and enlightening critique of *Spearing Tool*. In answering the question we posed before the opinion, he explains in depth what he believes to be the disastrous effect that this case has had on the long movement toward reducing debtor-name filing errors. IRS exceptionalism is well known and reluctantly tolerated in commercial law; here it will prove costly.

## 2.   THE FTLA'S GENERAL PRIORITY RULE

Federal law could have made the tax lien valid against both the taxpayer and all competitors whenever it arises. Such a rule would have given the federal tax lien complete priority. Section 3713, the general federal priority rule, in effect is such a rule. However, the FTLA doesn't adopt a "government always wins" rule. It instead determines priority essentially according to the order in time in which a competing interest in the taxpayer's property is obtained. In general, interests obtained before notice of the tax lien is filed prevail against the tax lien; interests obtained after filing notice of the tax lien occurs are subordinated to the tax lien. Although the FTLA's terminology differs from that of Revised Article 9, the FTLA's general priority rule gives priority only to security interests perfected before notice of a tax lien is filed.

Section 6323(a) states the FTLA's general priority rule. It provides in relevant part that the tax lien "shall not be valid against any purchaser, holder of a security interest, mechanic's lienor, or judgment lien creditor until notice thereof which meets the requirements of subsection (f) has been filed" by the IRS. As is often noted, § 6223(a) can't be read literally. Read literally, the subsection states that the federal tax lien has priority over the enumerated competitors when proper notice of the lien is filed. So read, a filed tax lien has retroactive effect: competitors lose to the federal tax lien once notice of the tax lien has been filed, even if the competing interests attached before filing notice was given. Because the literal reading conflicts with the FTLA's purpose to coordinate tax liens with other liens, § 6323(a) is understood nonliterally. Read nonliterally § 6323(a)'s general priority rule is that the federal tax lien primes the interests of purchasers, security interests, mechanic's liens, and judgment liens that come into existence after proper notice of the tax lien has been filed; these competitors have priority when their interests exist before filing notice of the tax lien occurs. Section 6323(a)'s general rule is subject to exceptions, discussed below. However, unless an exception applies, interests in the taxpayer's property that come into existence after the tax lien filing are subordinate to the tax lien.

Security interests are among the competing interests enumerated in § 6323(a). In order for a secured creditor to have priority over the tax lien under § 6323(a), the secured creditor must be a "holder of a security interest" at the time of the tax lien filing. Section 6323(h)(1) in turn defines "security interest." This important definition provides in relevant part that "[a] security interest exists at any time (A), if, at such time, the property is in existence and the interest has become protected under local law against a subsequent judgment lien arising out of an unsecured obligation, and (B) to the extent that, at such time, the holder has parted with money or money's worth." Thus, to hold a security interest at the time of the tax lien filing, three requirements must be met: the collateral must exist, the security interest must be protected under local law against a subsequent judgment lien on an unsecured claim, and the creditor must have parted with money or money's worth. Failure to meet one or more of these requirements means that the claimant doesn't hold a "security interest" for purposes of the FTLA. As such it loses to the federal tax lien under § 6323(a)'s general rule.

Two points about 6323(h)(1)'s definition should be noted. First, because (A) requires that collateral be in existence at the time of the tax lien filing, § 6323(a)'s general rule doesn't protect perfected security interests in after-acquired property against a tax lien. Security interests in after-acquired property are protected, if at all, under one or more exceptions to § 6323. See § 6323(c). Second, (h)(1) uses the rights of a lien creditor under local law (i.e., non-FTLA law) as a baseline of sorts. If a security interest doesn't have priority over a lien creditor under local law, it isn't a "security interest" under the FTLA. If the security interest has priority under local law, it's a "security interest" under the FTLA as long as the other requirements of (h)(1) are satisfied. Revised Article 9 of course is a prominent sort of local law. Section 9–317 of the Revision determines the priority of a security interest against a lien creditor's rights. The problems below test an understanding of § 6323(a)'s general priority rule.

## PROBLEMS

**1.** On January 1 SP made a loan to D Corporation and D granted SP a security interest in its equipment in use in its factory in Virginia to secure the loan. The same day SP filed a financing statement in the proper office identifying D as "Dee Corp." On February 1, after D refused to pay payroll taxes it owed the federal government, the IRS properly filed notice of a tax lien in Virginia.

(a) In a contest between the IRS and SP over D's equipment in use, who prevails? 9–317(a)(2)(A), 9–502(a), 9–506(b), (c).

(b) Assume that SP's filed financing statement is such that under 9–317 SP is subordinated to the IRS. Is SP the "holder of a security interest" under § 6323(h)(1)? Under Revised Article 9?

(c) Assume that on January 1 the financing statement SP filed omitted D Corporation's address. Does the result in (a) change? 9–502(a), 9–516(b), 9–520(a), (c).

(d) Assume that on January 1 SP's financing statement identified D as "D Corporation" and included its address. The filing officer, however, rejected SP's financing statement when SP presented it along with a filing fee. Does the result in (a) change? 9–502(a), 9–516(d), 1–201(29).

**2.**   On January 1 SP had D execute a security agreement covering D's equipment in use and at the same time properly filed a financing statement. The security agreement gave SP the right to refuse to make loans to D. On February 1 the IRS properly filed notice of a tax lien covering D's equipment. The next day SP loaned D funds.

(a) If a contest arises between SP and the IRS over D's equipment, who will prevail under § 6323(a)? § 6323(h)(1)(B), 9–317(a)(2)(B), 26 C.F.R. § 301.6323(h)–1(a)(3) (2003); cf. § 6323(d), 9–323(b).

(b) Would the result under § 6323(a) change if on January 1 SP agreed to loan D funds on February 2, which it subsequently did? § 6323(h)(1)(B), 1–204, 26 C.F.R. § 301.6323(h)–1(a)(3) (2003).

**3.**   On January 1 D Corporation purchased from Seller on credit a piece of equipment for its factory. To secure the purchase price owed, D executed on that date a security agreement granting Seller a security interest in the equipment purchased as well as in equipment it owned at the time. Seller delivered the piece of equipment to D on January 8. On January 10 the IRS properly filed a tax lien arising from unpaid payroll taxes owed by D. Seller filed a valid financing statement covering D's equipment on January 15. In a contest between the IRS and Seller over D's equipment, who has priority?

## 3.   § 6323(c) AND (d)S' EXCEPTIONS: POST-LIEN TRANSACTIONS

Sections 6323(c) and (d) contain important exceptions to § 6323(a)'s general priority rule. Section 6323(c) addresses both future advances and floating liens, and § 6323(d) concerns future advances. By its terms, § 6323 only gives priority to holders of security interests at the time filing notice of the tax lien is given. A post-notice advance creates a security interest not in existence at the time of the tax lien filing. Similarly, a post-notice acquisition by the debtor of collateral covered by an after-acquired property clause creates a security interest that didn't exist at the time of the filing of the tax lien. Without § 6323(c) or (d), all post-notice advances and post-notice acquisitions of collateral therefore would be subordinate to the IRS's tax lien under § 6323(a). Section 6323(c) protects a secured creditor's future advances and after-acquired property against subordination to a tax lien, and § 6323(d) also protects its future advances from subordination. Both sections prescribe the conditions under which the tax lien is "*in*valid" against a security interest.

Section 6323(c)(1) protects a range of security interests that come into existence within 45 days after the tax lien filing through the taxpayer's acquisition of collateral. To be protected, the collateral acquired must be "qualified property" covered by a pre-notice "commercial transactions financing agreement," and protected under local law against a judgment lien creditor. Section 6323(c)(3)(B) defines "qualified property" as "commercial financial security" acquired by the taxpayer within 45 days after the date of the tax lien filing. Section 6323(c)(3)(C) in turn defines "commercial financial security" to include commercial paper, accounts receivable, real property mortgages and inventory. (Treasure Department regulations have extended the category of commercial paper to include commercial documents evidencing contract rights; 26 C.F.R. § 301.6323(c)–1(c)(1).) Thus, in plain English, § 6323(c)(1) protects security interests in certain types of after-acquired property when the property is collateral acquired by the taxpayer within 45 days of a tax lien filing.

Section 6323(d) gives priority against a tax lien to prescribed future advances. Under (d) the tax lien is subordinate to security interests that come into existence "by reason of a disbursement made" within 45 days of the tax lien filing. Future advances are disbursements. To have priority, the secured party must make the advance without actual knowledge of the tax lien filing, the advance must be secured by collateral existing at the time of the filing, and the advance must be protected under local law against the rights of judgment lien creditors. The first condition means that § 6323(d) treats future advances less favorably than under Revised Article 9. Under 9–317(a)(2) and 9–323(b), advances by a secured creditor who is perfected or has filed a financing statement and satisfied one of 9–203(b)(3)'s conditions has priority over a lien creditor are protected when made within 45 days of the lien. The secured creditor's knowledge of the intervening lien does not affect the advance's priority. Under § 6323(d) the secured creditor's actual knowledge of the tax lien filing cuts off the advance's priority over the intervening tax lien, even if the advance is made within the 45–day period.

Section 6323(c) and (d) overlap to some extent. By defining a "commercial transactions financing agreement" to cover advances under such agreements made within 45 days of the tax lien filing without knowledge of the filing, subsection (c) also protects some post-lien advances. However, the subsections generally give different protections. Section 6323(c) protects qualifying after-acquired collateral; (d) protects only future advances. Unlike (c) § 6323(d) does not restrict the type of collateral securing protected future advances. For its part, (c)'s protection of qualifying after-acquired property is unaffected by a secured creditor's actual knowledge of the tax lien filing.

Consider § 6323(c)'s application to the facts in the case below.

## McCord v. Petland, Inc.

United States Bankruptcy Court, N.D. West Virginia, 2001.
264 B.R. 814.

■ L. Edward Friend, II, Bankruptcy Judge.

This matter is before the Court pursuant to the Complaint to Determine Priority of Liens filed by the debtors, Harry K. McCord and Linda Susan McCord ("the McCords"). Defendant United States Department of Treasury, Internal Revenue Service ("IRS") and Defendant Petland, Inc. ("Petland") both claim a priority security interest in the same leasehold items, equipment, and inventory. The Court has jurisdiction by virtue of 28 U.S.C. § 1334 and the standing order of reference in this district. The matter before the Court is a core proceeding pursuant to 28 U.S.C. § 157(b).

### FACTS

The McCords owned and operated two pet stores in Maryland, initially as a sole proprietorship, and later as a corporation owned wholly by the McCords. The two stores were located in Lavale and in Hagerstown. Harry McCord obtained the Lavale store by assignment from a previous franchisee on June 1, 1992, and obtained the Hagerstown store by franchise agreement on February 4, 1993. On December 15, 1997, Harry McCord filed Articles of Incorporation of Brandywine Pets, Inc. ("Brandywine"). The McCords transferred the assets and liabilities of the pet stores to Brandywine sometime in 1998.

Prior to the incorporation, Petland obtained two liens on the McCords' pet stores. On December 4, 1997, the McCords executed two promissory notes in favor of the defendant Petland, Inc. ("Petland") in the amounts of $95,000 and $60,646.73. The notes were secured by a lien on all accounts, leasehold items, fixtures, inventory, equipment, proceeds, and after acquired collateral of the Hagerstown and Lavale stores, respectively. Petland filed a UCC–1 financing statement for the interest in the Lavale store with the Maryland Department of Assessments and Taxation on January 31, 1997, and filed a financing statement for the interest in the Hagerstown store on May 15, 1997.

Subsequent to Petland's filing of its UCC financing statements, the IRS filed two Notices of Federal Tax Liens in Berkeley County, West Virginia, the McCords' county of residence. These liens arose from unpaid federal Insurance Contribution Act ("FICA") taxes. The notices were filed on November 13, 1998, and on April 15, 1998.

The debtors filed a petition under Chapter 13 of the Bankruptcy Code on May 25, 1999. In their schedules, the McCords claimed to have $60,000 assets in real property and $91,803.05 in personal property. The McCords claim a personal property interest of $1,000 in fixtures and $10,000 in actual liquidation value of inventory in the two stores. During discovery, the McCords admitted that essentially all of the inventory on hand on the date of the bankruptcy filing came into existence after April 14, 1998 (the day before the first tax lien was filed); that there were no accounts receivable on April 14, 1998; and that all leasehold items, fixtures, and equipment were purchased prior to April 14, 1998. The McCords further stated that the fair market value of the leasehold items, fixtures, and equipment was $39,808 but could probably be sold for only $1,000 to $2,000.

Petland maintains that its liens have priority over those of the IRS by virtue of the fact that it perfected its liens before the IRS filed its notices of liens. The IRS contends that Petland's liens attached to property acquired by the McCords after the IRS filed its notices and that the IRS liens have priority. The IRS filed a secured claim for $70,817.79. Petland filed a secured claim for $237,175.42. On August 7, 2000, the McCords filed this adversary proceeding to determine the relative priority of these secured liens.

## DISCUSSION

The United States Supreme Court addressed similar issues in United States by & Through Internal Revenue Service v. McDermott, 507 U.S. 447, 123 L.Ed.2d 128, 113 S.Ct. 1526, (1993), holding that a federal tax lien filed before judgment debtors acquired real property had priority over the judgment creditor's previously recorded Utah state lien. On December 9, 1986, the IRS assessed the McDermotts for unpaid federal taxes for 1997 through 1981. *Id.* at 448. Upon that assessment, pursuant to 26 U.S.C. § 6321 and § 6322, a lien was created in favor of the IRS on all real and personal property of the McDermotts, including after-acquired property. *Id.* The IRS filed notice of the lien on September 9, 1987. *Id.* Prior to that, on July 6, 1987, Zions First National Bank had docketed a Utah state court judgment against the McDermotts, creating a judgment lien under Utah law on all of the McDermotts' real property then owned or thereafter acquired. *Id.*

Thereafter, on September 23, 1987, the McDermotts acquired title to a parcel of real property. *Id.* at 448–449. The McDermotts brought an interpleader action in state court to establish which lien was entitled to priority; the case was removed to District Court where Zions First National Bank was awarded priority. The Tenth Circuit Court of Appeals affirmed, and the United States Supreme Court granted certiorari and reversed and remanded.

The Court began its analysis by noting that "[f]ederal tax liens do not automatically have priority over all other liens. Absent provision to the contrary, priority for purposes of federal law is governed by the common law principle that 'the first in time is the first in right.' " *Id.* at 449, quoting United States v. New Britain, 347 U.S. 81, 85, 123 L.Ed.2d 128, 74 S.Ct. 367, 370 (1954). Noting that under 26 U.S.C. § 6323(a) the IRS' lien was "not valid ... until notice thereof ... has been filed," the Court deemed the IRS' lien "to have commenced no sooner than the filing of notice." 507 U.S. at 449.

Considering Zions First National Bank's lien, the Court stated that "[o]ur cases deem a competing state lien to be in existence for 'first in time' purposes only when it has been 'perfected' in the sense that 'the identity of the lienor, *the property subject to the lien*, and the amount of the lien are established.' " 507 U.S. at 449–450, (emphasis in original) quoting United States v. New Britain, 347 U.S. at 84, 74 S.Ct. at 369. As a result, establishment of priority hinged on whether the bank's judgment lien was "perfected in that sense" before the IRS had filed its tax lien on September 9, 1987. 507 U.S. at 450. The Court concluded that a lien in after-acquired property is not "perfected" until the debtor's acquisition of that property. 507 U.S. at 451–453. Therefore, the Court reasoned, Zions First National Bank's lien was not "first in time" even though it was filed prior to the IRS' filing. *Id.*

The IRS' lien in the after-acquired property also attached at the moment the McDermotts acquired the property. The Court noted that the two liens attached at exactly the same instant. 507 U.S. at 453. The Court concluded, however, that "under the language of § 6323(a) ('shall not be valid as against any ... judgment lien creditor until notice ... has been filed'), the filing of notice renders the federal tax lien extant for 'first in time' priority purposes regardless of whether it has yet attached to identifiable property."[2] 507 U.S. at 453.

In the instant case, the *McDermott* analysis is appropriate. First. the United States has a secured claim in all of the McCords' property, including the property subject to Petland's interest. A federal tax lien arose upon assessment and attaches to all property of the McCords. 26 U.S.C. §§ 6321,6322. The IRS filed a proof of claim for $70,817.79. Under 11 U.S.C. § 506(a), an allowed claim is secured to the extent of a debtor's interest in the property of the estate. Since the McCords indicate in their schedules that they have assets in excess of $70,817.79, the United States has an allowed secured claim. There is no dispute that Petland has a secured interest under Maryland law.

Next, the Court must determine when the relative security interests of the IRS and of Petland were perfected. Petland obtained an interest in all accounts, leasehold items, fixtures, inventory, equipment, proceeds, and after-acquired collateral by security agreement, with financing statements

---

**2.** The Supreme Court defends its position in part by noting that while a "first-to-record" presumption may be appropriate between two voluntary transactions involving after-acquired property, the Government "cannot indulge the luxury of declining to hold the taxpayer liable for taxes; notice of a previously filed security agreement covering after-acquired property does *not* enable the Government to protect itself." McDermott, 507 U.S. at 455, 113 S.Ct. at 1531.

filed pursuant to Maryland law on January 31, 1997, and May 15, 1997. The liens on the relevant property already acquired by the McCords were perfected on those dates. However, the liens on any after-acquired property were not perfected until the McCords' actual acquisition of that property. The United States' tax lien notices were filed on November 13, 1998, and April 15, 1998. These liens were perfected on those dates as far as property previously acquired by the McCords. The liens on any after-acquired property were not perfected until the McCords actually acquired the property.

## CONCLUSION

Under the *McDermott* analysis, the Court finds that Petland has priority over the IRS liens on any accounts, leasehold items, fixtures, inventory, equipment and proceeds of the two Maryland pet stores according to the security agreement so long as the McCords acquired that property prior to April 15, 1998. The IRS has priority on any accounts, leasehold items, fixtures, inventory, equipment and proceeds of the two Maryland pet stores acquired by the debtors on or after April 15, 1998.

It is accordingly so ordered.

## NOTES

**1.** The *McCord* court leaves unaddressed the effect of the McCords' transfer of assets to Brandywine, Inc. on the IRS's tax lien filing. The FTLA is silent on whether the IRS must refile in the transferee's name in order to preserve the effectiveness of its filing notice. In In re LMS Holding Co., 50 F.3d 1520 (10th Cir.1995), the court relied on former Article 9's analogous provisions not to require refiling of the tax lien notice in the transferee's name for assets transferred by the taxpayer. It required refiling with respect to assets acquired by the transferee after the initial tax lien filing. The McCords initially operated their business as a sole proprietorship and subsequently as a corporation, transferring assets and liabilities to the corporation. The IRS filed notice of its tax lien in the McCords' names prior to the change in business form. After the tax lien filing, the stores operated by the corporation acquired more assets. At the time of the dispute between the IRS and the McCords' secured creditor (Petland), the stores' assets consisted of leasehold items, fixtures, equipment and accounts receivables. If *In re LMS Holding* were followed, who would prevail?

**2.** The *McCord* court determines priority without mentioning § 6323(c). Isn't § 6323(c)'s protection relevant to the priority contest between the IRS and Petland? The court instead thinks that *McDermott* and the Supreme Court's application of the choateness doctrine in that case controls. It doesn't. Section 6323(c), which at least partially displaces the choateness doctrine, instead applies. *McDermott* involved a priority contest between a judgment lien creditor and the IRS in real estate acquired by the judgment debtor-taxpayer after notice of the tax lien was filed. State law created a judgment lien on real property owned or thereafter acquired. The Court, applying the choateness doctrine, found that the judgment creditor's interest in after-acquired realty attached at the time of the tax lien filing. Because the judgment lien on the realty didn't precede the filing, it wasn't "valid" against the tax lien under § 6323(a)'s general priority rule. The collateral at issue in *McCord* consists of existing and after-acquired personal property, not realty: leasehold rights, fixtures, equipment, inventory and accounts receivables. Thus, § 6323(c)'s protection for qualifying after-acquired property is available for at least some of the after-acquired collateral. For reasoning similar to *McCord*, see Old National Bank v. RH Electronics Systems, Inc., 56 UCC Rep. Serv.2d 468 (S.D. Ind. 2005).

The stores' accounts receivables and inventory are "commercial financial security." § 6323(c)(2)(C). According to the McCords, essentially all were acquired after the IRS's April 15 tax lien notice was filed. Section 6323(c) counts as "qualified property" of all of the accounts and inventory acquired within 45 days after April 15 and protects Petland's security interest in them. The McCords admitted that all of the other items of collateral were purchased before that date. Because Petland's security interest in them was perfected, its security interest was "valid" under § 6323(a) at the time of the April tax lien filing. Hence Petland would have priority over the IRS in the leasehold interests, fixtures and equipment.

## PROBLEMS

**1.** On January 1 SP and Debtor executed a security agreement covering Debtor's factory machinery in use and on January 2 SP properly filed a valid financing statement. The IRS on January 3 properly filed notice of a tax lien against Debtor. On January 4 SP made a secured loan to Debtor knowing of the tax lien filing.

   (a) If Debtor defaults on its obligations to SP under the security agreement, who has priority in the collateral described in SP and Debtors' security agreement: SP or the IRS?

   (b) Suppose SP had loaned Debtor $1,000 on a secured basis on January 2. It also made another $5,000 secured loan to Debtor on January 4 knowing of the IRS's tax lien filing. Who as priority in the collateral described in SP and Debtors' security agreement: SP or the IRS?

**2.** On January 1 SP and Debtor executed a security agreement covering Debtor's existing and after-acquired inventory. On January 2 SP loaned Debtor funds covered by the security agreement and properly filed a valid financing statement listing the collateral as inventory. On January 3 the IRS properly filed notice of its tax lien against Debtor. Debtor, with SP's knowledge, acquired two pieces of inventory, one on February 1 and the other on May 1.

   (a) In a priority dispute between the IRS and SP, who has priority in the two pieces of inventory?

(b) Suppose the collateral had been Debtor's machinery in use in its factory, Debtor acquiring one piece of machinery on February 1 and the other on May 1. Would the result in (a) change?

## 4.  PMSIs and Post-Lien Proceeds

Courts and the Internal Revenue Service have created exceptions to the FTLA protecting purchase money security interests and post-lien proceeds. Consider the exceptions in turn. In some circumstances the FTLA gives a PMSI priority over an intervening tax lien. For instance, suppose a creditor and debtor execute a security agreement on day 1, the creditor delivers the collateral the same day and the creditor's security interest is a purchase money security interest. On day 2 the IRS files notice of its tax lien against the debtor, and on day 15 the creditor files a financing statement covering the collateral. Under § 6323(h)(1) the creditor "holds a security interest" on day 1. This is because (h)(1)'s conditions are satisfied as of that date: the purchase money collateral is in existence as of the date notice of the tax lien is given since it was delivered on day 1; the creditor's purchase money security interest is protected under 9–317(e) against an intervening lien creditor's rights; and the creditor has parted with "money or money's worth." As the holder of a security interest, the purchase money creditor's security interest is "valid" against the tax lien and therefore has priority under § 6323(a).

However, in other circumstances PMSIs aren't protected. For instance, assume that a tax lien is filed on day 1 covering all of taxpayer's assets. On day 5 a purchase money creditor delivers the purchase money collateral to the taxpayer. The creditor has the taxpayer execute a security agreement and files a financing statement on day 8. The creditor isn't a "holder of a security interest" at the time the tax lien was filed. See § 6323(h)(1). Although it later became a holder of a security interest, neither § 6323(c) nor (d) allows the creditor priority over the tax lien because both sections require that a written security agreement be executed prior to the filing of the tax lien.

Under a judicially created exception to the FTLA, the purchase money creditor nonetheless has priority over the previously filed tax lien. This is so regardless of whether the security agreement creating the PMSI occurred before or after the tax lien was filed. See Slodov v. United States, 436 U.S. 238, 258 n. 23 (1978); First Interstate Bank of Utah, N.A. v. Internal Revenue Service, 930 F.2d 1521 (10th Cir.1991); Rev. Rul. 68–57, 68–1 C.B. 553 (1968). In *Slodov* the Supreme Court's justification is that the purchase money creditor's priority "reflects his contribution of property to the taxpayer's estate and therefore does not prejudice creditors who are prior in time." *Slodov*, 426 U.S. at 258 n. 23. Affected noncreditors, such as the taxpaying public, may feel differently when the reduction in tax revenues collected increases their tax rates. If the Court is right, why does 9–317(e) restrict purchase money priority over intervening lien creditors in the way it does? If the Court is wrong and there is prejudice, why isn't the judicially created exception tailored more precisely to the circumstances in which creditors are likely to be prejudiced?

The other judicially created exception to tax lien priority concerns proceeds of collateral. The FTLA doesn't address the priority in proceeds. Treasury Department regulations instead deal with the matter; 26 C.F.R. § 301.6323(c)–1 (2003). Obviously, pre-notice identifiable proceeds of pre-notice collateral don't cause a problem. If the proceeds are identifiable under 9–315(b), a security interest attaches to them under 9–315(a)(2). Further, under 9–315(c) a perfected security interest in collateral carries over to proceeds. Thus, a secured creditor with a pre-notice perfected security interest in proceeds is a "holder of a security interest" for § 6323(h)(1)'s purposes. Its security interest in proceeds therefore is "valid" against a tax lien filing under § 6323(a). However, the FTLA is silent about the priority treatment of proceeds in two other circumstances: when post-notice proceeds are realized from disposal of pre-notice collateral, and when post-notice proceeds are realized from the disposal of post-notice collateral that is "qualifying property" under § 6323(c). In the former circumstance the proceeds are not "in existence" as required by (h)(1) at the time notice of the tax lien is filed; in the latter case both the collateral and its proceeds are not "in existence" at that time as required by (h)(1). The following case raises the question of the priority of proceeds in the latter circumstance.

## Plymouth Savings Bank v. Internal Revenue Service

United States Court of Appeals, First Circuit, 1999.
187 F.3d 203.

■ Cudahy, Senior Circuit Judge.

Jordan Hospital ("Hospital") owed Shirley Dionne ("Dionne") $75,000. Dionne, in turn, was indebted to the Plymouth Savings Bank ("Bank") and the Internal Revenue Service ("IRS"), both of which held valid liens on the money the Hospital owed Dionne. The Hospital deposited the money with the district court, and we must now decide who is entitled to it. The problem is simply to determine which of the two liens has priority. We hold that the Bank's lien may trump the IRS's and therefore reverse the district court's grant of summary judgment in favor of the IRS.

Most of the facts are not in dispute. Dionne owned and operated the Greenlawn Nursing Home, a 47–bed state-licensed facility. On September 22, 1993 and apparently before extending credit, the Bank filed a financing statement with the state of Massachusetts describing and giving notice of its security interest in Greenlawn and other assets of Dionne. On April 13, 1994, Dionne executed an $85,000 promissory note in favor of the Bank. As security for the loan, Dionne granted the Bank a security interest in all of her tangible and intangible personal property individually, as well as in her capacity as a sole proprietor doing business as Greenlawn. Paragraph 2 of the agreement specifically granted the Bank: all cash and non-cash proceeds resulting or arising from the rendering of services by Dionne; all general intangibles including proceeds of other collateral; and all inventory, receivables, contract rights or other personal property of Dionne. On or about December 1, 1994, Dionne defaulted on her $85,000 obligation to the Bank, leaving some $65,465 unpaid.

Dionne's financial troubles did not end there. She failed to make Federal Insurance Contribution Act, 26 U.S.C. § 3101, *et seq.* (FICA), payments of $19,639 for the second quarter of 1994. The IRS assessed liability on September 19, 1994 and filed a federal tax lien in the district court on December 19. Dionne again failed to make FICA payments of $62,767 for the fourth quarter of 1994. Liability was assessed on February 2, 1995 and a lien was filed on February 14.

On March 31, 1995, Dionne signed a contract in which she agreed to help the Hospital obtain a license to operate a skilled nursing facility in exchange for $300,000, payable in three installments. Dionne would receive $25,000 when she signed a letter of intent, $200,000 when Massachusetts approved a license and the final $75,000 two years after the license-approval date. With Dionne's assistance, by mid-May 1995 the Hospital had received approval for its license and had paid Dionne the first two installments, totaling $225,000. (In practical effect, it appears that Dionne transferred her Greenlawn license to the Hospital.) The Hospital never paid Dionne the $75,000 balance.

The Bank sued the Hospital in Massachusetts state court to recover the unpaid balance of its loan to Dionne. Considering cross-motions for summary judgment, the state court ruled for the Bank. It found that, pursuant to the contract between Dionne and the Hospital, the $75,000 constituted cash proceeds arising from the rendering of personal services by Dionne. Because the security agreement between the Bank and Dionne expressly covered "proceeds" of services, the court held that the Bank had a secured interest in the money. The court rejected the Bank's argument that the security interest attached to the nursing home license or to proceeds of the transfer of that license. Instead of awarding the $75,000 to the Bank, however, the court directed the Bank to bring a declaratory judgment action to determine whether its interest in the money had priority over that of other lien-holders.

Ever diligent, the Bank brought such an action—this one—which the IRS subsequently removed to the district court. The Hospital, content to let the Bank and the IRS do battle, deposited the $75,000 with the district court and exited from the action. The Bank and the IRS filed cross-motions for summary judgment, each asserting that its lien trumped the other's. The court sided with the IRS. The Bank's right to recover as against the government depended on when Dionne had performed the services required by the contract, the district court stated. And, although the record on the timing of Dionne's performance was sparse, the court determined that it was undisputed that she had not helped the Hospital secure approval of a nursing home license within the 45 days following the tax lien filing as required by the Federal Tax Lien Act, 26 U.S.C. §§ 6321, 6323(c) (FTLA). Accordingly, the district court held that the IRS's two liens were superior to the Bank's lien. The Bank appeals this decision, and we review *de novo* the district court's grant of summary judgment in favor of the government. * * *

When an individual fails to pay her taxes after a demand has been made, the FTLA grants the United States a lien "upon all property and rights to property, whether real or personal, belonging to such person." 26 U.S.C. § 6321. The lien also attaches to property acquired by the delinquent taxpayer after the initial imposition of the lien. * * * Section 6323 of the FTLA, however, gives certain commercial liens priority over federal tax liens. Pursuant to § 6323(a) and as defined in § 6323(h), for example, tax liens are subordinate to security interests in a taxpayer's property that is "in existence" *before* the government files notice of the tax lien. (Subsection 6323(f) details the filing requirements.) And § 6323(c) extends the priority of these prior security interests to certain "qualified property" that the taxpayer acquires even *after* the government has filed a notice of the tax lien. The scope of this safe harbor for after-acquired property under § 6323(c) is at issue here. Mindful that we are entering "the tortured meanderings of federal tax lien law, intersected now by the somewhat smoother byway of the Uniform Commercial Code [UCC]," Texas Oil & Gas Corp. v. United States, 466 F.2d 1040, 1043 (5th Cir.1972), we lay out the pertinent provisions with as much specificity as we can apply.

To fall within § 6323(c)'s safe harbor for after-acquired property, a security interest must be in "qualified property covered by the terms of a written agreement entered into before tax lien filing," including "commercial transactions financing agreement[s]." 26 U.S.C. § 6323(c)(1)(A)(i). The security interest must also be superior, under local law, to a judgment lien arising out of an unsecured obligation. *See id.* at § 6323(c)(1)(B). A "commercial transactions financing agreement" is defined as "an agreement (entered into by a person in the course of his trade or business) ... to make loans to the taxpayer to be secured by commercial financing security acquired by the taxpayer in the ordinary course of his trade or business," *id.* at § 6323(c)(2)(A)(i), and must be entered into within 45 days of the date of the tax lien filing. *See id.* at § 6323(c)(2)(A). "Commercial financing security" can include, among other things, "paper of a kind ordinarily arising in commercial transactions" and "accounts receivable," *id.* at § 6323(c)(2)(C), and it must be "acquired by the taxpayer before the 46th day after the date of tax lien filing." *Id.* at § 6323(c)(2)(B).

The relevant Treasury regulations include still more definitions. "Paper of a kind ordinarily arising in commercial transactions" means "any written document customarily used in commercial transactions," and includes "paper giving contract rights." 26 C.F.R. § 301.6323(c)–1(c)(1). For purposes of the FTLA, a "contract right" is "any right to payment under a contract not yet earned by performance and not evidenced by an instrument or chattel paper." *Id.* at § 301.6323(c)–1(c)(2)(i). "An account receivable is any right to payment for goods sold or leased or for services rendered which is not evidenced by an instrument or chattel paper." *Id.* at § 301.6323(c)–1(c)(2)(ii).

Because Dionne signed the personal service contract with the Hospital exactly 45 days after the IRS filed notice of the second tax lien (February 14–March 31),[1] the fighting issue is whether by so doing she "acquired" rights to the $75,000, the money the Hospital owed Dionne and deposited with the district court. *See* 26 U.S.C. § 6323(c)(2)(B). If, by signing the contract, Dionne acquired rights to the money, then the Bank's lien trumps the IRS's. For, if that is the case, it is undisputed that the Dionne–Hospital contract is commercial financing security within § 6323(c)(2)(C) and that the Dionne–Bank agreement is a commercial transactions financing agreement within §§ 6323(c)(1)(A)(i) & (c)(2).[2] In this scenario, the Bank's security interest is in qualified property, and the $75,000 would fall within the safe harbor for after-acquired property. On the other hand, if Dionne did not acquire the rights to the money when she signed the contract, the IRS's lien takes priority.

The Treasury Department (of which the IRS is a part) has provided an answer. Recall that the potential qualified property here is the contract between Dionne and the Hospital, which granted Dionne certain rights to payments when she performed certain services. Before the 46th day after the tax lien was filed (that is, before April 1, 1995), if Dionne had acquired anything, she could only have acquired a contract right, not an account receivable, because she had yet to perform any services. See 26 C.F.R. §§ 301.6323(c)–1(c)(2)(i) & (ii). The regulations provide that a "contract right . . . is acquired by a taxpayer when the contract is made." *Id.* at § 301.6323(c)–1(d). So, Dionne acquired the right to be paid for services to be rendered in the future at the time she entered into that contract. In statutory terms, the commercial transactions financing agreement (the Dionne–Bank agreement), which was entered into well before the tax lien filing, covers the Bank's loan (the $85,000) to the taxpayer (Dionne). The loan in turn was secured by commercial financing security (the Dionne–Hospital contract). The Dionne–Hospital contract conferred contract rights (the right to be paid $75,000 two years after Massachusetts approved a nursing home license for the Hospital) and was acquired by the taxpayer within 45 days of the tax lien filing. See 26 U.S.C. §§ 6323(c)(2)(A) & (B). The contract, and the rights (even if conditional) under it, are therefore qualified property covered by the Bank's security interest and protected by § 6323(c)'s safe harbor.

Of course, the Bank is interested in the money, not the contract right. The regulations again point the way. "Proceeds" are "whatever is received when collateral is sold, exchanged, or collected." 26 C.F.R. § 301.6323(c)–1(d). The regulations further provide: "Identifiable proceeds, which arise

---

**1.**   The Bank does not claim that its lien should take priority over the first tax lien, filed on December 19, 1994. The duel here is between only the second tax lien (filed on February 14, 1995 and covering FICA payments of $62,767 for the fourth quarter of 1994) and the Bank's lien.

**2.**   For purposes of the following discussion, we assume that if Dionne acquired the rights to the $75,000 within 45 days of the tax lien filing, she did so in the ordinary course of her trade or business as required by § 6323(c)(2)(B). The IRS challenges this assumption, and we discuss the issue later. *See infra* at 14–16.

from the collection or disposition of qualified property by the taxpayer, are considered to be acquired at the time such qualified property is acquired if the secured party has a continuously perfected security interest in the proceeds under local law." *Id.* Recall that the commercial financing security (the Dionne–Hospital contract and the rights under it) is simply collateral for the loan (the Bank's $85,000 loan to Dionne). So, where the collateral is a contract giving contract rights, the proceeds of those rights, like the rights themselves, are considered to have been acquired at the time the contract was made. This is so even though the right to proceeds under the contract does not become unconditional until the contract is performed. Pursuant to the Treasury regulations, the conditional right to the proceeds relates back to the time the contract was formed and executed. Therefore, Dionne acquired the rights to the proceeds of the contract right on March 31, 1995, exactly 45 days from the date of the tax lien filing.

In this case, however, the proceeds of the contract right are simply an account receivable, the right to payment of $75,000 for services rendered by Dionne. See 26 C.F.R. § 301.6323(c)–1(c)(2)(ii). And herein lies the rub. The IRS argues that, pursuant to the regulations, a taxpayer acquires an account receivable "at the time, and to the extent, a right to payment is earned by performance." Echoing the district court, the IRS correctly points out that Dionne did not earn a *right to payment* before the 45 days. But the contract and the rights under it, rather than the account receivable, are the qualified property at issue here, and the regulations provide that the proceeds of qualified property are deemed to be acquired at the time the qualified property is acquired. The regulations do not distinguish between forms of proceeds. Well then, the IRS parries, the account receivable cannot be "proceeds" because the contract was not "sold, exchanged, or collected." See 26 C.F.R. § 301.6323(c)–1(d). Had Dionne sold the contract, the IRS says, the Bank's lien would reach the proceeds of that sale; but performance (rendering the services) does not amount to a sale. This ingenious quibble is unconvincing. Dionne's rendering of the contract-ed-for services effectively "exchanged" her contract right, converting it into an account receivable. *See* 26 C.F.R. § 301.6323(c)–1(d). The IRS has given us no good reason, nor can we find any basis in commercial reality, to distinguish between a "sale" or an "exchange" and a conversion by performance for this purpose. In fact, performance would seem to be necessary for the production of proceeds even if there were a sale or exchange of the contract. We therefore conclude that the account receivable, the right to the $75,000, is the proceeds of the contract right.

To this, the IRS responds by complaining that we have expanded too far § 6323(c)'s safe harbor for after-acquired property. It cites legislative history which it claims suggests that Congress intended § 6323(c)'s protections to extend only to property that was *collected* within 45 days of the tax lien filing. We find this argument unpersuasive. As an initial matter, this Senate Report does not directly address commercial financing secured by contract rights, the precise issue here. The Report does indicate, however, that the FTLA was "an attempt to conform the lien provisions of the internal revenue laws to the concepts developed in [the UCC]." S.Rep. No.

1708, 89th Cong., 2d Sess., at 2. The Treasury regulations reflect this intent by providing definitions for FTLA terms that closely track UCC definitions of like terms. For example, the FTLA definitions of "contract right" and "account receivable" match the pre–1972 revision definitions of "contract" and "account," *compare, e.g.*, 26 C.F.R. §§ 301.6323(c)–1(c)(i) & (ii) *with* Mass. Gen. Laws Ann. ch. 106, § 9–106 (West 1998) (Official Reasons for 1972 Changes), and the two definitions of the term "proceeds" are almost identical, *compare* 26 C.F.R. § 301.6323(c)–1(d) *with* Mass. Gen. Laws Ann. ch. 106, § 9–306(a) (West 1988) (defining "proceeds" as "whatever is received upon the sale, exchange, collection or other disposition of collateral or proceeds"). Our conclusion that the Bank's security interest in the contract rights covers the proceeds of those rights—even if the proceeds are accounts receivable—is compatible with still other provisions of the UCC. *See, e.g.*, Mass. Gen. Laws Ann. ch. 106, § 9–306(2) (West 1980) (providing that security interests extend to the proceeds of all secured property). In all events, whatever Congress intended, the regulations make it clear that, so long as the contract was entered into within 45 days of the tax lien filing, the rights under that contract and *all of the proceeds* of those rights fall within § 6323(c)'s protective bounds. * * *

One issue remains. The IRS, reminding us that we "can affirm a correct judgment on any ground," Appellee's Br. at 20 (citing Levy v. FDIC, 7 F.3d 1054, 1056 (1st Cir.1993)), argues that Dionne did not enter into the contract with the Hospital "in the ordinary course of [her] trade or business" as required by § 6323(c)(2)(A)(i). Normally, we will consider only those issues that the district court considered below * * *, and can "affirm a correct district court's ruling on any ground *supported in the record . . .*," *Levy*, 7 F.3d at 1056 (emphasis added) (internal quotation and citation omitted). In this case, not only did the district court fail to address the "ordinary course of business" element, both parties also acknowledge that the record is undeveloped on this point. Because the record is so undeveloped, and because trade-or-business determinations are highly fact-intensive, *see, e.g.*, Higgins v. Commissioner, 312 U.S. 212, 217, 85 L.Ed. 783, 61 S.Ct. 475 (1941); Deputy v. du Pont, 308 U.S. 488, 496, 84 L.Ed. 416, 60 S.Ct. 363 (1940), we decline the IRS's invitation to affirm the district court on this ground. However, the parties are free to develop the factual record on remand to the district court. * * *

Because we find that the Bank's lien may trump the IRS's, we reverse the district court's grant of summary judgment in favor of the IRS. The case is remanded to the district court for proceedings consistent with this opinion.

NOTE

*Plymouth Savings Bank* is typical in relying heavily on Treasury Department Regulation § 301.6323(c)–1 to determine the priority of post-notice proceeds. Treasury Department regulations have the force of law. Regulation § 301.6323(c)–1 provides that accounts receivable are acquired when the right to payment is earned by performance. Contract rights, as defined by the regulation, are acquired at the time the contract is made. Finally, inventory is acquired when title is passed to the taxpayer. The regulation considers identifiable proceeds of qualified property to be acquired at the time the qualified property is acquired.

Regulation § 301.6323(c)–1 doesn't address priority in the taxpayer's acquisition of post-notice proceeds arising from the disposition of pre-notice collateral. Such collateral isn't "qualified property." In this circumstance, mentioned above, courts have treated a continuously perfected security interest in proceeds as a security interest "in existence" for purposes of § 6323(h)(1). The continuously perfected security interest in post-notice proceeds has priority over the tax lien under § 6323(a). See, e.g., PPG Industries, Inc. v. Hartford Fire Insurance Co., 531 F.2d 58 (2d Cir.1976). Forced by (h)(1)'s "in existence" restriction, courts taking this position in effect treat post-notice proceeds as "in existence" when the taxpayer acquires the pre-notice collateral.

### PROBLEM

Debtor manufacturers truck trailers. Bank loaned money to Debtor and took a duly perfected security interest in "all items of personal property, wherever situated, including but not limited to: cars, trucks, inventory, accounts receivable, equipment used in connection with manufacturing, tools, finished products, work in progress, now owned or purchased as a replacement, or purchased as new equipment in the future." Later the IRS filed a tax lien against the Debtor in the appropriate place. On the 45th day after the filing of the tax lien Debtor had in its possession some finished and some unfinished truck trailers. After this date it sold some of the finished trailers and took in exchange trade-ins and cash which it segregated in a deposit account. Debtor expended labor and added parts after the 45th day to complete the unfinished trailers. The added parts were acquired by the Debtor after the 45th day. What are the priorities of Bank and the IRS in (1) the deposit account holding the proceeds, (2) the trailers traded-in, and (3) the trailers finished after the 45–day period? See Donald v. Madison Industries, Inc., 483 F.2d 837 (10th Cir.1973).

# CHAPTER 4

# DEFAULT AND ENFORCEMENT

## A. INTRODUCTION

In this Chapter we will see that a secured party has formidable remedies to enforce its security interest against a defaulting debtor under Part 6 of Article 9. It can take possession of tangible collateral such as goods, sell them to satisfy the secured debt and hold the debtor for any deficiency. In the case of rights to payment such as accounts and chattel paper, it can collect directly from the account debtors the amounts they owe the debtor, or sell the rights to payment. Thus, the secured party may deprive the business debtor of assets that it must have to operate its business and the consumer debtor of property essential to her lifestyle. In short, Article 9 allows a secured party to put a defaulting business debtor out of business in most cases and to lower the consumer debtor's standard of living by depriving her of such necessities of contemporary life as automobiles, furniture and appliances. Deficiency judgments allow the creditor to take the consumer debtor's unencumbered property and future earnings, to the extent the property and earnings are nonexempt.

Frequently, both business and consumer debtors when threatened by enforcement action on the part of secured parties turn to bankruptcy for protection. We will examine the impact of bankruptcy on secured transactions in Chapter 9 of the casebook. Suffice it to say at this point that the Bankruptcy Code provides an alternative body of law on the enforcement of secured transactions. Once the debtor files in bankruptcy, all creditor action to enforce a security interest is automatically stayed and brought under the control of the bankruptcy court. No longer is the secured party free to repossess collateral and conduct its own foreclosure sale; it must seek the approval of the court before doing so. In liquidation bankruptcy, the trustee in bankruptcy will sell the debtor's assets and distribute proceeds of the sale to creditors having claims against the estate, with secured claims receiving a priority. When the debtor has no equity in property subject to a secured claim, the bankruptcy court may abandon the property to the debtor and allow the secured party to proceed to foreclose under Article 9 rules. If the debtor is proceeding under Chapter 11 to reorganize a business, under Chapter 12 to adjust the debts of a farm family, or under Chapter 13 to rehabilitate an individual, the secured party may be completely barred from retaking its collateral if the debtor's reorganization or rehabilitation plan calls for payments to be made to the secured party that the court will approve as compensating it for the loss of its right to repossess and foreclose on the collateral. Thus, the debtor's petition in bankruptcy changes the rules of enforcement of security interests drastically.

## B.  DEFAULT

### 1.  MEANING OF DEFAULT

The event that triggers a secured party's rights to enforce its security interest under 9–601(a) is the debtor's default. Article 9 does not define default, leading Professor Gilmore to observe that "default is, within reason, . . . whatever the security agreement says it is." 2 Gilmore, Security Interests in Personal Property § 43.3, at 1193 (1965). Comment 3 to 9–601 observes: "[T]his Article leaves to the agreement of the parties the circumstances giving rise to a default."

The great variety of commercial and consumer transactions falling within Article 9's broad scope yields almost infinite variations in the kinds of events that the security agreement may define as defaults. In all instances agreements make failure to meet required payments a default. Other commonly found events of default are the death, dissolution, insolvency or bankruptcy of the debtor, and the debtor's breach or failure to perform any of the agreements, covenants, representations, or warranties contained in the agreement. See Loan Agreement 9.1 (Events of Default), Appendix I. If the collateral is tangible personal property, the debtor will typically agree to insure the collateral, maintain it in good condition, not remove or transfer the collateral, and not permit its loss, theft, damage, or destruction, or levy, seizure, or attachment. See Loan Agreement 6.5 (Taxes and Premiums), 6.6 (Insurance), and 7 (Negative Covenants), Appendix I. If the collateral is accounts, the debtor may affirm that it owns all accounts free and clear of any claims of others, that the account debtor has accepted delivery of the goods giving rise to the account, and that all accounts are binding obligations of the account debtor. See Loan Agreement 1.21 (Eligible Accounts), Appendix 1. In commercial lending transactions, events of default may include the debtor's failure to maintain net worth or working capital ratios or any other material adverse change in the debtor's financial position. See Loan Agreement 6.11 (Financial Tests), Appendix 1. If the creditor is concerned that its enumeration of specific events of default is not adequate to protect against unforeseen occurrences that might impair the debtor's prospect of payment, it may contract for the right to declare a default whenever it deems itself insecure. See 1–309. The CNB form provides: "Notwithstanding any other provisions of this Agreement, upon the occurrence of any event, action or inaction by Borrower, or if any action or inaction is threatened which CNB reasonably believes will materially affect the value of the Collateral, CNB may take such legal actions as it deems necessary to protect the Collateral, including, but not limited to, seeking injunctive relief and the appointment of a receiver, whether an Event of Default or Potential Event of Default has occurred under this Agreement." Loan Agreement 9.4 (Additional Remedies), Appendix I.

In failing to define default, Article 9 leaves for resolution by agreement the crucial issue of when a creditor may proceed against the collateral. As we have said, in commercial transactions, seizure of the collateral may effectively close the debtor's business. In consumer cases, repossession of the debtor's automobile, furniture, or appliances may alter drastically the debtor's standard of living. In most instances economic considerations restrain creditors from proceeding against collateral as other than a last resort, utilized only after all other collection efforts by way of workout arrangements have failed. Creditors understandably prefer payment from debtors, even though delayed, to the expense of foreclosing on collateral.

In leaving the definition of default to the agreement of the parties, Article 9 assumes that debtors and creditors can look after their own interests. However, the consumer movement of the 1960s and 1970s rejected this assumption in consumer transactions on the ground that there was a disparity in bargaining position between creditors and consumer debtors. For example, § 5.109 of the Uniform Consumer Credit Code (1974) defines default as follows:

An agreement of the parties to a consumer credit transaction with respect to default on the part of the consumer is enforceable only to the extent that:

(1) the consumer fails to make a payment as required by agreement; or

(2) the prospect of payment, performance, or realization of collateral is significantly impaired; the burden of establishing the prospect of significant impairment is on the creditor.

Only a dozen states have adopted the UCCC, either in its original or revised versions. State consumer protection legislation has for the most part not regulated contractual definitions of default.

## 2.   ACCELERATION

### a.   FUNCTION OF ACCELERATION

Since a security interest secures the performance of an obligation, usually to pay money, the extent to which the secured party can resort to the collateral upon default depends on the amount of the obligation. If the debt is payable in installments, the agreement between the creditor and the debtor commonly provides that upon default by the debtor the creditor may accelerate the due date of the debt not yet payable, so that the entire debt becomes immediately payable. Thus, default in one installment payment could lead to acceleration of the entire unpaid debt. But if the debtor is in default on one or more installments and the agreement does not provide for acceleration, the secured party may sell or otherwise dispose of the collateral under 9–610(a) only to the extent of the amount of the overdue installments. General Electric Credit Corp. v. Bankers Commercial Corp., 429 S.W.2d 60 (Ark. 1968). Moreover, in such a case the debtor may redeem the collateral under 9–623 by paying only the amount of the overdue installments plus other amounts required by the statute. If the default is other than a failure to make a payment, there may be no amount then due, absent an acceleration clause. Hence, failure to include an acceleration clause may be very costly to a secured creditor. If, in such a case, the collateral is repossessed and sold before all installments are due, the proceeds of sale can be applied to satisfy only the amount of the installments then due, and the surplus must be returned to the debtor. See 9–615(a)(2) and (d)(1). Although the secured creditor would retain a security interest in the money returned to the debtor as proceeds of the disposition of the collateral (9–315(a)), the practical difficulty of tracing cash proceeds renders the creditor effectively unsecured after foreclosure. The equally unappealing alternative is for the creditor to wait until all payments are due before repossessing. See the acceleration clause in Loan Agreement 9.3 (CNB's Remedies), Appendix I. It is apparent that omission of an acceleration clause in a loan agreement has malpractice implications if the drafter is a lawyer.

### b. INSECURITY CLAUSES

A commonly litigated issue under former Article 9 concerned acceleration in secured transactions involving insecurity clauses. If a creditor is given the right by agreement to accelerate "at will" or "when it deems itself insecure," 1–309 provides that the creditor "has the power to do so only if that party in good faith believes that the prospect of payment or performance is impaired." The burden of establishing the creditor's lack of good faith is imposed on the debtor. Section 1–201(b)(20) defines "good faith" as "honesty in fact and the observance of reasonable commercial standards of fair dealing."

The Comment to 1–309 cautions: "This section is intended to make clear that despite language that might be so construed and which further might be held to make the agreement void as against public policy or to make the contract illusory or too indefinite for enforcement, the option is to be exercised only in the good faith belief that the prospect of payment or performance is impaired." Given the potentially disastrous consequences to the business debtor of having its debt accelerated and its collateral seized, the need for barring arbitrary action on the part of the creditor in making the crucial acceleration decision is great. Much turns on the meaning of "good faith."

Former 1–201(19) defined good faith merely as "honesty in fact." Pre–Revision case law divided on whether this definition posed solely a subjective test or whether some degree of objectivity could be read into the definition. The principal drafter encouraged an objective interpretation: "The creditor has the right to accelerate if, under all the circumstances, a reasonable man, motivated by good faith, would have done so." 2 Grant Gilmore, Security Interests in Personal Property § 43.4, at 1197 (1965). A number of courts declined to read former 1–201(19) and 1–208 as they were written and injected some degree of objectivity into the meaning of good faith, but others purported to apply a subjective meaning.

Reading the decisions taking both views, one is struck by the difficulty of saying with any certainty whether the results in any of these cases would have changed whether a subjective or objective definition of good faith were employed. Farmers Co-op. Elevator, Inc., Duncombe v. State Bank, 236 N.W.2d 674 (Iowa 1975), is a leading case for the subjective standard of good faith. In that case the bank decided to accelerate the debtor's secured loan on the basis of an insecurity clause and to set off against the debtor's deposit account. The court strongly rejected the debtor's contention that the bank should be held to a standard of reasonableness. But, in showing that the bank had acted honestly, the court listed enough factors to lead one to believe that the bank had acted quite reasonably as well.

The commercial law establishment that shaped the UCC in the late 1940s probably intended in drafting former 1–201(19) and 1–208 that creditors acting under insecurity clauses should be granted much leeway so long as they acted honestly. See Robert Braucher, The Legislative History of the Uniform Commercial Code, 58 Colum.L.Rev. 798, 812–813 (1958). Several decades later, however, ideas about creditor responsibility to deal fairly with debtors have changed. The redefinition of "good faith" in 1–201(b)(20) as meaning not only "honesty in fact" but also "the observance of reasonable commercial standards of fair dealing," takes an important step toward an appropriate solution to the issue of the latitude granted creditors under insecurity clauses. The fair-dealing prong of the definition should preclude creditors from whimsical or capricious use of insecurity clauses.

## 3.   LENDER LIABILITY

We have seen that acceleration of the balance due on the loan, allowing a secured creditor repossess, can spell disaster for a debtor. Sometimes a creditor can have the same effect by refusing to make a further advance of credit vital to the debtor's business. If default is what the security agreement says it is, and if, as is commonly the case, the creditor writes the security agreement, what safeguards does the law offer debtors who believe that they are being taken advantage of by secured parties? One might conclude that an important strand in the fabric of debtor-creditor law over the years has been the creation by courts of various doctrines designed to make creditors treat debtors fairly: good faith, fair dealing, material breach, waiver, estoppel, and the like. In the latter third of the 20th century, debtor representatives were so successful in persuading courts to adopt these doctrines in various hardship cases that a body of law called "lender liability" grew. The common issue in these cases was challenge by debtors of conduct by creditors that was, arguably, authorized by the contract of the parties. The expansion of punitive damages during this period played a major role in inducing lawyers to represent debtors in these case.

In the following case and notes we briefly discuss some of the legal doctrines utilized by debtors in lender liability cases. The following case is considered by some to be the high-water mark of the judicial enforcement of the implied covenant of good faith and fair dealing.

# K.M.C. Co. v. Irving Trust Company

United States Court of Appeals, Sixth Circuit, 1985.
757 F.2d 752.

■ CORNELIA G. KENNEDY, CIRCUIT JUDGE.

Irving Trust Company (Irving) appeals from a judgment entered against it in this diversity action for breach of a financing agreement. K.M.C. is a Tennessee corporation headquartered in Knoxville and engaged in the wholesale and retail grocery business. In 1979, Irving and K.M.C. entered into a financing agreement, whereby Irving held a security interest in all of K.M.C.'s accounts receivable and inventory and provided K.M.C. a line of credit to a maximum of $3.0 million, increased one year later to $3.5 million at a lower rate of interest, subject to a formula based on a percentage of the value of the inventory plus eligible receivables. On March 1, 1982, Irving refused to advance $800,000 requested by K.M.C. This amount would have increased the loan balance to just under the $3.5 million limit. K.M.C. contends that Irving's refusal without prior notice to advance the requested funds breached a duty of good faith performance implied in the agreement and ultimately resulted in the collapse of the company as a viable business entity. Irving's defense is that on March 1, 1982, K.M.C. was already collapsing, and that Irving's decision not to advance funds was made in good faith and in the reasonable exercise of its discretion under the agreement.

Trial was conducted by a Magistrate on consent of the parties pursuant to 28 U.S.C. § 636(c). Although the financing agreement contained a jury trial waiver clause, the Magistrate ordered a jury trial over defendant's objection. He based his decision upon the statement of plaintiff's president Leonard Butler, that Butler was told by a representative of Irving prior to signing the agreement that absent fraud, which was not present in the instant case, the waiver provision would not be enforced. The jury found Irving liable for breach of contract and fixed damages at $7,500,000 plus pre-judgment interest. Defendant's motions to dismiss and for a directed verdict and post-trial motions for judgment n.o.v., a new trial or a remittitur were denied.

Irving has raised several issues on appeal. * * * Third, it argues that it did not in fact breach the financing agreement with K.M.C., and that the jury's verdict is not supportable in law and is contrary to the weight of the evidence. * * *

* * *

Irving contends that the Magistrate erred in instructing the jury with respect to its obligations under the financing agreement, that K.M.C. failed to sustain its burden of showing that Irving acted in bad faith and that the jury's verdict was against the weight of the evidence. We conclude that the jury instructions were not in error and that the jury's verdict was supported by substantial evidence.

## A. INSTRUCTIONS

The essence of the Magistrate's instruction to the jury was that there is implied in every contract an obligation of good faith; that this obligation may have imposed on Irving a duty to give notice to K.M.C. before refusing to advance funds under the agreement up to the $3.5 million limit; and that such notice would be required if necessary to the proper execution of the contract, unless Irving's decision to refuse to advance funds without prior notice was made in good faith and in the reasonable exercise of its discretion. Irving contends that the instruction with respect to notice gave undue emphasis to K.M.C.'s theory of the case and was an erroneous explanation of its contractual obligations, in that the decision whether to advance funds under the financing agreement was solely within the bank's prerogative. It reasons further that an implied requirement that the bank provide a period of notice before discontinuing financing up to the maximum credit limit would be inconsistent with the provision in the agreement that all monies loaned are repayable on demand.

As part of the procedure established for the operation of the financing agreement, the parties agreed in a supplementary letter that all receipts of K.M.C. would be deposited into a "blocked account" to which Irving would have sole access. Consequently, unless K.M.C. obtained alternative financing, a refusal by Irving to advance funds would leave K.M.C. without operating capital until it had paid down its loan. The record clearly established that a medium-sized company in the wholesale grocery business, such as K.M.C., could not operate without outside financing. Thus, the literal interpretation of the financing agreement urged upon us by Irving, as supplemented by the "blocked account" mechanism, would leave K.M.C.'s continued existence entirely at the whim or mercy of Irving, absent an obligation of good faith performance. Logically, at such time as Irving might wish to curtail financing K.M.C., as was its right under the agreement, this obligation to act in good faith would require a period of notice to K.M.C. to allow it a reasonable opportunity to seek alternate financing, absent valid business reasons precluding Irving from doing so. Hence, we find that the Magistrate's instructions were an accurate statement of the applicable law. * * *

* * *

Nor are we persuaded by Irving's reasoning with respect to the effect of the demand provision in the agreement. We agree with the Magistrate that just as Irving's discretion whether or not to advance funds is limited by an obligation of good faith performance, so too would be its power to demand repayment. The demand provision is a kind of acceleration clause, upon which the Uniform Commercial Code and the courts have imposed limitations of reasonableness and fairness. See § 1–208; Brown v. AVEM-

CO Investment Corp., 603 F.2d 1367, 1375–80 (9th Cir.1979). The Magistrate did not err in refusing the requested charge on the demand provision.

\* \* \*

## B.  SUFFICIENCY OF THE EVIDENCE

\* \* \*

Irving contends that the sole factor determinative of whether it acted in good faith is whether it, through its loan officer Sarokin, *believed* that there existed valid reasons for not advancing funds to K.M.C. on March 1, 1982. It quotes Blaine v. G.M.A.C., 82 Misc.2d 653, 655, 370 N.Y.S.2d 323, 327 (1975), for the proposition that under applicable New York law, it is the bank's "actual mental state" that is decisive. The Magistrate observed that there was competent evidence that a personality conflict had developed between Sarokin and Butler of K.M.C. He suggested that the jury may have concluded that Sarokin abused his discretion in refusing without notice to advance funds despite knowing that he was fully secured because of his disapproval of Butler's management philosophy.

Were the outcome of this case solely dependent upon Sarokin's *subjective* state of mind, we might feel constrained, despite the conclusions of the Magistrate above, to hold that the evidence was insufficient to support the verdict.[11] However, to a certain extent the conduct of Irving must be measured by objective standards. While it is not necessary that Sarokin have been correct in his understanding of the facts and circumstances pertinent to his decision not to advance funds for this court to find that he made a valid business judgment in doing so, there must at least be *some* objective basis upon which a reasonable loan officer in the exercise of his discretion would have acted in that manner. The court in *Blaine* did state that

> [t]he test as to the good faith of the creditor in accelerating under an insecurity clause is a matter of the creditor's actual mental state and this is not negatived by showing there was no basis for the creditor's belief, Sheppard Federal Credit Union v. Palmer [408 F.2d 1369 (5th Cir.1969)], supra, and it is immaterial whether the information upon which the creditor based his determination was in fact not true or the creditor was negligent in not examining to determine whether it was true. Van Horn v. Van De Wol, Inc., 6 Wash.App. 959, 497 P.2d 252 (1972).

370 N.Y.S.2d at 327 (emphasis added). However, this definition followed the court's statement that "[t]he criterion for permissible acceleration . . . has the *dual* elements of (1) *whether a reasonable man would have accelerated the debt under the circumstances,* and (2) whether the creditor acted in good faith." Id. (emphasis added) (citation omitted). There is

---

**11.** We do not understand the Magistrate to have relied upon this point alone. Rather, as we read his opinion, the alleged personality conflict between Butler and Sarokin was cited as just one of several relevant factors that may have persuaded the jury.

ample evidence in the record to support a jury finding that no reasonable loan officer in the same situation would have refused to advance funds to K.M.C. without notice as Sarokin did on March 1, 1982.

\* \* \*

In fact, counsel for Irving conceded in his summation to the jury that the bank was adequately secured on March 1, 1982. He argued, however, that what is important is not the amount of security, but the capacity of the debtor to pay back the loan. The jury was entitled to find that a reasonable notice period would not change the ability of K.M.C. to pay the loan. The nature of the security was such that the loan would rapidly be paid down on demand. Irving's quarterly audits and other memoranda regarding K.M.C. consistently stated that the strength of its position was in the inventory, which was readily marketable. As late as two months before the events in question, the quarterly audit had concluded that even in the event of a liquidation of the company no loss would be sustained by Irving.

Generally, there was ample evidence in the record from which the jury could have concluded that March 1 simply was not that unusual a day in the history of the relationship between Irving and K.M.C. Such factors as payables and receivables, cited by Sarokin as the basis for his conclusion that K.M.C. was in a state of financial collapse, were closely monitored by Irving. Moreover, three days later, on March 4, Sarokin agreed to advance $700,000 to K.M.C., increasing its outstanding balance to $3.3 million. While the evidence was in conflict whether K.M.C.'s overall financial condition was deteriorating or improving, there is ample evidence belying Irving's characterization that on March 1, Sarokin was faced with a sudden crisis of unprecedented proportions. On this basis alone, the jury could have found that Irving did not fulfill its obligation of good faith performance to K.M.C. when it cut off financing without prior notice.

\* \* \*

Finally, Irving contends that even if a period of notice were required, it would be unreasonable to impose upon it an obligation to continue financing K.M.C. for the length of time that would have been necessary to arrange alternative financing or a sale of the company. If Irving had given K.M.C. 30 days, 7 days, even 48 hours notice, we would be facing a different case.[13] However, no notice was given. Until Sarokin told Butler on the phone the afternoon of March 1 that the $800,000 requested would not be advanced, not even Calloway of the Park Bank or Lipson, who had been sent down to Knoxville by Sarokin the previous Friday to gather information, both of whom lunched with Butler immediately before the call to New York, had any inkling that Sarokin might act as he did. Based upon the reasoning above, whether alternative financing could have been found or a

---

**13.** If during that period a tentative commitment was made with respect to a sale or alternative financing, since either of those once completed would result in the immediate repayment of Irving's loan, it might well be that it would be arbitrary and capricious for Irving to terminate financing at the expiration of the notice period if that period was insufficient to permit completion of the contemplated transaction.

sale arranged is pertinent to causation rather than whether Sarokin acted reasonably and in good faith, and there was ample evidence in the record from which the jury could find that either would have been possible.

\* \* \*

The judgment is affirmed.

## PROBLEM

*KMC* became a famous case. The $7.5 million, plus interest, judgment handed down in *KMC* caught the attention of bank lawyers all over the country. ABA institutes on lender liability became popular. Where does this opinion leave banks in Irving's position that have concluded that they do not wish to make further optional advances to a sinking debtor? Must they "throw good money after bad"?

## NOTES

**1.** A spate of lender liability suits in the 1980s and 90s involved alleged promises by lenders to continue financing debtors; when debtors began to fail, lenders denied that any such undertakings had been made and debtors sued. A significant factor in the popularity of lender liability cases of the 1980s and 90s was the success of debtors in imposing punitive damages on lenders. The barrier was that ordinarily punitive damages are not appropriate in breach of contract cases. Nonetheless a number of cases found sufficient tortious conduct on the part of lenders to justify punitive damages. Other cases found punitive damages inappropriate.

In Walker v. First Commercial Bank, noted in 8 Bank. L. Rep. (BNA) 287 (Ark. Cir. Ct. Mar. 13, 1996), an Arkansas state court jury awarded debtors $12.5 million in compensatory damages and $10 million in punitive damages in their suit against a bank that allegedly drove the debtors out of business by refusing to honor a pledge to provide long-term financing. The debtors contended that the bank tortuously interfered with their business and engaged in fraud and deceit by promising long-term financing and not providing it. The trial consumed five and one-half weeks, and the jury deliberated only three hours in handing down the largest jury award in Arkansas history. The case was eventually reversed, First Commercial Bank v. Walker, 969 S.W.2d 146 (Ark. 1998). California lenders were so disturbed by such suits that they secured passage of an amendment to the Statute of Frauds, Cal. Civ. Code § 1624(a)(7), making contracts to grant credit for business purposes in amounts greater than $100,000 invalid unless in writing.

**2.** In Brown v. AVEMCO Investment Corp., cited in *KMC*, the debtor breached a clause in the agreement expressly prohibiting lease of the collateral without the secured party's consent. This was clearly a default under the contract, but the Ninth Circuit held the secured party's acceleration and repossession to be wrongful because there was no basis for a belief on the part of the secured party that its prospect of payment was impaired. The court relied on former 1–208 (now 1–309) even though the secured party was relying on a clear breach of a specific provision of the agreement and not on an "insecurity" or "at will" clause. *Brown* has been rejected on the reach of former 1–208 by Greenberg v. Service Business Forms Industries, Inc., 882 F.2d 1538 (10th Cir.1989), but debtors have found other sources of law to safeguard them from what they conceive to be improper acts of acceleration and repossession by creditors. Section 1–304 imposes an obligation of good faith in the performance or enforcement of every contract within the UCC. Moreover, Restatement of Contracts (Second) § 205 (1981) provides that every contract imposes upon each party a duty of good faith and fair dealing in its performance and enforcement. Section 9–102(a)(43) defines "good faith" as including "observance of reasonable commercial standards of fair dealing."

**3.**   Lender liability cases are highly fact-sensitive, and in this Note we summarize the facts of two of the cases in which debtors prevailed on the issue. In both cases the debtors were awarded damages from creditors for economic harm for action apparently permitted by the contract between the parties but which was deemed to be arbitrary and unfair to the debtor and thus in violation of former 1–203. In Alaska Statebank v. Fairco, 674 P.2d 288 (Alaska 1983), a toy store was in default on its debt to a bank. After negotiations were entered into for a workout, the bank without notice seized its collateral, the inventory of the store, and refused to honor the debtor's checks. The debtor was allowed to reopen its business only by agreeing to terms it had previously rejected. Alleging that the bank had breached its duty of good faith under former 1–203 in closing the store in order to coerce the debtor into putting up additional security, the debtor sued for wrongful repossession and dishonor of checks. Although the debtor was clearly in default when the bank acted, the trial court, sitting without a jury, held for the debtor on the ground that the existence of negotiations between the parties modified the written agreement so as to require the bank to give notice to the debtor before closing its business and dishonoring its checks. Punitive damages were awarded. The Supreme Court of Alaska affirmed.

A similar view was expressed in Duffield v. First Interstate Bank, 13 F.3d 1403 (10th Cir.1993). In that case Bank lent Debtor $2 million secured by Debtor's interest in oil and gas wells. When Debtor got behind in his payments, Bank agreed that Debtor could sell a portion of the collateral and apply the proceeds to the debt, but, according to Bank, the proceeds of the sale were not enough to cure the default. Hence, Bank exercised its rights under the security agreement to direct the operators of Debtor's wells to make their payments to Bank rather than to Debtor. This action put Debtor out of business, and he eventually lost all his oil and gas interests. The court approved a jury verdict of $6 million for Debtor on the ground that Bank breached its covenant of good faith and fair dealing. Although under the contract, upon Debtor's default, Bank had the discretion to direct the operators to make their payments to Bank, Debtor's legitimate expectation was that Bank would take this action only on reasonable belief that Debtor was in default and after giving Debtor an opportunity to cure the default. In such a case the implied covenant of good faith and fair dealing protects Debtor from an unexpected and unwarranted use of this discretionary right on the part of Bank. The court rejected Bank's contention that the doctrine of good faith and fair dealing applies only to ambiguous terms of the contract and held that it applies "in all situations—including when a contract's express terms do not limit either party's right to act unreasonably." 13 F.3d at 1405.

**4.** Quite a different view of the role of good faith in lender liability cases is presented in Kham & Nate's Shoes No. 2, Inc. v. First Bank, 908 F.2d 1351 (7th Cir.1990). Bank gave Debtor a $300,000 line of credit reserving the right to cancel at its discretion. After Bank had advanced $75,000 it refused to advance more funds and Debtor failed. The lower court held Bank's refusal was inequitable conduct and justified equitable subordination of its claim in bankruptcy. In reversing the lower court, Judge Easterbrook, speaking for the court, said:

> Firms that have negotiated contracts are entitled to enforce them to the letter, even to the great discomfort of their trading partners, without being mulcted for lack of "good faith." Although courts often refer to the obligation of good faith that exists in every contractual relation, e.g., UCC § 1–203; Jordan v. Duff & Phelps, Inc., 815 F.2d 429, 438 (7th Cir.1987), this is not an invitation to the court to decide whether one party ought to have exercised privileges expressly reserved in the document. "Good faith" is a compact reference to an implied undertaking not to take opportunistic advantage in a way that could not have been contemplated at the time of drafting, and which therefore was not resolved explicitly by the parties. When the contract is silent, principles of good faith—such as the UCC's standard of honesty in fact, UCC § 1–201(19), and the reasonable expectations of the trade, UCC § 2–103(b) (a principle applicable, however, only to "merchants", which Bank is not)—fill the gap. They do not block use of terms that actually appear in the contract.

> We do not doubt the force of the proverb that the letter killeth, while the spirit giveth life. Literal implementation of unadorned language may destroy the essence of the venture. Few people pass out of childhood without learning fables about genies, whose wickedly literal interpretation of their "masters' " wishes always leads to calamity. Yet knowledge that literal enforcement means some mismatch between the parties' expectation and the outcome does not imply a general duty of "kindness" in performance, or of judicial oversight into whether a party had "good cause" to act as it did. Parties to a contract are not each others' fiduciaries; they are not bound to treat customers with the same consideration reserved for their families. Any attempt to add an overlay of "just cause"—as the bankruptcy judge effectively did—to the exercise of contractual privileges would reduce commercial certainty and breed costly litigation. The UCC's requirement of "honesty in fact" stops well short of the requirements the bankruptcy judge

thought incident to contractual performance. "[I]n commercial trans-actions it does not in the end promote justice to seek strained interpretations in aid of those who do not protect themselves." James Baird Co. v. Gimbel Bros., 64 F.2d 344, 346 (2d Cir.1933) (L. Hand, J.). 908 F.2d at 1357.

The Comment to 1–304 responds to concerns about the role of good faith under Article 9: "This section does not support an independent cause of action for failure to perform or enforce good faith.... [T]he doctrine of good faith merely directs a court towards interpreting contracts within the commercial context in which they are created, performed, and enforced, and does not create a separate duty of fairness and reasonableness which can be independently breached."

**5.** Lender liability cases present two common issues: whether the source of the obligation of good faith is contractual or extra-contractual, and the operative standard of good faith. Daniel Fischel summarizes the difficulty of defining a workable standard of good faith: "[N]otwithstanding the extensive literature on the subject, no consensus exists on precisely the duty of good faith means. At one extreme, commentators have argued that the duty should be limited to a prohibition of intentional dishonesty. Under this view, the duty of good faith adds little to the prohibition against fraud other than a vague exhortation for moral behavior. At the other extreme, several commentators have concluded that good faith should be interpreted expansively to incorporate community standards of fairness and decency. The obvious difficulty with this position is the lack of any accepted understanding of the meaning of these terms. Moreover, this lack of content creates an added risk that the fairness and decency standard will be applied arbitrarily to the detriment of lenders and borrowers alike." Daniel R. Fischel, The Economics of Lender Liability, 99 Yale L. J. 131, 140–41 (1989) (references omitted).

**6.** Does the obligation of good faith under 1–309 limit a creditor's right to call a loan if the promissory note is "payable on demand"? Not according to the Comment to that section: "Obviously this section has no application to demand instruments or obligations whose very nature permits call at any time with or without reason." In Centerre Bank v. Distributors, Inc., 705 S.W.2d 42 (Mo.App.1985), the court rejected the debtor's contention that former 1–203 limited the creditor's discretion in calling the note:

> The imposition of a good faith defense to the call for payment of a demand note transcends the performance or enforcement of a contract and in fact adds a term to the agreement which the parties had not included. The additional term would be that the note is not payable at any time demand is made but only payable when demand is made if such demand is made in good faith. The parties by the demand note did not agree that payment would be made only when demand was made in good faith but agreed that payment would be made whenever demand was made. Thus [former] 1–203 has no application because it does not relate to the performance or enforcement of any right under

the demand note but in fact would add an additional term which the parties did not agree to.

This court is not willing to rewrite the agreement which Distributors made that the demand note which it executed could be called for payment at any time by adding a provision that payment could only be demanded in good faith.

705 S.W.2d at 48. Larson v. Vermillion State Bank, 567 N.W.2d 721 (Minn.App.1997), agrees with *Centerre*. However, in Reid v. Key Bank of Southern Maine, Inc., 821 F.2d 9 (1st Cir.1987), the court, faced with what appeared to be an unambiguous demand clause, invoked the good faith doctrine to limit the creditor's discretion in calling the loan because other terms of the contract indicated that the parties did not intend a true demand note. *Reid* is disapproved in PEB Commentary No. 10.

## 4.   WAIVER AND ESTOPPEL

A secured party's enforcement remedies arise only after the debtor's default. But what if the secured party has not insisted on the debtor's compliance with the terms of the agreement? The secured party's conduct can be interpreted in two ways, both adverse to it. One interpretation is that the debtor's actions were part of a course of dealing, understood under 1–303 as an element of the parties' agreement. 1–303(a), (d). As part of a course of dealing, the debtor's actions don't constitute a default. The other, more plausible interpretation is that the secured party's conduct constitutes waiver of the debtor's default. Litigation on the waiver issue has flourished, and secured parties have attempted to deal with the problem by including nonwaiver clauses in the agreement like the one quoted in the case below. Comment 3 to 9–601 states that Article 9 takes no position on the kind of conduct that constitutes waiver or the effect of nonwaiver clauses. Hence, pre-Revision case law is still good precedent. The following case is a good example of trend of authority on this issue.

## Moe v. John Deere Company

Supreme Court of South Dakota, 1994.
516 N.W.2d 332.

■ MOSES, CIRCUIT JUDGE.

This is an appeal by Ted Moe (Moe) from a summary judgment granted by Third Judicial Circuit Court in favor of John Deere Company (Deere) and Day County Implement Company (Implement). We reverse.

### FACTS

On September 29, 1983, Moe bought a farm tractor from Day County Equipment in Watertown, South Dakota. He purchased a John Deere D8850 for a cash price of $121,268. In financing the transaction, Moe traded in two old tractors for the amount of $77,543 and agreed to pay the $59,802 difference in five equal installments of $11,960 each due on

October 1st for the years 1984, 1985, 1986, 1987 and 1988. After the contract was completed it was assigned to Deere on September 30, 1983.

Moe was two months late in paying his first installment. Rather than paying $11,960 on October 1, 1984, Moe paid $12,212 on December 3, 1984. On October 1, 1985, Moe was again unable to timely pay his second installment. Deere waived full payment and extended the time in which Moe was to make this payment. On January 13, 1986, Moe made a partial payment in the amount of $6,200, over three months late. Moe and Deere agreed that Moe was to pay a second amount on March 1, 1986 in the amount of $6,350 to complete the second installment. On March 10, 1986, Deere sent a notice to Moe indicating that Moe's second installment was past due and that he had until March 20, 1986 to pay $6,389 to bring his account current. Again Moe missed this payment deadline.

Deere did not follow up on the delinquent payment until a representative from Deere contacted Moe sometime in May or the first part of June 1986, over seven months after the second installment was originally due. Deere's representative and Moe agreed that Moe would pay $2,000 of the $6,389 plus interest owing to Deere and Deere would allow Moe to pay the balance when he started to harvest. Deere's representative and Moe failed to specify the due date for either the $2,000 payment or when the balance was due. Moe had no further conversations with the representative from Deere about the $2,000 until after Deere repossessed the tractor on July 30, 1986.

Moe, who was in Oklahoma at the time of repossession, did not receive any notice from Deere's representative that the tractor was going to be repossessed because his payments were delinquent. Deere reassigned Moe's contract to Implement following the repossession. On August 1, 1986, Deere mailed from Minneapolis, Minnesota a certified letter dated July 31, 1986 to Moe which indicated that Deere "[found] it necessary to gain possession of the equipment involved." This letter apparently was returned to Deere undelivered to Moe. Thus, Deere hand-addressed a new letter and sent it to Moe who picked it up on August 18, 1986. The letter indicated:

> We intend to reassign your contract to the above named dealer. Once we reassign it, two weeks from the date of this letter, you will contact them on all matters concerning the disposition of the equipment or the amount owed under the contract. They intend to dispose of said collateral by public or private sale. If you wish to redeem this equipment, you must pay to John Deere Company $37,591 plus any expenses incurred from this repossession, in cash certified funds, before we reassign the contract.

> We hope you will be able to pay this amount within the prescribed period. If you have any questions regarding this matter please contact us. M.K. Mehus, Manager Financial Services.

Implement sold the tractor on August 19, 1986 for $44,000. Implement paid Deere in full on the contract and applied the proceeds to the debt and turned over the excess proceeds to Moe's lender by mailing two (2) checks totaling $2,616 to the Farmers and Merchants Bank on December 1, 1986.

Moe sued Deere and Implement on the following causes of action: (1) wrongful repossession; (2) fraudulent repossession; (3) commercially unreasonable sale; and (4) failure to account for the surplus.

Deere moved for partial summary judgment on the third and fourth issues of commercially unreasonable sale and failure to account for surplus. The trial court granted Deere's motion. Then, Deere moved for summary judgment on the first and second issues of wrongful repossession and fraudulent repossession. On February 5, 1993, the trial court issued an order granting Deere's summary judgment motion on both issues. Moe appeals.

\* \* \*

ISSUE

\* \* \*

We recognized in First Nat. Bank of Black Hills v. Beug, 400 N.W.2d 893, 896 (S.D.1987), that "[t]he term 'default' is not defined in the Uniform Commercial Code, thus we must look to other sources for a definition." Id. at 895. Then, we turned to hornbook law for a definition of default:

> "Default" triggers the secured creditor's rights under Part Five of Article Nine. But what is "default?" Article Nine does not define the word; instead it leaves this to the parties and to any scraps of common law lying around. Apart from the modest limitations imposed by the unconscionability doctrine and the requirement of good faith, default is "whatever the security agreement says it is."

Id. at 896 (quoting J. White & R. Summers, Uniform Commercial Code § 26–22 at 1085–86 (2d ed. 1980)).

\* \* \*

Here, the promissory note provided a definition of default:

> The borrower shall be in default upon the occurrence of any one or more of the following events: (1) the Borrower shall fail to pay, when due, any amount required hereunder, or any other indebtedness of the borrower to the Lender of any third parties; (2) the Borrower shall be in default in the performance of any covenant or obligation under the line of credit or equivalent agreement for future advances (if applicable) or any document or agreement related thereto; (3) any warranty or representation made by the Borrower shall prove false or misleading in any respect; (4) the Borrower or any Guarantor of this promissory note shall liquidate, merge dissolve, terminate its existence, suspend business operations, die (if individual), have a receiver appointed for all or any part of its property, make an assignment for the benefit of creditors, or file or have filed against it any petition under any existing

or future bankruptcy or insolvency law; (5) any change that occurs in the condition or affairs (financial or otherwise) of the Borrower or any Guarantor of this promissory note which, in the opinion of the Lender, impairs, the Lender's security or increases its risk with respect to this promissory note or (6) an event of default shall occur under any agreements intended to secure the repayment of this promissory note. Unless prohibited by law, the Lender may, at its option, declare the entire unpaid balance of principal and interest immediately due and payable without notice or demand at any time after default as such term is defined in this paragraph.

Technically, there was a breach of the security agreement and the promissory note when Moe did not make his payment on October 1, 1984, but instead paid it on December 3, 1984. One could find Moe in default, and under § 9–503, Deere would have had a right to repossess the tractor. However, Deere's right to a default or remedies under breach of contract can be modified or waived by the conduct of the parties.

The trial court's memorandum opinion indicated that "The terms of the written contract should control. Further the 'course of dealing' between the parties is not persuasive." However, here there is a question of fact. Did the oral statements and conduct of the parties modify the written agreement? In Alaska Statebank v. Fairco, 674 P.2d 288 (Alaska 1983), the issue was if the parties' oral statements and conduct between September 15, 1978 and November 6, 1978 modified the written agreement so that pre-possession notice was required. The court held:

> [M]odification of a written contract may be effected either through subsequent conduct or oral agreements. Whether a modification has occurred is a question of fact. The superior court found that the parties had agreed to such modification, "[g]iven the course of dealings between the parties...."

Id. at 292 (quoting Nat. Bank of Alaska v. J.B.L. & K. of Alaska, Inc., 546 P.2d 579, 586–87 (Alaska 1976)). * * *

The record reveals through affidavits and depositions that the oral statements and conduct of the parties herein between October 1, 1984 and July 30, 1986 appear to modify the written agreement. Deere sent notice to Moe that he had until March 20, 1986 to pay $6,389 including late charges. Moe admits that in May or the first week of June 1986 he agreed to pay the March installment in two parts. He agreed to pay $2,000 with the balance due in August 1986 when he commenced his wheat harvest. There was no date certain by which Moe was to pay the $2,000. In determining if there was a default on the part of Moe in complying with this contract, all statements and conduct of the parties are essential in determining whether there was an oral modification or waiver of the promissory note or security agreement by John Deere.

* * *

The second issue that needs to be addressed is whether the "non-waiver clause" is enforceable in this contract. Deere's brief refers to this clause as an "anti-waiver" clause but we will refer to it as a "non-waiver" clause. See Lewis v. National City Bank, 814 F.Supp. 696, 699 (N.D.Ill. 1993) (referring to the clause dealing with waiver provisions as a "non-waiver" clause). The security agreement between Moe and Deere contained the following provisions:

> In the event of default (as defined on the reverse side hereof), holder may take possession of the Goods and exercise any other remedies provided by law.

> This contract shall be in default if I (we) shall fail to pay any installment when due....

> In any such event (default) the holder may immediately and without notice declare the entire balance of this contract due and payable together with reasonable expenses incurred in realizing on the security interest granted hereunder, including reasonable attorney's fees.

> Waiver or condonation of any breach or default shall not constitute a waiver of any other or subsequent breach or default.

> We now turn to other jurisdictions' interpretations of the "non-waiver" clause.

Courts have adopted two basic rules for interpreting situations where repeated late payments have been accepted by a creditor who has the contractual (i.e., "non-waiver" clauses) and the statutory right (i.e., § 9–503) to repossess the collateral without notice. Some courts have held that the acceptance of late payments does not waive or otherwise affect the right of a creditor to repossess without notice after subsequent late payment defaults. * * * Other courts have imposed a duty on the creditor to notify the debtor that strict compliance with the time for payment will be required in the future or else the contract remedies may be invoked. * * * See also 2 J. White & R. Summers, Uniform Commercial Code, § 27–2 at 563–65 (3d ed. 1988).

Deere urges us to adopt the position that the acceptance of late payments does not waive or otherwise affect the right of a creditor to repossess without notice after subsequent late payment defaults stating to do so would mean that the "non-waiver" clause is a nullity.

A majority of states who have considered the issue adhere to the general rule that "a secured party who has not insisted upon strict compliance in the past, who has accepted late payments as a matter of course, *must*, before he may validly rely upon such a clause to declare a default and effect repossession, *give notice* to the debtor ... that strict compliance with the terms of the contract will be demanded henceforth if repossession is to be avoided." [Nevada National Bank v.] Huff, 582 P.2d 364, 369 [Nev.1978] (citations omitted) (emphasis in original).

The basis for imposing this duty on the secured party is that the secured party is estopped from asserting his contract rights because his conduct has induced the debtor's justified reliance in believing that late payments were acceptable. § 1–103 preserves the law of estoppel. The acts which induced reliance are the repeated acceptance of late payments. The reliance is evidenced by the continual pattern of irregular and late payments.

The debtor has the right to rely on the continuation of the course of performance and that right to rely is sufficient to satisfy the reliance element. See Ford Motor Credit Co. v. Waters, 273 So.2d 96 (Fla.App.1973). This right to rely is supported by the policy of the Uniform Commercial Code which encourages the continual development of "commercial practices through, custom, usage, and agreement between the parties." See § 1–102(2). South Dakota's adaptation of the Uniform Commercial Code is found in Title 57A of the South Dakota Code. The purpose of Title 57A is found in § 1–102 and states in pertinent part as follows:

(1) This title shall be liberally construed and applied to promote its underlying purposes and polices.

(2) Underlying purposes and polices of this title are

(a) To simplify, clarify and modernize the law governing commercial transactions;

(b) To permit the continued expansion of commercial practices, through custom, usage and agreement of the parties;

§ 1–102(1)B(2). The Uniform Commercial Code should be liberally construed and applied to promote its underlying purposes and policies. First Nat. Bank v. John Deere Co., 409 N.W.2d 664 (S.D.1987).

Adopting the rule that a creditor must give pre-possession notice upon modification of a contract results in both the debtor and the creditor being protected. The debtor would be protected from surprise and from a damaging repossession by being forewarned that late payments would no longer be acceptable. Likewise, the creditor would be protected utilizing the device of "one letter." The creditor can totally preserve his remedies so that if the account continues in default, repossession could be pursued as provided in the contract without further demand or notice. It is recognized that this rule does place the creditor in a slightly worse position because if a creditor sends out a letter to preserve his rights and then once again accepts late payments another notice would be required. The second notice would be required because the acceptance of the late payment after the initial letter could again act as a waiver of the rights asserted in the letter.

We hold that the repeated acceptance of late payments by a creditor who has the contractual right to repossess the property imposes a duty on the creditor to notify the debtor that strict compliance with the contract terms will be required before the creditor can lawfully repossess the collateral.

The dispositive issue is if the plaintiff was in default. Whether a default exists is a factual question not properly resolved on a motion for summary judgment. * * * We reverse this order and the judgment of the circuit court and remand for trial.

## NOTES

**1.** In Gaynor v. Union Trust Co., 582 A.2d 190 (1990) (Peters, C.J.), the court enforced a nonwaiver clause in a consumer repossession case. In this case the debtors had repeatedly been late with their payments. In April the secured party warned the debtors by letter that their defaults put them at the risk of repossession. In early July the debtors agreed to make payments of $300 at the beginning of each month to make their account current. They made the July payment but missed the payment due on August 1; the secured party repossessed on August 15. The contract said: "Waiver of Notice. If you do not repay this loan when it becomes due or do not keep your other promises in this agreement, we do not have to make a protest or give you any notice." Another clause said: "Delay in Enforcement. We can delay in enforcing any of our rights without losing them. If on any occasion we should waive one of our rights, it does not necessarily mean that we will waive that right in the future. We will still have that right." In holding for the secured party the court said:

> The essence of the [debtors'] contention is that no creditor should be allowed to invoke formal contractual provisions that a consumer debtor had reason to believe would not be enforced. Whatever the merits of this legal principle might be in the abstract, it cannot prevail in the light of two crucial findings of fact by the trial court in this case. One finding is that the repossession was precipitated by the [secured party's] failure to receive a $300 payment that the [debtors] had expressly agreed to pay on August 1, 1987, in accordance with the work-out plan to make their indebtedness more current. This case therefore cannot be characterized as one in which a creditor without warning retakes goods following its silent acceptance of one or more belated installment payments on the part of the debtor. The second finding is that the [debtors] were not lulled into any misapprehensions about the jeopardy that they faced because of their lateness in making payments. We conclude, accordingly, that the defendant had the contractual authority to repossess the plaintiff's car.

582 A.2d at 196.

**2.** See the nonwaiver clause in Loan Agreement 10.3 (* * * No Waiver), Appendix I.

### PROBLEM

Your creditor client has heard about decisions like *Moe* but she finds it hard to turn down late payments from financially stressed debtors. Something is better than nothing. She asks you to suggest a procedure for dealing with such debtors that will not result in the kind of trouble in which Deere found itself. What is your advice?

## C.  ENFORCEMENT

### 1.  CUMULATIVE REMEDIES

Most overdue debts are collected—if they are collected at all—without litigation through negotiation and settlement. But it is fair to assume that debtors are more amenable to voluntary repayment because of the existence of powerful legal remedies that creditors can inflict on them if they refuse payment. And, increasingly, in an information world the ability of unpaid creditors to stain the credit reputation of debtors by reporting defaults to private credit reporting agencies is a powerful stimulant to voluntary repayment.

If voluntary payments are not forthcoming, Article 9 offers secured parties a broad array of enforcement remedies that are summarized in 9–601. Section 9–601(a)(1) recognizes that the secured party can disregard its in rem rights against its collateral and proceed outside Article 9 to obtain an in personam judgment against the debtor as though the debt were unsecured. ("Debtor" is defined as the person who owns the collateral in 9–102(a)(28); "obligor" is defined as the person who owes the debt in 9–102(a)(59). Since in most cases, the debtor and the obligor are the same person, for ease of communication we will refer to this person as a debtor unless the reference is only to the obligor.) The secured party may sue the debtor on the obligation and obtain a judgment for the amount of the debt, and may collect the judgment by whatever means available under state law: e.g., obtaining a writ of execution on the debtor's nonexempt assets, real or personal, selling the property at a public sale presided over by a judicial officer, and applying the sale proceeds to satisfaction of the judgment. Other common judgment satisfaction remedies are levying on the debtor's deposit accounts and garnishing an individual debtor's wages. If a secured creditor levies on the collateral pursuant to its judgment against the debtor, 9–601(e) provides that the lien of the levy relates back to the earlier of the date of filing or perfection of the security interest. Thus, the secured party enjoys the priority of the first-to-file-or-perfect rule with respect to property that is collateral.

The downside of using judicial process is that court proceedings may be expensive and time-consuming. The upside is that all the debtor's nonexempt property can be levied on, not just the collateral, and the judgment obtained will allow the judgment creditor to sell off the debtor's property piecemeal without further court proceedings until the judgment debt is satisfied, with any deficiency remaining serving as the basis for further executions against the debtor's subsequently obtained property. Foreclosure by judicial sale avoids having to comply with the commercial reasonableness standard applicable to all Article 9 dispositions. Moreover, the judgment creditor can buy at its own judicial sale, as can foreclosing creditors in most nonjudicial dispositions.

In the great majority of cases, secured parties choose to proceed against the collateral by the extra-judicial procedures authorized by Article 9, which are cheap and fast. These procedures fall within two general categories: sale or other disposition of the collateral and collection of rights to payment. The two prototypic cases are: (1) under 9–610 the secured party may make a commercially reasonable sale of collateral consisting of goods at either a public or private sale and, under 9–615, apply the proceeds of the sale to satisfaction of the obligation secured by the security interest, with any surplus going to the debtor; or (2) in the case of a right to payment, such as an account, the secured party may proceed in a commercially reasonable manner under 9–607 to collect the amount owing by notifying the account debtor to make payment to the secured party. In the alternative, instead of disposing of the collateral the secured party may opt to accept the collateral in full or partial satisfaction of the amount owing under 9–620, but only if the debtor consents to the acceptance in the manner prescribed by the statute.

We emphasize that secured parties can proceed to repossess and sell collateral or collect rights to payment without going to court. The secured party, not judicial officers, conducts the sale of property or collects the payments on accounts and other rights to payment. Not until the secured party has established that the debtor is liable for a deficiency does it have to bring a lawsuit in order to obtain a judgment for the amount of the deficiency.

A question that has traditionally arisen in both real and personal property security law is whether a creditor can use both avenues of recovery—money judgment and extra-judicial sale—simultaneously, so long as only one satisfaction is obtained, or whether, once the creditor chooses one track it has, by the doctrine of election of remedies, waived any right to proceed by the other. Courts, and to some extent legislatures, have sometimes reasoned that if a creditor has encumbered a debtor's asset with a security interest, fairness requires that it must proceed first against that asset instead of levying on the debtor's unencumbered assets which are available to satisfy the claims of the debtor's other creditors. Or, if a secured creditor has proceeded by the money judgment route, it waives its security interest in the debtor's assets.

Article 9 addresses this question in 9–601(c): "The rights under subsections (a) and (b) are cumulative and may be exercised simultaneously." Comment 5 states: "Moreover, permitting the simultaneous exercise of remedies under subsection (c) does not override any non-UCC law, including the law of tort and statutes regulating collection of debts, under which the simultaneous exercise of remedies in a particular case constitutes abusive behavior or harassment giving rise to liability."

## PROBLEM

Debtor is in default on a secured loan to SP. The principal collateral is the machinery used in Debtor's shoe repair store. SP proceeded to take possession of the machinery and placed it in a warehouse. This seizure put Debtor out of business. While holding the collateral, SP sued Debtor for the full amount of the indebtedness and obtained a personal judgment against Debtor. SP recorded an abstract of judgment in the county where Debtor's house was located, thus clouding the title to the real property. Finally, SP acted to satisfy its judgment by levying on some personal property of Debtor that was not collateral for SP's loan and proposing to sell the property at a judicial sale. May Debtor stop the judicial sale because of SP's repossession of the collateral? If the sale is not stopped and there is still a balance owing after the sale, may SP proceed to sell the repossessed collateral? The devastated Debtor seeks your advice on his rights in this case. What advice do you offer?

## 2.   REPOSSESSION

### a.   SELF–HELP REPOSSESSION

A secured creditor has a property right in collateral. The property right includes the right to repossess the collateral upon the debtor's default without judicial assistance. The right of extra-judicial self-help repossession set out in 9–609 is a traditional remedy in this country. Europeans tend to see it as another example of American barbarism: "You mean that the creditor can just go out and steal the property back?" Yes, but not without risk. In 1994 a Texas debtor whose truck was being repossessed killed the repo man with a .30–30 rifle as he was hooking his tow truck to the debtor's vehicle. Police declined to arrest the debtor because of a frontier-era law that gives considerable leeway in dealing with nighttime thieves and intruders. New York Times, Mar. 8, 1994, at A16. The Times article notes that one or two repo men are killed each year; in 1990 the number was four.

The revolution in creditor's remedies law occasioned by Sniadach v. Family Finance Corp., 395 U.S. 337 (1969) ("due process for debtors"), threatened the legality of self-help repossession. Since creditor groups cherished the remedy as one of their most important weapons—probably for its in terrorem effect on debtors—and debtor groups detested it as being subject to abuse, both sides threw maximum resources into a series of test cases that raged across the country throughout the 1970s. But the courts could find no state action in self-help repossessions and the creditors won all the battles in the federal appeals courts. The great debtor-creditor issue of the decade never reached the Supreme Court. See William M. Burke & David J. Reber, State Action, Congressional Power and Creditors' Rights: An Essay on the Fourteenth Amendment, 47 S. Cal. L. Rev. 1 (1973); James R. McCall, The Past as Prologue: History of the Right to Repossess, 47 S. Cal. L. Rev. 58 (1973).

### PROBLEM

Debtor granted a security interest in its fishing boat to Bank to secure a loan. Bank was aware that Debtor was a lobster fisherman and that it was his practice to leave lobster pots at sea for several days. Debtor was behind in his payments, and Bank notified him in writing that he must come in and discuss with his loan officer at Bank ways of bringing his account current. When Debtor failed to respond to this notice, Bank repossessed the boat without notifying Debtor of its intent to do so. Debtor had several lobster pots at sea that were never recovered. Debtor sued Bank for conversion on the ground that the repossession was wrongful because he was entitled to notice of Bank's intention to repossess. Bank had not referred to the possibility of repossession in any of its prior communications with Debtor. Had he been given notice of the repossession he would have voluntarily surrendered possession after recovering his lobster pots. Is there any basis in 9–609 for a court to impose a duty on Bank to give notice of intention to repossess? Since there was no risk that Debtor would abscond with the fishing boat—such boats are hard to hide and slow to flee—should 1–304 be read to require that notice of repossession be given in any case in which there is no danger of a debtor's removing, concealing, or dissipating the collateral?

Some consumer protection statutes prevent the creditor from accelerating or repossessing until the debtor is notified of the right to cure a default within a stated number of days. See, e.g., Uniform Consumer Credit Code § 5.110 and § 5.111 (1974); Wis.Stat.Ann. § 425.104 and § 425.105 (1998).

### b.  BREACH OF PEACE

Under 9–609(b) a secured party may repossess without judicial process only if it can do so "without breach of the peace." The breadth and uncertainty of the meaning of this language, coupled with the potential for significant liability, have severely limited the use of self-help repossession by secured parties. In the great majority of cases in which the secured party retakes possession, it does so with the expressed consent of the debtor, who knows it is in default and wishes to avoid the heavy costs of judicial actions for possession. If the secured party cannot take possession without risking a breach of the peace, and the debtor will not voluntarily relinquish possession, it may have judicial officers seize possession under a replevin action or the like, with the costs passed on to the debtor under 9–608(a).

Under 9–609(a)(2), a secured creditor need not take possession of the collateral in order to sell it; it may render the collateral unusable and sell it on the debtor's premises. This procedure may be necessary in cases in which the collateral is bulky and removal is impractical or unduly expensive. See Comment 6. Section 9–609(c) authorizes a secured party to require a debtor in default to "assemble the collateral and make it available to the secured party at a place to be designated by the secured party which is reasonably convenient to both parties." Loan agreements invariably include provisions covering the right of self-help repossession, sale without removal, and assembly of the collateral. In reality, no matter what the statute or agreement says about the secured party's right to require the debtor to assemble the collateral at another place, the debtor's cooperation is needed; if the debtor is recalcitrant, it may have incurred further liability, but the secured party may have to go to court to enforce its rights. The same may be true with respect to the secured party's efforts to conduct a sale on the debtor's premises.

If a breach of the peace occurs in a self-help repossession case, 9–625(b) subjects the secured party to liability for damages in the amount of any loss suffered by the debtor. In consumer transactions, 9–625(c)(2) provides for statutory damages "not less than the credit service charge plus 10 percent of the principal amount of the obligation or the time-price differential plus 10 percent of the cash price." In cases in which the consumer goods are expensive automobiles or boats, these damages can be substantial. Anecdotal evidence tends to show that a comparable provision under former Article 9 has rarely been used.

Debtors often seek recovery outside Article 9 for repossessions that result in a breach of the peace. Wrongful repossession is the tort of conversion, and Comment 3 to 9–625 recognizes that "principles of tort law supplement" recovery for a breach of the peace under 9–609. The typically more generous statute of limitations in tort is attractive to debtors. More important, the potential for punitive damages is present if the repossessing party's conduct falls within whatever the law of the jurisdiction requires, e.g., malice, oppression, or fraud. Section 1–305 states that "penal damages" are not recoverable under the UCC unless specifically provided "or by other rule of law." Presumably, every jurisdiction has a body of law, whether judge-made or statutory, on punitive damages.

Case law has struggled with the meaning of the ancient term "breach of the peace." Courts often recite that the standard includes a risk of violence. See, e.g., Ford Motor Credit Co. v. Herring, 589 S.W.2d 584 (Ark. 1979). The difficulty in the cases, of course, is to identify the circumstances in which the risk exists. The large body of case law on the subject suggests that a secured party breaches the peace by entering an enclosed area without consent: a house, apartment, garage, or office. No breach occurs with respect to unattended vehicles parked on streets or driveways. A growing body of case law indicates that a secured creditor cannot avoid liability for breach of the peace by employing an independent contractor to serve as the repo agent. 1 Clark, The Law of Secured Transactions Under the Uniform Commercial Code & 4.05[2][c] (Rev. ed. 2005). And if the agent misbehaves, the secured party has even been hit with punitive damages, e.g., Williamson v. Fowler Toyota, Inc., 956 P.2d 858 (Okla.1998). Hence, self-help repossession is used most commonly with respect to unattended motor vehicles parked on streets or in unenclosed areas. In other instances, if the debtor's consent to the retaking cannot be obtained, the creditor must proceed by judicial process.

## PROBLEM

SP repossessed a bus in which it had a purchase money security interest from Debtor who was in default. Debtor sued SP for wrongful repossession and alleged that: (i) The bus was parked in a fenced-in area with a "No Trespassing" sign in plain view. (ii) In order to enter the lot, SP broke the lock on the entry gate. SP countered by stating that even if these allegations were true, its conduct was protected by a provision in the security agreement that said: "It shall be lawful for [SP] to take possession of the [collateral] at any time where it may be and to enter any premises without liability for trespass." The repossession took place at night and there was no threat of violence to any person. Does SP's conduct amount to a breach of the peace under 9–609? See 9–602(6) and 9–603. These facts are based on Wombles Charters, Inc. v. Orix Credit Alliance, Inc., 39 UCC Rep. Serv.2d 599, 1999 WL 498224 (S.D. N.Y. 1999).

The following case addresses the oft-litigated issue of the legality of repossession of a vehicle when the owner is present.

## Williams v. Ford Motor Credit Co.

United States Court of Appeals, Eighth Circuit, 1982.
674 F.2d 717.

■ BENSON, CHIEF JUDGE.

In this diversity action brought by Cathy A. Williams to recover damages for conversion arising out of an alleged wrongful repossession of an automobile, Williams appeals from a judgment notwithstanding the verdict entered on motion of defendant Ford Motor Credit Company (FMCC). In the same case, FMCC appeals a directed verdict in favor of third party defendant S & S Recovery, Inc. (S & S) on FMCC's third party claim for indemnification. We affirm the judgment n.o.v. FMCC's appeal is thereby rendered moot.

In July, 1975, David Williams, husband of plaintiff Cathy Williams, purchased a Ford Mustang from an Oklahoma Ford dealer. Although David Williams executed the sales contract, security agreement, and loan papers, title to the car was in the name of both David and Cathy Williams. The car was financed through the Ford dealer, who in turn assigned the paper to FMCC. Cathy and David Williams were divorced in 1977. The divorce court granted Cathy title to the automobile and required David to continue to make payments to FMCC for eighteen months. David defaulted on the payments and signed a voluntary repossession authorization for FMCC. Cathy Williams was informed of the delinquency and responded that she was trying to get her former husband David to make the payments. There is no evidence of any agreement between her and FMCC. Pursuant to an agreement with FMCC, S & S was directed to repossess the automobile.

On December 1, 1977, at approximately 4:30 a.m., Cathy Williams was awakened by a noise outside her house trailer in Van Buren, Arkansas.[2] She saw that a wrecker truck with two men in it had hooked up to the Ford Mustang and started to tow it away. She went outside and hollered at them. The truck stopped. She then told them that the car was hers and asked them what they were doing. One of the men, later identified as Don Sappington, president of S & S Recovery, Inc., informed her that he was repossessing the vehicle on behalf of FMCC. Williams explained that she had been attempting to bring the past due payments up to date and informed Sappington that the car contained personal items which did not even belong to her. Sappington got out of the truck, retrieved the items

---

**2.** Cathy Williams testified that the noise sounded like there was a car stuck in her yard.

from the car, and handed them to her. Without further complaint from Williams, Sappington returned to the truck and drove off, car in tow. At trial, Williams testified that Sappington was polite throughout their encounter and did not make any threats toward her or do anything which caused her to fear any physical harm. The automobile had been parked in an unenclosed driveway which plaintiff shared with a neighbor. The neighbor was awakened by the wrecker backing into the driveway, but did not come out. After the wrecker drove off, Williams returned to her house trailer and called the police, reporting her car as stolen. Later, Williams commenced this action.

The case was tried to a jury which awarded her $5,000.00 in damages. FMCC moved for judgment notwithstanding the verdict, but the district court, on Williams' motion, ordered a nonsuit without prejudice to refile in state court. On FMCC's appeal, this court reversed and remanded with directions to the district court to rule on the motion for judgment notwithstanding the verdict. The district court entered judgment notwithstanding the verdict for FMCC, and this appeal followed.

§ 9–503 provides in pertinent part:

Unless otherwise agreed, a secured party has on default the right to take possession of the collateral. In taking possession, a secured party may proceed without judicial process if this can be done without breach of the peace. . . .[4]

In Ford Motor Credit Co. v. Herring, 27 U.C.C.Rep. 1448, 267 Ark. 201, 589 S.W.2d 584, 586 (1979), which involved an alleged conversion arising out of a repossession, the Supreme Court of Arkansas cited § 9–503 and referred to its previous holdings as follows:

In pre-code cases, we have sustained a finding of conversion only where force, or threats of force, or risk of invoking violence, accompanied the repossession. * * *

The thrust of Williams' argument on appeal is that the repossession was accomplished by the risk of invoking violence. The district judge who presided at the trial commented on her theory in his memorandum opinion:

Mrs. Williams herself admitted that the men who repossessed her automobile were very polite and complied with her requests. The evidence does not reveal that they performed any act which was oppressive, threatening or tended to cause physical violence. Unlike the situation presented in Manhattan Credit Co. v. Brewer, supra, it was not shown that Mrs. Williams would have been forced to resort to physical violence to stop the men from leaving with her automobile.

---

**4.** It is generally considered that the objectives of this section are (1) to benefit creditors in permitting them to realize collateral without having to resort to judicial process; (2) to benefit debtors in general by making credit available at lower costs * * *; and (3) to support a public policy discouraging extrajudicial acts by citizens when those acts are fraught with the likelihood of resulting violence * * *.

In the pre-Code case Manhattan Credit Co. v. Brewer, 232 Ark. 976, 341 S.W.2d 765 (1961), the court held that a breach of peace occurred when the debtor and her husband confronted the creditor's agent during the act of repossession and clearly objected to the repossession, 341 S.W.2d at 767–68. In *Manhattan*, the court examined holdings of earlier cases in which repossessions were deemed to have been accomplished without any breach of the peace, id. In particular, the Supreme Court of Arkansas discussed the case of Rutledge v. Universal C.I.T. Credit Corp., 218 Ark. 510, 237 S.W.2d 469 (1951). In *Rutledge*, the court found no breach of the peace when the repossessor acquired keys to the automobile, confronted the debtor and his wife, informed them he was going to take the car, and immediately proceeded to do so. As the *Rutledge* court explained and the *Manhattan* court reiterated, a breach of the peace did not occur when the "Appellant [debtor-possessor] did not give his permission but he did not object." *Manhattan*, supra, 341 S.W.2d at 767–68; *Rutledge*, supra, 237 S.W.2d at 470.

We have read the transcript of the trial. There is no material dispute in the evidence, and the district court has correctly summarized it. Cathy Williams did not raise an objection to the taking, and the repossession was accomplished without any incident which might tend to provoke violence. * * *

Appellees deserve something less than commendation for the taking during the night time sleeping hours, but it is clear that viewing the facts in the light most favorable to Williams, the taking was a legal repossession under the laws of the State of Arkansas. The evidence does not support the verdict of the jury. FMCC is entitled to judgment notwithstanding the verdict.

The judgment notwithstanding the verdict is affirmed.

■ HEANEY, CIRCUIT JUDGE, dissenting.

The only issue is whether the repossession of appellant's automobile constituted a breach of the peace by creating a "risk of invoking violence." See Ford Motor Credit Co. v. Herring, 267 Ark. 201, 589 S.W.2d 584, 586 (1979). The trial jury found that it did and awarded $5,000 for conversion. Because that determination was in my view a reasonable one, I dissent from the Court's decision to overturn it.

Cathy Williams was a single parent living with her two small children in a trailer home in Van Buren, Arkansas. On December 1, 1977, at approximately 4:30 a.m., she was awakened by noises in her driveway. She went into the night to investigate and discovered a wrecker and its crew in the process of towing away her car. According to the trial court, "she ran outside to stop them * * * but she made no *strenuous* protests to their actions." (Emphasis added.) In fact, the wrecker crew stepped between her and the car when she sought to retrieve personal items from inside it, although the men retrieved some of the items for her. The commotion created by the incident awakened neighbors in the vicinity.

Facing the wrecker crew in the dead of night, Cathy Williams did everything she could to stop them, short of introducing physical force to meet the presence of the crew. The confrontation did not result in violence only because Ms. Williams did not take such steps and was otherwise powerless to stop the crew.

The controlling law is the UCC, which authorizes self-help repossession only when such is done "without breach of the peace * * *." § 9–503. The majority recognizes that one important policy consideration underlying this restriction is to discourage "extrajudicial acts by citizens when those acts are fraught with the likelihood of resulting violence." Supra, at 719. Despite this, the majority holds that no reasonable jury could find that the confrontation in Cathy Williams' driveway at 4:30 a.m. created a risk of violence. I cannot agree. At a minimum, the largely undisputed facts created a jury question. The jury found a breach of the peace and this Court has no sound, much less compelling, reason to overturn that determination.

Indeed, I would think that sound application of the self-help limitation might require a directed verdict in favor of Ms. Williams, but certainly not against her. If a "night raid" is conducted without detection and confrontation, then, of course, there could be no breach of the peace. But where the invasion is detected and a confrontation ensues, the repossessor should be under a duty to retreat and turn to judicial process. The alternative which the majority embraces is to allow a repossessor to proceed following confrontation unless and until violence results in fact. Such a rule invites tragic consequences which the law should seek to prevent, not to encourage. I would reverse the trial court and reinstate the jury's verdict.

NOTES

**1.** What would the court have Cathy Williams do to show her lack of consent? In Hollibush v. Ford Motor Credit Co., 508 N.W.2d 449 (Wis.App. 1993), when the repo man hooked the debtor's Bronco up to his tow truck, the debtor's fiancé, in debtor's presence, said: "You are not going to take the Bronco." Despite this admonition, the tow truck drove off with the Bronco. The court held that a breach of the peace had taken place and stated: "Cases interpreting [former] § 9–503 also support [debtor's] assertion that 'no means no.'" 508 N.W.2d at 453. In Dixon v. Ford Motor Credit Co., 391 N.E.2d 493, 497 (Ill. App. 1979) (citing J. White & R. Summers, Uniform Commercial Code § 26–6, at 972 (1st ed. 1972)), the court said: "'When a creditor repossesses in disregard of the debtor's unequivocal oral protest, the repossession may be found to be in breach of the peace.'"

Chrysler Credit Corp. v. Koontz, 661 N.E.2d 1171 (Ill.App.1996), the case of the demure debtor, rejects the "just-say-no" test. Koontz, fearing repossession, parked his car in his front yard, so that he could see it by the porch light. When the repossessor arrived, Koontz ran out and shouted "Don't take it." The repossessor made no verbal or physical response while removing the vehicle. Koontz testified that although he was close enough to the repossessor to run over and get into a fight, he elected not to do so because he was in his underwear. The court stated that the term breach of the peace "connotes conduct which incites or is likely to incite immediate public turbulence, or which leads to or is likely to lead to an immediate loss of public order and tranquility." 661 N.E.2d at 1173. The probability of violence is sufficient to constitute a breach of the peace, the court stated, but nothing Koontz did would indicate to the repossessor that violence was likely to ensue if he continued to repossess the vehicle. Thus, the court found no breach of the peace: "We note that to rule otherwise would be to invite the ridiculous situation whereby a debtor could avoid a deficiency judgment by merely stepping out of his house and yelling once at a nonresponsive repossessor. Such a narrow definition of the conduct necessary to breach the peace would, we think, render the self-help repossession statute useless. Therefore, we reject Koontz's invitation to define 'an unequivocal oral protest,' without more, as a breach of the peace." 661 N.E.2d at 1174. Presumably, if Koontz had not been so modest and had duked it out with the repossessor, a breach of the peace would have occurred. Does the court wish to encourage such conduct?

**2.**   In Thompson v. Ford Motor Credit Company, 550 F.2d 256 (5th Cir.1977), the automobile sought by the seller was found in a repair garage. The garageman refused to allow the seller to take the vehicle unless he had obtained the debtor's consent. The seller lied in telling the garageman that he had the debtor's consent. The court stated that "[m]erely to connive to repossess does not make [the seller] liable * * *" On similar facts the same result was reached in K.B. Oil Co. v. Ford Motor Credit Co., Inc., 811 F.2d 310 (6th Cir.1987). In Reno v. General Motors Acceptance Corp., 378 So.2d 1103 (Ala.1979), the finance company repossessed an automobile from the parking lot of a grocery supermarket where the debtor worked by use of a duplicate key obtained from the dealer who had sold the installment contract to the finance company. The court held that there was no breach of the peace because possession was obtained without fraud, artifice, stealth, or trickery. The same court found a breach of the peace when the repo agent induced the debtor to drive his car to the dealer's office to discuss whether his payments were in arrears. While the debtor was inside discussing the account, his car was removed. See Ford Motor Credit Co. v. Byrd, 351 So.2d 557 (Ala.1977).

## PROBLEM

Seller sold Buyer a tractor and Buyer fell in default. When Seller demanded payment, Buyer was unable to pay and said that he would not give up possession of the tractor unless Seller established his right to repossess by judicial proceedings. He said that "someone would get hurt" if an attempt was made to repossess without "proper papers." Seller filed suit in Washington but was unable to locate the tractor. Later he located the tractor in Oregon and contacted the local sheriff, requesting him to accompany him in retaking the tractor. Proceeding to the site of the tractor was a convoy made up of Seller's car, his mechanic in a pickup, a lo-boy truck to transport the tractor, and the sheriff's official car. The sheriff was in uniform, wearing his badge and sidearms. The sheriff, who had seen the contract, informed Buyer that Seller had the right to repossess and said, "We come to pick up the tractor." Buyer asked whether the sheriff had the proper papers to take the tractor and the sheriff replied, "No." Buyer protested the repossession but offered no physical resistance because, as he later testified, he didn't think he could disregard the order of a sheriff. Seller testified that he had the sheriff present to prevent anticipated violence. Is Seller liable in conversion? See Stone Machinery Co. v. Kessler, 463 P.2d 651 (Wash. App. 1970).

### c.   JUDICIAL ACTION

As we saw in the previous section, self-help repossession is problematic owing to the liability a secured party may incur in cases in which the debtor will not consent to the repossession. Under 9–609(a) the secured party is entitled to take possession of the collateral when the debtor defaults, and it may do so by judicial action under 9–609(b)(1). Depending on state law outside Article 9, it may bring an action in replevin or, in some states, claim and delivery, and obtain a writ of possession. The levying officer (sheriff or marshal) may seize the property and deliver it to the secured party, who may then dispose of the property pursuant to Article 9. Another course of action is for the secured party to reduce its claim to judgment, levy on the collateral, and execute on its judgment by a judicial sale under 9–601(a). The sale is conducted by judicial officers, under the same rules that govern other execution sales pursuant to a money judgment in the jurisdiction. Section 9–601(f) and Comment 8 make clear that an execution sale is an appropriate method of foreclosure. Still another alternative is for the secured creditor to bring a judicial foreclosure proceeding in which a court sells the collateral under a judicial sale, similar to the execution sale on a money judgment. See 4 White & Summers, Uniform Commercial Code § 34–9 (5th prac. ed. 2002), for a discussion of these alternatives. Judicial actions offer secured parties important advantages. If the collateral is either repossessed or sold by judicial officers, Article 9 limitations do not apply to the removal or sale. The requirements of a commercially reasonable disposition are inapplicable, and whether a secured party may bid at the judicial sale is governed by other state law. Comment 8 to 9–601. Judicial sales that meet the procedural requirements of state statutes as to notice, location, bidding and the like are virtually invulnerable to debtor attack. Of course, judicial actions may be costly, and the fact that these costs can be shifted to the debtor's obligation (9–615(a)) is no guaranty that they will be collectible.

An important advantage to secured parties in opting for judicial action is revealed in the next case.

## Cla–Mil E. Holding Corp. v. Medallion Funding Corp.

Court of Appeals of New York, 2006.
6 N.Y.3d 375.

■ ROSENBLATT, J.

A secured creditor, Medallion Funding Corp., obtained a court order directing the New York City marshal to recover collateral located on property belonging to Cla–Mil East Holding Corp. Cla–Mil, the judgment debtor's landlord, has alleged that the marshal negligently damaged its real estate, and has sued Medallion and its law firm under a variety of theories. The only one it seriously argues here is that it was entitled to reimbursement under UCC 9–604 (d).* We must now decide whether Medallion's court-ordered use of the marshal, rather than self-help, insulates it from Cla–Mil's claim. We hold that it does.

The present dispute began when a tenant of Cla–Mil's who had operated a laundromat on his leased space defaulted on his rent. About the same time, the tenant defaulted on payments he owed Medallion, which had provided him with a loan to purchase the laundry equipment, including large washers and dryers. The loan was secured by the equipment itself as collateral. Cla–Mil evicted the tenant. Medallion then obtained a judgment against its debtor (the tenant) and an ex parte order from Supreme Court, based on that judgment, directing the city marshal to recover possession of the collateral.

Pursuant to the Supreme Court decree and without notice to Cla–Mil, the marshal broke the landlord's seal on the premises (which, perhaps ironically, had also been placed there by the city marshals) and removed the washers, dryers and associated equipment. To accomplish the removal, the marshal severed air vents, unplugged power lines, and disconnected hot and cold water pipes.

Cla–Mil has sued Medallion and its law firm, alleging that the damage to the premises was caused by the marshal's negligence in performing these disconnections. Cla–Mil alleged trespass, abuse of process and negligence. Supreme Court denied Medallion's motion for summary judgment and granted Cla–Mil partial summary judgment on the question of liability, reasoning in part that Medallion had an obligation to notify Cla–Mil before sending the marshal to repossess the collateral. The Appellate Division reversed and granted summary judgment in Medallion's favor. We now affirm.

UCC 9–604 (d) specifies that "[a] secured party that removes collateral shall promptly reimburse" the owner of real property damaged by the removal (other than the debtor). Here, the party that "remove[d] collateral" was not the secured party, nor any employee, contractor, or agent of the secured party. The New York City marshals are government officers appointed by the Mayor (CCA 1601), neutral and free of any conflict of interest concerning the removal of collateral (CCA 1601–a [a]), and subject to discipline by appropriate authorities (*id.*). Marshals do not owe allegiance to or take orders from the secured creditors whose collateral they recover; rather, they act under the direction of a court, as the marshal did here.

---

* The Appellate Division correctly awarded Kramer & Shapiro, P.C. summary judgment. The firm acted properly in seeking a court order on behalf of its client.

(1) The marshal's actual and legal independence from the secured party suggests to us that the UCC reference to a "secured party that removes collateral" does not include secured parties who arrange for marshals to remove collateral under court order. Policy reasons support a distinction between marshals and secured parties, and we see no reason to conflate their identities under the UCC. If the marshal here damaged the real property, as Cla–Mil alleges, Cla–Mil should have brought an action against the marshal, rather than against Medallion. Indeed, marshals are bonded for just that purpose (*see* CCA 1604), and the Legislature has expressly authorized such actions in the New York City Civil Court (CCA 1605). We see no link between Medallion and the marshal sufficient to make Medallion liable for the marshal's alleged negligence.

(2) Furthermore, we reject Cla–Mil's claims to the extent they allege any direct wrongdoing by Medallion. Medallion obtained a judgment against the debtor, returned to court to get an order executing the judgment, and brought the order to a marshal to carry out the execution. At each stage, Medallion avoided self-help and appropriately relied on the legal system to recover its collateral with no breach of peace. Far from abusing legal process, Medallion submitted to legal authority at every step. Such conduct is consistent with public policy disfavoring parties taking matters into their own hands.

Accordingly, the order of the Appellate Division should be affirmed, with costs.

Chief Judge Kaye and Judges G.B. Smith, Ciparick, Graffeo, Read and R.S. Smith concur.

Order affirmed, with costs.


NOTES

**1.** Removal of collateral may cause damage either to the collateral or to the premises where the collateral is located. We saw in the previous section that a secured party cannot avoid liability by employing an agent, but we find in this case that the secured party is not liable for the damage caused by judicial officers in a removal. Here the Marshals allegedly damaged the real property of the debtor's landlord in removing the washers and dryers and related equipment by severing air vents, unplugging of power lines and disconnecting water pipes. The debtor's landlord brought suit against the secured party, Medallion, for damage to its property, for which it relied on 9–604(d) for reimbursement. The debtor was not involved. The collateral in this case is classified under Article 9 as fixtures, and we will give further attention to the law of fixtures in Chapter 8.

**2.** The court's advice to the landlord is to sue the Marshals, who are bonded. If liability is to fall on the judicial officers, there will be resistance on the part of these officers to making removals that will cause damage. Note how the California provisions set out below deal with this issue. The following provisions are found in the California Code of Civil Procedure § 514.010:

(c) If the specified property or any part of it is in a private place, the levying officer shall at the time he demands possession of the property announce his identity, purpose, and authority. If the property is not voluntarily delivered, the levying officer may cause any building or enclosure where the property may be located to be broken open in such a manner as he reasonably believes will cause the least damage and may call upon the power of the county to aid and protect him, but, if he reasonably believes that entry and seizure of the property will involve a substantial risk of death or serious bodily harm to any person, he shall refrain from seizing the property and shall promptly make a return to the court from which the writ issued setting forth the reasons for his belief that the risk exists. In such case, the court shall make such orders as may be appropriate.

(d) Nothing in this section authorizes the levying officer to enter or search any private place not specified in the writ of possession or other order of the court.

## 3.   DISPOSITION OF COLLATERAL

The law has long struggled with the problem of how to strike a fair balance between the interest of the foreclosing creditor in being able to realize on collateral quickly and cheaply and the rights of the defaulting debtor in having a disposition of the property that brings a fair price. The traditional view was to require a public auction sale to the highest cash bidder after public notice of the sale. As in the foreclosure of real estate mortgages, if the creditor complied with all of the procedural requirements, the sale was a valid termination of all the debtor's rights in the collateral even though the price obtained for the property might be only a fraction of what the debtor thought the property was worth. The Uniform Conditional Sales Act was an example of the assimilation of the procedures for disposition on default of personal property to the rigid procedures long used in the foreclosure of real property mortgages.

The drafters of the Code wanted something better than a "sale on the courthouse steps" held before a listless audience of courthouse loiterers or, still worse, before a conniving group of professional public sale bidders colluding to keep the bids down. In Part 6 of Article 9, they strove to loosen up the disposition process and make it more businesslike in order to get a better return. They encourage the creditor to resell in private sales at market prices. But as a balance to this freedom of action the creditor is held to an ex post standard of "commercial reasonableness" in all aspects of the realization process with strict accountability for failure to meet this flexible standard. The adoption of the commercially reasonable standard and the introduction of dispositions by private sale by the 1962 version of Article 9 constituted a revolution in foreclosure of security interests and raised many issues unresolved by the language of the rather terse provisions of the Act. Revised Article 9 moved to address these issues and, in doing so, has posed a new set of questions.

Section 9–610(a) allows the foreclosing creditor to "sell, lease, license or otherwise dispose" of the collateral. Since most dispositions are by sale of the collateral, we have often used this form of disposition in our discussion in the following sections on disposition of collateral.

### a. NOTIFICATION BEFORE DISPOSITION

Debtors usually know whether they are in default; what they don't know is what the secured party intends to do about it. Although creditors have very likely communicated with defaulting debtors about the range of remedies available, the UCC does not require creditors to inform debtors of their intentions until they decide either to foreclose on the collateral or to accept it in satisfaction of the debt. If the secured party chooses to foreclose by extra-judicial sale, 9–611(b) and (c) provide that the secured party "shall send * * * a reasonable authenticated notification of disposition" to the debtor, any secondary obligor, such as a guarantor, and, in nonconsumer cases, to certain other enumerated parties. The authentication requirement (9–102(a)(7)) resolves the question under former Article 9 whether oral notice sufficed, and use of the term "send" (9–102(a)(74)(A)) continues the rule that the secured party need only prove the notice was dispatched, not that it was received. Section 9–613 prescribes the contents of the notification in nonconsumer goods transactions and offers secured creditors a safe-harbor notification form. Section 9–614 does the same for consumer goods transactions. The drafters have done a commendable job of using easily understood language in the consumer goods form.

Both 9–613 and 9–614 require the information contained in 9–613(1): the method of intended disposition must be stated, as well as the time and place of a public disposition or the time after which any other disposition is to be made, such as a private sale. The differences in the information required by the two sections show that creditors are cut more slack in commercial transactions than in consumer transactions. The major differences are:

(i) Section 9–613(2) provides that whether a notification that lacks any of the information required by paragraph (1) is sufficient is a question of fact. Section 9–614(1) provides that for a notification to be sufficient, it must contain all the information stated in that subsection.

(ii) Section 9–613(3)(B) provides that a notification may be sufficient even though it includes "minor errors that are not seriously misleading." No such provision is found in 9–614. Section 9–614(5) excuses errors only with respect to information not required by paragraph (1).

(iii) In consumer goods transactions, 9–614(1)(B) requires a description of any liability of the debtor for a deficiency.

One of the aspects of former Article 9 that particularly irritated creditors was the absence of any specific directions on the timeliness of notice. Pre–UCC statutes had always set definite deadlines. Revised Article 9 responded to creditor complaints. Section 9–611(b) requires the secured party to send a "reasonable authenticated notification of disposition." Comment 2 explains that this includes timeliness ("a reasonable time before the disposition is to take place"). Section 9–612(a) says that whether a notification is sent within a reasonable time "is a question of fact." But 9–612(b) gives creditors in commercial cases the safe harbor protection they had long sought by providing that a notification of disposition sent after default and at least 10 days before the earliest time of disposition is sent within a reasonable time. It is important to note that the safe harbor provision does not apply to consumer transactions; here the only guidance provided secured parties is that the notice must be sent within a reasonable time under 9–612(a). The drafters offer no justification for the different treatment of consumer transactions and only scant assistance in determining what they mean by a reasonable time. Comment 2 says: "A notification that is sent so near to the disposition date that a notified person could not be expected to act on or take account of the notification would be unreasonable." Does this quotation require secured parties to anticipate what kind of action the debtor wishes to take? Not much notice is needed to allow the debtor to attend the sale and observe whether all goes well; more might be required if the debtor intends to attempt to raise the money to redeem before the sale.

## PROBLEM

If a secured party fails to give timely notice before the foreclosure sale or even fails to give notice at all, how is the debtor injured? What can the debtor do to protect its interests if it receives timely notification? Hustle up prospective bidders? (Hasn't the debtor in a commercial case probably been trying to sell the collateral since it learned that it would have to default on its loan, with no success?) Redeem from the secured party before the sale? See 9–623(a). How much would it have to pay to do so? See 9–623(b) and the description of the right to redeem found in the safe-harbor form in 9–614 ("You can get your property back * * *"). How often do you believe redemption is used by defaulting debtors?

---

In the following opinion the court briefly addresses the issue raised in the Problem above. See the next to last paragraph. Did BMW overlook passage of Revised Article 9?

## In re Downing

United States Bankruptcy Court, W.D. Missouri, 2002.
286 B.R. 900.

■ ARTHUR B. FEDERMAN, CHIEF JUDGE.

Debtor Steven L. Downing objected to the unsecured deficiency claim of creditor BMW Financial Services, N.A., LLC (BMW) in this Chapter 13 bankruptcy case * * *

## ISSUE PRESENTED

On April 4, 2002, BMW notified Mr. Downing that it intended to sell his vehicle pursuant to state law on a date no sooner than 10 days after the date of the notice. The letter was sent to Mr. Downing at his address in Kansas City, Missouri. On August 1, 2002, the vehicle was sold at a commercial auction in Milwaukee, Wisconsin. Missouri law requires that, in order to obtain a deficiency judgment after the sale of collateral, the creditor must provide "a reasonable authenticated notification of disposition,"[1] including "the method of intended disposition, ... the time and place of public sale, or the time after which any other disposition is to be made," and debtor's right to an accounting of any unpaid indebtedness.[2] In addition, if the creditor is disposing of consumer goods, it must provide a description of any liability for a deficiency.[3] Was the notice provided by BMW sufficient as to these requirements?

## DECISION

A notice that fails to inform the debtor that the intended method of disposition is a private sale, that the debtor has a right to an accounting, and that debtor will be liable for any deficiency following the sale is not sufficient to preserve the creditor's right to a deficiency claim.

## FACTUAL BACKGROUND

On September 25, 2000, Mr. Downing purchased a 1999 BMW 528i from BMW, and granted BMW a lien on the car. On June 11, 2001, the Downings filed a Chapter 13 bankruptcy petition. Debtors' proposed plan provided for the surrender of the 1999 BMW and for the payment of 100 percent of the allowed claims. On March 27, 2002, after this Court granted BMW relief from the automatic stay, Mr. Downing surrendered the vehicle to BMW. On April 4, 2002, BMW notified Mr. Downing that it intended to sell the car, as allowed under state law, no sooner than 10 days after the date of the notice. On August 1, 2002, BMW sold the car at a commercial auction in Milwaukee, Wisconsin. After the sale, BMW filed an unsecured deficiency claim in this case in the amount of $18,517.24. Mr. Downing objected to the claim, on the grounds that BMW did not provide him with proper notice of the sale as required by Missouri's version of Revised Article 9 of the Uniform Commercial Code (the UCC).

## DISCUSSION

In Missouri, compliance with the notice provisions of Article 9 is a prerequisite to the recovery of a deficiency following the sale of repossessed

**1.** Mo. Stat. Ann. § 400.9–611(b) (Supp. 2002).

**2.** *Id.* at § 400.9–613(1)(C), (D), and (E).

**3.** *Id.* at § 400.9–614(1)(B).

collateral. * * * The party seeking the deficiency judgment has the burden of proving the sufficiency of the notice. Any doubt as to what constitutes strict compliance with the statutory requirements must be resolved in favor of the debtor.

The parties agree that the adequacy of the notice is governed by sections 9–613 and 9–614 of the Missouri's Revised Statutes.[8] Section 9–613 provides the contents and form of notification prior to the disposition of non-consumer goods.

Except in a consumer-goods transaction, the following rules apply:

(1) The contents of a notification of disposition are sufficient if the notification:

    (A) Describes the debtor and the secured party;

    (B) Describes the collateral that is the subject of the intended disposition;

    (C) States the method of intended disposition;

    (D) States that the debtor is entitled to an accounting of the unpaid indebtedness and states the charge, if any, for an accounting; and

    (E) States the time and place of a public sale or the time after which any other disposition is to be made.

Section 9–614 applies those same requirements to consumer-goods dispositions. In addition, when disposing of consumer goods, the creditor must provide a "description of any liability for a deficiency of the person to which the notification is sent,"[11] and a "telephone number from which the amount that must be paid to the secured party to redeem the collateral under section 9–623 is available."[12] The pertinent distinction between the two provisions is that in nonconsumer-goods dispositions, the question of whether the contents of a notification that lacks any of the required information are nevertheless sufficient is a question of fact.[13] Since an automobile is a consumer good,[14] however, the sufficiency of the notice sent by BMW must be evaluated pursuant to both sections 9–613 and 9–614.

The notice sent by BMW was in the form of a letter dated April 4, 2002. The letter identified the debtor as Steven L. Downing, the creditor as BMW, and the collateral as a 1999 BMW 528i, WBADP5340XBR95304. It then stated as follows:

---

**8.** Mo. Stat. Ann. §§ 9–613 and 9–614 (Supp.2002). Note that revised Article 9 became effective in Missouri as of July 1, 2001. Since this action was commenced after that date, revised Article 9 governs my decision. Mo. Stat. Ann. § 9–702.

    **11.** *Id.* at § 9–614(1)(B).

    **12.** *Id.* at § 9–614(1)(C).

**13.** 9–613(2). In consumer-goods transactions, a notification that lacks any of the required information is insufficient as a matter of law. *Id.*, UCC Comment, ¶ 2.

**14.** *See* Mo. Stat. Ann. § 9–102(23), which defines consumer goods as goods that are used or bought for use primarily for personal, family, or household purposes.

This letter confirms you have rejected and/or terminated your loan due to the filing of bankruptcy. BMW Financial Services NA, LLC has taken possession of the Vehicle.

You are notified that BMW Financial Services NA, LLC intends to sell the vehicle as allowed under state law, but no sooner than 10 days after the date of this letter.

This letter is not being sent in violation of the discharge injunction of 11 U.S.C. § 727 and/or 1328(e), if any, but is merely an attempt to comply with requisite notice requirements under the contract/lease and applicable law. If you have received a discharge in bankruptcy, this letter is an attempt to collect a debt solely from the vehicle pledged to secure payment of the contract/lease and not from you personally and any information obtained will be used for that purpose.

Should you have any questions, call us at the number referenced below, Monday through Friday, 9:00 a.m. to 5:00 p.m. ET or at either address listed below.

At the hearing, BMW represented that it sold the 1999 BMW at a commercial auction in Milwaukee, Wisconsin attended only by automobile dealers. As such, BMW argues that the sale was a private sale to commercial buyers, therefore, it was not required to provide Mr. Downing with the exact time and place of the auction. While BMW offered no support for this contention, in fact, other courts have held that a dealers-only auction is not public in character. Professor Barkley Clark, likewise, posits that where a sale is open only to automobile dealers, it is closed to some aspect of the market; therefore, it is a private sale.[18] Nonetheless, the UCC clearly required BMW to inform Mr. Downing as to whether it would sell the car at either a private sale or public sale. Mr. Downing rightly points out in his brief that the notice sent by BMW did not inform him of the type of sale contemplated, or that he would be responsible for any deficiency. It also failed to inform Mr. Downing of his right to an accounting of the exact amount of his indebtedness, or what BMW claimed the indebtedness to be at the time of the sale. The burden of proof is on BMW to demonstrate that it has in all respects complied with the notice provisions of the UCC. By the express terms of the statute, that includes the method of disposition. BMW did not specify the nature of the sale, it did not inform Mr. Downing of his potential liability, and it did not inform him of his right to an accounting. For all of these reasons, I find that the notice did not strictly comply with the requirements of section 9–613 of Missouri's Revised Statutes, as made applicable to consumer-goods transactions by section 9–614.

BMW also argues that since the Downings' plan provided that Mr. Downing intended to surrender the vehicle, Missouri law does not require it to advise him of his right to redeem the vehicle. But that is not the sole purpose served by the notice. If a debtor is given the terms of the private

---

**18.** Barkley Clark, Law of Secured Transactions Under the Uniform Commercial Code, § 4,08(2) at 4–98 (1988).

sale, he has the opportunity to offer better terms. If a debtor is told the time and place of a public sale, he has an opportunity to appear at the sale, or have someone appear on his behalf, and bid. In any event, Missouri has long held that the right to a deficiency exists only if the creditor strictly complies with the statutory requirements of the UCC, regardless of whether there was any resulting harm to the debtor from the failed notice.

The notification was not sufficient, therefore, under Missouri law, BMW loses its right to a deficiency judgment. Debtors' objection to the claim of BMW will be sustained. An Order consistent with this Memorandum Opinion will be entered this date.

## NOTE

If the secured party decides to dispose of the collateral, it may do so either by "public or private proceedings." See 9–610(b). The method of disposition selected must itself be commercially reasonable. 9–609(b); see 9–627(b). There are two procedural consequences of the secured party's choice. First, if a public sale is selected, the notification must state the time and place of the public sale, but if a private sale is chosen, only the time after which the sale will be made. See 9–613(1)(E). The second is that in most instances a secured party may not purchase at a private sale, but it may do so at a public sale. See 9–610(c). The term "public or private proceeding" is not defined in the text of Article 9, but Comment 7 to 9–610 speaks to the issue: "[A]s used in this Article, a 'public disposition' is one at which the price is determined after the public has had a meaningful opportunity for competitive bidding. 'Meaningful opportunity' is meant to imply that some form of advertisement or public notice must precede the sale (or other disposition) and that the public must have access to the sale (disposition)." The requirements of public notice and opportunity to participate are consistent with the understanding under former Article 9; see William E. Hogan, The Secured Party and Default Under the UCC, 47 Minn. L. Rev. 205, 226–27 (1962).

## PROBLEMS

**1.** Look carefully at the kind of sale made in *Downing*. Was the court correct in saying that the sale was not a public sale? We usually think of a public sale as an auction to which the public is invited. Why wasn't that true here?

**2.** The case in which a secured party is allowed to buy at a private sale is one in which the collateral is of a kind that "is customarily sold on a recognized market or the subject of widely distributed standard price quotations." 9–610(c)(2). Given the existence of Kelley Blue Books and the like that contain widely followed estimates of the value of automobiles, would BMW have been able to buy Downing's automobile at the sale in this case? See Comment 9 to 9–610.

**3.** (a) Debtor signed a security agreement granting Finance a security interest in a new automobile. This agreement contained the following clause: "Debtor agrees that upon a default of this agreement that is not cured within 10 days of notice of default sent by Finance to Debtor, Finance may repossess and resell the automobile without further notification at the weekly car auction held each Friday afternoon at 2:00 p.m. at the Auto Barn, open to all automobile dealers of Corcoran County." Has Debtor effectively waived its right to notification before disposition? See 9–602(7), 9–624(a).

(b) Debtor had been in default on its auto loan to Finance a number of times. In each case, Debtor cured the default by back payments. After the last default, Finance required Debtor to sign an agreement that if he fell into default in the future Finance was authorized to repossess and resell the automobile without further notification to Debtor. After Debtor signed the agreement, Finance waived the existing default. Has Debtor effectively waived his right to notification before disposition with respect to a future default? See 9–624(a).

## NOTE

The equitable doctrine of marshaling, applicable via 1–103(b), sometimes can prevent a secured party from disposing of collateral. Disposing of an item of collateral generally harms other creditors in that they can no longer satisfy their claims from the item. For instance, when a senior secured party disposes of collateral in which a junior secured party has a security interest, the junior party must look to other assets from which to satisfy its claim. The junior party might be unsecured with respect to these assets. The doctrine of marshaling allows a junior secured creditor to require a senior secured party to proceed against collateral other than assets in which the junior secured party has a security interest. The doctrine applies when three conditions are satisfied: (1) the two parties are creditors of the same debtor; (2) two funds are owned by debtor; and (3) one of the creditors can satisfy its entire claim from either or both of the funds, while the other creditor can satisfy its claim from only one of the funds. See Meyer v. United States, 375 U.S. 233, 237 (1963). Marshaling is permitted only when the creditor wouldn't be prejudiced or inconvenienced by being required to proceed against one of the funds. In addition, the doctrine only applies to creditors with liens on assets, such as secured parties. It also can't be used by one junior secured creditor having another junior secured creditor. Some bankruptcy courts have extended the doctrine to allow the bankruptcy trustee, representing unsecured creditors, to require marshaling against secured creditors. A few other courts relax the "debtor ownership" requirement, allowing marshaling as long as a creditor has the right to proceed against two or more funds (whoever owns them). Comment 5 to 9–610 leaves to courts the determination as to when marshaling is appropriate.

## b. COMMERCIALLY REASONABLE DISPOSITION

We explained earlier that one of the principal goals of the 1962 Code was to increase the return on dispositions of collateral. The drafters strove to make the disposition process more "business-like" and to get away from the rigidities of the old "sale on the courthouse steps" methods of foreclosing on collateral. The 1962 Code encouraged creditors to sell by private negotiations rather than at public sales. The thrust was to have collateral disposed of in the same manner as other property of the same kind so that something approaching market value could be obtained. Revised Article 9 carries on this policy: 9–610(a) provides broadly that disposition may be by sale, lease, license or otherwise, and 9–610(b) allows either a public or private disposition.

The tradition in secured transactions in both real and personal property law had been that the defaulting debtor was entitled to a public sale in order to protect its "equity" in the property. That is, the property might be worth more than the debt, and a public sale was necessary to test the value of the property. If the sale price was greater than the amount of the debt, plus the expenses of the disposition, the surplus would go to the debtor, but if the price was less than the amount of the debt the interest of the secured party was protected by allowing it a judgment for the amount of the deficiency. Old fashioned statutes like the Uniform Conditional Sales Act prescribed rigid procedures for the disposition of collateral, modeled on those governing judicial foreclosures. Everyone agreed that these statutes didn't work for debtors, but how could the flexibility needed to sell collateral in a business-like manner at near market prices be achieved without giving up the protections the debtor had under the old statutes? The drafters of the 1962 Code attempted to solve this problem by introducing to secured transactions law the overriding concept of commercial reasonableness. The secured party should be allowed to dispose of the collateral in almost any manner so long as "[e]very aspect of a disposition of collateral, including the method, manner, time, place, and other terms, must be commercially reasonable." 9–610(b).

When former Article 9 was being drafted in the 1950s, creditors were appalled by this new-fangled idea of commercial reasonableness. The old foreclosure statutes may not have been perfect, but for creditors they provided a safe harbor: if the creditor met all the notice and sale requirements, it was very difficult for debtors to attack the legality of the sale, however paltry the price paid for the collateral. Now, under the commercial reasonableness rubric, every disposition was open to attack. Creditors noted that debtors will always contend that the proceeds of a sale do not represent the true value of the property. There will be a lot of lawsuits, they predicted. And they were right; there were many lawsuits about the meaning of commercial reasonableness under former Article 9. Revised 9–627(b)(3) offers a safe-harbor definition of the crucial term similar to that in former 9–507(2): a disposition is commercially reasonable if it is "in conformity with reasonable commercial practices among dealers in the type of property that was the subject of the disposition." The drafters focused on procedure rather than the price obtained at the disposition, which is what debtors are most interested in. Section 9–627(a) spells this out: the fact that a higher price could have been obtained at a different time or in a different method from that selected by the secured party "is not of itself sufficient to preclude the secured party from establishing that the * * * disposition was made in a commercially reasonable manner." As we will see, however, if the price is too low, 9–615(f) applies in limited situations. Comment 2 to 9–627. Section 9–626(c) offers secured parties another safe-harbor of sorts by providing that a disposition is commercially reasonable if it has been approved by a court or creditors' committee.

We include the following case, decided under former Article 9, to demonstrate how one of the most sophisticated creditors in America, GECC, deals with the commercially reasonable resale standard in a case in which it contemplates going for a deficiency judgment and knows that the debtors are going to put up a fight. Note the time and money that GECC devotes to publicizing the sale. The case would be decided the same way under Revised Article 9. 9–610(b), 9–613, 9–627.

## General Electric Capital Corporation v. Stelmach Construction Company

United States District Court, D. Kansas, 2001.
45 UCC Rep.Serv.2d 675.

■ MURGUIA.

This is an action brought by a creditor to recover a deficiency judgment against two debtors after the repossession and sale of collateral securing the loan at issue. Plaintiff General Electric Capital Corporation ("GECC") is the creditor in this action and defendants Stelmach Construction Company and Christopher S. Stelmach are the debtors. * * *

[P]ending before the court is plaintiff GECC's motion for summary judgment on damages. Plaintiff seeks to recover the full amount of its deficiency, including interest, attorneys' fees, and costs against defendant Stelmach Construction Company on a promissory note and against defendant Christopher S. Stelmach on his personal guaranty. As set forth in detail below, plaintiff's motion for summary judgment is granted.

### I.  FACTS

#### Breach of Agreements

Plaintiff and defendant Stelmach Construction entered into a promissory note, a master security agreement, and several related agreements (the "Agreements") on or about June 30, 1998. Defendant Stelmach Construction signed the Agreements. Pursuant to the Agreements, defendant Stelmach Construction agreed to repay to plaintiff the principal sum of $400,000, plus interest at 9.32% in forty-two consecutive monthly installments to begin August 25, 1998. The Agreements also provide for interest at the rate of 18% per annum upon default and a 5% late payment charge on delinquent payments. Also, on or about June 30, 1998, defendant Christopher Stelmach executed an individual guaranty of the amount loaned to defendant Stelmach Construction.

As the term of the note progressed, Stelmach Construction failed to make the required principal and interest payments due under the Agreements. Accordingly, plaintiff and defendant Stelmach Construction entered into a modification agreement, thereby modifying the terms of payment. Defendant Stelmach Construction executed the modification agreement. Although defendants waived notice, presentment, and other defenses in the Agreements and the guaranty, on April 7 and June 9, 1999, plaintiff sent both defendants notices of default with respect to payments due by defendant Stelmach Construction.

Subsequently, on or about June 24, 1999, plaintiff and defendants entered into a voluntary surrender agreement, wherein defendant Stelmach Construction retained all of its rights as a debtor, including but not limited to the right to challenge the commercial reasonableness of the sale of the collateral.

Following plaintiff's motion for summary judgment on liability, on August 31, 2000 the court entered an order finding defendants breached the Agreements entered into between the parties and that amounts are due and owing by defendants to plaintiff as a result of such breach.

## Sale of Collateral

Pursuant to a voluntary surrender agreement, defendants voluntarily surrendered the collateral with the understanding that plaintiff would sell it. Plaintiff notified defendants that the sale of the collateral would occur on or after August 6, 1999.

Plaintiff hired Elcor, Inc. to repossess, appraise and sell the collateral. Elcor inspected and evaluated the condition of each piece, and prepared a condition report and approximate value for each piece of equipment. When analyzing the collateral piece by piece, Elcor's approximate values totaled $258,200.00. In contrast, defendants present the report of Kenneth Fowler—their designated expert in the area of construction appraisal—who opines that the value of the collateral as of August 6, 1999 was $457,400.

Plaintiff advertised the sale through publications in two nationally recognized trade magazines, and on two internet sites known by the trade. The advertisements gave a complete description of the make, model, and year of each piece of collateral, and identified where the collateral could be viewed. None of the advertisement specified whether the collateral would be sold by the lot or individually. GECC also advertised the sale of collateral through mass mailing, targeting potential purchasers.

The collateral was stored in the Lee's Summit, Missouri area during the advertisement period and was available for inspection by interested bidders. Plaintiff received six (6) bids for the collateral from third party bidders. All of the bids were made for the entire lot. The bids ranged in price from $225,000 to $311,000.

Plaintiff accepted the highest bid, selling the collateral for $311,000, with costs to plaintiff of $6,800 for obtaining possession of the collateral, evaluating the collateral and properly preparing the collateral for sale, and costs of $31,100 for commission expenses with respect to the sale. When the collateral was sold on August 24, 1999, the principal amount due by defendants was $389,710.68. Interest and delinquency charges at that time totaled $31,355.56. Additional interest accrued after August 24, 1999 at the contract rate of $54.91 per diem. Pursuant to the terms of the Agreements, defendants agreed to pay plaintiff's attorneys fees and costs incurred in collecting under the Agreements.

As of August 24, 1999 (the sale date of the collateral), the amount due and owing to plaintiff, after crediting all payments made and the proceeds from the sale of collateral, totaled:

- Remaining principal balance after sale of collateral ($389,710.68 (principal) less $311,000 (proceeds from sale of collateral)) $78,710.68

- Interest and delinquency charges (Additional interest accrued after August 24, 1999 at the contract rate of $54.91 per diem.) $31,355.56

- Costs to repossess/recondition collateral $6,800

- Commission expenses on sale $31,100

- Amount due and owing by defendants (attorneys' fees obligations not included) $147,966.24

The parties dispute the total amount due by defendants to plaintiff as a result of the breach. Plaintiff asserts the sale of the collateral was conducted in accordance with the Agreements between the parties and in accordance with Article 9 of the Uniform Commercial Code. Defendants, however, argue that the sale of collateral conducted by plaintiff was not commercially reasonable.

\* \* \*

## III.  MOTION FOR SUMMARY JUDGMENT

\* \* \*

### Commercially Reasonable

As liability in this case has been resolved, the issue that remains is whether the sale of the collateral securing the loan to defendants was conducted in a commercially reasonable manner.[9] Determination of wheth-

---

**9.** It is unclear, based upon the papers presented to the court, which state law's Uniform Commercial Code governs the Agreements between the parties in this diversity action. The parties have not addressed the issue directly, nor have they pointed to portions of the record providing guidance on this matter to the court. Because all parties cite to the Kansas Uniform Commercial Code in presenting their arguments to the court, the court assumes it is the Kansas code that governs the Agreement between the parties.

In addition, the court notes that the provisions of the revised version of the Kansas UCC, effective July 1, 2001, do not govern this action. See Uniform Commercial Code Secured Transactions, ch. 142, § 9–702(c),

er a sale has been held in a commercially reasonable manner is a question of fact to be determined by the trier of fact. *Westgate State Bank v. Clark*, 231 Kan. 81, 91, 642 P.2d 961, 969 (1982).

Plaintiff, as the secured creditor, has the burden to establish that the sale of the collateral at issue was conducted in a commercially reasonable manner. *Id.* ("in an action for a deficiency judgment, the secured creditor has the burden of proof to show that the disposition or sale of the collateral was made in a commercially reasonable manner"). Accordingly, to prevail on its summary judgment motion, plaintiff must set forth evidence demonstrating an absence of a genuine issue of material fact and entitlement to judgment as a matter of law in its favor in the amount of $147,966.24, for principal and interest through August 24, 1999, plus pre-judgment and post-judgment interest accruing after that time at a per diem rate of $54.91, plus reasonable attorneys fees and costs. *Celotex*, 477 U.S. at 331. Plaintiff must support its motion with uncontroverted evidence which would entitle it to a directed verdict at trial. *Id.*

The Kansas Uniform Commercial Code (UCC) provides that "every aspect of the disposition [of collateral] including the method, manner, time, place and terms must be commercially reasonable." Kan. Stat. Ann. § 84–9–504(3) (1996). When determining whether the sale of collateral was conducted in a commercially reasonable manner, "the trial court should consider all of the relevant factors together as part of a single transaction." *Westgate*, 231 Kan. at 91, 642 P.2d at 969. In Westgate, the Kansas Supreme Court identified nine factors relevant to determining whether a sale has been conducted in a commercially reasonable manner, including: (1) the duty to clean, fix up, and paint the collateral; (2) public or private disposition; (3) wholesale or retail disposition; (4) disposition by unit or in parcels; (5) the duty to publicize the sale; (6) length of time collateral held prior to sale; (7) duty to give notice of the sale to the debtor and competing secured parties; (8) the actual price received at the sale; and (9) other methods, including the number of bids received and the method employed in soliciting bids, the time and place of the sale. 231 Kan. at 91–94, 642 P.2d at 970–971. This list of factors is not exclusive and a court should consider other factors, where relevant in a particular case. *Id.*

\* \* \*

[Eds. The court concluded that Plaintiff gave proper notice of sale.]

### Piecemeal Sale

Second, defendants contend that, in order for the sale to have been commercially reasonable, the collateral should have been disposed of on a piecemeal basis, rather than in bulk. Specifically, defendants argue the plaintiff's advertisements for the collateral implied that the collateral was offered only in bulk.

2000 Kan. Sess. Laws 949, 1046–47 (2001) ("Pre-effective date proceedings. This act does not affect an action, case, or proceeding commenced before this act takes effect.").

As noted above, the Kansas UCC allows that the "sale or other disposition [of repossessed collateral] may be as a unit or in parcels ..." However, "the linchpin remains commercial reasonableness." *Id.* § 84–9–504, 1996 Kansas Comment, subsection (3). Accordingly, "the secured party may have a duty to dispose of collateral on a piecemeal basis if such a method would generate a higher price."

Reviewing plaintiff's advertisements, the court does not find that a reasonable fact finder could conclude that potential bidders were misled into believing that the collateral was available only as a lot, rather than individually. Plaintiff's advertisements for the sale of the collateral list each item of collateral and indicate that they are "accepting bids." The advertisements do not indicate the collateral may be purchased only in its entirety.

Defendants emphasize that each of the six bids received for the collateral was for the entire lot, rather than for a single item. However, an examination of the bids reveals that although each bidder did seek to purchase the entire lot, they did not use identical language, as may have been done where the advertisements limited purchase to the "entire lot." For example, the bidders placed bids on "your schedule of equipment," "entire package of equipment (16 pieces)," the "entire lot," the "total package," and the "package of equipment."

Moreover, although defendants' expert report places the fair market value of the collateral as a whole at $457,400, compared to the $311,000 received for the collateral by plaintiff, the expert did not opine that selling the collateral individually, rather than in bulk, would have been more likely to generate the fair market value of the collateral.

Accordingly, the court finds the plaintiff's advertisements and the plaintiff's acceptance of one of six bids for the entire lot, did not render the sale commercially unreasonable.

### Price Received for Collateral at Sale

Finally, defendants contend that the price received for the collateral indicates the sale was commercially unreasonable. Specifically, defendants argue the difference between defendants' expert's assessment of the fair market value of the collateral ($457,400) and the price plaintiff obtained from the sale ($311,000) demonstrates the commercial unreasonableness of the sale. That is, defendants argue the $146,400 difference makes the sale presumptively commercially unreasonable.

Although the court must examine the price obtained for the collateral in determining the commercial reasonableness of a sale, "[t]he fact that a better price could have been obtained by a sale at a different time or in a different method from that selected by the secured party is not of itself sufficient to establish that the sale was not made in a commercially reasonable manner." *Id.* § 84–9–507(2). "If the secured party either sells the collateral in the usual manner in any recognized market therefor or if he sells at the price current in such market at the time of his sale or if he has otherwise sold in conformity with reasonable commercial practices among dealers in the type of property sold he has sold in a commercially reasonable manner." *Id.*

Defendants do not argue that the collateral was not sold in a recognized market for the equipment or that the collateral was not sold in the usual manner for the sale of such equipment. Nor do defendants contend that plaintiff did not follow reasonable commercial practices among dealers in the type of equipment sold when selling the collateral. Instead, defendants contend the price obtained for the collateral was not the current price in the market at the time of the sale.

"[C]ourts will frown at a sale which yields a shockingly low price unless the secured creditor can offer a valid explanation...." *Id.* § 84–9–504, 1996 Kansas Comment, subsection (3). Here, plaintiff's agent set forth a valuation of the collateral at the time of repossession of $258,200. In contrast, defendants' expert valued the collateral at the time of the sale at $457,400. Plaintiff obtained a price of $311,000 upon sale of the collateral. The difference between the price obtained and the presumptively correct valuation of the collateral by defendants' expert is large. However, as noted in the Kansas UCC and in Kansas case law, simply because a higher price could have been obtained does not establish a sale was not commercially reasonable. As noted herein, the court finds that each of the remaining factors regarding commercial reasonableness weigh in favor of plaintiff. Therefore, even though a low price was obtained from the sale, because the court has found all procedures regarding the sale of the collateral were handled in line with section 84–9–504 of the Kansas UCC, the court finds the low price, on its own, does not render the sale of the collateral commercially unreasonable. See *id.* § 84–9–504, 1996 Kansas Comment, subsection (3) ("However, if a low price is obtained in a sale for which all procedures were handles in line with this subsection [Kan. Stat. Ann. § 84–9–504], the creditor has a much stronger argument that the sale should not be considered commercially unreasonable.").

### Remaining Factors

Plaintiff argues that, in addition to the three factors discussed above, the five additional relevant factors set forth in Westgate demonstrate the commercial reasonableness of the sale of the collateral. First, plaintiff contends it satisfied its duty to prepare the collateral for sale by hiring Elcor, Inc. to assess, prepare and clean each piece of collateral prior to the sale. Plaintiff invested $6,800 preparing the collateral in order to maximize the ultimate sale price. Second, plaintiff contends it chose the method of disposition—a private sale—most likely to result in a higher return. See *Westgate*, 231 Kan. at 92, 642 P.2d at 970 (noting that a private sale should be used whenever such a disposition is likely to result in a higher return). Third, plaintiff advertised the sale in multiple national trade publications and on several internet sites commonly used by the construction industry. Plaintiff also conducted direct mail solicitations all over the country to likely purchasers. Plaintiff made the collateral available for inspection prior to any sale. Fourth, plaintiff held the collateral for approximately one month prior to agreeing to a sales price. And fifth, plaintiff received six bids from third party bidders prior to accepting the highest bid.

Defendants do not dispute the facts set forth by plaintiff supporting these five factors. Accordingly, the court finds plaintiff has set forth evidence sufficient to establish no genuine issue of material fact exists as to these five factors.

## CONCLUSION

Accordingly, given the above analysis, the court finds plaintiff has met its burden to establish entitlement to judgment as a matter of law on its damages claim. That is, plaintiff has met its burden to establish the commercial reasonableness of the sale of the collateral at issue. Therefore, plaintiff's motion for summary judgment on damages is granted. Plaintiff is granted judgment in the amount of $147,966.24, for principal and interest through August 24, 1999, plus pre-judgment and post-judgment interest accruing after that time at a per diem rate of $54.91, plus reasonable attorneys' fees and costs in an amount to be approved by the court.

\* \* \*

## NOTE

It is difficult to generalize on how courts deal with the commercially reasonable test. Some courts have imposed standards of conduct on secured creditors that would have been unthinkable under pre-Code procedure-oriented foreclosure laws. An example is Liberty National Bank & Trust Co. v. Acme Tool Division of Rucker Co., 540 F.2d 1375 (10th Cir.1976), referred to in the principal case. The court described Liberty Bank's actions in selling an oil rig as follows:

It had no previous experience in selling an oil rig and so the officers inquired or investigated as to the usual manner of such sales. Liberty was told that the ordinary method for selling a drilling rig was to employ an auctioneer to move the rig to a convenient location to clean and paint it and then notify interested persons and, in addition, advertise the sale in trade journals and newspapers. The bank followed none of these suggestions. Indeed, it sold the rig without any professional help. Notices were sent to 16 creditors, including Taurus, and to some 19 other companies. Mrs. Bailey did not receive notice except information furnished by her son-in-law. The rig was neither cleaned, painted nor dismantled. Liberty did not move it to a convenient site, but sold it at the place where it had been near Perryton, Texas. The sale was conducted by an attorney for Liberty who had never conducted an auction of an oil rig or oil field equipment and who lacked experience in the oil business. The attorney was assisted by a Liberty Bank officer who knew something about oil production, but was not acquainted with the drilling of wells. Some 40 or 50 people appeared for the sale, but few made bids. In fact, after the price reached $37,000, there were only two bidders. The final sale price, $42,000, was sufficient to pay off the Taurus note and pay the expenses of the sale, but left little for the other creditors. The rig had been appraised at $60,000 to $80,000.

The successful bidder was Raymond Hefner of Bonray Oil Company and Miller & Miller Auctioneers. In June 1972, Miller & Miller sold the equipment for $77,705.50.

540 F.2d at 1377–78.

In deciding that the sale was not conducted in a commercially reasonable manner (it was held in a snowstorm in Perryton, Texas), the court quoted the District Court's finding of fact:

> The proper way to sell the rig and related equipment would have been to contract with a professional auctioneer, or to follow the same steps and procedures a professional auctioneer follows in disposing of equipment of this type which is to clean and paint the equipment, prepare a brochure and mail it to the proper people; advertise in trade journals, regional newspapers and the Wall Street Journal; move the equipment to a convenient location, and offer the equipment on a piece by piece basis as well as in one lot. The Court finds that the rig and related equipment were not sold by Liberty Bank in the usual manner in a recognized market, nor in conformity with reasonable commercial practices among oil field equipment dealers.

540 F.2d at 1378 n.l.

## PROBLEM

In the paragraph quoted immediately above, the court in *Liberty Bank* says that one of the aspects of conducting a commercially reasonable sale of the equipment in question is to clean and paint it. But former 9–504(1) seemed to give secured parties an option whether to refurbish or not, and Revised 9–610(a) merely paraphrases former 9–504(1) ("in its present condition *or* following any commercially reasonable preparation or processing"). However, Comment 4 is new. How would you advise a creditor client with respect to refurbishing in the light of 9–610(a) and Comment 4?

## c.   LIABILITY FOR DEFICIENCY

### (1)   NONCONSUMER TRANSACTIONS

Prudent creditors think twice before seeking deficiency judgments. A secured party can conduct an extra-judicial foreclosure sale without hiring lawyers and going to court, but they can obtain a deficiency judgment only through a lawsuit, and lawsuits and lawyers are expensive. This means the debtor will also have to hire counsel who may challenge the commercial reasonableness of the foreclosure or assert lender liability claims. Another question is whether a judgment obtained against a debtor who has defaulted on a significant debt is worth anything. The debtor's other assets, if any, may be hard to reach or already encumbered by others. Then, too, in the case in which the debtor is an individual, as in guarantor cases that we will discuss later, a deficiency judgment is dischargeable in bankruptcy. But if, after weighing all these factors, the secured party wishes to pursue a deficiency, the provisions of Revised Article 9 offer reasonably clear guidance.

Section 9–615(d) provides that after disposition of the collateral by the secured party any surplus from the sale goes to the debtor, and the obligor (who is usually, but not always, the debtor) is liable for any deficiency. Of course, if the underlying transaction is an outright sale of, rather than a security interest in, accounts, chattel paper, payment intangibles or promissory notes, 9–615(e) provides that the debtor receives no surplus and the obligor is not liable for a deficiency.

What is the debtor's remedy if the secured party seeking the deficiency fails to comply with the disposition provisions of Article 9? The only remedy, other than injunction, set out in former Article 9 for noncompliance in nonconsumer cases was recovery of damages from the secured party for any loss caused by the failure to comply. Former 9–507(1). But merely awarding compensatory damages for failure of the secured party to give notification before sale, for example, was likely to be of small benefit to debtors because actual damages of any significance were hard to prove and of little deterrence to secured parties. Hence, courts almost unanimously viewed the damages remedy under former Article 9 as inadequate in cases in which the secured party sought a deficiency, and imposed their own sanctions that limited the secured party's right to a deficiency judgment.

The decisions divided among three rules: the "absolute bar," "rebuttable presumption" and "setoff" rules. See Comment 4 to 9–626. The "absolute bar" rule denied the noncomplying secured party a deficiency judgment altogether. It was easy to apply and gave secured creditors the maximum incentive to comply strictly with the statute. It was also grossly unfair in cases in which the secured party's transgression was minor and the deficiency amount was large. Other courts limited the liability of the secured party to the amount by which debt exceeded the amount that would have been recovered at the sale of the collateral had it been disposed of in compliance with the statute. This was called the "rebuttable presumption" rule. The presumption was that the proceeds of the sale were equal to the amount of the debt, leaving no deficiency, unless the secured party could rebut the presumption by proving that a complying sale of the collateral would have brought less than the debt. A majority of courts adopted this rule. A minority followed the "setoff" rule. The rule allows the debtor to deduct from the deficiency owed the amount of its loss caused by the secure party's transgression.

In 9–626(a)(3) and (4), Revised Article 9 adopts the rebuttable presumption rule in nonconsumer transactions. Comment 3 states the rule:

> Unless the secured party proves that compliance with the relevant provisions would have yielded a smaller amount, under paragraph (4) the amount that a complying collection, enforcement, or disposition

would have yielded is deemed to be equal to the amount of the secured obligation, together with expenses and attorney's fees. Thus, the secured party may not recover any deficiency unless it meets this burden.

Thus, if the debtor places in issue the secured party's compliance with Part 6 of Article 9, under 9–626(a)(2) the secured party has the burden of establishing that it has complied with the requirements of Part 6. But, even if it cannot prove, for example, that it gave the required notification before sale, it can still recover a deficiency judgment by proving that the price obtained at the sale was that which would have been produced at a commercially reasonable resale. The secured party's proof consists of showing that the disposition complied with 9–627(b): that it was made in the usual manner on a recognized market, at the price current in that market, and conformed to reasonable commercial practices among dealers in the type of property sold. *GECC* is an example of such a disposition.

### (2) CONSUMER TRANSACTIONS

Both the rebuttable presumption and the absolute bar rules demonstrate judicial hostility toward deficiency judgments. Perhaps one of the unspoken reasons why courts were so willing to curtail deficiency judgments under case law interpreting former Article 9 is the harshness of deficiency judgments in cases in which there is no ready secondhand market for the goods. This is particularly true in the case of used consumer goods like furniture, appliances, and clothing, with respect to which the price on resale may be so low in relation to the value of the item to the debtor and the expenses of resale so high that the embittered debtor ends up without the property but owing a deficiency in excess of the original price. The relatively low balances owing in cases of most consumer goods other than motor vehicles often mean that the cost of resale may be disproportionately great in relation to the amount owing on the contract. No wholly satisfactory solution to the deficiency judgment problem has been worked out. Some states prohibit deficiency judgments in all consumer sales except those of motor vehicles for which the used market is usually good. See, e.g., Cal. Civ. Code 1812.5.

Deficiency judgments in consumer transactions are problematic for creditors as well because they are likely to pose collection problems. The debtor's other assets, if any, may be exempt from judgment under state exemption law, and attempts to garnish the debtor's earnings may drive the debtor into Chapter 7 bankruptcy, in which judgments are dischargeable. Moreover, pursuing deficiency judgments against a consumer debtor forces the consumer to hire counsel who may, if noncompliance is found, recover statutory damages under 9–625(c)(2) for the amount of the finance charge plus 10 percent of the principal amount, which can be a considerable. These statutory damages are easy for debtors to prove.

If, in spite of all this, the secured party seeks a deficiency, 9–626(a) (preamble) and (b) leave to the courts the determination of the proper deficiency rules in consumer transactions. The exclusion of consumer transactions was done at the request of consumer advocates, presumably, to allow courts to continue to apply the absolute bar rule in the many jurisdictions that applied that rule before Revised Article 9 was enacted. Section 9–626(b) reflects the compromise reached between advocates for consumers and secured parties. It prohibits courts from drawing a negative inference in consumer transactions from 9–626(a)'s rebuttable presumption rule to nonconsumer transactions. The prohibition still allows courts to rely on other law to determine the appropriate deficiency rule in consumer transactions.

Section 9–616 is a commendable attempt to tell the hapless consumer who has lost her goods by repossession what her rights are after foreclosure. Under 9–616(b)(1) in consumer goods transactions, if after disposition the debtor is either entitled to a surplus or liable for a deficiency, the secured party may have to give the debtor a detailed explanation of how the surplus or deficiency was calculated. 9–616(c). However, if the debtor or obligor is neither entitled to a surplus nor liable for a deficiency, this explanation need not be made, and even if the obligor is liable for a deficiency the explanation need not be made if the secured party sends the consumer obligor a record waiving its right to a deficiency. 9–616(b)(2). Section 9–625(e)(5) goes easy on secured parties who fail to comply with 9–616. See Comment 4 to 9–616. See also 9–628(d) which frees secured parties who fail to comply with 9–616 from the statutory damages prescribed by 9–625(c)(2).

### d. CRITIQUE OF PUBLIC SALE

Is it possible that in some instances a disposition by public sale cannot be commercially reasonable? Since secured creditors cannot purchase at their own private disposition, they have strong incentive to get the highest price obtainable. But secured parties can buy at their public sales and, like all buyers, their incentive is to bid as little as possible. If there are no higher bids the secured creditor may acquire the property without laying out any cash, merely by credit-bidding (offsetting) the amount of the debt. The creditor may then dispose of the property in any manner. Although Comment 2 to 9–610 states that 9–610(b) "encourages private dispositions on the assumption that they frequently will result in higher realization on collateral for the benefit of all concerned," the option granted to secured parties by 9–610(c) to buy at their public sales encourages public dispositions. In fact, creditors are often the purchasers at their own public sales, sometimes because they are the only bidder.

If Article 9 allows, in fact encourages, the creditor to opt for a public sale, aren't we back where we started before the Code: a funereal auction on the courthouse steps with the only people present being the local public-sale vultures and the secured creditor prepared to bid the amount of the debt? Not if courts take to heart the admonition of 9–610(b) that "[e]very aspect of a disposition of collateral, including the method, manner, time, place, and other terms must, be commercially reasonable." In Farmers Bank v. Hubbard, 276 S.E.2d 622 (Ga. 1981), the creditor sold a tractor and trailer at public sale after advertisement and notice. The creditor sued for a deficiency judgment. The court said:

> In passing, however, we note that it was not shown that selling a tractor-trailer on the courthouse steps was commercially reasonable, where there was no evidence that tractor-trailers are customarily sold on the courthouse steps where the sale occurred. We note further that there was no evidence as to what a dealer in used tractor-trailers would have paid for the tractor-trailer or what an auctioneer would have been able to sell it for. That is to say, courthouse sales may not be commercially reasonable as to all types of collateral, especially where there are better recognized means of marketing the particular collateral involved.

276 S.E.2d at 627. See also In re Frazier, 93 B.R. 366 (Bankr.M.D.Tenn. 1988) (public sale inappropriate for sale of Lear Jet). But if the sale is held at a place convenient for bidders who are interested in collateral of the type sold, and if adequate publicity has been given about the sale, a public sale can be commercially reasonable.

### e.  SECTION 9–615(f)

A method of curtailing deficiency judgments in real property mortgage financing that grew out of the economic depression of the 1930s was to limit the amount of the deficiency to the difference between the amount of the debt and the "fair value" of the land sold on foreclosure. No definition of fair value was stated in these laws, and courts tended to find that the fair value of the land and the amount of the debt were the same, thus protecting mortgagors from both losing their land and being burdened by large deficiency judgments. The traditional safeguards of a noticed public auction were unsuccessful in protecting mortgagors from socially and politically unacceptably large deficiency judgments in those years of economic crisis.

Section 9–615(f) appears to have a similar mission. It is intended to protect debtors by limiting deficiency judgments in cases in which a commercially reasonable, procedurally correct foreclosure sale (i) is made either to the secured party, a person related to the secured party (such as an affiliate), or a secondary obligor (such as a guarantor of the debt), and (ii) the price obtained at the sale is "significantly below the range of proceeds that a complying disposition to a person other than the secured party * * * would have bought." In such a case the deficiency is based on the amount of proceeds that would have been realized by a commercially reasonable disposition to a person other than the secured party, a related person or a secondary obligor. The underlying assumption of the provision is that a secured party or its affiliates lack incentive to bid at a price that equals the value of the collateral. See Comment 6 to 9–615. How would 9–615(f) apply to the outrageous facts in the Problem below, suggested by Williams v. Regency Financial Corp., 309 F.3d 1045 (8th Cir.2002)?

From the standpoint of efficiency, 9–615(f) has three defects. First, secured parties in effect can shift back to debtors ex ante by higher interest charges the risk of an "excessively low" price yielded ex post in a procedurally correct sale. In a world of adjusting secured creditors, 9–615(f) therefore doesn't produce efficiency-gains. Second, the subsection induces transaction costs by encouraging litigation (or settlement) over prices yielded even in some procedurally correct sales. Third, 9–615(f) lacks a workable standard of price disparity. It requires determining the price that a person other than the secured party or one related to it would have paid in a complying disposition. To which set of counterfactual complying dispositions and purchasers does the subsection refer? When a sale to a secured party is commercially reasonable, by definition the proceeds yielded fall within the range of feasible bids for the collateral. Otherwise, the secured party's winning bid makes the sale commercially unreasonable under 9–615(f)(2). Thus, contrary to 9–615(f)'s assumption, it is impossible for a commercially reasonable disposition to the secured party to yield proceeds significantly below those that would have been realized in a sale to bidders unrelated to the secured party. The absence of a workable legal standard for an "excessively low" price again induces litigation or other transaction costs.

## PROBLEM

Sales and Finance were owned by the same company. Sales sold used cars at retail to buyers with sub-prime credit ratings for about twice their cost and charged 18 percent interest. Sales sold all its installment contracts to Finance at a 35 percent discount. When buyers defaulted, their cars were repossessed by Finance and resold to Seller at a low price that created a substantial deficiency. Sales placed the cars back in its inventory, and the process started all over again. Finance employed an attorney to file lawsuits to obtain and collect deficiency judgments. Records showed that Finance had filed more than 1800 such lawsuits in the county, and Sales and Finance were colloquially described as running a "repossession churning mill."

(a) Since 9–615(f) applies only in cases in which there has been a commercially reasonable disposition, does it apply to this case? Does it apply to any case? Is it possible to have a commercially reasonable disposition if the proceeds are "significantly below the range of proceeds that a complying deposition to a person other than the secured party * * * would have brought"? The court in In the Matter of Excello Press, 890 F.2d 896, 905 (7th Cir.1989) (Easterbrook, J.), opined: "The price obtained in a commercially reasonable sale is not *evidence* of the market value * * * It *is* the market value."

(b) How do we know when a sale price is "significantly below the range of proceeds" when neither the Code nor the comments provide guidance on the issue? Could a debtor establish this fact in a sale of collateral to the secured party if: (1) the secured party bid the full amount of the obligation and resold the collateral for twice the price two months later? (2) some other bidders made bona fide bids at the sale?, or (3) other people attending the sale testified that they would have bid but that they assessed the collateral's value below the amount of the secured party's bid?

PROBLEMS

**1.** Debtor is a retail automobile dealer and Secured Party finances Debtor's inventory. The following clause appears in the security agreement: "Debtor further agrees that if Secured Party shall solicit bids from three or more other dealers in the type of property repossessed by Secured Party hereunder, any sale by Secured Party of such property to the bidder submitting the highest cash bid therefor shall be deemed to be a commercially reasonable means of disposing of the same." Debtor contends the clause is an invalid attempt at a waiver barred by 9–602(7). Secured Party asserts that it is a valid exercise of 9–603(a). Who is right? See Ford Motor Credit Co. v. Solway, 825 F.2d 1213 (7th Cir.1987).

**2.** On August 1, Debtor purchased a used car from Dealer for $1,595 plus finance charges, payable under an installment sale contract under which Dealer was granted a security interest in the car. The car immediately developed mechanical problems and Debtor had to return the car several times for repairs. On August 25, after paying only one partial installment Debtor refused to make additional payments and surrendered the car to Dealer. After making a demand for payment which was ignored, Dealer sent written notice to Debtor that after October 15 the car would be sold at private sale. The car was purchased by Dealer at a private sale to itself on October 16. The sale took place by means of an interoffice exchange of papers by which Debtor was credited with $900, the proceeds of the sale. Debtor was also credited with the amount of the down payment and first installment payment totaling $95. Dealer then brought an action against Debtor for a deficiency judgment of $600 ($1,595–$995).

Dealer testified that the $900 value was based on the wholesale value for used cars of the same model, year etc. stated in the then-current market reporter or "blue book" used by used car dealers in the area. Dealer resold the car to a retail customer for $1,495 a few weeks after Debtor surrendered the car.

How much is Dealer entitled to recover from Debtor? Would your answer differ if Dealer had sold the car surrendered by Debtor to another used car dealer for $900 and used that sale as the basis for its deficiency judgment claim? See Vic Hansen & Sons, Inc. v. Crowley, 203 N.W.2d 728 (Wis. 1973).

f.  TRANSFER STATEMENTS

If foreclosure sales are to bring something approximating the value of the collateral, the secured party who conducts the sale must be able to pass good title to the transferee (the purchaser at the sale). But the secured party doesn't own the collateral. In Motors Acceptance Corp. v. Rozier, 597

S.E.2d 367, 367 (Ga. 2004), the court stated: "The question * * * in this case is whether, under Georgia law, ownership of collateral passes from a debtor to a creditor upon repossession. * * * [W]e hold that ownership remains with the debtor until the creditor disposes of or elects to retain the collateral in accordance with the procedures of the" UCC; accord In re Vaughn, 2006 WL 44261 (E.D. Mich. 2006) (majority of courts follow *Rozier*). However, 9–617(a)(1) empowers the selling secured party to pass "all of the debtor's rights in the collateral" to the transferee, and warranties of title, possession, quiet enjoyment, and the like, are made unless disclaimed. See 9–610(c) and (d).

Problems arise if the collateral, such as a motor vehicle, is subject to a certificate of title statute, and the name on the title is that of a buyer as the record owner who won't voluntarily indorse the title and deliver it to the secured creditor. This precludes the transferee from having a new certificate of title issued to it by the state DMV. Before Revised Article 9, some states addressed this problem by allowing the secured party to obtain a title-clearing transfer statement vesting title in either the secured party or the transferee, which the transferee at the disposition sale could submit with its application for issuance of title in its name. Section 9–619 brings this title-clearing solution into Article 9. It contemplates a transfer of title to the secured party if the statement is sought before disposition, or to the transferee if obtained after disposition. The pre-Revision cases had been divided on whether a title-clearing transfer was a disposition under Article 9. Section 9–619(c) makes clear that it is not; the secured party retains its duties under Article 9.

## 4.   SECONDARY OBLIGORS

Under 9–102(a)(28) "debtor" includes "a person having an interest, other than a security interest or other lien, in the collateral, whether or not the person is an obligor." Typically, the interest would be an ownership interest. "Obligor" under 9–102(a)(59) includes a person who "owes payment or other performance" of the secured obligation. Usually the obligor is also the debtor. Section 9–102(a)(71) defines "secondary obligor" as meaning an obligor to the extent that "the obligor's obligation is secondary" or "the obligor has a right of recourse with respect to an obligation secured by collateral against the debtor, another obligor, or property of either." See the brief discussions of these terms in Comment 2a to 9–102. The Restatement (Third) of Suretyship and Guaranty § 1 (1996), in general terms, speaks of a secondary obligation as one in which the secondary obligor is liable to the obligee but, as between the principal obligor and the secondary obligor, it is the principal obligor who is ultimately liable. Under § 17 of the Restatement, when a secondary obligor has paid the obligee, it is subrogated to all rights of the obligee against the principal obligor. Guarantors and sureties are secondary obligors. There is no definition of "guarantor" and the word is not used in Article 9.

Case #1. D grants a security interest to SP in its equipment to secure a loan made by SP to D. D is a debtor and an obligor. This is the most common case.

Case #2. D grants a security interest to SP in its equipment to secure a loan made by SP to D, and G signs a separate agreement promising to pay D's debt if D defaults. D is a debtor and obligor. G is a secondary obligor.

Case #3. D grants a security interest in its equipment to SP to secure a loan by SP to D, and G cosigns D's promissory note, which evidences D's obligation to SP, as an accommodation party under 3–419. G is a secondary obligor. These cases are discussed in Comment 2a to 9–102.

Two issues concerning guarantors were widely litigated before enactment of Revised Article 9. One issue was whether a guarantor was entitled to receive notification before disposition. Under former Article 9 this turned on whether a guarantor was a debtor. The majority view was that guarantors were debtors for these purposes. Revised Article expressly provides in 9–611(c) that secondary obligors, as well as debtors, are entitled to notification of disposition.

The second issue was whether guarantors could make effective pre-default waiver of their rights under Article 9 to notification and a commercially reasonable disposition. The traditional rule is that guarantors may make effective waivers of their defenses, and the PEB Study Group Report, Recommendation 31.B, at 226–27, favored validating a guarantor's pre-default waiver of the right to notification of disposition of the collateral.

The Committee members sense that the principal effect of not permitting pre-default waivers of notifications of dispositions of collateral by debtors (including guarantors) has been to confer undeserved windfalls. In many cases in which the failure to notify is simply an inadvertent administrative lapse, it is likely that the guarantor knows about the debtor's default and is in a position to protect its interests in advance of the secured party's disposition of collateral. In the experience of the Committee members, creditors normally make demand for payment against guarantors long before resorting to a disposition of collateral. Moreover, an uncompensated guarantor of payment, whether the guarantor is an individual acting in a consumer transaction or a business entity participating in a commercial transaction, typically has some affiliation with the principal obligor or an interest in the underlying transaction. Consequently, if the guarantor so wishes, it can obtain the principal obligor's contractual undertaking to notify the guarantor of any default, any repossession, any proposed disposition of collateral, or any other circumstance of which the guarantor wishes to have notice.

Early drafts of Revised Article 9 followed the PEB recommendation, but 9–602(7) provides that neither debtors nor obligors may waive the right to a commercially reasonable disposition under 9–610(b) or notification of disposition under 9–611. Comment 4 to 9–602 observes that this resolves the issue that arose under former Article 9 of whether secondary obligors could make effective pre-default waivers of their Article 9 rights.

PROBLEM

Section 9–611(c) requires the secured party to send notification of disposition to "any secondary obligor," as well as to the debtor. Has notification been sent to the guarantor in the following common fact situation? Bank sent a notification of sale to Debtor, a corporation, giving adequate notice of the time after which Bank would conduct a private sale of Debtor's collateral. Although no such notice was sent to Volpe, a guarantor, she, as the chief executive officer of Debtor, was shown the notice as soon as it arrived at Debtor's place of business and clearly had actual knowledge of the contents of the notice. Volpe contends that these facts do not comply with the statutory requirement that notification of the sale must be sent to her. Is she correct? United Missouri Bank v. Gagel, 815 F.Supp. 387 (D.Kan.1993). See 1–201(b)(36) ("Send"), 1–202 ("Notice; Knowledge"). If she is correct, is this the kind of windfall that the PEB had in mind?

## 5. ACCEPTANCE OF COLLATERAL IN SATISFACTION OF DEBT

*Strict foreclosure.* Article 9 provides a secured party alternate procedures for cutting off the debtor's rights in the collateral after default: disposition under 9–610 and acceptance by the secured party of the collateral in satisfaction of the secured obligation under 9–620. The latter procedure is known as "strict foreclosure." The drafters of the revision made expansion and clarification of this procedure one of their imperatives. It may be mutually advantageous to the secured party and the debtor to choose strict foreclosure. Under this procedure, the secured party receives the collateral without the expense and delay of a foreclosure sale as well as the uncertainties of complying with the commercially reasonable standard in disposing of the collateral. The secured creditor can then market the returned collateral in any manner it wishes. The defaulting debtor, who concedes that it cannot pay the secured debt, escapes any further liability for a deficiency, which would be even greater with addition of the expenses of disposition. This procedure may be especially attractive to secured parties in the all-to-frequent case in which recovery of a deficiency from the defaulting debtor is unlikely. Thus, the drafters promote strict foreclosure as a cheaper and faster way of realizing on collateral.

*Consent to acceptance in full satisfaction.* Secured parties can enjoy the benefits of strict foreclosure only if the debtor after default consents to the acceptance in satisfaction. With respect to cases in which the secured party is offering full satisfaction, the debtor may consent by expressly agreeing to the terms of the acceptance in a record authenticated after default. 9–620(c)(2) Alternatively, it may consent by its silence. The secured party may send the debtor a proposal to accept the collateral in full satisfaction of the secured obligation. If the secured party has not received an authenticated notification of the debtor's objection within 20 days after the proposal is sent, the debtor is deemed to have accepted the secured party's proposal. 9–620(c)(2).

In real property law, if the parties wish to avoid a foreclosure sale, a common practice is for the mortgagor and mortgagee to expressly agree that the mortgagor will deed the property to the mortgagee, who will then release the debtor from any further liability on the debt. This is commonly referred to as a "deed in lieu of foreclosure." Real property law has never embraced acceptance by silence as a method of agreement, and one might ask why Article 9 does so. Certainly, acceptance by silence under Article 9 has raised problems.

## PROBLEM

In Reeves v. Foutz & Tanner, Inc., 617 P.2d 149 (N.M. 1980), two uneducated Navajos with limited ability to understand English pawned jewelry with a lender as security for a thirty-day loan. The jewelry was worth much more than the amount borrowed. The debtors defaulted and the lender sent each of them a notice of intent to retain the collateral. Neither debtor objected and the lender sold the jewelry in the regular course of its business for more than the amount of the debt. In selling the jewelry, the lender treated the jewelry as belonging to it through the debtors' acceptance by silence. The debtors contended that the lender could not sell the collateral as its own property without complying with the requirements for a commercially reasonable resale, which would result in a surplus to be returned to the debtors. The trial court found that the secured party acted in bad faith in disposing of the collateral. What remedy is appropriate? See 1–304 and Comment 11 to 9–620.

---

Professor Gilmore's prescience is shown by his comment on the acceptance-by-silence provision in former Article 9:

> Now what is to happen when a secured party makes a proposal to retain, say, a million dollars' worth of collateral in satisfaction of a hundred-thousand-dollar debt—or a thousand dollars' worth of collateral in satisfaction of a hundred-dollar debt—and, through oversight in the million-dollar case or ignorance in the thousand-dollar case, no one who is qualified to object does so within the statutory time limits? The courts will do what they always have done and always will do. If fraud is alleged by someone who has standing to complain of it, the allegation will be inquired into. If the fraud is proved, the offending transaction will be set aside and the court will devise an appropriate remedy.

2 Grant Gilmore, Security Interests in Personal Property § 44.3, at 1226–1227 (1965).

*Acceptance in partial satisfaction.* A debtor may consent to acceptance of collateral in partial satisfaction only if the debtor expressly agrees to the terms of the acceptance in a record authenticated after default. 9–620(c)(1). Acceptance by silence is not allowed.

Case #1. Debtor is in default on a $100,000 obligation owing to SP that is secured by an interest in Debtor's equipment, now in SP's possession. Debtor is unsure how much the collateral would bring at a foreclosure sale. Under 9–620(c)(2), Debtor can consent to SP's proposal that it agrees accept the collateral in full satisfaction by failing to object within 20 days after the proposal is sent.

Case #2. Same facts except that SP's proposal is that it agrees to accept the collateral in satisfaction of $50,000 of the debt. In this case, Debtor can consent only by an express agreement under 9–620(c)(1).

Why is Debtor's silence considered adequate evidence of its best interest in the case of full satisfaction but not in the case of partial satisfaction? In both cases Debtor's decision will rest on its assessment of the value of the collateral. Debtor should object to SP's proposal in Case #1 if it believes the collateral is likely to bring more than $100,000 on a commercially reasonable disposition. In Case #2 it should object if it believes the collateral would bring more than $50,000. What's the difference? Is it that if Debtor underestimates the value of the collateral, in Case #1, it can only lose a surplus, but in Case #2 it may be liable for a greater deficiency?

*Consumer debtors.* Section 9–620(g) forbids a secured party from accepting collateral in partial satisfaction of the obligation it secures in a consumer transaction. Nor is acceptance in satisfaction of consumer goods effective if possession of the collateral is still with the debtor. 9–620(a)(3). Apparently the latter limitation is based on the concerns expressed in the PEB Study Group Report, Recommendation 34.A., at p. 241 that until the secured party has repossessed consumers may not take acceptance-in-satisfaction notices seriously.

Out of an abundance of caution, 9–620(e) requires that a secured party in possession of consumer goods collateral must foreclose by disposition under 9–610 if the debtor has paid either 60 percent of the cash price of the collateral or 60 percent of the obligation secured by the goods. The belief is that if the debtor has paid this much, it is entitled to have the possibility of a surplus tested by a disposition. Section 9–620(f) requires the mandated disposition to take place within 90 days after taking possession. Both mandated dispositions and the ban on partial strict foreclosure are mandatory terms that can't be altered by agreement. 9–602(10). However, Comment 3 to 9–610 allows the parties to "settle" claims arising from breach of these mandatory terms.

*Intangibles.* Former Article 9 allowed strict foreclosure only with respect to collateral in the possession of the secured party. This called into question any attempt at strict foreclosure in cases involving intangibles, such as accounts. The PEB Study Group Report, Recommendation 34.A, sought deletion of the possession requirement, and 9–620 follows this recommendation by dropping any mention of possession, except in the consumer case covered by 9–620(a)(3). Comment 10 to 9–620 explains that a consequence of allowing satisfaction by acceptance of collateral like accounts, chattel paper, payment intangibles and promissory notes is that the secured party's acceptance is a sale to the secured party which would normally give rise to a new security interest in that party under 1–201(b)(35) and 9–109(a)(3).

Sections 9–605 and 9–628 are exculpation provisions that protect foreclosing secured parties from liability to unknown persons. Comment 2 to 9–605 explains: "[A] secured party may be unaware that the original debtor has sold the collateral subject to the security interest and that the new owner has become the debtor. If so, the secured party owes no duty to the new owner (debtor) or to a secured party who has filed a financing statement against the new owner." Accordingly, 9–628 provides that the secured party is not liable to these persons.

*"Constructive" strict foreclosure.* The most litigated issue in pre-Revision case law in the area of acceptance in satisfaction was whether a secured party's retention of possession of repossessed collateral for a long period without either foreclosing by sale or proposing acceptance in satisfaction amounted to a "constructive" acceptance in satisfaction, which deprived the secured party of the right to a deficiency. This issue focused on the nature of the secured party's interest in the collateral after repossession but before sale.

PROBLEM

Seller sold his appliance business, including all inventory, receivables, and furnishings, to Buyer for $300,000. Buyer paid $50,000 down, signed a note to Seller for the remaining $250,000 secured by a security interest in all the property acquired from Seller, and took possession of these assets at the place of business. The note was payable in monthly installments over a period of five years. Seller perfected his security interest in the collateral by filing. After six months, Buyer found that she was unable to make her payments; she called Seller and told him that she "would have to ask him to call off the deal and take back his business." Soon after, she vacated the premises and enrolled in business school. Seller went back into possession, where he found to his dismay that the assets were currently worth no more than $200,000. After brooding about the matter for several months, Seller sent Buyer a demand that she pay him the difference, $50,000, between the value of the assets that he had sold her (less her down payment) and the value of the goods that she returned to him. Buyer replied that she thought the deal was that Seller would keep the $50,000 down payment and take back his collateral, and that she was released from any further liability. (i) What are Seller's rights with respect to the collateral after repossession? Does Seller own the collateral or must he cut off Buyer's rights in the collateral by either disposition or acceptance in satisfaction? (ii) Some pre-Revision cases held that Seller in this case would have no right to a deficiency judgment because, owing to Seller's delay, there has been a "constructive" acceptance in satisfaction by Seller. Would this be true under 9–620(b)?

## 6.   EFFECT OF DISPOSITION OR ACCEPTANCE ON THIRD PARTIES

### a.   TRANSFEREES

A person who buys at a foreclosure sale is called a transferee by 9–617. The popular usage of "purchaser" for such a person is not technically correct because, as Comment 2 explains, the transfer is not voluntary with respect to the debtor. Although the selling secured party does not "own" the collateral after repossession, 9–617(a)(1) empowers it to make a transfer of all the debtor's rights to the transferee. Unless disclaimed by the secured party, such a transfer includes warranties relating to title, possession, quiet enjoyment and the like. 9–610(d) and (e).

### PROBLEM

SP sold Debtor's collateral to Transferee for value at a public auction sale that met all the requirements for a commercially reasonable disposition, but for the fact that SP gave Debtor no notification of sale. Transferee had no knowledge of SP's error. What are Debtor's rights against Transferee and SP? See 9–617(b), Comment 2 to 9–617, and 9–625(b).

### b.   JUNIOR SECURITY INTERESTS OR LIENS

#### (1)   DISPOSITIONS

If buyers are to be induced to bid at a foreclosure sale, they must be able to buy the property free of any security interests or liens that are junior to the security interest that is being foreclosed. Section 9–617(a)(3) affords them this protection. Since foreclosure sales cut off the rights of junior lien holders in the collateral sold, these parties have a strong interest in having the sale made for a price that will leave a surplus to be distributed to them under 9–615(a), for if there is no surplus they are relegated to the status of being unsecured creditors of the debtor. Thus, they want notification of sale and a method of claiming any surplus resulting from the disposition.

Under former Article 9, the duty of senior secured parties to notify junior secured parties was controversial. Should notice be given only to those who gave written request for notice, or should the secured party have the duty to notify any junior secured party whose security interest was on file? The developments on this issue over the life of former Article 9 are described in Comment 4 to 9–611. Section 9–611(c)(3) requires notification of sale to be given (i) to a person who has given the secured party before sale notification of a claim to the collateral, and (ii) any other secured party or lienholder whose interest was perfected by a filing statement indexed in the debtor's name in the proper filing office. Hence, the burden is placed on the secured party to search the files. Some of the difficulties likely to arise under this requirement are ameliorated by 9–611(e). See Comment 4 to 9–611. Even though a junior secured party whose financing statement is properly filed is entitled to notification of the disposition, this person is entitled to share in any surplus from the sale only if the foreclosing secured party receives from the junior "an authenticated demand for proceeds before distribution of the proceeds is completed." 9–615(a)(3)(A).

## PROBLEM

SPA, who held the senior security interest in Debtor's collateral, sold the collateral to Transferee for value at a public auction sale that met all the requirements for a commercially reasonable sale. However, SPA failed to give the notification of sale required by 9–611(c)(3)(B) to SPB, who held a junior security interest in the same collateral that had been perfected by filing several months before the sale. Transferee knew of SPB's interest but had no knowledge that SPA had failed to give the requisite notice to SPB. (i) Does Transferee take the property subject to SPB's security interest? See 9–617(a)(3). (ii) What are SPB's rights against SPA? See 9–625(b) and (c)(1).

------------

What is the loss that must be shown in order for a junior secured party to recover damages under 9–625(b)? In McGowen v. Nebraska State Bank, 427 N.W.2d 772 (Neb. 1988), the senior secured party failed to notify the junior secured party of the sale of the collateral. The junior contended that it was damaged by the lack of notice because it was deprived of the profit that could have been realized by buying the collateral at the senior's sale and subsequently selling it at a higher price. The court decided in favor of the senior:

> We hold that the "loss" envisioned by [former] 9–507(1), as to junior lienholders, refers to the loss of any surplus proceeds due to an improper disposition of the collateral. Surplus proceeds in this case means the difference between the fair market value of the collateral, if sold at a proper sale, and the amount required to satisfy the senior lien. Thus, a junior lienholder can only be said to suffer a loss due to lack of notice if a commercially reasonable sale would have produced an amount in excess of the senior lien.

427 N.W.2d at 775. River Valley State Bank v. Peterson, 453 N.W.2d 193 (Wis. App.1990), is in accord. See Steve H. Nickles, Rights and Remedies Between U.C.C. Article 9 Secured Parties with Conflicting Security Interests in Goods, 68 Iowa L. Rev. 217 (1983).

## (2) ACCEPTANCE IN SATISFACTION

The most ambitious reform in this area proposed by the Revision is to state the effect of acceptance in satisfaction on the rights of others. Section 9–622(a) provides that a secured party's acceptance of collateral in full or partial satisfaction of debt not only transfers to the secured party all of the debtor's rights in the collateral but also cuts off all rights of junior lienors and other subordinate interests. This resolves for Article 9 purposes a controversy that has cast a cloud over real property deed-in-lieu transactions. That is, if the debtor deeds the property to the mortgagee in satisfaction of the mortgage debt, does the mortgagee take the property subject to any junior liens under the nefarious doctrine of merger, which holds that the mortgagee's lien is discharged by merging into ownership? Ann M. Burkhart, Freeing Mortgages of Merger, 40 Vand.L.Rev. 283 (1987). After all, the junior lienors didn't consent to the transfer and no court order has foreclosed their interests. In consequence, real property mortgagees will usually not enter into a deed-in-lieu transaction if there are junior lienors.

Since 9–622(a)(4) allows an acceptance of collateral by the secured party with the consent of the debtor to cut off all junior liens, fairness requires that junior parties be allowed to prevent this from happening by objecting. Accordingly, 9–621(a) provides that the secured party must send notification of its proposal not only to parties who notify the secured party that they claim an interest but also to holders of security interests who have perfected by filing financing statements or who have otherwise perfected by compliance with certificate of title acts. These parties can halt the secured party's attempt at strict foreclosure by objecting within the periods set out in 9–620(d). Even though no proposal need be sent to the debtor if it agrees to an acceptance in an authenticated record, a proposal must be sent to third parties entitled to notification, whether or not there was agreement between the secured party and debtor, allowing them to object to the acceptance in satisfaction. Comment 4 to 9–620. What if the secured party fails to notify junior lienors or otherwise fails to comply with the Act? Section 9–622(b) provides that the secured party still takes the property free of their interests, but these parties may sue for damages pursuant to 9–625(b) for any loss resulting from the secured party's noncompliance with this section.

## 7. COLLECTION OF RIGHTS TO PAYMENT

Comment 2 to 9–607 explains the advantages creditors have in realizing on collateral consisting of rights to payment over creditors whose collateral is tangible property. We have seen the difficulties encountered in realizing on tangible personal property. The selling creditor must be concerned about refurbishing or repairing the property, selling it in the proper market, and getting a decent price even though the liquidation value of used goods may be disproportionately low compared to their original cost. In short, the selling creditor must make sure that goods were disposed of in a manner that a reviewing court years later will deign to call commercially reasonable. Contrast the position of a creditor having a security interest in accounts, chattel paper, payment intangibles or promissory notes. If the financing arrangement calls for account debtors to pay the secured party directly, the secured party continues to collect after the default of the debtor assignor. If the security agreement calls for account debtors to pay the debtor assignor, 9–607(a)(1) (and invariably the security agreement) allows the secured party to notify the account debtors to make their payments directly to the secured party in the future. See Loan Agreement 8.2 (Notification of Account Debtors), Appendix I. Under 9–406(a), the account debtors must comply. There is no requirement that the secured party must notify the debtor before it collects directly from the account debtors. If the accounts are good, the secured party collects one hundred cents on the dollar and does so with very little additional expense. If the secured party does not choose to collect the accounts, it may dispose of the collateral by sale under 9–610.

In Parvez v. Bigelman, 58 UCC Rep. Serv.2d 475 (Mich. App. 2005), after the apparent default of the debtor-assignor, secured party sent letters to the account debtors stating that secured party had a perfected security interest in all debtor's accounts and that, owing to debtor's default, the account debtors were to directed pay to secured party any amounts owing to debtor. Debtor sued secured party for tortuous interference with its business relationship, alleging it was not in default and that secured party had acted in bad faith by sending the letters without investigating whether default had occurred and without first obtaining a judgment of default. Debtor claimed that as a result of the letters debtor's customers assumed that debtor was going into bankruptcy and ceased doing business with debtor. The court granted the secured party summary judgment; debtor had come forward with no evidence contravening secured party's assertions that it had only legitimate business purposes in mind when it distributed the letters. It held that if default had occurred, the secured party had no duty to investigate the existence of the default or to obtain a judgment of default before sending the letters to the account debtors. If debtor's business was disrupted, so be it. Although the case was decided under former 9–502(1), 9–607(a) confirms the court's decision.

In some cases account debtors may be somewhat reluctant to voluntarily make their payments to the secured party. But under 9–607(a)(3) the secured party may actively enforce the obligations of the account debtor or obligor to pay the debtor and exercise the rights and remedies of the debtor with respect to these obligations. Thus, a secured party may collect whatever is owed on the collateral directly from the account debtor or obligor whether the security agreement provides for the account debtor or obligor to pay the debtor, as in "nonnotification" financing, or to pay the secured party, as in "notification" financing.

What duties does the secured party owe the debtor in the collection process? Under 9–607(c), the question of whether a secured party must proceed in a commercially reasonable manner in collecting from account debtors is determined by whether the assignee of the right to payment has a right of recourse against the debtor. The debtor's right to a commercially reasonable collection under 9–607(c) may not be waived. 9–602(3). In all cases in which the assignment secures a debt there will be a right of recourse. But, as Comment 9 to 9–607 assures us, in most true sales the assignee will have no right of recourse against the debtor. In fact, the existence of the right of recourse is a strong factor that many courts invoke to characterize a transaction as a security assignment. See In re De–Pen Line, Inc., 215 B.R. 947 (Bankr.E.D.Pa.1997); Thomas E. Plank, The True Sale of Loans and the Role of Recourse, 14 Geo. Mason U. L. Rev. 287 (1991). Section 9–607(c) imposes the duty of commercial reasonableness on buyers in true sales only in unusual cases in which there is a right of recourse. Comment 9 explains why the commercially reasonable duty should apply in such a case: "The obligation to proceed in a commercially reasonable manner arises because the collection process affects the extent of the seller's recourse liability, not because the seller retains an interest in the sold collateral (the seller does not)."

Section 9–608(b) provides: "If the underlying transaction is a sale of accounts, chattel paper, payment intangibles, or promissory notes, the debtor is not entitled to any surplus, and the obligor is not liable for any deficiency." But Comment 4 to 9–109 concedes that even though in some cases Article 9 distinguishes between outright sales of receivables and sales that secure an obligation, it does not provide a test for the distinction. "That issue is left to the courts." One of the leading decisions on that issue follows.

# Major's Furniture Mart, Inc. v. Castle Credit Corp.

United States Court of Appeals, Third Circuit, 1979.
602 F.2d 538.

■ GARTH, CIRCUIT JUDGE:

This appeal requires us to answer the question: "When is a sale not a sale, but rather a secured loan?" The district court held that despite the form of their Agreement, which purported to be, and hence was characterized as, a sale of accounts receivable, the parties' transactions did not constitute sales. Major's Furniture Mart, Inc. v. Castle Credit Corp., 449 F.Supp. 538 (E.D.Pa.1978). No facts are in dispute, and the issue presented on this appeal is purely a legal issue involving the interpretation of relevant sections of the Uniform Commercial Code * * * and their proper application to the undisputed facts presented here.

The district court granted plaintiff Major's motion for summary judgment. Castle Credit Corporation appeals from that order. We affirm.

Major's is engaged in the retail sale of furniture. Castle is in the business of financing furniture dealers such as Major's. Count I of Major's amended complaint alleged that Major's and Castle had entered into an Agreement dated June 18, 1973 for the financing of Major's accounts receivable; that a large number of transactions pursuant to the Agreement took place between June 1973 and May 1975; that in March and October 1975 Castle declared Major's in default under the Agreement; and that from and after June 1973 Castle was in possession of monies which constituted a surplus over the accounts receivable transferred under the

Agreement. Among other relief sought, Major's asked for an accounting of the surplus and all sums received by Castle since June 1, 1976 which had been collected from the Major's accounts receivable transferred under the Agreement.

The provisions of the June 18, 1973 Agreement which are relevant to our discussion provide: that Major's shall from time to time "sell" accounts receivable to Castle, and that all accounts so "sold" shall be with full recourse against Major's. Major's was required to warrant that each account receivable was based upon a written order or contract fully performed by Major's.[3] Castle in its sole discretion could refuse to "purchase" any account. The amount paid by Castle to Major's on any particular account was the unpaid face amount of the account exclusive of interest[4] less a fifteen percent "discount"[5] and less another ten percent of the unpaid face amount as a reserve against bad debts.[6]

Under the Agreement the reserve was to be held by Castle without interest and was to indemnify Castle against a customer's failure to pay the full amount of the account (which included interest and insurance premiums), as well as any other charges or losses sustained by Castle for any reason.

In addition, Major's was required to "repurchase" any account "sold" to Castle which was in default for more than 60 days. In such case Major's was obligated to pay to Castle

> an amount equal to the balance due by the customer on said Account plus any other expenses incurred by CASTLE as a result of such default or breach of warranty, less a rebate of interest on the account under the "Rule of the 78's"....[7]

---

**3.** The parties do not dispute that their rights are governed by the law of Pennsylvania. The Pennsylvania Uniform Commercial Code, and in particular § 9–105, classifies the accounts receivable which are the subject of the agreement as "chattel paper."

**4.** According to Major's brief, the "face amount" of its customers' installment payment agreements included (1) the retail cost of the furniture purchased (amount financed), (2) the total amount of interest payable by the customer over the life of the customer's installment payment agreement, and (3) insurance charges.

**5.** The 15% "discount" was subsequently increased unilaterally by Castle to 18% and thereafter was adjusted monthly to reflect changes in the prime rate (Appellee's Supplemental Appendix 3b–4b).

**6.** It becomes apparent from a review of the record that the amount which Castle actually paid to Major's on each account transferred was the unpaid face amount ex-

clusive of interest *and* exclusive of insurance premiums less 28% (18% "discount" and 10% reserve).

In its brief on appeal, Castle sets out the following summary of the transactions that took place over the relevant period. It appears that the face amount of the accounts which were "sold" by Major's to Castle was $439,832.08, to which finance charges totaling $116,350.46 and insurance charges totaling $42,304.03 were added, bringing the total amount "purchased" by Castle to $598,486.57. For these "purchases" Castle paid Major's $316,107. Exclusive of any surplus as determined by the district court Castle has retained $528,176.13 which it has received as a result of customer collections and repurchases by Major's. Collection costs were found by the district court to be $1,627.81.

**7.** The Rule of 78 is "the predominant method used to determine refunds of unearned finance charges upon prepayment of

Thus essentially, Major's was obligated to repurchase a defaulted account not for the discounted amount paid to it by Castle, but for a "repurchase" price based on the balance due by the customer, plus any costs incurred by Castle upon default.

As an example, applying the Agreement to a typical case, Major's in its brief on appeal summarized an account transaction of one of its customers (William Jones) as follows:

> A customer Jones of Major's (later designated Account No. 15,915) purchased furniture from Major's worth $1700.00 (or more). [H]e executed an installment payment agreement with Major's in the total face amount of $2549.88, including interest and insurance costs.... Using this piece of chattel paper, ... Major's engaged in a financing transaction with Castle under the Agreement.... Major's delivered the Jones' chattel paper with a $2549.88 face amount of Castle together with an assignment of rights. Shortly thereafter, Castle delivered to Major's cash in the amount of $1224.00. The difference between this cash amount and the full face of the chattel paper in the amount of $2549.88, consisted of the following costs and deductions by Castle:
>
> 1. $180.00 discount credited to a "reserve" account of Major's.
> 2. $300.06 "discount" (actually a prepaid interest charge).
> 3. $30.85 for life insurance premium.
> 4. $77.77 for accident and health insurance premium.
> 5. $152.99 for property insurance premium.
> 6. $588.27 interest charged to Jones on the $1700 face of the note.

Thus, as to the Jones' account, Castle received and proceeded to collect a piece of chattel paper with a collectible face value of $2549.88. Major's received $1224.00 in cash.

As we understand the Agreement, if Jones in the above example defaulted without having made any payments on account, the very least Major's would have been obliged to pay on repurchase would be $1,700 even though Major's had received only $1,224 in cash on transfer of the account and had been credited with a reserve of $180. The repurchase price was either charged fully to reserve or, as provided in the Agreement, 50% to reserve and 50% by cash payment from Major's. In the event of bankruptcy, default under the agreement or discontinuation of business, Major's was required to repurchase all outstanding accounts immediately.
\* \* \*

consumer debts." Hunt, James H., "The Rule of 78: Hidden Penalty for Prepayment in Consumer Credit Transactions," 55 B.U. L. Rev. 331, 332 (1975). That article points out that the Rule of 78 allocates a disproportionately large portion of finance charges to the early months of a credit transaction which produces a hidden penalty for prepayment, although the extent of the penalty diminishes as the term of the debt nears expiration.

Apparently a rebate of insurance premiums was provided as well as a rebate of interest.

Under the Agreement, over 600 accounts were transferred to Castle by Major's of which 73 became delinquent and subject to repurchase by Major's. On March 21, 1975, Castle notified Major's that Major's was in default in failing to repurchase delinquent accounts. Apparently to remedy the default, Major's deposited an additional $10,000 into the reserve. After June 30, 1975, Major's discontinued transferring accounts to Castle. On October 7, 1975 Castle again declared Major's in default.

Major's action against Castle alleged that the transaction by which Major's transferred its accounts to Castle constituted a financing of accounts receivable and that Castle had collected a surplus of monies to which Major's was entitled. We are thus faced with the question which we posed at the outset of this opinion: did the June 18, 1973 Agreement create a *secured interest* in the accounts, or did the transaction constitute a *true sale* of the accounts? The district court, contrary to Castle's contention, refused to construe the Agreement as one giving rise to the sales of accounts receivable. Rather, it interpreted the Agreement as creating a security interest in the accounts which accordingly was subject to all the provisions of Article 9 of the U.C.C. It thereupon entered its order of June 13, 1977 granting Major's' motion for summary judgment and denying Castle's motion for summary judgment. This order was ultimately incorporated into the court's final judgment entered May 5, 1978 which specified the amount of surplus owed by Castle to Major's. It was from this final judgment that Castle appealed.

Castle on appeal argues (1) that the express language of the Agreement indicates that it was an agreement for the sale of accounts and (2) that the parties' course of performance and course of dealing compel an interpretation of the Agreement as one for the sale of accounts. Castle also asserts that the district court erred in "reforming" the Agreement and in concluding that the transaction was a loan. In substance these contentions do no more than reflect Castle's overall position that the Agreement was for an absolute sale of accounts.

Our analysis starts with Article 9 of the Uniform Commercial Code which encompasses both *sales* of accounts and *secured interests* in accounts. Thus, the Pennsylvania counterpart of the Code "applies . . . (a) to any transaction (regardless of its form) which is intended to create a security interest in . . . accounts . . .; and also (b) to any sale of accounts . . ." § 9–102. The official comments to that section make it evident that Article 9 is to govern *all* transactions in accounts. Comment 2 indicates that, because "[c]ommercial financing on the basis of accounts . . . is often so conducted that the distinction between a security transfer and a sale is blurred," that "sales" as well as transactions "intended to create a security interest" are subject to the provisions of Article 9. Moreover, a "security interest" is defined under the Act as "any interest of a buyer of accounts." § 1–201(37). Thus even an outright buyer of accounts, such as Castle claims to be, by definition has a "security interest" in the accounts which it purchases.

Article 9 of the Pennsylvania Code is subdivided into five parts. Our examination of Parts 1–4, §§ 9–101 to 9–410, reveals no distinction drawn between a sale and a security interest which is relevant to the issue on this appeal. However, the distinction between an outright sale and a transaction intended to create a security interest becomes highly significant with respect to certain provisions found in Part 5 of Article 9. That part pertains to default under a "security agreement." § 9–501, et seq.

The default section relevant here, which distinguishes between the consequences that follow on default when the transaction *secures an indebtedness* rather than a *sale*, provides:

A secured party who by agreement is entitled to charge back uncollected collateral or otherwise to full and limited recourse against the debtor and who undertakes to collect from the account debtors or obligors must proceed in a commercially reasonable manner and may deduct his reasonable expenses of realization from the collections. *If the security agreement secures an indebtedness, the secured party must account to the debtor for any surplus*, and unless otherwise agreed, the debtor is liable for any deficiency. But, *if the underlying transaction was a sale of accounts*, contract rights, or chattel paper, *the debtor is entitled to any surplus* or is liable for any deficiency *only if the security agreement so provides*.

§ 9–502(2) (emphasis added).

Thus, if the accounts were transferred to Castle *to secure Major's indebtedness*, Castle was obligated to account for and pay over the surplus proceeds to Major's under § 9–502(2), as a debtor's (Major's) right to surplus in such a case cannot be waived even by an express agreement. § 9–501(3)(a). On the other hand, if a *sale of accounts* had been effected, then Castle was entitled to all proceeds received from all accounts because the June 18, 1973 Agreement does not provide otherwise.

However, while the Code instructs us as to the consequences that ensue as a result of the determination of "secured indebtedness" as contrasted with "sale," the Code does not provide assistance in distinguishing between the character of such transactions. This determination, as to whether a particular assignment constitutes a sale or a transfer for security, is left to the courts for decision. § 9–502, Comment 4. It is to that task that we now turn.

\* \* \*

The comments to § 9–502(2) (and in particular Comment 4) make clear to us that the presence of recourse in a sale agreement without more will not automatically convert a sale into a security interest. Hence, one of Major's arguments which is predicated on such a *per se* principle attracts us no more than it attracted the district court. The Code comments however are consistent with and reflect the views expressed by courts and commentators that "[t]he determination of whether a particular assignment constitutes a [true] sale or a transfer for security is left to the courts." § 9–502, Comment 4. The question for the court then is whether the *nature* of the recourse, and the true nature of the transaction, are such that the legal rights and economic consequences of the agreement bear a greater similarity to a financing transaction or to a sale.

[The court's discussion of other cases is omitted.]

Hence, it appears that in each of the cases cited, despite the express language of the agreements, the respective courts examined the parties' practices, objectives, business activities and relationships and determined whether the transaction was a sale or a secured loan only after analysis of the evidence as to the true nature of the transaction. We noted earlier that here the parties, satisfied that there was nothing other than the Agreement and documents bearing on their relationship...., submitted to the court's determination on an agreed record. The district court thereupon reviewed the Agreement and the documents as they reflected the conduct of the parties to determine whether Castle treated the transactions as sales or transfers of a security interest. In referring to the extremely relevant factor of "recourse"[12] and to the risks allocated, the district court found:

> In the instant case the allocation of risks heavily favors Major's claim to be considered as an assignor with an interest in the collectibility of its accounts. It appears that Castle required Major's to retain all conceivable risks of uncollectibility of these accounts. It required warranties that retail account debtors—e.g., Major's customers—meet the criteria set forth by Castle, that Major's perform the credit check to verify that these criteria were satisfied, and that Major's warrant that the accounts were fully enforceable legally and were "fully and timely collectible." It also imposed an obligation to indemnify Castle out of a reserve account for losses resulting from a customer's failure to pay, or for any breach of warranty, and an obligation to repurchase any account after the customer was in default for more than 60 days. Castle only assumed the risk that the assignor itself would be unable to fulfill its obligations. Guaranties of quality alone, or even guarantees of collectibility alone, might be consistent with a true sale, but Castle attempted to shift all risks to Major's, and incur none of the risks or obligations of ownership. It strains credulity to believe that this is the type of situation, referred to in Comment 4, in which "there may be a true sale of accounts ... although recourse exists." When we turn to the conduct of the parties to seek support for this contention, we find

---

**12.** Gilmore, in commenting on the Code's decision to leave the distinction between a security transfer and a sale to the courts, would place almost controlling significance on the one factor of recourse. He states:

> If there is no right of charge-back or recourse with respect to uncollectible accounts and no right to claim for a deficiency, then the transaction should be held to be a sale, entirely outside the scope of Part 5. If there is a right to

charge back uncollectible accounts (a right, as § 9–502 puts it, of "full or limited recourse") or a right to claim a deficiency, then the transaction should be held to be for security and thus subject to Part 5 as well as the other Parts of the Article.

II Gilmore, Security Interests in Personal Property, § 44.4 at 1230.

Here, of course, the Agreement provided Castle with full recourse against Major's.

instead that Castle, in fact, treated these transactions as a transfer of a security interest.

449 F.Supp. at 543.

Moreover, in looking at the conduct of the parties, the district court found one of the more significant documents to be an August 31, 1973 letter written by Irving Canter, President of Castle Credit, to Major's. As the district court characterized it, and as we agree:

> This letter, in effect, announces the imposition of a floating interest rate on loans under a line of credit of $80,000 per month, based upon the fluctuating prime interest rate. The key portion of the letter states:

> Accordingly, your volume for the month of September cannot exceed $80,000. Any business above that amount will have to be paid for in October. I think you'll agree that your quota is quite liberal. The surcharge for the month of September will be 3% of the principal amount financed which is based upon a 9 1/2% prime rate. On October 1, and for each month thereafter, the surcharge will be adjusted, based upon the prime rate in effect at that time as it relates to a 6 1/2% base rate. . . .

> This unilateral change in the terms of the Agreement makes it obvious that Castle treated the transaction as a line of credit to Major's—i.e., a loan situation. Were this a true sale, as Castle now argues, it would not have been able to impose these new conditions by fiat. Such changes in a sales contract would have modified the price term of the agreement, which could only be done by a writing signed by all the parties.

449 F.Supp. at 543.

It is apparent to us that on this record none of the risks present in a true sale is present here. Nor has the custom of the parties or their relationship, as found by the district court, given rise to more than a debtor/creditor relationship in which Major's debt was secured by a transfer of Major's customer accounts to Castle, thereby bringing the transaction within the ambit of § 9–502. To the extent that the district court determined that a surplus existed, Castle was obligated to account to Major's for that surplus and Major's right to the surplus could not be waived, § 9–502(2). Accordingly, we hold that on this record the district court did not err in determining that the true nature of the transaction between Major's and Castle was a secured loan, not a sale.

\* \* \*

The judgment of the district court will be affirmed.

## NOTES

**1.** *Major's* assumes that under Article 9 the debtor can either transfer absolute ownership of, or create a security interest in, accounts and chattel paper. This commonly held premise has been challenged in Octagon Gas Systems, Inc. v. Rimmer, discussed in Chapter 3. As stated in that

Chapter, 9–318(a) rejects *Octagon* by making it clear that the debtor's sale transfers all of its interests in the accounts or chattel paper sold. See Comment 1 to 9–318 and Comment 5 to 9–109.

**2.** As noted, distinguishing a sale of accounts or chattel paper from a security interest in them can be difficult. A sale connotes a transfer of ownership; a security interest does not. However, the notion of ownership itself can be as difficult to characterize as the difference between a sale and a secured transaction. The hallmarks of ownership are elusive even in some tolerably complex transactions. Two extreme cases are easy: the case where the transferor continues to bear all upside and downside risks associated with the asset transferred, and the case where it bears none of these risks. Examples of upside risk are increases in the value of the asset or beneficial changes in the suitability of the asset for particular uses. Decreases in asset value or damage or risk of loss are examples of downside risk. A good indication of ownership is the bearing of all upside and downside risk around the asset. Where the transferor continues to bear them, as in the first extreme case, no change in ownership and therefore no sale has occurred. In the second extreme case, where the transferee bears both upside and downside risks, ownership has changed and therefore a sale has occurred.

The trouble is that upside and downside risks can be split and divided even within themselves. Where this occurs, it can be indeterminate as to whether the transfer or transferee owns the financial asset. For instance, a right of recourse places the risk of the account debtor's default ("collectibility risk") on the assignor, not the assignee. It is the equivalent of a warranty given by the seller in the ordinary sale of goods, the warranty allocating the risk of nonconformity in the goods to the seller. See, e.g., In re De–Pen Line, Inc., 215 B.R. 947 (Bankr. E.D.Pa.1997). In both cases the transferor bears the risk of the asset not performing according to the terms of the underlying contract. A limited right of recourse divides the collectibility risk between the assignor and assignee. It corresponds to a restricted warranty or remedy limitation in the case of the sale of goods. Thus, the allocation of downside risk through a right of recourse does not alone identify ownership in the account assigned. This is why the *Major's* court observes that "[g]uarantees of quality alone, or even guarantees of collectibility alone, might be consistent with a true sale," 602 F.2d at 545, and that it is the "nature of the recourse" that distinguishes a sale from a financing transaction.

The allocation of upside risks also does not decisively determine ownership. A paradigmatic owner derives revenues directly from the owned assets; a lender's return typically is fixed and unrelated to the asset's performance. Fixed returns or returns unrelated to the account debtor's actual payment under the account or chattel paper might appear to mark the transferee of the account or chattel paper as a lender. See Peter V. Pantaleo et al., Rethinking the Role of Recourse in the Sale of Financial Assets, 52 Bus. Law. 159 (1996); Peter L. Mancini, Bankruptcy and the UCC as Applied to Securitization: Characterizing a Mortgage Loan Transfer as a Sale or a Secured Loan, 73 B. U. L. Rev. 873, 881–82 (1993). However, these revenue streams can be split to give a fixed or variable share to a transferee. For instance, amounts collected from the account debtor above a stipulated sum can be divided between the assignor and assignee. Alternatively, the assignor and assignee can agree to readjust the "price" of an account to reflect the account debtor's performance over time. In both cases, the transaction can be characterized either as a sale of a divisible portion of an account or as a loan with a floating rate of interest. The notion of ownership probably is not up to the job of distinguishing sales from secured loans in such transactions. Rather, characterization must be based directly on efficiency gains in the form of transaction cost savings or risk reduction produced by transfers of accounts or chattel paper with recourse, holdbacks, divisible interests and the like.

## 8.   REDEMPTION

Section 9–623 recognizes the debtor's traditional right to redeem the collateral by paying the secured party before foreclosure the full amount owing on the debt plus the expenses incurred by the secured party in repossessing and preparing the property for sale. In consumer goods transactions, the debtor must be given information about its right to redeem. See 9–614(1)(C) and safe-harbor notification form. We can assume that by the time the secured party is ready to foreclose, it has accelerated the debt and the whole amount is due. The debtor probably doesn't need a statute to force the secured party to take full payment; creditors will always make this deal. But if the debtor can afford to pay the total debt owed, it probably wouldn't have defaulted on the installment payments that are now overdue.

Bankruptcy offers some help. Under BC 722, a Chapter 7 debtor can redeem consumer goods in some cases by paying the secured party the value of the collateral; any deficiency remaining becomes an unsecured claim of the creditor and is discharged. This is a better deal than that offered by 9–623, but BC 722, as amended by BAPCPA, still requires the debtor to come up with the cash in a lump sum at the time of redemption. The basic shortcoming of both 9–623 and BC 722 is that the debtor is broke and at best can pay the amount necessary to redeem only in installments. But if the debtor is an individual who is eligible for Chapter 13, 1325(a)(5) allows the debtor to do what a debtor cannot do under 9–623 or BC 722: redeem the property by paying the creditor its present value in installments. See In re Robinson, 285 B.R. 732 (Bankr. W.D. Okla. 2002). However, as we will see later in Chapter 9 of the Casebook, BAPCPA places limitations on 1325(a)(5) in purchase money transactions involving motor vehicles.

Why should a consumer have to go into Chapter 13 bankruptcy in order to reinstate a loan in default? Earlier drafts of Revised Article 9 provided that in a case in which 60% of the cash price has been paid, a consumer debtor or guarantor could cure a default by paying the amount due at the time of tender, without acceleration, plus a performance deposit

# CHAPTER 5

# Leases and Consignments

In this Chapter we treat two transactions that are used as alternatives to secured transactions. Leases compete vigorously with secured transactions as methods for equipment and consumer goods financing. Consignments are a traditional method of inventory financing. Both leases and consignments are types of bailments. Although both transactions raise troubling issues of ostensible ownership, Article 9 deals with the two in very different ways. Leases are governed by law outside Article 9, but commercial consignments are brought into Article 9.

## A. Leases

The distinction between leases and sales in which the seller reserves a purchase money security interest has long perplexed American commercial law. The objective similarities between the two transactions are great. In both leases and purchase money secured transactions, the transferee is in possession of the goods and makes periodic payments to the transferor. The periodic payments made to the transferor may either be rental payments or installment payments on the purchase price. In both, the transferor has an interest in the goods, but the transferee may appear to be the owner of the goods, using them in its business or personal affairs, maintaining them, paying taxes on them, and insuring them. It's difficult for an outside observer to be sure whether the person in possession is a debtor under a secured transaction or a lessee under a lease without further investigation.

> Some legal scholars go so far as to deny that there is such a distinction:
>
> The theoretical proposition of this Article concerns the supposed distinction between "lease" and "sale." An enormous amount of scholarly effort has gone into the task of seeking to elucidate the distinction. I am of the opinion that the enterprise is chimerical: for all practical purposes no such distinction exists. This assertion is not, strictly speaking, new. Maitland suggested it a century ago * * *.

John D. Ayer, On the Vacuity of the Sale/Lease Distinction, 68 Iowa L. Rev. 667 (1983). Other commentators disagree. Amelia Boss suggests that Professor Ayer is "misguided." Amelia H. Boss, Leases and Sales: Ne'er or Where Shall the Twain Meet?, 1983 Ariz. St. L.J. 357, 358 (herein Boss, Leases & Sales). An extensive analysis of the sale/lease distinction is found in Corinne Cooper, Identifying a True Lease under U.C.C. Section 1–201(37), in Equipment Leasing Ch. 4 (Jeffrey J. Wong, ed. 1995) (herein Cooper, Identifying a True Lease).

Current law treats leases and security interests very differently. Each occupies its own legal space; Article 2A applies to leases, Article 9 to secured transactions. In a lease transaction, the lessor has a residual interest in the property and is entitled to get the property back when the term of the lease is over. In a secured transaction, when the debtor pays its debt to the secured party, the security interest ends and the former debtor owns the property unencumbered. Despite the lessee's ostensible ownership, the lessor need give no public notice of its interest, and third party claimants of the lessee—creditors, trustees in bankruptcy and buyers—are subject to the lessor's prior interest in the property. Section 2A–307(1); Comment 2 to 2A–301. However, as we have seen, the secured party must perfect its security interest, usually by filing; if it does not, its security interest may be subject to third party claimants of the debtor. There are many other differences in the legal treatment of the two transactions under the UCC and the Bankruptcy Code, some of which we will encounter in this chapter.

There are significant business differences between leases and sales as well. The tax and accounting treatment of leases and security interests vary significantly. A lessee may deduct total rent payments as business expenses; a debtor in a secured transaction may deduct only depreciation and interest payments. For accounting purposes, operating leases are off the balance sheet, enabling lessees to maintain more favorable debt-to-equity ratios. Moreover, bank lending standards make it easier for one wishing to acquire goods to lease them through a bank rather than to borrow the money from the bank and buy the goods. Leasing often provides 100% financing, while banks usually will not lend money to purchase goods unless the borrower makes a down payment on the purchase. The general assumption is that leasing goods is more expensive than borrowing to buy them.

The parties to goods acquisition transactions will make business decisions in the light of the consequences outlined above in reaching an acquisition agreement. The question that has engendered so much litigation over the years is whether the transaction agreed upon amounts in substance to a so-called "true lease" or a sale with retention of a security interest. The first statutory attempt to distinguish security interests from leases was found in Section 1 of the Uniform Conditional Sales Act, promulgated in the 1920s, which treated as a conditional sale any lease or bailment under which "the bailee or lessee contracts to pay as compensation a sum substantially equivalent to the value of the goods, and by which it is agreed that the bailee or lessee is bound to become, or has the option of becoming the owner of such goods upon full compliance with the terms of the contract."

Under the UCC, the 1962 version of former 1–201(37) was patterned on the UCSA provision: " 'Security interest' means an interest in personal property or fixtures which secures payment or performance of an obligation. * * * Unless a lease or consignment is intended as security, reservation of title thereunder is not a 'security interest' * * *. Whether a lease is intended as security is to be determined by the facts of each case; however, (a) the inclusion of an option to purchase does not of itself make the lease one intended for security, and (b) an agreement that upon compliance with the terms of the lease the lessee shall become or has the option to become the owner of the property for no additional consideration or for a nominal consideration does make the lease one intended for security.''

In the late 1980s Article 2A on Leases was added to the Code, and ''lease'' was defined as excluding a transaction creating a security interest. 2A–103(1)(j). At this time it was decided to redraft former 1–201(37) in an effort to provide clearer guidelines on the lease/security interest distinction. The amendment to former 1–201(37) is discussed in Corinne Cooper, Identifying a Personal Property Lease under the UCC, 49 Ohio St. L.J. 195 (1988), and Edwin E. Huddleson III, Old Wine in New Bottles: UCC Article 2A—Leases, 39 Ala. L. Rev. 615 (1988). The efficacy of the lease/security interest distinction is debated in John D. Ayer, supra; John D. Ayer, Further Thoughts on Lease and Sale, 1983 Ariz. St. L.J. 341; and Charles W. Mooney Jr., The Mystery and Myth of ''Ostensible Ownership'' and Article 9 Filing: A Critique of Proposals to Extend Filing Requirements to Leases, 39 Ala. L. Rev. 683 (1988). In 2001 former 1–201(37) was divided into two sections: 1–201(b)(35) and 1–203. Section 1–201(b)(35) defines ''security interest'' to reflect the expanded scope of Revised Article 9. Section 1–203 contains, with no change in substance, former 1–201(37)'s rules for distinguishing a lease from a security interest. It is the key provision for the discussions to follow.

## 1. LEASE WITH OPTION TO PURCHASE OR RENEW

In the following case the court guides the reader step-by-step through the intricacies of former 1–201(37) (now 1–201(b)(35) and 1–203) in order to determine whether a transaction creates a security interest. When you understand the analysis explained in this case, you should be prepared to deal with the more challenging situation posed by the Problem following the case.

## In re Zaleha

United States Bankruptcy Court, D. Idaho, 1993.
159 B.R. 581.

■ ALFRED C. HAGAN, CHIEF JUDGE.

Toyota Motor Credit Corporation (''TMCC'') moves, under 11 U.S.C. § 365, to require Daniel Zaleha, the debtor in this chapter 11 case (''debtor''), to assume or reject an unexpired lease. The debtor defends on the ground the transaction is not a true lease, but is in fact a disguised security interest.

The lease at issue is for a 1991 Toyota 4WD Deluxe ExtraCab Pickup. The lease has a term of five years, and calls for 60 monthly payments of

$323. The debtor could become owner of the vehicle at the end of the lease term for $5,390, which the lease defines as both the "Purchase Option Price" and the "Estimated Residual Value." The debtor contends this amount undervalues the vehicle. The debtor presented copies of the current Blue Book, which indicates a five-year old Toyota pickup with comparable options and mileage has an average retail value of $8,275. Based on this, debtor argues the vehicle will have an expected value at lease termination of at least $8,275.

The determination of whether a transaction is a true lease or a disguised security interest is determined by state law. * * * Traditionally, this court has relied upon a list of seven factors in determining whether a transaction is a true lease or a disguised sale. These are:

1.  Whether the option price is nominal;

2.  Whether the lessee obtains equity in the property leased;

3.  Whether the lessee bears the risk of loss;

4.  Whether the lessee pays the tax, licensing and registration fee;

5.  Whether the lessor may accelerate payment;

6.  Whether the property is purchased specifically for lease to the lessee; and

7.  Whether the lease contains a disclaimer of warranties.

In re Maritt, 155 B.R. 12, 13 (Bankr.D.Idaho 1993). This list of factors was based upon interpretation of [former] 1–201(37). * * * However, the Idaho Legislature has recently amended [former] 1–201(37) to include a much more detailed discussion of whether a transaction is a lease or a sale. Thus, the express language of the statute in determining the status of the lease agreement at issue here must first be considered.

Section 1–201(37) defines the term "security interest." * * *

* * *

1–201(37) [1–203].[2] This amendment became effective on July 1, 1993. * * * No reported Idaho cases have considered the interpretation of this section.

This statute consists of several different standards to be used in the lease/security interest issue. The proper manner in which these tests are to be applied was set forth in In re Lerch, 147 B.R. 455 (Bankr.C.D.Ill.1992) interpreting the same statute:

**2.** This quote omits the language of the first paragraph of § 1–207(37), which is not directly relevant to the discussion here. The paragraphs of subsection (37) are not numbered, as can be seen in the portion quoted above. In order create uniformity in the manner in which references are made to the different paragraphs, the paragraphs shall be referred to by number, counting the first, unquoted paragraph. Thus, the paragraph beginning "Whether a transaction creates a lease or security interest" shall be referred to as the second paragraph; the paragraph beginning "A transaction does not create a security interest" shall be referred to as the third paragraph; etc.

The initial portion of the first sentence of the second unnumbered paragraph contains the basic direction that the determination is made based on the facts of each case. The latter portion of the first sentence of the second unnumbered paragraph starting with the word "however" creates an exception to the basic direction that the determination is made on the facts of each case, as it provides that without looking at all the facts, a lease will be construed as a security interest if a debtor cannot terminate the lease, and if one of the four enumerated terms is present in the lease.

Absent a mandated classification, the determination is based on the facts of the case. At this point the third unnumbered paragraph comes into effect. Focusing on the economics of the transaction, it states that a security interest is not created merely because it contains any of the five terms enumerated in the third unnumbered paragraph.

147 B.R. at 460.

It must first be determined whether the transaction in this case falls within the mandated definition of security interest set forth in the second paragraph of 1–201(37) [1–203(b)]. The first element of the test is that the lessee must be obligated to perform for the full length of the lease, without being able to voluntarily terminate the lease [1–203(b)(preamble)]. That condition is met here. Second, one of four conditions must also be met. The fourth, subsection (d) [1–203(b)(4)], is the only one of the four possibly applicable here; namely, whether "the lessee has an option to become the owner of the goods for no additional consideration or nominal additional consideration upon compliance with the lease agreement." The consideration required to exercise the option in this instance is not nominal. Accordingly, the transaction does not meet the *mandatory* conditions under which it is deemed a disguised security interest.

The nature of this transaction must therefore be determined on the facts of the case. The manner, however, in which 1–201(37) [1–203] has been amended indicates the prior seven-point test must be reconsidered. Factors previously relied upon by this Court in determining whether a transaction is in fact a disguised security interest include, as noted previously, whether the lessee bears the risk of loss (factor 3), and whether the lessee pays tax, licensing, and registration fees (factor 4). Subsection (b) of the third paragraph of amended section 1–201(37) [1–203(c)(2) and (3)] states that none of these facts of necessity creates a security interest. In addition, the seventh factor of the prior test of a disguised security interest was a disclaimer of warranties. At the same time that section 1–201(37) was amended, the Idaho Legislature adopted Article 2A of the Uniform Commercial Code, governing leases. The new provisions specifically contemplate that a lease of personal property may include disclaimers of warranties. 2A–214.

> These inconsistencies reflect the fact that courts have relied upon factors that were thought to be more consistent with sales or loans than leases. Most of these criteria, however, are as applicable to true leases as to security interests. Examples include the typical net lease

provisions, a purported lessor's lack of storage facilities or its character as a financing party rather than a dealer in goods.

U.C.C. 1–201(37) Official Comment (1987 amendment). [Comment 2, paragraph 8, to 1–203.]

It makes sense that a lessee would provide insurance on the property while in possession of it under a lease; it seems perfectly reasonable for a lessee to agree to undertake some of the risks of loss or damage while the lessee enjoys possession and use of the property. The same holds true for taxes and maintenance.

Basic Leasing, Inc. v. Paccar, Inc., 1991 WL 117412, at *4 (D.N.J.1991). "Costs such as taxes, insurance and repairs are necessarily borne by one party or the other. They reflect less the true character of the transaction than the strength of the parties' respective bargaining positions." In re Marhoefer Packing Co., Inc., 674 F.2d 1139, 1146 (7th Cir.1982).

The key distinction between a lease and a security interest is suggested by the tests set out in the second paragraph of 1–201(37) [1–203(b)].

In each situation where a security interest is deemed to exist under [the second paragraph], the "lessor" cannot reasonably expect to receive back anything of value at the end of the lease. Either the goods will have reached the end of their economic life or the "lessee" will be compelled, contractually or economically, to purchase the goods or renew the "lease" to the end of the economic life of the goods. Commentators have labelled this key factor distinguishing a lease from a security interest as the lessor's retention of a "meaningful residual interest."

Woodson v. Ford Motor Credit Corp. (In re Cole), 100 B.R. 561, 564 (Bankr.N.D.Okl.1989), aff'd, 114 B.R. 278 (N.D.Okl.1990) (footnote omitted).

By placing more emphasis upon what happens at the termination of the original lease, the drafters of Article 2A have attempted to reestablish the significance of residual value as an economic rationale for a lease transaction, the argument being that absent a concern for the value or expectant return of the goods upon the conclusion of the lease term the lessor, at the inception of the lease, had really formulated no further anticipation of an investment return from the leased goods, an anticipation more historically associated with an intent to transfer a title interest in the goods (with lease terms designed to protect against the failure of that intent). Hence, the need for some form of security.

Gregory J. Naples, "A Review and Analysis of the New Article 2A—Leases Amendment to the UCC and its Impact on Secured Creditors, Equipment and Finance Lessors," 93 Comm.L.J. 342, 350 (Fall 1988).

It is important to note that the term "meaningful residual interest" refers to more than just a legal reversionary interest retained by a lessor. As suggested above, the term looks to the value retained by the leased goods after completion of the transaction. See Corinne Cooper, "Identifying a Personal Property Lease Under the UCC," 49 Ohio St.L.J. 195, 204 n.31 (1988).

The notion that the key aspect of a true lease is whether the lessor retains a meaningful residual interest is not new. If a lease contains an option to purchase for no or nominal consideration (factor 1 of the seven-point test), it suggests that the lessor does not care, in an economic sense, whether or not the option is exercised. If the lessee develops equity in the leased property such that the only sensible decision economically for the lessee is to exercise the option (factor 2 of the test, also known as the "economic realities" test), it suggests the lessor did not expect the return of the leased goods. As a result, these two factors, in contrast to the others, have been recognized as the more important in determining the lease/security interest distinction. * * *

Because the seven-factor test incorporated the consideration of whether a lessor retains a meaningful residual interest, prior precedent remains helpful in establishing circumstances under which a lessor retains such an interest. However, the seven factors previously used by this Court are both inadequate and contrary to the language of 1–201(37) [1–203]. The seven-factor test also distracts from consideration of the true issue, that is, whether at the time of contracting the lessor retained a meaningful residual interest. It is accordingly held that, where a transaction must be evaluated on its facts because the mandatory elements of the second paragraph of 1–201(37) [1–203] are not met, the proper standard of evaluation is whether the transaction left the lessor with a meaningful residual interest in the leased property. This incorporates consideration of whether the lessee develops equity in the leased goods, without distracting from other elements of the transaction that may also bear on the central issue of whether the transaction is a true lease.

Debtor argues that he has accumulated equity in the truck. As already discussed, debtor has presented evidence to show the truck will have an average retail value on termination of the lease of at least $8,275, while he may purchase the vehicle at that time for $5,390. This represents an accumulation of $2,885 in what may be termed equity, or 54% of the option price.

Debtor's evidence addresses only the value of the truck as calculated from the present date, nearly 2½ years after the option price was set. This is not the proper point to determine whether the option price was set low in order to force the debtor to buy the truck. As the Seventh Circuit held under the prior version of U.C.C. § 1–201(37), "in determining whether an option price is nominal, the proper figure to compare it with is not the actual fair market value of the leased goods at the time the option arises, but their fair market value at that time as anticipated by the parties when the lease is signed." *Marhoefer*, supra, 674 F.2d at 1144–45. In *Marhoefer*, for example, high inflation rates over the term of the lease had resulted in an option price significantly less than the actual fair market value at the time the option would have been exercised.

Commentators support the conclusion that the date of the transaction, rather than a future date, is the more appropriate point to determine the adequacy of the option price. White and Summers reach such a conclusion in their discussion of the "economic realities" test.

> Intending a true lease, parties might at the outset select an option price that they believe will equal the fair market value of the property at the end of the lease. The value may be substantially higher or lower than their estimate when the lease ends. If the option were "nominal" at the conclusion of the lease (because the property had not depreciated as expected), but would have been equal to the fair price had the parties' estimate proved true, should the agreement be termed a lease or a security interest? We believe it should be termed a lease.

> Parties make the agreement at the outset. It is only there that they have the common intention to create a lease or security agreement, and it is at that time we should measure the economic realities to determine their true intention. If subsequent events make the option price "nominal" at the end of the lease, so be it. That fact does not change what was once a true lease into a security agreement. The courts have not always been careful to distinguish between the predicted value established at the outset and the actual value to determine the economic realities; our view is supported by the newly proposed uniform law on leasing [U.C.C. Article 2A and the amendments to section 1–201(37)].

James J. White & Robert S. Summers, Uniform Commercial Code § 21–3, at 934 (3d ed. 1988) (footnote omitted). "Any other timing for this evaluation permits a lease which was believed by the parties at its inception to be a true lease, to be 'transubstantiated' into a security interest if the residual turns out to be more valuable than the parties anticipated at the inception of the transaction." Cooper, supra, 49 Ohio St.L.J. at 212 n. 58.

In applying these standards to the present case, labels used by the parties are not determinative of the situation. However, where the transaction is denominated a lease, the burden is upon the debtor to demonstrate that the transaction is in fact a disguised security interest rather than a true lease. The debtor has not carried that burden here. The agreement here is denominated a lease, and contains provisions entirely consistent with the terms of a true lease. No evidence has been presented to show that the "Estimated Residual Value" was not a reasonable estimate, at the time the contract was signed, of the truck's value after five years of use. The agreement limits the number of miles that the truck may be driven in a year, and imposes a penalty of ten cents per mile if that limit is exceeded, suggesting that TMCC wishes to preserve the residual value of the truck. There is no indication that TMCC, as lessor, had effectively bargained away to the debtor the residual economic value of the truck on termination of the lease.

A separate order will be entered.

PROBLEM

Supplier offered to sell or lease a food processing machine to Customer. For a cash sale the purchase price was $33,225. For a credit sale, the terms were $7,225 down and 24 monthly installments of $1,224, for a total purchase price of $36,601. However, Customer chose a third alternative which was designated a lease. The terms were: Lessor leased the machine to Lessee for four years at $665 per month, a total of $31,920. At the end of the four-year term Lessee had the option of (1) returning the equipment to Lessor, (2) purchasing the equipment for $9,968, or (3) renewing the lease for four more years at an annual rental of $2,990. If Lessee chose the third option, it could purchase the machine for $1 at the end of the second four-year term. The useful life of the machine was eight to ten years. The $9,968 option price was arrived at by estimating that at the end of four years the machine would have a market price of 30% of its original $33,225 cash price. Lessee filed in bankruptcy only a year after the lease was entered into. Since Lessor did not file a financing statement, the trustee in bankruptcy moved to sell the property free of Lessor's interest. The issue was whether the lease created a security interest or whether it was a true lease which would be valid in bankruptcy without a filing. At the hearing on Lessor's motion, the trustee introduced expert testimony that the value of the property at the end of four years would be $18,000 to $20,000. On this basis the trustee contended that the option to buy for $9,968 was actually nominal consideration. The facts are based on Matter of Marhoefer Packing Co., 674 F.2d 1139 (7th Cir.1982). Comment 2, final paragraph, to 1–203 states: "[T]his section could have stated a rule to govern the facts of In re Marhoefer Packing Co. * * * This was not done because it would unnecessarily complicate the definition. Further development of this rule is left to the courts."

(a) Does this "lease" create a security interest under 1–203?

(b) In the above "lease," the purported lessee is not obligated to renew the lease for a second four-year period. Therefore, it is not obligated to make payments necessary to exercise the $1 purchase option. On the same facts the *Marhoefer* court found this decisive in characterizing the transaction as a true lease; see *Marhoefer*, 674 F.2d 1139. Do you agree? Suppose the "lessee" were obligated to renew the "lease" for a second four-year term, but it also had the right to terminate the "lease" one day prior to the end of the second period. Would the transaction still be a true lease? What statement would express a defensible rule to govern both the facts above as well as the altered facts concerning termination?

NOTE

How would 1–203 deal with facts like those in *Zaleha* if the $5,390 option price, viewed at the inception of the transaction, was below the predictable fair market value of the goods at the end of the first four-year term of the lease? Comment 2 to 1–203, paragraph 9, states: "A fixed price purchase option in a lease does not of itself create a security interest. This is particularly true if the fixed price is equal to or greater than the reasonably predictable fair market value of the goods at the time the option is to be performed. A security interest is created only if the option price is nominal * * *. There is a set of purchase options whose fixed price is less than fair market value but greater than nominal that must be determined on the facts of each case to ascertain whether the transaction in which the option is included creates a lease or a security interest." Professor Cooper, in Identifying a Personal Property Lease under the UCC, 49 Ohio St.L.J. 195 (1988), criticizes this Comment:

> The second unresolved issue is the absence of any guidance in the Proposed Amendment describing when the amount of an option to buy or renew is nominal. An option payment that is less than the anticipated fair market value is not necessarily nominal under the Proposed Amendment. The troubling language in the Official Comment, which notes that there is a category of options whose price is less than fair market value but greater than nominal, pinpoints this problem, but offers little guidance. The comment merely provides that these must be determined "on the facts of each case." Given what the courts have done when left with this slim guidance under the current version of Section 1–201(37), this gap in the definition of nominal value could create the same problems which the Proposed Amendment is intended to resolve.
>
> Remember that nominal value is only relevant when there is an option to purchase the goods, or to renew the lease to the end of economic life. In other words, we need a definition of nominal that will address a transfer of all remaining residual value, and recognize that transfer of this value for sufficient payment does not make the initial transaction a disguised security interest. For example, it would be preferable to provide that an option payment less than the anticipated fair market rent or value is nominal when it would not induce a reasonable lessor to transfer the residual outside of the context of the lease agreement. If no reasonable lessor would transfer the entire residual in exchange for the option payment, absent a prior lease relationship between the lessor and lessee, then the option payment is not compensating the lessor for the value of the residual, but is completing payment, and the transaction is a security interest, and was from the inception. This test, or any similar test which gives the courts guidance as to the operation of the section, is better than the "other facts" guidance offered by the Official Comment.

49 Ohio St. L.J. 245–246. In In re Super Feeders, Inc., 236 B.R. 267 (Bankr. D. Neb. 1999), the court held that an option to buy for $46,250 was nominal when the purchase price was $925,000, the total rental payments were $1,281, 987, and the predicted value at the end of the seven-year lease was $225,000. The option purchase price was five percent of the predicted value of the asset. According to the court, the percentage made the option price "nominal." In *Marhoefer* the court characterized an option purchase price of almost 50 percent of the estimated value of the asset as "not

nominal." Suppose the relevant percentage had been 23, 50 or 75 in these cases. At what point does the percentage of purchase option price to predicted value make the option price "nominal"?

The preamble paragraph to subsection 1–203(d) provides that "[a]dditional consideration is nominal if it is less than the lessee's reasonably predictable cost of performance under the lease agreement if the option is not exercised." Thus, if at the time of entering into the lease it appears that it would cost the lessee less to exercise the option than not to exercise it, the assumption is that the lessee will likely exercise the option and become owner of the goods. Under this assumption the lessor has retained no meaningful residual interest in the goods. Some cases and commentators see the new test as merely a recodification of the common law "economic realities" rule, which found a purchase option nominal if no reasonable person would fail to exercise it. The new test for nominality has had little effect in case law largely owing to uncertainty about what was intended to be included in the "cost of performance." See 1–203(e) provides only that "[the] cost of performance under the lease agreement must be determined with reference to the facts and circumstances at the time the transaction is entered into." In the absence of any helpful guidance in the Comments to 1–203 on the intended meaning of this phrase, no generally accepted meaning of the term has emerged in case law. See In re QDS Components, Inc., 292 B.R. 313 (Bankr. S.D. Ohio (2002)), for an extended discussion of the issue.

Edwin E. Huddleson III, Old Wine in New Bottles: UCC Article 2A— Leases, 39 Ala. L. Rev. 615, 628–631 (1988), describes the efforts of the drafters to agree on some percentage formula to define what is nominal consideration, e.g., no greater than 10 percent of the original value of the goods or less than 75 percent of the reasonably predictable fair market value of the goods at the time the option was to be exercised. Eventually efforts to arrive at a percentage formula were abandoned. In comparison, the efforts of accountants have been more successful. The Financial Accounting Standards Board's Statement No. 13 (1976) includes percentage tests among its tests for distinguishing capital from operating leases: for example, a lease must be treated as a capital lease if the net present value of minimum lease payments equal or exceed 90 percent of the fair market value of the leased asset as of the lease's inception. The court in *QDS Components*, supra, infers from 1–203's failure to mention the percentage test of nominality that the test is inapplicable to 1–203.

## PROBLEM

Leasing Corp. leased business machines with a cash price of $100,000 to Firm. The lease was for a term of three years, with an option on the part of Firm to purchase the equipment at the end of the term for the market value of the equipment at that time as determined by the semi-annual Industry Standards Manual (similar to Kelley Blue Book for automobiles). Rental payments were due monthly and Firm had no right to terminate during the three-year term. True lease or secured transaction? See 1–203(d)(2).

Note: Rent–to–Own Leases

A rent-to-own contract is a terminable lease with an option to purchase. No downpayment or security deposit is required and the credit history or financial state of the lessee is not checked. The term of the lease is typically short, from one week to a month, and the rent for the period is paid in advance. The lease permits the lessee to renew the lease for an additional term simply by paying in advance for the term. If the lessee continues to rent the asset for a stipulated period (usually about 78 weeks), it becomes the owner at the end of the period. RTOs typically also include an option allowing the lessee to purchase the asset within the period for a cash price determined in part by the amount of rental payments previously made. Small rental payments are usually required; the effective exercise price of becoming the owner under an RTO lease often is two to four times the retail cash price. The assets rented are mostly new and used furniture, appliances and electronic equipment. Although the RTO industry reports that most RTO customers do not end up owning the assets rented, an FTC survey finds that 70 percent of RTO customers purchase the merchandise. Federal Trade Commission Bureau of Economics Staff Report, Executive Summary (2000).

In the last 15 years RTOs have become the focus of legislative efforts, pitting consumer groups and bankruptcy trustees against the RTO industry. At the federal level, the National Bankruptcy Review Commission in 1994 recommended that the Bankruptcy Code be amended to characterize RTOs as installment sales contracts. The recommendation was not adopted. The RTO industry has prevailed at the state level. Almost all states have enacted statutes providing that RTOs terminable by the lessee are "true leases," not installment sales contracts. Even in the few states that have not enacted such legislation, 1–203[1–201(37)] arguably does not consider a terminable RTO a "security interest." In Perez v. Rent–A–Center, Inc., 892 A.2d 1255 (N.J. 2006), the New Jersey Supreme Court relied on its finding that a vast majority of RTO customers purchase the merchandise rented to conclude that a terminable RTO contract is a type of conditional sales contract. Although the *Perez* court did not consider 1–203 [1–201(37)], its "conditional sale" characterization commits it to characterizing the transaction as creating a security interest.

## 2. Lease Without Option to Purchase or Renew

We have concluded that the functional difference between a lease of goods and a sale of these goods with reservation of a security interest is whether the purported lessor has reserved a meaningful reversionary interest in the goods. We saw how 1–203(b) aids in this inquiry by stating four factors, the presence of any one of which mandates the existence of a security interest. Three of these factors relate to options to purchase or renew and the other goes to the term of the lease. All four relate to the existence of a reversionary interest in the purported lessor. What guidance does 1–203 offer in a case, like the one below, in which none of these factors is present? Section 1–203(a) seems to be punting when it blandly tells us to look to the "facts of each case." But for what are we supposed to be looking?

# In re Pillowtex, Inc.

United States Court of Appeals, 3d Cir., 2003.
349 F.3d 711.

■ FUENTES, CIRCUIT JUDGE.

Duke Energy Royal LLC ("Duke") appeals from an order of the District Court denying a motion to compel Pillowtex Corporation ("Pillowtex" or "debtor") to make lease payments owing under the Master Energy Services Agreement ("MESA"), an agreement its predecessor entered into with Pillowtex. The District Court denied Duke's motion on the grounds that the MESA was not a true lease, but rather a secured financing arrangement. The sole issue in this appeal is whether the District Court correctly determined that the MESA entered into between Pillowtex and Duke prior to Pillowtex's bankruptcy filing was a secured financing arrangement rather than a true lease. We affirm because we agree with the District Court that, based on the economic realities of the underlying transaction, the MESA was a secured financing arrangement.

## I. Facts and Procedural Background

Because the nature of the MESA is at issue, we first turn to its provisions and the transaction underlying the agreement. Pillowtex and Duke entered into the MESA on June 3, 1998. Pursuant to the MESA, Duke agreed to install certain equipment "for the purpose of improving the efficiency of energy consumption or otherwise to reduce the operating costs" incurred by Pillowtex at its facilities. (MESA § 2.5, App. at 299). The MESA covered two different sets of energy services projects, one involving production equipment and the other energy-savings equipment. The production equipment was provided to Pillowtex by Duke pursuant to separate stand-alone agreements, which were recorded as true leases on Pillowtex's books, and which the parties agree constituted true leases. Therefore, only the nature of the parties' arrangements concerning the energy-savings equipment is at issue in this appeal.

The energy-savings equipment included certain lighting fixtures, T8 lamps and electronic ballasts (collectively the "lighting fixtures"), which were installed in nine of Pillowtex's facilities and a new wastewater heat recovery system that included hot water heating equipment (the "wastewater system" and together with the lighting fixtures, the "energy fixtures"), which was installed at Pillowtex's Columbus, Georgia plant. The lighting fixtures were selected, and the wastewater system was constructed, specifically for Pillowtex's facilities.

In order to induce Pillowtex to enter into the energy services projects, Duke offered to originate funding for the production equipment "on a two-to-one basis (*i.e.*, for every $1 million of energy projects Duke would originate $2 million for funding of equipment) with a minimum of $28 million in funding for equipment leasing or financing." Another incentive Pillowtex had for entering into the agreement was "that the energy projects would be cost neutral to Pillowtex for the term of the agreement; that is, Pillowtex's payments to Duke would be equivalent to Pillowtex's actual savings . . . and Pillowtex would then reap the benefits from the cost savings after the end of the term of the project." (App. at 153). In keeping with this arrangement, Pillowtex accounted for its payments to Duke under the MESA as a utility expense.

The MESA provided that the cost of acquiring and installing the energy fixtures would be paid by Duke, which incurred total costs of approximately $10.41 million. (MESA § 5, App. at 302; 339). Of this amount, approximately $1.66 million was for material and labor costs for the wastewater system. Approximately $4.46 million was for labor to install the lighting fixtures and $4.29 million was for material costs for the lighting fixtures, which is to say that the cost of labor to install the fixtures was higher than the cost of the actual materials themselves. Also, Duke paid approximately $223,000 to dispose of light fixtures and related equipment that it removed from Pillowtex's facilities.

In exchange, Pillowtex was to pay Duke on a monthly basis one-twelfth of Pillowtex's annual energy savings, in an amount the parties agreed to in advance, until the end of the MESA's 8 year term. (MESA § 7.0). In addition, the parties agreed that the simple payback of all of Duke's costs was not to exceed 5 years. (MESA § 4.1(f)). "Simple payback" is synonymous with "payback period," an accounting term which refers to "[t]he length of time required to recover a venture's initial cash investment, without accounting for the time value of money." BLACK'S LAW DICTIONARY 1150 (7th ed. 1999). In other words, the payments were structured to ensure that Pillowtex would make predetermined, equal monthly payments and that Duke would recover its costs 3 years prior to the end of the term of the MESA. Although the MESA was for an 8 year term, the parties agree that the useful life of the energy fixtures was 20–25 years.

It is undisputed that Duke and Pillowtex intended to structure the MESA to have the characteristics of a lease and that the parties were trying to create a true lease. Indeed, Pillowtex's counsel conceded during oral argument before the District Court, "I don't disagree that [the MESA] was structured to have those characteristics for tax purposes and, you know, to [the] extent they could, the parties were trying to create a true lease, I would admit that." The parties intended for the MESA to be structured as a true lease, in large part, because Pillowtex was subject to capital expenditure limitations under its senior credit facility and did not wish to have the energy-savings equipment count as capital expenditures under that facility. Nevertheless, the MESA is not labeled a lease and it does not refer to the parties as lessee and lessor. * * *

In keeping with their intent to structure the transaction as a lease, the MESA provides that title to the equipment would remain with Duke. (MESA § 11.0). Also, Pillowtex agreed not to claim ownership of the equipment for income tax purposes, (MESA § 9.13(ii)), and Pillowtex was not obligated to purchase the equipment at the end of the term of the MESA. Rather, the MESA provided the following four options to Duke at the conclusion of its term, if Pillowtex was not then in default:

(i) remove the Equipment installed and replace those [sic] Equipment with equipment comparable to those originally in place, provided that no such replacement shall be required with respect to Production Equipment; or,

(ii) abandon the Equipment in place; or,

(iii) continue this Agreement until the expiration of the term hereof and then extend the term of this Agreement for such additional period(s) and payment terms as the parties may agree upon; or,

(iv) [g]ive the Customer the option of purchasing all (but not less than all) of the Equipment at a mutually agreed upon price.

(MESA § 8.3). If Duke elected to exercise option (I), it was bound to "be responsible for all costs and expenses in removing such Equipment, including costs to repair any damage to [Pillowtex's] Facility caused by such removal." (*Id.*)[2] Despite the existence of the option for Duke to repossess the equipment, Pillowtex's Vice President for Engineering, Michael Abba, testified that in his understanding, there was no chance of that option being exercised:

It was clearly my understanding that Duke would abandon the Lighting Fixtures and the Wastewater System at the conclusion of the MESA and in fact statements were made to me by Duke sales personnel to that effect. Moreover, because the energy projects were of no economic benefit to Pillowtex until the end of the term when Pillowtex would reap the energy savings going forward, I would not have signed off on the projects if the Lighting Fixtures and Wastewater System were not to be abandoned. I also believe that, based on the prohibitive cost of removing and replacing the Lighting Fixtures and the Wastewater System for Pillowtex, Duke [had] no choice but to abandon the Lighting Fixtures and the Wastewater System at the end of the term of the MESA.

Abba Affidavit at ¶ 6. * * *

[*Eds.* After Duke and Pillowtex executed the MESA, Duke made a collateral assignment agreement with General Electric Capital Corporation (GECC) under which it agreed to finance the purchase of lighting fixtures at four of the nine Pillowtex facilities. Duke then granted GECC a security interest in all its rights and interests under

---

**2.** In the event of a default by Pillowtex, Duke would have the right to remove the equipment at Pillowtex's expense, without being obligated to replace it, and could terminate the MESA. (MESA § 13.2, App. at 309).

the MESA, including Duke's right to payment under the MESA. Shortly thereafter, GECC assigned all its rights under the MESA to Southtrust.]

On November 14, 2000, Pillowtex and certain of its subsidiaries filed petitions for relief under Chapter 11 of the Bankruptcy Code. Thereafter, Pillowtex stopped making payments due under the MESA. On February 21, 2002, Duke filed a motion under section 365(d)(10) of the Bankruptcy Code to compel Pillowtex to make lease payments on the equipment it had provided to Pillowtex under the MESA. Section 365(d)(10) requires debtors-in-possession, such as Pillowtex, to "timely perform all of the obligations of the debtor . . . first arising from or after 60 days after the order for relief in a case under Chapter 11 . . . under an unexpired lease of personal property . . . until such lease is assumed or rejected. . . ." § 365(d)(10).[3] In response to Duke's motion, Pillowtex filed an objection in which it argued that Duke was not entitled to payment of post-petition monthly obligations, which Pillowtex represented amounted to $1.8 million, because the MESA was not a true lease. After a hearing on the matter, the District Court, sitting in Bankruptcy, denied Duke's motion. Duke timely appealed. * * *

### III.  Analysis

Whether an agreement is a true lease or a secured financing arrangement under the Bankruptcy Code is a question of state law. * * * In this case, the parties agreed that the MESA would be interpreted, performed, and enforced in accordance with the laws of the State of New York. (MESA, Appendix A, § 17.7). Accordingly, we turn to New York law in order to resolve whether the MESA constitutes a secured financing arrangement or a lease. * * *

Section 1–201(37) of the U.C.C. provides that a security interest "means an interest in personal property or fixtures which secures payment or performance of an obligation." N.Y. U.C.C. § 1–201(37). After defining the term "security interest," section 1–201(37) sets out a test for determining whether a transaction creates a lease or a security interest. Section 1–201(37) begins by noting that whether a transaction creates a lease or a security interest is to be determined on a case-by-case basis. After indicating that courts are to examine the facts of each case in order to characterize a transaction, the statute sets out a bright-line test, sometimes referred to as a per se rule, for determining whether a transaction creates a security interest as a matter of law. Specifically, section 1–201(37) provides:

> (a) Whether a transaction creates a lease or security interest is determined by the facts of each case; however, a transaction creates a security interest if the consideration the lessee is to pay the lessor for the right to possession and use of the goods is an obligation for the term of the lease not subject to termination by the lessee, **and:**

---

**3.** Although § 365(d)(10) refers to the obligation of a trustee to make lease payments, its provisions apply to Pillowtex because the Bankruptcy Code provides that debtors-in-possession, such as Pillowtex, are to perform all of the functions and duties of a Chapter 11 trustee. See 11 U.S.C. § 1107(a).

(i) the original term of the lease is equal to or greater than the remaining economic life of the goods,

(ii) the lessee is bound to renew the lease for the remaining economic life of the goods or is bound to become the owner of the goods,

(iii) the lessee has an option to renew the lease for the remaining economic life of the goods for no additional consideration or nominal additional consideration upon compliance with the lease agreement, *or*

(iv) the lessee has an option to become the owner of the goods for no additional consideration or nominal additional consideration upon compliance with the lease agreement.

N.Y. U.C.C. § 1–201(37) (emphasis added). Thus, under the two-part test set out in New York's U.C.C., if Pillowtex did not have the right to terminate the MESA prior to the end of its term, *and* any of the four factors set out in section 1–201(37)(a)(i)–(iv) are met, then the MESA would be considered to create a security interest as a matter of law. *See In re Owen*, 221 B.R. at 60–61. If, on the other hand, it is determined that "the transaction is not a disguised security agreement per se, [we] must then look at the specific facts of the case to determine whether the economics of the transaction suggest such a result." *In re Taylor*, 209 B.R. 482, 484 (Bankr.S.D.Ill.1997) (citation omitted). *See also In re Murray*, 191 B.R. 309 (Bankr.E.D.Pa.1996); *In re American Steel Prod.*, 203 B.R. 504, 506–07 (Bankr.S.D.Ga.1996) (describing the standards for determining whether a disguised security arrangement exists).[8] In this case, the District Court went directly to the economic realities of the transaction memorialized in the MESA. In doing so the Court seems to have implicitly held that the MESA was not a disguised security agreement under the bright-line test of section 1–201(37). We agree. * * *

[*Eds*: The court determined that none of the four factors set out in 1–201(37)(a)(i)–(iv) was met.]

The parties agree that, where none of the four factors set out in section 1–201(37) are present, courts are to consider the economic reality of the transaction in order to determine, based on the particular facts of the case, whether the transaction is more fairly characterized as a lease or a secured financing arrangement. They also agree that the District Court applied the correct standard for evaluating the economic reality of their transaction. As the District Court explained:

Under relevant case law, courts will look to various factors in evaluating the "economic reality of the transaction ... in determining whether there has been a sale or a true lease," *Pactel Fin. v. D.C. Marine*

**8.** Because N.Y. U.C.C. § 1–201(37) is based on the Uniform Commercial Code, decisions from other jurisdictions interpreting this same uniform statute are instructive. *See, e.g., In re Edison Bros. Stores, Inc.*, 207 B.R. 801, 809 n. 7 (Bankr.D.Del.1997) (applying the reasoning of cases from a variety of jurisdictions to analysis of N.Y. U.C.C. § 1–201(37)); *In re Owen*, 221 B.R. at 61 n. 6.

*Serv. Corp.*, 136 Misc.2d 194, 518 N.Y.S.2d 317, 318 (N.Y.Dist.Ct.1987), including the following: "[a] whether the purchase option is nominal; [b] whether the lessee is required to make aggregate rental payments having a present value equaling or exceeding the original cost of the leased property; and [c] whether the lease term covers the total useful life of the equipment." *In re Edison Bros. Stores, Inc.*, 207 B.R. 801, 809–10 and n. 8, 9, 10 (Bankr.D.Del.1997). *See also* [N.Y. U.C.C.] § 1–201(37) (McKinney Supp.1996). "In this regard, courts are required to examine the intent of the parties and the facts and circumstances which existed at the time the transaction was entered into." *In re Edison*, 207 B.R. at 809.

\* \* \* The District Court found that the MESA was substantively better characterized as a security agreement than a true lease because the second *Edison Bros.* factor clearly weighed in Pillowtex's favor, and the first and third factors were largely neutral. We agree with the District Court's conclusion in this regard.

Specifically, with respect to the second factor, Duke concedes that the aggregate rental payments owing by Pillowtex under the MESA had a present value equal to or exceeding the cost of the energy fixtures. The *Edison Bros.* court cogently explained the importance of such a fact in showing the existence of a security agreement:

The rationale behind this second factor is that if the alleged lessee is obligated to pay the lessor a sum equal to or greater than the full purchase price of the leased goods plus an interest charge over the term of the alleged lease agreement, a sale is likely to have been intended since what the lessor will receive is more than a payment for the use of the leased goods and loss of their value; the lessor will receive a consideration that would amount to a return on its investment.

*Edison Bros.*, 207 B.R. at 814 (*quoted in Owen*, 221 B.R. at 61–62). Applying that logic to this case, Duke has already been well-compensated for the transferral of the lighting fixtures to Pillowtex, undercutting the proposition that the fixtures were merely leased.

Like the District Court, we are unpersuaded by Duke's attempt to rely on the first and third *Edison Bros.* factors. With respect to the first factor, Duke points out that the MESA provides that it "has the option to . . . give [Pillowtex] the option of purchasing all (but not less than all) of the Equipment at a *mutually agreed price*." App. at 304 (emphasis added). Based on this provision of the MESA, Duke asserts that "Pillowtex does not have the option to purchase the Equipment unless Duke offers it such option, and even then only if Pillowtex agrees on a satisfactory price with Duke." Duke's Br. at 21. Duke concludes that, therefore, the first economic realities factor weighs in favor of a finding that the MESA is a lease. We agree, however, with Pillowtex's contention that, although the MESA nominally required Pillowtex to bargain for an option price, Pillowtex could essentially ensure a nominal option price by refusing to bargain. This refusal would "effectively compel Duke to abandon the [e]nergy [f]ixtures to avoid the exorbitant expense of acquiring and installing replacements."

Pillowtex's Br. at 28. Thus, as an economic reality the option price at the end of the MESA was illusory, nullifying the weight of this factor.

With respect to the third factor, Duke observes that the useful life of the energy fixtures is longer than the term of the MESA, and cites to *Edison Bros.* for the proposition that the long life of the fixtures is indicative of a true lease. In relevant part, the *Edison Bros.* court explained that:

> An essential characteristic of a true lease is that there be something of value to return to the lessor after the term. Where the term of the lease is substantially equal to the life of the lease property such that there will be nothing of value to return at the end of the lease, the transaction is in essence a sale. Conversely, if the lessor expected a remaining useful life after the expiration of the lease term, it can be reasonably inferred that it expected to retain substantial residual value in the leased property at the end of the lease term and that it therefore intended to create a true lease.

207 B.R. at 818 (citations omitted). We agree that under certain circumstances, the fact that transferred goods have a useful life extending beyond the term of the transferring agreement could reveal the transferor's expectation of retaining residual value in those goods. Such an inference would only be proper, however, where the evidence showed a plausible intent by the transferor to repossess the goods.

The economic realities of the particular transaction in this case belie any such intent. Although the useful life of the lighting fixtures is 20–25 years, eclipsing the MESA's 8–year term, it would be unreasonable for Duke to incur the high costs necessary to repossess the fixtures: namely, the costs associated with removing, scrapping, and replacing the fixtures. Also, the uncontroverted evidence in this case establishes that there is little (if any) market value for used lighting fixtures. In short, it would have made no economic sense for Duke to spend large amounts of money to reclaim the fixtures, especially in the face of poor resale prospects. We therefore conclude that the District Court did not err by discounting the significance of the useful life of the lighting fixtures as compared to the length of the MESA when conducting its analysis of the economic realities of the transaction underlying the MESA. On balance, then, applying the three *Edison Bros.* factors to this case leads us to conclude that the MESA was not a true lease.

Beyond reiterating its arguments on the three factors, Duke argues that (1) the mutual subjective intent of the parties was to structure the MESA as a lease; (2) Pillowtex's accounting for the MESA payments as a utility expense is evidence that it did not treat the MESA as a repayment of debt incurred to purchase the energy fixtures; (3) it is of no consequence that the MESA is not labeled a lease; and (4) Duke maintained a meaningful reversionary interest in the fixtures at the end of the MESA's term. None of these arguments is persuasive to us.

First, Duke argues that the District Court erred by failing to analyze the intent of the parties. Duke asserts that the record shows that the parties structured the MESA so that it would qualify as a lease under relevant accounting standards. That way, Pillowtex would not reduce the amount of credit available to it under its senior credit facility. Duke also cites a statement that counsel for Pillowtex made to the District Court, which Duke characterizes as a concession: "I don't disagree that it was structured to have that, those characteristics for tax purposes and, you know, to the extent that they could, the parties were trying to create a lease, I would admit that."

Duke's intent argument fails, however, because the New York U.C.C. no longer looks to the intent of the drafting parties to determine whether a transfer is a lease or a security agreement. Specifically, the 1992 version of § 1–201(37) directed courts to determine "[w]hether a lease *is intended* as security" (emphasis added); this language was amended in 1995 to read "[w]hether a transaction *creates* a lease or security interest" (emphasis added). In this way, the reference to parties' intent was explicitly omitted. The Official Comment to the amended version confirms the importance of the changed language:

> Prior to this amendment, [s]ection 1–201(37) provided that whether a lease was intended as security (i.e., a security interest disguised as a lease) was to be determined from the facts of each case ... Reference to the intent of the parties to create a lease or security agreement has led to unfortunate results. In discovering intent, courts have relied upon factors that were thought to be more consistent with sales or loans than leases. Most of these criteria, however, are as applicable to true leases as to security interests ... Accordingly, amended section 1–201(37) deletes all references to the parties' intent.

U.C.C. § 1–201(37), Official Cmt.; *accord In re Murray*, 191 B.R. at 314 (stating that "judicial opinions construing U.C.C. § 1–201(37) and the Official Uniform Commercial Code Comments ... clearly place the focus of the inquiry under the revised statute on the economics of the transaction rather than on the intent of the parties as had been the emphasis previously").

Duke relies on *Edison Bros.*, 207 B.R. at 809, for the proposition that "[c]ourts are required to examine the intent of the parties and the facts and circumstances which existed at the time the transaction was entered into." *Edison Bros.*, however, explicitly relied on the 1992 version of the statute in looking at intent, and therefore has been superseded by the 1995 version of the U.C.C. Indeed, Judge Walsh, the author of *Edison Bros.*, noted in a later opinion: "I am persuaded by th[e] clear weight of authority that the intent of the parties, no matter how clearly spelled out in the parties' representations within the agreement, can not control the issue of whether the agreement constitutes a true lease or a security agreement." *In re Homeplace Stores*, 228 B.R. 88, 94 (Bankr.D.Del.1998). Judge Walsh observed that the shift away from intent had been remarked upon by various commentators. *Id.* (citing Richard L. Barnes, *Distinguishing Sales* *and Leases: A Primer on the Scope and Purpose of UCC Article 2A*, 25 U. Mem. L. Rev. 873, 882 (1995) ("What had been a test of intention has become a test of economic realities; that is, intention has been dropped from section 1–201(37) ... Thus, the parties to a transaction may create a secured transaction under the revised definition even though their every intention was to create a lease")). * * *

Duke goes on to insist that it had a "meaningful residual interest" in the fixtures, such an interest being "the fundamental characteristic distinguishing a lease from a security interest." *E.g., In re Thummel*, 109 B.R. 447, 448 (Bankr.N.D.Okla.1989). As discussed earlier, however, Duke only has a nominal residual interest, not a *meaningful* one: the combination of the cost of retrieving the fixtures and their poor market value renders the residual interest negligible. Duke claims that we should not "speculate" as to what it might do for economic reasons at the end of the MESA's term, and instead look to the parties' intent at the time of drafting the agreement. As we have mentioned above, however, Duke's argument is backwards: the Court must subordinate the parties' intent to the economic reality that Duke would not have plausibly reclaimed the fixtures at the end of the MESA's term. This is not mere speculation on our part. The uncontroverted evidence shows that removal of the fixtures would be prohibitively expensive, and that the fixtures' value on the market would not make it worth Duke's while to reclaim them. In short, the economic realities analysis not only permits, but *requires* us to examine the state of affairs at the end of the MESA's term. * * *

### IV.   *Conclusion*

After carefully considering the arguments discussed above and all other arguments advanced by appellant, we conclude that the District Court correctly determined that the MESA was not a lease and, therefore, that Duke was not entitled to lease payments under 11 U.S.C. § 365(10). We will remand this case to the District Court so that it may determine whether Duke is entitled to adequate protection.

NOTES

**1.** The courts in *Pillowtex* and *Zaleha* answer the question posed by the introductory text in this section as to what 1–203(a) intends us to look for in the "facts of each case." It is whether the purported lessor has a meaningful reversionary interest. And in order to determine the existence of such a reversionary interest, the court goes back one of the earliest tests used to distinguish leases from security interests: an economic realities analysis. At the inception of the transaction, it was understood by both Duke and Pillowtex that at the end of the 8–year lease the economic reality was that Duke had no choice but to abandon the equipment even though it had many more years of useful life. Thus, Duke had no meaningful reversionary interest in the equipment. The bankruptcy consequences of this holding are that Duke could not compel Pillowtex within 60 days of filing either to reject or to assume the lease by making all payments due on the lease under BC 365(d)(10). Moreover, Duke's security interest became vulnerable to cramdown under Pillowtex's Chapter 11 plan under BC 1129(b).

**2.**   In re Grubbs Const. Co., 319 B.R. 698 (Bankr. M.D. Fla. 2005), is a particularly ardent embrace of the economic realities test, which goes so far as to state in the course of the opinion that a transaction may create a security interest notwithstanding the inclusion of a fair value purchase option if the economic realities otherwise indicate. It is as though 1–203(b)(3) and (d)(2) had not been adopted. The case collects the authorities and cites *Pillowtex* with approval. It notes that the economic realities test has been known colloquially as the "no sensible person" or "no person in its right mind" test. In *Pillowtex* the purported lessee had no options at the end of the lease but the purported lessor did have options, and the court believed that no sensible person in Duke's position would have exercised any option other than abandonment of the equipment in Pillowtex's possession. Hence, under the economic realities test, Duke had no meaningful reversionary interest.

## 3.   OPEN-END LEASE

The equipment and consumer leasing business is a huge enterprise with innumerable legal problems. In our brief treatment we have concentrated on how to distinguish true leases from credit sales. But even in this relatively narrow segment of the field we find ourselves engulfed, not by cases, though there are plenty of them, but by the infinite variations found in leasing contracts. This is nowhere more evident than with respect to the issue raised by the following case regarding what has come to be known as the "terminal rent adjustment clause" or TRAC. These clauses are particularly common in motor vehicle leases. The subject is treated in Cooper, Identifying a True Lease, supra, ¶ 4.08; and in Boss, Leases & Sales at 371 et seq.

## In re Tulsa Port Warehouse Co.

United States Court of Appeals, Tenth Circuit, 1982.
690 F.2d 809.

■ SEYMOUR, CIRCUIT JUDGE.

We are once again called upon to consider a question proven to be a prime source of litigation in the field of commercial law: when is a purported lease in fact a security agreement subject to the requirements of Article 9 of the Uniform Commercial Code (UCC)?

In this case, Tulsa Port Warehouse Company (bankrupt or lessee) entered into four automobile "Non–Maintenance Lease Agreements" with defendant Chuck Naiman Buick Company (lessor), which were subsequently assigned to defendant General Motors Acceptance Corporation (GMAC). Following the bankruptcy of the lessee, the trustee in bankruptcy and GMAC engaged in the classic battle to determine the priority of their interests in the vehicles. It is undisputed that GMAC did not comply with the requirements of Article 9 relating to the perfection of a security interest. If the leases are in fact security agreements, GMAC's interest in the automobiles is subordinate to that of the trustee under * * * § 9–301(1)(b), (3). The bankruptcy court resolved the issue in favor of the trustee, and the district court affirmed that decision.

Under the open-end leases[1] at issue, which are identical in all pertinent respects, the bankrupt leased the automobiles for commercial or business use for either a twenty-four or thirty-six month period. The monthly charge was determined as follows: first, the agreed depreciated value of the vehicle at the end of the lease term was deducted from the original value; second, to this remainder, designated "total amount of fixed monthly rentals for the lease term to be credited against original value," was added the item "total amount of fixed monthly rentals *not* to be credited against original value." The lease agreements did not further identify this latter amount or indicate how it was calculated.[2] Finally, the sum of these two items was divided by the number of months in the lease term to produce the amount due monthly.[3]

The open-end leases contain no option to purchase. Each lease includes termination and default provisions under which the lessee is obligated at termination to return the vehicle to the lessor. At that time, the lessor is required to dispose of the vehicle at wholesale in a commercially reasonable manner. If the amount realized at this sale exceeds the agreed depreciated value, the lessee receives the surplus. If the sale amount is less than the agreed depreciated value, the lessee is liable to the lessor for the deficit.

In Oklahoma, "[w]hether a lease is intended as security is to be determined by the facts of each case." 1–201(37) [1–203(a)]. This court has recently set out the analytical framework for determining whether an agreement is a true lease or a secured transaction. Steele v. Gebetsberger (*In re Fashion Optical, Ltd.*), 653 F.2d 1385, 1388–89 (10th Cir.1981). We

---

**1.**   The lessor uses closed-end and open-end leases. Under the closed-end leases, the lessee returns the vehicle to the lessor at the end of the lease term and the obligations of both come to an end. Under the open-end lease, however, the relationship between the lessor and lessee does not end. Rather, it involves the sale of the vehicle and an adjustment between the lessor and lessee based on the sales price, as more fully described hereinafter.

**2.**   The bankruptcy court held that this item "euphemistically describes ordinary interest without disclosure as to its rate." The district court also found the amount to constitute interest. [[Place chart here]]

**3.**   For example, under one of the 36 month leases for a Buick Regal, the monthly rental was computed as follows:

| | |
|---|---|
| 1. Original value of vehicle | $7,798.00 |
| 2. Agreed depreciated value at end of lease term | 3,450.00 |
| 3. Total amount of fixed monthly rentals for the full base term to be credited against original value | 4,348.00 |
| 4. Total amount of fixed monthly rentals *not* to be credited against original value | 1,730.96 |
| 5. Fixed monthly rental charges | 6,078.96 |
| 6. Sales or use tax | 243.00 |
| 7. Total monthly rental charge | $6,321.96 |
| 8. Monthly rental payments | $175.61 |

pointed out that when a lease does not contain a purchase option, the lease "will still be deemed one intended as security if the facts otherwise expose economic realities tending to confirm that a secured transfer of ownership is afoot." Id. at 1389.

In considering the persistent lease versus secured transfer question, the courts have identified a number of significant factors tending to suggest that a sale has occurred: (1) whether the lease creates an equity in the lessee * * *; (2) whether the lessee is obligated to provide comprehensive insurance in favor of the lessor * * *; (3) whether the lessee pays sales tax * * *; (4) whether the lessee pays all taxes, maintenance, and repairs * * *; and (5) whether the lessee holds the lessor harmless * * *.

With respect to the creation of an equity interest in the lessee in this case, the bankruptcy court and the district judge approved the discussion in Bill Swad Leasing Co. v. Stikes (In re Tillery), 571 F.2d 1361 (5th Cir.1978). In Tillery, the court considered an open-end lease agreement substantially similar to the ones before us and concluded that "[t]he termination formula recognizes the equity of the 'Lessee,' in the vehicle because he is required to bear the loss or receive the gain from its wholesale disposition." Id. at 1365. Although defendants argue vigorously on appeal that Tillery was wrongly decided, we agree with its analysis on this issue.

Moreover, many of the other factors tending to indicate that a lease is in reality a secured transaction are present in this case. The lessee is required to obtain comprehensive insurance in favor of the lessor; pay sales tax and all other licenses, registration, and title fees; pay for all maintenance and repairs; and indemnify the lessor against all loss. As a practical matter, the lessee holds all the incidents of ownership except bare legal title.

Defendants conceded at oral argument that there is no economic difference to the lessor between the lease arrangement here and a secured transfer of property. Under the lease, the lessor is assured of receiving the entire original value of the vehicle plus an amount that realistically must be viewed as interest. The fact that a portion of the original value may be paid by a third party wholesale purchaser after termination of the lease is of no economic significance to the lessor, particularly when the surplus or deficit from this sale is borne by the lessee. We agree with the trial judge's conclusion that "[t]he practical effect of this arrangement is the same as if lessee purchased the car, then sold it two or three years later and used the proceeds to pay off the note."

In sum, we conclude that the agreements were transfers of property subject to a security interest. One purpose of Article 9 of the UCC is to provide notice of such prior interests to third parties dealing with personal property. To promote that end, buyer and seller should be prevented "from masquerading their secured installment sale as a 'lease,' thereby placing it beyond the reach of UCC provisions governing secured transactions." Fashion Optical, 653 F.2d at 1388.

Judgment affirmed.

NOTES

**1.** Industry representatives wanted former 1–201(37) [1–203] to provide that open-end leases are true leases, but the drafters decided not to include special provisions on TRAC leases. Edwin E. Huddleson III, Old Wine in New Bottles: UCC Article 2A—Leases, 39 Ala. L. Rev. 615, 638–641 (1988). How would *Tulsa Port Warehouse* be decided under 1–203?

Motor vehicle and trailer lessors apparently form a compact interest group whose activities are affected by 1–203. They have successfully lobbied in about half the states for a nonuniform amendment to 1–203. Sometimes the amendments appear in a state's certificate of title rules, not the UCC. Typical nonuniform amendments provides that in the case of motor vehicles or trailers "a transaction does not create a sale or a security interest merely because it provides that the rental price is permitted or required to be adjusted under the agreement either upward or downward by reference to the amount realized upon sale or other disposition of the motor vehicle or trailer." See, e.g., Va. Code Ann. § 46.2–640.1 (2003). The operative language is "merely because." The language is intended to make characterization turn on factors other than the rent adjustment clause. A purported lessor's hope is that, without the clause being taken into account, the TRAC lease will be characterized as a true lease. However, the result is not guaranteed. The language of typical nonuniform legislation doesn't require courts to ignore the rent adjustment clause. It only prevents them from treating a TRAC lease as a sale or security interest "merely" because of the clause's presence. Courts therefore still can consider the clause in determining its affect on risk allocations around residual asset values. This determination in turn could affect characterization.

**2.** Case law is still divided. In Sharer v. Creative Leasing, Inc., 612 So.2d 1191 (Ala.1993), the court held an open-end lease to be a true lease. The court opined that in order to create a security interest a lease must give the lessee some ownership in the leased property. An open-end lease does not transfer an ownership interest or create an equity in the lessee but merely shifts the risk of fluctuations in market value to the lessee. "Therefore, it cannot be said that such a shifting of the risk of loss in value of the item alone is sufficient to hold that any lease agreement containing such a clause necessarily was intended to create a security interest." 612 So.2d at 1196. Is there any important analytical difference between owning an asset and bearing the downside and upside risks with respect to it? Sometimes the argument is made that the kind of TRAC in *Tulsa Port Warehouse* is merely incentive for the lessee to take good care of the vehicle and is not inconsistent with the existence of a true lease. Is this a persuasive argument? Cooper, Identifying a True Lease, supra, ¶ 4.08[2].

**3.** Each year new cases appear on the issue whether a lease creates a security interest. Has the UCC taken the correct approach in making filing depend on the sometimes difficult issue of when a lease creates a security interest under 1–203? With respect to consignments we will find that the Code requires filing in most cases to protect the consignor's interest against the consignee's creditors even though no security interest is created. 9–102(a)(20). Article 9 covers in a similar manner both security interests in and outright sales of accounts and other rights to payment. 9–109(a)(3). Should the same approach be taken in the leasing area with filing required for all leases of personal property in which the term of the lease exceeds a certain period of time? See the Uniform Consumer Credit Code definition of "consumer lease" as a "lease of goods * * * which is for a term exceeding four months." UCCC § 1.301(14) (1974). The issue was extensively debated in the course of drafting Article 2A and the decision was made not to require filing for true leases. See Charles W. Mooney Jr., The Mystery and Myth of "Ostensible Ownership" and Article 9 Filing: A Critique of Proposals to Extend Filing Requirements to Leases, 39 Ala. L. Rev. 683 (1988). The PEB Study Group Report recommended no change in the current law on this issue and the Drafting Committee proposed none.

## PROBLEMS

**1.** Drive and Smith enter into an agreement described as a "lease." It calls for Smith to lease a car from Drive for a period of two years. The lease payments are based on the difference between the car's estimated residual value at the end of the period and the original purchase price. (The estimated value is based on the figures given in the current Industry Standards Manual.) At the end of the two-year period Drive is required to sell the vehicle in a commercially reasonable manner. The car has a useful life of 10 years. If the sale proceeds are less than the car's estimated residual value, Smith must pay Drive the deficiency. If the sale proceeds exceed the estimated residual value, Drive must credit Smith for the surplus. Smith doesn't have the right to cancel or extend the agreement, or purchase the car from Drive. Is this transaction a true lease or a disguised secured sale?

**2.** Assume that Drive and Smith enter into a different agreement. This agreement contains an estimated number of miles the car is to be driven over the two-year period. Drive is to retain the car at the end of the term. If the car is driven more than the estimated miles, the excess mileage is charged to Smith at a per mile charge of 50 cents. If fewer miles are driven than the estimate, Smith is given a credit on the same per mile basis. The mileage charge is called a "rent readjustment" and the credit a "rent rebate." True lease or disguised secured sale?

**3.** Assume that Drive and Smiths' agreement states an estimated residual value of the car at the end of the two-year period. It also provides that at the end of the period, Drive is to retain the car and obtain a commercially reasonable appraisal of its fair market value at that time. Smith is liable for any deficiency between the estimated and appraised values of the car, and is to be credited for any surplus. True lease or disguised secured sale?

**4.** Assume that Drive and Smiths' agreement requires Drive to sell the car in a commercially reasonable manner at the end of the two-year period. Drive is to receive a maximum of $1000 of the sale proceeds. Any amounts above that maximum are surplus, to be credited to Smith as a "rent rebate." If the sale proceeds are less than $1000, Smith is liable to the extent of the deficiency. The deficiency is to be considered a "rent adjustment." The current Industry Standards Manual puts a $5000 resale price on two-year old cars of the sort Smith "leased." True lease or secured sale? Would the result change if the Manual put a $1000 resale price on the car?

## B.   CONSIGNMENTS

### 1.   COMMON LAW CONSIGNMENTS

Commercial consignments have long been used as an alternative to secured transactions in financing merchant inventories. The basic consignment is a simple transaction that is described in the following quotation.

> Under a "true" consignment, the owner of goods delivers them to a consignee for sale. If the consignee sells them, he must account to the owner-consignor for the proceeds of sale less his commission. If he does not sell the goods, he must return them, but he does not in any case become liable to the consignor for the price of the goods if they are not sold. Title to the goods remains in the consignor during the consignment and passes, when the goods are sold, directly to the purchaser. * * * The consignment was never thought of as a security device, and indeed, since there is no obligation to be secured, it is not. * * * [A]s a matter of common law the consignor was protected against the consignee's creditors and on insolvency was entitled to reclaim the goods from the consignee's trustee in bankruptcy.

1 Grant Gilmore, Security Interests in Personal Property § 3.5, at 73–74 (1965).

In short, at common law a consignment was a bailment for the purpose of sale. The bailee-consignee did not own the goods and its creditors could not reach the ownership interest of the bailor-consignor. Consignments were used for a variety of purposes, among them, to induce dealers to stock inventory untested in the market place, maintain the supplier's control of the dealer's resale prices, or, in most cases, make it possible for dealers to stock merchandise by allowing them to acquire inventory without having to invest their own capital.

### 2.   CONSIGNMENTS UNDER ARTICLE 9

Since commercial consignments function as a form of purchase money financing, they create an ostensible ownership problem for the consignee's creditors and purchasers. Potential lenders may assume that the merchant owns the inventory that it possesses. A consignee's senior inventory financer might rely on the consignee's unencumbered ownership of incoming consigned goods to extend subsequent credit to it. Article 9 has addressed the ostensible ownership issue by assimilating commercial consignments to

purchase money secured transactions and by dealing with them accordingly. But it has done so to only a restricted class of consignment transactions
that fall within the definition of "consignment" in 9–102(a)(20) below. We
will refer to this as an "Article 9 consignment." Article 9 consignments are
a type of bailment sometimes referred to as a "true consignment."

Consignment means a transaction, regardless of its form, in which a
person delivers goods to a merchant for the purpose of sale and:

> (A) the merchant:
>
>> (i) deals in goods of that kind under a name other than the name
>> of the person making the delivery;
>>
>> (ii) is not an auctioneer; and
>>
>> (iii) is not generally known by its creditors to be substantially
>> engaged in selling the goods of others;
>
> (B) with respect to each delivery, the aggregate value of the goods is
> $1,000 or more at the time of the delivery;
>
> (C) the goods are not consumer goods immediately before delivery; and
>
> (D) the transaction does not create a security interest that secures an
> obligation.

If the transaction falls within this definition, it is covered by Article 9
under 9–109(a)(4). As Comment 6 to 9–109 explains, this definition is more
restrictive than the popular use of the term "consignment," but whenever
the term "consignment" is used in Article 9, it refers only to the transaction described in 9–102(a)(20). Comment 14 to 9–102 explains: "The
definition of 'consignment' excludes, in subparagraphs (B) and (C), transactions for which filing would be inappropriate or of insufficient benefit to
justify the costs. * * * The definition also excludes, in subparagraph (D),
what have been called 'consignments intended for security'. These 'consignments' are not bailments but secured transactions. Accordingly, [under 9–
109(a)(1)] all of Article 9 applies to them."

Section 1–201(b)(35) provides: " 'Security interest' includes any interest of a consignor * * * that is subject to Article 9." This provision tells us
that those consignments defined in 9–102(a)(20) ("Article 9 consignments")
are treated as creating security interests within Article 9 even though they
do not meet the test of the first sentence of 1–201(b)(35) of securing an
obligation. Since an Article 9 consignment creates a security interest, it
must be perfected by filing under 9–310(a), and, since 9–103(d) treats the
consignor's security interest as a purchase money security interest in
inventory, the consignor must comply with the filing and notification
requirements of 9–324(b) for protection against a prior filed security
interest.

Under a genuine consignment, title to the goods remains in the
consignor and the consignee is only a bailee of the goods for the purpose of
sale. Since the bailee-consignee has no ownership rights in the consigned
goods, how can creditors of, or purchasers from the consignee reach the
owner-consignor's rights in these goods? Section 9–319(a) deals with this by

legislative fiat: "for purposes of determining the rights of creditors of, and purchasers for value of goods from, a consignee, while the goods are in the possession of the consignee, the consignee is deemed to have the rights and title to the goods identical to those the consignor had or had the power to transfer." Thus, creditors of, and purchasers from the consignee can take judicial liens and security interests in the consigned goods even though they belong to the consignor. Comment 2 to 9–319.

Article 9 determines rights only between the consignee's creditors and purchasers and the consignor, with respect to goods in the possession of the consignee. It does not deal with the relationship between the consignor and consignee. In keeping with this, 9–601(g) states "this part imposes no duties upon a secured party that is a consignor * * *." The "part" mentioned is Part Six that governs the rights of secured parties upon default by a debtor. The remedies of an Article 9 consignor against a consignee are left to the agreement of the parties or other law. There is no requirement that upon default by the consignee the consignor dispose of the collateral or collect obligations in a commercially reasonable manner, nor are there deficiency limitations.

## 3.   SECURITY CONSIGNMENT EXCLUSION

Article 9 applies to two different transactions that may be referred to by the parties as consignments. The first of these is what we call an "Article 9 consignment," narrowly defined in 9–102(a)(20), which cannot under subparagraph (D) secure an obligation. The second sentence of 1–201(b)(35) provides that this transaction creates a security interest. The second is a transaction in the form of a consignment that secures an obligation. We will call this a security consignment because it secures an obligation and therefore creates a security interest under the first sentence of 1–201(b)(35). This transaction is never referred to in Article 9 as a consignment, and is treated merely as creating a security interest in inventory. See Comment 6 to 9–109. Thus, we find Article 9 applying to two kinds of transactions that the parties may have labeled "consignments." Under 9–109(a)(4), Article 9 applies to "consignments," as defined in 9–102(a)(20), but, because of 9–601(g), only the first five Parts apply. However, under 9–109(a)(1), all of Article 9 applies to transactions in which the consignment secures an obligation. Does 9–102(a)(20) include the transaction in the following Problem?

## PROBLEM

In an agreement termed a "consignment," Manufacturer (M) entrusted his new line of road bicycles ("Roadsters") to Dealer for sale at his Bicycle Shop. Demand for Roadsters is strong, and the deal M and Dealer reached was: (i) Dealer must account to M at the end of each month for the agreed wholesale price of M's bikes sold that month; (ii) in the unlikely case that a bike fails to sell within a six-month period, at the end of this period Dealer must account to M for the wholesale price of the bike and can then deal with the bike in any way it wishes. See 9–102(a)(20)(D), 1–201(b)(35) "security interest."

---

Case law on the differences between true consignments and security consignments was confusing and unsatisfactory under former Article 9. Revised Article 9 helps somewhat by having a clear definition of an "Article 9" consignment in 9–102(a)(20), but nothing in the text of 1–201(b)(35) offers assistance on when a consignment secures an obligation. Gilmore sensibly read the language to mean that for a transaction labeled a consignment to create a security interest the consignee must owe an obligation to pay for the goods after a period of time, whether they were sold or not. But the cases have gone far beyond that. For instance, in Mann v. Clark Oil & Refining Corp., 302 F.Supp. 1376 (E.D.Mo. 1969), an oil company consigned gasoline to a dealer; if it failed to sell the gasoline it had to return the gasoline to the oil company. The court found the existence of a security interest: reservation of title to the gasoline secured the payment for the gasoline that was delivered. If the court is holding that a security interest is created if the consignment agreement reserves title to the consigned goods and requires the consignee to pay for the goods when sold, then any consignment creates a security interest. In In re Gross Mfg. & Importing Co., Inc., 328 F.Supp. 905 (D.N.J. 1971), the agreement required the consignee either to sell the goods and pay for them within 30 days or return the unsold goods. The court found a security interest even though there was no obligation to pay for the goods in any event.

How do consignors cope with this uncertainty? In matters of attachment, perfection and priority, it usually doesn't matter whether there is a true consignment or security consignment if the consignor has filed an appropriate financing statement. Prudent commercial consignors have been filing financing statements since the 1962 Code was enacted, and they will continue to do so under Revised Article 9. Consignors may use the terms "consignor" and "consignee" instead of "secured party" and "debtor" in financing statements. 9–505(a). The filing of a financing statement is not a factor in determining whether the transaction is a true consignment or a security consignment, and, if the transaction is found to secure an obligation, a financing statement using consignment terminology is effective to perfect the security interest. 9–505(b). But filing does not solve the consignor's problem of whether, on default, it must comply with Part 6 by disposing of the consigned goods in a commercially reasonable manner. Whether the consignment is a security consignment or a true consignment usually does not arise in what is probably most likely default case, that of the bankruptcy of the consignee. If the trustee in bankruptcy undertakes to liquidate the collateral, Part 6 does not matter. In other disposition cases, consignors may find some comfort in giving the consignee notification of intent to sell by a private sale before disposition.

---

The following case demonstrates the application of the consignment provisions of Revised Article 9 to a common transaction.

# In re Georgetown Steel Co., LLC

United States Bankruptcy Court, D. South Carolina, 2004.
318 B.R. 352.

■ JOHN E. WAITES, BANKRUPTCY JUDGE.

This matter comes before the Court upon cross Motions for Summary Judgment filed by Georgetown Steel Company, LLC ("Georgetown Steel" or "Debtor") and Progress Rail Services Corporation ("Progress Rail" or "Defendant"). The controversy in this matter is the determination of which party is entitled to the proceeds of certain inventory that was in Debtor's possession on the date of the bankruptcy filing. After examining the record of the case and considering the arguments of counsel, the Court believes that before it can rule on the ultimate issue of which party is entitled to the proceeds of the inventory, it must first determine the nature of the transaction between the Debtor and Progress Rail. After reviewing the parties' pleadings and arguments, the Court makes the following findings of fact and conclusions of law relating to the nature of the transaction between the Debtor and Progress Rail.

## *FINDINGS OF FACT*

1.  Hot briquetted iron, also known as HBI in the steel industry, is a raw material commodity used in the production of steel. Debtor processed HBI in order to produce steel.

2.  Progress Rail supplied HBI and other raw materials to Debtor.

3.  On October 10, 2003, Debtor and Progress Rail entered into an agreement titled "Consignment Agreement" (the "Agreement").

4.  During the period between October 10, 2003 and October 20, 2003, Progress Rail delivered HBI to Debtor at its facility in Georgetown, South Carolina as required by the Agreement.

5.  Pursuant to the terms of the Agreement, Progress Rail maintained title to the HBI delivered to Debtor. Debtor stored the HBI in a segregated location from its other inventory, and removed and used the HBI from the location on an as-needed basis. Once a week Debtor reported the HBI usage to Progress Rail and paid Progress Rail for the HBI that it consumed during the prior week.

6.  The parties do not dispute that Progress Rail did not file a UCC–1 financing statement to evidence its interest in the inventory of HBI in Debtor's possession.

7.  It is also undisputed that on October 20, 2003, Progress Rail sent a written notice to Debtor stating that it was terminating the Agreement and sent an additional written notice demanding reclamation of certain goods in Debtor's possession. Progress Rail's written notice terminating the Agree-

ment advised Debtor that the Agreement was to be terminated effective October 21, 2003, and Debtor was directed to immediately stop withdrawing and consuming HBI.

8.   Progress Rail's reclamation demand provided that the demand was for all goods received by Debtor from Progress Rail within the applicable reclamation period, regardless of whether such goods were included in the exhibit to the reclamation demand.

9.   On October 21, 2003 (the "Petition Date"), Debtor filed its voluntary petition for relief under Chapter 11 of the Bankruptcy Code. Debtor is operating its business and managing its properties as debtor-in-possession pursuant to Sections 1107(a) and 1108 of title 11 of the United State Code, 11 U.S.C. § 101, *et seq.* (the "Bankruptcy Code").

10.   After the Petition Date, Debtor no longer had an immediate use for the HBI because of the closure of the mill.

11.   On the Petition Date, the CIT Group/Business Credit Inc. ("CIT") claimed a first priority perfected security interest in Debtor's entire inventory, including the HBI, based on its loan documents with Debtor and as further set forth in the Cash Collateral Orders entered by the Court in the bankruptcy case. MidCoast Industries, Inc. ("MidCoast") claimed a second perfected security interest in Debtor's inventory.[4]

12.   After the Petition Date, Debtor and Progress Rail entered into a Stipulation (the "Stipulation"), which provided for the sale of HBI in Debtor's possession. Both Debtor and Progress Rail wanted to liquidate the inventory of HBI because the market price of HBI at that time was high and was expected to decrease in the near future.

13.   Furthermore, the Stipulation provided that this Court would resolve all claims and disputes concerning ownership of the proceeds generated by the sale of the HBI. Moreover, Debtor and Progress Rail also agreed that the sale would not affect any party's interest in the HBI and that any interest in the HBI would attach to the proceeds produced from the sale.

14.   The HBI was sold in December 2003 pursuant to the terms of the Stipulation. The sale of the HBI generated $1,381,435.01 in proceeds. The proceeds of the sale are currently being held in trust pending the outcome of this adversary proceeding.

15.   On December 22, 2003, Debtor filed a Complaint seeking a declaratory judgment that Debtor's interest in the HBI is superior and senior to Progress Rail's interests in the HBI and asserting its rights as a lien creditor pursuant to 11 U.S.C. § 544.

16.   Debtor contends that the Agreement is a consignment pursuant to Article 9 of the Uniform Commercial Code ("UCC") as enacted by the state of Alabama under Title 7 of the Alabama Code (the UCC provisions enacted under Title 7 of the Alabama Code shall generally be referred to as

---

**4.** Debtor acknowledges the claims of CIT and MidCoast Industries, Inc. have now been paid or otherwise satisfied from other resources of the Debtor.

the "Alabama Commercial Code"). However, Progress Rail contends that the Agreement represents a sales transaction governed by the provisions of Article 2 of the Alabama Commercial Code.[5] In light of the parties' competing views, the Court must determine which alternative best describes this transaction.

## CONCLUSIONS OF LAW

The question before the Court, as stipulated by the parties, is whether the Agreement is a consignment governed under Article 9 of the Uniform Commercial Code (Article 9A of Title 7 of the Alabama Code) or is more in the nature of a sale or transaction in goods in which Article 2 expressly applies.

## ARTICLE 9 CONSIGNMENT

Prior to the 1999 revisions to the UCC, most of the law concerning consignment transactions was governed by Article 2 of the UCC. Following the revisions, most provisions governing consignments are now contained in Article 9. White & Summers, Uniform Commercial Code, § 30–4 (5th ed., 2002); Official Comment 4 to Ala. Code § 7–2–326. Additionally, the definition of a "security interest" under the revised UCC now includes an interest of a consignor pursuant to Article 9. *See id.*; UCC § 1–201(37); Ala. Code § 7–1–201(37) (West, WESTLAW through 2004 Legis. Sess.). Alabama has adopted the 1999 revisions to the UCC.

In order to determine whether the Agreement is a consignment governed by Article 9, it is necessary to examine whether the transaction between Debtor and Progress Rail meets the definition of consignment under the Alabama Commercial Code. If the transaction falls outside the definition, it is likely governed by Article 2. *See* White & Summers, Uniform Commercial Code, § 30–4 (5th ed., 2002).

Section 7–9A–109 of the Alabama Commercial Code states that Article 9A (Alabama's enactment of revised 1999 version of Article 9 of the UCC) applies to:

(1) a transaction, regardless of its form, that creates a security interest in personal property or fixtures by contract; . . . [and]

(4) a consignment.

According to the changes in the Alabama Commercial Code, the provisions describing a consignment under former § 7–2–326(3) are now largely incorporated into the definition of consignment pursuant to Ala. Code § 7–9A–102(a)(20). Section 7–9A–102(a)(20) of the Alabama Commercial Code defines a consignment as follows:

**5.** To the extent Progress Rail argued at the hearing that the transaction between it and Debtor was of another type, such as a common law consignment or a consignment not within the purview of Article 9, because it fails to meet the technical definition of a consignment provided in Article 9, Progress Rail appears to have abandoned that position by failing to brief the matter in its proposed order, instead relying on the argument that the transaction is a sale under Article 2.

"Consignment" means a transaction, regardless of its form, in which a person delivers goods to a merchant for the purpose of sale and:

(A) the merchant:

    (i) deals in goods of that kind under a name other than the name of the person making delivery;

    (ii) is not an auctioneer; and

    (iii) is not generally known by its creditors to be substantially engaged in selling the goods of others;

(B) with respect to each delivery, the aggregate value of the goods is $1,000 or more at the time of delivery;

(C) the goods are not consumer goods immediately before delivery; and

(D) the transaction does not create a security interest that secures an obligation.

In order to be a consignment agreement solely governed by Article 9A of the Alabama Commercial Code, the transaction at issue must fall within the definition set forth above. Debtor contends that the Agreement meets all of the elements of a consignment pursuant to Ala. Code § 7–9A–102(a)(20). Progress Rail concedes that the transaction meets most of the above criteria but argues that the Agreement is not a consignment because (A) the goods were not delivered to a merchant "for the purpose of sale"; (B) Debtor does not "deal in goods of that kind;" and (C) the Agreement creates a security interest that secures an obligation.

*A.   Did Progress Rail Deliver the HBI to Debtor "For the Purpose of Sale"?*

The goods under a "consignment" transaction as defined by § 7–9A–102(a)(20) must be delivered "for the purpose of sale." The Agreement between Debtor and Progress Rail provides that title to the HBI shall remain with Progress Rail and that Debtor "[s]hall purchase [HBI] only for its own use." While there is no evidence indicating that Debtor sold HBI as a commodity to others, the Agreement contemplates the processing and incorporation of HBI into Debtor's manufactured steel products, which Debtor sells to its customers. Thus, the issue here is whether Debtor must sell HBI in its raw and unadulterated form to others in order to find that Progress Rail's delivery of HBI was "for the purpose of sale."

This issue is not new. When determining whether goods were delivered "for sale" under the provisions of former UCC § 2–326(3), the courts in *Pearson Industries, Inc.* and *BFC Chemicals, Inc.* rejected similar arguments to that made by Progress Rail in the matter before the Court. The court in *Pearson Industries* concluded that manufacturers selling component goods incorporated into products are delivered for sale as "component parts" of the product that the manufacturer sold to its customers. *Barber v. McCord Auto Supply, Inc. (In re Pearson Industries, Inc.)*, 147 B.R. 914, 928 (Bankr.C.D.Ill.1992). In addressing the same issue, the Court in *BFC Chemicals, Inc.* concluded that in order to apply former UCC § 2–326(3), debtor-consignee is not required to sell the raw form of goods delivered by a vendor for such goods to be delivered "for sale." *BFC Chemicals, Inc. v. Smith–Douglass, Inc.*, 46 B.R. 1009, 1019 (E.D.N.C.1985).

Further, the current version of the Alabama Commercial Code and commentary on the UCC lend support to Debtor's argument that the delivery was "for the purpose of sale." Official Comment 14 to Ala. Code § 7–9A–102, the statutory provision that defines a "consignment," provides that:

> The definition of "consignment" requires that goods be delivered "to a merchant for the purpose of sale." If the goods are delivered for another purpose as well, *such as milling or processing*, the transaction is a consignment nonetheless because a purpose of delivery is "sale."

(emphasis added). Finally, the leading commentary on the Uniform Commercial Code contemplates transactions such as that between Debtor and Progress Rail and concludes:

> If despite their processing and commingling the goods are to be returned to the owner and not sold to a third person, the transaction is not a consignment under the 1999 Article 9.... If, on the other hand, the goods are to be processed and then sold by the processor to persons to be selected by him, *the transaction is a consignment even though the processor is both processing and selling.*

White & Summers, Uniform Commercial Code, § 30–5 (5th ed., 2002) (emphasis added). In the matter before the Court, Debtor processed the HBI delivered by Progress Rail and incorporated the HBI into steel. The HBI is an integral component of the steel that Debtor sells to its customers. Therefore, this Court concludes that Progress Rail delivered HBI to Debtor "for the purpose of sale."

### B.  Does Debtor "Deal in Goods of that Kind"?

The Alabama Commercial Code does not specifically provide for the precise meaning of "dealing in goods of the kind." Additionally, the Court was unable to find, and the parties did not cite, Alabama case law specifically defining the phrase "deals in goods of the kind." However, a survey of other jurisdictions provided some measure of guidance. In *Marvin Lumber & Cedar Co. v. PPG Indus., Inc.*, 223 F.3d 873, 883–84 (8th Cir.2000), the Eighth Circuit, in determining whether Minnesota's economic loss doctrine applied to a specific transaction, addressed the issue of whether a manufacturer that incorporated a component good into its end product may be considered a merchant that deals in that particular component good. Under the facts of *Marvin Lumber & Cedar Co.*, a manufacturer and seller of customized wooden windows and doors incorporated a wood preservative into his final products. In light of the manufacturer's expertise in selling the wooden products and incorporating the wood preservative into those products, the Eighth Circuit held that the manufacturer dealt in wood preservatives. *Id.* In so holding, the Eighth Circuit stated that "[w]here a manufacturer with sophisticated knowledge of a component purchases and incorporates that component into its product, the manufacturer is a[sic] not merely a dealer with respect to finished product, but with respect to the component part as well." *Id.*

In *Pearson Industries, Inc.*, the debtor received tires and incorporated them into machinery that it manufactured and then sold. The vendor that supplied the tires argued that former UCC § 2–326, as adopted by the state of Illinois, did not apply to the transaction because the debtor did not sell the tires individually. The court in that case rejected the vendor's argument and concluded that debtor maintained a place of business at which it dealt with the tires delivered by vendor by incorporating the tires into the equipment that debtor manufactured and sold. The Court went on to conclude that despite the fact that debtor did not retail the component tires individually and apart from its manufactured product, former UCC §§ 2–326(2) & (3) applied nonetheless. 147 B.R. at 928.

In *BFC Chemicals*, as in this case, a debtor-consignee purchased goods from the creditor-consignor, processed and transformed the goods, and then resold the processed and transformed goods. 46 B.R. at 1019. The Court in *BFC Chemicals* noted that the goods that were the subject of the consignment agreement between debtor-consignee and creditor-consigner would normally be in the inventory of a manufacturer such as the debtor-consignee. Notwithstanding the transformation of the purchased goods, the court in *BFC Chemicals* held that the buyer dealt in the goods of the kind involved in the transaction. *Id.*

In this case, Debtor received the HBI from Progress Rail, and through its manufacturing process, combined it with other materials to produce steel. HBI is a processed metal used to manufacture Debtor's product and, in fact, is an integral component part of Debtor's final product. Moreover, HBI appears to be a raw material normally maintained in the inventory of manufacturers such as Debtor. Despite the fact that further processing of HBI is required to incorporate HBI into the steel that Debtor sells, HBI is a component of the steel produced and sold by Debtor; thus, it appears that Debtor deals in goods of the kind delivered by Progress Rail. Therefore, the Court finds that Debtor "deals in goods of the kind" for purposes of applying § 7–9A–102(a)(20) to the transaction between Debtor and Progress Rail.

*C. Did the Agreement Create a Security Interest "that Secures an Obligation?"*

In determining the last element of Article 9's definition of a consignment, a distinction can be made between a "conventional" commercial consignment—as defined in UCC § 9–102(a)(20)—and an "unusual" commercial consignment. *See* White & Summers, Uniform Commercial Code, § 30–4 (5th ed., 2002). The "conventional" commercial consignment is also typically a security interest, while the "unusual" commercial consignment creates a security interest "that secures an obligation." *Id.* The latter is still treated under Article 9 (even though it does not meet part D of UCC

§ 9–102(a)(20)), but is restricted to the recovery rules set forth in Part 6 of Article 9. *Id.*[10]

Whether an interest "secures an obligation" has been described as dependent upon whether there is a duty to pay for unsold goods. *Id.* In the matter before the Court, it is clear that Debtor only owed Progress Rail a debt for the goods it consumed. The Agreement does not reference any accompanying broader debt or obligation Debtor owes to Progress Rail. Although the Agreement states, "[t]o the extent it may be necessary or appropriate under applicable law or regulation, [Debtor] grants [Progress Rail] a security interest in the [HBI]," the conditional nature of the language indicates that the terms of the Agreement do not create a clear and express grant of a security interest *that secures an obligation* in the HBI to Progress Rail. Thus, the Court concludes that the Agreement does not create a security interest that secures an obligation. Accordingly, the transaction meets all of the elements of the definition of a consignment set forth in § 7–9A–102(a)(20) of the Alabama Commercial Code.

\* \* \*

### IV.   *CONCLUSION*

In light of the provisions of the Agreement and the definition of "consignment" provided by Ala. Code § 7–9A–102(a)(20), the Court determines that the Agreement between Debtor and Progress Rail is a consignment transaction as defined by the provisions of Article 9A of the Alabama Commercial Code.

Therefore, for the reasons set forth hereinabove, it is hereby

**ORDERED** that the Agreement between Debtor and Progress Rail is a consignment transaction pursuant to Ala. Code § 7–9A–102(a)(20) \* \* \*

## 4.   NON-ARTICLE 9 CONSIGNMENTS AND NON-ARTICLE 9 LAW

PROBLEM

Knight was broke and needed to raise money to pay her taxes. She took her valuable gold charm bracelet to The Alamo, a store that sold western clothing and accessories. The agreement was that the bracelet was on consignment from Knight and that the store would attempt to sell it for her for no less than $1,200; if it sold it for more than that amount the store could keep the surplus. The Alamo did very little consignment selling, and both Knight and The Alamo were ignorant of any filing requirements regarding consignments. But The Alamo hadn't been paying *its* taxes, and the IRS seized the store's inventory, including the bracelet, under a jeopardy assessment and levy. The facts are based on Knight v. United

---

**10.** In essence, if a transaction satisfies UCC § 9–102(a)(20) A through C, the consignor's interest is a security interest treated under Article 9. Those transactions that fall outside of the scope of 9–102(a)(20) by failing to satisfy 9–102(a)(20)A through C will likely be treated under revised Article 2–326(1). White & Summers, Uniform Commercial Code, § 30–4 (5th ed., 2002).

States, 838 F.Supp. 1243 (M.D.Tenn.1993). See John Dolan, The UCC's Consignment Rule Needs an Exception for Consumers, 44 Ohio St.L.J. 21 (1983). See 9–102(a)(20)(C). See "consumer goods" 9–102(a)(23). Is this case within 9–102(a)(20)? Should Knight get her bracelet back?

———————

This case raises three questions: (1) does this consignment transaction describe an Article 9 consignment?; (2) if not, what law governs a non-Article 9 consignment?; and (3) what does that law provide with respect to the rights of the consignor against the consignee's creditors? As to the first question, this is true consignment because the transferor continues to bear the risks in market price around the value of the asset. The Alamo's right to return the bracelet allocates market declines to Knight; The Alamo's entitlement to a surplus (or commission) limits its opportunity to benefit from increases in the bracelet's market price. However, the transaction is not an Article 9 consignment; see 9–102(a)(20)(A) and (C). This means that none of Article 9's filing requirements apply to the non-Article 9 consignor, and the rights of the consignee's creditors against the consigned goods are not controlled by Article 9 (e.g., 9–319(a)).

As to the second question, if this case is not within Article 9, what law governs? Section 2–326(2) provides that goods held on sale or return are subject to the claims of the buyer's creditors while in the possession of the buyer. Comment 1 to 2–326 describes a "sale or return" transaction: "A sale or return * * * typically is a sale to a merchant whose unwillingness to buy is overcome by the seller's engagement to take back the goods * * * in lieu of payment if they fail to be resold. A sale or return is a present sale of goods which may be undone at the buyer's option." Is the transaction in the Problem a sale or return within 2–326? If the consignment transaction isn't covered by Article 9 or Article 2, the applicable state's extra-Code law on the subject of consignments controls.

This raises the third question: what does the applicable state's controlling extra-Code law on the subject generally provide? There are three possible positions that can be taken on the matter. One position is that the pre-Code common law of bailments applies. Under it the consignor prevails against the consignee's creditors even when it fails to give public notice of its consignment interest. A second position is that non-Code common law developed while former Article 9 was in effect applies, and under it the consignor might lose to the consignee's creditors. In re Haley & Steele, 58 UCC Rep. Serv.2d 394 (Super. Ct. Mass. 2005). The third (just "possible") position is that courts will mistakenly consider non-Article 9 consignments "sale or return" transactions and treat them accordingly under 2–326(2). For a discussion of these issues, see In re Morgansen's LTD, 302 B.R. 784 (Bankr. EDNY 2003). See Jean Wegman Burns, New Article 9 of the UCC: The Good, the Bad, and the Ugly, 2002 U. Ill. L. Rev. 29, 56 n.210.

## 5.   KNOWLEDGE-OF-CREDITORS EXCLUSION

If the consignee is generally known by its creditors to be "substantially engaged in selling the goods of others," there is no ostensible ownership issue and, presumably, its creditors and purchasers will not rely on the consignee's ownership of the goods. Therefore, 9–102(a)(20)(A)(iii) excludes the transaction. Is the transaction in the following Problem excluded on this basis?

### PROBLEM

Maude Thaxton, a woman of means, decided to sell her Archipenko bronze—long coveted by her undeserving son—through the SoHo gallery owned and operated by Jacques DeBus, whom Maude had found to be such a charming young man at society gatherings. They worked out an agreement under which Maude entrusted the sculpture to SoHo for sale at a price no less than $200,000; SoHo's commission was to be 15%. Although Maude successfully managed her substantial estate, she had never heard of a financing statement and Jacques did not enlighten her on the subject. Jacques' creditors did not find him charming at all, and one of them levied on all of the art objects at SoHo's premises pursuant to a large money judgment against Jacques. Can this judgment creditor take rights in the Archipenko prior to those of a sadder-but-wiser Maude under Article 9? Doesn't everyone know that art galleries don't own the art on display? Or do they? See 9–102(a)(20)(A). Is this transaction one involving "consumer goods"? See In re Haley & Steele, 58 UCC Rep. Serv.2d 394 (Super. Ct. Mass. 2005).

## 6.   BAILMENTS OTHER THAN LEASES AND CONSIGNMENTS

### PROBLEMS

**1.**  Debtor both sells and stores grain. Farmer stored grain with Debtor who agreed to deliver the grain to any buyer to whom Farmer sold the grain. Debtor had no authority to sell Farmer's grain. Before Farmer found a buyer for his grain, Debtor filed in bankruptcy. Farmer had not filed a financing statement because he was merely storing grain with Debtor. Debtor's trustee maintained that 9–102(a)(20) applied to this case because the purpose of the bailment was the sale of Farmer's grain, and whether Debtor sold the grain or Farmer did was immaterial. Since Debtor was a seller of grain, Debtor's creditors were misled by Debtor's possession of Farmer's grain. Is this a case in which "a person delivers goods to a merchant for the purpose of sale"?

**2.**  Sight Inc., a manufacturer of television sets, and Ace, a large advertiser, agreed that Sight would produce and deliver 100 sets to Ace. Because Sight was low on working capital and could not purchase the components needed to produce the sets, Ace agreed to buy the components and have them delivered to Sight. Sight, in turn agreed to assemble the televisions with them, deducting from the contract price of doing so the cost of the components. Sight sells only completed units. Unknown to Ace, a year earlier Sight had granted Bank a security interest in all its existing and after-acquired inventory, in which Bank perfected its interest by filing a financing statement. Subsequently Sight defaults on the loan from Bank and Bank seizes all of Sight's components, including those Ace had delivered. Ace's components, although identifiable as delivered by it, were unmarked. Ace gave no public notice of its arrangement with Sight, and Sight had never previously entered into a similar arrangement. Bank refuses to turn over the components to Ace. Who has paramount rights in the television components Ace delivered: Bank or Ace? Does 9–102(a)(20) resolve the question? Cf. Welding Metals, Inc. v. Foothill Capital Corp., 1997 WL 289671 (D.Conn.1997); In re Medomak Canning Co., 25 UCC Rep. Serv. 437 (Bankr. D.Me. 1977).

# CHAPTER 6

# SECURITY INTERESTS IN INTELLECTUAL PROPERTY

## A. INTRODUCTION

Intellectual property usually falls within the definition of "general intangible" in 9–102(a)(42). Obvious examples are copyrights, trademarks, patents and trade secrets. Comment 5d. to 9–102 notes that the reference to "things in action" in the definition of general intangible includes rights that arise under a license of intellectual property, including the right to exploit the intellectual property without liability for infringement. The definition specifically includes "software," which is defined under 9–102(a)(75) as meaning a computer program, when software isn't embedded in goods.

As we have seen, the perfection and priority rules under Article 9 with respect to general intangibles are simple. In order to perfect a security interest in general intangibles, the secured creditor need only reasonably identify the collateral in the security agreement (9–108(a)) and file a financing statement indicating the collateral covered (9–502(a)). Creditors will usually be safe if they describe the collateral in both the security agreement and the financing statement as "all general intangibles." The secured creditor can enjoy the benefits of the floating lien by including after-acquired property and future advances clauses. 9–204. Moreover, the secured creditor need file in only one jurisdiction, that of the location of the debtor (9–301(1)), which, if the debtor is a registered organization, such as a corporation, is its state of organization (9–307(e)). Hence, only the filing records of that jurisdiction need be searched preparatory to the credit extension.

However, the idyllic Article 9 environment for secured creditors who rely on intellectual property collateral is greatly altered by the existence of federal statutes on copyrights, trademarks and patents. Section 9–109(c)(1) provides that Article 9 does not apply to the extent that "a statute, regulation, or treaty of the United States preempts this article." The meaning and extent of the federal preemption is the principal issue addressed in this chapter.

The Article 9 "step-back" provisions that we will discuss co-exist uneasily with federal statutes on copyrights, trademarks and patents that appear to have been drafted with no regard to state laws like the Code and its precedent statutes. As we see in the following materials, courts have had a great deal of difficulty in deciding the extent to which the federal statutes on intellectual property preempt the Code provisions on general intangibles. These difficulties have been highlighted in recent years by the astonishing growth in the value of intellectual property.

In today's high-tech world, it is quite common for a firm's intellectual property—copyrights, patents, trademarks and trade secrets—to be worth much more than its tangible assets. Moreover, the trend toward the internationalization of business has greatly enhanced the value of trade names like Marlboro, Coca-Cola or Sony, trade secrets like Coke's secret formula, character rights like "Winnie the Pooh," or software like Microsoft's Windows. If businesses cannot reliably use their intellectual property as collateral for loans, their ability to finance their operations is greatly curtailed, for one of the greatest sources of wealth today is intellectual property. The following section shows that, with respect to the use of intellectual property as collateral for loans, the law is critically deficient; reform is badly needed. Among the articles calling for reform are Shawn K. Baldwin, Note, "To Promote the Progress of Science and Useful Arts": A Role for Federal Regulation of Intellectual Property as Collateral, 143 U. Pa. L. Rev. 1701 (1995); Patrick R. Barry, Note, Software Copyrights as Loan Collateral: Evaluating the Reform Proposals, 46 Hastings L.J. 581 (1995). For a review of the whole field of financing intellectual property, see Jonathan C. Lipson, Financing Information Technologies: Fairness and Function, 2001 Wisc. L. Rev. 1067.

## B.   COPYRIGHTS

Our simple inquiry is how to perfect a security interest in a copyright and the proceeds stemming from the exploitation of the copyright. Since 1978, a copyright arises when a work is "fixed in any tangible medium of expression," and not when it is later registered or published. 17 U.S.C. § 102(a). The copyright "notice" (the letter C in a circle or the word "Copyright") need not be placed on the work until publication. 17 U.S.C. § 401. Thus copyrights abound. You have a copyright in your seminar papers as well as in your novel of law school life that the publishers have been so unreasonable about. These garden variety copyrights are called unregistered copyrights. For the most part, the basic protections of the Copyright Act apply without respect to whether the copyright is registered, e.g., the exclusive right of the copyright owner to copy, publish, or, in the case of dramatic works, to perform the work. 17 U.S.C. § 106. But in some instances benefits accrue from registration, an act that can be accomplished at any time during the life of the copyright by sending to the Copyright Office an application, fee, and the requisite number of copies of the work. 17 U.S.C. § 408. Registration is necessary when a security interest is granted in a copyright because a copyright must be registered before a security interest can be recorded in the Copyright Office and become effective against third parties. 17 U.S.C. § 205(c).

The relevant provisions of the Copyright Act are:

Section 205(d). "As between two conflicting transfers, the one executed first prevails if it is recorded, in the manner required to give constructive notice under subsection (c), within one month after its execution in the United States or within two months after its execution outside the United States, or at any time before recordation in such manner of the later transfer. Otherwise the later transfer prevails if recorded first in such manner, and if taken in good faith, for valuable consideration or on the basis of a binding promise to pay royalties, and without notice of the earlier transfer."

Section 101. "A 'transfer of copyright ownership' is an assignment, mortgage, exclusive license, or any other conveyance, alienation, or hypothecation of a copyright or of any of the exclusive rights comprised in a copyright, whether or not it is limited in time or place, of effect but not including a nonexclusive license."

The following case, *Peregrine Entertainment*, shook the world of intellectual property financing to its foundation. Former Article 9 contained two "step-back" provisions: 9–104(a) and 9–302(3), (4). By their terms, Article 9 deferred to federal law ("stepped back") when the provisions applied. Revised 9–109(c)(1) and 9–311(a) and (b) replace former 9–104(a) and 9–302(3), (4) respectively. We set out below the former Article 9 "step-back" provisions that were in force at the time of both this decision and the next case, *World Auxiliary*. After each provision, we set out its Revised Article 9 replacement.

Former 9–104(a): "[This Article does not apply] to a security interest subject to any statute of the United States, to the extent that such statute governs the rights of parties to and third parties affected by transactions in particular types of property."

Revised 9–109(c)(1): "This article does not apply to the extent that a statute, regulation, or treaty of the United States preempts this article."

Former 9–302(3): "The filing of a financing statement otherwise required by this Article in not necessary or effective to perfect a security interest in property subject to (a) a statute or treaty of the United States which provides for a national or international registration * * * or which specifies a place of filing different from that specified in this Article for filing of the security interest."

Revised 9–311(a): "[T]he filing of a financing statement is not necessary or effective to perfect a security interest in property subject to: (1) a statute, regulation, or treaty of the United States whose requirements for a security interest's obtaining priority over the rights of a lien creditor with respect to the property preempt Section 9–310(a) [requiring filing of a financing statement]."

Former 9–302(4): "Compliance with a statute or treaty described in subsection (3) is equivalent to the filing of a financing statement under this Article, and a security interest in property subject to the statute or treaty can be perfected only by compliance therewith * * *."

Revised 9–311(b): "Compliance with the requirements of a statute, regulation, or treaty described in subsection (a) for obtaining priority over the rights of a lien creditor is equivalent to the filing of a financing statement under this article * * *."

# In re Peregrine Entertainment, Ltd.

United States District Court, C.D.Cal., 1990.
116 B.R. 194.

■ Kozinski, Circuit Judge. [Sitting by designation pursuant to 28 U.S.C. § 291(b) (1982).]

This appeal from a decision of the bankruptcy court raises an issue never before confronted by a federal court in a published opinion: Is a security interest in a copyright perfected by an appropriate filing with the United States Copyright Office or by a UCC–1 financing statement filed with the relevant secretary of state?

I

National Peregrine, Inc. (NPI) is a Chapter 11 debtor in possession whose principal assets are a library of copyrights, distribution rights and licenses to approximately 145 films, and accounts receivable arising from the licensing of these films to various programmers. NPI claims to have an outright assignment of some of the copyrights; as for the others, NPI claims it has an exclusive license to distribute in a certain territory, or for a certain period of time.[1]

In June 1985, Capitol Federal Savings and Loan Association of Denver (Cap Fed) extended to American National Enterprises, Inc., NPI's predecessor by merger, a six million dollar line of credit secured by what is now NPI's film library. Both the security agreement and the UCC–1 financing statements filed by Cap Fed describe the collateral as "[a]ll inventory consisting of films and all accounts, contract rights, chattel paper, general intangibles, instruments, equipment, and documents related to such inventory, now owned or hereafter acquired by the Debtor." Although Cap Fed filed its UCC–1 financing statements in California, Colorado and Utah, it did not record its security interest in the United States Copyright Office.

---

**1.** According to NPI, valid copyrights exist in all of the motion pictures in its library by virtue of either (1) originality and fixation with respect to the works created after January 1, 1978, the effective date of the Copyright Act of 1976, or (2) publication and notice with respect to films created prior to 1978, and, thus governed by the Copyright Act of 1909. See Brief of Appellants at 6 n. 6 (citing 17 U.S.C. § 10 (1909 Act); 17 U.S.C. §§ 102(a), 302(a) (1976 Act)). Cap Fed, however, contends that NPI failed to offer any proof in its motion for summary judgment

that any of these works were protected under either Act. The court need not resolve this dispute, however. For purposes of presenting the legal issues raised by this appeal, it is sufficient if at least one of the films in NPI's library is the subject of a valid copyright. Cap Fed has stipulated that there is at least one such film, the unforgettable "Renegade Ninjas," starring Hiroki Matsukota, Kennosuke Yorozuya and Teruhiko Aoi, in what many consider to be their career performances. * * *

NPI filed a voluntary petition for bankruptcy on January 30, 1989. On April 6, 1989, NPI filed an amended complaint against Cap Fed, contending that the bank's security interest in the copyrights to the films in NPI's library and in the accounts receivable generated by their distribution were unperfected because Cap Fed failed to record its security interest with the Copyright Office. NPI claimed that, as a debtor in possession, it had a judicial lien on all assets in the bankruptcy estate, including the copyrights and receivables. Armed with this lien, it sought to avoid, recover and preserve Cap Fed's supposedly unperfected security interest for the benefit of the estate.

The parties filed cross-motions for partial summary judgment on the question of whether Cap Fed had a valid security interest in the NPI film library. The bankruptcy court held for Cap Fed. * * * NPI appeals.

## II

### A.   Where to File

The Copyright Act provides that "[a]ny transfer of copyright owner-ship or other document pertaining to a copyright" may be recorded in the United States Copyright Office. 17 U.S.C. § 205(a); see Copyright Office Circular 12: Recordation of Transfers and Other Documents (reprinted in 1 Copyright L.Rep. (CCH) & 15,015) [hereinafter "Circular 12"]. A "trans-fer" under the Act includes any "mortgage" or "hypothecation of a copyright," whether "in whole or in part" and "by any means of convey-ance or by operation of law." 17 U.S.C. §§ 101, 201(d)(1); see 3 Nimmer on Copyright § 10.05[A], at 10–43C10–45 (1989). The terms "mortgage" and "hypothecation" include a pledge of property as security or collateral for a debt. See Black's Law Dictionary 669 (5th ed. 1979). In addition, the Copyright Office has defined a "document pertaining to a copyright" as one that has a direct or indirect relationship to the existence, scope, duration, or identification of a copyright, or to the ownership, division, allocation, licensing, transfer, or exercise of rights under a copyright. That relation-ship may be past, present, future, or potential.

37 C.F.R. § 201.4(a)(2); see also Compendium of Copyright Office Practices II & & 1602–1603 (identifying which documents the Copyright Office will accept for filing).

It is clear from the preceding that an agreement granting a creditor a security interest in a copyright may be recorded in the Copyright Office. See G. Gilmore, Security Interests in Personal Property § 17.3, at 545 (1965). Likewise, because a copyright entitles the holder to receive all income derived from the display of the creative work, see 17 U.S.C. § 106, an agreement creating a security interest in the receivables generated by a copyright may also be recorded in the Copyright Office. Thus, Cap Fed's security interest *could* have been recorded in the Copyright Office; the parties seem to agree on this much. The question is, does the UCC provide a parallel method of perfecting a security interest in a copyright? One can answer this question by reference to either federal or state law; both inquiries lead to the same conclusion.

1. Even in the absence of express language, federal regulation will preempt state law if it is so pervasive as to indicate that "Congress left no room for supplementary state regulation," or if "the federal interest is so dominant that the federal system will be assumed to preclude enforcement of state laws on the same subject." Hillsborough County v. Automated Medical Laboratories, Inc., 471 U.S. 707, 713, 105 S.Ct. 2371, 2375, 85 L.Ed.2d 714 (1985) (internal quotations omitted). Here, the comprehensive scope of the federal copyright act's recording provisions, along with the unique federal interests they implicate, support the view that federal law preempts state methods of perfecting security interests in copyrights and related accounts receivable.

The federal copyright laws ensure "predictability and certainty of copyright ownership," "promote national uniformity" and "avoid the practical difficulties of determining and enforcing an author's rights under the differing laws and in the separate courts of the various States." Community for Creative Non–Violence v. Reid, 490 U.S. 730, 109 S.Ct. 2166, 2177, 104 L.Ed.2d 811 (1989); H.R.Rep. No. 1476, 94th Cong., 2d Sess. 129 (1976), U.S.Code Cong. & Admin.News 1976, p. 5659. As discussed above, section 205(a) of the Copyright Act establishes a uniform method for recording security interests in copyrights. A secured creditor need only file in the Copyright Office in order to give "all persons constructive notice of the facts stated in the recorded document." 17 U.S.C. § 205(c).[7] Likewise, an interested third party need only search the indices maintained by the Copyright Office to determine whether a particular copyright is encumbered. * * *

A recording system works by virtue of the fact that interested parties have a specific place to look in order to discover with certainty whether a particular interest has been transferred or encumbered. To the extent there are competing recordation schemes, this lessens the utility of each; when records are scattered in several filing units, potential creditors must conduct several searches before they can be sure that the property is not encumbered. * * * UCC § 9401, Official Comment & 1. It is for that reason that parallel recordation schemes for the same types of property are scarce as hens' teeth; the court is aware of no others, and the parties have cited none. No useful purposes would be served—indeed, much confusion would result—if creditors were permitted to perfect security interests by filing with either the Copyright Office or state offices. See G. Gilmore, Security Interests in Personal Property § 17.3, at 545 (1965); see also 3 Nimmer on Copyright § 10.05[A] at 10–44 (1989) ("a persuasive argument . . . can be made to the effect that by reasons of Sections 201(d)(1), 204(a), 205(c) and 205(d) of the current Act . . . Congress has preempted the field with respect

---

**7.** For a recordation under section 205 to be effective as against third parties, the copyrighted work must also have been registered pursuant to 17 U.S.C. §§ 408, 409, 410. See 17 U.S.C. § 205(c)(2). Of course, registration is also a prerequisite to judicial enforce-ment of a copyright, except for actions for infringement of copyrights in foreign works covered by the Berne Convention. 17 U.S.C. § 411; International Trade Management, Inc. v. United States, 553 F.Supp. 402, 402–03, 1 Cl.Ct. 39 (1982).

to the form and recordation requirements applicable to copyright mortgages'').

If state methods of perfection were valid, a third party (such as a potential purchaser of the copyright) who wanted to learn of any encumbrances thereon would have to check not merely the indices of the U.S. Copyright Office, but also the indices of any relevant secretary of state. Because copyrights are incorporeal—they have no fixed situs—a number of state authorities could be relevant. * * * Thus, interested third parties could never be entirely sure that all relevant jurisdictions have been searched. This possibility, together with the expense and delay of conducting searches in a variety of jurisdictions, could hinder the purchase and sale of copyrights, frustrating Congress's policy that copyrights be readily transferable in commerce.

This is the reasoning adopted by the Ninth Circuit in Danning v. Pacific Propeller, Inc. [620 F.2d 731 (9th Cir.1980)]. *Danning* held that 49 U.S.C.App. § 1403(a), the Federal Aviation Act's provision for recording conveyances and the creation of liens and security interests in civil aircraft, preempts state filing provisions. 620 F.2d at 735–36. According to *Danning*, the predominant purpose of the statute was to provide one central place for the filing of [liens on aircraft] and thus eliminate the need, given the highly mobile nature of aircraft and their appurtenances, for the examination of State and County records.

620 F.2d at 735–36. Copyrights, even more than aircraft, lack a clear situs; tangible, movable goods such as airplanes must always exist at some physical location; they may have a home base from which they operate or where they receive regular maintenance. The same cannot be said of intangibles. As noted above, this lack of an identifiable situs militates against individual state filings and in favor of a single, national registration scheme.

Moreover, as discussed at greater length below * * *, the Copyright Act establishes its own scheme for determining priority between conflicting transferees, one that differs in certain respects from that of Article Nine. Under Article Nine, priority between holders of conflicting security interests in intangibles is generally determined by who perfected his interest first. UCC § 9312(5). By contrast, section 205(d) of the Copyright Act provides:

As between two conflicting transfers, the one executed first prevails if it is recorded, in the manner required to give constructive notice under subsection (c), *within one month after its execution in the United States or within two months after its execution outside the United States*, or at any time before recordation in such manner of the later transfer....

17 U.S.C. § 205(d) (emphasis added). Thus, unlike Article Nine, the Copyright Act permits the effect of recording with the Copyright Office to relate back as far as two months.

Because the Copyright Act and Article Nine create different priority schemes, there will be occasions when different results will be reached depending on which scheme was employed. The availability of filing under the UCC would thus undermine the priority scheme established by Congress with respect to copyrights. This type of direct interference with the operation of federal law weighs heavily in favor of preemption. * * *

The bankruptcy court below nevertheless concluded that security interests in copyrights could be perfected by filing either with the copyright office or with the secretary of state under the UCC, making a tongue-in-cheek analogy to the use of a belt and suspenders to hold up a pair of pants. According to the bankruptcy court, because either device is equally useful, one should be free to choose which one to wear. With all due respect, this court finds the analogy inapt. There is no legitimate reason why pants should be held up in only one particular manner: Individuals and public modesty are equally served by either device, or even by a safety pin or a piece of rope; all that really matters is that the job gets done. Registration schemes are different in that the *way* notice is given is precisely what matters. To the extent interested parties are confused as to which system is being employed, this increases the level of uncertainty and multiplies the risk of error, exposing creditors to the possibility that they might get caught with their pants down.

A recordation scheme best serves its purpose where interested parties can obtain notice of all encumbrances by referring to a single, precisely defined recordation system. The availability of parallel state recordation systems that could put parties on constructive notice as to encumbrances on copyrights would surely interfere with the effectiveness of the federal recordation scheme. Given the virtual absence of dual recordation schemes in our legal system, Congress cannot be presumed to have contemplated such a result. The court therefore concludes that any state recordation system pertaining to interests in copyrights would be preempted by the Copyright Act.

2.  State law leads to the same conclusion. Article Nine of the Uniform Commercial Code establishes a comprehensive scheme for the regulation of security interests in personal property and fixtures. By superseding a multitude of pre-Code security devices, it provides "a simple and unified structure within which the immense variety of present-day secured financing transactions can go forward with less cost and greater certainty." UCC § 9101, Official Comment. However, Article Nine is not all encompassing; under the "step back" provision of UCC § 9104, Article Nine does not apply "[t]o a security interest subject to any statute of the United States to the extent that such statute governs the rights of parties to and third parties affected by transactions in particular types of property."

For most items of personal property, Article Nine provides that security interests must be perfected by filing with the office of the secretary of state in which the debtor is located. See UCC §§ 9302(1), 9401(1)(c). Such filing, however, is not "necessary or effective to perfect a security interest in property subject to ... [a] statute or treaty of the United States which provides for a national or international registration ... or which specifies a place of filing different from that specified in [Article Nine] for filing of the security interest." UCC § 9302(3)(a). When a national system for recording security interests exists, the Code treats compliance with that system as "equivalent to the filing of a financing statement under [Article Nine,] and a security interest in property subject to the statute or treaty can be perfected only by compliance therewith...." UCC § 9302(4).

As discussed above, section 205(a) of the Copyright Act clearly does establish a national system for recording transfers of copyright interests, and it specifies a place of filing different from that provided in Article Nine. Recording in the Copyright Office gives nationwide, constructive notice to third parties of the recorded encumbrance. Except for the fact that the Copyright Office's indices are organized on the basis of the title and registration number, rather than by reference to the identity of the debtor, this system is nearly identical to that which Article Nine generally provides on a statewide basis.[10] And, lest there be any doubt, the drafters of the UCC specifically identified the Copyright Act as establishing the type of national registration system that would trigger the section 9302(3) and (4) step back provisions:

> Examples of the type of federal statute referred to in [UCC § 9302(3)(a)] are the provisions of [Title 17] (copyrights)....

UCC § 9302, Official Comment & 8; see G. Gilmore, Security Interests in Personal Property § 17.3, at 545 (1965) ("[t]here can be no doubt that [the Copyright Act was] meant to be within the description of § 9–302(3)(a)").[11]

---

**10.** Moreover, the mechanics of recording in the Copyright Office are analogous to filing under the UCC. In order to record a security interest in the Copyright Office, a creditor may file either the security agreement itself or a duplicate certified to be a true copy of the original, so long as either is sufficient to place third parties on notice that the copyright is encumbered. See 17 U.S.C. §§ 205(a), (c); 37 C.F.R. § 201.4(c)(1). Accordingly, the Copyright Act requires that the filed document "specifically identif[y] the work to which it pertains so that, after the document is indexed by the Register of Copyrights, it would be revealed by a reasonable search under the title or registration number of the work." 17 U.S.C. § 205(c); see also Compendium of Copyright Office Practices II & & 1604–1612; Circular 12, at 8035–4.

That having been said, it's worth noting that filing with the Copyright Office can be much less convenient than filing under the UCC. This is because UCC filings are indexed by owner, while registration in the Copyright Office is by title or copyright registration number. See 17 U.S.C. § 205(c). This means that the recording of a security interest in a film library such as that owned by NPI will involve dozens, sometimes hundreds, of individual filings. Moreover, as the contents of the film library changes, the lienholder will be required to make a separate filing for each work added to or deleted from the library. By contrast, a UCC–1 filing can provide a continuing, floating lien on assets of a particular type owned by the debtor, without the need for periodic updates. See UCC § 9204.

This technical shortcoming of the copyright filing system does make it a less useful device for perfecting a security interest in copyright libraries. Nevertheless, this problem is not so serious as to make the system unworkable. In any event, this is the system Congress has established and the court is not in a position to order more adequate procedures. If the mechanics of filing turn out to pose a serious burden, it can be taken up by Congress during its oversight of the Copyright Office or, conceivably, the Copyright Office might be able to ameliorate the problem through exercise of its regulatory authority. See 17 U.S.C. § 702.

**11.** Cap Fed points to a portion of the official commentary that suggests the contrary conclusion:

> Although the Federal Copyright Act contains provisions permitting the mortgage

The court therefore concludes that the Copyright Act provides for national registration and "specifies a place of filing different from that specified in [Article Nine] for filing of the security interest." UCC § 9302(3)(a). Recording in the U.S. Copyright Office, rather than filing a financing statement under Article Nine, is the proper method for perfecting a security interest in a copyright. * * *

## CONCLUSION

The judgment of the bankruptcy court is reversed. The case is ordered remanded for a determination of which movies in NPI's library are the subject of valid copyrights. The court shall then determine the status of Cap Fed's security interest in the movies and the debtor's other property. To the extent that interest is unperfected, the court shall permit NPI to exercise its avoidance powers under the Bankruptcy Code.

## PROBLEM

In *Peregrine* the court states that step-back under former 9–302(3) depends on whether a federal statute "provides for a national or international registration * * * or which specifies a place of filing different from that specified in this Article for filing of the security interest." And whether the federal statute also provides a priority scheme different from that in Article 9 is a separate issue. "Compliance with a national registration scheme is necessary for perfection regardless of whether federal law governs priorities." 116 B.R. at 204. How does Revised 9–311(a)(1) and (b) affect the court's holding?

————————

Revised Article 9's "step-back" provisions are different from former Article 9's counterpart provisions, and potentially affect the law governing the perfection of security interests in copyrights. Under the predominant understanding of former 9–104(a) and 9–302(3), state law filing requirements applied unless federal law either preempted state law or state law otherwise deferred to federal filing requirements. Revised Article 9's "step-back" provisions do not otherwise defer to federal law. Rather, Article 9 and its filing requirements are inapplicable only when federal law preempts them. See 9–109(c)(1), Comment 8 to 9–109, and Comment 2 to 9–311. In other words, Revised Article makes state filing unnecessary and ineffective only when it has to: when federal law preempts state filing requirements. Revised Article 9 therefore makes irrelevant *Peregrine*'s inquiry into whether Article 9 defers to federal law even if it does not preempt state

of a copyright and for the recording of an assignment of a copyright [Title 17] such a statute would not seem to contain sufficient provisions regulating the rights of the parties and third parties to exclude security interests in copyrights from the provisions of this Article.

UCC § 9104, Official Comment & 1 * * *.

filing requirements. Of course, it remains a matter of federal law as to when preemption occurs.

Under Revised 9–311(a)(1), a UCC filing is neither necessary nor effective to perfect a security interest only when the relevant federal statute requires a federal filing in order to obtain priority over a lien creditor. The standard is one of federal preemption against a baseline of a lien creditor's rights. Section 9–311(a)(1) is unclear in one detail: the explicitness with which federal law must preempt state filing requirements. The subsection's terms refer to the "requirements" of the relevant federal law, and the question is whether federal filing "requirements" must expressly displace state filing requirements or whether less explicit displacing provisions are sufficient. If the former, the Copyright Act doesn't preempt a UCC filing requirement because it doesn't expressly deal with the priority of lien creditors or displace state filing requirements. If the latter, the Act's priority provisions might be sufficiently explicit for 9–311(a)(1)'s purposes. Section 9–311(a)(1) seemingly doesn't require explicit displacement of state filing requirements. It can't. After all, federal preemption is a matter of federal law over which state law, including Article 9, has no say. This is required by the Supremacy Clause of the Constitution. If federal law filing requirements preempt state filing requirements, state filing is neither necessary nor effective, even if federal law doesn't explicitly say so. This is simply a consequence of preemption.

The question now is how 9–311(a)(1) applies in the case of the Copyright Act. Arguably the Act's filing requirements make UCC filings neither necessary nor effective. Section 9–311(a)(1) makes state filing requirements inapplicable when the relevant federal statute's filing requirements preempt state filing requirements for priority over a lien creditor's rights. The preemptive effect of the Copyright Act's priority rule (section 205(d)) therefore is at issue. The rule doesn't expressly mention the rights of lien creditors. Further, the Act's definition of "transfer" (section 101), although broad, doesn't mention involuntary conveyances. More important, the Act doesn't expressly preempt state filing requirements for priority over a lien creditor. It says nothing about state filing requirements. However, the Act's priority rule (section 205(d)) is sufficiently comprehensive in its ordering of interests that it's unlikely that the rule doesn't apply against lien creditor's rights as well. And 9–311(a)(1) seemingly doesn't require relevant federal law filing requirements to expressly preempt state filing requirements. Thus, following *Peregrine*'s preemption analysis, under 9–311(a)(1) UCC filings are neither necessary nor effective with respect to copyrights.

## NOTES

**1.** Recordation of a document in the Copyright Office gives notice only if "the document * * * specifically identifies the work to which it pertains * * *" 17 U.S.C. § 205(c)(1). Hence, recording a security agreement, even one that purports to cover after-acquired copyrights, gives constructive notice only with respect to the work as it was at the time it was registered and not future copyrights. See Footnote 10 of *Peregrine* and Paul Heald, Resolving Priority Disputes in Intellectual Property Collateral, 1 J. Intellectual Prop. L. 135 (1993). In short, although state law has recognized after-acquired property clauses for more than 100 years, they are ineffective under federal law for security interests in copyrights.

> * * * [In the 1976 Copyright Act] Congress temporally expanded federal copyright back from the point of publication under the 1909 Copyright Act to the point in time where the work was "fixed in a tangible medium of expression" under the Copyright Act. If as we believe, Peregrine and AEG Acquisition are correct interpretations of congressional intent, much of the copyright financing that used to be controlled by state law and Article 9 of the UCC is now controlled by federal law and, therefore, by more primitive principles. . . .
>
> [O]ne result of this expansion may be to sharply reduce or eliminate the possibility of using creative work in progress as collateral for a loan. Consider, for instance, a debtor that creates valuable intellectual property in stages, for example, an author whose work is produced over time or through different drafts, or a movie studio that produces a film from daily shootings.

Harold R. Weinberg & William J. Woodward, Jr., Legislative Process and Commercial Law: Lessons from the Copyright Act of 1976 and the Uniform Commercial Code, 48 Bus. Law. 437, 475 (1993). But see the next case.

**2.** In a second holding, equally as important as the first, *Peregrine* decided that a Copyright Office recording is also the exclusive method for perfecting a security interest with respect to copyright receivables, that is, the proceeds from licensing the showing of the debtor's films. Though the court was on solid ground in deciding that recording pursuant to the federal Copyright Act is the exclusive means of perfecting a security interest in a copyright, the basis for its holding on proceeds is not as clear. The court describes the debtor's right to collect these fees as "accounts receivable." This is correct under 9–102(a)(2) ("accounts"). Under 9–315(a)(2) and (d), a security interest in these proceeds would be perfected by perfecting a security interest in the films. Certainly a security interest in a copyright is much less valuable if it doesn't cover the return from the exploitation of the copyrighted work. The Copyright Act has no specific provisions on proceeds. Judge Kozinski based his holding on § 106(5) which doesn't mention proceeds but gives a copyright owner the exclusive right to display the copyrighted work. Thus "a copyright entitles the holder to receive all income derived from the display of the creative work * * *." 116 B.R. at 199. He apparently reasons from this that since the receivables flow from the copyrighted work, the manner of perfecting a security interest in the copyrighted work should control for the receivables as well.

The implications of this holding for lenders who rely on receivables for collateral are ominous. Suppose a lender finances the operations of a retailer, who sells computers together with copyrighted software, by taking a security interest in the receivables that arise from the sale of the computers (accounts) and software (general intangibles). The software developer has registered a copyright in the software; retail customers receive a diskette and are licensed to make limited use of the program that it contains. Lender complies with Article 9 with respect to perfecting its security interest in all present and future accounts and general intangibles of the retailer. What additional burdens does *Peregrine* impose on the lender to perfect a security interest in the software receivables? Since these receivables are proceeds of a copyrighted software program, must the lender file its security interest in the Copyright Office to perfect as to these receivables? If so, given the inapplicability of after-acquired property clauses in copyright law, must it refile each time it acquires a security interest in additional receivables? Until the law is clarified, these problems may dissuade lenders from relying on receivables arising out of the marketing of copyrightable intellectual property. These issues are discussed in Patrick R. Barry, Note, Software Copyrights as Loan Collateral: Evaluating the Reform Proposals, 46 Hastings L.J. 581, 594–98 (1995); Haemmerli, 96 Colum. L. Rev., at 1694–1695; Steven Weinberger, Perfection of Security Interests in Copyrights: The *Peregrine* Effect on the Orion Pictures Plan of Reorganization, 11 Cardozo Arts & Ent. L.J. 959, 980 (1993).

**3.** Arguably *Peregrine*'s holding discussed in Note 2 has been overruled by Broadcast Music, Inc. v. Hirsch, 104 F.3d 1163 (9th Cir.1997). In that case Debtor, a songwriter, received royalties on his compositions through BMI which licenses performances of copyrighted musical compositions and collects and pays royalties to composers. In payment of debts he owed to Creditors, Debtor assigned his rights to future royalties to them to satisfy his debts. They neither recorded the assignments with the Copyright Office nor, apparently, did they attempt to perfect under the UCC. Before the debts were paid, the IRS asserted a tax lien for Debtor's unpaid taxes. The Ninth Circuit, interpreting the Copyright Act and New York assignment law, held that the Creditors' rights in the royalties were superior to those of the IRS. No recording in the Copyright Office was required because there was no "transfer of copyright ownership or other document pertaining to a copyright." 17 U.S.C. § 205(a). An assignment of royalties is not, the court opined, an assignment of a copyright or an interest in a copyright. The court distinguished *Peregrine* on the ground that this case does not involve the creation of a security interest; it is a case of "outright assignments of a right to receive royalties for the purpose of satisfying a debt." 104 F.3d at 1166.

Where does *Broadcast Music* leave the law on security interests in rights to payment, like royalties or license fees, arising from the exploitation of copyrighted works? Distinguishing *Broadcast Music* from *Peregrine* on the ground that a security interest was created in the latter while an outright assignment was present in the former is too glib. It's also inaccurate. Under the definition of a security interest in 1–201(b)(35) (an interest in personal property that secures payment of an obligation), in a case in which a debtor grants a creditor the right to collect payments due the debtor from an account debtor until the obligation is paid, it seems extremely unlikely that a court would distinguish between a debtor's granting a security interest in the payments to the creditor and the debtor's assigning the payments. In each case the creditor would have only the right to collect until its debt is paid; it doesn't "own" the future payments. Thus, a security interest has been created. Restatement (Third) of Property, Mortgages, § 4.2, Reporters' Notes to Comment a. (1997) takes the position that an "absolute" assignment of rents to a creditor that will terminate upon satisfaction of the debt is merely security for an obligation and does not confer absolute ownership in the creditor.

A more fundamental distinction between *Peregrine* and *Broadcast Music* is that the court in the latter case reads the statute narrowly to say that recordation in the Copyright Office is necessary only in the case of transfers (assignments and security interests) in ownership of the copyright itself. Recordation indicates to prospective creditors and buyers who owns rights in the copyright itself. Transfer of royalties resulting from licensing of the copyright has nothing to do with ownership of the copyright itself; therefore, recordation is unnecessary. If this interpretation were to be accepted in the future, it could be the basis for a regime in which federal law recordation would apply to assignments of and security interests in copyrights, but Article 9 would apply to receivables arising out of copyright exploitation, thus greatly diminishing the operational problems discussed in Note 2. Alice Haemmerli, Insecurity Interests: Where Intellectual Property and Commercial Law Collide, 96 Colum.L.Rev. 1645, 1692 (1996), contends that requiring Copyright Office recording for copyright receivables is not defensible under either federal or state law.

**4.** Although some secured lenders apparently continue to make UCC filings, the *Peregrine* decision has greatly increased the number of recordings of security interests in intellectual property in the Copyright Office. It has also focused critical attention on the antiquated system prescribed by federal law for protection of security interests in copyrights. The "tract" system of recording security interests in copyrights, described by Judge Kozinski in Footnote 10 of the opinion, in which the security interests are indexed not by the name of the debtor but by the registration number or title of the copyright, has been improved in recent years by the practice of cross-indexing in the name of the debtor. But we understand that the cross-indexing has not been done for older copyrights. Even when the searcher ascertains that no security agreement has been recorded regarding a given copyright, the relation-back provisions of 17 U.S.C. § 205(d) (one month after execution of the security agreement if executed within the U.S. or two months if executed outside the U.S.) may still allow a later recorded interest to take priority over an earlier recorded one. Matters have been hopelessly complicated in past years by the practice of the Copyright Office of delaying recording documents submitted to it for a period of months, making reliance on the record impossible. Craig Joyce, et al., Copyright Law 297 (2d. ed. 1991).

The following decision is a welcome clarification of the law on security interests in unregistered copyrights.

# In re World Auxiliary Power Company

United States Court of Appeals, Ninth Circuit, 2002.
303 F.3d 1120.

■ KLEINFELD, CIRCUIT JUDGE:

In this case we decide whether federal or state law governs priority of security interests in unregistered copyrights.

## FACTS

Basically, this is a bankruptcy contest over unregistered copyrights between a bank that got a security interest in the copyrights from the owners and perfected it under state law, and a company that bought the copyrights from the bankruptcy trustees after the copyright owners went bankrupt. These simple facts are all that matters to the outcome of this case, although the details are complex.

Three affiliated California corporations—World Auxiliary Power, World Aerotechnology, and Air Refrigeration Systems—designed and sold products for modifying airplanes. The FAA must approve modifications of civilian aircraft by issuing "Supplemental Type Certificates." The three companies owned copyrights in the drawings, technical manuals, blueprints, and computer software used to make the modifications. Some of these copyrighted materials were attached to the Supplemental Type Certificates. The companies did not register their copyrights with the United States Copyright Office.

The companies got financing from Silicon Valley Bank, one of the appellees in this case. Two of the companies borrowed the money directly, the third guaranteed the loan. The security agreement, as is common, granted the bank a security interest in a broad array of presently owned and after-acquired collateral. The security agreement covered "all goods and equipment now owned or hereafter acquired," as well as inventory, contract rights, general intangibles, blueprints, drawings, computer programs, accounts receivable, patents, cash, bank deposits, and pretty much anything else the debtor owned or might be "hereafter acquired." The security agreement and financing statement also covered "[a]ll copyright rights, copyright applications, copyright registrations, and like protections in each work of authorship and derivative work thereof, whether published or unpublished, now owned or hereafter acquired."

The bank perfected its security interest in the collateral, including the copyrights, pursuant to California's version of Article 9 of the Uniform Commercial Code, by filing UCC–1 financing statements with the California Secretary of State. The bank also took possession of the Supplemental Type Certificates and the attached copyrighted materials. But the copyrights still weren't registered with the United States Copyright Office, and the bank did not record any document showing the transfer of a security interest with the Copyright Office.

Subsequently, the three debtor companies filed simultaneous but separate bankruptcy proceedings. Their copyrights were among their major assets. Aerocon Engineering, one of their creditors (and the appellant in this case), wanted the copyrights. Aerocon was working on a venture with another company, Advanced Aerospace, and its President, Michael Gilsen, and an officer and director, Merritt Widen (all appellees in this case), to engineer and sell aircraft modifications using the debtors' designs. Their prospective venture faced a problem: Silicon Valley Bank claimed a security interest in the copyrights. To solve this problem, Aerocon worked out a deal with Gilsen, Widen, and a company named Erose Capital (not a party in this case) to buy the debtors' assets, including their copyrights, from the bankruptcy trustees along with the trustees' right to sue to avoid Silicon Valley Bank's security interest. Once Aerocon owned the copyrights, it planned to exercise the trustees' power to avoid Silicon Valley Bank's security interest[7] so that the venture would own the copyrights free and clear.

The transaction to purchase the copyrights and the trustees' avoidance action worked as follows. First, Aerocon paid the bankruptcy trustees $90,000, $30,000 for each of the three bankruptcy estates. Then, the trustees, with the bankruptcy court's approval, sold the estates' assets and avoidance action to Erose Capital, Gilsen, and Widen. Gilsen and Widen then sold their two-thirds interest to their company, Advanced Aerospace.

After this transaction was completed, for reasons not relevant to this appeal, Aerocon's planned joint venture with Advanced Aerospace and Gilsen and Widen fell through. In the aftermath, Erose Capital sold its one-third interest to Aerocon and Advanced Aerospace sold its two-thirds interest to Airweld. These transactions meant that Aerocon and Airweld owned the debtors' copyrights and the trustees' avoidance action as tenants in common.

Meanwhile, Silicon Valley Bank won relief from the bankruptcy court's automatic stay and, based on its security interest, foreclosed on the copyrights. Then the bank sold the copyrights to Advanced Aerospace (Gilsen's and Widen's company) which then sold the copyrights to Airweld. Had Aerocon's joint venture with Gilsen and Widen gone through, buying off the trustees' and the bank's interests in the copyrights would have been a sensible, if expensive, way to ensure that the venture owned the copyrights free and clear. But, of course, the venture did not go through, and Gilsen and Widen's affiliations had changed. Thus Gilsen and Widen's purchase from the bank and sale to Airweld meant that Aerocon, which had paid $90,000 for the copyrights and had owned them as a tenant in common with Airweld, now had a claim adverse to Airweld's, which purportedly owned the copyrights in fee simple.

___

**7.** *See* 11 U.S.C. § 544(a) (2000).

Aerocon brought an adversary proceeding in each of the three bankruptcy proceedings against Silicon Valley Bank, Advanced Aerospace, Gilsen, Widen, and Airweld. (These adversary proceedings were later consolidated.) Aerocon sued to avoid Silicon Valley Bank's security interest and to recover the copyrights or their value from subsequent transferees Advanced Aerospace, Gilsen, Widen, and Airweld.[9] The bankruptcy court granted the subsequent transferees' motion to dismiss Aerocon's claims against them as time-barred.[10] The bankruptcy court then granted summary judgment to Silicon Valley Bank on all of Aerocon's claims on the ground that the bank had perfected its security interest in the copyrights under California's version of Article 9 of the Uniform Commercial Code. Aerocon appealed to the Ninth Circuit Bankruptcy Appellate Panel. Silicon Valley Bank objected, and the appeal was transferred to the district court, which affirmed the bankruptcy court. Aerocon appeals from the district court's order.

## ANALYSIS

Copyright and bankruptcy law set the context for this litigation, but the legal issue is priority of security interests. The bankruptcy trustees sold Aerocon their power to avoid any security interest "that is voidable by a creditor that extends credit to the debtor at the time of the commencement of the case, and that obtains, at such time and with respect to such credit, a judicial lien...."[15] Under this "strong-arm" provision, Aerocon has the status of an "ideal creditor" who perfected his lien at the last possible moment before the bankruptcy commenced, and if this hypothetical creditor would take priority over Silicon Valley Bank's lien, then Aerocon may avoid the bank's security interest.

Whether Aerocon's hypothetical lien creditor would take priority turns on whether federal or state law governs the perfection of security interests in unregistered copyrights. The bank did everything necessary to perfect its security interest under state law, so if state law governs, the bank has priority and wins. The bank did nothing, however, to perfect its interest under federal law, so if federal law governs, Aerocon's hypothetical lien creditor arguably has priority, although the parties dispute whether Aerocon might face additional legal hurdles.

We are assisted in deciding this case by two opinions, neither of which controls, but both of which are thoughtful and scholarly. The first is the bankruptcy court's published opinion in this case, *Aerocon Engineering Inc. v. Silicon Valley Bank (In re World Auxiliary Power Co.)*, which we affirm largely for the reasons the bankruptcy judge gave. The second is a published district court opinion, *National Peregrine, Inc. v. Capitol Federal Savings & Loan Association (In re Peregrine Entertainment, Ltd.)*, the holdings of which we adopt but, like the bankruptcy court, distinguish and limit.

Our analysis begins with the Copyright Act of 1976. Under the Act, "copyright protection subsists ... in original works of authorship fixed in

---

**9.** *See id.* § 550(a).

**10.** *See id.* § 550(f).

**15.** *See* 11 U.S.C. § 544(a).

any tangible medium of expression...."[20] While an owner must register his copyright as a condition of seeking certain infringement remedies, registration is permissive, not mandatory, and is not a condition for copyright protection.[22] Likewise, the Copyright Act's provision for recording "transfers of copyright ownership"[23] (the Act's term that includes security interests)[24] is permissive, not mandatory: "Any transfer of copyright ownership or other document pertaining to copyright may be recorded in the Copyright Office...."[25] The Copyright Act's use of the word "mortgage" as one definition of a "transfer"[26] is properly read to include security interests under Article 9 of the Uniform Commercial Code.[27]

Under the Copyright Act,

[a]s between two conflicting transfers, the one executed first prevails if it is recorded, in the manner required to give constructive notice ... within one month after its execution ... or at any time before recordation ... of the later transfer. Otherwise the later transfer prevails if recorded first in such manner, and if taken in good faith, for valuable consideration ... and without notice of the earlier transfer.[28]

The phrase "constructive notice" refers to another subsection providing that recording gives constructive notice but only if—

(1) the document, or material attached to it, specifically identifies the work to which it pertains so that, after the document is indexed by the Register of Copyrights, it would be revealed by a reasonable search under the title or registration number of the work; and

(2) registration has been made for the work.[29]

A copyrighted work only gets a "title or registration number" that would be revealed by a search if it's registered.[30] Since an unregistered

---

**20.** *Id.* § 102(a).

**22.** *Id.* § 408(a) ("[T]he owner of copyright ... may obtain registration of the copyright claim.... Such registration is not a condition of copyright protection.").

**23.** *Id.* §§ 101, 205(a).

**24.** *See id.* §§ 101, 201(d).

**25.** *Id.* § 205(a) (emphasis added).

**26.** *Id.* § 101 ("A 'transfer of copyright ownership' is an assignment, mortgage, exclusive license, or any other conveyance, alienation, or hypothecation of a copyright....").

**27.** *See* Grant Gilmore, 1 *Security Interests in Personal Property* § 13.3, at 415 (1965) ("The phrase 'may be mortgaged' in [the Copyright Act of 1909] should be read as equivalent to 'may be transferred for security.' ... A copyright would not in any case seem to be within the category of intangible property which can be pledged; under Article 9 of the [Uniform Commercial] Code it would

be a 'general intangible.' "). *See also In re Cybernetic Services, Inc.*, 252 F.3d 1039, 1056 (9th Cir.2001) ("[T]he Copyright Act, by its terms, governs security interests."); *National Peregrine, Inc.*, 116 B.R. at 199 ("It is clear ... that an agreement granting a creditor a security interest in a copyright may be recorded in the Copyright Office.").

**28.** 17 U.S.C. § 205(d) (emphasis added).

**29.** *Id.* § 205(c) (emphasis added).

**30.** *See id.* § 409 ("The application for copyright registration shall ... include ... the title of the work...."); *id.* § 410(a) ("When ... the Register of Copyrights determines that ... the material deposited constitutes copyrightable subject matter ... the Register shall register the claim and issue ... a certificate of registration.... The certificate shall contain the information given in the application, together with the number and effective date of the registration.").

work doesn't have a title or registration number that would be "revealed by a reasonable search," recording a security interest in an unregistered copyright in the Copyright Office wouldn't give "constructive notice" under the Copyright Act, and, because it wouldn't, it couldn't preserve a creditor's priority. There just isn't any way for a secured creditor to preserve a priority in an unregistered copyright by recording anything in the Copyright Office. And the secured party can't get around this problem by registering the copyright, because the secured party isn't the owner of the copyright, and the Copyright Act states that only "the owner of copyright . . . may obtain registration of the copyright claim. . . ."[31]

Aerocon argues that the Copyright Act's recordation and priority scheme exclusively controls perfection and priority of security interests in copyrights. First, Aerocon argues that state law, here the California U.C.C., by its own terms "steps back" and defers to the federal scheme. Second, whether or not the U.C.C. steps back, Aerocon argues that Congress has preempted the U.C.C. as it applies to copyrights. We address each argument in turn.

## A.   U.C.C. Step Back Provisions

Article 9 of the Uniform Commercial Code, as adopted in California, provides that unperfected creditors are subordinate to perfected, and as between perfected security interests, the first perfected interest prevails. The bank perfected first under state law by filing a financing statement with the California Secretary of State on existing and after-acquired copyrights. The U.C.C. treats copyrights as "general intangibles." Security interests in general intangibles are properly perfected under the U.C.C. by state filings such as the one made by the bank in this case.

To avoid conflict with the federal law, the U.C.C. has two "step-back provisions," by which state law steps back and out of the way of conflicting federal law. The first, more general "step-back" provision says that Article 9 "does not apply . . . [t]o a security interest subject to any statute of the United States to the extent that such statute governs the rights of parties to and third parties affected by transactions in particular types of property. . . ."[35] As applied to copyrights, the relevant U.C.C. Official Comment makes it clear that this step-back clause does not exclude all security interests in copyrights from U.C.C. coverage, just those for which the federal Copyright Act "governs the rights" of relevant parties:

> Although the Federal Copyright Act contains provisions permitting the mortgage of a copyright and for the recording of an assignment of a copyright such a statute would not seem to contain sufficient provisions regulating the rights of the parties and third parties to exclude security interests in copyrights from the provisions of this Article.[36]

The second step-back provision[37] speaks directly to perfection of security interests. It exempts from U.C.C. filing requirements security interests

---

**31.**  *Id.* § 408(a).

**35.**  Cal. Comm.Code § 9104(a).

**36.**  *Id.* Official Comment 1.

**37.**  *Id.* § 9302(3)(a).

in property "subject to . . . [a] statute . . . of the United States which provides for a national . . . registration . . . or which specifies a place of filing different from that specified in this division for filing of the security interest."[38] Compliance with such a statute "is equivalent to the filing of a financing statement . . . and a security interest in property subject to the statute . . . can be perfected only by compliance therewith. . . ."[39]

Under the U.C.C.'s two step-back provisions, there can be no question that, when a copyright has been registered, a security interest can be perfected only by recording the transfer in the Copyright Office. As the district court held in *Peregrine*, the Copyright Act satisfies the broad U.C.C. step-back provision by creating a priority scheme that "governs the rights of parties to and third parties affected by transactions" in registered copyrights and satisfies the narrow step-back provision by creating a single "national registration" for security interests in registered copyrights. Thus, under these step-back provisions, if a borrower's collateral is a registered copyright, the secured party cannot perfect by filing a financing statement under the U.C.C. in the appropriate state office, or alternatively by recording a transfer in the Copyright Office. For registered copyrights, the only proper place to file is the Copyright Office. We adopt *Peregrine*'s holding to this effect.

However, the question posed by this case is whether the U.C.C. steps back as to unregistered copyrights. We, like the bankruptcy court in this case, conclude that it does not. As we've explained, there's no way for a secured creditor to perfect a security interest in unregistered copyrights by recording in the Copyright Office. The U.C.C.'s broader step-back provision says that the U.C.C. doesn't apply to a security interest "to the extent" that a federal statute governs the rights of the parties. The U.C.C. doesn't defer to the Copyright Act under this broad step-back provision because the Copyright Act doesn't provide for the rights of secured parties to unregistered copyrights; it only covers the rights of secured parties in *registered* copyrights. The U.C.C.'s narrow step-back provision says the U.C.C. doesn't apply if a federal statute "provides for a national . . . registration . . . or which specifies a place of filing different from that specified in this division for filing of the security interest." The U.C.C. doesn't defer to the Copyright Act under this narrow step-back provision because the Copyright Act doesn't provide a "national registration": unregistered copyrights don't have to be registered, and because unregistered copyrights don't have a registered name and number, under the Copyright Act there isn't any place to file anything regarding unregistered copyrights that makes any legal difference. So, as a matter of state law, the U.C.C. doesn't step back in deference to federal law, but governs perfection and priority of security interests in unregistered copyrights itself.

## B. Federal Preemption

It wouldn't matter that state law doesn't step back, however, if Congress chose to knock state law out of the way by preemption. Federal

---

**38.** Cal. Comm.Code § 9302(3)(a).        **39.** *Id.* § 9302(4).

law preempts state law under three circumstances. The first is "express preemption," where Congress explicitly preempts state law. The second is "field preemption," where Congress implicitly preempts state law by "occupy[ing] the entire field, leaving no room for the operation of state law" The third is "conflict preemption," where we infer preemption because "compliance with both state and federal law would be impossible, or state law stands as an obstacle to the accomplishment and execution of the full purposes and objectives of Congress." We presume that federal law does not preempt "state law in areas traditionally regulated by the States."

Aerocon argues, relying on *Peregrine*, that Congress intended to occupy the field of security interests in copyrights. Aerocon also argues that the U.C.C. actually conflicts with the Copyright Act's text and purpose.

Because Aerocon relies so heavily on *Peregrine* and its progeny, we will briefly review the facts and holding of that case. In *Peregrine*, a bank had secured a loan with the debtor's copyrights in a library of films licensed out for exhibition and related accounts receivable and attempted to perfect its security interest by filing a U.C.C. financing statement. The debtor later filed for bankruptcy and, as debtor-in-possession, sued in the bankruptcy court to avoid the bank's lien on the ground that the bank had failed to perfect its lien by failing to record it with the Copyright Office. The bankruptcy court held for the bank, and the debtor-in-possession appealed to the district court. The district court reversed, holding that "the comprehensive scope of the Copyright Act's recording provisions, along with the unique federal interests they implicate, support the view that federal law preempts state methods of perfecting security interests in copyrights. . . ." The district court reasoned that federal law preempts state law because "the Copyright Act establishes a uniform method for recording security interests in copyrights" and creates a different priority scheme than state law, and because "competing recordation schemes . . . lessen [] the utility of each."

Although *Peregrine* did not specify whether the copyrights at issue were registered, it is probably safe to assume that they were, and that the *Peregrine* court did not have a case involving unregistered copyrights, because the collateral at issue was a movie library that got licensed out to exhibitors[57] and, in the ordinary course, copyrights in such films would be registered. Also, as the bankruptcy judge in the case at bar pointed out, *Peregrine*'s "analysis only works if the copyright was registered." The district court in *Peregrine* held that Congress had preempted state law because of "the comprehensive scope of the Copyright Act's recording provisions." As applied to registered copyrights, the Act's recording scheme is comprehensive; it doesn't exclude any registered copyright from its coverage. But as applied to unregistered copyrights, the Act doesn't have comprehensive recording provisions. Likewise, *Peregrine* notes that "[t]o the extent there are competing recordation schemes, this lessens the utility of each." This holds true for registered copyrights. But there aren't two

---

**57.** *Id.* at 197.

competing filing systems for unregistered copyrights. The Copyright Act doesn't create one. Only the U.C.C. creates a filing system applicable to unregistered copyrights. *Peregrine* reasoned that creditors could get conflicting results under the U.C.C. and the Copyright Act, because each provides a different priority scheme. That's true only for registered copyrights. The Copyright Act wouldn't provide a conflicting answer as to unregistered copyrights because it wouldn't provide any answer at all. *Peregrine*'s holding applies to registered copyrights, and we adopt it, but as the bankruptcy court reasoned in the case at bar, it does not apply to unregistered copyrights.

We accordingly reject two other lower court opinions, *Zenith Productions, Ltd. v. AEG Acquisition Corp. (In re AEG Acquisition Corp.)*[63] and *In re Avalon Software Inc.*,[64] that extended *Peregrine*'s holding to unregistered copyrights. No circuit court has come to that erroneous conclusion.[66] In both cases, the courts held that security interests in unregistered copyrights may not be perfected under the U.C.C.; perfection could be obtained only by registering the copyrights and recording the security interest with the Copyright Office. We reject these opinions because they miss the point made by the bankruptcy judge in this case, and discussed above, that *Peregrine*'s analysis doesn't work if it's applied to security interests in unregistered copyrights. Moreover, such extensions of *Peregrine* to unregistered copyrights would make registration of copyright a necessary prerequisite of perfecting a security interest in a copyright. The implication of requiring registration as a condition of perfection is that Congress intended to make unregistered copyrights practically useless as collateral, an inference the text and purpose of the Copyright Act do not warrant.

In the one instance where the Copyright Act conditions some action concerning a copyright on its registration—the right to sue for infringement—the Act makes that condition explicit.[70] Nowhere does the Copyright Act explicitly condition the use of copyrights as collateral on their registration. Second, the Copyright Act contemplates that most copyrights will not be registered. Since copyright is created every time people set pen to paper, or fingers to keyboard, and affix their thoughts in a tangible medium,[71] writers, artists, computer programmers, and web designers would have to have their hands tied down to keep them from creating unregistered copyrights all day every day. Moreover, the Copyright Act says that

---

**63.** 161 B.R. 50 (9th Cir.BAP 1993), *affirming* 127 B.R. 34 (Bankr.C.D.Cal.1991).

**64.** 209 B.R. 517 (D.Ariz.1997).

**66.** In *In re Cybernetic Services, Inc.*, 252 F.3d 1039 (9th Cir.2001), we held that state law governs perfection of security interests in patents. *Id.* at 1059. We distinguished *Peregrine* because the Patent Act, unlike the Copyright Act, doesn't contemplate the recordation of security interests. *See id.* at 1056. We neither approved nor disapproved *Peregrine* because patent law, not copyright law,

was at issue. *Id. See also Broadcast Music, Inc. v. Hirsch*, 104 F.3d 1163, 1166 (9th Cir. 1997) (distinguishing *Peregrine* on the ground that an assignment of royalties was not a "transfer" of an interest in copyright).

**70.** *See* 17 U.S.C. § 411(a).

**71.** *See id.* § 102(a) ("[C]opyright protection subsists ... in original works of authorship fixed in any tangible medium of expression....").

copyrights "may" be registered, implying that they don't have to be, and since a fee is charged and time and effort is required, the statute sets up a regime in which most copyrights won't ever be registered.

Though Congress must have contemplated that most copyrights would be unregistered, it only provided for protection of security interests in registered copyrights. There is no reason to infer from Congress's silence as to unregistered copyrights an intent to make such copyrights useless as collateral by preempting state law but not providing any federal priority scheme for unregistered copyrights. That would amount to a presumption in favor of federal preemption, but we are required to presume just the opposite. The only reasonable inference to draw is that Congress chose not to create a federal scheme for security interests in unregistered copyrights, but left the matter to States, which have traditionally governed security interests.

For similar reasons, we reject Aerocon's argument that congressional intent to preempt can be inferred from conflict between the Copyright Act and the U.C.C. There is no conflict between the statutory provisions: the Copyright Act doesn't speak to security interests in unregistered copyrights, the U.C.C. does.

Nor does the application of state law frustrate the objectives of federal copyright law. The basic objective of federal copyright law is to "promote the Progress of Science and useful Arts"[75] by "establishing a marketable right to the use of one's expression" and supplying "the economic incentive to create and disseminate ideas."[76] Aerocon argues that allowing perfection under state law would frustrate this objective by injecting uncertainty in secured transactions involving copyrights. Aerocon conjures up the image of a double-crossing debtor who, having gotten financing based on unregistered copyrights, registers them, thus triggering federal law, and gets financing from a second creditor, who then records its interest with the Copyright Office and takes priority. We decline to prevent this fraud by drawing the unreasonable inference that Congress intended to render copyrights useless as collateral unless registered.

Prudent creditors will always demand that debtors disclose any copyright registrations and perfect under federal law and will protect themselves against subsequent creditors gaining priority by means of covenants and policing mechanisms. The several *amici* banks and banking association in this case argue that most lenders would lend against unregistered copyrights subject to the remote risk of being "primed" by subsequent creditors; but no lender would lend against unregistered copyrights if they couldn't perfect their security interest. As we read the law, unregistered copyrights have value as collateral, discounted by the remote potential for priming. As Aerocon reads the law, they would have no value at all.

---

**75.**  U.S. Constitution, article 1, section 8.

**76.**  *Harper & Row Publishers v. Nation Enterprises*, 471 U.S. 539, 558, 105 S.Ct. 2218, 85 L.Ed.2d 588 (1985).

Aerocon's argument also ignores the special problem of copyrights as after-acquired collateral. To use just one example of the multi-industry need to use after-acquired (really after-created) intangible intellectual property as collateral, now that the high-tech boom of the 1990s has passed, and software companies don't attract equity financing like tulips in seventeenth century Holland, these companies will have to borrow more capital. After-acquired software is likely to serve as much of their collateral. Like liens in any other after-acquired collateral, liens in after-acquired software must attach immediately upon the creation of the software to satisfy creditors. Creditors would not tolerate a gap between the software's creation and the registration of the copyright. If software developers had to register copyrights in their software before using it as collateral, the last half hour of the day for a software company would be spent preparing and mailing utterly pointless forms to the Copyright Office to register and record security interests. Our reading of the law "promote[s] the Progress of Science and useful Arts" by preserving the collateral value of unregistered copyrights, which is to say, the vast majority of copyrights. Aerocon's reading of the law—which would force producers engaged in the ongoing creation of copyrightable material to constantly register and update the registrations of their works before obtaining credit—does not.

## CONCLUSION

Regarding perfection and priority of security interests in unregistered copyrights, the California U.C.C. has not stepped back in deference to federal law, and federal law has not preempted the U.C.C. Silicon Valley Bank has a perfected security interest in the debtors' unregistered copyrights, and Aerocon, standing in the bankruptcy trustees' shoes, cannot prevail against it.

*AFFIRMED.*

## NOTE

The importance of *World Auxiliary* is shown in the fluid context of a field like film making. Take the elementary case in which a shell corporation (Production) is set up to make a single feature film to be distributed by Studio. Bank is willing to finance the picture solely because Studio has given Production an iron-clad agreement (the negative pick-up agreement) to buy the film (the negative) at an agreed purchase price when the film is completed. Bank is covered in case the film is not finished by a completion bond from Insurer, payable to Bank. Although Studio is functionally the debtor in this transaction, Studio doesn't want the loan on its balance sheet, and the deal is structured so that Bank makes its loan to Production, which assigns to Bank its right to be paid the purchase price by Studio when the film is completed. The purchase price will equal the amount of the loan made by Bank to Production plus interest. Thus, if the film is completed and Studio honors the negative pick-up agreement, Bank is paid; if the film is not completed, Bank is paid by Insurer. Clearly, Bank's credit risk is Studio's solvency; if it files in bankruptcy before paying the purchase price of the film, Bank is going to have collection problems.

If Bank doesn't get paid by Studio, it at least wants possession of the film from Production. Banks usually aren't happy about involuntarily becoming equity participants in the entertainment business, but having a completed film may be better than having a claim in Studio's bankruptcy. Hence, before Bank disburses the loan proceeds to Production, Bank will take a security interest in whatever rights it can get in the, as yet, unmade film. It will, for what it is worth, perfect a security interest under Article 9 in all Production's assets, now owned or hereafter acquired, including all the existing and future intellectual property such as the script and the eventual film. Under *Peregrine*, it must also perfect under the Copyright Act. But at the inception of the transaction, there may be at most a script; Bank may require registration of a copyright in the script and any other copyrightable property that Production has at that time so that it can promptly record its security agreement. But, as the film progresses, each new version of the script and each new print of the film would be "fixed in a tangible medium of expression" and covered by the 1976 Copyright Act. Under *Peregrine* the Copyright Office is the place to record a security interest in such rights and the recording can have no effect until the copyright is registered. In re AEG Acquisition Corp., 161 B.R. 50 (B.A.P. 9th Cir.1993). But Alice Haemmerli, in Insecurity Interests: Where Intellectual Property and Commercial Law Collide, 96 Colum. L. Rev. 1645, 1695 (1996), points out that obtaining registration "is a matter of many months." Since the copyright for the film is usually not registered until the film is ready for release, Bank's security interest in the film could be jeopardized if Production filed in bankruptcy before the copyright was registered and recorded; moreover, preference law might be implicated if registration and recording took place within 90 days before Production filed. *World Auxiliary* solves Bank's problems by allowing it to take an effective Article 9 security interest in the unregistered copyrighted material that is created before the film is finished. This security interest is valid in Production's bankruptcy and against subsequent buyers or secured parties.

## PROBLEMS

**1.** Assume the facts in the preceding Note. Under *World Auxiliary*, Bank can take an Article 9 security interest in all of the unregistered copyright material involved in the film that will protect Bank until it has Production register the completed film and Bank records its security interest, if it has not been paid by then. But suppose Production, after it has registered the film, fraudulently grants a security interest in the film to Lender, who records its security interest in the Copyright Office before Bank. Before making the loan to Production, Lender searched the Copyright Office records and found nothing. When Bank is ready to record its security interest, it discovers that Lender had recorded three months earlier. Is Lender prior to Bank with respect to the intellectual property associated with the film?

**2.** In *Peregrine* the court held that a Copyright Office recording is the exclusive method for perfecting a security interest in copyright receivables, the proceeds of the exploitation of the copyright. How does *World Auxiliary* affect this holding?

## C.  TRADEMARKS

A trademark is a distinctive mark, symbol or emblem used by a producer or manufacturer to identify and distinguish that person's products from those of others. Educational Development Corp. v. Economy Co., 562 F.2d 26 (10th Cir.1977). The name "Coke" distinguishes one soft drink from another soft drink, "Pepsi," which looks and tastes almost the same. Trademark protection arises from either federal or state law. The owner of a trademark may register it at the U.S. Patent and Trademark Office (PTO), and certain benefits flow from such registration. But federal registration is permissive, and the owner can also register the trademark in the states where it is used or can choose not to register the trademark at all and rely on a common law trademark based on its status as a first user.

The Lanham Act provides: "A registered mark or mark for which application to register has been filed shall be assignable with the good will of the business in which the mark is used, or with that part of the goodwill of the business connected with the use of and symbolized by the mark. * * * An assignment shall be void as against any subsequent purchaser for a valuable consideration without notice, unless the prescribed information reporting the assignment is recorded in the Patent and Trademark Office within three months after the date of the subsequent purchase or prior to the assignment." 15 U.S.C. § 1060. Thus, for federally registered trademarks, recording of assignments is mandatory, but, unlike the Copyright Act, nothing is said about security interests. In the comprehensive revision of the Lanham Act in 1988, consideration was given to providing that recording a security interest in a trademark in the PTO would establish the secured party's priority against subsequent claimants, but this proposal was not enacted.

Working with a fragmentary federal statute and a somewhat ambiguous UCC, the court in the following case decides the issue of how to perfect a security interest in a trademark.

## In re Together Development Corporation

United States Bankruptcy Court, D. Massachusetts, 1998.
227 B.R. 439.

■ JAMES F. QUEENAN, BANKRUPTCY JUDGE.

This case presents the question of the proper method of perfecting a security interest in trademarks. The subject involves a trap for the unwary.

By previous order, the court authorized Together Development Corporation (the "Debtor") to sell substantially all its assets, including its trademark "Together Dating Service", free of the security interest of Horace Trimarchi ("Trimarchi"). The order attached the security interest to the sales proceeds. The order also set down an evidentiary hearing so the court could adjudicate the validity and perfection of Trimarchi's security interest. Set forth here are my findings of fact and conclusions of law following that hearing.

The case was submitted on agreed exhibits and an oral stipulation of facts. Trimarchi is a former shareholder of the Debtor. By agreement dated May 13, 1986, the Debtor purchased all its shares owned by Trimarchi (and two others). The price for Trimarchi's shares was $200,000, which was represented by the Debtor's promissory note in that amount bearing interest at 10% per annum and payable in 780 weekly installments of $500. In consideration of other indebtedness owed Trimarchi, the Debtor gave him its promissory note in the sum of $30,372.12, also bearing interest at 10% and payable in 780 weekly installments. Both notes were secured by the Debtor's "accounts receivable, it's [sic] Trademark, Franchise Fees and Royalties." In furtherance of that security interest, the Debtor executed and delivered to Trimarchi a separate assignment which described the assigned property as the Debtor's "Trademark (Together Dating Service) . . . which is registered under Certificate Number 1,145,365 in the United States Patent Office transfer said mark [sic], along with the goodwill of the business connected with that mark. . . ." The Debtor also gave to Trimarchi a signed financing statement (UCC–1) covering the following described collateral: "All fixtures, office furniture, files, etc., accounts receivable, Franchise Fees, Royalties, License Fees, Franchise Agreements, License Agreements, and 'TOGETHER' Trademark–Registration number 1,145,-365."

Trimarchi did not make a filing with the Secretary of State of Connecticut, where the Debtor's principal office was then located, nor with any other state. Instead, he filed the financing statement by mail with the United States Patent and Trademark Office ("PTO"), which sent back a written acknowledgment of the filing. There is no dispute that Trimarchi's security interest in items of property other than the trademark is unperfected for lack of recording with the appropriate state authority. The question is whether the filing with the PTO was sufficient to perfect his security interest in the trademark.

The parties' agreement provides that it "shall be interpreted under the Laws of the State of New York. . . ." The agreement does not state it shall be "governed" by New York law. Because there is no essential difference among the states on the point at issue, I assume, as urged by Trimarchi, that the agreement is governed by New York law in all respects. If a federal statute contains filing requirements for particular collateral, U.C.C. § 9–302(3) defers to the federal statute. As in effect in New York, § 9–302(3) provides as follows:

(3) The filing of a financing statement otherwise required by this Article is not necessary or effective to perfect a security interest in property subject to

    (a) a statute or treaty of the United States which provides for a national or international registration or a national or international certificate of title or which specifies a place of filing different from that specified in this Article for filing of the security interest

   . . .

(4) Compliance with a statute or treaty described in subsection (3) is equivalent to the filing of a financing statement under this Article, and a security interest in property subject to the statute or treaty can be perfected only by compliance therewith except as provided in Section 9–103 on multiple state transactions. Duration and renewal of perfection of a security interest perfected by compliance with the statute or treaty are governed by the provisions of the statute or treaty; in other respects the security interest is subject to this Article.

The "Lanham Act," chapter 22 of Title 15 of the United States Code, governs trademarks. Its provision on the transfer of an interest in a trademark reads in relevant part as follows:

A registered mark or a mark for which application to register has been filed shall be assignable with the goodwill of the business in which the mark is used, or with that part of the goodwill of the business connected with the use of and symbolized by the mark[,]. However, no application to register a mark under section 1(b) [15 U.S.C. § 1051(b)] shall be assignable prior to the filing of the verified statement of use under section 1(d) [15 U.S.C. § 1051(d)], except to a successor to the business of the applicant, or portion thereof, to which the mark pertains, if that business is ongoing and existing. . . . An assignment shall be void as against any subsequent purchaser for a valuable consideration without notice, unless it is recorded in the Patent and Trademark Office within three months after the date thereof or prior to such subsequent purchase. . . .

15 U.S.C. § 1060.

The Lanham Act contains no definition of "assignment," thereby casting doubt on whether the term includes the grant of a security interest. The question therefore is this: Is its provision on transfer a statute which, in the words of § 9–302(3), "specifies a place of filing different from that specified in this Article for filing of the security interest"?

I have been directed to no pertinent legislative history. In the abstract, the term "assignment" is broad enough to include the granting of a consensual lien. See BLACK'S LAW DICTIONARY 1342 (5th ed.1979) (defining term as "[a] transfer . . . of the whole of any property . . . or any estate or right therein."). It is helpful, however, to have some history in mind. The Lanham Act was passed in 1946, prior to the general passage by the states of the Uniform Commercial Code, which uses the phrases "security agreement" and "security interest" to describe the granting of a consensual lien in personal property. In 1946, a "chattel mortgage" or "conditional sale" was the vehicle through which most consensual personal property liens were granted. Outside the sales context, to describe the grant of a security interest it was then common to refer to the grant of a "mortgage" rather than an "assignment," the term used in the Lanham Act. The term "hypothecation" was often used with respect to receivables. Thus ordinary language usage points away from treating the grant of a security interest as an "assignment" under the Lanham Act.

Two other considerations indicate the statute does not apply to security interest filings. First, its reference to the "successor to the business" suggests Congress had in mind an outright assignment in the context of the sale of an entire business of which the trademark is a part. Second, and perhaps more persuasive, Congress has expressly included consensual liens in the copyright recording system, thereby demonstrating its awareness of the possibility of such liens and its inclination to make manifest an intention to require their recording when that intention is present. See 17 U.S.C.S. § 205 (providing for recording of "transfer" of copyright); 17 U.S.C.S. § 101 (defining "transfer" to include "mortgage" or "hypothecation").

I therefore conclude that Trimarchi's security interest in the trademark is unperfected. The case law appears to be in uniform agreement.
\* \* \*

Pointing to the national filing requirement for security interests in copyrights, Trimarchi suggests that a similar requirement for trademarks makes a great deal of sense. He cites a copyright case, National Peregrine, Inc. v. Capitol Federal Savings and Loan Association (In re Peregrine Entertainment, Ltd.), 116 B.R. 194 (C.D.Cal.1990). In that case, in the process of holding that filing with the United States Copyright Office is the proper method for perfection of security interests in copyrights, the district court espoused the virtues of mandatory national filing of such security interests. Those virtues may also be present as to trademarks. A proposed purchaser or lender might well find it more convenient and reliable to have just one filing office at which to ascertain both the registered ownership of a trademark and the existence of encumbrances on it. But my job is to apply the statute as Congress has written it. The *Peregrine* court was careful to point out the absence of any reference to security interests in the trademark statute and the consequent irrelevance of trademark cases. See 116 B.R. at 204, n. 14. See also In re Avalon Software Inc., 209 B.R. 517 (Bankr.D.Ariz.1997) (holding PTO proper place for filing for security interest in copyright).

It is of course unfortunate that the trademark statute is sufficiently vague to require judicial interpretation. This produced the understandable mistake made here. Security interests in patents present the same difficulty. See 35 U.S.C. § 261 (requiring recording for "assignment" of patents without furnishing definition of "assignment"); In re Transportation Design and Technology, Inc., 48 B.R. 635 (Bankr.S.D.Cal.1985) (ruling that filing with state, not PTO, perfects security interest in patents against subsequent lien creditor, but not against subsequent bona fide purchaser). Not even the copyright statute is totally consistent with the Uniform Commercial Code. All three statutes should be amended to place them in better harmony with the Code. See Alice Haemmerli, Insecurity Interests: Where Intellectual Property and Commercial Law Collide, 96 Colum. L. Rev. 1645 (1996) (noting difficulties and various proposals for reform). The problem was emphasized long ago in a leading treatise. See 1 Grant Gilmore, Security Interests in Personal Property § 13.1 (1965) (stating statutes such as copyright and patent statutes "pose intricate and difficult problems with respect to the interrelationship of state and federal law and the jurisdiction of state and federal courts—problems which remain largely unsettled and indeed unexplored.").

Being unperfected, Trimarchi's security interest is "subordinate" to a "person who becomes a lien creditor before the security interest is perfected." § 9–301(1). As debtor in possession, the Debtor has the "rights" and "powers" of a trustee. 11 U.S.C.S. § 1107. A trustee, in turn, has the "rights and powers of, or may avoid any transfer of property of the debtor ... that is voidable ... by a [lien creditor]." 11 U.S.C.S. § 544(a)(1). Hence Trimarchi's security interest is subordinate to the Debtor's rights as a lien creditor, and the Debtor may avoid that security interest. Avoidance should normally be accomplished through an adversary proceeding. Fed. R. Bankr.P. 7001(2). For the sake of simplicity, however, at the hearing on the Debtor's sales motion, to which Trimarchi was an objecting party, I dispensed with the necessity of further pleadings. Trimarchi has not objected to this procedure.

An order has accordingly issued declaring Trimarchi's security interest in the trademark (as well as other collateral covered by the parties' agreement) invalid by reason of lack of perfection.

NOTE

Notwithstanding an unbroken line of precedent taking the same view as *Together Development*, commentators recommend, as a precaution, filing a copy of a security agreement and the requisite cover sheet in the PTO for security interests in registered trademarks. Morris W. Hirsch, Taking Security Interests in Personal Property 26 (Cal. CEB Action Guide 1993). In George C. Yu, Security Interests in Federally Registered Trademarks: The Double Filing Problem and a Proposal for a State–Based Perfection System (1996) (unpublished paper in possession of the Editors), the author found that double filing was the norm. Alice Haemmerli, Insecurity Interests: Where Intellectual Property and Commercial Law Collide, 96 Colum. L. Rev. 1645, 1716–1721 (1996), views the trademark scene and sees that "the potential for trouble lurks just beneath the surface."

## D.   PATENTS

Federal statutes on copyrights, trademarks and patents are not so comprehensive as to completely exclude coverage of security interests in these kinds of collateral from the provisions of Article 9. Section 9–109(c)(1) aggressively states that Revised Article 9 defers to federal law only when and to the extent that federal law preempts it. See Comment 8 to 9–109. But whether filing under the federal statute is the exclusive manner of perfection under 9–311(a) and (b), is answered differently with respect to each of the federal statutes. We saw that federal filing is the exclusive method of perfecting a security interest in copyrights, and Article 9 filing is the exclusive manner of perfecting a security interest in trademarks. In the following case we find that with respect to patents, federal and state law offer parallel systems governing perfection of security interests: for one set of claimants the secured party can perfect under Article 9; for another it must perfect under federal law. The federal statute is set out in the opinion.

## In re Cybernetic Services, Inc.

United States Court of Appeals Ninth Circuit, 2001.
252 F.3d 1039.

■ GRABER, CIRCUIT JUDGE:

As is often true in the field of intellectual property, we must apply an antiquated statute in a modern context. The question that we decide today is whether 35 U.S.C. § 261 of the Patent Act, or Article 9 of the Uniform Commercial Code (UCC), as adopted in California, requires the holder of a security interest in a patent to record that interest with the federal Patent and Trademark Office (PTO) in order to perfect the interest as against a subsequent lien creditor.[1] We answer "no"; neither the Patent Act nor Article 9 so requires. We therefore affirm the decision of the Bankruptcy Appellate Panel (BAP).

The parties stipulated to the relevant facts: Matsco, Inc., and Matsco Financial Corporation (Petitioners) have a security interest in a patent developed by Cybernetic Services, Inc. (Debtor). The patent is for a data recorder that is designed to capture data from a video signal regardless of the horizontal line in which the data is located. Petitioners' security interest in the patent was "properly prepared, executed by the Debtor and timely filed with the Secretary of State of the State of California," in accordance with the California Commercial Code. Petitioners did not record their interest with the PTO.

---

**1.** A "security interest" is an interest in personal property that secures a payment or the performance of an obligation. Cal. Com.Code § 1201(36)(a). We refer to a person who holds a security interest in property but who does not hold title to that property as a "lien creditor." * * *

After Petitioners had recorded their security interest with the State of California, certain creditors filed an involuntary Chapter 7 petition against Debtor, and an order of relief was granted. The primary asset of Debtor's estate is the patent. Petitioners then filed a motion for relief from the automatic stay so that they could foreclose on their interest in the patent. The bankruptcy Trustee opposed the motion, arguing that Petitioners had failed to perfect their interest because they did not record it with the PTO.

The bankruptcy court ruled that Petitioners had properly perfected their security interest in the patent by following the provisions of Article 9. Furthermore, the court reasoned, because Petitioners had perfected their security interest before the filing of the bankruptcy petition, Petitioners had priority over the Trustee's claim in the patent and deserved relief from the stay. Accordingly, the bankruptcy court granted Petitioners' motion. The BAP affirmed.

Petitioners then filed this timely appeal. * * *

### DISCUSSION

Article 9 of the UCC, as adopted in California, governs the method for perfecting a security interest in personal property. Article 9 applies to "general intangibles," a term that includes intellectual property. Cal. Com.Code § 9106. The parties do not dispute that Petitioners complied with Article 9's general filing requirements and, in the case of most types of property, would have priority over a subsequent lien creditor. The narrower question in this case is whether Petitioners' actions were sufficient to perfect their interest when the "general intangible" to which the lien attached is a patent. The parties also do not dispute that, *if* Petitioners were required to file notice of their security interest in the patent with the PTO, then the Trustee, as a hypothetical lien creditor under 11 U.S.C. § 544(a)(1), has a superior right to the patent.

The Trustee makes two arguments. First, the Trustee contends that the Patent Act preempts Article 9's filing requirements. Second, the Trustee argues that Article 9 itself provides that a security interest in a patent can be perfected only by filing it with the PTO. We discuss each argument in turn. * * *

### A.  PREEMPTION

#### 1.  The Analytical Framework

* * * The Trustee argues that the recording provision found in 35 U.S.C. § 261 requires that the holder of a security interest in a patent record that interest with the PTO in order to perfect as to a subsequent lien creditor. Section 261 provides:

Ownership; assignment

Subject to the provisions of this title, patents shall have the attributes of personal property.

Applications for patent, patents, or any interest therein, shall be assignable in law by an instrument in writing. The applicant, patentee, or his assigns or legal representatives may in like manner grant and convey an exclusive right under his application for patent, or patents, to the whole or any specified part of the United States.

A certificate of acknowledgment under the hand and official seal of a person authorized to administer oaths within the United States, or, in a foreign country, of a diplomatic or consular officer of the United States or an officer authorized to administer oaths whose authority is proved by a certificate of a diplomatic or consular officer of the United States, or apostle of an official designated by a foreign country which, by treaty or convention, accords like effect to apostles of designated officials in the United States, shall be prima facie evidence of the execution of an assignment, grant or conveyance of a patent or application for patent.

*An assignment, grant or conveyance shall be void as against any subsequent purchaser or mortgagee for a valuable consideration, without notice, unless it is recorded in the Patent and Trademark Office within three months from its date or prior to the date of such subsequent purchase or mortgage.*

(Emphasis added.)

If the Trustee's reading of the relevant portion of § 261 is correct, then to the extent that Article 9 allows a different method of perfection, it would be preempted under either a "field" or "conflict" preemption theory. That is because recording systems increase a patent's marketability and thus play an integral role in the incentive scheme created by Congress. Recording systems provide notice and certainty to present and future parties to a transaction; they work "by virtue of the fact that interested parties have a specific place to look in order to discover with certainty whether a particular interest has been transferred." *Nat'l Peregrine, Inc. v. Capitol Fed. Savs. & Loan Ass'n (In re Peregrine Entm't, Ltd.),* 116 B.R. 194, 200 (C.D.Cal.1990) * * *. If, as the Trustee argues, the Patent Act expressly delineates the place where a party must go to acquire notice and certainty about liens on patents, then a state law that requires the public to look elsewhere unquestionably would undercut the value of the Patent Act's recording scheme. If, on the other hand, § 261 does not cover liens on patents, then Article 9's filing requirements do not conflict with any policies inherent in the Patent Act's recording scheme.

Article 9 itself recognizes the existence of preemption principles. California Commercial Code § 9104(a) expressly subordinates Article 9's requirements to those of federal law. That section provides that Article 9 does not apply to any "security interest subject to any statute of the United States to the extent that such statute governs the rights of parties to and third parties affected by transactions in particular types of property." Section 9104(a) may be broader than federal preemption doctrine under the Patent Act. The text of § 9104(a) implies that Article 9's requirements are inapplicable to the extent that a federal law *governs* the rights of a party to a secured transaction, with or without a *conflict* between the state law and the scheme created by Congress in the Patent Act. * * *

This possible difference in scope does not affect the result in the present case, however. As noted, the Trustee argues that § 261 *required* Petitioners to record their interest with the PTO. If that is true, then the Trustee has priority to the patent's proceeds, either because there is a clear conflict between the state and federal schemes and the state scheme is preempted, or because the Patent Act "governs the rights of parties" to the transaction and § 9104(a) operates to nullify Article 9's filing requirements. We turn to that issue now.

### 2. The Patent Act Requires Parties to Record with the PTO Only Ownership Interest in Patents.

As noted, the Patent Act's recording provision provides that an "assignment, grant or conveyance shall be void as against any subsequent purchaser or mortgagee for a valuable consideration, without notice, unless it is recorded in the [PTO]." 35 U.S.C. § 261. In order to determine whether Congress intended for parties to record with the PTO the type of interest that is at issue in this case, we must give the words of the statute the meaning that they had in 1870, the year in which the current version of § 261 was enacted. * * *

With that history in mind, we must determine whether Congress intended to include the kind of transaction at issue in this case within the scope of 35 U.S.C. § 261. The first phrase in § 261's recording provision— "assignment, grant or conveyance"—refers to different types of transactions. The neighboring clause—"shall be void as against any subsequent purchaser or mortgagee"—refers to the status of the party that receives an interest in the patent. Therefore, for the Trustee to prevail in this case, (1) Petitioners' transaction with Debtor must have been the type of "assignment, grant or conveyance" referred to in § 261, and (2) the Trustee, who has the status of a hypothetical lien creditor, must be a "subsequent purchaser or mortgagee." We hold that neither condition is met.

As we will discuss next, our conclusion finds support in the text of § 261, keeping in view the historical definitions of the terms used in the recording provision; the context, structure, and policy behind § 261; Supreme Court precedent; and PTO regulations. We will begin by analyzing the statute's text and context, as interpreted by the Supreme Court. For the sake of clarity, we will discuss the two relevant phrases in the recording provision of § 261 separately.

### a. The phrase "assignment, grant or conveyance" concerns transfers of ownership interests only.

The historical meanings of the terms "assignment, grant or conveyance" all involved the transfer of an ownership interest. A patent "assignment" referred to a transaction that transferred specific rights in the patent, all involving the patent's title. * * *

A "grant," historically, also referred to a transfer of an ownership interest in a patent, but only as to a specific geographic area. * * *

Although older cases defining the term "conveyance" in the context of intangible property are sparse, and its historic meaning tended to vary, the common contemporaneous definition was "to transfer the legal title . . . from the present owner to another." *Abendroth v. Town of Greenwich*, 29 Conn. 356 (1860) * * *

In summary, the statute's text, context, and structure, when read in the light of Supreme Court precedent, compel the conclusion that a security interest in a patent that does not involve a transfer of the rights of ownership is a "mere license" and is not an "assignment, grant or conveyance" within the meaning of 35 U.S.C. § 261. And because § 261 provides that only an "assignment, grant or conveyance shall be void" as against subsequent purchasers and mortgagees, only transfers of ownership interests need to be recorded with the PTO. * * *

In the present case, the parties do not dispute that the transaction that gave Petitioners their interest in the patent did not involve a transfer of an ownership interest in the patent. Petitioners held a "mere license," which did not have to be recorded with the PTO.

> b. The phrase "subsequent purchaser or mortgagee" does not include subsequent lien creditors.

The Trustee's argument fails not only because a security interest that does not transfer ownership is not an "assignment, grant or conveyance," but also because he is not a subsequent "purchaser or mortgagee." Congress intended for parties to record their ownership interests in a patent so as to provide constructive notice only to subsequent holders of an ownership interest. Again, we derive our conclusion from the historical definitions of the words, from the context and structure of § 261, and from Supreme Court precedent.

The historical meaning of "purchaser or mortgagee" proves that Congress intended for the recording provision to give constructive notice only to subsequent holders of an ownership interest. For the sake of convenience, we begin with the definition of "mortgagee."

Historically, a "mortgagee" was someone who obtained title to property used to secure a debt. * * * A "mortgage" must be differentiated from a "pledge," a term that is absent from the Patent Act. Professor Gilmore, in his treatise, Security Interests in Personal Property § 1.1, at 8, notes that the historical distinction between a pledge and a mortgage was that "the mortgagee got title or an estate whereas the pledgee got merely possession with a right to foreclose on default." * * *

That the Patent Act refers to securing a patent through a "mortgage" but not through a "pledge" is significant, for both were common methods of using a patent as collateral. * * * Generally, the inclusion of certain terms in a statute implies the exclusion of others. * * * It seems then, that by using the term "mortgagee," but not "lien" or "pledge," Congress intended in 1870 for the Patent Act's recording provision to protect only those who obtained title to a patent.

The term "purchaser" does not detract from this conclusion. Section 261 instructs that an unrecorded "assignment, grant or conveyance" shall be void as against a subsequent "purchaser ... for a valuable consideration, without notice." The historical definition of a "purchaser for value and without notice" was a *bona fide* purchaser. A purchaser ... who takes a conveyance purporting to pass the entire title, legal and equitable," who pays value and does not have notice of the rights of others to the property. Bouvier's Law Dictionary 1005 (Baldwin's Century ed.1926). * * *

Congress, by stating that certain transactions shall be void as against a subsequent "purchaser or mortgagee" intended for the words to be read together: A "purchaser" is one who buys an ownership interest in the patent, while a "mortgagee" is one who obtains an ownership interest in a patent as collateral for a debt.

Our previous comments about the context and structure of § 261 support our conclusion that Congress intended to protect only subsequent holders of an ownership interest. As noted, the title of § 261 is "Ownership; assignment," which suggests that the recording provision is concerned only with ownership interests.

Similarly, the second paragraph delineates the types of transactions that § 261 covers—(1) the assignment of a patent, and (2) the grant or conveyance of an exclusive right in the patent to the whole or any specified part of the United States—each involving the transfer of an ownership interest in a patent. It follows that, when Congress referred to a "subsequent purchaser or mortgagee," it was simply describing the future recipients of those transactions. In one case the recipient bought the interest (purchaser), while in the other the recipient loaned money and received the interest as collateral (mortgagee). In either case, an ownership interest was transferred.

Precedent confirms our reading of the statute. The Supreme Court has endorsed the view that Congress intended to provide constructive notice only to subsequent recipients of an ownership interest in a patent. In *Waterman*, the Court observed, as we do, that the Patent Act refers to a "mortgage" but not to a "pledge." * * *

In summary, the historical definitions of the terms "purchaser or mortgagee," taken in context and read in the light of Supreme Court precedent, establish that Congress was concerned only with providing constructive notice to subsequent parties who take an ownership interest in the patent in question. *See In re Transp. Design & Tech., Inc.*, 48 B.R. 635, 639–40 (1985) (interpreting *Waterman* as holding that the Patent Act is concerned only with transactions that transfer title) * * *.

The Trustee is not a subsequent "mortgagee," as that term is used in § 261, because the holder of a patent mortgage holds title to the patent itself. * * * Instead, the Trustee is a hypothetical lien creditor. The Patent Act does not require parties to record documents in order to provide constructive notice to subsequent lien creditors who do not hold title to the patent.

> 3.   Public Policies that Underlie Recording Provisions
> Cannot Override the Text of the Patent Act.

The Trustee argues that requiring lien creditors to record their interests with the PTO is in line with the general policy behind recording statutes. It may be, as the Trustee argues, that a national system of filing security interests is more efficient and effective than a state-by-state system. However, there is no statutory hook upon which to hang the Trustee's policy arguments. Moreover, we are not concerned with the policy behind recording statutes generally but, rather, with the policy behind § 261 specifically.

* * * [Section] 261, as we have demonstrated and as its label suggests, is concerned with patent ownership. In that provision Congress gave patent holders the right to transfer their ownership interests, but only in specific ways. The congressional policy behind that decision was to protect the patent holder and the public for, as the Supreme Court put it,

> it was obviously not the intention of the legislature to permit several monopolies to be made out of one, and divided among different persons within the same limits. Such a division would inevitably lead to fraudulent impositions upon persons who desired to purchase the use of the improvement, and would subject a party who, under a mistake as to his rights, used the invention without authority, to be harassed by a multiplicity of suits instead of one, and to successive recoveries of damages by different persons holding different portions of the patent right in the same place.

*Gayler v. Wilder*, 51 U.S. (10 How.) 501, 519–20 (1850) * * *. The recording provision, if read to include ownership interests only, is perfectly aligned with that policy. By contrast, a security interest in a patent does not make "several monopolies . . . out of one, . . . divided among different persons within the same limits." 51 U.S. at 519.

We must interpret § 261 in the light of the purposes that Congress was seeking to serve. * * * Congress simply was not concerned with nonownership interests in patents, and this limitation was well understood at the time. As explained in a venerable treatise on the law of patents:

> A license is not such a conveyance of an interest in the patented invention as to affect its ownership, and hence is not required to be recorded. . . . The value of the patented invention to the vendee may be impaired by such outstanding licenses, but of this he must inform himself at his own risk as best he may. The record of a license, not being legally required, is not constructive notice to any person for any purpose.

2 Robinson § 817, at 602–03 (footnotes omitted).

The Patent Act was written long before the advent of the "unitary" Article 9 security interest. But we must interpret § 261 as Congress wrote it. The Constitution entrusts to Congress, not to the courts, the role of ensuring that statutes keep up with changes in financing practices. It is notable that Congress has revised the Patent Act numerous times since its enactment, most recently in 1999, *see* Pub.L. 106–113, but it has not updated the Act's recording provision. We decline the Trustee's invitation to do so in Congress' place. * * *

### 6.   There is no Conflict Between the Patent Act and Article 9 in this Case.

Because the Patent Act does not cover security interests or lien creditors at all, there is no conflict between 35 U.S.C. § 261 and Article 9. Petitioners did not have to file with the PTO to perfect their security interest as to a subsequent lien creditor.

### B.   ARTICLE 9's STEP–BACK PROVISION

The Trustee's second major argument is that Article 9 itself requires that a creditor file notice of a secured transaction with the PTO in order to perfect a security interest. California Commercial Code § 9302(3)(a) states that the filing of a financing statement pursuant to Article 9 "is not necessary or effective to perfect a security interest in property subject to . . . [a] statute . . . which provides for a national or international registration . . . or which specifies a place of filing different from that specified in" Article 9. If § 9302(3)(a) applies, then a party *must* utilize the federal registration system in order to perfect its security interest. Cal. Com.Code § 9302(4).

The question, then, is whether the Patent Act is "[a] statute . . . which provides for a national or international registration . . . or which specifies a place of filing different from that specified in" Article 9. Cal. Com.Code § 9302(3)(a). The Patent Act is clearly a statute that provides for a national registration. But that begs the more focused question: a national registration *of what*? Courts have tended to use the context of the statute to amplify the bare text and to answer the focused question: a national registration *of security interests*. For example, in *Aerocon Engineering, Inc. v. Silicon Valley Bank (In re World Auxiliary Power Co.)*, 244 B.R. 149, 155 (1999), the bankruptcy court observed that § 9302(3)(a), if read literally, would be absurd. It would provide that, whenever a particular type of collateral may be registered nationally, regardless of whether the federal statute specifies a place for filing a security interest different than that provided by the UCC, filing a UCC–1 financing statement would be neither necessary nor effective to perfect a security interest in the collateral.

Courts have thus read § 9302(3)(a) as providing that federal filing is necessary only when there is a statute that "provides for" a national registration *of security interests*. * * * We agree with that interpretation.

Under that more restrictive definition, it is clear that the Patent Act is outside the scope of § 9302(3)(a). As we have explained, a transaction that grants a party a security interest in a patent but does *not* effect a transfer of title is *not* the type of "assignment, grant or conveyance" that is referred to in 35 U.S.C. § 261. The transaction in this case did not transfer an ownership interest. Therefore, § 9302(3)(a) did not require that Petitioners record their security interest with the PTO.

The Comments to Article 9 of the UCC support this view. Comment 8 states that § 9302(3)

> exempts from the filing provisions of this Article transactions as to which an adequate system of filing, state or federal, has been set up outside this Article and subsection (4) makes clear that when such a system exists perfection of a relevant security interest can be had only through compliance with that system.

The Comments instruct that "17 U.S.C. §§ 28, 30 (copyrights), 49 U.S.C. § 1403 (aircraft), [and] 49 U.S.C. § 20(c) (railroads)" are examples of the "type of federal statutes" referred to in § 9302(3). Each of the statutes listed in the Comments refers expressly to security interests. *See* 17 U.S.C. § 101; 49 U.S.C. § 44107; 49 U.S.C. § 11301. The Patent Act is not among them.

## C.   CONCLUSION

Because § 261 concerns only transactions that effect a transfer of an ownership interest in a patent, the Patent Act does not preempt Article 9, and neither California Commercial Code § 9104(a) nor § 9302(3) applies. Consequently, Petitioners perfected their security interest in Debtor's patent by recording it with the California Secretary of State. They have priority over the Trustee's claim because they recorded their interest before the filing of the bankruptcy petition.

*AFFIRMED.*


NOTES

**1.**   Case #1. Debtor is a patent holder. It granted a security interest in the patent to SP to secure a debt owed by Debtor to SP, who filed an Article 9 financing statement in the filing office of the State of Debtor's residence. Later, Debtor filed in bankruptcy and its trustee (T) asserted that, in its capacity as a hypothetical lien creditor, it was entitled to avoid SP's security interest under BC 544(a). *Cybernetic Services* held that SP would prevail even though it had not recorded its interest under section 261, which applies only to assignments of ownership to the patent (not present here) and protects only purchasers and mortgagees (not present here) against unrecorded assignments. Hence, former Article 9 applies and protects SP with a perfected security interest against T because its step-back provisions do not apply. The same would be true under 9–311(a)(1). See In re Pasteurized Eggs Corporation, 296 B.R. 283 (Bankr. D. N.H. 2003).

Case #2. If SP files only an Article 9 financing statement, how safe is it in cases having facts different from those in Case #1? (i) Before SP filed its security interest, Debtor assigned the patent to Assignee (A), who recorded the assignment in the PTO? Or failed to record in the PTO? (ii) After SP filed its security interest, Debtor assigned the patent to A, who recorded in the PTO? Or failed to record in the PTO? Section 261 has nothing to say about these cases because, in the court's view, an Article 9 security interest does not affect ownership in the collateral and SP is not a subsequent purchaser or mortgagee within the court's understanding of those terms. Section 9–317(d) has something to say about both cases. The section's apparent assumption is that state law governs the matter.

**2.** Unease about these questions has driven creditors taking security interests in patents to record in the PTO as well as file under Article 9. The obstacle they face in attempting to record a security interest is the prevailing assumption in patent law that the terms "assignment, grant or conveyance" do not contemplate the bare grant of a security interest. Shreen Danamraj, Note, Priority Disputes Involving Security Interests in Patents: Case Law and Current Proposals, 2 Tex. Intell. L.J. 257 (1994). The practice today is to cast a security agreement covering a patent in the form of an assignment, either a "collateral assignment" (absolute present assignment defeasible by repayment of the debt) or "conditional assignment" (assignment worded as a present transfer that takes effect only on the happening of a future event). But some forms we have seen merely say: "Grantor does hereby collaterally assign and grant to Grantee a lien and security interest in all of Grantor's right, title and interest to [the described patent]." Or: "Assignor assigns and grants to Assignee a security interest in and mortgage on [rights in the patent] to secure payment of the obligations." Such language can be dangerous. According to *Cybernetic Services*, the grants create "mere licenses," not a security interest created by assignment or mortgage. Because the grants don't transfer an ownership interest, the Patent Act doesn't govern the secured interests created. Alice Haemmerli, Insecurity Interests: Where Intellectual Property and Commercial Law Collide, 96 Colum. L. Rev. 1645, 1696–1716 (1996), has an extensive discussion of patents and the many difficulties associated with perfecting a reliable security interest in them. In the course of her discussion she comments on the issues raised by use of the various kinds of assignments. Id. at 1710–16. She concludes that under the present law one can never be completely confident that perfection has been achieved and that reform is essential.

**3.** The lien creditor test of step-back under 9–311(a)(1) supports the holding of *Cybernetic Services*. Section 261 is not a statute that deals with priority with respect to lien creditors. But the court's opinion raises eyebrows with its definition of lien creditors in footnote 1: "We refer to a person who holds a security interest in property but who does not hold title to that property as a 'lien creditor.'" Compare this with 9–102(a)(52)(A): "a creditor that has acquired a lien on the property involved by attachment, levy, or the like;". Recall that under 9–202 title is immaterial under Article 9. One wonders whether the court's misconception of the meaning of lien creditor will come home to roost someday.

**4.** In re AvCentral, Inc., 289 B.R. 170 (Bankr. D. Kan. 2003), applied 9–311(a)(1)'s step-back provision to the Federal Aviation Act. There the debtor granted a security interest in aircraft it acquired to sell as spare parts. The secured creditor recorded its security interest in accordance with the Federal Aviation Act (FAA) but didn't make a UCC filing. In the debtor's bankruptcy proceeding, the court found that a UCC filing was neither necessary nor effective under 9–311(a)(1). The asset purchased by debtor either was an "aircraft" under the FAA or inventory. In either case, according to the court, the FAA's filing requirements preempted state law filing requirements for priority over a lien creditor's rights in aircraft or its components. Section 44108(b) of the FAA provides in relevant part that "[w]hen a conveyance, lease or instrument is recorded . . . the conveyance, lease or instrument is valid from the date of filing against all persons . . ." Since a lien creditor is a "person," the court concluded that the secured creditor's FAA filing was the equivalent of a UCC filing under 9–311(b).

---

# E.   SOFTWARE

We include this brief section on software, in part, as a means of introducing one of the more intractable provisions of the UCC, 9–408. Some software is copyrighted; some is patented. Thus, the discussions above on perfecting security interests in copyrights and patents apply to software as well. However, the definition of "transfer of copyright ownership" in 17 U.S.C. § 101 excludes taking a security interest in a nonexclusive license— the usual interest in software marketed to users. Thus, thus Copyright Office recordation is not required under § 205.

"General Intangible" is defined in 9–102(a)(42) as including "software."

"Software" is defined in 9–102(a)(75) as meaning "a computer program and any supporting information provided in connection with a transaction relating to the program. The term does not include a computer program that is included in the definition of goods."

"Goods" is defined in 9–102(a)(44) as including "a computer program imbedded in goods * * * if (i) the program is associated with the goods in such a manner that it customarily is considered part of the goods, or (ii) by becoming the owner of the goods, a person acquires a right to use the program in connection with the goods. The term does not include a computer program embedded in goods that consist solely of the medium in which the program is embedded." Comment 4a. to 9–102. Hence, automobiles that feature computer-activated brakes and acceleration are goods but plastic CD–roms designed as anti-virus devices are software.

As Ronald Mann points out in his seminal article, Secured Credit and Software Financing, 85 Cornell L.Rev. 134, 151 (1999), the basic assumption of modern commercial law—that a debtor can always grant security interests in its assets and that a foreclosure will transfer these assets to the creditor—is entirely foreign to participants in the intellectual property field who believe that transfers by a licensee should be made only with the consent of the licensor. As they see it, not only must the licensor be able to control the number of licenses by limiting sublicensing but also the identity of the licensees, lest the license go to a competitor of the licensor. This policy is enthusiastically supported by the court in *In re CFLC, Inc.*, 89 F.3d 673, 679 (9th Cir.1996):

> Allowing free assignability—or, more accurately, allowing states to allow free assignability—of nonexclusive patent licenses would undermine the reward that encourages invention because a party seeking to use the patented invention could either seek a license from the patent holder *or* seek an assignment of an existing patent license from the licensee. In essence, every licensee would become a potential competitor with the licensor-patent holder in the market for licenses under the patents. And while the patent holder could presumably control the absolute *number* of the licensees, it would lose the very important ability to control the *identity* of its licensees. Thus, any license a patent holder granted—even to the smallest firm in the product market most remote from its own—would be fraught with the danger that the licensee would assign it to the patent holder's most serious competitor, a party to whom the patent holder itself might be absolutely unwilling to license. (Emphasis in original.)

## PROBLEM

Developer licenses its copyrighted UCC Magic program to law firms, with the amount of the license fee determined by the number of computer work-stations at the licensee firms. UCC Magic's unique capacity for offering instantaneous but well-founded solutions to problems of interpretation of UCC provisions has made the product popular in the legal world. Developer has been able to take advantage of the success of the program by charging high license fees. A finance company, Computer Finance (CP), is interested in moving into this field by financing the licensing of UCC Magic to those firms that are either unable or unwilling to pay Developer the full amount of the license charge at the inception of the transaction. CP wishes to take a security interest in the licensee's interest in UCC Magic to secure its obligation to CP and consults you about how it would go about perfecting its security interest and enforcing it if a licensee defaulted on its payments to CP. Developer's licensing agreement prohibits the assignment of, or creation of a security interest in the licensee's interest without the consent of the licensor. Assume that such a license would be classified as nonexclusive. The usual view under copyright law is that a licensee cannot create a security interest in a nonexclusive license without the consent of the licensor. 17 U.S.C. § 201(d) (Transfer of Ownership), § 101 (definition of Transfer of Copyright Ownership); 3 Melville B. and David Nimmer, Nimmer on Copyright § 10.02[B][4] (1998). What advice do you offer CP under 9–408?

It was unclear under former law whether security interests could be created in nonassignable intangible assets. Section 9–406 allows the free assignability of payment intangibles, and 9–408 allows the same with respect to all other intangibles, including software licenses. Both sections achieve this by rendering contractual and noncontractual restrictions on assignments "ineffective" in most instances. At the same time the nondebtor's interest in an intangible is protected against the debtor's grant of a security interest in it. Comment 2 to 9–408 explains free assignability and the Example is helpful in illustrating its operation under 9–408. The discussion below focuses only on 9–408.

Section 9–408 is generally seen as a compromise between licensors, who don't want their licensees to be able to assign to third parties, and secured creditors who wish to be able to take effective security interests in the vast wealth represented by software. Which side prevailed? In applying 9–408, you must grasp that on the facts set out above the licensor is the account debtor and the licensee's interest is a general intangible. Comment 5 explains that even though the licensee will be obligated to pay royalties to the licensor, the licensor is the account debtor for purposes of applying 9–408 because it is obligated to render performance in exchange for payment.

Section 9–408(c)(1) renders "ineffective" contractual and noncontractual restrictions on assignments "to the extent" that they "impair the creation, attachment or perfection of a security interest." Given 9–408(c)(1), antiassignment provisions don't prevent attachment of a security interest in a software licensee's license, for instance. As to perfection, for the reason pointed out in the second paragraph of this section, we don't see any reason for a secured creditor (CP) of the licensee to record in the Copyright Office. However, with respect to enforcement, the secured creditor's rights are eliminated. Under 9–408(d), the security interest is unenforceable against the licensor, the licensee's security agreement doesn't impose any obligations on the licensor, and the secured creditor cannot use the license. 9–408(d)(1), (2) and (4). Thus, the secured creditor cannot enforce its security interest in the license by foreclosing and selling the licensee's interest. In this way 9–408(d) eliminates one of the important rights normally associated with a security interest.

Professor Mann in his article reports that secured creditors believe that they have enough protection if they have the right to terminate the debtor-licensee's power to use the license. He thinks that this might be accomplished by including terms in the loan agreement that give the secured party the right to stop the licensee from further use of the license by court order or by installing a self-help termination switch on the computers. This is uncharted territory, and we can't predict what might happen on this issue in the courts. Such provisions might run afoul 9–408(d). We question whether a secured party can use 9–609(a)(2) and (c) to support self-help efforts; such efforts might violate (d)(6) as enforcing the security interest. Uncertainties in the free assignment of intangibles are described in Steven D. Walt, Uncertainty about Free Assignment: Payment and General Intangibles Under Article 9, 2 J. Payment Sys. L. 4 (2006).

What, then, is the value of having a security interest that cannot be enforced on default? That is, how does 9–408 increase the value of intangible assets as collateral above zero? To understand how, realize that the value of collateral to the secured party is a function of the expected distributions on the collateral it receives either outside or inside the debtor's bankruptcy. Given 9–408(d)'s elimination of enforcement rights, the value of the intangible collateral to the secured party outside of bankruptcy is very close to zero. Example 5 in Comment 8 to 9–408 is unrealistically optimistic in its assessment. The Example proposes a nondebtor franchisor who consents to the debtor-franchisee's assignment of its rights to create a security interest. Consent of course overrides a default rule against assignability, and one wonders why the franchisor wouldn't have consented to the assignment initially. The scenario, although possible, isn't likely or frequent. It certainly isn't likely or frequent enough to justify a new Code section.

The value to the secured creditor instead comes from expected distributions on the collateral in the debtor's bankruptcy. Under prescribed conditions, BC 365(f) allows the bankruptcy trustee to assign the debtor's rights under an executory contract, notwithstanding nonbankruptcy restrictions on its assignment. Essentially this means that antiassignment provisions in executory contracts generally are invalid in bankruptcy. A software license is a type of executory contract, and 9–408(c) enables a security interest to attach to the licensee's rights in the license. BC 365(f) allow the licensee's trustee to sell the licensee's interest, overriding relevant attendant antiassignment provisions. The sale yields proceeds, and the licensee's secured party is entitled to them under BC 552(b) as postpetition proceeds of prepetition collateral. Comment 8 to 9–408 recognizes this outcome; see infra Chapter 9. A debtor's prospects of bankruptcy can be substantial and expected to change over the life of a loan. Thus, while the secured party might receive nothing on the debtor's default outside of bankruptcy, it might well receive a distribution from liquidation of the debtor's license interest in the debtor's bankruptcy. Section 9–408(c) therefore increases the ex ante value of the debtor's intangible assets above zero. The prospect of a bankruptcy payout from these assets provides the added value. Comment 9 to 9–408 politely recommends that applicable federal law, including presumably bankruptcy law, treat 9–408 as valid.

CHAPTER 7

# SECURITY INTERESTS IN INVESTMENT SECURITIES

## A. INTRODUCTION

In this Chapter we offer a primer on secured transactions in securities under Revised Article 8, promulgated in 1994 by the American Law Institute and the National Conference of Commissioners on Uniform State Laws. For illustrations throughout we will use simple transactions, familiar to commercial law generalists, in which individuals use their stocks, bonds, mutual funds, and the like, as collateral for loans. In the business these are called retail transactions. We make no attempt to cover other transactions affected by Revised Article 8 involving devices like repos, hedges, swaps, derivatives and other more exotic financial vehicles that characterize the global and ever-changing securities industry.

The following material is taken from Revised Article 8 Prefatory Note, "Investment Securities" I.A–I.D (1994). This was prepared by Professor James Steven Rogers, who served as Reporter for the revision of Article 8.

> The present version of Article 8 is the product of a major revision made necessary by the fact that the prior version of Article 8 did not adequately deal with the system of securities holding through securities intermediaries that has developed in the past few decades. Although the prior version of Article 8 did contain some provisions dealing with securities holding through securities intermediaries, these were engrafted onto a structure designed for securities practices of earlier times. The resulting legal uncertainties adversely affected all participants. The revision is intended to eliminate these uncertainties by providing a modern legal structure for current securities holding practices.

> I. EVOLUTION OF SECURITIES HOLDING SYSTEMS

> A. The Traditional Securities Holding System

> The original version of Article 8, drafted in the 1940s and 1950s, was based on the assumption that possession and delivery of physical certificates are the key elements in the securities holding system. Ownership of securities was traditionally evidenced by possession of the certificates, and changes were accomplished by delivery of the certificates.

Transfer of securities in the traditional certificate-based system was a complicated, labor-intensive process. Each time securities were traded, the physical certificates had to be delivered from the seller to the buyer, and in the case of registered securities the certificates had to be surrendered to the issuer or its transfer agent for registration of transfer. As is well known, the mechanical problems of processing the paperwork for securities transfers reached crisis proportions in the late 1960s, leading to calls for the elimination of the physical certificate and development of modern electronic systems for recording ownership of securities and transfers of ownership. That was the focus of the revision effort that led to the promulgation of the 1978 amendments to Article 8 concerning uncertificated securities.

### B.   The Uncertificated Securities System Envisioned by the 1978 Amendments

In 1978, amendments to Article 8 were approved to establish the commercial law rules that were thought necessary to permit the evolution of a system in which issuers would no longer issue certificates. The Drafting Committee that produced the 1978 amendments was given a fairly limited charge. It was to draft the revisions that would be needed for uncertificated securities, but otherwise leave the Article 8 rules unchanged. Accordingly, the 1978 amendments primarily took the form of adding parallel provisions dealing with uncertificated securities to the existing rules of Article 8 on certificated securities.

The system of securities holding contemplated by the 1978 amendments differed from the traditional system only in that ownership of securities would not be evidenced by physical certificates. It was contemplated that changes in ownership would continue to be reflected by changes in the records of the issuer. The main difference would be that instead of surrendering an indorsed certificate for registration of transfer, an instruction would be sent to the issuer directing it to register the transfer. Although a system of the sort contemplated by the 1978 amendments may well develop in the coming decades, this has not yet happened for most categories of securities. Mutual funds shares have long been issued in uncertificated form, but virtually all forms of publicly traded corporate securities are still issued in certificated form. Individual investors who wish to be recorded as registered owners on the issuers' books still obtain and hold physical certificates. The certificates representing the largest portion of the shares of publicly traded companies, however, are not held by the beneficial owners, but by clearing corporations. Settlement of securities trading occurs not by delivery of certificates or by registration of transfer on the records of the issuers or their transfer agents, but by computer entries in the records of clearing corporations and securities intermediaries. That is quite different from the system envisioned by the 1978 amendments.

### C.   Evolution of the Indirect Holding System

At the time of the "paperwork crunch" in the late 1960s, the trading volume on the New York Stock Exchange that so seriously strained the capacities of the clearance and settlement system was in the range of 10 million shares per day. Today, the system can easily handle trading volume on routine days of hundreds of millions of shares. This processing capacity could have been achieved only by the application of modern electronic information processing systems. Yet the legal rules under which the system operates are not the uncertificated securities provisions of Article 8. To understand why this is so, one must delve at least a bit deeper into the operations of the current system.

If one examines the shareholder records of large corporations whose shares are publicly traded on the exchanges or in the over the counter market, one would find that one entity—Cede & Co.—is listed as the shareholder of record of somewhere in the range of sixty to eighty percent of the outstanding shares of all publicly traded companies. Cede & Co. is the nominee name used by The Depository Trust Company ("DTC"), a limited purpose trust company organized under New York law for the purpose of acting as a depository to hold securities for the benefit of its participants, some 600 or so broker-dealers and banks. Essentially all of the trading in publicly held companies is executed through the broker-dealers who are participants in DTC, and the great bulk of public securities—the sixty to eighty per cent figure noted above—are held by these broker-dealers and banks on behalf of their customers. If all of these broker-dealers and banks held physical certificates, then as trades were executed each day it would be necessary to deliver the certificates back and forth among these broker-dealers and banks. By handing all of their securities over to a common depository all of these deliveries can be eliminated. Transfers can be accomplished by adjustments to the participants' DTC accounts.

Although the use of a common depository eliminates the needs of physical deliveries, an enormous number of entries would still have to be made on DTC's books if each transaction between its participants were recorded one by one on DTC's books. Any two major broker-dealers may have executed numerous trades with each other in a given security on a single day. Significant processing efficiency has been achieved by netting all of the transactions among the participants that occur each day, so that entries need be made on the depository's books only for the net changes in the positions of each participant at the end of each day. This clearance and netting function might well be performed by the securities exchanges or by the same institution that acts as the depository, as is the case in many other securities markets around the world. In the United States, however, this clearance and netting function is carried out by a separate corporation, National Securities Clearing Corporation ("NSCC"). All that needs to be done to settle each day's trading is for NSCC to compute the net receive and deliver obligations and to instruct DTC to make the corresponding adjustments in the participants' accounts.

The broker-dealers and banks who are participants in the DTC–NSCC system in turn provide analogous clearance and settlement functions to their own customers. If Customer A buys 100 shares of XYZ Co. through Broker, and Customer B sells 100 shares of XYZ Co. through the same Broker, the trade can be settled by entries on Broker's books. Neither DTC's books showing Broker's total position in XYZ Co., nor XYZ Co.'s books showing DTC's total position in XYZ Co., need be changed to reflect the settlement of this trade. One can readily appreciate the significance of the settlement function performed at this level if one considers that a single major bank may be acting as securities custodian for hundreds or thousands of mutual funds, pension funds, and other institutional investors. On any given day, the customers of that bank may have entered into an enormous number of trades, yet it is possible that relatively little of this trading activity will result in any net change in the custodian bank's positions on the books of DTC.

Settlement of market trading in most of the major U.S. securities markets is now effected primarily through some form of netted clearance and depository system. Virtually all publicly traded corporate equity securities, corporate debt securities, and municipal debt securities are now eligible for deposit in the DTC system. Recently, DTC has implemented a similar depository settlement system for the commercial paper market, and could, but for limitations in present Article 8, handle other forms of short-term money market securities such as bankers' acceptances. For trading in mortgage-backed securities, such as Ginnie Mae's, a similar depository settlement system has been developed by Participants Trust Company. For trading in U.S. Treasury securities, a somewhat analogous book-entry system is operated under Treasury rules by the Federal Reserve System.

### D. Need for Different Legal Rules for the Direct and Indirect Holding Systems

Both the traditional paper-based system, and the uncertificated system contemplated by the 1978 amendments, can be described as "direct" securities holding systems; that is, the beneficial owners of securities have a direct relationship with the issuer of the securities. For securities in bearer form, whoever has possession of the certificate thereby has a direct claim against the issuer. For registered securities, the registered owner, whether of certificated or uncertificated securities, has a direct relationship with the issuer by virtue of being recorded as the owner on the records maintained by the issuer or its transfer agent.

By contrast, the DTC depository system for corporate equity and debt securities can be described as an "indirect holding" system, that is, the issuer's records do not show the identity of all of the beneficial owners. Instead, a large portion of the outstanding securities of any given issue are recorded on the issuer's records as belonging to a depository. The depository's records in turn show the identity of the banks or brokers who are its members, and the records of those securities intermediaries show the identity of their customers.

Even after the 1978 amendments, the rules of Article 8 did not deal effectively with the indirect holding system. The rules of the 1978 version of Article 8 were based on the assumption that changes in ownership of securities would still be effected either by delivery of physical certificates or by registration of transfer on the books of the issuer. Yet in the indirect holding system, settlement of the vast majority of securities trades does not involve either of these events. For most, if not all, of the securities held through DTC, physical certificates representing DTC's total position do exist. These "jumbo certificates," however, are never delivered from person to person. Just as nothing ever happens to these certificates, virtually nothing happens to the official registry of stockholders maintained by the issuers or their transfer agents to reflect the great bulk of the changes in ownership of shares that occur each day.

The principal mechanism through which securities trades are settled today is not delivery of certificates or registration of transfers on the issuer's books, but netted settlement arrangements and accounting entries on the books of a multi-tiered pyramid of securities intermediaries. Herein is the basic problem. Virtually all of the rules of the prior version of Article 8 specifying how changes in ownership of securities are effected, and what happens if something goes awry in the process, were keyed to the concepts of a transfer of physical certificates or registration of transfers on the books of the issuers, yet that is not how changes in ownership are actually reflected in the modern securities holding system.

---

Further explication of Professor Rogers' views are found in his article, Policy Perspectives on Revised U.C.C. Article 8, 43 UCLA L. Rev. 1431 (1996) (hereinafter Rogers, Policy Perspectives). A detailed critique of Revised Article 8 is found in Jeanne L. Schroeder, Is Article 8 Finally Ready this Time? The Radical Reform of Secured Lending on Wall Street, 1994 Colum. Bus. L. Rev. 291.

As Professor Rogers' note explains, much of the impulse for revising Article 8 stemmed from the need to deal with the current practice of having most securities held by intermediaries rather than by the beneficial owners of the securities. The assumption made by the 1978 revision was that the solution to the "back office paper crunch" problems, that caused the certificate-based system to break down in the 1960s under the burden of greatly increased trading volume, would be the development of uncertificated securities. This proved incorrect. In fact the securities industry chose to meet the problems raised by paper-based securities by the further development of the indirect holding system, and today, for the most part, uncertificated stocks are issued only by mutual funds. Most stocks and corporate bonds are still certificated, but the certificates are commonly held by intermediaries. As described in the Prefatory Note above, the usual pattern is that the Depository Trust Corporation holds "jumbo certificates" for its over 600 customers, who are securities intermediaries like broker-dealers and banks, which, in turn, hold securities for their customers, the owners of the securities, in the "street name." A major contribution that the Article 8 revision is expected to make is to further unlock the enormous value of these indirectly held securities so that the very large number of individuals and organizations that own these securities can use them more effectively as collateral to obtain financing from creditors.

## B.   BASIC RULES

We introduce you to the UCC rules governing security interests in investment securities in the following simplified summary. Attachment, perfection and priority of security interests in investment securities are governed by Article 9, but important rules and definitions are found in Article 8. If the other requirements of 9–203(b) are met, attachment occurs with respect to certificated securities when delivered to the secured party (9–203(b)(3)(C)) and with respect to other investment property when the secured party has control (9–203(b)(3)(D)). Perfection occurs either by control (9–314(a)) or by filing (9–312(a)). Under 9–106(a), a person has control of a certificated security, uncertificated security or security entitlement as stated in 8–106. A security interest perfected by control is prior to one perfected by filing, whether or not the control party had knowledge of the filing. 9–328(1). Priority among security interests perfected by control is on a first-in-time basis. 9–328(2). Security interests held by brokers or banks in securities held by them (the common margin loan situation) are prior to security interests held by other parties. 8–106(e), 9–328(3).

The drafters of Revised Article 8, conceived the control doctrine to meet the problems raised both by indirect holding of securities by securities intermediaries and by uncertificated securities. For a secured party to gain control with respect to a security interest in certificated securities held by a securities intermediary, it must either become the entitlement holder or enter into in a three-party agreement with the debtor and the broker or bank holding the securities that gives the secured party the power to have the securities sold or transferred without further action by the debtor. 8–106(d). And for control with respect to a security interest in an uncertificated security, such as a mutual fund, the secured party must either become the registered owner or reach an agreement with the debtor and the issuer that gives the secured party the power to sell or transfer without the consent of the owner. 8–106(c).

Working definitions of some of the terms that we will be dealing with in this chapter follow:

As we will see more fully in the next section, "security" is defined in 8–102(a)(15) as including stocks, bonds and the like that are traded in the markets.

A "certificated security" is one that is represented by a certificate. 8–102(a)(4). An "uncertificated security" is one that is not. 8–102(a)(18).

A "securities account" is an account to which financial assets such as stocks, bonds, and mutual funds are credited. 8–501(a).

A "securities intermediary" means a broker or bank that maintains securities accounts for others. 8–102(a)(14).

A "security entitlement" means the rights of the customers of the brokers or banks in their securities accounts. 8–102(a)(17). These customers are described as "entitlement holders." 8–102(a)(7).

"Investment property" is defined in 9–102(a)(49) to include securities, whether certificated or not, security entitlements and securities accounts. This catch-all phrase is used throughout Article 9 as a convenient way to refer to the kinds of property that are subject to the special rules set out above with respect to security interests. This collateral would otherwise fall within the definition of general intangible, from which they are specifically excluded. 9–102(a)(42).

The "issuer" of a bond is the obligor. The "issuer" of stock is the enterprise or property whose equity interest the shares of stock represent. 8–102(a)(15), 8–201.

---

## C.   WHAT IS A SECURITY?

It is not our task in this brief treatment to probe the fringes of investment securities; we will deal with familiar examples: stocks and bonds. The "functional" prong of the definition of security in 8–102(a)(15) provides that for the property to be a "security," it must, among other requirements, be an obligation or share of ownership:

(iii) which:

(A) is, or is of a type, dealt in or traded on securities exchanges or securities markets; or

(B) is a medium for investment and by its terms expressly provides that it is a security governed by this Article.

Comment 15 to 8–102 is helpful on the meaning of a security. First, the interest (stock) or obligation (bond) must be fully transferable either on transfer books or by bearer or registered certificate. Second, the interest or obligation must be divisible as one of a class or series. Even though a clearing corporation (like DTC) may hold the only certificate, the underlying intangible interest is divisible. Third, the interest or obligation must function as a security by being dealt with or traded on securities exchanges or markets, or, at least, be of a type that is so dealt or traded.

NOTE

Comment 15 to 8–102 explains: "[T]he functional test in subparagraph (iii), provides flexibility while ensuring that the Article 8 rules do not apply to interests or obligations in circumstances so unconnected with the securities markets that parties are unlikely to have thought of the possibility that Article 8 might apply." Two cases that generalist commercial lawyers are likely to run across are shares in close corporations and interests in limited liability companies (LLCs). In close corporations the shares of stock are usually wholly owned by the promoters of the company and are not traded on securities markets. Comment 2 to 8–103 makes clear that these shares are securities under 8–102(a)(15) by stating that corporate stock is a security whether or not the issue is traded on securities exchanges. But interests in LLCs are usually not securities under 8–103(c) because members' interests are commonly uncertificated and are rarely traded on securities markets. Section 8–103(c) provides that unless an interest in a LLC is traded on securities exchanges or its terms "opt-in" to Article 8, the interest is not a security. Hence, these interests are usually treated as general intangibles, and security interests are perfected by filing. In the unlikely event that a LLC interest were to be held in a securities account with a securities intermediary, the interest becomes investment property and a security interest must be perfected accordingly. 8–103(c). For a discussion of the status of LLCs under the UCC, see 2 Barkley Clark, The Law of Secured Transactions Under the Uniform Commercial Code ¶ 14.07 (Rev. ed. Supp. 2005).

## D.   Certificated Securities

### 1.   Held by Owner

A word should be said about why some investors choose to be listed on the company's books as the registered owner, with a stock or bond certificate issued to them, while, in recent years, most have opted to have their certificated securities in publicly traded companies held by an intermediary like a broker-dealer or bank. Stock certificates for shares in close corporations are usually held by owners. The probable explanation for the greater popularity of the indirect holding method is its convenience. The intermediary provides consolidated records of all sales, purchases, margin loans, dividends and interest payments, reinvestments, and the like. Tax reporting information is given. When sales are made there is no need to hunt around for the securities certificates which must be promptly delivered to the broker. There are no certificates to be lost or stolen. In addition many intermediaries offer an asset management service, to be discussed later, which automatically sweeps all of the dividends, interest and sale proceeds into a money market account, on which the investor can draw by check or credit card.

But there are some advantages in possessing the stock or bond certificates. Under the indirect holding system, the investor is locked into one broker when it wishes to sell the securities, but an investor who holds the certificates can call a number of brokers to see which offers the most favorable commission rate. Lenders can make loans immediately if a debtor has a stock certificate to pledge; under an indirect holding system it will take more time to arrange a loan on the security of the debtor's brokerage account from any lender other than the intermediary itself. Moreover, some companies offer investors dividend reinvestment plans in which investors are allowed to reinvest their dividends in additional shares without having to pay a brokerage commission. In order to participate in one of these plans, the investor must have the stock registered in its name. A growing number of companies now sell their shares directly to investors; the advantage to the investor is that there is no brokerage commission to pay. Another reason given to explain why investors are willing to endure the inconvenience of holding certificates is that they are concerned about the safety of securities left with brokerage houses. Since the Securities Investor Protection Corporation now insures customers against loss owing to the failure of intermediaries up to $500,000, this concern has been allayed in most instances. Securities Investor Protection Act, 15 U.S.C. §§ 78aaa–111.

## a.   CONTROL IN PLEDGE TRANSACTIONS

The following Problems concern the oldest type of lending transaction involving securities collateral: the pledge.

## PROBLEMS

**1.**   Eleanor owns 1,000 shares of Amalgamated, Inc., worth approximately $200,000, and possesses a security certificate (8–102(a)(16)) registered on the books of the company in her name (8–102(a)(13)). She wishes to borrow $100,000 from Bank as a short term loan to allow her to make a down payment on a new residence while awaiting the sale of her old residence. Bank required security for the loan, and, pursuant to an agreement, she delivered possession of the stock certificate to Bank to secure the loan on the date Bank advanced the funds to her. The stock certificate contained her indorsement (8–102(a)(11)), that is, she signed the transfer form on the back of the certificate, leaving the name of the transferee blank. Although her indorsement entitled Bank to have the shares registered in its name on the books of the company, it merely retained possession of the certificate without acting to have the registration changed to its name or notifying Amalgamated of its security interest. What are Bank's rights with respect to the stock pledged as against Eleanor's creditors and, if she subsequently files in bankruptcy, her trustee in bankruptcy? Work you way through the following provisions. 9–203(b)(3)(C) (attachment) and Comment 4 to that section; 9–313(a) (perfection by delivery under 8–301); 8–301(a)(1) (possession is delivery to purchaser); a pledgee is a purchaser under 1–201(b)(29), (30); 9–314(a) (perfection by control); 9–106(a) (control) refers to 8–106(b)(1) which defines control of a certificated security as delivery of indorsed certificate to purchaser; and 9–310(b)(7) (no filing required to perfect if certificated security delivered to secured party).

Although the facts stated above are adequate to raise the issue to be decided in this Problem, it should be pointed out that the elementary manner in which Eleanor indorsed the certificate by signing the transfer form is not the usual way of proceeding. Lenders anticipate that pledges will be redeemed by the debtors and the stock certificate will be returned to the debtor. If this happened in this case, Eleanor would find herself holding a certificate indorsed with her name but blank as to the transferee. The effect would be a blank indorsement creating a situation in which any bearer of the certificate, including a thief, could claim ownership. The preferred method is to have Eleanor sign a separate stock power appointing the pledgee as attorney to transfer the stock certificate if there is default; however, the name of the person to act as attorney is usually left blank to be filled in by the transferee if transfer is called for. The definition of "indorsement" in 8–102(a)(11) includes a signature on a separate stock power. See John F. Dolan, Commercial Law: Essential Terms and Transactions § 14.3 (2d ed. 1997).

**2.** Change the facts in Problem 1 to these: Bank did not take possession of the certificate but did require Eleanor to sign a security agreement and authorize a financing statement describing the stock as collateral. Bank promptly filed the financing statement.

(a) If Eleanor files in bankruptcy, what are Bank's rights against her trustee in bankruptcy? See 9–312(a) (perfection by filing); 9–317(a) (priority of security interest against lien creditor).

(b) While her debt to Bank was still unpaid, Eleanor indorsed and delivered the certificate to Lender as security for a loan of $120,000 which Lender made to her. There is good reason to believe that Lender knew of Eleanor's transaction with Bank. What are Bank's rights with respect to the stock as against Lender? See 8–106(b)(1) (control by possession); 9–328(1) (priority).

NOTE

The basic priority rule in Revised Article 8 is that a secured party who obtains control (8–106) has priority over other claimants who do not obtain control. 9–328(1). As explained by Comment 1 to 8–106, a person obtains control by taking whatever steps are necessary, given the manner in which the securities are held, to place itself in a position in which it can have the securities sold, without further action by the owner. In the case of a certificated security, the control principle is consistent with the traditional rule that a secured party with possession of the certificate has a perfected security interest that is prior to other claims. Comment 3 to 9–328 states:

> The control priority rule does not turn on either temporal sequence or awareness of conflicting security interests. Rather, it is a structural rule, based on the principle that a lender should be able to rely on the

collateral without question if the lender has taken the necessary steps to assure itself that it is in a position where it can foreclose on the collateral without further action by the debtor. * * * As applied to the retail level, the control priority rule means that a secured party who obtains control has priority over a conflicting security interest perfected by filing without regard to inquiry into whether the control secured party was aware of the filed security interest. Prior to the 1994 revisions to Articles 8 and 9, Article 9 did not permit perfection of security interests in securities by filing. Accordingly, parties who deal in securities have never developed a practice of searching the UCC files before conducting securities transactions. Although filing is now a permissible method of perfection, in order to avoid disruption of existing practices in this business it is necessary to give perfection by filing a different and more limited effect for securities than for some other forms of collateral. The priority rules are not based on the assumption that parties who perfect by the usual method of obtaining control will search the files. Quite the contrary, the control priority rule is intended to ensure that, with respect to investment property, secured parties who do obtain control are entirely unaffected by filings. To state the point another way, perfection by filing is intended to affect only general creditors or other secured creditors who rely on filing.

b.   DIVIDENDS

The facts in the following Problem raised difficulties under former Article 9. How does Revised Article 9 deal with cash and stock dividends in pledge cases?

PROBLEM

Change the facts in Problem 1 above so that while the certificate was still in the possession of Bank and Eleanor's debt was unpaid, Amalgamated declared its usual quarterly cash dividend and sent a check for the amount to Eleanor. Does Bank's security interest cover the cash dividend? Would your answer be the same if Amalgamated declared a stock dividend and sent Eleanor a certificate for 1,000 additional shares? See 9–102(a)(64)(B) and Comment 13a. to 9–102.

c.   PLEDGEE'S DUTY OF REASONABLE CARE

The pledgor will ordinarily be required by the pledgee to execute a stock power which allows the pledgee to transfer the stock represented by the certificate held by the pledgee if it forecloses. The pledgee may sell the stock if the pledgor is in default. 9–610(a). If the stock "is of a kind that is customarily sold on a recognized market or the subject of widely distributed standard price quotations," the pledgee may buy the stock at a private sale or sell it to another, without prior notification to the pledgor of the time and place of sale. 9–610(c), 9–611(d). This allows pledgees to move quickly in realizing on shares listed on stock exchanges.

Section 9–207(a) imposes on a pledgee the duty to use reasonable care in the custody and preservation of collateral in its possession. The question has arisen about the nature of pledgee's duty in cases in which the value of the stock is declining. In the following case the Sixth Circuit deals with the duty of care of a pledgee under § 9–207 in the context of the bursting of the IP bubble in 2001 that left paper millionaires reluctant to part with the shares in their doomed enterprises that they had pledged with banks to cover their loans. The opinion traces, e-mail by e-mail, the grim descent of their expectations regarding their pledged shares, which they had clung to in the forlorn hope that, somehow, the bubble would reinflate and they would be rich again. In the end, they are left with nothing but a suit against the pledgee bank that sold them out. Do they have a good case?

## Layne v. Bank One, Kentucky, N.A.

United States Court of Appeals, 6th Cir., 2005.
395 F.3d 271.

■ Moore, Circuit Judge.

Plaintiff–Appellant, Charles E. Johnson, Jr. ("Johnson"), appeals the district court's grant of summary judgment in favor of Defendants–Appellees, Bank One, Kentucky, N.A. and Banc One Securities Corporation (collectively, "Bank One"). The district court found that under Kentucky law, Bank One was not liable for the depreciation in value of the shares it held as collateral for a loan to Johnson. Furthermore, the district court found that by selling the stock on a national stock exchange, Bank One acted in a commercially reasonable way in disposing of the collateral. On appeal, Johnson asserts that the district court erred in these findings. * * * We conclude that the district court did not err on any of these issues, and thus, the grant of summary judgment to the defendants is **AFFIRMED**.

### I.  BACKGROUND

This case arises out of two loan transactions made by Bank One to plaintiffs Johnson and Geoff Layne ("Layne").[1] Johnson was the founder and CEO of PurchasePro.com, Inc. ("PurchasePro"); Layne served as the national marketing director of the company. Following a successful initial public offering, both Johnson and Layne had considerable net worth, though their PurchasePro shares were subject to securities laws restricting their sale.[2] To increase their liquidity, Johnson and Layne entered into separate loan agreements with Bank One for an approximately $2.8 million

---

**1.** On March 29, 2004, Bank One and Layne entered into a settlement agreement of all of their claims. As a result, Layne agreed to voluntarily dismiss his appeal pursuant to Fed. R.App. P. 42(b). Johnson's appeal remains before us for determination.

**2.** Johnson and Layne were considered "affiliates" of PurchasePro as defined under SEC Rule 144 and therefore, their shares in the company were restricted. 17 C.F.R. § 230.144. Pursuant to Rule 144, an affiliate may not sell restricted securities unless certain conditions are met, including a minimum holding period, a limitation on the amount to be sold, and the manner of the sale. 17 C.F.R. § 230.144(d)–(f).

and $3.25 million line of credit respectively, secured by their shares of PurchasePro stock. The loan agreements included a Loan-to-Value ("LTV") ratio, which conditioned default on the market value of the collateral stock. The LTV ratio was calculated as the outstanding balance on the line of credit over the market value of the collateral stock. Specifically, Layne's loan agreement had a 50% LTV ratio, which meant that the market value of the collateral stock must be at least twice the outstanding balance on the line; Johnson's loan agreement had a 40% LTV ratio, which meant that the market value must remain two and a half times the outstanding balance.[4] The credit agreements provided that if the LTV ratio exceeded those specified percentages, Johnson and Layne had five days to notify Bank One and either increase the collateral or reduce the outstanding balance such that the target LTV ratios were met. Failure to remedy the situation would be an immediate default and Bank One "*may exercise* any and all rights and remedies" including, "*at Lender's discretion*," selling the shares (emphasis added). If Bank One intended to sell the shares, it had to give Johnson written notice ten days prior to the sale. Pursuant to these agreements, Johnson and Layne entered into trade authorization agreements that enabled Bank One to sell the shares without their consent. Though Bank One had the option of selling the collateral shares if the LTV ratios were not met, nothing in the loan agreements obligated it to do so.

In February 2001, along with the rest of the Internet sector, the stock price of PurchasePro fell considerably, such that both loans exceeded their respective LTV ratios.[5] Rather than selling the collateral stock, Bank One entered into discussions with Johnson and Layne to pledge more collateral. The record reveals that Layne and Johnson repeatedly stated their intentions to pledge additional collateral to meet the LTV requirements. On March 6, 2001, Layne wrote that he had "been able to hold [Bank One] off from calling it in because of additional collateral that I have pledged." (Email from Layne to Lichtenberger). On March 19, 2001, Johnson sent an email to Layne inquiring about whether Bank One was "hanging in there." (Email from Johnson to Layne). On March 22, 2001, Bank One sent a letter to Layne informing him that the loan was in default. (Letter from Holton to Layne). That same day, in a conversation with Bank One, Layne stated that "[you] guys have been great ... holding on for this long," but he indicated he would like to begin selling some of the collateral stock. (Tr. of call between Layne and Thompson). After this conversation, Bank One began taking steps to liquidate the collateral stock for both loans. Later that same day, however, Johnson sent an email to Layne under the subject heading "Bank 1" which stated "they want to sell our shares and I want to

**4.** For example, if Johnson utilized the entire line of credit, approximately $2.8 million, the market value of his collateral stock would need to be approximately $6.9 million to comply with the required LTV ratio of 40%.

**5.** Because the loans were over-collateralized, though the market value of the stock was below the required LTV level, it was still greater than the outstanding loan balances. Thus, Bank One could have sold the stock in February, recouped the value of the loans, and returned the surplus proceeds to Layne and Johnson.

stop it with additional collateral—pls call." (Email from Johnson to Layne). Later that night, Layne sent an email to Burr Holton ("Holton"), Bank One's loan officer, under the heading "[h]old off on selling" which stated that "[Johnson] is putting together a collateral package (real estate, additional shares, etc.) to secure the note at acceptable levels." (Email from Layne to Holton). Early the next morning, Layne left a voicemail for Doug Thompson, Bank One's senior trader, stating "[i]t's a possibility that . . . [Johnson]'s gonna put up some additional securities to secure his note and my note and maybe we don't sell right now. So I just wanna put a hold on any . . . trading activity until [Johnson] talks with [the loan officer]." (Voice Message from Layne to Thompson). On April 3, 2001, Layne called Holton and stated that "he was ready to sell his [collateral] stock as soon as possible" and that "he has decided not [to work] with Mr. Johnson on combining their loans and adding additional collateral, which would have cured their default." (Memo. from Holton to File). The next day, April 4, 2001, Layne faxed a letter to Holton which stated that he would not be able to provide additional collateral to satisfy the loan agreement. (Letter from Layne to Holton); 634 (Layne Dep.). The following day, however, Layne changed his mind again and faxed Holton a letter which stated:

> [Johnson] and myself are putting together a collateral package to secure our notes with Bank One. I DO NOT wish for the bank to proceed with any liquidation whatsoever of my PurchasePro stock at this time. I believe we have a strong company and that market conditions will improve, thus enabling the stock to recover to a price that allows me to pay my debt to Bank One in it's [sic] entirety. And that is certainly in everybody's best interest.

(Letter from Layne to Holton). The same day, Layne sent an email to Holton which stated "[Johnson] will be back this afternoon and we will firm the plan then. I would like to have time to discuss this [sic] him before we start liquidation." (Email from Layne to Holton). The record reveals that Johnson and Bank One were involved in discussions in the end of April and May to pay down the balance or pledge additional collateral including his house in Las Vegas. At the end of May, the proposed deal fell through and Bank One sent letters to Johnson notifying him of his continued default on the loans. Throughout the entire time from February to May 2001, Layne and Johnson continued to make principal and interest payments under the terms of the agreement, but both loans significantly exceeded their respective LTV ratios. Bank One finally sold Johnson's PurchasePro shares over four days in July, recovering $524,757.39 in net proceeds to pay down his debt, leaving approximately a $2.2 million unpaid balance.[6]

Layne and Johnson separately filed suit against Bank One in the United States District Court for the Eastern District of Kentucky on a

---

**6.** If the full $2.8 million credit line was used, the market price of the 410,000 shares would need to be approximately $16.89 in order to maintain an LTV ratio of 40%. In July, the shares were sold at an average price of $1.28 over the four-day period. The LTV ratio at the time the collateral was sold was approximately 530%.

number of counts. On January 30, 2002, the cases were consolidated. Bank One filed counterclaims against Johnson and Layne, seeking payment for the deficiencies on the loans. On November 1, 2002, Bank One filed a motion for summary judgment on all counts as well as its counterclaims. On March 26, 2003, the district court granted Bank One's motion. Johnson appeals from that ruling.

## II.  ANALYSIS

\* \* \*

B.   Duty to Preserve Collateral

We first consider Johnson's argument that Bank One violated a duty under Kentucky law to preserve the value of the collateral held in its possession. With respect to the regulation of secured transactions, Kentucky has adopted the Uniform Commercial Code ("U.C.C."), which states that "a secured party shall use reasonable care in the custody and preservation of collateral in the secured party's possession. In the case of chattel paper or an instrument, reasonable care includes taking necessary steps to preserve rights against prior parties unless otherwise agreed." Ky.Rev.Stat. Ann. § 355.9–207. Whether a secured party's duty to preserve collateral applies to pledged shares is an issue of first impression in Kentucky. \* \* \* As the district court noted below, although Kentucky courts have not reviewed the matter, several courts around the country have addressed the issue of whether § 9–207 applies to pledged stock. Before analyzing their holdings, however, we begin our analysis with the U.C.C. itself.

The comment to § 9–207 states that the provision "imposes a duty of care, similar to that imposed on a pledgee at common law, on a secured party in possession of collateral," and cites to §§ 17–18 of the Restatement of Security. U.C.C. § 9–207 cmt. 2. Section 17 of the Restatement is essentially identical to the first sentence of § 9–207, and its accompanying explanatory comment states that "[t]he rule of reasonable care expressed in this Section is confined to the *physical care* of the chattel, whether an object such as a horse or piece of jewelry, or a negotiable instrument or document of title." Restatement of Security § 17 cmt. a (1941) (emphasis added). Section 18 of the Restatement mirrors the second sentence of § 9–207 and addresses "instruments representing claims of the pledgor against third persons." Restatement of Security § 18. Though it deals with negotiable instruments rather than equity investments, § 18 sheds light on the topic of preserving collateral value. Specifically, the explanatory comment accompanying the section states "[t]he pledgee is not liable *for a decline in the value* of pledged instruments, even if timely action could have prevented such decline." Restatement of Security § 18 cmt. a (1941) (emphasis added). In the context of pledged stock, courts have used this language from the Restatement to hold that "a bank has no duty to its borrower to sell collateral stock of declining value." *Capos v. Mid–Am. Nat'l Bank*, 581 F.2d 676, 680 (7th Cir.1978). *See also Tepper v. Chase Manhattan Bank, N.A.*, 376 So.2d 35, 36 (Fla.Dist.Ct.App.1979) (holding that "a pledgee is not liable for a decline in the value of pledged instruments"); *Honolulu*

*Fed. Sav. & Loan Ass'n v. Murphy*, 7 Haw.App. 196, 753 P.2d 807, 816 (1988) (finding that a lender has no duty to preserve the value of pledged securities by financially supporting the issuing company); *FDIC v. Air Atl., Inc.*, 389 Mass. 950, 452 N.E.2d 1143, 1147 (1983) (finding a lender not liable for the "ruinous" decline in the market value of pledged stock); *Marriott Employees' Fed. Credit Union v. Harris*, 897 S.W.2d 723, 728 (1995) (holding that the duty of reasonable care "refers to the physical possession of the stock certificates" and does not impose liability for depreciation in value); *Dubman v. N. Shore Bank*, 85 Wis.2d 819, 271 N.W.2d 148, 151 (1978) (concluding that "our law does not hold a pledgee responsible for a decline in market value of securities pledged to it as collateral for a loan absent a showing of bad faith or a negligent refusal to sell after demand"). As the Seventh Circuit stated, "[i]t is the borrower who makes the investment decision to purchase stock. A lender in these situations merely accepts the stock as collateral, and does not thereby itself invest in the issuing firm." *Capos*, 581 F.2d at 680. "Given the volatility of the stock market, a requirement that a secured party sell shares . . . held as collateral, at a particular time, would be to shift the investment risk from the borrower to the lender." *Air Atl., Inc.*, 452 N.E.2d at 1147.

We agree with the reasoning of these courts and believe that the Kentucky Supreme Court would adopt a similar approach with regards to Ky.Rev.Stat. Ann. § 355.9–207. Specifically, we conclude that under Kentucky law a lender has no obligation to sell pledged stock held as collateral merely because of a market decline. If the borrower is concerned with the decline in the share value, it is his responsibility, rather than that of the lender, to take appropriate remedial steps, such as paying off the loan in return for the collateral, substituting the pledged stock with other equally valued assets, or selling the pledged stock himself and paying off the loan.[8]

---

**8.** Johnson argues that these options were not available to him in this case because he did not have other assets to substitute and was unable to sell the stock on his own because of his insider status. Appellant's Reply Br. at 13–14. Particularized facts of the borrower's situation, however, are insufficient to alter the law and burden the lender with the responsibility of being an investment adviser. The fact that the borrower adopted a risky investment strategy does not transform the legal obligations of the lender unless explicitly specified in the contract. Moreover, the record does not support Johnson's contention that he could not avail himself of other options to preserve the value of his collateral. Johnson had other assets which he could have substituted for the collateral stock. In his deposition, Johnson stated that his house in Las Vegas was valued at around $5.0 million and was free of any mortgages and encumbrances. J.A. at 591–92 (Johnson Dep.). Discussions were held between Bank One and Johnson during the months of April and May specifically about using the Las Vegas house as additional collateral. Furthermore. despite the fact that he was an insider, Johnson could have sold his restricted stock through a Rule 144 transaction so long as he ensured the sale was not a result of any material, non-public information. 17 C.F.R. § 230.144(b). *See, e.g.*, J.A. at 513–16 (Layne's Stock Selling Plan). Johnson stated in his deposition that he was intending to sell his restricted shares pursuant to a selling plan, the proceeds of which he would use "to pay [Bank One] off one hundred percent." J.A. at 591 (Johnson Dep.). Unfortunately, the sale of Johnson's shares under the plan was triggered by the stock reaching a certain price, which it never did.

In his brief, Johnson attempts to distinguish his case from the several cases outlined above, by arguing that in the situation where a loan is *over-secured*, the pledgee has a duty to preserve the surplus. Johnson argues that where a loan is over-secured, the amount of collateral greater than the loan value belongs to the borrower and a duty should be imposed on the secured party to protect that surplus because the secured party has no incentive to do so on its own. By contrast, Johnson argues, where a loan is *under-secured*, the secured party's incentive is the same as that of the borrower, and thus no statutory duty to preserve the value of the collateral is necessary. In support of his argument, Johnson cites to two district court opinions which distinguish between over-secured and under-secured loans. Unfortunately, his theory is neither supported by these cases nor compelling on its own.

Generally, the dual purpose of collateral is to secure financing for the borrower and hedge against credit risk for the lender. Where a lender extends credit solely on the basis of *over-secured* collateral, it is because of perceived heightened risk, and therefore over-collateralization provides the lender with more flexibility. In this case, Bank One agreed to loan Johnson $2.8 million dollars only if he pledged two-and-a-half times that value in PurchasePro stock, or $6.9 million. The underlying rationale was that unless the surplus value was included, the collateral may be insufficient at the time of any default. The LTV ratio was to provide a cushion so that Bank One could either wait for the stock to rebound, restructure the loan, solicit additional collateral, or call the loan with enough time to sell the stock to recoup the value. If accepted, Johnson's argument would bifurcate the collateral amount between the actual value of the loan and the surplus value, and impose a duty upon the lender to preserve the latter. Requiring preservation of the surplus value, however, leaves only the actual value of the loan to serve as collateral and wipes out any flexibility for the lender. Under Johnson's theory, Bank One would have had only $2.8 million worth of stock as collateral for the $2.8 million loan and would have been required to preserve the remaining $4.1 million of surplus. On the first day the market value of the stock fell below the LTV requirement, Bank One would have called the loan or risked liability under § 9–207. Imposing automatic liability for the decreased value of the surplus defeats the inherent purpose of requiring over-collateralization in the first place.

The two cases Johnson cites for support do not stand for the proposition that over-collateralization necessarily implies a duty of the lender to preserve, but rather suggest that the borrower does have a valid interest in the surplus value and therefore his wishes should not be ignored in over-collateralized situations. In *Fidelity Bank & Trust Co. v. Production Metals Corp.*, 366 F.Supp. 613, 618 (E.D.Pa.1973), the district court found that "where the value of the collateral exceeds the amount of the debtor's entire obligation ... there is no justification for a rule authorizing the pledgee to disregard [the pledgor's] interest in the collateral and deprive him of the right to control its disposition for the benefit of both parties." The district court noted that where the pledgee, "*upon request of the pledgor*" fails to take steps to preserve the value of the collateral, "a question should properly be raised as to whether the pledgee has exercised reasonable care under the circumstances." *Id.* (emphasis added). The *Fidelity* court noted, however, that "where the entire obligation of the pledgor exceeds the value of the collateral held by the pledgee . . . the pledgee's refusal to sell the collateral upon request of the pledgor would not, as a matter of law, constitute a breach of his duty to preserve its value." *Id.* at 619. Similarly, in *FDIC v. Caliendo*, 802 F.Supp. 575, 583–84 (D.N.H.1992), the district court, citing *Fidelity Bank*, ruled that a pledgor could bring a claim under § 9–207, where there is an over-collateralized loan, a default by the pledgor, and "the receipt of a reasonable request by the pledgor/borrower to either sell or have the stock redeemed." These two cases do not provide any support for Johnson's argument that a duty to preserve collateral arises simply because of an over-collateralized situation; rather, where there is over-collateralization *and the pledgor has requested liquidation*, the pledgee should respect the pledgor's interest in the surplus value. These two cases are inapposite to Johnson's case, because the record is clear that he never made a request to the bank to sell the collateral to preserve his surplus, but rather urged Bank One as late as May 1, 2001, to do the opposite.

In sum, we conclude that, under Kentucky law, a lender is not under any duty or obligation to sell collateral in its possession merely because the collateral is declining in value, regardless of whether the loan is over-collateralized. Therefore, the district court's grant of summary judgment on this issue is affirmed.

\* \* \*

### III.  CONCLUSION

In summary, we conclude that none of issues Johnson raises on appeal are compelling, and therefore we **AFFIRM** the grant of summary judgment in favor of Bank One.

NOTE

In a deleted portion of *Layne*, the court considered Pledgors' claim that Pledgee bank had failed to conduct a commercially reasonable disposition of the collateral under 9–610 because of its delay in selling the stock. Comment 3 to 9–610 says: "[I]f a secured party \* \* \* holds collateral for a long period of time without disposing of it, and if there is no good reason for not making a prompt disposition, the secured party may be determined not to have acted in a 'commercially reasonable' manner." The court held that the time of the sale was commercially reasonable under the circumstances in this case: the parties were still negotiating until the end of May; Pledgee had to make sure that Rule 144 was complied with; and the timing of the sale was influenced by the thin market volume. Moreover, Johnson never demanded a sale. The opinion noted that courts have been reluctant to second-guess the timing of stock dispositions; pledgees, like pledgors may reasonably believe that the market price of the stock may revive and both parties have incentive for getting the highest price for the stock on resale. See the discussion below.

———————

Both former 9–207(1) and Rev. 9–207(a) leave unspecified the precise nature of the pledgee's duty with respect to collateral, and the case law does not help to specify the duty. In defining the pledgee's duty of reasonable care, two factors are present: disparities in information about the value of the collateral, and the extent to which the secured debt is collateralized. Consider them in turn. With tangible assets, the pledgor and pledgee usually have the same knowledge about its value and what measures would preserve or increase value. Both parties know that leaving a pledged piece of equipment unattended or maintained, for example, is likely to diminish its value. With intangible assets such as investment securities, there is asymmetric information: the pledgor knows about its own investment goals and strategies, and the effect of market changes in a security on the value of its investment portfolio; the pledgee often does not have the same knowledge. Requiring the pledgee to take measures to preserve or increase the value of intangible collateral imposes a duty on the party in an inferior informational position. Thus, the predominant rule that a pledgee's duty with respect to pledged securities is limited to maintaining physical possession is understandable. The few cases in which the pledgee's duty extends to preserving or increasing their value are cases in which the asymmetry in information has been eliminated. These are instances in which the pledgor has demanded that the securities be sold or kept. See Reed v. Central National Bank of Alva, 421 F.2d 113 (10th Cir.1970); Fidelity Bank & Trust Co. of N.J. v. Production Metals Corp., 366 F.Supp. 613 (E.D.Pa.1973); cf. Grace v. Sterling, Grace & Co., 289 N.Y.S.2d 632 (App. Div. 1968) (demand not required; even without communication from pledgor, pledgee knew consequences of failure to convert debentures). The demand conveys to the pledgee information about the pledgee's valuation of the collateral.

The extent of collateralization also is crucial to the pledgee's duty. This is because it affects the secured creditor's incentives to take action that preserves or increases the value of collateral. Where the creditor is overcollateralized, by definition there is sufficient collateral to satisfy the secured debt held. Since the creditor's interest in the collateral is limited by the amount of its debt, any benefit produced by preserving or increasing collateral value above that amount goes to the debtor. The creditor receives none of it. Thus, when the loan is overcollateralized, the creditor has no incentive to take value-preserving or -increasing measures with respect to the collateral. In the circumstances, the debtor and creditor's interests diverge. (True, under former 9–207(2)(a) and 9–207(b)(1), amounts expended by the creditor in preserving the collateral are chargeable to the debtor and are secured by the collateral. However, this at most makes the creditor indifferent between taking and not taking action to do so.) Case law imposing a duty with respect to maintaining or increasing collateral value has done so only when the creditor is overcollateralized and the debtor requests liquidation of the collateral. See In re Solfanelli, 203 F.3d 197 (3d Cir.2000); Dubman v. North Shore Bank, 271 N.W.2d 148 (Wis. 1978) (dicta). The court in FDIC v. Caliendo, 802 F.Supp. 575 (D. N.H. 1992), expressly conditioned the creditor's duty on this fact. Where a creditor is undercollateralized, the creditor and debtor's incentives are aligned: the benefit of preserving or increasing collateral value (up to the amount of the secured debt held) flows to the creditor because it can avoid looking to the debtor to satisfy the debt. The debtor too is benefited because the outstanding deficiency it owes is reduced or at least not increased. There is no need therefore to impose a duty on the pledgee with respect to collateral value.

## 2.   CERTIFICATE IN POSSESSION OF SECURITIES INTERMEDIARY

### a.   CONTROL TEST

By a wide margin the most common form of holding securities today is by an intermediary like a broker or a bank. The control concept was conceived to deal with security interests in certificates held by intermediaries. The following Problems show how it works. As you work through these Problems, ask yourself why more familiar priority rules, such as first-to-file or first-to-notify the intermediary, were abandoned in favor of the novel and complicated control test.

### PROBLEMS

**1.** Seth opened a securities account (8–501(a)), designated Account Number 987654321, with a broker-dealer firm (Firm), a securities intermediary (8–102(a)(14)), which buys, sells and holds securities on behalf of its customers, as well as for its own account. Seth placed a buy order with Firm for 1,000 shares of Consolidated, Inc. When the trade was completed, Firm credited the stock to Seth's account, giving Seth a security entitlement (8–102(a)(17), 8–501(b)) with respect to the stock. Seth is now an entitlement holder (8–102(a)(7)). All of Consolidated's shares are represented by security certificates (8–102(a)(16)), most of which are in the possession of Depository Trust Corporation, a clearing corporation (8–102(a)(5)) and a securities intermediary, as registered owner. Firm is one of DTC's many customers, and the trade in question was cleared through DTC which holds the shares in Firm's account. Settlement through DTC was on a net basis by book entries. At the time Seth opened his account, he granted Firm a security interest in his account and all of the financial assets (8–102(a)(9)) held in the account to secure any future advances made by Firm to Seth. Later Seth borrowed $10,000 from Bank. He executed a security agreement describing the collateral as "1,000 shares of Consolidated, Inc. stock."

a.   Bank promptly filed a financing statement containing the description of the collateral in the security agreement. Subsequently, Seth filed in Chapter 7 bankruptcy. In a contest between Bank and Seth's trustee in bankruptcy with respect to the stock, who is prior? See 9–108(d) (sufficiency of description); 9–312(a) (perfection by filing); and 9–317(a)(2) (priority of lien creditor).

b. Bank promptly filed a financing statement containing the description of the collateral in the security agreement. Subsequently Seth borrowed $30,000 from Lender and executed a security agreement granting Lender a security interest in "Acct. No. 987654321 held by Firm." Lender promptly filed a financing statement authorized by Seth containing that description of the collateral. If Seth defaults on both loans, which creditor is prior with respect to the stock, Bank or Lender? See 9–308(f) (perfection of security interest in securities account); 9–328(7) (priority of security interests in investment property); and 9–322(a) (residual priority rule). See also 9–108(d) referred to in Problem a. above.

c. Bank promptly filed a financing statement containing the description of the collateral in the security agreement. In addition Bank sent Firm a copy of the security agreement and financing statement, as well as the number of Seth's account.

(i) Subsequently, Firm advanced Seth a margin loan of $15,000. If Seth defaults on both loans, which creditor is prior with respect to the stock, Bank or Firm? See 8–106(e) (control by securities intermediary); 9–106 (control); 9–328(1) (priority of secured party having control) and (3) (priority of securities intermediary).

(ii) With Seth's authorization, Firm agreed to comply with any orders by Bank regarding transfer or redemption of the stock without further consent by Seth. Subsequently Firm advanced Seth $15,000. If Seth defaults on both loans, which creditor is prior with respect to the stock, Bank or Firm? See 8–106(d) (control by purchaser) and (e); 9–106 (control); 9–328(3) (priority of securities intermediary.) See Comment 4 to 9–328. How could Bank ever be prior to Firm? See 9–339.

**2.** Debtor grants Bank One a security interest in an account Debtor holds with Broker containing 1,000 shares of ABC stock. Bank One and Debtor agree that Bank's attorney can foreclose on the account only if Debtor defaults on the terms of the loan. Broker agrees to the arrangement. Later, Debtor grants Bank Two a security interest in the same account with Broker. Bank Two and Debtor's agreement allows Bank Two to foreclose on Debtor's account only if Debtor has defaulted on Bank Two's loan, and again Broker agrees to the arrangement. In both cases Debtor retains the right to trade the assets in its account. Neither Bank One nor Two files a financing statement covering Debtor's account with Broker. If Debtor files a petition in bankruptcy and its trustee alleges that it has priority in Debtor's account over both Bank One and Two, who will prevail? See 8–106(d)(3); Comment 7 to 8–106, Example 11; 9–317(a)(2).

**3.** Debtor holds an account with Broker containing bonds issued by the ABC Corporation. The bonds are backed by a letter of credit issued by a bank. The bank undertakes in the letter to pay to the owner of the bond the face amount of the bond plus accrued interest in the event ABC fails to do so when the bond matures. On January 1 Debtor grants SP1 a security interest in the account administered by Broker. At the same time SP1 files a proper financing statement covering the account and has the bank agree to pay over to it proceeds of the letter of credit if the letter is drawn upon. On February 1 SP2 obtains a security interest in Debtor's account with Broker. SP2, Debtor and Broker agree that SP2 can dispose of the assets in the account only if Debtor defaults on the terms of the loan. As between SP1 and SP2, if Debtor defaults on its loan obligations to SP1 and SP2, who has priority in Debtor's account? 9–328(2). In the proceeds from the letter of credit? 9–102(a)(77), 9–107, 9–322(c), 9–322(f)(1), 9–329.

### NOTE

Why the control priority rule? Professor Rogers explains in his Policy Perspectives article, 43 UCLA at 1437–1449, that the impetus for the 1994 revision was growing concern about the adequacy of the existing system of securities clearance and settlement. What if, owing to an unanticipated excess in trading volume or the failure of a major brokerage house, sellers do not get paid and buyers do not receive the securities they have purchased? In short, trades do not clear and settlements are not made. The failure of some trades to clear might, in a chain reaction, prevent others from clearing; the failure of one brokerage firm might have a domino effect on the solvency of other firms unpaid in their trades with that firm; systemic collapse might result that would bring stock exchanges to a stop. Liquidity is essential to the securities market; an investor's nightmare is being unable to unload securities in a rapidly falling market like the one-day 1987 crash. In a systemic crisis, the value of the stocks and bonds in which trillions of dollars are invested would be at great risk.

But what do mundane rules about the priority of security interests in securities have to do with the potential for meltdown of the clearance and settlement system? After a discussion of the importance of the control principle at the highest industry level, the clearing corporation, Professor Rogers relates the issue to retail transactions:

> The control priority rule works in essentially the same fashion to facilitate settlement of transactions involving investors at the retail level. * * * Consider the case of an individual investor who purchases a few thousand dollars worth of securities through her broker. Once the broker executes the trade on her behalf in the relevant market or exchange, the broker itself is obligated to settle, that is, receive and pay for the securities. As in the clearing bank-dealer arrangement described above, the broker in this retail level transaction may well make payment for the customer's purchase in advance of completion of final funds transfer arrangements by the customer to pay the broker, for instance, if the broker permits the customer to pay for the purchase by check. Accordingly, either by general law or by specific agreement, the securities that the broker has received and paid for on behalf of the

customer should be subject to a lien in favor of the broker to secure the obligation of the customer to make payment. Under the control priority rule of 9–115(5)(a) [Rev.9–328(3)], the broker can rely with confidence on such an arrangement. When a customer purchases securities through a broker and holds the securities through a securities account with that broker, it will be the case that the broker will be holding the securities in such fashion that the broker has the power to have the securities sold off without further action by the customer; that is, the broker, qua secured party, has control. Thus, the broker can safely permit its customer to make payment for securities purchased by check or in some other fashion that does not assure the broker of receipt of immediately available funds, because the broker can be assured that it will be able to realize upon its security interest in the event of a default by the customer without concern that the customer may have entered into transactions with others that might be thought to give the others conflicting security interests in that property.

The control priority principle that underlies the secured transactions rules of the 1994 revision is equally well-suited to routine commercial finance transactions. It provides the basis for clear and simple rules covering such transactions ranging from the simple physical pledge of certificated securities to more complex arrangements in which securities and other financial assets held though a securities account are used as collateral. Though the control concept may, at first examination, seem novel, it is, in fact fully consistent with basic principles of the law of secured transactions; indeed, the control concept can usefully be regarded as merely a generalization from several specific rules that have long been part of the law of securities and secured transactions.

Rogers, Policy Perspectives, 43 UCLA L. Rev. at 1437–1449.

The Revision expands the role of control in perfection and priority beyond just investment property. Sections 9–104–9–107 respectively define when control occurs with respect to deposit accounts as original collateral, electronic chattel paper, investment property, and letter-of-credit rights. Section 9–322(a)'s basic priority rules, are made subject, via 9–322(f)(1), to the control priority rules of 9–327–9–329 governing deposit accounts, investment property, and letter-of-credit rights. Why the Revision expands the role of control priority is uncertain. As we indicated above, security interests in investment property don't appear to have the potential to produce externalities on the order of meltdowns in the clearance and settlement network. Even if they did, the same isn't true of assets other than investment property such as deposit accounts and letter-of-credit rights. Comment 3 to 9–328 justifies control priority for investment property by settled practice: before 1994 filing was not a permissible method of perfection, and control priority preserves the expectations of parties who perfect by taking control of investment property. Again, even if so, this doesn't justify expanding control priority to types of collateral in which control wasn't a perfection method under former Article 9.

An interesting case on whether a secured party has achieved control of investment property follows. This case was decided before Revised Article 9 was enacted, and the references to former 9–115 are now found in several provisions of Article 9 that we have considered.

# First Nat. Bank of Palmerton v. Donaldson, Lufkin & Jenrette Securities Corp.

United States District Court, E.D. Pa., 1999.
38 UCC Rep.Serv.2d 564.

■ Yohn, J.

Plaintiff First National Bank of Palmerton ("the bank") has brought suit against Donaldson, Lufkin & Jenrette Securities Corporation ("DLJ"), claiming negligence, breach of fiduciary duty, and fraud. The suit arises out of a security interest taken by the bank in marketable securities held for the debtor in a DLJ brokerage account. Pending before the court is defendant's motion to dismiss. The court finds that the bank has failed to plead the necessary elements to state a cause of action for negligence, breach of fiduciary duty, or fraud. Therefore, plaintiff's complaint will be dismissed.

On May 15, 1996, the bank entered into a loan agreement with Pankesh Kadam and Alka Patel ("first loan"). As part of this agreement, Kadamand Patel signed a promissory note in the amount of $50,000. The parties to the loan agreement also signed a security agreement in which the borrowers granted the bank a security interest in, among other things, marketable securities registered in Patel's name and held by DLJ in Account Number 219–141298. The securities were valued at $56,350.

On the same day that Patel and Kadam entered into the loan agreement, the bank sent a letter to DLJ explaining that Patel had "pledged the marketable securities" and "she agreed to have the bank perfect its interest in the stocks." In the letter, the bank requested that DLJ either "forward the stock certificates or an agreement from [DLJ] that the securities will remain in the account until notification from the bank." At the end of the letter, Patel had signed an acceptance and acknowledgment whereby she "consented to the stock certificates being forwarded to The First National Bank of Palmerton." DLJ forwarded the stock certificates to the bank.

Some time after the Bank received the certificates from DLJ, Patel allegedly requested that the stocks be returned to her brokerage account to enable her to trade them. The bank agreed and on August 20, 1996, sent the stock certificates back to DLJ. Accompanying the stocks was a transmittal letter in which the bank's vice-president stated, "The stocks are being returned to you to be retained in Ms. Patel's account. It is our understanding that she will trade the stocks, however, maintain the principal balance in her account #219–141298." The complaint contains no allegation that DLJ ever responded to this letter.

On June 6, 1997, Patel individually executed a second promissory note for $25,000 ("second loan"). Collateral for the loan consisted of the DLJ brokerage account Number 219–141298 then valued at $60,520.52. Patel signed a security agreement and a collateral pledge agreement which granted the bank an assignment and security interest in the account. On May 22, 1997, prior to the execution of the promissory note and security agreement, the bank sent DLJ a copy of the collateral pledge agreement. The bank also requested that DLJ sign and return an acknowledgment form whereby it would agree that the bank, as the secured party, would have the sole right to make withdrawals from the collateral. The acknowledgment form was signed by the bank's vice-president and Patel. DLJ, however, did not sign the form or return it to the bank.

Seven months later, on December 15, 1997, Kadam and Patel defaulted on the first loan. At the same time, Patel defaulted on her payments under the second loan. When the bank tried to liquidate the securities in the collateral brokerage account in order to apply the funds toward the borrowers' outstanding debt, it learned that Patel had liquidated the account the previous month. Plaintiff alleges that Patel liquidated the account without obtaining express written consent from the bank. In an effort to recover its loss, the bank has brought suit against DLJ claiming that by allowing Patel to liquidate the brokerage account, DLJ was negligent, breached its fiduciary duty, and committed fraud.

DLJ argues that the bank has failed to plead facts sufficient to state a cause of action for negligence, breach of fiduciary duty, or fraud. With regard to the negligence and breach of contract claims, DLJ asserts that it had no duty to act on behalf of the bank. * * * As such a duty is a required element of the claims of negligence and breach of fiduciary duty, DLJ contends that plaintiff's complaint is deficient with regard to these causes of action. * * *

## A. NEGLIGENCE AND BREACH OF FIDUCIARY DUTY CLAIMS

To state a cause of action for either breach of fiduciary duty or negligence, the bank must allege the existence of a duty owed to it by DLJ. * * * DLJ claims that the bank did not perfect its security interest in the securities held in the DLJ account in accordance with the Pennsylvania Uniform Commercial Code. Because the bank failed to perfect its security interest, defendant asserts that it "had no duty under the UCC to act for the benefit of the Bank." Absent this duty, DLJ contends, the allegations in the complaint do not support the bank's claims of negligence and breach of fiduciary duty.

Sections eight and nine of the Uniform Commercial Code [as revised 1994] ("UCC"), as codified in the Pennsylvania statutes, set forth the rights and duties of parties participating in secured transactions involving marketable securities such as those maintained in Patel's account with DLJ. For purposes of the UCC, the collateral at issue here falls into the category of investment property, which includes certificated and uncertificated securities, security entitlements, and security accounts. The term "security entitlement" is defined as "the rights and property interest of a person who holds securities or other financial assets through a securities intermediary." Title 13, section 8102(a), UCC Comment ¶ 17. The UCC defines a "securities intermediary" as "a bank or broker.... that in the ordinary course of its business maintains securities accounts for others and is acting in that capacity." Title 13, section 8102(a). Both parties agree that DLJ qualifies as a securities intermediary who maintained Patel's securities in her brokerage account. Patel's interest in these securities in her account constituted a security entitlement and Patel was the entitlement holder or the "person identified in the records of a securities intermediary as the person having a security entitlement against the securities intermediary." Title 13, section 8102(a).

In the instant case, Patel granted to the bank a security interest in her security entitlements. In and of itself, this transaction did not establish a duty between DLJ, the securities intermediary, and the bank, the secured party. Although Pennsylvania courts do not appear to have considered this issue yet, the drafters of the Uniform Commercial Code have stated that a "securities intermediary owes no duties to the secured party, unless the intermediary has entered into a 'control' agreement in which it agrees to act on entitlement orders originated by the secured party." Uniform Commercial Code § 8–507, 2C U.L.A. 147 (Supp.1998) (citing to UCC § 8–106). A "control agreement" is created when "the securities intermediary has agreed that it will comply with entitlement orders originated by the purchaser without further consent by the entitlement holder." Id. § 8106(d). Thus, the legal duty owed by DLJ to the bank that is necessary to support claims of negligence and breach of fiduciary duty, could arise only if the bank, Patel, and DLJ all agreed that the bank had the power "to have the securities sold or transferred without further action by [Patel]." Title 13, section 8106(d)(2), UCC Comment 7.

Control of a security entitlement can be achieved in one of two ways: through a control agreement or by having the secured party become the entitlement holder. See Title 13, section 8106(d). To acquire a securities entitlement and thus become the entitlement holder, the bank would have needed to establish a separate securities account to which DLJ would credit Patel's securities. See id. § 8501(b). Plaintiff does not allege that this occurred and, thus, it cannot claim to be the entitlement holder. This leaves a control agreement as the sole means by which the bank could have perfected its security interest.

Consequently, in this particular case, whether the bank perfected its security interest and whether DLJ owes any duty to the bank both depend on whether the bank controlled the securities and account by means of a control agreement.

To obtain control through an agreement in conformance with section 8106(d)(2), a secured party cannot simply notify the intermediary of the secured party's interest and the debtor's willingness to allow entitlement orders to issue from the secured party—"it is essential that the.... securities intermediary.... actually be a party to the agreement." Title 13, section 8106(d)(2), UCC Comment 5; see William D. Hawkland et al., Uniform Commercial Code Series § 8–106:04 (Main Volume 1996) (stating that sending notice of security interest to intermediary is insufficient to establish control through agreement). While the intermediary must "specifically agree" to allow the secured party to issue entitlement orders, the statute does not require that the intermediary agree in writing. See Title 13, section 8106(d)(2), UCC Comment 5; Hawkland, supra (noting that asserting existence of unwritten agreement likely would occur as "a rescue effort in litigation for a transaction in which someone made some fairly obvious blunders in practical planning"). The bank acknowledges that no written control agreement exists in this case. Instead, the bank claims that DLJ's conduct in response to three separate letters from the bank evidences its assent to follow entitlement orders from the bank without concurrence from Patel.

The first of these letters sent to DLJ on May 15, 1996, stated in relevant part:

> "As per our prior discussions, Alka P. Patel has pledged the marketable securities in Account #219–141298 to the First National Bank of Palmerton for a loan. As a result, she agreed to have the bank perfect its interest in the stocks. Please forward the stock certificates or an agreement from your firm that the securities will remain in the account until notification from the bank."

Below the closing and signature of the bank's vice-president, the letter included the following paragraph:

> "ACCEPTANCE: I acknowledge that I have pledged the securities in my stock Account #219–141298 and hereby consent to the stock certificates being forwarded to the First National Bank of Palmerton."

Patel's signature appeared beneath this paragraph. In response to this letter, DLJ sent the stock certificates to the bank.

The bank claims that "it clearly thought that [DLJ's forwarding of the stock certificates to the bank] implied DLJ's agreement to the terms of the security arrangement generally." The complaint, however, contains no allegation that DLJ was in possession of or had knowledge of the security agreement such that it could have agreed with all or any of its terms. Furthermore, DLJ's conduct evidences only that it complied with Patel's explicit authorization which extended exclusively to delivering the stock certificates to the bank. Thus, despite what the bank says it "thought", the complaint contains no evidence of a control agreement having been entered into at this point.

On August 20, 1996, the bank sent the certificates back to DLJ accompanied by a transmittal letter in which the bank stated:

> "Enclosed please find the following stock certificates in the name of Alka Patel:

> "2000 shares Hospitality Properties Trust

> "1175 shares Q Sound Labs, Inc.

"The stocks are being returned to you to be retained in Ms. Patel's account. It is our understanding that she will trade the stocks, however, maintain the principal balance in her account #219–141298."

Complaint, Attachment D. DLJ credited Patel's account with the securities.

In its memorandum in opposition to DLJ's motion to dismiss, the bank states that "when [it] returned the certificates to DLJ...., it relied on its understanding that DLJ would be bound by the terms of the parties' agreement, which was that, in the absence of a possessory pledge, DLJ would undertake to see that the principal balance in the account would remain in its custody." Plaintiff's claim appears somewhat disingenuous, however, given that the complaint contains no allegations that any agreement to that effect between DLJ and the bank actually existed at the time the bank sent the certificates to DLJ. Perhaps in the alternative, the bank also contends that DLJ's acceptance of the returned certificates demonstrated its agreement to maintain the balance in the account.

Neither the UCC nor Pennsylvania contract law require that acceptance of an offer be in writing or even be an express oral acknowledgment-conduct can suffice. see Hawkland supra (stating that nothing in UCC requires that control agreement be in writing); Occidental Chem. Corp. v. Environmental Liners, Inc., 859 F.Supp. 791, 794 (E.D.Pa.1994) (stating that offer may be accepted through conduct of offeree); Schreiber v. Olan Mills, 627 A.2d 806, 808 (Pa.Sup.Ct.1993) (noting that "one may look to the 'conduct' of the parties to ascertain the acceptance of the agreement"). Whatever form the acceptance takes, however, it must be "unconditional and absolute." O'Brien v. Nationwide Mut. Ins. Co., 689 A.2d 254, 258 (Pa.Super.Ct.1997); see Schreiber, 627 A.2d at 808 (holding that no contract existed where "[t]here was no 'unconditional' manifestation on the part of [the defendant] that a contract was acknowledged by behavior of the defendant"). DLJ's "conduct" in receiving the returned certificates and crediting them to Patel's account does not meet this standard. * * *

DLJ contends that, as with the first loan and security interest, no agreement existed between DLJ, Patel, and the bank such that the bank had control of the account pursuant to § 8106(d)(2) In response, the bank argues that, because a security agreement was already in place with respect to the securities, and the bank had agreed to maintain the principal balance regardless of which securities were held in the account, the bank "perfected" its security interest in the account when it "forwarded to DLJ the collateral pledge agreement signed by the debtor." In essence, the bank seems to be arguing that a control agreement existed with respect to the entire contents of the account as a result of DLJ's having accepted the securities back from the bank, and consequently, a control agreement was in place with regard to the account itself.

If a control agreement had already existed between the parties and Patel, plaintiff's argument would have some merit. See Title 13, [former] section 9115 (stating that with regard to control, "a secured party has control over a securities account.... if the secured party has control over all security entitlements.... in the securities account"). As discussed above, however, no control agreement was in place at the time the bank negotiated the second loan.

Taken individually, the actions of DLJ do not support a finding that a control agreement existed pursuant to section 8106(d)(2). Nevertheless, the bank argues that DLJ became "obligated to recognize the security interest because of the pattern of dealings among the parties during the whole course of the transactions." DLJ's alleged conduct during this period amounts to the following: (1) not creating and forwarding a written agreement regarding the certificates pursuant to the bank's first letter on May 15, 1996; (2) placing the stock certificates into the brokerage account of Patel, the registered owner and entitlement holder; (3) not signing and returning to the bank an acknowledgment of Patel's assignment of a second interest in her account; (4) following Patel's order to liquidate the account. None of these alleged actions, viewed individually or as a whole, evidence an intent to enter into an agreement with the bank and Patel such that DLJ would accept entitlement orders emanating solely from the bank. As no agreement existed, no duty arose between DLJ and the bank. Because the bank cannot allege the existence of a duty, I must dismiss plaintiff's negligence and breach of fiduciary duty claims. * * *

IT IS HEREBY ORDERED that the motion to dismiss is GRANTED and plaintiff's complaint is dismissed with prejudice.

NOTES

**1.**  Suppose Patel, DJF and Bank had agreed that DJF would comply with Bank's orders to sell without further consent by Patel, but the agreement also allowed Patel to continue to trade the stock held by DLJ. This means that if Patel issued an "entitlement order" (8–102(a)(8)) to DLJ directing it to transfer stock, it would have to comply. Would Patel's power to transfer stock without further consent of Bank invalidate Bank's control status? How can Bank be said to have control if Patel can order DLJ to sell the property Bank supposedly controls? See 8–106(f) and Comment 7. How does this practice differ from what happened in the principal case?

**2.**  Control agreements with security intermediaries usually are detailed documents, not the somewhat skeletal agreement alleged by the bank in *Palmerton*. Common clauses include the intermediary's obligation not to agree to comply with entitlement orders by third parties without the secured creditor's consent, a subordination of specific existing and after-acquired liens in favor of the intermediary, specification of the conditions under which the creditor can exercise control and the means of doing so, and the indemnification of the intermediary against liability arising from its compliance with the control agreement. Form control agreements appear in Sandra M. Rocks & Robert A. Wittie, Getting Control of Control Agreements, 31 UCC L. J. 318 (1999).

### b.   ASSET MANAGEMENT ACCOUNTS

Asset management accounts, like the one in the Problem below, have become a common feature of brokerage accounts. The fact that they resemble a bank account is no accident. They contain a great deal of wealth, but there have been problems on how to categorize them. Are they "deposit accounts" (9–102(a)(29)) or "investment property" (9–102(a)(49))? See 8–501(a) and (b), and Comments 1 and 2.

### PROBLEM

Customer holds stocks and bonds in an account with Royce Hall Securities (RHS), a broker-dealer and securities intermediary. The account also contains a Liquid Asset Fund (LAF), a money market fund that RHS maintains in the accounts of each of its customers. Customers may acquire shares (each share is maintained at the price of $1) in their LAFs by depositing cash in the fund; moreover all bond interest and stock dividends, as well as all proceeds from sales of securities, are automatically poured over into the fund. The cash flowing into the LAF is invested by RHS for Customer's benefit in corporate commercial paper (obligations of corporations with 90 to 120 day maturities) and short term U.S. Treasuries; hence, the return on the fund is at relatively low money market rates. Money may be withdrawn by Customer at any time by (i) a written order or an oral order made through authorized telephone access, (ii) a check drawn on RHS Bank & Trust, a subsidiary of RHS, or (iii) use of a Visa card issued by RHS Bank & Trust. Customer has found the account extremely convenient. Not only may it be used to "park" cash but also it obviates the need to have a local bank account. The return on the LAF is always higher than the interest paid on checking accounts by commercial banks, and no per-check charges are made. At times, between securities transactions, Customer has very large sums of money in the LAF. How would Bank perfect a security interest in the LAF and of what use would a security interest be in an asset management account, the proceeds of which Customer can withdraw by writing a check anytime it wishes? The definition of "deposit account" in 9–102(a)(29) excludes "investment property." See 8–501(a) and (b) and Comments 1 and 2.

Asset management accounts, the generic term for the arrangement described in the Problem, are discussed in In re *Van Kylen*, 98 B.R. 455 (Bankr. W.D.Wis. 1989), at 459, n.2:

> 2.   Cash Management Accounts Have Been Noted as an Instance of "Competition From Non-bank Financial Institutions" With Conventional Banking Entities.
>
> Other non-bank financial institutions also compete with commercial banks and savings institutions to some extent. In the recent period of high interest rates, competition from money-market funds for the savings of depositors who otherwise would use the services of commercial banks and savings institutions has been intense. Moreover, there appears to be a growing tendency for these non-bank institutions to

offer services similar to those offered by banks and savings institutions. Major brokerage houses offer their customers diverse financial services. For example, Merrill Lynch, Pierce, Fenner and Smith has a Cash Management Account in which the customer receives interest on balances maintained, checking facilities, a charge card, and lending privileges.

F. Beutel & Milton R. Schroeder, Bank Officer's Handbook of Commercial Law 5–45 (5th ed. 1982). Merrill Lynch pioneered these accounts in the 1970s, and "Cash Management Account" is their registered trademark.

## E.   UNCERTIFICATED SECURITIES

### 1.   MUTUAL FUNDS

The movement of investors, particularly individual investors, away from holding individual securities and into mutual funds has been pronounced for several years. In the 1990s it became a tidal wave. Traditional brokerage houses like Merrill Lynch, which 40 years ago did not offer mutual funds, have fought competition from giant mutual fund providers like Fidelity and Vanguard by offering a full range of mutual funds. Today trillions of dollars are invested in American mutual funds.

There are two types of mutual funds. By far the most common is the open-end fund which will issue as many shares as investors wish to purchase, except in unusual cases in which the fund is temporarily closed to new investors because of a perceived lack of attractive securities in which to invest new funds. Open-end fund issuers will redeem shares from their shareholders at net asset value as a matter of right. Closed-end funds are much less popular. They issue a fixed number of shares at the inception of the fund and do not redeem shares from shareholders. Thus, shareholders who wish to liquidate must find buyers for their shares; by the same token new investors must find shareholders willing to sell. However, since closed-end funds are usually listed on securities exchanges, thereby creating a secondary market for them, trading shares in closed-end funds is usually as simple as trading other listed securities. A characteristic of closed-end funds is that, after the initial issuance of shares, the shares tend to trade at a discount to the net asset value of the securities held by the fund. Sometimes the discount is a substantial one. Open-end funds are securities under 8–102(a)(15), and 8–103(b) considers close-end funds securities.

PROBLEM

Barbara wearied of attempting to pick the right stock for her investment portfolio and decided to make all her investments in the future through mutual funds. "Let the experts pick the stock," became her creed. Her procedure was to scan financial publications for information on well managed, "no load" (no sales commission charged) stock and bond funds.

When she had made her selection, she would call the fund and ask for a prospectus and an application to purchase. She followed this course with the Oak Growth Fund, a member of the Oak Family of Funds, whose portfolio included mostly mid-cap growth stocks. She sent the application, along with her check for $25,000, to this fund. In her application she agreed that all dividends would be reinvested. She received a document informing her that she was the owner of 2,280 shares of the Oak Growth Fund and that her account number was 123456789. Periodic statements of her account would be sent to her quarterly.

Barbara applied for a loan from Bank. In the past, when Barbara had invested in stocks or bonds, she always insisted on having the securities registered in her name with the stock or bond certificate in her possession. When she wished to borrow money from Bank, it was a simple matter to take the certificate out of her safe deposit box and pledge it with Bank. But when she wished to borrow money on the security of her position in the Oak Growth Fund, she had nothing to offer Bank for security but the document referred to above. Before making the loan, Bank had Barbara sign a security agreement granting Bank a security interest in "all debtor's shares of the Oak Growth Fund, now owned and hereafter acquired, in Account Number 123456789 of the Oak Family of Funds." Bank promptly filed a financing statement.

a.   How would Bank perfect by control in this case? See 8–103(b), 8–106(c); 8–301(b); Comment 3 to 8–301 (discussing "delivery").

b.   How would Bank perfect by control if instead of buying the mutual funds directly from the issuer, Barbara bought them through her broker who held them as a securities intermediary in her securities account? Does Bank obtain control pursuant to 8–106(c) for an uncertificated security (8–102(a)(18)) or under 8–106(d) for a security entitlement (8–102(a)(17))? See Comment 3 to 8–106.

NOTE

Mutual funds are almost entirely uncertificated, and corporate bonds are also mostly held in electronic book entry form. Issuance of corporate stock in an uncertificated form through a direct registration system would offer investors a third option, in addition to the traditional ones of having a certificate issued directly to the investor or having stock held in the street name of a securities intermediary. Historically state corporate law frequently has prevented the practice by requiring that shares be represented by certificates; see Egon Guttman, Modern Securities Transfers 1.04[2] (3d ed. 1987). Most state corporate statutes now permit issuance of uncertificated shares. This option would allow the investor to have its name registered on the issuer's records as the owner, but, instead of sending the investor a stock certificate, the issuing company would make an electronic book entry in its records and send the investor the kind of statement that mutual fund investors now receive. This method offers the investor both the convenience of having the issuing company (through its transfer agent) do all of the record keeping that investors who have their securities held in a street name or who hold mutual funds now enjoy, as well as the advantages of being the registered owner and having (i) the power to select the broker through which the stock is sold, and (ii) the opportunity to participate in corporate dividend reinvestment programs open only to registered owners. If the issuer is a close corporation, an uncertificated share relieves the investor of having to keep track of a stock certificate.

The posture of the direct registration stockholder is similar but not identical to that of the mutual fund investor. The rules that apply in the above Problem for security interests in uncertificated mutual fund securities would apply in direct registration cases. However, a major difference between mutual funds and direct registration systems lies in the fact that mutual fund investors, at least with respect to open-end funds, do not need to sell their shares in order to withdraw their investment because mutual funds agree to redeem the owner's shares at any time. Stock issuers make no such agreement. A direct registration investor who wishes to sell would instruct the issuing company's transfer agent to route the shares to a broker of the investor's choice who would sell them for the investor. Transfers would be by electronic book entries, and the investor could engage in whatever negotiations it chooses with the broker about the terms of the sale. Presumably, such a system would result in more competition between brokers and better service and rates to investors.

In the following case, we see the mechanics of perfecting a security interest in a mutual fund and the function of the transfer agent.

## In re Pfautz

United States Bankruptcy Court, W.D. Mo., 2001.
264 B.R. 551.

■ ARTHUR B. FEDERMAN, CHIEF JUDGE.

The Chapter 7 trustee (the Trustee) filed a motion to compel Liberty Bank to turn over certain uncertificated securities, owned by debtors Jerry and Suzanne Pfautz, in which Liberty Bank claims a security interest. * * *

Debtors granted Liberty Bank a security interest in uncertificated securities. Liberty Bank and the debtors established a loan collateral account to hold the securities. The loan collateral account is administered by a transfer agent designated by the issuer of the securities. The transfer agent will only release the securities upon instructions from Liberty Bank. In order to perfect a security interest in uncertificated securities under Missouri law the secured party must exercise control over the securities. Control is defined as having the power to sell the securities without the consent of the owners. The Third Party Pledge Agreement grants Liberty Bank the authority to dispose of the securities in the event of default, but does not specifically say that Liberty Bank can sell the securities without the consent of the debtors. Did debtors agree to allow Liberty Bank to sell the securities without their consent when they signed the Third Party Pledge Agreement, thus granting Liberty Bank control of the securities?

The language in the Third Party Pledge Agreement authorizes the secured party to dispose of the collateral in the event of default. By signing the Agreement, the debtors agreed to allow Liberty Bank to sell the uncertificated securities without their consent. Thus, Liberty Bank properly perfected its security interest.

Sometime prior to January of 1998, debtors acquired 289.786 shares of Guardian Park Avenue Fund–A (Guardian), Account Number 52576–3, in the form of uncertificated securities (the Uncertificated Securities). On January 14, 1998, debtors executed a "Third Party Pledge Agreement" in which they granted Liberty Bank a security interest in the Uncertificated Securities. On May 1, 1998, debtors, Liberty Bank, and State Street Bank and Trust Company (State Street), as the transfer agent for Guardian, established a separate Loan Collateral Account by executing a Loan Collateral Account Establishment Request for Recording of Assignment as Security (The Request). The debtors, a vice-president of Liberty Bank, and the Client Relations Officer for State Street signed the Request.

On January 23, 2001, debtors filed a Chapter 7 bankruptcy petition. As of December 31, 2000, the Uncertificated Securities had a market value of $11,933.39. On February 14, 2001, Liberty Bank filed a motion to lift the automatic stay to allow it to foreclose its security interest in the Uncertificated Securities. The Trustee filed a response in which he claimed that Liberty Bank had failed to prove its security interest was perfected. On March 21, 2001, this Court held a hearing on Liberty Bank's motion, which it then continued at the request of the parties to allow counsel for Liberty Bank to obtain additional documentation of perfection. * * * On June 6, 2001, the Trustee and counsel for Liberty Bank deposed Traci Connery. Ms. Connery is a division manager for National Financial Data Services (NFDS), a subsidiary of State Street, and the servicing agent, or record-keeping agent, for Guardian. Ms. Connery testified that NFDS maintains Guardian's mutual fund accounts. Ms. Connery also testified as to the procedures NFDS uses to establish a loan collateral account, and the procedure for redeeming any uncertificated securities subject to a security interest. Ms. Connery stated that NFDS transferred the Uncertificated Securities into the loan collateral account on June 9, 1998, and that, since that time, the loan collateral account has contained a "stop transfer," which freezes the assets. Ms. Connery also testified that NFDS would only act upon instructions from Liberty Bank to release the collateral held in the account. She further stated that the release does not require the signature of the debtors. The Trustee objected to some of Ms. Connery's replies. On June 11, 2001, counsel for Liberty Bank submitted the transcript, and this Court is now prepared to rule.

Uncertificated securities are securities that are not represented by certificates. Pursuant to the Uniform Commercial Code, uncertificated securities are defined as investment property:

(f) "Investment property" means:

(i) A security, whether certificated or uncertificated. [Rev. 9–102(a)(49)]

A secured party perfects its security interest in uncertificated securities by controlling the securities:

(4) Perfection of a security interest in investment property is governed by the following rules:

(a) A security interest in investment property may be perfected by control. [Rev. 9–314(a)]

A purchaser, or secured party, has control of an uncertificated security if it has accepted delivery, or if the issuer agrees to comply with the purchaser's instructions without consent from the registered owner:

(c) A purchaser has "control" of an uncertificated security if:

(1) The uncertificated security is delivered to the purchaser; or

(2) The issuer has agreed that it will comply with the instructions originated by the purchaser without further consent by the registered owner. [8–106]

Liberty Bank does not contend that it has accepted delivery of the Uncertificated Securities by becoming the registered owner. The issue, therefore, is whether Liberty Bank can demand that Guardian, or its transfer agent, redeem or dispose of the Uncertificated Securities without regard to the Pfautzes' wishes. The Trustee contends that neither the Third Party Pledge Agreement nor the Loan Collateral Account contains a provision wherein the issuer agrees to comply with instructions from Liberty Bank without consent of the debtors. Liberty Bank argues that it controls the loan collateral account and is, therefore, perfected, since the issuer will respond only to its instructions.

I begin with the exhibits from both the trial and the deposition. The Third Party Pledge Agreement is signed by Jerry and Suzanne Pfautz, and it purports to grant Liberty Bank a security interest in "MUTUAL FUND ACCT #52576." No one disputes that Mutual Fund Acct. #52576 is the Guardian Fund Account. The Pledge Agreement spells out the rights of Liberty Bank as the secured party and provides that:

> Pledgor agrees that Secured Party may at any time, whether before or after the occurrence of an Event of Default and without notice or demand of any kind, (i) notify the obligor on or issuer of any Collateral to make payment to Secured Party of any amount due or distributable thereon, (ii) in Pledgor's name or Secured Party's name enforce collection of any Collateral by suit or otherwise, or surrender, release or exchange all or any part of it, or compromise, extend or renew for any period any obligation evidenced by the Collateral, (iii) receive all proceeds of the Collateral, and (iv) hold any increase or profits received from the Collateral as additional security for the Obligations, except that any money received from the Collateral shall, at Secured Party's option, be applied in reduction of the Obligations, in such order of applications as Secured Party may determine, or be remitted to Debtor.

In this document the debtors grant to Liberty Bank alone the right to instruct Guardian, as the issuer of the collateral, to sell the Uncertificated Securities.

Ms. Connery testified that in order to perfect a security interest in Uncertificated Securities, both the registered owner and the secured party must request the establishment of a loan collateral account. It is undisputed that Liberty Bank and the Pfautzes made such a Request. The Request identifies the collateral as the Guardian Park Avenue Fund, Account Number 52576–3. In the Request, the Pfautzes instruct State Street, as the Fund's transfer agent, to record the Guardian shares pledged, along with Liberty Bank's security interest, on the books and records of the Fund and on the initial transaction statement. The Request also contains the following instructions:

transfer such shares into separate Loan Collateral Account ... registered on the books and records of the Fund in the following manner:

1) LOAN COLLATERAL ACCOUNT

2) LIBERTY BANK PLEDGEE

3) JERRY A. PFAUTZ AND SUZANNE PFAUTZ Sharehold(s)/Pledgor(s)

4) 4133 N HAVEN SPRINGFIELD MO 65803

The Request states that the instructions contained within the Request cannot be amended or terminated without the prior written consent of Liberty Bank, and that Liberty Bank's rights shall be in accordance with the procedures established and in effect between the Fund and State Street. The Request directs the issuer to distribute the Uncertificated Securities to a Loan Collateral Account. Finally, the Request provides that "[e]xecution and return of this Request of Assignment as Security by State Street shall serve as notice that State Street has recorded the Pledge and security interest herein referenced on the books and records of the Fund as required under the applicable provisions of the Uniform Commercial Code." The Request contains the signature of one Wilma Collado, Client Relations Officer for State Street.

During Ms. Connery's deposition, she testified that Wilma Collado is her manager at NFDS, and that Ms. Collado is also a vice-president of Boston Financial Services, a parent company of NFDS. She also testified that NFDS follows the written procedures of their parent company, Boston Financial, when establishing a loan collateral account. * * *

At Ms. Connery's deposition, Liberty Bank offered a document titled "ASSIGNMENT OF ACCOUNT AND ESTABLISHMENT OF LOAN COLLATERAL ACCOUNT." Part I of this document sets forth the procedure for assigning an account or establishing a loan collateral account. It provides as follows:

The shareholder(s) and account officer of the lending institution ... [shall] complete three copies of the *Assignment of Securities Account and Control Agreement* and the *Request for Recording of Assignment as*

*Security*, Section One, and return three signed originals to Boston Financial. These forms serve as a request from the shareholder to transfer the indicated number of shares into a separate Loan Collateral Account and to record the security interest on the books and records of the Fund. All signatures must be guaranteed. * * *

[T]he issuer's transfer agent apparently recognizes the procedures established by Boston Financial, as Ms. Connery testified that the loan collateral account is frozen, and only Liberty Bank can release the freeze. According to the procedure set forth, the Request must identify the account, the name of the pledgee, the shareholder's name, and the shareholder's address. I find that Trial Ex. #1 contains this information. Finally, upon receipt of the documents, the issuer shall:

1a) Establish a Loan Collateral Account.

1b) Reinvest distributions to the Loan Collateral Account or establish a special mail file to the shareowner as indicated on the Request for Recording form.

1c) No privileges are carried over or established.

1d) Transfer shares from the assignor's account to the Loan Collateral Account.

1e) Place a Stop Transfer on the Loan Collateral Account.

1f) Code the assignor's original account Non Purge Y so that it will be available for transfer deposit when the collateral shares are released.

Ms. Connery testified that NFDS followed all of these procedures. She stated, "[W]e transferred the account into the loan collateral account on June 9, 1998, and we have had a stop transfer, which freezes the assets in that account since that time, and have not removed it." She further testified that NFDS would only release the collateral in the loan collateral account upon instructions of Liberty Bank. Based upon the language in the Request and the Third Party Pledge Agreement, I find that the Pfautzes granted Liberty Bank the right to sell the Uncertificated Securities upon their default, and, thus, they consented to the possibility of such a sale. That constitutes control pursuant to section 400.8–106(c) of Missouri's Revised Statutes. I, therefore, find that Liberty Bank properly perfected its security interest in the Uncertificated Securities, and I will deny the Trustee's motion for turnover.

An Order in accordance with this Memorandum Opinion will be entered this date.

## 2.   TREASURY SECURITIES

The vast debt of the United States is evidenced by debt securities issued by the Treasury, ranging from 30–year government bonds to very short term Treasury bills or notes. All of these securities are uncertificated, with ownership rights shown on the "books" of the Federal Reserve Banks in favor of "participants," typically banks, that have a securities account relationship directly with a Federal Reserve Bank. In turn broker-dealers and banks hold Treasuries entitlements in securities accounts with the participants, and individual holders have Treasuries entitlements in securities accounts with the broker-dealers or banks. Under this system, participants, broker-dealers and banks, and individual holders have securities entitlements and are entitlement holders. Federal Reserve Banks, participants, and broker-dealers and banks are securities intermediaries. Transfers of Treasury securities are done on a book-entry basis.

Federal law governs the creation of security interests in Treasury securities. Treasury rules effectively incorporate Revised Article 8 as the federal law governing the creation of security interests in Treasury securities. 61 Fed. Reg. 43626 (1996), 31 C.F.R. pt. 357. They do this by providing that state law governs in states that have already adopted Revised Article 8 and, in states that have not yet adopted it, the official text of Article 8 applies "as though the State had adopted Revised Article 8." 31 C.F.R. § 357.11(d). All states have adopted Article 8.

Although mutual funds and Treasuries are both uncertificated securities, there is an important difference in the manner in which they are held. A very substantial percentage of mutual funds are directly held by individual holders, and as to these the provisions of Article 8 and 9 on the perfection and priority of security interests in uncertificated securities apply. In contrast, only a very small percentage of Treasury securities are directly held by beneficial owners; these are called Treasury Direct accounts. These are held on the records of the Treasury through its agents the Federal Reserve Banks in a direct account relationship between the beneficial owner of the Treasury security and the Federal Reserve Bank. The vast majority of Treasury securities are held by securities intermediaries under the system described in the first paragraph of this section, and perfection and priority of security interests in these securities are determined by the rules concerning security interests in securities accounts. A discussion of perfection of security interest in Treasury securities, see 2 Barkley Clark, The Law of Secured Transactions Under the Uniform Commercial Code, ¶ 14.04 (Rev. ed. Supp. 2005).

# CHAPTER 8

# SECURITY INTERESTS IN FIXTURES

---

## A.  WHAT IS A FIXTURE?

Section 9–102(a)(41) states: " 'Fixtures' means goods that have become so related to particular real property that an interest in them arises under real property law." Related how? The drafters of Revised Article 9, like the drafters of the previous versions, have declined to go beyond a definition that refers us to local real property law for the answer. Comment 3 to 9–334 observes: "[T]his section recognizes three categories of goods: (1) those that retain their chattel character entirely and are not part of the real property; (2) ordinary building materials that have become an integral part of the real property and cannot retain their chattel character for the purpose of finance; and (3) an intermediate class that has become real property for certain purposes, but as to which chattel financing may be preserved." Using a simple residential example, a lamp plugged into a wall socket would probably be in class 1; bricks and mortar used in the walls of the house would surely be in class 2; a heating and air-conditioning unit may be in either class 3 or class 1. Goods falling in class 3 are called fixtures, and priorities with respect to claims in fixtures are determined by 9–334 rather than by 9–322, as for class 1 goods, or by the law of real property for property in class 2.

Although 9–334's uniform priority rules for fixture claimants now prevail throughout the land, the key variable in applying these rules is whether the collateral is a fixture under the law of the state. The courts of the different states have varied wildly on what they find to be a fixture. For instance, a five-room house built by a lessee is personal property in Nebraska, Bank of Valley v. U.S. National Bank, 341 N.W.2d 592 (Neb. 1983). But carpets and pads, nailed to the floor and easily removable, are fixtures in Pennsylvania, In re Kriger, 169 B.R. 336 (Bankr. W.D.Pa. 1994). A machine weighing 45,000 pounds, 124 inches wide by eight feet in length, anchored securely by leg screws and connected by a 220 volt electric line, which could "easily be removed in one hour without material physical damage to the building" (by how many people we are not told), is personal property in New Jersey, In re Park Corrugated Box Corp., 249 F.Supp. 56 (D.N.J. 1966). Go figure.

These differences have been so great and unpredictable that commentators question whether any universal, one-size-fits-all definition is possible, or even desirable. Before the 1962 Code was enacted, Professor Harold W. Horowitz pointed out, prophetically, in The Law of Fixtures in California—A Critical Analysis, 26 S. Cal. L. Rev. 21, 22 (1952): " * * * There is no separate universe of the law in which objects are either fixtures or not * * *. Terms such as 'realty,' 'personalty' and 'fixtures' should be recognized to be not only descriptions of fact but also convenient but confusing descriptions of the nature of legal relations between persons in various factual situations." In short, the term "fixture" is perhaps less a description of an object that it is a legal conclusion about who should win the lawsuit. However uncertain the meaning of this term, courts must decide the cases before them. As Lord Lindley said in Viscount Hill v. Bullock, (1897) 2 Ch. 482, in which it was claimed that certain stuffed birds were fixtures: "After all there is such a thing as common sense, and it must be brought to bear upon the question whether these birds are or are not fixtures." Quoted from Wyoming State Farm Board, 759 P.2d at 1241. Over the years courts have tended to coalesce around some formulaic criteria, however vague, that they can cling to for guidance. In 1853 the court in Teaff v. Hewitt, 1 Ohio St. 511, prescribed three elements for the recognition of a fixture: (1) physical annexation to the land; (2) adaptation for use with the land; and (3) annexation made with the intention to make a permanent addition to the land. Teaff has been cited in many cases, but however common the use of this three-prong test, you will not be surprised to learn that the law remains unsettled and nonuniform on how to identify a fixture.

## B.  Fixture and Other Filings

A good that becomes a fixture retains its character as a type of good. A factory machine bolted to the floor still is equipment even if it also becomes a fixture. Fixture status simply means that a real estate interest in the good can arise. Correspondingly, an ordinary filed financing statement that perfects a security interest in a good continues to perfect the security interest after the good becomes a fixture. These filings often are called "UCC" or "chattel" filings. A security interest in a fixture also can be perfected by making a "fixture filing." Section 9–102(a)(40) defines a fixture filing as "the filing of a financing statement covering goods that are or are to become fixtures and satisfying Section 9–502(a) and (b)." Article 9 doesn't require that a fixture filing be made to perfect a security interest in fixtures. See 9–501(a)(1)(B) ("the filing is filed as a fixture filing"). A UCC filing suffices. Finally, a security interest in a fixture can be perfected under applicable realty law, usually by recording a mortgage that covers the fixture. An appurtenances clause or similar language in the mortgage instrument is enough to extend the mortgage to fixtures. Section 9–502(c) refers to the recorded mortgage as "effective" as a fixture filing. Thus, there are three sorts of filings that can perfect security interests in goods that are fixtures: a UCC filing, a fixture filing, and a recorded mortgage.

A fixture filing differs from a UCC filing both in the information required in the financing statement and the place at which the financing statement must be filed. As to required information, in addition to the information demanded by 9–502(a), the financing statement must contain the information described by 9–502(b). 9–102(a)(40). Section 9–502(b) requires, among other information, a description of the reality to which the collateral is or will be affixed as well as the somewhat formalistic demand that the financing statement "indicate" that it is being filed in the realty records. 9–502(b)(2), (3). UCC filings need not satisfy 9–502(b)'s informational demands. As to the place of filing, 9–501(1)(B) requires a local filing in the office designated for the filing of mortgages on realty. This is typically the register of deeds. (Section 9–301(3)(A) selects as the applicable law for perfecting security interests in fixtures the local law of the jurisdiction in which the affixed good is located.) A UCC filing is made centrally, usually in the office of the secretary of state. 9–501(a)(2). A filing in the office where mortgages are recorded saves realty interests the cost of conducting a dual search: one search to detect UCC filings and another to detect mortgage interests in fixtures.

A fixture filing is ineffective against a secured creditor who has perfected a security interest in the affixed good by making a UCC filing. Fixture filings are effective only against realty interests that extend to the fixture. In most of these cases a creditor claiming a security interest only in fixtures (e.g., as in the common purchase money case) must make a fixture filing. A UCC filing has only limited effect against realty interests. The filing is effective against a lien creditor's rights in the fixture arising from its lien on the real estate; 9–334(e)(3). It is also effective as to fixtures that fall within the restricted class of readily removable goods described by 9–334(e)(2). In all other cases the UCC filing is ineffective against realty interests. Thus, to be protected against both realty and competing security interests in most goods that are fixtures, a prudent secured creditor must make both a fixture and a UCC filing covering the goods. Of course, if the goods described in the mortgage records aren't fixtures, recording the mortgage is not a filing with respect to the goods. The priority problems below describe the protection given by UCC and fixture filings.

## C.  PRIORITY

### 1.  BASIC RULES

Section 9–334 provides the priority rules governing contests between secured creditors and realty interests in goods that have become fixtures. Contests between secured creditors over the goods continue to be governed by 9–322's basic priority rules. The classic conflict addressed by 9–334 is between the holder of a security interest in goods that are attached to real property and the mortgagee of the real property to which the goods are attached. Typically, the security agreement will provide that the goods remain personal property even though attached to realty, and the mortgage will cover all fixtures and other appurtenances to the realty. The thrust of 9–334 is to subordinate a security interest in fixtures to the conflicting interest of the real property mortgagee unless the secured party brings its interest into the real property recording system by making a "fixture filing." 9–334(c).

In the following Problems, we examine the priority rules set out in 9–334.

## PROBLEMS

**1.** Seller (S) sold Debtor a heating/cooling unit that was installed in Debtor's building by attaching pipes, vents, and electrical conduits. Seller took a security interest in the unit in a written security agreement that specifically provided that the unit remained personal property after installation and that Seller had a right to remove it upon default by Debtor. Mortgagee (M) recorded a record of a mortgage covering Debtor's real property and all fixtures and appurtenances attached to the property in the county recorder's office. You may assume that the unit is a fixture under the law of the relevant jurisdiction.

(a) Assume that M's mortgage was on record when S sold the unit to Debtor. What steps must S take to protect its interest from subordination to the interest of the mortgagee under 9–334(c)? See 9–334(d) and (e).

(b) At the time S took its security interest in the unit, there was no mortgage on Debtor's property. What steps should S take to be sure that no subsequent mortgage on D's land could subordinate S's interest in the unit? See 9–334(e).

(c) At the time S took its security interest in the unit, there was no mortgage on Debtor's property. S made a regular filing covering the unit in the central filing office of the State. Subsequently, Debtor filed a bankruptcy petition and its bankruptcy trustee sought to avoid S's interest under BC 544(a)(1) as a hypothetical lien creditor. Should the trustee succeed? See 9–334(e)(3) and 9–501(a)(2). See Comment 9 to 9–334. See Mark S. Scarberry, Fixtures in Bankruptcy, 16 Cap. U. L. Rev. 403, 441–478 (1987), for a general treatment of the subject.

**2.** Suppose we have a case like In re Park Corrugated Box Corporation, cited above, in which the Seller (S) made a fixture filing with respect to a machine because it believed, with some justification, that the machine was a fixture. The machine weighed 45,000 pounds, was 124 inches wide by eight feet in length, was anchored securely by leg screws and connected by a 220 volt electric line. Subsequently, Debtor, the buyer of the machine and owner of the structure to which the machine was affixed, filed a bankruptcy petition. Its trustee in bankruptcy sought to avoid S's interest under BC 544(a) as a hypothetical lien creditor. The court held that the machine was not a fixture. Should the trustee succeed? See 9–334(e)(3).

**3.** First Mortgagee (M1) held a duly recorded mortgage on Debtor's (D) real property and fixtures securing D's obligation to M1. After M1 recorded its mortgage, Seller (S) sold a heating unit to D on credit and took a security interest in the unit to secure the unpaid purchase price. You may assume that the unit fell within the definition of a fixture in the relevant jurisdiction. Six weeks after S installed the unit, it made a fixture filing covering the unit. Subsequently, interest rates were falling and D wished to refinance its mortgage through Second Mortgagee (M2). The refinancing was carried out by M2's advancing the money to D, D's paying off M1, M1's returning D's promissory note to D, marked "paid," and recording a satisfaction statement that terminated its mortgage, and D's signing a new promissory note payable to M2 and granting M2 a mortgage on the real property and the fixtures, which M2 promptly recorded. Is S's security interest in the unit subordinated to M2's mortgage? See 9–334(e)(1).

## 2.   CONSTRUCTION MORTGAGES

Construction lending often involves an agreement by a lender to advance money to a developer in a series of "progress payments" to be made at various stages in the construction of a project. The lender customarily records its mortgage on the premises before the work of improvement commences. If the developer buys goods on credit which may become affixed to the improvement and the seller retains a security interest in the goods sold, a priority contest may arise upon the developer's default between the lender, claiming a prior security interest in the entire improvement, and the seller who seeks to remove the attached goods.

Pre–UCC law favored the construction lender over the fixture financer, but the 1962 version of Article 9 omitted this priority. Having been told that Article 9 had no effect on real property law, the powerful real property finance industry was not much involved in the drafting of Article 9. When it discovered this omission, fears rose that the new UCC would allow a supplier of air-conditioning units for a housing development in Arkansas to remove the units in mid-summer and render the development unmarketable. The industry lobbied for restoration of the old rule and prevailed in the 1972 version of Article 9. The revision continues this rule in 9–334(h).

We illustrate this priority with the following facts:

Bank agreed to advance $5 million to Developer (D), the owner of the real property, to enable D to build a structure on the land. The money was to be paid out in under a schedule that allowed D to receive advances as the work of improvement reached certain stages of completion. Before construction began, Bank recorded a record of the mortgage, which included fixtures, securing D's obligations, which stated that it was a construction mortgage. Instead of paying cash for the heating and cooling equipment for the structure out of the proceeds of the construction loan, as the loan agreement required, D induced Seller to sell D the equipment on credit, secured by a purchase money security interest in the equipment that was perfected by a fixture filing. Assume that under the law of the jurisdiction this equipment would be classified as a fixture. Under 9–334(h), S's interest is subordinated to that of Bank.

(a) What is the policy basis justifying the traditional priority rule that protects the Bank in this case? Do construction lenders need this priority?

(b) Once S learns that Bank is advancing funds to D pursuant to a construction mortgage, how can S take a security interest in fixtures it sells to D on credit that will be protected against Bank's 9–334(h) priority? See 9–334(f) and 9–602.

## 3.   Manufactured Homes

Courts have had difficulties in classifying mobile homes for fixtures purposes. When wheels are placed under them, they are, indeed, mobile. Personal property? But when they come to rest they are placed on foundations, hooked up to water pipes and power wires, telephone and cable connections, and they stay put. Fixtures? Over time, with more built-ons and attachments, they become more and more a part of the real property. How do they differ from prefabricated or modular homes that are assembled on the owner's land? Real property?

Article 9 has undertaken to clarify the status of mobile homes as collateral. See 9–334(e)(4). The term "manufactured home" is ambiguous. Was it intended to mean what used to be called "trailer homes" and for several decades has been known as "mobile homes"? These are small, relatively inexpensive housing boxes that are usually restricted by zoning to trailer parks and are occupied by people who can't afford traditional housing. Or is the intention to cover prefabricated homes, now called "modular homes," that are manufactured in components in factories and shipped to the building site where they are assembled? Prefabs started with the Sears' build-your-own-home kit in 1908—the Goldenrod, three rooms, no bath (outhouse sold separately) cost $445 in 1925—and have progressed to modern modular homes that have architectural pretensions and $200,000 price tags. See Daniel Akst, The Very Model of a Modern Modular House, Wall St.J., May 29, 2003 at D8. Now the Sears' homes are collectors' items; a large version sold in 2005 for $900,000. Sara Schaefer Munoz, Historians and Fans are Racing to Catalog Homes Sold by Sears, Wall St. J., May 15, 2006 at A1. The definition of "manufactured home" in 9–102(a)(53) makes clear that the term means a mobile home and not a modular home.

Although pre-Revision judicial opinions differed on their nature for purposes of perfection of security interests, the likelihood that mobile homes would be classified as either fixtures or real property led financers to be sure to record their security interest in the real property records. But the insatiable quest of state governments for money has led to widespread inclusion of mobile homes in certificate-of-title statutes, with the requirement that security interests be indicated on the certificate. Under such a statute, is indication of a security interest on the certificate the exclusive means of perfection of security interests in mobile homes? In re Kroskie, 315 F.3d 644 (6th Cir.2003), held that it is, and banks stopped financing mobile homes in Michigan. The legislature promptly responded by providing that recording in real property records is an alternative method of perfection. See In re Oswalt, 318 B.R. 817 (W.D. Mich. 2004). Some states provide that perfection under their certificate-of-title law is the exclusive method of perfection. See, e.g., In re Renaud, 302 B.R. 280 (Bankr. E.D. Ark. 2003).

Section 9–334(e)(4) gives a security interest in a manufactured home perfected under a state certificate-of-title statute priority over conflicting interests of encumbrancers or owners of the real property, if the security interest is created in a manufactured-home transaction. The detailed definition of "manufactured home" in 9–102(a)(53) is taken from the federal Manufactured Housing Act, 42 U.S.C. §§ 5401 et seq. See Comment 4b. to 9–102. It means a structure of 320 or more square feet, "which is built on a permanent chassis and designed to be used as a dwelling with or without a permanent foundation...." This definition excludes smaller trailer-type units, but the limits of its meaning may puzzle participants in mobile home financing for years to come. See 4 James J. White & Robert S. Summers, Uniform Commercial Code 303–304 (5th Prac. Ed. 2002), for a discussion of some of the uncertainties.

A "manufactured-home transaction" is defined in 9–102(a)(54) to mean a purchase money security interest in a manufactured home or a security interest in which the manufactured home is the primary collateral. It excludes manufactured homes held in inventory. Under 9–515(b) an initial filing with respect to a manufactured home transaction is effective for 30 years if it indicates that it is filed in connection with a manufactured-home financing.

## 4.   CIRCULAR PRIORITIES

### PROBLEM

Debtor operated a plant on a piece of land it also owned. The plant contains a spare sprinkler system housed in concrete struts. Requiring working capital for the plant, Debtor obtained a loan from First Bank secured by a mortgage on the land and plant. The mortgage instrument contained the usual appurtenances clause, and First Bank recorded its mortgage interest in the proper registry of deeds. A year before, Debtor had granted Second Bank a security interest in the sprinkler system in the plant to secure a loan Second Bank made to it. Second Bank filed a valid Article 9 financing statement in both the proper location for filing Article 9 financing statements and the registry of deeds. The financing statement, however, did not recite that it was filed as a fixture filing. Two months later, Third Bank made a loan to Debtor also secured by Debtor's sprinkler system and filed a valid financing statement in both places. The statement filed in the registry of deeds recited that it was being filed as a fixture filing. Debtor subsequently defaulted on the loans from the three banks. Assuming that the spare sprinkler system is worth $100,000 and Debtor owes each bank $100,000, who has priority in the system? See 9–102(a)(40), 9–322(a), (f)(1), 9–334, Comment 2 to 9–334(e)(1), and 9–502(b).

### NOTE

This Problem involves a circular priority: a contest involving three or more creditors in which Creditor 1 has priority over Creditor 2; Creditor 2 has priority over Creditor 3; and Creditor 3 has priority over Creditor 1. A circular priority is produced when different priority rules apply in pairwise contests among different creditors, so that the final result of combining them is an intransitive order of priority of claims. Since a circular priority describes an intransitive ordering of claimants, the scheme of priority rules does not give a consistent sequence in which claims are to be paid. This is a serious problem because a priority scheme must determine who is paid first. Circular priorities, although rarely found in case law controlled by Article 9, are possible in contexts other than priority contests over fixtures. In general, circular priorities are possible when a priority rule contains a "knowledge" component or when different priority schemes, such as the Bankruptcy Code, the Federal Tax Lien Act or realty law, apply to different claimants. There are solutions to them, ranging from a pro rata share to "equitable" devices for subordinating one creditor to the others, see 2 Gilmore, Security Interests in Personal Property 1120–46 (1965); M. Stuart Sutherland, Note, Circular Priority Systems Within the Uniform Commercial Code, 61 Tex. L. Rev. 517 (1982), but they are controversial and not compelled by Article 9's provisions. At the very least, it is wise not to create a circular priority that needs resolving in the first place.

Revised Article 9 gets mixed marks on this score. It eliminates some sources of circular priorities present in former Article 9 but leaves intact some rules that allow for circular priorities and add others that create them where not previously possible. Section 9–316(b) provides that, when a financing statement becomes ineffective under stipulated conditions, it is deemed never to have been effective "against a purchaser of the collateral for value." The negative implication is that the statement remains effective against nonpurchasers such as lien creditors. Thus, because a financing statement can be ineffective against a secured creditor but still effective against a lien creditor, the Revision allows the following priority order: Secured Creditor 1 over Lien Creditor via 9–317(a)(2) and 9–316(b)'s negative implication; Lien Creditor over Secured Creditor 2 via 9–317(a)(2); and Secured Creditor 2 over Secured Creditor 1 via 9–316(b) and 9–322(a). In another change, 9–515(c) amends former 9–402(5) so that a lapsed financing statement is ineffective only "against a purchaser of the collateral for value." (Under former 9–402(5), a lapsed financing statement rendered the security interest unperfected against all competing interests.) The change makes 9–515(c) consistent with 9–316(b), but at the price of now allowing a circular priority to arise where none could arise under 9–402(5).

The Revisers are fairly sanguine about allowing circular priorities to continue, estimating that the bankruptcy consequences of not doing so are more serious. See Comment 3 to 9–316 (another approach would create significant and unjustifiable preference risks). Their estimate can be questioned. Adverse bankruptcy consequences faced by a creditor give it an additional incentive to maintain perfection, by monitoring the location of collateral and updating the financing statement. This might not be a bad thing. At least the creditor then can calculate accurately the marginal benefits and costs of updating the statement or monitoring the collateral.

Because resolutions of circular priorities are nonuniform, controversial and have no explicit statutory basis, circular priorities can create a good deal of legal uncertainty. Creditors incur socially wasteful costs in planning transactions to avoid the uncertainty of the prospect of circularity.

## D.   ENFORCEMENT

If a creditor's security interest in fixtures has priority over encumbrancers and owners of real property, 9–604(c) allows the secured party to remove the fixture from the real property. However, under 9–604(d), the secured party must reimburse an encumbrancer or owner of the real property "for the cost of repair of any physical injury caused by the removal," and the person entitled to reimbursement may demand adequate assurance of reimbursement as a condition of its permission to remove. The difficulties facing the fixture financer in using the removal remedy are obvious. In cases like *Maplewood*, which follows, Sears would incur costs of removal, together with the expense of reimbursement for physical injuries to the house, that might well exceed the second-hand value of the kitchen equipment removed. Tearing out built-in fixtures will inevitably leave damage to walls and floors as well as enraged home owners not likely to welcome the repossessors into their kitchen. Haggling over the amount of injury caused by the removal and the adequacy of the reimbursement proffered by the fixture financer seems inevitable.

If Sears cannot share in the proceeds of foreclosure of the real property, it may well choose to write off the debt unless it can make a deal with the bank. The basis for the deal would be that the bank's interest in the home is probably more valuable with the Sears fixtures left in than with a denuded kitchen requiring the foreclosure buyer to install new fixtures. As we suggest in Note 2 following *Maplewood*, Sears has a bargaining position that might lead to a settlement with the bank.

Given the inadequacies of the right of removal, fixture financers have long sought remedies that would allow them access to the proceeds of the mortgagee's foreclosure sale to compensate them for the value of the fixtures. The following pre-Revision case is the best judicial discussion of the differing points of view on this issue.

## Maplewood Bank and Trust v. Sears, Roebuck and Co.

Superior Court of New Jersey, Appellate Division, 1993.
625 A.2d 537, aff'd, 638 A.2d 140 (N.J. 1994).

■ COLEMAN, J.H., P.J.A.D.

This appeal requires us to decide whether a first mortgage lender or a fixture financier is entitled to priority in the funds realized from a foreclosure sale of the mortgaged premises. We hold that a first mortgagee is entitled to priority in such funds.

Plaintiff Maplewood Bank and Trust is the holder of a first purchase money mortgage dated September 20, 1988 and recorded on October 5, 1988 on premises owned by defendants Edward and Terre Capers. The original mortgage debt was for $121,000. On May 31, 1989, Sears, Roebuck and Company (Sears) filed a Financing Statement covering a completely new kitchen, consisting of "new countertops, cabinets, sinks, disposal unit, dishwasher, oven, cooktop and hood," installed in the mortgaged premises at the request of the Capers after they executed a Security Agreement. The Financing Statement, known as the UCC–1 form, filed by Sears gave notice that Sears had a security interest in the new kitchen installed in the mortgaged premises in the sum of $33,320.40.

On August 18, 1989 the Capers executed a second mortgage on the previously mortgaged premises to defendant New Jersey Savings Bank for the sum of $34,000. That mortgage was recorded on August 23, 1989.

When the Capers eventually defaulted in the payments due plaintiff and Sears, plaintiff declared the entire unpaid balance on the mortgage was due. Nonpayment of the entire balance plus interest prompted plaintiff to file its complaint for foreclosure on November 5, 1990 and an amended complaint on or about December 6, 1990. Sears filed an answer and a counterclaim. Sears sought a declaration that its debt was "prior to the mortgage of the plaintiff" and, among other things, to compel plaintiff to "pay [Sears] the amount due on its Agreement." The essence of the counterclaim was that under § 9–313, Sears was entitled to priority over the plaintiff in the funds realized from the anticipated foreclosure sale. Sears' answer and counterclaim were stricken on July 26, 1991, and the matter proceeded as an uncontested foreclosure action. A final judgment in foreclosure was entered on February 28, 1992.

Sears has appealed the dismissal of its counterclaim. It argues that the priority given Sears as a purchase money security interest holder under the Uniform Commercial Code "applies to the proceeds of a judicial sale instituted" by a purchase money mortgagee. This is the same issue Sears raised in Orange Savings Bank v. Todd, 48 N.J. 428, 430, 226 A.2d 178 (1967), wherein Sears asserted that it was entitled to priority over the purchase money mortgagee "in the funds realized on foreclosure." Ibid. The Supreme Court concluded that although the briefs raised "interesting and important questions under the secured transactions provisions of the Uniform Commercial Code, we find no present occasion to deal with any of them in view of the position now taken by the parties." Ibid. In the present case, we have considered the contention raised by Sears and conclude that it is unsound and must be rejected.

It is undisputed that the new kitchen Sears installed and financed satisfies the definition of a fixture under § 9–313(1)(a). It is also undisputed that Sears obtained a purchase money security interest in the fixture to secure full payment. See § 9–107(a). Sears perfected its security interest by filing a financing statement (UCC–1) covering the fixtures in the Hunterdon County Clerk's Office where the first mortgage held by plaintiff was recorded. § 9–313(1)(b) and § 9–402(5).

The purchase money security interest of Sears attached to the goods or chattels before they became affixed to the realty as fixtures. § 9–313(4)(a). By perfecting the security interest, Sears was able to make its security interest in the fixtures permanent, or until paid or discharged. The point to be made is that Sears' security interest is limited to the fixtures and does not extend to the realty otherwise.

By statute, Sears' purchase money security interest, when perfected, "has priority over the conflicting interest of an encumbrancer or owner of the real estate...." § 9–313(4). This concept was expressed more clearly in the version of the statute which predated the 1981 amendments. The prior version of § 9–313(2) provided "A security interest which attaches to goods before they become fixtures takes priority as to the goods over the claims of all persons who have an interest in the real estate except as stated in subsection (4)." This means the purchase money security interest of Sears in the goods or chattels which became fixtures gives it a "super priority" as to those goods or chattels which became fixtures.

Next we must focus upon the remedies available to a purchase money security interest lienholder upon default by the debtor. Sears contends it should be entitled to receive from the proceeds obtained at the foreclosure sale, the difference between the value of the realty with the new kitchen and the value of the realty after the new kitchen has been removed. We reject this entire approach as an inappropriate remedy absent authorization by statute.

The Uniform Commercial Code, as adopted in New Jersey, provides at § 9–313(8) that:

> When the secured party has priority over all owners and encumbrancers of the real estate, he may, on default, subject to the provisions of subchapter 5, remove his collateral from the real estate but he must reimburse any encumbrancer or owner of the real estate who is not the debtor and who has not otherwise agreed for the cost of repair of any physical injury, but not for any diminution in value of the real estate caused by the absence of the goods removed or by any necessity of replacing them.... (Emphasis added).

Thus based on the plain language of § 9–313(8), Sears has two options: removal of the fixtures or foregoing removal of the fixtures.

New York, the only other jurisdiction which has addressed the issue, rejected Sears' argument. In Dry Dock Savings Bank v. DeGeorgio, 61 Misc.2d 224, 305 N.Y.S.2d 73 (1969) the defense asserted a lien superior to the mortgage by reason of a properly filed fixture financial statement covering aluminum siding on a house which was the subject of a foreclosure action. The mortgage was recorded prior to the time the fixture financial statement was filed.

The court held that under § 9–313 the purchase money security interest holder may remove his fixtures from the real estate, but must reimburse any owner or encumbrancer for the cost of repair. Id. 305 N.Y.S.2d at 75. The court observed:

He merely has the right to remove the goods after posting security to repair any damage. This may turn out to be a somewhat Pyrrhic victory, giving the lienor a pile of dubious scrap not worth the labor of getting it off the house, repairing nail holes, etc. . . . [Removal] may hurt the mortgagee without doing the lienor any corresponding good. However, that is something for the parties to consider and beyond the control of the court. Ibid.

In Nu–Way Distributing Corp. v. Schoikert, 44 A.D.2d 840, 355 N.Y.S.2d 475, 14 UCC Rep.Serv. 1058 (N.Y.App.Div.1974), plaintiff instituted an action to recover the price of fixtures (kitchen cabinets, etc.) sold by plaintiff, after the goods or chattels had been installed in the realty as fixtures. The Appellate Division construed § 9–313 "as merely providing the creditor with the statutory right of repossession, provided that he first comply with the security provision of the statute." Id. 355 N.Y.S.2d at 476.

The Appellate Division opined that even if the purchase money security interest holder failed or did not desire to repossess the fixtures upon default, that lienholder was not entitled to maintain an action for the purchase price against a subsequent purchaser of the real property. Ibid. The court further held that the same rule would apply even in cases where the fixtures are custom-made and would be of no use or value should they be repossessed. The underlying rationale for the rule was that such a lienholder as the one involved in Nu–Way must be assumed to have known and understood the risk he was taking.

Sears' approach has been adopted only in Louisiana and there it was based on the legislature's definitive modification of § 9–313(8) by adding the following language:

A secured party may also demand separate appraisal of the fixtures to fix his interest in the receipts of the sale thereof in any proceedings in which the real estate is sold pursuant to execution upon it by a mortgagee or other encumbrancer. [Uniform Commercial Code § 9–313, 3 U.L.A. 332 to 23 (1992) (Action in Adopting Jurisdictions)].

The most compelling authority supportive of Sears' position is an article "An Integrated Financing System for Purchase Money Collateral: A Proposed Solution to the Fixture Problem Under Section 9–313 of the Uniform Commercial Code" by Morris G. Shanker. 73 Yale L.J. 795 (1964). In this article, Professor Shanker states "[w]here the fixture secured debt is not paid, removal of the fixture seems to be the favorite means of foreclosing on the fixture security interest." Id. at 804.

The article goes on to cite certain instances where the fixture secured party may prefer not to exercise his removal rights. For example, if an elevator was designed for a specific building, it would have little or no value apart from that building. Ibid. Other cited examples include situations where a fixture secured party should be required to use judicial foreclosure proceedings even though he has the right of removal. For example a secured party should not be free to remove a heating system in a large apartment building in the dead of winter, even where the debtor defaulted.

Shanker opines that "the Code, as it now stands, probably authorizes the fixture secured party to employ judicial foreclosure proceedings to enforce his security interest" in lieu of removal of the fixtures. Ibid. He states that limiting the remedy to the right to remove or choosing not to remove, in no way detracts from the fixture secured party's paramount security interest in his collateral; it merely requires him to enforce his security interest in a sensible and equitable fashion. Id. 805.

We decline to adopt the creative approach articulated by Professor Shanker. Such action, in our view, would be legislating. We prefer the approach followed in Louisiana where the legislature, upon its preference and initiative, provided the innovative remedy sought by Sears. To adopt Sears' argument in the absence of legislation, would mean that a mortgagee's security interest could be impaired substantially without the Legislature pronouncing an intention to do so. Any modification of long established fundamental property rights of purchase money mortgagees, must be done in some straight forward manner and may not be implied from the existing statute. The fact that fixtures may be custom made does not require any different result. See Nu–Way, supra, 355 N.Y.S.2d at 476.

We are also persuaded that Sears is not entitled to any remedy, other than removal of the fixtures, based on equitable principles. Sears knew its remedy was limited to removal upon default. Indeed, the Retail Installment Contract and Security Agreement prepared by Sears and signed by the Capers provided that the Capers were giving Sears a "security interest under the Uniform Commercial Code in all merchandise purchased under this contract ... [and] the security interest allows Sears to repossess the merchandise" in the event the Capers did not make payments as agreed. (Emphasis added).

Summary judgment in favor of plaintiff is affirmed.


NOTES

**1.** Section 9–604(b) expands the remedies of the fixture financer by providing: "Subject to subsection (c), if a security agreement covers goods that are or become fixtures, a secured party may proceed (1) under this part; or (2) in accordance with the rights with respect to real property, in which case the other provisions of this part do not apply." This provision is explained in the Comment 3 to 9–604: "Subsection (b) is new. It makes clear that a security interest in fixtures may be enforced either under real-property law or under any of the applicable provisions of Part 6, including sale or other disposition either before or after removal of the fixtures (see subsection (c)). Subsection (b) also serves to overrule cases holding that a secured party's only remedy after default is the removal of the fixtures from the real property. See, e.g., Maplewood Bank & Trust v. Sears, Roebuck & Co., 625 A.2d 537 (N.J.Super.App.Div.1993)."

What does 9–604(b) mean when it allows a fixture financer to proceed against a defaulting debtor under either Article 9 or real property law? The Article 9 remedies would include suing the debtor for a personal judgment under 9–601(a)(1) and removal of the fixture under 9–604(c). The right to foreclose and dispose of collateral under 9–610(a) surely would not entitle the fixture claimant to foreclose on the real property to which the fixture is attached, and foreclosure and disposition of the fixture in place hardly seems a feasible remedy. Nothing new here.

The change in law is found in allowing the fixture claimant to proceed "in accordance with the rights with respect to real property." We are not told what this means. The real property law of the jurisdiction is likely to have provisions on the right of a real property mortgagee to proceed in a case in which its mortgage lien covers fixtures as well as land, but that's not our case. However, it may have no provisions governing the rights of a fixture financer to proceed against its fixture collateral, and it almost surely will have no law allowing such a claimant to compel the sale of the real property to which the fixture is appurtenant. So what does it mean? A hint is found in Comment 3 to 9–604, which states that 9–604(b) is intended to overrule *Maplewood*. In that case, the court denied the fixture financer's right to share in the proceeds of the foreclosure sale of the real property. Presumably, subsection (b)(2) gives the fixture financer this right. The courts are left with deciding how this can be done. The fixture financer may be allowed to join in a judicial foreclosure and, depending on the priority of the security interest in the fixtures, to share the proceeds of the foreclosure on the ratio between the values of the fixtures and the real property without the fixtures. If the mortgage lien is prior to the fixture security interest, the fixture interest would share only after the mortgage lien is satisfied. Some mechanism would have to be worked out for fixture financers to participate in the non-judicial foreclosures that predominate in many states. The right of the fixture party to share in the proceeds of foreclosure of the real property is meaningless if the mortgagee is not foreclosing. Here the fixture financer seems to be left with the right of removal, imperfect as that remedy may be.

**2.**   Another way of viewing the plight of the fixture claimant in a more favorable light is to recognize that its right to remove fixtures gives it a bargaining position that might allow it to share in the proceeds of foreclosure without jumping over the legal hurdles described in the previous Note. Sears' security interest in the kitchen fixtures is prior to that of the bank under 9–334(d). Since Sears perfected its security interest by a fixture filing in the real estate records, a title examiner will note the fixture security interest and a purchaser at the foreclosure sale will take subject to Sears' right to remove the kitchen fixtures. See 9–604(c). If the mortgagee finds it more advantageous to sell a house with a kitchen rather than a house without one, either the mortgagee and Sears or the mortgagee and the prospective purchaser may well find some basis for compromise. Section 9–604 can affect the compromise reached.

To see this, recognize that 9–604 gives the fixture financer the right to remove the fixture or proceed "in accordance with [its] rights with respect to real property." 9–604(c), (b)(2). These are remedies provided by Article 9. However, 9–604 does not require the fixture financer to pursue legal remedies in order to satisfy its claim. An obvious alternative "remedy" is contractual: the mortgagee and the fixture financer can bargain ex post to allocate a portion of the proceeds of a foreclosure sale to the financer. Section 9–604(b)(2) and (c) together therefore in effect create a default rule, which the parties can alter by agreement. The default rule is that the fixture financer can remove the fixture or proceed against the realty in accordance with real property law, unless the parties agree otherwise. The question is whether this default rule is a good one. This depends on an assessment of the costs associated with operating under 9–604 as compared to feasible alternative rules. In making an assessment, recognize that the fixture financer and mortgagee's situation describes a bilateral monopoly. In order to obtain some of the foreclosure proceeds of a sale without removing the fixture or wrestling with mysteries of unresponsive real property law, the fixture financer has to reach agreement with the mortgagee. Correspondingly, to sell the realty with the fixture, the mortgagee must purchase the fixture financer's right to remove it. Neither party can obtain its requirements from an alternative source. The trouble is that the transaction costs of reaching agreement are high where a bilateral monopoly exists, because competition isn't present to provide credible information about price. They may exceed the surplus realized from selling the realty with the fixture.

For instance, assume that a dual default occurs: the debtor defaults on its obligations to both its fixture financer and its mortgagee. Suppose too that the realty with the fixture can be sold for $100,000 and for $80,000 without it. Suppose too that the fixture, if removed, can be sold for $10,000 and that there are no costs associated with its removal. A $10,000 surplus therefore is realized if the parties can agree to sell the realty with the fixture ($100,000 less the sum of $80,000 if the realty is sold without the fixture plus $10,000 realized by the fixture financer from the sale of the fixture alone), but to do so the distributional issue of how it will be split must be solved. $80,000 plus one cent makes the mortgagee better off than if the realty is sold without the fixture, the fixture financer receiving $9,999.99 of the surplus. Alternatively, $10,000 plus one cent gives the fixture financer more than it would receive if it removes the fixture, $9,999.99 going to the mortgagee. Thus, the possible distributions that can be bargained for range between one cent and $9,999.99. The allocation actually agreed to apparently depends on factors such as the relative bargaining positions of the parties, the psychological salience of a particular allocation and the likelihood of repeated bargains of a similar sort in the future. See generally Alvin E. Roth, Bargaining Experiments, in The Handbook of Experimental Economics 253–348 (John H. Kagel & Alvin E. Roth eds. 1995); Sidney Siegel & Lawrence E. Fouraker, Bargaining and Group Decision Making: Experiments in Bilateral Monopoly (1960). The transaction costs of negotiating a particular allocation can exceed $10,000.

The former law, which afforded only the remedy of removal, reinforced the bilateral monopoly just described more than does 9–604. Because the fixture financer's only remedy was removal, it had to bargain with the mortgagee for part of the surplus realized by selling the realty with the fixture. Bargaining costs are a consequence of restricting the financer's remedy. Section 9–604(b) does not require the financer to bargain. Instead, the financer may proceed "in accordance with the rights with respect to real property." In the case of a foreclosure sale following debtor's dual default, these "rights" could include having the realty sold subject to its fixture interest. See 9–604(b)(2); Comment 3 to 9–604. Even if real property law doesn't allow the financer to compel a sale of realty, Comment 3 to 9–604's rejection of *Maplewood* apparently allows the financer to share in the proceeds of the sale attributable to the fixture. Since the offers of bidders at the foreclosure sale reflect their valuation of the fixture, the financer has available alternatives to having the mortgagee "purchase" the financer's right to remove the fixture. The financer therefore need not reach agreement with the mortgagee. Even if it bargains with the mortgagee, the presence of potential bids provides credible information about the price of the fixture. In both ways the transaction costs associated with bargaining with the mortgagee are reduced. Section 9–604(b)(2) and (c) therefore arguably is a better default rule than the former law.

# SECURITY INTERESTS IN BANKRUPTCY

---

## A.   OVERVIEW OF BANKRUPTCY

## 1.   INTRODUCTION

No lawyer can competently advise on the planning of secured transactions or on the enforcement of security interests arising from these transactions without a detailed understanding of the Bankruptcy Code's impact on Article 9 security interests. Our coverage of this broad subject is roughly divided into two parts. First, we briefly discuss how Article 9 security interests are treated by the Bankruptcy Code. Here we offer an overview of bankruptcy law, note the effect of the automatic stay, and discuss the status of secured claims under Chapters 7, 11 and 13 of the Bankruptcy Code. Second, we deal with the trustee's avoiding powers and the effect of bankruptcy on secured interests. Here we discuss the ''strong arm'' clause, preferences and fraudulent transfers. In the following overview, we offer more material than you can absorb at first, but you may find it useful to refer to this background material as we go through this chapter.

Bankruptcy law is federal law. The applicable statute is the Bankruptcy Reform Act of 1978, 11 U.S.C. §§ 101, et seq., which went into effect in 1979 replacing the Bankruptcy Act of 1898. We will refer to the 1978 Act as the Bankruptcy Code, and its provisions will be cited as, for example, BC 544(a). Amendments to the Bankruptcy Code occur frequently. The most significant amendment to the 1978 Act is the Bankruptcy Abuse Prevention and Consumer Protection Act (BAPCPA), enacted in 2005. The Bankruptcy Code is supplemented by the Bankruptcy Rules, which govern procedures in the United States Bankruptcy Courts.

Although bankruptcy is federal law, the rights in bankruptcy of debtors and creditors are governed in large part by rights under applicable state law. Liens, which are created by state law, are of paramount importance in bankruptcy. The creditor whose debt is secured by a lien in the debtor's property has absolute priority with respect to that property over other creditors who have no liens, or whose liens are of lower priority. Usually bankrupts are insolvent, i.e., the value of their assets is less than their debts, and the debtor's property is often encumbered. The result in many of these cases is that the bulk of the bankrupt's assets is applied to the payment of secured debts. Much of bankruptcy law is concerned with striking an equitable balance between the rights of secured and unsecured creditors to the debtor's assets. Toward this end bankruptcy law allows some liens that are valid outside bankruptcy to be invalidated in the bankruptcy proceedings, thus demoting the lienholder from the status of secured creditor to that of unsecured creditor. Sometimes the bankruptcy law recognizes the validity of a lien but the rights of the lienholder are restricted in some fashion in order to enhance the rights of unsecured creditors.

Under the early law, bankruptcy was exclusively a creditor's remedy, and in modern times bankruptcy is still an important, though little used, creditor's remedy. Some creditors who would receive little or nothing in payment of their claims outside bankruptcy may be able to obtain substantial payment if the debtor is in bankruptcy. Creditors can, under some circumstances, force a debtor into bankruptcy by filing a petition in involuntary bankruptcy against a debtor. The most common ground for obtaining involuntary bankruptcy is that "the debtor is generally not paying such debtor's debts as such debts become due * * *." BC 303(h)(1). Involuntary bankruptcy, however, is uncommon. Bankruptcy today is most important as a debtor's remedy. The overwhelming majority of bankruptcies are initiated by voluntary filing by debtors who are seeking immediate relief from the demands of their creditors.

Outside of bankruptcy there is often little relief for a debtor who is unable to pay creditors. Creditors with security interests may be threatening to sell collateral. Other creditors may have obtained, or are threatening to obtain, judicial liens in the debtor's property. Although state law may allow the debtor to protect exempt property from execution or attachment, that law may not apply to some property that the debtor vitally needs. Most debtors that are not natural persons are not allowed to protect any property from creditors though exemptions. For debtors beset by creditors, bankruptcy can provide instant and dramatic relief. The paragraphs that follow provide a brief description of the principal characteristics of voluntary bankruptcy proceedings.

The United States is divided into 91 judicial districts. Each of these districts comprises either a state or a part of a state, the District of Columbia, or Puerto Rico. In each district there is a United States Bankruptcy Court with one or more bankruptcy judges. There are also United States Trustees, each of whom is assigned to one or more of the judicial districts. The function of the United States Trustee, who is a salaried employee appointed by the Attorney General, is to supervise the administration of bankruptcy cases. The duties of a United States Trustee are stated in 28 U.S.C. § 586.

## 2.   TYPES OF BANKRUPTCY

The debtor can choose two types of bankruptcy. The first, and most simple, is liquidation under Chapter 7 of the Bankruptcy Code. In a liquidation bankruptcy all of the property of the debtor owned at the date of bankruptcy becomes part of the bankruptcy estate. BC 541. A debtor who is an individual is entitled to exempt certain property from the bankruptcy estate. The exempt property is released to the debtor by the trustee in bankruptcy. The property that may be exempted is in most cases determined by the law of the state of the debtor's domicile and consists of property that is exempt from judicial liens in that state. In some cases the debtor has the option of electing to exempt property listed in BC 522(d). The trustee must also dispose of property in which a lienholder or other person such as a co-owner has a property interest. In some cases that property is abandoned by the trustee to the debtor. In other cases the property is sold by the trustee and the property interest of the lienholder or other person is satisfied from the proceeds of sale. Any remaining property of the estate is sold by the trustee and the proceeds are applied to payment of claims of the debtor's creditors and the expenses of the bankruptcy proceedings. A debtor who is an individual normally will be discharged of personal liability on all or most prebankruptcy debts. The ability of an individual to obtain a discharge of prebankruptcy debts is one of the most important characteristics of modern bankruptcy law. The overextended debtor can get a "fresh start" by having personal liability on prebankruptcy debts wiped out while being allowed to retain all exempt property. Debtors other than individuals, such as corporations and partnerships, do not need this fresh start. An insolvent organization can simply be dissolved and liquidated by distributing all its assets to creditors. Thus, in Chapter 7, only an individual can be discharged. BC 727(a)(1). The Bankruptcy Abuse Prevention and Consumer Protection Act limits an individual debtor's access to Chapter 7. Individuals whose income prior to the bankruptcy exceeded applicable state median family income are subject to a "means test" that is designed to force individuals who are deemed to have sufficient future income to obtain relief in Chapters 13 or 11 rather than Chapter 7.

In the second type of bankruptcy the assets of the debtor need not be liquidated. This type of bankruptcy is usually referred to as reorganization or rehabilitation bankruptcy and is governed by Chapter 11, Chapter 12, or Chapter 13 of the Bankruptcy Code. Chapter 13 can be used only by a debtor who is "an individual with regular income that owes, on the date of the filing of the petition, noncontingent, liquidated, unsecured debts of less than $307,675 and noncontingent, liquidated, secured debts of less than $922,975 * * *." BC 109(e). The amounts are subject to periodic adjustment under an escalator clause. The great advantage of Chapter 13 is that the debtor can get the benefits of discharge without losing nonexempt property. The debtor is required to formulate a plan under which the debtor proposes to pay, in whole or in part, some or all prebankruptcy debts over a period of time, usually five years. Creditors are paid in accordance with the plan, normally from postbankruptcy earnings, although the plan can provide for a liquidation of some assets. The plan need not be approved by creditors. If the plan is confirmed by the bankruptcy court, creditors are bound by its terms. BC 1327(a). But a plan cannot be confirmed over the objection of a creditor unless certain requirements are met. If the plan does not propose payment in full of unsecured claims, the plan must provide for all of the debtors "projected disposable income" for the period of the plan. BC 1325(b)(1). In most cases, disposable income means total income received by the debtor less the amount reasonably necessary for the maintenance or support of the debtor and the debtor's dependents. BC 1325(b)(2). But for debtors whose incomes exceed applicable state family medians, this amount is limited by certain standards that rely on statistical medians published by the Internal Revenue Service and the Bureau of the Census. BC 1325(b)(3). When all payments are completed, the debtor is entitled to a discharge of those debts (with some exceptions) that are provided for in the plan. BC 1328(a). Under some circumstances the debtor can obtain a discharge even if payments under the plan have not been completed if the failure to complete the plan is not the fault of the debtor. BC 1328(b). The treatment of secured claims in Chapter 13 will be discussed in detail later in this chapter when we take up the BAPCPA amendments to BC 1325.

Chapter 11 can be used by both individuals and organizations, whether or not the debtor is engaged in business, but it is designed primarily for business organizations. It resembles Chapter 13 in that the debtor is normally allowed to retain its assets and to continue operation of its business. The debtor proposes a plan of reorganization under which creditors will be paid, often over a period of time, from assets of the estate or postconfirmation earnings of the debtor. Unlike Chapter 13, confirmation of a plan in Chapter 11 is usually made only after it has been accepted by the various classes of creditors and stockholder interests of the debtor. Acceptance by a class is accomplished by a vote of members of the class in specified majorities. Under some circumstances a plan can be confirmed even though not all classes accept the plan. Upon confirmation of the plan the debtor, whether an individual or an organization, is normally given a discharge of all preconfirmation debts. In return, creditors and stockholder interests have rights that are given to them by the plan. There are various provisions in Chapter 11 designed to protect the interests of creditors and stockholder interests who do not accept the plan.

Chapter 12 was added to the Bankruptcy Code in 1986 to provide for the rehabilitation of "family farmers" defined in BC 101. Chapter 12 is similar to Chapter 13, but it incorporates some elements of Chapter 11. It is specifically designed to make it easier for family farmers who are threatened with loss of their farms to restructure their debts in bankruptcy while continuing to operate their farms.

### 3. PETITION IN BANKRUPTCY AND THE AUTOMATIC STAY

Voluntary bankruptcy, or a "voluntary case" as it is called in the Bankruptcy Code, is commenced by the debtor's filing a petition in bankruptcy in the Bankruptcy Court. BC 301. In addition to the petition, the debtor must file various statements and schedules of information, including a statement of assets and liabilities with descriptions of each and a list of creditors identified by name and address.

This filing operates as an automatic stay against a variety of acts taken against the debtor or with respect to property of the bankruptcy estate. BC 362(a). Among the most important acts that are stayed are the following: the commencement or continuation of judicial proceedings against the debtor to recover a prebankruptcy claim; the enforcement of any prebank-ruptcy judgment against the debtor or against property of the estate; any act to obtain possession of property of the estate or property held by the estate; and any act to create, perfect or enforce any lien against property of the estate. The stay applies even to informal acts to collect a prebankruptcy debt such as dunning letters, telephone calls and the like. There are many exceptions to the very broad scope of the stay, but the stay effectively insulates the debtor from any kind of action to collect prebankruptcy debts. The effect of the stay is to require all collection action to be made through or with the consent of the bankruptcy court. Under BC 362(d), a creditor can get relief from the stay in some cases. The importance of the automatic stay cannot be overemphasized. Frequently the primary purpose of the filing of a bankruptcy petition is to obtain the benefit of the stay.

## 4.   TRUSTEE IN BANKRUPTCY

In a Chapter 7 bankruptcy the bankruptcy estate is administered by a trustee in bankruptcy who can be either an individual or a corporation. BC 321. The duties of the trustee are listed in BC 704. The principal duty of the trustee is to collect the property of the estate, reduce it to money by selling it, and apply the proceeds to payment of expenses of the bankruptcy and claims of creditors. The collecting of the property of the estate sometimes requires the trustee to recover property of the debtor that was transferred before bankruptcy in transactions that are avoidable in bank-ruptcy because they violate some bankruptcy policy. These "avoidance powers" of the trustee are one of the most important aspects of bankrupt-cy. In asserting these powers the trustee acts primarily for the benefit of unsecured creditors. The trustee also has wide powers of investigation of the financial affairs of the debtor and may oppose discharge of the debtor if the circumstances warrant. The trustee may also examine the validity of claims of creditors and may oppose improper claims. The trustee, who must be a disinterested person, is a fiduciary although the Bankruptcy Code does not specify the nature of the fiduciary relationship. The trustee's duties, particularly those of collecting, holding and disposing of property of the estate, are exercised on behalf of creditors generally, but often the trustee must oppose some creditors to benefit others. Basically the job of the trustee is to maximize the assets available for payment to general unse-cured creditors.

Promptly after a Chapter 7 case is commenced, an interim trustee in bankruptcy is appointed by the United States Trustee. In each district there is a panel of persons qualified to serve as trustees. The interim trustee is appointed from this panel. BC 701.

There is a trustee in bankruptcy in a case under Chapter 12 or Chapter 13, but the trustee's duties are somewhat different. The only property of the bankruptcy estate that normally comes into the hands of the trustee is the earnings of the debtor that are the source of the payments under the plan. The primary duty of the trustee is to disburse to creditors payments due under the plan. The trustee is either appointed by the bankruptcy court to serve in the particular case or is a "standing trustee" appointed by the court to act generally in Chapter 12 or Chapter 13 cases filed in the district. Normally there is no trustee in bankruptcy in a Chapter 11 case. Rather, the debtor continues in possession of its property as a "debtor in possession" that exercises the powers of a trustee in bankruptcy. BC 1107(a) and BC 1108. A trustee in bankruptcy is appointed in a Chapter 11 case only in unusual cases such as those involving fraud or gross misman-agement by the debtor. BC 1104(a).

## 5.   CLAIMS IN BANKRUPTCY

In Chapter 7, after the trustee in bankruptcy has collected the bank-ruptcy estate and has sold it, the proceeds are applied to the payment of bankruptcy expenses and the claims of creditors. A claim is the basis for a distribution from the bankruptcy estate. A "proof of claim," which is a written statement setting forth a creditor's claim, is normally filed by the creditor. BC 501 and Bankruptcy Rule 3001. "Creditor" is defined by BC 101(10) to mean an entity (also defined in BC 101(15)) holding a claim that arose before the filing of the petition in a voluntary case. Thus, rights against the debtor that arise after bankruptcy are not treated as claims in bankruptcy. There are a few exceptions to this statement.

A claim can be paid only if it is "allowed." Allowance of a claim means simply that it has been recognized by the court as valid in the amount claimed. If there is a dispute concerning a claim, the court must determine whether the claim should be allowed. BC 502 contains detailed provisions governing allowance and disallowance. Any claim can be paid within bankruptcy except to the extent that a claim is specifically excepted. The exceptions are stated in BC 502(b), (d), and (e).

Claims are classified as either secured or unsecured. Suppose the debtor owes Bank $20,000 and the debt is secured by a security interest in collateral of the debtor on which there are no other liens. The collateral, because it was owned by the debtor, is part of the bankruptcy estate. BC 541(a)(1). If Bank's security interest is valid in bankruptcy, Bank has a secured claim to the extent that its debt is covered by value of the collateral. To the extent that its debt is not covered by value of the collateral, Bank has an unsecured claim. BC 506(a)(1). For example, if the collateral has a value of $30,000 Bank is oversecured and it has a secured claim of $20,000; if the collateral has a value of $15,000 Bank is underse-cured and it has a secured claim of $15,000 and an unsecured claim of $5,000. The value of the collateral is determined by the bankruptcy court.

## 6.   DISTRIBUTION OF ASSETS TO UNSECURED CREDITORS

In Chapter 7, after the trustee has disposed of property of the estate in satisfaction of secured claims, the remaining property will be distributed pursuant to BC 726, which states an order of priority among the various claimants. First to be paid are the ten priority claims set out in BC 507 in the order of priority prescribed in that provision. The first priority is domestic support obligations, defined in BC 101(14A). Second priority is administrative expenses described in BC 503. Other priority claims are ranked in an ever-growing list of additional categories by BC 507(a)(3)–

(10). The most important are certain claims of employees of the debtor that have a fourth and fifth priority and taxes with an eighth priority. After all priority claims have been paid in their order of priority, distribution is made pursuant to BC 726 to the remaining creditors. With some exceptions these claims are paid on a pro rata basis to the extent of the property available.

The BC 507 priorities also apply to cases under Chapters 11, 12 and 13. Under Chapters 12 and 13 the plan must provide for payment in full of all priority claims, but deferred payment can be made, with interest, over the period of the plan. A Chapter 11 plan must provide for payment in full of all priority claims. Some priority claims must be paid in cash on the effective date of the plan and some can be paid, with interest, over time.

## 7.   DISCHARGE

In Chapter 7, a debtor who is an individual will normally receive a discharge from prebankruptcy debts. BC 727(b). For individuals the primary purpose of filing a petition in Chapter 7 bankruptcy is to obtain this discharge. In some cases, however, the debtor is not entitled to a discharge. The various grounds for denying a discharge to a debtor in Chapter 7 are set forth in BC 727(a). A debtor is not entitled to a discharge if the debtor has received a discharge under Chapter 7 in a case commenced within eight years of the time the current case was commenced. The other grounds stated for denying discharge refer to misconduct by the debtor. This reflects the fact that bankruptcy is an equitable proceeding and that a debtor guilty of certain inequitable conduct should not enjoy the benefit of a discharge. Even in cases in which the debtor is entitled to discharge, not all debts are dischargeable. Discharge is a benefit to the debtor and a concomitant loss to the creditor. While a debtor is generally entitled to a discharge of prepetition debts, in some cases the creditor may have equities that are greater than those of the debtor. In those cases the law provides that the debt of that creditor is nondischargeable. In effect, that creditor can participate in the distribution of the debtor's property, but to the extent that the creditor's debt has not been satisfied, the creditor will have a claim against the debtor that survives bankruptcy. Debts that are excepted from a Chapter 7 discharge are described in BC 523(a). Chapters 11, 12 and 13 have their own discharge provisions. Corporations and partnerships may be discharged in Chapter 11 and Chapter 12, but not in Chapter 7. The Chapter 11 discharge for non-individual debtors is extremely broad and is not subject to the special exceptions to dischargeability applicable under BC 523(a).

## B.   SECURED CLAIMS IN BANKRUPTCY

## 1.   MEANING OF SECURED CLAIM

As we saw in the introductory material, when a debtor whose property is subject to an Article 9 security interest files in bankruptcy, the secured party enters a new legal world. The governing law is now federal law, the

Bankruptcy Code, and all cases and controversies in bankruptcy are heard by bankruptcy judges. Even the creditor's label changes: instead of being a secured party it is now the holder of a "secured claim" under BC 506(a)(1). The collateral is now property of the debtor's estate under BC 541(a) and subject to the jurisdiction of the bankruptcy court. In fact, BC 506(a)(1) defines a "secured claim" broadly to include claims secured by any lien on property, not just consensually created liens. In the preceding chapters, you have learned how to create, perfect and enforce a security interest under Article 9. In this chapter we will see that bankruptcy law modifies the rights of the parties under Article 9 to such an extent that no business lawyer working with Article 9 transactions can competently plan these transactions without an understanding of the effect of bankruptcy law.

In the competition among creditors to share in the debtor's assets in bankruptcy, a secured claim is the gold standard, for it is prior to unsecured claims, however meritorious those claims may be. Secured claims "take off the top." We find this principle in BC 725, which says that before final distribution of the estate to the unsecured creditors "the trustee * * * shall dispose of any property in which an entity other than the estate has an interest, such as a lien * * * " That entity is the secured party. Article 9 makes it very easy for a creditor to take a perfected security interest in all of the tangible and intangible personal property that a debtor now owns or will acquire in the future, leaving nothing for unsecured creditors. We have seen that the only public notice a secured party need give to establish this powerful priority is a brief indication in a financing statement that it may claim a security interest in all the debtor's personal property. Some respected academics were so incensed by Revised Article 9's "secured-creditors-uber-alles" approach that they proposed that either Article 9 or the Bankruptcy Code contain a "carve out" of 20% of secured assets to be set aside for unsecured claims, at least in bankruptcy. This proposal was never seriously considered by the drafters of Revised Article 9. (English bankruptcy law recently has adopted a "carve-out" provision applicable to floating liens when collateral exceeds a stipulated minimum value.) But bankruptcy lawyers have been battling with the holders of secured claims for many years, and, as we will see, the "avoidance powers" of the Bankruptcy Code give them some ammunition to work with.

Before going further in this chapter, you must be sure that you understand BC 506(a)(1). By way of review, suppose that at the time D files in bankruptcy, SP has a perfected security interest in an item of D's personal property securing a debt of $100,000.

Case #1. If the collateral has a value of $150,000, what is the amount of SP's secured claim? Of its unsecured claim?

Case #2. If the collateral has a value of $50,000, what is the amount of SP's secured claim? Of its unsecured claim?

## PROBLEM

At the time D files in bankruptcy, SP has a perfected security interest in an item of D's personal property securing a debt of $100,000 that has a value of only $50,000. After D's trustee in bankruptcy (T) examined the collateral, T chose not to take possession of the collateral and, pursuant to BC 554(a) abandoned the property and left it in D's possession, subject to SP's existing security interest. Under BC 704(1), the duty of a trustee is "to collect and reduce to money the property of the estate." In view of this provision, was T's action in abandoning the property appropriate?

## 2.   THE AUTOMATIC STAY

The first barrier facing the holder of a secured claim who wishes to enforce its security interest against a debtor's property in bankruptcy is the automatic stay of BC 362(a). The filing of the bankruptcy petition automatically operates as a stay; no formal order of a stay need be entered. The automatic stay is a form of an injunction; violators may in the discretion of the court be held in contempt and assessed damages. In a special provision, BC 362(k)(1) allows an "individual" injured by a willful violation of the stay to recover actual damages, costs and attorney's fees, and, under appropriate circumstances, punitive damages. Although the courts are divided on its meaning in BC 362(k)(1), the term "individual" is consistently used elsewhere in the Bankruptcy Code to refer to natural persons in contrast to legal entities such as corporations and partnerships.

BC 362(a)(5) stays any act of a prepetition secured creditor to enforce its security interest in property of the estate or of the debtor. Accordingly, a creditor having an Article 9 security interest in personal property is barred by the stay from availing itself of its rights under 9–609 to repossess by either self-help or judicial process. If the creditor is a pledgee or has retaken possession of the collateral before the debtor's petition, it may not realize on the collateral by either a judicial sale or nonjudicial creditor's sale under Article 9 after the petition. If the sale of the property had already been completed before the petition, the debtor has no right under 9–623 to redeem; the stay is inapplicable because property sold is no longer property of the estate or of the debtor, and the stay with respect to that property has ended. BC 362(c)(1).

The automatic stay ends when the case is closed or dismissed, BC 362(c)(2), but, as noted above, it may end earlier with respect to property that is no longer property of the estate. BC 362(c)(1). The holder of a secured claim may seek relief from the stay under BC 362(d), which allows the court to terminate or modify the stay on certain grounds.

## PROBLEMS

**1.** SP has a perfected security interest in an item of D's personal property securing a debt of $100,000. On Day 1, SP sent to D, who was in default, a notice that the collateral would be sold at a public sale to be held on Day 21. D received the notice and called SP, urging that the sale be postponed. SP declined. On Day 20, D filed in Chapter 7 bankruptcy, without notifying SP, who conducted the sale on Day 21 and purchased at its own sale by making a credit bid of $100,000. The sale was well advertised but no bid exceeded SP's bid, and you may assume that the sale was commercially reasonable in every respect. D's trustee in bankruptcy (T) attacked the sale as void in violation of BC 362(a). The sale did not involve the action of any court or judicial officer. Is T correct?

**2.** Debtor Corporation (D) sought a loan from Bank, which agreed to make the loan only if D granted a security interest in all its assets to Bank and obtained the signature of Garrison (G), who was the CEO and principal stockholder in D, as a guarantor. D complied with Bank's conditions. D ultimately defaulted on the loan and filed a petition in Chapter 7. Since Bank was stayed from proceeding against D by BC 362(a), it proceeded against G, as D's guarantor. Does BC 362(a) prevent Bank from suing G on her guaranty? Does it stay only claims against the debtor and property of the estate, or does it protect others? You may assume that if G is has to pay Bank, she will have recourse against D for reimbursement.

## 3. EFFECT OF DISCHARGE ON SECURED CLAIMS

Under 9–601(a), a secured party has two rights after default of the debtor: to hold the debtor personally liable on the secured obligation and to enforce its security interest by proceeding against the collateral. If an individual debtor in Chapter 7 is granted a discharge under BC 727(b), the effect is to discharge the debtor from any further personal liability on the obligation, but the security interest in the collateral remains unaffected. In other words, a discharge in effect transforms a recourse into a nonrecourse debt. BC 524(a). The theory of discharge has always been that it affects only the personal liability of the debtor. It does not affect the debt itself which remains unpaid. If third parties are liable on the debt they remain liable. For example, a surety or other guarantor is liable even through the principal debtor is released as a result of the discharge. This is specifically recognized in BC 524(e). Nor is an insurance carrier's liability affected by the discharge of the insured. Similarly, if the debt is secured by property of a third party that property can be reached to the full extent of the security agreement. The same rule applies if the discharged debt was secured by a lien in the debtor's property. The debt and the lien continue to exist after bankruptcy even though the debtor may have been discharged from personal liability to pay the debt and even though the creditor did not file a proof of claim in bankruptcy. This principle was recognized in Long v. Bullard, 117 U.S. 617 (1886), a case antedating the Bankruptcy Act of 1898. In that case, Long received a discharge in bankruptcy and retained as exempt property a homestead that was subject to a mortgage in favor of Bullard, who did not file proof of the mortgage debt in the bankruptcy. After bankruptcy, Bullard brought a foreclosure action. Long defended on the ground that the discharge prevented foreclosure under the mortgage. This defense was rejected in the state court, which stated that "there could be no personal recovery against [Long] upon the note, but that the property could be subjected to the payment of the amount due, as the discharge of Long in bankruptcy did not release the lien of the mortgage." The court entered a decree for sale of the property. The Supreme Court of the United States affirmed the decree.

BC 506(d), which was amended in the 1984 Amendments, is meant to preserve the rule of Long v. Bullard, but its wording is difficult to follow. The House Report on the Bankruptcy Reform Act of 1978 states with respect to the original version of BC 506(d): "Subsection (d) permits liens to pass through the bankruptcy case unaffected. However, if a party in interest requests the court to determine and allow or disallow the claim secured by the lien under section 502 and the claim is not allowed, then the lien is void to the extent that the claim is not allowed." 1978 U.S.C.C.A.N. 5963, 6313. BC 506(d) in both its original and amended form is phrased negatively. It states when a lien is void. Only by negative inference does it indicate that a lien not void under BC 506(d) will survive bankruptcy. It assumes that the rule of Long v. Bullard preserves a lien if the lien is not void under BC 506(d) and is not avoided by some other provision of the Code. The text of BC 506(d) follows:

> (d) To the extent that a lien secures a claim against the debtor that is not an allowed secured claim, such lien is void, unless—
>
> > (1) such claim was disallowed only under section 502(b)(5) [an unmatured claim for spousal or child support, etc.] or 502(e) [a claim for reimbursement or contribution] of this title; or
> >
> > (2) such claim is not an allowed secured claim due only to the failure of any entity to file a proof of such claim under section 501 of this title.

## PROBLEMS

**1.** Debtor (D), an individual, borrowed $100,000 from Bank to buy equipment and granted Bank a security interest in the equipment to secure the obligation. Later D defaulted on the obligation and filed Chapter 7 bankruptcy. At the time of D's bankruptcy, her obligation to Bank was $90,000, but the equipment was valued at only $60,000. D's trustee in bankruptcy (T) abandoned the equipment to D under BC 554. Bank filed an unsecured claim in D's bankruptcy for the $30,000 deficiency. After T had liquidated all D's other assets, unsecured claims, including Bank's deficiency claim, were paid 10% of the amount of the claims. Bank received $3,000. What are Bank's rights against D and the equipment after D receives a discharge?

**2.** If D were a corporation in Problem 1, it could not be granted a discharge under 727(a)(1). What is the policy basis for denying D a discharge in Chapter 7 but allowing it in Chapter 11? See BC 1141(d). What are Bank's rights in this case against D and the collateral?

## C.   TREATMENT OF SECURED CLAIMS IN CHAPTERS 7, 11 AND 13

In this section we use some specific examples to show how the rights of the debtor and the holder of a secured claim change depending on which chapter of the Bankruptcy Code the debtor chooses for relief.

## 1.   CONSUMER DEBTORS

Assume in the following discussion that Debtor owns an auto that is subject to a security interest in favor of Bank. The balance of the debt is $20,000 but the car is worth only $13,000. Debtor's financial position is precarious. She owes a good deal on her three credit cards and is in default on several other unsecured debts. She is two payments behind on her car but desperately needs to retain it in order to drive to work; there is no available public transportation, and if she loses her car she loses her job.

### a.   IN CHAPTER 7

If the car were property that Debtor did not wish to retain, the procedure in Chapter 7 would be simple. The trustee has two choices. It can sell the vehicle for, say, $13,000, free of Bank's security interest (BC 363(f)), and turn the money over to Bank. Bank may credit bid at the trustee's sale (BC 363(k)), that is, offset the balance of the debt against the purchase price and, if no one bids more, Bank will own the car. Bank will have an unsecured claim (BC 506(a)) for the $7,000 deficiency and can share with the other unsecured creditors in Debtor's unencumbered assets. The other alternative is more likely to be chosen by the trustee in this case. Since Bank has a secured claim equal to the value of the car ($13,000), the foreclosure sale is entirely for the benefit of Bank. The unsecured creditors will not benefit from it, and thus the trustee has no incentive to spend the time and money necessary to conduct the foreclosure sale. Hence, the court may grant a motion by Bank to lift the stay (BC 362(d)) or allow the trustee to abandon the auto to Debtor under BC 554(a). In either case Bank may then proceed to repossess and conduct a creditor's sale under Article 9. If the car is sold for $13,000, Bank may file a claim in Debtor's bankruptcy for the $7,000 deficiency. Bank may receive little or nothing for this claim, but Debtor will be discharged from any further liability to Bank.

If Debtor wishes to retain the auto, Chapter 7 offers two alternatives, neither of which is particularly appealing to Debtor. BC 722 empowers Debtor to redeem the property from Bank by paying only the amount of the allowed secured claim (the value of the collateral, BC 506(a)(1)), $13,000, leaving Bank with an unsecured claim for the balance. Although this is not a happy result for Bank because Debtor will be able to retain her car by paying less than the contract obligation, it is unattractive to the cash-strapped Debtor as well, for it offers her a remedy that she can avail herself of only if she can come up with the amount of the secured claim, $13,000, "in full at the time of redemption." BC 722.

The other alternative for Debtor is to enter into a postpetition agreement with Bank to reaffirm the debt under BC 524(c). By this agreement, Debtor undertakes to comply with the terms of the original contract—pay the balance owing on the $20,000 obligation—and, in effect, gives up her right to be discharged with respect to the debt reaffirmed. If Debtor again defaults and the property is resold for less than the amount of the debt then owed, Debtor is liable for the deficiency as though there had been no bankruptcy. Whether a debtor should be allowed to relinquish the right to a discharge with respect to a reaffirmed debt is a controversial policy matter. BC 524 was extensively amended by BAPCPA to provide better disclosure and enforcement for the protection of debtors in reaffirmation cases. Perhaps the very case that moved the drafters to allow reaffirmations to continue under the 1978 Code is the one we consider here: Debtor wishes to keep the car more than she wishes to be discharged from the debt.

Understandably, what debtors usually want in these cases is to keep the car without either redeeming or reaffirming. They would like to get back into the good graces of Bank by making up any back payments and to continue to use the auto while staying current on their payments. This is called a "ride-through." There has been a long-running battle between debtors and secured creditors in the courts over whether a debtor who is not in default on an installment contract can hold onto the car in a Chapter 7 bankruptcy *without the creditor's consent* and without either reaffirming or redeeming. BAPCPA effectively ended the "ride through" option that had been enjoyed by debtors in some jurisdictions by terminating the automatic stay under BC 362(h)(1) if the debtor fails to file within a prescribed period a statement of intention either to surrender or redeem or reaffirm. With the stay ended, the secured creditor may proceed under nonbankruptcy law to enforce its security interest. The debtor's contention that there has been no default since she is current on her payments will fail if the contract contains a provision declaring filing in bankruptcy an act of default. Resolving divided authority on the validity of such "ipso facto" clauses in bankruptcy, BC 521(d) provides that nothing in the Bankruptcy Code "shall prevent or limit the operation of" such provisions. Doubtless in many cases financers, reluctant to get involved in a bankruptcy and happy to be getting paid, allow debtors to retain possession as long as they are current in their payments.

## PROBLEMS

What does Bank have to lose in allowing Debtor a "ride-through"? If Debtor defaults again, Bank may repossess and dispose of the car. If Debtor doesn't default, Bank is paid the contract amount. So what's the cost to Bank in being big-hearted?

## b.  IN CHAPTER 13

Pre–2005 Chapter 13 gave Debtor what she wanted, that is, the right to retain the car, without Bank's consent, and to pay Bank in installments from her postpetition income. She could keep all her property, including her indispensable car, if she proposed a confirmable plan calling for her to pay all her disposable earnings over a three-year period to a standing trustee to be distributed to her creditors. The plan had to be approved by the court, but the consent of creditors was not necessary. In order for the plan to be approved by the court, Bank, as a secured creditor, had to receive payment of the present value of its secured claim ($13,000) in installments over the three-year life of the plan. Former BC 1325(a)(5). Debtor's unsecured creditors shared in what was left, but they had to receive as much in Chapter 13 as they would have received in Chapter 7, taking into account the fact that payment in Chapter 13 is on a deferred basis. Former BC 1325(a)(4). Thus, if Debtor's earnings were enough to pay off in installments the $13,000 secured claim with interest over a three-year period, she could hold on to her car. The $7,000 deficiency claim, along with other unsecured claims, would be paid only to the extent that Debtor had disposable income in excess of the amount needed to pay off the secured claims relating to property that Debtor wished to retain. Usually these payments were minimal. At the end of the three-year period, Debtor received a broad discharge. The power of debtors to strip-down security interests in assets they wished to retain, as in this case, was a major attraction of Chapter 13 for debtors: a debtor could keep her car by paying only its depreciated value in monthly installments and discharge her deficiency debt by paying pennies on the dollar. Good deal.

Too good, the creditors contended, and BAPCPA made major changes that substantially reduced the attraction of Chapter 13 for debtors. It arguably limits lien-stripping with respect to purchase money security interests in motor vehicles, as well as certain other collateral, by making inapplicable the bifurcation effect of BC 506(a)(1), in which an undersecured claim is divided into a secured claim for the value of the collateral and an unsecured claim for the remainder of the debt. The following language was added at the end of BC 1325(a):

> For the purposes of paragraph (5), section 506 shall not apply to a claim described in that paragraph if the creditor has a purchase money security interest securing the debt that is the subject of the claim, the debt was incurred within the 910–day [period] preceding the filing of the petition, and the collateral for that debtor consists of a motor vehicle * * * acquired for the personal use of the debtor, or if collateral for that debt consists of any other thing of value, if the debt was incurred during the 1–year period preceding that filing.

This provision is not well drafted and is open to a conflicting interpretation. Although its probable effect is to prevent the bifurcation of undersecured claims under 506(a)(1), there is another possibility. The provision states that "section 506 shall not apply . . ." to claims described in the paragraph quoted above. If BC 506 does not apply to a described claim, then the claim is not a "secured claim." After all, BC 506(a)(1) defines a "secured claim." Accordingly, if the claim is not a secured claim because 506 is inapplicable to it, then the entire claim apparently is unsecured. Thus, on this reading of the above provision, the provision turns qualifying undersecured claims into entirely unsecured claims. As such liens securing these claims can be stripped completely. The early trend in relevant case law interprets the provision to prevent lien-stripping of qualifying undersecured claims; compare In re Johnson, 337 B.R. 269 (Bankr. M.D.N.Y. 2006); In re Robinson, 338 B.R. 70 (Bankr. M.D. Ala. 2006) (representing majority view that entire claim secured) with In re Carver, 338 B.R. 521 (Bankr.

S.D. Ga. 2006); In re Wampler, 345 B.R. 730 (Bankr. D. Kan. 2006) (representing minority view that entire claim unsecured). The authorities are marshaled in In re Green, 2006 WL 2531531 (Bankr. M.D. Ga.).

According to the probable effect of this amendment, if Debtor wishes to retain her car by making installment payments to Bank under a Chapter 13 plan, the balance she must pay (with interest) over the life of the plan is $20,000 rather than $13,000, the value of the secured claim under BC 506(a). Treating undersecured purchase money automobile loans as fully secured reduces the amount of debtor's income payable to unsecured creditors to the great advantage of secured auto lenders. The effect is similar to reaffirmation of such debts. Moreover, under BC 1325(a)(5)(B)(iii), unless the debtor completes her plan (something that happens in only about one-third of the cases), the secured creditor retains a lien for the remaining unpaid balance. There is little incentive for buyers to retain their cars under such circumstances, and these measures remove a major incentive for debtors to opt for Chapter 13.

The following case examines Revised Article 9 provisions on repossession, transfer statements and redemption in the context of Chapter 13. Moreover, it shows the importance of the basic bankruptcy concept of property of the estate under BC 541.

# In re Robinson

United States Bankruptcy Court, W.D. Oklahoma, 2002.
285 B.R. 732.

■ NILES L. JACKSON, BANKRUPTCY JUDGE.

On September 26, 2001, Eldorado financed Debtor's purchase of a 1996 Cadillac automobile (hereinafter the "Vehicle") in return for which Debtor granted to Eldorado a security interest therein. When Debtor became delinquent on payments under the note, Eldorado exercised its right to self-help repossess the Vehicle pursuant to Okla. Stat. Ann. tit. 12A, § 9–609(a)(1) & (b)(2)(West 2001). Thereafter, Eldorado sent to Debtor a document entitled "Notice After Repossession or Voluntary Surrender" dated July 31, 2002 (hereinafter the "Notice of Sale"). See id. §§ 9–611–614. The Notice of Sale stated, inter alia, that Eldorado had obtained Debtor's Vehicle by repossession and would be offering it for private sale beginning August 13, 2002. Further, the Notice of Sale informed Debtor she could still redeem her Vehicle by paying in full the amount due under the contract up until the time the Vehicle was actually sold. See id. § 9–623. In contemplation of the disposition sale of Debtor's Vehicle, Eldorado applied for and obtained from the Oklahoma Tax Commission a "Repossession Title." This Repossession Title is in Eldorado's name and does not reflect any liens on the Vehicle.

On August 12, 2002, Debtor filed her voluntary chapter 13 petition. That same day, Debtor's attorney notified Eldorado of the bankruptcy filing and provided to Eldorado verification of liability, casualty, and comprehensive insurance coverage on the Vehicle. On August 13, 2002, Debtor's attorney provided similar notice to Eldorado's counsel and requested return of the Vehicle. Eldorado refused to surrender the Vehicle.

On August 15, 2002, Debtor filed her Motion for Turnover, Motion for Determination of Willful Violation of Automatic Stay, for Costs and Attorney Fees seeking return of her Vehicle and damages against Eldorado for willful violation of the automatic stay under § 362(h) (hereinafter the "Motion for Turnover"). Eldorado responded, asserting the Vehicle was not property of Debtor's bankruptcy estate, thus the automatic stay was not applicable. Eldorado alternatively asked, if the Court determined the stay was applicable, that the Court find it had not violated such stay, and that the Court terminate the stay so Eldorado could retain the Vehicle. At Debtor's request, the Court conducted an expedited hearing on the Motion for Turnover. At the conclusion of the hearing the Court ruled Eldorado's Repossession Title did not convey ownership of the Vehicle to Eldorado. Based upon that finding, the Court granted Debtor's Motion for Turnover and denied both parties' requests for costs.

Subsequently, Eldorado timely filed a Motion for Reconsideration of [its] Response to Debtor's Motion for Turnover (hereinafter the "Motion to Reconsider"). The Court conducted a hearing on Motion to Reconsider, at the conclusion of which the Court took the matter under advisement. The Court has reviewed the pleadings and the law applicable to the facts herein, and has considered the arguments of the parties, and rules as follows.

During the hearing on the Motion for Turnover, counsel for Eldorado argued that the fact Eldorado had obtained a Repossession Title meant that ownership of the Vehicle had been transferred to Eldorado. Based upon this argument, Eldorado asserted the Vehicle could not be property of Debtor's bankruptcy estate subject to the automatic stay. According to Eldorado, the nature and extent of Debtor's interest in the Vehicle at the time of bankruptcy filing was limited to the right to redeem under state law.

While counsel for Debtor conceded that Eldorado's pre-petition repossession was legal and proper, he argued that so long as the Vehicle had not been sold prior to Debtor's bankruptcy filing it must be returned to Debtor upon the filing of her Chapter 13. He pointed out that if the Court sustained Eldorado's position, then every creditor who repossessed a vehicle would immediately obtain a Repossession Title and thereby defeat all rights of debtors to bring their vehicles back into the bankruptcy estate.
* * *

Debtor's counsel argued that according to Oklahoma law, the title held by Eldorado was simply for the purpose of facilitating the transfer at a subsequent disposition sale.

In analyzing in the bankruptcy context the relative rights of the parties with respect to repossessed collateral, the Supreme Court's seminal decision in United States v. Whiting Pools, Inc., 462 U.S. 198, 103 S.Ct. 2309, 76 L.Ed.2d 515 (1983) is instructive. Much as in this case, in Whiting Pools the secured creditor seized the debtor's property pre-petition in order to enforce its lien, but had not sold the property as of the date the debtor filed its bankruptcy petition. The Supreme Court emphasized the broad scope of § 541(a)(1), noted that it "is intended to include in the estate any property made available to the estate by other provisions of the Bankruptcy Code," noted that § 542 "requires an entity (other than a custodian) holding any property of the debtor that the trustee can use under § 363 to turn that property over to the trustee," and concluded "that the reorganization estate includes property of the debtor that has been seized by a creditor prior to the filing of a petition for reorganization." Id., 462 U.S. at 209, 103 S.Ct. at 2313–2315.

Unlike this case, Whiting Pools involved a Chapter 11 reorganization. * * * However, numerous courts have applied the Whiting Pools analysis to Chapter 13 cases. * * * This Court concurs with the courts that have extended Whiting Pools to the Chapter 13 context.

In applying Whiting Pools to the instant case, the Supreme Court's statement that § 542(a) may not apply where a seizure transfers ownership of the property to the creditor becomes relevant. While a determination of whether the debtor's interest is property of the estate is a matter of federal law * * * the nature and existence of a debtor's interest in property is determined in accordance with state law.

Pursuant to Oklahoma law, the transaction at issue, which created a security interest in personal property and occurred after July 1, 2001, comes within the scope of revised UNIFORM COMMERCIAL CODE ("UCC") Article 9 which has been enacted in Oklahoma and became effective July 1, 2001. Okla. Stat. Ann. tit. 12A, § 9–108 (West 2001). * * * Thus, the primary question before the Court is whether the Repossession Title obtained by Eldorado transferred legal ownership of the Vehicle from Debtor to Eldorado.

In order to make that determination, it is necessary to review the repossession procedure. Section 9–609 authorizes a secured creditor to self-help repossess its collateral, without a breach of the peace, after there is a default by the debtor. Thereafter, the secured party may dispose of the collateral by sale, lease, license, or other means, so long as every aspect of the disposition is commercially reasonable. § 9–610(a) & (b). In order to effect such disposition sale, it may be necessary for the secured creditor to seek transfer of record or legal title pursuant to § 9–619. Under this section, the secured creditor prepares a "transfer statement" * * *

> (c) A transfer of the record or legal title to collateral to a secured party under subsection (b) of this section or otherwise is not of itself a disposition of collateral under this article and does not of itself relieve the secured party of its duties under this article.

§ 9–619 (emphasis added). The Oklahoma Comments to this section [Comment 2] add clarification:

> [u]nder subsection (c), a transfer of record or legal title (under subsection (b) or under other law) to a secured party prior to the exercise of those remedies merely puts the secured party in a position to pass legal

or record title to a transferee at foreclosure. A secured party who has obtained record or legal title retains its duties with respect to enforcement of its security interest, and the debtor retains its rights as well.
* * *

What, then, are the relative rights of the parties herein? As of the petition date, Debtor's rights included the right to notice of the sale of the repossessed collateral, the right to the surplus proceeds, if any, from the sale of the collateral, and the right to redeem the collateral prior to sale by tendering "fulfillment of all obligations secured by the collateral" and payment of reasonable expenses and attorney fees. §§ 9–611, 615(d)(1) & 623. These are the very rights possessed by the debtor in the Whiting Pools case, where the Supreme Court found the debtor to be the owner of the property. 462 U.S. at 211, 103 S.Ct. at 2317. The Supreme Court further determined that "[o]wnership of the property is transferred only when the property is sold to a bona fide purchaser...." Id. "Until such a sale takes place, the property remains the debtor's and thus is subject to the turnover requirement of § 542(a)." Id.

Eldorado's interest in the Vehicle, as of the petition date, was therefore limited to enforcement of its security interest or lien, as it is only upon consummation of a disposition sale of the collateral that all of the debtor's rights in the collateral are transferred and the security interest is discharged. § 9–617(a)(1) & (2). * * * Therefore, as of the petition date, Debtor retained an interest in the Vehicle, subject to Eldorado's lien, and this interest was included among property of the bankruptcy estate. Based upon the foregoing, the Court reaffirms its Order Granting Debtor's Motion for Turnover.

Even though the parties have disagreed on the ownership issue, there is no dispute that Debtor's right of redemption is property of the bankruptcy estate. Eldorado has argued that if Debtor desires to redeem her Vehicle, she must do so in accordance with state law, which would require her to tender "fulfillment of all obligations secured by the collateral" along with payment of certain expenses and fees. § 9–623(b). Oklahoma law requires that where, as here, the creditor has accelerated the entire balance of the obligation, the debtor must tender the entire balance. Id. at UCC Comment 2. Based upon the cases submitted after the hearing on reconsideration, it appears Eldorado's position is that Debtor's sole remaining remedy consists of her right to redeem the Vehicle in accordance with state law. * * *

However * * * in this case in which the disposition sale of the collateral has not yet occurred, Debtor is not limited to the state law right of redemption * * *. Debtor also retains the rights conferred upon her by § 1322(b)(2) to modify the rights of holders of secured claims, and by § 1322(b)(3) to cure the default and thereby negate the effect of Eldorado's acceleration clause. Anderson v. Associate Comm'l Corp. (In re Anderson), 29 B.R. 563 (Bankr.E.D.Va.1983) (citation omitted). As so cogently expressed by the Anderson court:

> [t]he right to cure default and reinstate an accelerated note is granted by federal bankruptcy law and cannot be frustrated by the law of any

state. In re Taddeo, 685 F.2d 24, 28 (2d Cir.1982). By allowing debtors to cure defaults in cases in which there is still a right of redemption under state law, this section furthers the intent of Chapter 13 which is to facilitate debtor rehabilitation while protecting the rights of creditors. Taddeo at 29; . . . . Other courts with factual situations identical to that found in the instant case are in accord. . . . In each of these cases the courts concluded that the debtor's right to redeem their property was a part of the bankruptcy estate.

Anderson, 29 B.R. at 565 (some citations omitted). Debtor's proposed Chapter 13 Plan complies with the applicable provisions of the Bankruptcy Code, preserves Eldorado's lien, and provides for pro rata payments of Eldorado's allowed secured claim with interest. According to the latest information available to the Court, the Vehicle is insured and Debtor is current on her payments to the Chapter 13 Trustee. Eldorado has not argued that it is not adequately protected, and Debtor has represented that the Vehicle is necessary for her to keep her job. Thus, for the reasons so persuasively articulated by the Anderson court, this Court concludes that Debtor's proposed plan is a permissible method of retaining her Vehicle in Chapter 13.

Eldorado's Motion to Reconsider is granted. The Court having duly reconsidered, finds that Debtor retains an interest in the Vehicle subject to Eldorado's lien, and the Vehicle therefore is included among the property of the bankruptcy estate. Based upon that finding, the Court reaffirms its prior Order Granting Debtor's Motion for Turnover. This ruling will necessitate re-issuance of the certificate of title to reflect Debtor as the legal owner of the Vehicle and Eldorado as the lienholder.

Further, the Court concludes that Debtor is entitled to exercise the rights conferred upon her by § 1322(b), and that Debtor's proposed plan is a permissible method of retaining her Vehicle in Chapter 13, subject to confirmation of her proposed plan which is currently set for hearing December 17, 2002.


NOTE

Would Debtor's plan comply with the amended version of BC 1325(a)(final paragraph)?

## 2.   BUSINESS DEBTORS

Assume in the following discussion that Hospital (H), a corporation, is unsuccessfully struggling with the exigencies of the new managed care regime that governmental agencies and insurance companies have imposed on it. H's cash flow is inadequate to meet its obligations and its creditors are pressing for payment. One of the creditors is Lender, which holds a purchase money security interest in H's only Magnetic Resonance Imaging (MRI) machine, an important diagnostic device. Although the value of the machine has shrunk to $1 million, H's obligation to Lender that is secured by the machine is $1.5. Lender is threatening to repossess. H owes several hundred thousand dollars to various unsecured trade creditors, as well as to unpaid attending physicians who have performed services for H.

### a.   IN CHAPTER 7

Assume that H is hopelessly insolvent and has been attempting, without success, to sell its business for some time. H's aging management has decided to give up and liquidate in Chapter 7. The analysis here is not unlike that above for the consumer debtor, except that, for the reasons discussed above, H cannot be discharged in Chapter 7. So there is no issue in corporate Chapter 7s of a debtor's retaining assets of the estate; the business must dissolve, and everything must go to its creditors. Here again the trustee has its choice of conducting the foreclosure sale of the collateral or, as is likely here, of lifting the stay or abandoning the property to H and leaving it to Lender to proceed under Article 9. In either instance, Lender can credit bid the amount of its debt and file an unsecured claim for the deficiency.

### b.   IN CHAPTER 11: CONFIRMATION

Suppose H's board of directors won't give up; they hire new management and try to reorganize under Chapter 11. Usually no trustee will be appointed and H, meaning its board, will serve as debtor in possession with the powers of a trustee in bankruptcy. BC 1107. H will have two major tasks in the months following filing. First, it must improve its business operations so that it can create cash flow adequate to meet its current expenses of operation. This may entail downsizing and often involves obtaining some postpetition financing. If H is unable to right the sinking ship, it will have to go into Chapter 7, as a very large percentage of small enterprises that attempt to reorganize under Chapter 11 ultimately do. Second, H must deal with its unhappy prepetition creditors by seeking to achieve confirmation of a plan of reorganization. It has the exclusive right to propose a plan for 120 days (BC 1121(b)) after filing and to obtain acceptance of it within an additional 60 days (BC 1121(c)). The court has discretionary authority to grant extensions of these periods (BC 1121(d)), and often does, but since 2005 the period of exclusivity has been limited to 18 months after filing. After the period of exclusivity has ended, creditors and others may propose their own plans. In a small case like this one, it's likely that only the debtor in possession will propose a plan and that the 18-month limitation on exclusivity will not pose difficulties.

Typically the plan will provide for retention by the debtor of property needed by the reorganized enterprise and for payment, in full or in part, of secured and unsecured claims under the terms of the plan, often over a period of years, or the conversion of some debt claims into equity interests in H. A Chapter 11 plan can be confirmed by the court only if (1) all classes of impaired claims vote to accept the plan (BC 1129(a)), or (2) the plan complies with the requirements of BC 1129(b), in which case the court must confirm the plan even though one or more classes of impaired claims have not accepted the plan. The latter case is popularly referred to as "cramdown." The great majority of cases in which Chapter 11 plans are confirmed are consensual plans under BC 1129(a), in which all classes of impaired claims have accepted the plan. In large cases, this acceptance by creditors is sometimes obtained only after prolonged bargaining.

Secured parties, like Lender, have a strong position from which to bargain. Since each secured creditor is usually the only member of its class, by withholding its consent it can bar confirmation of the plan under BC 1129(a). If a secured party does not accept the plan, cramdown can occur under BC 1129(b)(2)(A) only if the secured party receives the economic value of its secured claim under the terms of the plan. Hence, Lender may go into negotiations demanding full payment of its claim of $1.5 million upon confirmation, but, if agreement cannot be reached between Lender and H, Lender will either (1) receive in cramdown the present value of its secured claim ($1 million), plus whatever distribution it receives for its unsecured deficiency claim ($500,000), which may be minimal, or (2), if a BC 1111(b)(2) election is made, the value of its secured claim ($1 million), paid in installments totalling $1.5 million. We leave an explanation of BC 1111(b) to a course in bankruptcy.

## 3.  VALUING COLLATERAL IN BANKRUPTCY

Collateral must be valued in a bankruptcy proceeding for a number of purposes. For instance, the amount of a secured claim is the value of the collateral securing the claim. BC 506(a)(1). And whether a secured creditors' security interest is adequately protected depends on the whether the debtor's use of collateral affects its value. More controversial is whether adequate protection requires compensating the secured creditor for the time value of the money: in this case the returns on proceeds the creditor could have realized had it foreclosed and disposed of the collateral. BC 362(d). For each of these purposes, the value of collateral must be determined. Finally, to be confirmable, repayment plans under Chapter 11 and Chapter 13 plans must promise secured creditors amounts at least equal to their secured claims. BC 1129(b)(2)(A), 1325(a)(5). BC 506(a)(1) in turn defines a secured claim by the value of collateral securing the claim ("to the extent of the value of such creditor's interest in the estate's interest in such property"). Thus, the confirmation of a repayment plan depends indirectly on valuations of the collateral.

There are two questions in play here: what is the secured creditor's "interest" in the collateral? And how is the value of that interest measured? In United States Savings Ass'n v. Timbers of Inwood Assoc., 484 U.S. 365 (1988), the Supreme Court answered the first question by holding that the secured creditor's interest in collateral did not include returns on the reinvestment of proceeds of collateral. Focusing on the first sentence of BC 506(a)(1), the Court construed the secured creditor's "interest in property" to exclude its right to repossess and dispose of collateral on default. Thus, BC 506(a)(1) doesn't protect the secured creditor's right to compensation for foregone interest on proceeds of collateral over the course of the bankruptcy case. BC 506(b) protects an oversecured creditor's right to postfiling interest on collateral to the extent that its value is enough to cover the interest claim. According to *Timbers of Inwood*, the Bankruptcy Code doesn't do the same for an undersecured creditor.

The second question asks how the security interest in collateral is valued. In a Chapter 7 case collateral value is easy to determine because liquidation provides a market test of value. The collateral is disposed of, often by sale at auction, and the winning bid establishes the value of the asset purchased. In these circumstances the value of the collateral is the amount the secured creditor realizes from its orderly disposal. In Chapter 11 and Chapter 13 cases, where the debtor's plan proposes to retain the collateral, market tests of value aren't available. The Bankruptcy Code still requires that the collateral be valued, and some measure of value must be set. BC 506(a)(1) doesn't explicitly set the measure of value. The first sentence of 506(a)(1) only defines the secured creditor's interest in collateral, as *Timbers of Inwood* found. It doesn't measure that value. BC 506(a)(1)'s second sentence instead measures the value of collateral: "Such value shall be determined in light of the purpose of the valuation and of the proposed disposition or use of such property, and in conjunction with any hearing on such disposition or use or on a plan affecting such creditor's interest." Chapter 11 or 13 plans often propose that the debtor "use" the collateral by retaining it. How is the value of the collateral measured in these cases? The Supreme Court answers the question in the following case. In reading *Rash* consider whether the Court's interpretation of BC 506(a)(1) gives the secured creditor more than it is entitled to outside of bankruptcy. Also consider, taking into account footnote 6 of the opinion, whether the "replacement value" measure adopted by the Court is easily applied by bankruptcy courts.

## Associates Commercial Corporation v. Rash

Supreme Court of the United States, 1997.
520 U.S. 953.

■ JUSTICE GINSBURG delivered the opinion of the Court.*

We resolve in this case a dispute concerning the proper application of § 506(a) of the Bankruptcy Code when a bankrupt debtor has exercised the "cram down" option for which Code § 1325(a)(5)(B) provides. Specifically, when a debtor, over a secured creditor's objection, seeks to retain and use the creditor's collateral in a Chapter 13 plan, is the value of the collateral to be determined by (1) what the secured creditor could obtain through foreclosure sale of the property (the "foreclosure-value" standard); (2) what the debtor would have to pay for comparable property (the "replacement-value" standard); or (3) the midpoint between these two measurements? We hold that § 506(a) directs application of the replacement-value standard.

* Justice Scalia joins all but footnote 4 of this opinion.

## I

In 1989, respondent Elray Rash purchased for $73,700 a Kenworth tractor truck for use in his freight-hauling business. Rash made a downpayment on the truck, agreed to pay the seller the remainder in 60 monthly installments, and pledged the truck as collateral on the unpaid balance. The seller assigned the loan, and its lien on the truck, to petitioner Associates Commercial Corporation (ACC).

In March 1992, Elray and Jean Rash filed a joint petition and a repayment plan under Chapter 13 of the Bankruptcy Code (Code), 11 U.S.C. §§ 1301–1330. At the time of the bankruptcy filing, the balance owed to ACC on the truck loan was $41,171. Because it held a valid lien on the truck, ACC was listed in the bankruptcy petition as a creditor holding a secured claim. Under the Code, ACC's claim for the balance owed on the truck was secured only to the extent of the value of the collateral; its claim over and above the value of the truck was unsecured. See 11 U.S.C. § 506(a).

To qualify for confirmation under Chapter 13, the Rashes' plan had to satisfy the requirements set forth in § 1325(a) of the Code. The Rashes' treatment of ACC's secured claim, in particular, is governed by subsection (a)(5).[1] Under this provision, a plan's proposed treatment of secured claims can be confirmed if one of three conditions is satisfied: The secured creditor accepts the plan, see 11 U.S.C. § 1325(a)(5)(A); the debtor surrenders the property securing the claim to the creditor, see § 1325(a)(5)(C); or the debtor invokes the so-called "cram down" power, see § 1325(a)(5)(B). Under the cram down option, the debtor is permitted to keep the property over the objection of the creditor; the creditor retains the lien securing the claim, see § 1325(a)(5)(B)(i), and the debtor is required to provide the creditor with payments, over the life of the plan, that will total the present value of the allowed secured claim, i.e., the present value of the collateral, see § 1325(a)(5)(B)(ii). The value of the allowed secured claim is governed by § 506(a) of the Code.

The Rashes' Chapter 13 plan invoked the cram down power. It proposed that the Rashes retain the truck for use in the freight-hauling business and pay ACC, over 58 months, an amount equal to the present value of the truck. That value, the Rashes' petition alleged, was $28,500. ACC objected to the plan and asked the Bankruptcy Court to lift the automatic stay so ACC could repossess the truck. ACC also filed a proof of

---

**1.** Section 1325(a)(5) states: "(a) Except as provided in subsection (b), the court shall confirm a plan if—

. . . . .

"(5) with respect to each allowed secured claim provided for by the plan—

"(A) the holder of such claim has accepted the plan;

"(B)(i) the plan provides that the holder of such claim retain the lien securing such claim; and

"(ii) the value, as of the effective date of the plan, of property to be distributed under the plan on account of such claim is not less than the allowed amount of such claim; or

"(C) the debtor surrenders the property securing such claim to such holder."

claim alleging that its claim was fully secured in the amount of $41,171. The Rashes filed an objection to ACC's claim.

The Bankruptcy Court held an evidentiary hearing to resolve the dispute over the truck's value. At the hearing, ACC and the Rashes urged different valuation benchmarks. ACC maintained that the proper valuation was the price the Rashes would have to pay to purchase a like vehicle, an amount ACC's expert estimated to be $41,000. The Rashes, however, maintained that the proper valuation was the net amount ACC would realize upon foreclosure and sale of the collateral, an amount their expert estimated to be $31,875. The Bankruptcy Court agreed with the Rashes and fixed the amount of ACC's secured claim at $31,875; that sum, the court found, was the net amount ACC would realize if it exercised its right to repossess and sell the truck. See *In re Rash*, 149 B.R. 430, 431–432 (Bkrtcy.Ct.E.D.Tex.1993). The Bankruptcy Court thereafter approved the plan, and the United States District Court for the Eastern District of Texas affirmed.

A panel of the Court of Appeals for the Fifth Circuit reversed. *In re Rash*, 31 F.3d 325 (1994). On rehearing en banc, however, the Fifth Circuit affirmed the District Court, holding that ACC's allowed secured claim was limited to $31,875, the net foreclosure value of the truck. *In re Rash*, 90 F.3d 1036 (1996).

In reaching its decision, the Fifth Circuit highlighted, first, a conflict it perceived between the method of valuation ACC advanced, and the law of Texas defining the rights of secured creditors. See *id.*, at 1041–1042 (citing Tex. Bus. & Com.Code Ann. §§ 9.504(a), (c), 9.505 (1991)). In the Fifth Circuit's view, valuing collateral in a federal bankruptcy proceeding under a replacement-value standard—thereby setting an amount generally higher than what a secured creditor could realize pursuing its state-law foreclosure remedy—would "chang[e] the extent to which ACC is secured from what obtained under state law prior to the bankruptcy filing." 90 F.3d, at 1041. Such a departure from state law, the Fifth Circuit said, should be resisted by the federal forum unless "clearly compel[led]" by the Code. *Id.*, at 1042.

The Fifth Circuit then determined that the Code provision governing valuation of security interests, § 506(a), does not compel a replacement-value approach. Instead, the court reasoned, the first sentence of § 506(a) requires that collateral be valued from the creditor's perspective. See *id.*, at 1044. And because "the creditor's interest is in the nature of a security interest, giving the creditor the right to repossess and sell the collateral and nothing more[,] . . . the valuation should start with what the creditor could realize by exercising that right." *Ibid.* This foreclosure-value standard, the Fifth Circuit found, was consistent with the other relevant provisions of the Code, economic analysis, and the legislative history of the pertinent provisions. See *id.*, at 1045–1059. Judge Smith, joined by five other judges, dissented, urging that the Code dictates a replacement-value standard. See *id.*, at 1061–1075.

Courts of Appeals have adopted three different standards for valuing a security interest in a bankruptcy proceeding when the debtor invokes the cram down power to retain the collateral over the creditor's objection. In contrast to the Fifth Circuit's foreclosure-value standard, a number of Circuits have followed a replacement-value approach. See, *e.g., In re Taffi,* 96 F.3d 1190, 1191–1192 (C.A.9 1996) (en banc), cert. pending *sub nom. Taffi v. United States,* No. 96–881;[2] *In re Winthrop Old Farm Nurseries, Inc.,* 50 F.3d 72, 74–75 (C.A.1 1995); *In re Trimble,* 50 F.3d 530, 531–532 (C.A.8 1995). Other courts have settled on the midpoint between foreclosure value and replacement value. See *In re Hoskins,* 102 F.3d 311, 316 (C.A.7 1996); cf. *In re Valenti,* 105 F.3d 55, 62 (C.A.2 1997) (bankruptcy courts have discretion to value at midpoint between replacement value and foreclosure value). We granted certiorari to resolve this conflict among the Courts of Appeals, see 519 U.S. 1086, 117 S.Ct. 758, 136 L.Ed.2d 694 (1997), and we now reverse the Fifth Circuit's judgment.

## II

The Code provision central to the resolution of this case is § 506(a), which states:

> "An allowed claim of a creditor secured by a lien on property in which the estate has an interest . . . is a secured claim to the extent of the value of such creditor's interest in the estate's interest in such property, . . . and is an unsecured claim to the extent that the value of such creditor's interest . . . is less than the amount of such allowed claim. Such value shall be determined in light of the purpose of the valuation and of the proposed disposition or use of such property. . . ." 11 U.S.C. § 506(a).

Over ACC's objection, the Rashes' repayment plan proposed, pursuant to § 1325(a)(5)(B), continued use of the property in question, *i.e.,* the truck, in the debtor's trade or business. In such a "cram down" case, we hold, the value of the property (and thus the amount of the secured claim under § 506(a)) is the price a willing buyer in the debtor's trade, business, or situation would pay to obtain like property from a willing seller.

Rejecting this replacement-value standard, and selecting instead the typically lower foreclosure-value standard, the Fifth Circuit trained its attention on the first sentence of § 506(a). In particular, the Fifth Circuit relied on these first sentence words: A claim is secured "to the extent of the value of such *creditor's interest* in the estate's interest in such property." See 90 F.3d, at 1044 (emphasis added) (citing § 506(a)). The Fifth Circuit

---

**2.** In *In re Taffi,* the Ninth Circuit contrasted replacement value with fair-market value and adopted the latter standard, apparently viewing the two standards as incompatible. See 96 F.3d, at 1192. By using the term "replacement value," we do not suggest that a creditor is entitled to recover what it would cost the debtor to purchase the collateral brand new. Rather, our use of the term replacement value is consistent with the Ninth Circuit's understanding of the meaning of fair-market value; by replacement value, we mean the price a willing buyer in the debtor's trade, business, or situation would pay a willing seller to obtain property of like age and condition. See also *infra,* at 1886–1887, n. 6.

read this phrase to instruct that the "starting point for the valuation [is] what the creditor could realize if it sold the estate's interest in the property according to the security agreement," namely, through "repossess[ing] and sell [ing] the collateral." *Ibid.*

We do not find in the § 506(a) first sentence words—"the creditor's interest in the estate's interest in such property"—the foreclosure-value meaning advanced by the Fifth Circuit. Even read in isolation, the phrase imparts no valuation standard: A direction simply to consider the "value of such creditor's interest" does not expressly reveal *how* that interest is to be valued.

Reading the first sentence of § 506(a) as a whole, we are satisfied that the phrase the Fifth Circuit considered key is not an instruction to equate a "creditor's interest" with the net value a creditor could realize through a foreclosure sale. The first sentence, in its entirety, tells us that a secured creditor's claim is to be divided into secured and unsecured portions, with the secured portion of the claim limited to the value of the collateral. See *United States v. Ron Pair Enterprises, Inc.*, 489 U.S. 235, 238–239, 109 S.Ct. 1026, 1029, 103 L.Ed.2d 290 (1989); 4 L. King, Collier on Bankruptcy ¶ 506.02[a], p. 506–6 (15th ed. rev.1996). To separate the secured from the unsecured portion of a claim, a court must compare the creditor's claim to the value of "such property," *i.e.*, the collateral. That comparison is sometimes complicated. A debtor may own only a part interest in the property pledged as collateral, in which case the court will be required to ascertain the "estate's interest" in the collateral. Or, a creditor may hold a junior or subordinate lien, which would require the court to ascertain the creditor's interest in the collateral. The § 506(a) phrase referring to the "creditor's interest in the estate's interest in such property" thus recognizes that a court may encounter, and in such instances must evaluate, limited or partial interests in collateral. The full first sentence of § 506(a), in short, tells a court what it must evaluate, but it does not say more; it is not enlightening on how to value collateral.

The second sentence of § 506(a) does speak to the *how* question. "Such value," that sentence provides, "shall be determined in light of the purpose of the valuation and of the proposed disposition or use of such property." § 506(a). By deriving a foreclosure-value standard from § 506(a)'s first sentence, the Fifth Circuit rendered inconsequential the sentence that expressly addresses how "value shall be determined."

As we comprehend § 506(a), the "proposed disposition or use" of the collateral is of paramount importance to the valuation question. If a secured creditor does not accept a debtor's Chapter 13 plan, the debtor has two options for handling allowed secured claims: surrender the collateral to the creditor, see § 1325(a)(5)(C); or, under the cram down option, keep the collateral over the creditor's objection and provide the creditor, over the life of the plan, with the equivalent of the present value of the collateral, see § 1325(a)(5)(B). The "disposition or use" of the collateral thus turns on the alternative the debtor chooses—in one case the collateral will be surrendered to the creditor, and in the other, the collateral will be retained and used by the debtor. Applying a foreclosure-value standard when the cram down option is invoked attributes no significance to the different consequences of the debtor's choice to surrender the property or retain it. A replacement-value standard, on the other hand, distinguishes retention from surrender and renders meaningful the key words "disposition or use."

Tying valuation to the actual "disposition or use" of the property points away from a foreclosure-value standard when a Chapter 13 debtor, invoking cram down power, retains and uses the property. Under that option, foreclosure is averted by the debtor's choice and over the creditor's objection. From the creditor's perspective as well as the debtor's, surrender and retention are not equivalent acts.

When a debtor surrenders the property, a creditor obtains it immediately, and is free to sell it and reinvest the proceeds. We recall here that ACC sought that very advantage. See *supra*, at 1882. If a debtor keeps the property and continues to use it, the creditor obtains at once neither the property nor its value and is exposed to double risks: The debtor may again default and the property may deteriorate from extended use. Adjustments in the interest rate and secured creditor demands for more "adequate protection," 11 U.S.C. § 361, do not fully offset these risks. See 90 F.3d, at 1066 (Smith, J., dissenting) ("vast majority of reorganizations fail ... leaving creditors with only a fraction of the compensation due them"; where, as here, "collateral depreciates rapidly, the secured creditor may receive far less in a failed reorganization than in a prompt foreclosure" (internal cross-reference omitted)); accord, *In re Taffi*, 96 F.3d, at 1192–1193.[3]

Of prime significance, the replacement-value standard accurately gauges the debtor's "use" of the property. It values "the creditor's interest in the collateral in light of the proposed [repayment plan] reality: no foreclosure sale and economic benefit for the debtor derived from the collateral equal to ... its [replacement] value." *In re Winthrop Old Farm Nurseries*, 50 F.3d, at 75. The debtor in this case elected to use the collateral to generate an income stream. That actual use, rather than a foreclosure sale that will not take place, is the proper guide under a prescription hinged to the property's "disposition or use." See *ibid.*[4]

The Fifth Circuit considered the replacement-value standard disrespectful of state law, which permits the secured creditor to sell the

---

**3.** On this matter, *amici curiae* supporting ACC contended: " 'Adequate protection' payments under 11 U.S.C. §§ 361, 362(d)(1) typically are based on the assumption that the collateral will be subject to only ordinary depreciation. Hence, even when such payments are made, they frequently fail to compensate adequately for the usually more rapid depreciation of assets retained by the debtor." Brief for American Automobile Manufacturers Association, Inc., et al. as *Amici Curiae* 21, n. 9.

**4.** We give no weight to the legislative history of § 506(a), noting that it is unedifying, offering snippets that might support either standard of valuation. The Senate Report simply repeated the phrase contained in the second sentence of § 506(a). See S.Rep. No. 95–989, 95th Cong. 2nd Sess. p. 68 (1978) U.S.Code Cong. & Admin.News 1978, pp. 5787, 5854. The House Report, in the Fifth Circuit's view, rejected a "replacement cost" valuation. See *In re Rash*, 90 F.3d 1036, 1056 (C.A.5 1996) (quoting H. Rep. No. 95–595, 95th Cong. 2nd Sess. p. 124 (1977) U.S.Code Cong. & Admin.News 1978, pp. 5963, 6085). That Report, however, appears to use the term " 'replacement cost' " to mean the cost of buying new property to replace property in collateral, thereby obtaining its net foreclosure value "and nothing more." See 90 F.3d, at 1044. In allowing Chapter 13 debtors to retain and use collateral over the objection of secured creditors, however, the Code has reshaped debtor and creditor rights in marked departure from state law. See, *e.g.*, Uniform Commercial Code §§ 9–504, 9–505, 3B U.L.A. 127, 352 (1992). The Code's cram down option displaces a secured creditor's state-law right to obtain immediate foreclosure upon a debtor's default. That change, ordered by federal law, is attended by a direction that courts look to the "proposed disposition or use" of the collateral in determining its value. It no more disrupts state law to make "disposition or use" the guide for valuation than to authorize the rearrangement of rights the cram down power entails.

Nor are we persuaded that the split-the-difference approach adopted by the Seventh Circuit provides the appropriate solution. See *In re Hoskins*, 102 F.3d, at 316. Whatever the attractiveness of a standard that picks the midpoint between foreclosure and replacement values, there is no warrant for it in the Code.[5] Section 506(a) calls for the value the property possesses in light of the "disposition or use" in fact "proposed," not the various dispositions or uses that might have been proposed. Cf. *BFP v. Resolution Trust Corporation*, 511 U.S. 531, 540, 114 S.Ct. 1757, 1762, 128 L.Ed.2d 556 (1994) (court-made rule defining, for purposes of Code's fraudulent transfer provision, "reasonably equivalent value" to mean 70% of fair market value "represent[s][a] policy determinatio[n] that the Bankruptcy Code gives us no apparent authority to make"). The Seventh Circuit rested on the "economics of the situation," *In re Hoskins*, 102 F.3d, at 316, only after concluding that the statute suggests no particular valuation method. We agree with the Seventh Circuit that "a simple rule of valuation is needed" to serve the interests of predictability and uniformity. *Id.*, at 314. We conclude, however, that § 506(a) supplies a governing instruction less complex than the Seventh Circuit's "make two valuations, then split the difference" formulation.

In sum, under § 506(a), the value of property retained because the debtor has exercised the § 1325(a)(5)(B) "cram down" option is the cost the debtor would incur to obtain a like asset for the same "proposed . . . use."[6]

\* \* \*

which a creditor had a security interest. See *ibid.* In any event, House Report excerpts are not enlightening, for the provision pivotal here—the second sentence of § 506(a)—did not appear in the bill addressed by the House Report. The key sentence originated in the Senate version of the bill, compare H.R. 8200, 95th Cong., 1st Sess., § 506(a) (1977), with S. 2266, 95th Cong., 1st Sess., § 506(a) (1977), and was included in the final text of the statute after the House–Senate conference, see 124 Cong. Rec. 33997 (1978).

**5.** As our reading of § 506(a) makes plain, we also reject a ruleless approach allowing use of different valuation standards based on the facts and circumstances of individual cases. Cf. *In re Valenti*, 105 F.3d 55, 62–63 (C.A.2 1997) (permissible for bankruptcy courts to determine valuation standard case-by-case).

**6.** Our recognition that the replacement-value standard, not the foreclosure-value standard, governs in cram down cases

For the foregoing reasons, the judgment of the Court of Appeals is reversed, and the case is remanded for further proceedings consistent with this opinion.

It is so ordered.

## NOTES

**1.** How would *Rash* be decided under the current version of BC 506(a)(2) quoted below?

> (2) If the debtor is an individual in a case under chapter 7 or 13, such value with respect to personal property securing an allowed claim shall be determined based on the replacement value of such property as of the date of filing the petition without deduction for costs of sale or marketing. With respect to property acquired for personal, family, or household purpose, replacement value shall mean the price a retail merchant would charge for property of that kind considering the age and condition of the property at the time value is determined.

Since BC 506(a)(2) doesn't apply to cases concerning corporate or partnership debtors or to Chapter 11 or 12 cases, *Rash* presumably remains good authority in commercial cases. What guidance does that case offer on how to determine the ''replacement value'' of important types of collateral in business reorganization cases involving inventory or accounts?

**2.** In footnote 5 of the opinion the Court rejects a ''ruleless approach'' and adopts the ''replacement value'' measure of value when the debtor's repayment plan proposes to retain the collateral. The Court in footnote 6 refuses to identify replacement value with retail or wholesale price, or some other prevalent measure. However, in the same note, the Court finds in the context of the case that replacement cost should not include the cost of such items as warranty coverage, inventory storage and reconditioning. These costs should be deducted from the retail price. The difference between retail and wholesale price is the additional costs of items such as inventory storage, advertising and the like. Isn't the Court therefore in fact finding that replacement value is wholesale price? If replacement value can vary with the context of a case, sometimes being retail price and sometimes wholesale, has the Court in fact announced a ''rule'' for valuation of collateral?

leaves to bankruptcy courts, as triers of fact, identification of the best way of ascertaining replacement value on the basis of the evidence presented. Whether replacement value is the equivalent of retail value, wholesale value, or some other value will depend on the type of debtor and the nature of the property. We note, however, that replacement value, in this context, should not include certain items. For example, where the proper measure of the replacement value of a vehicle is its retail value, an adjustment to that value may be necessary: A creditor should not receive portions of the retail price, if any, that reflect the value of items the debtor does not receive when he retains his vehicle, items such as warranties, inventory storage, and reconditioning. Cf. 90 F.3d, at 1051–1052. Nor should the creditor gain from modifications to the property—*e.g.,* the addition of accessories to a vehicle—to which a creditor's lien would not extend under state law.

**3.** In dissent Justice Stevens acknowledged that BC 506(a)(1) wasn't "entirely clear" but on policy grounds found that "... the foreclosure standard best comports with economic realty. Allowing any more than the foreclosure value simply grants a general windfall to undersecured creditors at the expense of unsecured creditors." *Rash*, 520 U.S. at 967. Friends of undersecured creditors might respond that the windfall compensates undersecured creditors for the shortfall caused by the loss of pendency interest under *Timbers of Inwood*'s holding.

## 4. EFFECT OF BANKRUPTCY ON AFTER-ACQUIRED PROPERTY CLAUSE

In previous chapters we learned that in Article 9 secured parties can obtain security interests that apply not only to property currently owned by the debtor but also to after-acquired property. 9–204(a). We saw that in inventory or accounts financing, in which the collateral turns over frequently, after-acquired property clauses are vital to the effectiveness of floating liens. But we find that in bankruptcy—the very situation in which the secured party most needs the protection of a perfected security interest—after-acquired property clauses are severely limited by BC 552. Property acquired by the debtor after filing in Chapter 11 that would otherwise have been covered by the security agreement's after-acquired property clause becomes available under BC 552(a) for the debtor-in-possession who is operating a business to use as collateral to obtain postpetition credit. What is the reach of BC 552? Note that the definition of "proceeds" in former 9–306(1) included the proceeds of proceeds.

### PROBLEM

Secured Party (SP) lent Debtor (D) $500,000 secured by a security interest in D's inventory, accounts, equipment, and general intangibles "now owned or hereafter acquired and the proceeds from said collateral." When D later filed in Chapter 11, the unpaid debt was still about $500,000 and the value of D's inventory was $750,000. After filing, D continued in business as a debtor in possession. At the time D filed, it owned inventory that it had acquired prepetition and accounts that had arisen prepetition. After filing, it sold prepetition inventory and collected prepetition accounts. With the funds resulting from the sale of the inventory and the collection of the accounts, D purchased postpetition inventory. You may assume that all the postpetition inventory was purchased with these funds. D contends that SP has no security interest in the postpetition inventory because it is after-acquired property and therefore no longer subject to SP's security interest under BC 552(a). SP replies that the postpetition inventory was second-generation proceeds of the property D acquired before bankruptcy and therefore within the exception to BC 552(a) that is found in BC 552(b). Which party is correct? Assume that the bankruptcy court would rely on the definition of "proceeds" found in 9–102(a)(64). Note the definition of "collateral" in 9–102(a)(12)(A) includes proceeds. For the result when the secured party is unable to trace the proceeds of collateral, see In re Skagit Pacific Corp., 316 B.R. 330 (9th Cir. BAP 2004).

NOTE

BC 552(a) eliminates liens on postpetition property that are not proceeds of prepetition collateral. It therefore refuses to give effect to after-acquired property clauses in security agreements. Why does BC 552(a) do so? It is surprisingly difficult to give a completely satisfactory answer to this very basic question. The section presents a problem for both of two opposing views about the justification and purpose of bankruptcy law: "traditionalism" and "proceduralism." See Douglas G. Baird, Bankruptcy's Uncontested Axioms, 108 Yale L. J. 573 (1998) (discussing rival approaches to evaluating bankruptcy law). Traditionalists view bankruptcy law as pursuing a range of goals, including rehabilitative, distributional and paternalistic values, that are implicated when insolvency occurs. They are less concerned about the effect of substantive bankruptcy rules on the financial incentives of parties prior to bankruptcy. Proceduralists, because they are primarily concerned about incentive effects, evaluate bankruptcy rules by how closely they preserve the value of the parties' prebankruptcy entitlements. Since BC 552(a) cuts off security interests in postpetition property without regard to the debtor or creditors' circumstances, doing so is unlikely to promote distributive or rehabilitative goals systematically. It is just too rough a rule to justify the "equitable purpose" which courts find BC 552(a) to support; see, e.g., Financial Security Assurance, Inc. v. Days California Limited Partnership, 27 F.3d 374, 377 (9th Cir.1994).

Although a bright-line rule often is useful, its usefulness depends on the rule being probabilistically related to a specified purpose, and such a relation is unlikely in BC 552(a)'s case. Thus, traditionalists cannot convincingly justify the section.

Proceduralists also have a difficult time with BC 552(a). Cutting off a security interest in postpetition property seemingly reduces the value of the creditor's security interest as compared to the creditor's prebankruptcy entitlement. Without bankruptcy, the creditor has a security interest in after-acquired property; in bankruptcy, it does not. True, if a bankruptcy petition had not been filed and the debtor had defaulted, the creditor could have foreclosed on the collateral. In that case the debtor probably would have been unable to continue business and therefore would not have purchased further assets. However, the creditor and debtor might well have renegotiated the payment terms of the loan after the debtor's default, leaving the other terms in place and without the creditor seizing the debtor's assets. The debtor then would have acquired further assets subject to the creditor's after-acquired property clause. BC 552(a) gratuitously assumes that the renegotiated terms would cutoff the creditor's security interest in after-acquired property.

## D.   AVOIDANCE POWERS OF THE TRUSTEE

The purpose of this chapter is to offer an introduction to what business lawyers should know about how security interests in personal property are treated under the Bankruptcy Code. Lawyers planning secured transactions must know how to structure those transactions so that they will stand up in bankruptcy. This requires an understanding of the trustee's powers to avoid transfers of the debtor. The trustee not only succeeds to the assets owned by the debtor at the time of filing (BC 541(a)(1)) but also has the power to enhance the value of the debtor's estate by reaching back and nullifying prepetition transfers of the debtor that are subject to some infirmity (BC 541(a)(3)). We can summarize the most important of these powers in simple terms: Under BC 544(a), the "strong arm clause," if the security interest isn't perfected at the time the debtor files in bankruptcy, it may be set aside in its totality. Under BC 547, if an insolvent debtor pays an unsecured creditor in preference to other creditors within 90 days before filing in bankruptcy, the payment may be recovered as a voidable preference. Under BC 548, if an insolvent debtor within two years of filing in bankruptcy transfers property to another person without receiving reasonably equivalent value in exchange, the property transferred may be recovered as a fraudulent transfer, even though no true fraud was involved. And under 544(b), fraudulent transfers are recoverable by the trustee using state fraudulent transfer law. These may seem simple rules, but even in our brief treatment of them we will see how complex and pervasive their application can be.

## 1.   STRONG ARM CLAUSE: BC 544(a)

Earlier in the course we discussed the role of BC 544(a) in empowering trustees to avoid unperfected security interests. This provision is commonly called the "strong arm" clause, and strong it is, for we have already seen how the trustee can use it to turn secured creditors, who are otherwise entitled to the economic value of their collateral in bankruptcy, into unsecured creditors, who often take little or nothing from the debtor's estate. Section 544(a)(1) arms a trustee with the power to avoid any transfer of property of the debtor that is "voidable" by a hypothetical judicial lien creditor at the date of bankruptcy. The rights of a lien creditor are not granted by the Bankruptcy Code. To determine what they are, resort must be had to state law, in this case, 9–317(a)(2). But that section doesn't speak of avoiding; it says that an unperfected security interest is "subordinate" to the rights of a lien creditor. This has been treated by courts as allowing the trustee, invoking the powers of a lien creditor, to set aside a security interest in its entirety that is subordinated to a judicial lien by 9–317(a)(2). BC 546(b) allows perfection after bankruptcy to defeat the rights of the trustee under BC 544(a) in cases in which the applicable nonbankruptcy law, Article 9, gives retroactive effect to the perfection.

PROBLEMS

**1.** On Day 1, SP, after having examined D's finances, was sufficiently interested in accepting D's application for a loan to have D sign a security agreement and for SP to file a financing statement. After checking the UCC filings, on Day 9 SP advanced the funds to D that were called for in the agreement. Later SP was astonished to learn from D's trustee in bankruptcy (T) that D had filed in bankruptcy on Day 8 without informing SP of that fact. Can T set aside SP's security interest under BC 544(a)? See 9–317(a)(2)(B). Why the change in law? See Comment 4. Are you convinced that the reason given justifies the change in law?

**2.** On Day 1, Seller sold and delivered to D several units of equipment. On that date, D signed a security agreement granting a security interest in the equipment to Seller to secure the unpaid balance of the purchase price. On Day 10, D filed in bankruptcy. When Seller learned of D's bankruptcy, it perfected its security interest by filing on Day 19.

(a) Can D's trustee in bankruptcy set aside Seller's security interest under BC 544(a)? See 9–317(e) and BC 546(b)(1).

(b) Did Seller violate the automatic stay by filing a financing statement? See BC 362(b)(3).

## 2.   SUBROGATION OF TRUSTEE UNDER BC 544(b)

BC 544(b) provides:

(1) * * * [T]he trustee may avoid any transfer of an interest of the debtor in property or any obligation incurred by the debtor that is voidable under applicable law by a creditor holding an unsecured claim that is allowable under section 502 of this title or that is not allowable only under section 502(e) of this title.

The meaning of this provision is that if the trustee can find one *actual unsecured creditor* at the time of bankruptcy against whom the debtor's transfer is voidable, the trustee can set aside the entire transfer for the benefit of all the debtor's estate under BC 541(a)(3) and BC 550(a). In effect, the trustee is subrogated to the rights of an unpaid creditor in existence at the time of the debtor's filing against whom under state law the transfer is voidable.

The origin of BC 544(b) is found in the celebrated case of Moore v. Bay, 284 U.S. 4 (1931) (Holmes, J.). That case involved the validity of a chattel mortgage that had not been promptly recorded. Under the applicable state law some unsecured intervening creditors of the mortgagor had priority over the mortgagee's claim because of its late recording and the failure to give advance public notice of the mortgage required by existing law. Some of these creditors had claims in bankruptcy. Other unsecured creditors with claims in the bankruptcy did not, under the state law, have priority over the mortgagee. The Supreme Court held that the chattel mortgage was void in its entirety in bankruptcy. By this decision all creditors, whether or not they had rights under the state law, got the benefit of the avoidance.

Although the opinion in Moore v. Bay is cryptic, the case is understood to articulate a two-part principle: a right voidable under state law is voidable in its entirety under bankruptcy law, and all creditors share in the benefit if the right is avoided. The principle of Moore v. Bay—often described as "void against one, void against all"—was first codified by the enactment of § 70e of the Bankruptcy Act, and subsequently by the enactment of BC 544(b) and BC 550(a) of the Bankruptcy Code.

Potentially the principle of Moore v. Bay, as codified by BC 544(b), can have devastating effects. Assume the debtor makes a transfer of property worth $1 million and that under the state law one creditor, with a claim of $100, can avoid the transfer because some duty to that creditor had not been performed. Assume no other creditor has the right under the state law to attack the transfer, that under the state law the creditor with the $100 claim is entitled to have that claim paid from the property transferred, and that the transfer is otherwise valid. The effect in bankruptcy, if the $100 debt exists at the time of bankruptcy, is that the entire $1,000,000 transfer is voidable by the trustee under BC 544(b). Under BC 550(a), the $1,000,000 worth of property recovered benefits the entire estate. This means that all creditors share in the $1,000,000 recovered, including the creditor whose interest in the property was avoided. The following Problems raise the crucial issue of whether BC 544(b) acts to avoid Article 9 security interests.

PROBLEMS

On Day 1 Debtor (D) granted a security interest in personal property to Secured Party (SP) to secure a loan of $1,000,000 made by SP to D. Although SP's security interest attached on Day 1, it did not file a financing statement until Day 30. On Day 25, Creditor (C), having checked the filings on D's property, granted unsecured credit to D in the amount of $1,000 in the belief that there were no security interests in D's property. On Day 180 D defaulted on both loans, which remain unpaid.

**1.** If D is not in bankruptcy, what are C's rights with respect to SP's collateral on which C relied when it made its unsecured loan? See 9–201(a) and 9–317(a).

**2.** If D is in bankruptcy, what are the rights of D's trustee in bankruptcy to avoid SP's security interest under BC 544(b)(1)? You may assume that C has an allowed unsecured claim for $1,000 at the time D files in bankruptcy.

---

## E.  Preferences: BC 547

## 1.  Elements of a Preference

An insolvent debtor who is unable to pay all unsecured creditors in full may prefer one over the others by paying that creditor or granting it a security interest in the debtor's property. Consumer debtors, skating on the edge of insolvency, make preferential payments every month when they choose, for obvious reasons, to pay the utilities bill or the landlord and leave the bill from the health club until next month. Sometimes the preferential transfer is involuntary. This might occur if one of the creditors acquires a judicial lien in the debtor's property under a writ of execution or pursuant to a statute allowing prejudgment attachment; the creditor is paying itself out of the debtor's property. For the most part, preferences are valid under state law. Under the common law a transfer by an insolvent debtor in payment of a debt was not a fraudulent conveyance even if the effect or the purpose of the transfer was to make it more difficult for other creditors to obtain payment of their debts. See, e. g., Shelley v. Boothe, 73 Mo. 74, 77 (1880). A preferential payment of a bona fide debt does not violate UFTA § 4(a)(1) (actual fraud). Nor does it violate UFTA § 4(a)(2) (without reasonably equivalent value) because satisfaction of an antecedent debt is "value." UFTA § 3(a).

State debt collection law is a race of diligence among creditors. Priority goes to the first creditor to receive payment or obtain a judicial lien in the debtor's property. But the rule in bankruptcy is different: for the most part unsecured claims are paid on a pro rata basis. Preference law prevents debtors from frustrating this "equality of distribution" rule by making payments to preferred creditors on the eve of bankruptcy. BC 547 allows the trustee in bankruptcy to avoid these prebankruptcy transfers of the debtor's property, known as voidable preferences. BC 550(a) allows the trustee to recover the payment or property transferred.

The five elements of a voidable preference are set forth in subsection (b) of BC 547.

Except as provided in subsections (c) and (i) of this section, the trustee may avoid any transfer of an interest of the debtor in property

(1) to or for the benefit of a creditor;

(2) for or on account of an antecedent debt owed by the debtor before such transfer was made;

(3) made while the debtor was insolvent;

(4) made

(A) on or within 90 days before the date of the filing of the petition; or

(B) between 90 days and one year before the date of the filing of the petition, if such creditor at the time of such transfer was an insider; and

(5) that enables such creditor to receive more than such creditor would receive if

(A) the case were a case under chapter 7 of this title;

(B) the transfer had not been made; and

(C) such creditor received payment of such debt to the extent provided by the provisions of this title.

## 2.  BASIC APPLICATIONS OF PREFERENCE LAW

The fundamental principles of voidable preference law are illustrated by the following Problems. Study them carefully. Problem 2 is very important for its illustration of the operation of BC 547(b)(5).

PROBLEMS

**1.**  On May 1 Debtor was indebted to Creditor on an overdue unsecured loan made the previous year. On that date Debtor paid Creditor cash equal to the amount due on the loan. At the time of payment Debtor had other debts that were not being paid and that exceeded Debtor's assets. On July 15 Debtor filed a petition in bankruptcy under Chapter 7. Answer the following questions on the basis of BC 547(b) without considering whether an exception under BC 547(c) applies.

(a) Is the trustee in bankruptcy entitled to recover from Creditor the amount received from Debtor? BC 547(b) and 550(a). Does it matter whether or not Creditor knew of Debtor's financial condition at the time payment was received? Who has the burden of proving that Debtor was insolvent? BC 101 ("insolvent"), and BC 547(f) and (g)?

(b) Would your answers to (a) be different if Debtor had filed in bankruptcy on August 15? BC 101 ("insider" and "relative").

(c) Suppose that on May 1 Debtor had not paid the loan and that Creditor on that date had obtained a prejudgment attachment lien on business property of Debtor with a value exceeding the amount due on the loan. When the petition in bankruptcy was filed on July 15, Debtor's assets included the property on which Creditor had an attachment lien. What are the rights of the trustee in bankruptcy? BC 547(b) and 101 ("transfer").

**2.**  Bank made a one-year loan of $10,000 to Debtor on September 1, 2007, and to secure the loan Debtor granted Bank a security interest in equipment owned by Debtor. Bank promptly perfected by filing a financing statement. On November 1, 2008 Debtor paid Bank $10,000 plus interest in discharge of the debt. Debtor filed a petition in bankruptcy on December 1, 2008. Debtor was insolvent on November 1, 2008 and at all times thereafter. Was the payment to Bank on November 1, 2008 a transfer on account of an antecedent debt? BC 547(b)(2). Can the transfer be avoided by the trustee in bankruptcy under BC 547(b)? What is the effect of BC 547(b)(5)? Assume that the value of the equipment was greater than the payment made to Bank and that there were no other security interests or liens in the equipment superior to the security interest of Bank. Would the outcome of the case be different if Bank had been undersecured at the time it received payment from Debtor?

## 3.   WHY PREFERENCE LAW?

Questions arise with respect to the justification of the large and intrusive body of law that has grown up around preferences. Why does the Bankruptcy Code invalidate transfers that are valid outside bankruptcy? Why have a provision such as BC 547 that operates to disadvantage efficient creditors who are able to receive voluntary payment from a debtor before that debtor files in bankruptcy and to benefit less efficient creditors who have not collected their claims. Egalitarian notions, such as the pro rata distribution rule, are not common in business transactions. What are the transaction costs of allowing trustees to reopen completed transactions and grab back payments on which the creditor had relied? What incentive is there for creditors to help debtors stay in business through workout agreements calling for rescheduling of overdue debts if payments made pursuant to those agreements can be recovered under BC 547 if the debtor files in bankruptcy within 90 days after the payment? Perhaps if we understand more fully the policies underlying BC 547, we will be better able to predict how this provision will apply to the myriad situations in which it has been invoked.

The oft-quoted House Committee Report explanation follows. We have referred to the goal of equality of distribution above, but we see from this quotation that Congress had more in mind.

> A preference is a transfer that enables a creditor to receive payment of a greater percentage of his claim against the debtor than he would have received if the transfer had not been made and he had participated in the distribution of the assets of the bankrupt estate. The purpose of the preference section is two-fold. First, by permitting the trustee to avoid prebankruptcy transfers that occur within a short period before bankruptcy, creditors are discouraged from racing to the courthouse to dismember the debtor during his slide into bankruptcy. The protection thus afforded the debtor often enables him to work his way out of a difficult financial situation through cooperation with all of his creditors. Second, and more important, the preference provisions facilitate the prime bankruptcy policy of equality of distribution among creditors of the debtor. Any creditor that received a greater payment than others of his class is required to disgorge so that all may share equally. The operation of the preference section to deter "the race of diligence" of creditors to dismember the debtor before bankruptcy furthers the second goal of the preference section—that of equality of distribution.

H.R.Rep. No. 95–595, at 177–78 (1977), reprinted in 1978 U.S.C.C.A.N. 5963, 6138.

Congress is telling the creditor of a failing debtor not to worry if it sees other creditors dismembering the debtor; BC 547 will come to the rescue. But this is true only if the debtor files in bankruptcy within 90 days after making its transfers to the preferred creditors. The Bankruptcy Code offers creditors a remedy in these cases by allowing them to force the debtor into involuntary bankruptcy under BC 303 in cases in which the debtor is "generally not paying" its debts. BC 303(h)(1). In Problem 1(c) above, if Debtor doesn't voluntarily file in bankruptcy within the 90–day period, the other creditors can get rid of Creditor's judicial lien only by forcing Debtor into involuntary bankruptcy before the end of that period. Throughout this section, consider whether the applications of the provisions of BC 547 that we will deal with bear any discernible relation to the noble goals stated above.

## 4.   EFFECT OF AVOIDANCE

If the trustee in bankruptcy avoids a preferential transfer under BC 547(b), the property transferred by the debtor to the creditor or its value can be recovered for the benefit of the estate. BC 550(a). If the preference occurred when the debtor paid a debt in cash, the trustee is entitled to recover an equivalent amount, which then becomes part of the bankruptcy estate. BC 541(a)(3). Suppose the preference occurred when the creditor obtained a lien in the debtor's property to secure the debt either by voluntary act of the debtor or against the will of the debtor as in the case of a judicial lien. Assume that the property to which the lien applies is property of the bankruptcy estate. In that case avoidance of the preference usually means that the creditor's lien is nullified. The effect of nullification is to increase the value of property of the estate in the amount of the value of the nullified lien. But sometimes simple nullification of a lien will not benefit the estate.

### PROBLEM

Suppose property of the estate worth $10,000 is burdened by two liens, valid outside of bankruptcy, in favor of Creditor A and Creditor B, each of whom is owed $10,000. Assume that under the nonbankruptcy law the lien of Creditor A has priority over the lien of Creditor B, but that the lien of Creditor A is avoidable under BC 547(b) while the lien of Creditor B is indefeasible in bankruptcy. If the lien of Creditor A is nullified, the effect is to benefit Creditor B. The junior lien of Creditor B had no value before nullification but it has a value of $10,000 after nullification. We have seen that the purpose of allowing the trustee to recover preferential transfers is to benefit the estate, i.e., to increase the value of the estate for the benefit of creditors generally. If the effect of avoidance of a lien is simply to shift the benefit of the preference from one creditor to another creditor, this bankruptcy purpose is frustrated. How does BC 551 prevent this result?

## 5.   PREFERENCE PERIOD

Under BC 547(b)(4) a transfer cannot be a voidable preference unless it occurs within what is called the "preference period." The preference period can be one of two lengths depending upon the identity of the recipient of the transfer. If the transferee is an insider, defined in BC 101, the preference period is one year before the date of the filing of the petition in bankruptcy. If the transferee is not an insider, the preference period is only

90 days before the filing of the petition. Why does BC 547(b)(4)(A) extend the preference period to one year for transfers to insiders? Judge Easter-brook explains:

> How long should [the] preference-recovery period be? If one outside creditor knows that the firm is in trouble, others will too. Each major lender monitors both the firm and fellow lenders. If it perceives that some other lender is being paid preferentially, a major lender can propel Firm into bankruptcy. Reasonably alert lenders can act with sufficient dispatch to ensure that the perceived preference is recoverable even when the preference period is short. Section 547(b) makes 90 days the rule, time enough (Congress concluded) for careful creditors to protect themselves (and when one does, small unsecured trade creditors get the benefits too).
>
> Insiders pose special problems. Insiders will be the first to recognize that the firm is in a downward spiral. If insiders and outsiders had the same preference-recovery period, insiders who lent money to the firm could use their knowledge to advantage by paying their own loans preferentially, then putting off filing the petition in bankruptcy until the preference period had passed. Outside creditors, aware of this risk, would monitor more closely, or grab assets themselves (fearing that the reciprocity that is important to the pooling scheme has been destroyed), or precipitate bankruptcy at the smallest sign of trouble, hoping to "catch" inside preferences before it is too late. All of these devices could be costly. An alternative device is to make the preference-recovery period for insiders longer than that for outsiders. With a long period for insiders, even the prescient managers who first see the end coming are unlikely to be able to prefer themselves in distribution.

Levit v. Ingersoll Rand Financial Corp., 874 F.2d 1186, 1194–1195 (7th Cir.1989). Before 1984, the one-year period applied only if the insider transferee had "reasonable cause to believe that the debtor was insolvent at the time of such transfer." We briefly discuss this discarded requirement later.

Uniform Fraudulent Transfer Act § 5(b) treats insider preferences as fraudulent transfers. The term "insider" is defined in UFTA § 1(7) to "include" the persons stated. The definition is based on BC 101 ("insider") although there are minor differences between the two sections. The official comment to UFTA § 1(7) makes clear that that section, like BC 101 ("insider"), is not meant to be limited to the persons stated. A court would be free to find that other persons are insiders if they "have the kind of close relationship intended to be covered by the term 'insider.' " Avoidability under UFTA § 5(b) depends upon the insider's having had "reasonable cause to believe that the debtor was insolvent," and there being a creditor whose claim arose before the transfer was made, requirements that no longer exist under BC 547(b). Since the statute of limitations for causes of action arising under § 5(b) is only one year (§ 9(c)), it adds nothing to the rights that a trustee enjoys under BC 547 with respect to insider preferences.

## 6. TRANSFERS TO OR FOR BENEFIT OF A CREDITOR

### a. TRANSFER OF DEBTOR'S PROPERTY

Cutting through the complexities of BC 547, we must conclude that preference law when viewed from the position of the people it is supposed to protect, the creditors, is designed to prevent an insolvent debtor from depleting its estate on the eve of bankruptcy by transfers to other creditors. Thus, a basic requirement of BC 547(b) is that the property transferred must be that of the debtor. A simple illustration of the kinds of problems that can arise in determining whose property has been transferred follows.

### PROBLEM

Debtor's obligation to Creditor was guaranteed by Guarantor. Under the law of the jurisdiction, if Guarantor had to make good on its guaranty by paying Creditor, it had a right to reimbursement from Debtor. When Debtor became insolvent and defaulted on its obligation, Guarantor paid Creditor. Within 90 days of the payment, Debtor filed in bankruptcy. Guarantor promptly filed a claim in Debtor's bankruptcy for reimbursement of the amount of the payment. Since Creditor was paid when other creditors of Debtor were not, Debtor's trustee sought to avoid the transfer to Creditor. BC 547(b) allows avoidance of "any transfer of an interest of the debtor in property * * *." Was there a voidable preference in this case? Matter of Corland Corporation, 967 F.2d 1069 (5th Cir.1992).

### b. TO OR FOR THE BENEFIT OF A CREDITOR

Preference law varies from fraudulent transfer law in that a fraudulent transfer is voidable whoever the recipient is, but a preference is voidable only if the transfer is made to or for the benefit of a creditor of the debtor-transferor. BC 547(b)(1). Take the guaranty hypothetical in the previous problem. Change the facts so that Debtor, instead of Guarantor, pays the obligation within 90 days of bankruptcy. Can Debtor's trustee pursue Guarantor as the recipient of a voidable preference? Clearly there has been a preference in favor of Creditor, but Debtor's payment also benefited Guarantor, who is now released from the guaranty because Creditor has been paid. Thus, although Debtor's payment is *to* Creditor it is *for the benefit of* Guarantor as well as Creditor, there is no voidable preference to Guarantor unless Guarantor is a creditor of Debtor. Under BC 101(10)(A) a "creditor" is person with a "claim" against a debtor, and BC 101(5)(A) defines claim broadly to include a contingent right to payment. Guarantor has a contingent right to be reimbursed by Debtor because if Creditor collects from Guarantor, Guarantor can collect from Debtor. Hence, Debtor's payment to Creditor is voidable under BC 547(b), and Debtor's trustee has a choice under BC 550(a)(1) of recovering the money from either "the initial transferee of such transfer [Creditor] or the entity for whose benefit such transfer was made [Guarantor]."

## 7.   CONTEMPORANEOUS EXCHANGES

BC 547(b) expands preferences law so broadly that virtually every payment or other transfer made by an insolvent debtor to a creditor within the preference period is called into question. BC 547(c) sets out nine exceptions that limit the reach of preferences law and bring it more into harmony with its professed purposes. In the next few sections we will consider the more important of these exceptions.

BC 547(b)(2) states as one element of a voidable preference that the transfer be "for or on account of an antecedent debt." Thus, if an insolvent buyer buys goods and pays for them at the time of sale by transferring money or other property to the seller, there is no preference because the buyer's obligation to pay for the goods and the transfer of the property to satisfy the obligation arise contemporaneously. But suppose there is a short delay between the time the obligation is incurred and the transfer of property in payment of the obligation. Does the short delay make the debt antecedent? The issue was considered by the Supreme Court in the case of Dean v. Davis, 242 U.S. 438 (1917). On September 3 the debtor obtained a loan from Dean on the debtor's promise to secure the loan by a mortgage on all of his property. The proceeds of the loan were used by the debtor to pay a debt owed to a bank. The mortgage was executed on September 10 and recorded the next day. Within a few days a petition for involuntary bankruptcy was filed against the debtor. The trustee in bankruptcy brought an action to set aside the mortgage. Both the district court and the court of appeals held that the mortgage was voidable as a fraudulent conveyance. The court of appeals also held that the mortgage could be avoided as a preference under Section 60b of the Bankruptcy Act. The Supreme Court, in reversing the court of appeals on the latter point stated: "The mortgage was not voidable as a preference under § 60b. Preference implies paying or securing a pre-existing debt of the person preferred. The mortgage was given to secure Dean for a substantially contemporary advance. The bank, not Dean, was preferred. The use of Dean's money to accomplish this purpose could not convert the transaction into a preferring of Dean, although he knew of the debtor's insolvency." 242 U.S. at 443.

BC 547(c)(1) codifies the part of this holding concerning the timing of the transfer. If a bank advances funds to a debtor who intends to secure the loan by granting the bank a security interest in the debtor's property, and the granting of the security interest is delayed only a short time, the exchange is substantially contemporaneous and the security interest cannot be avoided. If a buyer gives a seller an ordinary check in payment, the exchange is contemporaneous even though the seller doesn't actually receive the funds until a few days later when the check clears. Does this analysis apply to the problems that follow?

PROBLEMS

**1.**   Bank made an unsecured demand loan to Debtor on the morning of April 1. Bank believed that Debtor was financially sound. Later that day

Bank received a credit report indicating that Debtor was in financial difficulty and might be insolvent. Bank immediately talked to Debtor who acknowledged the truth of the credit report. When Bank demanded immediate repayment of the loan, Debtor offered instead to secure the loan by a mortgage on real property worth more than the amount of the loan. Bank agreed and the mortgage was executed on the evening of April 1 and recorded the next day. If Debtor was insolvent on April 1 and filed a petition in bankruptcy on June 1, can the mortgage be avoided as a preference? BC 547(b) and BC 547(c)(1). National City Bank v. Hotchkiss, 231 U.S. 50 (1913).

**2.** On April 1, Bank lent $10,000 to Debtor by crediting that amount to Debtor's checking account. The loan agreement signed on that day provided that the $10,000 would be used to buy certain described equipment in which Debtor granted a security interest to Bank. Bank filed a financing statement covering equipment of Debtor on April 1. On April 7, Debtor bought the equipment described in the loan agreement. On June 20, Debtor filed a petition in bankruptcy. Under BC 547(e)(2) and (3), when did a transfer of property of Debtor occur? If Debtor was insolvent on April 1 and at all times thereafter, can Bank's security interest be avoided under BC 547(b)? Is avoidance prevented by BC 547(c)(1)? Is avoidance prevented by BC 547(c)(3)? Would your answers be different if Debtor had acquired the equipment on April 30?

## 8.   ORDINARY COURSE PAYMENTS

One vital goal of any commercial law regime is certainty and finality of transactions. If large numbers of ordinary commercial transactions are subject to being upset by later legal proceedings, all transactions of that type become more expensive. Creditors must charge for the increased risk and expense incident to those transactions. There is general consensus in favor of avoiding preferences made in out-of-the-ordinary transactions in which a creditor seeks, and is given, favored treatment by a debtor in obvious financial difficulty. It is not so clear that transactions by an insolvent debtor in paying debts as they mature should be avoided solely because an incidental result is that the creditors have been preferred over others who did not have the good fortune of being paid before bankruptcy. If a doctrine designed to obtain equality for all creditors interferes with normal commercial practices and significantly adds to the cost of ordinary commercial transactions, the cost of the equality may be too high.

One traditional limitation on avoidance of preferences was to allow avoidance only if the transferee had reasonable cause to believe that the debtor was insolvent. This principle stemmed from the early characterization of preferences in terms of unconscionability or fraud, as in the case in which a preferred creditor relies on a special relationship with the debtor to obtain a advantage not obtainable by others. Another limitation was to allow payments made to trade creditors on short term credit to remain unassailable under preference law. Both these limitations are rejected in the current version of BC 547(c), and reliance is placed on one very specific provision, BC 547(c)(8), to cover small consumer debts, and one very general one, BC 547(c)(2), which has been broadly interpreted to cover both long-term and short-term credit. See Union Bank v. Wolas, 502 U.S. 151 (1991).

BC 547(c)(2) bars the trustee from avoiding a transfer:

(2) to the extent that such transfer was in payment of a debt incurred by the debtor in the ordinary course of business or financial affairs of the debtor and such transfer was—

(A) made in the ordinary course of business or financial affairs of the debtor and the transferee; or

(B) made according to ordinary business terms;

This is a major limitation on voidable preferences law, and the question that has puzzled courts is when are transfers not in ordinary course. Are payments in ordinary course when made by a business debtor that is struggling to stay in business by paying only essential creditors during the preference period? Suppose the recipients of these payments know of the debtor's financial condition. Is any policy served by taking payments back from creditors willing to work with a debtor trying to save its business? These are troublesome issues.

A few patterns in the case law have emerged. When a creditor becomes concerned about the debtor's financial condition and the medium of payment, say, ordinary checks, is changed to cashier's checks or wire transfers to give the creditor greater security, the payments may no longer be in ordinary course. See, e.g., In re Spirit Holding Co., Inc., 153 F.3d 902 (8th Cir.1998) (medium changed from checks to wire transfers). Perhaps the most litigated issue is whether late payments are in ordinary course of business. Failure to make payments when called for by the contract seems presumptively "nonordinary." But if the prior course of conduct shows that late payments were customarily accepted, those payments might qualify as ordinary under BC 547(c)(2)(A). See, e.g., In re Yurika Foods Corp., 888 F.2d 42 (6th Cir.1989) (87% of debtor's payments were late). Under the pre–2005 version of BC 547(c)(2) the question arose what if the parties' ordinary practice in making and accepting late payments seems extraordinary by usual commercial standards in the business. The meaning of ordinary course of business is addressed in the *Tolona* opinion below.

# Matter of Tolona Pizza Products Corp.

United States Court of Appeals, Seventh Circuit, 1993.
3 F.3d 1029.

■ POSNER, CIRCUIT JUDGE.

When, within 90 days before declaring bankruptcy, the debtor makes a payment to an unsecured creditor, the payment is a "preference," and the trustee in bankruptcy can recover it and thus make the creditor take pot luck with the rest of the debtor's unsecured creditors. § 547. But there is an exception if the creditor can show that the debt had been incurred in the ordinary course of the business of both the debtor and the creditor, § 547(c)(2)(A); that the payment, too, had been made and received in the ordinary course of their businesses, § 547(c)(2)(B); and that the payment had been "made according to ordinary business terms." § 547(c)(2)(C). The first two requirements are easy to understand: *of course* to defeat the inference of preferential treatment the debt must have been incurred in the ordinary course of business of both debtor and creditor and the payment on account of the debt must have been in the ordinary course as well. But what does the third requirement—that the payment have been "made according to ordinary business terms"—add? And in particular does it refer to what is "ordinary" between this debtor and this creditor, or what is ordinary in the market or industry in which they operate? The circuits are divided on this question * * *.

Tolona, a maker of pizza, issued eight checks to Rose, its sausage supplier, within 90 days before being thrown into bankruptcy by its creditors. The checks, which totaled a shade under $46,000, cleared and as a result Tolona's debts to Rose were paid in full. Tolona's other major trade creditors stand to receive only 13¢ on the dollar under the plan approved by the bankruptcy court, if the preferential treatment of Rose is allowed to stand. Tolona, as debtor in possession, brought an adversary proceeding against Rose to recover the eight payments as voidable preferences. The bankruptcy judge entered judgment for Tolona. The district judge reversed. He thought that Rose did not, in order to comply with § 547(c)(2)(C), have to prove that the terms on which it had extended credit to Tolona were standard terms in the industry, but that if this was wrong the testimony of Rose's executive vice-president, Stiehl, did prove it. The parties agree that the other requirements of § 547(c)(2) were satisfied.

Rose's invoices recited "net 7 days," meaning that payment was due within seven days. For years preceding the preference period, however, Tolona rarely paid within seven days; nor did Rose's other customers. Most paid within 21 days, and if they paid later than 28 or 30 days Rose would usually withhold future shipments until payment was received. Tolona, however, as an old and valued customer (Rose had been selling to it for fifteen years), was permitted to make payments beyond the 21–day period and even beyond the 28–day or 30–day period. The eight payments at issue were made between 12 and 32 days after Rose had invoiced Tolona, for an average of 22 days; but this actually was an improvement. In the 34 months before the preference period, the average time for which Rose's invoices to Tolona were outstanding was 26 days and the longest time was 46 days. Rose consistently treated Tolona with a degree of leniency that made Tolona (Stiehl conceded on cross-examination) one of a "sort of exceptional group of customers of Rose ... fall[ing] outside the common industry practice and standards."

It may seem odd that paying a debt late would ever be regarded as a preference to the creditor thus paid belatedly. But it is all relative. A debtor who has entered the preference period—who is therefore only 90 days, or fewer, away from plunging into bankruptcy—is typically unable to pay all his outstanding debts in full as they come due. If he pays one and not the others, as happened here, the payment though late is still a preference to that creditor, and is avoidable unless the conditions of § 547(c)(2) are met. One condition is that payment be in the ordinary course of both the debtor's and the creditor's business. A late payment normally will not be. It will therefore be an avoidable preference.

This is not a dryly syllogistic conclusion. The purpose of the preference statute is to prevent the debtor during his slide toward bankruptcy from trying to stave off the evil day by giving preferential treatment to his most importunate creditors, who may sometimes be those who have been waiting longest to be paid. Unless the favoring of particular creditors is outlawed, the mass of creditors of a shaky firm will be nervous, fearing that one or a few of their number are going to walk away with all the firm's assets; and this fear may precipitate debtors into bankruptcy earlier than is socially desirable. * * *

From this standpoint, however, the most important thing is not that the dealings between the debtor and the allegedly favored creditor conform to some industry norm but that they conform to the norm established by the debtor and the creditor in the period before, preferably well before, the preference period. That condition is satisfied here—if anything, Rose treated Tolona more favorably (and hence Tolona treated Rose less preferentially) before the preference period than during it.

But if this is all that the third subsection of 547(c)(2) requires, it might seem to add nothing to the first two subsections, which require that both the debt and the payment be within the ordinary course of business of both the debtor and the creditor. For, provided these conditions are fulfilled, a "late" payment really isn't late if the parties have established a practice that deviates from the strict terms of their written contract. But we hesitate to conclude that the third subsection, requiring conformity to "ordinary business terms," has no function in the statute. We can think of two functions that it might have. One is evidentiary. * * * If the debtor and creditor dealt on terms that the creditor testifies were normal for them but that are wholly unknown in the industry, this casts some doubt on his (self-serving) testimony. Preferences are disfavored, and subsection C makes them more difficult to prove. The second possible function of the subsection is to allay the concerns of creditors that one or more of their number may have worked out a special deal with the debtor, before the preference period, designed to put that creditor ahead of the others in the event of bankruptcy. It may seem odd that allowing late payments from a debtor would be a way for a creditor to make himself more rather than less assured of repayment. But such a creditor does have an advantage during the preference period, because he can receive late payments then and they will still be in the ordinary course of business for him and his debtor.

The functions that we have identified, combined with a natural reluctance to cut out and throw away one-third of an important provision of the Bankruptcy Code, persuade us that the creditor must show that the payment he received was made in accordance with the ordinary business terms in the industry. But this does not mean that the creditor must establish the existence of some single, uniform set of business terms, as Tolona argues. * * * Not only is it difficult to identify the industry whose norm shall govern (is it, here, the sale of sausages to makers of pizza? The sale of sausages to anyone? The sale of anything to makers of pizza?), but there can be great variance in billing practices within an industry. Apparently there is in this industry, whatever exactly "this industry" is; for while it is plain that neither Rose nor its competitors enforce payment within seven days, it is unclear that there is a standard outer limit of forbearance. It seems that 21 days is a goal but that payment as late as 30 days is generally tolerated and that for good customers even longer delays are allowed. The average period between Rose's invoice and Tolona's payment during the preference period was only 22 days, which seems well within the industry norm, whatever exactly it is. The law should not push businessmen to agree upon a single set of billing practices; antitrust objections to one side, the relevant business and financial considerations vary widely among firms on both the buying and the selling side of the market.

We conclude that "ordinary business terms" refers to the *range* of terms that encompasses the practices in which firms similar in some general way to the creditor in question engage, and that only dealings so idiosyncratic as to fall outside that broad range should be deemed extraordinary and therefore outside the scope of subsection C. * * * Stiehl's testimony brought the case within the scope of "ordinary business terms" as just defined. Rose and its competitors pay little or no attention to the terms stated on their invoices, allow most customers to take up to 30 days to pay, and allow certain favored customers to take even more time. There is no single set of terms on which the members of the industry have coalesced; instead there is a broad range and the district judge plausibly situated the dealings between Rose and Tolona within it. These dealings are conceded to have been within the normal course of dealings between the two firms, a course established long before the preference period, and there is no hint either that the dealings were designed to put Rose ahead of other creditors of Tolona or that other creditors of Tolona would have been surprised to learn that Rose had been so forbearing in its dealings with Tolona.

Tolona might have argued that the district judge gave insufficient deference to the bankruptcy judge's contrary finding. The district judge, and we, are required to accept the bankruptcy judge's findings on questions of fact as long as they are not clearly erroneous. * * * But since Tolona did not argue that the district judge had applied an incorrect standard of review, we need not decide whether the district judge overstepped the bounds. Which is not to say that he did. While he did not intone the magic words "clear error," he may well have believed that the record as a whole left no doubt that Tolona's dealings with Rose were within the broad band of accepted practices in the industry. It is true that Stiehl testified that Tolona was one of an exceptional group of Rose's customers with whom

Rose's dealings fell outside common industry practice. But the undisputed evidence concerning those dealings and the practices of the industry demonstrates that payment within 30 days is within the outer limits of normal industry practices, and the payments at issue in this case were made on average in a significantly shorter time.

The judgment reversing the bankruptcy judge and dismissing the adversary proceeding is

AFFIRMED.

■ FLAUM, CIRCUIT JUDGE, dissenting. [opinion omitted]

NOTE

*Tolona* minimizes the inquiry that a court must make into "ordinary business terms," and BAPCPA goes further by giving the debtor the option of proving *either* that payment was made in ordinary course of the debtor's business *or* that it was made according to ordinary business terms. The latter is a good change: A payment made either in the ordinary course of the debtor's business or according to ordinary business terms probably is not a strategic ploy by the creditor to be paid in advance of a bankruptcy proceeding. So long as the debtor is making payments in ordinary course of its business relationship with the creditor, preference law is not offended; it should not grab back normal payments.

## 9. FLOATING LIEN AS A PREFERENCE

The battle over the validity of floating liens in bankruptcy was the cause celebre of commercial law in the years immediately after enactment of the UCC. The bankruptcy bar had stood by, largely ignored, while Article 9 was drafted in a manner that seemed to give every advantage to the secured creditor: abrogation in 9–205 of the prohibition on the debtor's retention of unrestricted dominion over collateral; automatic future advance and after-acquired property clauses in 9–204; first-to-file priority rule in 9–322; notice filing in 9–502. Taken together, these provisions allowed the secured party to take a security interest in all of a debtor's personal property now owned or thereafter acquired to secure both present and future advances. If the floating lien were upheld in bankruptcy without limitations, there would be nothing left in a debtor's estate to distribute among unsecured trade creditors who had provided goods and services to the failed debtor.

But bankruptcy counsel believed that the drafters of the 1962 version of Article 9, none of whom was experienced in the nether world of bankruptcy law, had painted themselves into a corner, and that security interests in inventory acquired and accounts that arose during the preference period were potentially voidable as preferences. This view if accepted would have destroyed the inventory and accounts financing industry. And these lawyers had a solid basis for their opinion. Test cases followed.

As we will see in more detail in the following section, the time of the transfer for security interests in bankruptcy is the time of perfection of the security interest, not its attachment. BC 547(e). Suppose Debtor, an appliance retailer, signed a security agreement on February 1 granting a security interest to Bank to secure a loan made at the same time. The collateral was all of Debtor's inventory then owned or thereafter acquired. Bank immediately filed a financing statement covering inventory. Under Article 9 the security interest attached, with respect to any item of inventory, when all of the following conditions were met: (1) there was an authenticated security agreement; (2) Bank gave value to Debtor; and (3) Debtor had rights in the item of inventory. 9–203(b). The first two conditions were satisfied on February 1 when the loan was made and the agreement signed. The third condition was satisfied at various times. With respect to inventory owned on February 1 it was satisfied on that date. With respect to after-acquired inventory it was satisfied when the inventory was acquired. Section 9–308(a) states that a security interest is perfected when it has attached and when all of the applicable steps required for perfection have been taken. The step normally taken to perfect a security interest in inventory is the filing of a financing statement. Thus, under Article 9 whenever Debtor acquired an item of inventory after February 1, a security interest in that item attached and was perfected. Filing of the financing statement occurred on February 1 but perfection with respect to the inventory covered by the financing statement could not occur until the inventory was acquired.

Suppose in our example that Debtor's inventory completely turned over every 60 days and that Debtor filed in bankruptcy on December 1. Under this assumption, all inventory on hand at the date of bankruptcy had been acquired during the preference period. Assume further that Bank did not make additional loans to Debtor after February 1 and that the original loan was unpaid at the date of bankruptcy. Under Article 9 the security interest of Bank in inventory at the date of bankruptcy attached and was perfected during the preference period and secured a debt that arose on February 1. Under Bankruptcy Act § 60a(2) (now found in BC 547(e)), the apparent result was that the transfer of Debtor's property represented by the security interest was made when the security interest attached and was perfected during the preference period. Thus, if Debtor was insolvent at the time of the transfer, the security interest was voidable as a preferential transfer under Bankruptcy Act § 60b.

For our purposes, it is enough to say that in Grain Merchants of Indiana, Inc. v. Union Bank & Savings Co., 408 F.2d 209 (7th Cir.1969), the court, in a highly unorthodox reading of the law, upheld the validity of floating lien security interests in inventory and accounts in bankruptcy. The reasoning of this opinion was sufficiently questionable to drive all parties to resolve the issue by a compromise amendment to the Bankruptcy Code. This provision is now BC 547(c)(5). It was drafted against a background that assumed the following: accounts receivable and inventory normally turn over within a short period of time. It is likely that at the date of bankruptcy some receivables or inventory on hand were acquired by the debtor within the 90–day period. Since a security interest in this new collateral was, by virtue of BC 547(e)(3), a transfer to the secured party when it was acquired by the debtor, there might have been a voidable preference under BC 547(b) if the debtor was insolvent at the time. BC 547(c)(5), set out below, is a limited exemption from this rule.

(c) The trustee may not avoid under this section a transfer

(5) that creates a perfected security interest in inventory or a receivable or the proceeds of either, except to the extent that the aggregate of all such transfers to the transferee caused a reduction, as of the date of the filing of the petition and to the prejudice of other creditors holding unsecured claims, of any amount by which the debt secured by such security interest exceeded the value of all security interests for such debt on the later of

(A)(i) with respect to a transfer to which subsection (b)(4)(A) of this section applies, 90 days before the date of the filing of the petition; or

(ii) with respect to a transfer to which (b)(4)(B) of this section applies, one year before the date of the filing of the petition; or

(B) the date on which new value was first given under the security agreement creating such security interest;

## PROBLEM

How does this provision work? Secured Party is secured by all accounts receivable of Debtor. At the beginning of the 90–day period the debt was $100,000 and at the date of bankruptcy the debt was $90,000; at the beginning of the 90–day period there were $60,000 in receivables. During the 90–day period Debtor increased its receivables so that on the date of bankruptcy they amounted to $70,000. The test is stated in terms of the amount of the reduction of the amount by which the debt exceeded the value of the security interest from the beginning of the 90–day period to the date of bankruptcy.

(a) What result would it give in this case?

(b) What result if Secured Party's $100,000 debt was secured by $120,000 in account receivables at the beginning of the 90–day period and $70,000 in receivables on the date of bankruptcy all obtained by Debtor within the 90–day period?

Section 547(c)(5) is a variation of the substitution theory, which was one of the more persuasive bases of the *Grain Merchants* decision. It says in effect that it is not important whether the items making up the mass of inventory or accounts receivable at bankruptcy were identical to the items making up the mass at the beginning of the 90–day period so long as the volume has not changed. Within that limitation any new item that came into existence within the 90–day period is treated as a substitute for an item that was disposed of by the debtor during the same period.

## 10.   FALSE PREFERENCES: DELAYED PERFECTION OF SECURITY INTERESTS

*Delayed Attachment.* In the section on contemporaneous exchange we dealt with cases in which there is a delay between the time when credit is granted and the security interest intended to secure that credit attaches. Since the subsequent attaching of the security interest is a transfer of property of the debtor on account of the antecedent debt arising from the credit, there is a prima facie voidable preference if the other elements of BC 547(b) are present. If the delay is very short the security interest may, under some circumstances, be saved by BC 547(c)(1). If the credit was for the purpose of enabling the debtor to acquire the collateral which secures the debt the security interest may be saved if there was compliance with BC 547(c)(3). In all of these cases the problem arises because of a delay in the creation of the security interest.

*Delayed Perfection.* A superficially similar but entirely distinct problem arises when the granting of the credit and the creation of the security interest are contemporaneous, but there is a delay between the creation, or attachment, of the security interest and the subsequent perfection of the security interest by filing. There is no true preference in these cases because the grant of the security interest to the creditor was not on account of an antecedent debt. The problem of delayed perfection is the evil of the secret lien. The classic case is that of a debtor in financial difficulty who wishes to conceal from general creditors the true state of its financial condition. The debtor obtains an emergency loan from a creditor and grants to that creditor a mortgage on real property or a security interest in personal property to secure the loan. The property involved might well be most of the debtor's previously unencumbered assets. If public notice of the transaction were given by recording the mortgage or filing a financing statement with respect to the security interest, the result might be that other creditors would be deterred from giving to the debtor further unsecured credit because of the absence of unencumbered assets. To avoid this result the creditor might be induced not to record the mortgage or file the financing statement.

Essentially the issue is fraud on creditors, not preference. Usually, an unrecorded mortgage of real property has priority over the claim of a creditor who subsequently levies on the property. The holder of an unperfected security interest in personal property takes a greater risk by not promptly perfecting because an unperfected Article 9 security interest does not have priority over a subsequent judicial lien. But in either case the creditor can protect the lien by promptly perfecting at the first sign that other creditors may either levy on assets of the debtor or file a petition for involuntary bankruptcy against the debtor. In the classic case, the creditor is an insider with access to information that provides some assurance that the creditor will have sufficient advance notice of facts that will allow the creditor to perfect in time.

It is understandable that there should be a policy against secret liens, and such a policy was expressed in the Bankruptcy Act. However, the technique used in the Bankruptcy Act to address the evil was unusual. Instead of dealing with the problem directly as a case of fraud on creditors, Congress discouraged the secret lien by a provision in the Bankruptcy Act preference section. This 1950 provision was the culmination of a series of amendments dating as far back as 1903, designed to deal with the problem of secret liens. The effect was to convert what was not in fact a preferential lien into a preferential lien by a conclusive presumption that the lien became effective at the time it was perfected rather than at the time it was actually created. Certain grace periods were allowed for the creditor to perfect. If the creditor didn't perfect within these periods. the lien was treated as having been given for an antecedent debt. This technique of turning secret liens into false preferences was carried over into the Bankruptcy Code. The relevant provision is BC 547(e)(2). The meaning of BC 547(e)(2) is clarified in BC 547(e)(1), which defines the term ''perfected,'' and limited in BC 547(e)(3), which defines the earliest time a transfer can occur.

BC 547(e)(2) was designed to eliminate the evils of the secret lien, and it is effective in that regard. Unfortunately, it also ensnared many hapless secured creditors who, through no fault of their own, were unable to perfect within the former ten-day time limit. This is particularly true in cases involving motor vehicles. Unhappy with the harsh results in these cases, several states have attempted to deal with the problem by making special rules for security interests in motor vehicles by providing that if proper documentation is presented to the relevant state agency within a given period of time (usually from 15 to 30 days) after the security interest has attached, the security interest is deemed to have been perfected at the time it attached. Courts divided over whether an extended relation-back period under a state statute could prevail over the former ten-day period in BC 547(e)(2). The Supreme Court resolved the issue in *Fidelity Financial Services, Inc. v. Fink*, 522 U.S. 211 (1998), by holding that the time period provided in BC 547(e)(2) trumped any more expansive relation-back period under state law. In BAPCPA, the periods in BC 547(e)(2)(A), (B) and (C) for refinancing transactions and in BC 547(c)(3)(b) for purchase money transactions are extended to 30 days. These amendments should lessen the difficulties posed for secured creditors by the Code's policy of dating the time of transfer at the time of perfection. Article 9 has extended the relation-back period for purchase money security interests to 20 days, 9–317(e).

## F.   FRAUDULENT TRANSFERS: BC 548

## 1.   BASIC RULES

This large and ancient body of law, codified at the federal level by BC 548 and at the state level by the Uniform Fraudulent Transfer Act (UFTA), provides that trustees may avoid certain transfers or obligations deemed fraudulent that are made or entered into by debtors within two years of bankruptcy. "Transfer" in BC 101(54) includes the grant of a security interest. The UFTA, enacted in most states, contains provisions similar to those in BC 548. These laws are not as important in personal property secured transactions as are BC 544(a), the strong arm clause, or BC 547, voidable preferences law. Thus, our treatment of fraudulent transfer law is limited to the few instances in which it affects Article 9 secured transactions.

a.   ACTUAL FRAUD

BC 548 provides:

(a)(1) The trustee may avoid any transfer of an interest of the debtor in property, or any obligation incurred by the debtor, that was made or incurred on or within two years before the date of filing of the petition, if the debtor voluntarily or involuntarily

(A) made such transfer or incurred such obligation with actual intent to hinder, delay, or defraud any entity to which the debtor was or became, on or after the date that such transfer was made or such obligation was incurred, indebted;

Courts have sought for centuries to decide the illusive issue of when the transferor has "actual intent to hinder, delay, or defraud" another. Sometimes it is obvious, as in the case in which a debtor attempts to shield her assets from her unsecured creditors by granting a phony security interest in her assets to a relative. But in other cases it is not so obvious, and in these cases, the First Circuit, like many other courts, relies on factors known as the "badges of fraud" announced in a famous decision of the Star Chamber, Twyne's Case, (1601) 76 Eng. Rep. 234 (1601), which was decided under the Act Against Fraudulent Deeds, Gifts, Alienations, [etc.] 13 Elizabeth c. 5 (1570)(Eng.). Most courts subject a showing of actual fraud to an enhanced standard of proof.

Given the practical difficulty of mounting direct evidence of the debtor's intent, few cases turn on such proof. Instead, looking to the circumstances surrounding the transfer, courts have identified several objective indicia that, taken together, strongly indicate fraudulent intent. Those indicia include: (1) insider relationships between the parties; (2) the retention of possession, benefit or use of the property in question; (3) the lack or inadequacy of consideration for the transfer; (4) the financial condition of the party sought to be charged both before and after the transaction at issue; (5) the existence or cumulative effect of the pattern or series of transactions or course of conduct after the incurring of debt, onset of financial difficulties, or pendency or threat of suits by creditors; (6) the general chronology of the events and transactions under inquiry; * * * and (7) an attempt by the debtor to keep the transfer a secret; * * *. In re Watman, 301 F.3d 3, 8 (1st Cir.2002). That court adds a 21st century factor to these 17th century indicia: "The shifting of assets by the debtor to a corporation wholly controlled by him is another badge of fraud." Ibid. The UFTA § 4(b) includes a list of the traditional badges of fraud.

### b.   CONSTRUCTIVE FRAUD

Of greater significance to secured transactions law is what is generally called "constructive fraud," which requires no fraudulent intent. BC 548(a)(1)(B) states this alternative ground for avoiding a transfer or obligation. It provides that the trustee may do so if the debtor:

(B)(i) received less than a reasonably equivalent value in exchange for such transfer or obligation; and

(ii)(I) was insolvent on the date that such transfer was made or such obligation was incurred, or became insolvent as a result of such transfer or obligation;

(II) was engaged in business or a transaction, or was about to engage in business or a transaction, for which any property remaining with the debtor was an unreasonably small capital; or

(III) intended to incur, or believed that the debtor would incur, debts that would be beyond the debtor's ability to pay as such debts matured.

This ground for avoidance has nothing to do with actual fraud. It states a simple rule that an insolvent debtor must receive "reasonably equivalent value" in exchange for a transfer or obligation. Subparagraphs (ii) and (iii) are proxies for insolvency. As is sometimes said, an insolvent debtor must be just before it can be generous. Such a debtor cannot deplete its estate at the expense of its creditors in order to benefit others. An insolvent debtor may transfer its assets or enter into obligations, so long as it doesn't prejudice its creditors in doing so. If it receives reasonably equivalent value, its creditors are not harmed.

## 2.   REASONABLY EQUIVALENT VALUE

In most secured transactions there is no issue regarding whether a debtor who grants a security interest in its property receives reasonably equivalent value. Suppose Debtor has an estate consisting of personal property valued at $500,000. Debtor grants Secured Party a security interest in this property to secure a $100,000 advance made by Secured Party to Debtor. Debtor's estate has not been reduced: after the transaction, it has $100,000 in cash and a $400,000 interest—its "equity," in common parlance—in the personal property. The value of the property available to Debtor's creditors is the same.

However, the reasonably equivalent value issue does arise when the loan proceeds go to a person other than one granting the security interest in its own property. Throughout our discussion of Article 9, we have assumed in most cases that the "obligor" (9–102(a)(59)), the person who owes the debt, and the "debtor" (9–102(a)(28)), the person who owns the collateral in which the security interest is created, are the same person, as they usually are. When they are different persons, and the loan proceeds go to the obligor rather than to the debtor creating the security interest, there are fraudulent transfer implications that can subject the transaction to avoidance under BC 548.

### a. INDIRECT BENEFIT

What if the debtor is the indirect beneficiary of the loan proceeds that went to the obligor, as in the following case?

## In re Northern Merchandise, Inc.

United States Court of Appeals, Ninth Circuit, 2004.
371 F.3d 1056.

■ WARDLAW, CIRCUIT JUDGE:

Frontier Bank ("Frontier") appeals a decision of the Bankruptcy Appellate Panel ("BAP") affirming in part the bankruptcy court's summary judgment in favor of Ronald G. Brown, Chapter 7 Trustee ("Trustee"), in the Trustee's action alleging that Frontier received a fraudulent transfer from Chapter 7 Debtor Northern Merchandise, Inc. ("Debtor"). Specifically, Frontier challenges the BAP's ruling that Debtor did not receive reasonably equivalent value under 11 U.S.C. § 548(a)(1)(B) in exchange for a security interest it granted to Frontier and, thus, Frontier was not protected under 11 U.S.C. § 548(c). We have jurisdiction pursuant to 28 U.S.C. § 1291. Reviewing the bankruptcy court's decision to grant summary judgment de novo * * * we reverse.

### I. Background

In 1997, Debtor, a company that sold general merchandise to grocery stores, was incorporated by Paul Weingartner, Gary David, and Paul Benjamin. In February 1998, Frontier loaned $60,000 to the newly formed company. The loan was evidenced by a promissory note in the amount of $60,000, secured by a commercial financing agreement granting Frontier a security interest in Debtor's inventory, chattel paper, accounts, equipment, and general intangibles. The security interest was later perfected by the filing of a Uniform Commercial Code financing statement on February 24, 1998.

In October 1998, Debtor sought a second loan of $150,000 from Frontier to provide Debtor with working capital. Frontier refused to give such a loan to Debtor after determining that Debtor's financial performance did not support an additional direct loan to the company. However, Frontier agreed to loan $150,000 (the "October Loan") to Paul Weingartner, Paul Benjamin, and Stephen Comer, Debtor's shareholders (collectively, "Shareholders"), whose credit warranted such a loan.[1] Frontier understood that the Shareholders would, in turn, allow Debtor to utilize the money to fund its business operations. In fact, the loan transaction was structured so that Frontier deposited the proceeds of the October Loan

---

**1.** Shareholders were also officers and/or directors of Debtor.

directly into Debtor's checking account. However, while the funds themselves were transferred directly from Frontier to Debtor, the transaction was documented as a loan to Shareholders, who then turned the funds over to Debtor. The October Loan was evidenced by a promissory note in favor of Frontier executed by Shareholders. However, on the same day that Shareholders entered into the October Loan with Frontier, Debtor executed a commercial security agreement granting Frontier a security interest in its inventory, chattel paper, accounts, equipment, and general intangibles.

On March 5, 1999, Debtor ceased doing business, leaving approximately $875,000 in unsecured debt. At the time, Debtor had approximately $400,000 worth of inventory. Debtor transferred the $400,000 worth of inventory to Benjamin News Group, a company owned by shareholder Paul Benjamin, for $125,000.[2] On March 19, 1999, Benjamin News Group paid Frontier, not Debtor, the $125,000, which amount was credited to the October Loan. The remaining $25,000 due on the October Loan was paid to Frontier by the Safeway Corporation from the proceeds of prior sales of inventory to the Safeway Corporation.

On March 22, 1999, creditors filed an involuntary Chapter 7 petition against Debtor, and a trustee was appointed. Debtor scheduled assets of $4,116.17 and debts of $875,847.32. On February 9, 2001, Trustee filed a complaint against Frontier, and thereafter a motion for partial summary judgment, arguing that the grant of the security interest and the $125,000 transfer were fraudulent conveyances under 11 U.S.C. § 548(a). The bankruptcy court granted the motion for summary judgment, holding that a fraudulent conveyance had occurred. On appeal before the BAP, Frontier argued, *inter alia*, that the bankruptcy court erred in finding a fraudulent conveyance because (1) Debtor received reasonably equivalent value for the security interest and (2) Frontier was a good faith transferee with respect to receipt of the security interest. The BAP ruled in favor of Trustee on both issues.

## II.   Reasonably Equivalent Value

§ 548(a)(1) provides:

> The trustee may avoid any transfer of an interest of the debtor in property, or any obligation incurred by the debtor, that was made or incurred on or within one year before the date of the filing of the petition, if the debtor voluntarily or involuntarily ... received less than a reasonably equivalent value in exchange for such transfer or obligation.

It is well settled that "reasonably equivalent value can come from one other than the recipient of the payments, a rule which has become known as the indirect benefit rule." *Harman v. First Am. Bank (In re Jeffrey*

---

**2.** Trustee filed a fraudulent convey-    and ultimately recovered $45,000.
ance action against Benjamin News Group

*Bigelow Design Group, Inc.*), 956 F.2d 479, 485 (4th Cir.1992). For example, in *Rubin v. Manufacturers Hanover Trust Co.*, the court explained:

> a debtor may sometimes receive "fair" consideration even though the consideration given for his property or obligation goes initially to a third person ... although transfers solely for the benefit of third parties do not furnish fair consideration ... the transaction's benefit to the debtor need not be direct; it may come indirectly through benefit to a third person.... If the consideration given to the third person has ultimately landed in the debtor's hands, or if the giving of the consideration to the third person otherwise confers an economic benefit upon the debtor, then the debtor's net worth has been preserved, and [the statute] has been satisfied-provided, of course, that the value of the benefit received by the debtor approximates the value of the property or obligation he has given up.

661 F.2d 979, 991–92 (2d Cir.1981) (internal quotation marks and citations omitted).

*Jeffrey Bigelow* is such an example. In *Jeffrey Bigelow*, shareholders of a debtor entered into a line of credit agreement with First American Bank for $1,000,000. 956 F.2d at 481. Although the shareholders were the makers of the line of credit, "only the debtor received the draws and all payments were made directly from the debtor to First American." *Id.* Subsequently, "the debtor executed a note for $1,000,000 to [the shareholders] with substantially the same terms as the line of credit between First American and [the shareholders]." *Id.* As the debtor directly repaid First American, its liability on the note to the shareholders likewise decreased. *Id.* Holding that the payments made by the debtor on the shareholders' line of credit did not constitute fraudulent conveyances, the Fourth Circuit reasoned:

> [T]he proper focus is on the net effect of the transfers on the debtor's estate, the funds available to the unsecured creditors. As long as the unsecured creditors are no worse off because the debtor, and consequently the estate, has received an amount reasonably equivalent to what it paid, no fraudulent transfer has occurred.

*Id.* at 484. Because it was "apparent that the transfers [had] not resulted in the depletion of the bankruptcy estate," but rather "served simply as repayment for money received," the Fourth Circuit held that "no fraudulent transfer occurred." *Id.* at 485.

As *Jeffrey Bigelow* illustrates, the primary focus of Section 548 is on the net effect of the transaction on the debtor's estate and the funds available to the unsecured creditors. *See id.* ("the focus is whether the net effect of the transaction has depleted the bankruptcy estate"); *see also Nordberg v. Republic Nat'l Bank (In re Chase & Sanborn Corp.)*, 51 B.R. 739, 740 (Bankr.S.D.Fla.1985) ("the indirect benefit cases are bottomed upon the ultimate impact to the debtor's creditors"); *Rubin*, 661 F.2d at 992 ("decisions in [indirect benefit cases] turn on the statutory purpose of conserving the debtor's estate for the benefit of creditors."). Trustee contends that Debtor's grant of the security interest to Frontier resulted in a $150,000 loss to Debtor's estate and thus the funds available to the unsecured creditors. Trustee reasons that because the transfer of $150,000 from Shareholders to Debtor was technically a capital contribution, rather than a loan, Debtor was under no legal obligation to grant a security interest to Frontier. Therefore, Trustee argues, Debtor would have been justified to not grant the security interest to Frontier, which would have resulted in an additional $150,000 in Debtor's estate.

We reject this formalistic view. Although Debtor was not a party to the October loan, it clearly received a benefit from that loan. In fact, Frontier deposited the $150,000 proceeds of the October Loan directly into Debtor's checking account. Because Debtor benefited from the October Loan in the amount of $150,000, its grant of a security interest to Frontier to secure Shareholder's indebtedness on that loan, which totaled $150,000, resulted in no net loss to Debtor's estate nor the funds available to the unsecured creditors. To hold otherwise would result in an unintended $150,000 windfall to Debtor's estate. Accordingly, Debtor received reasonably equivalent value in exchange for the security interest it granted to Frontier. * * *

### IV.  Conclusion

For the foregoing reasons, the BAP erred in holding that Debtor did not receive reasonably equivalent value under § 548(a)(1)(B) in exchange for the security interest it granted to Frontier and that Frontier was not protected under § 548(c).

**REVERSED**

### b.  LEVERAGED BUYOUT

A person may want to buy a corporation but lacks the money or collateral necessary to finance the purchase. If the target corporation has unencumbered assets, it may be possible to use those assets to provide most of the capital necessary to make the purchase. Doing so, however, may violate fraudulent transfer law with serious consequences if the acquired firm subsequently files in bankruptcy. Corporate acquisitions in which assets of the acquired firm are encumbered require careful attention to the fraudulent transfer issues raised by the transaction.

### PROBLEMS

**1.** Shareholder agrees to sell the stock of Target Corporation to Acquirer who is unable to pay for the stock out of its own assets. Acquirer offers Shareholder a security interest in the stock of Target to secure the unpaid amount of the purchase price. Shareholder isn't interested in this because under the absolute priority rule debt must be paid before equity, and creditors of Target would come ahead of Shareholder in any liquidation. Shareholder will sell on credit only if it can have a security interest in Target's assets. Acquirer agrees, and Target grants Shareholder a security interest in Target's assets to secure Acquirer's debt to Shareholder. If the transfer rendered Target insolvent or left it with unreasonably small capital to engage in business and Target filed in bankruptcy within a year, may the trustee of Target avoid the security interest under BC 548?

**2.** Same facts, except that instead of Shareholder financing the deal Acquirer borrows the money to buy the stock from Bank and causes Target to grant Bank a security interest in its assets to secure the loan. Bank advances the loan proceeds to Acquirer who pays the money to Shareholder for the stock. Has Acquirer avoided the infirmity present in Problem 1?

**3.** Same facts. But Bank is wise to the problem posed by the Problem 2 transaction, and its loan officers are taught to be sure that the loan proceeds go to the entity that grants Bank the security interest. The transaction is structured so that the loan goes to Target, which grants Bank a security interest in its assets. Target then re-lends the money to Acquirer, an acquisition entity without significant assets, and Acquirer uses the money to pay Shareholder for the stock in Target. Now Bank believes that it is safe; it received a security interest in Target's assets and gave Target hard cash in exchange. What Target does with the loan proceeds is its own business. Surely this meets the requirements of "reasonably equivalent value" under BC 548(a)(1)(B)(i). Does it?

When United States v. Tabor Court Realty Corp., 803 F.2d 1288 (3d Cir.1986) (often referred to by its district court title, *"Gleneagles"*), held that under the facts of Problem 3 Bank was the recipient of a fraudulent transfer, the ancient law of fraudulent transfers became required reading for mergers and acquisitions lawyers throughout the land. The court invalidated Bank's security interest as a fraudulent transfer on the ground that although Bank had given value to Target at the time it received the security interest, the money "merely passed through" Target to Acquirer and ultimately to the shareholders of Target. Acquirer's note to Target was worthless because Acquirer had virtually no assets other than the stock of now insolvent Target; hence, Target's loan to Acquirer was a gratuitous transfer. Bank countered by insisting that there were two separate transactions, first, its loan to Target and, second, Target's loan to Acquirer. Bank gave good value to Target and what Target chose to do with the proceeds of the loan was a decision that should not affect the legitimacy of Bank's security interest. The court rejected this argument; since Bank knew the purpose of the loan, the two transactions were in fact "part of one integrated transaction." This holding made leveraged buy-out transactions more risky and focused the attention of lenders on the solvency of the entities being acquired.

### c.   SECURITIZATION

We discussed asset securitization earlier in Chapter 3 with respect to sale of rights to payment. The following Problem addresses the fraudulent transfer risk that may be present in these transactions.

### PROBLEM

At the urging of its shareholders, Originator Corporation decided to securitize some of its intangible assets. Accordingly, it created a separately incorporated special purpose vehicle (SPV) whose only assets are those to be transferred to it by Originator. Originator subsequently transfers to the SPV its existing account receivables in exchange for an agreed price. The SPV undertakes to bear all of the risks of payment by the account debtors of the accounts transferred as well as the responsibility for collecting payments from them. The SPV pays Originator for the transferred accounts with funds received from the issuance and sale of securities in it to investors. At the same time the SPV files a proper financing statement covering Originator's account receivables, listing Originator as "debtor" and itself as "creditor." Originator pays out to its shareholders as a dividend the sum received from the SPV. If Originator files a bankruptcy petition within two years of the transaction, may Originator's trustee avoid the SPV's interest in the account receivables? May the trustee recover amounts from Originator's shareholders?

# CHAPTER 10

# LETTERS OF CREDIT

## A. INTRODUCTION

Letters of credit are ubiquitous and important financial instruments. They have a wide variety of uses, such as paying for goods, guaranteeing commercial paper and municipal and corporate bonds, and backing up the performance of nonfinancial contracts. Simply put, a letter of credit is an undertaking in a writing or other record by one person to pay or deliver an item of value to a named person on that person's satisfaction of documentary conditions, if any, stipulated in the record. 5–102(a)(10). In its most basic form the instrument involves three parties: the issuer, the applicant (or "customer") and the beneficiary. The issuer is the party making the record undertaking, the applicant is the party requesting the issuer to make the record undertaking (almost always for a fee), and the beneficiary is the party who is to receive payment or deliver an item of value. The letter of credit provides that the issuer will pay the beneficiary a stipulated amount upon the beneficiary's satisfaction of stipulated documentary conditions by a specified date. It may even provide that the issuer will deliver an item of value to the beneficiary, such as stock certificates. The legal relationship between the beneficiary and applicant may vary, as can their identity. The beneficiary and applicant may be, respectively, a seller and buyer in a sales contract, a contractor and owner in a construction contract, a creditor and debtor, or a donee and donor. Although the relationship between parties and the transactions can change, the elementary form of the letter of credit is the same: an issuer's record undertaking, made at the request of an applicant, to give specified value to a beneficiary upon its satisfaction of documentary conditions, if any, stated in the record.

A letter of credit may involve additional parties. The issuer can engage a party, called the adviser, to notify the beneficiary of the existence and terms of the credit. 5–102(a)(1), 5–107(c). Another party, called the confirmer, may be engaged by the issuer to pay the beneficiary upon the beneficiary's presentation of documents required by the confirmation. 5–102(a)(4). A confirmed letter of credit is a separate instrument from the issuer's letter of credit. 5–107(a). Often the same party may undertake both to advise and confirm the issuer's letter of credit. Letters of credit issued in international transactions frequently involve advisers and confirmers. This is because applicants and beneficiaries often are strangers to each other. An advisor local to the beneficiary can vouch reliably for the genuineness and accuracy of the terms of a foreign letter of credit. A local confirmer provides a convenient and reliable source of payment as well as other advantages such as avoidance of foreign currency exchange controls. Where an advice and confirmed letter of credit is warranted, a prudent beneficiary will require them as part of the terms of transaction that calls for the issuance of a letter of credit.

Letter of credit contracts are traditionally called commercial or mercantile "specialties." They are contracts subject to special rules, not the ordinary rules that apply to other contracts. Some commentators and courts describe the letter of credit as a "unique" or "idiosyncratic" instrument. For instance, the issuer's obligation to the beneficiary is not the product of the beneficiary's acceptance of an offer by the issuer. The issuer's obligation also is enforceable without consideration, although typically consideration will support its obligation. See 5–105. Essential to letter of credit law is the rule that the issuer's payment obligation to the beneficiary is conditioned only on the documentary terms described in the credit. Only these terms govern the issuer's obligation to the beneficiary. Terms or facts bearing on the relationship or contracts between the beneficiary and the applicant, or between the applicant and issuer, have no effect on the issuer's obligation to the beneficiary. In this sense the issuer's obligation to the beneficiary is "primary": it is independent of facts or terms bearing on relationships between other parties. The issuer's undertaking to the beneficiary alone controls its payment obligation to the beneficiary. Thus, a letter of credit isn't a guarantee because the issuer's obligation isn't conditional on the default of the principal obligor; the issuer's liability isn't "secondary." In contrast, the guarantor's liability is secondary. See Restatement (Third) of Suretyship and Guaranty § 34 (1995). The letter of credit contract also doesn't give the issuer or applicant rights of a third party beneficiary: neither can use the rights of others to affect the issuer's payment obligation to the beneficiary. Legally, the insulation of the issuer's payment obligation from other transactions makes the letter of credit a distinctive financial instrument. See Comment 1 to 5–102.

In a typical transaction involving a letter of credit, three separate contracts are involved: (1) the contract between the beneficiary and the applicant that calls for the establishment of the credit or gives rise to it; (2) the contract between the issuer and beneficiary requiring payment against presentation of the documents; and (3) the contract of reimbursement between the issuer and the applicant. It is standard to refer to contract (1) as the underlying contract, contract (2) as the letter of credit contract, and contract (3) as the reimbursement contract. The distinctiveness of letter of a credit as a financial instrument derives from the independence of the letter of credit contract from the other two sorts of contract. Thus, issuer's obligations to the beneficiary under the letter of credit are "primary" and therefore unaffected by the underlying or reimbursement contracts.

There are two types of letters of credit: commercial and standby letters of credit. They are distinguished by their intended financial purposes and the sorts of documentary conditions specified credits. A commercial letter of credit serves as a mechanism for payment owed on the underlying contract. For instance, a contract for the sale of goods might require the buyer-applicant to establish a letter of credit naming the seller as the beneficiary. The terms of the credit require the issuer to pay a specified amount equal to the contract price to the beneficiary upon the beneficiary's presentation to it of documents described in the credit. The described documents can be of any sort. They typically include a draft drawn by the seller on the buyer, a commercial invoice, a bill of lading or other document of title, and certificates of origin or inspection certificates. Where the underlying contract involves a sale of assets other than goods, such as real estate or securities, different documentation will be required. The seller is paid the contract price by the issuer if the seller-beneficiary presents documents to it that comply with the terms of the credit. Because the issuer undertakes to pay the seller-beneficiary, the commercial credit adds the issuer's obligation to that of the buyer. Thus, the seller won't receive the contract price only if both the buyer and issuer are unable or unwilling to pay it. Because issuers frequently are banks with low risks of insolvency and a great concern for their reputations as reputable financial intermediaries, a commercial credit reduces the seller-beneficiary's risk of nonpayment significantly. The use of commercial credits in sales transactions is discussed in Clayton P. Gillette and Steven D. Walt, Sales Law: Domestic and International 406–454 (2d ed. 2002).

A standby letter of credit has a different purpose and specifies different documentary conditions. Standby letters of credit function to guarantee performance of an underlying contract or transaction. They do not serve as a risk-reducing device for payment of the contract price. Typically a standby credit provides that the issuer will pay the beneficiary if the beneficiary presents specified documentary evidence of default by the applicant or some other party in an underlying contract or transactions. Unlike the commercial letter, the issuer of a standby credit does not usually expect the beneficiary to draw on the credit. ("Direct pay" credits are variant standby credits in which the credit serves as a payment mechanism for discharging financial obligations, and the issuer expects to pay upon the beneficiary's presentation of a draft or documentary demand.) Required documents generally include a draft and noncommercial documents, typically a certificate of default of specified content. Thus, presentation of documentary evidence of default allows the beneficiary to obtain payment from the issuer. In this way the issuer's obligation backs up the applicant or another's obligation under the underlying contract or transactions. The standby credit thereby shifts the risk of the applicant's insolvency, nonpayment or nonperformance from the beneficiary to the issuer. Standby credits that back up financial obligations owed in an underlying transaction are called "financial" standby credits. "Performance" standby credits back up nonmonetary obligations owed in the underlying transaction. As a standby credit, the issuer's obligation to the beneficiary in each case depends only on the beneficiary's presentation of documentary evidence of default in an underlying transaction, not on nondocumentary facts bearing on default.

Standby credits serve a guarantee function in a variety of underlying transactions. Issuers of commercial paper can market the paper at a higher price by backing it up with letters of credit. The credits can be drawn upon by the holders of the paper if the paper isn't paid at maturity. Purchasers of limited partnerships on credit can guarantee their partnership interests by having issued a credit that undertakes to pay the beneficiary-sellers upon certification of the purchasers' default on its payment obligations. In securitization transactions standby credits serve to enhance the credit rating of securities issued by the securitization vehicle: the credit guarantees the payment of interest and principal on securities the vehicle issued. Finally, a standby credit might serve as an alternative to withholding progress payments under a construction contract. Rather than withhold progress payments, the owner can have the contractor-applicant establish a standby credit in the owner's favor. The credit can allow the owner-beneficiary to draw stipulated amounts if the owner presents documentary evidence to the issuer of the contractor's default. The same sort of scheme can allow the buyer-beneficiary in a sales of goods contract to prepay for the goods and draw on credit upon documentary presentation of the seller-applicant's default under the sales contract. Its wide range of uses and the comparatively low fees charged by issuers of standby credits apparently make the standby credit an attractive financial instrument. In 2001 U.S. FDIC-insured depository banks issued approximately 296.2 billion dollars in standby credits. During the same period they issued about 23.3 billion dollars in commercial credits. See FDIC Statistics on Banking C–12 (Table RC–6) (2001). A form standby letter of credit and reimbursement agreement appear at the end of this Chapter.

## B.   SOURCES OF LETTER OF CREDIT LAW

Most letter of credit law consists of domestic law and institutional rules, and much of it is uniform across jurisdictions. Letter of credit law has five sources: (1) In the United States Article 5 of the UCC and extra-Code common law; (2) Publication Number 500 of the Uniform Customs and Practice for Documentary Credits of the International Chamber of Commerce ("UCP 500" or "UCP"); (3) the Uniform Law for Demand Guarantees of the International Chamber of Commerce; (4) the International Standby Practices of the International Chamber of Commerce ("ISP 98"); and (5) the United Nations Convention on Independent Guarantees and Standby Letters of Credit ("U.N. Convention"). To date, six countries have ratified the U.N. Convention; the United States has not done so. Thus, domestic law such as Article 5 and the International Chamber of Commerce's institutional rules remain the most important rules governing credits. Treatises describing the sources of letter of credit law include John F. Dolan, The Law of Letters of Credit: Commercial and Standby Credits (rev. ed. 2003) (herein Dolan, Letters of Credit); 3 James J. White & Robert S. Summers, Uniform Commercial Code, Chapter 26 (4th prac. ed. 1995) (herein White & Summers; prac. ed.); and Brooke Wunnicke et al., Standby and Commercial Letters of Credit (3d ed. 2003). A brief summary appears in Boris Kozolchyk, Commercial and Standby Letters of Credit, in 3 United States Law of Trade and Investment, Chapter 24 (B. Kozolchyk & J.F.

Molloy eds. 2001). This Chapter focuses almost exclusively on Article 5 and the UCP.

Article 5 of the UCC governs both commercial and standby letters of credit. Since the International Chamber of Commerce has no legislative authority, its institutional rules apply only if the credit incorporates them. Credits frequently incorporate UCP 500 in particular as a source for principles governing letter of credit transactions. To be applicable, both UCP 500 and ISP 98 require that the incorporation be express. UCP 500 art. 1; ISP 98 art. 1.01(b). Almost all international credits and many domestic commercial credits issued in New York, for instance, are made subject to the UCP. Over half of the standby credits currently issued by Citibank and J.P. Morgan Chase are reported to be governed by the ISP 98. A few courts have held that the UCP can apply to a credit by virtue of trade usage even when the credit does not refer to the UCP. Article 5 governs credits issued by banks or other persons, but excludes credit undertakings issued by consumers. UCP 500 applies to both commercial and standby credits issued only by banks. The ISP 98 applies to standby credits issued by any person. See UCP 500 art. 2; ISP 98 art. 1.04. Both UCP 500 and ISP 98 allow parties to opt-in to the respective rules by incorporation in the credit when the credit would not otherwise be covered. UCP 500 art. 1; ISP 98 art. 1.01(b); cf. U.N. Convention art. 1(2).

Incorporation of institutional rules in most cases displaces conflicting default rules under Article 5. Section 5–116(c) is clear that if a credit is made subject to the UCP or other "rules of custom or practice," the UCP or other rules of custom or practice displace Article 5 only if there is a conflict and the conflict involves a default rule of Article 5. See Comment 3 to 5–116. If Article 5's conflicting rule is mandatory, its rule continues to apply. Article 5's rules, default or mandatory, also continue to apply when they have no counterpart under UCP 500, such as rules concerning fraud or standards of documentary compliance. In these cases there is no conflict between rules. For the most part, Article 5's very few mandatory rules are consistent with the UCP 500's rules, the current version of the UCP. The exceptions bearing on comparatively nuanced rules concerning the expiration of a credit, and the assignment of credit proceeds are isolated. Cf. 5–106(c), UCP 500 art. 42; 5–114(c), UCP 500 art. 49. Thus, although future versions of the UCP might contain rules in conflict with Article 5, at present there are few conflicts. Article 5 therefore effectively allows parties to select between its rules and the UCP.

Article 5, along with most other domestic letter of credit law, allows parties virtually unrestricted freedom of choice over the terms of the credit. Almost all of Article 5's rules are default rules: they apply unless the parties agree to vary them. As just noted, very few of Article 5's rules are mandatory. Section 5–103(c)'s lists the following mandatory rules: the exclusion of consumer-issuers and noncredit undertakings from Article 5, restrictions on the stipulated expiration date for a credit, regulation of the issuer's withholding of consent to the assignment of credit proceeds, obligations of good faith, and subrogation rights. See 5–102(a)(8), (10), 5–

106(d), 5–114(d), 1–302(b), 5–117(d). All of Article 5's other rules are default rules. In fact, even Article 5's mandatory rules are in effect default rules too. This is because Article 5 allows parties to select law governing the letter of credit, without restriction. Section 5–116(a) provides that the law of the jurisdiction chosen by the "affected parties" controls the liability of the issuer, nominated person or adviser, and the law selected "need not bear any relation to the transaction." Parties therefore can select applicable law that does not contain Article 5's mandatory rules. Thus, Article 5's mandatory rules apply only if affected parties fail to select the law of a jurisdiction that does not contain the same rules. See Comment 2 to 5–103 (second paragraph).

## C.  FORMAL REQUIREMENTS

Under 5–106(a), a letter of credit is enforceable when issued. The credit in turn is issued when the issuer sends or transmits the credit to the beneficiary. Because a credit is "sent" when it is mailed or delivered for transmission by the usual means, 1–201(36)(A), the credit becomes enforceable upon dispatch. Article 5 does not explicitly provide when a confirmed credit becomes enforceable. However, Comment 1 to 5–107 instructs us to treat the terms "confirmation" and "letter of credit" interchangeably throughout Article 5. Thus, the same rules concerning issuance and dispatch apply to confirmed letters of credit. Under 5–106(a), UCP 500 art. 6(c), and ISP 98 art. 1.06(a), a letter of credit is irrevocable unless it states otherwise. Irrevocability means that the issuer cannot cancel or amend the credit without the beneficiary's consent. 5–106(b). This default rule makes sense for the vast majority of beneficiaries, who might want to rely on the credit in advance of drawing on it. Section 5–106(c) provides that if there is no stated expiration date in a credit, it expires one year after issuance, and 5–106(d) provides that if the credit purports to be perpetual, it expires five years after issuance. The latter is a mandatory rule.

To be a letter of credit, a financial instrument must take a certain form. Section 5–104 sets out the formal requirements a credit must satisfy. However, to be a letter of credit in the first place, the financial instrument must contain a particular sort of undertaking. Since the essential feature of a letter of credit is that the credit is independent of the underlying contract, the instrument must reflect this fact. Form must reflect function. Thus, an instrument is a letter of credit only if it conditions the issuer's obligation on satisfaction of documentary conditions. Section 5–102(a)(10) defines a letter of credit as a "definite undertaking ... to honor a documentary presentation by payment...." This definition describes a mandatory rule (5–103(c)), and an agreement to treat an instrument that is not a letter of credit under 5–102(a)(1) therefore is ineffective. In the following case, Notes and Problems, we inquire after the conditions in a written undertaking that undermine the writing's character as a letter of credit. The Problems following the case also investigate 5–104's formal requirements.

## Wichita Eagle and Beacon Publishing Company, Inc. v. Pacific National Bank of San Francisco

United States Court of Appeal, Ninth Circuit, 1974.
493 F.2d 1285.

■ Before Chambers and Browning, Circuit Judges, and King, District Judge.

■ Per Curiam:

The facts are summarized in the district court's opinion, 343 F.Supp. 332 (N.D.Cal.1971).

\* \* \*

[Summary by Eds. Lessors leased a site on which Lessee (Circular Ramp Garages), under the terms of the lease, undertook to build a parking garage. In order to assure Lessors that Lessee would perform, Lessee obtained from Bank (Pacific National Bank) a writing addressed to Lessors in which Bank established its "Letter of Credit No. 17084" in favor of Lessors for payment of $250,000 "available by drafts drawn at sight on the Pacific National Bank providing that all of the following conditions are met at the time said draft is received by the undersigned." The conditions were (1) that Lessee has failed to perform the terms of the lease; (2) that Lessors have given Bank an affidavit stating that it has given notice to Lessee and its contractor specifying how Lessee has failed to perform its lease; and (3) that either Lessee or its contractor has failed to cure defaults under the lease during a period of thirty days after receiving Lessor's notice. Lessee failed to obtain the financing necessary to build the parking garage and defaulted on the lease. Lessors' assignee (Plaintiff) presented to Bank a draft for $250,000 drawn upon Letter of Credit No. 17084, together with the required documents. When Bank refused payment, Plaintiff brought suit against Bank. The district court concluded that "Although the question is not free from doubt, the Instrument denominated 'Letter of Credit No. 17084' should be treated as a letter of credit and be subject to the law respecting letters of credit to the extent applicable and appropriate." 343 F.Supp. at 339.]

We do not agree with the district court that the instrument sued upon is a letter of credit, though it is so labeled. Rather, the instrument is an ordinary guaranty contract, obliging the defendant bank to pay whatever the lessee Circular Ramp Garages, Inc., owed on the underlying lease, up to the face amount of the guaranty. Since the underlying lease clearly contemplated the payment of $250,000 in case of default, and since this provision appears to be a valid liquidated damages clause, the judgment below must be modified to award the plaintiff $250,000 plus interest.

We do not base our holding that the instrument is not a letter of credit on the fact that payment was triggered by default rather than performance or on the fact that the instrument was written in a lease context, for we recognize that the commercial use of letters of credit has expanded far beyond the international sales context in which it originally developed.
\* \* \*

The instrument involved here strays too far from the basic purpose of letters of credit, namely, providing a means of assuring payment cheaply by eliminating the need for the issuer to police the underlying contract. * * * The instrument neither evidences an intent that payment be made merely on presentation on a draft nor specifies the documents required for termination or payment. To the contrary, it requires the actual existence in fact of most of the conditions specified: * * * for payment, that the lessee have failed to perform the terms of the lease and have failed to correct that default, in addition to an affidavit of notice.

True, in the text of the instrument itself the instruments is referred to as a "letter of credit," and we should, as the district court notes, "giv[e] effect wherever possible to the intent of the contracting parties." 343 F.Supp. at 338. But the relevant intent is manifested by the terms of the agreement, not by its label. * * * And where, as here, the substantive provisions require the issuer to deal not simply in documents alone, but in facts relating to the performance of a separate contract (the lease, in this case), all distinction between a letter of credit and an ordinary guaranty contract would be obliterated by regarding the instrument as a letter of credit.

It would hamper rather than advance the extension of the letter of credit concept to new situations if an instrument such as this were held to be a letter of credit. The loose terms of this instrument invited the very evil that letters of credit are meant to avoid—protracted, expensive litigation. If the letter of credit concept is to have value in new situations, the instrument must be tightly drawn to strictly and clearly limit the responsibility of the issuer.

* * *

NOTES

**1.** The conceptual issue presented in *Wichita Eagle* concerns the character of the instrument issued by the Bank: is it a guarantee or a standby letter of credit? The issue is important as a matter of bank regulation. Banks in the United States generally are not permitted to issue guarantees. They are permitted, however, to issue letters of credit, subject to regulation. As noted above, in function guarantees and standby letters of credit are indistinguishable, both involving the enhancement of an obligor's promise by adding the promise of a creditworthy third party. In fact, European banking terminology sometimes refers to standby credit as "bank guarantees." Conceptually they are distinguishable by the nature of the issuer's obligation and the conditions under which its obligation attaches. As to the issuer's obligation, it is primary: the issuer cannot invoke defenses against the beneficiary available to the applicant to resist honoring the credit. A guarantor's obligation is secondary: it can invoke defenses available to the obligor to resist payment to the obligee. Because banks generally can only issue letters of credit, the conceptual distinction between credits and guarantees is crucial.

The Office of the Comptroller of the Currency regulates the issuance of letters of credit by focusing on documentary conditions. By the Comptroller's interpretive ruling, national banks may issue letters of credit, including standby letters of credit, only if the obligation to honor "depends upon the presentation of specified documents and not upon nondocumentary conditions or resolution of questions of fact or law at issue between the account party and the beneficiary." 12 C.F.R. 7.1016(a) (1998). State chartered banks usually are subject to a similar sort of regulation.

An important question is the effect of a bank issuing a guarantee in violation of bank regulations. Issuing banks or applicants sometimes adopt the odd litigation posture of urging the illegal issuance of a guarantee as a defense to enforcement of the guarantee. This is the "ultra vires" defense to honor. See Republic National Bank v. Northwest National Bank, 578 S.W.2d 109 (Tex.1978); *Wichita Eagle*. Although a few courts have accepted the ultra vires defense, the majority of case law has rejected it. See, e.g., Federal Dep. Ins. Corp. v. Freudenfeld, 492 F.Supp. 763 (E.D.Wis.1980); First American National Bank v. Alcorn, Inc., 361 So.2d 481 (Miss.1978); Dolan, Letters of Credit & 12.03[2]. In *Wichita Eagle*, for instance, the court enforced the instrument as a guarantee. The rejection of the ultra vires defense makes a good deal of sense. The issuer or applicant almost always is in a better position than the beneficiary to avoid violating applicable bank regulations or detecting their violation. Bank regulating agencies also are better positioned than beneficiaries to monitor issuers and applicants. Accordingly, not allowing the defense to enforcement increases the cost to issuers of violating the regulation against the issuance of guarantees. It serves as a partial substitute for closer monitoring of a bank's investment activities by bank regulating agencies.

**2.**   *Wichita Eagle* was decided under the version of Article 5 in effect before its revision in 1995. How would this case be decided under current version of Article 5? See 5–102(a)(10) ("letter of credit") and Comment 6 to 5–102. How could the document in *Wichita Eagle* be rewritten to remove all doubt about its status as a letter of credit? Does 5–108(g) allow the court in this case to find that the writing is a valid letter of credit by disregarding the two nondocumentary conditions? Comment 9 to 5–108. See Dolan, Letters of Credit & 2.05; 3 White & Summers, Prac. ed. § 26–2. If the undertaking is a letter of credit, the disregard of nondocumentary conditions does not mean that the issuer can ignore them. As a matter of the reimbursement agreement between the applicant and the issuer, their honor might be required. Section 5–108(g)'s injunction only means that the issuer's obligations to the beneficiary under the letter of credit do not depend on the satisfaction of nondocumentary conditions. See Comment 9 to 5–108.

**3.**   The cardinal principle of letter of credit law, the "independence principle," is codified in 5–103(d). Section 5–104 recognizes that the day of an exclusively paper-based system of letter of credit transactions has long since passed. Comment 3 notes: "Many banking transactions, including the issuance of many letters of credit, are now conducted mostly by electronic means. * * * By declining to specify any particular medium in which the letter of credit must be established or communicated, Section 5–104 leaves room for future developments." See the definitions of "document" (5–102(a)(6)) and "record" (5–102(a)(14)).

**4.** The documents to be presented to the issuer of the letter of credit to obtain payment are usually accompanied by a draft drawn by the beneficiary (5–102(a)(3)) on the issuing bank (5–102(a)(9)) payable "at sight" (that is on presentment) to the order of the beneficiary. A sight draft is merely a demand for payment that may be negotiable in form, thus conferring upon the beneficiary the power to transfer the draft to a third person who may take the rights of a holder in due course. Comment 11 to 5–102.

## PROBLEMS

**1.** Paysaver Credit Union executed the following writing at the request of Wells and Titan Tool, which owed Transparent Products $33,000 on open account:

Transparent Products Corporation

Bensenville, IL 60101

RE: Thomas Wells

Gentlemen:

We hereby establish our letter of credit at the request of Thomas Wells of 1315 South 3rd Avenue, Maywood up to the aggregate amount of fifty-thousand dollars ($50,000).

Titan wanted to buy more plastics from Transparent and obtained Paysaver's issuance of the writing directed to Transparent to bolster Titan's creditworthiness. Wells is an employee of Titan who was not indebted to Transparent. It was Wells' $50,000 certificate of deposit with Paysaver that apparently persuaded Paysaver to issue this writing. Transparent ultimately declined to extend more credit to Titan and, when the latter filed in bankruptcy, Transparent demanded payment under Paysaver's "letter of credit" to defray the remaining $33,000 debt. Is the quoted writing sufficiently "definite" to be a letter of credit under 5–102(a)(10)? See Comment 6 to Rev. 5–102. If it is not, is the instrument effective as a guaranty? A guarantor undertakes to pay the debt of another and can raise the principal debtor's defenses; the issuer of a letter of credit is primarily liable and cannot set up defenses of the applicant. The facts are based on Transparent Products Corp. v. Paysaver Credit Union, 864 F.2d 60 (7th Cir.1988). Comment 1 to 5–104 states: " * * * a letter of credit will typically specify the amount available, the expiration date, the place where presentation should be made, and the documents that must be presented to entitle a person to honor."

**2.** (a) What would be the result in Problem 1 if the body of the writing had said: "We hereby establish our letter of credit at the request of

Thomas Wells of 1315 South 3rd Avenue, Maywood up to the aggregate amount of fifty-thousand dollars ($50,000) on which Transparent Products Corporation may draw at any time within the next year by presentation of a draft payable at sight for any amount up to the credit limit"? See 5–102(a)(6) ("document"), (10) ("letter of credit") and (12) ("presentation").

(b) What would be the result in Problem 1 if the body of the writing had said: "This is a guarantee, not a letter of credit. At the request of Thomas Wells of 1315 South 3rd Avenue, Maywood, we hereby undertake to pay Transparent Products Corporation up to the aggregate amount of fifty-thousand dollars ($50,000) at any time within the next year upon the following three conditions: (1) Transparent presents a written demand for payment; (2) Transparent not make the presentation before 1 p.m. eastern standard time; and (3) Transparent recites to our representative that the writing represented is a written demand for payment"?

## D. ISSUER'S DUTY TO HONOR OR DISHONOR

### 1. THE STRICT COMPLIANCE STANDARD

A letter of credit is a highly efficient instrument in which banks or others issue suitably definite undertakings to honor complying documentary presentations and the beneficiaries present the prescribed documents and are paid. Indirect evidence of the credit's efficiency is the comparatively low fees issuers charge compared to fees charged for other comparable financial instruments. Central to the credit's cost advantage is the issuer's duty to honor complying documentary presentations. Under 5–108(a), the standard of documentary compliance is strict: ". . . [A]n issuer shall honor a presentation that, as determined by the standard practice referred to in subsection (e), appears on its face strictly to comply with the terms and conditions of the letter of credit." The domestic law of most legal systems apparently also adopts the strict compliance standard. See Boris Kozolchyk, Commercial Letters of Credit in the Americas 72, 259 (1966). Neither the UCP nor ISP 98 expressly adopts a standard of documentary compliance. See UCP 500 art. 13(a); ISP 98 art. 4.01. Accordingly, in credits governed by the UCP or ISP 98 that otherwise do not address the standard of compliance, domestic law standards continue to apply. The strict compliance standard therefore likely will control under applicable law in these cases.

The importance of a documentary discrepancy is irrelevant under the standard. As a Law Lord put it in Equitable Trust Co. of New York v. Dawson Partners Ltd., [1927] 27 Lloyd's List. L. R. 49, 52 (Summer L.), a leading letter of credit case, "[t]here is no room for documents which are almost the same, or which will do just as well." Of course, facts about the underlying transaction also are irrelevant to the issuer's duty to the beneficiary. If the documents presented correspond to the terms of the credit, the issuer must pay. Otherwise, not. As we will discuss below, an issuer who honors a noncomplying documentary presentation risks not being reimbursed by the applicant.

The strict compliance standard resists an informative and precise statement. Strict compliance does not require literal, letter-for-letter correspondence between the contents of prescribed documents and the credit's terms. Comment 1 to 5–108 states that the standard does not mean "slavish conformity to the terms of the credit." On the other hand, both the strict compliance standard and Comment 1 reject a substantial compliance standard, which judges compliance by an undefined measure of the degree to which documents comply with the credit's terms. Thus, the standard seems to treat documents as complying if they less than literally comply, but more than substantially comply, with the credit's terms. Courts and commentators have had trouble identifying the permissible range of less than perfect compliance. Even courts that do not insist on absolute compliance sometimes disagree on what is strict but less than literal compliance. A rough working notion of compliance under 5–108(a) finds that documents strictly comply when the issuer, using standard practices of issuers, determines that they correspond on their face with the credit's terms. Put another way, the notion is that the documents comply if a reasonable issuer, examining only the documents and the credit, and charged with knowledge of the practices of issuers, would decide that a documentary discrepancy is substantial. For a brief history of applications of the standard, see Peter Ellinger, The Doctrine of Strict Compliance: Its Development and Current Construction, in Lex Mercatoria: Essays on International Commercial Law in Honour of Francis Reynolds 187–198 (Francis D. Rose ed. 2000). The strict compliance standard and related issues are extensively discussed in 2 Barkley Clark & Barbara Clark, The Law of Bank Deposits, Collections and Credit Cards 14.05 (rev. ed. 2005); Dolan, Letters of Credit Ch. 6; and 3 White & Summers, Prac. ed. § 26–6.

In this section we examine perhaps the most litigated issue in the letter of credit law: the duty of the issuer to both the beneficiary and applicant to honor or dishonor a presentation. At issue in most of the litigation is the application of the strict compliance standard in the face of documentary discrepancies. Strict compliance tests documentary presentations by the standard practice of financial institutions that regularly issue credits. Using slightly different terms, 5–108(a) and (e), UCP 500 art. 13(a) and ISP 98 art. 4.01(b) refer to such practice. Did the court in the following case rely on evidence of the standard practice of financial institutions to determine the appropriate compliance standard?

## Carter Petroleum Products, Inc. v. Brotherhood Bank & Trust Company

Court of Appeals of Kansas, 2004.
97 P.3d 505.

■ GREEN, P.J.

This action involves a bank's wrongful refusal to honor a letter of credit. Carter Petroleum Products, Inc. (Carter) sued Brotherhood Bank &

Trust Company (Bank) for its failure to honor a letter of credit. The Bank appeals from a judgment of the trial court granting summary judgment in favor of Carter on the letter of credit. On appeal, the Bank contends that the untimely presentment of the letter of credit and the noncompliance of the submitted documents with the letter of credit relieved the Bank of its duty to honor the letter of credit. We disagree and affirm.

Carter is in the petroleum business and sells fuel products to Highway 210, LLC (Highway 210), which operates a gas station. Highway 210 is also a customer of the Bank. On October 19, 2001, the Bank issued a letter of credit, No. 2001–270, in the aggregate amount of $175,000, for the benefit of Carter on the account of Highway 210.

By its terms, the letter of credit authorized Carter to draw on the Bank on the account of Highway 210, to the aggregate amount of $175,000 available by Carter's draft at sight accompanied by the following document: "STATEMENT SIGNED BY CARTER PETROLEUM PRODUCTS STATING THAT HIGHWAY 210, LLC HAS FAILED TO PAY OUTSTANDING INVOICES IN ACCORDANCE WITH TERMS OF PAYMENT."

The letter of credit further provided that "[e]ach draft must state that it is 'Drawn under Brotherhood Bank & Trust Company's Letter of Credit #2001–270 dated July 26, 2001.' This credit must accompany the draft(s)." The date of "July 26, 2001" in the aforementioned quotation was a typographical error because the letter of credit at issue was dated October 19, 2001. This letter of credit was a renewal of one of a series of previous letters of credit which were referenced in the lower margin of the letter of credit. The October letter of credit replaced the letter of credit dated July 26, 2001, in the amount of $125,000.

Additionally, the letter of credit stated "that all draft(s) drawn under and in compliance with the terms of this credit will be duly honored on delivery of documents as specified if presented at this office in Shawnee, KS no later than June 26, 2002." The letter of credit was also subject to the Uniform Customs and Practice for Documentary Credits, International Chamber of Commerce Publication No. 500 (1993 Revision) (UCP).

Hal O'Donnell, Carter's credit manager, delivered a draft request to the Bank for payment on June 26, 2002. Carter's draft request contained the following statement:

> "Pursuant to the terms stated in the Letter of Credit #2001–270 dated October 19, 2001 (copy attached), Carter Petroleum Products, Inc., hereby exercises its option to draw against said Brotherhood Bank and Trust Company's Letter of Credit in the amount of $175,000 due to non-payment of invoices in accordance with terms of payment (copies also attached)."

The account name listed on the draft request was Highway 210 Texaco Travel Plaza, LLC, not Highway 210, LLC, as listed on the letter of credit. In addition, the draft request contained a statement that Highway 210 had failed to pay outstanding invoices and contained a statement that Carter was exercising its rights under the letter of credit. Carter's draft request was accompanied by the letter of credit and copies of Carter's outstanding invoices to Highway 210.

O'Donnell arrived at the Bank at approximately 5 p.m. on June 26, 2002, to present the draft request. When O'Donnell arrived at the Bank, the lobby doors were locked, but after O'Donnell knocked on the door, an employee of the Bank admitted O'Donnell into the lobby. O'Donnell indicated he was there to see Ward Kerby, the assistant vice president of the Bank. Upon meeting Kerby, O'Donnell handed him the draft request accompanied by the letter of credit and unpaid Carter invoices of Highway 210. The draft request was then stamped received on June 26, 2002, and was signed by Kerby with a notation that it was received at 5:05 p.m.

When O'Donnell delivered Carter's draft request to the Bank, the drive-through window was still open for business. O'Donnell maintained that had the employee of the Bank not opened the lobby, he would have delivered the draft request along with the attachments to the drive-through window attendant.

June 26, 2002, was a Wednesday. There is no dispute that the lobby of the Bank closed at 5 p.m. on Wednesdays. Similarly, there is no dispute that the drive-through lane at the Bank was open until 7 p.m. on Wednesdays. Additionally, inside the Bank there were several signs which alerted customers that any transactions occurring after 2 p.m. would be posted on the next business day.

The Bank dishonored Carter's draft request on the letter of credit on June 28, 2002. The Bank's dishonor notice stated two reasons: (1) The draft request was presented to the Bank after regular banking hours of the Bank on the date the letter of credit expired, and (2) the request failed to contain the specific language required by the letter of credit: "Drawn under Brotherhood Bank & Trust Company's Letter of Credit #2001–270 dated July 26, 2001."

Carter sued the Bank for its failure to honor the letter of credit. Both parties both moved for summary judgment. The trial court ruled in favor of Carter and granted its motion for summary judgment. The Bank requested time to conduct further discovery concerning Highway 210's current debt to Carter. Carter furnished the Bank's counsel with copies of documents including an acknowledgment by Highway 210 that its debt to Carter exceeded the $175,000 face amount of the letter of credit. Later, the trial court entered its judgment in favor of Carter in the amount of $175,000, plus interest, costs, and attorney fees. * * *

On appeal, the Bank relies on two theories. First, the Bank contends that the attempted presentment of the draft request was untimely. The Bank makes two separate arguments. It argues that the presentment was untimely either because it occurred past 2 p.m. and, thus, should be considered on the next day's business or because the presentment occurred past 5 p.m., after the regular banking hours of the Bank. Second, the Bank argues that the draft request did not strictly comply with the terms of the letter of credit.

Letters of credit are governed by Article 5 of the Uniform Commercial Code (UCC), K.S.A. 84–5–101 *et seq.* The pertinent statute is K.S.A. 84–5–108. It states, in relevant part:

> "(a) Except as otherwise provided in K.S.A. 84–5–109, an issuer shall honor a presentation that, as determined by the standard practice referred to in subsection (e), appears on its face strictly to comply with the terms and conditions of the letter of credit. Except as otherwise provided in K.S.A. 84–5–113 and unless otherwise agreed with the applicant, an issuer shall dishonor a presentation that does not appear so to comply.
>
> . . . .
>
> "(e) An issuer shall observe standard practice of financial institutions that regularly issue letters of credit. Determination of the issuer's observance of the standard practice is a matter of interpretation for the court. The court shall offer the parties a reasonable opportunity to present evidence of the standard practice."

Strict compliance and standard practice are explained in the Official UCC Comment 1 to K.S.A. 84–5–108. The comment states:

> "The standard of strict compliance governs the issuer's obligation to the beneficiary and to the applicant. By requiring that a 'presentation' appear strictly to comply, the section requires not only that the documents themselves appear on their face strictly to comply, but also that the other terms of the letter of credit such as those dealing with the time and place of presentation are strictly complied with. . . .
>
> . . . .
>
> "The section adopts strict compliance, rather than the standard that commentators have called 'substantial compliance[.]' . . . Strict compliance does not mean slavish conformity to the terms of the letter of credit. For example, standard practice (what issuers do) may recognize certain presentations as complying that an unschooled layman would regard as discrepant. . . .
>
> "Identifying and determining compliance with standard practice are matters of interpretation for the court, not for the jury. . . . Granting the court authority to make these decisions will also encourage the salutary practice of courts' granting summary judgment in circumstances where there are no significant factual disputes."

The Kansas Comment to K.S.A. 84–5–108, as it pertains to strict compliance and standard practice, mirrors the sentiments presented in the official comment.

Turning first to the issue of timeliness, we notice that there is no dispute that the letter of credit was subject to the UCP. Both parties agree that Article 45 of the UCP provides that "[b]anks are under no obligation to accept presentation of documents outside their banking hours."

Letters of credit are governed by the rules applicable to the construction of ordinary contracts. *Sports, Inc. v. The Sportshop, Inc.*, 14 Kan. App.2d 141, 142, 783 P.2d 1318 (1989). The document must be construed from its four corners and all provisions must be considered together and not in isolation. When an ambiguity appears in a document, the language is construed against the party who prepared the instrument. *Amoco Production Co. v. Wilson, Inc.*, 266 Kan. 1084, 1088, 976 P.2d 941 (1999). In the instant case, the Bank prepared the letter of credit.

The letter of credit first stated that $175,000 was available by Carter's draft at "sight" accompanied by certain documents. It then stated that the letter of credit would be honored "if presented at this office in Shawnee, KS no later than June 26, 2002." The only office referred to in the letter of credit is the Bank's office at 7499 Quivira, Shawnee, Kansas.

O'Donnell arrived at the Bank just after 5 p.m., and the lobby was closed. The drive-through window at the Bank, located at 7499 Quivira, was still open. The letter of credit made no reference that the sight draft must be presented before the lobby closed on June 26, 2002. Similarly, it did not state that the draft needed to be presented before 2 p.m. or before 5 p.m. The letter of credit did not state that the draft needed to be presented to a loan officer, a vice president, or any particular person. The letter of credit simply stated that the money was available by draft at "sight" and would be honored "if presented at this office in Shawnee, KS no later than June 26, 2002."

Under the rules of construction, the presentment of the draft did comply with the requirements set forth for the time and place of presentment. The draft was presented at the Bank on June 26, 2002, at a time when the Bank was still open for business. Although the lobby was closed, by the terms of the letter of credit, anyone working at the Bank was authorized and could have accepted the draft, including the drive-through teller who was open for business.

Although the Bank may have intended to limit the presentment of a sight draft to either before 2 p.m. or 5 p.m. on June 26, 2002, the Bank did not specify in the letter of credit that presentment was to be conducted in this way. This was the source of the confusion; other than the date, no specific time of day was mentioned as to when it must be presented. For example, the letter of credit could have stated that it must be presented "no later than 5 p.m., June 26, 2002, at which date and time the letter of credit expires." The letter of credit failed to contain such language or any similar language to that effect. "Any ambiguity in a letter of credit must be resolved against the party drafting it." *East Girard Sav. Ass'n v. Citizens Nat. Bank & Trust Co. of Baytown*, 593 F.2d 598, 602 (5th Cir.1979). The Bank was the sole drafter of the letter of credit. Accordingly, if the Bank wanted more specificity as to when and where Carter had to make presentment, the Bank could have included such provisions in its letter of credit. The ambiguities or lack of explicitness in the letter of credit stemmed from the Bank's own pen. As a result, the Bank's argument fails.

Next, we must consider whether the draft request strictly complied with the terms of the letter of credit. When do documents comply with the terms of the letter of credit so that a bank is forced to pay the draft is a difficult legal question. The UCC furnishes no easy answer to this question.

The Bank was to make funds available to Carter under its sight draft when it was accompanied by a "statement signed by Carter Petroleum Products stating that Highway 210, LLC has failed to pay outstanding invoices in accordance with terms of payment."

Additionally, the letter of credit required that "[e]ach draft must state that it is 'Drawn under Brotherhood Bank & Trust Company's Letter of Credit #2001–270 dated July 26, 2001.' This credit must accompany the draft(s)."

On June 26, 2002, Carter presented to the Bank a sight draft in the amount of $175,000. The account name on the draft was Highway 210 Texaco Travel Plaza, LLC. The draft contained the following statement:

"Pursuant to the terms stated in the Letter of Credit #2001–270 dated October 19, 2001 (copy attached), Carter Petroleum Products, Inc., hereby exercises its option to draw against said Brotherhood Bank and Trust Company's Letter of Credit in the amount of $175,000 due to non-payment of invoices in accordance with terms of payment (copies also attached)."

The draft was accompanied by the letter of credit and Carter's outstanding invoices to Highway 210.

On appeal, the Bank contends that the demand was not in strict compliance because (1) the draft request stated the account name as "Highway 210 Texaco Travel Plaza, LLC," not "Highway 210, LLC," and (2) the draft request did not contain the exact language from the letter of credit.

In support of its contentions, the Bank cites *American Coleman v. Intrawest Bank of Southglenn*, 887 F.2d 1382 (10th Cir.1989). The defendant bank in *Coleman* was to make funds available to plaintiff under its sight drafts to be accompanied by the " '[o]riginal Letter of Credit and your signed written statement that Jim Gammon and Associates is in default on the Note and Security Agreement dated November 21, 1984, between American Coleman and Jim Gammon and Associates.' " 887 F.2d at 1383. Plaintiff tendered to the bank a sight draft with the following attached statement: "[T]he American Coleman Company informs you that Jim Gammon and Associates is in default on the Note and Security Agreement dated November 21, 1984, *and the Promissory Note dated November 16, 1984*, between American Coleman and Jim Gammon and Associates." (Emphasis added.) 887 F.2d at 1384.

The bank dishonored the draft. In finding in favor of the bank, the trial judge stated:

"In the present case, it is clear that [plaintiff's] request for payment presented November 13, 1986 was not in technical or literal compliance with the terms of the letter of credit. [Plaintiff's] reference to two different notes could easily have caused the bank's documents examiner some confusion. Accordingly, because I conclude that the rule of strict compliance, as it is applied in Colorado, requires literal compliance with the terms and requirements set forth in the letter of credit, and there was no such literal compliance in this case." 887 F.2d at 1385.

In affirming the decision of the trial court, the Tenth Circuit Court of Appeals stated:

"While it is apparent from the cases that minute discrepancies which could not possibly mislead a document examiner are usually disregarded, this does not constitute a retreat from the strict compliance standard applicable in this case inasmuch as the district court found that '[plaintiff's] reference to two different notes could easily have caused the bank's documents examiner some confusion.' " 887 F.2d at 1386.

The *Coleman* court then held that the trial court did not err in applying the strict compliance standard. 887 F.2d at 1386. In rejecting plaintiff's argument that reference to the second note was mere surplusage, the *Coleman* court declared:

"The apparent existence of two promissory notes supports the district court's finding that Bank could have been misled by [plaintiff's] November 13, 1986, draft. [Plaintiff's] contention that Bank could not have been misled by the draft because Bank drafted the letter of credit is without support in this record." 887 F.2d at 1386–87.

Thus, the *Coleman* court's decision was largely based upon whether the defendant bank could have been misled by the discrepancy in the draft.

In *American Airlines, Inc. v. Federal Deposit Ins.*, 610 F.Supp. 199 (D.Kan.1985), a bank had issued a letter of credit No. G–301, to American Airlines, Inc. (American). Unfortunately, American delivered a sight draft to the bank referring to the letter of credit No. G0391. The cover letter, however, correctly referred to the letter of credit as G–301. The bank refused to pay on the letter of credit. The bank maintained that the typographical error on the sight draft indicated that American had failed to strictly comply with the terms of the letter of credit. As a result, American was not entitled to payment.

In ruling in favor of American, the *American Airlines* court stated:

"In the case at hand, we conclude that there was no possibility that the Bank could have been misled by the documents submitted to it by [plaintiff]. Even under the rule of strict compliance, a beneficiary may establish compliance with the terms of a letter of credit via documents submitted in conjunction with the disputed draft. [Citation omitted.] Here, the documents submitted along with [plaintiff's] draft clearly indicated the correct letter of credit reference number and the proper drawee (the Bank)." 610 F.Supp. at 202.

Because the bank could not have been misled, even with the typographical error, the *American Airlines* court determined that the documents did strictly comply with the terms of the letter of credit. As a result, American was entitled to payment. 610 F.Supp. at 202.

In the instant case, although the draft request submitted by Carter was not in complete conformity with the letter of credit issued by the Bank, it did contain all the necessary information requested by the letter of credit. Moreover, the Bank could not have been misled by the nonconformity.

Although the draft request listed the account name as "Highway 210 Texaco Travel Plaza, LLC," not "Highway 210, LLC" as requested in the letter of credit, the draw request was accompanied by the letter of credit which properly named the account. Obviously, there was no confusion caused by the different name referred to in the draft request because the Bank did not rely on this ground in rejecting the letter of credit. Moreover, the Bank failed to raise this particular argument before the trial court. Issues not raised before the trial court cannot be raised on appeal. *Board of Lincoln County Comm'rs v. Nielander*, 275 Kan. 257, 268, 62 P.3d 247 (2003).

The draft request also contained all of the other pertinent information requested in the letter of credit. The letter of credit accompanied the draft, the draft stated it was drawn under Brotherhood Bank and Trust Company's letter of credit, and the draft contained the correct letter of credit number: #2001–270. Additionally, as required by the letter of credit, the draft stated that Carter was exercising its option to draw against the Bank due to nonpayment of invoices in accordance with the terms of payment.

The draft request differed from the requirements stated in the letter of credit in that the letter of credit mistakenly referred to the letter of credit dated July 26, 2001. In its draft request, Carter properly referred to the letter of credit dated October 19, 2001. Had Carter referred to the incorrect date as specified in the letter of credit, it would have been likely to cause confusion on the part of the Bank because the October 19, 2001, letter of credit was for a different amount and superceded [sic] the July 26, 2001, letter of credit. As a result, the Bank's argument fails. * * *

Affirmed.

## NOTES

**1.** With respect to the timeliness issue, is the court saying that presentation of the $175,000 letter of credit in *Carter Petroleum* would have been timely if made to the bank's drive-through teller at 6:59 on June 26, 2002? Might the court have found the presentation untimely had Carter Petroleum drafted the letter of credit? What does this case teach banks to do in drafting letters of credit with respect to time and place of presentation?

With respect to the compliance issue, is the court saying that, in the absence of proof of standard practice to the contrary, the test of compliance under 5–108(a) is whether the error in compliance (here "October 19, 2001" in the draft instead of "July 26, 2001") is "misleading"? How does a "misleading" test vary from a substantial compliance standard? See Comment 1 to 5–108. The court says that it takes this standard from *American Coleman*, in which the triggering event for the bank's obligation to pay was presentation to the bank of a sight draft accompanied by a written statement by the beneficiary that the "Note and Security Agreement dated November 21, 1984" were in default. Even though there was no such note, the beneficiary's statement contained the required representation. However, out of an abundance of caution and because of its unease about representing that the customers were in default on a nonexistent note, the beneficiary *added* the fatal words "and the Promissory Note dated November 16, 1984," which described the true note on which the customers were actually in default. The court held that under former Article 5 the documentary presentation was not in compliance owing to the additional language, which could have caused the bank's documents examiner some confusion and misled the bank. Wasn't the potential for confusion just as great in *Carter Petroleum*?

**2.** Section 5–108(a)'s strict compliance standard is a default rule. As with most aspects of the letter of credit, it can be varied by the reimbursement agreement between the applicant and the issuer when their interests and capabilities favor doing so. See 5–103(c); Comment 2 to 5–103; Comment 1 to 5–108. Reimbursement agreements sometimes are altered accordingly. For example, see ¶ 8 of the Letter of Credit Agreement form reprinted at the end of this Chapter. Another example is ISP 98 art. 4.09(c), which requires exact compliance in the documentary presentation when the credit calls for "exact" or "identical" wording in documents. Even when the parties do not opt out of the default rule, 1–102(3) allows the reimbursement agreement to set standards of documentary compliance. Thus, whether a strict compliance standard is preferable to an alternative compliance standard depends on the preferences and capacities of typical parties to a letter of credit. Which rule is likely to minimize the costs of effecting payment under a credit for the typical applicant?

In his article, Letters of Credit, 44 Bus. Law. 1567, 1589 (1989), Albert J. Givray, an experienced bank counsel, contended that the strict compliance rule is essential to the efficient operation of the letter of credit department of banks. The document examiner must lay the draft against the letter of credit in the bank's files. If there is a discrepancy the examiner is ill-equipped to deal with it: she is not a lawyer and may know nothing of the circumstances surrounding the transaction. The examiner's task should merely be to ask: do the presented documents *on their face* meet all the letter of credit's requirements? Do you agree with this view of the examiner's function?

**3.** Section 5–108(e) states that "[a]n issuer shall observe standard practice of financial institutions that regularly issue letters of credit.

Determination of the issuer's observance of the standard practice is a matter of interpretation for the court." Under both 5–108(a) and UCP 500 art. 13(a), the degree of documentary compliance is determined by the "standard practice" of issuers. However, although close in meaning, the two provisions are not identical. They differ in the "practice" referred to: 5–108(e)'s "standard practice" is that of financial institutions that regularly issue credits; UCP 500 art. 13(a)'s "practice" is that of international banking practice. Given the number of non-bank issuers of domestic credits in the United States, the difference might be potentially important. Comment 8 to 5–108 discusses the intended meaning of "standard practice."

The ICC has attempted to describe some of the specific "best practices" for examining documents among international banks. See ICC Document No. 645, International Standard Banking Practice (ISBP) (2003). For example, ISBP para. 69 finds acceptable a description of the quantity of goods in the invoice that varies by $+-5\%$ from the quantity required by the credit. ISBP para. 32 requires that each document be presented in at least one original, unless the credit allows otherwise. ISBP para. 28 considers misspellings or typographical errors in a document nondiscrepant as long as they do not alter the meaning of the word or sentence in which they occur.

Section 5–108(e) allocates to the court the determination of the issuer's observance of standard practice. Comment 1 explains, "... it is hoped that there will be more consistency in the outcomes and speedier resolution of disputes if the responsibility for determining the nature and scope of standard practice is granted to the court, not to a jury." Does this unconstitutionally deprive the parties of a jury trial? See Margaret L. Moses, The Uniform Commercial Code Meets the Seventh Amendment: The Demise of Jury Trials Under Article? 5, 72 Ind. L. J. 681 (1997). Compare also §§ 1–205(2), 2–202, 2–302 and 4A–202(c) which use a similar approach. Section 5–108(e)'s treatment of the issue of standard practice as a question of law is controversial. Three states have adopted nonuniform amendments to the subsection eliminating the offending portion of subsection (e). See N.Y. U.C.C. § 5–108(e) (McKinney 2003); Pa. Stat. Ann. 13 § 51–8(e) (2003); Wyo. Stat. Ann. § 34.1–5–108(e) (2003).

**4.** Does the strict compliance standard enhance the reliability of letters of credit as payment mechanisms? Or does it encourage an issuing bank to find a minor defect in the documents in cases in which the bank doesn't want to pay, such as cases in which the applicant has gone into bankruptcy and reimbursement of the bank's claim against the applicant may be difficult? Observers consistently have found a high frequency of noncomplying documentary presentations, typically exceeding 50%. In an informal survey of selected banks issuing commercial credits, the issuers reported that 73% of the documentary presentations contained discrepancies. See Ronald J. Mann, The Role of Letters of Credit in Payment Transactions, 98 Mich. L. Rev. 2494 (2000). Concerned about the number of discrepant presentations, the ICC has tried to create uniformity in international banking practices for handling documentary discrepancies by publishing a set of "best practices." See Document No. 645, ISBP.

In assessing the wisdom of the strict compliance standard, recognize three points. First, in most commercial credits the beneficiary doesn't care if the documents presented contain discrepancies, because the issuer will honor the presentation anyway. Where the market price of goods contracted for in the underlying transaction is stable or rising, the applicant-buyer will want the goods and therefore will have the issuer waive its right to insist on conforming documents. Alternatively, under these markets conditions the issuer may waive the discrepancy at its own risk. Thus, most of the time obtaining conforming documents isn't cost-justified for beneficiary-sellers. See John F. Dolan, Why High Discrepancy Rates Do Not Discourage L/C Use, 2003 Ann. Survey Let. Credit L. & Prac. 36. The few beneficiaries who are concerned about the prospect of a falling market can opt-out of strict compliance by insisting that the reimbursement agreement provide a more forgiving standard of compliance.

Second, there is a powerful market mechanism controlling strategic rejections of discrepant documents by issuers. Issuers operate in a market in which reputation matters. Because issuance fees are comparatively low, an issuer's profit from operating a credit department depends on it generating a high volume of credits. The issuer therefore must both obtain repeat business and attract potential applicants and beneficiaries. The number of issuers is relatively small, and information about their handling of credits often can be obtained from other issuers. An issuer may seize on a discrepancy to avoid honor because it fears not being reimbursed or is undercollaterized or wants to avoid involvement in the applicant's bankruptcy or simply wants to placate its applicant. But doing so risks a loss of credit business since potential beneficiaries will insist that credits be issued by issuers that are reliable sources of payment. The presenting beneficiary also is unlikely to do business with the issuer again. Thus, prospect of a loss in reputation often suffices to prevent issuers from strategic rejections even under a strict compliance standard.

Third, less stringent standards of compliance require judicial intervention, and courts are poorly positioned to intervene effectively. For instance, the court in Voest–Alpine Trading USA Corp. v. Bank of China, 167 F.Supp.2d 940 (S.D.Tex. 2000), considers and rejects a standard that finds documentary discrepancies when the deviation in the document risks harming the applicant in the underlying transaction. Application of this standard encourages parties to litigate the issuer's decision to honor or dishonor a documentary presentation. Courts (and issuers) are unfamiliar with the facts necessary to make this determination of harm at the time the issuer must decide to honor the presentation. They know nothing about industry practices bearing on the underlying transaction. Standards less stringent than strict compliance therefore undermine the credit's efficient payment function. Professor White reaches the same conclusion and states, without remorse, that "the issuer may examine the documents microscopically and may assert small discrepancies to excuse its duty to pay." 3 White & Summers, Prac. ed. § 26–5, at 140–41.

**5.** Under 5–108(a), an issuing bank must honor a conforming presentation. Must it dishonor a nonconforming presentation? Suppose in the case of questionable documentation like that in *American Coleman*, the bank called the applicant and asked its consent to the bank's payment of the credit. If the applicant gave its consent, (1) may the bank safely pay the credit? (2) May it safely decline to pay the credit? 5–108(a) and Comment 7 to 5–108. (3) Does the issuer have a duty to seek a waiver from the applicant in the case of a nonconforming presentation? Comment 2 to 5–108; see Bombay Industries, Inc. v. Bank of N.Y., 649 N.Y.S.2d 784 (N.Y.App.Div.1996).

**6.** Matter of Coral Petroleum, Inc., 878 F.2d 830 (5th Cir.1989), presented the issue of whether impossibility excuses strict compliance with a letter of credit. Seller sold Buyer 31,000 barrels of West Texas Intermediate crude oil for $880,400 and required Buyer to obtain a standby letter of credit in a form acceptable to Seller for the price. Bank issued the letter of credit under Buyer's instructions that the credit would be payable upon receipt of certain documents including (1) a statement by Seller that West Texas Intermediate oil had been delivered to Buyer and (2) a copy of the shipper's transfer order showing transfer to Buyer of 31,000 barrels of "WTNM SO or SR." Buyer's instructions were mistaken. West Texas Intermediate crude is a sweet oil (meaning not containing certain undesirable elements found in sour oil), but "WTNM SO or SR" refers to sour oil. Thus, the letter of credit required two documents that were contradictory: a shipper's order showing transfer of sour oil to Buyer and a statement that sweet oil had been delivered to Buyer. After Buyer filed in bankruptcy under Chapter 11, Seller demanded payment under the letter of credit. Bank refused to pay because Seller's demand was accompanied by a shipper's order showing transfer of sweet oil to Buyer. Seller had inspected the letter of credit before accepting it and did not ask that the erroneous description be corrected. Seller argued that the terms of the credit were impossible to perform. Seller could not deliver sweet oil to Buyer and procure a shipper's transfer order showing that sour oil had been delivered. Seller also argued that the letter of credit was ambiguous and the ambiguity should be construed against Bank. The court held that the letter of credit was not ambiguous. The fact that it was impossible for Seller to comply did not excuse compliance by Seller. Bank is not required to know the meaning of technical trade terms used in the letter of credit. If Seller finds the terms of a shipping agreement impossible to fulfill, it should attempt to renegotiate them beforehand or refuse to sign the letter of credit. BM Electronics Corporations v. LaSalle, 59 UCC Rep. Serv. 2d 280 (N.D. Ill. 2006). See also In re Sanders–Langsam Tobacco Co., Inc., 224 B.R. 1 (Bankr.E.D.N.Y.1998). Moreover, Seller was negligent in accepting a letter of credit with requirements that could not be met. Accord: First State Bank v. Diamond Plastics Corp., 891 P.2d 1262 (Okla.1995).

In Albert J. Givray, Letters of Credit, 44 Bus. Law. 1567, 1587 (1989), it is suggested that issuers add a conspicuous legend stating "Please examine this letter of credit at once. If you feel unable to meet any of its requirements, either singly or together, please contact customer immediately to see if the letter of credit can be amended. Otherwise, you risk losing payment under this letter of credit for failure to comply strictly with its terms as written." Would the suggested legend be likely to help parties in Seller's position in *Coral Petroleum*? If Seller discovered the inconsistency after Buyer had filed a bankruptcy petition and Buyer were willing to have the credit amended to remove the inconsistency, the automatic stay could prevent it from doing so. See Bankruptcy Code § 362(a)(3). If the discovery and amendment were made prior to Buyer's bankruptcy filing, preference law could be implicated.

## 2.   NOTICE OF DISCREPANCIES: WAIVER AND PRECLUSION

An issuer can respond to a documentary presentation in either of two ways: by honoring or dishonoring it. Both Article 5 and the UCP describe the steps that an issuer must take when documents are presented under a credit and the consequence of failing to take them. The two sets of rules prescribe the same steps. If the documents appear to comply with the credit's terms, both 5–108(a) and UCP 500 art. 13(b) require the issuer to honor the presentation. If the documents are discrepant and the discrepancy allows the issuer to refuse honor, the issuer has a choice: it can waive its right to insist on a complying presentation and honor the discrepant presentation or it can dishonor the presentation. (An issuer who waives the discrepancy does so at its own risk, unless the customer has agreed to the waiver.) Under both 5–108(b) and UCP 500 art. 13(b), 14(c) and (d), the issuer must honor or dishonor a presentation within a reasonable time after the documentary presentation, but not beyond seven business days after receipt of the documents, unless the credit provides otherwise. Comment 2 to 5–108 notes that this seven-day period is not a safe harbor: the issuer must act within a reasonable period, but no later than the end of the seven-day period. The failure to decide to honor or dishonor within the prescribed "reasonable period" constitutes dishonor by the issuer. See Comment 2 to 5–108.

Waiver is an intentional relinquishment of a known legal right and applies to Article 5 via 1–103(a), as a supplementing principle of extra-UCC common law. A waiver can be oral, unless the reimbursement agreement requires otherwise. Paragraph 11 of the Letter of Credit Agreement form at the end of the Chapter requires that waivers be in writing. UCP 500 art. 14(c) explicitly allows the issuer to waive its rights against the applicant. The UCP is silent as to the issuer's waiver against the beneficiary. A few courts have divided over whether common law doctrines such as waiver apply to credits subject to the UCP. Compare Banco General Runinahui, S.A. v. Citibank Int'l, 97 F.3d 480 (11th Cir.1996), with Alaska Textile Co., Inc. v. Chase Manhatten Bank, N.A., 982 F.2d 813 (2d Cir.1992).

In deciding whether to waive a documentary discrepancy, prudent issuers usually approach their applicants to obtain their consent. This is because the applicant's consent modifies the reimbursement agreement to allow for the issuer's reimbursement if it honors the presentation. Sometimes issuer's waive discrepancies at their own risk, without the consent of their applicants. In all cases, waiver is a right of the issuer that it can exercise within its discretion. The issuer has no obligation to waive a discrepancy, even if the applicant consents to the waiver. See Suntex Industrial Corp., Ltd. v. The CIT Group/BBC, Inc., 2001 WL 34401367 (D.Del.). It need not even approach the applicant to elicit the applicant's consent. See Note 6 above. ISP 98 arts. 5.05 and 5.06(a) are to the same effect. Comment 7 to 5–108 construes waiver narrowly, so that waiver of one or more presentations does not waive subsequent discrepant presentations.

The issuer's second alternative is to dishonor a discrepant documentary presentation. Article 5 follows the UCP's approach both to the sufficiency of notice that must be given to the presenter and the effect of the failure to give timely notice and sufficient notice of dishonor. Section 5–108(b) requires that, in the case of dishonor, the issuer must communicate both the fact and grounds of dishonor to the presenter. See Comment 2 to 5–108 (second paragraph); cf. UCP 500 art. 14(d)(i), (ii). Thus, 5–108(b) contemplates two possibilities: either the issuer fails to make a timely decision to honor or dishonor, or the issuer's timely decision fails to give timely notice of the grounds for dishonor. In both cases 5–108(c) precludes the issuer from relying as a ground for dishonor on discrepancies it has delayed communicating to the presenter within 5–108(b)'s prescribed time limit. (Strictly, the UCP 500s preclusion rule only applies to the failure to give timely notice of the grounds for dishonor; see UCP 500 art. 14(e). It does not apply to the failure to make a timely decision to honor the presentation; see UCP 500 art. 13(b).)

Section 5–108(b)'s preclusion rule is not a rule concerning waiver or estoppel. Courts tend to mix waiver and estoppel together, and sometimes treat both as preclusion. See, e.g., *American Coleman*, 887 F.2d at 1387 ("waiver-estoppel rule"); *Banco General Runinahui, S.A.*, 97 F.3d at 485 n.11 (preclusion as "strict estoppel"). The notions are distinct. Preclusion isn't waiver because it doesn't require the issuer to intentionally relinquish its right to a complying presentation. Section 5–108(b)'s preclusion rule applies when the issuer simply fails to give timely notice of the grounds for dishonor within the prescribed period. Preclusion also isn't estoppel, because estoppel requires detrimental reliance and 5–108(b)'s rule does not require reliance. It therefore requires no showing that the presenter has been harmed by the issuer's failure to give timely notice of the fact, or grounds, of dishonor. For the same reasons, UCP 500 art. 14(e)'s preclusion rule isn't a waiver or estoppel rule. See Toyota Tsusho Corp. v. Comerica Bank, 929 F.Supp. 1065 (E.D.Mich. 1996). Unlike waiver and estoppel, Article 5 and the UCP 500's preclusion rules avoid the proof costs associated with litigating over relinquishment of a right to a complying presentation (waiver) or detrimental reliance on a failure to give timely notice of a discrepancy (estoppel).

Both 5–108(b) and UCP 500 art. 14(d)'s prescribed time periods set an outer limit of seven business days, but requires the decision to honor or dishonor be within a "reasonable time" within the seven-day period. The issue what is a "reasonable time" to decide or give notice of discrepancies has troubled courts construing the UCP. Courts under former Article 5 treated the three-day period prescribed by former 5–112(1) as a safe harbor: notice of dishonor given by the end of the period is effective, even if the decision to dishonor has been made at the beginning of the period. 3 White & Summers, Prac. Ed. § 26–9(c). Because the seven-day period under 5–108(b) is not a safe harbor, only an outer limit, courts applying the subsection face the same issues concerning the time for giving notice of discrepancies as courts face in applying UCP 500. ISP 98 art. 5.01(a)(i) resolves some of the uncertainty, when applicable, by deeming notice given within three business days "not unreasonable." The following UCP case discusses these matters. Although application of an earlier version of the UCP's preclusion rule is at issue in the case (UCP 400 art. 16(c)), the interpretation of a "reasonable time" in the rule remains relevant under UCP 500's art. 14(d)'s time period.

# Esso Petroleum Canada v. Security Pacific Bank

United States District Court, D. Oregon, 1989.
710 F.Supp. 275.

■ FRYE, DISTRICT JUDGE:

The matters before the court are the motion for summary judgment (#45) of defendant, The Oregon Bank (the Bank), on all claims brought by plaintiff, Esso Petroleum Canada (Esso), and Esso's motion for partial summary judgment on its first and third claims for relief (#).

Esso alleges that the Bank wrongfully dishonored its irrevocable standby letter of credit by failing to specify the discrepancies which caused the Bank to reject the documents submitted by Esso or to notify Esso of the discrepancies in a timely fashion.

UNDISPUTED FACTS

Esso is a division of Imperial Oil Limited, a company organized and existing under the laws of Canada, with its principal place of business in Toronto, Canada. The Bank, presently known as Security Pacific Bank, is a banking corporation organized and existing under the laws of the State of Oregon.

Prior to October 22, 1987, Esso entered into a contract with Valley Oil Co., Inc. (Valley Oil) to sell to Valley Oil amounts of aviation gasoline for a total purchase price of $1,196,580. As a condition of sale, Esso required Valley Oil to obtain a standby letter of credit naming Esso as the beneficiary. As a condition to issuing the standby letter of credit, the Bank required Valley Oil to obtain a backup letter of credit from Western Pioneer, Inc., dba Delta Western (Delta), Valley Oil's customer. On October 21, 1987, Delta transferred by wire $1,288,140 to the Bank for deposit to Valley Oil's account.

On October 22, 1987, the Bank executed and delivered to Esso an irrevocable standby letter of credit, a copy of which is attached as Exhibit "A." On November 1, 1987, Esso delivered the aviation fuel to Delta.

The letter of credit issued by the Bank to Esso on October 22, 1987 provides that it is subject to the Uniform Customs and Practice for Documentary Credits (1983 Revision) International Chamber of Commerce (Publication 400) (the UCP). Article 48 of the UCP provides that letters of credit expiring on a day on which the issuing bank is not open for business do not expire until the end of the following day on which the bank is open for business. Therefore, since November 15, 1987 fell on a Sunday, the letter of credit did not expire until Monday, November 16, 1987.

At approximately 1:00 p.m. on Friday, November 13, 1987, Esso presented its draft for $1,218,116.90, drawn on the Bank under the letter of credit, and documents fulfilling the terms and conditions of the letter of credit. Esso demanded immediate payment.

At 5:15 p.m. on Friday, November 13, 1987, the Bank informed Esso that it would not honor Esso's draft and demand for payment due to certain discrepancies. In a Memorandum for Credit Files dated November 16, 1987, Fred Hammack, commercial loan officer for the Bank, states that although Fulvio Santin, supervisor for foreign crude oil supply and scheduling for Esso, demanded a list of these discrepancies on November 13, 1987, the Bank did not inform Esso of them at that time. This memorandum reads as follows:

On 11/13/87 at approximately 5:15 p.m., I informed Mr. Santin that the Bank had uncovered discrepancies in the documents and would give to him by 9:00 am on 11/16/87 a written response stating what these discrepancies were.

Mr. Santin asked me if I could tell him what those discrepancies were. I told Mr. Santin and the other representatives that the discrepancies involved the supporting documents but that I could not give him specifics since it was the obligation of the International Banking Department who is responsible for the review process to give the written response. I further stated that this response per Bank policy must be signed by the Head of the International Banking Department. He would be back in his office by 7:30 on 11/16/87 and would be available to sign the letter in order to meet the 9:00 am delivery time. The Head of the International Banking Department was not in the office today.

In a deposition dated August 30, 1988, Hammack states that on behalf of the Bank he informed Esso's representatives on November 13, 1987 that they would have to wait for a written response by the Bank to discover the discrepancies in the documents they had submitted to the Bank on that date. The relevant portion of this deposition states:

Q What was their response?

A They wanted to know what the discrepancies were.

Q What was your response?

A I said, I did not know.

Q What did they say?

A They implored me again about the discrepancies, and if they could talk, I believe, to someone upstairs.

Q What was your response?

A My response was they had to wait for the written response by the bank.

Q Did that satisfy them?

A I think the conversation ended, I don't think it satisfied them.

The Bank sent Esso a list of the discrepancies in a letter dated Monday, November 16, 1987. This letter stated that Esso's draft under the letter of credit:

> remains unpaid due to the following discrepancies:
>
> —Invoice does not show beneficiary as stated in Letter of Credit.
>
> —Merchandise description on invoice not per Letter of Credit.
>
> —Applicant name and address on invoice not per Letter of Credit.
>
> —Documentary requirement number 2 as stated in the Letter of Credit not presented.

On November 16, 1987, Esso attempted to correct these discrepancies and again presented its draft for $1,218,116.90 drawn on the Bank under the letter of credit demanding immediate payment. The Bank again refused to honor Esso's draft on the grounds of uncorrected discrepancies.

On January 20, 1988, various creditors of Valley Oil filed a petition in the United States Bankruptcy Court for the District of Oregon, naming Valley Oil as the debtor.

On February 10, 1988, Esso filed this action against the Bank seeking money damages in the amount of $1,218,116.90 plus interest, $935,000 in punitive damages, and costs incurred in this action.

The second amended complaint states several claims for relief in contract, equity and tort. The contract and equity claims are as follows:

(1) that the Bank wrongfully dishonored its irrevocable standby letter of credit;

(2) that the Bank failed to specify the discrepancies which caused it to reject the draft and documents submitted by Esso;

(3) that the Bank failed to notify Esso of the discrepancies in a timely fashion;

(4) that the Bank wrongfully set off amounts owed to it by Valley Oil against funds from the special deposit made by Delta;

(5) that the Bank's conduct in this matter amounted to a waiver of its opportunity to claim that the alleged discrepancies were not in accordance with the letter of credit; and

(6) that the Bank's conduct estops it from asserting the alleged discrepancies as a defense in this action.

Esso also seeks punitive damages on the grounds that the Bank tortiously breached its obligation to deal in good faith by wrongfully, deliberately, or recklessly disregarding Esso's rights under the letter of credit.

\* \* \*

## DISCUSSION

I.   Dishonor of Letter of Credit—(Claims for Relief 1, 2, 3, 5, 6 and 7).

Esso alleges that the Bank wrongfully dishonored the Bank's irrevocable standby letter of credit when Esso properly presented Esso's draft drawn on the Bank under the letter of credit for payment. Esso contends that Article 16(e) of the UCP precludes a bank from dishonoring the letter of credit once the Bank failed to timely notify Esso of the specific discrepancies on November 13, 1987.

The Bank responds that it properly dishonored the letter of credit on both November 13, 1987 and on November 16, 1987 because the documents presented by Esso on those dates contained numerous discrepancies. In addition, the Bank contends that the letter of credit is subject to the Oregon Commercial Code, arguing that the Bank gave Esso sufficient and timely notice of the discrepancies under O.R.S. 75.1120, which grants banks three days to determine whether to dishonor letters of credit.

Both parties concede that they are bound by the UCP. Article 16 of the UCP provides, in pertinent part, that:

c.   The issuing bank shall have a reasonable time in which to examine the documents and to determine ... whether to take up or to refuse the documents.

d.   If the issuing bank decides to refuse the documents, it must give notice to that effect without delay by telecommunication or, if that is not possible, by other expeditious means, to the bank from which it received the documents (the remitting bank), or to the beneficiary, if it received the documents directly from him. such notice must state the discrepancies in respect of which the issuing bank refuses the documents and must also state whether it is holding the documents at the disposal of, or is returning them to the presentor (remitting bank or the beneficiary, as the case may be). The issuing bank shall then be entitled to claim from the remitting bank refund of any reimbursement which may have been made to that bank.

e.   If the issuing bank fails to act in accordance with the provisions of paragraphs (c) and (d) of this article and/or fails to hold the documents at the disposal of, or to return them to, the presentor, the issuing bank shall be precluded from claiming that the documents are not in accordance with the terms and conditions of the credit.

UCP Article 16(c)–(e) (emphasis added).

The issue is not whether the Bank had cause to reject the documents presented by Esso, but whether, once the Bank made its decision to reject those documents, it properly notified Esso of its decision by specifying the alleged discrepancies in accordance with Article 16(d).

In Bank of Cochin v. Manufacturers Hanover Trust Co., 808 F.2d 209 (2d Cir.1986), the Second Circuit held that an issuing bank was estopped under the UCP from asserting the confirming bank's noncompliance with the terms of a letter of credit where the issuing bank delayed twelve to thirteen days in notifying the confirming bank of specific defects in the presented documents and of its intent to return those documents. The court stated that " '[w]ithout delay' is defined neither in Article 8 nor in any case law dealing with international letters of credit. However, the phrase is akin to 'immediate (at once), instant, instantaneous, instantly, prompt.' W. Burton, Legal Thesaurus 1053 (1980). All of these synonyms connote a sense of urgent action within the shortest interval of time possible." Id. at 213.

In Datapoint Corp. v. M & I Bank, 665 F.Supp. 722 (W.D.Wis.1987), the United States District Court held that a bank was precluded from claiming that a draft varied from the terms of the letter of credit where it failed to notify the beneficiary of the dishonor by telecommunication or other expeditious means. The court found that "[u]nder the provisions of the Uniform Customs and Practice, incorporated by the Letter of Credit, once defendant decided to refuse the Original Draft, it was obligated to notify plaintiff to that effect without delay by telecommunication or, if that was impossible, by other expeditious means." Id. at 727.

In the present action, Esso presented its draft for $1,218,116.90, drawn on the Bank under the letter of credit, at 1:00 p.m. on November 13, 1987. The Bank notified Esso of its decision to dishonor the letter of credit by 5:15 p.m. that afternoon. Under Article 16(d) of the UCP, the Bank was required to state the discrepancies in respect of which it refused the documents at the time it notified Esso of its refusal to honor the letter of credit. Since the Bank's notice did not state these discrepancies at that time, under UCP Article 16(e), the Bank is now precluded from claiming that the documents were not in accordance with the terms and conditions of credit. Esso is, therefore, entitled to collect funds from the Bank under the terms of the letter of credit.

Esso's motion for partial summary judgment on its first and third claims for relief is granted. Since the court has granted Esso summary judgment under its claim of wrongful dishonor of the letter of credit, it need not address Esso's equitable claim for money had and received.

\* \* \*

NOTE

How would this case be decided under 5–108? See Comments 2 and 4 to 5–108. In Rhode Island Hospital Trust Nat. Bank v. Eastern General Contractors, Inc., 674 A.2d 1227 (R.I.1996), a UCP case, the beneficiary made presentation on Thursday, September 26, 1985. On Friday, September 27, the bank did not open for business owing to Hurricane Gloria. Monday, September 30 was the expiry date. On Tuesday, October 1, the bank notified the beneficiary of certain discrepancies and stated that it would hold the documents for beneficiary's disposal. The court concluded that the trial court erred in directing a verdict for the bank. Expert testimony was to the effect that the bank did not act within a reasonable time; if the date of receipt of the presentation to the issuing bank is close to the expiry date of the credit, common banking procedure is to act expeditiously, presumably so that any discrepancy can be cured before expiration of the credit.

PROBLEMS

**1.** Over the period of a year, Beneficiary presented three drafts for payment to Issuer. Each presentation contained the same discrepancy. The first two times Issuer paid the draft without objection after receiving permission of the Applicant to pay despite the nonconformity. The third time Applicant refused to consent to payment and Issuer dishonored the draft on the ground that the presentation was nonconforming. Has Issuer wrongfully dishonored? Comment 7 to 5–108. 3 White & Summers, Prac. ed. § 26–9(a).

**2.** Bank issued a letter of credit subject to the UCP 500 and with an expiration date of January 9. The credit undertook to pay Beneficiary $100,000 (U.S.) upon Beneficiary's presentation of three documents: a commercial invoice, a bill of lading and a certificate of inspection. The terms of the credit required the documents to cover "100 pounds of widgets," and invoice and certificate of inspection to state that the widgets were "quality 100%." On January 1, Beneficiary presented all three documents to Bank. The commercial invoice described the goods as "105 pounds of widgets of 95% quality." The bill of lading described the goods as "105 pounds of widgit . . . all received on board for shipment." The certificate of origin described them as "105 pounds of WGS," "WGS" being an abbreviation for widgets commonly used in the widget trade.

Bank notified Beneficiary on January 2 to the effect that it "finds discrepancies in the invoice presented by you going to the quantity and quality of widgets described." On January 5 it notified Beneficiary that it "rejects the bill of lading based on the failure of the description of the goods in the bill ('105 pounds of widgit') to conform to the terms of the credit." Bank gave notice to Beneficiary on January 6 that it "rejects the certificate of inspection because the description of goods ('WGS') fail to conform to the terms of the credit." Each notice was accompanied by Bank's statement that it was returning the documents to Beneficiary, and

Bank did so. This did Beneficiary no good because Beneficiary was unable make another presentation by January 9, the date on which the credit expired. Bank refused to pay Beneficiary $100,000.

(1) Did Beneficiary's documentary presentation comply with the terms of the credit? Consult ISBP paras. 28 and 69 reproduced below. (2) If not, is Bank entitled to dishonor Beneficiary's noncomplying documentary presentation? See UCP 500 arts. 14(d)(i), (ii), (e).

ICC, International Standard Banking Practices (ISBP) (2003)

28.   Misspellings or typing errors that do not affect the meaning of a word or the sentence in which it occurs, do not make a document discrepant.... However, a description as "model 123" instead of "model 321" would not be regarded as a typing error and would constitute a discrepancy.

69.   The quantity of the goods required in the credit may vary within a tolerance of $+/-5\%$. This does not apply if the a credit stipulates that the quantity must not be exceeded or reduced, or if a credit stipulates the quantity in terms of a stated number of packing units or individual items.

## 3.   ISSUER'S RIGHT TO REIMBURSEMENT AND OTHER REMEDIES

### a.   REIMBURSEMENT

Section 5–108(i) arms the issuer with a statutory right of reimbursement against the applicant. Credits usually also provide for reimbursement, as in the opening paragraph of the Letter of Credit Agreement at the end of this Chapter.

The credit risk that an issuer takes with respect to payment of a letter of credit depends on whether the transaction involves a commercial or a standby letter of credit. Commercial letters of credit are payment mechanisms and are meant to be paid in every case, usually upon presentation of the seller-beneficiary's bill of lading covering the goods sold to the buyer-applicant. When the issuer has paid, it receives possession of the bill of lading which the applicant must obtain from the issuer in order to receive the goods from the carrier that issued the bill of lading. 5–108(i)(2). The issuer can secure its claim for reimbursement by holding the bill of lading until the applicant either pays or arranges for credit.

A standby letter of credit functions as a guaranty and is usually meant to be paid only in case of the applicant's failure to perform the underlying contract. When the issuer pays a standby letter of credit, it receives no bill of lading or similar document that can be used to induce the applicant to pay. Functionally, a letter of credit is a conditional loan made to the applicant by the issuer, and issuing banks treat it as such. Since it is a loan that will usually not have to be funded unless the applicant is in financial difficulty, as when the applicant is in bankruptcy, the statutory reimbursement right under 5–108(i) is invariably supplemented with an express reimbursement agreement between the issuer and applicant containing the usual terms of commercial loans with respect to security, interest rates, setoff, and the like. See ¶ ¶ 4,5 and 9 of the Letter of Credit Agreement form reprinted at the end of this Chapter.

As we have said before, if obligees are able to obtain standby letters of credit from their obligors, they are in a position far superior to that of secured parties under Article 9. Upon default by their obligor, they can go to the issuing bank and obtain prompt payment of the obligation. They do not need to engage in the expensive and time-consuming exercise of collecting the debt by repossessing and foreclosing on collateral, with all the attendant problems that we raised in the preceding chapters of this book, problems that are exacerbated by the obligor's bankruptcy. If no rational obligee would take a security interest in preference to a standby letter of credit, does this mean the death of security interests? Not at all; it merely changes the identity of the secured party from the obligee to the bank issuing the letter of credit. Unless the applicant is a customer who could borrow money on unsecured credit, banks will usually not issue standby letters of credit without receiving a security interest in the applicant's property. Efficiencies flowing from this tripartite arrangement have contributed to the great popularity of standby letters of credit. The creditworthiness of the obligor is determined by the bank, a professional credit grantor, rather than by the obligee who may be a seller of goods, a centerfielder, or others who are not in the business of credit granting. In this respect, the efficiency of the standby letter of credit resembles that present in the consumer bank credit card transaction. Retail stores, hotels, restaurants and others who sell goods and services can rely on a credit card issued by a bank that will guarantee payment on transactions made pursuant to the card; they don't need to maintain credit departments making costly credit evaluations of their customers. Banks will make the determination of the consumer's creditworthiness in deciding whether to issue the credit card.

### b.   STANDARD OF COMPLIANCE

Under 5–108(i), an issuer is entitled to reimbursement from the applicant only if it "has honored a presentation as permitted or required by this article." Under 5–108(a) an issuer must dishonor a presentation that does not strictly comply with the terms of the letter of credit. Comment 1 to 5–108 says that "[t]he standard of strict compliance governs the issuer's obligation to the beneficiary and to the applicant." The view adopted by Article 5 that an issuing bank that pays on a presentation that does not strictly comply with the terms of the letter of credit cannot receive reimbursement from the applicant was rejected by some cases under the old law which applied a "bifurcated" standard of compliance. This approach applied a strict compliance standard for the issuer's liability to the beneficiary for wrongful dishonor but a substantial compliance standard for the issuer's liability to the applicant for wrongful honor. The bifurcation view was thought to be justified by an appreciation of the difficulty an issuing bank experiences in a case in which the applicant is demanding that the bank dishonor while the beneficiary is threatening suit if the bank does not pay.

In rejecting the bifurcated approach, Article 5 takes the realistic position that institutions issuing letters of credit, usually commercial banks, are sophisticated parties which are eminently capable of looking out for themselves. Section 5–108(a) recognizes that an issuing bank can safely pay on a noncomplying presentation if the applicant will waive the discrepancy and consent to the payment. But what if the bank is uncertain about whether there is a discrepancy in the presentation and the applicant will not waive the potential discrepancy? Section 5–103(c) allows the parties to contract around 5–108(a)'s standard of compliance as it applies to the issuer's right to reimbursement. Prudent issuers will safeguard themselves against liability for wrongful payment by including exculpatory clauses in the reimbursement agreement designed to allow them to obtain reimbursement, even when they honor a credit in which a discrepant presentation has been made. See ¶ 8 of the Letter of Credit Agreement form reprinted at the end of this Chapter. Provisions imposing a standard of only substantial compliance on issuing banks with respect to their duty to dishonor are clearly enforceable. Comment 2 to 5–103. However, under the last sentence of 5–103(c), terms "generally excusing liability or generally limiting remedies for failure to perform obligations" are unenforceable.

## c.   SUBROGATION, RESTITUTION AND BREACH OF WARRANTY

As we have seen, the prudent issuer of a standby letter of credit makes sure that if it has to pay the credit the applicant will be able to reimburse it. This is usually done by requiring that the applicant give security for its reimbursement obligation. However, if the security proves worthless and the applicant is insolvent, the issuer is unable to obtain reimbursement from the applicant. In these cases the issuer will explore alternative remedies. If the applicant has given the beneficiary security, the issuer may seek to be subrogated to the beneficiary's rights to the security. If the issuer can claim to have paid because of fraud or mistake, it may demand restitution from the beneficiary. Or the issuer may claim that the beneficiary has breached its presentation warranties to the issuer. In the materials below we will examine the availability of these remedies.

Whether an issuer, having paid the beneficiary of a letter of credit, is entitled to the equitable remedy of subrogation has been much litigated. For reasons discussed in *Ochoco Lumber Company* below, a majority of courts have denied issuers the right to subrogation. Section 5–117(a) recognizes subrogation for issuers: "An issuer that honors a beneficiary's presentation is subrogated to the rights of the beneficiary to the same extent as if the issuer were a secondary obligor of the underlying obligation owed to the beneficiary and of the applicant to the same extent as if the issuer were the secondary obligor of the underlying obligation owed to the applicant." The subsection does not itself give an issuer a right of subrogation. It instead gives the issuer whatever rights a secondary obligor would have in the same circumstances ("as if the issuer were a secondary obligor

..."). Thus, 5–117(a) removes a doctrinal barrier based on the issuer's "primary obligation" to granting issuers rights of subrogation. *Ochoco Lumber Company*, below, rehearses and adopts Judge Becker's dissenting opinion in Tudor Development Group, Inc. v. United States Fidelity & Guaranty Company, 968 F.2d 357 (3d Cir.1992). Professor White, the Reporter of Revised Article 5, states in 3 White & Summers, Prac. ed. § 26–15, at 212–14 that Judge Becker's dissenting opinion in *Tudor* is the correct analysis of the problem, and Comment 1 to 5–117 indorses the Becker position. *Ochoco Lumber Company* shares this understanding of 5–117(a).

## Ochoco Lumber Company v. Fibrex & Shipping Company, Inc.

Court of Appeals of Oregon, 2000.
994 P.2d 793.

■ KISTLER, J.

The trial court ruled that neither the applicant nor the issuer on a standby letter of credit can be subrogated to the beneficiary's claims. The court accordingly granted defendants' motion to dismiss plaintiff's equitable subrogation claims, denied plaintiff leave to replead, and entered judgment on those claims. We reverse and remand.

In 1993, defendant Fibrex & Shipping Co., Inc., entered into an agreement to purchase timber in Montana. To fund the purchase, Fibrex borrowed $3,900,000 from West One Idaho Bank.[1] West One imposed two conditions on the loan. First, it required that Fibrex's sole shareholder, Akira Saheki, and his wife, Saeko Saheki, personally guarantee the loan. Second, "[a]s security for repayment of [Fibrex's] note," West One required a standby letter of credit "in an amount no less than the amount of the principal balance of th[e] note."

Fibrex obtained the letter of credit by entering into an agreement with plaintiff Ochoco Lumber Company. Fibrex agreed to sell and Ochoco agreed to buy up to six and one-half million board feet of harvested ponderosa pine logs. As part of their agreement, Ochoco provided for an irrevocable standby letter of credit for $3,900,000, which First Interstate Bank issued for the benefit of West One. The letter of credit both served as security for Ochoco's performance under its agreement with Fibrex and also "was used by Fibrex to fulfill its obligations under [its loan from West One]."[2]

In 1994 and 1995, Fibrex failed to fulfill its obligations under its agreement with Ochoco. In May 1995, Ochoco and Fibrex renegotiated their agreement. In August 1995, Fibrex, Ochoco, and the persons who owned the timber entered into an amended timber purchase agreement. In

---

**1.** West One Idaho Bank has since been acquired by U.S. Bank.

**2.** Fibrex agreed to use the funds it received from Ochoco's log purchases to reduce the balance on its loan with West One and thus reduce Ochoco's exposure on the letter of credit.

September 1996, Fibrex's loan from West One came due. Fibrex failed to pay the loan, and West One drew over two million dollars on First Interstate's letter of credit. Ochoco reimbursed First Interstate Bank in full.[3] Ochoco then demanded repayment from Fibrex. After Fibrex refused to repay Ochoco, Ochoco notified West One that it was subrogated to West One's rights against both Fibrex and the Sahekis, the guarantors of Fibrex's loan.

When West One refused to acknowledge Ochoco's equitable subrogation rights, Ochoco brought an action alleging, among other things, four claims for relief that were based on equitable subrogation. Ochoco sought a declaration that it is subrogated to West One's rights, it sued Fibrex on the note that Fibrex had given West One, and it sued the Sahekis on their guarantee. Ochoco also sought injunctive relief against Fibrex and the Sahekis.[4] Defendants moved to dismiss Ochoco's claims for relief that were based on equitable subrogation. Relying on *Tudor Dev. Group, Inc. v. U.S. Fid. & Guar. Co.*, 968 F.2d 357 (3d Cir.1992), and *Shokai v. U.S. National Bank of Oregon*, 126 F.3d 1135 (9th Cir.1997), defendants argued that equitable subrogation is not available to the parties on a standby letter of credit. The trial court agreed. It dismissed Ochoco's subrogation claims without leave to replead and entered judgment on those claims pursuant to ORCP 67 B.

On appeal, defendants advance two arguments. They argue initially that equitable subrogation is available only to persons who are secondarily liable for a debt. They reason that the issuer's contractual obligation to pay on a standby letter of credit[5] [previous fn is in wrong place] means that the issuer is primarily, not secondarily, liable. They argue alternatively that, in any event, the particular facts of this transaction make subrogation inap-

---

**3.** The complaint does not allege specifically that Ochoco reimbursed First Interstate. Ochoco acknowledged this oversight at the Rule 21 hearing and stated that it would replead to include that allegation. The trial court, however, dismissed Ochoco's subrogation claims without leave to replead, thereby preventing Ochoco from alleging that it had reimbursed First Interstate pursuant to its obligations under the letter of credit. Fibrex neither objected to Ochoco's request to replead at the Rule 21 hearing nor disputes Ochoco's contention on appeal that it reimbursed First Interstate in full. We accordingly assume that Ochoco has paid First Interstate the amount it paid West One.

**4.** Ochoco alleged other claims for relief, but only its first, second, and third claims for relief and the first count of its thirteenth claim for relief are based on equitable subrogation and are at issue here.

**5.** A letter of credit "is an engagement by an issuer, usually a bank, made at the request of the [applicant] for a fee, to honor a beneficiary's drafts or other demands for payment upon satisfaction of the conditions set forth in the letter of credit." *Tudor Dev. Group, Inc.*, 968 F.2d at 360; *accord* Peter R. Jarvis, *Standby Letters of Credit—Issuers' Subrogation and Assignment Rights*, 9 UCC LJ 356, 356–60 (1977). There are two major types of letters of credit transactions. A commercial letter of credit is typically used when the seller is unfamiliar or uncertain about the buyer's credit history. *Id.* The beneficiary of a commercial letter of credit (usually the seller) may draw upon the letter by showing that it has performed and is entitled to the funds. *Id.* A standby letter of credit, on the other hand, typically requires the production of documents showing that the applicant has defaulted on its obligation to the beneficiary, which triggers the beneficiary's right to draw on the letter. *Id.*

propriate. Ochoco responds that a standby letter of credit is no different from a surety bond or a guarantee in that the issuer's obligation to pay on a standby letter of credit does not arise until there is a default. It follows, Ochoco reasons, that equitable subrogation should be equally available to the parties to a standby letter of credit; the transactions are in substance no different.

We begin with the statutes that govern letters of credit. When First Interstate issued the letter of credit in this case, the Oregon statutes did not address whether equitable subrogation was available on a standby letter of credit. Nothing should be inferred from that omission, however. ORS 75.1020(3) (1991) specifically recognized that "ORS 75.1010 to 75.1170 deal with some but not all the rules and concepts of letters of credit as such rules or concepts have developed * * * or may hereafter develop." It added: "The fact that ORS 75.1010 to 75.1170 state a rule does not by itself require, imply or negate application of the same or a converse rule to a situation not provided for * * * by ORS 75.1010 to 75.1170." ORS 75.1020(3) (1991). The statute thus explicitly left to judicial development those rules that were not codified in ORS chapter 75.

In 1997, the legislature authorized issuers of and applicants for letters of credit to seek equitable subrogation but made the new statute applicable to letters of credit issued on or after January 1, 1998.[6] Or. Laws 1997, ch. 150, §§ 20, 27 & 29. The Ninth Circuit has concluded that because Oregon's 1997 law applies prospectively, the Oregon legislature must have believed that prior law did not allow subrogation. *See Shokai*, 126 F.3d at 1136. Defendants find the Ninth Circuit's reasoning "instructive" and urge us to follow it. We decline to do so.

The 1997 Legislature amended many of the provisions in ORS chapter 75 governing letters of credit. *See* Or. Laws 1997, ch. 150, §§ 3–20. The fact that the legislature provided that all those amendments would apply prospectively hardly reflects a judgment on the existing state of the law with respect to each or any of them. *See* Or. Laws 1997, ch. 150, § 27. The inference the Ninth Circuit drew is, at best, a weak one and is at odds with the long-standing principle that one legislature's view on an earlier state of the law is entitled to little or no weight. *Cf. DeFazio v. WPPSS*, 296 Or. 550, 561, 679 P.2d 1316 (1984) ("[t]he views legislators have of existing law

---

**6.**  Oregon Laws 1997, chapter 150, section 20, provides:

"(1) An issuer that honors a beneficiary's presentation is subrogated to the rights of the beneficiary to the same extent as if the issuer were a secondary obligor of the underlying obligation owed to the beneficiary and of the applicant to the same extent as if the issuer were the secondary obligor of the underlying obligation owed to the applicant.

"(2) An applicant that reimburses an issuer is subrogated to the rights of the issuer against any beneficiary, presenter or nominated person to the same extent as if the applicant were the secondary obligor of the obligations owed to the issuer and has the rights of subrogation of the issuer to the rights of the beneficiary stated in subsection (1) of this section."

By its terms, this law applies only to letters of credit issued on or after January 1, 1998. Or. Laws 1997, ch. 150, §§ 27 & 29.

may shed light on a new enactment, but it is of no weight in interpreting a law enacted by their predecessors"). Even if, however, the inference that defendants urge were textually permissible, it is not required and the legislative history points in the opposite direction. The Oregon Bankers' Association, which sponsored the 1997 legislation, told the legislature that the courts had not agreed on the availability of equitable subrogation, giving rise to confusion in the law. Testimony, Senate Committee on Business, Law and Government, SB 246, January 22, 1997, Ex H (statement of Frank E. Brawner). Although the legislature sought to clarify the law for letters of credit issued after the effective date of the act, the text, context, and the legislative history of the 1997 act do not suggest that the legislature made any judgment about the parties' right to equitable subrogation for letters of credit issued before the act's effective date. We are accordingly left to resolve that issue under common law principles.

The court has explained that subrogation is " 'the substitution of another person in place of the creditor to whose rights he succeeds in relation to the debt, and gives to the substitute all of the rights, priorities, remedies, liens and securities of the party for whom he is substituted.' " *Maine Bonding v. Centennial Ins. Co.*, 298 Or. 514, 521, 693 P.2d 1296 (1985) (quoting *United States F. & G. Co. v. Bramwell*, 108 Or. 261, 277, 217 P. 332 (1923)). The purpose of subrogation is to prevent unjust enrichment. *See Barnes v. Eastern & Western Lbr. Co.*, 205 Or. 553, 596, 287 P.2d 929 (1955). Simply stated, subrogation is an equitable device used " 'to compel ultimate discharge of a debt by [the person] who in equity and good conscience ought to pay it * * *.' " *Maine Bonding*, 298 Or. at 521, 693 P.2d 1296 (quoting *United States F. & G. Co.*, 108 Or. at 277, 217 P. 332).

As a general rule, the courts have required that the party seeking subrogation must have paid a debt for which it was secondarily liable. *Wasco Co. v. New England E. Ins. Co.*, 88 Or. 465, 469–71, 172 P. 126 (1918); *accord Tudor Dev. Group, Inc.*, 968 F.2d at 361. The party must not have acted as a volunteer but must have paid to protect its own interests. *Id.* Finally, equitable subrogation "will not be enforced where it will work injustice to those having equal equities." *Id.* The Oregon courts have not specifically addressed how these requirements apply to standby letters of credit.[7] A handful of courts and commentators have done so, although their decisions have not been uniform. *See Tudor Dev. Group, Inc.*, 968 F.2d at 361–62 (collecting cases).

The majority and minority views are perhaps best illustrated by the two opinions in *Tudor Dev. Group, Inc.* The majority in *Tudor* focused on whether the issuer is primarily or secondarily liable for the debt. 968 F.2d at 362. It reasoned, as a majority of courts have, that the issuer is primarily liable because a letter of credit imposes an independent obligation on the

---

**7.** In *Marshall–Wells Co. v. Tenney*, 118 Or. 373, 244 P. 84 (1926), the court used the terms letter of credit and guarantee interchangeably, but its reasoning reveals that it was considering the parties' rights under a guarantee, not a letter of credit. *See* Jarvis, 9 UCC LJ at 375.

issuer to pay. *Id.* The majority reasoned that the issuer is "satisfying its own absolute and primary obligation to make payment rather than satisfying an obligation of its customer." *Id.* The majority recognized that the issuer's obligation on a standby letter of credit is secondary in the sense that it does not arise until the applicant has defaulted, but it still declined to view an issuer as comparable to a guarantor.

The dissent in *Tudor* responded that the majority's reasoning proved too much. A surety also has a contractual obligation to pay, but that fact neither means that the surety is primarily liable nor prevents it from seeking equitable subrogation. In the dissent's view, the fact that there is a contractual obligation to pay provides no basis for saying that the issuer of a standby letter of credit is not secondarily liable. Rather, like a surety or guarantor, the issuer of a standby letter of credit only has an obligation to pay if and when there is a default. In this case, for example, the note between West One and Fibrex required Fibrex to obtain a letter of credit as "security for repayment of [Fibrex's] note."

The relevant question, in the dissent's view, was whether allowing equitable subrogation would defeat the independence principle that distinguishes letters of credit from guarantees and suretyships. Guarantors generally may assert defenses available to the party whose obligation is guaranteed. *Tudor Dev. Group, Inc.*, 968 F.2d at 366. Under the independence principle, however, the issuer of a standby letter of credit may not assert those defenses. Rather, it must pay if the documents presented by the beneficiary satisfy the conditions set out in the letter of credit. *Id.*

In the dissent's view, once the issuer has honored the letter of credit, the purpose of the independence principle—ensuring prompt payment on the letter of credit according to its terms—has been satisfied. *Id.* at 368. The dissent reasoned that denying equitable subrogation after the issuer had paid the letter of credit would not advance the purposes of the one principle that distinguishes letters of credit from guarantees. *Id.* Rather, in the dissent's view, denying subrogation after payment amounts to "[i]nsistence on * * * pointless formalism." *Id.* Although the dissent's view has only gained minority support among the courts, it has been generally supported by the commentators. *See* James J. White & Robert S. Summers, *Uniform Commercial Code* § 26–15 (4th ed. 1995); Peter R. Jarvis, *Standby Letters of Credit, Issuers' Subrogation and Assignment Rights*, 10 UCC LJ 38 (1977); *cf.* Task Force on the Study of U.C.C. Article 5, *An Examination of U.C.C. Article 5 (Letters of Credit)* 21 (Sept. 29, 1989), *reprinted in* 45 Bus.L. 1527 (1990).

Faced with these two positions, we conclude that the minority view is more persuasive. It recognizes that First Interstate was a *de facto* surety for Fibrex's obligations and is thus consistent with the long-standing principle in Oregon law that equity looks to the substance of the transaction rather than its form. *General Electric Co. v. Wahle*, 207 Or. 302, 317, 296 P.2d 635 (1956); *Decker v. Berean Baptist Church*, 51 Or.App. 191, 199,

624 P.2d 1094 (1981).[8] It is also consistent with the general practice on standby letters of credit—that the issuer's obligation to pay on the letter of credit only arises if there is a default. *See* Jarvis, 9 UCC LJ at 368–71 (comparing standby letters of credit and guarantees). More importantly, it is consistent with our legislature's recognition that having paid the beneficiary, the issuer (and the applicant if it has reimbursed the issuer) should be able to step into the beneficiary's shoes and assert its rights. Accordingly, we hold that equitable subrogation is available to both the issuer and the applicant on a standby letter of credit. * * *

Reversed and remanded.

## NOTE

The most common case in which the subrogation issue is litigated concerns the applicability of Bankruptcy Code 509(a), which states: "Except as provided in subsection (b) or (c) of this section, an entity that is *liable with the debtor* on, or that has secured, a claim of a creditor against the debtor, and that pays such claim, is subrogated to the rights of such creditor to the extent of such payment" (emphasis added). In CCF, Inc. v. First National Bank & Trust, 69 F.3d 468 (10th Cir.1995), the court held that the independence principle under which an issuer is not "liable with the debtor" precluded subrogating an issuer to the beneficiary's right to setoff against funds of the applicant that the beneficiary had collected on behalf of the applicant. Accord Hamada v. Far East National Bank, 291 F.3d 645 (9th Cir.2002). Although 5–117 was not yet law in the jurisdiction in question, the court was aware of it and said: "Although the revised Article Five provides an issuer with the remedy of subrogation, the UCC does not determine the availability of subrogation in a bankruptcy proceeding. Rather, § 509 of the Bankruptcy Code governs an entity's eligibility for subrogation in a bankruptcy proceeding. Thus, the effect of the Rev. 5–117 on § 509 subrogation is presently undecided, and suitable for resolution by a future court." 69 F.3d at 476 n.7.

Courts remain uncertain about whether BC 509 provides the exclusive source of subrogation in bankruptcy or whether equitable subrogation instead continues to be available. The issue is one of bankruptcy law and is unaffected by nonbankruptcy law such as 5–117(a). In concluding that the issuer lacked subrogation rights in bankruptcy, the *Hamada* court analyzed the issuer's rights under both BC 509 and state law of equitable subrogation. In re AGF Direct Gas Sales & Servicing, Inc., 47 UCC Rep. Serv.2d

---

**8.** Defendants argue that the court's reasoning in *Newell v. Taylor*, 212 Or. 522, 532–33, 321 P.2d 294 (1958), supports a contrary position, but the court's reasoning in that case cannot be divorced from the statutory rights established by the workers' compensation laws. As the court explained, the Workers' Compensation Commission had a statutory obligation to pay the injured worker, regardless of whether the injury was due to a third party's negligence. *Id.* at 532, 321 P.2d 294. This case is far closer to the court's later. decision in *Jenks Hatchery v. Elliott*, 252 Or. 25, 30–31, 448 P.2d 370 (1968), where the court held, under common law principles, that an accommodation maker that had paid on a note could sue on it.

445 (D.N.H. 2002), offered the same analysis, adding in passing that it is not "apparent" that a ruling to the effect that BC 509 preempted state law of equitable subrogation would constitute legal error. Id. at 449. The court's analysis didn't rely on this observation.

## NOTE: RESTITUTION AND BREACH OF WARRANTY

Issuers who have honored a draft drawn under a letter of credit but have been unable to obtain reimbursement from the applicant may attempt to get their money back from the beneficiary under doctrines of restitution or breach of warranty. The applicable common law of restitution may allow one who has paid out under mistake or who has honored a forged or fraudulent presentation to recover the payment. Former Article 5 was silent on the subject. Section 5–108(i)(4) provides that an issuer who has honored a presentation is "except as otherwise provided in Sections 5–110 and 5–117, precluded from restitution of money paid or other value given by mistake to the extent the mistake concerns discrepancies in the documents or tender which are apparent on the face of the presentation * * *." Section 5–110 states: "(a) If its presentation is honored, the beneficiary warrants: (1) to the issuer, any other person to whom presentation is made, and the applicant that there is no fraud or forgery of the kind described in § 5–109(a); and (2) to the applicant that the drawing does not violate any agreement between the applicant and beneficiary or any other agreement intended by them to be augmented by the letter of credit."

Under 5–110, after its presentation has been honored, the beneficiary makes two warranties. One warranty, created by 5–110(a)(1), is to the applicant, issuer and persons who received the presentation. The beneficiary warrants that there is no forgery or material fraud. As is made clear below, forgery involves a document presented whereas material fraud need not. Material fraud may involve fraud in the nondocumentary aspects of the underlying transaction. A party protected by 5–110(a)(1)'s warranty might prefer to recover under it even when the party can recover on some other basis, such as in tort. This is because forgery or documentary fraud typically presents fewer problems of proof than other bases of recovery.

A second warranty, created by 5–110(a)(2), runs only to the applicant. The beneficiary warrants that the drawing did not violate either an agreement between the applicant and beneficiary or any other agreement underlying the credit. Section 5–110(a)(2)'s warranty is more complicated than 5–110(a)(2)'s warranty, and leaves some uncertainty. It applies to any agreement that is part of the transaction underlying the letter of credit. Thus, even if the applicant isn't a party to the underlying agreement, the beneficiary breaches its 5–110(a)(2) warranty to the applicant if its draw "violates" the agreement. For instance, the warranty applies when an applicant has a credit issued at the request of a party to underlying agreement other than beneficiary. Usually, of course, the applicant has no need for 5–110(a)(2)'s warranty when it is a party to the agreement with the beneficiary. It can rely on warranties created by the underlying agreement. See Comment 2 to 5–110.

An uncertainty remains with respect to the "violations" referred to in 5–110(a)(2). Does a draw following any breach of the underlying agreement constitute a "violation" or must the breach rise to the level of seriousness on par with forgery or material fraud? Comment 2 (last sentence) to 5–110 suggests the former: the beneficiary warrants that it has performed all acts under the underlying agreement necessary for it to demand honor. If so, a beneficiary's draw upon presentation of documents indicating "due performance" of the underlying contract breaches the beneficiary's 5–114(a)(2) warranty to the applicant when the beneficiary has breached the underlying contract. Professor White agrees; 3 White & Summers, Prac. Ed. at 164. The position has a lot going for it. After the issuer has honored a presentation and paid, none of the concerns about disturbing the credit's payment function apply. Finality of payment by the issuer isn't jeopardized by the beneficiary's warranty against "violations," because the warranty runs only to the applicant against the beneficiary. In any case, finality of payment isn't a first principle of letter of credit law. Its principle, if any, is "pay first, litigate later." Both of 5–110's warranties arise only if honor has occurred. Thus, there seems to be no good reason to restrict 5–110(a)(2)'s warranty to breaches ("violations") of the underlying agreement on the order of forgery or material fraud. For an argument reaching the opposite conclusion, see Richard F. Dole, Jr., Warranties by Beneficiaries of Letters of Credit Under Revised Article 5 of the UCC: The Truth and Nothing But the Truth, 39 Houston L. Rev. 375, 394–97 (2002).

The UCP contains no warranties. Professor White, the Reporter for Revised Article 5, notes that of the "hotly debated issues" in Article 5's drafting, 5–110(a)'s warranty provision was the only one that "went against" the UCP. See James J. White, The Influence of International Practice on the Revision of Article 5 of the UCC, 16 Nw. J. Int'l L. & Bus. 189, 207 (1995). This does not mean that the UCP conflicts with 5–110(a)'s warranties. It merely means that the ICC's representatives preferred that warranty provisions not apply to a credit also subject to the UCP. They were disappointed. Given 5–110(a), its warranties apply to credits subject to the UCP, unless Article 5 is otherwise inapplicable or the credit excludes 5–110(a)'s application.

## PROBLEMS

In the following Problems assume the following facts: Applicant, a movie producer with limited assets, engaged Beneficiary to appear in a new film, entitled "Legal Nights." In order to induce Beneficiary to agree to perform, Applicant caused Bank to issue a standby letter of credit to her payable on presentation to Bank of the letter of credit, a draft drawn on Bank payable 15 days after the date of presentation, and an affidavit that Beneficiary had satisfactorily completed the film and had not been paid by Applicant. Upon presentation by Beneficiary, Bank honored the draft but was unable to obtain reimbursement from Applicant. Bank proceeded against Beneficiary invoking the remedies of restitution and breach of warranty. What result in the following two cases under Article 5? The issues in these Problems are discussed in 3 White & Summers, Prac. ed. § 26–8 (warranties), § 26–9(e) (restitution).

**1.**   The documents presented by Beneficiary included a draft drawn on Bank "at sight," meaning at the time of presentation. Bank did not notice that the draft did not comply with the documents specified by the letter of credit and paid the draft according to its terms. Had the draft complied with the terms of the credit, Bank might not have paid it at all because during the 15–day period Applicant filed in bankruptcy and Bank's right of reimbursement became virtually worthless.

**2.**   The documents presented by Beneficiary complied with the requirements of the credit, including the affidavit of completion. After honoring the draft, Bank learned that Beneficiary had not completed the film and had breached her contract with Applicant.

## 4.   DAMAGES FOR WRONGFUL DISHONOR

As we have seen, it is fundamental that the letter of credit undertaking between an issuer and a beneficiary is independent of the underlying contract between the beneficiary and the applicant. 5–103(d). Does it follow that if the issuer wrongfully dishonors a draft presented under a letter of credit, the beneficiary can recover the full amount of the draw from the issuer, leaving the applicant to litigate with the beneficiary in a separate action over any amount the beneficiary has received in excess of its rights on the underlying contract? Yes. Under 5–111(a), the beneficiary or any other presenter can recover from the issuer the face amount of the draw under the credit if the issuer wrongfully dishonors the draw. The presenter also can recover incidental damages, but not consequential damages. Section 5–111(a) doesn't require the presenter to mitigate its damages in these circumstances. Because the issuer will have paid the presenter according to the credit's terms, as required by 5–111(a) (the dishonor was wrongful), the issuer's reimbursement agreement requires the applicant to reimburse it. The applicant in turn is left to recover from the beneficiary or other presenter in a separate action.

Section 5–111(b) governs the remedies of an applicant against the issuer. Under 5–111(b), the applicant can recover damages from the issuer who wrongfully dishonors a draft or other presentation under the credit. As under 5–111(a), incidental damages are recoverable but not consequential damages. Unlike 5–111(a)'s recovery, the applicant is required to mitigate its damages under 5–111(b). Article 5 does not provide a remedy in cases of improper honor by the issuer. Instead, recoverable damages are left to the courts. See Comment 2 to 5–111.

Section 5–111(e) requires courts to award reasonable attorney's fees and other litigation expenses to the prevailing party for any action in which a remedy is obtained under Article 5. The subsection overrules the "American rule" under which each party bears its own litigation costs. Section 5–111(e)'s mandatory award is not limited to remedies available under 5–111. The operative language of 5–111(e) is "under Article 5." Thus, a party prevailing on a breach of warranty claim against a beneficiary under 5–110, for instance, must be awarded reasonable attorney's fees and other litigation expenses. Would an injunction issued to prevent a materially fraudulent draw, discussed below, be a "remedy ... obtained under Article 5"? Unsurprisingly, both 5–111(e) and the exclusion of consequential damages have proven controversial. Connecticut and Louisiana have adopted nonuniform amendments to 5–111 allowing recovery of consequential damages, and several states have enacted nonuniform versions of 5–111(e). New Jersey and Texas, for instance, simply allow the award of attorney's fees and litigation expenses. New York's enactment of Article 5, significantly, omits 5–111(e) entirely. See 2B U.L.A. § 5–111 (2003). How would you apply 5–111 to the following Problems?

## PROBLEMS

**1.** Seller in New York agreed to sell goods to Buyer in Los Angeles by rail shipment with payment to be made pursuant to a commercial letter of credit. Buyer obtained issuance of a letter of credit by Issuer, Buyer's bank. The credit was payable to Seller on presentation to Issuer of a bill of lading, invoice, inspection and insurance certificates, sight draft drawn on Issuer, and the letter of credit. Issuer sent the letter of credit to Seller in New York (this is usually done through an "adviser" bank; 5–102(a)(1)). Seller shipped the goods and obtained an order bill of lading from the carrier. Seller then assembled the required documents and sent them through banking channels to Issuer for payment. Buyer decided that it had made a bad bargain and urged Issuer to dishonor the credit. Buyer threatened that if Issuer honored the letter of credit, Buyer would take its business elsewhere. Issuer reluctantly dishonored. When the goods arrived in Los Angeles, Seller ordered the carrier to store them in a warehouse. Several months later, Seller sold the goods for only a fraction of their invoice price. Seller sued Issuer for wrongful dishonor and sought the face amount of the draft drawn pursuant to the letter of credit in damages. Issuer contended that Seller should have mitigated damages, and that the goods should have been sold for a much higher price; moreover, at the very least, Seller must offset the amount actually recovered from the resale against its claim on the letter of credit.

(a) What result under 5–111(a)? See Comment 1 to 5–111. (b) What incentive does an Issuer have not to dishonor wrongfully? Comment 6 to 5–111. The explanation of the phrase "expenses of litigation" in that comment should be enough to chill the blood of any banker. (c) When might Seller have an incentive to seek recovery under law other than Article 5? See 5–111(e).

**2.** Applicant planned to develop a recreational community. County approval of Applicant's subdivision was conditional on Applicant's agreement to provide a standby letter of credit payable to the County as beneficiary to ensure that Applicant would complete roads and related improvements in accordance with subdivision design specifications. The required letter of credit was obtained from Issuer. Applicant never commenced construction of the roads or other improvements. Issuer wrongfully dishonored the letter of credit upon presentation. The County sued Issuer for the face amount of the credit plus interest from the date of the demand for payment. Issuer defended on the ground that the County would receive a windfall since it had not expended or committed itself to expend any funds to complete the improvements. The facts are based on Colorado National Bank v. Board of County Commissioners, 634 P.2d 32 (Colo.1981). What result under 5–111(a)? Dolan, Letters of Credit & 9.02[5][b][ii] and 3 White & Summers, Prac. ed. § 26–14(b), at 207 & 207 n.15., discuss the existing law.

**3.**  Sport manufactured running shoes for various retail chains. It made the shoes to the specifications of retailers who sold the shoes under their own brand names. Sport was thinly capitalized and the business was highly competitive. Sport had contracts for large deliveries to Retailer A on March 1, Retailer B on June 1, and Retailer C on September 1. Sport required A to obtain a standby letter of credit for the invoice price of the goods on which Sport could draw if A failed to pay for the goods within 15 days of delivery. When the shoes arrived, A contended that they were defective and ordered Issuer not to honor the letter of credit. Sport made timely presentation to Issuer of the required documents and Issuer wrongfully dishonored. Sport immediately implored Issuer to pay, explaining that without the proceeds of this large sale it would be unable to fulfill its obligations to B and C and would lose the profits that it anticipated making on these contracts. When Issuer continued to refuse payment, Sport sued Issuer for wrongful dishonor and claimed damages measured by the face amount of the credit plus the amount of lost profits on its contracts with B and C. What result under 5–111(a)? Do you believe that this is a desirable result? See Comment 4 to 5–111.

## E.  FORGERY AND FRAUD

The influential pre-Code case, Sztejn v. J. Henry Schroder Banking Corp., 31 N.Y.S.2d 631 (N.Y.Sup.Ct.1941), was a concession to the reality that the independence principle, however important, must have limits. The facts of *Sztejn* are summarized as follows: In brief, the contract of sale between the applicant and beneficiary was for the beneficiary to ship bristles to the applicant. Payment was to be made by a letter of credit calling for presentation of a draft along with a bill of lading describing the goods as bristles. The beneficiary's agent presented these documents to the issuer. However, the applicant had discovered that the beneficiary had actually shipped what the court described as rubbish before the issuer honored the draft. It sought to enjoin the issuer from honoring the draft on the ground of fraud. On the pleadings, assuming the applicant was correct about the fraud, the court held for the applicant. Although the documents were in compliance on their face, they were not genuine and therefore the issuer did not have to honor.

This case seemed to undermine the independence principle in that it allowed the court to look outside the documents presented to determine whether the issuer must honor. Would this mean that honor could be enjoined if the applicant could make a showing that the goods shipped by the beneficiary were defective in a degree amounting to a breach of warranty of quality? Or if the applicant could show that it had been induced to enter into the underlying sale transaction by misrepresentations by the beneficiary about the goods? Former 5–114 attempted to codify and delimit *Sztejn*. It allowed the applicant to obtain an injunction against honor even though the documents appear on their face to be in compliance so long as a required document "is forged or fraudulent or there is fraud in the transaction." The breadth of the "fraud in the transaction" test seemed to place the independence principle in peril.

Intraworld Industries, Inc. v. Girard Trust Bank, 336 A.2d 316 (Penn. 1975), is the leading case in interpreting former 5–114 in a manner that preserved the independence principle by limiting "fraud in the transaction" to cases in which the beneficiary had no bona fide claim to payment or that its claim had absolutely no basis in fact. It required that the beneficiary's alleged wrongdoings had so vitiated the transaction that the legitimate ends of the independence principle would no longer be served. Comment 1 to 5–109 incorporates the *Intraworld* standards as the intended meaning of "material fraud."

There are two conceptual problems inherent in the test: describing behavior that constitutes fraud, and identifying the transaction in which fraud occurs. In part to clarify the "fraud in the transaction" test, 5–109 to Revised Article 5 redrafts former 5–114. The following case discusses and applies the test in connection with a request for a preliminary injunction against honor. For an extensive discussion of fraud in the transaction, see Dolan, Letters of Credit ¶ 7.04.

## Levin v. Meagher

Court of Appeals, First District, California, 2004.
54 UCC Rep. 2d 224.

■ MARGULIES, J.

Plaintiffs Adam Levin and Credit.Com, Inc. obtained a preliminary injunction that prevents defendant Todd A. Meagher from drawing on a letter of credit. Defendant contends that the trial judge "misunderstood and misapplied" the statutory fraud standard governing the issuance of an injunction against drawing on a letter of credit, that plaintiffs failed to demonstrate irreparable harm, and that the preliminary injunction is overbroad. We affirm.

### BACKGROUND

Todd Meagher and Adam Levin are former business partners. Until early 2003, Meagher, Levin and Levin's wife owned 100 percent of the stock of Credit.Com, Inc. (Credit.Com). In 2002, however, Meagher and

Levin had a falling out, which they resolved by agreeing that Levin would purchase Meagher's interest in Credit.Com. The various agreements associated with the buyout were signed in March 2003. Levin paid the purchase price partially in cash and partially by way of a $331,000 promissory note to Meagher, secured by a letter of credit. The promissory note provided that upon certain events of default, Meagher could declare the entirety of its unpaid principal immediately due and payable and draw down the letter of credit.

At the time of the buyout, Credit.Com was obligated on a line of credit extended by Wells Fargo Bank on which Meagher was a guarantor. Although Meagher had long since "closed" the line of credit, meaning that it could no longer be drawn upon, an outstanding balance of over $70,000 remained. To assure Meagher of a safe release from his guarantee, section 7.2.1 of the buyout agreement required Credit.Com to "either pay off and terminate its line of credit with Wells Fargo Bank, or . . . . arrange for the release of [Meagher] as a guarantor thereof, as soon as practicable, and in any event not later than" April 21, 2003. Failure to satisfy this obligation within the applicable time period was included as an event of default under the promissory note. Accordingly, a breach of section 7.2.1 would permit Meagher to declare the note due and draw on the line of credit.

On the morning of April 17, 2003, four days before the deadline for paying off the line of credit, Levin visited a San Francisco branch of Wells Fargo. Working with Megan Taub–Smith, the Premier Banking Manager at the branch, Levin drew against his personal line of credit sufficient funds to pay off the Credit.Com line of credit. Ms. Taub–Smith transferred these funds into the Credit.Com checking account and then applied them against the line of credit, paying it off in full.

The next day, Friday, April 18, Meagher encountered Levin at the offices of Credit.Com, which Meagher continued to share. Meagher asked whether the line of credit had been paid off, and Levin said that it had. Apparently not trusting Levin's assurance, later that day Meagher went to a Wells Fargo branch in the City of Alameda and asked whether the loan balance had been paid off. An employee there reported that the bank's computer continued to show an open balance. The employee recommended that Meagher talk to Mike Tonelli, who worked at the bank's Business Direct division in Phoenix. The employee then called Tonelli and handed the telephone to Meagher. Meagher confirmed with Tonelli that the bank's computer continued to display an outstanding balance on the line of credit.

The disparity resulted from internal bank accounting procedures. Wells Fargo may take several days to "process" a loan payment and reflect the payment in its computer records, even though (as in this case) the bank is merely taking money from one of its own pockets and putting it in another. As a result, while Levin in fact paid off the loan on April 17, employees of the bank other than Taub–Smith would not have known of the payment because the bank did not immediately process that payment and "post" it to the computer system. In fact, the payment was not posted to the bank's computers until April 28.

Early in the afternoon of April 18, Meagher's attorney, George Hisert, sent an e-mail to Levin's attorney, J. Anthony Vittal, noting that Meagher had received mixed information regarding payment of the line of credit and asking whether the line of credit had been paid off. Vittal responded, "[Y]ou may rest assured that the release of Mr. Meagher from his guaranty obligations. . . . will be effective before the contractual deadline." Presented with this equivocal response, Hisert concluded in a responsive e-mail that afternoon that "the Wells Fargo business line on which [Meagher] is the guarantor has not been paid," although he acknowledged that Levin had stated the contrary. To resolve the confusion, Hisert asked for written confirmation of the payment. Although Vittal responded promptly, his e-mail merely noted that he would "endeavor to obtain" written proof of the payoff by April 21, leaving the then-current status of the line uncertain. Vittal did not commit to supplying such proof by the 21st, noting, "[I]f it takes a few days to generate the proof you request, I trust you will understand."

Meagher could have confirmed that the line of credit had been paid if he had called Taub–Smith, but because Vittal did not confirm that the payment had been made or explain in what manner, it appears that neither Meagher nor his attorney knew that it was Taub–Smith who had received payment. Moreover, Meagher and his counsel believed they had reason to doubt Levin's word as a result of Vittal's equivocal messages and the apparently contrary information from Tonelli of Wells Fargo.

The day after the deadline for payment passed, April 22, Meagher called Tonelli again and was again told that there was an outstanding balance on the line of credit, which Tonelli confirmed in a letter. During this conversation with Tonelli, Meagher did not mention that Levin claimed to have paid off the line of credit already. Tonelli later asserted that if he had known about "even the allegation of such a pay off," he would have referred Meagher to another banking division to find out the true current status of the line.

Meagher's counsel then delivered a letter from Meagher to Levin declaring Levin to be in default and the full amount under the promissory note immediately due, demanding payment, and providing wire transfer instructions for the payment. Levin's counsel, Vittal, became aware of the letter of default that afternoon. At the same time, he also discovered that he had received a facsimile of a letter from Taub–Smith confirming in writing that the line of credit had been paid off and inviting any questions to be directed to her. Vittal responded to Meagher's default notice with his own letter disputing the default, describing when and how Levin paid off the line of credit, and enclosing the letter from Taub–Smith. The facsimile receipt shows that Vittal's letter was received by Meagher's counsel's office at approximately 8:20 p.m. on April 22.

In order to draw on the letter of credit, its terms required Meagher to present a draft to Wachovia Bank accompanied by a dated certificate from Meagher made under penalty of perjury that (1) he was the payee on the letter of credit, (2) Levin had defaulted in his obligations under the promissory note, and (3) neither Meagher nor his company, Credit 411, Inc., was in material breach of any of the covenants under paragraph 6.1 of the stock purchase agreement, relating to Meagher's and Levin's obligations after the closing. Meagher signed such a certification, stating that Levin had defaulted on his contractual obligations and that Meagher was entitled to the full amount due under the promissory note. Meagher's counsel, Hisert, had instructed a North Carolina attorney to present this certification to the home office of Wachovia Bank, the issuer of the letter of credit, along with a demand that Meagher be paid over $330,000 on the letter of credit. The North Carolina attorney took the documents to the bank at approximately 10:00 a.m. Eastern Daylight Time on April 23, 2003. Although Hisert is vague about the time at which he authorized the delivery of these documents, it appears that after delivery of the notice of default he made no further inquiry of Vittal regarding written proof that Levin had paid off the line of credit or Levin's response to the notice of default, and he gave no warning to Levin or Vittal that the letter of credit was to be drawn on. It was not until "[l]ater on the morning of April 23" that Hisert learned that, the night before, Vittal had provided the written proof of payment that had been promised.

Despite receiving a copy of Taub–Smith's confirmation that the line of credit had been paid, neither Meagher nor his counsel called Taub–Smith for an explanation. Instead, they reported the discrepancy to Tonelli, who himself called Taub–Smith. Later on April 23, Tonelli told Meagher's counsel that Taub–Smith had confirmed that full payment had been made. Tonelli noted, however, that the payment had yet to be reflected in the bank's computer system and expressed his opinion that Meagher remained guarantor on the loan until the payment had posted. Based upon this information, on April 24, Meagher's counsel wrote a letter to Vittal claiming that Tonelli told them that "the loan was still outstanding," that "Mr. Meagher had not been released as guarantor," and that "no payment had been posted." The letter did not mention that Taub–Smith had confirmed to Tonelli that full payment had been made a week before, despite the fact that the payment had not "posted."

Although Tonelli confirmed Taub–Smith's report that the line of credit had been paid off by midday on April 23, Meagher continued, through his counsel, to assert that the bank's failure internally to post the payoff transaction by April 21 created a default. In addition to the April 24 letter noted above, Hisert took the same position in an e-mail of April 25, despite his hearing directly from Taub–Smith, who told him in a voicemail that the failure of the bank to post the transaction was due to "an internal accounting error." In light of Meagher's refusal to withdraw his request to draw on the letter of credit, on April 29, 2003, Levin filed a complaint and an ex parte application for a temporary restraining order (TRO) to prevent Meagher from drawing on the letter of credit. The TRO was granted the same day. Following further briefing and a hearing, the trial court entered a preliminary injunction enjoining Meagher "from making any draw request or 'presentation' to Wachovia Bank or taking possession of or control over any draw on the Letter of Credit without prior leave from this Court." Meagher appeals entry of the preliminary injunction.

## DISCUSSION

### A.   The Standard of Review

. . . . . .

### B.   Likelihood of Success on the Merits

The first half of the "interrelated" standard for grant of a preliminary injunction is a likelihood of success on the merits. (Hunt v. Superior Court, supra, 21 Cal.4th at p. 999.) Of the various express requirements for an injunction under California Uniform Commercial Code section 5109, subdivision (b), Meagher challenges only the trial judge's conclusion that Levin is likely to succeed in demonstrating that Meagher committed a "material fraud" on the issuer. * * *

Under the so-called "independence principle," the issuer's decision to honor a draft on a letter of credit must be based solely on compliance with the requirements of the presentation terms of the letter of credit itself, rather than on the parties' compliance (or lack thereof) with their obligations under the underlying contract. (Mitsui Manufacturers Bank v. Texas Commerce Bank–Fort Worth (1984) 159 Cal.App.3d 1051, 1955.) As summarized in Intraworld Industries, Inc. v. Girard Trust Bank (1975) 336 A.2d 316, "unless otherwise agreed, the issuer deals only in documents. If the documents presented conform to the requirements of the credit, the issuer may and must honor demands for payment, regardless of whether the goods conform to the underlying contract between beneficiary and customer. Absent its agreement to the contrary, the issuer is, under the general rule, not required or even permitted to go behind the documents to determine if the beneficiary has performed in conformance with the underlying contract." (Id. at p. 323.) Accordingly, the issuer of a letter of credit is required to honor a draft that "appears on its face strictly to comply with the terms and conditions of the letter of credit." (Cal.U.Com.Code, § 5108, subd. (a).)

There is one narrow exception to the independence principle. An issuer is not required to honor a draft if "a required document is forged or materially fraudulent, or honor of the presentation would facilitate a material fraud by the beneficiary on the issuer or applicant." (Cal.U.Com. Code, § 5109, subd. (a).) Where such fraud exists, a third party can obtain an injunction against the issuer's honor of the presentation, as Levin did here. (Cal.U.Com.Code, § 5109, subd. (b).)

This case demonstrates that the term "fraud" in section 5109 is ambiguous. It can be argued that the term incorporates the elements of the common law tort of "fraud," one of which requires the maker of a false statement to possess an active intent to deceive. On the other hand, it can also be argued that any time an issuer releases funds under a letter of credit in reliance on false statements, there has been a "material fraud. . . . on the issuer" because the funds were released under false pretenses. The latter is true regardless of whether the maker of the statements knew they were false and intended to deceive. Meagher argues that the standard governing his submission to Wachovia Bank should incorporate the subjective "intent" element of common law fraud. In support of this legal argument, Meagher cites TMTI v. Empresa Nacional de Comercializacion (9th Cir.1987) 829 F.2d 949, 956 (TMTI), which held that a finding of "active intentional fraud" or "evil intent" was required before an injunction could issue under a similar provision of the California Uniform Commercial Code that preceded section 5109.

The fraud exception of California Uniform Commercial Code section 5109, enacted in its current form in 1996, has yet to be construed by a California appellate court, but the official code comment to section 5109, citing to several decisions from other jurisdictions, provides guidance regarding the proper legal standard for fraud. It is these cases that must guide our decision in interpreting section 5109, and TMTI, supra, is not cited in the official code comment. What unifies the various standards formulated in the cases cited in the official code comment is their requirement that fraud be determined by an objective examination of the circumstances, rather than by reference to the subjective beliefs of the beneficiary. The leading case in the area, recognized as such in the official code comment, is Intraworld Industries, Inc. v. Girard Trust Bank, supra, 336 A.2d 316, which construes the predecessor to section 5109. Intraworld Industries held that an injunction would not issue to prevent a draw on a letter of credit unless the beneficiary's presentation "had absolutely no basis in fact" or there was "no bona fide claim to payment under the [underlying contract]." (Id. at pp. 325, 327.) This standard requires the court to make an evaluation of the beneficiary's entitlement to payment under the letter of credit, rather than to inquire into the beneficiary's state of mind. No injunction will issue if the circumstances demonstrate that the beneficiary has a "colorable" (or stronger) claim of entitlement to draw. (Itek Corp. v. First Nat. Bank of Boston (1st Cir.1984) 730 F.2d 19, 25.) * * * The most recent decision on this issue, 3Com Corp. v. Banco do Brasil, S.A. (2d Cir.1999) 171 F.3d 739, similarly adopts an objective standard, precluding an injunction unless the beneficiary's claim to payment is "clearly untenable." (Id. at p. 747.)[3]

The issue before us is therefore whether there is substantial evidence in the record to support the conclusion that Levin is likely to demonstrate that Meagher has no colorable claim of default under the promissory note. (14859 Moorpark Homeowner's Assn. v. VRT Corp., supra, 63 Cal.App.4th at p. 1402.) That standard is satisfied on this record. Levin's obligation under the parties' agreement was to "either pay off and terminate [the line

---

**3.** The adoption of an objective standard is consistent with the contractual nature of letters of credit. Under such contracts, a beneficiary has the right to draw on the letter of credit only if certain conditions are met. If there is "no bona fide claim" that those conditions have been met—in other words, if it is clear that the beneficiary has no right to draw on the letter of credit—the beneficiary should not be permitted to draw on the line of credit merely because the beneficiary has formed a good faith but mistaken belief that conditions permitting a draw do exist.

of credit] or.... arrange for the release of [Meagher] as a guarantor.'' (Italics added.) Because the line of credit had already been terminated by Meagher months before, Levin could satisfy this obligation merely by paying off the line of credit by April 21, regardless of whether Meagher remained a guarantor. The evidence that Levin did so is undisputed. Accordingly, Levin was never in default under the promissory note.

Tonelli's repeated mistaken statements that a balance remained on the line of credit, based on the fact that the bank's accounting system did not accurately reflect the payment that had been made, are simply irrelevant. Under the express terms of the promissory note, Levin's obligation was to pay off the line of credit by April 21, not to cause the bank's accounting system to reflect that payment—a process over which Levin had no control. Tonelli's apparent insistence that Meagher remained liable on the note is similarly irrelevant to the issue of default, since Levin's obligation was stated in the alternative: either to pay off the line or secure a release of liability. When Levin paid off the note, he satisfied his contractual obligation, regardless of whether Meagher continued as a guarantor. Finally, the equivocal messages of Levin's attorney, Vittal, and his failure to obtain written confirmation of the payoff prior to April 22, while they contributed to Meagher's suspicion that a default had occurred, were similarly irrelevant. Levin's obligation was merely to pay off the line of credit, not to inform Meagher or provide written proof that payoff had occurred. Because there is no truth to Meagher's statement that Levin had defaulted in his obligations under the promissory note, Levin is virtually certain to demonstrate that Meagher's claim to payment under the letter of credit was not even "colorable." The trial court's conclusion on this issue was therefore fully supported by the evidence and the law.

### C. The Balance of Interim Harms

The second element of the "two interrelated factors" governing the issuance of a preliminary injunction is "the relative interim harm to the parties from the issuance or nonissuance of the injunction." (Hunt v. Superior Court, supra, 21 Cal.4th at p. 999.) "An evaluation of the relative harm to the parties upon the granting or denial of a preliminary injunction requires consideration of: '(1) the inadequacy of any other remedy; (2) the degree of irreparable injury the denial of the injunction will cause; (3) the necessity to preserve the status quo; [and] (4) the degree of adverse effect on the public interest or interests of third parties the granting of the injunction will cause.' '' (Vo v. City of Garden Grove (2004) 115 Cal.App.4th 425, 435, quoting Cohen v. Board of Supervisors (1985) 40 Cal.3d 277, 286, footnote 5; 14859 Moorpark Homeowner's Assn. v. VRT Corp., supra, 63 Cal.App.4th at p. 1402.)

Of these various factors, Meagher challenges only Levin's showing of irreparable injury. "Irreparable injury" is harm that cannot be fully compensated by money damages. (Tahoe Keys Property Owners' Assn. v. State Water Resources Control Bd. (1994) 23 Cal.App.4th 1459, 1471.) Although a showing of irreparable injury is "ordinarily" a requirement for preliminary injunctive relief (Intel Corp. v. Hamidi (2003) 30 Cal.4th 1342, 1352), irreparable injury is only one element of the calculus required of the trial court in its balance of the hardships. Moreover, "[t]he more likely it is that plaintiffs will ultimately prevail, the less severe must be the harm that they allege will occur if the injunction does not issue. This is especially true when the requested injunction maintains, rather than alters, the status quo. [Citation.]" Thus, ". . . . if the party seeking the injunction can make a sufficiently strong showing of likelihood of success on the merits, the trial court has discretion to issue the injunction notwithstanding that party's inability to show that the balance of harms tips in his favor. [Citation.]" (14859 Moorpark Homeowner's Assn. v. VRT Corp., supra, 63 Cal.App.4th at p. 1407.) It is important to remember that "[t]he ultimate goal of any test to be used in deciding whether a preliminary injunction should issue is to minimize the harm which an erroneous interim decision may cause. [Citation.]" (White v. Davis (2003) 30 Cal.4th 528, 554, quoting IT Corp. v. County of Imperial (1983) 35 Cal.3d 63, 73.)

Measured by the proper objective standard, Levin's likelihood of success is very great, lowering the degree of harm necessary to sustain the balance of hardships in his favor. In addition, the injunction as entered maintains the status quo, similarly lowering the standard for harm. Particularly in light of these two mitigating factors, Levin's demonstration of irreparable injury was adequate. It is true that some of the potential harm cited by Levin appears compensable in damages, such as the acceleration of his liability under the note and Meagher's possible violation of a noncompetition clause, but some is not. The potential loss of investment gains in the securities that would be liquidated to fund the payout and the harm to the business reputation and interests of Levin and his company as a result of a draw on the letter of credit, while plausible consequences of a wrongful draft, are sufficiently difficult to quantify that they would be difficult, if not legally impossible, to compensate in damages. Both of these types of damage have been held to constitute irreparable harm. (See, e.g., Heckmann v. Ahmanson (1985) 168 Cal.App.3d 119, 136; Hubbard Business Plaza v. Lincoln Liberty Life Ins. (D.Nev.1986) 649 F.Supp. 1310, 1317, affd. (9th Cir.1988) 844 F.2d 792 [damage to business reputation and interests from allegedly fraudulent draw of letter of credit constitutes irreparable injury supporting preliminary injunction]; but cf. Foxboro Co. v. Arabian American Oil Co. (1st Cir.1986) 805 F.2d 34, 37 [rejecting damage to business reputation as a basis for enjoining allegedly fraudulent draw on a letter of credit].) Although Meagher objected to evidence of certain of these possible harms as speculative, it is the degree and impact of these events that is speculative, not the fact that they pose a realistic risk. Weighed against these possible harms is the relative lack of harm to Meagher from grant of the preliminary injunction. In spite of the injunction, the letter of credit remains in place to secure Meagher's recovery under the promissory note. All he has lost through entry of the preliminary injunction is the acceleration of that debt, which remains payable according to its terms. Accordingly, the trial court did not abuse its discretion in finding that Levin provided sufficient evidence of irreparable injury, viewed in the context of the other factors relevant to the balance of harms.

\* \* \*

NOTES

**1.**   As *Levin* shows, applicants seeking to enjoin honor by issuers have more than the tough *Intraworld* standards to contend with. The applicant must show that it is more likely than not to succeed on the merits of the fraud or forgery issue (5–109(b)(4)), and it must also comply with the law of the jurisdiction on granting injunctions (5–109(b)(3)). This normally requires a showing of irreparable harm. An equitable suit for an injunction is not appropriate if there is an adequate remedy at law. Since the remedy would usually be an action by the applicant against the beneficiary for a money judgment, an injunction would usually be inappropriate if the beneficiary were solvent and subject to service of process. See Hendricks v. Bank of America, 408 F.3d 1127 (9th Cir.2005) (injunction granted where beneficiary is insolvent). *Levin* has a sophisticated analysis of irreparable injury that balances the applicant's likelihood of success in proving fraud with the degree of harm that must be shown. The damage to the applicant's business reputation in having to liquidate securities in order to pay the draft may be difficult if not impossible to quantify.

**2.**   Professor White concedes that the Drafting Committee was unable to agree on a definition of fraud. 3 White & Summers, Prac. ed. § 26–10, at 185. Section 5–109(a) adopts the standard of "material fraud." Comment 1 states: "Material fraud by the beneficiary occurs only when the beneficiary has no colorable right to expect honor and where there is no basis in fact to support such a right to honor." Does the addition of the adjective "material" make the inquiry as to fraud any more manageable? Without a working notion of fraud, 5–109(a)'s requirement that the fraud be material is unhelpful. The U.N. Convention on Independent Guarantees tries, without using the term, to make the fraud inquiry more manageable. It does not obligate an issuer to pay when it is "manifest and clear" that payment is not due on the basis asserted in the demand or documents presented. See U.N. Convention art. 19(1).

The *Sztejn* court distinguished between what it called "active fraud" and a "mere" breach of warranty without precisely characterizing the distinction. See *Sztejn*, 31 N.Y.S.2d at 634–635. To see the difficulty, consider a sales contract calling for Seller to deliver new widgets and a letter of credit requiring documents describing the goods delivered as "new widgets." Is there fraud in Seller's performance of the sales contract in the following four circumstances? (1) Seller intentionally delivers an automobile, not new widgets. (2) Seller intentionally delivers new widgets with very minor scratches. (3) The same as (2) except the market price for widgets has increased so that scratched widgets sell for more than new widgets were previously sold. (4) Seller intentionally delivers seriously malfunctioning new widgets. Notice that Seller has breached an express warranty in all four circumstances. Circumstance (4) arguably is an easy case: deliberately delivering seriously defective goods is egregious behavior characteristic of fraud. The extent of breach differs in the other three circumstances, and a standard is needed to find fraud nonarbitrarily in one or more of them. Article 5 apparently decided not to provide one.

Section 5–109(a) also abandons the "fraud in the transaction" formulation that had led scholars and courts to differ on whether the transaction meant was only the credit transaction or whether it extended to the underlying transaction as well. A critique of the differing positions on this issue appears in 3 White & Summers, Prac. ed. § 26–10, at 179–80. With the addition of "or honor of the presentation would facilitate a material fraud by the beneficiary on the issuer or applicant," 5–109(a) expressly applies to fraud in the underlying transaction. Prevailing authority finds that Article 5's fraud exception continues to apply to credits governed by the UCP. See Mid–America Tire, Inc. v. PTZ Trading Ltd., 768 N.E.2d 619 (Ohio 2002).

**3.**  Section 5–109(a)'s fraud provision is not limited to forgery or fraud by the beneficiary. By its terms, 5–109(a) applies when "a required document is forged or materially fraudulent." Thus, if 5–109(b)'s conditions for injunctive relief are satisfied, an applicant can enjoin an issuer from honoring a draw by the beneficiary even if the beneficiary has not perpetrated the forgery or fraud.

In some cases applicants have attempted to forestall payment under a letter of credit by seeking to enjoin the beneficiary from making presentation to the issuer. An occasional opinion has applied a lesser standard for granting an injunction in such a case than in the usual case of an injunction against the issuer. Dolan, Letters of Credit ¶ 7.04[4][f]. Section 5–109(b) makes clear that the same standards must apply to limit injunctions in both cases by the addition of the language: "or grant similar relief against the issuer or other persons." Comment 5 to 5–109.

**4.**  Article 5 distinguishes between two classes of presenters: presenters whose conforming documentary presentations the issuer must honor even if there is fraud in the transaction and presenters whose conforming presentations the issuer in good faith is permitted to honor or dishonor when there is fraud. See 5–109(a)(1), (b). The former class of presenters are protected against dishonor: fraud does not allow the issuer to dishonor their conforming presentations. Under 5–109(b)(4), the issuer also cannot be enjoined from honoring the draw. Protected presenters are all transferees of documents under the letter of credit. See 5–109(a)(1)(i)–(iv). (Recognizing developments in letter of credit practice, 5–109(a)(1)(iv) protects an assignee under a deferred obligation credit, a relatively recent type of credit first issued in Southeast Asia.) For instance, a negotiating bank, holder of a draft, or good faith purchaser of documents can be protected purchasers. To be protected, the presenter must take the documents or draft in good faith and without notice of the fraud. See 5–109(a)(1). All other presenters are not protected, and the issuer therefore in good faith can dishonor conforming presentations by them. Because a beneficiary under the credit does not purchase the draft or documents, it is a not transferee and therefore not a protected presenter.

Section 5–109(a)(2) deals with the rights of the issuer against unprotected presenters. It allows the issuer to honor ("may honor") presentations by them, even when the presentation involves forgery or material fraud, as long as the issuer does so in good faith. Is an issuer acting in good faith if it honors after the applicant has given it notice of the fraud or forgery? A common tactic used by applicants is to send a barrage of evidence to the issuer in advance of honor documenting the alleged fraud. The purpose is to present a risk to the issuer that a judge or jury ex post will find the issuer to have honored the draw in bad faith. Prudent practice sometimes leads issuers to resort to interpleader in these and other circumstances. See Dolan, Letters of Credit 7.04[4][g]. White & Summers, Prac. ed. § 26–10 at, 183 disapproves of the practice.

Notice how 5–109 allocates the risk of the beneficiary's fraud. In the case of a protected presenter, the applicant bears this risk. This is because the issuer honoring the draw is entitled to be reimbursed by the applicant either by contract or by statute, or both. 5–108(i)(1). The applicant therefore must recover from the beneficiary. Because the issuer can dishonor an unprotected presenter's conforming presentation, the presenter bears the risk of the beneficiary's fraud when dishonor occurs. It must recover from the beneficiary (or its transferor, who ultimately must recover from the beneficiary). Thus, the unprotected presenter bears the risk of the beneficiary's fraud. Article 5's implicit judgment is that protected presenters are in an inferior position to the applicant or issuer to detect the beneficiary's fraud. Allocating fraud risk to either the applicant or unprotected presenters but never to protected presenters is thought to be the cost-minimizing solution. Is the judgment sound? In support, it is usually observed that the applicant has dealt with the beneficiary whereas a presenter may have purchased a draft or documents from a remote transferor and never have dealt directly with the applicant. See United Bank Ltd. v. Cambridge Sporting Goods, 360 N.E.2d 943, 949 n. 6 (N.Y.1976). The applicant's costs in taking appropriate precautions therefore are thought generally to be lower than those facing the ultimate transferee's precaution costs. The observation has no force when the presenter purchases directly from the beneficiary. Consider also that often issuers or confirmers are local banks who know the beneficiary or can easily acquire information about it. Article 5's allocation of fraud risk is justifiable only if most documentary drafts are discounted in markets to strangers to the underlying contract. Neither the Comments to 5–109 nor its drafting history discuss this assumed empirical generalization.

**5.** "Good faith" is defined in 5–102(a)(7) as "honesty in fact." This is a subjective standard. Section 1–201(20) contains the operative standard of good faith in the Articles of the UCC: " 'Good faith,' except as otherwise provided in Article 5, means honesty in fact and the observance of commercially reasonable standards." The generally applicable definition includes both subjective and objective elements. Why is the "commercially reasonable standards'' language not included in the Article 5 definition of good faith? See Comment 3 to 5–102. Professor White reports that in Article 5's drafting representatives of a banking industry trade group argued that "Europeans and other nonAmericans were frightened by the threat of a runaway good faith doctrine, particularly by American courts' applying good faith in unforeseen cases.'' James J. White, The Influence of International Practice on the Revision of Article 5 of the UCC, 16 Nw. J. Int'l L. & Bus. 189, 205 (1995).

Comment 3 finds 5–102(a)(7)'s subjective standard of good faith appropriate because it "creates greater certainty'' in the issuer's obligations. The finding goes against the usual assessment of the effects of subjective standards. Standards such as "honesty in fact'' make potentially relevant large bodies of evidence, encourage prelitigation coaching of witnesses, and potentially extend the course of judicial proceedings going to the issue of good faith. Objective standards of good faith, by contrast, typically involve more limited evidence, less prelitigation jockeying, and more truncated proceedings. The usual assessment is that subjective standards produce indeterminacy and high costs in the application of otherwise clear rules. See, e.g., Richard A. Epstein, Simple Rules for a Complex World (1995); Robert D. Cooter & Edward L. Rubin, A Theory of Loss Allocation for Consumer Payments, 66 Tex. L. Rev. 63 (1987). Comment 3's different assessment depends on a confidence that the requisite showing of "honesty in fact'' is so easy (and a showing of "dishonesty in fact'' so hard) as to discourage investment in litigation of the issue.

### PROBLEM

At Buyer's request Bank One issued a letter of credit in Beneficiary's favor. At Beneficiary's–Seller's insistence, Buyer also asked Bank One to have a bank known to Beneficiary, Bank Two, confirm the credit, and Bank One did so. Bank Two accordingly notified Beneficiary of its confirmation. Later, Buyer learns that Beneficiary has intentionally breached the underlying sales contract by shipping nothing but will present documents to Bank Two for payment under Bank Two's credit. The documents will evidence shipment in accordance with the sales contract, as required under the credit. (a) At Buyer's urging, can Bank One obtain an injunction to prevent Bank Two from honoring Beneficiary's presentation? See 5–107(a), 5–109(b). (b) Can Buyer obtain an injunction against Bank Two in these circumstances? See 5–109(b); 5–107(a); Comment 1 to 5–107 (third paragraph); International Trade Relationship & Export v. Citibank, N.A., 41 UCC Rep. Serv.2d 626 (S.D.N.Y. 2000).

## F.   Transfer, Assignment and Security Interests

### 1.   Transfer and Assignment

There are two ways to transfer rights in a letter of credit: by "transferring'' the credit and by assigning the proceeds of the credit. The two notions are different. Section 5–112(a) defines "transfer" to mean the transfer of the beneficiary's right to draw on the letter of credit. Transferring the credit changes the party who must present documents to the issuer for honor. See also UCP 500 art. 48(a). Section 5–114 defines "proceeds of a letter of credit" to mean cash, checks or other items of value paid by the issuer upon honor of the letter of credit. Thus, assignment of the proceeds merely changes the party entitled to receive them. Assignment doesn't change the party who must present the documents for honor.

Letter of credit law treats transfer of the credit very differently from assignment of the credit's proceeds. Under 5–112(a) transfer conveys to a third party the beneficiary's right to draw on the credit by signing and presenting its own draft and other documents. See UCP 500 art. 48(i). Further, in the words of Comment 2 to 5–112, "[i]t contemplates not merely payment to but also performance by the transferee." That is, the beneficiary's duties are delegated to the transferee, and it may submit documents showing that it rather than the beneficiary performed the underlying contract. The applicant loses control over the identity of the person who will perform. In short, it is analogous to a novation. Comment 2 to 5–112.

Transfer of the right to draw is a radical change in the original deal in which an applicant obtained an issuer's undertaking to pay a beneficiary, who is usually a party to whom the applicant is or will be indebted for performance. In the commercial letter of credit setting, the applicant is usually a buyer and the beneficiary a seller. Since after the transfer, the issuer's undertaking is to pay another person who may perform the beneficiary's contract, how are the applicant's rights protected in transfer cases? A letter of credit can be transferred only if the credit provides that it is transferable. 5–112(a); see also UCP 500 art. 48(b). Section 5–112(a) sets the default rule against transfer to reflect the preferences of most applicants. If the applicant doesn't want to give the beneficiary the right to transfer, it must be sure that the credit it procures from the issuer does not permit transfer. In this case the issuing bank must dishonor any presentation of invoices of third persons; the applicant bargained for performance by its beneficiary and only its invoices will do. But if the credit is transferable on its face, Comment 2 to 5–112 states: "The issuance of a transferable letter of credit with the concurrence of the applicant is ipso facto an agreement by the issuer and applicant to permit a beneficiary to transfer its drawing right and permit a nominated person to recognize and carry out that transfer without further notice to them." Issuing banks may counter this by a requirement in the letter of credit that the beneficiary obtain the bank's permission before transfer so that the bank can anticipate who will make the presentation. 5–112(b)(2).

Transferable credits often are used by intermediate sellers to finance sales to their buyers. In the simplest form of such transactions the intermediate seller has its buyer have issued a transferable credit in the amount of the contract price naming the seller as the beneficiary. Typically the credit requires the seller to present its invoice and draft. The seller in turn asks the issuer to transfer part of the credit to the supplier of the goods it is selling to its buyer. This is called a "partial transfer" of the credit because the issuer is being asked to allow the transferee to draw less than the full amount payable under the credit. The issuer notifies the supplier of the terms of the transfer, agreeing to pay the amount of the supplier's invoice and draft upon the supplier's presentation of conforming documents. If the documents comply with the notice of transfer, the issuer pays the supplier the face amount of the supplier's draft. It also pays over to the intermediate seller the difference between the amount it paid to the supplier and the amount of the credit—the seller's profit from the sale to its buyer. The issuer substitutes the intermediate seller's invoice, draft and other documents it has received from the seller for the supplier's documents. This is done in order to avoid disclosing to the buyer the supplier's identity and its lower invoice price. See UCP 500 art. 48(i). The issuer then delivers the substituted documents to the buyer. Transferable credits usually involve more parties such as advisers of the credit, who may themselves undertake to allow transfer.

The notion of assignment is straightforward. It simply means assignment by the beneficiary of the proceeds that it is entitled to receive upon honor of the credit by the issuer. Proceeds are always assignable. Assignment of proceeds does not include the beneficiary's drawing rights. 5–114(a). The right to draw on the credit remains in the beneficiary, and the assignee's rights are contingent upon whether the beneficiary's presentation for honor complies with the terms and conditions of the credit. See Comment 2 to 5–112 and 5–114(b). Further, the issuer and the beneficiary can amend the credit without the assignee's consent. The beneficiary may assign its rights to part or all of the proceeds, and it may do so after the credit is established but before presentation. Presumably the beneficiary may also assign the proceeds even after presentation if the issuer wrongfully dishonors. In re XYZ Options, Inc., 154 F.3d 1276 (11th Cir.1998), so held, interpreting former Article 5. Comment 1 to 5–114 appears to support this sensible holding by its statement that assignments of proceeds are valid if made after the credit is established "but before the proceeds are realized." Section 5–114(a)'s default rule allowing assignment presumably reflects the preferences of most beneficiaries under credits.

Section 5–114(c) provides that an issuing bank can ignore an assignment of proceeds "until it consents to the assignment." Professor White, Reporter for the 1995 Revision to Article 5, describes this as a "significant concession" to issuing banks. 3 White & Summers, Prac. ed. § 26–12, at 200. Comment 3 to 5–114 states that the requirement of the issuer's consent conforms to "recognized national and international letter of credit practices." Common practice is for the beneficiary to sign a form giving the issuer notice of the assignment and instructing the issuer to pay the assignee directly upon presentation. Noting that it is always advisable for assignees to obtain the consent of the issuer, the Comment says: "When notice of an assignment has been received, issuers normally have required signatures on a consent form. This practice is reflected in the revision. By unconditionally consenting to such an assignment, the issuer or nominated person becomes bound * * * to pay the assignee the assigned letter of credit proceeds that the issuer or nominated person would otherwise pay to the beneficiary or another assignee."

Thus does banking practice become law. Some amelioration is found in 5–114(d), which provides that though an issuer is not obliged to consent, "consent may not be unreasonably withheld if the assignee possesses and exhibits the letter of credit and presentation of the letter of credit is a condition to honor." The assignee's exhibition to the issuer of a letter of credit presumably gives the issuer sufficient evidence of the assignment to make unreasonable its refusal to consent. Presumably the issuer may consent in advance to assignments by a provision in the letter of credit. Dolan, Letters of Credit, Ch. 10 contains an extensive discussion of transfer and assignment of letters of credit. The subject is also treated in Barkley Clark, The Law of Secured Transactions Under the Uniform Commercial Code, Ch. 7 (rev. ed. 2003), and 3 White & Summers, Prac. Ed. § 26–12.

## PROBLEMS

Beneficiary transferred a letter of credit payable on presentation of the draft without further documents, designated as transferable, to its supplier, Transferee. On a false pretext, Beneficiary retained the letter of credit and, later, fraudulently assigned the proceeds to Assignee who took delivery of the letter of credit for value without knowledge of the previous transfer.

**1.** Transferee made timely presentation of its draft to Issuer, together with the papers documenting the transfer from Beneficiary. The draft was honored. Later, Assignee presented the letter of credit, papers showing the assignment, and a draft drawn by Beneficiary. Issuer dishonored because the credit had already been paid to Transferee. Is Issuer liable to Assignee? See 5–114(e) and Comment 2 to 5–114.

**2.** Assignee presented the letter of credit, papers showing the assignment, and a draft drawn by Beneficiary. Issuer, who knew nothing of the previous transfer to Transferee, honored the draft. Later, Transferee presented its own draft. Issuer informed Transferee that it had not known of the transfer and had previously honored beneficiary's draft. Is Issuer liable to Transferee?

**3.** How should the parties guard by contract and conduct against the risks inherent in a system like that in Revised Article 5 in which Transferee has the right to draw on a letter of credit that is in the possession of Assignee? See 5–112(b)(2) and Comment 1 to 5–112.

## 2. SECURITY INTERESTS

The most common reason for a beneficiary to assign the proceeds of a letter of credit is to secure the beneficiary's obligation to a creditor. Security interests in the proceeds of a credit fall within Article 9. Section 5–114(f) provides that "[t]he mode of creating and perfecting a security interest in or granting an assignment of a beneficiary's rights to proceeds is governed by Article 9 or other law." Article 9 governs only the right to proceeds of the credit. It does not control rights in the letter of credit itself. Article 9 calls the right to proceeds of the credit "a letter-of-credit right." Comment 5(e) to 5–102. Under 9–102(a)(51) a letter-of-credit right is "a right to payment or performance under the letter of credit . . . The term does not include the right of the beneficiary to demand payment or performance under a letter of credit." Thus, the term does not include the right to draw on the credit. The transfer of rights to draw is controlled by Article 5. 5–114(e).

To obtain a property right in a letter-of-credit right, the creditor's security interest must attach to it. Attachment allows enforcement of the right against the debtor. It occurs when three conditions are satisfied. § 9–203(b). Two of the conditions are easily met in letter of credit contexts involving a loan or other value provided to the beneficiary: that the creditor give value to the debtor-beneficiary, and that the debtor-beneficiary have a right to the letter of credit proceeds. The third condition is disjunctive: the debtor must either authenticate a security agreement describing the letter-of-credit right or the secured creditor obtain "control" of the right pursuant to the debtor's security agreement or the secured creditor obtain a security interest in collateral for which the letter-of-credit right is a "supporting obligation." 9–203(b)(3).

Thus, under the third condition, a security interest can attach to the letter-of-credit right in either of two different ways. Attachment occurs if the right is described in a security agreement authenticated by the debtor or the creditor obtains control of the letter-of-credit right pursuant to the debtor's security agreement. Alternatively, the security interest attaches to the letter-of-credit right if it attaches to collateral for which the letter-of-credit right is a "supporting obligation." The next section discusses the letter-of-credit right as a "supporting obligation." Section 9–409(a) treats as ineffective restrictions on the creation of security interests in letter of credit proceeds. This allows a security interest to attach when the restriction otherwise would prevent attachment. Comment 2 to 9–409.

Perfection of a security interest allows enforcement of a security interest against third parties. It requires attachment plus the secured creditor to take steps, usually acts of public notice, prescribed by Article 9. 9–308(a), 9–310. Under 9–312(b)(2) a security interest in a letter-of-credit right as original collateral may be perfected only by "control." Thus, control is a particularly effective (but sometimes costly) means of attachment because a security interest that attaches by control also is perfected. Control, according to 9–107, occurs when the issuer "has consented to an assignment of proceeds of the letter of credit under Section 5–114(c)." Section 5–114(c) in turn provides that an issuer need not recognize an assignment of credit proceeds until it consents to the assignment. Where the assignee possesses and exhibits the credit to the issuer, the issuer cannot withhold its consent unreasonably. Article 5 gives no further guidance on obtaining the issuer's consent, and Comment 2 to 9–107 states that the details of the consenting issuer's duty to pay the assignee are left to the parties' agreement.

Article 9's use of the concept of control is borrowed from Article 8. First used in Article 8 to govern the rights of purchasers and secured parties in investment property, Article 9 adapts and applies the concept to security interests in deposit accounts, electronic chattel paper, letter-of-credit rights, and investment property. It replaces the old system of requiring possession of the credit by the assignee in order to perfect a security interest in the credit proceeds. The requirement of possession was cumbersome, contrary to industry practice and in the case of partial assignments of the credit sometimes impossible to satisfy. See Barkley Clark, The Law of Secured Transactions Under the Uniform Commercial Code 7.14[1] (rev. ed. 2003). Control doesn't require possession of the credit.

In the two cases below determine whether the secured parties have control over the described letter-of-credit proceeds.

Case #1. Beneficiary assigned 1/3 of the credit proceeds to A1, its secured creditor, and delivered possession of the letter of credit to A1. Subsequently Beneficiary assigned 1/3 of the letter-of-credit proceeds to each A2 and A3. Beneficiary notified the issuer of all three assignments.

Case #2. Foreign Buyer had issued a letter of credit for $1,000,000 from Foreign Issuer payable to US Seller. Issuer sent the letter of credit to its US correspondent bank to serve as an advising and confirming bank, which delivered Issuer's letter of credit to Seller. Seller granted a security interest to SP Bank in the credit proceeds to secure a loan of $500,000, and a second security interest to US Distributor to secure an existing $250,000 obligation. Advising Bank's invariable practice when notified of assignments of letter-of-credit rights was to demand and retain possession of the credit and note on it the terms of the assignment. It followed the practice in this case. When Seller filed a bankruptcy petition, its trustee sought to avoid the security interests of SP Bank and Distributor in the proceeds of the letter of credit. Seller's trustee can avoid their security interests if the interests are unperfected.

Revised Article 9 leaves unaddressed the rights and priority of a secured creditor when it becomes the transferee of a letter of credit. A transferee acquires all of the beneficiary's rights under the letter of credit, and therefore transferring the credit is a good way to secure the beneficiary's obligations. Section 9–109(c)(4) makes Article 9 inapplicable to the rights of a transferee beneficiary given priority under 5–114(e). And Section 5–114(e) in turn gives the transferee priority over the assignee's right to credit proceeds as well as over claims of competing secured creditors in the proceeds. See Comment 3 to 9–329. Thus, Article 9 leaves undisturbed 5–114(e)'s grant of paramount rights in the letter of credit proceeds to the transferee beneficiary, even when the transferee is a secured creditor. Article 9 therefore does not govern at least two situations: (1) the rights of a beneficiary-debtor against the transferee beneficiary-secured creditor; and (2) the priority of the transferee beneficiary-secured creditor against competing secured creditors. In situation (1), a distinction between an outright transfer and the grant of a security interest has to be made. In situation (2), a conflict between Article 9's priority rules and 5–114(e)'s priority rule is possible. Section 9–329's "control priority" rule gives priority to the security party first obtaining control of the letter of credit right. Section 5–114(e), however, gives priority to the transferee beneficiary over competing claimants to the letter of credit proceeds. Suppose Secured Creditor 1 obtains control over credit proceeds of a transferable letter of credit. Later, Secured Creditor 2 becomes a transferee beneficiary under the same letter. It never obtains control over the credit proceeds. Section 9–329(1) awards priority to Secured Creditor 1. Section 5–114(e) awards it to Secured Creditor 2. Comment 4 to 9–329 recognizes the two unaddressed situations and simply counsels courts to give "appropriate consideration to the policies and provisions of Article 5 and letter-of-credit practice as well as Article 9."

### 3.   LETTERS OF CREDIT AS SUPPORTING OBLIGATIONS

Article 9 has special rules that apply to letter-of-credit rights when the letter of credit is a "supporting obligation" under 9–102(a)(77). This term "means a letter-of-credit right or secondary obligation that supports the payment or performance of an account, chattel paper, a document, a general intangible, an instrument, or investment property." Collateral described in (a)(77) is the "supported obligation," and the letter-of-credit right is the "supporting obligation." When a letter-of-credit right "supports" the sort of collateral described in 9–102(a)(77), it serves to enhance the value of the supported collateral. Given the frequent use of standby credits as credit enhancement devices, our guess is that in the great majority of cases letter-of-credit rights will be supporting obligations. If a sports franchise assures a basketball player that if its promissory note for the athlete's salary is not paid, the athlete can rely on a standby letter of credit, the letter of credit is a supporting obligation. The same is true when a dealer assigns its accounts to a financer and backs the accounts by a letter of credit. The examples are endless.

Article 9's special rules for attachment, perfection and priority of a security interest in a letter-of-credit right treat the right as an incident of the collateral it supports. Comment 5f. to 9–102. Accordingly, the secured creditor's rights in the credit proceeds derive from its rights in the collateral supported by the credit proceeds. Thus, under 9–203(f) a security interest automatically attaches to the letter-of-credit right when it attaches to the supported collateral. So, for example, there is no need for an authenticated security agreement describing the supported obligation to describe or contain any reference to the letter-of-credit right supporting it. Under 9–308(d) perfection in the supported collateral is perfection in the letter-of-credit right. And under 9–322(c), with one significant exception, priority in the supported collateral is priority in the letter-of-credit right.

Article 9's control concept must be understood taking into account its special rules for supporting obligations. Two points are important. First, the role of control is significantly qualified for letter-of-credit rights when they are supporting obligations. If a letter-of-credit right is not a supporting obligation, 9–312(b)(2) provides that perfection may be achieved only by control. But the requirement doesn't apply to supporting obligations. In this case perfection of the security interest in the supported collateral automatically perfects a security interest in the supported obligation. Some commercial and most standby transactions letter-of-credit rights are supporting obligations. Thus, in many cases attachment and perfection in these rights is automatic. Control isn't necessary and will be a more expensive alternative.

Second, and by far more important, are Article 9's special priority rule for supporting obligations. Section 9–322(b)(2) describes Article 9's basic priority rule for supporting obligations. Under it the time for filing and perfection as to the supported obligation is also the time of filing and perfection as to the supported obligation. This priority rule treats priority in the supporting obligation as derivative: the priority of the supporting obligation is the priority of the supported collateral. However, 9–322(b)(2)'s basic rule is subject to an important exception contained in 9–322(c). Section 9–322(c)(1) provides in relevant part that the rule that a security interest in the supporting obligation takes the priority of a security interest in the supported collateral, subject to 9–329(1). Section 9–329(1) in turn provides that if there are conflicting security interests in the same letter-of-credit right, the security interest of the secured party having control has priority over a security interest of a secured party that does not have control. Hence, for example, if a bank files first against accounts, it is perfected with respect to a supporting letter-of-credit right. However, it will not be prior as to that right if a financer who filed second against the same accounts but perfected its security interest in the supporting letter of credit right by control. Thus, to be sure of their priority, secured parties claiming security interests in letter-of-credit rights that are supporting obligations must obtain control. Control remains the central tenet of the law of secured transactions in letter-of-credit rights.

## G. Letters of Credit in Bankruptcy

If a standby letter of credit is to be useful as the functional equivalent of a guaranty, it must pass muster in bankruptcy. So far it has. Discharge of the applicant in bankruptcy does not affect the liability of the issuer on a letter of credit. BC 524(e). The initial question is whether the automatic stay of BC 362(a) restrains the beneficiary from drawing on the issuer after the applicant's bankruptcy. If it does, the utility of letters of credit is greatly impaired because the beneficiary would be forced to go through the expensive and time-consuming procedure to lift the stay under BC 362(d). As we have shown, the usual letter of credit transaction involves three undertakings: the letter of credit between the issuer and the beneficiary;

the underlying contract between the applicant and the beneficiary; and the reimbursement contract between the applicant and the issuer. There is no question that the automatic stay precludes any action by the beneficiary against the applicant on the underlying contract as well as any action by the issuer against the applicant on the reimbursement agreement.

That BC 362(a) does not stay the beneficiary's draw against the issuer was decided in In re Page, 18 B.R. 713 (D.D.C.1982), and has been widely accepted. Accord In re War Eagle Construction Co., Inc., 283 B.R. 193 (S.D.Va. 2002). The applicant in *Page* granted security interests in its assets to issuer to secure its obligation to reimburse the issuer if the issuer had to pay the letter of credit. Later the applicant filed in bankruptcy and the beneficiary presented the letter of credit for honor. The bankruptcy court held that unless payment of the letter of credit were stayed, the issuer, after payment, would be able to realize on its security interest in debtor's property, thereby reducing the assets available to the other creditors. The district court reversed on the ground that before the applicant had filed in bankruptcy the issuer already had a perfected security interest in the applicant's assets to secure its contingent claim for reimbursement. In its payment of the letter of credit, the issuer merely liquidated its claim against the applicant for reimbursement, and applicant's other creditors are no worse off because the property of the applicant's bankruptcy estate has not been depleted. The letter of credit was not, of course, property of the applicant's estate. The court demonstrated its respect for the importance of the independence principle of letter of credit law: "Moreover, enjoining the payment of the letter of credit, even temporarily, would frustrate the commercial purposes of letters of credit to the detriment of financial institutions as well as their customers. * * * If payment on a letter of credit could be routinely delayed by the filing of a Chapter 11 petition the intended substitution of a bank for its less credit-worthy customer would be defeated." 18 B.R. at 717.

The more difficult problems concerning letters of credit in bankruptcy have arisen in the area of voidable preferences law as illustrated in the following case.

## Matter of Compton Corp.

United States Court of Appeals, Fifth Circuit, 1987.
831 F.2d 586.

■ JERRE S. WILLIAMS, CIRCUIT JUDGE:

This is a bankruptcy preference case in which a bankruptcy trustee seeks to recover a transfer made via a letter of credit for the benefit of one of the debtor's unsecured creditors on the eve of bankruptcy. The bankruptcy court and the district court found there to be no voidable preference. We reverse.

### I.  FACTUAL BACKGROUND

In March 1982, Blue Quail Energy, Inc., delivered a shipment of oil to debtor Compton Corporation. Payment of $585,443.85 for this shipment of oil was due on or about April 20, 1982. Compton failed to make timely payment. Compton induced Abilene National Bank (now MBank–Abilene) to issue an irrevocable standby letter of credit in Blue Quail's favor on May 6, 1982. Under the terms of the letter of credit, payment of up to $585,443.85 was due Blue Quail if Compton failed to pay Blue Quail this amount by June 22, 1982. Compton paid MBank $1,463.61 to issue the letter of credit. MBank also received a promissory note payable on demand for $585,443.85. MBank did not need a security agreement to cover the letter of credit transaction because a prior 1980 security agreement between the bank and Compton had a future advances provision. This 1980 security agreement had been perfected as to a variety of Compton's assets through the filing of several financing statements. The most recent financing statement had been filed a year before, May 7, 1981. The letter of credit on its face noted that it was for an antecedent debt due Blue Quail.

On May 7, 1982, the day after MBank issued the letter of credit in Blue Quail's favor, several of Compton's creditors filed an involuntary bankruptcy petition against Compton. On June 22, 1982, MBank paid Blue Quail $569,932.03 on the letter of credit after Compton failed to pay Blue Quail.

In the ensuing bankruptcy proceeding, MBank's aggregate secured claims against Compton, including the letter of credit payment to Blue Quail, were paid in full from the liquidation of Compton's assets which served as the bank's collateral. Walter Kellogg, bankruptcy trustee for Compton, did not contest the validity of MBank's secured claim against Compton's assets for the amount drawn under the letter of credit by Blue Quail. Instead, on June 14, 1983, trustee Kellogg filed a complaint in the bankruptcy court against Blue Quail asserting that Blue Quail had received a preferential transfer under § 547 through the letter of credit transaction. The trustee sought to recover $585,443.85 from Blue Quail pursuant to § 550.

Blue Quail answered and filed a third party complaint against MBank. On June 16, 1986, Blue Quail filed a motion for summary judgment asserting that the trustee could not recover any preference from Blue Quail because Blue Quail had been paid from MBank's funds under the letter of credit and therefore had not received any of Compton's property. On August 27, 1986, the bankruptcy court granted Blue Quail's motion, agreeing that the payment under the letter of credit did not constitute a transfer of debtor Compton's property but rather was a transfer of the bank's property. The bankruptcy court entered judgment on the motion on September 10, 1986. Trustee Kellogg appealed this decision to the district court. On December 11, 1986, the district court affirmed the bankruptcy court ruling, holding that the trustee did not establish two necessary elements of a voidable transfer under § 547. The district court agreed with Blue Quail and the bankruptcy court that the trustee could not establish that the funds transferred to Blue Quail were ever property of Compton. Furthermore, the district court held that the transfer of the increased security interest to MBank was a transfer of the debtor's property for the sole benefit of the bank and in no way benefitted Blue Quail. The district court therefore found no voidable preference as to Blue Quail. The trustee is appealing the decision to this Court.

## II.   THE LETTER OF CREDIT

It is well established that a letter of credit and the proceeds therefrom are not property of the debtor's estate under § 541. * * * When the issuer honors a proper draft under a letter of credit, it does so from its own assets and not from the assets of its customer who caused the letter of credit to be issued. * * * As a result, a bankruptcy trustee is not entitled to enjoin a post petition payment of funds under a letter of credit from the issuer to the beneficiary, because such a payment is not a transfer of debtor's property (a threshold requirement under § 547(b)). A case apparently holding otherwise, In re Twist Cap., Inc., 1 B.R. 284 (Bankr.Fla.1979), has been roundly criticized and otherwise ignored by courts and commentators alike.

Recognizing these characteristics of a letter of credit in a bankruptcy case is necessary in order to maintain the independence principle, the cornerstone of letter of credit law. Under the independence principle, an issuer's obligation to the letter of credit's beneficiary is independent from any obligation between the beneficiary and the issuer's customer. All a beneficiary has to do to receive payment under a letter of credit is to show that it has performed all the duties required by the letter of credit. Any disputes between the beneficiary and the customer do not affect the issuer's obligation to the beneficiary to pay under the letter of credit.

Letters of credit are most commonly arranged by a party who benefits from the provision of goods or services. The party will request a bank to issue a letter of credit which names the provider of the goods or services as the beneficiary. Under a standby letter of credit, the bank becomes primarily liable to the beneficiary upon the default of the bank's customer to pay for the goods or services. The bank charges a fee to issue a letter of credit and to undertake this liability. The shifting of liability to the bank rather than to the services or goods provider is the main purpose of the letter of credit. After all, the bank is in a much better position to assess the risk of its customer's insolvency than is the service or goods provider. It should be noted, however, that it is the risk of the debtor's insolvency and not the risk of a preference attack that a bank assumes under a letter of credit transaction. Overall, the independence principle is necessary to insure "the certainty of payments for services or goods rendered regardless of any intervening misfortune which may befall the other contracting party." In re North Shore, 30 B.R. at 378.

The trustee in this case accepts this analysis and does not ask us to upset it. The trustee is not attempting to set aside the post petition payments by MBank to Blue Quail under the letter of credit as a preference; nor does the trustee claim the letter of credit itself constitutes debtor's property. The trustee is instead challenging the earlier transfer in which Compton granted MBank an increased security interest in its assets to obtain the letter of credit for the benefit of Blue Quail. Collateral which has been pledged by a debtor as security for a letter of credit is property of the debtor's estate. In re W.L. Mead, 42 B.R. at 59. The trustee claims that the direct transfer to MBank of the increased security interest on May 6, 1982, also constituted an indirect transfer to Blue Quail which occurred one day prior to the filing of the involuntary bankruptcy petition and is voidable as a preference under § 547. This assertion of a preferential transfer is evaluated in Parts III and IV of this opinion.

It is important to note that the irrevocable standby letter of credit in the case at bar was not arranged in connection with Blue Quail's initial decision to sell oil to Compton on credit. Compton arranged for the letter of credit after Blue Quail had shipped the oil and after Compton had defaulted in payment. The letter of credit in this case did not serve its usual function of backing up a contemporaneous credit decision, but instead served as a back up payment guarantee on an extension of credit already in jeopardy. The letter of credit was issued to pay off an antecedent unsecured debt. This fact was clearly noted on the face of the letter of credit. Blue Quail, the beneficiary of the letter of credit, did not give new value for the issuance of the letter of credit by MBank on May 6, 1982, or for the resulting increased security interest held by MBank. MBank, however, did give new value for the increased security interest it obtained in Compton's collateral: the bank issued the letter of credit.

When a debtor pledges its assets to secure a letter of credit, a transfer of debtor's property has occurred under the provisions of § 547. By subjecting its assets to MBank's reimbursement claim in the event MBank had to pay on the letter of credit, Compton made a transfer of its property. The broad definition of "transfer" under § 101 is clearly designed to cover such a transfer. Overall, the letter of credit itself and the payments thereunder may not be property of debtor, but the collateral pledged as a security interest for the letter of credit is.

Furthermore, in a secured letter of credit transaction, the transfer of debtor's property takes place at the time the letter of credit is issued (when the security interest is granted) and received by the beneficiary, not at the time the issuer pays on the letter of credit. * * *

The transfer to MBank of the increased security interest was a direct transfer which occurred on May 6, 1982, when the bank issued the letter of credit. Under § 547(e)(2)(A), however, such a transfer is deemed to have taken place for purposes of § 547 at the time such transfer "takes effect" between the transferor and transferee if such transfer is perfected within 10 days. The phrase "takes effect" is undefined in the Bankruptcy Code, but under Uniform Commercial Code Article 9 law, a transfer of a security interest "takes effect" when the security interest attaches. Because of the future advances clause in MBank's 1980 security agreement with Compton, the attachment of the MBank's security interest relates back to May 9, 1980, the date the security agreement went into effect. The bottom line is that the direct transfer of the increased security interest to MBank is artificially deemed to have occurred at least by May 7, 1981, the date MBank filed its final financing statement, for purposes of a preference attack against the bank.[4] This date is well before the 90 day window of § 547(b)(4)(A). This would protect the bank from a preference attack by the trustee even if the bank had not given new value at the time it received the increased security interest.* MBank is therefore protected from a preference attack by the trustee for the increased security interest transfer under either of two theories: under § 547(c)(1) because it gave new value and under the operation of the relation back provision of § 547(e)(2)(A). The bank is also protected from any claims of reimbursement by Blue Quail because the bank received no voidable preference.

The relation back provision of § 547(e)(2)(A), however, applies only to the direct transfer of the increased security interest to MBank. The indirect transfer to Blue Quail that allegedly resulted from the direct transfer to MBank occurred on May 6, 1982, the date of issuance of the letter of credit. The relation back principle of § 547(e)(2)(A) does not apply to this indirect transfer to Blue Quail. Blue Quail was not a party to the security agreement between MBank and Compton. So it will not be able to utilize the relation back provision if it is deemed to have received an indirect transfer resulting from the direct transfer of the increased security interest to MBank. Blue Quail, therefore, cannot assert either of the two defenses to a preference attack which MBank can claim. Blue Quail did not give new value under § 547(c)(1), and it received a transfer within 90 days of the filing of Compton's bankruptcy petition.

## III. DIRECT/INDIRECT TRANSFER DOCTRINE

The federal courts have long recognized that "[t]o constitute a preference, it is not necessary that the transfer be made directly to the creditor." *National Bank of Newport v. National Herkimer County Bank*, 225 U.S.

---

4. UCC § 9–312(7) specifies that for purposes of priority among competing secured parties, the security interest for a future advance has the same priority as the security interest for the first advance. Conflicting security interests rank according to priority in time of filing or perfection. UCC § 9–312(5).

* [Editors' Note: The "relation back" theory of the Court is not supported by the Bankruptcy Code. The Court is correct in stating that the phrase "at the time such transfer takes effect" in § 547(e)(2)(A) refers to the time the security interest "attaches" under the UCC. The time of attachment is governed by UCC § 9–203. In this case attachment occurred when three events occurred: (1) value was given by MBank; (2) the debtor had rights in the collateral; and (3) the debtor signed a security agreement providing for the security interest. The second and third events occurred before May 6, but MBank did not give value with respect to the transfer challenged by the trustee in bankruptcy until the letter of credit was issued on May 6. Thus, under § 547(e)(2)(A), the transfer could not have occurred before May 6. Under UCC § 9–303, the security interest that attached on May 6 was perfected at the time it attached because the filing of a financing statement—the applicable step required for perfection—had already occurred before May 6. Because May 6 is the day of both attachment and perfection, the result under § 547(e)(2)(A) is that the transfer from the debtor to MBank occurred on May 6. It is irrelevant under § 547 that UCC § 9–312(5) and (7) date the priority of MBank with respect to the May 6 transaction from the time MBank filed its financing statement. § 547(e)(2)(A) refers to the time of attachment and perfection, not to the date of priority. There is no avoidable preference in this case, however. The Court correctly holds that the giving of value by MBank and the transfer by the debtor to MBank were a contemporaneous exchange under § 547(c)(1).]

178, 184 (1912). "If the bankrupt has made a transfer of his property, the *effect* of which is to enable one of his creditors to obtain a greater percentage of his debt than another creditor of the same class, circuity of arrangement will not avail to save it." Id. (Emphasis added). To combat such circuity, the courts have broken down certain transfers into two transfers, one direct and one indirect. The direct transfer to the third party may be valid and not subject to a preference attack. The indirect transfer, arising from the same action by the debtor, however, may constitute a voidable preference as to the creditor who indirectly benefitted from the direct transfer to the third party.

This is the situation presented in the case before us. The term "transfer" as used in the various bankruptcy statutes through the years has always been broad enough to cover such indirect transfers and to catch various circuitous arrangements. Katz v. First National Bank of Glen Head, 568 F.2d 964, 969 n. 4, (2d Cir.), cert. denied, 434 U.S. 1069 (1978). The new Bankruptcy Code implicitly adopts this doctrine through its broad definition of "transfer."[6] Examining the case law that has developed since the *National Bank of Newport* case yields an understanding of what types of transfers the direct/indirect doctrine is meant to cover.

In Palmer v. Radio Corporation of America, 453 F.2d 1133 (5th Cir.1971), a third party purchased from the debtor a television station for $40,000 cash and the assumption of certain liabilities of the debtor, including unsecured claims by creditor RCA. This Court found the direct transfer from the debtor to the third party purchaser constituted an indirect preferential transfer to creditor RCA. We found that the assumption by the third party purchaser of the debt owed by the debtor to RCA and the subsequent payments made thereunder constituted a voidable transfer as to RCA. The court noted that such indirect transfers as this had long been held to constitute voidable preferences under bankruptcy laws. 453 F.2d at 1136.

\* \* \*

In Virginia National Bank v. Woodson, 329 F.2d 836 (4th Cir.1964), the debtor had several overdrawn accounts with his bank. The debtor talked his sister into paying off $8,000 of the overdrafts in exchange for an $8,000 promissory note and an assignment of some collateral as security. The debtor's sister made the $8,000 payment directly to the bank. The $8,000 technically was never part of the debtor's estate. The court, however, held that the payment of the $8,000 by the sister to the bank was a preference as to the bank to the extent of the value of the collateral held by the sister. The court noted that the measure of the value of a voidable preference is

**6.** "Transfer" means every mode, direct or *indirect*, absolute or conditional, voluntary or involuntary, of disposing of or parting with property or with an interest in property, including retention of title as a security inter- est and foreclosure of the debtor's equity of redemption. § 101(50) (emphasis added). See also the Notes of the Committee on the Judi- ciary under 11 U.S.C. 101 ("The definition of transfer is as broad as possible.")

diminution of the debtor's estate and not the value of the transfer to the creditor.

In the *Woodson* case the sister was secured only to the extent the pledged collateral had value; the remainder of her loan to her brother was unsecured. Swapping one unsecured creditor for another unsecured creditor does not create any kind of preference. The court held that a preference in such a transaction arises only when a secured creditor is swapped for an unsecured creditor. Only then is the pool of assets available for distribution to the general unsecured creditors depleted because the secured creditor has priority over the unsecured creditors. Furthermore, the court held that the bank and not the sister had received the voidable preference and had to pay back to the trustee an amount equal to the value of the collateral.

\* \* \*

## IV.   THE DIRECT/INDIRECT DOCTRINE IN THE CONTEXT OF A LETTER OF CREDIT TRANSACTION

The case at bar differs from the cases discussed in Part III supra only by the presence of the letter of credit as the mechanism for paying off the unsecured creditor. Blue Quail's attempt to otherwise distinguish the case from the direct/indirect transfer cases does not withstand scrutiny.

In the letter of credit cases discussed in Part II supra, the letters of credit were issued contemporaneously with the initial extension of credit by the beneficiaries of the letters. In those cases the letters of credit effectively served as security devices for the benefit of the creditor beneficiaries and took the place of formal security interests. The courts in those cases properly found there had been no voidable transfers, direct or indirect, in the letter of credit transactions involved. New value was given contemporaneously with the issuance of the letters of credit in the form of the extensions of credit by the beneficiaries of the letters. As a result, the § 547(c)(1) preference exception was applicable.

The case at bar differs from these other letter of credit cases by one very important fact: the letter of credit in this case was issued to secure an antecedent unsecured debt due the beneficiary of the letter of credit. The unsecured creditor beneficiary gave no new value upon the issuance of the letter of credit. When the issuer paid off the letter of credit and foreclosed on the collateral securing the letter of credit, a preferential transfer had occurred. An unsecured creditor was paid in full and a secured creditor was substituted in its place.

The district court upheld the bankruptcy court in maintaining the validity of the letter of credit issued to cover the antecedent debt. The district court held that MBank, the issuer of the letter of credit, could pay off the letter of credit and foreclose on the collateral securing it. We are in full agreement. But we also look to the impact of the transaction as it affects the situation of Blue Quail in the bankrupt estate. We hold that the bankruptcy trustee can recover from Blue Quail, the beneficiary of the letter of credit, because Blue Quail received an indirect preference. This result preserves the sanctity of letter of credit and carries out the purposes of the Bankruptcy Code by avoiding a preferential transfer. MBank, the issuer of the letter of credit, being just the intermediary through which the preferential transfer was accomplished, completely falls out of the picture and is not involved in this particular legal proceeding.

MBank did not receive any preferential transfer—it gave new value for the security interest. Furthermore, because the direct and indirect transfers are separate and independent, the trustee does not even need to challenge the direct transfer of the increased security interest to MBank, or seek any relief at all from MBank, in order to attack the indirect transfer and recover under § 550 from the indirect transferee Blue Quail.

We hold that a creditor cannot secure payment of an unsecured antecedent debt through a letter of credit transaction when it could not do so through any other type of transaction. The purpose of the letter of credit transaction in this case was to secure payment of an unsecured antecedent debt for the benefit of an unsecured creditor. This is the only proper way to look at such letters of credit in the bankruptcy context. The promised transfer of pledged collateral induced the bank to issue the letter of credit in favor of the creditor. The increased security interest held by the bank clearly benefitted the creditor because the bank would not have issued the letter of credit without this security. A secured creditor was substituted for an unsecured creditor to the detriment of the other unsecured creditors.

\* \* \*

The precise holding in this case needs to be emphasized. We do not hold that payment under a letter of credit, or even a letter of credit itself, constitute preferential transfers under § 547(b) or property of a debtor under § 541. The holding of this case fully allows the letter of credit to function. We preserve its sanctity and the underlying independence doctrine. We do not, however, allow an unsecured creditor to avoid a preference attack by utilizing a letter of credit to secure payment of an antecedent debt. Otherwise the unsecured creditor would receive an indirect preferential transfer from the granting of the security for the letter of credit to the extent of the value of that security. Our holding does not affect the strength of or the proper use of letters of credit. When a letter of credit is issued contemporaneously with a new extension of credit, the creditor beneficiary will not be subject to a preferential attack under the direct/indirect doctrine elaborated in this case because the creditor will have given new value in exchange for the indirect benefit of the secured letter of credit. Only when a creditor receives a secured letter of credit to cover an unsecured antecedent debt will it be subject to a preferential attack under § 547(b).

\* \* \*

## NOTES

**1.** The trustee in *Compton* elected to recover from Blue Quail, the beneficiary of Compton's grant of a security interest to Mbank. In dicta the court suggested that the trustee could not recover from Mbank because it did not receive a preference. This conflicts with Levit v. Ingersoll Rand Financial Corp., 874 F.2d 1186 (7th Cir.1989), as well as four other circuits. These courts have held that a transfer voidable as a preference under BC 547(b) can be recovered from a transferee who was not preferred as the "initial transferee of such transfer" under BC 550(a)(1). Because the creation of a security interest is a transfer under the Bankruptcy Code and Mbank is the "initial transferee," they would allow recovery from Mbank under BC 550(a)(1) in the circumstances described in *Compton*. (Further, BC 550(b)'s good faith defense to recovery does not apply to initial transferees to protect Mbank.) The 1994 Bankruptcy Reform Act altered BC 550 in response to *Levit*, adding BC 550(c) to limit recovery from an insider transferee of an indirect preference. However, Congress left BC 550(a)(1) untouched. Congress' action arguably signals approval of *Levit*'s literal reading of the subsection, to the effect that if a transfer is preferential as to anyone, the trustee may recover from the initial transferee.

**2.** In *Compton* we see that a debtor who already owes a debt makes a voidable preference to the creditor if it causes a bank to issue a letter of credit to the creditor to secure the debt within 90 days of bankruptcy. If the debtor had paid the creditor or had granted the creditor a security interest in the debtor's property during the 90–day period, there would clearly be a preference. The debtor cannot alter this result by use of a letter of credit. But letters of credit are not normally used to secure antecedent debts. The usual case is one in which the letter of credit is issued to the creditor at the inception of the credit transaction between the beneficiary and applicant. An example is one in which the beneficiary sells goods to the debtor-applicant on credit and takes a standby letter of credit to protect itself against the debtor-applicant's failure to pay. Here the seller-beneficiary gives new value at the time it receives the letter of credit. Is it possible for a preference problem to arise in such a case?

Take two cases:

Case #1. Beneficiary sold goods to Applicant on 60–day credit for $100,000 and demanded a letter of credit to secure it against Applicant's default. Applicant induced Bank to issue the letter of credit by granting Bank a security interest in its property worth in excess of $100,000 to secure its agreement to reimburse Bank. Applicant was unable to pay for the goods at the end of the credit period but induced Beneficiary not to draw on the letter of credit for a month. At the end of the month Applicant, though thoroughly insolvent, paid $100,000 to Beneficiary in satisfaction of the debt. Within 90 days of the payment, Applicant filed in bankruptcy and its trustee sought to recover the payment as a voidable preference. There should be no preference in this case under BC 547(b)(5), and it shouldn't matter if payment to Beneficiary came from Bank or Applicant. The transfer of assets from Applicant's estate occurred when the security interest was granted to Bank, and Bank gave new value for that transfer by undertaking to pay Beneficiary. If Bank pays Beneficiary, Bank has a valid secured claim in Applicant's bankruptcy for $100,000. If Applicant pays, Bank's claim to the security is released and, although Applicant's unsecured creditors have lost $100,000 in the cash payment Applicant made to Beneficiary, they have gained the same amount in the release of Bank's claim against Applicant's property. The transfer of assets that depleted Applicant's estate to the detriment of its creditors took place before the beginning of the 90–day period.

Case #2. Difficulties arise when we change only one fact in the case above. Assume that Applicant either granted no security interest in its property to Bank or, more realistically, granted a security interest in property that eventually turned out to be worth much less than $100,000. Let's assume for purposes of discussion that the collateral became worthless. If Bank pays Beneficiary on the letter of credit, there is no preference because Bank's payment does not transfer property of Applicant's estate. Before payment Applicant owed $100,000 to Beneficiary on an unsecured claim; after payment Applicant owes the same amount to Bank on an unsecured claim. The problem arises if Applicant, rather than Bank, pays the Beneficiary. Here $100,000 in cash has been taken from Applicant's estate for the benefit of Beneficiary during the 90–day period. We look at preferences from the point of view of the debtor's unsecured creditors. Are they worse off after the transfer than before? True, Applicant has been relieved of Bank's unsecured contingent claim for reimbursement, but that does not put money into the Applicant's estate for the benefit of its creditors. In re Powerine Oil Co., 59 F.3d 969 (9th Cir.1995), held that payment by the Applicant in such a case is preferential, even though payment by the Bank in the same case would not be. Noting that the result of this case makes Beneficiary better off if its debtor, the Applicant, defaults, the court observed that "law can be stranger than fiction in the Preference Zone." 59 F.3d at 971. The Bankruptcy Appellate Panel had held that the payment was not a preference because it did not enable the Beneficiary to obtain more than it would in a Chapter 7 bankruptcy. If Applicant hadn't paid it, Bank would have had to. Could you contend that Bank rather than Beneficiary is the recipient of the preference in *Powerine*?

## FORM.   LETTER OF CREDIT APPLICATION AND AGREEMENT

When an applicant requests a standby letter of credit, banks require completion of the following form which states the agreement between the applicant and issuing bank and the terms under which the bank must honor upon presentation of the letter of credit.

 **CITY NATIONAL BANK**

# INTERNATIONAL OPERATIONS CENTER

606 South Olive Street, Suite 300                               Date:
CABLE ADDRESS "CINABANK LSA"                      Los Angeles, California 90014
                                                                TELEX 825717

| IRREVOCABLE STANDBY LETTER OF CREDIT APPLICATION AND LETTER OF CREDIT AGREEMENT |
|---|

TO: CITY NATIONAL BANK (CNB)

☐ Cable

We (Applicant) request you to establish by     ☐ Overnight courier service     an irrevocable standby Letter of Credit on

☐ Same day messenger service

the following terms and conditions:

| ADVISING BANK (name and address) | APPLICANT (name and address) |
|---|---|
| BENEFICIARY (name and address) | AMOUNT — indicate currency—i.e., U.S. $—and specify amount in figures and words |
| EXCEPT SO FAR AS OTHERWISE EXPRESSLY STATED THIS CREDIT WILL BE SUBJECT TO INTERNATIONAL STANDBY PRACTICES 1998 (ISP98), INTERNATIONAL CHAMBER OF COMMERCE PUBLICATION AS IN FORCE AS OF THE DATE OF ISSUANCE OF THE LETTER OF CREDIT | EXPIRY DATE<br><br>AT CNB'S ISSUING OFFICE |

available by Draft(s) at sight on CNB and accompanied by the following:

## APPLICANT'S AGREEMENT TO PAY CNB

Applicant agrees immediately upon CNB's demand or if no demand is made then on _____, to repay to CNB the total amount of each disbursement by CNB under this Letter of Credit, together with interest thereon at the rate of __ percent per year in excess of the Prime Rate. The "Prime Rate" shall mean the floating loan rate of CNB announced from time to time as its "Prime Rate". Any change in the interest rate resulting from a change in the Prime Rate shall be effective on the effective date of change in the Prime Rate. Interest shall be calculated on a basis of a 360-day year and actual days elapsed. We further authorize you to charge, without further notice, our account, (or an account of any of us) for all such amounts when and as such are due and payable.

**THE OPENING OF THIS CREDIT IS SUBJECT TO THE TERMS AND CONDITIONS AS SET FORTH IN THE LETTER OF CREDIT AGREEMENT APPEARING ON THE REVERSE HEREOF TO WHICH WE AGREE. WE FURTHER AGREE THAT THE CREDIT AS ISSUED SHALL INCLUDE SUCH REVISIONS OF THE LANGUAGE SET FORTH ABOVE AS YOU DEEM NECESSARY.**

(APPLICANT)

FIRM NAME

AUTHORIZED SIGNATURE

SOCIAL SECURITY/TAXPAYER I.D. NO.

**FOR BANK USE ONLY:**
**APPROVAL OF CREDIT:**

Lending Officer

Sr. Loan Officer (when applicable)

Branch

**ACCOUNT TO BE DEBITED:**
(  )  Branch G/L No. 11305000
(  )  Customer Acct. No.

### LETTER OF CREDIT AGREEMENT

In consideration of your opening, at our request, a letter of Credit (herein called "the Credit"), the terms and conditions of which appear on the reverse side hereof we hereby agree as follows:

1. As to drafts under or purporting to be under the Credit, which are payable in lawful United States funds, we agree to pay you on demand at your issuing office in lawful United States funds, the amount of such draft(s) on the presentment to you thereof or, at your request in advance.

2. As to drafts under or purporting to be under the Credit, which are payable in foreign currency, we agree to pay you at your office on demand, the equivalent of each such draft in lawful United States funds at your then prevailing rate of exchange effective for sales of that other currency for cable transfer to the country of which it is the currency.

3. We also agree to pay to you any attorneys' fees incurred in the enforcement of this Letter of Credit Agreement, your service charge in accordance with your Schedule of Fees and Charges now existing or as hereafter adopted, and all other charges and expenses paid or incurred by you in connection therewith.

4. We agree to reimburse you for any losses and charges incurred by you or made against you in connection with this Agreement and related to the reevaluation or fluctuations in the exchange rate of any currency whether United States or any other.

5. We hereby convey and transfer to you a security interest in all goods, documents and instruments which shall come into your control or into your possession or that of any of your correspondents as the result of opening or in connection with any transactions under the Credit, which goods, documents and instruments are and shall be granted to you as security (a) for all payments made or to be made by you or your correspondents under the Credit; (b) for any interest, commission or other customary charges in relation to the Credit and (c) for any other obligations or liabilities (absolute or contingent) of us to you, which now exist or are hereafter created. Upon any default by us in any of the undertakings set forth in this Letter of Credit Agreement, you are authorized to sell, under the provisions of the Commercial Code of the State of California, any or all goods, documents and instruments; in the event of any deficiency, we will pay the same to you immediately or in the event of any surplus, you shall pay the same to us or to the persons entitled thereto. In the event such described property should suffer any decline in value we will upon demand, deliver to you additional collateral to your satisfaction.

6. We agree that your rights and duties under the Credit are, except as otherwise provided herein, governed by the International Standby Practices 1998 (ISP98), International Chamber of Commerce Publication as in force on the date of issuance of the Credit.

7. We agree that in the event of any amendments or modifications of the terms of the Credit, this Agreement shall be binding upon us with regard to the Credit so amended. You may (at your option) issue the requested Credit through a correspondent of your choice.

8. The users of the Letter of Credit shall be deemed our agents and we assume all risks of their acts of omissions. Neither you nor your correspondents shall be responsible for/or: the validity, sufficiency, or genuineness of documents, even if such documents should in fact prove to be in any or all respects invalid, insufficient, fraudulent or forged; the solvency or responsibility of any party issuing any documents; delay in arrival or failure to arrive of any documents; delay in giving or failure to give notice of arrival or any other notice; failure of any draft to bear adequate reference to the Credit; failure of documents to accompany any draft at negotiation, or failure of any person to note the amount of any draft on the reverse of the Credit, to surrender or take up the Credit or to send documents apart from drafts as required by the terms of the Credit, each of which provisions, if contained in the Credit itself, it is agreed may be waived by you; errors, or omissions, or interruptions or delays in transmission or delivery of any message by mail, cable, telegraph, wireless or otherwise; nor shall you be responsible for any error, neglect, or default of any of your correspondents; and none of the above shall affect, impair, or prevent the vesting of any of your rights or powers hereunder. In furtherance and extension and not in limitation of the specific provisions hereinbefore set forth, we agree that any action taken by you or any correspondent of you under or in connection with the Credit or relative drafts or documents, if taken in good faith, shall be binding on us and shall not put you or your correspondent under any resulting liability to us.

9. We agree at any time and from time to time, on demand, to deliver, convey, transfer, or assign to you, as security for any and all of our obligations and liabilities hereunder, and also for any and all other obligations and liabilities, absolute or contingent, due or to become due, which are or may at any time hereafter be owing to you, additional security of a value and character satisfactory to you, or to make such cash payment as you may require. We agree that all property belonging to us, or in which we may have an interest, conveyed, transferred, assigned, or paid to you, or coming into your possession or into the possession of anyone for you in any manner whatsoever, whether expressly as security, or for safekeeping or otherwise including any items received for collection or transmission and the proceeds thereof, whether or not such property is in whole or in part released to us on trust of bailee receipt, is security for each and all such obligations and liabilities. We agree that upon our failure at all times to keep a margin of security with you satisfactory to you, or upon the making by us of any assignments for the benefit of creditors, or upon the filing of any voluntary or involuntary petition in bankruptcy by or against us, or upon any application for the appointment of a receiver of any of our property, or upon any act of bankruptcy or state of insolvency of us, or if you in good faith deem yourself insecure at any time, or upon the death of any of us, all of such obligations and liabilities shall become and be immediately due and payable without demand or notice notwithstanding any credit or time allowed to us, or any instrument evidencing any such obligation or otherwise; and each of us, and all of us, as to property in which we may have any interest, expressly authorize you in any such event, or upon our failure to pay any of such obligations or liabilities when it or they shall become or be made due, to sell all such property, in accordance with the Commercial Code of the State of California and to apply the

net proceeds of such sale or sales, together with any balance of deposits and any sum credited by or due from you to us, in general accounts or otherwise, to the payment of all of our obligations or liabilities to you however arising.

10. Your rights specified in this Agreement are in addition to any created by statute or rule of law. You are expressly given the right to execute and file and record endorsements, assignments, financing statements, and other instruments in the name of any of us with respect to documents, property and interests relative to the Credit or any property of any of us in which you have a security interest which may at any time come into your possession under the Credit or by virtue of this Agreement. We agree to pay all expenses, filing fees and other charges incurred by you relative to the perfection or enforcement of your rights and security interests hereunder.

11. You shall not be deemed to have waived any of your rights hereunder, unless you or your authorized agent shall have signed such waiver, in writing. No such waiver unless expressly stated therein shall be effective as to any transaction which occurs subsequent to the date of such waiver, nor as to any continuance of a breach after such waiver.

12. We understand that any credit issued pursuant to this Agreement is the direct obligation of you established in favor of our designated beneficiaries. Once established, such credit is irrevocable and is not subject to recall or stop payment, and any claim or demand by us to stop payment thereunder is void and of no effect.

13. The word "property" as used in this Agreement includes goods, merchandise, securities, funds, choses in action, and any and all other forms of property, whether real, personal or mixed and any right or interest therein.

14. This Agreement incorporates the provisions on the reverse hereof. Time is of the essence. Acceptance by you of partial or delinquent payments or your failure to exercise any right, power or remedy shall not waive any obligation of us or modify this Agreement. You, your successors and assigns have all rights, powers and remedies herein and as provided by law, and may exercise the same and effect any set-off and proceed against any security for the obligations of us at any time notwithstanding any cessation of our liability or running of any statute of limitations, which we hereby waive to the fullest extent permitted by law. Notice to you must be given at the office of City National Bank to which this Credit and Agreement is addressed.

15. We hereby agree to pay all reasonable fees and costs incurred by you and arising out of any act or action you may take to enforce any provision of this Agreement or to enforce collection of any sums, payments or obligations owing from us to you.

16. If this Agreement is signed by one individual the terms, "we", "our", "us", shall be read throughout as "I", "my", "me", as the case may be. If this Agreement is signed by two or more parties, it shall be the joint and several Agreement of such parties.

\*

PART II

# PAYMENTS AND CREDITS

CHAPTER 11

# NEGOTIABILITY AND HOLDERS IN DUE COURSE

---

## A. INTRODUCTION

We introduce the materials on payments and credits by a treatment in this chapter of two traditional doctrines unique to negotiable instruments. We will refer to these as the merger doctrine (the instrument reifies the obligation to pay; the holder of the instrument is entitled to payment) and the holder-in-due-course doctrine (the holder of an instrument may take free of claims and defenses on the instrument). As we shall see, the holder-in-due-course doctrine, conceived long ago under different social and economic conditions, has been under attack for years by courts, legislatures and commentators. The policy justification for this harsh doctrine is so questionable that there was debate on whether what now remains of the doctrine should be retained in Revised Article 3. However, under the drafting-by-consensus regime that prevails in the writing of uniform state laws the doctrine was retained. In recent years the merger doctrine has come under criticism for the results it yields in real estate transactions that participants in that field believe are unjust. We will inquire throughout this chapter whether the decision to retain these doctrines in Revised Article 3 was sound. Whatever the merit of these rules, an understanding of them is essential to those planning and executing payment and credit transactions, and we treat them in this chapter. A review of the cases decided under Revised Article 3 shows a surprising number raising holder-in-due-course issues. Since adoption of Revised Articles 3 and 4 has been widespread, citation of the provisions of these articles in the text of the following chapters will not be prefaced by "revised." Citation of the provisions of the pre-revision statutes will be prefaced by "former."

The law of negotiable instruments is based in large part on common law doctrines developed primarily in the last half of the eighteenth century and the first half of the nineteenth century. This law was codified in Great Britain in 1882 in the Bills of Exchange Act and in 1896 in the United States in the Uniform Negotiable Instruments Law, usually referred to as the NIL. In 1952 the American Law Institute and the National Conference of Commissioners on Uniform State Laws promulgated the Uniform Commercial Code. Article 3 of the Code eventually displaced the NIL as the primary statute governing negotiable instruments. Article 4 of the Code complements Article 3 with respect to collection of negotiable instruments by banks and also governs the bank-customer relationship with respect to some matters relating to instruments. In 1990 Revised Article 3 was promulgated to take the place of the original Article 3. At the same time conforming amendments to Articles 1 and 4 were promulgated. Revised Article 3 and the conforming amendments to Articles 1 and 4 have been enacted in all but one state. In 2002 several amendments to these Articles were promulgated. Revised Article 3 is not a radical departure from the earlier statute; the principal concepts of traditional negotiable instruments law have been preserved. But Revised Article 3 differs from former Article 3 with respect to a number of important substantive areas. In addition, no attempt was made to preserve the language of former Article 3. As a result, the drafting style reflected in Revised Article 3 is quite different from that of the previous statute.

We have included a number of cases interpreting Revised Articles 3 and 4, but in those negotiable instruments cases decided under former Article 3 or 4, we include the text of the particular section involved to the extent reference to the statutory language is necessary to understand the point at issue. Revised Article 3 is accompanied by a "Table of Disposition of Sections in Former Article 3" that indicates the section of Revised Article 3 governing the issue addressed by a section of former Article 3. In reading cases reprinted in this book, this table should be consulted because the result reached in the case may be different if the same facts are governed by Revised Article 3.

## B. CONCEPT OF NEGOTIABILITY

## 1. HISTORICAL ORIGIN

Professor Gilmore sketches the background of negotiable instruments law in the following quotation from his article "Formalism and the Law of Negotiable Instruments," 13 Creighton L. Rev. 441, 446–450 (1979):

> Our law of negotiable instruments dates from the late eighteenth century. * * * Lord Mansfield and his colleagues in the late eighteenth century were faced with radically new problems for which they devised radically new solutions.

> The radically new problems all stemmed from the industrial revolution and the vastly increased number of commercial transactions which it spawned. When goods were shipped, they had to be paid for. The idea that the payments could be made in metallic currency, chronically in short supply, was ludicrous. The primitive banking system could not cope with the situation: the bank check which—a hundred years later—became the universal payment device was unknown. In effect the merchants and the bankers invented their own paper currency. The form which they used was an old one: the so-called bill of exchange which was an order issued by one person (the drawer) to a second person (the drawee) directing the drawee to pay a specified sum of money at a specified time to a third person (the holder). Frequently these bills, drawn by sellers on buyers, represented the purchase price of goods sold. In a more sophisticated and somewhat later variant a

mercantile banking house issued what came to be called a letter of credit to a customer. The letter authorized the customer to draw on the bankers for the purchase price of goods which he intended to buy: Through the first half of the nineteenth century Yankees trading out of Boston, armed with their letters of credit which were frequently issued by English houses, roamed the Far East assembling their precious and fabulously profitable cargoes of silks and teas and spices, paying for them with drafts on London. For half a century these bills or drafts were an indispensable supplement to the official currencies and were indeed used as currency: the bills which showed up in litigation had, as the case reports tell us, passed from hand to hand in a long series of transactions. And a draft on a ranking London house was a much safer as well as a much more convenient thing to have than a bag-full of clipped Maria Theresa dollars. These bills moved in a world-wide market, typically ending up in the possession of people who knew nothing about the transaction which had given rise to the bill, had no way of finding out anything about the transaction and, in any case, had not the slightest interest in it.

Against that background, the courts, English and American, put together, in not much more than half a century, the law of negotiable instruments almost exactly as we know it today. Indeed anyone who has mastered the current American formulation of the subject in Article 3 of the Uniform Commercial Code will have a startling sense of *deja vu*—I suppose this is *deja vu* in reverse—if he then goes back to the mid-nineteenth century treatises: time seems to have been suspended, nothing has changed, the late twentieth century law of negotiable instruments is still a law for clipper ships and their exotic cargoes from the Indies. The *deja vu* is false, a sort of floating mirage—but I will return to that later.

In putting together their law of negotiable instruments, the courts assumed that the new mercantile currency was a good thing whose use should be encouraged. Two quite simple ideas became the foundation pieces for the whole structure. One was the good faith purchase idea. The stranger who purchased the bill in the market was entitled to do so without inquiry into the facts of the underlying transaction or of previous transfers of the bill and without being affected by them: if he bought the bill for value, in good faith and in the ordinary course of business, he held it free both of underlying contract defenses and of outstanding equities of ownership. The other idea which, the first time you run into it, sounds like nonsense—the legal mind at its worst—was even more basic to the structure and indeed was what gave the completed edifice its pure and almost unearthly beauty. That was the idea that the piece of paper on which the bill was written or printed should be treated as if it—the piece of paper—was itself the claim or debt which it evidenced. This idea came to be known as the doctrine of merger—the debt was merged in the instrument. At one stroke it drastically simplified the law of negotiable instruments, to the benefit of both purchasers and the people required to pay the instruments.

Under merger theory the only way of transferring the debt represented by the bill was by physical delivery of the bill itself to the transferee. The courts also worked out an elaborate set of rules on when the transferor was required to endorse, as well as deliver, the bill and on what liabilities to subsequent parties he assumed by endorsing. When these formalities—delivery and endorsement—had been accomplished—but not until then—the transfer became a negotiation and the transferee a holder. Only the holder—the person physically in possession of the bill under a proper chain of endorsements—was entitled to demand payment of the bill from the party required to pay it; only payment to such a holder discharged the bill as well as the underlying obligation. Merger theory was also of immense importance from the point of view of the paying party: not only did he know whom he was supposed to pay—the holder—but, under another aspect of the theory, he was entitled to pay (and get his discharge) even if he knew, to state an extreme case, that the holder he paid had acquired the bill by fraud or trickery from a previous holder. Parties with claims adverse to the holder were required to fight their own battles; they could not involve the payor by serving notice on him not to pay.

See also James S. Rogers, The Early History of the Law of Bills and Notes (1995).

A 21st century business or consumer lawyer is wise to consider the doctrine of negotiability to be a legal landmine. In the next two chapters, we will learn how to protect your clients from it. In Grant Gilmore's sketch on the background of negotiability, we learn that it emerged centuries ago as a substitute for money. There surely is no shortage of money in circulation now, but when the law of payments was restated in 1990 in UCC Articles 3 and 4, the ancient doctrine of negotiability survived— limited somewhat but still around. And, as we will see, causing a lot of trouble.

We need a few preliminary working definitions in order to communicate.

A "note," often referred to as a "promissory note," is *promise* to pay another person, a "payee." 3–104(e). This is a two-party transaction. A note is a negotiable instrument if it complies with the requirements of 3–104(a) (unconditional promise to pay money to a bearer or order, etc.).

A "draft" is an *order* by a "drawer" (3–103(a)(5)) to a "drawee" (3–103(a)(4)) to pay a payee. 3–104(e). This is a three-party transaction. A "check" is the most common form of draft. 3–104(f). The person signing the check is the drawer and the bank on which the check is drawn is the drawee.

In most cases, a "holder" is the possessor of an instrument that is either payable to that person or indorsed to that person. But the possessor of a bearer instrument is also a holder. This is a very important definition because we will be dealing with the rights of holders in due course, and a person must be a holder before it can be a holder in due course. 1–201(b)(21).

## 2.  MERGER DOCTRINE

### a.  NEGOTIATION AND TRANSFER

#### (1)  NEGOTIATION

The merger doctrine described by Professor Gilmore determines two important issues: (i) who can enforce the instrument against the obligor, and (ii) whom does the obligor pay to be discharged on the instrument. We discuss the first of these issues in this section on "Negotiation and Transfer," and the second in the next section on "Discharge."

The basic rule on enforcement is stated in 3–301:

"[P]erson entitled to enforce" an instrument means (i) the holder of the instrument, (ii) a nonholder in possession of the instrument who has the rights of a holder, or (iii) a person not in possession of the instrument who is entitled to enforce the instrument pursuant to Section 3–309 [lost instrument] or 3–418(d) [dishonored instrument]. A person may be a person entitled to enforce the instrument even though the person is not the owner of the instrument or is in wrongful possession of the instrument.

This provision implements the merger doctrine as described by Professor Gilmore by stating that, with minor exceptions, the right to enforce an instrument belongs to the holder of the instrument. The following elementary cases illustrate 3–301 and some basic concepts and terminology regarding negotiation and transfer of instruments.

Case #1. John signs a note and delivers it to Rachel. The note reads as follows:

I promise to pay $1,000 on April 1, 2007 to the bearer of this note.

The note is "issued" by John, the "maker," when it is delivered to Rachel. 3–105(a) and 3–103(a)(5). The note is "payable to bearer." 3–109(a). When Rachel receives possession, she becomes the bearer of the note as well as its holder. 1–201(5) and (20). Normally, Rachel is also the owner of the note. But the right of Rachel to receive or enforce payment is based on the fact that Rachel is the holder of the note, not on Rachel's ownership. 3–301.

Suppose Rachel loses the note and it is found by Peter who takes possession of it. By obtaining possession Peter does not become the owner of the note, but he becomes the holder of the note and thereby obtains the right to enforce it. 3–301. The transfer of possession which resulted in Peter's becoming a holder is described in 3–201(a) as "negotiation" of the note. Typically, negotiation is the result of a voluntary transfer of possession, but 3–201(a) applies to any transfer of possession, voluntary or involuntary.

Case #2. John signs a note and delivers it to Rachel. The note reads as follows:

> I promise to pay $1,000 on April 1, 2007 to the order of Rachel.

In this case the note is not payable to bearer. Rather, it is "payable to order" because it is "payable to the order of an identified person." 3–109(b). Upon delivery of the note to Rachel, she becomes its holder because she has possession and she is the person identified in the note as its payee. 1–201(20). In Case #1 we saw that a finder or thief can obtain the right to enforce a note payable to bearer simply by obtaining possession of it. That rule does not apply if an instrument is payable to an identified person. Negotiation of such an instrument also requires transfer of possession, but an indorsement by the holder is necessary as well. 3–201(b). (Note the UCC spelling, or misspelling, of "indorse.") Thus, the note payable to Rachel cannot be negotiated unless she indorses it; no one else can become its holder until then.

Suppose Rachel does not lose the note. Rather, she sells it to Peter for cash and delivers the note to him. In this case no negotiation to Peter occurs unless Rachel indorses the note. Indorsement is defined in 3–204(a) and can be made for several purposes. The most important purpose is to negotiate the instrument. An indorsement is normally made on the reverse side of the instrument and can consist of a signature alone or a signature accompanied by other words. An indorsement by Rachel consisting of her signature preceded by the words "Pay to Peter" identifies a person to whom it makes the note payable and is called a "special indorsement." 3–205(a). An indorsement by Rachel consisting solely of her signature does not identify a person to whom the note is payable and is called a "blank indorsement." 3–205(b). The effect of a blank indorsement is to make the note payable to bearer. 3–205(b) and 3–109(c). If either indorsement is made, Peter becomes the holder when he obtains possession of the note (1–201(20)) and may enforce the note as holder. If Rachel indorses in blank, Peter can negotiate the note to somebody else either by delivery alone or by delivery plus Peter's indorsement. 3–205(b) and 3–109(c). If Rachel indorses specially, Peter must indorse the note in order to negotiate it and may indorse either specially or in blank. 3–205(a).

By way of a reality check, we will see that the fact that a finder or a thief may be the correct person to sue on a note doesn't necessarily mean that this person will recover. If the maker can prove that the instrument was lost or stolen, she has a valid defense under 3–305(c) unless the person suing on the note can prove holder-in-due-course status. 3–302.

## (2) TRANSFER

Although the right to enforce an instrument is normally obtained as a result of negotiation, the right to enforce an instrument can also be obtained in some transactions in which negotiation does not occur. Suppose Rachel delivers the note in Case #2 to Peter without indorsing it. What rights does Peter obtain? Because Rachel's purpose in delivering the note is to give Peter the right to enforce it, Rachel has "transferred" the note to Peter. 3–203(a). Transfer means that there has been a conveyance by the transferor to the transferee of the transferor's right to enforce the instrument. This transfer can occur only by "delivery," a voluntary transfer of possession (1–201(b)(15)), plus an intent by the transferor to give to the transferee the right to enforce. Since the note was not indorsed by Rachel, Peter cannot enforce the note in his own right as holder and cannot negotiate the note to somebody else. But as a result of the transfer from Rachel, Peter obtains Rachel's right as holder to enforce the note. 3–203(b). This result is commonly referred to as the "shelter doctrine." Armed with that right and possession of the note, Peter becomes a person entitled to enforce the note under clause (ii) of the first sentence of 3–301. In addition Peter, as a buyer of the note for value, obtains a specifically enforceable right to have Rachel indorse the note so that Peter can become its holder. 3–203(c).

If, by transfer, Peter acquires Rachel's right as holder to enforce the note, why is it important whether Peter, in enforcing the note, is asserting his own right as holder or a right to enforce derived from Rachel's right as holder? The answer is burden of proof under 3–308, as illustrated in Problem 1 below. Read Comments 2 through 4 to 3–203 as well as 3–308(b) and the first two paragraphs of Comment 2 to 3–308.

### PROBLEMS

**1.** Mark signed a note and delivered it to Patricia for value; she, in turn, delivered it to Teresa for value. The note reads as follows:

I promise to pay $1,000 to the order of Patricia on November 1, 2008.

Mark defaulted on the note and Teresa brought an action to enforce the note against him. In his pleadings Mark did not deny the authenticity of his signature or raise any defense to his liability on the note. Teresa introduced the note into evidence and rested. Mark sought a directed verdict. Is he entitled to one under 3–203, 3–301 and 3–308 if the following facts obtained:

a. When Patricia delivered the note to Teresa she indorsed the instrument?

b. When Patricia delivered the note to Teresa she intended to pass ownership to Teresa but failed to indorse the instrument?

White & Summers, Uniform Commercial Code § 13–4b (burden of proof) (5th ed. 2000).

**2.** Pete fraudulently induced Maria to issue a note to him. The note reads as follows:

I promise to pay $1,000 to the order of Pete on July 1, 2008.

In May 2008 Pete indorsed and delivered the note to Helen who gave value, was in good faith and had no notice of any claims or defenses on the instrument. In June Maria discovered that she had been defrauded, notified Helen of the fraud, and stated her intention to refuse payment of the note. Helen, a busy executive, had no interest in incurring the litigation expenses needed to enforce the note, and, in August 2008, out of sympathy, gave the note, without indorsement, to her former husband, David, now an impecunious law student and desperate for money. She told him the circumstances surrounding the note and said that if he could recover anything on the note he could keep the recovery "for old-time's sake." May David recover on the note from Maria free of her defense of fraud? 3–203(b). What policy is furthered by Article 3 in this case? Comment 2 to 3–203.

## b.   DISCHARGE

A corollary to the merger doctrine that the right to enforce an instrument is the exclusive right of the holder is that the person obliged to pay the instrument discharges the obligation only by paying the holder. Until 2002, Revised Article 3 reflected this corollary in 3–602. The obligor who pays the holder is assured that nobody else can obtain a right to enforce the instrument if the obligor obtains surrender of the instrument from the holder at the time of payment. 3–501(a) and (b)(2). But there is also a corollary to the discharge rule: payment to a person who is not the holder might not result in discharge. This result raised the issue that caused the real property finance industry to vigorously challenge the traditional discharge rule.

## PROBLEM

Debtor bought a home from Seller in part with money that she borrowed from Bank. In order to secure her $100,000 obligation, evidenced by a negotiable promissory note, she granted Bank a mortgage on the property. The agreement was that payments on the note would be made to Bank each month. Bank immediately negotiated the note and assigned the mortgage to Assignee. Neither Bank nor Assignee notified Debtor about the assignment. Bank deliberately withheld notice for the purpose of defrauding Debtor by continuing to receive Debtor's payments after the assignment. After a number of payments were made to Bank, Assignee notified Debtor that she was in default and that unless she cured her default Assignee would initiate foreclosure proceedings. Bank has "suspended payments" (closed) and its owners have absconded. Should Debtor receive credit for the payments made to Bank after it had negotiated the note and assigned the mortgage to Assignee? What result under 3–602(a) before the 2002 amendment? How could Debtor have protected herself in this case? Should she have demanded to see her note each month before making her payment?

The traditional doctrine of former 3–602 that payment had to be made to the holder to achieve discharge was disapproved in Restatement (Third) of Property (Mortgages) § 5.5 (1996). It states:

> § 5.5   Effect of Performance to the Transferor After Transfer of an Obligation Secured by a Mortgage
>
> [A]fter transfer of an obligation secured by a mortgage, performance of the obligation to the transferor is effective against the transferee if rendered before the obligor receives notice of the transfer.

The effect of former 3–602 was to impose the burden on the mortgagor to be sure that payments go to the note holder or its agent. This may be appropriate in commercial cases, but the Restatement view has much to commend it in cases involving mortgages on residential real estate. In these cases, as the Restatement commentary points out, it is unrealistic to require that consumer mortgagors ascertain the identity of the holder of their notes, either in the case of periodic payments or even for the final payment, given the practice in the industry of notifying the mortgagor at the time of payoff that the note and mortgage will be returned a month or six weeks later. Imposing the burden on the transferee of the mortgage note to notify the mortgagor of the transfer in these cases seems fair.

Virtually all real estate mortgage notes are immediately assigned by the loan originator (a bank, savings and loan association, or the like) and eventually are securitized. That is, an entity pools large numbers of mortgage notes and issues bonds secured by the mortgage receivables, i.e., the rights to future payments. The proceeds of the bond issue are then used to buy more mortgages. Fanny Mae (Federal National Mortgage Association) and Freddie Mac (Federal Home Loan Mortgage Corporation), among others, are in the business of arranging for pooling of mortgages. So, you might expect that the issue raised in the Problem is an important one. Actually, the issue hasn't caused much trouble. First, the real property finance industry is scrupulously careful to see that the mortgagor is notified of any assignment; assignees have great incentive to make sure that they receive their payments. Second, the loan originator usually becomes the agent of the assignee to "service" the loan, that is collect the payments and remit them to the assignee. In the Problem, Bank would usually be Assignee's agent and any payments made to Bank would be treated as though they had gone to Assignee. Nevertheless, in cases that fall outside the standard institutional loan transactions, litigation does arise, e.g., Aquaduct, L.L.C. v. McElhenie, 116 S.W.3d 438 (Tex. App. 2003); Lambert v. Barker, 348 S.E.2d 214 (Va. 1986).

After a decade of debate, the Permanent Editorial Board, charged with oversight of the UCC, promulgated in 2002 an amended version of 3–602, set out below, which revokes the traditional rule that only payments to a holder discharge instruments. This change is a broad rejection of the discharge rule that prevailed for hundreds of years: it is not restricted to real estate, and applies to commercial as well as consumer transactions.

Section 3–602.

(a) Subject to subsection (e), an instrument is paid to the extent payment is made by or on behalf of a party obliged to pay the instrument, and to a person entitled to enforce the instrument.

(b) Subject to subsection (e), a note is paid to the extent payment is made by or on behalf of a party obliged to pay the note to a person that formerly was entitled to enforce the note only if at the time of the payment the party obliged to pay has not received adequate notification that the note has been transferred and that the payment is to be made to the transferee. A notification is adequate only if it is signed by the transferor or the transferee; reasonably identifies the transferred note; and provides an address at which payments subsequently are to be made. Upon request, a transferee shall seasonably furnish reasonable proof that the note has been transferred. Unless the transferee complies with the request, a payment to the person that formerly was entitled to enforce the note is effective for purposes of subsection (c) even if the party obliged to pay the note has received a notification under this paragraph.

(c) Subject to subsection (e), to the extent of payment under subsections (a) and (b), the obligation of the party obliged to pay the instrument is discharged even though payment is made with knowledge of a claim to the instrument under Section 3–306 by another person.

(d) Subject to subsection (e), a transferee, or any party that has acquired rights in the instrument directly or indirectly from a transferee, including any such party that has rights as a holder in due course, is deemed to have notice of any payment that is made under subsection (b) after the date that the note is transferred to the transferee but before the party obliged to pay the note receives adequate notification of the transfer.

The traditional rule worked well if the transferor and transferee were honest parties. When they were not, obligors, particularly consumer obligors could be damaged. Does the new rule adequately protect obligors against dishonest parties? See the Problem below.

## PROBLEM

Maker issued a note payable to the order of Payee, which Payee indorsed and delivered to Transferee. The note was payable in 60 monthly installments.

(a) Neither Payee nor Transferee notified Maker of the transfer and Maker made six payments to Payee after the transfer before discovering that Payee no longer held the note. Must Transferee credit Maker for the amount of the six payments made to Payee? If so, is Payee liable to Transferee for the payments under this statute?

(b) Payee did not notify Maker of the transfer but Transferee gave adequate notification to Maker. Maker, a financially unsophisticated person, was not familiar with Transferee, and, since she had heard nothing from Payee, was suspicious about sending any money to Transferee. Maker first phoned, then wrote Payee asking what she should do. Payee, a crook, told Maker to continue making payments to it because it was Transferee's agent for collection. Must Transferee credit Maker for the payments made to Payee after its notice to Maker?

## 3. HOLDER IN DUE COURSE: FREEDOM FROM CLAIMS AND DEFENSES

The most dramatic aspect of negotiability is the holder-in-due-course rule. The Restatement (Second) of Contracts § 336(1) (1981) provides that the assignment of a contract gives the assignee rights against the obligor "only to the extent that the obligor is under a duty to the assignor." And § 336(2) provides that the right of an assignee is subject to any defense or claim that the obligor had against the assignor. In other words, when the obligee of an ordinary contract assigns the contract, assignee gets only the rights of the obligee. Why has a different rule prevailed for negotiable instruments for centuries? Under Article 3, a holder in due course (3–302) takes free of some defenses of the obligor (3–305(b)) as well as claims of ownership (3–306). As a counselor, you cannot assume that either your business or consumer clients understand what a negotiable instrument is, much less how much trouble they can get into by becoming a party to one in any of several different capacities. The holder-in-due-course rule is counter-intuitive and difficult to justify to an irate client that has been victimized by it. We see it in action in a contemporary setting in the following Problem.

### PROBLEM

Mark is one of 20 limited partners of a limited partnership (LP) in which Parker is the general partner. At the inception of the partnership, each limited partner contributed $100,000 in cash and gave Parker a negotiable promissory note for another $50,000, payable on demand. The understanding was that Parker would hold these notes until LP needed more funds and then would request each limited partner to contribute $50,000 more. Upon receipt of the money from each partner, Parker would return the note to the partner. The notes were made payable to the order of LP, and Parker had express authority to receive and indorse all instruments made payable to the LP. Without informing the limited partners of his intentions, which were entirely fraudulent, Parker indorsed the notes of all the limited partners to Bank and delivered them to Bank, which knew nothing of Parker's fraud and purchased the notes for 85% of the face value of each note. Parker took the money and ran. When Bank demands payment of his note, Mark heatedly informed Bank that Parker had no authority to do what he did and that Bank was at fault in dealing with a crook, therefore Bank should take the loss. Bank disagreed, explaining that before it bought the notes it had diligently inquired into the creditworthiness of the general and limited partners.

(a) On which party does the UCC impose the loss, Mark or Bank? What is the policy basis for this result? Why wouldn't the rules of Restatement § 336(1) and (2) serve as well in this case?

(b) How does Mark discover whether he is dealing with a negotiable note? See 3–104(a) (formalities). If by any chance you didn't know about these formal requirements before you took this course, why is Mark expected to know about them under the UCC? Should negotiable instruments bear legends warning of the consequences of negotiability? See our discussion of formalities later.

_____

We will first examine the claims and defenses that holders in due course take free of, and then we will go into detail on the issue of who qualifies as a holder in due course.

## a.   CLAIMS OF OWNERSHIP

Lord Mansfield created the doctrine that a good faith purchaser for value takes better rights than its assignor in two seminal 18th century cases involving claims of ownership: Miller v. Race, 1 Burr. 452, 97 Eng. Rep. 398 (K.B. 1758), and Rhodes v. Peacock, 99 Eng. Rep. 402 (1781). In the latter case, he said: "The holder of a bill of exchange [a draft], or promissory note, is not to be considered in the light of an assignee of the payee. An assignee must take the thing assigned, subject to all the equity to which the original party was subject. If this rule applied to bills and promissory notes, it would stop their currency. The law is settled, that a holder, coming fairly by a bill or note has nothing to do with the transaction between the original parties * * *." The doctrine was later applied to defenses.

Lord Mansfield's doctrine on claims of ownership is found in 3–306. Defenses and claims of recoupment arise between the original parties to the instrument, e.g., between the maker of a note and the payee. Claims of ownership arise between the owner of the instrument and subsequent transferees, e.g., between the payee and a subsequent takers of the instrument. The Comment to 3–306 construes "claims" broadly, so that claims to the instrument includes a lien or a possessory right in it. Thus, 3–306's rule applies to these interests in the instrument as well.

## PROBLEM

In October 2006, for valuable consideration, Maurice made and delivered a negotiable promissory note to Patricia for $25,000, payable in annual installments of $5,000, at 10% interest. The first payment was due in October 2007. Patricia, a member of the Ohio National Guard, was called for active duty in January 2007, and requested that Alice, a family friend, hold the note and collect the payments until Patricia returned from abroad. In order to allow Alice to make the collections, Patricia indorsed the note to Alice by writing "Pay to Alice" on the back of the note. Alice was down on her luck and, in breach of her agreement with Patricia, wrongfully indorsed and delivered the note to Harry in February 2007, who paid 85% of the face amount of the note to Alice. When Patricia returned from duty in 2008, she learned of Alice's wrongdoing, and sued Harry to retake possession of the note and to recover the $5,000 payment that Harry had collected from Maurice in October 2006. If Harry is a holder in due course, does he take free of Patricia's claim of ownership with respect to the note? With respect to the $5,000? See 3–306 and its Comment.

### b.   ORDINARY DEFENSES

The extent to which a holder takes free of defenses is governed by 3–305(a) and (b). Subsection (a) states that the right to enforce an instrument is subject to defenses described in paragraphs (1) and (2) of that subsection and claims in recoupment described in paragraph (3). Subsection (b) of 3–305 is a limitation on subsection (a). The right of a holder in due course to enforce an instrument is subject to the defenses stated in subsection (a)(1)—the so-called "real defenses"—but is not subject to the "ordinary" defenses stated in subsection (a)(2) or claims in recoupment described in subsection (a)(3).

Section 3–305(a)(2) refers to defenses that are specifically stated in other sections of Article 3. Those defenses and the sections in which they are found are listed in the first paragraph of Comment 2 to 3–305. Subsection (a)(2) also refers to the common law defenses applicable to simple contracts which are not enumerated. The principal common law defenses are fraud, misrepresentation, and mistake in the issuance of the instrument.

### c.   REAL DEFENSES

Section 3–305(a)(1) lists the defenses that may be asserted against even a holder in due course. These defenses are discussed in Comment 1 to 3–305. With the exception of the defense of discharge in bankruptcy, all of the real defenses refer to an instrument that is made unenforceable in order to carry out some public policy of the state not related to the law of negotiable instruments (illegality), or to an instrument that does not represent a contract of the person who signed the instrument (infancy, duress, fraud in the factum).

### d.   CLAIMS IN RECOUPMENT

Restatement (Second) of Contracts § 336(2) (1981) states: "The right of an assignee is subject to any defense or claim of the obligor which accrues before the obligor receives notification of the assignment, but not to defenses or claims which accrue thereafter * * *." Suppose A promises to pay $1,000 to B in return for a promise by B to deliver goods to A. B assigns to C the right of B to receive $1,000 from A. A receives no notification of the assignment. If A's promise to pay B was induced by B's fraud or if B failed to deliver the goods as promised, A has a defense to the obligation to pay B. The defense can be asserted against C, the assignee. Change the facts. Suppose there was no fraud by B and B tendered the goods to A, who accepted them. A has no defense to the obligation to pay for the goods. But suppose A has a claim against B to receive $600. If C demands payment of $1,000 from A, A can assert the $600 claim as a reduction of the amount owing to C from $1,000 to $400.

If A's promise to pay is a negotiable instrument and the instrument is negotiated to C, 3–305 rather than the Restatement governs the rights of A and C. Subsection (a)(2) of 3–305 applies to the defense of fraud or failure to deliver the goods. Subsection (a)(3) applies to A's $600 claim against B if A's claim arose from the transaction that gave rise to the instrument and is therefore a claim in recoupment. Furthermore, the rights of C depend upon whether C is a holder in due course. 3–305(b). Claims in recoupment are discussed in Comment 3 to 3–305.

### PROBLEM

Merchant sold and delivered goods to Plumber who accepted them and, as payment of the price, delivered to Merchant a negotiable note of Plumber to pay $10,000 to the order of Merchant. The note was payable one year after the date it was issued. Merchant immediately negotiated the note to Finance Co. A month after the sale and delivery of the goods by Merchant, Plumber, at the request of Merchant, repaired and replaced water pipes and plumbing fixtures at Merchant's place of business. Plumber's bill for this work was $8,000. When Plumber's note became due, Finance Co. demanded payment. Plumber refused to pay for the following reasons: (1) Merchant had not paid the $8,000 owed for the work performed by Plumber; (2) some of the goods sold by Merchant to Plumber were defective and, as a result of the defects, Plumber incurred losses of over $4,000. How much is Finance Co. entitled to recover from Plumber if Finance Co. is a holder in due course? How much is Finance Co. entitled to recover if Finance Co. is not a holder in due course?

## C.   FORMAL REQUISITES OF NEGOTIABLE INSTRUMENTS

The consequences of the use of negotiable instruments vary greatly from those of ordinary contracts. What kinds of contracts qualify for the special treatment accorded negotiable instruments? Under Article 3, as under the common law, form follows function.

Merger theory and the ability of a good faith purchaser for value to take free of claims and defenses with respect to the instrument were based on a separation of the right to payment represented by the instrument from the underlying transaction giving rise to the instrument. But merger theory assumed that the terms of the instrument were not inconsistent with separation from the underlying transaction, and that the terms of the right to receive payment could be determined simply by examination of the instrument itself. Thus, the consequences of negotiability were applied by the common law courts only if the instrument met certain criteria that satisfied these assumptions. The definition of negotiable instrument is found in Article 3 in 3–104(a), and this definition differs only slightly from the requisites for negotiability stated in the NIL and the original Article 3.

The definition of "negotiable instrument" in 3–104 defines the scope of Article 3. 3–102(a). The most important elements of that definition can be briefly described. Only an "order" or "promise" can qualify as a negotiable instrument. "Order" is defined in 3–103(a)(6) as a written instruction to pay money signed by the person giving the instruction. "Promise" is defined in 3–103(a)(9) as a written undertaking to pay money signed by the person undertaking to pay. Thus, a negotiable instrument is always a signed writing that promises or orders payment of money. Negotiable instruments fall into two categories: drafts and notes. An instrument is a draft if it is an order and is a note if it is a promise. 3–104(e). Checks are the most common examples of drafts. 3–104(f). Certificates of deposit are considered to be notes. 3–104(j). Representative simple Note Forms are set out at the end of this chapter. More complex Forms are found in the Appendix.

Because the rules applicable to negotiable instruments and the rules applicable to ordinary contracts can produce dramatically different results in some cases, it is imperative that both the person issuing a promise or order to pay money and the person to whom the promise or order is issued be able to know in advance whether Article 3 or ordinary contract law will apply. The various requirements of 3–104(a) are designed to provide mechanical tests to allow that determination to be made. One particularly important requirement is that the order or promise be "payable to bearer or to order," a term explained in 3–109. Thus, a technical and wholly formal distinction is made between a promise to pay "to John Doe" and a promise to pay "to the order of John Doe." The second promise may be a negotiable instrument if it otherwise qualifies under 3–104. The first promise cannot be a negotiable instrument. Because of this distinction, the issuer of a promissory note payable to an identified person can easily avoid the consequences of negotiability by avoiding use of the words of negotiability: "to order" or "to bearer," sometimes called the "magic words." Another device for avoiding the effects of Article 3 is provided by 3–104(d). These devices for excluding an order or promise from Article 3 are discussed in Comments 2 and 3 to 3–104.

Three of the requisites of a negotiable instrument relate to the certainty of the obligation to pay. First, the order or promise to pay must be "unconditional," a term explained in 3–106. An examination of that provision discloses that some promises or orders that are in fact conditional are deemed to be unconditional while others that are in fact unconditional are deemed to be conditional for the purposes of 3–104(a). The Comment to 3–106 is a guide to the rather arbitrary distinctions and refinements of 3–106. Second, the order or promise must be payable on demand or at a definite time, a requirement explained in 3–108. Third, the order or promise must be to pay a "fixed amount of money, with or without interest or other charges described in the promise or order." 3–104(a). The quoted language differs from 3–104(1)(b) of the original Article 3, which used the phrase "sum certain in money." *Taylor v. Roeder*, which follows, discusses the problem of variable interest rates under the original Article 3. It is fair to say that this case and several others like it shook the real property finance world. How is this issue resolved under Revised Article 3? 3–112(b).

# Taylor v. Roeder

Supreme Court of Virginia, 1987.
234 Va. 99, 360 S.E.2d 191.

■ RUSSELL, JUSTICE.

The dispositive question in this case is whether a note providing for a variable rate of interest, not ascertainable from the face of the note, is a negotiable instrument. We conclude that it is not.

The facts are undisputed. VMC Mortgage Company (VMC) was a mortgage lender in Northern Virginia. In the conduct of its business, it borrowed funds from investors, pledging as security the notes secured by deeds of trust which it had obtained from its borrowers. Two of these transactions became the subject of this suit. Because they involve similar facts and the same question of law, they were consolidated for trial below and are consolidated in a single record here * * *.

In the first case, Olde Towne Investment Corporation of Virginia, Inc., on September 11, 1979, borrowed $18,000 from VMC, evidenced by a 60–day note secured by a deed of trust on land in Fairfax County. The note provided for interest at "[t]hree percent (3.00%) over Chase Manhattan Prime to be adjusted monthly." The note provided for renewal "at the same rate of interest at the option of the makers up to a maximum of six (6) months in sixty (60) day increments with the payment of an additional fee of [t]wo (2) points." The note was renewed and extended to November 11, 1980, by a written extension agreement signed by Olde Towne and by VMC.

In May 1981, Frederick R. Taylor, Jr., as trustee for himself and other parties, entered into a contract to buy from Olde Towne the land in Fairfax County securing the $18,000 loan. Taylor's title examination revealed the VMC deed of trust. He requested the payoff figures from VMC and forwarded to VMC the funds VMC said were due. He never received the cancelled Olde Towne note, and the deed of trust was not released.

In the second case, Richard L. Saslaw and others, on December 31, 1979, borrowed $22,450 from VMC evidenced by a 12–month note secured by deed of trust on Fairfax County land. This note also bore interest at

"3% over Chase Manhattan prime adjusted monthly." Interest was to be "payable quarterly beginning April 1, 1980." In November 1980, Virender and Barbara Puri entered into a contract to purchase from Saslaw, et al., the land subject to the last-mentioned deed of trust. The Puris designated the same Frederick R. Taylor, Jr., as their settlement attorney. Taylor's title examination revealed VMC's deed of trust. Taylor again requested a payoff figure from VMC. At settlement, Saslaw objected to the figure, communicated with VMC and received VMC's agreement to an adjusted figure. Taylor paid the adjusted amount to VMC. Again, Taylor failed to receive the cancelled Saslaw note, and the Saslaw deed of trust was not released.

Cecil Pruitt, Jr., was a trustee of a tax-exempt employees' pension fund. He invested some of the pension fund's assets with VMC, receiving as collateral pledges of certain secured notes that VMC held. The Saslaw note was pledged and delivered to him on January 25, 1980; the Olde Towne note was pledged and delivered to him on September 12, 1980. No notice was given to the makers, or to Taylor, that the notes had been transferred, and all payments on both notes were made to and accepted by VMC.

VMC received and deposited in its account sufficient funds to pay both notes in full, but never informed Pruitt of the payments and made no request of him for return of the original notes. In February 1982, VMC defaulted on its obligation to Pruitt for which both notes had been pledged as collateral. In May 1982, VMC filed a bankruptcy petition in federal court.

Learning that the properties securing both notes had been sold, Pruitt demanded payment from the respective original makers as well as the new owners of the properties, contending that he was a holder in due course. The makers and new owners took the position that they had paid the notes in full. Pruitt caused William F. Roeder, Jr., to qualify as substituted trustee under both deeds of trust and directed him to foreclose them. Taylor and the Puris filed separate bills of complaint against Roeder, trustee, seeking to enjoin the foreclosure sales. The chancellor entered a temporary injunction to preserve the *status quo* and heard the consolidated cases *ore tenus*. By letter opinion incorporated into a final decree entered February 3, 1984, the chancellor found for the defendant and dissolved the injunctions. We granted the complainants an appeal. The parties have agreed on the record that foreclosure will be withheld while the case is pending in this Court.

Under the general law of contracts, if an obligor has received no notice that his debt has been assigned and is in fact unaware of the assignment, he may, with impunity, pay his original creditor and thus extinguish the obligation. His payment will be a complete defense against the claim of an assignee who failed to give him notice of the assignment. * * *

Under the law of negotiable instruments, continued in effect under the Uniform Commercial Code, the rule is different: the makers are bound by their contract to make payment to the *holder*. * * * Further, a holder in due course takes the instrument free from the maker's defense that he has made payment to the original payee, if he lacks notice of the payment and has not dealt with the maker. UCC § 3–305. Thus, the question whether the notes in this case were negotiable is crucial.

UCC § 3–104(1) provides, in pertinent part:

Any writing to be a negotiable instrument within this title must . . .

    (b) contain an unconditional promise or order to pay a sum certain in money. . . .

The meaning of "sum certain" is clarified by UCC § 3–106:

    (1) The sum payable is a sum certain even though it is to be paid

        (a) with stated interest or by stated installments; or

        (b) with stated different rates of interest before and after default or a specified date; or

        (c) with a stated discount or addition if paid before or after the date fixed for payment; or

        (d) with exchange or less exchange, whether at a fixed rate or at the current rate; or

        (e) with costs of collection or an attorney's fee or both upon default.

    (2) Nothing in this section shall validate any term which is otherwise illegal.

Official Comment 1, which follows, states in part:

It is sufficient [to establish negotiability] that at any time of payment the holder is able to determine the amount then payable *from the instrument itself* with any necessary computation. . . . The computation must be one which can be made *from the instrument itself without reference to any outside source*, and this section does not make negotiable a note payable with interest "at the current rate."

(Emphasis added.) UCC § 3–107 provides an explicit exception to the "four corners" rule laid down above by providing for the negotiability of instruments payable in foreign currency.

We conclude that the drafters of the Uniform Commercial Code adopted criteria of negotiability intended to exclude an instrument which requires reference to any source outside the instrument itself in order to ascertain the amount due, subject only to the exceptions specifically provided for by the U.C.C. * * *

The appellee points to the Official Comment to UCC § 3–104. Comment 1 states that by providing criteria for negotiability "within this Article," * * * "leaves open the possibility that some writings may be made negotiable by other statutes or by judicial decision." The Comment continues: "The same is true as to any new type of paper which commercial practice may develop in the future." The appellee urges us to create, by judicial decision, just such an exception in favor of variable-interest notes.

Appellants concede that variable-interest loans have become a familiar device in the mortgage lending industry. Their popularity arose when lending institutions, committed to long-term loans at fixed rates of interest to their borrowers, were in turn required to borrow short-term funds at high rates during periods of rapid inflation. Variable rates protected lenders when rates rose and benefitted borrowers when rates declined. They suffer, however, from the disadvantage that the amount required to satisfy the debt cannot be ascertained without reference to an extrinsic source—in this case the varying prime rate charged by the Chase Manhattan Bank. Although that rate may readily be ascertained from published sources, it cannot be found within the "four corners" of the note.

Other courts confronted with similar questions have reached differing results. See, e.g., A. Alport & Son, Inc. v. Hotel Evans, Inc., 65 Misc.2d 374, 376–77, 317 N.Y.S.2d 937, 939–40 (1970) (note bearing interest at "bank rates" not negotiable under U.C.C.); Woodhouse, Drake and Carey, Ltd. v. Anderson, 61 Misc.2d 951, 307 N.Y.S.2d 113 (1970) (note providing for interest at "8½% or at the maximum legal rate" was not usurious. Inferentially, the note was negotiable.); Farmers Production Credit Ass'n v. Arena, 145 Vt. 20, 23, 481 A.2d 1064, 1065 (1984) (variable-interest note not negotiable under U.C.C.).

The U.C.C. introduced a degree of clarity into the law of commercial transactions which permits it to be applied by laymen daily to countless transactions without resort to judicial interpretation. The relative predictability of results made possible by that clarity constitutes the overriding benefit arising from its adoption. In our view, that factor makes it imperative that when change is thought desirable, the change should be made by statutory amendment, not through litigation and judicial interpretation. Accordingly, we decline the appellee's invitation to create an exception, by judicial interpretation, in favor of instruments providing for a variable rate of interest not ascertainable from the instrument itself.

In an alternative argument, the appellee contends that even if the notes are not negotiable, they are nevertheless "symbolic instruments" which ought to be paid according to their express terms. Those terms include the maker's promises to pay "to VMC Mortgage Company *or order*," and in the event of default, to make accelerated payment "at the option of the *holder*." The emphasized language, appellee contends, makes clear that the makers undertook an obligation to pay any party who held the notes as a result of a transfer from VMC. Assuming the abstract correctness of that argument, it does not follow that the makers undertook the further obligation of making a monthly canvass of all inhabitants of the earth in order to ascertain who the holder might be. In the absence of notice to the makers that their debt had been assigned, they were entitled to the protection of the rule in *Evans v. Joyner* in making good-faith payment to the original payee of these non-negotiable notes.

Accordingly, we will reverse the decree and remand the cause to the trial court for entry of a permanent injunction against foreclosure.

■ COMPTON, JUSTICE, dissenting.

The majority views the Uniform Commercial Code as inflexible, requiring legislative action to adapt to changing commercial practices. This overlooks a basic purpose of the Code, flexibility and adaptability of construction to meet developing commercial usage.

According to § 1–102(1), the UCC "shall be liberally construed and applied to promote its underlying purposes and policies." One of such underlying purposes and policies is "to permit the continued expansion of commercial practices through custom, usage and agreement of the parties." § 1–102(2)(b). Comment 1 to this section sets out clearly the intention of the drafters:

> "This Act is drawn to provide flexibility so that, since it is intended to be a semi-permanent piece of legislation, it will provide its own machinery for expansion of commercial practices. *It is intended to make it possible for the law embodied in this Act to be developed by the courts in light of unforeseen and new circumstances and practices.* However, the proper construction of the Act requires that its interpretation and application be limited to its reason." (Emphasis added).

The majority's rigid interpretation defeats the purpose of the Code. Nowhere in the UCC is "sum certain" defined. This absence must be interpreted in light of the expectation that commercial law continue to evolve. The § 3–106 exceptions could not have been intended as the exclusive list of "safe harbors," as the drafters anticipated "unforeseen" changes in commercial practices. Instead, those exceptions represented, at the time of drafting, recognized conditions of payment which did not impair negotiability in the judgment of businessmen. To limit exceptions to those existing at that time would frustrate the "continued expansion of commercial practices" by freezing the Code in time and requiring additional legislation whenever "unforeseen and new circumstances and practices" evolve, regardless of "custom, usage, and agreement of the parties."

> "The rule requiring certainty in commercial paper was a rule of commerce before it was a rule of law. It requires commercial, not mathematical, certainty. An uncertainty which does not impair the function of negotiable instruments in the judgment of business men ought not to be regarded by the courts.... The whole question is, do [the provisions] render the instruments so uncertain as to destroy their fitness to pass current in the business world?" *Cudahy Packing Co. v. State National Bank of St. Louis*, 134 F. 538, 542, 545 (8th Cir.1904).

Instruments providing that loan interest may be adjusted over the life of the loan routinely pass with increasing frequency in this state and many others as negotiable instruments. This Court should recognize this custom and usage, as the commercial market has, and hold these instruments to be negotiable.

The majority focuses on the requirement found in Comment 1 to § 3–106 that a negotiable instrument be self-contained, understood without reference to an outside source. Our cases have interpreted this to mean that reference to terms in another agreement which materially affect the instrument renders it nonnegotiable. See, e.g., McLean Bank v. Nelson, Adm'r, 232 Va. 420, 350 S.E.2d 651 (1986) (where note was accepted "pursuant" to a separate agreement, reference considered surplusage and the note negotiable); Salomonsky v. Kelly, 232 Va. 261, 349 S.E.2d 358 (1986) (where principal sum payable "as set forth" in a separate agreement, all the essential terms did not appear on the face of the instrument and the note was nonnegotiable).

The commercial market requires a self-contained instrument for negotiability so that a stranger to the original transaction will be fully apprised of its terms and will not be disadvantaged by terms not ascertainable from the instrument itself. For example, interest payable at the "current rate" leaves a holder subject to claims that the current rate was established by one bank rather than another and would disadvantage a stranger to the original transaction.

The rate which is stated in the notes in this case, however, does not similarly disadvantage a stranger to the original agreement. Anyone coming into possession could immediately ascertain the terms of the notes; interest payable at three percent above the prime rate established by the Chase Manhattan Bank of New York City. This is a third-party objective standard which is recognized as such by the commercial market. The rate can be determined by a telephone call to the bank or from published lists obtained on request. * * *

Accordingly, I believe these notes are negotiable under the Code and I would affirm the decision below.

NOTES

**1.** See 3–104(a), 3–112(b) and Comment 1 to 3–112.

**2.** Since the scope of Article 3 (3–102(a)) is determined by the definition of negotiable instrument in 3–104, it is not surprising that this definition was the subject of a great deal of debate in the revision of Article 3. There were a number of proposals either to restrict or enlarge the kinds of instruments to which the harsh doctrine of negotiability would apply by changes in the definition of negotiable instrument. At one extreme was the view that the concept of negotiability was no longer needed; let the parties contract for whatever terms they can agree on for credit and payment instruments. A recurring suggestion for reform was to discard the "magic words"—"order" and "bearer"—as prerequisites of negotiability. Then too, a number of proposals were made to junk the traditional formal requirements of negotiability in favor of a functional test along the lines of that suggested in Fred H. Miller and Alvin C. Harrell, The Law of Modern Payment Systems 2.01, at [2][c] (2003):

(1) Any writing to be a negotiable instrument within this article must be

(a) signed by the maker or drawer;

(b) for the payment, or evidence a right to the payment, of money; and

(c) of a type which in the ordinary course of business is transferred by delivery with any necessary endorsement or assignment.

This is similar to the definition of "instrument" in 9–102(a)(47).

After five years of discussion, the Drafting Committee decided to retain the traditional, somewhat mechanical tests similar to those developed at common law and codified in both the NIL and the 1962 version of Article 3. The strongest reason for this was the elusive quest for a "bright line." Comment 2 to 3–104 explains:

> Total exclusion from Article 3 of other promises or orders that are not payable to bearer or order serves a useful purpose. It provides a simple device to clearly exclude a writing that does not fit the pattern of typical negotiable instruments and which is not intended to be a negotiable instrument. If a writing could be an instrument despite the absence of "to order" or "to bearer" language and a dispute arises with respect to the writing, it might be argued that the writing is a negotiable instrument because the other requirements of subsection (a) are somehow met. Even if the argument is eventually found to be without merit it can be used as a litigation ploy. Words making a promise or order payable to bearer or to order are the most distinguishing feature of a negotiable instrument and such words are frequently referred to as "words of negotiability." Article 3 is not meant to apply to contracts for the sale of goods or services or the sale or lease of real property or similar writings that may contain a promise to pay money. The use of words of negotiability in such contracts would be an aberration. Absence of the words precludes any argument that such contracts might be negotiable instruments.

**3.** Why then is a check that says "Pay to Payee" a negotiable instrument under 3–104(c) while a promissory note with this language is not? The reason for this distinction is that, as we shall see, banks deal with the billions of checks issued each year almost entirely on an automated basis. They pay checks drawn on them largely on the basis of machine-readable information encoded on the bottom of the check. Virtually all checks are printed with the words "Pay to the order of." If a drawer scratches out the word "order," the depositary and drawee banks have no feasible way of detecting that they are taking a nonnegotiable instrument. Section 3–104(c) largely relieves them of the burden of having to look at the face of each check to know whether it is negotiable. Comment 2 to 3–104.

**4.** The justification for retaining the "words of negotiability"—"bearer" or "order"—stated in Note 2 is that they describe a bright line test for negotiability. Certainly most creditors know what these words mean, but is this true of most debtors? There is nothing about this 18th century formalism that would indicate to an unsophisticated debtor that its inclusion means a debtor who is defrauded by a payee is, nevertheless, liable to a good faith purchaser of the instrument. This is a harsh consequence to visit upon a debtor who has no way of learning what these words mean short of consulting a lawyer. During the Drafting Committee discussions, a strong view was pressed that if the doctrine of negotiability was to be retained (and not all were in favor of doing so), then any note that purported to be negotiable should bear a legend warning of the consequences of negotiability. Such a provision was carried in a number of drafts until late in the drafting process. When it was finally dropped in the last year of the project, the justification for doing so was that business debtors should be held to know what business documents mean and, as we shall see, the doctrine of negotiability has been severely circumscribed in consumer transactions.

## D. REQUIREMENTS FOR HOLDER IN DUE COURSE

Section 3–302. Holder in Due Course

(a) * * * "[H]older in due course" means the holder of an instrument if:

(1) the instrument when issued or negotiated to the holder does not bear such apparent evidence of forgery or alteration or is not otherwise so irregular or incomplete as to call into question its authenticity; and

(2) the holder took the instrument (i) for value, (ii) in good faith, (iii) without notice that the instrument is overdue or has been dishonored or that there is an uncured default with respect to payment of another instrument issued as part of the same series, (iv) without notice that the instrument contains an unauthorized signature or has been altered, (v) without notice of any claim to the instrument described in Section 3–306, and (vi) without notice that any party has a defense or claim in recoupment described in Section 3–305(a).

## 1. GOOD FAITH AND NOTICE

To qualify as a holder in due course under 3–302 a holder must, among other requirements, have taken the instrument in good faith and without notice of any defense against or claim to it on the part of any person. The meaning of good faith as applied to negotiable instruments has varied over the years. The definition of "good faith" in former Article 3 was purely subjective: "honesty in fact." In Revised Article 3, the definition was changed to "honesty in fact and observance of reasonable commercial standards of fair dealing." This definition is now found in 1–201(b)(20) and applies to all Articles except Article 5. There is no definition of "fair dealing." Section 3–302(a)(2) continues the previous Article 3 requirement that the instrument be taken both in good faith and without notice of claims or defenses. "Notice" is defined in 1–202(a):

(a) * * * [A] person has "notice" of a fact if the person

(1) has actual knowledge of it:

(2) has received a notice or notification of it; or

(3) from all the facts and circumstances known to the person at the time in question, has reason to know that it exists.

Clearly, there are aspects of both subjectivity and objectivity in the standards Article 3 requires for holder-in-due-course status. We include two opinions in this section. The first, *Kaw Valley*, decided under the former statute, is one of the few decisions in which a court discusses the difference between good faith and notice. It involves a very common transaction, inventory financing. The second, *Maine Family Federal*, is one of the first cases to consider the meaning of "fair dealing" in the amended definition of good faith in Revised Article 3. It is a much discussed opinion.

## Kaw Valley State Bank & Trust Co. v. Riddle

Supreme Court of Kansas, 1976.
549 P.2d 927.

■ FROMME, JUSTICE.

This action was brought by The Kaw Valley State Bank and Trust Company (hereinafter referred to as Kaw Valley) to recover judgment against John H. Riddle d/b/a Riddle Contracting Company (hereafter referred to as Riddle) on two notes and to determine the priority of conflicting security agreements. The two notes were covered by separate security agreements and were given to purchase construction equipment. The Planters State Bank and Trust Company (hereinafter referred to as Planters) held a note and security interest on the same and other construction equipment acquired by Riddle. Kaw Valley had acquired the two notes and the security agreements by assignment from Co–Mac, Inc. (hereinafter referred to as Co–Mac), a dealer, from whom Riddle purchased the construction equipment.

In a trial to the court Kaw Valley was found not to be a holder in due course of one of the notes. Its claim on said note, totaling $21,904.64, was successfully defended on the grounds of failure of consideration. It was stipulated at the trial that none of the construction equipment for which the note was given had ever been delivered by Co–Mac. Kaw Valley has appealed.

\* \* \*

Prior to the transactions in question Riddle had purchased construction equipment and machinery from the dealer, Co–Mac. A number of these purchases had been on credit and discounted to Kaw Valley by Co–Mac. Including the Riddle transactions, Kaw Valley had purchased over 250 notes and security agreements from Co–Mac during the prior ten year period. All were guaranteed by Co–Mac and by its president personally.

In May, 1971, Riddle negotiated for the purchase of a model 6–c Caterpillar tractor, a dozer and a used 944 Caterpillar wheel tractor with a two yard bucket. Riddle was advised that this machinery could be delivered but it would first be necessary for Co–Mac to have a signed note and security agreement to complete the transaction. An installment note, security agreement and acceptance of delivery of the machinery was mailed to Riddle. These were signed and returned to Co–Mac. Ten days later, the machinery not having been delivered, Riddle called Co–Mac and inquired about purchasing a D–8 Caterpillar and a #80 Caterpillar scraper in place of the first machinery ordered. Co–Mac agreed to destroy the May 11, 1971 papers and sell this larger machinery to Riddle in place of that previously ordered.

The sale of this substitute machinery was completed and the machinery was delivered after the execution of an additional note and security agreement. However, the May 11, 1971 papers were not destroyed. The note had been discounted and assigned to Kaw Valley prior to the sale of the substitute machinery. Thereafter Co–Mac, who was in financial trouble, made regular payments on the first note to Kaw Valley. The note was thus kept current by Co–Mac and Riddle had no knowledge of the continued existence of that note. The 6–c Caterpillar tractor, dozer and the used 944 Caterpillar wheel tractor were never delivered to Riddle. Riddle received no consideration for the May 11, 1971 note and no lien attached under the security agreement because the machinery never came into possession of Riddle. (See UCC § 9–204.) The debtor never had rights in any of the collateral.

On February 24, 1972, representatives of Riddle, Co–Mac and Kaw Valley met for the purpose of consolidating the indebtedness of Riddle on machinery notes held by Kaw Valley and guaranteed by Co–Mac. Riddle was behind in some of his payments and wanted to consolidate the notes and reduce his monthly payments to $4,500.00. Kaw Valley disclosed eight past due machinery notes, each representing separate purchase transactions by Riddle. Riddle objected to one of these notes dated July 16, 1971, because the machinery purchased under this particular transaction had been previously returned to Co–Mac.

It was agreed by Kaw Valley that Riddle did not owe for this machinery because of the previous settlement between Co–Mac and Riddle. Kaw Valley cancelled the $5,000.00 balance shown to be due from Riddle.

Thereupon a renewal note and security agreement for $44,557.70 dated February 24, 1972, was drawn consolidating and renewing the seven remaining notes. Riddle then asked Kaw Valley if this was all that it owed the bank and he was assured that it was. The renewal note was then executed by Riddle.

It was not until March 12, 1972, that Riddle was advised by Kaw Valley that it held the note and security agreement dated May 11, 1971, which Riddle believed had been destroyed by Co–Mac. This was within a week after a receiver had been appointed to take over Co–Mac's business affairs. Riddle explained the machinery had never been delivered and Co–Mac promised to destroy the papers. No demand for payment of the May 11, 1971 note was made on Riddle until this action was filed.

Prior to the time this action was filed, Riddle executed a note and granted a security agreement in all of its machinery and equipment to Planters. This included the machinery covered in the previous consolidation transaction of February 24, 1972, with Kaw Valley and Co–Mac.

Subsequently Kaw Valley obtained possession of the machinery covered by the February 24 transaction by court order. Thereupon by agreement in writing between Kaw Valley, Planters and Riddle an immediate sale of the collateral covered in the February 24 transaction was held. By the terms of this agreement the first $22,200.00 in proceeds was to be paid to Kaw Valley in full satisfaction of the note of February 24, 1972. The money received from the sale in excess of this amount was to be paid to the Merchants National Bank to hold as escrow agent, awaiting a determination of entitlement by the court.

At the time of the trial the $22,200.00 had been received by Kaw Valley and the balance of the proceeds of the agreed sale amounting to $25,371.15 was in the hands of the escrow agent.

In the court's memorandum of decision filed November 19, 1974, the court found:

"That the proceeds remaining in plaintiff's possession from the agreed equipment sale are $25,371.15. The plaintiff claims $21,904.64 of same is due on the transaction of May 11, 1971. The parties agree that the excess of $3,466.51 should be paid to defendant Planters State Bank to apply on its August 28, 1972 claim;"

On December 20, 1974, the court entered the following pay-out order:

"TO THE CLERK OF THE DISTRICT COURT:

"Now on this 20th day of December 1974, you are ordered to pay to The Planters State Bank and Trust Company the sum of $3,466.51 now in your hands, having been paid by the Kaw Valley State Bank and Trust Company, pursuant to the Journal Entry of Judgment entered herein on November 19, 1974."

Although it does not appear who initiated the order, the $3,466.51 was paid to and accepted by Planters leaving the disputed proceeds of the sale ($21,904.64) in the hands of either the escrow agent or the court.

\* \* \*

The primary point on appeal questions the holding of the trial court that Kaw Valley was not a holder in due course of the note and security agreement dated May 11, 1971.

UCC § 3–306 provides that unless a holder of an instrument is a holder in due course he takes the instrument subject to the defenses of want or failure of consideration, nonperformance of any condition precedent, nondelivery or delivery for a special purpose. It was undisputed in this case that Riddle received no consideration after executing the note. The machinery was never delivered and he was assured by Co–Mac that the papers would be destroyed. The parties so stipulated. If Kaw Valley was not a holder in due course the proven defense was a bar to recovery by Kaw Valley.

UCC § 3–302 states that a holder in due course is a holder who takes the instrument (1) for value, (2) in good faith and (3) without notice of any defense against it. It was not disputed and the court found that Kaw Valley took the note for value so the first requirement was satisfied. The other requirements were subject to dispute. The trial court concluded:

> "Kaw Valley State Bank and Trust Company is not a holder in due course of the note and security agreement, dated May 11, 1971 for the reason that it did not establish in all respects that it took said instruments in good faith and without notice of any defense against or claimed to it on the part of John H. Riddle, and Kaw Valley State Bank and Trust Company therefor took said instruments subject to the defense of failure of consideration. [Citations omitted.]"

So we are confronted with the question of what is required for a holder to take an instrument "in good faith" and "without notice of defense." We will consider the two parts of the question in the order mentioned.

"Good faith" is defined in UCC § 1–201(19) as "honesty in fact in the conduct or transaction concerned." The first draft of the Uniform Commercial Code (U.C.C.) as proposed required not only that the actions of a holder be honest in fact but in addition it required the actions to conform to *reasonable commercial standards*. This would have permitted the courts to inquire as to whether a particular commercial standard was in fact reasonable. (See Uniform Commercial Code, Proposed Final Draft [1950], § 1–201, 18, p. 30.) However, when the final draft was approved the test of reasonable commercial standards was excised thus indicating that a more rigid standard must be applied for determining "good faith." * * *

From the history of the Uniform Commercial Code it would appear that "good faith" requires no actual knowledge of or participation in any material infirmity in the original transaction.

The second part of our question concerns the requirement of the U.C.C. that a holder in due course take the instrument without notice of any defense to the instrument. UCC § 1–201(25) provides:

> "A person has 'notice' of a fact when
>
> "(a) he has actual knowledge of it; or
>
> "(b) he has received a notice or notification of it; or
>
> "(c) from all the facts and circumstances known to him at the time in question he has reason to know that it exists. A person 'knows' or has 'knowledge' of a fact when he has actual knowledge of it. 'Discover' or 'learn' or a word or phrase of similar import refers to knowledge rather than to reason to know. The time and circumstances under which a notice or notification may cease to be effective are not determined by this act."

As is apparent from reading the above statute the standard enunciated is not limited to the rigid standard of actual knowledge of the defense.

Reason to know appears to be premised on the use of reasonable commercial practices. * * * Since "good faith" and "no notice of defense" are both required of a holder to claim the status of a holder-in-due course it would appear that the two standards are not in conflict even though the standards of conduct may be different.

There is little or no evidence in the present case to indicate that Kaw Valley acted dishonestly or "not in good faith" when it purchased the note of May 11, 1971. However, as to "notice of defense" the court found from all the facts and circumstances known to Kaw Valley at the time in question it had reason to know a defense existed. The court found:

> "During the period 1960 to May, 1971, plaintiff purchased from Co–Mac over 250 notes and secured transactions and held at any given time between $100,000.00 and $250,000.00 of such obligations. All of which were guaranteed by Co–Mac and personally guaranteed by D. J. Wickern, its president. Conant Wait personally handled most if not all of such transactions for plaintiff. Mr. Wait was aware that Co–Mac was making warranties and representation as to fitness to some purchasers of new and used equipment. Mr. Wait further knew that some transactions were in fact not as they would appear to be in that the money from Kaw Valley would be used by Co–Mac to buy the equipment that was the subject matter of the sale. Further, that delivery to the customer of said purchased equipment was sometimes delayed 60 to 90 days for repairing and/or overhauling of same. The plaintiff obviously on many transactions was relying on Co–Mac to insure payment of the obligations and contacted Co–Mac to collect delinquent payments. Some transactions involved delivery of coupon books to Co–Mac rather than the debtor so Co–Mac could bill service and parts charges along with the secured debt. Co–Mac collected payments directly from debtors in various transactions and paid plaintiff. Plaintiff did not concern itself with known irregularities in the transactions as it clearly was relying on Co–Mac;

> "The coupon book on the May 11, 1971 transaction was not sent to defendant Riddle; no payments on same were made by defendant Riddle; the payments were made by Co–Mac until January 25, 1972; prior to early March, 1972, defendant Riddle did not know plaintiff had the May 11, 1971 secured transaction; knowledge of said transaction came to defendant Riddle on March 12, 1972 when Mr. Wait contacted defendant Riddle's manager; that Co–Mac had shortly before been placed in receivership; that no demand for any payment on said transaction was made by plaintiff to defendant Riddle until September 1972."

To further support its holding that Kaw Valley had reason to know that the defense existed the court found that when Kaw Valley, Co–Mac and Riddle met on February 24, 1972, to consolidate all of Riddle's past due notes Kaw Valley recognized Co–Mac's authority to act for it. Co–Mac had accepted return of the machinery on one of the eight transactions and Kaw

Valley recognized its authority as their agent to do so and cancelled the $5,000.00 balance remaining due on the note held by the bank.

The cases dealing with the question of "reason to know a defense exists" seem to fall into four categories.

The first includes those cases where it is established the holder had information from the transferor or the obligor which disclosed the existence of a defense. In those cases it is clear if the holder takes an instrument having received prior or contemporaneous notice of a defense he is not a holder-in-due course. (Billingsley v. Mackay, 382 F.2d 290 (5th Cir. 1967)). Our present case does not fall in that category for there is no evidence that Co–Mac or Riddle informed Kaw Valley that the machinery had not been delivered when the note was negotiated.

The second group of cases are those in which the defense appears in an accompanying document delivered to the holder with the note. For example, when a security agreement is executed concurrently with a note evidencing an indebtedness incurred for machinery to be delivered in the future. In such case the instrument may under certain circumstances disclose a defense to the note, such as nondelivery of the machinery purchased. (See also Commerce Trust Company v. Denson, 437 S.W.2d 94 [Mo. App. 1968], and HIMC Investment Co. v. Siciliano, 103 N.J. Super. 27, 246 A.2d 502, for other examples.) Our present case does not fall in this category because Riddle had signed a written delivery acceptance which was handed to Kaw Valley along with the note and security agreement.

A third group of cases are those in which information appears in the written instrument indicating the existence of a defense, such as when the note on its face shows that the due date has passed or the note bears visible evidence of alteration and forgery or the note is clearly incomplete. (See E. F. Corporation v. Smith, 496 F.2d 826 [10th Cir. 1974]; Srochi v. Kamensky, 118 Ga. App. 182, 162 S.E.2d 889; and Winter & Hirsch, Inc. v. Passarelli, 122 Ill. App.2d 372, 259 N.E.2d 312.) In our present case the instrument assigned bore nothing unusual on its face and appeared complete and proper in all respects.

In the fourth category of cases it has been held that the holder of a negotiable instrument may be prevented from assuming holder in due course status because of knowledge of the business practices of his transferor or when he is so closely aligned with the transferor that transferor may be considered an agent of the holder and the transferee is charged with the actions and knowledge of the transferor.

Under our former negotiable instruments law containing provisions similar to the U.C.C. this court refused to accord holder in due course status to a machinery company receiving notes from one of its dealers because of its knowledge of the business practices of the dealer and the company's participation and alignment with the dealer who transferred the note. (International Harvester Co. v. Watkins, 127 Kan. 50, Sly. & 3, 272 P. 139, 61 A.L.R. 687.)

In Unico v. Owen, 50 N.J. 101, 232 A.2d 405, the New Jersey court refused to accord holder in due course status to a financing partnership which was closely connected with the transferor and had been organized to finance the commercial paper obtained by the transferor and others. The financing partnership had a voice in setting the policies and standards to be followed by the transferor. Under such circumstances the court found that the holder must be considered a participant in the transaction and subject to defenses available against the payee-transferor. In United States Finance Company v. Jones, 285 Ala. 105, 229 So.2d 495, it was held that a finance company purchasing a note from a payee for fifty percent of its face value did not establish holder in due course status and must be held subject to defenses inherent in the original transaction. Other jurisdictions have followed the rationale of Unico. See American Plan Corp. v. Woods, 16 Ohio App.2d 1, 240 N.E.2d 886, where the holder supplied forms to the payee, established financing charges and investigated the credit of the maker of the note; Calvert Credit Corporation v. Williams, 244 A.2d 494 (D.C.App. 1968), where the holder exerted total control over payee's financial affairs; and Jones v. Approved Bancredit Corp., 256 A.2d 739 (Del.1969), where ownership and management of the holder and payee were connected.

In the present case Kaw Valley had worked closely with Co–Mac in over 250 financing transactions over a period of ten years. It knew that some of these transactions were not for valuable consideration at the time the paper was delivered since the bank's money was to be used in purchasing the machinery or equipment represented in the instruments as already in possession of the maker of the note. Kaw Valley had been advised that delivery to Co–Mac's customers was sometimes delayed from 60 to 90 days. Kaw Valley continued to rely on Co–Mac to assure payment of the obligations and contacted it to collect delinquent payments. Some of these transactions, including the one in question, involved the use of coupon books to be used by the debtor in making payment on the notes. In the present case Kaw Valley did not notify Riddle that it was the holder of the note. It delivered Riddle's coupon book to Co–Mac as if it were the obligor or was authorized as its collection agent for this transaction.

Throughout the period from May 11, 1971, to February 25, 1972, Kaw Valley received and credited the monthly payments knowing that payments were being made by Co–Mac and not by Riddle. Then when Riddle's loans were consolidated, the May 11, 1971 transaction was not included by Kaw Valley, either by oversight or by intention, as an obligation of Riddle. Co–Mac occupied a close relationship with Kaw Valley and with its knowledge and consent acted as its agent in collecting payments on notes held by Kaw Valley. The working relationship existing between Kaw Valley and Co–Mac was further demonstrated on February 24, 1972, when the $5,000.00 balance due on one of Riddle's notes was cancelled when it was shown that the machinery for which the note was given had previously been returned to Co–Mac with the understanding that no further payments were due.

UCC § 3–307(3) provides:

"After it is shown that a defense exists a person claiming the rights of a holder in due course has the burden of establishing that he or some person under whom he claims is in all respects a holder in due course."

In the present case the court found that the appellant, Kaw Valley, had not sustained its burden of proving that it was a holder in due course. Under the evidence in this case the holder failed to advise the maker of the note of its acquisition of the note and security agreement. It placed the payment coupon book in the hands of Co–Mac and received all monthly payments from them. A close working relationship existed between the two companies and Co–Mac was clothed with authority to collect and forward all payments due on the transaction. Agency and authority was further shown to exist by authorizing return of machinery to Co–Mac and terminating balances due on purchase money paper. We cannot say under the facts and circumstances known and participated in by Kaw Valley in this transaction it did not at the time in question have reason to know that the defense existed. This was a question of fact to be determined by the trier of fact which if supported by substantial competent evidence must stand.

\* \* \*

The judgment is affirmed.

NOTE

Is the court telling us that the doctrine of holding in due course performs no legitimate function in inventory and sales financing?

PROBLEMS

**1.** On October 16, 1969, $8,000,000 of United States Treasury Bills in bearer form were stolen from Morgan Bank. On October 28, 1969, when the theft was discovered, Morgan Bank sent a "notice of lost securities," describing the stolen bills by serial number, to bankers and brokers throughout the country. Third Bank, upon receiving the notice, placed the notice in its lost securities file. On January 30, 1970 Third Bank made loans totaling $82,000 to Bialkin. As collateral for the loans it took two treasury bills each with a face amount of $50,000. The two bills were among those stolen from Morgan Bank and were listed in the notice of lost securities. The officer of Third Bank who approved the loan to Bialkin did not check the lost securities file of Third Bank. He testified that he was not aware of its existence. Third Bank later discovered that the treasury bills had been stolen and reported it to law enforcement authorities. Morgan Bank then sued to recover the bills.

Treasury bills come within the definition of "security" (8–102(a)(15)) that are governed by Article 8 of the UCC rather than Article 3. 3–102(a). In this case Third Bank would defeat the claim of Morgan Bank if it qualified as a "protected purchaser." 8–303. The treasury bills in this case are now known as "security certificates." 8–102(d)(16). A protected purchaser of a security certificate is essentially the same as a holder in due course of a negotiable instrument. Although he 1995 revision of Article 8 changed the notice test under that statute (8–105), would Third Bank have notice of the claim of Morgan Bank under 1–202? This problem is based on the facts, slightly modified, of Morgan Guaranty Trust Co. of New York v. Third National Bank of Hampden County, 529 F.2d 1141 (1st Cir.1976).

**2.** In December 1957 Fazzari was induced by fraud to sign a promissory note for $400 payable to the order of Wade. After discovering the fraud, in January 1958, Fazzari notified all of the local banks of the fraud. He personally spoke to the cashier of Odessa Bank and advised him not to purchase the note because he had been "tricked" by Wade. Three months later Odessa Bank, acting through its cashier, purchased the note. The cashier admitted that Fazzari had told him about the note in January but testified that at the time the note was purchased in April he had forgotten the incident. Did Odessa Bank take the note as a holder in due course? See 1–202. In the Comment to that provision, under the heading "Changes from former law," the following sentence appears: "The reference to the 'forgotten notice' doctrine has been deleted." The statement refers to a sentence in the former definition of "notice" that said: "The time and circumstances under which notice or notification may cease to be effective are not determined by this Act." The Comment to that section explained there was no intention of overruling a 1935 Supreme Court holding that notice that is forgotten is no longer notice. This problem is based on the facts of First National Bank of Odessa v. Fazzari, 10 N.Y.2d 394, 223 N.Y.S.2d 483, 179 N.E.2d 493 (N.Y. 1961).

## Maine Family Federal Credit Union v. Sun Life Assurance Co.

Supreme Judicial Court of Maine, 1999.
727 A.2d 335.

■ SAUFLEY, J.

We are called upon here to address the concept of "holder in due course" as defined by recent amendments to the negotiable instruments provisions of the Maine Uniform Commercial Code. We conclude that, pursuant to those amendments, the Superior Court (Cumberland County, Calkins, J.) did not err when it entered a judgment based on the jury's finding that the Maine Family Federal Credit Union was not a holder in due course. * * *

### I. FACTS

Daniel, Joel, and Claire Guerrette are the adult children of Elden Guerrette, who died on September 24, 1995. Before his death, Elden had purchased a life insurance policy from Sun Life Assurance Company of Canada, through Sun Life's agent, Steven Hall, and had named his children as his beneficiaries. Upon his death, Sun Life issued three checks, each in the amount of $40,759.35, to each of Elden's children.[1] The checks were drawn on Sun Life's account at Chase Manhattan Bank in Syracuse, New York.[2] The checks were given to Hall for delivery to the Guerrettes.

The parties have stipulated that Hall and an associate, Paul Richard, then fraudulently induced the Guerrettes to indorse the checks in blank and to transfer them to Hall and Richard, purportedly to be invested in "HER, Inc.," a corporation formed by Hall and Richard.[3] Hall took the checks from the Guerrettes and turned them over to Richard, who deposited them in his account at the Credit Union on October 26, 1995.[4] The Credit Union immediately made the funds available to Richard.

The Guerrettes quickly regretted having negotiated their checks to Hall and Richard, and they contacted Sun Life the next day to request that Sun Life stop payment on the checks. Sun Life immediately ordered Chase Manhattan to stop payment on the checks.[5] Thus, when the checks were ultimately presented to Chase Manhattan for payment, Chase refused to pay the checks, and they were returned to the Credit Union.

The Credit Union received notice that the checks had been dishonored on November 3, 1995, the sixth business day following their deposit.[6] By that time, however, Richard had withdrawn from his account all of the funds represented by the three checks. The Credit Union was able to

---

**1.**  " 'Issue' means the first delivery of an instrument by the maker or drawer, whether to a holder or nonholder, for the purpose of giving rights on the instrument to any person." § 3–105(a).

**2.**  Accordingly, Sun Life was the drawer of the checks. " 'Drawer' means a person who signs or is identified in a draft as a person ordering payment." § 3–103(a)(3). Chase Manhattan was the "drawee." " 'Drawee' means a person ordered in a draft to make payment." § 3–103(a)(2). More specifically, Chase Manhattan was also the "payor bank." " 'Payor bank' means a bank that is the drawee of a draft." § 4–105(3).

**3.**  " 'Indorsement' means a signature, other than that of a signer as maker, drawer or acceptor, that alone or accompanied by other words is made on an instrument for the purpose of: (a) Negotiating the instrument; (b) Restricting payment of the instrument; or (c) Incurring indorser's liability on the instrument." § 3–204(a).

**4.**  Maine Family Federal Credit Union is a "federally chartered credit union," regulated by the National Credit Union Administration. See 12 U.S.C.A. § 1752a (Law.Co-op.1996). It qualifies as an "insured credit union" under the Federal Credit Union Act, 12 U.S.C.A. §§ 1751–1795k (Law. Co-op.1996 & Supp.1998), and is therefore subject to the provisions of Regulation CC. 12 C.F.R. § 229 (1998).

By accepting the checks for deposit, Maine Family Federal Credit Union became the "depositary bank." Under Maine law, " '[d]epositary bank' means the first bank to take an item ... unless the item is presented for immediate payment over the counter." § 4–105(2).

**5.**  "A customer ... may stop payment of any item drawn on the customer's account ... by an order to the bank describing the item or account with reasonable certainty received at a time and in a manner that affords the bank a reasonable opportunity to act on it before any action by the bank with respect to the item...." § 4–403(a). Thus, Sun Life, as the customer of Chase Manhattan Bank, had the right to order Chase Manhattan to stop payment on the three checks deposited by Paul Richard at the Maine Family Federal Credit Union.

**6.**  "Notice of dishonor may be given by any person and by any commercially reasonable means, including an oral, written or electronic communication, and is sufficient if it reasonably identifies the instrument and indicates that the instrument has been dishonored or has not been paid or accepted." § 3–503(b).

recover almost $80,000 from Richard, but there remained an unpaid balance of $42,366.56, the amount now in controversy.

The Credit Union filed a complaint against Sun Life alleging that Sun Life was liable as drawer of the instruments, and that Sun Life had been unjustly enriched at the Credit Union's expense. * * *

The Credit Union moved for summary judgment. The Superior Court held, as a matter of law, that Daniel Guerrette had raised a "claim of a property or possessory right in the instrument or its proceeds," § 3–306, and therefore that Sun Life was entitled to assert that claim as a "defense" against the Credit Union. See § 3–305(c). The court found, however, that a genuine issue of material fact remained as to whether the Credit Union had acted in "good faith" when it gave value for the checks—a fact relevant to determining whether the Credit Union was a holder in due course. See § 3–302(a)(2)(ii). Accordingly, the court denied the Credit Union's motion for summary judgment, and the matter proceeded to trial.

At trial, the only issue presented to the jury was whether the Credit Union had acted in "good faith" when it gave value for the checks, thus entitling it to holder in due course status.[10] At the close of evidence, the Credit Union made a motion for a judgment as a matter of law, which the Superior Court denied. The jury found that the Credit Union had not acted in good faith and therefore was not a holder in due course. Therefore, the Superior Court entered judgment in favor of Sun Life * * * against the Credit Union. The court denied the Credit Union's renewed motion for judgment as a matter of law and motion to amend the judgment, and the Credit Union filed this appeal.

## II.   OBLIGATIONS OF THE PARTIES

At the heart of the controversy in this case is the allocation of responsibility for the loss of the unpaid $42,366.56, given the fact that Paul Richard and Steven Hall, the real wrongdoers, appear to be unable to pay. Maine, like the other forty-nine states, has adopted the Uniform Commercial Code. Under the Maine U.C.C., Articles 3 and 4 deal with "Negotiable Instruments" and "Bank Deposits and Collections." * * * It is these statutes that govern the parties' dispute.

Pursuant to Article 4 of the Maine U.C.C., the Credit Union, as a depositary bank, is a "holder" of the instruments, see § 4–205(1),[12] making

---

**10.** The parties stipulated to the fact that Daniel, Joel, and Claire were defrauded by Hall and Richard, and Paul Richard consented to the entry of judgment against him in the amount of $42,366.56 on the Credit Union's cross-claim against him. In addition, the parties stipulated that the Credit Union had incurred damages in the amount of $42,366.56. The parties' cooperation in crafting the stipulations appropriately allowed the court and the jury to focus on the only issue in dispute.

**12.** § 4–205(1) provides that a depositary bank becomes a holder of an item if the item was deposited by a customer who was also a holder. The Credit Union's customer, Paul Richard, became a holder of the checks when Daniel, Joel, and Claire indorsed them in blank and transferred them to Richard and Hall. See § 3–201(a) (" 'Negotiation' means a transfer of possession, whether voluntary or involuntary, of an instrument by a person other than the issuer to a person who there-it a "person entitled to enforce" the instrument under § 3–301(i). Upon producing an instrument containing the valid signature of a party liable on the instrument, a person entitled to enforce the instrument is entitled to payment, unless the party liable proves a defense or claim in recoupment, see § 3–308(b), or a possessory claim to the instrument itself. See § 3–306.

Because their signatures appear on the backs of the checks, Daniel, Joel, and Claire are "indorsers" of the checks. See § 3–204(a), (b). As indorsers, they are obligated to pay the amounts due on each dishonored instrument "[a]ccording to the terms of [each] instrument at the time it was indorsed." § 3–415(a)(i). This obligation is owed "to a person entitled to enforce the instrument or to a subsequent indorser who paid the instrument under this section." § 3–415(a).

As drawer of the checks, Sun Life is obligated to pay each dishonored instrument "[a]ccording to its terms at the time it was issued." § 3–414(b)(i). Again, this obligation is owed to a person entitled to enforce the instrument or to an indorser who paid the draft under § 3–415. See § 3–414(b). Chase Manhattan, as drawee of these checks, was not obligated to accept them for payment, see § 3–408, and therefore has not been made a party to this action.

Unless the Credit Union is a holder in due course, its right to enforce the obligations of the drawer and indorsers of the instruments is subject to a variety of defenses, including all those defenses available "if the person entitled to enforce the instrument[s] were enforcing a right to payment under a simple contract." See § 3–305(a)(2). In addition, its right to enforce is subject to any claims in recoupment, see § 3–305(a)(3), or claims to the instruments themselves. See § 3–306. If, however, the Credit Union establishes that it is a "holder in due course," it is subject to only those few defenses listed in § 3–305(a)(1). See § 3–305(b). None of those specific defenses is applicable here. Thus, the Credit Union argues that because it is entitled as a matter of law to holder in due course status, it is entitled to enforce the instruments against the Guerrettes and Sun Life.

## III.   HOLDER IN DUE COURSE

### A.   Burden of Proof and Standard of Review

A holder in due course is a holder who takes an instrument in good faith, for value, and without notice of any claims or defenses. See § 3–302(a). * * *

\* \* \*

The Credit Union argues that the court erred in failing to find, as a matter of law, that it was a holder in due course. * * * The question before us, therefore, is whether any reasonable view of the evidence, along with any justifiable inferences therefrom, can possibly support the jury's conclu-

by becomes its holder."); § 3–202(a)(ii) ("Negotiation is effective even if obtained ... [b]y fraud.").

sion that the Credit Union did not act in good faith and therefore was not a holder in due course. Alternatively stated, the question is whether the evidence compelled a finding that the Credit Union was a holder in due course. If there is any rational basis for the jury's verdict, we must affirm the judgment.

## B.   Good Faith

We therefore turn to the definition of "good faith" contained in Article 3 of the Maine U.C.C. In 1990, the National Conference of Commissioners on Uniform State Law recommended substantial changes in the U.C.C. The Maine Legislature responded to those recommendations in 1993 by repealing the entirety of Article 3 and enacting a new version [of Article 3], which contains a new definition of "good faith." While the previous version of the good faith definition only required holder to prove that it acted with "honesty in fact," the new definition provides:

> "Good faith" means honesty in fact *and the observance of reasonable commercial standards of fair dealing.*

§ 3–103(a)(4) (emphasis added). Because the tests are presented in the conjunctive, a holder must now satisfy both a subjective and an objective test of "good faith."

### 1.   Honesty in fact

Prior to the changes adopted by the Legislature in 1993, the holder in due course doctrine turned on a subjective standard of good faith and was often referred to as the "pure heart and empty head" standard. See M.B.W. Sinclair, Codification of Negotiable Instruments Law: A Tale of Reiterated Anachronism, 21 U. TOL. L. REV. 625, 654 (1990); see also Seinfeld v. Commercial Bank & Trust Co., 405 So.2d 1039, 1042 (Fla.Dist.Ct.App.1981) (noting that the U.C.C. "seem[s] to protect the objectively stupid so long as he is subjectively pure at heart"). That standard merely required a holder to take an instrument with "honesty in fact" to become a holder in due course.

Courts interpreting this language have routinely declared banks to be holders in due course, notwithstanding the failures of these banks to investigate or hold otherwise negotiable instruments, when they took the instruments with no knowledge of any defects, defenses, or stop payment orders. See, e.g., UAW–CIO Local #31 Credit Union v. Royal Ins. Co., 594 S.W.2d 276, 279 (Mo.1980) (en banc); Bank of New York v. Asati, Inc., 15 U.C.C. Rep. Serv.2d (CBC) 521, 1991 WL 322989 (N.Y.Sup.Ct. July 8, 1991). This approach has been understood to promote the negotiability of instruments, particularly checks, in the stream of commerce. Rejecting a contrary approach, one court put it bluntly:

> The requirement urged by defendant would bring the banking system to a grinding halt. A stop payment order issued by the drawer to the drawee which is unknown to the paying-collecting bank cannot fasten upon the paying bank any legal disability; particularly it cannot reduce the status of the collecting bank to a mere assignee of the instrument

or a holder of a non-negotiable instrument, or a mere holder of a negotiable instrument.

Mellon Bank, N.A. v. Donegal Mutual Ins. Co., 29 U.C.C. Rep. Serv. (CBC) 912, 1980 WL 98414 (Pa. Ct. C.P. Alleghany County, Jan. 8, 1980).

Although courts were often urged to engraft an objective reasonableness standard onto the concept of "honesty in fact," most refused to do so. Their refusals recognized that: "[T]he check is the major method for transfer of funds in commercial practice. The maker, payee, and endorsers of a check naturally expect it will be rapidly negotiated and collected.... The wheels of commerce would grind to a halt [if an objective standard were adopted]." Bowling Green, Inc. v. State St. Bank & Trust, 425 F.2d 81, 85 (1st Cir.1970).

Moreover, under the purely subjective standard, a bank was not expected to require the presence of offsetting collected funds in the customers' account in order to give value on newly deposited checks: "A bank's permitting its customers to draw against uncollected funds does not negate its good faith." Asati, Inc., 15 U.C.C. Rep. Serv.2d at 521; accord * * *.

Application of the "honesty in fact" standard to the Credit Union's conduct here demonstrates these principles at work. It is undisputed that the Credit Union had no knowledge that Richard obtained the Sun Life checks by fraud. Nor was the Credit Union aware that a stop payment order had been placed on the Sun Life checks. The Credit Union expeditiously gave value on the checks, having no knowledge that they would be dishonored. In essence the Credit Union acted as banks have, for years, been allowed to act without risk to holder in due course status. The Credit Union acted with honesty in fact.

Thus, had the matter at bar been decided before the Legislature's addition of the objective component of "good faith," there can be little question that the Credit Union would have been determined to have been a holder in due course. Because it took the instruments without notice of any possible dishonor, defect, fraud, or illegality, it could have given value immediately and yet have been assured of holder in due course status. * * * Today, however, something more than mere subjective good faith is required of a holder in due course.

### 2. Reasonable commercial standards of fair dealing

We turn then to the objective prong of the good faith analysis. The addition of the language requiring the holder to prove conduct meeting "reasonable commercial standards of fair dealing" signals a significant change in the definition of a holder in due course.[19] While there has been little time for the development of a body of law interpreting this new objective requirement, there can be no mistaking the fact that a holder may no longer act with a pure heart and an empty head and still obtain holder

---

**19.** "The new definition of good faith *substantially affects* ... the requirements for holder in due course status." Hawkland & Lawrence UCC Series § 3–103:05 (Rev. Art. 3) (emphasis added).

in due course status.[20] The pure heart of the holder must now be accompanied by reasoning that assures conduct comporting with reasonable commercial standards of fair dealing.

The addition of the objective element represents not so much a new concept in the doctrinal development of holder in due course status, but rather a return, in part, to an earlier approach to the doctrine. See JAMES J. WHITE & ROBERT S. SUMMERS, UNIFORM COMMERCIAL CODE § 14–6, at 628–29 (3d ed. 1988) (discussing the objective test of good faith in England, first applied by the King's Bench in Gill v. Cubitt, 3 B & C 466, 107 Eng.Rep. 806 (K.B. 1824)). The concept of an objective component of good faith has been part of the discussion regarding the holder in due course doctrine since the first enactment of the U.C.C. See id. (noting that "[t]he good faith requirement has been the source of a continuing and ancient dispute"). The early drafters debated the need and wisdom of including such an objective component and ultimately determined *not* to include it in the definition of good faith because of its potential for freezing commercial practices. * * * The "new" element of good faith requiring the holder to act according to reasonable commercial standards of fair dealing is actually a more narrow version of the "reasonable person" standard considered and rejected by the drafters of the 1962 Code.

The new objective standard, however, is not a model of drafting clarity. Although use of the word "reasonable" in the objective portion of the good faith test may evoke concepts of negligence, the drafters attempted to distinguish the concept of "fair" dealing from concepts of "careful" dealing:

> Although fair dealing is a broad term that must be defined in context, it is clear that it is concerned with the fairness of conduct rather than the care with which an act is performed. Failure to exercise ordinary care in conducting a transaction is an entirely different concept than failure to deal fairly in conducting the transaction.

U.C.C. § 3–103 cmt. 4 (1991).

Unfortunately, the ease with which the distinction between "fair dealing" and "careful dealing" was set forth in the comments to the U.C.C. revisions belies the difficulty in applying these concepts to the facts of any particular case, or in conveying them to a jury. The difficulty is exacerbated by the lack of definition of the term "fair dealing" in the U.C.C.[21] The most obvious question arising from the use of the term "fair" is: fairness to

---

**20.** The objective requirement, however, has generated a number of articles and commentaries on the reason, meaning, and anticipated interpretations of the changes. See, e.g., Patricia L. Heatherman, Comment, Good Faith in Revised Article 3 of the Uniform Commercial Code: Any Change? Should There Be? 29 WILLAMETTE L. REV. 567 (1993); Kerry Lynn Macintosh, Liberty, Trade, and the Uniform Commercial Code, When Should Default Rules be Based on Business Practices? 38 WM. & MARY L. REV. 1465, 1466 (1997).

**21.** One commentator has suggested that fair dealing refers to "playing by the rules." See Heatherman, supra, at 585. Yet "the rules" ordinarily define the parameters of reasonable conduct, a concept which sounds much like a negligence analysis.

whom? Transactions involving negotiable instruments have traditionally required the detailed level of control and definition of roles set out in the U.C.C. precisely because there are so many parties who may be involved in a single transaction. If a holder is required to act "fairly," regarding all parties, it must engage in an almost impossible balancing of rights and interests. Accordingly, the drafters limited the requirement of fair dealing to conduct that is reasonable in the commercial context of the transaction at issue. In other words, the holder must act in a way that is fair according to commercial standards that are themselves reasonable.

The factfinder must therefore determine, first, whether the conduct of the holder comported with industry or "commercial" standards applicable to the transaction and, second, whether those standards were reasonable standards intended to result in fair dealing. Each of those determinations must be made in the context of the specific transaction at hand. If the factfinder's conclusion on each point is "yes," the holder will be determined to have acted in good faith even if, in the individual transaction at issue, the result appears unreasonable. Thus, a holder may be accorded holder in due course status where it acts pursuant to those reasonable commercial standards of fair dealing—even if it is negligent—but may lose that status, even where it complies with commercial standards, if those standards are not reasonably related to achieving fair dealing.

Therefore the jury's task here was to decide whether the Credit Union observed the banking industries' commercial standards relating to the giving of value on uncollected funds, and, if so, whether those standards are reasonably designed to result in fair dealing.

The evidence produced by the Credit Union in support of its position that it acted in accordance with objective good faith included the following: The Credit Union's internal policy was to make provisional credit available immediately upon the deposit of a check by one of its members. In certain circumstances—where the check was for a large amount and where it was drawn on an out-of-state bank—its policy allowed for a hold to be placed on the uncollected funds for up to nine days. The Credit Union's general written policy on this issue was reviewed annually—and had always been approved—by the National Credit Union Administration, the federal agency charged with the duty of regulating federal credit unions. See 12 U.S.C.A. § 1752a (Law. Co-op. 1996). In addition, the policy complied with applicable banking laws, including Regulation CC. See 12 C.F.R. §§ 229.12(c), 229.13(b) (1998).

The Credit Union also presented evidence that neither Regulation CC nor the Credit Union's internal policy *required* it to hold the checks or to investigate the genesis of checks before extending provisional credit. It asserted that it acted exactly as its policy and the law allowed when it immediately extended provisional credit on these checks, despite the fact that they were drawn for relatively large amounts on an out-of-state bank.[22] Finally, the Credit Union presented expert testimony that most credit unions in Maine follow similar policies.

---

**22.** The Credit Union could also have withheld provisional credit under the law and its own internal policy if there were other reasons to doubt the validity of the checks. See 12 C.F.R. § 229.13(e) (1998).

In urging the jury to find that the Credit Union had not acted in good faith, Sun Life and the Guerrettes argued that the Credit Union's conduct did not comport with reasonable commercial standards of fair dealing when it allowed its member access to provisional credit on checks totalling over $120,000 drawn on an out-of-state bank without either: (1) further investigation to assure that the deposited checks would be paid by the bank upon which they were drawn, or (2) holding the instruments to allow any irregularities to come to light.

The applicable federal regulations provide the outside limit on the Credit Union's ability to hold the checks. Although the limit on allowable holds established by law is evidence to be considered by the jury, it does not itself establish reasonable commercial standard of fair dealing. The factfinder must consider all of the facts relevant to the transaction. The amount of the checks and the location of the payor bank, however, are relevant facts that a bank, observing reasonable commercial standards of fair dealing, takes into account when deciding whether to place such a hold on the account. The jury was entitled to consider that, under Regulation CC, when a check in an amount greater than $5,000 is deposited, or when a check is payable by a nonlocal bank, a credit union is permitted to withhold provisional credit for longer periods of time than it is allowed in other circumstances. See 12 C.F.R. § 229.13(b), (h) (1998). Therefore, the size of the check and the location of the payor bank are, under the objective standard of good faith, factors which a jury may also consider when deciding whether a depositary bank is a holder in due course.

The Credit Union's President admitted the risks inherent in the Credit Union's policy and admitted that it would not have been difficult to place a hold on these funds for the few days that it would normally take for the payor bank to pay the checks. He conceded that the amount of the checks were relatively large, that they were drawn on an out-of-state bank, and that these circumstances "could have" presented the Credit Union with cause to place a hold on the account. He also testified to his understanding that some commercial banks followed a policy of holding nonlocal checks for three business days before giving provisional credit.[23] Moreover, the Credit Union had no written policy explicitly guiding its staff regarding the placing of a hold on uncollected funds. Rather, the decision on whether to place a temporary hold on an account was left to the "comfort level" of the teller accepting the deposit. There was no dispute that the amount of the three checks far exceeded the $5,000 threshold for a discretionary hold established by the Credit Union's own policy.

On these facts the jury could rationally have concluded that the reasonable commercial standard of fair dealing would require the placing of a hold on the uncollected funds for a reasonable period of time and that, in

---

**23.** There was evidence that, on the second business day after he deposited the checks, Paul Richard notified the Credit Union that there may have been a problem with his deposit.

giving value under these circumstances, the Credit Union did not act according to commercial standards that were reasonably structured to result in fair dealing.

We recognize that the Legislature's addition of an objective standard of conduct in this area of law may well have the effect of slowing the "wheels of commerce."[24] As one commentator noted:

> Historically, it was always argued that if negotiable instruments were to be usefully negotiable a subsequent holder should not have to investigate the transaction giving rise to the paper. The paramount necessity of negotiability has dominated thinking and legislation on negotiable instruments law. Drafts and promissory notes, it has been believed, must be able to change hands freely, without investigation beyond the face of the instrument, and with no greater requirement than the indorsement of the holder.

Sinclair, supra, at 630 (footnotes omitted). Notwithstanding society's oft-cited need for certainty and speed in commercial transactions, however, the Legislature necessarily must have concluded that the addition of the objective requirement to the definition of "good faith" serves an important goal. The paramount necessity of unquestioned negotiability has given way, at least in part, to the desire for reasonable commercial fairness in negotiable transactions.

\* \* \*

### NOTES

**1.** Is the court's interpretation of "fair dealing" consistent with Comment 4 to 3–103? As we will see later, the purpose of Regulation CC is to allow depositors to withdraw funds from their bank accounts more rapidly. However, it permits depositary banks to place holds on checks in specified cases to protect the banks. In this case the credit union could have placed a nine-day hold on the check, but Reg. CC does not require that banks place maximum holds on checks, and we will find that in most cases banks allow their depositors to withdraw the proceeds of checks much more quickly as a convenience. If a check is dishonored and the drawer later raises defenses on the check, banks have been able to recover from the drawer as holders in due course.

In *Maine Family Federal*, everything on the face of the checks paid by the credit union (CU) was regular ("in order," as bankers say). They were drawn by a large insurance company, Sun Life, on one of the largest banks in the world at that time, Chase, payable to the beneficiaries of an insurance policy in satisfaction of legitimate claims. The payees properly indorsed the checks and they were deposited by a customer of CU, Paul

---

**24.** The new definition of "good faith" has been forecasted by some to bring possible "undesirable changes" to the law of negotiable instruments. See Henry J. Bailey, New 1990 Uniform Commercial Code: Article 3, Negotiable Instruments, and Article 4, Bank Deposits and Collections, 29 WILLAMETTE L. REV. 409, 415 (1993).

Richard, in his account. There was no basis for CU to have the slightest suspicion about the transaction. The fraud giving rise to the beneficiaries' claim of ownership arose entirely from activities about which CU knew nothing. CU got into trouble when it accommodated the wishes of its customer by allowing him to draw on the checks on the date of deposit. The strongest argument Sun Life had was that CU acted imprudently because these were checks of substantial amounts. But large checks from insurance companies are not unusual, and the fact they were drawn on an out-of-state bank in no way makes them appear unreliable; this would probably be normal for insurance checks. How this arguably imprudent conduct led the court to hold that the jury could have rationally concluded that CU did not act according to commercial standards of fair dealing is a stretch. CU dealt only with its customer, Richard, and whether its accommodation to him constituted dealing unfairly is highly problematic.

What effect will *Maine Family Federal* have on the practice of granting early withdrawal privileges to bank customers that has proved so popular? If this case is followed, where will courts draw the line on the size of checks that can be paid out by the depositary bank promptly? Will every payment by a depositary bank on an uncollected check be subject to scrutiny on fair-dealing grounds. The Clarks in Bank Deposits and Payments Monthly, Vol.7, No.10 (April 1999), describe the Maine decision as "dead wrong." But some cases purport to have adopted its analysis, e.g., Any Kind Checks Cashed, Inc. v. Talcott, 830 So.2d 160 (4th Dist.Fla.App. 2002). Others do not, e.g., Wachovia Bank, N.A. v. Federal Reserve Bank of Richmond, 338 F.3d 318 (4th Cir. 2003) ("To determine whether Wachovia acted in conformity with reasonable commercial standards of fair dealing, we consider the fairness of Wachovia's actions, rather than any negligence on its part. * * * [There must be] evidence in the record indicating that Wachovia acted in an unfair or dishonest manner, rather than in a negligent manner." 338 F.3d at 323); State Bank of the Lakes v. Kansas Bankers Surety Co., 328 F.3d 906 (7th Cir. 2003) (["G]ood faith is in a different phylum from 'due care.' * * * Article 3 of the UCC, which contains a definition of 'good faith' * * * links commercial reasonableness to 'fair dealing.' Avoidance of advantage-taking, which this section is getting at, differs from due care." 328 F.3d at 909.).

**2.**   The fair-dealing prong of good faith was enshrined in American contract law by Restatement (Second) Contracts § 205 (1981), which provides: "Every contract imposes upon each party a duty of good faith and fair dealing in its performance and its enforcement." Comments b. and d. draw an important distinction in the application of fair dealing between good faith purchase cases and those involving the performance of contracts. They explain that in determining whether one is a good faith purchaser the focus is on the honesty of the purchaser but in cases of performance of contracts fair dealing may require more than honesty. Thus, in performing a contract, one party may not take unfair advantage of another. Since the principal use of the good faith definition in Article 3 involves whether the taker of an instrument is, in effect, a good faith purchaser, should Article 3 have omitted the fair-dealing prong of the good faith definition? Cf.

Comment 3 to 5–102, in which the drafters explain why they rejected the fair-dealing prong of the good faith definition with respect to letters of credit.

## 2.   Overdue or Irregular Instruments

### PROBLEM

In payment of goods, Maker signed a negotiable note in the amount of $10,000 and mailed it to Payee. The note should have been payable in the amount of $20,000. Payee noticed the discrepancy and called Maker's attention to it. Maker told Payee to change the $10,000 to $20,000. Payee did so by erasing and typing over. The alteration was crudely done and very obvious. Payee then sold the note to Holder. Holder noticed the alteration but accepted Payee's truthful explanation of the circumstances under which it was made. When Holder demanded payment Maker refused, stating that Payee failed to deliver the goods for which the note was given. Assuming that Maker had a valid defense against Payee under 3–305(a)(2) relating to Payee's failure to perform the contract, is Holder subject to the defense? Suppose Holder, before completing the transaction, had called Maker and that Maker had verified that the $20,000 figure was correct. How does this affect your answer? See 3–302(a)(1) and Comment 1 to 3–302.

---

Section 3–302(a) incorporates two traditional rules: holder-in-due-course status cannot be attained if the instrument is taken with notice that it is overdue or if the instrument is so irregular or incomplete as to call into question its authenticity. These doctrines are rooted in the law of good faith and may be viewed as special applications of the suspicious circumstances rule of Gill v. Cubitt. But for a long time they have enjoyed independent status, and NIL § 52 adopted them as separate requirements for holder-in-due-course status in addition to the good faith requirement.

Under the common law view, the fact that an instrument was overdue or irregular or incomplete was notice that something was wrong. But the fact that an instrument is overdue does not point to any particular defense or claim or, for that matter, to the existence of any defense or claim at all. Most notes are probably overdue because the makers can't pay them. Most checks that are still out more than 90 days (3–304(a)(2)) have not been collected because the holder hasn't deposited them. In the range of possibilities raised in the mind of one purchasing an overdue instrument, it is doubtful that the likelihood of a defense rises very high or that the possibility of a claim of ownership by a prior party is considered at all. The fact that an instrument bears an obvious alteration does warn a taker of the possibility of a fraudulent alteration but not of defenses or claims wholly unrelated to the alteration.

Why shouldn't a purchaser who is willing to pay good money for an overdue or irregular or incomplete instrument be entitled to holder-in-due-course status? Perhaps the question is better phrased in terms of why such a purchaser should be accorded that status. The answer to these questions may depend upon whether one looks upon holder-in-due-course status to be the norm or whether it should be seen as something unusual to be given only when a clear commercial benefit is achieved. If negotiability is a doctrine to promote the free flow of instruments, what social or economic gain is achieved by encouraging the currency of stale, irregular or incomplete instruments?

## PROBLEMS

**1.**   S agreed to sell real property to B for $58,000, of which $6,500 was to be a down payment. When making the down payment, B insisted that S execute a promissory note to B's order for the amount of $6,500 as evidence of indebtedness for any sums B might be called upon to expend to pay off any claims or liens with respect to the property of which B was not aware. In time B expended $4,244 in paying these claims. The note, which was executed by S on March 25 and due 75 days after date, was indorsed without recourse to Plaintiff on September 1 for a total consideration of $3,067. S refused to pay the note and Plaintiff brought suit. How much is Plaintiff entitled to recover—$6,500, $4,244, or $3,067? See 3–203(b), 3–302(a), 3–117, and 3–305(a). See also Brock v. Adams, 79 N.M. 17, 439 P.2d 234 (1968).

**2.**   Payee sold a house to Maker and as partial payment of the price took a promissory note for $5,000 payable in monthly installments over a five-year period. When Payee's reserve army unit was called to active duty Payee asked Banker to collect the note during Payee's indefinite absence. Banker insisted that Payee indorse the note in blank and turn over possession of both the note and mortgage. Later Maker fell in default on the payments and Banker, who was also in financial difficulties, sold the note to Purchaser for value. Purchaser knew that four payments had not been made but had no knowledge of the circumstances under which Banker had taken the note. After Payee returned and learned of Banker's actions, Payee asserted a claim of ownership against Purchaser and sued to retake possession of the note. What result? Justice v. Stonecipher, 267 Ill. 448, 108 N.E. 722 (1915). See 3–304(b)(1) and 3–306.

## 3.   NEGOTIABILITY IN CONSUMER TRANSACTIONS

### a.   INTRODUCTION

## Universal C.I.T. Credit Corp. v. Ingel

Supreme Judicial Court of Massachusetts, Worcester, 1964.
196 N.E.2d 847.

■ SPIEGEL, JUSTICE.

This is an action of contract on a promissory note by the assignee of the payee against the maker. The case was first tried in the District Court of Fitchburg, to which it had been remanded by the Superior Court. There was a finding for the plaintiff in the sum of $1,630.12. At the request of the defendants, the case was retransferred to the Superior Court for trial by jury. Upon conclusion of the evidence the court allowed a motion by the plaintiff for a directed verdict to which the defendants excepted. They also excepted to the exclusion of certain evidence.

At the trial the plaintiff introduced in evidence the note,[1] a completion certificate signed by the defendants, and the District Court's finding for the plaintiff. The defendants admitted the authenticity of the signatures on the note and the completion certificate. As a witness for the defendants, one Charles D. Fahey testified that he was the plaintiff's Boston branch manager at the time the defendants' note was purchased, and that the plaintiff purchases instalment contracts regarding automobile and property

---

**1.** "This Is A Negotiable Promissory Note

$1890.00 (Total Amount of Note)

Fitchburg, Mass. (City, State)

6/22, 1959 (Date)

I/WE JOINTLY AND SEVERALLY PROMISE TO PAY TO ALLIED ALUMINUM ASSOCIATES, INC. OR ORDER THE SUM OF EIGHTEEN HUNDRED NINETY DOLLARS IN 60 SUCCESSIVE MONTHLY INSTALMENTS OF $31.50 EACH, EXCEPT THAT THE FINAL INSTALMENT SHALL BE THE BALANCE THEN DUE ON THIS NOTE. COMMENCING THE 25 DAY OF JULY, 1959, AND THE SAME DATE OF EACH MONTH THEREAFTER UNTIL PAID, with interest after maturity at the highest lawful rate, and a reasonable sum (15% if permitted by law) as attorney's fees, if this note is placed in the hands of any attorney for collection after maturity. Upon nonpayment of any instalment at its maturity, all remaining instalments shall at the option of the holder become due and payable forthwith. Charges for handling late payments, of 5per $1 (maximum $5), are payable on any instalment more than 10 days in arrears. * * * *Notice of Proposed Credit Life Insurance*: Group credit life insurance will be obtained by the holder of this instrument, without additional charge to customer, subject to acceptance by the insurer, Old Republic Life Insurance Company, Chicago, Illinois. Such insurance will cover only the individual designated and signing below as the person to be insured (who must be an officer if customer is a corporation, a partner if partnership), except that no individual 65 years of age or older on the date the indebtedness is incurred will be eligible for such insurance. Such insurance will become effective, upon acceptance by the insurer, as of the date the indebtedness is incurred, and will terminate when the indebtedness terminates or upon such default or other event as terminates the insurance under the terms of the group policy. The amount of such insurance will be equal to the amount of customer's indebtedness hereunder at any time but not to exceed $10,000; proceeds will be applicable to reduction or discharge of the indebtedness. The provisions of this paragraph are subject to the terms of the group policy and the certificate to be issued.

PLEASE PRINT MAILING ADDRESS

Customer acknowledges receipt of a completed copy of this promissory note, including above Notice.

ALBERT T. INGEL

Customer (Person on whose life group credit life insurance will be obtained, if applicable.)

DORA INGEL

(Additional Customer, if any)

ORIGINAL"

improvement purchases. He described the procedures by which purchases of commercial paper are arranged by the plaintiff; these procedures included a credit check on the "customer," i. e., the maker of the note which the plaintiff is planning to purchase. The defendants attempted to introduce through Fahey a credit report obtained by the plaintiff on Allied Aluminum Associates, Inc. (Allied), the payee of the note. The defendants excepted to the exclusion of this evidence. They offered to prove that the excluded report, which was dated "3–31–59," contained the following statement: "The subject firm is engaged in the sale of storm windows, doors, roofing, siding, and bathroom and kitchen remodeling work. The firm engages a crew of commission salesmen and it is reported they have been doing a good volume of business. They are reported to employ high pressure sales methods for the most part. They have done considerable advertising in newspapers, on radio, and have done soliciting by telephone. They have been criticized for their advertising methods, and have been accused of using bait advertising, and using false and misleading statements. The Boston Better Business Bureau has had numerous complaints regarding their advertising methods, and have reported same to the Attorney General. *FHA has had no complaints other than report of this from Better Business Bureau and have warned the firm to stop their practice.*"

The defendants excepted to the exclusion of testimony by the defendant Dora Ingel concerning certain of her negotiations with Allied. An offer of proof was made which indicates that this testimony might have been evidence of fraud or breach of warranty on the part of Allied. They also excepted to the exclusion of a letter[2] from the plaintiff to the defendant Albert.

## I.

The defendants contend that the note was nonnegotiable as a matter of law and, therefore, any defence which could be raised against Allied may also be raised against the plaintiff. * * *

We thus conclude that the note in question is a negotiable instrument.

---

**2.** "October 27, 1959 Identification 'B'

Mr. Albert Ingel

115 Belmont

Fitchburg, Massachusetts

Re: 200–12–51767

Dear Sir.

We are sorry to learn that the Aluminum Siding on which we hold your promissory note, is giving you cause for complaint. Our part in the transactions consisted of extending the credit which you desired, and arranging to accept prepayment of the advance on terms convenient to you. We did not perform any of the work, and any questions in connection with materials and workmanship should be adjusted with the dealer from whom you made your purchase. Therefore, we have passed your report along to Allied Aluminum and we are confident that everything reasonably possible will be done to correct any faulty conditions which may exist.

In the meantime, we shall appreciate your continuing to make payments on your note as they fall due so that your account may be kept in current condition.

Very truly yours,

UNIVERSAL C. I. T. CREDIT CORPORATION

C. KEVENY Collection Man"

## II.

* * * The defendants' answer denies that the plaintiff is "a holder in due course" of the note on which the action is brought; accordingly, this must be regarded as a matter "put in issue by the pleadings." We are satisfied that the finding of the District Court was prima facie evidence that the plaintiff took the note for value and without notice, and * * * the burden was on the defendants to rebut the plaintiff's prima facie case.

## III.

The trial judge correctly excluded the evidence offered by the defendants to show that the plaintiff and Allied had worked together on various aspects of the financing and that the plaintiff was aware of complaints against Allied by previous customers. We are of opinion that there was nothing in this evidence by which the plaintiff had "reason to know" of any fraud. The letter of October 27, 1959, from the plaintiff to the defendant Albert was also properly excluded; it is immaterial that the plaintiff may have found out about Allied's alleged fraudulent representations after the note had been purchased.

Exceptions overruled.

### NOTE

This 1964 case is the most recent authoritative opinion that we can find holding a consumer financer to be a holder in due course. Since this opinion, all courts have found some basis for denying financers that status. If you were representing the consumers in this case, what arguments would you make on Universal C.I.T.'s status as a holder in due course? Why has the doctrine of holding in due course disappeared from consumer credit transactions? For a broad indictment of the holder-in-due-course doctrine in consumer cases, based on public policy and the outrage of the Supreme Court of New Jersey, see Unico v. Owen, 232 A.2d 405 (N.J. 1967).

––––––––––––

Whether the doctrine of negotiability in all its vigor is necessary or even desirable when applied to modern negotiable instruments such as promissory notes and checks has been challenged in Grant Gilmore, The Good Faith Purchase Idea and the Uniform Commercial Code: Confessions of a Repentant Draftsman, 15 Ga. L. Rev. 605 (1981). Consider the following observations of Professor Albert J. Rosenthal taken from his article, "Negotiability—Who Needs It?," 71 Colum. L. Rev. 375, 378–381 (1971):

> The negotiable promissory note of today is quite a different instrument, serving different purposes, and the consequences of its negotiability are quite different in impact. By far the most commonly employed variety of the species today is the note given by the installment purchaser of goods to reflect the unpaid portion of the purchase price.

Typically, such a note is transferred just once, from the dealer to the lender (usually either a finance company or a bank), and thereafter remains in the possession of the latter or its lawyers until it is either paid off or offered in evidence in court. Its negotiable character is of no importance with respect to claims of ownership, as it is unlikely to be lost or stolen. Even if it is, the last indorsement will have been a special indorsement to the order of the lender; without the genuine further indorsement of the latter there can be no subsequent holder, much less a holder in due course.

The only significant consequence of the negotiability of such a note is that it cuts off the defenses of the maker. If, for example, the purchaser gives the note in payment for a refrigerator, the finance company is entitled to full payment regardless of whether the refrigerator fails to work or whether its sale was accomplished through fraudulent misrepresentations or, indeed, whether it was ever delivered at all. And it may be small comfort to the buyer, forced to pay the finance company in full, to know that he has a cause of action against the seller, which may at best be collectible with difficulty and may in many cases be worthless because the seller is insolvent or has left town.

A promissory note of this kind, and a consequence of negotiability that works in this fashion, are a far cry from the stolen Bank of England note, and the protection accorded its purchaser, in Miller v. Race. Whether the finance company should be allowed to prevail free of the maker's defenses raises questions that ought to be decided on their own merits, and not merely through the absent-minded application of a doctrine created to meet an entirely different situation.

The social evils flowing from negotiability in this circumstance have become manifest, and there has been a clear trend in both the courts and the legislatures toward amelioration of its consequences. In particular, the unfairness to the poorest members of the community of the law governing consumer installment purchases has generated a reaction that is giving rise to a major alteration in it. This departure is being accomplished, not by modification of the provisions of Article 3 of the Code, but by legislative action forbidding the use of negotiable instruments in consumer installment transactions and by judicial attempts to stretch the facts to deny holder in due course status to finance companies. Since the installment buyer can be similarly harmed even without a negotiable instrument if there is a clause in his purchase contract waiving, as against an assignee of his obligation, any defenses on the contract that he may have, legislatures and courts have also been moving in the direction of declaring such clauses invalid.

It is not clear whether the apparent weakness in the opposition to these changes springs from a lack of genuine need on the part of sellers or lenders for continuation of the power to cut off buyers' defenses. While there has been ground to believe that where this protection is denied, credit nevertheless will remain available, a recent study suggests that this may not be so.

If an exception is carved out, should it be limited to consumer paper, or should it be applied to promissory notes across the board? Thus far, the demand for reform has been confined largely to the former. While there may be small commercial purchasers also in need of similar protection, and while there may be other situations in which unfair advantage seems to be taken of makers of promissory notes, there does not appear in such cases to be a resulting social problem of comparable dimension. On the other hand, we need to know more about the range of other uses to which promissory notes are put in today's economy, and about the circumstances in which the cutting off of claims and defenses in connection with such notes serves legitimate needs or works undue hardship.

b.  THE LEGISLATIVE RESPONSE

The drafters of former Article 3 could not agree on a suitable consumer exception to the holder-in-due-course rule, and the solution to the issue eventually agreed upon in the Uniform Consumer Credit Code (UCCC) (1964–1974), discussed below, after years of debate was not widely enacted. However, by the time Revised Article 3 was drafted there was a large body of state statutory and case law restricting the use of the holder-in-due-course doctrine in consumer transactions, and the drafting committee finally settled on 3–302(g), which has the effect of subordinating Article 3 to that law, and not only to existing law but to similar law that may evolve in the future. See Comment 7 to 3–302.

(1)  CONSUMER CREDIT SALES

By the early 1960s the handwriting was on the wall with respect to the judicial enforceability of notes against consumers who had valid defenses. One way or another, courts allowed consumers to assert their defenses. Indeed, many creditors had long since given up the use of negotiable instruments and contract clauses cutting off defenses upon assignment. Nevertheless, the issue of negotiability occupied more time and caused more rancor in the drafting of the UCCC than any other issue. Creditor representatives saw negotiability as an issue of freedom of contract and wanted the UCCC to turn back the clock. To consumer advocates negotiability was a symbol of creditor overreaching, and they saw the UCCC as the instrumentality for finally driving a stake through the heart of negotiability in consumer cases. As we see below, the consumers won, but not before years of wrangling and equivocation. While these bitter debates were going on as late as the early 1970s, consumer credit was being revolutionized by the growth of the bank credit card which, in all but larger consumer purchases, replaced promissory notes and rendered the negotiability issue largely irrelevant.

Consumer credit sales are regulated in most states by statute. Most states have taken the position that the holder-in-due-course doctrine should be abrogated with respect to notes given by buyers to sellers of consumer goods or services. One approach taken is to prohibit the taking of a negotiable note from the buyer and to invalidate waiver of defenses clauses in the installment sale contract. The Uniform Consumer Credit Code, in effect in 11 jurisdictions, is an example of this kind of legislation. The 1974 Official Text provides as follows:

### Section 3.307 [Certain Negotiable Instruments Prohibited]

With respect to a consumer credit sale or consumer lease, [except a sale or lease primarily for an agricultural purpose,] the creditor may not take a negotiable instrument other than a check dated not later than ten days after its issuance as evidence of the obligation of the consumer.

### Section 3.404 [Assignee Subject to Claims and Defenses]

(1) With respect to a consumer credit sale or consumer lease [, except one primarily for an agricultural purpose,] an assignee of the rights of the seller or lessor is subject to all claims and defenses of the consumer against the seller or lessor arising from the sale or lease of property or services, notwithstanding that the assignee is a holder in due course of a negotiable instrument issued in violation of the provisions prohibiting certain negotiable instruments (Section 3.307).

(2) A claim or defense of a consumer specified in subsection (1) may be asserted against the assignee under this section only if the consumer has made a good faith attempt to obtain satisfaction from the seller or lessor with respect to the claim or defense and then only to the extent of the amount owing to the assignee with respect to the sale or lease of the property or services as to which the claim or defense arose at the time the assignee has notice of the claim or defense. Notice of the claim or defense may be given before the attempt specified in this subsection. Oral notice is effective unless the assignee requests written confirmation when or promptly after oral notice is given and the consumer fails to give the assignee written confirmation within the period of time, not less than 14 days, stated to the consumer when written confirmation is requested.

\* \* \*

(4) An agreement may not limit or waive the claims or defenses of a consumer under this section.

The Federal Trade Commission has promulgated rules (16 C.F.R. Part 433—Preservation of Consumers' Claims and Defenses) (the "Holder Rule") designed to negate the holder-in-due-course doctrine in sales of consumer goods or services. The rules also apply to leases of consumer goods. References to "seller" also include a lessor. Any "consumer credit contract," a term which includes a promissory note, arising out of such a sale or lease must contain a bold-faced notice stating in effect that any holder of the contract is subject to all claims and defenses that the debtor has against the seller of the goods or services.

NOTICE

ANY HOLDER OF THIS CONSUMER CREDIT CONTRACT IS SUBJECT TO ALL CLAIMS AND DEFENSES WHICH THE DEBTOR COULD ASSERT AGAINST THE SELLER OF THE GOODS OR SERVICES OBTAINED PURSUANT HERETO OR WITH THE PROCEEDS HEREOF. RECOVERY HEREUNDER BY THE DEBTOR SHALL NOT EXCEED AMOUNTS PAID BY THE DEBTOR HEREUNDER.

The effect of the notice is to cause any assignee of the note or sales contract to take subject to the buyer's claims and defenses against the seller. Failure by a seller to include the notice is an unfair or deceptive act or practice under Section 5 of the Federal Trade Commission Act. Under that Act, the seller is subject to a civil suit by the FTC in which the court may "grant such relief as the court finds necessary to redress injury to consumers * * * resulting from the rule violation * * *. Such relief may include, but shall not be limited to, rescission or reformation of contracts, the refund of money or return of property, the payment of damages, and public notification respecting the rule violation * * * except that nothing in this subsection is intended to authorize the imposition of any exemplary or punitive damages." 15 U.S.C. § 57b(b). Under Revised Article 3, a promissory note bearing the FTC notice can be a negotiable instrument if it otherwise complies with 3–104(a) but there cannot be a holder in due course of the note. 3–106(d) and Comment 3 to 3–106.

### (2) PURCHASE MONEY LOANS

Under traditional law, a financer who lends money to a buyer for the purpose of buying goods or services is not subject to claims or defenses the buyer may have against the seller. However, the purchase money loan transaction bears a close functional resemblance to the assigned paper transaction discussed above. In both cases the seller desires to be paid as soon as possible; the buyer chooses not to pay cash; and the financer is willing to provide the money. In the purchase money loan, the financer makes a loan to the buyer; in the assigned paper case, the seller retains a security interest in the goods sold and the financer buys the buyer's credit contract from the seller. Customs differ among the states: in some, consumer goods financing is done by purchase money loans, but in most the assigned-paper transaction predominates.

If financers are subject to consumer defenses in assigned-paper transactions, an incentive is present to convert to purchase money loans to free financers of consumer defenses. By the latter part of the 1960s consumer representatives began to advocate subjecting purchase money lenders to consumer claims and defenses in situations in which there was a sufficiently close relationship between the seller and the lender to warrant doing so. But how close must this relation be? The task of defining the requisite relationship has been difficult.

Under the FTC rule referred to above, the seller is guilty of an unfair or deceptive act if it accepts the proceeds of a purchase money loan (§ 433.2(b)) unless the loan agreement between the debtor and the purchase money lender contains the requisite notice. If the loan agreement contains the notice, the lender thereby subjects itself to defenses arising out of the sale. Section 433.1(d) defines purchase money loan to include two cases: (1) the seller refers the buyer to the lender, or (2) the seller is affiliated with the lender by common control, contract or business arrangement (defined in Section 433.1(g) as "[a]ny understanding, procedure, course of dealing, or arrangement, formal or informal, between a creditor and a seller, in connection with the sale of goods or services to consumers or the financing thereof"). It is not at all clear what constitutes affiliation by business arrangement. In the very common case of the secured loan, the loan is made for a particular purpose and the lender will be aware that a particular seller is involved in the transaction, but, without more, this should not mean that the lender's right to repayment is subject to any defenses that the borrower has against the seller. There is no problem in the case in which the seller steers the buyer to the lender or the case in which the lender will make loans only if the proceeds are used to purchase from the particular seller. Suppose the buyer of an automobile from a dealer shows that the lender has made numerous loans to borrowers who used the proceeds to purchase automobiles from the same dealer. Have the lender and the dealer become affiliated by an informal course of dealing? Must the seller in each case inquire about the buyer's source of funds to determine whether the required notice was required and was in fact made? 2 White & Summers, Uniform Commercial Code § 17–9 b. (5th Prac. ed. 2002).

Compare the following provision of the Uniform Consumer Credit Code (1974 Official Text) dealing with the same problem.

### Section 3.405 [Lender Subject to Claims and Defenses Arising from Sales and Leases]

(1) A lender, except the issuer of a lender credit card, who, with respect to a particular transaction, makes a consumer loan to enable a consumer to buy or lease from a particular seller or lessor property or services [, except primarily for an agricultural purpose,] is subject to all claims and defenses of the consumer against the seller or lessor arising from that sale or lease of the property or services if:

(a) the lender knows that the seller or lessor arranged for the extension of credit by the lender for a commission, brokerage, or referral fee;

(b) the lender is a person related to the seller or lessor, unless the relationship is remote or is not a factor in the transaction;

(c) the seller or lessor guarantees the loan or otherwise assumes the risk of loss by the lender upon the loan;

(d) the lender directly supplies the seller or lessor with the contract document used by the consumer to evidence the loan, and the seller or lessor has knowledge of the credit terms and participates in preparation of the document;

(e) the loan is conditioned upon the consumer's purchase or lease of the property or services from the particular seller or lessor, but the lender's payment of proceeds of the loan to the seller or lessor does not in itself establish that the loan was so conditioned; or

(f) the lender, before he makes the consumer loan, has knowledge or, from his course of dealing with the particular seller or lessor or his records, notice of substantial complaints by other buyers or lessees of the particular seller's or lessor's failure or refusal to perform his contracts with them and of the particular seller's or lessor's failure to remedy his defaults within a reasonable time after notice to him of the complaints.

(3)  NEW SUBSECTION 3–305(e)

Under the FTC Holder Rule, inclusion of the notice gives notice: if a contract containing the notice is assigned to a financer, the assignee is bound by the terms of the notice and cannot take free of claims and defenses. The reason for the notice approach is that, in general, the FTC has no jurisdiction over banks and cannot prohibit banks that buy consumer notes from being holders in due course by a rule, as the UCCC does by statute. But can the Holder Rule apply when the consumer note omits the notice? Commentators conclude that compliance with the Holder Rule by lenders in including the notice on their notes has been poor. Clarks' Secured Transactions Monthly, Vol. 18, No. 5, p.2 (July 2002). One of the reasons for this is uncertainty over whether the lender in question qualifies as a purchase money lender under the FTC rule.

Gonzalez v. Old Kent Mortgage Company, 2000 WL 1469313 (E.D. Pa. 2000), an obscure, unreported decision, addressed the effect of omitting the notice and came up with the novel concept of virtual notice. Citing no authority, the court concluded that it must treat a case in which the consumer contract did not contain the legend *as though it did*. The court laconically justified its legerdemain by saying, "[I]t would turn the law on its head to allow [the bank] to avoid the consequences of this language by its own failure * * * to include the Holder Rule Notice on the loan documents." The decision has been followed by other cases, and when the issue of omitted notice came before the Permanent Editorial Board group drafting the 2002 amendments the following provision was added to 3–305.

(e) In a consumer transaction, if law other than this article requires that an instrument include a statement to the effect that the rights of a holder or transferee are subject to a claim or defense that the issuer could assert against the original payee, and the instrument does not include such a statement:

(1) the instrument has the same effect as if the instrument included such a statement;

(2) the issuer may assert against the holder or transferee all claims and defenses that would have been available if the instrument included such a statement; and

(3) the extent to which claims may be asserted against the holder or transferee is determined as if the instrument included such a statement.

See Comment 6 to 3–305.

## 4. PAYEE AS HOLDER IN DUE COURSE

We don't usually think of a payee as being a holder in due course because the defenses that a maker or drawer raises are commonly based on the conduct of the payee such as fraud, misrepresentation, lack of consideration and the like. Since the payee perpetrated these wrongs on the obligor, the payee can hardly qualify as one who takes the instrument in good faith and without knowledge of the defense. But there are a few situations in which a payee should be allowed holder-in-due-course status; these involve more than two parties. Former 3–302(2) expressly stated: "A payee may be a holder in due course." This provision was omitted in the revision of Article 3. Comment 4 to 3–302 states: "Former Section 3–302(2) has been omitted in revised Article 3 because it is surplusage and may be misleading. The payee of an instrument can be a holder in due course, but use of the holder-in-due-course doctrine by the payee of an instrument is not the normal situation." We will look at two situations, one involving recoupment and one a defense.

*Recoupment.* Seller (S) sold goods to Buyer (B). B issued a promissory note payable to the order of S to evidence B's obligation to pay for the goods. At the time S took the note, it had no reason to believe that there were any defects in the goods. Later it was clear that the goods were defective and that B had a claim in recoupment against S for breach of warranty. S sued B on the note claiming that it had been in good faith at the time the note was taken and had no reason to believe at that time that there was anything wrong with the goods, and, therefore, was a holder in due course. It would be absurd in this case to allow S to take free of B's claim based on breach of warranty on the ground that S was a holder in due course. Section 3–305(b) states that the right of a holder in due course to enforce an obligation is not subject to "claims in recoupment * * * against a person other than the holder." Here the claim of recoupment can be asserted because it is against the holder. Comment 3 to 3–305 states: "It is obvious that the holder-in-due-course doctrine cannot be used to allow Seller to cut off a warranty claim that Buyer has against Seller."

*Defenses.* In Kane v. Kroll, 196 Wis.2d 389, 538 N.W.2d 605 (Wis.Ct. App.1995), the facts, somewhat altered, were these. Seller (S) sold cows to Buyer (B) on credit. B induced his Mother (M) to pay his debt to S by falsely representing to her that he was about to sell enough hay to come up with the money. M wrote a check to S for the debt. The next day B disclosed his fraud to M and she promptly stopped payment on the check.

When S presented the check to the drawee bank it was dishonored because of the stop order. S sued M on the check, claiming to be a holder in due course because S had no reason to know of the fraud that B had perpetrated on M.

Under the old law we would need more facts to decide the case. Former 3–305(2) provided that a holder in due course "takes the instrument free from all defenses of any party to the instrument with whom the holder has not dealt." Thus, if M had given the check to B and B had delivered the check to S, S would be a holder in due course because there were no dealings with M. But if M had delivered the check to S, S would most likely not be a holder in due course because S had dealt with M. This distinction makes no sense; in both cases S knew nothing of B's fraud on M. Why make a distinction based on an irrelevant fact, such as which party handed the check to S, determinative of S's status as a holder in due course?

Under Revised Article 3, the language in former 3–305(2) is deleted. Comment 2 to 3–305 explains: "The meaning of this language was not at all clear and if read literally could have produced the wrong result." Examples of cases in which payees may be holders in due course are set out in Comment 4 to 3–302. Case #1 is comparable to *Kane*. Comment 2 to 3–305 concludes: "The [holder-in-due-course] doctrine applies only to cases in which more than two parties are involved. Its essence is that the holder in due course does not have to suffer the consequences of a defense of the obligor on the instrument that arose from an occurrence with a third party." Although it is quite clear from the comments to 3–302 and 3–305 that payees can be holders in due course in three-party transactions coming within the ambit of the language quoted in the previous sentence, it is not so clear whether Article 3 offers specific guidance on cases in which payees cannot become holders in due course, other than the general rule that a taker with notice of a defense cannot qualify as a holder in due course. Comment 2 to 3–305 says that the "with whom the holder has not dealt" language of old 3–305(2) was dropped because "It is not necessary." White & Summers, Uniform Commercial Code § 14–8 (5th ed. 2000), contends that 3–305(b) serves the function of determining when payees cannot become holders in due course. It provides that the rights of a holder in due course are not subject "to defenses of the obligor stated in subsection (a)(2) or claims in recoupment stated in subsection (a)(3) against a person other than the holder." If the "against" clause at the end of the section applies to defenses as well as recoupment, the implication is that even if the payee is a holder in due course that person cannot take free of the defenses that a maker or drawer has against the payee-holder. This interpretation gives a sensible result, but nowhere do the voluminous comments to 3–302 and 3–305 refer to the "against" clause as applying in any case but recoupment.

### 5.  TRANSACTIONS WITH FIDUCIARIES

Under 3–306 a holder in due course of an instrument takes free of "a claim of a property or possessory right in the instrument or its proceeds." For example, a claim to the instrument or its proceeds may arise if a fiduciary, in breach of fiduciary duty, negotiates the instrument for value. The negotiation of the instrument may be the means used by the fiduciary to misappropriate funds of the person to whom the fiduciary duty is owed. The claim of that person falls within the language of 3–306. Under 3–302(a)(2), the person to whom the instrument is negotiated cannot be a holder in due course if the instrument was taken with notice of the claim. Section 3–307 governs cases of negotiation of instruments in breach of fiduciary duty. It states rules for determining when the person taking the instrument has notice of breach of fiduciary duty. It also states that notice of breach of fiduciary duty is notice of the claim of the person to whom the fiduciary duty was owed. The scope of 3–307 is narrowed by (b)(ii) to cases in which "the taker has knowledge of the fiduciary status of the fiduciary." "Knowledge" is defined in 1–202(b) as actual knowledge, and Comment 2 to 3–307 points out that: "In many cases, the individual who receives and processes an instrument on behalf of the organization that is the taker of the instrument 'for payment or collection or for value' is a clerk who has no knowledge of any fiduciary status of the person from whom the instrument is received. In such cases, Section 3–307 doesn't apply because, under [1–202(f)], knowledge of the organization is determined by the knowledge of the 'individual conducting that transaction,' i.e., the clerk who receives and processes the instrument."

## PROBLEM

Fiscus is the guardian ad litem for a minor child, Welty, who has won a judgment for $25,000 in a personal injury case. A check for this amount was issued payable to the order of "Fred Fiscus, Guardian ad Litem for Roy Welty." In which of the following cases does Bank have notice of a breach of fiduciary duty on the part of Fiscus under 3–307 (b)?

Case #1. When Fiscus indorsed the check and delivered it to Bank, he requested that it be applied in partial payment of his overdue loan obligation to Bank. Bank followed his directions.

Case #2. When Fiscus indorsed the check and delivered it to Bank, he completed a deposit slip directing that the check be credited to his personal account. His direction was carried out. It was on this issue, that pre-revision cases were divided. The different views are set out in *Smith v. Olympic Bank*, below, and *Matter of Knox*, discussed in the Note following the *Smith* opinion. Which view is adopted by 3–307(b)(2)? Why?

Case #3. Fiscus delivered the check to Bank, indorsed "Fred Fiscus, Guardian ad Litem for Roy Welty," and deposited it in a guardianship account that he had opened in Bank for Welty earlier. A month later, Fiscus drew a check on the guardianship account, purporting to act in his fiduciary capacity, payable to the order of "Fred Fiscus." He deposited the check in his personal account in Bank and later misappropriated the proceeds of the check for his personal benefit.

# Smith v. Olympic Bank

Supreme Court of Washington, 1985.
693 P.2d 92.

■ DORE, JUSTICE.

We hold that, where a bank allows a check that is made payable to a guardian to be deposited in a guardian's personal account instead of a guardianship account, the bank is not a holder in due course under the Uniform Commercial Code (UCC) because it has notice that the guardian is breaching his fiduciary duty.

Charles Alcombrack was appointed guardian for his son Chad Stephen Alcombrack who was then 7 years old and the beneficiary of his grandfather's life insurance policy. The insurance company issued a check for $30,588.39 made payable to "Charles Alcombrack, Guardian of the Estate of Chad Stephen Alcombrack a Minor". The attorney for the son's estate directed the father to take the check, along with the letters of guardianship issued to the father, to the bank and open up a guardianship savings and checking account. The father, however, did not follow the attorney's instructions. Instead, he took the check, without the letters of guardianship, to the bank and opened a personal checking and a personal savings account. The following was printed on the back of the check:

> By endorsement of this check the payee acknowledges receipt of the amount thereof in full settlement of all claims resulting from the death of Roy Alcombrack, certificate holder under Group Life Policy No. 9,745,632
>
> /s/ Charles Alcombrack
>
> Guardian of the Estate of Chad Stephen Alcombrack, a minor

Despite the above written notice that the check was payable to the father in his guardianship capacity, the bank allowed the father to place the entire amount in newly opened personal accounts. On the same day that the father opened his accounts, the attorney for the guardian called a trust officer from Olympic Bank and inquired as to the fees the bank charged for maintaining guardianship accounts. Responding to the attorney's questions, the trust officer wrote the attorney, specifically mentioning the "Estate of Chad Alcombrack".[1]

---

**1.** The following is the letter sent by the trust officer to the guardian's attorney:

"October 30, 1975

"Mr. Charles A. Schaaf, Attorney

"Reference: Estate of Chad Alcombrack

"Dear Mr. Schaaf:

"This is a follow up to our telephone conversation of October 28, 1975. The information you requested on the performance of our common trust funds will be available in about four weeks. October 31st is the end of our fiscal year. If this is not too long for you to wait, please let me know and I will send you a copy of our annual report.

"Our fee for handling a Guardianship account is, eight tenths ($\frac{8}{10}$) of one percent (1%), minimum of $350.00 per year."

The father, and later his new wife, used all but $320.60 of the trust money for their own personal benefit. Bank records disclosed how the estate money was withdrawn: five withdrawals were made to cash or into the father's checking account (total—approximately $16,000); one withdrawal paid off an unsecured personal loan made by the bank to the father (approximately $3,000); seven debits to the account were made by the bank exercising its right of offset to make payments on or pay off personal loans by the bank to the father (total—approximately $12,500).

After the depletion of the son's estate, J. David Smith was appointed successor guardian. He received a judgment against the father and instituted this suit against the bank. The trial court granted summary judgment in favor of the bank. The Court of Appeals reversed and remanded, holding that the trial court should determine the factual issue whether the bank was a holder in due course.

Olympic Bank claims that it is a holder in due course (HIDC) and, as such, is not subject to the claims of the petitioner. In order to qualify as a HIDC, the bank must meet five requirements. It must be (1) a holder (2) of a negotiable instrument, (3) that took the instrument for value (4) in good faith and (5) without notice that it was overdue, dishonored, or of any defense or claim to it on the part of any person. * * * We need not decide whether the bank met the first four conditions as we hold that the bank took the check with notice of an adverse claim to the instrument and, therefore, is not a holder in due course. Consequently, the bank is liable to the petitioner.[4]

A purchaser has notice of an adverse claim when "he has knowledge that a fiduciary has negotiated the instrument in payment of or as security for his own debt or in any transaction for his own benefit or otherwise in breach of duty." UCC 3–304(2). Thus, the issue raised by this case is whether the bank had knowledge that the guardian was breaching his fiduciary duty when it allowed him to deposit a check, made payable to him in his guardianship capacity, into his personal accounts. As to this issue, Von Gohren v. Pacific Nat'l Bank, 8 Wash.App. 245, 505 P.2d 467 (1973) is persuasive and controlling. In *Von Gohren*, it was held that a bank had notice that an employee was breaching her fiduciary duty when it allowed her to deposit third-party checks payable to her employer in her personal account. The bank was put on notice despite the fact that the employer had authorized the employee to draw checks against his account and also to endorse checks made payable to him and deposit such checks into his account. The court held that notice need not always consist of actual knowledge of a breach of a fiduciary duty, but can be predicated upon reasonable commercial standards. The court concluded by stating:

**4.**   UCC § 3–306 sets forth the liabilities of one who accepts a check and who is not a holder in due course.

"Unless he has the rights of a holder in due course any person takes the instrument subject to

"(a) all valid claims to it on the part of any person; and

"(b) all defenses of any party which would be available in an action on a simple contract; . . ."

It is our view that since defendant had notice of the claim by virtue of UCC § 3–304(2), and since it is undisputed that defendant did nothing to investigate Mrs. Martin's authority to negotiate checks payable to her employer, we must hold as a matter of law it did not act in accordance with reasonable commercial standards.

*Von Gohren*, at 255, 505 P.2d 467. The same conclusion is mandated in the present case.

Here, the bank knew it was dealing with guardianship funds. The check was payable to the father as guardian and not to him personally. The father endorsed it in his guardianship capacity. The bank received a call from the guardian's attorney inquiring about the fee the bank charged for guardianship accounts, and a trust officer for the bank replied in a letter referring to the "Estate of Chad Alcombrack".

Reasonable commercial practices dictate that when the bank knew that the funds were deposited in a personal account instead of a guardianship account, it also knew that the father was breaching his fiduciary duty. The funds lost the protection they would have received in a guardianship account when they were placed in a personal account. If the funds had been placed in a guardianship account, the bank would not have been allowed to exercise its set-off rights which amounted to approximately $12,500. * * * Nor would it have been permitted to accept a check, drawn on the guardianship account, from the father in satisfaction of the father's unsecured personal loan in the amount of approximately $3,000. Nor could the father, or bank, have authorized his new wife to write checks against the guardianship account without court approval. * * * A fiduciary has a duty to ensure that trust funds are protected. * * * Here, the father breached his duty.

While this is the first time, under the Uniform Commercial Code, that we have held a bank liable for allowing a guardian to deposit trust funds in a personal account, we have held a bank liable in a pre-Code case for allowing a trustee to breach his fiduciary duty. * * * In addition, other jurisdictions have held banks liable under similar circumstances using the Code * * * and without using the Code * * *. The policy reasons for holding a bank liable are compelling—especially in the situation presented in this case. The ward has no control of his own estate. He must rely on his guardian and on the bank for the safekeeping of his money. In order to protect the ward, the guardian and bank must be held to a high standard of care. For the guardian, this means that he must deposit guardian funds in a guardianship account. For the bank, it means that when it receives a check made payable to an individual as a guardian, it must make sure that the check is placed in a guardianship account. This will not place an undue burden on either banks or guardians and will have the beneficial effect of protecting the ward.

* * *

NOTE

In Matter of Knox, 64 N.Y.2d 434, 488 N.Y.S.2d 146, 477 N.E.2d 448 (1985), a pre-Revision case, rejects 9–307(b)'s imputation of notice when a bank allowed a guardian to deposit a check payable to him as guardian in his personal account. Knox involved a father who was guardian of the property of a minor son. Robert, the son, was injured when he was four years old. An action brought on behalf of Robert for damages was settled and a check was issued to the father as guardian of the property of the son. The check was negotiated to a bank and $11,000 of the proceeds of the check was deposited in the personal account of the father in the bank. The amount deposited in the account was eventually spent in the purchase of a house for the family and for other family expenses. The family included three other children besides Robert and the parents. The family was impoverished and the father stated that the money was spent to "give Robert as well as the rest [of the family] the same kind of normal life that any family enjoys." Eventually an action was brought against the father by a guardian ad litem appointed for Robert to recover the funds that had been misappropriated by the father. The bank was joined in the action and the trial court entered judgment against both. The bank appealed and the Appellate Division reversed the judgment against the bank. In affirming the Appellate Division, the Court of Appeals, one judge dissenting, stated:

> In Bradford Trust Co. v. Citibank, 60 N.Y.2d 868, 470 N.Y.S.2d 361, 458 N.E.2d 820, we held that "there is no requirement that a check payable to a fiduciary be deposited to a fiduciary account, and the fact that the instrument was not so deposited may not, without more, be relied upon as establishing a wrongful payment on the part of the depositary bank" * * *. Our decision was grounded upon the Uniform Commercial Code which provides that "[a]n instrument made payable to a named person with the addition of words describing him * * * as [a] fiduciary for a specified person or purpose is payable to the payee and may be negotiated, discharged or enforced by him" (Uniform Commercial Code § 3–117[b]), and that mere knowledge that the "person negotiating the instrument is or was a fiduciary" does not of itself give the purchaser of a negotiable instrument notice of any claims or defenses (Uniform Commercial Code § 3–304[4][e]). The conduct with which [the bank] is charged—having negotiated a check payable to [the father] in a fiduciary capacity without requiring deposit of the check in a fiduciary account—is thus permissible.

> In general, a bank may assume that a person acting as a fiduciary will apply entrusted funds to the proper purposes and will adhere to the conditions of the appointment * * *. A bank is not in the normal course required to conduct an investigation to protect funds from possible misappropriation by a fiduciary, unless there are facts—not here present—indicating misappropriation * * *. In this event, a bank may be liable for participation in the diversion, either by itself acquiring a benefit, or by notice or knowledge that a diversion is intended or being executed * * *. No facts are before this court suggesting that

[the bank] had notice that [the father] intended to, or did in fact, use the settlement proceeds for improper purposes. Consequently, [the bank] cannot be charged with the misappropriation.

Section 3–307(b)(2)(iii) has been controversial. Some states did not enact it, e.g., Alabama, and others that enacted it repealed it a few years later, e.g., Missouri.

## PROBLEM

Assume the same facts as set out in Case #2 in the Problem at the beginning of the section, except that Fiscus deposited the check in his personal account until he could open a guardianship account at a bank in another locality. Three days after Fiscus deposited the check in his account, he wrote a check on the account for the entire $25,000 amount and deposited the check in the guardianship account in the other bank. He subsequently used the proceeds of this account for his personal benefit in breach of his fiduciary duty. In Richards v. Seattle Metropolitan Credit Union, 68 P.3d 1109 (Wash. App. 2003), the court held that although Bank was liable in conversion for breach of its fiduciary duty by allowing the funds to be deposited in an account other than the fiduciary account, Bank's breach was not the proximate cause of the child's loss and no damages were assessed. The loss occurred when the funds were taken from a guardianship account in another bank. Do you agree with this result?

## NOTE: UNIFORM FIDUCIARIES ACT

When the National Conference approved the final draft of Revised Article 3, the Commissioners did so knowing that 3–307 took positions contrary to those of another uniform act, the Uniform Fiduciaries Act, that had been promulgated by the National Conference in the 1920s and adopted in about half of the states. The inconsistency between the two acts was before the court in County of Macon v. Edgcomb, 274 Ill.App.3d 432, 654 N.E.2d 598 (Ill. App. Ct. 1995), in which a county treasurer, Edgcomb, embezzled over $400,000 in county funds by stealing checks made to the county, endorsing them and depositing them in his personal account in Bank. Under UFA § 9, Bank had no liability in the absence of knowledge of the breach of fiduciary obligation or bad faith, but under 3–307(b)(2) Bank would be liable. Conceding that when choosing between conflicting statutes the more recent enactment will prevail as the later expression of legislative intent, the court applied the UFA to the case because Revised Article 3 was not in effect at the time of the embezzlement and amendatory acts should be construed as prospective unless the act indicates otherwise. In Bradley v. First National Bank of Walker, 59 UCC Rep. Serv. 2d 240 (Minn. App. 2006), the court held that the UCC preempted the UFA on the length of the statute of limitations. The National Conference has issued an "Addendum to Revised Article 3, Notes to Legislative Counsel. * * * 2. If Revised Article 3 is adopted in your state and the Uniform Fiduciaries Act is also in effect in your state, you may want to consider amending Uniform Fiduciaries Act § 9 to conform to Section 3–307(b)(2)(iii) and (4)(iii). See Official Comment 3 to Section 3–307.''

---

## PROBLEM

Little Corporation has about 100 stockholders and conducts its manufacturing operations in Centerville, a small city. Little has a checking account in Centerville Bank. The agreement between Little and the bank provides that the bank is authorized to honor checks drawn on the account if signed in the name of Little by either the president or treasurer of Little. Della, the president of Little, was involved in the following transactions:

Case #1. Della's personal credit card was used to pay for automobile rentals, restaurant meals, and hotel accommodations. All of the credit card charges were incurred for her personal benefit and were not related to any business purpose of Little. Della wrote a check drawn on Little's checking account and sent it to Issuer of the credit card to pay the monthly bill that included the charges.

Case #2. Della bought a small but expensive rug from Merchant and paid for it by writing a check drawn on Little's checking account. The rug was delivered to Della at the store.

Case #3. Della went to Clothier's store and ordered several dresses that were to be custom made for her. Della paid by writing a check drawn on Little's checking account. Before accepting the check, Clothier asked her why a check of the corporation was being used to pay for the clothing. She answered, ''The dresses are a present from a grateful employer for five years of faithful service by yours truly.''

Case #4. Della wrote a $1,000 check drawn on Little's account payable to her. She indorsed the check in blank and deposited it to her account in Depositary Bank by delivering it to a teller who knew her personally and knew that she was president of Little.

In each of the foregoing cases, Della committed a breach of fiduciary duty to Little in writing the check on Little's account. When Little discovered the defalcations it brought actions to recover the proceeds of the checks written by Della and paid from Little's account. The actions were brought against Issuer of the credit card in Case #1, against Merchant in Case #2, against Clothier in Case #3, and against Centerville Bank in Case #4. State your opinion whether Little is entitled to recover in each case. 3–306, 3–307, 1–202(a) (''notice'') and (b) (''knowledge''), and Comment 2 to 3–307.

## 6. VALUE

### a. INTRODUCTION

If Thief steals a negotiable instrument from Owner and sells it to unsuspecting Holder, it may make sense to give Holder rights in the instrument at the expense of Owner. One or the other must bear a loss. Although each is equally innocent, the negotiability doctrine tips the scales in favor of Holder in order to carry out a policy objective of encouraging free commerce in instruments. But if Holder has paid nothing for the instrument, denial of the right to defeat Owner's title results in no loss to Holder except missing out on a windfall. Thus, if Thief makes a gift of the instrument to Holder it seems unfair to allow Holder to profit at the expense of Owner. Since it is not necessary to impose a loss on Owner in order to carry out the objective of encouraging free commerce in instruments, Holder loses. Section 3–302(a)(2)(i) provides that only a holder who takes the instrument for value can be a holder in due course. Taking for value is defined in 3–303(a). Although the requirement of taking for value can be explained in part by distinguishing between loss and windfall, this distinction is not always clearly apparent in the cases covered by 3–303(a). The elementary problems that follow illustrate some cases covered by that section. In each problem, and the cases that follow, you might ask yourself whether the holder-in-due-course doctrine is necessary to protect some interest of the holder or whether the doctrine simply confers on the holder a windfall. If there is a windfall, is the result justified by commercial necessity? You might also ask whether, if the doctrine did not exist, the taking of the instrument in the particular transaction would have been discouraged.

## PROBLEMS

In each of the following problems make these assumptions: Maker gave to Payee a negotiable note in the amount of $1,000 payable on a stated date. Maker's issuance of the note was induced by Payee's fraudulent promise to deliver goods that were never delivered. In each case, Payee, prior to the due date, negotiated the note to Holder who had no notice of the fraud. On the due date Holder demanded payment of Maker who refused and asserted the defenses of fraud and failure of consideration.

**1.** Payee negotiates the note to Holder in consideration of Holder's agreement to perform services for Payee. Before Holder is obligated to begin performance of the promised services the note falls due. Was there consideration for the transfer of the note from Payee to Holder? 3–303(b). Was the note taken for value by Holder? 3–303(a)(1).

**2.** Payee negotiates the note to Holder who pays $900 cash for the note. Is Maker's defense good against Holder? What provision in 3–303(a) applies to this case? If Maker is liable, how much can Holder recover? 3–302(a)(2). Suppose Holder paid $600 cash for the note and promised to pay an additional $300 cash in 60 days. After paying the $600, Holder learned of the fraud and paid no more. How much can Holder recover? See O. P. Ganjo, Inc. v. Tri–Urban Realty Co., 108 N.J.Super. 517, 261 A.2d 722 (N.J. Super. Ct. Law Div. 1969). Comment 6, Case #5, to 3–302(d).

**3.** Payee was indebted to Holder on a loan past due. Holder demanded payment but Payee was unable to pay. In order to forestall legal action by Holder, Payee negotiated Maker's note to Holder as collateral for payment of Payee's loan. When the note became due, Payee was still unable to repay the loan. Holder thereupon demanded payment of the note by Maker. Is Maker's defense good against Holder? 3–303(a)(3).

### b.   RIGHTS OF DEPOSITARY BANK IN DEPOSITED CHECK

The material in this section examines one of the most common applications of the holder-in-due-course doctrine: when does a bank in which a check is deposited become a holder in due course of that check? Does it give value as soon as the depositor is given a provisional credit in the deposit account, or only when it pays out the proceeds of the check to the depositor? The answer to this question influences the bank's decisions on when to allow its depositors to draw on recently deposited checks. If the bank is a holder in due course, it takes free of any defenses between the drawer and the payee of the check, and if it is unable to recover from the depositor for money paid out on a check that the drawee bank refuses to pay, it can count on the liability of the drawer. As we explain below, Article 4 has its own rules for determining when a depositary or other collecting bank has given value for a check. These rules are stated in 4–210 and 4–211, and they complement 3–303; they do not displace it.

Checks are usually deposited by the payee in the payee's bank. That bank of first deposit is a "depositary bank." 4–105(2). The payee's bank is also referred to as a "collecting bank" if the check is not drawn on the payee's bank. 4–105(5). The depositary bank normally credits the account of the depositor for the amount of the check and forwards the check to the drawee for payment. The drawee is referred to in 4–105(3) as the "payor bank." The depositary bank is considered to be acting as the agent of the depositor in obtaining payment of the deposited check. 4–201. The credit to the depositor's account is normally provisional in nature. When the check is paid by the payor bank, this provisional credit becomes final, i.e., the credit represents a debt owed by the depositary bank to the depositor, 4–215(d). If the check is not paid by the payor bank, the depositary bank has the right to "charge back," i.e., cancel the provisional credit. 4–214(a).

Frequently, the depositary bank will also be a creditor of the depositor because of a past transaction such as a loan. If a debt owing by the depositor to the depositary bank is past due, the depositary bank may exercise a common law right to set off against the debt any amounts which the bank owes the depositor. For example, if the depositor owes the depositary bank $1,000 on a past-due loan and there is an $800 final credit balance in the depositor's checking account, the depositary bank may simply wipe out the $800 balance by applying it to reduce the $1,000 loan balance.[1] In addition to this right of setoff a depositary bank has a closely-related common law right known as a banker's lien. See Restatement, Security § 62.

---

**1.** The bank's right of setoff may be limited by statute. For example, Calif. Financial Code § 864 limits setoffs with respect to certain consumer-type installment debt owed to the bank.

For example, if the depositor owes the depositary bank $1,000 on a past-due loan and deposits a check to the depositor's account in the regular course of business, the depositary bank has a lien in the check as security for the $1,000 debt. Although the bank acts as agent for the depositor when it forwards the check to the payor for payment, it also has a property interest in the check represented by the lien. Thus, the depositary bank can collect the check and apply the proceeds to the debt owed by the depositor. Since the taking of an instrument for an antecedent debt is value, the depositary bank could attain the rights of a holder in due course. These two related but separate common law rights—setoff and banker's lien—are preserved under 1–103. Comment 1 to 4–210. The two common law rights are frequently confused. It is not uncommon for a court to refer to the banker's lien as a right of setoff or to refer to the right of setoff as a banker's lien. When a depositary bank is asserting a right in an uncollected check it is relying on a lien. A setoff can occur only if there are mutual debts. There can be no present right of setoff with respect to an uncollected check because until collected the check does not represent a debt of the depositary bank to the depositor. Restatement, Security § 62.

Depositary banks may acquire rights as holders in due course under other provisions of the UCC. Suppose there is no debt owing by the depositor when the check is deposited. Whether the depositary bank has given value for the check is determined under 4–211, which states that the bank has given value to the extent it has a security interest in the check. Section 4–210 states rules for determining when a security interest arises. This security interest is in addition to the bank's common law banker's lien. Comment 1 to 4–210. By virtue of 4–210 the depositary bank has a security interest under subsection (a)(1) if the check is deposited and the resulting credit is withdrawn, under subsection (a)(2) if the check is deposited and the depositor is given the right to withdraw the credit, and under (a)(3) if the bank makes a loan or cash payment based on the check. In these cases the bank is treated as though it were a lender to the depositor taking as security a security interest in the check. In the case in which the depositor is not allowed to withdraw the funds, the bank does not have a security interest and is not a holder in due course. It has committed no funds and is fully protected by its ability to charge back the depositor's account in the event the check is not paid by the payor bank.

In most cases the depositor has an existing credit balance in the account when a deposit is made and there may be a series of deposits and withdrawals from the account. In those cases, whether credit for a particular check has been withdrawn cannot be determined except by applying some mechanical tracing rule. Such a rule is provided by the last sentence of 4–210(b), which states that "credits first given are first withdrawn." This rule is usually referred to as the first-in-first-out or FIFO rule.

## PROBLEM

The table shows debits and credits made to Depositor's checking account in Depositary Bank. Withdrawals were made by payment by

Depositary Bank of checks drawn by Depositor on the account. Deposits were made either in cash or by third-party checks payable to Depositor as indicated.

| Date | Debit | Credit | | Balance |
|------|-------|--------|---|---------|
| Nov. 1 | Existing balance | | | 4,000 |
| Nov. 2 | Deposit by check | 5,000 | | 9,000 |
| Nov. 3 | Withdrawal | | 4,000 | 5,000 |
| Nov. 4 | Deposit in cash | 6,000 | | 11,000 |
| Nov. 5 | Withdrawal | | 5,000 | 6,000 |
| Nov. 6 | Received notice of dishonor of check deposited on Nov. 2 | | | |
| Nov. 7 (A.M.) | Withdrawal | | 3,000 | 3,000 |
| Nov. 7 (P.M.) | Charge-back of Nov. 2 credit | | 5,000 | –2,000 |

The check deposited on November 2 was not paid by the payor bank because the drawer had stopped payment. 4–403(a). Depositary Bank received notice of dishonor of the check on November 6. Depositor is insolvent. Depositary Bank brings an action against the drawer of the November 2 check to recover the amount of the check. 3–414(b). The drawer defends by asserting that no consideration was given for the check. 3–303(b). Assume that Depositary Bank is a holder in due course if it gave value for the check. Did Depositary Bank give value? 4–210(a)(1) and (b). Is the result in this Problem consistent with the case discussed in Comment 2 to 3–303? That case is governed by 3–303(1)(a), under which the unperformed promise of performance is not value. The rationale is that until performance is made the promisor will not suffer any out-of-pocket loss and dishonor of the check excuses performance by the promisor. In this Problem, is holder-in-due-course status necessary to protect Depositary Bank against an out-of-pocket loss when Depositary Bank received notice of dishonor on November 6? 4–214(a).

———————

Section 4–210(a)(1) refers not only to cases in which a credit has been withdrawn, but also to cases in which the credit has been "applied." The latter term refers to cases in which the credit has been used by the bank to pay an obligation to itself or to make a payment to a third party.

## NOTE

Earlier, when we were discussing the concept of negotiability, we quoted from Professor Rosenthal's article questioning the desirability of the doctrine of negotiability. Here we include another section of that article in which he considers the negotiability of checks. This is from Albert J. Rosenthal, "Negotiability—Who Needs It?," 71 Colum. L. Rev. 375, 382–385 (1971). Bankers disagree with Professor Rosenthal's view on the importance of holder-in-due-course status as to checks.

To begin with, negotiability normally plays almost no part with respect to checks. While some checks are cashed at a grocery store or across the counter at a bank, the overwhelming majority of checks are deposited by the payee for collection at his own bank, which, acting merely as the depositor's agent for that purpose, sends the check through banking channels to the drawee bank where it is presented for payment. If paid, the check is so marked and is ultimately returned to the drawer along with his monthly statement; if the check is dishonored, a slip setting forth the reason is attached to it and goes with it back through banking channels to the payee.

There is no holder in due course (except perhaps the payee himself) of such a check since, even though such other requirements as good faith and lack of notice may be met, the bank would not have given value for the check. Any dispute between drawer and payee will, therefore, simply be between themselves, with no one else in a position to assert special rights.

Let us now modify the case of a relatively poor buyer purchasing a refrigerator on installments, and substitute a middle-class consumer paying for it with his personal check. If the refrigerator fails to work properly, if its defect is immediately apparent, if the buyer's attempts to get redress from the seller prove unavailing, and if the buyer moves with sufficient alacrity, he can often stop payment on his check before it has cleared through his own bank. The buyer and seller will then be in a position themselves to resolve their dispute on the merits, with the buyer having the tactical advantage that the seller will have to bring suit in order to collect if the matter cannot be resolved without litigation.

Suppose, however, the bank in which the seller-payee deposits the check allows him to draw against it before it has been collected. This is not standard practice, but it does occur with some frequency. When the check is presented to the drawee bank for payment, it is dishonored because of the stop payment order. This time, however, the depositary bank is given the status of holder in due course "to the extent to which credit for the item has been withdrawn or applied," or "if it makes an advance on or against the item." To this extent, the drawer cannot assert against the bank the defense that the sale of the refrigerator was fraudulent. Although the stop payment order is effective, its utility to the drawer is defeated, since he is liable to the depositary bank.

\* \* \*

If the depositary bank were to grant credit to the payee by allowing withdrawals before collection, and if it were to do this in reliance upon its knowledge of the *drawer's* financial standing or reputation, there might be good reason to protect the depositary bank in this fashion. Typically, however the depositary bank pays no attention to the identity of the drawer; in fact, it does not even know whether the drawer's signature is genuine. It will often allow or refuse to allow withdrawals against the check before collection solely on the basis of its relations with and knowledge of the creditworthiness of its own customer, the payee. If payment is stopped, and the depositary bank cannot recover its advances by charging the amount back against the payee's account, but is permitted to hold the drawer liable, the bank receives a windfall: in such cases, it picks up the liability of the drawer, which by hypothesis it had not counted upon when it made its decision to allow withdrawals before collection.

The fact that the depositary bank would not normally be relying upon the drawer's credit may be seen in the improbable combination of circumstances that have to coincide for the drawer's liability to matter. First, the bank's customer, the payee, must have allowed his account to drop to the point at which some of his withdrawals cannot be charged against other funds in the account but must be regarded as advances against the uncollected check. Second, the payee must be insolvent, or at least his assets must not be readily amenable to collection. Third, the drawer has to be solvent and available, and his signature genuine. Fourth, the check must be dishonored. Finally, for the doctrine to make any ultimate difference, the drawer must have a legitimate defense on the check that is good against the payee, but is not of a type that can be asserted against a holder in due course. Only if all of these elements coincide is the bank's position improved by virtue of its becoming a holder in due course. It must therefore be a rare case indeed in which the bank's decision to extend credit before the check is collected can be regarded as having been made in reliance upon its ability to cut off the defenses of the drawer. Neither banks specifically, nor commerce in general, seem to need the rule declaring the bank to be a holder in due course. Where the bank relies entirely on the identity and credit of the payee in allowing withdrawals, it should shock no one's conscience if the bank were limited to the payee as a source of reimbursement.

\* \* \*

## c.   ARTICLE 9 SECURITY INTEREST AS VALUE

Those who have studied Article 9 know that much asset-based financing in which the collateral consists of inventory, accounts and their proceeds, which may include negotiable instruments, is done on what is called a "floating lien" basis. That is, a lender takes a security interest in all the debtor's personal property, now owned or thereafter acquired, to secure all present and future obligations of the debtor. As soon as the debtor acquires an item of collateral, the lender's security interest automatically attaches to it as security for the outstanding loan balance. In the following case, Bank had a floating lien on Bowl–Mor's assets and their proceeds. The SBA check was proceeds of Bowl–Mor's chattel paper collateral, and as soon as Bowl–Mor acquired the check, Bank's security interest attached. See footnote 1. Can it be that Bank's Article 9 security interest, which first attached when the check was in the possession of Bowl–Mor, is value within the meaning of 4–211 even though it does not comply with 4–210? See 3–303(a). If so, banks having Article 9 floating liens could become holders in due course of checks the instant they take possession on deposit because their security interest attached to the checks even before deposit. *Bowling Green* was the first authoritative holding on this issue.

# Bowling Green, Inc. v. State Street Bank & Trust Co.

United States Court of Appeals, First Circuit, 1970.
425 F.2d 81.

■ COFFIN, CIRCUIT JUDGE.

On September 26, 1966, plaintiff Bowling Green, Inc., the operator of a bowling alley, negotiated a United States government check for $15,306 to Bowl–Mor, Inc., a manufacturer of bowling alley equipment. The check, which plaintiff had acquired through a Small Business Administration loan, represented the first installment on a conditional sales contract for the purchase of candlepin setting machines. On the following day, September 27, a representative of Bowl–Mor deposited the check in defendant State Street Bank and Trust Co. The Bank immediately credited $5,024.85 of the check against an overdraft in Bowl–Mor's account. Later that day, when the Bank learned that Bowl–Mor had filed a petition for reorganization under Chapter X of the Bankruptcy Act, it transferred $233.61 of Bowl–Mor's funds to another account and applied the remaining $10,047.54 against debts which Bowl–Mor owed the Bank. Shortly thereafter Bowl–Mor's petition for reorganization was dismissed and the firm was adjudicated a bankrupt. Plaintiff has never received the pin-setting machines for which it contracted. Its part payment remains in the hands of defendant Bank.

Plaintiff brought this diversity action to recover its payment from defendant Bank on the grounds that the Bank is constructive trustee of the funds deposited by Bowl–Mor. In the court below, plaintiff argued that Bowl–Mor knew it could not perform at the time it accepted payment, that the Bank was aware of this fraudulent conduct, and that the Bank therefore received Bowl–Mor's deposit impressed with a constructive trust in plaintiff's favor. The district court rejected plaintiff's view of the evidence, concluding instead that the Bank was a holder in due course * * * and was therefore entitled to take the item in question free of all personal defenses. Bowling Green, Inc., etc. v. State Street Bank and Trust Co., 307 F.Supp. 648 (D.Mass.1969).

\* \* \*

Plaintiff's first objection arises from a technical failure of proof. The district court found that plaintiff had endorsed the item in question to Bowl–Mor, but there was no evidence that Bowl–Mor supplied its own endorsement before depositing the item in the Bank. Thus, we cannot tell whether the Bank is a holder within the meaning of § 1–201(20), which defines holder as one who takes an instrument endorsed to him, or to bearer, or in blank. But, argues plaintiff, once it is shown that a defense to an instrument exists, the Bank has the burden of showing that it is in all respects a holder in due course. This failure of proof, in plaintiff's eyes, is fatal to the Bank's case.

We readily agree with plaintiff that the Bank has the burden of establishing its status in all respects. UCC § 3–307(3), on which plaintiff relies to establish the defendant's burden, seems addressed primarily to cases in which a holder seeks to enforce an instrument, but Massachusetts courts have indicated that the policy of § 3–307(3) applies whenever a party invokes the rights of a holder in due course either offensively or defensively. Cf. Elbar Realty Inc. v. City Bank & Trust Co., 342 Mass. 262, 267–268, 173 N.E.2d 256 (1961). The issue, however, is not whether the Bank bears the burden of proof, but whether it must establish that it took the item in question by endorsement in order to meet its burden. We think not. The evidence in this case indicates that the Bank's transferor, Bowl–Mor, was a holder. Under UCC § 3–201(a), transfer of an instrument vests in the transferee all the rights of the transferor. As the Official Comment to § 3–201 indicates, one who is not a holder must first establish the transaction by which he acquired the instrument before enforcing it, but the Bank has met this burden here.

We doubt, moreover, whether the concept of "holder" as defined in § 1–201(20) applies with full force to Article 4. Article 4 establishes a comprehensive scheme for simplifying and expediting bank collections. Its provisions govern the more general rules of Article 3 wherever inconsistent. UCC § 4–102(1). As part of this expediting process, Article 4 recognizes the common bank practice of accepting unendorsed checks for deposit. * * * § 4–201(1) provides that the lack of an endorsement shall not affect the bank's status as agent for collection, and § 4–205(1) authorizes the collecting bank to supply the missing endorsements as a matter of course. In practice, banks comply with § 4–205 by stamping the item "deposited to the account of the named payee" or some similar formula. * * * We doubt whether the bank's status should turn on proof of whether a clerk employed the appropriate stamp, and we hesitate to penalize a bank which accepted unendorsed checks for deposit in reliance on the Code, at least when, as here, the customer himself clearly satisfies the definition of "holder". Section 4–209 does provide that a bank must comply "with the requirements of section 3–302 on what constitutes a holder in due course," but we think this language refers to the enumerated requirements of good faith and lack of notice rather than to the status of holder, a status which § 3–302 assumes rather than requires. We therefore hold that a bank which takes an item for collection from a customer who was himself a holder need not establish that it took the item by negotiation in order to satisfy § 4–209.

\* \* \*

This brings us to plaintiff's final argument, that the Bank gave value only to the extent of the $5,024.85 overdraft, and thus cannot be a holder in due course with respect to the remaining $10,047.54 which the Bank credited against Bowl–Mor's loan account. Our consideration of this argument is confined by the narrow scope of the district court's findings. The

Bank may well have given value under § 4–208(1)(a) when it credited the balance of Bowl–Mor's checking account against its outstanding indebtedness. See Banco Espanol de Credito v. State Street Bank & Trust Co., 409 F.2d 711 (1st Cir.1969). But by that time the Bank knew of Bowl–Mor's petition for reorganization, additional information which the district court did not consider in finding that the Bank acted in good faith and without notice at the time it received the item. We must therefore decide whether the Bank gave value for the additional $10,047.54 at the time the item was deposited.

Resolution of this issue depends on the proper interpretation of § 4–209, which provides that a collecting bank has given value to the extent that it has acquired a "security interest" in an item. In plaintiff's view, a collecting bank can satisfy § 4–209 only by extending credit against an item in compliance with § 4–208(1). The district court, on the other hand, adopted the view that a security interest is a security interest, however acquired. The court then found that defendant and Bowl–Mor had entered a security agreement which gave defendant a floating lien on Bowl–Mor's chattel paper. Since the item in question was part of the proceeds of a Bowl–Mor contract, the court concluded that defendant had given value for the full $15,306.00 at the time it received the deposit.[1]

With this conclusion we agree. Section 1–201(37) defines "security interest" as an interest in personal property which secures payment or performance of an obligation. There is no indication in § 4–209 that the term is used in a more narrow or specialized sense. Moreover, as the official comment to § 4–209 observes, this provision is in accord with prior law and with § 3–303, both of which provide that a holder gives value when he accepts an instrument as security for an antecedent debt. Reynolds v. Park Trust Co., 245 Mass. 440, 444–445, 139 N.E. 785 (1923). Finally, we note that if one of the Bank's prior loans to Bowl–Mor had been made in the expectation that this particular instrument would be deposited, the terms of § 4–208(1)(c) would have been literally satisfied. We do not think the case is significantly different when the Bank advances credit on the strength of a continuing flow of items of this kind. We therefore conclude that the Bank gave value for the full $15,306.00 at the time it accepted the deposit.

We see no discrepancy between this result and the realities of commercial life. Each party, of course, chose to do business with an eventually irresponsible third party. The Bank, though perhaps unwise in prolonging its hopes for a prospering customer, nevertheless protected itself through security arrangements as far as possible without hobbling each deposit and

---

**1.** [Ed]s. The bank secured its loan to Bowl–Mor by a security interest in Bowl–Mor's installment sale contracts (defined as chattel paper by § 9–105(1)(b)). Its security interest applied not only to the chattel paper but also to any proceeds of the chattel paper. § 9–306. Bowling Green's check to Bowl– Mor, since it was in payment of the first installment of its sales contract, was proceeds. Under § 9–306 and § 9–203 the bank automatically obtained a security interest in this check as soon as Bowl–Mor obtained "rights" in the check, which in this case was when Bowl–Mor received the check.

withdrawal. Plaintiff, on the other hand, not only placed its initial faith in Bowl–Mor, but later became aware that Bowl–Mor was having difficulties in meeting its payroll. It seems not too unjust that this vestige of caveat emptor survives.

Affirmed.

## NOTES

**1.** The conclusion in *Bowling Green* that a depositary bank could become a holder in due course of a check which did not bear the indorsement of the depositor was very controversial and was not supported by the text of Article 3 and Article 4 then in effect. Some courts refused to follow *Bowling Green*. But Revised Article 4 follows *Bowling Green* in this regard. Section 4–205 states that a depositary bank receiving a check for collection becomes a holder when it receives the check if the customer was then a holder regardless of whether the check is indorsed by the customer. It goes on to state that the bank becomes a holder in due course if it satisfies the other requirements of 3–302.

**2.** Acquisition of a lien by a depositary bank does not depend upon the bank's making any accounting entries to "apply" the check to the outstanding debt. See Maryland Casualty Co. v. National Bank of Germantown & Trust Co., 320 Pa. 129, 182 A. 362 (1936). By contrast 4–210(a)(1) states that the bank gets a security interest in the deposited check at the time that credit given for it is "applied." In *Bowling Green* the court indicates that this refers to the time when Bowl–Mor's deposit account, which had been credited with the amount of the check, was charged $10,047.54 in reduction of the loan. Suppose a check payable to Customer was indorsed by Customer to Depositary Bank and delivered to one of its officers in reply to a demand by Depositary Bank to immediately cover an overdraft. Thereafter, but before the check was deposited to Customer's account, the drawer of the check told the officer handling the transaction that the check was issued without consideration. At what time was "credit given for the item * * * applied"? 4–210(a)(1). At what time did Depositary Bank take the instrument "as payment of, or as security for, an antecedent claim"? 3–303(a)(3). At what time did Depositary Bank acquire a "lien in the instrument other than a lien obtained by judicial proceeding"? 3–303(a)(2). Peoria Savings & Loan Association v. Jefferson Trust & Savings Bank of Peoria, 81 Ill.2d 461, 43 Ill.Dec. 712, 410 N.E.2d 845 (1980).

## FORM.   PROMISSORY NOTE–FIXED MATURITY

 CITY NATIONAL BANK

PROMISSORY NOTE - FIXED MATURITY
(INTEREST FIXED)

For value received, the undersigned, * ("Borrower"), promises to pay to the order of City National Bank, a national banking association ("CNB"), at its office in this city, in lawful money of the United States of America and in immediately available funds, the principal sum of * Dollars ($*), with interest thereon from the date of disbursement at the rate of * percent (*%) per year (computed on the basis of a 360–day year, actual days elapsed).

Interest accrued on this Note shall be payable on the * day of each *, commencing *, *. The minimum interest charge for the term of this Note shall in no event be less than One Hundred Dollars ($100.00).

Principal and any interest remaining unpaid shall be payable in full on *, *.

The occurrence of any of the following with respect to any Borrower or any guarantor of this Note or any general partner of such Borrower or guarantor, shall constitute an "Event of Default" hereunder:

1. The failure to make any payment of principal or interest when due under this Note;

2. The filing of a petition by or against any of such parties under any provisions of the *Bankruptcy Code*;

3. The appointment of a receiver or an assignee for the benefit of creditors;

4. The commencement of dissolution or liquidation proceedings or the disqualification of any such parties which is a corporation, partnership, joint venture or any other type of entity;

5. The death or incapacity of any of such parties who is an individual;

6. Any financial statement provided by any of such parties to CNB is false or misleading;

7. Any default in the payment or performance of any obligation, or any default under any provisions of any contract or instrument pursuant to which any of such parties has incurred any obligation for borrowed money, any purchase obligation or any other liability of any kind to any person or entity, including CNB;

8. Any sale or transfer of all or a substantial or material part of the assets of any of such parties other than in the ordinary course of business; or

9. Any violation, breach or default under any letter agreement, guaranty, security agreement, deed of trust or any other contract or instrument executed in connection with this Note or securing this Note.

Upon the occurrence of any Event of Default, the holder of this Note, at the holder's option, may declare all sums of principal and interest outstanding hereunder to be immediately due and payable without presentment, demand, protest or notice of dishonor all of which are expressly waived by each Borrower. Each Borrower agrees to pay all costs and expenses, including reasonable attorneys' fees, expended or incurred by the holder (or allocable to the holder's in-house counsel) in connection with the enforcement of this Note or the collection of any sums due hereunder and irrespective of whether suit is filed. Any principal or interest not paid when due hereunder shall thereafter bear additional interest from its due date at a rate of five percent (5.0%) per year higher than the interest rate as determined and computed above, and continuing thereafter until paid.

Should more than one person or entity execute this Note as a Borrower, the obligations of each such Borrower shall be joint and several.

This Note and all matters relating thereto, shall be governed by the laws of the State of California.

*, a

* corporation

BY: _____

ITS: _____

## FORM.  DEMAND NOTE

 **CITY NATIONAL BANK**                **DEMAND NOTE**
                                        (INTEREST TIED TO PRIME)

On demand, or if no demand is made, then on *, *, for value received, the undersigned * ("Borrower"), promises to pay to the order of City National Bank, a national banking association ("CNB"), at its Office in this city, in lawful money of the United States of America and in immediately available funds, the principal sum of * Dollars ($*), plus interest thereon at a rate computed on the basis of a 360–day year, actual days elapsed, equal to the "Prime Rate" of CNB as it exists from time to time, plus * percent (*%) per year. "Prime Rate" shall mean the rate most recently announced by CNB at its principal office in Beverly Hills as its "Prime Rate." Any change in the Prime Rate shall become effective on the same business day on which the Prime Rate shall change, without prior notice to Borrower.

Interest accrued on this Note shall be payable on the * day of each *, commencing *, *. The minimum interest charge for the term of this Note shall in no event be less than One Hundred Dollars ($100.00).

In the event the interest is not paid as it becomes due, or in the event there occurs any material default in the payment or performance of any obligation owing by any Borrower to CNB, then the holder of this Note, at the holder's option, may declare all sums of principal and interest outstanding hereunder to be immediately due and payable without presentment, demand, protest or notice of dishonor all of which are expressly waived by each Borrower. If principal or interest is not paid on the agreed or accelerated date of maturity, then the interest rate provided for under this Note shall, at CNB's option, and without notice, be increased to an amount 5.0% per year higher than the interest rate as determined and computed above, effective from the day following the time that such payment of principal or interest became overdue and continuing thereafter until paid.

Each Borrower agrees to pay all costs and expenses, including reasonable attorneys' fees, expended or incurred by CNB (or allocable to CNB's in-house counsel) in connection with the enforcement of this Note or the collection of any sums due hereunder and irrespective of whether suit is filed.

Should more than one person or entity execute this Note as a Borrower, the obligations of each such Borrower shall be joint and several.

This Note and all matters relating thereto shall be governed by the laws of the State of California.

\*, a

\* corporation

By: _____

Its: _____

# CHAPTER 12

# LIABILITY OF PARTIES TO NEGOTIABLE INSTRUMENTS

## A. LIABILITY OF MAKER

An understanding of the liability of the parties to negotiable instruments is essential to counseling clients in planning transactions as well as at the litigation stage. The obligations of the parties are set out in four sections: the obligation of a maker in 3–412, of an acceptor in 3–413, of a drawer in 3–414, and of an indorser in 3–415.

The person primarily obliged to pay a promissory note is the maker, who has expressly agreed to do so. The relevant statutory provisions are: 3–103(a)(5), which defines "maker" as "a person who signs or is identified in a note as the person undertaking to pay;" 3–412, which states, "[t]he issuer of a note * * * is obliged to pay the instrument (i) according to its terms at the time it was issued * * *;" and 3–105(a), which defines "issue" as "the first delivery of an instrument by the maker or drawer, whether to a holder or nonholder, for the purpose of giving rights on the instrument to any person."

### PROBLEM

New Movies Incorporated (NMI) produces films. It has rounded up 20 wealthy backers for a new motion picture, each of whom has agreed to contribute $1 million to the project. Now NMI wishes to obtain some bank financing before signing the talent for the film. In order to do this, NMI has persuaded all the backers to sign a single negotiable promissory note payable to NMI for $20 million that NMI can show banks and others to induce them to commit to the picture. Before production commenced, some of the backers wished to withdraw because of the economic recession. In order to keep them committed, NMI warned the backers that any signer of the note can be sued for the full amount of the note. Your client, a wealthy plastic surgeon, is one of the backers. She calls you and asks (1) whether NMI is correct is asserting that she can be sued for the full $20 million, and (2) if NMI is correct, what rights does she have against the other signers. What do you tell her (besides telling her to call you *before* she signs her name, not *after*)? See 3–412 and 3–116(a) and (b).

## B.    DRAWERS, DRAWEES AND ACCEPTORS

How do you answer the Problems below on the basis of the discussion in the text following these Problems? We use ordinary bank checks to illustrate the issues treated in this section.

PROBLEMS

Drawer signed and delivered a check for $1,000 to Payee in payment for goods purchased. The check was drawn on Drawee bank where Drawer maintains a deposit account.

**1.** When Payee presented the check to Drawee for payment, Drawee dishonored the check because Drawer had stopped payment on the check owing to its dissatisfaction with the goods delivered.

(a) Is Drawee liable on the check to Payee?

(b) Is Drawer liable on the check to Payee?

**2.** When Payee presented the check to Drawee for payment, Drawee dishonored the check even though no stop payment order had been received and Drawer had sufficient funds in its account to pay the check.

(a) Is Drawee liable on the check to Payee?

(b) Is Drawee liable to Drawer?

**3.** When Payee presented the check to Drawee for acceptance, Drawee certified the check. Later Payee presented the certified check to Drawee for payment. Drawee dishonored the check because after it had certified the check it received a stop order from Drawer.

(a) Is Drawee liable to Payee?

(b) Is Drawer liable to Payee?

**4.** When Payee presented the check to Drawee for acceptance, Drawee refused to certify the check, even though Drawer had sufficient funds in its account to cover the check. Is Drawee liable to Payee if Payee can show that when it presented the check to Drawee for payment ten days later, the check was dishonored because there were no longer funds in the account to pay the check?

---

When a drawer orders a drawee to pay an amount of money to the payee, nobody has expressly agreed to make the payment. A draft normally arises out of a pre-existing creditor-debtor relationship between the drawer and the drawee. For example, a seller ships goods to a buyer who is located in a distant market. The contract of sale provides for payment of the price of the goods by a draft drawn by the seller on the buyer or the buyer's bank acting on behalf of the buyer. The seller draws a draft ordering the drawee to pay to the order of a named payee a sum of money equal to the price of the goods. The named payee may be the seller's bank which buys the draft from the seller for the face amount less a discount to compensate the bank for its services. In that case, the draft is delivered to the bank, which then becomes its holder. The draft is then "presented" to the drawee for payment. "Presentment" is defined in 3–501(a). In this case, presentment is simply a demand made on the drawee to pay. Subsection (b) of 3–501 states rules regarding the place, time, and manner of presentment. In our example, presentment might be made by the bank named as payee of the draft, but often the draft will be negotiated to another bank located near the buyer and that bank will present the draft to the drawee for payment. When the draft is paid the buyer has discharged the obligation to the seller to pay the price of the goods.

The most common example of a draft is the ordinary check which is a draft drawn on a bank and payable on demand. 3–104(f). Payment of checks is also normally based on a creditor-debtor relationship. A check is drawn by a customer of a bank who has a checking account in the bank; the credit balance in the account represents a debt of the bank to the customer. When the bank pays the check, the bank's debt to the customer is reduced by the amount of the check.

Since the drawee of a draft has made no promise in the instrument to pay the payee or other holder, the holder has no action on the instrument against the drawee to enforce payment. 3–408. Sometimes the drawee will obligate itself, by a letter of credit or other separate contract, to pay a draft. In that case failure by the drawee to pay the draft may result in liability to the holder for breach of the letter of credit, but there is no liability based on an obligation created by the draft. In the absence of a separate contract of the drawee such as a letter of credit, payment by the drawee will normally depend upon the drawee's obligation to the drawer arising from an express or implied contract between them. For example, in opening a checking account for a customer, the bank incurs an obligation to the customer to pay properly payable checks drawn on the account. Failure to pay a properly payable check may result in liability to the customer for wrongful dishonor (4–402), but the holder of the check has no cause of action against the drawee bank. Before codification of negotiable instruments law by the NIL in the late 19th century, a minority of states took the view that a check created a direct liability on the part of the drawee bank to the holder. The theory was that a check amounted to an equitable assignment of the drawer's funds on deposit, but NIL § 189 took the majority view that the check is not itself an assignment. Article 3 follows the NIL in that respect.

Although a draft, by its stated terms, is simply an order of the drawer to the drawee to pay, it is also an obligation of the drawer to pay the draft if the draft is dishonored. 3–414(b). "Dishonor" occurs if the drawee fails to make timely payment when the draft is presented for payment. Dishonor of ordinary checks and drafts is defined in 3–502(b) and (e). The drawer of a draft other than a check can avoid liability under 3–414(b) if the signature of the drawer is accompanied by words that disclaim liability such as "without recourse." 3–414(e). Disclaimer of the drawer's liability is normally limited to documentary drafts. Comment 5 to 3–414. With respect to checks, disclaimer is not effective. 3–414(e). A relatively unimportant limitation on drawer's liability is provided by 3–414(f). This provision is explained in Comment 6 to 3–414.

Section 3–408 states that "the drawee is not liable on the instrument until the drawee accepts it." Section 3–409(a) defines "acceptance" as "the drawee's signed agreement to pay a draft as presented." The acceptance "must be written on the draft and may consist of the drawee's signature alone." A drawee that accepts a draft is known as the "acceptor" and is obliged to the holder to pay the draft. 3–413(a). To understand the concept of acceptance better, it is appropriate to distinguish between two types of drafts. The most common type of draft is the demand draft or "sight draft." It contemplates that the amount of the draft will be paid by the drawee upon presentation or "on sight." A draft that does not specify a time of payment is payable on demand. 3–108(a). A check is the most common example of a demand draft. Another type of draft, called a "time draft" does not contemplate immediate payment by the drawee. For example, suppose the draft reads as follows: "Pay $1,000 to the order of Jane Doe sixty days after presentment of this draft." Here, two steps are contemplated. Jane Doe, or some subsequent holder, will initially present the draft to the drawee to start the running of the 60 days, and when that period of time has passed a second presentment will be made for payment. The first presentment is known as a "presentment for acceptance." Its purpose is to allow the holder to know whether the drawee is agreeable to honoring the draft. Agreement of the drawee is manifested by acceptance, i.e., the drawee's signing of the draft with or without the addition of the word "accepted" or other words indicating an intention to accept. The date of acceptance is normally included but is not required. 3–409(a) and (c). The drawee's acceptance is equivalent to a promise to pay the amount of the draft to the holder. Thus, the obligation of an acceptor is like that of the maker of a note.

Another example of an accepted draft is the certified check. If the payee of an ordinary check wants assurance of payment, one way of getting it is to insist that the drawer obtain the acceptance of the drawee bank before the check is taken by the payee. This is done by the drawee bank's signing the check in much the same way as described in the case of a time draft. But the terminology differs. The bank's signature is called "certification" but it is identical to acceptance. 3–409(d). Certification is normally obtained by the drawer before delivery of the check to the payee, but in unusual cases the holder of an uncertified check may prefer to obtain the drawee bank's agreement to pay rather than payment itself. This can be done by asking the drawee bank to certify the check. The drawee of a check may certify it as a courtesy to the drawer or to the holder, but is not obliged to do so. Nor is refusal to certify a dishonor of the check. 3–409(d). Because certification of a check is treated by the bank as the equivalent of payment insofar as the drawer is concerned, the account of the drawer will be debited in the amount of the check at the time of certification. The effect of certification is to transform the check, which originally represented an order to pay of the drawer, into a promise of the drawee to pay the amount of the check to its holder. This transformation is reflected in 3–414(c), which states that acceptance of a draft by a bank discharges the drawer's obligation to pay the draft.

### PROBLEM

Seller contracted to sell real property to Buyer for $150,000 cash to be paid on the settlement date by a certified check. Buyer arrived at the settlement with an uncertified check drawn on her funds in Drawee Bank. When Seller refused to take the check, Buyer induced Seller to call Drawee Bank and inquire about the balance of her account. An authorized person at the bank assured Seller that there were funds in the account sufficient to cover the check. "But," Seller countered, "will there be funds there when the check is presented?" The bank representative replied in the affirmative, and when asked to confirm this in writing, sent an immediate fax to Seller stating: "This letter is to verify that the funds are available in Buyer's account. There is a hold on the funds for the check that was given you." When Seller presented the check for payment, Drawee Bank dishonored on the ground of insufficient funds in the account. The bank representative had mistakenly misstated the balance of the account. Is Drawee Bank liable to Seller on the check? The facts are based on those in *Harrington v. MacNab*, 163 F.Supp.2d 583 (D.Md. 2001). See also *Call v. Ellenville Nat'l Bank*, 774 N.Y.2d 76 (Sup. Ct. App. Div. 2004) (bank not bound by oral representation that check had "cleared.")

## C.   LIABILITY OF INDORSER

In the previous chapter, we examined the function of an indorsement in the negotiation of an instrument. Indorsement also has the additional function of causing the indorser to incur liability on the instrument. The obligation of the indorser, stated in 3–415(a), is to pay the instrument if the instrument is dishonored, but indorser's liability may be avoided by appropriate words accompanying the signature that disclaim liability. The most commonly used words indicating disclaimer are "without recourse." 3–415(b). An indorsement containing such language is called a "qualified indorsement." As we see in Problem 2 below, indorser's liability can be an unpleasant surprise to holders who believe that they are indorsing merely to transfer the instrument.

### PROBLEMS

**1.** Employer sent Peter his paycheck in the amount of $5,000, drawn on Bank One. Peter indorsed the check in blank and deposited it in his depositary bank, Bank Two. Bank Two gave Peter immediate credit for the check in his account, and Peter withdrew the amount of the credit before Bank Two learned that Bank One had dishonored the check because Employer had previously withdrawn all the money from the account. Employer went out of business, costing Peter his job, and several months later an impecunious Peter heard from Bank Two that it wanted $5,000 from him, long after Peter had closed his account in that bank. (i) If Bank Two chooses not to proceed against insolvent Employer on the check, is Peter personally liable to Bank Two for $5,000? (ii) If Peter has to pay, may he enforce the check against Employer? 3–414(b).

**2.** Seller sold residential real property to Buyer for the price of $100,000. Buyer was able to borrow $75,000 from a bank, secured by a first mortgage on the property. But Buyer didn't have enough cash to come up with the remaining $25,000. In order to make the sale, Seller agreed to take a second mortgage on the property from Buyer that secured a negotiable promissory note, payable in installments over ten years, in the amount of $20,000 made by Buyer to Seller. Buyer paid Seller the remaining $5,000 balance in cash. In State A, where the land was located, there is a secondary market for second mortgage notes, and Investor was willing to pay Seller $15,000 in cash for the note. Seller indorsed in blank the note to Investor and assigned the mortgage. Buyer defaulted on the payments on the $20,000 note, but under State A's real property anti-deficiency law Buyer is not personally liable on a purchase money note. Thus, Investor had no right to sue Buyer on the note, so it brought suit against Seller as an indorser. Is Seller liable to Investor on the note even though the maker, Buyer, was not liable? Had Seller talked to you before indorsing the note, what advice would you have given him? See 3–415(b).

---

### Drafts

The obligation of the indorser to pay an instrument arises upon its dishonor. With respect to unaccepted drafts, dishonor usually requires presentment for payment and a failure of the drawee to pay. 3–502(b)(1) through (3). With respect to some time drafts, dishonor requires presentment for acceptance and failure of the drawee to accept. 3–502(b)(4). In some cases, dishonor can occur without presentment. 3–502(e) and 3–504(a).

The obligation of an indorser of an unaccepted draft is subject to discharge in two situations. First, if the draft is a check and collection of the check is not initiated within 30 days of the indorsement, the indorser is discharged. 3–415(e). Second, discharge can occur as the result of a failure to give timely notice of dishonor to the indorser. 3–415(c) and 3–503(a). The manner and time for giving notice are stated in 3–503(b) and (c). Notice of dishonor need not be given if it is excused. 3–504(b). Delay in giving notice may also be excused in some cases. 3–504(c).

Indorser's liability with respect to checks has very limited importance because most checks are deposited by the payee with a depositary bank for collection. The depositary bank gives the depositor provisional credit for the check. Under 4–214(a), if the check is dishonored, the depositary bank may revoke the credit or otherwise obtain refund from the depositor. Normally, the depositary bank will use this remedy rather than the remedy provided by 3–415(a).

If a draft is accepted by a bank after the draft is indorsed, the indorser is discharged. 3–415(d). The rule is similar to 3–414(c) with respect to the liability of a drawer. Thus, with respect to an accepted draft, an indorser has liability under 3–415(a) only if the indorsement is made after the acceptance or if the acceptor is not a bank. Rules with respect to dishonor of accepted drafts are stated in 3–502(d).

NOTES

Dishonor of a note payable at a definite time does not normally require presentment unless the note is payable at or through a bank. 3–502(a)(2) and (3). In the case of notes that do not require presentment, indorser's liability under 3–415(a) arises automatically if the note is not paid when due. If a note is payable on demand, is payable at or through a bank, or the terms of the note require presentment, dishonor requires presentment and a failure to pay by the maker. But the requirements in 3–502(a) with respect to presentment can be waived. 3–504(a). Notice of dishonor required by 3–503(a) also can be waived, and waiver of presentment is also waiver of notice of dishonor. 3–504(b). Since most promissory note forms contain a clause waiving presentment and notice of dishonor, these formalities have little importance with respect to indorser liability in note cases. See the Promissory Note and Demand Note forms at the end of Chapter 11.

# D.  LIABILITY OF TRANSFEROR

Work the following Problem on the basis of the discussion in the text following the Problem.

PROBLEM

Maker signed and delivered a promissory note for $1,000 payable to the order of Payee one year after date. Shortly after receiving the note, Payee, who had fraudulently induced Maker to issue the note, indorsed the note "without recourse" and sold it to Holder for $600. When Holder presented the note to Maker for payment, Maker refused to pay because she had learned that Payee had defrauded her. Does Holder have rights against Payee? See 3–415(b) and 3–416(a)(4). Comment 5 to 3–416.

If goods are sold, the law gives to the buyer the benefit of certain warranties of the seller that are implied by reason of the sale and which apply unless they are disclaimed in the contract between the parties. For example, the seller warrants that the buyer is receiving good title to the goods and, if the seller is a merchant, that the goods are fit for the ordinary purposes for which such goods are used. 2–312(1) and 2–314. If an instrument is sold the law gives to the buyer the benefit of implied warranties that are comparable to sale of goods warranties, but which are expressed in terms appropriate to what the buyer is buying—a right to receive payment from the person obliged to pay the instrument. These warranties are known as "transfer warranties" and are stated in 3–416(a).

Two of the transfer warranties relate to the authenticity of the instrument; the transferor warrants that all signatures are authentic and authorized, and the instrument has not been altered. 3–416(a)(2) and (3). The other three warranties relate to the enforceability of the instrument. Under 3–416(a)(1) there is a warranty that the transferor is a person entitled to enforce the instrument. If the transferor is a person entitled to enforce the instrument, transfer will give the transferee that right. 3–203(b). The 3–416(a)(1) warranty, in practice, serves as a warranty that there are no unauthorized or missing indorsements that prevent the transferor from giving to the transferee the right to enforce the instrument. Under 3–416(a)(4) there is a warranty that the right to enforce the instrument is not subject to defenses that can be asserted against the transferor. Finally, there is a warranty of no knowledge of bankruptcy or other insolvency proceedings initiated against the person obliged to pay the instrument. 3–416(a)(5).

The transfer warranties are of very limited importance because in most cases the transferor is also an indorser and, as such, guarantees payment of the instrument. 3–415(a). In those cases the transfer warranties are redundant because the guarantee of payment gives greater rights to the transferee than do the warranties. Thus, the transfer warranties are important only in cases in which the transfer is made without indorsement or there is an indorsement without recourse. If the payee of a note indorsed the note without recourse, the transferee is assured of receiving an authentic and enforceable instrument but takes the risk that the maker will be unwilling or unable to pay the note.

## E. CASHIER'S CHECKS AND TELLER'S CHECKS

In this section we give detailed treatment to the rights of parties under cashier's checks and teller's checks. Our objective is to help you deal with one of the contemporary dilemmas facing business lawyers: how to take payment when the deal closes. Since the obligor side is not likely to lug sacks of money to the closing, the obligee should obtain agreement in advance on how payment is to be made. The ordinary uncertificated check leaves the payee vulnerable on several grounds: the drawer may stop payment on the check, thereby placing the burden on the payee to come after the drawer for payment; the drawer may have no money in its account in the bank; or, in rare cases, the bank on which payment is drawn may suspend payments before the check is paid because of insolvency, leaving the payee with a claim against the bank not covered by deposit insurance because the bank has no liability on the check (3–408) and therefore the payee has no "deposit" insured by the Federal Deposit Insurance Act. 12 U.S.C. § 1813(*l*) ("deposit"). On the other hand, we will see that no one can stop payment under 4–403 on a cashier's check; the payee can be sure that a cashier's check will not be returned marked "not sufficient funds;" and, even if the bank fails, the holder of the check is protected, at least to the extent of $100,000, by federal deposit insurance. 12 U.S.C. § 1813(*l*)(4). So why is it that in some cases even when the parties are across the street from each other, the obligee will insist on a wire transfer, which we will study in a later chapter, instead of a cashier's check? But first we have more to learn about cashier's checks.

## 1. USE IN PAYMENT OF OBLIGATIONS

In some transactions a creditor is unwilling to take the personal check of the debtor in payment of the obligation owed to the creditor. Instead, the creditor may insist on delivery by the debtor of the obligation of a bank as payment. The debtor can comply by delivering a cashier's check, a teller's check, or a check of the debtor that has been certified by the drawee. We have already discussed the certified check. Some banks have discontinued the practice of certifying checks. Cashier's checks and teller's checks have become the principal means of allowing a debtor to pay a debt with a bank obligation.

A cashier's check is a rather strange instrument. It is always issued by a bank and is in the form of an ordinary check, except that the drawer and the drawee are the same bank. Thus, Bank A orders itself to pay a sum of money to the payee stated in the instrument. One can justly argue that an order to oneself to pay money is fundamentally different from an order by one person to another person to pay money. The liability of the "issuer" (3–105(c)) of a cashier's check is not stated in 3–414(b), which applies to drawers of drafts (3–414(a)), but in 3–412, and is identical to the obligation of the maker of a note. However, 3–104(f) follows the universal banking practice of referring to a cashier's check as a check. This practice is also reflected in legislation other than Articles 3 and 4. Section 3–103(a)(6) defines "order" as a "written instruction to pay money" and artificially states that the "instruction may be addressed to any person, including the person giving the instruction." Thus, a cashier's check is an order and, under 3–104(e) and (f), is a draft and a check. The purpose of the artificiality in the definition of "order" was to allow references to drafts and checks in Article 3 to include cashier's checks.

A teller's check, like a cashier's check, is always issued by a bank. The difference between the two is that a cashier's check is drawn on the issuing bank while a teller's check typically is drawn on another bank. In some cases a teller's check is drawn on a nonbank but is payable at or through a bank. 3–104(h). A typical use of teller's checks is the practice of credit unions or small banks of maintaining deposits in regional or city banks from which to make payments. The issuer of a teller's check is obliged to pay the check as drawer of the check. 3–414(b). If a teller's check is issued by Bank A and the check is drawn on Bank B, presentment for payment of the check is made to Bank B, the drawee. As in the case of the drawee of an ordinary check, Bank B as drawee of a teller's check has no obligation to the payee to pay the check. 3–408. If the check is dishonored, the remedy of the payee is against Bank A. Thus, a teller's check represents an obligation of the bank that issues the check, not of the bank on which it is drawn.

One of the aspects in which cashier's checks differ from ordinary checks is the effect of taking a check on the underlying obligation for which the check was given. Section 3–310(b)(1) provides that if an uncertified check is taken for an obligation, the obligation is suspended "until dishonor of the check or until it is paid or certified." If the check clears, the obligation is discharged; if it is dishonored, the payee has a choice whether to take action against the drawer on the check or on the underlying obligation. Usually, there is no advantage to the payee in being able to pursue the drawer on the underlying transaction, but in a few instances there may be. However, if the obligee takes a cashier's check for an obligation, the obligation is discharged (3–310(a)) and the payee is restricted to its rights on the check against the issuing bank. As we explained above, if the bank has failed, the holder is insured by federal deposit insurance to the extent of $100,000.

## PROBLEM

Seller contracted to sell goods to Buyer with payment by cashier's check to be made at the time of delivery. Buyer purchased a cashier's check in the amount of $10,000 from Bank made payable to Seller. Bank delivered the check to Buyer who held it pending Seller's performance. Before delivering the cashier's check to Seller, Buyer learned that Seller did not intend to comply with the contract. Buyer asked Bank to return the money that it paid to Bank to issue the check, but Bank delayed in doing so. Is Buyer, the remitter, a person entitled to enforce the instrument under 3–301? The prevailing view in case law is that since a remitter is not a party to an instrument it cannot enforce the instrument under 3–301. The authorities are marshaled in Perrino v. Salem, Inc., 243 B.R. 550 (D. Me. 1999), which states that although Article 3 does not directly address the issue in the text, Comment 1 to 3–312 expressly says that a remitter is not a person entitled to enforce a check. How do you reconcile this Comment with the 2002 addition to the Comment to 3–301? What is the statutory basis for this language?

## 2.   Payment With Notice of Adverse Claim

### a.   RIGHT TO STOP PAYMENT

The right of a buyer who has paid a seller with a cashier's check or a teller's check and who has either been defrauded or has received defective goods to stop payment on the check are considered in the following Problems and the text following the Problems.

## PROBLEMS

**1.** Seller agreed to sell goods to Buyer but insisted on immediate payment by means of a cashier's check or teller's check. Buyer had an account in Bank A. At the request of Buyer, Bank A issued a cashier's check payable to the order of Seller and delivered it to Buyer. Bank A debited the account of Buyer in the amount of the cashier's check. Buyer delivered the check to Seller, but Seller failed to deliver the promised goods stating that they would be delivered as soon as they became available. Buyer, fearing fraud on the part of Seller, stated that Seller had promised immediate delivery and demanded return of the check but Seller refused. Buyer ordered Bank A to stop payment on the check. Since the funds to pay for the cashier's check were withdrawn from Buyer's account, must Bank A comply with Buyer's stop payment order under 4–403(a)?

**2.** Assume the same facts as in Problem 1 except that at the request Buyer, Bank A issued a teller's check drawn on Bank B payable to the order of Seller. Bank A debited the account of Buyer in the amount of the teller's check. Buyer delivered the check to Seller. Buyer ordered Bank B to stop payment of the check. Must Bank B comply with Buyer's stop payment order under 4–403(a)? What is Bank A's liability on the check?

---

Suppose a buyer pays for goods by delivering the buyer's uncertified personal check to the seller. Shortly after the goods are delivered, the buyer examines them and decides that they are unsatisfactory. The buyer seeks to return the goods to the seller and obtain return of the check. The seller denies that the goods are defective and refuses to return the buyer's check. Or, suppose there is a fraudulent sale. The seller took the buyer's check after promising to deliver the goods, but the seller had no intention of carrying out the promise. No goods were ever delivered to the buyer. In either of these two cases the best remedy of the buyer is to prevent the drawee of the check from paying the check. Without that remedy the buyer has the burden of bringing an action against the seller. If the buyer can prevent payment of the check, it is the seller who has the burden of bringing an action. The buyer can prevent payment of an uncertified check of the buyer if the buyer can act very quickly. The check issued by the buyer to the seller functions as an order by the buyer to the buyer's bank to pay money to the seller. Section 4–403 allows the buyer to countermand that order by what is referred to as a "stop-payment order," which is simply an instruction to the bank not to pay the check. A stop-payment order may be given orally or in writing and must describe the check with reasonable certainty so that the bank can identify the check. The bank is obliged to carry out the order if it is received in time to allow the bank a reasonable opportunity to act on the order before the check is paid. 4–

403(a). Failure to carry out the order can give rise to an action for damages. 4–403(c).

The remedy provided by 4–403 is not available, however, if the buyer pays for the goods with a certified check, cashier's check, or teller's check. Section 4–403 applies only to an "item [check] drawn on the customer's [buyer's] account." What are the rights of the buyer under 4–403 if a certified check is delivered to the seller? A certified check, in form, is drawn on the customer's account, but it is not treated that way under 4–403(a). The right of a customer to stop payment of a check is conditioned upon receipt by the bank of a stop-payment order "before any action by the bank with respect to the item described in Section 4–303." One of the actions referred to in 4–303 is payment of the check. 4–303(a)(2). Another is certification. 4–303(a)(1). So far as the rights and obligations of the drawer are concerned, certification of a check is treated as the equivalent of payment. When the check is certified it is treated as an obligation of the certifying bank rather than an item drawn on the drawer's account. Thus, if the buyer delivers a certified check to the seller, no right to stop payment of the check ever arises.

If the buyer delivered a cashier's check or teller's check to the seller, the analysis under 4–403 is somewhat different. A cashier's check or teller's check is not drawn on the buyer's account even though the buyer may have bought the check from the buyer's bank which obtained payment for it by debiting the buyer's account. Section 4–403 allows the buyer to stop payment of a check of the buyer, but does not allow the buyer to stop payment of a check issued by the buyer's bank. Comment 4 to 4–403. Section 4–403 does not apply at all to a cashier's check because the obligation of the issuer is the same as the obligation of the issuer of a note. 3–412. There is no instruction by one person to another that can be countermanded. Section 4–403 does apply to a teller's check. The issuer of a teller's check is like the drawer of an ordinary check. The bank issuing the teller's check draws the check on the account of the issuer in the drawee bank. The issuer is a customer of the drawee bank. § 4–104(a)(5). Thus, under 4–403, the issuer of the teller's check has a right to stop payment by the drawee bank. But that right belongs only to the issuer of the check; the buyer has no right to stop payment.

### b.  ISSUING BANK DELAYS PAYMENT

Cashier's checks are usually issued by banks at the request of customers of the bank. Some customers may be big institutions that provide a large volume of business for the bank. If a such a valued customer of an issuing bank wishes to have payment stopped on a cashier's check, a patient explanation by the bank of why it cannot stop payment on the check under the law may not satisfy the customer. "Just do it," the angry customer says as he slams down the receiver. The following Problem addresses this issue and Revised Article 3's solution.

PROBLEM

Seller agreed to sell goods to Buyer but insisted on immediate payment by means of a cashier's check before it would deliver the goods. Buyer had an account in Bank, and, at the request of Buyer, Bank issued a cashier's check payable to the order of Seller and delivered it to Buyer. Buyer delivered the check to Seller who promised shipment of the goods the following day. Overnight, Buyer developed a common commercial affliction known as "buyer's remorse," and pleaded with Seller to call the deal off and return the check. When Seller proved unreasonable, Buyer demanded that Bank not pay the check ("Just do it!"), promising to reimburse it for any litigation expenses if Seller pressed its claim. Buyer assured Bank that Seller probably didn't want a lawsuit and would just drop the whole matter. Assuming that Buyer is a very good customer of Bank, would you advise Bank that in view of passage of 3–411 Bank should go ahead and pay Seller? See 3–411(b) and Comment 2 to 3–411.

## 3.   ISSUING BANK'S RIGHT TO RAISE OWN CLAIMS OR DEFENSES

In our inquiry into the question whether you would advise a client to accept a cashier's check in payment, we have seen that the person obtaining a cashier's check has no right to stop payment on the check under 4–403. The issuing bank also cannot assert defenses of others (3–305(c)) unless they are impleaded by the issuer in the holder's action against it (3–305(c)). This leaves a third issue to be resolved: can the issuing bank raise its own claims or defenses when a cashier's check is presented to it for payment? Before enactment of Revised Article 3 there was a split of authority in the cases, as well as a lively disagreement among commentators, on the matter. The initial article on the subject was Lary Lawrence, Making Cashier's Checks and Other Bank Checks Cost–Effective: A Plea for Revision of Articles 3 and 4 of the Uniform Commercial Code, 64 Minn. L. Rev. 275 (1980), which advocated making cashier's checks "cash equivalents" by prohibiting issuing banks from raising any defenses to payment even against non-holders in due course. Flatiron Linen, Inc. v. First American State Bank, 23 P.3d 1209 (Colo. 2001), states the policy basis for the cashier's-check-as-cash view: "[W]e look to and take guidance from the nature and usage of cashier's checks. The commercial world treats cashier's checks as the equivalent of cash. People accept cashier's checks as a substitute for cash because the bank, not an individual, stands behind it. By issuing a cashier's check, the bank becomes the guarantor of the value of the check and pledges its resources to the payment of the amount represented upon presentation. 'To allow the bank to stop payment on such an instrument would be inconsistent with the representation it makes in issuing the check. Such a rule would undermine the public confidence in the bank and its checks and thereby deprive the cashier's check of the essential incident which makes it useful.' " 23 P.3d at 1213. The court in *Flatiron Linen* states that its holding is in accord with the majority rule.

The cash equivalent theory found no support in Revised Article 3, and 3–411(c) allows the "obligated bank" to refuse payment with impunity if it "asserts a claim or defense of the bank that it has reasonable grounds to believe is available against the person entitled to enforce the instrument." The following Problem probes the meaning of this language.

### PROBLEM

Rolando requested that Bank One issue a cashier's check for $10,000, which he intended use to pay for goods that Parsons agreed to sell Rolando. Roland paid for the cashier's check by giving Bank One an ordinary check for $10,000 drawn on his account in Bank Two. At Rolando's request, Bank One made the check payable to Rolando, who indorsed and delivered it to Parsons, who then delivered the goods to Rolando. When Parsons presented the cashier's check to Bank One for payment, it dishonored the check because Rolando's check was returned by Bank Two for insufficient funds. Bank One refused to pay the cashier's check on the ground that it had been fraudulently induced to issue the check and was protected from expenses or consequential damages by 3–411(c)(ii). Does Bank One have "reasonable grounds to believe" that the defense is "available" against Parsons even though it knew that Parsons might be able to prove that he is a holder in due course. See State Bank & Trust v. First State Bank of Texas, 242 F.3d 390 (10th Cir. 2000).

## 4.   LOST INSTRUMENTS

### a.   LOST INSTRUMENTS UNDER SECTION 3–309

We have seen that the person obliged to pay an instrument can obtain discharge by paying the holder even if some other person has a claim to the instrument. The discharge can be asserted against anyone other than a person with rights of a holder in due course who took the instrument without notice of the discharge. 3–601(b). If the instrument is surrendered when payment is made, there is no risk that the instrument will be negotiated to a holder in due course. But we have also seen that in some cases the person entitled to enforce the instrument is not in possession of the instrument. 3–301. Although payment to a person entitled to enforce who does not have possession results in discharge (3–602(a)), there is the possibility that the instrument is in existence and has or will come into the possession of a holder in due course. Section 3–309 deals with enforcement of lost instruments. Suppose the payee indorses the instrument in blank and then loses it. The payee can enforce the instrument, but 3–309(b) requires the court to find that the person required to pay the instrument is "adequately protected against loss that might occur by reason of a claim by another person to enforce the instrument." The predecessor of 3–309 was 3–804 of former Article 3, which provided that "[t]he court may require security indemnifying the defendant against loss by reason of further claims on the instrument." The quoted language in 3–804 was not uniformly adopted. Some states, including New York, as we see in *Diaz* below, changed the language in their versions of former Article 3.

The 2002 amendment to 3–309 is illustrated by the following Problem.

## PROBLEM

Maker borrowed $100,000 from Bank and evidenced its loan by a promissory note payable to the order of Bank. When Bank failed, the Federal Deposit Insurance Corporation (FDIC) acquired the note when it became receiver for Bank. FDIC sold the note in a batch of several hundred notes to Pooler, which planned to securitize the notes and issue bonds backed by the note pool. Later FDIC disclosed to Pooler that it had lost the original of the note before the sale and that possession of the note had never been delivered to Pooler. Pooler now brings suit against Maker on the note under 3–309 as a lost note. Maker defended on the ground that Pooler never had possession of the note and could not have lost it. What does Pooler have to prove to recover under 3–309? The facts are suggested by those in Dennis Joslin Company, LLC v. Robinson Broadcasting Corporation, 977 F.Supp. 491 (D. D. C. 1997).

## NOTE

In the contemporary world in which notes are pooled by the FDIC and sold in bulk to others for securitization, it is likely that the assignee's first step on learning that it didn't receive the note would be to proceed against the FDIC under warranties contained in the assignment to assure the assignee that it received all the notes described in the assignment documents. Since in large portfolio purchases "due diligence" may not extend to examining each file for a note, the transferee should bargain for a blanket warranty that protects it if a note is missing by requiring the transferor to repurchase the rights to missing notes. The transfer warranty of 3–416 does not apply because the note was not delivered under 3–203(a).

### b.   LOST CASHIER'S, TELLER'S OR CERTIFIED CHECKS UNDER SECTION 3–312

Although 3–309 and its predecessor, former 3–804, apply to any instrument, most lost instrument problems arise with respect to cashier's checks, teller's checks, and certified checks. Section 3–312, which has no predecessor, applies only to these bank obligations and can be used as an alternative to 3–309. But in some cases a person with rights under 3–312 does not have rights under 3–309 because the person is not a person entitled to enforce the instrument. In that category are remitters of cashier's checks or teller's checks and drawers of certified checks who cannot enforce the lost check but who can use 3–312 to obtain refund from the bank that issued or certified the check. See Comment 1 to 3–312. Cf. Comment to 3–301.

*Diaz*, which follows, was decided under the New York version of 3–804 of the original Article 3. It involved loss of a certified check by the payee of the check. Section 3–312 was a direct response to the hardship suffered by people in the position of Ms. Diaz in the following case.

# Diaz v. Manufacturers Hanover Trust Co.

New York Supreme Court, Queens County, Special Term, 1977.
92 Misc.2d 802, 401 N.Y.S.2d 952.

■ Martin Rodell, Justice.

The petitioner moves by order to show cause to require the respondent Manufacturers Hanover Trust Company to pay the sum of $37,000 or in the alternative to require the respondent Al Newman to issue a new negotiable instrument to her in the same amount.

The facts are uncontroverted. The petitioner posted the sum of $37,000 as security for a bond in behalf of a defendant in a criminal proceeding. Said security was posted with the respondent Newman, a licensed bail bondsman.

The aforementioned criminal action was concluded on July 20, 1977. Subsequently, the petitioner made demand upon the respondent Newman for the sum of $37,000, which she had heretofore posted with him. On August 4, 1977 the respondent Newman dutifully delivered to the petitioner two certified checks, in the amounts of $12,000 and $25,000, drawn on the respondent Manufacturers Hanover Trust Company. Shortly thereafter, the petitioner lost, misplaced, or was criminally relieved of the said certified checks and has to this date been unable to locate them.

The petitioner notified the respondent Newman, who, in turn, requested that the respondent Manufacturers Hanover Trust Co. stop payment. To this date, the checks have not been presented to Manufacturers Hanover Trust Co. for payment.

The petitioner also contacted an unnamed officer of the respondent Manufacturers Hanover Trust Co., who informed her that the bank would not honor any replacement checks issued by the respondent Newman unless an indemnity bond was posted in twice the amount of the original checks. The petitioner avers that this is an onerous and unjust burden; justifiably so, as it would require the posting of $74,000 as security.

* * * When a bank certifies a check, it accepts that check and has the obligation to pay the amount for which it is drawn. * * * The bank in certifying a check obligates itself to an innocent holder in due course to pay the amount for which the check is drawn. Thus, the respondent Manufacturers Hanover Trust Co., through its act of certification, assumed liability on the instruments.

> The owner of an instrument which is lost, whether by destruction, theft or otherwise, may maintain an action in his own name and recover from any party liable thereon upon due proof of his ownership, the facts which prevent his production of the instrument and its terms. The court shall require security, in an amount fixed by the court not less than twice the amount allegedly unpaid on the instrument, indemnifying the defendant, his heirs, personal representatives, successors and assigns against loss, including costs and expenses, by reason of further claims on the instrument, but this provision does not apply

where an action is prosecuted or defended by the state or by a public officer in its behalf. L.1962, c. 553; amended L.1963, c. 1003, § 9, eff. Sept. 27, 1964 (Uniform Commercial Code, § 3–804.)

While it is clear that the petitioner has the right to recover the amount of the checks upon sufficient proof that in fact the checks did at one time exist, were payable to her and cannot be produced, the issue to be decided is presented to this court as follows:

May the court order payment on a lost negotiable instrument without requiring the payee to post security as required in Uniform Commercial Code, § 3–804? In 487 Clinton Avenue v. Chase Manhattan, 63 Misc.2d 715, 313 N.Y.S.2d 445 (1970, Supreme Court, Kings County), the payee of a certified check was robbed of same at gun point and offered to pay the proceeds into an account controlled by the certifying bank. The court held that it had discretion to fix the security and that the security offered by the plaintiff was adequate.

The court notes that no appeal has been taken from the above decision, and thus no Appellate Court guidance is available. However, the Supreme Court in New York County in Guizani v. Manufacturers Hanover Trust, N.Y.L.J. October 12, 1971, p. 2, col. 5, held that under New York's version of this section (Uniform Commercial Code, § 3–804), the furnishing of the security is mandatory and not discretionary.

The section, as drawn by the drafters of the Uniform Commercial Code, and found in the Official Text and Official Commentaries, made the requirement for security discretionary with the court by the use of the word *"may."* The Official Commentaries to the Uniform Commercial Code state as follows:

"There may be cases in which so much time has elapsed, or there is so little possible doubt as to the destruction of the instrument and its ownership that there is no good reason to require the security."

The court, in 487 Clinton Avenue v. Chase Manhattan, supra, predicated its decision on the above reasoning. However, the New York version of section 3–804 of the Uniform Commercial Code pointedly changed the word "may" to "shall," and the Legislature in 1964 further amended this section to fix the amount of security to be not less than twice the amount allegedly unpaid on the instrument. * * * Thus, our Legislature appears to have considered the matter and amended the statute to make the furnishing of security not only mandatory but has also set the minimal amount at not less than twice the amount allegedly unpaid on the instrument.

* * *

The New York Commission Commentaries on section 3–804 of the Uniform Commercial Code leave little doubt that the express purpose of the Legislature was to make the furnishing of security mandatory rather than discretionary and thus conform to section 333 of the old Civil Practice Act.

* * *

If the court is to have the authority to determine the amount of security to be furnished, it would seem on the basis of the legislative history of this section that the change must come from the Legislature.

The court notes additionally that this section, as enacted by our Legislature, while being most positive in regard to the requirement of security and the amount thereof, fails to set any limit whatsoever as to the amount of time the security shall remain posted. The problem of the longevity of a certified check no doubt rendered the Legislature unable to fix a time limit. There being no legislative scheme to either limit the life of a certified check or the duration of time for which a bond must be posted, an unfortunate gap exists into which the petitioner's prayer must fall. It is the opinion of this court that further revision of this section of the Uniform Commercial Code is mandated, or in the alternative, legislation dealing with the valid life of certified checks must be enacted. Simple justice cries out for remedial legislation at the next session of the Legislature. The petitioner is being deprived of her life savings; the bank receives no benefit from the funds which are necessarily frozen. Under the present posture of the law, the funds will remain in that condition until the end of time or it escheats to the state, whichever comes first.

In light of the above, the court is constrained to reject the petitioner's application for recovery without posting of security as required by section 3–804 of the Uniform Commercial Code.

\* \* \*

PROBLEMS

How does 3–312 resolve the following problems? Comment 4 to 3–312.

Claimant lives in New York and has her life savings amounting to almost $100,000 in First Bank. She decided to retire and move to Miami Beach to be near her sister. In anticipation of the move she obtained a cashier's check, dated January 2, from First Bank for $90,000 payable to her order. Her deposit account was immediately debited for $90,000.

**1.** Thief stole Claimant's purse on January 5 and it contained the cashier's check. The check was not indorsed by Claimant. She immediately called First Bank and asked that payment be stopped. An employee explained to her that if she would come in and sign a form asserting a claim to the check she could get her money back 90 days after the date of the check, but if she wanted her money immediately she would have to provide a bond to protect the bank. 3–309. Having no resources to obtain a bond, Claimant went to First Bank on January 6 and signed a form asserting her rights under 3–312(b). Included in the form was a declaration of loss complying with 3–312(a)(3). Thief forged Claimant's signature as an indorsement of the cashier's check and deposited the check in his account in Second Bank on January 8. The check was promptly presented to First Bank for payment. First Bank paid the check. Thief withdrew the proceeds of the check from his account in Second Bank and absconded. Ninety days after the date of the check, Claimant demanded payment of $90,000 from First Bank. What are Claimant's rights against First Bank if it refuses to pay? If First Bank pays, what are its rights against Second Bank?

**2.** Change the facts in Problem 1. When First Bank issued the check to Claimant, she indorsed the check by writing her name on the back. She then mailed the check to her sister in Miami Beach who had agreed to deposit it in her account until Claimant could arrive and open her own account. The check was stolen from the mail by Thief who deposited it in his account in Second Bank. By January 10, Claimant realized that something had happened to the check. On that date she went to First Bank and requested that payment be stopped. She was given the same information that was given in Problem 1 and on January 10 executed the necessary form to claim her rights under 3–312(b). On January 11 Second Bank presented the check to First Bank for payment. First Bank paid the check. Ninety days after the date of the check, Claimant sought $90,000 from First Bank and it refused to pay. What are Claimant's rights against First Bank?

**3.** Change the facts in Problem 2 in one respect. The check was deposited by Thief in Second Bank on May 10. Second Bank promptly presented the check to First Bank for payment. At the time the check was presented for payment First Bank had already paid $90,000 to Claimant because 90 days had elapsed since the date of the check. First Bank dishonored the check. What are Second Bank's rights against First Bank and Claimant?

# F.   ACCOMMODATION PARTIES

## 1.   LIABILITY OF ACCOMMODATION PARTY AND RIGHTS AGAINST ACCOMMODATED PARTY

### a.   ACCOMMODATED PARTY IS INDIVIDUAL

The issues raised in this basic Problem are discussed in the text following the Problem.

PROBLEM

Bank would lend Son the $25,000 that he needed to start his own business only if his Mother would "co-sign" the note. Mother reluctantly did so by signing her name on the face of the note in the lower right hand corner beneath that of Son. Bank advanced the money to Son. Mother was paid nothing by Son for her cooperation and she received none of the proceeds of the loan. When Son went into default in his payments on the note, Bank asked Mother to pay the note. Mother, who had broken with Son by this time, was reluctant to do so. When Bank threatened to sue her, she demanded that Bank sue Son first, and only if he could not pay the judgment should Bank be allowed to sue her. (1) Is Mother correct on this issue? In what capacity did Mother sign within the meaning of 3–419(b)? (2) If Mother pays the note, what are her rights against Son? (3) If Son pays the note, what are his rights against Mother?

---

A creditor taking the promissory note of a debtor who is not a good credit risk may require that a third party act as guarantor of the debtor's obligation to pay the note. Sometimes this guaranty is expressly stated. In many cases, however, a person who intends to act as guarantor does not expressly state that intention and signs the note as co-maker or indorser. For example, Son wants to buy equipment from Dealer for use in Son's business venture. Dealer is willing to sell to Son on credit only if Mother signs the note as co-maker along with Son. Two people who sign a note as co-makers are jointly and severally liable to pay the note. 3–412 and 3–116(a). Thus, if the note is not paid at the due date, Dealer as holder can enforce payment for the full amount against either Son or Mother or both. If two people are jointly and severally liable to pay an obligation and one of the obligors pays the entire amount, the normal rule, in the absence of a contrary agreement between the two obligors, is that the burden is shared equally by the two obligors. This principle of equal sharing is expressed as a right of the obligor who pays the obligation to receive "contribution" from the other obligor. 3–116(b). The contribution rule is based on the assumption that the joint obligation was incurred for the joint benefit of the two obligors and that each should contribute equally in the payment of the obligation. But this assumption is not true if Mother did not have any property interest either in Son's business venture or in the equipment for which the note was given. There is a suretyship relationship between Son and Mother. Generically, Mother is referred to as the "surety" and Son is referred to as the "principal" or "principal debtor." In Article 3, the terminology is different. Mother is the "accommodation party," Son is the "accommodated party," and the note is signed by Mother "for accommodation." 3–419(a).

Mother, as accommodation party, has certain rights against Son. If Son doesn't pay the note when due and Mother has to pay, it is only fair that she be entitled to recover from Son the full amount that she paid. He got the full benefit of the transaction that gave rise to the note and therefore should have to bear the full burden. Otherwise, Son would be unjustly enriched at the expense of Mother. Instead of having the normal right of contribution from a co-obligor, Mother has a right of "reimbursement" for the amount she paid and has subrogation rights as well. By subrogation she succeeds to the rights that Dealer had against Son on the note. 3–419(e). When she pays the note she can require its surrender by Dealer (3–501(b)(2)) and becomes the person entitled to enforce the note. 3–301. Thus, if a note is secured by a security interest in collateral, the accommodation party who pays the note succeeds to the rights of the creditor with respect to the security interest (9–618(a)) and is entitled to a formal transfer of the note and security interest. Reimann v. Hybertsen, 275 Or. 235, 550 P.2d 436 (1976).

If Son pays the note when due, Son has no right of contribution against Mother because she did not benefit from the transaction. 3–419(f) and 3–116(b).

Any type of instrument can be signed for accommodation, and an accommodation party could sign as maker, drawer, acceptor, or indorser. In the typical case the instrument is a note and the accommodation party signs either as maker or indorser. We have examined the function of indorsement in the negotiation of an instrument and that is its primary function, but an indorsement can also be made for the purpose of incurring liability on the instrument. 3–204(a). In most cases, the negotiation and liability purposes coincide, but in some cases only one is present. For example, if an instrument is payable to an identified person, negotiation requires indorsement by the holder. 3–201(b). But the holder can negotiate the instrument without incurring liability as an indorser by indorsing without recourse. 3–415(b). The purpose of the indorsement is negotiation, not liability. An indorsement for accommodation is the converse. Because it is not made by the holder of the instrument, it has no negotiation function and is referred to in 3–205(d) as an "anomalous indorsement." Its only purpose is to impose liability on the indorser.

## PROBLEM

Bob and Ted borrowed money from Bank to set up their own business. Bank required that their wives, Carol (Bob) and Alice (Ted), and Bob's parents, Bill and Mildred, cosign the note. All signed the note in the lower right-hand corner. When Bob and Ted defaulted on the note, Bank demanded and received payment from Bill and Mildred. Neither Bill, Mildred, Carol nor Alice played any part in the business, and the property of the business was in the name of Bob and Ted. The facts in this Problem are based on Fithian v. Jamar, 410 A.2d 569 (Md. 1979).

(a) In a state that does not recognize community property, what are the rights of Bill and Mildred against Bob? Ted? Carol? Alice? See 3–116 and 3–419.

(b) Would your answer change in a community property state?

## b.  ACCOMMODATED PARTY IS BUSINESS ORGANIZATION

## PROBLEM

X owned 50% of the capital stock of Corporation and was its President. Y and Z each owned 25%. Corporation needed money for working capital and borrowed it from Bank which insisted as a condition to the loan that X sign the note because of the precarious financial condition of Corporation. The note was signed as follows:

Corporation

By X, President

X, individually

The loan, which is unsecured, was made by crediting the entire principal amount to Corporation's account with Bank and was used entirely for corporate purposes. Corporation has defaulted on the loan. After Corporation's default on the loan to Bank, X paid Bank the entire unpaid balance amounting to $10,000. Is X an accommodation party? Is X entitled to reimbursement from Corporation for the $10,000 paid to Bank or are X's rights limited to a claim for contribution? Would X's rights be any different if X owned 100% of the stock of Corporation rather than 50%? What do you learn about these questions from the following case?

## Plein v. Lackey

Supreme Court of Washington, Third District, 2003.
149 Wash.2d 214, 67 P.3d 1061.

■ MADSEN, J.

Lee Cameron signed a promissory note both in his corporate capacity and individually, secured by a deed of trust, to purchase property from Sunset Investments for his corporation, Alpen Group, Inc. Later, Cameron paid off the Sunset note. He then sought to enforce the instrument and foreclose the deed of trust when Alpen defaulted. He claims he signed the note as an accommodation party and was therefore entitled to foreclose. We agree. . . . We reverse the Court of Appeals and reinstate the trial court's grant of summary judgment in favor of Cameron.

### FACTS

In 1997, Paul Plein, Bruce White, and Lee Cameron formed Alpen Group Inc. to buy and sell real estate (the group formerly operated as a partnership). In April 1997, Alpen purchased a lot from Sunset Investments, issuing a promissory note for $75,000 to Sunset with the promise to pay stated: "For value received, ALPEN GROUP, INC., A WASHINGTON CORPORATION, promise(s) to pay to SUNSET INVESTMENTS. . . ." The note was secured by a deed of trust naming Sunset as the beneficiary and Alpen as the grantor. It was signed by Cameron as "Secretary/Treasurer" and by White as "Vice–President". Cameron, his wife, Plein (who was president), and his wife each signed "individually."

Alpen also borrowed $136,500 from Columbia State Bank, executing a promissory note also secured by a deed of trust. Columbia loaned the money in part on Sunset's agreement to subordinate its interest in the property to Columbia's. Alpen commenced constructing a log home on the lot. However, more funds were needed, and Cameron advanced $30,000. The money was still insufficient to complete the project and trade creditors were owed an additional $45,000. Cameron declined to loan any more money to Alpen. The parties state that Plein, as president of Alpen, issued deeds of trust against the log home to secure the debt to the trade creditors.

At some point thereafter, Plein was ousted and Cameron became president. Alpen issued a promissory note for the $30,000 that Cameron had advanced to Alpen, secured by another deed of trust on the property. Then, one of the trade creditors sued Alpen in Thurston County Superior Court. The record does not contain any information about that suit beyond the parties' brief descriptions, but it evidently involved a number of claims and cross-claims resulting in payment to the creditor who sued and a judgment entered against Alpen in favor of Plein for $45,000, which Plein recorded. In addition, Cameron received all the stock in Alpen.

At this point, the creditors, in order of their secured interests in the log home property, were (1) Columbia, (2) Sunset, (3) the unpaid trade creditors, (4) Cameron, and (5) Plein. Any equity remaining in the property would be that of Alpen.

According to plaintiffs, "around the time the Thurston County suit was being litigated," the note to Columbia Bank came due and Columbia refused to extend the loan. Clerk's Papers (CP) at 105. In October 1998, Cameron paid the amount due to Columbia with his personal funds and Columbia endorsed the note to Cameron. In addition, Columbia assigned the beneficial interest in its deed of trust to Cameron. Then, in December 1998, the pivotal transaction in this case occurred. Cameron paid the amount due Sunset, Sunset endorsed the promissory note for this loan to Cameron, and Sunset assigned its beneficial interest in its deed of trust to Cameron.

By these two transactions, Cameron, as beneficiary of the two deeds of trust originally issued to Columbia Bank and Sunset, claimed secured interests in the property superior to all other secured interests. He also continued to have a secured interest junior to the trade creditors based on his loan of $30,000 to Alpen.

In October 1999, Cameron, as assignee of the Sunset note, hired attorney Chester Lackey to begin nonjudicial foreclosure proceedings as a result of Alpen's default on the Sunset note. All of the secured creditors received notice of the foreclosure informing them that the trustee's sale of the property would be held on March 31, 2000.

On February 7, 2000, Plein and the trade creditors (hereafter Plein) brought this suit against Cameron and Lackey (hereafter Cameron), seeking a permanent injunction barring the trustee's sale and a declaration that the deed of trust was void because the underlying debt had been paid, i.e., there was no default on the underlying debt. Plein did not seek a preliminary injunction or any other order restraining the sale. On March 28, three days before the scheduled sale, Plein filed a motion for summary judgment, claiming that undisputed facts showed that Cameron paid off the Sunset note on behalf of Alpen, thus extinguishing the debt. Plein further claimed that he was entitled to an order declaring that his and the trade creditors security interests were superior to Cameron's and that the foreclosure proceedings were void.

Plein did not obtain a preliminary injunction or restraining order restraining the sale, and on March 31, the trustee's sale occurred. Cameron, the only bidder, bought the property for $245,312.35 (approximately the total of the Columbia, Sunset, and Cameron notes).

On May 1, 2000, Cameron filed a cross-motion for summary judgment. He argued there was no evidence supporting Plein's motion for summary judgment because Mr. Plein's declaration, the only material submitted by Plein, was not made on personal knowledge. Cameron also argued he was entitled to summary judgment because the evidence indisputably established that Cameron purchased the Sunset and Columbia notes and obtained valid assignments of the promissory notes and deeds of trust for his personal benefit, rather than paying on behalf of Alpen. Cameron also argued that Plein failed to timely and properly object to the sale, pointing out Plein did not seek a preliminary injunction or a restraining order in time to restrain the trustee's sale.

The trial court granted Cameron's motion and dismissed Plein's complaint. Plein appealed and the Court of Appeals reversed. That court reasoned that where a person is individually liable on a note and pays it, the individual cannot also foreclose because the debt has been extinguished. The court held that there are disputed facts regarding Cameron's personal liability on the Sunset note that preclude summary judgment. In addition, the Court of Appeals reasoned that if Cameron was personally liable on the note, then Plein's failure to obtain an order restraining the foreclosure sale would make no difference because the debt would have been extinguished, Cameron would have nothing on which to foreclose, and the trustee's sale would be null and void.

Cameron petitioned for review by this court; his petition was granted. For the first time, he specifically relies on RCW 62A.3–419, a provision in the Uniform Commercial Code, to argue that he signed the Sunset note as an accommodation party, and that as such he had the right, once he paid the note, to enforce the instrument against Alpen and to foreclose the deed of trust. * * *

## ANALYSIS

Application of RCW 62A.3–419 resolves the first issue in this case, whether Cameron signed the Sunset note as an accommodation party. * * *

Section 3–419(1) provides that

[i]f an instrument is issued for value given for the benefit of a party to the instrument ("accommodated party") and another party to the instrument ("accommodation party") signs the instrument for the purpose of incurring liability on the instrument without being a direct beneficiary of the value given for the instrument, the instrument is signed by the accommodation party "for accommodation."

The comments to the statute explain that "[a]n accommodation party is a person who signs an instrument to benefit the accommodated party either by signing at the time value is obtained by the accommodated party or later, and who is not a direct beneficiary of the value obtained." RCWA 62A.3–419, cmt. 1, at 161. The issue whether a party is an accommodation party is a question of fact, comment 3 to section 3–419, and the party asserting accommodation party status bears the burden of proof.

Comment 1 to section .3–419 gives an example of accommodation party status that parallels the facts of this case:

> For example, if X cosigns a note of Corporation that is given for a loan to Corporation, X is an accommodation party if no part of the loan was paid to X or for X's direct benefit. This is true even though X may receive indirect benefit from the loan because X is employed by Corporation or is a stockholder of Corporation, or even if X is the sole stockholder so long as Corporation and X are recognized as separate entities.[2]

Here, the promissory note states that for value received, *Alpen* promised to repay the borrowed amount. The direct beneficiary of the loan was the corporation. As a stockholder of Alpen, any benefit obtained by Cameron was derivative and indirect. *See* Neil B. Cohen, *Suretyship Principles in the New Article 3: Clarifications and Substantive Changes*, 42 ALA. L.REV. 595, 600 (1991). Thus, Cameron received no proceeds from and no direct benefit from the loan.

In addition to the direct/indirect benefit inquiry, another factor that serves to establish accommodation party status is that the lender would not have made the loan in the absence of the party's signature on the note giving rise to liability. *Hendel v. Medley*, 66 Wash.App. 896, 899, 833 P.2d 448 (1992) (decided under former UCC provisions regarding accommodation parties); 11 AM.JUR.2D *Bills and Notes* § 85 (2002) (two primary factors that indicate accommodation party status are that the party received no direct benefit from the proceeds of the instrument and that the loan would not have been made unless the party signed the instrument). Here, Plein's complaint itself asserts that Sunset would not have loaned the money to Alpen, which had no assets, unless the corporate officers signed individually, thus incurring personal liability. Plein repeats this factual statement in his appellate brief. ("[b]ecause Alpen had virtually no other assets, as is customary in the business, Sunset demanded and obtained the personal guaranties of Alpen's owners"). Plein has repeatedly insisted that Cameron was a personal guarantor of the loan.

Because there are no disputed material questions of fact as to Cameron's status, we conclude as a matter of law that Cameron signed the Sunset note as an accommodation party.[3] Cameron obtained no direct benefit from

---

**2.** There is no suggestion in this record or the briefing that Cameron and Alpen Group, Inc., were not separate entities.

**3.** An accommodation party may be a maker, a drawer, an acceptor, or an indorser. Section .3–419(b). He or she is liable on the note in the capacity in which he or she

the loan, and Plein has conceded that the loan would not have been made unless the individual stockholders were subject to personal liability on the note.

\* \* \*

The Court of Appeals is reversed and the trial court's grant of summary judgment in favor of Cameron is reinstated.

## 2. SURETYSHIP DEFENSES

A surety, in addition to having rights against the principal debtor, also has certain rights which can be asserted against the creditor seeking enforcement of the surety's obligation to pay the debt. These rights are usually referred to as "suretyship defenses." Suretyship defenses relate to changes in the obligation of the principal debtor without the consent of the surety. For example, a surety guarantees performance of the principal debtor as buyer under a contract of sale of coal to be supplied on credit by a seller. The seller and the principal debtor agree to amend the contract so that it refers to fuel oil rather than coal. The surety didn't agree to the amendment. If the principal debtor fails to pay for fuel oil purchased under the amended contract and the seller demands payment, the surety has a complete defense. The surety's obligation related to a contract of the principal debtor to buy coal not fuel oil. The seller and the principal debtor cannot impose a new contract on the surety.

However, in some cases it cannot be said that the creditor and the principal debtor have attempted to impose an entirely new contract on the surety. There might be only some modification of the contract. In those cases the existence of a defense may be justified only if the modification causes loss to the surety. A few examples illustrate the problem. The principal debtor borrows money from a lender. The debt is payable with interest and is secured by a security interest in personal property of the principal debtor. After the suretyship relationship arises, the lender agrees with the principal debtor to an amendment of the debt obligation as follows: (1) the amendment changes the interest rate; or (2) it extends the due date of the debt; or (3) it releases some of the collateral that secures the debt; or (4) it releases the principal debtor from any personal obligation to pay the debt. In each of these cases, if the surety does not agree to the change it may be unfair to allow the lender to enforce the surety's obligation to pay if, at the time the change was made, the lender had knowledge of the suretyship relationship. The suretyship defenses are intended to protect the surety by providing that in some cases a change in the terms of the debt may result in a total or partial discharge of the

signed, usually as a maker or indorser. Cmt. 4, § .3–419. However, the nature of the liability on the note does not dictate whether Cameron was an accommodation party. Instead, the absence of direct benefit, and the fact that Sunset would not have made the loan without individual liability on the part of the stockholders dictate that he signed as an accommodation party.

surety. See Restatement (Third) of Suretyship and Guaranty §§ 39–44 (1995).

Restatement § 4(1) provides that to the extent negotiable instruments law governs, it takes precedence over otherwise applicable rules in the Restatement. The suretyship defenses with respect to negotiable instruments are stated in 3–605. In 2002 this section was substantially rewritten to bring it into harmony with the principles of the Restatement. Readers of 3–605 will profit from having a copy of the Restatement at hand; frequent references are made to it in the Comments. However, 3–605 applies to some transactions beyond those covered in the Restatement, including indorsers of notes and checks, as well as co-makers, who are not accommodation parties.

We have eschewed an analysis of the complexities of 3–605 because suretyship defenses are almost always waived in instruments prepared by creditors. The most important provision in 3–605 is subsection (f), which authorizes waivers. Comment 9 says:

> The importance of the suretyship defenses provided in Section 3–605 is greatly diminished by the fact that the right to discharge can be waived as provided in subsection (f). The waiver can be effected by a provision in the instrument or in a separate agreement. It is standard practice to include such a waiver of suretyship defenses in notes prepared by financial institutions or other commercial creditors. Thus, Section 3–605 will result in the discharge of an accommodation party on a note only in the occasional case as in which the note does not include such a waiver clause and the person entitled to enforce the note nevertheless takes actions that would give rise to a discharge under this section without obtaining the consent of the secondary obligor.

Even general language "indicating that the parties waive defenses based on suretyship or impairment of collateral" will suffice. 3–605(f). However, some note forms do not contain such waivers. This omission may be explained by 3–605(e), which provides that certain suretyship defenses cannot be asserted unless the creditor has knowledge of the accommodation. If this knowledge is present, the creditor may ask the accommodation party to sign a separate guaranty contract that contains the waivers.

Section 3–605 applies to only a narrow category of transactions, those in which the payment obligation is a negotiable instrument and the secondary obligor is a party to the instrument, such as an indorser or co-maker. The separate guaranty contracts that are more common in most commercial lending are not covered. The implied suretyship in the familiar real property transaction in which a grantee assumes existing financing is not covered because the assuming grantee is not a party to the instrument. See Comment 2.

The Restatement is generally regarded as a major advance in modernizing and clarifying the law of suretyship. A case can be made for the 2002 revisions of 3–605 on the ground that the Restatement rules constitute the prevailing law of the great majority of suretyship transactions. Since 3–605 applies to only narrow segment of suretyship transactions, conformity with the Restatement, when appropriate, is a desirable simplification.

## G.   Signatures by Representatives

A person is not liable on an instrument unless the instrument is signed personally by that person or by a representative who is authorized to sign for that person. 3–401(a). Whether a representative is authorized to sign for a represented person is determined by general principles of the law of agency. 3–402(a). Consider this case: Employer, an individual, has a checking account in Bank that is used to pay obligations incurred in Employer's business. Employer follows the practice of personally signing all checks, except that Employer authorizes Employee to sign Employer's name to checks during extended absences of Employer. Bank has paid all checks drawn on Employer's account whether Employer's name was written in Employer's handwriting or that of Employee. Employer never objected to the payment by Bank of any check on which Employer's name was written by Employee. On one occasion Employer was about to leave town and instructed Employee to pay all invoices arriving during Employer's absence except invoices of John Doe. In violation of these instructions Employee writes a check on Employer's account to John Doe in payment of a bill that Doe submitted. Employee's act of signing Employer's name to that particular check is not authorized by Employer in the sense that Employer never assented to it, but Employer nevertheless may be bound by the signature. The question of whether the signature is binding on Employer is determined by the law of agency. In our example, the probable result under agency law is that Employer is bound because Employee, although lacking actual authority to sign the Doe check, had apparent authority to do so because Employee had general authority to sign checks. In that event, under 3–401(a) and 3–402(a), the signature by Employee is effective as the authorized signature of Employer.

Signatures by agents on behalf of principals occur most often with respect to the obligations of organizations such as corporations whose signatures are made by its officers or employees. Two problems arise: Whether the corporation is bound by the signature of the officer or employee and whether the officer or employee also becomes a party to the instrument by signing it on behalf of the principal. If it is clear that an agent is signing on behalf of a named principal, only the principal is bound. But sometimes it is not clear whether the agent's signature is in behalf of the principal or whether it is made to impose liability on the officer as an accommodation party.

## 1.   Liability of Agent on Notes

The problem of ambiguous signatures on notes by representatives is governed by 3–402(b). How does this provision resolve the cases in the following Problem?

PROBLEMS

Your client, Carolyn Park, has been appointed Treasurer of New Corp., Inc., a new enterprise. She is authorized to sign promissory notes on behalf of the company.

**1.** Before taking up her duties she consults you about personal liabilities that she might incur in her new position. Among these is her concern about signing her name on notes given to evidence substantial bank loans and other credit extensions made to the company. Her fear is that if later on her new employer should fail and have to file in bankruptcy, holders of these notes might come after her as personally liable on the notes. How should she sign the company's notes to gain full protection from personal liability under 3–402(b)?

**2.** Are the following signatures "unambiguous" within the meaning of 3–402(b)?

(a) New Corp. Inc., by Carolyn Park

(b) New Corp. Inc., Carolyn Park, Treasurer

(c) Carolyn Park, Treasurer

(d) New Corp. Inc., Carolyn Park

**3.** Carolyn signed a note authorized by New Corp. Inc. merely by writing her name, "Carolyn Park."

(a) Is New Corp. Inc. liable on this note? See 3–401(a).

(b) This signature is clearly ambiguous. What would she have to prove under 3–402(b)(2) to avoid personal liability on the note against a non-holder in due course?

**4.** In order to evidence a loan obligation incurred by New Corp. to Lender, Carolyn signed on the front of the note: "New Corp., Inc., by Carolyn Park, Treasurer." On the back of the instrument, she signed "Carolyn Park." When New Corp. filed in bankruptcy, Lender sued Carolyn as indorser of the note. The usual reason one signs on the back of the note is to guarantee payment. Are there any facts that could be admitted into evidence to save Carolyn from personal liability against a non-holder in due course? Comment 2 to 3–402.

## 2.  LIABILITY OF AGENT ON CHECKS

Section 3–402(c) states a different rule for checks than we saw in the prior section for notes. Why was this done?

## Triffin v. Ameripay, LLC

Superior Court of New Jersey, Appellate Division, 2004.
847 A.2d 628.

■ AXELRAD, J.T.C. (temporarily assigned).

Defendant, Ameripay, LLC, a payroll services company for Nu Tribe Radio Networks, Inc. (NTRN) appeals from a judgment entered, following a bench trial, in favor of plaintiff, Robert Triffin, an assignee of several dishonored payroll checks. The issue before us is not whether a holder in due course who purchases dishonored checks has recourse against the drawer of the dishonored checks but, rather, the identification of the drawer who should be held liable. More specifically, the novel issue is whether a payroll services company that opened an account and signed and issued the checks in its representative capacity should be held liable for payment of the dishonored checks, rather than the employer in whose name the checks were drawn and whose identity and location were fully disclosed on the face of the checks. We hold that the Uniform Commercial Code (UCC) imposes liability for the dishonored checks on the disclosed principal, not the agent. Accordingly, we reverse.

The testimony at trial was as follows. As a payroll services company, Ameripay determines withholding obligations, calculates amounts required to be withheld, and issues payroll checks to employees of its clients. It also handles related tax filings for the employer. In July 2002, NTRN, a company located in New York City, retained Ameripay to perform payroll services. Under its agreement, Ameripay established an account on behalf of NTRN for all amounts required to be paid for employee compensation. NTRN wired funds to the account as necessary to cover its payroll obligations, and Ameripay issued payroll checks from the account to NTRN's employees. No Ameripay funds or funds of other clients were commingled in the NTRN account. Paul Bultmeyer, one of Ameripay's partners, testified as to the arrangement:

> [T]he situation is that the client funds this account, this is not an account that is funded by us. It's an account that we establish as an agent, if you will, for the client to pay their payroll, and it's their obligation to fund it. When they fail to fund it, and a check or direct deposit is returned, . . . the client would have to pay it if it's paid at all, because we don't pay it.

According to Bultmeyer, in accordance with its standard practices, Ameripay opened an account at Commerce Bank as an agent for NTRN, bearing account number 3450032895. As part of the bank's standard operating procedures for opening accounts, Bultmeyer and his partner, Arthur Piacentini, the owners of Ameripay, signed an account card as authorized signatories on the account. Because all payroll functions were to be handled by Ameripay with funds provided by NTRN, no representatives of NTRN were authorized signatories or co-signers on the account. On the bank's signature card, the title of the account holder was designated as "Account Holder Name(s): Ameripay LLC Client Payroll NRN." Bultmeyer testified that "NRN" represented "Nu Tribe Radio Network."

Ameripay submitted the required certificate of authority for a limited liability company to the bank, identifying the account holder at the top of the document as "Ameripay LLC Client Payroll NRN," consistent with the signature card. Further down on the document the account holder is identified as "Ameripay, L.L.C." On the face of the checks, NTRN's name, address, and telephone number were imprinted in the top left corner. Other than Commerce Bank as the paying bank, NTRN was the only company identified on the check. The payroll checks also contained a signature line, without any identification of the status of the signatory. The identity of Ameripay is not contained anywhere on the checks except in the faint watermark, which establishes authenticity.

On or about July 26, 2002, Ameripay issued payroll checks on behalf of NTRN, signed by Piacentini, based on NTRN's authorization for electronic transfer into the account of the amount necessary to cover the checks. Four NTRN employees cashed their payroll checks at A–1 Check Cashing Emporium, Inc., (A–1 Check Cashing).[1] A–1 Check Cashing then deposited the eight checks, which were returned dishonored with the notation "return to maker." According to its standard procedure, A–1 Check Cashing's employee had verified with the bank that there were sufficient funds in the account to pay the checks. The only reason Ameripay stopped payment on the checks is because it did not receive the funds from NTRN for disbursement through the NTRN account. According to Bultmeyer, Jonathan Harris, NTRN's principal, told him that NTRN's funds had been dishonored by its bank because the forms he filled out did not allow for electronic funds transfer. Harris represented that the funds were in its PNC bank account and would be transferred into the payroll account the next day.

After the checks were returned, Alex Neu, A–1 Check Cashing's president, contacted a representative from NTRN and was told the funds for the checks had been placed with Ameripay. Bultmeyer relayed to Neu the information he had received from Harris about the problem with the electronic transfer and assured that Ameripay would honor the checks if it received the funds from NTRN to cover them. NTRN failed to transfer the necessary funds into the payroll account and the checks continued to be dishonored.

On August 22, 2002, A–1 Check Cashing assigned its interest in the checks to Triffin, who is in the business of purchasing dishonored negotiable instruments from licensed check cashers. * * * Triffin knew the checks had been dishonored when he purchased them from A–1 Check Cashing. Triffin commenced this action against Ameripay and the payees for collection of the dishonored checks, totaling $4400, along with pre-judgment interest and costs.[2] Triffin did not join NTRN as a defendant. Apparently, the payees were not served with the complaint and the matter was tried solely as to Ameripay.

The judge found that A–1 Check Cashing was a holder in due course— one who takes an instrument for value, in good faith, and without notice of dishonor or any defense against or claim to it on the part of any person—at the time the checks were cashed. N.J.S.A. 12A:3–302a(2). Triffin acquired the same status by the assignment under the shelter provision of the UCC,

---

**1.** Each employee cashed two checks.

**2.** Triffin did not sue Piacentini, as signatory on the check, in his personal capacity.

which provides that "[t]ransfer of an instrument, whether or not the transfer is a negotiation, vests in the transferee any right of the transferor to enforce the instrument, including any right as a holder in due course...." N.J.S.A. 12A:3–203b; *Triffin v. Cigna Ins. Co.*, 297 N.J.Super. 199, 202, 687 A.2d 1045 (App.Div.1997) (emphasis omitted).

The judge found persuasive that the bank records identify Ameripay as the account holder. He concluded that the signature on the checks controlled, and because Ameripay's representative signed the checks, Ameripay was liable as a drawer to a holder in due course, or its assignee, for the amount of the dishonored checks. Moreover, the court adopted Triffin's argument that, as between two innocent parties, Ameripay and Triffin, the person who should be "blamed for ... [NTRN's fraud] or the one who takes the loss, is the party who initiated the action," which the court found to be Ameripay as a result of Piacentini issuing and signing the checks. Accordingly, the court entered judgment in Triffin's favor for the sum of $4,609.74.

The status of Triffin as a holder in due course, although disputed by Ameripay at trial, is not an issue on appeal. On appeal, Ameripay asserts it should not be held liable for payment of the checks it issued for NTRN because it did so solely in a representative capacity as a payroll agent. We agree.

This matter is governed by Article 3 of New Jersey's version of the UCC pertaining to negotiable instruments, as implemented in New Jersey in N.J.S.A. 12A:3–101 to–605. A check is considered a draft under the Code. N.J.S.A. 12A:3–104f. A drawer includes a person who signs a check. *See N.J.S.A.* 12A:3–103a(3). If an unaccepted check is dishonored, the drawer is obligated to make payment to a person entitled to enforce the check. *See N.J.S.A.* 12A:3–414b. As the assignee of a holder in due course to the dishonored checks, Triffin is entitled to enforce the instruments against the maker. N.J.S.A. 12A:3–301; N.J.S.A. 12A:3–308b; *see also Somerset Valley Bank, supra*, 343 N.J.Super. at 83–84, 777 A.2d 993.

The trial judge acknowledged that he adopted in their entirety the arguments advanced by Triffin at trial. Triffin did not dispute the fact that Ameripay was an authorized representative of NTRN with the authority to issue payroll checks on its behalf. Nor did he dispute that the represented party was prominently disclosed on the face of these checks and, in fact, was the only entity identified on the checks. Triffin's arguments focused on the status of Ameripay as the sole account holder. He emphasized that the signature card and certificate of authority on file with the bank listed Ameripay, LLC as the account holder, though the account was clearly designated as a payroll account for NTRN. Most importantly, Triffin relied on the fact that the only signature on the checks belonged to Piacentini, Ameripay's managing partner. He argued, therefore, based on Piacentini's signature, that Ameripay was a drawer under N.J.S.A. 12A:3–103a(3). According to Triffin,

> [U]nder the Uniform Commercial Code the only party that can be liable [on a] negotiable instrument is the party whose signature ap-

pears thereon. And in this instance as the drawer [it] would be the person who is the account holder.

The court accepted Triffin's conclusion that Ameripay was the drawer of the dishonored checks and, therefore, was liable to him for their payment. \* \* \*

The new definitional section recognizes that the drawer of a check is not limited to the signatory and defines "drawer" as "a person who signs *or is identified in a draft as a person ordering payment.*" N.J.S.A. 12A:3–103a(3) (emphasis added). N.J.S.A. 12A:3–401(1) previously provided that "[n]o person is liable on an instrument unless his signature appears thereon." The revised version provides two instances where a person is liable on a negotiable instrument, where "the person signed the instrument" or "the person is represented by an agent or representative who signed the instrument and the signature is binding on the represented person under 12A:3–402." N.J.S.A. 12A:3–401a.

The Legislature also added § 3–402, which clarified liability for the obligation to pay a negotiable instrument when the signature is that of a representative. N.J.S.A. 12A:3–402 achieves two important goals. First, the statute explicitly provides that a represented party is liable on an instrument to the same extent as a represented party would be bound on a simple contract executed by its agent, even though its signature never appears on the instrument:

a. If a person acting, or purporting to act, as a representative signs an instrument by signing either the name of the represented person or the name of the signer, the represented person is bound by the signature to the same extent the represented person would be bound if the signature were on a simple contract. If the represented person is bound, the signature of the representative is the authorized signature of the represented person and the represented person is liable on the instrument, whether or not identified in the instrument.

Second, the statute provides for a "representative capacity defense," in which the maker may avoid personal liability in certain instances, even where the agency is not disclosed on the face of the instrument:

b. If a representative signs the name of the representative to an instrument and the signature is an authorized signature of the represented person, the following rules apply:

(1) If the form of the signature shows unambiguously that the signature is made on behalf of the represented person who is identified in the instrument, the representative is not liable on the instrument.

(2) Subject to subsection c. of this section, if the form of the signature does not show unambiguously that the signature is made in a representative capacity or the represented person is not identified in the instrument, the representative is liable on the instrument to a holder in due course that took the instrument without notice that the representative was not intended to be

liable on the instrument. With respect to any other person, the representative is liable on the instrument unless the representative proves that the original parties did not intend the representative to be liable on the instrument.

At trial, the evidence was undisputed that Ameripay and NTRN had formed a contractual relationship. In retaining Ameripay to administer its payroll account, NTRN explicitly or implicitly gave Piacentini authority to sign checks on its behalf and bind NTRN on the instruments. In opening the payroll account and signing and issuing payroll checks, Ameripay acted as an agent of NTRN. NTRN, not Ameripay, owed the compensation to its employees that was paid by the checks. NTRN, not Ameripay, was obligated to provide the funds to cover the checks. NTRN, not Ameripay, ordered the payments to its employees. Thus, under agency principles, NTRN would be bound for the acts that it authorized Piacentini to undertake. * * * Normally, a principal is responsible for the actions of an agent who is acting within the scope of his authority. * * * Accordingly, had Piacentini signed a simple contract instead of the checks, NTRN would have been required to perform. Thus, Piacentini's signature on the checks was an authorized signature of the represented person within the meaning of N.J.S.A. 12A:3–402a.

We need not determine whether Piacentini's signature on the checks showed "unambiguously" that it was made on behalf of NTRN or whether Ameripay was otherwise entitled to the general "representative defenses" for a negotiable instrument under N.J.S.A. 12A:3–402b. We find that Ameripay is immune from liability under the specific provisions of N.J.S.A. 12A:3–402c pertaining to checks. Subsection c, also implemented as part of the 1995 revisions to the UCC, changed the statutory provisions regarding who shall be liable on a dishonored check payable from an account of a represented person and expanded a representative's defenses. The agent is no longer liable on the check simply because he or she signed for the principal. Subsection c now provides, with respect to an authorized representative who signs his or her name on a check in which the represented person is identified, an additional exception from liability as a drawer:

> c.   If a representative signs the name of the representative as drawer of a check without indication of the representative status and the check is payable from an account of the represented person who is identified on the check, the signer is not liable on the check if the signature is an authorized signature of the represented person.

In comment 3 to revised N.J.S.A. 12A:3–402, the drafters express a clear intent to reverse decisions that imposed liability on agents for the obligations of their principals:

> 3.   Subsection (c) is directed at the check cases. It states that if the check identifies the represented person the agent who signs on the signature line does not have to indicate agency status. Virtually all checks used today are in personalized form which identify the person on whose account the check is drawn. In this case, nobody is deceived into thinking that the person signing the check is meant to be liable.

This subsection is meant to overrule cases decided under former Article 3 such as *Griffin v. Ellinger*, 538 S.W.2d 97 (Texas 1976).[4]

We have not found any reported case in New Jersey interpreting these new provisions. Because we adopted the Uniform Laws, which were also adopted verbatim in most states in the United States, decisions by other states adopting revised Article 3 of the UCC, specifically § 3–402, are instructive. These cases have insulated from personal liability an authorized representative who signs a check imprinted with the corporate name, on behalf of the represented entity, where the check is returned for insufficient funds, even though the instrument does not indicate on its face that it is being signed in a representative capacity on behalf of the drawer, pursuant to UCC 3–402(c). *See, e.g., Medina v. Wyche*, 796 So.2d 622 (Fla.Dist.Ct.App.2001) (corporate officer is not liable to landlord for amount of dishonored corporate rent check); *Helmer v. Rumarson Techs., Inc.*, 245 *Ga.App.* 598, 538 S.E.2d 504 (2000) (corporate officers are not personally liable to payee creditor for amount of dishonored corporate check); *Peterson v. Holtrachem, Inc.*, 239 Ga.App. 838, 521 S.E.2d 648 (1999) (employee is not personally liable to payee creditor for amount of dishonored corporate check). As one prominent commentator noted, this modification of the UCC "puts the Code's legal stamp of approval on the obvious intent of the transaction—that the company's check binds only the company, even if an agent signs in her own name." *Medina, supra*, 796 So.2d at 623 (quoting 2 James J. White & Robert S. Summer, *Uniform Commercial Code* § 16–5, at 86 (4th ed. 1995)).

Piacentini's signature was clearly "an authorized signature of the represented person." Ameripay's representatives, Bultmeyer and Piacentini, were given authority to issue and sign checks on NTRN's behalf. Piacentini signed the checks in this case as a representative of NTRN. While Piacentini signed his name without indicating his agency status, the name and address of NTRN, the represented entity, appear prominently in the top left-hand corner of the check, which is the customary place for identification of the drawer.

The record further supports a finding that the funds were "payable from an account of the represented person." We first note that the requirement is not that the funds be payable from an account *in the name of* the represented person. It is not fatal to this defense that Ameripay opened and managed the account from which the checks were issued and that Ameripay's representatives were the only signatories on the account. With regard to the UCC defenses, for all intents and purposes, NTRN is the owner of the payroll account. \* \* \*

Although we rest our decision on N.J.S.A. 12A:3–402c rather than b, the same rationale applies. Bultmeyer's testimony, corroborated by the banking documents associated with the creation of the account, is that

---

**4.** In *Griffin v. Ellinger*, 538 S.W.2d 97 (Tex.1976), the president of a corporation who signed checks in payment of corporate obligations was held personally liable because the signature line did not indicate his corporate capacity, even though the checks were drawn on a corporate account and the name of the corporation was printed on the checks.

Ameripay held funds for NTRN in the account and maintained the account solely to satisfy NTRN's payroll obligations. The documents clearly identify the account as a client payroll account for NTRN. It is apparent that the second reference in the certificate to "Ameripay, L.L.C" as the account holder is a shorthand designation for the prior listing as "Ameripay LLC Client Payroll NRN." None of Ameripay's funds were commingled in the payroll account. The funds in the payroll account clearly belonged to NTRN, not to Ameripay. Had the electronic transfer of funds from NTRN been credited to the payroll account, neither Bultmeyer nor Piacentini would have been entitled to those funds for their personal use or for the use of Ameripay.

Moreover, our interpretation of subsection c is consistent with the spirit of this new provision as articulated in the official comment. A 1 Check Cashing, the holder in due course, was not deceived into thinking that Piacentini, as signatory on the check, or his LLC, Ameripay, was meant to be liable.

Based on the documents themselves, there was ample basis to assume they were payroll checks from NTRN to its employees and the checks were intended to be written on funds belonging to NTRN. Not only is the represented party's identity clearly disclosed but it is the only company identified on the checks. There is no basis on the face of the checks for A–1 Check Cashing to have reasonably assumed Piacentini's signature was not that of an authorized representative, whether corporate officer or otherwise, of NTRN. Accordingly, A–1 Check Cashing had no reasonable expectation when it cashed the checks that any entity other than NTRN would be liable for their dishonor.

Under N.J.S.A. 12A:3–402c, a holder in due course could not enforce the dishonored payroll checks against Ameripay. As assignee, Triffin is entitled to no greater rights. There is no basis in law for the trial court's adoption of a balancing of blame or loss allocation analysis as overriding the plain language of the UCC.

Reversed.

## NOTE

Section 3–403(c) relieves the drawer from liability on the check only if the check is payable from an account of the represented person "who is identified on the check." The provision does not provide what is required for the represented person to be "identified." Suppose the legal name of the represented person is XYZ Corp. XYZ Corp.'s agent, with authority, draws a check on XYZ's account that does not indicate that the agent is signing on XYZ Corp.'s behalf. The name "XYZ" and XYZ Corp.'s address appear on the check. Is the agent liable on the check? See Packaging Materials & Supply Co., Inc. v. Prater, 882 So.2d 861 (Ala. Ct. Civ. App. 2004). Would the result be different if XYZ Corp.'s trade name "ABC" appeared on the check? See Peterson v. Holtrachem, Inc., 521 S.E.2d 648 (Ga. Ct. App. 1999).

## H.  ACCORD AND SATISFACTION

Effectuating an accord and satisfaction of a disputed claim by a "full satisfaction" legend on a check is a cheap and fast way in which to settle a claim. Section 3–311(a) and (b) provide that, as a general rule, if the legend on the check is conspicuous and the claim is subject to a bona fide dispute, the claimant cannot receive payment of the check without agreeing to the accord and satisfaction. If the claimant wishes to avoid settlement for the amount of the check, it may not cash the check or deposit it for collection. However, accord and satisfaction is a two-edged sword. As Comment 1 to 3–311 points out, accord and satisfaction by use of notations on checks is useful to consumers in disputes about the quality of goods or services purchased, but it is also commonly employed by insurance companies to settle claims of insured parties.

Section 3–311(c)(1) addresses a problem encountered by organizations like large retailers and other high volume recipients of checks who find it burdensome and wasteful to conduct a visual search of tens of thousands of checks to see if a handful contain a proposed accord and satisfaction legend. This provision allows such an organization to notify its customers to send any communications concerning disputed debts, including checks containing full satisfaction legends, to a specified address at which these checks and other communications can be examined and decisions made with respect to whether to accept them as settlement of claims. This allows retailers to rapidly process other checks without sight examination to detect accord and satisfaction language. Section 3–311(c)(2) is an alternative to 3–311(c)(1), which is designed to ameliorate the consequences of an inadvertent accord and satisfaction. It is explained in Comment 6 to 3–311.

## IFC Credit Corporation v. Bulk Petroleum Corp.

United States Court of Appeals, Seventh Circuit, 2005.
403 F.3d 869.

■ CUDAHY, CIRCUIT JUDGE.

Plaintiff IFC Credit Corporation (IFC) brought suit alleging that Bulk Petroleum Corporation (Bulk) and its CEO, Darshan Dhaliwal, breached a lease agreement under which Bulk leased gasoline tanks and other equipment from IFC with an option to purchase them at the end of the lease. Bulk claims that the lease agreement has been concluded through an accord and satisfaction executed with the assignee of IFC's rights under the lease. The district court, through Magistrate Judge Aaron E. Goodstein, granted Bulk's motion for summary judgment, ruling that a valid accord and satisfaction had taken place. IFC now appeals that ruling, and we affirm.

## I.  FACTUAL BACKGROUND AND DISPOSITION BELOW

On or about June 21, 1995, Bulk and IFC entered into a series of agreements by which Bulk leased gasoline tanks and equipment from IFC to be used at various gas stations operated by Bulk. Under the terms of the agreements, Bulk was given an option to purchase the equipment at the end of the 72–month lease term. The purchase price was to be the greater of the fair market value of the equipment and $31,419.40, together with all applicable taxes. The lease documents also provided for extension of the lease term at a rate of $2,820.52 per month. The documents further required that any notices regarding the purchase of the equipment were to be sent to IFC at a designated address. Concurrent with the execution of the lease, Bulk's CEO, Darshan Dhaliwal, executed a personal guaranty of the agreements.

Less than two weeks later, on or about June 30, 1995, the Bulk lease was assigned by IFC to Finova Capital Corporation (Finova), giving Finova full right, title and interest in the lease, including the initial scheduled payments under the lease. Bulk's payments were to be sent to a Finova lockbox.

Beginning in November 2000, IFC's Patrick Witowski and Bulk's John Gerth engaged in negotiations concerning the termination of the lease and purchase of the equipment by Bulk. However, the two parties could not agree on a purchase price. On January 23, 2001, while these negotiations were ongoing, Finova notified Bulk in writing that all further negotiations regarding the purchase option were to be conducted with IFC (and with Witowski specifically). Finova then promptly filed for bankruptcy on March 7, 2001.

On June 18, 2001, Dhaliwal, who to that point had apparently not been involved in negotiations, sent a letter to Finova and a check for $31,419.40, made out to Finova Capital Corporation. The invoice attached to the check read "pay off lease 5613500," and the endorsement area on the back of the check stated "payment in full of lease and purchase option #5613500." The accompanying letter from Dhaliwal stated that the check represented "payment in full of the lease and the purchase option" and that "[a]cceptance of this check represents full satisfaction of the obligation of Bulk Petroleum to Finova Capital Corporation." *Id.* at 42A. The letter concluded by stating that if Finova did not accept the check, then it should inform Bulk as to where it should ship the leased equipment back to Finova. *Id.*

The parties dispute the exact date upon which IFC, via Witowski, received a copy of Dhaliwal's letter. They also dispute whether the letter and the check were sent together or separately,[1] and whether the check was sent to Finova's "automated lockbox" rather than to its office (though the letter does not appear to have been sent to a P.O. Box address). In any event, it is undisputed that Witowski (and hence IFC) received a copy of the

---

**1.** IFC's contention that they were sent separately is waived in any event. *See* discussion, *infra.*

letter and the check via fax from Bulk on June 22, 2001. The check was negotiated three days later by Finova on June 25, 2001. Following negotiation of the check, IFC did not return the tendered money or claim that Finova had negotiated the check in error. Instead, IFC retained the tendered money, claiming that it constituted only partial satisfaction of Bulk's outstanding obligations under the agreement (which IFC reckoned to be in excess of $200,000). Bulk refused to make further payments, contending that its contractual obligations under the lease had been fulfilled upon acceptance and negotiation of the $31,419.40 check to Finova.

IFC filed this action on December 15, 2002, seeking to recover $207,961.88 (plus holdover rent) that it claims is owed by Bulk due to the breach of the lease agreement. IFC also sued Dahliwal based upon the personal guaranty he executed contemporaneously with the lease. On October 22, 2003, Bulk and Dahliwal filed a motion for summary judgment, contending that IFC's claim was barred by a valid accord and satisfaction. The district court granted Bulk and Dahliwal's motion, ruling that there was no remaining question of fact that defendants had met all the requirements of an accord and satisfaction under the relevant Uniform Commercial Code (UCC) provisions and Illinois law, and there was no evidence that the check was tendered in bad faith. IFC's appeal now comes before this Court. Since Bulk's tender met all the requirements of a valid accord and satisfaction, and above all since IFC did not return the tendered money or attempt to "undo" the transaction, we affirm.

## II.  JURISDICTION

* * * The district court granted Bulk Petroleum's motion for summary judgment in an order resolving all claims on April 5, 2004. IFC timely filed its notice of appeal on April 23, 2004. Accordingly, we now have jurisdiction pursuant to 28 U.S.C. § 1291, which provides for appellate review of final orders issued by the district courts.

## III.  DISCUSSION

In proceedings below, the district court granted Bulk's motion for summary judgment on the ground that a valid accord and satisfaction had occurred. We review rulings on motions for summary judgment *de novo*.
* * *

Under both Illinois law and the relevant provisions of the UCC, an accord and satisfaction occurs when the "person against whom a claim is asserted proves that (i) that person in good faith tendered an instrument to the claimant as full satisfaction of the claim, (ii) the amount of the claim was unliquidated or subject to a bona fide dispute, and (iii) the claimant obtained payment of the instrument." 810 Ill. Comp. Stat. 5/3–311(a) (2004). *Accord Saichek v. Lupa*, 204 Ill.2d 127, 135, 272 Ill.Dec. 641, 787 N.E.2d 827, 832 (2003) ("An accord and satisfaction is a contractual method of discharging a debt or claim. To constitute an accord and satisfaction there must be: (1) a bona fide dispute, (2) an unliquidated sum, (3) consideration, (4) a shared and mutual intent to compromise the claim, and (5) execution of the agreement."). Additionally, 810 Ill. Comp. Stat. 5/3–311(b) requires that "the instrument or an accompanying written communication contain a conspicuous statement to the effect that the instrument was tendered as full satisfaction of the claim."

Clearly Bulk's tendered check and accompanying letter facially meet these criteria. The purchase price of the tanks was subject to a "bona fide dispute" (the parties could not agree on a price), the instrument and accompanying letter sent by Bulk contained highly "conspicuous statement[s]" that the check was tendered as full satisfaction of all obligations under the lease and purchase agreement, and Finova "obtained payment of the instrument" by negotiating the check on June 25, 2001. So far so good.

Paragraph (c) of section 5/3–311 adds a slight twist. It provides for an exception to these basic requirements which is designed to avoid inadvertent satisfaction of debts when a tender is sent to a large company. Under section (c), an otherwise valid tender to a claimant "organization" fails if "(i) within a reasonable time before the tender, the claimant sent a conspicuous statement to the person against whom the claim is asserted that communications concerning disputed debts, including an instrument tendered as full satisfaction of a debt, are to be sent to a *designated person, office, or place*, and (ii) the instrument or accompanying communication was not received by that designated person, office, or place." 810 Ill. Comp. Stat. 5/3–311(c) (emphasis added). This exception does not apply, however, if "within a *reasonable time before collection of the instrument* was initiated, the claimant or an agent of the claimant having direct responsibility with respect to the disputed obligation knew that the instrument was tendered in full satisfaction of the claim." 810 Ill. Comp. Stat. 5/3–311(d) (emphasis added).

In the present case, assuming that IFC and Finova qualify as "organizations" so as to trigger the provisions of paragraph (c), Witowski was the acknowledged "designated person" responsible for conducting communications regarding the lease/purchase agreement, and Bulk sent the disputed check to Finova rather than to IFC or Witowski directly. Had no further communications taken place, this circumstance could have thwarted any attempted accord and satisfaction under section 5/3–311(c). However, it is undisputed that Witowski eventually received notice of Bulk's tender no later than June 22, 2001—three days before the check was cashed by Finova. The transaction here thus falls squarely within the provisions of section 5/3–311(d): regardless of any initial misdirection in making the tender, notice was given to the correct party within a reasonable time before collection of the instrument. The special exception contained in paragraph (c) does not apply, and Finova's negotiation of the check presumptively suffices to conclude a valid accord and satisfaction.

IFC objects that there is a material question of fact as to whether Bulk tendered its check in good faith. The UCC comment provides that "good faith" implies "not only honesty in fact, but the observance of reasonable commercial standards of fair dealing. The meaning of 'fair dealing' will depend upon the facts in the particular case." U.C.C. § 3–311, cmt. ¶ 4

(2002). *See also Fremarek v. John Hancock Mut. Life Ins.*, 272 Ill.App.3d 1067, 1072, 209 Ill.Dec. 423, 651 N.E.2d 601, 605 (1995) (same). Here, IFC alleges that Bulk's failure to send the check directly to Witowski and its mailing of the check and explanatory letter separately, taken together, indicate that Bulk was surreptitiously attempting to induce IFC into an inadvertent accord and satisfaction. On this score we note first that the parties hotly contest whether the letter and check were sent separately or together, and in any case IFC has waived this particular argument since it did not advance it below. * * *

Moreover, IFC's allegations, even if credited, are probably not sufficient to obviate the tender in any event. Ordinarily the good faith requirement is violated where there is no bona fide mutual dispute concerning consideration, or the party tendering the payment affirmatively misleads the claimant. *See McMahon Food Corp. v. Burger Dairy Co.*, 103 F.3d 1307, 1313 (7th Cir.1996) (holding there was no good faith where debtor induces acceptance of payment by falsely leading creditor's agent to believe that creditor agreed to the terms of the payment). Here, by contrast, there was no misrepresentation or proactive deception; Bulk merely sent the check to the wrong party. Additionally, Bulk quickly notified Witowski of the tender verbally and via fax thereafter.

But in any event, IFC continues to retain the money sent to it by Bulk. This bare fact trumps any concerns we might have about the procedural specifics of the transaction itself. On the basis of this consideration alone IFC's claims must fail. Illinois courts have long held that, where there is a bona fide dispute as to the amount due, retention of a tender conspicuously identified as an accord and satisfaction effectively dooms a claimant's case. * * * An Illinois appellate court has recently applied this principle to a case analogous to the one at bar. In *Bankers Leasing Association, Inc. v. Pranno*, the debtor sent the creditor a check conspicuously marked as being in full satisfaction of all outstanding debts and accompanied by a letter to the same effect. The creditor, with full knowledge of the dispute as to the amount of the debt, promptly cashed the check and, just as IFC/Finova has done in this case, attempted to characterize the transaction as only partial satisfaction of outstanding debts. The court rejected this argument, however, holding that a valid accord and satisfaction had occurred:

> When Pranno [the creditor] cashed the check, however, he knew there was a dispute. He knew the parties did not agree on what amount Bankers owed him.... Pranno may have tried to hedge what he was agreeing to by stating in an affidavit that the check satisfied only part of the dispute, but "If there is a bona fide dispute as to the amount due, it makes no difference that the creditor protests that he does not accept the amount in full satisfaction. The creditor must either accept the payment with the condition or refuse." *Nelson v. Fire Insurance Exchange*, 156 Ill.App.3d 1017, 1020, 109 Ill.Dec. 516, 510 N.E.2d 137 (1987).

Both the check and letter Bankers sent Pranno clearly indicated that by cashing the check, Pranno agreed that all claims between Bankers and Pranno would be satisfied. If Pranno did not agree to these terms, he should not have cashed the check.

*Pranno*, 224 Ill.Dec. 46, 681 N.E.2d at 34. IFC attempts to distinguish *Pranno* by pointing out that there the tendered check and the explanatory letter arrived together, while in this case they were (allegedly) sent separately. Once again, IFC has waived any argument to this effect, and in any case such a minor factual quibble is irrelevant to the principle articulated here. The recipient of a conspicuously-marked tender proposing an accord and satisfaction may not keep the tender and simultaneously contend that no accord and satisfaction occurred.

### IV.   CONCLUSION

In light of the foregoing, we AFFIRM the district court's grant of summary judgment in favor of defendants Bulk Petroleum and Darshan Dhaliwal.

NOTES

**1.**   Before Revised Article 3, the UCC had no section on accord and satisfaction. One of the reasons for adding 3–311 was a deep division of authority over the meaning of 1–207 which provided that: "[a] party who, with explicit reservation of rights, performs or promises performance or assents to performance in a manner demanded or offered by the other party does not thereby prejudice the rights reserved. Such words as 'without prejudice', 'under protest' or the like are sufficient." The issue was whether under this section the recipient of a check marked "tendered in full satisfaction" could negate the effect of these words by merely writing "reserving all rights" or "under protest" on the check. The drafters of 3–311 took the position that the recipient of a full-satisfaction check could avoid an accord and satisfaction only by not cashing the check; words reserving rights were ineffective. This result was reached by adding a new subsection to 1–207: "(2) Subsection (1) does not apply to an accord and satisfaction." A new Comment 3 to 1–207 was added.

**2.**   The drafting of 3–311 was contentious; the final product is a series of compromises that can be detected by going through the section in the manner of an archeological dig. Stage 1. Subsections (a) and (b) codify the common law rule of accord and satisfaction. Ironically this was supported both by consumers, who saw it as the little person's way of settling disputes without having to litigate, as well as by insurance companies and other businesses who wanted to induce their customers to settle claims by sending them checks that they would be tempted to cash on the bird-in-the-hand principle. Stage 2. Department stores, utilities and others who receive a huge volume of checks objected that the unadorned common law rule meant that they had to sift through thousands of checks each day to reach the few that contained the full-satisfaction legend. This was unduly expensive, and, in consequence, the drafters were urged to get rid of the archaic rule that contract disputes can be settled by legends on checks. The drafters addressed their concerns in subsection (c)(1) which allows these organizations to require that customers send checks intended to pay disputed claims to a special office where the staff is trained to look for and deal with full-satisfaction checks. Subsection (c)(2) was a concession to companies that did not wish to use the somewhat cumbersome subsection (c)(1). Inadvertent accord and satisfaction could be avoided by allowing the claimant that had mistakenly deposited a full-satisfaction check to tender the money back to the drawer of the check within 90 days after payment. Organizations could opt for either (c)(1) or (c)(2), but not both. The second sentence in (c)(2) does not allow an organization that has set up a lockbox account under (c) (1) to escape an accord and satisfaction by returning money under (c)(2) if a full-satisfaction check had been sent to the lockbox account and deposited by the claimant. Stage 3. Subsection (c) looked too pro-business to consumer representatives and they posed this case: Suppose Big Store sends out the notice under subsection (c)(1) that all checks for disputed claims must be sent to a certain post office box. Although Big Store complied fully with the requirements for notice under subsection (c)(1), Customer delivered her full-satisfaction check to the credit manager for the branch of Big Stores where she had always shopped. She had talked with him by telephone and he was aware of the dispute on the balance of her account. Big Store cashed her check and did not avail itself of the escape valve in subsection (c)(2). Do you mean to tell me, the consumer representatives asked, that there should be no accord and satisfaction in this case merely because Customer hadn't read all the periodic statements she received from Big Store (do you read yours?), even though the person in charge of her account received the check bearing a conspicuous full-satisfaction legend and cashed the check? This was a persuasive argument and subsection (d) was added to address this concern. Reaching consensus on the wording of subsection (d) was very difficult. The *IFC* case, above, is the first decision we have seen that invokes subsection (d).

CHAPTER 13

# PAYMENT SYSTEMS: CHECKS AND CREDIT CARDS

## A. CHECK COLLECTION

Noncash payments are made by transferring funds from a transferor's deposit account to a transferee through banking channels. Payments may be made by paper checks, debit cards or electronic orders, or, increasingly, by a combination of these methods. In this chapter we will examine check-originated transfers and debit and credit card transactions. In the following chapter, we will deal with funds transfers originated by electronic orders: big-dollar funds transfers under UCC Article 4A and transfers made through the Automated Clearing House (ACH) system.

The United States is the only developed nation to use paper checks as its principal means of making noncash payments. The expense of processing check payments is enormous. In Lucinda Harper, American's Won't Stop Writing Checks, Wall St. J., Nov. 24, 1998, at A2, the cost of transporting and processing checks was estimated at more than $181 billion per year. The total transportation costs incurred by Federal Reserve Banks alone was about $150 million in 2005. Tons of checks are lugged around by trucks, helicopters and airplanes all over the nation. Some checks are stolen; others are lost. A courier plane carrying Bank of America deposits went down in the Pacific and some of the checks dredged up from the ocean had to be restored by hair dryers. In the digital age, why can't the enormous cost of transporting and processing paper checks be greatly reduced by communicating the information on checks electronically or, better still, by getting rid of checks in favor of electronic payments? The response to this rhetorical question is that the paper-based system is finally changing. Although paper checks are still the most common payment method in the United States, their popularity is finally declining: the number of paper checks paid dropped from 41.9 billion in 2000 to 36.7 billion in 2003. Federal Reserve Bulletin, Trends in the Use of Payment Instruments in the United States 181 (Spring 2005). The rapid growth of debit cards and the wide-spread conversion of checks into electronic payments through ACH, will be discussed in next chapter. Nonetheless, we will examine in detail the traditional check-oriented payment system set out in UCC Articles 3 and 4. The use of the banking system for transferring credits from an obligor's account to an obligee is the basis for all payment systems, and it is best learned through the study of checks.

## 1.   TIME CHECK IS PAID BY PAYOR BANK

Article 4 governs the rights and obligations of banks and their customers with respect to the collection of checks by the banking system. However, the Federal Reserve Board has always played a very important role in check collection. This role has been expanded by Regulation CC, 12 U.S.C. § 4001 et seq. We discuss the impact of Regulation CC later in this chapter.

The check collection process consists of the movement of the check from the depository bank to its presentation at the payor bank. 4–105(3), 4–105(2). Unsurprisingly, the process of returning the check operates in reverse: the check moves from the payor bank to the depository bank, and ultimately to the depositor. The check return process is important when the payor bank dishonors the check. To avoid liability for the check, the payor bank must return the dishonored check to the depository bank by the midnight deadline, which is midnight of the next day after the check is received. 4–104(a)(10). Failure to comply with the midnight deadline makes a settlement final. The amount paid can't be recovered. When settlement hasn't occurred timely, tardy settlement makes the payor bank liable ("accountable") for the face amount of the item.

### a.   THE MIDNIGHT DEADLINE

Solve the following Problems on the basis of the text following the Problems and statutory provisions provided.

### PROBLEMS

**1.**   Drawer wrote a check for $10,000 (Check) on its account in Bank A payable to the order of Payee who deposited it in its account in Bank B, the "depositary bank" 4–105(2). Bank B gave Payee a provisional credit for the amount of Check and sent it to Bank A for payment. Check was presented to Bank A on Monday at 8:30 a.m. in a bundle of checks itemized in a cash letter, which listed each check and the total dollar amount for the bundle. Bank A provisionally settled for the checks by sending Bank B a Fedwire for the total amount of the cash letter on Monday afternoon. The checks in the bundle went through Bank A's reader-sorter computer on Monday afternoon.

(a) The reader-sorter selected out Check because Drawer's account balance was insufficient to pay it. On Tuesday morning, Bank A reviewed Drawer's account to ascertain whether Drawer had added funds sufficient to pay Check by that time. Finding none, Bank decided to dishonor Check and sent it to its check-return office on Tuesday afternoon, but owing to a mix-up Check was not returned until the 3:00 a.m. courier on Wednesday. Check reached Bank B on Wednesday afternoon, and on Thursday Bank B erased the provisional credit in Payee's account and delivered Check to Payee on Friday. Did Bank A revoke its settlement with Bank B under the time limits of 4–301(a)? Is Bank A accountable to Payee for the amount of the check under 4–302(a) even if Payee has suffered no damage?

(b) Check was selected out for visual inspection because of its relatively large amount. After Check was inspected, Bank A decided to pay it, and Drawer's account was debited for the amount of Check at 1:00 p.m. on Tuesday. Check was then routed to a filing clerk whose responsibility it was to place it with Drawer's other cancelled checks to be mailed to Drawer at the end of the monthly billing cycle. At 5:00 p.m. on Tuesday, Bank A learned that a mistake had been made and that Drawer's account was insufficient to cover the amount of Check, but the file clerk had left and the employees could not locate Check until 9:00 p.m., an hour after the 8:00 p.m. motor courier had left. They placed it in the mail at 10:00 p.m. addressed to the presenting bank, Bank B, where it arrived on Friday. Did Bank A revoke its settlement under 4–301(a) and (d)(2) or was Check finally paid at 1:00 p.m. on Tuesday under 4–215(a) when Bank A completed its processing? "Send" is defined in 1–201(b)(36).

(c) Change the facts in question (b) by having Bank A send the Fedwire to Bank B on Tuesday afternoon. Bank B's loss from the one-day delay in settlement was only one day's interest on the $10,000. Would this change your answer in (b)?

**2.**   Drawer drew a check (Check) on its account in Bank payable to the order of Payee. Upon receipt of Check, Payee deposited it in its account, which was also in Bank, on Monday. Hence, Bank is both the payor and depositary bank. Bank gave Payee a provisional settlement in its account on Tuesday for the amount of Check. On Wednesday morning Bank discovered that Drawer's account was insufficient to pay Check. On Wednesday afternoon Bank erased the credit from Payee's account and returned Check to Payee. Did Bank properly revoke the credit in Payee's account under 4–301(a) and (b)? Is Bank liable to Payee for the amount of the check under 4–302(a)(1)?

---

The next case in this book discusses the issue of when, under Article 4, the bank on which a check is drawn is deemed to have paid the check. This issue is presented in its most simple form if the payee of a check takes it to the drawee bank and asks for payment in cash over the counter. The check is paid when the bank gives cash equal to the amount of the check to the payee. 4–215(a)(1). But that case is not at all typical. Most checks are not paid in cash but are deposited in a bank account of the holder of the check.

To understand how Article 4 applies to checks deposited in a bank, it is necessary to understand the concept of settlement in Article 4. 4–104(a)(11) and 4–213. Typically, in the check-collection process, each bank that takes a check pays for it at, or shortly after, the time that the check is taken. Article 4 uses the terms "settlement" and "settle" to refer to this act of paying for the check. But to say that a bank has settled or paid for a check is not the same as saying that the bank has paid the check. The bank on which a check is drawn is referred to in Article 4 as the payor bank. 4–105(3). Only a payor bank can pay the check; any other bank giving value for the check may be buying the check but is not paying it. And even in the case of the payor bank there is a distinction between the bank's settling for the check and paying the check. For example, suppose the payee of a check deposits it to the payee's account in Bank A. The drawer of the check also has an account in Bank A and the check is drawn on that account. In this case, Bank A is both the depositary bank with respect to the check and the payor bank. 4–105(2) and (3). Bankers refer to this kind of check as an "on us" item. At or shortly after the time Bank A receives the check from the payee, Bank A will credit the account of the payee for the amount of the check. By making that credit Bank A settles for the check. 4–104(a)(11) and 4–213(a)(2)(iii). This settlement, however, is provisional in nature because Bank A has the right to revoke it under certain circumstances.

At the time Bank A settles with the payee for the check, it usually does not know whether, as the payor bank, it should pay the check. For example, suppose the balance in the drawer's account in Bank A is not sufficient to cover the amount of the check. Bank A has no obligation to the payee of the check to pay the check (3–408) and, if Bank A is not assured of reimbursement from the drawer of the check, Bank A normally would refuse to pay the check. Under Article 4, Bank A is given a time-limited right to revoke or recover the payment that it made to the payee when the payee's account was credited. 4–301(a). The prescribed technique for accomplishing this result is to return the check to the payee and to debit ("charge-back") the payee's account in the amount of the check. As payor bank, Bank A "pays the check" if and when it has not exercised its right to recover a provisional payment that it has made and the right of recovery no longer exists. 4–215(a)(3) and 4–301(a). This practice of settle-first-take-back-later is in effect because it is operationally efficient. Since payor banks have reason to refuse payment with respect to only a tiny percentage of the vast number of checks that are processed each day for payment, it is sensible to pay for all checks as they are received ("settlement") and to deal later with the small number of checks that turn out to be bad by revoking the settlement and returning the checks. Although in Montana only one in every 192 checks is returned, in Los Angeles, where guilt is less oppressive, one in every 34 bounces. Roger Lowenstein, Behind the Teller Window, Wall St. J., Dec. 30, 1996, at A10.

A similar analysis applies with respect to the more common case in which the depositary bank is not also the payor bank. In that case the depositary bank is a "collecting bank" that acts as agent of the holder to obtain payment of the check. 4–105(5). The depositary bank will either present the check directly to the payor bank or it will negotiate the check to an "intermediary bank," which acts as a collecting bank to obtain payment of the check. 4–105(4) and (5). The intermediary bank is likely to be a Federal Reserve Bank and often there is more than one intermediary bank. Each collecting bank will give provisional settlement to the bank from which the check is received. The last collecting bank will present the check for payment to the payor bank, which will give provisional settlement to the presenting bank.

In transactions between banks, settlement is often made by a credit to the Federal Reserve account of the bank receiving the settlement. The payor bank may refuse payment of the check by returning it to the presenting bank and recovering the amount of the check from that bank. 4–301(a). In turn the presenting bank and each collecting bank may return the check to the bank from which it received the check and recover the provisional payment. 4–214(a). As we will see, Regulation CC requires payor and collecting banks to expedite the return of checks and authorizes them to return checks directly to the depositary bank or to any bank that has agreed to handle the checks for expeditious return to the depositary bank. Any bank returning the check may obtain the amount of the check from the bank to which the check is transferred. When the depositary bank receives the returned check, it may recover the provisional payment given to the holder from whom it took the check for collection. 4–214(a).

*Blake*, which follows, describes in more detail the time-limited right that Article 4 gives to a payor bank to return a check and recover any provisional settlement given for the check or to avoid liability to pay the check under 4–302. It also deals with one of the more common excuses for failing to meet the midnight deadline, delays recognized by 4–109 (formerly 4–108).

## Blake v. Woodford Bank & Trust Co.

Court of Appeals of Kentucky, 1977.
555 S.W.2d 589.

■ PARK, JUDGE.

This case involves the liability of * * * Woodford Bank and Trust Company on two checks drawn on the Woodford Bank and Trust Company and payable to the order of * * * Wayne Blake. Following a trial without a jury, the Woodford Circuit Court found that the bank was excused from meeting its "midnight deadline" with respect to the two checks. Blake appeals from the judgment of the circuit court dismissing his complaint. The bank cross-appeals from that portion of the circuit court's opinion relating to the extent of the bank's liability on the two checks if it should be determined that the bank was not excused from meeting its midnight deadline.

### BASIC FACTS

The basic facts are not in dispute. On December 6, 1973, Blake deposited a check in the amount of $16,449.84 to his account at the Morristown Bank, of Morristown, Ohio. This check was payable to Blake's order and was drawn on the K & K Farm Account at the Woodford Bank and Trust Company. The check was dated December 3, 1973.

On December 19, 1973, Blake deposited a second check in the amount of $11,200.00 to his account in the Morristown Bank. The second check was also drawn on the K & K Farm Account at the Woodford Bank and Trust

Company and made payable to Blake's order. The second check was dated December 17, 1973.

When Blake deposited the second check on December 19, he was informed by the Morristown Bank that the first check had been dishonored and returned because of insufficient funds. Blake instructed the Morristown Bank to re-present the first check along with the second check. Blake was a cattle trader, and the two checks represented the purchase price for cattle sold by Blake to James Knight who maintained the K & K Farm Account. Blake testified that he had been doing business with Knight for several years. On other occasions, checks had been returned for insufficient funds but had been paid when re-presented.

The two checks were forwarded for collection through the Cincinnati Branch of the Federal Reserve Bank of Cleveland. From the Federal Reserve Bank, the two checks were delivered to the Woodford Bank and Trust Company by means of the Purolator Courier Corp. The checks arrived at the Woodford Bank and Trust Company on Monday, December 24, 1973, shortly before the opening of the bank for business. The next day, Christmas, was not a banking day. The two checks were returned by the Woodford Bank and Trust Company to the Cincinnati Branch of the Federal Reserve Bank by means of Purolator on Thursday, December 27, 1973.

The two checks were received by the bank on Monday, December 24. The next banking day was Wednesday, December 26. Thus, the bank's "midnight deadline" was midnight on Wednesday, December 26. § 4–104(1)(h) [Revised § 4–104(a)(10)]. As the bank retained the two checks beyond its midnight deadline, Blake asserts that the bank is "accountable" for the amount of the two checks under § 4–302(1)(a) [Revised § 4–302(a)(1)].

## HISTORY OF PAYOR BANK'S LIABILITY FOR RETAINING CHECK

Under the Uniform Negotiable Instruments Law a payor bank was not liable to the holder of a check drawn on the bank until the bank had accepted or certified the check. * * * Because of the payor bank's basic nonliability on a check, it was essential that some time limit be placed upon the right of the payor bank to dishonor a check when presented for payment. If a payor bank could hold a check indefinitely without incurring liability, the entire process of collection and payment of checks would be intolerably slow. To avoid this problem, a majority of courts construing § 136 and § 137 of the Uniform Negotiable Instruments Law held that a payor bank was deemed to have accepted a check if it held the check for 24 hours after the check was presented for payment. * * * Thus, in a majority of jurisdictions, the payor bank had only 24 hours to determine whether to pay a check or return it. However, in Kentucky and a few other jurisdictions, the courts held that § 136 and § 137 of the Uniform Negotiable Instruments Law applied only to checks which were presented for acceptance. * * * Consequently, the payor bank would be liable on the check only if it held the check "for an unreasonable length of time" and could thus be deemed to have converted the check.

In order to bring uniformity to the check collection process, the Bank Collection Code was proposed by the American Bankers' Association. The Bank Collection Code was adopted by Kentucky in 1930. Under § 3 of the Bank Collection Code, a payor bank could give provisional credit when a check was received, and the credit could be revoked at any time before the end of that business day. The payor bank became liable on the check if it retained the item beyond the end of the business day received. * * *

Banks had only a few hours to determine whether a check should be returned because of insufficient funds. Banks were required to "dribble post checks" by sorting and sending the checks to the appropriate bookkeepers as the checks were received. This led to an uneven workload during the course of a business day. At times, the bookkeeping personnel might have nothing to do while at other times they would be required to process a very large number of checks in a very short time. * * * Because of the increasingly large number of checks processed each day and the shortage of qualified bank personnel during World War II, it became impossible for banks to determine whether a check was "good" in only 24 hours. The banks were forced to resort to the procedure of "paying" for a check on the day it was presented without posting it to the customer's account until the following day. See First National Bank of Elwood v. Universal C.I.T. Credit Corporation, 132 Ind.App. 353, 170 N.E.2d 238, at 244 (1960). To meet this situation, the American Banking Association proposed a Model Deferred Posting Statute. * * *

Under the Model Deferred Posting Statute, a payor bank could give provisional credit for a check on the business day it was received, and the credit could be revoked at any time before midnight of the bank's next business day following receipt. A provisional credit was revoked "by returning the item, or if the item is held for protest or at the time is lost or is not in the possession of the bank, by giving written notice of dishonor, nonpayment, or revocation; provided that such item or notice is dispatched in the mails or by other expeditious means not later than midnight of the bank's next business day after the item was received." * * * If the payor bank failed to take advantage of the provisions of the deferred posting statute by revoking the provisional credit and returning the check within the time and in the manner provided by the act, the payor bank was deemed to have paid the check and was liable thereon to the holder. * * *

The Model Deferred Posting Statute was the basis for the provisions of the Uniform Commercial Code. Under § 4–301(1) [Revised § 4–301(a)] of the Uniform Commercial Code (UCC), a payor bank may revoke a provisional "settlement" if it does so before its "midnight deadline" which is midnight of the next banking day following the banking day on which it received the check. Under the Model Deferred Posting Statute, the payor bank's liability for failing to meet its midnight deadline was to be inferred rather than being spelled out in the statute. Under UCC § 4–302 [Revised § 4–302], the payor bank's liability for missing its midnight deadline is explicit. If the payor bank misses its midnight deadline, the bank is "accountable" for the face amount of the check. * * *

Like the Model Deferred Posting Statute, the Uniform Commercial Code seeks to decrease, rather than increase, the risk of liability to payor banks. By permitting deferred posting, the Uniform Commercial Code extends the time within which a payor bank must determine whether it will pay a check drawn on the bank. Unlike the Bank Collection Code or the Uniform Negotiable Instruments Law as construed by most courts, the Uniform Commercial Code does not require the payor bank to act on the day of receipt or within 24 hours of receipt of a check. The payor bank is granted until midnight of the next business day following the business day on which it received the check.

### EXCUSE FOR FAILING TO MEET MIDNIGHT DEADLINE

UCC § 4–108(2) [Revised § 4–109(b)] provides:

"Delay by a * * * payor bank beyond time limits prescribed or permitted by this Act * * * is excused if caused by interruption of communications facilities, suspension of payments by another bank, war, emergency conditions or other circumstances beyond the control of the bank provided it exercises such diligence as the circumstances require."

The circuit court found that the bank's failure to return the two checks by its midnight deadline was excused under the provisions of UCC § 4–108.

The circuit court dictated its findings of fact into the record:

"From all of the evidence that was presented in this case, it would appear that there was no intentional action on the part of the bank to hold these checks beyond the normal course of business as an accommodation to its customer. In fact, the uncontroverted testimony of the bank officers was to the contrary. To say that the bank failed, through certain procedures, to return the checks by the midnight deadline does not, in the mind of this Court, imply or establish an intentional act on the part of the bank.

* * *

"In this instance we have the Christmas Holiday, which caused in the bank, as in all businesses, certain emergency and overloaded situations. This is not unique to the banking industry; but is true of virtually every business in a christian society, in which the holiday of Christmas is observed as the major holiday of the year. Special considerations are always given to employees as well as customers of these banking institutions.

" * * * On the Christmas Holiday, two machines were broken down for periods of time during this critical day in question. There was an absence of a regular bookkeeper."

Under CR 52.01, these findings of fact cannot be set aside by this court unless they are clearly erroneous. The foregoing findings are supported by the record, and are not questioned by Blake on the appeal.

After making findings of fact, the circuit court dictated the following conclusions into the record:

" * * * The entire cumulative effect of what happened would constitute diligence on the part of the bank, as circumstances required.

"It is the opinion of the Court and it is the Finding of the Court that the circumstances described by the banking officers, the standards of banking care, as described by expert witnesses, would bring the bank within 4–108(2), and the Court therefore, finds as a fact that there were circumstances here beyond the control of the bank, and that it exercised such diligence as those circumstances required."

When the circuit court concluded "that there were circumstances here beyond the control of the bank, and that it exercised such diligence as those circumstances required," the circuit court was doing no more than repeating the words of the statute. This court must determine whether the circuit court's findings of fact support these conclusions.

Before turning to the facts presented in this case, it is appropriate to discuss the only two cases involving the application of UCC § 4–108 to a payor bank's midnight deadline. In Sun River Cattle Co. v. Miners Bank of Montana, 164 Mont. 237, 521 P.2d 679 (1974), the payor bank utilized a computer in the adjacent town of Great Falls to process its checks. The checks were picked up at the Miners Bank by an armored car between 5:00 p.m. and 6:00 p.m. on the date of receipt. The checks would normally reach the computer center at Great Falls around 10:30 p.m. Ordinarily the checks would have been processed by 11:30 p.m., returned to the Miners Bank by 8:00 a.m. the next morning. The checks in question were received by the Miners Bank on May 11. On that day, the armored car broke down, and the checks did not reach the computer center at Great Falls until 1:30 a.m. the next morning, May 12. On that morning, the computer malfunctioned and the checks were not returned to the Miners Bank until 2:30 p.m. on May 12. There was no testimony as to what actually happened to the checks after they were received by the Miners Bank on the afternoon of May 12, but the Miners Bank failed to return the checks by midnight of May 12. The trial court held that the failure of the Miners Bank to meet its midnight deadline was excused by the provisions of UCC § 4–108(2). The Montana Supreme Court reversed, holding that the Miners Bank had failed to show the degree of diligence required under the circumstances. The Montana court pointed out that the Miners Bank had more than the normal interest in the activities in the account upon which the checks were drawn, and that due diligence could not be shown merely by following ordinary operating procedures.

In Port City State Bank v. American National Bank, 486 F.2d 196 (10th Cir.1973), the payor bank, American National, was changing from machine posting to computer processing of its checks commencing Monday, December 1, 1969. Two checks were in dispute. The first check arrived at American National on Friday, November 28, 1969. As Monday was the next banking day, the midnight deadline for the first check was December 1. The second check arrived on Tuesday, December 2, 1969, and the midnight deadline for that check was Wednesday, December 3. American National's new computer developed a "memory error" which rendered it unusable at 10:00 a.m. on December 1, the first day of computer operations. The computer manufacturer assured the bank that repairs would not take "too long." Unfortunately repairs and testing were not completed until the early hours of Tuesday, December 2. In the meantime, American National attempted to utilize an identical computer in a bank some two and a half hours away. Processing commenced at the other bank at 11:30 p.m. on December 1, and continued through the night. Although work proceeded to the point of "capturing" all of the items on discs, the backup computer was required by its owner, and the American National personnel returned to the bank to complete the printing of the trial balances. Another memory error developed in the new computer which again rendered the computer unusable. No further use could be made of American National's computer until a new memory module was installed on Thursday, December 4. The trial court held that the computer breakdown constituted a condition beyond the control of American National and that the bank had exercised due diligence. On appeal, the United States Court of Appeals affirmed, holding that the findings of the district court were not clearly erroneous.

* * *

The basic facts found by the circuit court can be summarized as follows: a) the bank had no intention of holding the checks beyond the midnight deadline in order to accommodate its customer; b) there was an increased volume of checks to be handled by reason of the Christmas Holiday; c) two posting machines were broken down for a period of time on December 26; d) one regular bookkeeper was absent because of illness. Standing alone, the bank's intention not to favor its customer by retaining an item beyond the midnight deadline would not justify the application of § 4–108(2). The application of the exemption statute necessarily will turn upon the findings relating to heavy volume, machine breakdown, and absence of a bookkeeper.

The bank's president testified that 4,200 to 4,600 checks were processed on a normal day. Because the bank was closed for Christmas on Tuesday, the bank was required to process 6,995 checks on December 26. The bank had four posting machines. On the morning of December 26, two of the machines were temporarily inoperable. One of the machines required two and one half hours to repair. The second machine was repaired in one and one half hours. As the bank had four bookkeepers, the machine breakdown required the bookkeepers to take turns using the posting machines for a time in the morning. One of the four bookkeepers who regularly operated the posting machines was absent because of illness on December 26. This bookkeeper was replaced by the head bookkeeper who had experience on the posting machines, although he was not as proficient as a regular posting machine operator.

Because of the cumulative effect of the heavy volume, machine breakdown and absence of a regular bookkeeper, the bank claims it was unable to process the two checks in time to deliver them to the courier from

Purolator for return to the Federal Reserve Bank on December 26. As the bank's president testified:

> "Because we couldn't get them ready for the Purolator carrier to pick them up by 4:00 and we tried to get all our work down there to him by 4:00, for him to pick up and these two checks were still being processed in our bookkeeping department and it was impossible for those to get into returns for that day."

\* \* \*

The increased volume of items to be processed the day after Christmas was clearly foreseeable. The breakdown of the posting machines was not an unusual occurrence, although it was unusual to have two machines broken down at the same time. In any event, it should have been foreseeable to the responsible officers of the bank that the bookkeepers would be delayed in completing posting of the checks on December 26. Nevertheless, the undisputed evidence establishes that no arrangements of any kind were made for return of "bad" items which might be discovered by the bookkeepers after the departure of the Purolator courier. The two checks in question were in fact determined by Mrs. Stratton to be "bad" on December 26. The checks were not returned because the regular employee responsible for handling "bad" checks had left for the day, and Mrs. Stratton had no instructions to cover the situation.

Even though the bank missed returning the two checks by the Purolator courier, it was still possible for the bank to have returned the checks by its midnight deadline. Under UCC § 4–301(4)(b) [Revised § 4–301(d)(2)] an item is returned when it is "sent" to the bank's transferor, in this case the Federal Reserve Bank. Under UCC § 1–201(38) an item is "sent" when it is deposited in the mail. 1 R. Anderson, Uniform Commercial Code § 1–201 pp. 118–119 (2d ed. 1970). Thus, the bank could have returned the two checks before the midnight deadline by the simple procedure of depositing the two checks in the mail, properly addressed to the Cincinnati branch of the Federal Reserve Bank.

This court concludes that circumstances beyond the control of the bank did not prevent it from returning the two checks in question before its midnight deadline on December 26. The circumstances causing delay in the bookkeeping department were foreseeable. On December 26, the bank actually discovered that the checks were "bad," but the responsible employees and officers had left the bank without leaving any instructions to the bookkeepers. The circuit court erred in holding that the bank was excused under § 4–108 from meeting its midnight deadline. The facts found by the circuit court do not support its conclusion that the circumstances in the case were beyond the control of the bank.

## RE–PRESENTMENT OF CHECK PREVIOUSLY DISHONORED BY NONPAYMENT

On its cross-appeal, the bank argues that the circuit court erred in holding that there was no difference in the status of the two checks. The bank makes the argument that it is not liable on the first check which had previously been dishonored by nonpayment. Blake received notice of dishonor when the first check was returned because of insufficient funds. The bank claims that it was under no further duty to meet the midnight deadline when the check was re-presented for payment.

The bank relies upon the decision of the Kansas Supreme Court in *Leaderbrand v. Central State Bank*, 202 Kan. 450, 450 P.2d 1 (1969). A check drawn on the Central State Bank was presented for payment on two occasions over the counter. On both occasions, the holder of the check was advised orally that there were not sufficient funds in the account to honor the check. Later, the holder deposited the check in his own account at the First State Bank. The First State Bank did not send the check through regular bank collection channels, but rather mailed the check directly to the Central State Bank for purposes of collection. The check arrived at the Central State Bank on March 21 or March 22, and the check was not returned by the Central State Bank to the First State Bank until April 5. The Kansas Supreme Court held that there was no liability under § 4–302 of UCC for a check which had previously been dishonored when presented for payment.

Relying on the provisions of UCC § 3–511(4), the Kansas Supreme Court held that "any notice of dishonor" was excused when a check had been "dishonored by nonacceptance" and was later re-presented for payment. The Kansas Supreme Court specifically held that § 3–511(4) [See Revised § 3–502(f)] applied to a check which was dishonored when presented for payment, stating:

> "While the language of 84–3–511(4), supra—'Where a draft has been dishonored by nonacceptance'—does not refer to a dishonor by nonpayment, we think reference to the dishonor of a 'draft' 'by nonacceptance' would, a fortiori, include the dishonor of a check by nonpayment."

The Kansas Supreme Court concluded that a payor bank was excused from giving any further notice of dishonor when a previously dishonored check was re-presented for payment and there were still insufficient funds in the drawer's account to cover the check.

\* \* \*

The decision of the Kansas Supreme Court in the *Leaderbrand* case has been criticized. As UCC § 3–511(4) applies by its terms to a "draft" which has been "dishonored by nonacceptance," most of the criticism has been directed to the Kansas court's application of § 3–511(4) to a check which had been dishonored by nonpayment. As stated in B. Clark and A. Squillante, The Law of Bank Deposits, Collections and Credit Cards at 71–72 (1970):

> "Use of this section to excuse retention under § 4–302 seems questionable, since the draftsmen are saying nothing more than dishonor by nonacceptance excuses notice of dishonor by nonpayment. If a time draft is not accepted, it is a useless act to present it for payment. On

the other hand, sending a check through a second or third time often yields results, since the depositor may have had time to make a deposit to his account. It is presumably for this reason that the Code drafts-men limited the excuse rule of § 3–511(4) to 'nonacceptance' of 'drafts' and did not by express language indicate 'nonpayment' of 'checks.' "

See also Note, Uniform Commercial Code—Nonapplicability of Payor Banks "Midnight Deadline" to Re–Presented Checks, 18 Kan.L. Rev. 679 (1970).

Two courts have refused to follow the *Leaderbrand* decision. In Wiley, Tate and Irby v. Peoples Bank and Trust Company, 438 F.2d 513 (5th Cir.1971), the United States Court of Appeals for the Fifth Circuit held:

"We disagree with *Leaderbrand* and hold § 3–511(4) inapplicable here. Acceptance applies only to time items. It has nothing to do with demand items."

In Sun River Cattle Co. v. Miners Bank of Montana, supra, the Montana Supreme Court rejected the *Leaderbrand* decision and followed the decision of the United States Court of Appeals in the *Wiley, Tate and Irby* case. The Montana Supreme Court held that § 3–511(4) of the UCC was inapplicable to checks payable on demand.

\* \* \*

A practical reason also exists for rejecting the *Leaderbrand* decision. In 1972, approximately 25 billion checks passed through the bank collection process. The Federal Reserve Banks handled 8 billion checks that year. \* \* \* An earlier study indicated that only one half of one percent of all checks were dishonored when first presented for payment. Of those initially dishonored, approximately one half were paid upon re-presentment. F. Leary, Check Handling Under Article Four of the Uniform Commercial Code, 49 Marq.L. Rev. 331, 333, n. 7 (1965). A significant number of previously dishonored checks are paid upon re-presentment in the regular course of the check collection process. Such checks are often presented through intermediate collecting banks, such as the Federal Reserve Bank in this case. Each collecting bank will have made a provisional settlement with its transferor, and, in turn, received a provisional settlement from the bank to which it forwarded the check. In this way, a series of provisional settlements are made as the check proceeds through the bank collection process.

Under UCC § 4–213(2) [Revised § 4–215(c)], final payment of a check "firms up" all of the provisional settlements made in the collection process. Under subsection (1)(d) of UCC § 4–213 [Revised § 4–215(a)(3)], a payor bank makes final payment of a check when it fails to revoke a provisional settlement "in the time and manner permitted by statute, clearing house rule or agreement." As to items not presented over the counter or by local clearing house, this means that a payor bank is deemed to have made final payment of a check when it fails to revoke a provisional settlement by its midnight deadline. See UCC § 4–213, Official Code Comment 6 [Comment 7 to Revised § 4–215]. In his article on check handling, Leary has described

§ 4–213 as the "zinger" section: "when provisional credit given by the payor bank becomes firm then—'zing'—all prior provisional credits are instantaneously made firm." Leary, op.cit., at 361. If a payor bank was not required to meet its midnight deadline with respect to previously dishonored items, then none of the other banks involved in the collection process could safely assume that the check had been paid. Consider the problems of the depository bank. It must permit its customer to withdraw the amount of the credit given for the check when provisional settlements have become final by payment and the bank has had "a reasonable time" to learn that the settlement is final. See UCC § 4–213(4)(a) [Revised § 4–215(e)(1)]. The depository bank will rarely receive notice that an item has been paid. In actual practice, the depository bank will utilize availability schedules to compute when it should receive the check if it is to be returned unpaid. Leary, op.cit., at 345–346. If a payor bank is not bound by its midnight deadline as to previously dishonored items, then there is no way for the depository bank to know whether a previously dishonored item has been paid upon re-presentment except by direct communication with the payor bank. Such a procedure would impose an unnecessary burden upon the check collection process.

This court concludes that the circuit court was correct in holding that there was no difference in the status of the two checks.

\* \* \*

NOTES

**1.** The court deals with the question of whether the first check, which was re-presented on December 24, should be treated differently from the second check which was presented for the first time on that date. Woodford Bank argued that because that check had been properly returned the first time that it was presented, it had no duty to return it in a timely manner a second time. A previous case, *Leaderbrand*, discussed in the opinion, supported this argument. The court in *Leaderbrand* relied on former 3–511(4). That provision was intended to apply to time drafts. It states the principle that if the draft is dishonored when presented for acceptance, it is not necessary to present it again for payment to charge secondary parties. Despite the clear language of former 3–511(4) restricting the provision to dishonor by nonacceptance, the court in *Leaderbrand* applied it to a check dishonored when presented for payment. Revised Article 3 dropped former 3–511(4) and replaced it with 3–502(f), which does not contain the language relied on in *Leaderbrand*. *Leaderbrand* has been widely criticized and the court in *Blake* declined to follow it.

Re-presentment of checks is common, and about one half are paid when presented the second time. The typical case is that of a customer who writes a check to be covered by a check contemporaneously deposited in the customer's account or which will be deposited in the very near future. If the customer's check is presented for payment before the deposited check is collected, the customer's check may be dishonored because of a temporary insufficiency of funds in the account. If the check is re-presented, it must be treated as a check presented for the first time because, if the midnight deadline does not apply to such checks, the depositary bank would have no basis for making a judgment whether the check was paid. The depositary bank receives notice that a check has been dishonored either by return of the check or by a separate notice of dishonor. But it is not told that a check has been paid. The bank normally determines that a check has been paid by the fact that it didn't receive the returned check or notice of dishonor within the normal time for receiving the check or notice.

**2.** Taken together 4–301(a) and 4–302(a) provide that if a check arrives on Day 1, Payor Bank may avoid being held accountable for, meaning liable for, the amount of the check by returning it before its "midnight deadline" (midnight of Day 2, 4–104(a)(10)), only if it had settled for the check before midnight of Day 1. We discussed settlement briefly in the text preceding *Blake*. In Hanna v. First National Bank of Rochester, 87 N.Y.2d 107, 637 N.Y.S.2d 953, 661 N.E.2d 683 (N.Y. 1995), checks arrived at Payor Bank on November 12 and were returned on November 13, but Payor Bank was held accountable on the checks because it offered no proof that it had settled for the checks on November 12. Payor Bank objected to this result on the ground that it should not be liable for the full amount of the checks, $44,503, when Depositary Bank's loss was minimal. The court stated:

> Some commentators have questioned the wisdom of imposing liability under UCC 4–302(a) for a payor bank's failure to settle for the item on the day it is received when the bank has dishonored or returned the item within the midnight deadline because if the item has been dishonored before payment of it has become final, the only apparent harm that results is that the depositary bank has been deprived of one day's interest on the amount of the item. They maintain that holding the payor bank accountable for the face value of the item in the light of such minimum damages is an unduly harsh penalty (see 6 Hawkland, Leary & Alderman, UCC Series, § 4–302:02). * * * We do not similarly view the matter.

661 N.E.2d at 688.

The unusual aspect of *Hanna* is how the issue of failure to settle on Day 1 ever arose. *Hanna* is the first reported case we have seen in which there was no settlement on the date of delivery. A large percentage of checks are presented by Federal Reserve Banks, and, as to these checks, there is always settlement on the day of presentment. This is true because the Fed will not present a check to a payor bank unless that bank or its correspondent bank has an account in the Fed; this account will be promptly debited by the Fed. With respect to checks not presented by the Fed, settlement may be made by the payor bank's sending a Fedwire credit to the presenting bank's Fed account before the close of Fedwire (6:30 p.m. ET) on the day of delivery. If, as in *Hanna*, a check is presented through a clearing house, the banks that are members of the clearing house usually have agreements (4–213(a)) providing that as each member exchanges checks at the clearing with each other member, the amounts are netted out with debit balances to be paid that day by wire transfers to the account of the creditor bank in the Fed by an agreed time or by entries in accounts each of the members holds in the others. In short, in clearing house transactions, payor banks must settle for checks on the day the checks are delivered to it. The court has little to say about why this result didn't follow in *Hanna*, other than to observe, laconically, that the payor bank had presented no admissible evidence of settlement on November 12.

### b.   WHAT IS A PAYOR BANK?

Under 4–302(a) presentment to the payor bank starts the running of the midnight deadline period. But in the branch banking system so common today, what is the payor bank? In a branch banking system, checks drawn by customers having accounts in a branch will usually not be sent to the branch for payment initially but will be routed through a processing center where the checks are run through a reader/sorter machine and drawers' balances are adjusted in the bank's electronic data storage system. Checks meeting the bank's standards for sight review of signatures (usually large balance checks) may then be delivered to the branch where the drawer has an account and signature cards are kept. Which is the payor bank for the purpose of the midnight deadline: any branch in the system, the branch where the drawer maintains its account whose address is on the check, or the processing center? Section 4–107 states: "A branch or separate office of a bank is a separate bank for the purpose of computing the time within which and determining the place at or to which action may be taken or notices or orders shall be given under this Article and under Article 3." Comment 1 suggests that this is the best the drafters can do given the infinitely varying practices in the huge banking industry, and the courts will have to sort out the proper results "on the basis of the facts of each case." See the extensive discussion on this issue in 2 White & Summers, Uniform Commercial Code 20–4c. (4th Prac. Ed. 1995).

### PROBLEMS

**1.** Bank has 20 branches in and around a large city and a central processing center (Center) to which all checks drawn on any branch of Bank are automatically routed for processing by directions encoded on the bottom of the check. These directions are pursuant to 4–204(c) that allows the payor bank to designate the place where presentment should be made. The check in question is received by Center at noon on Day 1 and run through Bank's computers. Because the check is for an amount larger than $5,000, it is then delivered to Branch, whose address is on the check, at 8:00 a.m. on Day 2 for sight review of signature. Branch decided at noon on Day 2 to dishonor the check and delivered it to Center at 5:00 p.m. on Day 2. At 3:00 a.m. on Day 3, Center dispatched the check by motor courier to the presenting bank. Did Bank meet its midnight deadline?

**2.** Show–Me Bank (SMB) has 100 branches in Missouri; most are clustered around either St. Louis or Kansas City. SMB maintains separate processing centers (Centers) in St. Louis for the eastern area (Eastern) and in Kansas City for the western area (Western). Checks drawn on eastern branches are routed to Eastern Center, and those drawn on western branches go to Western Center. Payee deposits a check drawn on an Eastern branch in her deposit account in a Western branch on Day 1. The check is delivered by Western branch to Western Center at 8 a.m. on Day 2, which sends it by air courier to Eastern Center where it arrives at noon on Day 3 and is run through that Center's computers. Because the check is for an amount larger than $5,000, at 8 a.m. on Day 4 the check is delivered to the Eastern branch whose address is on the check for sight review of the signature. Eastern Branch decided at noon on Day 4 to dishonor the check and returned it to Eastern Center at 5:00 p.m. on Day 4. At 11:00 p.m. on Day 4, Eastern Center dispatched the check by air courier to Western Center where it arrived at 1:00 a.m. on Day 5. Did SMB meet its midnight deadline?

## c.   CHECK KITING

The prevalence of check kiting scams in recent years has placed pressure on the strict accountability rule of 4–302(a). If a depositary bank, knowing that a kite is taking place, presents checks to a payor bank that doesn't know about the kite, is it fair to impose strict accountability on the payor bank that misses its midnight deadline on these checks? The depositary bank is trying to get paid before the kite crashes, while the payor bank ends up liable for the face amount of these "large item" checks that are drawn on uncollected, in fact, uncollectible, funds in the kiter's account. The following case is a good analysis of the problem under Revised Article 4. Check kiting is discussed in 1 Clark & Clark, The Law of Bank Deposits, Collections and Credit Cards, Chapter 9 (Rev. ed. 2006).

## First National Bank in Harvey v. Colonial Bank

United States District Court, N.D. Illinois, 1995.
898 F.Supp. 1220.

■ GRADY, DISTRICT JUDGE.

Before the court are the parties' cross-motions for summary judgment. For the reasons explained, plaintiff First National Bank in Harvey's motion is granted in part and denied in part. Defendant Colonial Bank's motion is granted in part and denied in part. Defendant Federal Reserve Bank of Chicago's motion is granted.

Check kiting is a form of bank fraud. The kiter opens accounts at two (or more) banks, writes checks on insufficient funds on one account, then covers the overdraft by depositing a check drawn on insufficient funds from the other account.

To illustrate the operation, suppose that the defrauder opens two accounts with a deposit of $500 each at the First National Bank and a distant Second National Bank. (A really successful defrauder will have numerous accounts in fictitious names at banks in widely separated states.) The defrauder then issues for goods or cash checks totaling $3000 against the First National Bank. But before they clear and overdraw the account, he covers the overdrafts with a check for $4,000 drawn on the Second National Bank. The Second National account will be overdrawn when the $4,000 check is presented; before that happens, however, the defrauder covers it with a check on the First National Bank. The process is repeated innumerable times until there is a constant float of worthless checks between the accounts and the defrauder has bilked the banks of a substantial sum of money.

John D. O'Malley, "Common Check Frauds and the Uniform Commercial Code," 23 Rutgers L. Rev. 189, 194 n. 35 (1968–69). By timing the scheme correctly and repeating it over a period of time, the kiter can use the funds essentially as an interest-free loan. Williams v. United States, 458 U.S. 279, 281 n. 1, 102 S.Ct. 3088, 3090 n. 1, 73 L.Ed.2d 767 (1982) (quoting Brief for the United States).

Check kiting is possible because of a combination of two rules found in Article 4 of the Uniform Commercial Code. Under § 4–208(a)(1) [4–210(a)(1)], a depositary bank may allow a customer to draw on uncollected funds, that is, checks that have been deposited but not yet paid. Second, under §§ 4–301 and 4–302, a payor bank must either pay or dishonor a check drawn on it by midnight of the second banking day following presentment. Barkley Clark, The Law of Bank Deposits, Collections and Credit Cards & 5.03[5] (3d ed. 1990). Thus, when a kite is operating, the depositary bank allows the kiter to draw on uncollected funds based on a deposit of a check. The depositary bank presents that check to the payor bank, which must decide whether to pay or return the check before the midnight deadline. The check may appear to be covered by uncollected funds at the payor bank, and so the payor bank may decide to pay the check by allowing the midnight deadline to pass.

A kite crashes when one of the banks dishonors checks drawn on it and returns them to the other banks involved in the kite. Clark, supra. Usually, such a dishonor occurs when one bank suspects a kite. Id. However, an individual bank may have trouble detecting a check kiting scheme. "Until one has devoted a substantial amount of time examining not only one's own account, but accounts at other banks, it may be impossible to know whether the customer is engaged in a legitimate movement of funds or illegitimate kiting." James J. White & Robert S. Summers, Uniform Commercial Code § 17–1 (3d ed. 1988 & Supp. 1994). But each bank is usually able to monitor only its own account, and "[t]here is no certain test that distinguishes one who writes many checks on low balances from a check kiter." White & Summers, supra, § 17–2. Even if a bank suspects a kite, it might decide not to take any action for a number of reasons. First, it may be liable to its customer for wrongfully dishonoring checks. § 4–202.

Second, if it reports that a kite is operating and turns out to be wrong, it could find itself defending a defamation suit. White & Summers, supra, § 17–1 (Supp. 1994). Finally, if it errs in returning checks or reporting a kite, it may risk angering a large customer. Id.

This case involves the fallout of a collapsed check kite. Two of the banks involved, First National Bank in Harvey ("First National") and Colonial Bank ("Colonial") are the parties to this litigation. The Federal Reserve Bank of Chicago (the "Reserve Bank"), through whose clearinghouse the relevant checks were processed, is also a party.

Shelly International Marketing ("Shelly") opened a checking account at First National in December 1989. The principals of Shelly also opened accounts at the Family Bank (a nonparty) in the names of Shelly Brokerage and Crete Trading around December 1990. On December 31, 1991, the principals of Shelly opened a checking account at Colonial Bank in the name of World Commodities, Inc. Shelly and World Commodities were related companies, with the same or similar shareholders, officers, and directors. The principals of Shelly and World Commodities began operating a check kiting scheme among the accounts at the three banks in early 1991.

The main events at issue in this case took place in February 1992. The checks that form the basis of this suit are thirteen checks totalling $1,523,892.49 for which First National was the depositary bank and Colonial was the payor bank (the "Colonial checks"). Also relevant are seventeen checks totalling $1,518,642.86 for which Colonial was the depositary bank and First National was the payor bank (the "First National checks").

On Monday, February 10, Shelly deposited the thirteen Colonial checks to its First National account. First National then sent those checks through the check clearing system. That same day, World Commodities deposited the seventeen First National checks to its Colonial account.

The next day, Tuesday, February 11, the Colonial checks were presented to Colonial for payment, and the First National checks were presented to First National for payment. That day, David Spiewak, an officer with First National's holding company, Pinnacle, reviewed the bank's records to determine why there were large balance fluctuations in Shelly's First National account. Spiewak began to suspect that a kite might be operating. He did not know whether Colonial had enough funds to cover the Colonial checks that had been deposited on Monday, February 10, and forwarded to Colonial for payment. Later that day, First National froze the Shelly account to prevent any further activity in it.

On the morning of Wednesday, February 12, Spiewak met with First National president Dennis Irvin and Pinnacle's chief lending officer Mike Braun to discuss the Shelly account. Spiewak informed the others of what he knew, and the three agreed that there was a possible kite. They concluded that further investigation was needed. The First National officers decided to return the First National checks to Colonial. First National says that the decision was made at this meeting, but Colonial says the decision was actually made the day before.

On Wednesday, First National returned the First National checks to Colonial. Under Regulation CC, a bank that is returning checks in excess of $2,500.00 must provide notice to the depositary bank either by telephone, actual return of the check, or Fed Wire before 4:00 p.m. on the second business day following presentment. First National notified Colonial by Fed Wire that it was returning the seventeen First National checks. Initially, the large item return form indicated that the reason for the return was "uncollected funds," but Spiewak changed that reason to "refer to maker."

Colonial received the Fed Wire notices at approximately 2:45 p.m. on Wednesday and routed them to its cashier, Joanne Topham. Randall Soderman, a Colonial loan officer, was informed of the large return, and immediately began an investigation. He realized that if the Colonial checks were not returned by midnight that same day, Colonial would be out the money. Returning the Colonial checks before midnight would protect Colonial from liability, but it would risk disappointing the customer. Anthony Schiller, the loan officer in charge of the World Commodities account, called World Commodities comptroller Charles Patterson and its attorney Jay Goldstein. Both assured Schiller that the First National checks were good and should be redeposited. Ultimately, Richard Vucich, Colonial's president, and Joanne Topham, Colonial's cashier, decided not to return the Colonial checks on Wednesday. They decided instead to meet on Thursday morning with Schiller to discuss the matter.

Schiller, Topham, and Vucich met on the morning of Thursday, February 13. At the conclusion of the meeting, they decided to return the thirteen Colonial checks to First National. At about 10:45 a.m., Colonial telephoned First National to say that it intended to return the Colonial checks. Colonial sent the Colonial checks back through the Reserve Bank as a return in a return cash letter. The Reserve Bank debited First National's Reserve Bank account in the amount of the Colonial checks. First National received the returned Colonial checks on Friday, February 14.

First National then resorted to the Fed's "challenge procedure" to contest the return of the Colonial checks after the midnight deadline. First National prepared and submitted to the Reserve Bank a "Sender's Claim of Late Return" form for each of the Colonial checks. The Reserve Bank processed the claim forms and credited the Reserve Bank account of First National $1,523,892.49 and debited the Reserve Bank account of Colonial in the same amount. On February 24, Colonial prepared and filed a "Paying Bank's Response to Claim of Late Return" form for each of the thirteen Colonial checks. As a consequence of the processing of the response forms, the Reserve Bank reversed the credit given to First National and the debit made to Colonial.

First National then filed this suit against Colonial and the Reserve Bank, alleging that Colonial wrongfully returned the Colonial checks after the midnight deadline and the Reserve Bank wrongfully accepted the late return. * * * Count V against Colonial alleges breach of UCC § 4–302 for Colonial's failure to return the checks by the midnight deadline. * * *

First National moved for partial summary judgment as to Count V. On August 27, 1993, this court denied the plaintiff's motion. First Nat'l Bank in Harvey v. Colonial Bank, 831 F.Supp. 637 (N.D.Ill.1993). The parties now have each moved for summary judgment on all counts. Along with deciding the remaining counts, today's opinion reconsiders portions of our earlier ruling on Count V. * * *

## I.   COUNT V: BREACH OF UCC § 4–302 AGAINST COLONIAL

### A.   Accountability

Article 4 of the Uniform Commercial Code adopts a policy of "final payment"; that is, a check is considered to be finally paid at some specific and identifiable point in time. § 4–215 Comment 1. Final payment is the "end of the line" in the check collection process. Section 4–301 sets up the "midnight deadline" in the process: a payor bank which intends to return a check presented to it must do so before midnight of the next banking day following receipt of the check. §§ 4–301(a), 4–104(a)(10). If a payor bank fails to return a check before the midnight deadline, final payment occurs. * * *

Section 4–302 spells out the payor bank's liability for its late return of an item, that is, return after the midnight deadline:

(a) If an item is presented to and received by a payor bank, the bank is *accountable* for the amount of:

(1) a demand item, other than a documentary draft, whether properly payable or not, if the bank ... does not pay or return the item or send notice of dishonor until after its midnight deadline. . . .

§ 4–302 (emphasis added). The operative word in this section is "accountable." Courts interpreting this section have nearly unanimously concluded that § 4–302 imposes strict liability on a payor bank for failing to adhere to the midnight deadline, and makes the measure of damages the face amount of the check. In an early decision, the Illinois Supreme Court held that "accountable" means "liable" for the amount of the item. Rock Island Auction Sales, Inc. v. Empire Packing Co., 32 Ill.2d 269, 204 N.E.2d 721, 723 (Ill. 1965). The Rock Island court contrasted the "accountability" language in § 4–302 with the language used to specify the measure of damages in what is now § 4–103(e). Section 4–103(e) makes a bank liable for failing to exercise ordinary care in the handling of a check in "the amount of the item reduced by an amount that could not have been realized by the exercise of ordinary care." § 4–103(e). The Official Comment to this section explains: "When it is established that some part or all of the item could not have been collected even by the use of ordinary care the recovery is reduced by the amount that would have been in any event uncollectible." In other words, § 4–103(e) imposes liability in the amount of the loss caused by the negligence, while § 4–302(a) imposes strict liability in the face amount of the check.

The *Rock Island* court reasoned that the special role of the payor bank in the check collection system justifies the imposition of liability regardless of negligence. The midnight deadline requires the payor bank—the bank in the best position to know whether there are funds available to cover the check—to decide whether to pay or return the check:

> The role of a payor bank in the collection process ... is crucial. It knows whether or not the drawer has funds available to pay the item. The legislature could have considered that the failure of such a bank to meet its deadline is likely to be due to factors other than negligence, and that the relationship between a payor bank and its customer may so influence its conduct as to cause a conscious disregard of its statutory duty.

*Rock Island*, 204 N.E.2d at 723.

The overwhelming majority of courts that have considered the meaning of § 4–302(a) have followed the *Rock Island* court in concluding that the liability of a payor bank that fails to return a check by the midnight deadline is strict and is in the face amount of the check. * * *

Even where the damage suffered by the payee is not caused by the lateness of the return, the midnight deadline still has been strictly enforced. For example, in Chicago Title Ins. Co. v. California Canadian Bank, 1 Cal. App. 4th 798, 2 Cal. Rptr.2d 422, 424 (Ct. App. 1991), the payor bank decided to return twenty-eight checks involved in a massive check fraud scheme. The checks left the bank before the midnight deadline, but did not arrive at the clearinghouse until the next day—after the midnight deadline had passed. The court held that the bank's return was late. It held the bank strictly accountable for the face amount of the checks, reasoning that the bank " 'may be held strictly liable for its failure to return the checks by the applicable deadlines, regardless whether [the other party] demonstrated it suffered actual damage solely as a result of [the Bank's] omission.' " Id. at 426–29 (quoting Los Angeles Nat'l Bank v. Bank of Canton, 229 Cal. App.3d 1267, 280 Cal. Rptr. 831, 838 (Ct. App. 1991)); see also American Title Ins. Co. v. Burke & Herbert Bank & Trust Co., 813 F.Supp. 423, 426 (E.D.Va.1993) ("[L]iability for the face amount of the check is imposed without regard to whether any damages have been sustained as a result of the payor bank's failure to make a timely return."), aff'd, 25 F.3d 1038 (4th Cir.1994).

* * *

But is it appropriate to enforce the accountability provision of § 4–302 where a check kiting scheme is involved? The Minnesota Supreme Court did in Town & Country State Bank v. First State Bank, 358 N.W.2d 387, 393–95 (Minn.1984). There, the court held that two payor banks that held kited checks beyond the midnight deadline made "final payment" on the checks and were therefore accountable for the amounts of those checks. * * *

* * *

This court's prior opinion held that First National could not recover under the accountability provision of § 4–302 if it would be unjustly enriched by the recovery. § 1–103; 831 F.Supp. at 641. On the undisputed evidence presented by First National on the present motion, however, we now see that it did suffer a loss. At some point during the check kiting scheme, funds were siphoned out of the banking system, causing a deficit in First National's assets. The important point is that First National will not be unjustly enriched by recovering from Colonial. It has suffered a loss at some point, and will not experience a windfall if it recovers from Colonial.

Therefore, we conclude that Colonial is absolutely liable in the face amount of the Colonial checks for missing the midnight deadline. This does not end the analysis, however, because Colonial raises the defenses of good faith and mistaken payment to defeat strict accountability.

## B. Good Faith

The general provisions of the Uniform Commercial Code state: "Every contract or duty within this Act imposes an obligation of good faith in its performance or enforcement." § 1–203 [1–304]. The Code defines "good faith" as "honesty in fact in the conduct or transaction concerned." § 1–201(19) [1–201(b)(20)]. Colonial argues that First National's lack of good faith defeats its § 4–302 claim of accountability, contending that First National orchestrated the events of the week of February 10 in order to cause Colonial to miss the midnight deadline for returning the Colonial checks.

The first question is whether we should even consider bad faith in this check kiting case. First National urges us to refrain from injecting notions of bad faith to reallocate the loss here. It contends that introducing the concept of bad faith will muddy the concepts of certainty and finality, which are central to the treatment of kites by Article 4. However, the UCC itself, in § 1–103, injects notions of good faith into every transaction covered by it, and we cannot simply ignore the statute.

Colonial charges that First National returned the seventeen First National checks to Colonial on Wednesday, February 12, under circumstances amounting to bad faith. Colonial argues that First National deliberately caused confusion in returning the First National checks, which caused Colonial to miss the midnight deadline for the Colonial checks.

Colonial offers the following facts to show First National's bad faith. On Tuesday, February 11, Spiewak thought that a kite was taking place and together with other First National officers decided that the First National checks would be dishonored and returned to Colonial. First National returned the checks the next day, Wednesday, a day on which it is closed for business. It also notified Colonial of the return late in the day (2:45 p.m.) by Fed Wire rather than by telephone, a practice that is rarely used and less desirable than telephone notice because a wire notice may not be picked up by an employee for some time, while telephonic notice is received directly by a bank employee who can take immediate action. Finally, First National changed the reason for the return from "uncollected funds" to "refer to maker." When Colonial received the wire transmittal, it attempted to contact First National to determine why First National returned the checks "refer to maker." No one at Colonial was able to talk to anyone at First National, however, because a recorded message informed Colonial employees that First National was closed on Wednesdays. First National's endorsement stamp contains only its general telephone number, not any other telephone number that would allow telephone calls to be made even when the switchboard is closed, as is the practice at most Chicago area banks.

In short, Colonial argues that First National's failure to advise Colonial of the kite, its delay in giving notice of the return, its use of Fed Wire to give notice of the return, its return of the checks marked "refer to maker," and its return of the checks on a day when it was closed for business caused Colonial to miss the midnight deadline for the Colonial checks. These facts amount to bad faith, Colonial contends; consequently First National may not recover any losses it suffered in the kite. And, in any event, whether First National's acts constitute bad faith is an issue of fact that precludes summary judgment in favor of First National.

Colonial's argument raises specific questions about whether First National's conduct amounts to bad faith. But it also raises more general questions about banks' conduct in check kiting schemes: Does a depositary bank that suspects a kite have a good faith duty to disclose its suspicions to the payor bank? Furthermore, does a bank act in bad faith if it discovers or suspects a kite and attempts to shift the loss to the other bank by returning checks drawn on it while at the same time forwarding checks that have been deposited with it for payment?

Courts that have dealt with these issues usually take the latter two questions together, and most have concluded that a bank has no good faith obligation to disclose a suspected kite or to refrain from attempting to shift the kite loss. These were the conclusions of the Mississippi Supreme Court in the leading case of Citizens Nat'l Bank v. First Nat'l Bank, 347 So.2d 964 (Miss.1977). In *Citizens*, a check kite was operating through accounts at Citizens National Bank and at First National Bank. First National discovered the kite, and returned all checks drawn on its account that Citizens had presented. At the same time, First National presented checks to Citizens that the kiter had drawn on Citizens and deposited with First National. First National also accepted deposits by the kiter and payments by Citizens. After the kite crashed, Citizens sued First National, charging that First National converted funds belonging to Citizens.

The Mississippi Supreme Court upheld the dismissal of the complaint, agreeing with the chancellor's opinion which stated, "I cannot find where FNB has been charged with doing anything other than acting as a prudent and careful bank should act." Id. at 967, 969. In holding that there was no duty on the part of First National to notify Citizens of its conviction that their mutual customer was kiting checks, the court reasoned:

> [T]hese two banks were competitors in the banking field and ordinarily banks deal with each other at arm's length. The bill does not allege any circumstances or facts that tend to show that a confidential or fiduciary relationship existed between these two banks, neither does it show

that there is any requirement in the banking field that one bank notify another of its discovery of a customer kiting checks. In the absence of a fiduciary or confidential relationship, or some other legal duty, First National Bank had no duty to inform Citizens National Bank that Duran was kiting checks. This being true, we are of the opinion that First National Bank had the legal right to continue to accept for deposit checks drawn by Duran on accounts at Citizens National Bank and present those checks for payment. At the same time, First National Bank had the legal right to refuse to pay checks drawn by Duran on accounts in First National Bank and deposited in Citizens National Bank.

Id. at 967.

In a more recent case, the district court in Connecticut similarly concluded that a bank's failure to tell another bank about a suspected kite, while returning checks drawn on it and accepting checks drawn on the other bank, is not bad faith. Cumis Ins. Society, Inc. v. Windsor Bank & Trust Co., 736 F.Supp. 1226, 1231–34 (D.Conn.1990). In *Cumis*, the insurer of a credit union that sustained a kite loss sued the winning bank. The facts are similar: the bank suspected a kite and began to dishonor checks drawn against it while continuing to collect on checks drawn on the credit union and deposited with the bank. The bank had even instituted an expedited check clearing procedure specifically to handle drafts drawn on the credit union. Id. at 1230. The court refused to impose a good faith duty to disclose the kite:

> There is thus no duty between competing institutions to inform one another of the existence of a check kiting scheme because these institutions deal at arms length, have their own means of detecting check kiting, and, realistically, need no protection from other institutions.

Id. at 1233. The court identified several exceptions to this general rule: (1) where a fiduciary or confidential relationship exists; (2) where a contractual relationship exists; (3) where there is a duty created by law; and (4) where there was fraud or misrepresentation by the defendant bank. * * *

The facts here amount to, at most, an attempt by First National to shift the kite loss to Colonial. First, as First National points out, wire notice is a legally permissible method of notifying another bank of a large return. 12 C.F.R. § 229.33(a). In addition, First National has presented evidence that notifying other banks of large returns by wire rather than by telephone was its usual practice.

Although Colonial makes much of the fact that First National returned the First National checks marked "refer to maker" rather than "uncollected funds," the parties agree that "refer to maker" is a legally permissible reason for returning a check. And Colonial had contacted the maker, World Commodities, and its counsel, receiving assurances that the checks were good. As to First National's delay in informing Colonial of the return, it is undisputed that First National notified a Colonial employee at 9:30 a.m. on

Wednesday, February 12, that it would be returning certain checks, although it notified the wrong employee and did not specify the number or dollar amounts of those checks. But First National sent the wire notice later the same day stating that seventeen checks totalling $1,518,642.86 were being returned "refer to maker." Even if, as Colonial contends, First National officers decided to return the checks on Tuesday rather than Wednesday, Colonial had notice more than twelve hours before the midnight deadline that checks drawn on the Shelly account were being returned. And even though Colonial was not able to contact First National on Wednesday, Colonial knew on that day that the First National checks were being returned and that the midnight deadline for the Colonial checks was rapidly approaching.

All of First National's conduct regarding the First National checks was proper under the applicable laws. First National had the right to present the Colonial checks for payment and the right to return the First National checks. At most, First National took advantage of these laws and regulations to attempt to shift the kite loss onto Colonial. But even if this is what happened, such conduct does not constitute bad faith.

First National and Colonial were faced with the same dilemma at the same time: a number of checks totaling a goodly sum of money drawn on the account of a customer with low collected funds balances. First National chose to return the checks unpaid, but Colonial chose to trust its customer to cover the checks. By the time Colonial realized that its decision was wrong, it was too late—the midnight deadline had passed and the checks were paid. Each bank made a business decision; First National's turned out to be the correct one. * * *

For the reasons explained, plaintiff First National's motion for summary judgment is granted as to Count V of the first amended complaint * * *. Colonial's motion for summary judgment is * * * denied as to Count V.

NOTES

**1.** The principal case states the prevailing rule, but Oregon courts have taken the view that a depositary bank may be in bad faith if it presents checks knowing of a check kite while dishonoring checks drawn on it. Farmers & Merchants State Bank v. Western Bank, 841 F.2d 1433 (9th Cir.1987), applies Oregon law and reviews the state court authorities. 1 Clark & Clark, The Law of Bank Deposits, Check Collections and Credit Cards ¶ 9.03 (Rev. ed. 2005). Should the "fair dealing" prong of the definition of "good faith" in 1–201(b)(20) have any effect on facts like those in *First National Bank in Harvey*?

**2.** In the 1990 revision of Article 4, after much discussion, a new defense to the accountability rule was added by 4–302(b): "The liability of a payor bank to pay an item pursuant to subsection (a) is subject to defenses based on * * * proof that the person seeking enforcement of the liability presented or transferred the item for the purpose of defrauding the payor bank." Comment 3 says: "A payor bank that makes a late return of an item should not be liable to a defrauder operating a check kiting scheme." Why didn't the court in the preceding case refer to 4–302(b) and the quoted Comment? The court was correct in not doing so; 4–302(b) was not intended to cover such a case. The presenting bank (First National) was not "operating a check kiting scheme" when it presented checks to Colonial and had no intention of defrauding that bank.

The first authoritative holding on the application of 4–302(b) to check kiting is found in Bank of America NT & SA v. David W. Hubert, P.C., 101 P.3d 409 (Wash. 2004). In that case, Principal, an incorporated law firm, gave Agent complete control over a large deposit account of Principal in Bank A in which the proceeds from real estate closings were deposited. Agent, who was running a check kite, stole large sums from the account in Bank A and replenished the balance in the account by writing checks payable to Principal on her empty account in Bank B, which she deposited in Principal's account in Bank A. When these checks were presented to Bank B for payment, they were returned for insufficient funds *after* Bank B's midnight deadline. Principal asserted that Bank B was accountable for the funds under 4–302 but the court held that 4–302(b) applied because Agent's fraudulent intent was imputed to the careless Principal.

### d.  EFFECT OF REGULATION CC ON THE MIDNIGHT DEADLINE

Regulation CC, 12 CFR pt. 229, § 229.30(c), is a major modification of the Article 4 midnight deadline. In this regulation the Fed attempts to speed the return of checks by extending the midnight deadline. How does this make returns swifter? The regulation is set out below.

(c) Extension of deadline. The deadline for return or notice of nonpayment under the U.C.C. * * * is extended to the time of dispatch of such return or notice of nonpayment where a paying bank uses a means of delivery that would ordinarily result in receipt by the bank to which is sent

(1) On or before the receiving bank's next banking day following the otherwise applicable deadline [the UCC midnight deadline], for all deadlines other than those described in paragraph (c)(2) of this section; this deadline is extended further if a paying bank uses a highly expeditious means of transportation, even if this means of transportation would ordinarily result in delivery after the receiving bank's next banking day; or

(2) Prior to the cut-off hour for the next processing day (if sent to a returning bank), or on the next banking day (if sent to the depositary bank), for a deadline falling on a Saturday that is a banking day (as defined in the applicable U.C.C.) for the paying bank.

An example of how these provisions operate is found in the following case.

# Oak Brook Bank v. Northern Trust Company

United States Court of Appeals, Seventh Circuit, 2001.
256 F.3d 638.

■ POSNER, CIRCUIT JUDGE.

A bank that dishonors a check presented to it for payment must return the check to the bank in which the check had been deposited (the "depositary" bank), either directly or via a "returning bank," which acts as a transmitting agent. (The bank to which the check is presented for payment is called, even if it dishonors the check, the "payor" bank—a confusing usage in this context since it has *refused* to pay the check.) Like the other federal reserve banks, the Federal Reserve Bank of Chicago is a returning bank; indeed, returning checks is the major conventional banking activity in which federal reserve banks engage. In the case at hand, a check kiter who had accounts in both Oak Brook Bank and Northern Trust Company deposited in his Oak Brook account checks (none for less than $2,500) totaling some $450,000 drawn on his Northern account, which had only a minute balance (exactly how much, the record does not disclose). The checks were presented to Northern for payment the next day, February 11, 1998. On February 13, Northern decided to dishonor them and it informed Oak Brook of that decision by phone shortly before 4 p.m. By that time, however, Oak Brook had credited the kiter's account and he had withdrawn all but about $7,000 of the money in the account. At 4:30 p.m., Northern sent the dishonored checks by courier to the Federal Reserve Bank, which received them sixteen minutes later.

Oak Brook sued the kiter and the kiter's company in federal district court under RICO and added a claim under the supplemental jurisdiction of the district court against Northern, charging that the dishonor was ineffective because the return of the checks was untimely and concluding that therefore Northern must make good Oak Brook's loss. The district court granted summary judgment for Northern and entered a Rule 54(b) judgment enabling Oak Brook to take an immediate appeal. The claim against the kiter and his company remain pending in the district court. The issue in this appeal, a novel one, is the meaning of "banking day" in regard to federal reserve banks.

The banking article of the Uniform Commercial Code requires the payor bank that wishes to dishonor a check to dispatch it (for example by putting it in the mail), either to the depositary bank or to a "returning" bank for forwarding to the depositary bank, by midnight on the next banking day after the banking day on which the payor bank had received the check; and failure to make the deadline requires the payor bank to pay the check. UCC §§ 4–104(a)(10), 4–302(a)(1). Northern missed this deadline, for remember that it received the checks on February 11 but didn't dispatch them to the Federal Reserve Bank until the thirteenth. No matter. In 1987, concerned about delay in depositors' access to funds that they deposited by check, Congress, in the Expedited Funds Availability Act, 12 U.S.C. §§ 4001–10, shortened the "hold period" of depositary banks, that is, the period after a check is deposited before the depositor can withdraw the money from his account. 12 U.S.C. § 4002. The shortening of the hold period increased the risk of nonpayment to these banks, and to deal with that problem the Act authorized the Federal Reserve Board to issue regulations governing the system of bank payments. 12 U.S.C. § 4008(c)(1). Pursuant to this grant of authority the Board issued Regulation CC, 12 C.F.R. pt. 229, which contains two provisions that bear on this case. The first requires prompt notice of dishonor in the case of any check for more than $2,500, such as the kiter's checks that Northern dishonored. 12 C.F.R. § 229.33(a). It is conceded that this provision was satisfied by Northern's phone call to Oak Brook on the thirteenth. But second—and this is critical—the regulation extends the UCC's deadline from midnight to when the payor bank dispatches the dishonored check on its return journey, provided the bank "uses a means of delivery that would ordinarily result in receipt by the bank to which it is sent . . . on or before the receiving bank's next banking day following the otherwise applicable deadline." 12 C.F.R. § 229.30(c)(1).

It may seem odd that delay in returning the checks should make the payor bank have to pay them in a case such as this, when it had notified the depositary bank that the checks had been drawn against insufficient funds in time for that bank to prevent any money from being withdrawn. Oak Brook seems to have been careless in allowing the kiter to withdraw "his" money so fast. Of course, it didn't know he was a kiter. But because of the size of the deposit, it could have refused withdrawal for seven business days, see 12 C.F.R. §§ 229.13(b), (h)(1), (h)(4), and thus until February 20; and had it done so it wouldn't have been left holding the bag, since it received notice of the dishonor on the thirteenth and the checks themselves back on the seventeenth. But all that is irrelevant. If Northern missed the extended deadline in Regulation CC, it must pay the checks. The reason for this severe sanction is that the depositary bank could get into serious trouble if it refused to allow a depositor to withdraw his money, or took other action against a depositor, without proof that the depositor had no right to the money. See UCC § 4–402.

And now we come at last to the nub of the case. The provision that we quoted from Regulation CC extending the deadline requires that the method of delivery used be calculated to get the check to the depositary or, as here, the returning bank by that bank's "next banking day following the otherwise applicable deadline." The "otherwise applicable deadline" was the UCC's deadline of midnight on February 12, the day after Northern received the checks. The "next banking day" was the thirteenth, and so Northern had to get the checks to the Federal Reserve Bank, the returning bank, by the end of the Federal Reserve Bank's "banking day" on the thirteenth; and the question is whether it made this deadline.

Regulation CC defines "banking day" as "that part of any business day on which an office of a bank is open to the public for carrying on *substantially all of its banking functions.*" 12 C.F.R. § 229.2(f) (emphasis added). (The UCC's definition of "banking day" is materially identical. See UCC § 4–104(a)(3).) Oak Brook argues that by 4:46 p.m. on February 13, the Federal Reserve Bank of Chicago was no longer carrying on "substantially all of its banking functions." More precisely, it argues that whether it was or not is a contestable issue and so the grant of summary judgment for Northern was premature.

The Federal Reserve Bank of Chicago is open 24 hours a day, but that is neither here nor there. Federal reserve banks perform many functions for the banking system that are not banking functions. The question is whether at 4:46 p.m. on February 13, 1998, it was still carrying on substantially all of its banking functions. The bank's main banking function is check processing (including returns) for other banks—and it turns out that we need not consider what if any other banking functions the Federal Reserve Bank of Chicago, or any other federal reserve bank, performs. For that matter, it is of no significance that check processing is the Chicago reserve bank's main banking activity. Regulation CC states that a federal reserve bank is a bank within the meaning of the regulation only insofar as it is a "paying bank," the definition of which, so far as pertains to federal reserve banks, appears to be limited to a bank that processes checks. See 12 C.F.R. §§ 229.2(e), (z). Given that definition and the fact that Regulation CC is concerned solely with check processing, we think that for purposes of the regulation "all of [a federal reserve bank's] banking functions" means check processing. For it is irrelevant to the purpose of the regulation whether the bank is performing some other banking function on a particular day or at a particular time of day; and it would impair the utility of the extended deadline if a payor bank (Northern here), in order to determine what the deadline was, had to familiarize itself with the daily schedule of a bank's banking operations unrelated to check processing. This point is not logically limited to federal reserve banks, but we need not decide its applicability to banks that provide a broader range of conventional banking services and, unlike federal reserve banks, are not defined in the regulation as limited-purpose banks.

So the issue narrows to whether the Federal Reserve Bank of Chicago was open to the public (Oak Brook concedes that this means to other banks, which are a federal reserve bank's only "public") at 4:46 p.m. on February 13 for processing checks. The bank's check-processing department employs about 100 persons, with half or even more working during the peak hours of midnight to 9 a.m. Between 4 and 5 on a Friday afternoon, however (February 13, 1998, was a Friday), only one or two persons are on duty in the department. The processing of returned checks includes receipting the checks, sorting them by type and region, dispatching them to the depositary bank, and confirming the amount returned. When only one or two employees are on duty in the department, only receipting is completed; sorting is begun but not completed; dispatching, crediting, and, of course, confirming are not even begun. If, therefore, as Oak Brook argues, all these are separate functions, it cannot be said that the Federal Reserve Bank of Chicago performs substantially all of its banking functions on Friday afternoons after 4, and therefore Northern missed the deadline and must pay the checks.

We reject the argument, primarily on practical grounds. It would be impractical for payor banks to monitor the internal operations of returning banks in order to make sure that sending a check by courier at a given hour on a given day would be an occurrence that was within the returning bank's "banking day." It is telling in this regard that Oak Brook's lawyer was unable to pinpoint the end of the Federal Reserve Bank's banking day on February 13, 1998. The end was earlier than 4:46 p.m., he told us, but he was unable to say how much earlier, though he thought it might have been at 2 p.m. To fix the precise time would require, he told us, an in-depth inquiry, and therefore a trial.

Faced with such uncertainty, payor banks would tend to go back to the old UCC deadline, which Regulation CC does not supersede but merely supplements. Had Northern placed Oak Brook's checks in the mail to the Federal Reserve Bank of Chicago shortly before midnight on February 12 (the old UCC deadline), the checks probably wouldn't have gotten to that bank until the seventeenth (Monday the sixteenth was a federal holiday), and processing would have begun then rather than been completed then and therefore Oak Brook might not have received the checks as soon as it did. The added delay would have made no difference in this case but could make a difference in other cases.

We hold, therefore, that a federal reserve bank is open to the public for substantially all of its banking functions whenever the check-processing department is open for the receipt of checks, which in the case of the Federal Reserve Bank of Chicago is 24 hours of every day that the bank is open. The few cases dealing with the meaning of "banking day" under the materially identical definition of the term in the UCC are in accord with our position * * * Northern's employment of a means of delivery calculated to get the checks to the Federal Reserve Bank by any time up to midnight on February 13 therefore beat the deadline, and so summary judgment in Northern's favor was rightly granted. We leave open the implications of our analysis for returning banks other than federal reserve banks, which we were told dominate the check-return function.

AFFIRMED.

NOTES

**1.** Judge Posner leaves open the meaning of banking day for returning banks other than Federal Reserve Banks. Comment 2 to 4–104 speaks to this issue: "Under [the definition of banking day in 4–104(a)(3)] that part of a business day when a bank is open only for limited functions, e.g., to receive deposits and cash checks, but with loan, bookkeeping and other departments closed, is not part of a banking day."

**2.** In determining whether a payor bank has returned an item by its midnight deadline, 4–301(d)(2) focuses on when the item was "sent or delivered" rather than on when it arrived. If an item is mailed to the presenting bank just before the midnight deadline, the payor bank has revoked settlement under 4–301(a) and is not accountable under 4–

302(a)(1), even though the item may not arrive for a week. In an effort to speed up returns, Regulation CC added an additional day for return of the item to allow the payor to use a more expeditious means of return, such as an early morning courier, that would get the check back much faster than mail dispatched before the midnight deadline. *Oak Brook Bank* is an example of what the Fed had in mind in expediting returns.

## 2. RIGHT OF COLLECTING BANK TO REVOKE SETTLEMENT ON DISHONORED CHECK

We saw in the preceding section that a payor bank may inadvertently pay a check by failing to return the check within its midnight deadline. A collecting bank, including a depositary bank, is also subject to a midnight deadline in the case of return of a dishonored check to the bank. If a check forwarded to the payor bank is not paid, the depositary bank may revoke the provisional credit that it gave to its customer with respect to the check. 4–214(a). But the depositary bank is required either to return the check to its customer or to give notice of dishonor to the customer before the bank's midnight deadline. The case below discusses the Revised Article 4 provisions on notice of dishonor and the consequences of the failure of the depositary bank to act within its deadline.

## Essex Construction Corporation v. Industrial Bank of Washington, Inc.

United States District Court, D. Maryland, 1995.
913 F.Supp. 416.

■ MOTZ, CHIEF JUDGE.

Plaintiff Essex Construction Corporation (Essex) claims violations of the * * * District of Columbia banking laws. Essex alleges that Defendant Industrial Bank of Washington, Inc. (Industrial) * * * failed to provide timely notice that the check had been dishonored. Plaintiff seeks the amount of the check as damages. Defendant moves to dismiss or for summary judgment, and plaintiff cross-moves for default or summary judgment.

The relevant facts are not in dispute. On March 31, 1995, plaintiff deposited into its account at Industrial a check in the amount of $120,710.70 from East Side Manor Cooperative Association (East Side). East Side's check was drawn against its account at Signet Bank (Signet). At the time of the deposit, Industrial provisionally credited Essex's account but provided written notice that all but $100 of the funds would not be available for withdrawal until April 6, 1995.

On April 6, Signet notified Industrial that East Side had stopped payment on the check. Industrial placed a permanent hold on the $120,710.70 deposit, effectively revoking the provisional credit to Essex's account. On April 7, Industrial mailed written notice (including the returned check itself) to Essex.

On April 7, Essex wrote two checks in the amount of $21,224 and $18,084.60 against the funds it thought were available in its account at Industrial. Essex received Industrial's written notice of dishonor on April 11.

* * * [A] depository bank's right to revoke or charge back an uncollectible deposit * * * must comply with applicable state law. The District of Columbia has adopted the Uniform Commercial Code's system for regulating check processing transactions. The U.C.C. observes a fundamental distinction between "payor" and "collecting" banks. A payor bank is the bank maintaining the account against which a check is drawn, in this case Signet. See § 4–105(3). A collecting bank is a bank handling a check for collection from the payor, in this case Industrial. See § 4–105(5).

Payor and collecting banks have distinct obligations. A payor bank must decide whether to reject a check by midnight on the day it receives a check for collection. Failure to respond by midnight constitutes "final payment," making the payor bank strictly liable for the amount of the check. See First Nat'l Bank in Harvey v. Colonial Bank, 898 F.Supp. 1220, 1226 (N.D.Ill.1995) (discussing U.C.C.'s "final payment" system and role of payor banks); see also § 4–302(a). A collecting bank, in contrast, retains the right to revoke or charge back funds that are provisionally credited to a customer until the collecting bank's settlement with the payor bank becomes final. See § 4–214(a). It is at the moment of "final payment" by the payor bank that the respective liabilities for a check become fixed: the payor bank is strictly liable to the collecting bank for the amount of the check, see § 4–302(a), and the collecting bank loses the ability to revoke a provisional settlement or charge back withdrawn funds. See §§ 4–215(d), 4–214(a).

Essex argues that on April 6 Industrial's provisional credit to its account became a final and irrevocable payment under § 4–215(a). This contention misunderstands the difference between payor and collecting banks. As discussed, a final payment occurs when a payor bank accepts or fails to promptly reject a check presented for collection by a collecting bank. Industrial was the collecting bank in this transaction. Essex's reliance on § 4–215(a) therefore is misplaced. See § 4–215(a) ("An item is finally paid by a *payor* bank when the bank has first done any of the following....") (emphasis added). Essex's right to the provisionally credited funds became irrevocable only upon "final payment" by Signet to Industrial, a condition that Essex does not allege occurred.

Essex also argues that Industrial's mailing of the returned check via first class mail on April 7 did not constitute timely notice of dishonor under D.C. law. § 4–214 provides in relevant part:

§ 4–214 Right of charge-back or refund; liability of collecting bank; return of item.

(a) If a collecting bank has made a provisional settlement with its customer for an item and fails by reason of dishonor ... to receive settlement for the item which is or becomes final, the bank may revoke the settlement given by it, charge back the amount of any credit given for the item to its customer's account, or obtain refund from its customer . . . if by its midnight deadline or within a longer reasonable time after it learns the facts it returns the item or sends notification of the facts. . . .

There is no dispute that Industrial failed by reason of dishonor to receive a final payment from Signet, the payor bank. Section 4–214(a) therefore provides that Industrial could revoke the provisional credit "if by its midnight deadline or within a longer reasonable time after it learn[ed] the facts it return[ed] the item or sen[t] notification of the facts." A bank's "midnight deadline" is defined as "midnight on its next banking day following the banking day on which it receives the relevant item or notice." § 4–104(a)(10); see also § 3–503(c)(i) ("[W]ith respect to an instrument taken for collection by a collecting bank, notice of dishonor must be given by the bank before midnight of the next banking day following the banking day on which the bank receives notice of dishonor of the instrument."). The parties do not dispute that Industrial received notice of dishonor from Signet on April 6, that Industrial mailed the returned check to Essex before midnight on April 7 via first class mail, but that Essex did not receive it until April 11.

Essex argues that merely mailing the notice of dishonor before midnight on April 7 was insufficient. Industrial attempts to rely on § 3–508(4) for the proposition that "[w]ritten notice is given when sent although it is not received." However, the District of Columbia Council repealed § 3–508 effective March 27, 1995. See An Act to revise Articles 3 and 4 of the Uniform Commercial Code, 1994 D.C.Laws 10–249. Industrial's position finds alternative support, however, in § 4–214. Section 4–214(a) requires a bank to "*send* notification of the facts" or "return" the dishonored item. (emphasis added). Section 4–214(b) defines an item as "returned" "when it is *sent* or delivered to the bank's customer." In addition, § 3–503(b) provides that notice of dishonor may be given by "any commercially reasonable means, including an oral, written, or electronic communication." Industrial did not unduly delay notifying Essex, but instead took the reasonable step of promptly mailing the returned check. Although immediately telephoning Essex may have constituted better customer service, Industrial complied with D.C. notice requirements by mailing the returned check to Essex on April 7.

Moreover, even were I to find that Industrial's method of notice was not sufficient, Essex would not be entitled to the damages it seeks. In a case involving directly analogous provisions of the U.C.C. as enacted in Illinois, the Seventh Circuit has held that a depositor is entitled only to the damages actually resulting from a bank's failure to provide timely notice of dishonor. See Appliance Buyers Credit Corp. v. Prospect Nat'l Bank, 708 F.2d 290, 292–95 (7th Cir.1983). Furthermore, although the Appliance Buyers court reached this well-reasoned conclusion by interpreting an

Illinois statute that was silent as to damages,[4] here the D.C. provision contains additional language which expressly so limits a depositor's remedies: a bank that fails to provide timely notice retains its right to charge back dishonored deposits "but is liable for any loss *resulting from the delay*." § 4–214(a) (emphasis added).[5] Plaintiff therefore may have been able to assert a claim for the bank charges associated with the two checks written on April 7, or for other foreseeable damages.[6] Essex, however, has made no showing of damages actually suffered.

A separate order granting defendant's summary judgment motion and entering judgment on its behalf is being entered herewith.

## NOTE

In Gordon v. Planters & Merchants Bancshares, Inc., 935 S.W.2d 544 (Ark.1996), a collecting bank charged back against a customer's account a check for which it had received final settlement in violation of 4–215(d). The customer sued for punitive damages and the trial court granted the bank a directed verdict. The Supreme Court of Arkansas (4 to 3) reversed and remanded for a new trial. In its view the customer had shown substantial evidence that the bank had acted in a willful or malicious manner, and the "other rule of law" language 1–106(1) [1–305(a)] allows punitive damages even if not specifically provided for in the UCC. The court noted the "bad faith" language in 4–103(e). The dissenting judges were outraged; two judges didn't participate.

## 3.   CHECK ENCODING

The conservatism of the banking profession is snickered at by the following oft-told anecdote: When a retiring banker was asked what the

---

**4.** In *Appliance Buyers*, the Seventh Circuit noted that because the charge-back provision at issue in that case did not expressly address damages—in contrast to other U.C.C. provisions that expressly do hold banks "accountable" for the amount of the check—the drafters could not have intended "that banks should be held strictly liable for the face value of dishonored checks." 708 F.2d at 293. Instead, the *Appliance Buyers* court turned to Illinois' general damages provision, which provided only for actual damages and which was identical to D.C.'s current provision. Compare § 4–103(e) with 708 F.2d at 293 (quoting Ill. Rev.Stat. ch. 26 § 4–103(5)).

**5.** In fact, prior to revisions that became effective on March 27, 1995, the predecessor to § 4–214(a) was largely identical to the Illinois statute at issue in *Appliance Buyers*. In 1995, however, the D.C. Council re-

vised its U.C.C. provisions to add, among other changes, the above-quoted language that expressly limits recovery to actual loss. See 1994 D.C.Laws 10–249.

**6.** To recover the $120,710.70 from Industrial, therefore, Essex would have had to show that, absent the delay from April 7 to April 11, it would have been able to take action to collect from East Side. See Alioto v. United States, 593 F.Supp. 1402, 1416–17 (N.D. Ill. 1984) (discussing cases). The record indicates, however, that East Side stopped payment on the check because of its ongoing dispute with Essex, not that East Side lacked funds on April 11 (or any time thereafter) that it had on April 7. In addition, defendant points out that in a separate proceeding East Side has alleged that it directly informed Essex of the stop payment order on April 6, the same day Signet notified Industrial.

single biggest change in banking had been during his long career, he replied: "air conditioning." In the 20th century, the biggest change in check collection to have gained wide-spread acceptance was an elementary technology invented in 1956 and known as Magnetic Ink Character Recognition (MICR) encoding. In order to permit electronic processing of checks for presentment for payment, almost all checks in use today are preprinted with a row of numerals and symbols along the bottom of the check (the "MICR line") that can be read by machines that process the checks for payment. The preprinted MICR encoding identifies the payor bank, the Federal Reserve district in which the bank is located, the Federal Reserve Bank or branch that serves the payor bank, the number of the check, and the number of the account at the payor bank on which the check is drawn. When the check is deposited, either the depositary bank or the next collecting bank that has encoding equipment will add to the MICR line numerals that indicate the amount of the check. In some cases the encoding of the amount of the check will be done by the payee of the check before the check is deposited in the depositary bank. This can occur if the payee is a person receiving a very large volume of checks that are processed in processing centers operated by the payee. Examples of such payees are public utilities, insurance companies, and large retailers.

Most checks that have been encoded with the amount of the check will be processed by automated equipment by the payor bank and by collecting banks on the basis of the encoded information without any examination of the check by a human being. What happens if a check is payable in the amount of $123.45 but the person encoding the amount of the check erroneously encodes the amount as $12,345? The misencoding does not change the amount of the check. There has been no alteration of the check. But if the check is read by machines on the basis of the encoded amount, the bank that processes the check will treat it as a check in the amount of $12,345. If the payor bank pays the check, it has paid out the encoded amount to the presenting bank but will be entitled to debit the account of the drawer of the check only for the actual amount of the check. Or, the payor bank might wrongfully dishonor the check because the balance in the drawer's account, although large enough to cover the actual amount of the check, is not enough to cover the encoded amount. Before the 1990 revision, Article 4 did not address the problem of misencoding because MICR encoding did not exist when Article 4 was drafted. Section 4–209 now addresses the consequences of misencoding.

## PROBLEM

Drayton drew a check on Bank One for $10,000 payable to the order of Park Company. Park deposited the check in its account in Bank Two and was given a provisional credit for the amount of the check. Bank Two forwarded the check to Bank One for payment; it arrived on May 1.

(a) Bank Two misencoded the check for $1,000, and on May 1 Bank One sent Bank Two a wire transfer for $1,000 intended as provisional settlement. Bank One debited Drayton's account for that amount and retained the check for mailing to Drayton at the end of the billing cycle with her other cancelled checks. When Bank Two received only $1,000 for the check, it reduced the credit in Park's account to that amount. Park complained to Bank Two about its failure to give $10,000 final credit for check. What are Bank Two's rights against Bank One under 4–302(a)? What are Bank One's rights against Bank Two under 4–209(a)? If Drayton's account exceeds $10,000, has Bank One suffered a loss under 4–209(c)? See Comment 2 to 4–209.

(b) The check was misencoded for $100,000. On May 1, Bank One provisionally settled for the check by sending Bank Two a wire transfer for $100,000.

(i) Drayton had more than $100,000 in her account and Bank One debited her account for $100,000. What are Drayton's rights against Bank One? 4–401(a). Bank One's rights against Bank Two? 4–209(a) and (c).

(ii) On May 2, Bank One discovered that Drayton had only $25,000 in her account and dishonored the check by returning it to Bank Two before midnight on that date. Does Drayton have rights against Bank One for wrongful dishonor under 4–402? If Bank One is liable for damages to Drayton, what is its recourse under 4–209(a) against Bank Two?

Courts have not warmed to 4–209. Although the following case concerns an under-encoding error of major proportions and was decided years after 4–209 became law, the court decided the case without a mention of the statute. In another case, Douglas Companies, Inc. v. Commercial Bank of Texarkana, 419 F.3d 812 (8th Cir. 2005), the district court was at least aware of 4–209 but, in its concern about confusing the jury by requiring them "to sift through the intricacies of the UCC," chose to instruct on negligence. The Eighth Circuit approved this paternalistic approach on the ground that no harm was done.

## First Union National Bank v. Bank One, N.A.

United States District Court, E.D. Pa., 2002.
47 UCC Rep.Serv.2d 645.

■ BUCKWALTER, J.

[Eds. First Union, the depository bank, under-encoded in the amount of $0.00 a check with a face amount of $507,598.30 and presented the check to Mellon, the intermediate collecting bank, for collection. Mellon in turn presented the check to Bank One, the payor bank, for payment. After settling with Mellon in the amount of $0.00, Bank One discovered the under-encoding error and paid Mellon the $507,598.30 face amount of the check. Mellon did not remit the amount to First Union. Later, after First Union presented Bank One with a photocopy of the check, Bank One paid it the face amount of the check. On Bank One's behalf, First Union sought to recover from Mellon Bank One's payment to it (Mellon).]

\* \* \* [T]he Court is presented with two separate but related sets of questions. The first is the liability of Mellon, as an intermediary collecting bank, for having remitted $0.00 to the depository bank when the face amount of the Check was $507,598.30, and the effect of First Union's encoding error on that liability. \* \* \*

## B. MELLON'S LIABILITY TO FIRST UNION

Plaintiff, First Union, moves for partial summary judgment against Mellon on Counts III and V of its complaint. Count III alleges breach of a collecting bank's duty to account to its customer under Article 4 of the UCC. Count V alleges unjust enrichment.

\* \* \*

Section 4–215(d) of the UCC provides:

If a collecting bank receives a settlement for an item which is or becomes final, the bank is accountable to its customer for the amount of the item and any provisional credit given for the item in an account with its customer becomes final.

First Union's argument is straightforward. Bank One, the drawee bank, made final payment on the subject Check, an item in the amount of $507,598.30. Final payment triggered accountability along the chain of collection. Therefore, Mellon, the collecting bank that received settlement for an item which became final, is accountable to First Union, its customer, for the amount of the item, $507,598.30. The fact that First Union encoded the item in the wrong amount is irrelevant, because once final payment occurred, the drawee bank and each collecting bank along the chain of collection is strictly accountable to its respective customer for the amount of the item, here $507,598.30.

Mellon argues that for purposes of § 4–215(d) the "amount of the item" for which a collecting bank is accountable is the encoded amount of the check, as long as the encoded amount is less than the face amount of the check or, alternatively, whichever is less. Therefore, because Bank One made final payment on the under-encoded check in the amount of $0.00 on January 13, 1998, that is the amount for which Mellon is accountable. Mellon further argues that the fact that Bank One subsequently issued an unexplained adjustment to Mellon does not alter the fact that final payment was made prior to that time and in an amount which valued the Check as $0.00.

Mellon finds support for its position in *First Nat'l Bank of Boston v. Fidelity Bank, N.A.*, 724 F.Supp. 1168 (E.D.Pa.1989). In that case, plaintiff bank under-encoded a $100,000 check as a $10,000 check. The defendant, the payor bank, charged the drawer's account in the lesser amount, and remitted that sum to plaintiff. When plaintiff bank made demand upon defendant bank for the $90,000 deficit, the drawer's account was insufficient to cover it. The *First Nat'l Bank of Boston* court held that "as between the encoding bank and all other banks in the collecting process, . . . the encoder is estopped from claiming more than the encoded amount of the check." *Id.* at 1172.

This appears to support Mellon's position, however, the court reasoned that this equitable defense was available "where plaintiff's encoding error caused the payor bank to suffer a loss which it could not avoid by charging its customer's account." *Id.* at 1171. In the case at bar, the drawee bank, Bank One, successfully charged its customer's account for the face amount of the Check and remitted that amount to Mellon, albeit without proper documentation. Mellon, in turn, held onto the funds relying on the fact that Bank One had made "final payment" the prior day in the encoded amount of $0.00. The holding of *First Nat'l Bank of Boston*, does not entitle Mellon to hold onto funds properly debited from the maker of a check midway along the chain of collection because of an encoding error made by the depository bank.

The equitable defense described in *First Nat'l Bank of Boston*, would only come into play if (1) Bank One charged its customer, LCI, the under-encoded amount; (2) Bank One remitted the under-encoded amount along the chain of collection to Mellon; and (3) upon First Union's demand to collect the higher, face amount of the check from either Mellon or Bank One, the maker of the check, LCI, had insufficient funds in its account to cover that higher amount. In this fictional scenario, First Union would be estopped from collecting the face amount of the check under *First Nat'l Bank of Boston* because First Union's encoding error caused the loss which could not be avoided by charging the drawer's account.

Mellon's reliance on Bank One's final payment on the encoded amount within the midnight deadline does not change the analysis under § 4–215(d). The midnight deadline provisions of § 4–302 and the final payment provisions of § 4–215(a) are only relevant with respect to the time at which a bank's accountability for the retained check is triggered. The rules of final payment and the midnight deadline do not dictate whether "the amount of the check" for purposes of § 4–215(d) is the encoded amount or the face amount when those two differ. As the case relied on by Mellon points out, there is no support for the broad proposition that final payment of the amount of an item for § 4–215 purposes is the encoded amount, rather than the face amount of the check. *See First Nat'l Bank of Boston*, 724 F.Supp. at 1172.

In another leading under-encoding case, which provides guidance, the Georgia Court of Appeals held that a depository bank could recover the amount of the deficiency from the drawee bank where the latter debited its customer's account only the encoded amount of an under-encoded check mis-encoded by the depository bank. *Georgia Railroad Bank & Trust Co. v. First Nat'l Bank & Trust Co. of Augusta*, 139 Ga.App. 683, 229 S.E.2d 482 (Ga.Ct.App.1976), *aff'd* 238 Ga. 693, 235 S.E.2d 1 (Ga.1977). In that case, plaintiff bank erroneously encoded a $25,000 check as a $2,500 check. The defendant, the drawee bank, charged the drawer's account in the lesser amount, and remitted that sum to plaintiff. The error was not discovered for several weeks, by which time the cancelled check had already been returned to the maker. When plaintiff made demand upon the defendant for the deficiency, the defendant brought the error to the maker's attention, but the latter refused to allow the defendant to charge his account the additional $22,500, despite the fact that sufficient funds existed in the account. The Georgia court held, without extended discussion, that the defendant was liable to the plaintiff for the face amount of the check. The court first reasoned that the defendant bank was accountable to the plaintiff bank for the amount of the item pursuant to two code sections: (1) under § 4–213(1),[2] defendant bank was accountable because it had made "final payment" by charging the maker's account, albeit in the wrong amount; and (2) under § 4–302, defendant bank was strictly accountable by retaining the check beyond the midnight deadline without completely settling for it. Thus, because the defendant was accountable to plaintiff for the item and, more significantly, because the drawer's account contained sufficient funds to cover the face amount of the check, which would allow the loss to be shifted from the shoulders of the drawee bank, the Georgia court held the defendant drawee bank liable to the plaintiff collecting bank for the full amount of the check and not the under-encoded amount.

The common denominator between *First Nat'l Bank of Boston* and *Georgia R.R. Bank and Trust Co.*, is the principle that ultimate liability for encoding errors should rest on the shoulders of the depository bank that makes the error when deciding who should bear the loss between the depository bank, the collecting bank and the drawee bank. However, in the usual case, such as the case at bar, the parties can be put back into their original positions, with no party sustaining a loss. In the instant case, the payee has been credited with the face amount of the check by the depository bank, which is awaiting to collect the funds through the collection chain. The drawer has been debited by the drawee bank in the face amount of the check. The drawee bank has remitted the face amount of the check to the intermediary collecting bank. All that is needed to complete the chain is for the intermediary collecting bank to remit the funds to the depository bank.

The Court finds that Mellon did not properly account to First Union after receiving final settlement on the face amount of the check in violation of § 4–215(d) and Orders Mellon to remit $507,598.30 to First Union. Because the Court has found Mellon liable for the face amount of the Check pursuant to § 4–215(d), it does not address First Union's claim of unjust enrichment.

\* \* \*

NOTE

Although the court relied on the two cases that formed the basis for the drafting of 4–209(a), it didn't rely on the statute for its decision? Was this merely an oversight? Would it have changed the result? The analysis?

**2.** Section 4–213 is the predecessor code section to 4–215.

## NOTE: MISENCODING OR LATE RETURN?

Case #1. Drawer issues check for $10,000 to Payee on its account in Payor Bank (PB). Payee deposits the check in Depositary Bank (DB), which presents the check for payment to PB. Since Drawer has insufficient funds in its account, PB acts to dishonor the check by mailing it to DB within its midnight deadline at an incorrect address. Under 4–302 PB is liable for the full amount of the check because it has not properly returned the check under 4–301(d)(1) ("sent"). Under 1–201(b)(36)(A) ("send"), PB has not sent the check before the midnight deadline because the letter was not "properly addressed."

Case #2. Same facts as above, except that PB attached a magnetic tape to the check that made the check a "qualified return check," returnable by the Federal Reserve's automated processing system under Regulation CC. But PB misencoded the check by failing to encode DB's correct routing number on the tape, and the check went to another bank. Payee contends that PB is accountable for $10,000 because it did not properly return the check within the midnight deadline under 4–301(d). PB argues that this is a misencoding under 4–209, and, since no one suffered a loss (the check was worthless) PB has no liability.

In NBT Bank, N.A. v. First National Community Bank, 393 F.3d 404 (3d Cir. 2004), on facts similar to Case #2, the court held that the provisions of Regulation CC applied to this case and damages under Subpart C of Regulation CC, which includes encoding standards, are limited to the amount of the loss incurred; hence, PB is not liable. 12 CFR § 229.30(a)(2)(iii) provides:

> A paying bank may convert a check to a qualified return check. A qualified returned check must be encoded in magnetic ink with the routing number of the depositary bank, the amount of the returned check, and a "2" in position 44 of the MICR line as a return identifier.

12 CFR § 229.38(a) provides:

> * * * A bank that fails to exercise ordinary care or act in good faith under this subpart may be liable * * * The measure of damages for failure to exercise ordinary care is the amount of the loss incurred, up to the amount of the check, reduced by the amount of the loss that party would have incurred even if the bank had exercised ordinary care.

Thus, even though the misencoding causing the check to be returned to an incorrect party might have been an ineffective return under the UCC 4–301(d) (the court didn't decide the issue), Regulation CC preempts the UCC's strict liability under 4–302 by its actual damages limitation set out above. Subpart C of Regulation CC, 12 C.F.R. §§ 229.30–.43 governs the collection, processing and return of checks, and the provisions of Subpart C "supersede any inconsistent provisions of the UCC as adopted in any state, or of any other state law, but only to the extent of the inconsistency." Hence, with respect to "qualified return checks," Regulation CC preempts UCC 3–401 and 4–302 in providing that damages for a misencoding, even one affecting the midnight deadline, are limited to actual loss caused by the error. This is the same measure of damages for miscoding under 4–209. See 4–103(e).

## 4.   ELECTRONIC PRESENTMENT

### a.   UNDER UCC

Illustration: Charles is an American Express cardholder and has a deposit account in the Bank of America. He used his Amex card to purchase goods for $875. When his Amex statement arrived, he was billed for $875, which he promptly paid by check number 2034 drawn on his BofA account. Later, when he returned from a hectic vacation trip, he was uncertain whether he had paid the $875 charge. His checkbook record showed that he had but when he looked through the cancelled checks that he had just received from the BofA and found no cancelled check for the Amex bill, he was concerned. However, when he examined the BofA statement that accompanied the cancelled checks, he found under the column marked "Withdrawals, Transfers and Account Fees" a line stating "American Express DES: Checkpayment ID: 2034" followed by "INDN" and a very long number. Under the next column marked "Reference Number" he found a six digit number, and in the final column marked "Amount" the amount of the check, $875, appeared. From this, Charles concluded that he had paid the Amex bill, but he didn't understand how his account could have been debited for the payment if the BofA apparently had no check to return to him. The following material explains how Charles' check-originated payment was converted into electronic presentment pursuant to an agreement between the BofA and Amex that allows Amex to collect all checks drawn on the BofA that are payable to Amex by electronic presentment. Amex's depositary bank sends to the BofA in digitalized form the information from the MICR line of the check or an image of the check. As we see below, this is a valid presentment within the provisions of the UCC. Conversion of paper checks to electronic presentment by agreement of the parties is becoming increasingly common.

With respect to collection of checks by a depositary bank, the present system depends upon transportation of checks through the banking system from the depositary bank to the payor bank. The number of checks processed by the banking system each day is huge; the transportation of this volume of paper to the payor bank is very expensive and delays payment. It is not surprising that the banking system, which has been aggressively seeking methods of cutting costs, has considered alternatives to flying and trucking tons of checks across the nation each day. One method discussed is often referred to by bankers as "truncation," but this is a confusing term because it is used to describe two quite different transactions. One use of the term describes the practice of payor banks of retaining checks after payment rather than returning them to the drawers who wrote them. Some banks are attempting to persuade their customers through differential pricing to agree to this practice. We will discuss this matter later.

It is the second use of the term, sometimes described as "radical truncation," that we are concerned with at this point. In order to avoid confusing it with the other meaning of truncation, Revised Articles 3 and 4 refer to this process as "electronic presentment." 4–110. Under this process most checks would be retained by the depositary bank for destruction after a relatively short period of time. Presentment for payment of a check would be made to the payor bank by electronic transmittal of essential information describing the check rather than by delivery of the check. After the check is destroyed, an image of the check would be stored electronically so that a copy of the check could be produced if needed at some later time.

Although under the present system the check itself is normally transported to the payor bank, most checks are not examined by anybody in the payor bank's process of payment. In these cases the check serves only as the carrier of the electronic encoding on the MICR line, which is read by the automated machinery of the payor bank. Use of the paper check itself to convey the information contained on the MICR line is both inefficient and unnecessary. It is technologically feasible to provide this information to the payor bank by electronic transmission. Since a system of electronic presentment was believed to be a possible solution to the banking industry's difficulties with the present check payment system, much discussion during the drafting of Revised Articles 3 and 4 centered on how the revision should deal with electronic presentment. The agreement reached was that it was not the role of the UCC to mandate business practices in the banking industry. Electronic presentment, if found economically feasible, should come by inter-bank agreements or through the Federal Reserve pursuant to its broad regulatory authority. Articles 3 and 4 should be revised to remove any legal barriers to a regime of electronic presentment. The assumptions under which the Drafting Committee proceeded are set out in Comments 2 and 3 to 4–110. The changes made in Articles 3 and 4 to accommodate electronic presentment are explained in the following paragraphs.

With respect to collection of checks, presentment is simply a demand made to the drawee to pay the check. 3–501(a). The demand may be made by an electronic communication. 3–501(b)(1). But Revised Article 3 follows the pre–1990 law in preserving the right of the drawee to demand exhibition of the check and its surrender as a condition to payment. 3–501(b)(2). This right of the drawee to require exhibition and surrender of the check is subject, however, to rules stated in Article 4 and may be waived by the drawee by agreement. Section 4–110 permits electronic presentment by means of a "presentment notice," which is defined as "transmission of an image of an item or information describing the item." The presentment notice is in lieu of delivery of the check itself. Presentment under 4–110 requires an "agreement for electronic presentment" which provides for the presentment notice. The quoted term includes not only an agreement between the drawee and the presenting bank, but also a clearing-house rule or Federal Reserve regulation or operating circular providing for electronic presentment.

Electronic presentment raises a number of problems. The payor bank will not be able to examine the signature of the drawer to detect a possible forgery, but this problem exists under current practice as well, because most checks are not examined for forgery. Under the current practice, payor banks look at the drawer's signature only on some checks such as those in large dollar amounts. This practice could continue under a regime of electronic presentment by a requirement that large checks be excluded from electronic presentment. Or, presentment of some checks might be made by transmitting an image of the check rather than information describing the check to allow examination of the drawer's signature. Current imaging technology allows depositary banks to send to payor banks miniature digitized images of checks, 15 or 20 to a page. The process, encouraged by 4–110(a), is described in 2 Clark & Clark, The Law of Bank Deposits, Check Collections and Credit Cards & 16.02[1] (Rev. ed. 2005). Imaging gives more information than that contained on the MICR line; the drawer's signature appears as well as the name of the payee. The Electronic Clearing House Association (ECCHO), a nonprofit national clearing house, promotes image presentation of truncated checks.

The agreement for electronic presentment would also have to provide for retention and destruction of the check in order to protect the drawer of the check against further negotiation of the check. Under present practice many payor banks return all cancelled checks to the drawer after the checks are paid. This will not be possible with respect to checks paid pursuant to electronic presentment. But this practice of returning checks to the drawer has become less prevalent in recent years. Many banks have induced customers to opt for checking-account plans in which cancelled checks are not returned and instead the customer is given a statement describing the checks paid. Under electronic presentment the payor bank would be able to obtain, at the request of a customer, a copy of any check paid for the customer's account for which the customer may have a particular need. The agreement for electronic presentment would provide for electronic storage of copies of checks presented electronically and would impose a duty on the storing bank to provide a copy of a check on request of the payor bank. 4–406(a) and (b).

### b.   UNDER FEDERAL LAW: "THE CHECK 21 ACT"

In the late 1980s the prospects of federally mandated electronic presentment seemed bright. The Expedited Funds Availability Act, discussed in the next section, mandated that the Fed "shall consider * * * requiring by regulation, that * * * the Federal Reserve banks and depositary institutions provide for check truncation." 12 U.S.C. § 4008(b). The Fed has the power to mandate electronic presentment with no further authorization from Congress because 12 U.S.C. § 4008(c) gives the Fed the power to regulate any aspect of the payment system with respect to checks in order to carry out expedited funds availability. But after its 1988 post-EFTA study, the Fed declined to mandate electronic presentment. Although it conceded that electronic presentment was feasible given the technology current at that time, the study concluded that the benefits of mandatory electronic presentment would be outweighed by the potential risks borne by the paying banks. It concluded that the matter should be left up to banks to choose to participate in voluntary inter-bank or multi-bank electronic presentment agreements with Reserve banks or other presenting banks.

Fifteen years later Congress acted on its own. On October 28, 2003, President Bush signed into law the Check Clearing for the 21st Century Act ("The Check 21 Act" or "Check 21"), with an effective date one year later. 12 U.S.C. §§ 5001–5018 (2006). Check 21 allows the use of electronic presentment and return of checks without electronic truncation agreements between banks. It does so by creating a new type of negotiable instrument: a "substitute check." A "substitute check" is a paper reproduction created from an electronic image of the original check and suitable for automated processing in the same manner as the original check. § 5002(a)(16). A substitute check is the legal equivalent of the original check for all purposes if it accurately represents the information on the original check and contains the requisite legend ("This is a legal copy of your check. You can use it in the same way you would use the original check."). § 5003(b). Check 21 requires a bank to handle a substitute check if warranties created by the legislation cover the check. Sec. 4(a). Banks are not required to accept presentation of checks in electronic form, unless required to do so under an electronic truncation agreement.

Check 21 imposes a nondisclaimable warranty on a bank's use of a substitute check. §§ 5004, 5013(b). The bank warrants to downstream parties handling the check that the check is the legal equivalent of the original check and that they will not receive requests to pay the original or substitute check already paid. The warranty continues to apply even if the substitute check is converted into electronic form or reconverted back from an electronic form into another substitute check. Sec. 5. Further, because the substitute check is the legal equivalent of the original check, any warranties that apply to the original check carry over to the substitute check. Check 21 also requires a bank transferring a substitute check to indemnify subsequent transferees for loss due to receipt of a substitute rather than original check. § 5006. The legislation contains some consumer protection provisions that require expedited recrediting of consumer deposit accounts. In 2004, the Federal Reserve Board promulgated implementing regulations in 12 C.F.R. Subpart D, §§ 229.51 through 229.59, as part of Regulation CC. Availability of Funds and Collection of Checks.

A prototypic case follows: Payee deposits a check for $1,000 in Bank A in New York. The check is drawn on Payor Bank in Los Angeles. Bank A indorses and delivers the check to Bank B in New York for collection. Bank B is called the "truncating bank" because it truncates the check: Bank B takes the check out of the collection chain, creates an electronic file containing the information on the check or an electronic image of the check and sends this information electronically to Bank C in Los Angeles. Bank C is called the "reconverting bank" because it reconverts the electronic information into a paper substitute check. Bank C presents the substitute check to Payor Bank by a Los Angeles courier service; Payor Bank pays the check. For this transaction to occur, Bank B and Bank C must have an agreement authorizing the actions taken by Bank C. But there need be no agreement by Payor Bank that it will accept the paper substitute check as the equivalent of the original check. Check 21 requires Payor Bank to treat the paper check as the equivalent of the original check and deal with it accordingly. Hence, any payor bank in the United States must accept a substitute check, just as it would the original. Bank C, the reconverting bank, must warrant that the substitute check contains an accurate image of the front and back of the original check and a legend stating that it is the legal equivalent of the original check. Moreover, it must warrant that no depositary, drawee, drawer or indorser will be asked to pay a check that it has already paid. Any bank that presents, or otherwise transfers, a substituted check is responsible for indemnifying any person that suffers a loss owing to the receipt of the substituted check instead of the original check.

In this case, the paper check will not have to be flown across the country for presentment. When the substitute check is created by Bank C in Los Angeles, it can be presented to the payor bank by the local courier service on the day it is created. Banks will have to invest in reconversion equipment only if they agree to enter into such transactions. Other banks need buy no new equipment because the paper substitute checks they receive may be processed in the same way as original checks. If the drawer requires the payor bank to deliver the cancelled checks to it at the end of each periodic account cycle, the paper substitute checks will serve as the cancelled checks. Of course, disclosure to customers of the nature of the substituted checks and of the customers' rights must be made.

Check 21's intended purpose is obscured by its provisions governing substitute checks. The legislation aims to facilitate electronic presentment without biasing the form check truncation might take. § 5001(a)(3). Electronic presentment transfers electronic images of checks without the physical transfer of checks themselves. See House Comm. On Fin. Serv., 108 Congr. 108–32 (Background and Need for Legislation). This does not require the creation and transfer of substitute checks. Check 21 facilitates electronic presentment merely by removing legal or contractual barriers that require transfer of original checks. It does this by giving substitute checks the same legal status as original checks. The legislation does not require banks to truncate checks electronically. § 5001(b)(2). Nor does it require banks to create or transfer substitute checks. Check 21 simply requires banks to accept substitute checks when created and sent for collection or return, if a bank has made substitute check warranties as to it. § 5003(a). In this way the legislation is consistent with the demand for medium-neutrality required by other recent federal legislation (e.g., The Electronic Signatures in Global and National Commerce Act).

Electronic presentment can proceed without the creation or transfer of a substitute check. A substitute check is useful only when an individual or bank prefers (and pays) to create or receive a paper check. For instance, a substitute check can be created from an electronic image of an original check and presented to a payor bank without an inter-bank electronic presentment agreement. After payment the payor bank can return the substitute check to the drawer with other cancelled checks. The same process can be used to return dishonored checks to the depository bank when the bank or the depositor insists on a paper check. Check 21 allows for the possibility that a demand for paper checks might remain as part of a market for electronic presentment. Its regulation of substitute checks is a way of accommodating this preference without interfering with the market for electronic presentment of checks. The unit cost of processing paper checks increases as the volume of paper checks processed declines. For banks and their customers who still want paper checks, substitute checks are cheaper to process than original checks. Electronic truncation has lower unit processing costs than both substitute and original (paper) checks, because it avoids use of paper checks entirely. Check 21 leaves to market participants the decision as to the optimal mix of electronic presentment and substitute checks.

Check 21's impact on the market for electronic presentment of checks is likely to be significant. By facilitating the settlement and return of checks electronically, the legislation reduces the time in which payees are denied access to deposited funds. According to the New York Fed, the experience with Check 21 in 2005, its first full year of application, was a success: during that year the volume of substitute checks and check images grew from 3.7 million per month to 60.3 million per month. Clarks' Bank Deposits and Payments Monthly, Vol. 14, No. 10 (March 2006). Two other effects are predicted within the next few years. One is the development of check imaging technologies and applications to better detect check fraud. A second effect is to bring forward to the point of sale or deposit check imaging applications. These can allow a merchant to capture a digital image of the customer's original check and transmit it to the payor bank in real time. A similar forward movement allows scanning and transmitting upon deposit in ATM machines, increasing revenues generated by their use. Steve Bills, Remote Capture Worth More to Clients Than Banks Think?, Amer. Banker, August 7, 2005, at 17.

## 5. FUNDS AVAILABILITY AND REGULATION CC

Suppose Father living in Sacramento, California, mails a check for $1,000, drawn on First Bank in Sacramento, to Daughter, attending school in College Town, New York, 80 miles from New York City. The check arrives on Monday morning. Daughter takes it to Second Bank's College Town branch and deposits it in her account. On Monday night the check is driven by a courier to Second Bank's central check processing center in New York City and is run through a reader-sorter machine. On Tuesday morning it is taken to the New York Fed where it goes through another reader-sorter and is sent by air courier on Tuesday night to the San Francisco Fed where it arrives early Wednesday morning. There it goes through a reader-sorter machine, and on Wednesday afternoon is driven by courier to First Bank in Sacramento. By early Thursday morning the check has been posted by automation to Father's account, which was then debited. When Daughter deposited the check in Second Bank she asked when she could withdraw her money; she was told it would be available for her in two weeks. She needed the money earlier and called Father to describe her plight. He was irritated to learn that although the banking system had withdrawn the amount of the check from his account on Thursday morning, Daughter would not be able to withdraw the funds until several days later.

Second Bank's action in placing a two-week "hold" period on Daughter's check was thought necessary to protect itself from the possibility that the check would not be paid by First Bank, owing to insufficient funds in the account, entry of a stop-payment order or other reasons. Relatively long hold periods were thought to be necessary because of the slow and inefficient system banks use for returning checks that have been dishonored. Second Bank may not learn whether the check has been dishonored until the unpaid check is physically returned to it. The forward collection of the check in this case from College Town to Sacramento was fairly prompt because the MICR line enabled the collecting banks to utilize an automated system for sorting checks and directing them to the banks on which they are drawn. But there is no automated system for the return of checks. Each must be processed manually by clerks who must attempt to return the check to the proper bank by deciphering the sometimes unintelligible indorsements on the back of the check. Moreover, before institution of the reforms discussed below, the system of provisional credits made it desirable to send the check back through the same chain of banks as in the forward collection of the check. Thus, had First Bank dishonored the check that arrived there after that bank's 2:00 p.m. cutoff hour on Wednesday, it could have waited until its Friday night midnight deadline to send the check back to the San Francisco Fed. That bank would probably need a second banking day after the banking day of receipt for the manual processing of the check. The same is true for the New York Fed. Although the check would probably be returned by truck and air courier services, returning banks could slow the process down even more by mailing the returns back. One study found that although the forward collection process for checks averaged 1.6 days, the return averaged 5.2 days. Barkley Clark & Barbara Clark, Regulation CC: Funds Availability and Check Collection 1–4 (1988).

### a.   FUNDS AVAILABILITY

Banks met the growing chorus of customer complaints about what seemed to be excessive hold periods by justifying their actions as necessary to protect them from bad check losses. But in the 1980s several states passed laws limiting hold periods, and in 1987 Congress enacted the Expedited Funds Availability Act of 1987, 12 U.S.C. § 4001 et seq. The Board of Governors of the Federal Reserve System implemented this statute by promulgating Regulation CC in 1988, 12 C.F.R. Pt. 229. Subpart B of Regulation CC prescribes mandatory availability schedules. Next day availability is required for "low risk" deposits for which a hold period is not needed to protect the depositary bank from risk. Examples are cashier's checks, certified checks, teller's checks, electronic payments (wire transfers and ACH credits), "on us" items, Treasury and state and local government checks. § 229.10. For local checks the funds must be made available to the depositor not later than the second day after the banking day of deposit. § 229.12(b). For nonlocal checks funds must be made available not later than the fifth business day following the banking day of deposit. § 229.12(c). But a depositor is allowed to withdraw up to $100 on the next banking day after deposit of either local or nonlocal checks. § 229.10(c). Section 229.13 sets out exceptions to these mandatory availability schedules with respect to new accounts, large deposits, redeposited checks, repeated overdrafts, and cases in which there is reasonable cause to doubt collectibility.

For some time the Fed has been considering shortening the five-day period for nonlocal checks to four days. According to the Fed, paper checks are moving more rapidly now. In 1999 it estimated that about 83% of checks arrive back at the payor bank on which they were drawn within five business days. This is up from 73% in 1990. Rick Brooks, High–Tech Tactics Let Banks Keep the "Float", Wall. St. J., June 3, 1999, at B1. This article contends that banks are sometimes given such wide latitude by the special exceptions to the mandatory availability schedules that customers, counting on a normal period of float, find themselves with bounced checks on which high fees can be charged. We will discuss the issue of dishonored checks in a later chapter.

A 1994 American Bankers Association study showed that banks were generally making funds available to depositors earlier than Regulation CC requires. For local checks drawn on consumer demand accounts, over 90% of the banks surveyed reported that they were making funds available on either the day of deposit or the next day. And over 50% of the banks were following the same practice for nonlocal checks on these accounts. 1 Clark & Clark, The Law of Bank Deposits, Collections and Credit Cards & 10.01[7] (Rev. ed. 2006). Anecdotal evidence indicates that these percentages are probably higher today. The reasons given for the banks' early availability policy are customer service and competition. Clark & Clark, supra. The operational difficulties of dealing with the multiple availability schedules of Regulation CC may be another factor. Moreover, as indicated above, in cases in which a bank has reason to question the collectibility of a check it can protect itself by withholding payment.

b. CHECK COLLECTION AND RETURN

Today the law of check collection and return is found in Regulation CC as well as in Article 4, to the extent that its provisions are not preempted by Regulation CC. Consideration in the revision of Article 4 was given to redrafting Article 4 in order to make it compatible with Regulation CC. This approach was rejected because of the likelihood that Regulation CC will continue to evolve, leaving inconsistencies between Article 4 and

Regulation CC. Compatibility was again considered in the amending process that yielded the 2002 amendments to Articles 3 and 4, and was again rejected.

To allow the banking system to meet the funds availability standards set by Regulation CC without exposing depositary banks to excessive bad check losses, it was necessary to expedite the return system. Subpart C of Regulation CC sets out a sweeping revision of the law of check collection and return in order to speed the return of dishonored checks, thereby preempting portions of Article 4.

In the early stages of the revision of Article 4, before the EFAA had been passed, the drafters had proposed several provisions designed to speed the return of dishonored checks. These provisions included: facilitating direct return of dishonored checks to depositary banks; reducing the number of returned checks by extending the payor bank's midnight deadline for checks under $100 (thus giving the drawer time to put enough money in the account to pay the check); requiring compliance with uniform indorsement standards governing the content and placement of bank indorsements; commencing the running of the midnight deadline for return from the time of delivery of checks to central bank processing centers; and imposing on payor banks the duty to give prompt notice of the nonpayment of items of $2,500 or more. Regulation CC incorporated all these provisions except the extension of the midnight deadline for small checks, which was not included in Regulation CC and dropped from later drafts of Article 4 because of the belief that it would slow the collection of checks; hence, all these provisions were deleted from Article 4.

But Regulation CC went far beyond these modest steps. In sections 229.30 and 229.31, it authorizes a payor or returning bank to return a check directly to the depositary bank or to any returning bank agreeing to handle the returned check for expeditious return to the depositary bank, regardless of whether the returning bank had handled the check for forward collection. The contemplation was that the banks most likely to agree to handle a returning check expeditiously were the regional Federal Reserve banks. The consequences of allowing a check presented by one bank to be returned by the payor bank to a different bank undermined the usual methods of interbank settlements. Under these methods, the payor bank gives the presenting bank a provisional settlement, which it revokes when it returns the dishonored check to that bank. If the payor bank returns the check to a bank that was not the presenting bank, the payor bank cannot obtain settlement for the returned check by revoking the settlement with the presenting bank. Rather, it must recover settlement from the bank to which it returned the check. But in order to give banks incentive to make expeditious returns, even if the payor bank does return the dishonored check to the presenting bank, section 229.31(c) forbids a payor bank to obtain settlement for the check by charging back against a credit it had previously given the presenting bank. The payor bank cannot recover settlement from a bank to which it has returned a check until the check has reached the returning bank, as though in forward collection. In harmony with these two provisions, section 229.36(d) provides that all settlements between banks for the forward collection of checks are final when made.

The inter-bank settlement provisions of Article 4 are stated in terms of provisional settlements. 4–201(1). Bank credit given by a settling payor or collecting bank is provisional in the sense that it can be revoked upon return of the item. The Fed's decision in Regulation CC to make all settlements final meant that now the conceptual approach of Article 4 to inter-bank settlements differed from that of Regulation CC, though, at least with respect to the issues addressed by Article 4, there is little functional difference between the two laws. The fact that under Regulation CC any credit given for a check is final rather than provisional was not intended by the drafters of Regulation CC to limit the right of a payor or collecting bank to return a check and recover the amount of the check from the bank to which it was returned. After stating that settlement under Regulation CC is final rather than provisional, the commentary to section 229.36(d) of Regulation CC explains: "Settlement by a paying bank is not considered to be final payment for the purposes of U.C.C. [4–215(a)], because a paying bank has the right to recover settlement from a returning or depositary bank to which it returns a check under this subpart." Appendix Commentary, 53 Fed. Reg. 19,372, 19,486 (1988). The check collection aspects of Regulation CC are discussed in detail in 1 Clark & Clark, Bank Deposits, Collections and Credit Cards, Chapter 8 (Rev. ed. 2006).

## B. CREDIT AND DEBIT CARDS

### 1. INTRODUCTION

#### a. CREDIT CARDS

##### (1) HOW CREDIT CARDS FUNCTION

Credit cards fall into two broad categories: "restricted use" and "universal" cards. In the first category are credit cards issued by a merchant as a means of identifying customers who have charge accounts with the merchant. They are particularly convenient for merchants who have numerous retail outlets located over a large geographical area. These cards originally could be used to make purchases only from the merchant that issued the card, but in some cases use of the card to purchase from a limited number of other merchants is also permitted. "Restricted use" cards include cards issued by oil companies for use at affiliated or independently owned service stations that sell products of the company that issued the card. The most important characteristic of this category of credit card is that the primary purpose of the issuer is to facilitate sales of goods or services of the issuer. Financial institutions have become involved in the merchant credit business by issuing "private-label" credit cards that appear to be issued by the merchant. The so-called co-branded card, bearing the names of both the merchant and the financer, have also become common.

"Universal" credit cards comprise cards issued by financial institutions that provide short-term credit, usually unsecured, to cardholders to allow them to make purchases from a multitude of merchants and other sellers of goods and services who are not related to the issuer of the card. These used to be called travel and entertainment cards; more often today they are referred to as bank cards because of the prominence of Visa and Master-Card in this category. This category of credit card has emerged as an important substitute for cash or personal checks in paying for goods or services. A merchant who accepts this type of credit card as the payment mechanism is party to a preexisting arrangement either directly with the issuer of the card or with an interbank system to which the issuer belongs, such as Visa USA or MasterCard Worldwide. Pursuant to this arrangement the merchant can obtain payment from the issuer for purchases made by use of the card. In a face-to-face purchase, the cardholder signs a credit card slip indicating the amount of the purchase and containing the card number and other information taken from the card.

The merchant is faced with several risks in honoring a credit card. First, the person using the card may not be a person authorized to use the card. Second, the card may have been revoked by the issuer. One common reason for revocation is a report to the issuer that the card has been lost or stolen. Third, the amount of credit given by the issuer to the cardholder may not be sufficient to cover the amount of the purchase. The merchant can normally avoid the last two risks. At the time a purchase is to be made, the merchant can determine, through telephonic or electronic access to a computer center having a record of the card, whether the card is valid and whether the charge is within the cardholder's line of credit. Through this process the merchant obtains approval of the charge before the purchase is made and has assurance of receiving payment in accordance with the arrangement to which the issuer and merchant are parties. Normally the merchant receives the amount of the charge less a discount to compensate the issuer for financing the purchase. The issuer obtains this compensation by obtaining payment of the full amount of the charge from the cardholder. Thus, the credit risk of nonpayment by the cardholder is taken by the issuer. The issuer normally sends a monthly statement of charges to the cardholder. Under most plans, the cardholder has the option of paying the full amount by a specified date without an interest charge or of making payment in installments with an interest charge.

The growth of credit cards issued by financial institutions has been phenomenal. The Bank of America first issued its BankAmericard in the 1950s. A consortium of banks formed an association to issue a competing card, MasterCharge, in 1960. The BankAmericard was later taken over by an association of banks, Visa USA. and renamed the Visa card. Master-Charge became MasterCard; its bank association is MasterCard Worldwide. Formerly these two companies were owned and funded by their thousands of member banks, but in 2006, MasterCard made a $2.5 billion initial public offering, about 46% of its equity and 82% of its voting power. Robin Sidel, MasterCard Sets IPO Terms, Names Board Members, Wall St. J., May 4, 2006, at C4. In past years, many American banks issued both cards, but increasingly banks are required to choose between them. In 2003 Visa USA passed the $1 trillion mark in transactions per year; it had reached the $1 billion level in 1971. Eileen Alt Powell, Use of "Plastic" Changing Rapidly, LA Times, Aug. 29, 2003, at C2. In mid–2003, Visa had 45% of the market, MasterCard had 33%, and American Express had 15%. Jathon Sapsford, American Express May Reap Rewards in Credit Card Suit, Wall St. J., July 7, 2003, at C1. According to Ron Lieber, A Bonus for Blowing Off Your Bills, Wall St. J., Sept. 16, 2003, at D1: 61% of Americans carry balances on their credit cards and pay an average of 13% interest on these balances; the 51 million households that carry balances on their credit cards have balances averaging $11,944; and two-thirds of the revenue of card companies comes from interest charges.

Visa USA and MasterCard Worldwide do not issue credit cards. They maintain networks of participating banks and handle the clearing and settlement of credit card debts. They are supported by periodic assessments on their member banks. The process by which the participants are paid is as follows: After the merchant authorized to honor Visa cards or Master-Cards has received the issuer of the credit card's approval of a purchase with the credit card, it will present to the "merchant bank" (or "acquiring bank") a credit card slip signed by the cardholder at the time of purchase. The merchant bank, which also will be a member of the Visa or Master-Card network, in turn will give the merchant a provision credit in the amount of the purchase, less a discount, in its account with the bank. The merchant bank then sends the slip through the Visa or MasterCard clearing system to the bank issuing the credit card to the cardholder (the "issuing bank"). As in the case of collection of paper checks, paper credit card slips have been largely replaced by electronic messages in many instances in the collection process. The issuing bank in turn transfers funds, usually less a small per transaction fee, for the slip to the merchant bank through the settlement process of Visa or MasterCard and bills the cardholder for the amount of its purchase. If the cardholder returns goods purchased, the issuing bank credits the cardholder's account and charges back this amount against the merchant bank.

To illustrate, if a merchant sells goods for the price of $100 to the cardholder, the issuing bank will bill the cardholder for $100, but, as noted above, the merchant bank will credit the merchant's account for the cash price less a discount. The discount (sometimes called the "merchant discount") is a fee for the merchant bank's services. It will be determined by agreement between the merchant and the merchant bank, depending largely on the volume of the merchant's business. Whatever the amount of the discount, the issuing bank is entitled to an "interchange fee," a nonnegotiable fee fixed by the credit card network. The interchange fee goes to the issuing bank and the merchant bank is entitled to the remainder of the discount, if any. For example, if the discount is 2.5% and the interchange fee set by the network is 1.5%, the merchant bank will be entitled to a payment from the issuing bank of $98.50 ($100 – $1.50 = $98.50). The merchant bank in turn will credit the merchant's account for $97.50 ($100 – $2.50 = $97.50). When the cardholder pays the issuing bank the $100 face amount of the charge as part of its credit card bill, the issuing bank obtains the $1.50 interchange fee. The issuing bank has earned a profit of $1.50: it paid the merchant bank $98.50 and is entitled to collect from the cardholder the $100 face amount of the charge. For its part, the merchant bank has earned a profit of $1.00: the issuing bank gave it a credit for $98.50 and the merchant bank paid the merchant $97.50.

Although interchange fees have declined over time, there is always controversy between credit card networks and merchants about their size. Interchange fees range between 0.5% and 1.9%, averaging about 1.75%. Because credit card markets are competitive, issuers pass on to cardholders much of the interchange fee through lower card fees and reward features. Merchants largely bear the cost of the interchange fee. The amount of interchange fees varies with the kinds of business and the type of network. High volume grocery or drugstore chains are charged less than luxury retailers or high-priced restaurants. According to industry estimates, interchange fees are bringing in about $25 billion in annual revenue for card issuing banks. Robin Sidel, Merchant Group Sues Visa Over Card–Use Fees, Wall St. J., July 15, 2005, at C3. In 2002, in response to the European Competition Commission's finding that Visa's interchange fees violated EU competition laws, Visa agreed to lower its fees. In 2003 the Reserve Bank of Australia judged interchange fees too high and subjected them to regulation.

## (2)  THE PERILS OF SUCCESS

Credit cards have been so wildly successful in expanding the volume of consumer credit that they are often viewed, particularly in the bankruptcy context, as posing a serious social problem for consumers. In little more than 50 years bank cards have completely replaced the traditional, highly inefficient, system in which merchants made their own decisions on the creditworthiness of their customers, relying on the often sketchy information the local credit bureau was able to gather on the prospective customer. For bank credit cards, the creditworthiness of the cardholder is determined by a professional credit grantor, the bank, at the time it issues the credit card, and it can impose spending limits consistent with the cardholder's credit record. The merchant is safe in relying on that decision of the bank and can devote its resources to selling rather than credit evaluation. The system is cheap and efficient.

At the beginning bank credit cards were restricted to middle or upper income groups, but over the years aggressive competition for market share led card issuers to lower their credit standards, sometimes with disastrous results for both card issuer and cardholder. Estimates are that in 2006 there were nearly 700 million general purpose cards in circulation in the United States, and the average American has more than five credit cards. Robin Sidel, Credit Card Issuers' Problem: People Are Paying Their Bills, Wall St. J., May 25, 2006, at A1. In recent years credit card issuers have broadened their market by focusing on small business: a business simplifies its accounts payable by using a credit or charge card to pay all its suppliers and makes a single payment each month to the card issuer. Even the sub-prime market has become a target of credit card issuers. Direct mail solicitation with low temporary teaser rates (sometimes zero), followed by much higher regular rates, became standard, as did "pre-approved" card offers. By 2001 38 percent of households in the bottom quintile of income held credit cards; two percent of these households held credit cards in 1970. David S. Evans & Richard Schmalensee, Paying With Plastic 88–89 (2d ed. 2005).

Horror stories abound of bankrupts with 15 or 20 credit cards, all maxed out, seeking discharge of debt totals far exceeding annual income. Card issuers frequently opposed bankruptcy discharges in such cases by alleging fraud under BC 523(a)(2)(A). Cardholders fought back by asserting that card issuers could not have justifiably relied on the cardholder's representation of intent to repay because of inadequate inquiry into the cardholder's financial position. For a good discussion of the issue, see In re Ellingsworth, 212 B.R. 326 (Bankr.W.D.Mo.1997). The abuse by some cardholders in excessive use of their cards was matched by the unwarranted lowering of credit standards by some card issuers in their relentless pursuit of market share.

Under the 2005 BAPCPA amendments, credit card issuers substantially improved their position in bankruptcy under BC 523(a)(2)(C), which presumes nondischargeable all consumer debts to a single creditor aggregating more than $500 (formerly $1,225) incurred on or within 90 (formerly 60) days of filing if for "luxury goods or services." The quoted term "does not include goods or services reasonably necessary for the support or maintenance of the debtor or dependent of the debtor or a dependent of the debtor." BC 523(a)(C)(ii)(II). There is no positive definition of "luxury," and the extent to which goods and services not reasonably necessary for support or maintenance should be deemed luxury goods or services is not clear. Cash advances aggregating more than $750 (formerly $1,225) obtained on or within 70 (formerly 60) days before filing are presumed nondischargeable, but only if made in an open end credit transaction, which is the kind of transaction used for cash advances on credit cards. So long as the loan transaction is an extension of consumer credit, that is, the loan was obtained for a personal, family or household purpose, there are no limits on the use of the loan proceeds. Thus, the original, sensible belief that credit card issuers deserve some protection against the excesses of a "credit card spree" that allowed debtors to acquire expensive luxuries on the eve of bankruptcy, now, as amended, applies to a huge swath of consumer sales transactions made by use of credit cards within three months before filing and cash advances made pursuant to credit cards within 70 days before filing.

### b.   DEBIT CARDS

Debit and credit cards transfer funds in different ways and are subject to different regulations. A working definition of the difference between a debit and credit transfer is found in Comment 4 to 4A–104: "In a credit transfer the instruction to pay is given by the person making the payment. In a debit transfer the instruction to pay is given by the person receiving the payment." Thus, a debit transfer may be an order from a creditor, authorized by the debtor, to the debtor's bank to pay the creditor. As it is sometimes put, debit transfers "pull" funds from the account of the payor (e.g., the debtor) to the payee (e.g., the creditor) on instruction by the payee. A common example is the authorization given by an insured person to the insurer to periodically withdraw premiums from the insured's bank account. Mortgage payments and many other periodic payments are made in this way. In contrast, credit transfers "push" funds from the payor's account to the payee on instruction by the payor. Article 4A does not cover debit wire transfers. 4A–103(a)(1) ("payment order"). But several kinds of consumer debit transfers are covered by the Electronic Fund Transfer Act, 15 U.S.C. § 1693 et seq. Regulation E, which implements the EFTA, defines "electronic fund transfer" as including "[t]ransfers resulting from debit card transactions, whether or not initiated through an electronic terminal." 12 CFR § 205.3(b)(5).

Debit cards have two common uses: to deposit and withdraw money from accounts and to transfer funds to a merchant as payment. The most popular use of debit cards is in the ubiquitous automated teller machine (ATM) system, as a means of depositing and withdrawing funds. These terminals are located in all manner of places convenient to customers: street corners, supermarkets, and, for safety, even in police stations. Their utility to customers is greatly enhanced by their around-the-clock availability. The customer can use the access card and a personal identification number (PIN) to make deposits and withdrawals from the customer's account in a bank or other financial institution. The cost of human teller-handled deposits and withdrawals is far more than the cost of deposits and withdrawals made by ATM.

One method by which debit cards are used to transfer funds as payment is the point-of-sale (POS) retail transaction. Here the buyer pays for goods or services by using a plastic coded card, called an access or debit card, inserted into an electronic terminal on the merchant's premises, which is linked to the banks of both the merchant and the cardholder, usually by means of an interbank network. The debit card contains a machine-readable identification of the buyer's bank account. When the card is inserted into the terminal, the amount of the transaction and the buyer's personal identification number (PIN) are also entered. The result is that the buyer's account is debited and the merchant's account is credited in that amount at the same time.

As the language quoted above from Regulation E indicates, debit cards may also be used in transactions with merchants who do not maintain electronic terminals. The card authorizes the merchant to draw on the buyer's account in the issuing bank for the amount of the sales price. The cardholder signs for the transaction, as in a credit card transaction, rather than using a PIN in an electronic terminal. If the debit card used is a Visa card or MasterCard in signature cases, the merchant sends the debit card slip through the more expensive Visa or MasterCard credit card clearing and settlement network to the issuing bank which immediately debits the cardholder's account, instead of billing as is done for credit cards. PIN-based clearing systems, like those operated by First Data Corporation, are cheaper. Jathon Sapsford, First Data Deal is Start of Fight in Debit Cards, Wall St. J., April 3, 2003, at C1. Estimates are that retailers pay about 15 cents for each PIN transaction but 60 cents for each signature transaction. Thus, the bank takes a larger interchange fee from the merchant's sale price in signature cases. For this reason merchants challenged the requirement of Visa USA and MasterCard that all merchants authorized to accept credit cards must also accept their debit cards, and, in a class-action antitrust suit, won a settlement freeing them from this rule in 2003. Jathon Sapsford & Kara Scannell, Visa, MasterCard to Pay Share of $3 Billion Pact Over 10 Years, Wall St. J., May 2, 2003, at C9.

In the United States credit card use exceeds debit card use. But the market for debit cards is growing faster than that for credit cards. Although the volume of the credit card market is still much larger than that for debit cards because the size of the transactions financed is greater, according to Jathon Sapsford's First Data article, cited above, debit card purchases are increasing 24% per year while credit card purchases were going up only 7%. According to Visa USA, 60% of those surveyed used debit cards so they could carry less cash, and 70% said that use of debit cards gave them a better sense of how they spend their money. Calmetta Coleman, Debit Cards Look to Give Credit Cards a Run for Consumers' Money, Wall St. J., Dec. 3, 2001, at B1. One factor in the debit card/credit card competition is that one doesn't need a bank account to have a credit card but must have one to be accessed for a debit card, which are increasingly being called "check cards" by issuers.

## 2. LIABILITY FOR UNAUTHORIZED USE OF CARDS

### a. CREDIT CARDS

Hurried retail cashiers have little time to examine credit cards to be sure that the person presenting them is the true cardholder or that the card is genuine rather than counterfeit. Billions of dollars of payments for gasoline are made each year by running credit cards through strip-reading devices on the pumps with no human examination of the credit card or its bearer. A thief or counterfeiter has a good chance of not being caught. Credit card fraud was estimated to cause $1.8 in losses in 2002, with 41% of that owing to lost or stolen credit cards. Paul Beckett & Jason Sapsford, As Credit–Card Theft Grows, A Tussle Over Paying to Stop It, Wall St. J., May 1, 2003, at A1. How should the loss be allocated in unauthorized credit card cases: on the careless merchant, on the card owner who is slow in reporting the loss or theft, or on the highly profitable credit card industry that has monitoring capacities that can stop multiple uses of lost, stolen or counterfeit cards?

In 1970 Congress decisively resolved this issue in the following statute. The provisions on credit cards are found in the Truth-in-Lending Act (TILA), 15 U.S.C. §§ 1601–1667(e), which is a grab-bag of consumer protection provisions. In § 1602(k) "credit card" is defined as "any card, plate, coupon book or other credit device existing for the purpose of obtaining money, property, labor, or services on credit." An "accepted credit card" means one "which the cardholder has requested and received or has signed or has used, or authorized another to use for the purpose of obtaining money, property, labor or, services on credit." § 1602(*l*). "The term 'cardholder' means any person to whom a credit card is issued or any person who has agreed with the card issuer to pay obligations arising from the issuance of a credit card to another person." § 1602(m). "The term 'unauthorized use,' as used in section 133 [§ 1643], means a use of a credit card by a person other than the cardholder who does not have actual, implied, or apparent authority for such use and from which the cardholder receives no benefit." § 1602(*o*).

### Section 1643. Liability of Holder of Credit Card

(a)(1) A cardholder shall be liable for the unauthorized use of a credit card only if

(A) the card is an accepted credit card;

(B) the liability is not in excess of $50;

(C) the card issuer gives adequate notice to the cardholder of the potential liability;

(D) the card issuer has provided the cardholder with a description of a means by which the card issuer may be notified of loss or theft of the card, which description may be provided on the face or reverse side of the statement required by section 1637(b) or on a separate notice accompanying such statement;

(E) the unauthorized use occurs before the card issuer has been notified that an unauthorized use of the credit card has occurred or may occur as the result of loss, theft, or otherwise; and

(F) the card issuer has provided a method whereby the user of such card can be identified as the person authorized to use it.

## PROBLEMS

**1.** Oscar paid for his meal at a restaurant by use of his credit card. The waiter surreptitiously copied the information on Oscar's card by a device that he concealed in his belt and sold this information to an enterprise that fraudulently produced plastic cards that were replicas of Oscar's card. These cards were used to make purchases at retail establishments. When these purchases appeared on Oscar's monthly statement, he protested to the credit card issuer that he had not made the purchases. How does § 1643(a) apply to this Problem? How can fraud loss be reduced in cases such as this?

**2.** Oscar is absent minded, and his condition worsened in the months before his bar examination. He had obtained a credit card from Bank A but had forgotten to sign the back of the card. He used it only a couple of times by inserting it in the slot on gasoline pumps to buy gas; the mechanism on the pump did not search for the presence of a signature. He left the card unsigned on the top of a table in his bedroom in the house where he roomed. He wasn't aware that it had disappeared even though he was billed monthly for purchases that he had not made. The cause of his inattention was that he was so preoccupied in the weeks immediately before his exam that he had stopped opening his mail. After his exam, he discovered that the card had been stolen and that Bank A was demanding payment of $5,000 for purchases made on the card, some as long as three months after disappearance of the card, all of which were noted on Bank A's statements that Oscar had received. Not until then did Oscar notify Bank A of the unauthorized use of his card. How would this case be resolved under the statute set out above? See § 1643(d).

---

What policy was Congress implementing in adopting the drastic limitation in § 1643(a) on the liability of cardholders? What incentive does a cardholder have to report the loss or theft of a credit card? Does the fact that the $50 limit on liability has not been changed since 1970 give you some insight on what Congress had in mind? For a discussion of a variety of explanations of the TILA's allocation of risk between cardholder and card issuer, see Clayton P. Gillette, Rules, Standards, and Precautions in Payment Systems, 82 Va. L. Rev. 181 (1996).

b. DEBIT CARDS

Debit cards are governed by the Electronic Fund Transfer Act (EFTA). 15 U.S.C. § 1693(a)–(r). Definitions appear in § 1693a and consumer liability is covered by § 1693g, which affords debit cardholders much less protection than the TILA gives credit cardholders. If the debit cardholder notifies the card issuer of loss or theft of the card within two days of learning of the loss, liability for unauthorized use is limited to $50, otherwise liability may go as high as $500. However, there is no limit for liability for an unauthorized charge if the cardholder fails to report the unauthorized charge appearing on a periodic statement within 60 days of transmittal of the statement. Why is the EFTA's limitation of the debit card liability different from, and less generous than, the TILA's limitation of the credit cardholder's liability? Questions have arisen about which statute applies in cases in which the same card may be used as both a debit and credit card. Regulation E addresses the issue in 12 CFR § 205.12, which provides that if an electronic fund transfer is involved the EFTA provisions apply; TILA applies if the card is used as a credit card without an electronic fund transfer. 2 Clark & Clark, The Law of Bank Deposits, Collections and Credit Cards, ¶¶ 15.03[2][c], 16.06[2] (Rev. ed. 2003). The problem has been alleviated by the pledge on the part of both Visa and

MasterCard in 1997 that they would voluntarily apply a "zero liability" policy to the unauthorized use of both kinds of cards. But this policy has only limited application to debit cards used for small business or commercial purposes.

## PROBLEM

How would the case posed in the Problem 2 above be resolved if Oscar's debit card had been stolen? Concerned that owing to his stressful preparation for the bar exam he would forget his PIN, Oscar had copied it on a post-it stuck to the card where it remained at the time of the theft.

---

A cardholder whose debit card is lost, stolen or counterfeited is in a somewhat less advantageous position than a credit card holder in comparable circumstances because the money has already been removed from the cardholder's account, with bounced checks as a possible consequence, and what can be a prolonged period before the card issuing bank restores the money taken. Despite bank promises of "zero liability" for customers victimized by ATM fraud, E. Scott Reckard reports that banks take a tough stance on refunds in cases in which there is no hard evidence of fraud. Consumers, Banks Clash as ATM Fraud Escalates, LATimes, April 15, 2003, at C1. During the delay, cardholders can be deprived of necessary funds. On the other hand, in the case of a lost, stolen or counterfeited credit card, the cardholder can merely refuse to pay for fraudulent transactions charged on her account until the issue is resolved.

## 3.   WHEN IS USE AUTHORIZED?

As we have seen, TILA's imposition of a $50 limit on liability shifts most of the risk of losses owing to unauthorized uses of credit cards from cardholders to card issuers. A use is unauthorized for the purpose of § 1643 if the card user lacks actual, implied or apparent authority to make a purchase with the card. § 1602(o). The card issuer bears the burden of proof as to unauthorized use. § 1643(b). The TILA allows state law to be more protective of cardholders, reducing their liability in such cases below $50. § 1643(c). Because the cardholder remains fully liable for charges from authorized use, it is no surprise that litigation focuses on whether card use is authorized.

Most unauthorized use cases raise issues of apparent authority rather than of actual or implied authority. The card issuer contends that the card user had apparent authority to make purchases on the cardholder's account owing to the user's status as a member of the cardholder's family or, as in the following case, as an employee of the cardholder. In the case below, the court allows for "apparent authority created through the cardholder's negligence." Does the court allow for liability based on authorized use under the TILA or instead on the cardholder's grossly negligent behavior?

In other words, does the court carefully distinguish between negligence by a cardholder which creates apparent authority for someone else's use of the credit card and negligent acts that enable someone else to use the credit card whether or not apparent authority existed?

## Minskoff v. American Express Travel Related Services Company, Inc.

United States Court of Appeals, Second Circuit, 1996.
98 F.3d 703.

■ MAHONEY, CIRCUIT JUDGE.

Plaintiffs-appellants Edward J. Minskoff and Edward J. Minskoff Equities, Inc. ("Equities") appeal from a final judgment entered September 15, 1995 in the United States District Court for the Southern District of New York, Robert P. Patterson, Jr., Judge, that granted the motion of defendant-appellee American Express Travel Related Services Company, Inc. ("American Express") for summary judgment dismissing plaintiffs-appellants' complaint. The complaint asserted claims under 15 U.S.C. § 1643, a provision of the Truth in Lending Act, 15 U.S.C. § 1601 et seq. (the "TILA"), and New York General Business Law § 512 for recovery of $276,334.06 paid to American Express through checks forged by an Equities employee to cover charges incurred by that employee on American Express credit cards that were fraudulently obtained and used by the employee. * * * The complaint also sought a declaratory judgment that plaintiffs-appellants were not liable for the balance of the unpaid charges outstanding on those credit cards, but the district court granted American Express summary judgment in the amount of $51,657.71 on its counterclaim for that balance.

We vacate the judgment of the district court and remand for further proceedings.

### BACKGROUND

Minskoff is the president and chief executive officer of Equities, a real estate holding and management firm. In 1988, Equities opened an American Express corporate card account (the "Corporate Account") for which one charge card was issued in Minskoff's name. Minskoff also maintained a personal American Express account, which was established in 1963.

In October 1991, Equities hired Susan Schrader Blumenfeld to serve as its assistant to the president/office manager. Blumenfeld was responsible for both the personal and business affairs of Minskoff, and her duties included screening Minskoff's mail, reviewing vendor invoices and credit card statements (including statements for the Corporate Account), and forwarding such invoices and statements to Equities' bookkeepers for payment. Prior to Blumenfeld's employment with Equities, Minskoff personally reviewed all Corporate Account statements; after hiring Blumenfeld, he no longer reviewed any of these statements.

In March 1992, defendant-appellee American Express received an application for an additional credit card to issue from the Corporate Account in Blumenfeld's name. The application had been pre-addressed by American Express and mailed to Minskoff at his business address. It had been completed and submitted by Blumenfeld without the knowledge or acquiescence of Equities or Minskoff. American Express issued the supplemental card and mailed it to Equities' business address. From April 1992 to March 1993, Blumenfeld charged a total of $28,213.88 on that card.

During this period, American Express sent twelve monthly billing statements for the Corporate Account to Equities' business address. Each statement listed both Blumenfeld and Minskoff as cardholders on the Corporate Account, and separately itemized Corporate Account charges for Minskoff and Blumenfeld. These twelve statements show a total of $28,213.88 in charges attributed to Blumenfeld and $23,099.37 in charges attributed to Minskoff, for a total of $51,313.25. Between April 1992 and March 1993, American Express received twelve checks, drawn on accounts maintained by Minskoff or Equities at Manufacturers Hanover Trust ("MHT"), in payment of these charges, with each check made payable to American Express and bearing Equities' Corporate Account number. Minskoff did not review any statements or cancelled checks received during 1992 and 1993 from either his personal account with MHT or the Equities account with MHT.

In July 1992, American Express sent Minskoff an unsolicited invitation to apply for a platinum card. Blumenfeld accepted the invitation on behalf of Minskoff, again without the knowledge or acquiescence of either Minskoff or Equities.[3] Blumenfeld also submitted a request for a supplemental card to issue from this new account (the "Platinum Account") in her name. When platinum cards arrived in both Minskoff's and Blumenfeld's names, Blumenfeld gave Minskoff his card, claiming that it was an unsolicited upgrade of his American Express card privileges. Minskoff proceeded to use his platinum card for occasional purchases, and Blumenfeld charged approximately $300,000 to the Platinum Account between July 1992 and November 1993.

Between August 1992 and November 1993, American Express mailed sixteen Platinum Account monthly billing statements to Equities' business address. Each statement named Blumenfeld and Minskoff as cardholders and itemized charges for each separately. These statements attributed a total of $250,394.44 in charges to Blumenfeld and $10,497.31 to Minskoff, for a total of $260,891.75. These bills were paid in full with checks drawn on the MHT accounts, made payable to American Express, and bearing the Platinum Account number.

---

**3.** It is not clear from the record whether the invitation to receive a platinum American Express card was directed to Minskoff in his individual capacity or in his official position as president of Equities. The solicitation was preprinted with Minskoff's home address, and the record does not reveal how it ended up in Blumenfeld's hands at the Equities office.

In November 1993, Equities' controller, Steven Marks, informed Minskoff that MHT had called to inquire about a check made payable to American Express for approximately $41,000 that had been written on Equities' MHT account. Minskoff stopped payment on the check, initiated an internal investigation of Equities' accounts that revealed the full extent of Blumenfeld's fraudulent activities, and gave notice to American Express of Blumenfeld's unauthorized charges to the Platinum and Corporate Accounts. Blumenfeld subsequently stated in an affidavit that she had forged approximately sixty checks drawn on Equities' MHT account and Minskoff's personal MHT account, including at least twenty payments to American Express for charges to the Platinum and Corporate Accounts. Although some of these checks were used to pay legitimate obligations of plaintiffs-appellants, an accounting analysis attributed losses totalling $412,684.06 to Blumenfeld's theft. In January 1994, Blumenfeld agreed to repay $250,000 to Minskoff and Equities in return for their promise not to institute legal action against her.

Plaintiffs-appellants initiated this action in the United States District Court for the Southern District of New York on February 15, 1994. As previously noted, they sought (1) to recover $276,334.06 that had been paid to American Express in satisfaction of unauthorized charges by Blumenfeld, and (2) a declaration that they were not liable for the outstanding balances on the Platinum Account. The district court, however, dismissed their complaint and awarded American Express $51,657.71 on its counterclaim for that balance. The district court reasoned that the $50 limit on a cardholder's liability for the unauthorized use of the cardholder's credit card specified in 15 U.S.C. § 1643(a)(1)(B), see supra note 1, did not apply to plaintiffs-appellants because their negligence in failing to examine credit card statements that would have revealed Blumenfeld's fraudulent charges "resulted in an appearance of authority [to use the cards] in Blumenfeld."

This appeal followed.

## DISCUSSION

\* \* \*

Plaintiffs-appellants contend that because Blumenfeld obtained the platinum and corporate credit cards through forgery and fraud, her use of the cards is *per se* unauthorized under section 1643, see supra note 1, and plaintiffs-appellants' liability is therefore limited to $50 by section 1643(a)(1)(B). Section 1643 applies, however, only in the case of an "unauthorized use" of a credit card. See § 1643(a)(1), (d). The term "unauthorized use" is defined as "a use of a credit card by a person other than the cardholder who does not have actual, implied, or apparent authority for such use and from which the cardholder receives no benefit." 15 U.S.C. § 1602(*o*). In determining whether a use is unauthorized, "Congress apparently contemplated, and courts have accepted, primary reliance on background principles of agency law in determining the liability of cardholders for charges incurred by third-party card bearers." Towers World Airways v.

PHH Aviation Systems, 933 F.2d 174, 176–77 (2d Cir.), cert. denied, 502 U.S. 823, 112 S.Ct. 87, 116 L.Ed.2d 59 (1991).

Under general principles of agency, the authority of an agent "is the power of the agent to do an act or to conduct a transaction on account of the principal which, with respect to the principal, he is privileged to do because of the principal's manifestations to him." Restatement (Second) of Agency (the "Restatement") § 7 cmt. a (1958). Such authority may be express or implied, but in either case it exists only where the agent may reasonably infer from the words or conduct of the principal that the principal has consented to the agent's performance of a particular act. See id. cmt. b.

Apparent authority is "entirely distinct from authority, either express or implied," id. § 8 cmt. a, and arises from the "written or spoken words or any other conduct of the principal which, reasonably interpreted, causes [a] third person to believe that the principal consents to have [an] act done on his behalf by the person purporting to act for him," id. § 27; see also Fennell v. TLB Kent Co., 865 F.2d 498, 502 (2d Cir.1989). Apparent authority, then, is normally created through the words and conduct of the principal as they are interpreted by a third party, and cannot be established by the actions or representations of the agent. See *Fennell*, 865 F.2d at 502 (collecting cases).

The existence of apparent authority is normally a question of fact, and therefore inappropriate for resolution on a motion for summary judgment. * * * However, a principal may be estopped from denying apparent authority if (1) the principal's intentional or negligent acts, including acts of omission, created an appearance of authority in the agent, (2) on which a third party reasonably and in good faith relied, and (3) such reliance resulted in a detrimental change in position on the part of the third party. See Restatement § 8–* * *.

Viewing the facts in the light most favorable to plaintiffs-appellants, it is clear that Blumenfeld acted without actual or implied authority when she forged the platinum card acceptance form and supplemental card applications. Accordingly, plaintiff-appellants cannot be held accountable for Blumenfeld's initial possession of corporate and platinum cards. As we stated in *Towers*:

> Though a cardholder's [voluntary] relinquishment of possession may create in another the appearance of authority to use the card, [15 U.S.C. §§ 1602(*o*) and 1643] clearly preclude[ ] a finding of apparent authority where the transfer of the card was without the cardholder's consent, as in cases involving theft, loss, or fraud. However elastic the principle of apparent authority may be in theory, the language of the 1970 Amendments [to the TILA] demonstrates Congress's intent that the category of cases involving charges incurred as a result of *involuntary* card transfers are to be regarded as unauthorized under sections 1602(*o*) and 1643.

*Towers*, 933 F.2d at 177.

This result is consistent with the underlying policy of the TILA to protect credit card holders against losses due to theft or fraudulent use of credit cards on the theory that the card issuer is in the better position to prevent such losses. * * * We accordingly disagree with the decision of the district court insofar as it imposed upon plaintiffs-appellants the entire burden of the unauthorized charges made by Blumenfeld to the Corporate and Platinum Accounts.

However, while we accept the proposition that the *acquisition* of a credit card through fraud or theft cannot be said to occur under the apparent authority of the cardholder, our statement in *Towers* should not be interpreted to preclude a finding of apparent authority for the subsequent *use* of a credit card so obtained. Under the rule urged by plaintiffs-appellants, a cardholder could disregard both credit card and bank statements indefinitely, or even fail to act upon a discovery that an employee had fraudulently obtained and was fraudulently using a credit card, and still limit his liability for an employee's fraudulent purchases to $50. Cf. Transamerica Ins. Co. v. Standard Oil Co., 325 N.W.2d 210, 215 (N.D.1982) ("[A]n unscrupulous cardholder could allow another to charge hundreds of dollars in goods and services and then attempt to limit his liability to 50 dollars."). Nothing in the TILA suggests that Congress intended to sanction intentional or negligent conduct by the cardholder that furthers the fraud or theft of an unauthorized card user. We therefore agree with the district court to the extent that it decided that the negligent acts or omissions of a cardholder may create apparent authority to use the card in a person who obtained the card through theft or fraud. Apparent authority created through the cardholder's negligence does not, however, retroactively authorize charges incurred prior to the negligent acts that created the apparent authority of the user.

Applying these principles to the case at hand, we address the district court's conclusion that plaintiffs-appellants' failure to examine credit card and bank statements amounts to negligence which created an appearance of authority in Blumenfeld to use the card. Under New York law, consumers are obligated to "exercise reasonable care and promptness to examine [bank] statement[s] . . . to discover [any] unauthorized signature or any alteration." § 4–406(1) * * *. This provision is derived from a common law obligation to examine bank statements and report forgeries or alterations, and it is based upon a determination that "the depositor [is] in the better position to discover an alteration of the check or forgery of his or her own signature." Woods v. MONY Legacy Life Ins. Co., 84 N.Y.2d 280, 284, 617 N.Y.S.2d 452, 453, 641 N.E.2d 1070, 1071 (1994) (extending application of § 4–406 to brokerage accounts).

This policy is no less applicable to credit card holders than it is to bank depositors. Once a cardholder has established a credit card account, and provided that the card issuer is in compliance with the billing statement disclosure requirements of 15 U.S.C. § 1637,[4] the cardholder is in a

---

**4.** Section 1637(b) requires "[t]he creditor of any account under an open end consumer credit plan [to] transmit to the obligor, for each billing cycle at the end of which

superior position to determine whether the charges reflected on his regular billing statements are legitimate. A cardholder's failure to examine credit card statements that would reveal fraudulent use of the card constitutes a negligent omission that creates apparent authority for charges that would otherwise be considered unauthorized under the TILA. * * *

It is undisputed that between April 1992 and November 1993, American Express mailed to Equities' business address at least twenty-eight monthly billing statements documenting charges made to the Platinum and Corporate Accounts. Each of those statements clearly lists Blumenfeld as a cardholder, and each specifically itemizes those charges attributable to her credit card. During that same period, MHT mailed to Equities' business address numerous bank statements showing that checks made payable to American Express had been drawn on Equities' business account and Minskoff's personal account to pay these American Express charges. Minskoff concedes that he failed to examine any of these statements until November 1993, and no other employee or agent of Equities (other than Blumenfeld) became aware of the disputed monthly payments to American Express prior to the inquiry by Bankers Trust in November 1993. These omissions on the part of plaintiffs-appellants created apparent authority for Blumenfeld's continuing use of the cards, especially because it enabled Blumenfeld to pay all of the American Express statements with forged checks, thereby fortifying American Express' continuing impression that nothing was amiss with the Corporate and Platinum Accounts.

Plaintiffs-appellants argue that summary judgment is inappropriate because they exercised reasonable care in the hiring and supervision of Blumenfeld and in the implementation and administration of internal accounting procedures designed to detect and prevent fraud. In this case, however, while American Express concedes that Equities employed bookkeepers who were responsible, *inter alia*, for reviewing credit card statements and arranging for their payment, as well as reviewing bank statements and cancelled checks, the inadequate manner in which these procedures were performed from April 1992 to November 1993 enabled Blumenfeld to acquire unauthorized American Express credit cards, run up more than $300,000 in invalid American Express charges, and pay for them with approximately twenty forged checks drawn on Equities' MHT account and Minskoff's personal MHT account, without detection.

A cursory review of any of the American Express statements would have disclosed charges by Blumenfeld made with an unauthorized credit card. A review of any MHT statement would have disclosed one or more payments to American Express (or, if the cancelled checks had previously been removed by Blumenfeld, charges that could not be matched to

there is an outstanding balance in that account or with respect to which a finance charge is imposed, a statement setting forth," *inter alia*, the outstanding balance in the account at the beginning and end of the statement period, the amount and date of each extension of credit during the period, the amount of any finance charge added to the account, and the date by which payment must be made to avoid finance charges.

cancelled checks) generally in amounts far exceeding Minskoff's habitual American Express charges. We are not dealing in this case with an occasional transgression buried in a welter of financial detail. In our view, once a cardholder receives a statement that reasonably puts him on notice that one or more fraudulent charges have been made, he cannot thereafter claim lack of knowledge. The district court was justified in determining that no reasonable jury could conclude that this standard had been satisfied as to plaintiffs-appellants on the record presented in this case, warranting summary judgment in favor of American Express to the extent that we have previously indicated.

In our view, the appropriate resolution in this case is provided by adapting the ruling in *Transamerica* to provide that

[American Express] is liable for [Blumenfeld's] fraudulent purchases [as to each credit card] from the time the credit card was issued until [plaintiffs-appellants] received the first statement from [American Express] containing [Blumenfeld's] fraudulent charges plus a reasonable time to examine that statement. After that time, [plaintiffs-appellants are] liable for the remaining fraudulent charges.

325 N.W.2d at 216. We accordingly vacate the judgment of the district court and remand for further proceedings to make this determination. We leave it to the district court in the first instance to ascertain whether, as the record is developed on remand, any issues require submission to a jury.

## NOTES

**1.** Most of the TILA's provisions govern only the consumer credit transactions, not business transactions. § 1603(1). An exception is the TILA's limitation on liability for unauthorized use, which applies to credit cards used for business purposes as well. § 1645. For business cardholders, the $50 limit on liability of § 1643(a) is a default rule. A business cardholder can assume greater liability for unauthorized card use by its employees if it does not impose liability on them for such use. See, e.g., American Express Travel Related Services Co. v. Web, Inc., 405 S.E.2d 652 (Ga.1991).

**2.** In defining "unauthorized use" to mean the lack of actual, implied or apparent authority, the TILA (and implementing federal regulations; see 12 C.F.R. § 226.12(b)(1) (1997)) employs concepts borrowed from the law of agency. See Mary Elizabeth Matthews, Credit Cards—Authorized and Unauthorized Use, 13 Ann. Rev. Bank L. 233 (1994). Agency law can work to restrict the efficient allocation of loss from unauthorized card use, as determined by a court. In such cases courts sometimes stretch agency principles or infer facts that make agency law consistent with efficient loss allocation. Apparent authority, for example, requires that the principal's acts create in third parties a reasonable belief that a designated person is acting on its behalf. See Restatement (Second) of Agency § 8 (1958). A finding of authorized credit card use by an agent therefore requires conduct by the cardholder that creates such beliefs in merchants. The question of whether the card issuer or the cardholder is in a superior position to control the designated person's conduct is not directly at issue. The *Minskoff* court took the cardholder's failure to examine its credit card statements as omissions which induced a belief that the charges were authorized. Stieger v. Chevy Chase Savings Bank, F.S.B., 666 A.2d 479 (D.C.App.1995), goes further, concluding that an employee had apparent authority to make charges when she signed her name only after the employer had authorized her to make other charges. The employers in both cases were in a superior position to control the use of their credit cards by employees. The TILA's incorporation of agency notions seems to demand more: conduct by the cardholder that leads a merchant to believe that the employee is authorized to act on the employer's behalf. D.B.I. Architects, Inc. v. Amex, 388 F.3d 886 (D.C. Cir. 2004), follows *Minskoff* in holding a corporate credit cardholder liable for employee fraud under apparent authority.

## PROBLEM

When Wife married Husband, she opened a credit card account with Bank and requested that Bank issue a credit card to her and a duplicate card to Husband in his name. When the marriage broke up, Wife notified Bank that she would no longer pay for Husband's charges on the credit card. The credit card agreement that Wife signed provided that an account could be closed by returning all cards. Bank immediately revoked both cards and gave numerous notifications to both parties of revocation and requests that the cards be returned. Both Wife and Husband continued to make charges on the cards. Wife contended that with respect to Husband's charges made after her notification to Bank, her liability should be limited to $50; the card should be treated as a lost or stolen card since she had no power to make her ungrateful spouse return it. Bank sued her for the balance of her account. What result? Which party was in the better position to prevent Husband's improper use of the card, Wife or Bank? These facts are based on Walker Bank & Trust Co. v. Jones, 672 P.2d 73 (Utah 1983).

## 4.  ASSERTION BY CARDHOLDER OF DEFENSES

In Chapter 11, with respect to a promissory note issued by a consumer to obtain goods or services, we saw that various doctrines of case law or provisions of statutory or administrative law have been used to allow the consumer to assert against a financial institution that holds the note claims and defenses that the consumer has against the seller of the goods or services. If a consumer uses a bank credit card to buy goods and the goods are either never delivered or are defective, should the cardholder be allowed to refuse to pay the issuer of the credit card to the extent that the cardholder would have been excused from paying the seller of the goods if the sale had been a credit sale by the seller? This question was hotly debated at the state level in the late 1960s. Financial institutions that were issuers of credit cards argued that they had only the most tenuous relationship with retailers honoring their cards, and should not be subjected to claims and defenses arising out of sales made pursuant to their cards. The card issuer, it was contended, should be no more involved in the sale transaction financed by a credit card than should a drawee bank in a sale paid for by a check drawn on the bank. Moreover, would not subjecting card issuers to sales defenses ultimately restrict the acceptability of credit cards by retailers? The concern of the retailer was that the card issuer would insist on a right to charge back against the retailer debts as to which the cardholder raised claims or defenses. Would a retailer in Maine feel secure in honoring a credit card presented by a cardholder who lives in California knowing that if the cardholder claims the goods are defective the retailer may end up with an unsecured claim against the debtor three thousand miles away?

In 1974 Congress enacted the Fair Credit Billing Act, stating rights and obligations of the cardholder and the issuer of the credit card with respect to the correction of a billing error that the cardholder believes has been made in the billing statement received from the issuer. These provisions now appear in the Consumer Credit Protection Act, "Correction of Billing Errors" in 15 U.S.C. § 1666. "Billing error" is defined in § 1666(b) and includes reflection on the statement of an extension of credit not made by the cardholder and reflection on the statement of goods or services not accepted by the cardholder or not delivered to the cardholder in accordance with the agreement made at the time of the sales transaction. The 1974 legislation covered a number of other aspects of the issuer-cardholder relationship in §§ 1666a–1666i. Section 1666i, addressed the issue of the extent to which the cardholder can assert, as a defense to the obligation to pay the issuer, claims and defenses of the cardholder arising from the transaction in which the credit card was used. It is set out below:

### Section 1666i. Assertion by Cardholder Against Card Issuer of Claims and Defenses Arising Out of Credit Card Transactions

(a) Subject to the limitation contained in subsection (b), a card issuer who has issued a credit card to a cardholder pursuant to an open end consumer credit plan shall be subject to all claims (other than tort claims) and defenses arising out of any transaction in which the credit card is used as a method of payment or extension of credit if (1) the obligor has made a good faith attempt to obtain satisfactory resolution of a disagreement or problem relative to the transaction from the person honoring the credit card; (2) the amount of the initial transaction exceeds $50; and (3) the place where the initial transaction occurred was in the same State as the mailing address previously provided by the cardholder or was within 100 miles from such address, except that the limitations set forth in clauses (2) and (3) with respect to an obligor's right to assert claims and defenses against a card issuer shall not be applicable to any transaction in which the person honoring the credit card (A) is the same person as the card issuer, (B) is controlled by the card issuer, (C) is under direct or indirect common control with the card issuer, (D) is a franchised dealer in the card issuer's products or services, or (E) has obtained the order for such transaction through a mail solicitation made by or participated in by the card issuer in which the cardholder is solicited to enter into such transaction by using the credit card issued by the card issuer. * * *

## PROBLEM

California tourist, Marcy Birkenstock, goes to Maine, loves the maple syrup, buys $1,500 of the precious stuff, pays with her Visa card, issued by a bank in South Dakota, has the syrup shipped to her LA home, but hates the stuff delivered to her. She is sure that she has been defrauded. First, she calls Seller who maintains that the syrup shipped was exactly what she sampled at his store in Maine and assures her that he won't take the syrup back if she returns it. In a surly mood Marcy calls your law office to find out what she can do. If the Seller won't take the syrup back, she doesn't want to have to pay the bank issuing the Visa card when she is billed. (1) What do you tell her? (2) What is the purpose of the same-state or 100–mile limitation in the statute? (3) Where did the sale take place in this case? (4) What if Marcy had ordered the syrup by telephone after she had returned home? Or bought it on the Internet?

---

Section 1666i regulates only the rights between the cardholder and card issuer. The credit card systems, e.g., Visa USA and MasterCard Worldwide, have agreements governing the relationships of merchants, merchant banks, and issuing banks. These agreements allow limited recourse by an issuing bank against a merchant in defective merchandise cases. The issuing bank sends a chargeback to the merchant bank, requiring it to refund the payment made to it by the issuing bank. The merchant bank then charges back against the merchant's account. If there are too many complaints against a merchant, the merchant may be required to adopt fair policies for adjustment and return of defective merchandise in order to be allowed to continue to accept credit cards. See 2 Clark & Clark, The Law of Bank Deposits, Collections and Credit Cards ¶ 15.07[2] (Rev. ed. 2005).

## Citibank (South Dakota) v. Mincks

Missouri Court of Appeals, 2004.
135 S.W.3d 545.

■ JEFFREY W. BATES, JUDGE.

Citibank (South Dakota), N.A. ("Citibank") sued defendant Mary Mincks ("Mary") for breach of contract after Mary refused to make any further payments on her Citibank credit card account.[1] Mary defended on

---

**1.** We will refer to Mary Mincks and her husband, Chuck Mincks, collectively as "the Mincks." We will refer to them individu-

the ground that: (1) the only unpaid charges on the account related to merchandise which was never delivered by the merchant; and (2) since her Citibank credit card was used to order the merchandise, she was entitled to assert the defense of non-delivery against Citibank in its action to recover the balance due on her credit card account. After a bench trial, judgment was entered in Mary's favor. On appeal, Citibank argues that the trial court's judgment should be reversed because it was not supported by substantial evidence, and it was based on an erroneous application of the provisions of the Truth-in-Lending-Act, 15 U.S.C. 1601, *et seq.* We affirm.
\* \* \*

## II. Factual and Procedural History

The facts in this case are relatively simple and virtually undisputed. The summary set forth below is a synthesis prepared from the pleadings, trial testimony and exhibits.

On September 18, 1999, Mary applied to have a credit card issued to her by Citibank. She filled out a document called a "Citibank Platinum Select Acceptance Form," which appears to be a typical application for personal credit. Nothing on the application indicates that credit was being sought by either a business or by an individual who intended to use the credit card for business purposes. The application listed Mary as the cardholder and showed her home address as the billing location. The form asked for the normal personal information (e.g., mother's maiden name, social security number, income) found in such personal applications. Mary applied for credit for herself, and she requested that her husband, Chuck, also be authorized to use her credit card account. The application contained the familiar exhortation, typically found in consumer credit applications, offering an introductory period of very low interest. Such offers tend to encourage consumers to transfer balances from other credit cards to the new account in order to obtain the benefit of a lower rate of interest.

Mary's application was accepted, and Citibank issued a credit card to her with an $8,000 line of credit. On October 26, 1999, Mary transferred the existing balances from two other credit cards, totaling $7,213.50, to her Citibank account.[4] There is no indication in the record that these balance transfers were comprised of purchases for anything other than personal, family or household purposes.

Between November 1999 and January 2000, Mary purchased a few additional items with her credit card and made several payments on her account. Once again, nothing in the record demonstrates that these purchases were made for anything other than personal, family or household purposes. On January 27, 2000, Mary made a large payment on her account that reduced the outstanding balance to approximately $20.00.

ally by their first names. We do so for purposes of clarity and intend no disrespect.

**4.** Mary transferred the $2,432.62 balance from her AT & T card and the $4,780.88 balance from her Discover card. On Mary's October 1999 Citibank statement, the line item entry for the two transactions noted that each was a balance transfer and stated "purchase charged to lower rate."

In February 2000, Chuck received a solicitation to order merchandise from Purchase Plus Buyers Group ("PPBG"). PPBG sold products like mailing cards, telephone cards and other similar items which could be used to promote a home business. After reviewing the solicitation, Chuck decided to order some high-definition, high-color postcards that he could use to contact potential customers for a home business that he had started about three months earlier. On February 24, 2000, Chuck placed an order with PPBG for 4,000 postcards. The order form was sent by fax from Lamar, Missouri, to PPBG's office in Westerville, Ohio. Chuck used Mary's Citibank credit card to pay the $7,600 purchase price for the postcards. The charge for this purchase first appeared on Mary's Citibank statement in March 2000.

Four weeks after placing the order, Chuck contacted PPBG by telephone to find out why he had not yet received the postcards. He was told that the merchandise was on backorder and would not be available for another month. Having no reason to doubt that explanation at the time, he waited another month. When he still had not received the postcards, he contacted PPBG again by telephone. The persons with whom he spoke were very positive and continued to assure him that he would receive the postcards in time. Thereafter, he called PPBG "innumerable times" by telephone, and PPBG personnel kept reiterating that he would ultimately receive the postcards he ordered. In mid-May 2000, Chuck first learned from PPBG that the type of postcards he ordered had been discontinued in December 1999, even though the product continued to be offered for sale until April 2000. On May 18, 2000, he faxed a letter to PPBG requesting that he be given some other type of product that he could use since the postcards he wanted were no longer available. He received no response. He faxed the same letter to PPBG's executive committee on July 13, 2000, and again received no response.

Around August 1, 2000, Chuck decided he was never going to receive the postcards he ordered from PPBG. On August 4, 2000, he faxed a written demand for a full refund to PPBG because the company had failed to deliver either the postcards or a satisfactory alternative product. He sent this fax because he still believed he could get a refund for the undelivered merchandise. This belief changed on September 1, 2000, when he received a fax from PPBG stating the company had ceased operations and permanently closed its doors that day. Chuck knew then he would not be able to get a refund from PPBG.

On September 28, 2000, the Mincks sent a letter to Citibank. In sum, the letter provided Citibank with the following information: (1) Chuck's $7,600 postcard order from PPBG had never been delivered; (2) the charge for this order first appeared on Mary's March 2000 statement; (3) the facts showing that Chuck had made a good faith effort to resolve the issue with PPBG were recounted with considerable specificity and detail; (4) PPBG committed a breach of contract and fraud by failing to deliver the ordered merchandise and by continuing to sell a discontinued product; and (5) the Mincks were invoking their rights under Regulation Z of the federal Truth-in-Lending-Act to have their account credited in the amount of $7,600 and to have this sum charged back to PPBG.

On October 9, 2000, Citibank responded in a letter sent to Mary. Citibank took the position that it was not able to assist the Mincks because it had not received their letter "within 60 days of the disputed charge." Citibank advised the Mincks to pursue the matter with the merchant or through some alternative means available to them.

After receiving the October 9, 2000, letter from Citibank, the Mincks continued to use Mary's credit card. They made a few additional purchases with the card, and they continued to make payments on the account. That changed in February 2002, when the Mincks stopped making any payments on the Citibank account. The outstanding account balance at this time was comprised solely of the remaining amount due for the undelivered post-cards ordered from PPBG, plus accrued interest and late charges.[6] Citibank continued to add interest charges, over credit limit fees, and late fees to Mary's credit card account until July 2002. As of that date, the outstanding account balance was $9,048.49.

On October 7, 2002, Citibank sued Mary for breach of contract and sought to recover the $9,048.49 then due, accrued interest at the rate of 24.99% per annum and a 15% attorney fee. Insofar as pertinent to the issues here, the petition alleged that: (1) Citibank had issued a credit card to Mary; (2) by acceptance and use of the credit card, Mary had agreed to make the monthly payments described in the Citibank Card Agreement attached to the petition; (3) Citibank had advanced credit to Mary, through the use of the credit card, to certain persons or firms shown on her account statements; (4) Citibank had made demand on Mary to pay the amount due on her account, but she refused to do so for more than 25 days; and (5) Citibank had "paid valuable consideration to each of said issuers of the credit to Defendant [Mary], and that as consideration therefore [sic] each of said issuers of credit has assigned to Plaintiff [Citibank] the rights to receive payment evidenced in each of the transactions making up the balance due...." Thus, it is apparent from Citibank's petition that it was suing as the assignee of the individual merchants from whom Mary or Chuck had made purchases using Mary's Citibank credit card. It is also undisputed that the entire account balance which Citibank sought to recover from Mary resulted from the direct and collateral charges associated with the single $7,600 transaction in which PPBG was the merchant. In Mary's answer, she specifically asserted non-delivery of the merchandise ordered from PPBG as a defense against Citibank's claim.[7]

---

**6.** At trial, Mary's monthly Citibank statements from October 1999 through October 2002 were admitted in evidence. The statements show that from September 2000 through August 2001, the Mincks used Mary's Citibank card to make $337 in new purchases. The Mincks continued to make payments on Mary's account from September 2000 through January 2002. The total amount of these payments was $2,194. The outstanding account balance shown in the January 2002 statement was $7,734.47.

**7.** Paragraph 3 of Mary's answer stated, in pertinent part, as follows: "[T]he goods and services purchased by Defendant were never delivered to Defendant and Defendant received nothing in consideration of the

At trial, the sole dispute was whether Mary was entitled to assert PPBG's non-delivery as a defense against Citibank, which sought to recover the purchase price of the postcards as PPBG's assignee. Citibank argued that the non-delivery defense should not be permitted on two grounds. First, the PPBG postcard order, which was the only transaction at issue, was not within the scope of Regulation Z since this specific purchase was for a business or commercial purpose. Second, even if Regulation Z did apply, non-delivery of merchandise constitutes a "billing error" within the meaning of the regulation. According to Citibank, Mary lost the ability to assert non-delivery as a defense in this lawsuit because she did not give Citibank notice of this "billing error" within 60 days after the charge first appeared on her credit card statement. In response, Mary argued that Regulation Z imposed no time limit that precluded her from asserting non-delivery as a defense in Citibank's lawsuit against her, and she denied that this was a "billing error" within the meaning of the regulation. At the conclusion of the case, the trial court made the following ruling from the bench:

> I think that Reg Z does apply, and I don't think this is a billing error. And I think that the provision of Reg Z that allows the cardholder to assert any differences—any defenses that they could assert against the provider of the product is against the—the [sic] credit card company. Court's going to find the issues in favor of the Defendant and enter a judgment for the Defendant against the Plaintiff.

Judgment was entered in accordance with the trial court's pronouncement, and Citibank appealed.

### III.   Discussion and Decision

Citibank's appeal presents two points for us to decide. Each point relied on is a rescript of the arguments Citibank made below.

### *Point I*

In Citibank's first point, it contends the trial court erred in permitting Mary to assert PPBG's non-delivery as a defense in Citibank's breach of contract action. Specifically, Citibank argues that the trial court's judgment is not supported by substantial evidence and is based on a misapplication of the law because "Regulation Z" should not have been applied in this lawsuit, in that the PPBG transaction was primarily for a business or commercial purpose. Citibank's argument is grounded upon on two implicit premises: (1) the Truth-in-Lending-Act and its implementing regulations do not apply to this lawsuit if the single PPBG transaction at issue was for a business purpose; and (2) Mary's ability to assert non-delivery as a defense against Citibank in this contract action is derived solely from the Truth-in-

charges. Defendant notified Plaintiff of the non-delivery of the items purchased as soon as it was apparent to Defendant she had been defrauded. Under Federal Law, Defendant has no liability to Plaintiff. Federal Reserve Board Regulation Z; 12 Code of Federal Regulations 226.12(c)."

Lending-Act and Regulation Z. Citibank's first point fails because neither implicit premise is correct.

### The Truth-in-Lending-Act and Regulation Z Do Apply to Mary's Open End Consumer Credit Plan

\* \* \*

The Truth-in-Lending-Act governs a number of different types of consumer credit, including one type described as an "open end consumer credit plan." *See* 15 U.S.C. § 1637. This phrase is derived from a combination of two other statutory definitions found in 15 U.S.C. § 1602:

(h) The adjective "consumer", used with reference to a credit transaction, characterizes the transaction as one in which the party to whom credit is offered or extended is a natural person, and the money, property, or services which are the subject of the transaction are primarily for personal, family, or household purposes.

(i) The term, "open end credit plan" means a plan under which the creditor reasonably contemplates repeated transactions, which prescribes the terms of such transactions, and which provides for a finance charge which may be computed from time to time on the outstanding unpaid balance. A credit plan which is an open end credit plan within the meaning of the preceding sentence is an open end credit plan even if credit information is verified from time to time.

\* \* \* We have previously summarized the evidence presented at trial concerning how Mary's account was established and used prior to the single PPBG purchase at issue here. We find this evidence sufficient to support the conclusion that Mary's account was an open end consumer credit plan within the meaning of the Truth-in-Lending-Act. Furthermore, Citibank's counsel forthrightly conceded during oral argument that Mary's account was this type of plan.

Since Mary's open end consumer credit plan involved the use of a credit card, the Truth-in-Lending-Act specifically preserves her right to assert defenses against Citibank arising out of the PPBG transaction. Section 1666i states, in pertinent part:

*(a) Claims and defenses assertible*

Subject to the limitation contained in subsection (b) of this section, a card issuer who has issued a credit card to a cardholder pursuant to an open end consumer credit plan shall be subject to all claims (other than tort claims) and defenses arising out of any transaction in which the credit card is used as a method of payment or extension of credit if (1) the obligor has made a good faith attempt to obtain satisfactory resolution of a disagreement or problem relative to the transaction from the person honoring the credit card; (2) the amount of the initial transaction exceeds $50; and (3) the place where the initial transaction occurred was in the same State as the mailing address previously provided by the cardholder or was within 100 miles from such address. . . .

*(b) Amount of claims and defenses assertible*

The amount of claims and defenses asserted by the cardholder may not exceed the amount of credit outstanding with respect to such transaction at the time the cardholder first notifies the card issuer or the person honoring the credit card of such claim or defense. . . .

15 U.S.C. § 1666i. This same rule is repeated in 12 C.F.R. § 226.12(c). Hereinafter, we generically refer to the consumer protections contained in this statute and regulation as the "claims and defenses rule."

At the trial, Mary presented substantial evidence proving that she met each statutory element necessary to successfully assert the defense of non-delivery against Citibank under the Truth-in-Lending-Act claims and defenses rule:

1.   The defense arose out of the PPBG transaction, and Mary's credit card was used as the method of payment for that purchase.

2.   The Mincks made a good faith attempt to resolve the issue with PPBG.

3.   The amount of this transaction greatly exceeded the $50 minimum.

4.   The PPBG transaction occurred in Missouri, which is the same state as the mailing address shown on Mary's billing statements from Citibank.[8]

5.   The non-delivery defense was used solely to extinguish the remaining indebtedness on Mary's Citibank account resulting from the single PPBG transaction at issue.

Therefore, we hold that the trial court committed no error in concluding Mary was entitled to assert the non-delivery defense against Citibank. The Truth-in-Lending-Act claims and defenses rule authorized Mary to assert non-delivery as a defense because her Citibank credit card account was an open end consumer credit plan, and her credit card was used to make the PPBG purchase at issue.

In so holding, we have given due consideration to Citibank's assertion that the Truth-in-Lending-Act claims and defenses rule does not apply because the single PPBG purchase was for a business or commercial purpose. Citibank's argument is based on the 15 U.S.C. § 1603(1), which

---

**8.**   Courts deem a contract to have been made where the parties to the contract perform the last act necessary to complete the contract. *Gash v. Black and Veatch*, 976 S.W.2d 31, 32 (Mo.App.1998). Here, Chuck accepted PPBG's offer to sell the postcards by (a) filling out the written order form, (b) including Mary's Citibank credit card information on the form for use as the method of payment, (c) signing the form and (d) faxing the order from Lamar, Missouri, to PPBG's offices in Ohio. Since acceptance of PPBG's offer occurred in Missouri, the contract is deemed to have been made in this state. *See Johnson Heater Corp. v. Deppe*, 86 S.W.3d 114, 119 (Mo.App.2002); *Whiteman v. Del-Jen Const., Inc.*, 37 S.W.3d 823, 831 (Mo.App. 2001); *Garrity v. A.I. Processors*, 850 S.W.2d 413, 416 (Mo.App.1993).

defines what transactions are exempted from the scope of the Truth-in-Lending-Act. This statute states, in pertinent part:

> This subchapter does not apply to the following: (1) Credit transactions involving extensions of credit primarily for business, commercial, or agricultural purposes, or to government or governmental agencies or instrumentalities, or to organizations.

We find this argument unpersuasive for two reasons.

First, Citibank's argument is inconsistent with the plain language of 15 U.S.C. § 1666i. When an open end consumer credit plan is involved, this statute explicitly authorizes a cardholder (*i.e.*, Mary) to assert a defense against the card issuer (*i.e.*, Citibank) "arising out of *any transaction* in which the credit card is used as a method of payment or extension of credit...." 15 U.S.C. § 1666i(a) (emphasis added.) Since we are required to liberally construe this language in Mary's favor, we interpret the phrase, "any transaction," to mean exactly what it says. So long as a credit card was used to make a purchase on an open end consumer credit plan, the claims and defenses rule in 15 U.S.C. § 1666i applies to "any transaction" meeting the other requirements set forth in the statute. Any less expansive interpretation of this phrase would constitute a strict, rather than a liberal, construction of this remedial statute. We decline Citibank's invitation that we do so.

Second, Citibank's argument ignores the fact that the relevant "transaction" here was the initial extension of credit to Mary when her Citibank account was opened, rather than the specific transaction involving the postcard purchase from PPBG. We find the initial transaction controlling because it resulted in the creation of an open end consumer credit plan for Mary. It was this occurrence which inexorably led us to conclude that Mary was authorized by statute and regulation to assert non-delivery as a defense against Citibank in its lawsuit.

We believe this result is entirely consistent with the discussion of the Truth-in-Lending-Act by the United States Supreme Court in *American Express Company v. Koerner*, 452 U.S. 233, 101 S.Ct. 2281, 68 L.Ed.2d 803 (1981), upon which Citibank relies. In *Koerner*, the Supreme Court acknowledged that there can be an extension of consumer credit when an open end consumer credit account is created or renewed, as well as when individual credit card transactions occur. *Id.* at 240–42, 101 S.Ct. 2281. For the purpose of determining when the provisions of the Truth-in-Lending-Act apply, the Supreme Court described three possible alternative tests:

> The language of does not distinguish between the two types of transactions included in the definition of "credit" or indicate which of them must satisfy the definition of "consumer" in order for the section to be applicable. There are several possibilities. The relevant extension of credit may be only the creation or renewal of the account. Under this view, adopted by the District Court, [*Koerner v. American Express Co.*, 444 F.Supp. at 340 (E.D.La.1977)], if an account is opened by a natural person, its overall purpose must be considered. If the account is opened

primarily for consumer purposes, applies, even if the cardholder uses the card for an occasional nonconsumer purchase. On the other hand, the language might be interpreted to call for a transaction-by-transaction approach. With such an approach, would apply if the transaction that is the subject of the dispute is a consumer credit transaction, regardless of the overall purpose of the account. A third alternative would be to combine the two approaches by holding applicable to all disputes that arise under an account that is characterized as a consumer credit account as well as to any dispute concerning an individual transaction that is an extension of consumer credit, even if the overall purpose of the account is primarily a business one.

*Id.* at. 242, 101 S.Ct. 2281. The Supreme Court, however, was not required to decide which approach should be used because it determined there had not been an extension of consumer credit under any of the alternative tests.

In the case at bar, we do reach the issue which was deferred in *Koerner* and conclude that the first of the three alternatives, which we denominate the "overall purpose" test, is the one that should be used when an open end consumer credit plan is involved. Under this test, the overall purpose of an account opened by a natural person must be considered. If the account was opened primarily for consumer purposes, the statutory and regulatory framework of the Truth-in-Lending-Act applies, even if the cardholder occasionally uses the card for a nonconsumer purchase.

We find support for this conclusion in the Official Staff Interpretations of Regulation Z. *See* Supplement I to part 226, 12 C.F.R. p. 357 (1–1–04 edition). The Official Staff Commentary dealing with 12 C.F.R. § 226.3 (exempt transactions) notes that a creditor must determine in each case whether the extension of credit "is primarily for an exempt purpose." Pt. 226, Supp. I p. 369. "Examples of business-purpose credit include:

.... A business account used occasionally for consumer purposes. Examples of consumer-purpose credit include:.... A personal account used occasionally for business purposes." *Id.* Therefore, we disagree with Citibank's contention that the use of Mary's Citibank credit card account to purchase nonconsumer goods on one occasion prevents her from taking advantage of the Truth-in-Lending-Act's claims and defenses rule in this case.

### Mary's Use of Non-delivery as a Defense Against *Citibank Also Is Authorized by State Law*

Even if we accepted Citibank's argument in Point I that the Truth-in-Lending-Act does not apply, our decision would not change. Like Ulysses' unfortunate sailors in *The Odyssey*, Citibank would successfully navigate past the Charybdis of federal law only to be devoured by the Scylla of state law. Expressed in less metaphorical terms, the trial court's decision to enter judgment for Mary is still correct, based exclusively on Missouri common law and statutory principles. We must affirm the judgment under any reasonable theory supported by the evidence, even if the reasons advanced by the trial court are wrong or insufficient. * * *

Citibank brought a breach of contract action against Mary for failing to pay her credit card account. The only unpaid charge on Mary's account was the PPBG purchase. As the petition expressly acknowledged, Citibank was suing Mary as PPBG's assignee.

"Missouri law is well-settled that an assignee acquires no greater rights than the assignor had at the time of the assignment." *Carlund Corp. v. Crown Center Redevelopment*, 849 S.W.2d 647, 650 (Mo.App.1993). * * * As a result, Citibank stands in PPBG's shoes and can occupy no better position than PPBG would if it sued Mary directly. * * * These common law principles compel the conclusion that any defense valid against PPBG is valid against its assignee, Citibank. * * * The same is true under Missouri statutory law. * * * Therefore, without regard to the provisions of the federal Truth-in-Lending-Act, Missouri law gave Mary a common law and statutory right to assert any defense against Citibank that she could have asserted against its assignor, PPBG.

Assuming PPBG had sued Mary for breach of contract and sought to recover the cost of the postcards, would she have had a valid defense against that claim? We answer this question affirmatively because PPBG never delivered the merchandise for which Mary was charged. * * * This defense is just as effective against Citibank as it would have been against PPBG.

Regardless of whether the trial court's decision is reviewed by using the federal Truth-in-Lending-Act or state law standards, the judgment is correct. The trial court committed no error by ruling in Mary's favor and denying Citibank any recovery on its action for breach of contract. Citibank's first point is denied.

### Point II

In Citibank's second point, it contends the judgment is not supported by substantial evidence and is based on a misapplication of the law because, even if Regulation Z does apply, PPBG's non-delivery of the postcards constituted a "billing error" within the meaning of the regulation. Assuming that to be true, Citibank then argues Mary could not avoid responsibility for the PPBG purchase unless she gave Citibank notice of the error within 60 days after the charge first appeared on her credit card statement. According to Citibank, failure to invoke the billing error provisions of the Truth-in-Lending-Act prohibits a consumer from thereafter relying on the claims and defenses rule if he or she is sued on the debt by the creditor.

The relevant statutory and regulatory provisions of the Truth-in-Lending-Act dealing with billing errors are found in 15 U.S.C. § 1666 and 12 C.F.R. § 226.13. Hereinafter, we generically refer to the consumer protections contained in this statute and regulation as the "billing error rule." The billing error rule gives a consumer the right, upon proper written notice, to request correction of billing errors. The notice must be received within 60 days after the creditor has sent the consumer a statement reflecting a billing error. *See* 15 U.S.C. § 1666(a); 12 C.F.R. § 226.13(b). If the consumer properly invokes the billing error rule by giving timely written notice, the creditor is required to investigate the claim. 15 U.S.C. § 1666(a); 12 C.F.R. § 226.13(b) and (c). While the investigation is pending, the consumer may withhold payment of the disputed sum, and the creditor is prohibited from both collection and adverse credit reporting activity. 15 U.S.C. § 1666(c); 12 C.F.R. § 226.13(d). As defined in 15 U.S.C. § 1666(b)(3) a billing error includes "[a] reflection on a statement of goods or services . . . not delivered to the obligor or his designee in accordance with the agreement made at the time of a transaction." Essentially the same definition of a billing error is found in 12 C.F.R. § 226.13(a)(3).

The trial court concluded that PPBG's failure to deliver the postcards did not constitute a "billing error" within the meaning of 15 U.S.C. § 1666 and 12 C.F.R. § 226.13. We interpret this decision to be a rejection of Citibank's position that the 60 day time limit for giving written notice began running in March 2000 when the PPBG charge first appeared on Mary's statement because the Mincks did not know, during any portion of this 60 day period, that they would never receive the postcards, an acceptable substitute product, or a refund from PPBG. In order to dispose of Citibank's second point on appeal, however, it is unnecessary for us to decide whether this ruling was in error. Assuming PPBG's non-delivery of the postcards did constitute a "billing error" within the meaning of the Truth-in-Lending-Act, Mary still was entitled to invoke the claims and defenses rule in 15 U.S.C. § 1666i and 12 C.F.R. § 226.12(c). This statute and regulation are stand-alone provisions that operate independently of 15 U.S.C. § 1666 and 12 C.F.R. § 226.13, which give a consumer separate and distinct rights and remedies when seeking to correct a billing error. We find support for our conclusion through a textual analysis of 15 U.S.C. § 1666 and an examination of the Official Staff Interpretations of Regulation Z.

The only obligation imposed upon a consumer by 15 U.S.C. § 1666 is the transmittal of an adequate written notice to the creditor within 60 days after receiving a statement containing a billing error.[14] Once the billing error process is properly initiated, the consumer may withhold payment of the disputed sum and obtain an abatement of collection and adverse reporting activity while the creditor investigates the issue. Nothing in the statute affirmatively imposes any penalty on the consumer for failing to take advantage of the benefits of this statute. The only penalty which can even be inferred is the loss of the abatement rights contained therein. We accept as accurate the way in which the Texas Court of Appeals summed up the purpose of 15 U.S.C. § 1666:

> The purpose of the protections afforded a consumer under section 1666 is not, after all, to change the substantive law with regard to his

---

**14.** The notice must identify the consumer by name and account number, indicate that a billing error has occurred and what the amount of the error is, and explain why the consumer believes the charge is a billing error. 15 U.S.C. § 1666(a)(1–3).

liability for the underlying debt, but to protect him from the intimidating process of bargaining over a disputed debt with a creditor in a superior bargaining position. Without such protections, the creditor may use that bargaining power to encourage payment of even an illegitimate debt by threatening to force the consumer to expend substantial time and money to protect his rights.

*Dillard Department Stores, Inc. v. Owens*, 951 S.W.2d 915, 918 (Tex.App. 1997).

In contrast, the statute does affirmatively impose a penalty upon *a creditor* that ignores the provisions of this statute. This conclusion follows from 15 U.S.C. § 1666(e), which states:

> *(e) Effect of noncompliance with requirements by creditor*
>
> Any creditor who fails to comply with the requirements of this section or section 1666a of this title forfeits any right to collect from the obligor the amount indicated by the obligor under paragraph (2) of subsection (a) of this section, and any finance charges thereon, except that the amount required to be forfeited under this subsection may not exceed $50.

Thus, § 1666 only affects the amount of the debt in the event of a creditor's noncompliance with the statute. When this occurs, however, the creditor may still sue on the debt if there is a remaining balance due after subtracting the $50 forfeiture sum. If we were to accept Citibank's argument, it would mean that a consumer who failed to utilize this billing error statute—through ignorance, inadvertence, or purposeful action—would completely forfeit his right to contest the debt owed in a collection lawsuit. The creditor, on the other hand, could knowingly and willfully ignore its responsibilities under this statute and only be penalized a maximum of $50. In our view, this interpretation of the statute leads to an absurd result and turns topsy-turvy our duty to liberally construe the Truth-in-Lending-Act in a consumer's favor. Again, we decline to do so.

Our construction of how the billing error rule operates also is supported by the Official Staff Interpretations of Regulation Z. As the United States Supreme Court stated in *Ford Motor Credit Company v. Milhollin*, 444 U.S. 555, 100 S.Ct. 790, 63 L.Ed.2d 22 (1980):

> At the very least, . . . caution requires attentiveness to the views of the administrative entity appointed to apply and enforce a statute. And deference is especially appropriate in the process of interpreting the Truth in Lending Act and Regulation Z. Unless demonstrably irrational, Federal Reserve Board staff opinions construing the Act or Regulation should be dispositive. . . .

*Id.* at 565, 100 S.Ct. 790. We wholeheartedly agree. In this very specialized area of law governing commerce in credit, we believe the Federal Reserve Board's interpretation of the Truth-in-Lending-Act and its implementing regulations are entitled to substantial deference as we analyze the issues presented in Citibank's appeal.

The regulation dealing with a consumer's right to correct billing errors is 12 C.F.R. § 226.13. The regulation dealing with a consumer's right to assert claims and defenses is 12 C.F.R. § 226.12. The Official Staff Commentary for 12 C.F.R. § 226.12 states, in pertinent part:

*12(c) Right of cardholder to assert claims or defenses against card issuer.*

*1. Relationship to § 226.13.* The § 226.12(c) credit card "holder in due course" provision deals with the consumer's right to assert against the card issuer a claim or defense concerning property or services purchased with a credit card, if the merchant has been unwilling to resolve the dispute. Even though certain merchandise disputes, such as non-delivery of goods, may also constitute "billing errors" under § 226.13, that section operates independently of § 226.12(c). The cardholder whose asserted billing error involves undelivered goods may institute the error resolution procedures of § 266.13; but whether or not the cardholder has done so, the cardholder may assert claims or defenses under § 226.12(c). Conversely, the consumer may pay a disputed balance and thus have no further right to assert claims and defenses, but still may assert a billing error if notice of that billing error is given in the proper time and manner. An assertion that a particular transaction resulted from unauthorized use of the card could also be both a "defense" and a billing error.

*See* Pt. 226, Supp. I p. 419. Thus, the Federal Reserve Board recognizes that the claims and defenses rule operates independently of the billing error rule. As the Board's analysis of the proper relationship between these two different rules and their respective remedies is not demonstrably irrational, we accept it as dispositive here.

For all of the foregoing reasons, we reject Citibank's argument that a consumer's failure to give a creditor timely notice of a billing error precludes the consumer from later invoking the claim and defense provisions of 15 U.S.C. § 1666i and 12 C.F.R. § 226.12(c) if the creditor sues on the debt. Citibank's second point is denied.

## IV.   Conclusion

Mary was entitled to assert non-delivery as a valid defense against Citibank in its action for breach of contract. The use of this non-delivery defense was authorized both by the Truth-in-Lending-Act and by state law. Furthermore, the use of this defense was not precluded by the billing error rule found in the Truth-in-Lending-Act. Therefore, the trial court ruled correctly when it denied Citibank any recovery and entered judgment in Mary's favor. The judgment is affirmed.

NOTES

**1.** 15 U.S.C. § 1666i's geographic limitation on the cardholder's use of defenses to payment against the card issuer does not specify where the "initial transaction occurred." The court in *Izraelewitz v. Manufacturers*

*Hanover Trust Co.*, 120 Misc.2d 125 (Civil Ct. of N.Y. Kings County, 1983), states that the determination instead is left to state law. In *Plutchok v. European American Bank*, 540 N.Y.S.2d 135 (N.Y.Dist.Ct.1989), the court determined that under New York state law a contract concluded by telephone occurs where the acceptance occurs.

**2.** Although an informal policy argument might prefer eliminating § 1666i's geographic limit, the case for doing so is far from decisive. A card issuer has an advantage over the cardholder at monitoring and gaining information about merchants who have accounts with it, wherever the merchant is located. Repeat business between the merchant and card issuer also reduces the merchant's incentive and ability to engage in sharp practice when it affects the issuer. These considerations favor always allowing the cardholder to use whatever defense it has against the merchant to resist paying the card issuer. Cf. *Singer v. Chase Manhattan Bank*, 890 P.2d 1305 (Nev.1995). Against this, sharp practice by cardholders in transactions in distant locations also must be considered. There is also the possibility that local merchants might be well positioned to share information about the patterns of behavior of remote cardholders purchasing in their locality. If cardholders tend to "misbehave" differently in transactions entered into far from home, where reputational constraints are slight and such transactions are sporadic enough to make monitoring by card issuers costly, for instance, eliminating the geographic limit increases the cost to remote merchants of accepting payment by credit card. Thus, the likely source of misbehavior (merchant or cardholder) as well as its costs do not unambiguously favor doing away with a limit.

### 5.   INTERNET FRAUD

Most Internet sales are paid for by credit cards, and security problems are mounting. Losses may result from counterfeit credit cards in which the information on the card (credit card number and name of cardholder) is stolen and a new plastic card is manufactured from that information that can be used in face-to-face transactions, or, more commonly, use of fraudulently obtained information in telephone, Internet sales or other remote transactions in which no plastic card is required. How are losses in Internet sales allocated? The following Problem raises the issue in a common fact situation.

### PROBLEM

Brentwood Books (BB) sells rare books all over the world on its Website. It accepts Visa, MasterCard and Amex in payment, but for sales over $250, BB checks with the relevant network to verify that a card bearing the name and number submitted by the buyer has in fact been issued to the buyer. BB received a $1,000 order on the Internet purportedly from Lin Jong in Hong Kong, China, a well known book dealer, which directed that the sale be charged to Lin Jong's Visa card, with the credit card number and expiration date stated. BB verified with Visa International that a card bearing the stated number and expiration date had been issued to Lin Jong. When BB shipped the goods, it sent a memorandum to Union Bank, its California merchant bank (MB), that a sale had been made to be charged to Lin Jong's Visa card; MB credited BB's account for the amount of the sale and sent a charge message through the Visa International network to Hong Kong Bank, Lin Jong's issuing bank (IB), which debited Lin Jong's account for the amount of the sale. When Lin Jong saw the $1,000 charge on his statement, he protested to IB that he had not purchased the goods and demanded a chargeback. IB complied and sent a chargeback to MB, which erased the credit for that amount in BB's account. It became apparent that someone had stolen the information from Lin Jong's credit card and had ordered the goods sent to a Hong Kong address different from that of Lin Jong's business. Who should bear the loss in this case? How can the parties avoid losses of this kind on Internet sales?

---

Brentwood Books' difficulty is that it can't prove that Lin Jong received the goods because it doesn't have his signature. A typical online sale is considered a "card-not-present" transaction as opposed to a "card-present" sale at a brick-and-mortar store, where shoppers sign receipts. Thomas E. Weber, What Do You Risk Using a Credit Card to Shop on the Net, Wall.St.J., Dec. 10, 2001, at B1, states the understanding to be: "When a consumer challenges a card-not-present charge, the merchant is liable for the loss." Julia Angwin, Credit–Card Scams Bedevil E–Stores, Wall St. J., Sept. 19, 2000, at B1, reports that more Internet transactions are charged back (1.25%) than catalog transactions by telephone (0.33%) or storefront retail transactions (0.14%). She notes that one survey of 156 of the largest retailers showed that 2.64% of their Internet transactions are charged back. She interviewed online retailers whose chargeback losses have driven them to require that all deliveries be made only to the address of the cardholder and, for larger orders, to telephone the cardholder to confirm the order. The assumption is that a large portion of Internet chargeback losses are caused by use of stolen credit card numbers. Software has been developed to spot potential fraud cases, and Visa and MasterCard have developed new systems, "Verified by Visa" and "MasterCard SureCode," under which the cardholder receives a password resembling a PIN that only the cardholder can use in online sales. These systems will be phased in over the next few years. The intent is to have the use of the password treated as the equivalent to the cardholder's signature. Paul Beckett & Jathon Sapsford, As Credit–Card Theft Grows, A Tussle Over Paying to Stop It, Wall St. J., May 1, 2003, at A1.

Identity theft has brought credit card fraud to a new level of criminal professionalism. Individuals are duped by fraudsters into divulging confidential information: account numbers, home addresses, Social Security numbers, date of birth, even driver's license numbers. This information is collected on Web sites that sell or share stolen credit card information. In a recent year the MasterCard Worldwide security office detected 35,045 MasterCard numbers for sale or trade on the Internet; these numbers can be used in telephone or Internet transactions. A technology research firm estimated in 2004 that the astonishing number of 980,000 consumers had encountered identity theft fraud in the prior year, at a cost of more than $1.2 billion in losses. Mitchell Pacelle, How MasterCard Fights Against Identity Thieves, Wall St. J., May 9, 2005, at B1. As Internet sales grow, identity fraud becomes more costly; it's hard for merchants to recognize crooks with stolen identities. As merchants and banks become more wary, fraudsters become more sophisticated. As a harassed merchant put it: "[I]t's a cat-and-mouse game. As we get better, they get better." Mitchell Pacelle, At Online Stores, Sniffing Out Crooks Is a Matter of Survival, Wall St. J., Aug. 4, 2005, at A1. In 2004 an alliance of international law-enforcement agencies coordinated a global crackdown on illegal trade in stolen credit card numbers on the Internet: "Operation Firewall." The results are shown by the title of the following article. Riva Richmond, Stolen–Credit–Card Market Recovers, Wall St. J., June 1, 2005, at B5A.

CHAPTER 14

# PAYMENT SYSTEMS: ELECTRONIC TRANSFERS

## A. ELECTRONIC FUNDS TRANSFERS UNDER ARTICLE 4A

### 1. THE BASIC TRANSACTION COVERED BY ARTICLE 4A

Article 4A was promulgated by ALI and National Conference in 1989. By 1996 it had been enacted in all 50 states. Representatives of the Federal Reserve Board and of the New York Federal Reserve Bank were very active in the four-year drafting process of Article 4A, and, after Article 4A was completed, Regulation J, which governs Fedwire (described below), was revised by the Federal Reserve Board to bring it into conformity with Article 4A. 12 C.F.R. § 210.25 et seq. The Fed's stated policy in doing so was to provide a "level playing field" in which the rights and obligations of the parties in all funds transfers would be governed by essentially the same set of rules. Ernest T. Patrikis, Thomas C. Baxter, Jr. and Raj K. Bhala, Wire Transfers 140 (1993) (hereafter Patrikis et al., Wire Transfers).

Section 4A–108 provides that Article 4A does not apply to consumer electronic funds transfers governed by the Electronic Fund Transfer Act, 15 U.S.C. § 1693 et seq., discussed later in this chapter. Typical transactions covered by the EFTA are: point-of-sale transactions in which retail customers pay for purchases by use of an access or debit card inserted in a terminal at a retail store that allows the bank account of the customer to be debited; automated teller machine transactions; direct deposit of paychecks in consumer accounts and preauthorized withdrawals from consumer accounts to pay consumer obligations like insurance premiums. 15 U.S.C. § 1693a(6). "Small dollar" wire transfers by Western Union and its competitors are not covered by Article 4A because payment orders are defined in 4A–103 as orders to banks and Western Union and its competitors are not banks.

The typical funds transfer transaction covered by Article 4A is a large payment of money from one business or financial organization to another made through the banking system by electronic means. The average size of a wire transfer is measured in the millions of dollars. Although checks and credit cards account for 98% of the volume of payment transactions, domestic wire transfers amount to 85% of the value of all payments. Finance: Trick or Treat?, The Economist, October 23, 1999, at 91. A common wire transfer might be: Los Angeles Seller is selling $100 million in property to a New York Buyer. The closing is in Buyer's counsel's office in New York. When negotiations are concluded and the deal is made, Buyer calls its office and requests that an instruction be given to its bank, New York Bank (NYB), to transfer $100 million to Seller's account in Seller's bank, Los Angeles Bank (LAB). Within a few hours, Seller receives a call from its office stating that it has been notified by LAB that the funds are now in Seller's account in LAB and available for withdrawal by Seller. The deal is done.

What went on behind the scenes to move $100 million from New York to Los Angeles in a few hours? Some of the alternative methods follow. These are described in detail in Patrikis et al., Wire Transfers, Chapter 2.

(a) *Two bank transfer.* Buyer, the "originator" (4A–104(c)), instructs NYB, the "originator's bank" (4A–104(d)), to send $100 million to LAB, the "beneficiary's bank" (4A–103(a)(3)), for the account of the Seller, the "beneficiary" (4A–103(a)(2)). The instruction is a "payment order" (4A–103(a)(1)) and it may be transmitted "orally [e.g., by telephone], electronically, or in writing." NYB "accepts" (4A–209(a)) the payment order when it "execute[s]" (4A–301(a)) that order by sending a payment order to LAB intended to carry out the payment order it received from Buyer. LAB accepts the payment order of NYB by crediting the Seller's account and notifying Seller of this fact. 4A–209(b)(1). When LAB accepted the payment order, the "funds transfer" (4A–104(a)) was completed. Since Seller has received payment, Buyer's obligation to pay Seller for the property is discharged. 4A–406.

This transaction involved two payment orders: the first, from Buyer to NYB and the second, from NYB to LAB. With respect to the first, Buyer is the "sender" (4A–103(a)(5)), and NYB is the "receiving bank" (4A–103(a)(4)). With respect to the second, NYB is the sender and LAB is the receiving bank. In crediting Seller's account, LAB was not sending a payment order.

It is important to understand that Article 4A prescribes the liability of the parties to a funds transfer. It does not mandate a mode of settlement. That is, when NYB accepted Buyer's payment order, Buyer, as sender, became liable to pay the amount of that payment order to NYB, the receiving bank. 4A–402(c). When LAB, the beneficiary's bank, accepted NYB's payment order, NYB became liable to pay the amount of the order to LAB. 4A–402(b). When LAB credited Seller's account and gave notice to Seller, LAB paid Seller and Seller can withdraw the funds.

How these debts are settled, that is, how the money changes hands, is not covered by Article 4A, which merely provides for a series of bank credits, usually ending in a credit in the beneficiary's account in the beneficiary bank. NYB became a creditor of Buyer when it accepted Buyer's payment order by sending its own order to LAB. Buyer will pay its debt to NYB either by having enough money in its account in NYB that NYB can debit to cover the payment or by depositing enough money into the account, usually by the end of the banking day, to cover the payment made on Buyer's behalf. If no satisfactory agreement has been reached in advance between Buyer and NYB to fund the payment order, NYB would probably not accept the order.

LAB became a creditor of NYB when it accepted NYB's payment order by crediting Seller's account. Unless NYB and LAB have some agreement on how NYB will pay this debt, LAB probably would not accept the payment order. Usually in two-bank cases, settlement will be accomplished either through "cross accounts" or a "common account." In a cross-account situation, each bank will have an account in the other. When NYB accepts Buyer's payment order, it will debit Buyer's account and credit LAB's account. When LAB accepts NYB's payment order, it will debit NYB's account and credit Seller's account. Common-account settlement is possible when both NYB and LAB have accounts in a common correspondent bank. The correspondent bank will debit NYB's account and credit that of LAB.

(b) *CHIPS*. If both NYB and LAB are participants in the Clearing House Interbank Payments System (CHIPS) of the New York Clearing House Association, they can utilize the CHIPS facilities for both transmission of the payment order and settlement of the ensuing obligations. CHIPS is one of the two major wire transfer systems in the nation; it handles a large volume of international transfers in dollars and a number of its participants are foreign banks. Under CHIPS, NYB will send its payment order to LAB through the central CHIPS clearing system. At the end of the day, CHIPS computers will net out the difference between the total value of payments orders NYB has sent to LAB on that day, and vice versa, and the net balance debtor will pay through Fedwire the amount of the debit balance to the CHIPS Settlement Account at the New York Federal Reserve Bank; the net balance creditor will receive the amount of the credit balance from this account through Fedwire sent by the FRBNY at the end of the day. Patrikis et al., Wire Transfers, Chapter 17.

(c) *Fedwire*. This system is owned and operated by the 12 Federal Reserve banks and is the other major domestic wire transfer system. It can be used only by banks in privity with Reserve banks. These banks must have accounts in the Fed. However, other banks can use Fedwire through correspondent banks that are in privity with the Fed. If both LAB and NYB have access to Fedwire, the transaction would go like this: Buyer instructs NYB to send the funds to LAB for credit to Seller's account. NYB instructs the New York Fed to send the funds to LAB, for Seller. The NY Fed will instruct the San Francisco Fed to send funds to LAB for Seller's account. The SF Fed will instruct LAB to credit Seller's account. LAB will notify Seller that the money is available for withdrawal. In this case four payment orders have been sent: from Buyer to NYB, from NYB to NY Fed, from NY Fed to SF Fed, and from SF Fed to LAB.

Fedwire is not only a communication system that receives and sends payment orders, but, like CHIPS, it is also a settlement system. However, there is a difference. Under Fedwire, as soon as the NY Fed sends the instruction to the SF Fed, it debits NYB's Federal Reserve account and credits the Federal Reserve account of the SF Fed. As soon as the SF Fed sends the instruction to LAB, it debits the NY Fed's Federal Reserve account and credits the Federal Reserve account of LAB. As they say in the business, with Fedwire "the message is the money." By the time LAB receives the payment order, all prior payment orders are settled. No end-of-day settlement, as in CHIPS, is necessary. Each sender's payment order is settled for at the time of acceptance by the receiving bank by debiting the Federal Reserve account of the sender and crediting the Federal Reserve account of the receiving bank.

(d) *SWIFT*. The Society For Worldwide Interbank Financial Telecommunications (SWIFT), a Belgium-based consortium, is owned and operated by some of the world's largest financial institutions: Bank of America, JPMorgan Chase & Co. and Citigroup and large European banks such as Deutsche Bank in Germany. The SWIFT network was founded in 1973 to replace telex and is used primarily for non-dollar transfers between financial institutions in more than 200 countries. It has almost 7,900 participating institutions. Only 16% of its traffic is American. Like CHIPS, SWIFT does not transfer funds between banks; it transmits payment orders and settlement takes place through the Fed and its international counterparts. Josh Meyer and Greg Miller, U.S. Secretly Tracks Global Bank Data, LATimes, June 23, 2006, A1.

At the time Article 4A was being written, the United Nations Commission on International Trade Law (UNCITRAL) was drafting the Model Law on International Credit Transfers which is intended to be a model for any nation that wishes to have legislation on the subject. Advisers who had been active in the Article 4A project served as members of the U.S. delegation to the Working Group which constituted the drafting committee for the Model Law. Article 4A and the Model Law bear many similarities but there are differences as well. As yet no nation has adopted the Model Law and it is exceedingly unlikely the U.S. will do so. The Model Law is discussed extensively in Patrikis et al., Wire Transfers, Chapters 19–23.

## 2. PAYMENT ORDERS

A funds transfer involves a series of payment orders, defined in 4A–103(a)(1) as meaning "an instruction of a sender to a receiving bank, transmitted orally, electronically, or in writing to pay, or cause another bank to pay, a fixed or determinable amount of money to a beneficiary * * *." Why did the customer's instructions to its bank in the following case not constitute a payment order?

## Trustmark Insurance Company v. Bank One, Arizona, NA, a National Banking Association

Court of Appeals of Arizona, 2002.
48 P.3d 485.

■ GEMMILL, JUDGE.

If a banking customer sends a bank a letter of instructions requesting wire transfers of funds upon future occurrences of a specified balance condition in the customer's account, does the letter of instructions constitute a "payment order" under Article 4A of Arizona's Uniform Commercial Code ("UCC")? We address this question, and others, in this decision.

Bank One, Arizona, NA ("Bank One") appeals from a jury verdict for Trustmark Insurance Company ("Trustmark") on Trustmark's claim under Article 4A of the UCC * * *. We reverse the judgment on the UCC claim * * *.

## *FACTUAL AND PROCEDURAL BACKGROUND*

This case involves a commercial dispute between Bank One and Trustmark over a wire transfer arrangement. In February 1995, Trustmark set up a deposit account ("Account One") at Bank One governed by Bank One's deposit account rules. At the same time, Trustmark executed a wire transfer agreement with Bank One.

In May 1995, Trustmark sent Bank One a letter (the "Letter of Instructions") regarding a second deposit account ("Account Two"). Account Two was subject to the same deposit account rules and wire transfer agreement as Account One. In the Letter of Instructions, Trustmark instructed Bank One to (1) retain a daily balance of $10,000 in Account Two and (2) transfer funds in Account Two automatically to a Trustmark account at the Harris Bank ("Harris Account") whenever Account Two reached a balance of $110,000 or more. In September 1995, Trustmark's Arizona agent began depositing funds into Account Two. Bank One began transferring funds to the Harris Account whenever the Account Two balance rose above $110,000. * * *

In September 1996, the Account Two balance rose above $110,000 for the first time since the July 19, 1996 deadline. Bank One did not transfer funds from Account Two into the Harris Account. Bank One sent regular account statements to Trustmark showing the balances in Account Two, but received no further instructions from Trustmark. The Account Two balance continued to grow until December 1997, when Bank One brought the balance to the specific attention of Trustmark's Arizona agent, who contacted Trustmark's management. Bank One transferred $19,220,099.80 to the Harris Account, leaving $10,000 in Account Two. In early 1998, Trustmark instructed Bank One to transfer Account Two's remaining funds to the Harris Account and thereafter closed Account Two.

Trustmark then filed this action against Bank One, alleging a claim under Article 4A of the UCC, as well as claims for unjust enrichment and negligence. Trustmark alleged that Bank One failed to complete wire transfers from Trustmark's non-interest bearing account at Bank One (Account Two) to Trustmark's investment account at Harris Bank (Harris Account), contrary to the Letter of Instructions. Trustmark asserted a loss of more than $500,000 in interest on its funds as a result of Bank One's inaction, and that Bank One reaped a corresponding windfall profit through interest Bank One earned on Trustmark's money. Trustmark did not assert a breach of contract claim. According to Bank One, the contractual documents eliminated recovery or significantly limited the amount recoverable for breach of contract. However, Article 4A—if applicable—

restricts the right of a bank to limit its liability regarding funds transfers. *See* A.R.S. § 47–4A305(F) (1997).[2]

Bank One filed motions to dismiss and for summary judgment on the UCC claim, arguing that the wire transfers at issue were not subject to Article 4A because the Letter of Instructions was not a "payment order" under Article 4A. The trial court denied Bank One's motions, and the case proceeded to a jury trial. At the close of evidence, the court granted Bank One's motion for judgment as a matter of law on the unjust enrichment claim, but continued to reject Bank One's argument that Article 4A of the UCC was not applicable. The court submitted Trustmark's UCC claim and its negligence claim to the jury.

The jury returned a verdict for Trustmark on the UCC claim and found damages of $573,197.02. * * * The trial court entered judgment for Trustmark with damages of $573,197.02, as well as pre-judgment interest, attorneys' fees, and taxable costs.

### ISSUES ON APPEAL AND CROSS APPEAL

Bank One argues on appeal that Trustmark's judgment should be reversed as a matter of law because Article 4A of the UCC is not applicable. According to Bank One, the Letter of Instructions was not a "payment order" under Article 4A, and the trial court should not have sent this UCC claim to the jury. * * *

### BANK ONE'S APPEAL

Bank One challenges the trial court's submission of the UCC claim to the jury on the basis that the Letter of Instructions is not a "payment order" under Article 4A; therefore the UCC is not applicable, and this claim should have been dismissed as a matter of law. * * *.

### As a Matter of Law, the UCC Does Not Apply Because the Letter of Instructions Was Not a "Payment Order" Under Article 4A

\* \* \*

Article 4A applies only to "funds transfers" as defined in the statute. A.R.S. § 47–4A102 (1997). A "funds transfer" is "the series of transactions, beginning with the originator's *payment order*, made for the purpose of making payment to the beneficiary of the order." A.R.S. § 47–4A104(1) (1997) (emphasis added). Accordingly, to fall within the scope of Article 4A, a transaction must begin with a "payment order."

A "payment order" is defined by the UCC, in pertinent part, as:

---

**2.** Section 47–4A305 specifies the liability of a bank under UCC Article 4A for late or improper execution of, or failure to execute, a payment order. *See* A.R.S. § 47– 4A305(A), (B), and (D). Trustmark sought recovery under A.R.S. §§ 47–4A305 and 47– 4A506 (1997). Bank One argued these provisions were not applicable.

[A]n instruction of a sender to a receiving bank, transmitted orally, electronically, or in writing, to pay, or to cause another bank to pay, a *fixed or determinable amount of money* to a beneficiary if:

(a) *The instruction does not state a condition to payment* to the beneficiary *other than time of payment.* . . .

A.R.S. § 47–4A103(A)(1) (1997) (emphasis added). A recent law review article explains:

By definition, an Article 4A payment order must be unconditional. Therefore, an important scope issue in determining whether Article 4A applies is whether the payment order in question is or is not conditional.

Alvin C. Harrell, *UCC Article 4A*, 25 Okla. City U.L.Rev. 293 (2000) (footnote omitted).

Bank One argues that the Letter of Instructions was not a payment order, because the Letter was not for a "fixed or determinable amount of money" and imposed two conditions other than time of payment: that the account balance always remain $10,000 ("balance condition") and that transfers not occur until subsequent deposits have raised the balance to $110,000 or more ("deposit condition").[4] Trustmark argues that the conditions at issue were merely conditions regarding the time of payment—that the balance and deposit conditions essentially determined when transfers were to be made. Trustmark asserts that time of payment need not be set by a specific date, but may be set by events such as the bank's receipt of an incoming wire or deposit. However, the amounts to be transferred did not relate to incoming wires for the same amounts or even wires received on the same day of each month. Rather, Trustmark's agent made deposits sporadically and in varying amounts. Therefore, the conditions in the Letter of Instructions required Bank One to continuously monitor Trustmark's account balance to determine whether sufficient deposits had been made to enable the bank to make a transfer that satisfied both the deposit and balance conditions.

Neither party has cited, nor has our own research revealed, any reported decision addressing the precise issue presented: whether a letter of instructions from an account holder to its bank, requesting automatic wire transfers of funds in excess of a minimum balance whenever the total balance equals or exceeds a specified amount, constitutes a "payment order" governed by UCC Article 4A. We conclude that the Letter of Instructions was not a "payment order," because the Letter subjected Bank One to a condition to payment other than the time of payment.

Article 4A applies to discrete, mechanical transfers of funds. Comment 3 to UCC § 4A–104 (A.R.S. § 47–4A104) provides:

---

**4.** Because we base our resolution on the definition of "payment order," we do not reach Bank One's argument that the Letter of Instructions was not for a "fixed or determinable amount of money."

The function of banks in a funds transfer under Article 4A is comparable to their role in the collection and payment of checks in that it is essentially mechanical in nature. The low price and high speed that characterize funds transfers reflect this fact. Conditions to payment ... other than time of payment impose responsibilities on [the] bank that go beyond those in Article 4A funds transfers.

*See also Centre–Point Merchant Bank v. Am. Express Bank*, 913 F.Supp. 202, 208 (S.D.N.Y.1996) (payment orders under Article 4A are not intended to require banks to "engag[e] in inquiries as to whether conditions have been satisfied.").

Bank One's obligation to make an ongoing inquiry as to Account Two's balance status removes the Letter of Instructions from the Article 4A definition of a "payment order." A.R.S. § 47–4A103(A)(1)(a); Comment 3 to UCC § 4A–104 (A.R.S. § 47–4A104), (quoted in, *supra*). Conditions other than time of payment "are anathema to [A]rticle 4A, which facilitates the low price, high speed, and mechanical nature of funds transfers." *Grabowski*, 997 F.Supp. at 121 (citing Mass. Gen. L. ch. 106, § 4A–104, cmt. 3). In their treatise on the UCC, James J. White and Robert S. Summers further explain:

A payment order must not "state a condition to payment of the beneficiary other than time of payment." Few transactions will include such conditions. The exception for "time of payment" means that a payment order need not order immediate payment, though most do. For example, a payment order may specify that a certain amount of money must be paid on a certain date to a particular beneficiary.

3 James J. White & Robert S. Summers, *Uniform Commercial Code* § 22–2 (4th ed.1995) (citation omitted). White and Summers then quoted the same language from Comment 3 that we quote in to explain that "the drafters did not wish to involve banks in [inquiries] into whether other conditions have occurred." *Id.*

Based on the language defining "payment order," the purpose of Article 4A, and the drafters' intent that payment orders be virtually unconditional, we conclude that requiring the bank to continually examine the account balance is a condition to payment other than time of payment under A.R.S. § 47–4A103(A)(1)(a). We perceive a qualitative difference between a condition requiring daily monitoring of the account balance and an instruction to wire funds on a specific day. * * *

We conclude, as a matter of law, that Trustmark does not have a claim under UCC Article 4A, because the Letter of Instructions is not an Article 4A "payment order." Therefore, we reverse the judgment against Bank One on Trustmark's UCC claim. * * *

### CONCLUSION

We reverse the judgment in favor of Trustmark on the UCC claim * * *.

## 3.   ACCEPTANCE OF PAYMENT ORDER

*By Receiving Bank.* "Acceptance," defined in 4A–209, is a core concept of Article 4A. The rights and obligations of the participants to a funds transfer under Article 4A arise as a result of acceptance. A payment order instructs a receiving bank to accept the payment order, but the receiving bank may either accept or reject. If a receiving bank accepts a sender's payment order, the sender becomes liable to the receiving bank for the amount of the payment order, 4A–402(c), and the receiving bank is obliged to issue a payment order complying with the sender's payment order. 4A–302(a)(1). A receiving bank, other than the beneficiary's bank, accepts the sender's payment order by executing the order, 4A–209(a), that is, by issuing a payment order intended to carry out the payment order received by the bank. 4A–301(a). An originator is a sender and an originator's bank is a receiving bank. When the originator's bank executes the payment order by sending it to a receiving bank, the originator's bank becomes a sender.

*By Beneficiary's Bank.* The last receiving bank in the chain is the beneficiary's bank, the one identified in the payment order as the bank in which the account of the beneficiary is to be credited. 4A–103(a)(3). Section 4A–209(b) spells out when a beneficiary's bank accepts a payment order. In the most common case, this occurs when the beneficiary's bank credits the beneficiary's account and notifies the beneficiary that it may withdraw the credit. 4A–405(a). At this point the beneficiary's bank becomes liable for the amount of the payment order to the beneficiary. 4A–404(a). The beneficiary has bank credit in its account in the amount of the funds transfer—"money in the bank"—that it can withdraw. The purpose of the funds transfer has been achieved: the beneficiary is paid and the underlying obligation that the originator owed the beneficiary is discharged. 4A–406(a) and (b). Bank credit has been transferred from the originator's bank to the beneficiary's bank. Settlement between the banks may occur later.

### PROBLEM

Beneficiary's Bank (BB) received a payment order for $10,000 and credited Beneficiary's (B) account for that amount. A few hours later BB notified B that the credit had been received, but said nothing about its availability. However, the evidence was uncontradicted that B had been given immediate access to the funds in its account at the time the account was credited. The issue before the court was whether payment was made at the time of the credit or at the time of the notice. Section 4A–405(a) states that payment is made "when ... (i) the beneficiary is notified of the right to withdraw the credit * * * or (iii) funds with respect to the order are otherwise made available to the beneficiary by the bank." The court in First Security Bank of New Mexico v. Pan American Bank, 215 F.3d 1147 (10th Cir. 2000), held that payment occurred as soon as B had immediate access to the funds under 4A–405(a)(iii) even though BB had not given B notice of its right to withdraw the funds. The only discussion in Article 4A of this provision appears in Comment 5 to 4A–209 and is not clearly on point. Do you agree with the court's decision? What position does *Aleo*, following, take on this issue?

## 4.   RECEIVER FINALITY

In Chapter 12 we discussed why obligees might not choose to take payment in uncertified checks or even in cashier's checks. At that point we suggested that they might demand to be paid by wire transfer in order to provide maximum safety. In the following case we see why this is so.

## Aleo International, Ltd. v. Citibank

Supreme Court, New York County, 1994.
160 Misc.2d 950, 612 N.Y.S.2d 540.

■ HERMAN CAHN, JUSTICE.

Defendant Citibank, N.A. ("Citibank") moves for an order, pursuant to CPLR 3212, granting it summary judgment dismissing the complaint.

Plaintiff Aleo International, Ltd. ("Aleo") is a domestic corporation. On October 13, 1992, one of Aleo's vice-presidents, Vera Eyzerovich ("Ms. Eyzerovich"), entered her local Citibank branch and instructed Citibank to make an electronic transfer of $284,563 US dollars to the Dresdner Bank in Berlin, Germany, to the account of an individual named Behzad Hermatjou ("Hermatjou"). The documentary evidence submitted shows that at 5:27 p.m. on October 13, 1992, Citibank sent the payment order to the Dresdner Bank by electronic message. Dresdner Bank later sent Citibank an electronic message: "Regarding your payment for USD 284.563,00 DD 13.10.92 [indecipherable] f/o Behzad Hermatjou, Pls be advised that we have credited A.M. beneficiary DD 14.10.92 val 16.10.92 with the net amount of USD 284.136,16." This information was confirmed by the Dresdner Bank by fax to Citibank on July 29, 1993: "Please be advised that on 14.10.92 at 09:59 o'clock Berlin time Dresdner Bank credited the account of Behzad Hermatjou with USD 284.136,16 (USD 284.563,00 less our charges)." It is undisputed that Berlin time is six hours ahead of New York time, and that 9:59 a.m. Berlin time would be 3:59 a.m. New York time. At approximately 9 a.m. on October 14, 1992, Ms. Eyzerovich instructed Citibank to stop the transfer. When Citibank did not, this action ensued.

Article 4A of the Uniform Commercial Code ("UCC") governs electronic "funds transfers." The Official Comment to UCC § 4A–102 states that the provisions of Article 4A

> are intended to be the exclusive means of determining the rights, duties and liabilities of the affected parties in any situation covered by particular provisions of the Article. Consequently, resort to principles of law or equity outside of Article 4A is not appropriate to create rights, duties and liabilities inconsistent with those stated in this Article.

Article 4A does not include any provision for a cause of action in negligence. Thus, unless Citibank's failure to cancel Ms. Eyzerovich's transfer order was not in conformity with Article 4A, plaintiff Aleo has failed to state a cause of action, and this action must be dismissed.

UCC 4A–211(2), which governs the cancellation and amendment of payment orders, provides that

> A communication by the sender cancelling or amending a payment order is effective to cancel or amend the order if notice of the communication is received at a time and in a manner affording the receiving bank a reasonable opportunity to act on the communication before the bank accepts the payment order.

"Acceptance of Payment Order" is defined by UCC 4A–209 (2), which provides that:

> a beneficiary's bank accepts a payment order at the earliest of the following times: (a) when the bank (i) pays the beneficiary . . . or (ii) notifies the beneficiary of receipt of the order or that the account of the beneficiary has been credited with respect to the order . . .

The documentary evidence shows that Hermatjou's account was credited on October 14, 1992 at 9:59 a.m. Berlin time. Thus, as of 3:59 a.m. New York time, the Dresdner Bank "paid the beneficiary" and thereby accepted the payment order. Because this payment and acceptance occurred prior to Ms. Eyzerovich's stop transfer order at 9 a.m. on that day, according to UCC 4A–211(2), Ms. Eyzerovich's attempt to cancel the payment order was ineffective, and Citibank may not be held liable for failing to honor it.

"Summary judgment is designed to expedite all civil cases by eliminating from the Trial Calendar claims which can properly be resolved as a matter of law. . . . [W]hen there is no genuine issue to be resolved at trial, the case should be summarily decided." Andre v. Pomeroy, 35 N.Y.2d 361, 364, 362 N.Y.S.2d 131, 320 N.E.2d 853.

Accordingly, defendant's motion is granted and this action is dismissed.

## NOTES

**1.** The attractions of the wholesale wire transfer system, as regulated by Article 4A, are that it is cheap, fast and final. After LAB accepted the payment order in the hypothetical case at the beginning of the chapter by crediting Seller's account and notifying Seller of its right to withdraw, Buyer could not stop payment by canceling the payment order unless LAB agreed to do so, and then only in the four cases set out in 4A–211(c)(2). These are that the payment order was (i) unauthorized; (ii) a duplicate; (iii) made to the wrong beneficiary; or (iv) in an excessive amount. "Buyer's remorse" is not listed. Since LAB will have little incentive to antagonize its customer, Seller, by agreeing to the cancellation of the payment order and may not be sure whether any of the four events has actually occurred, it is unlikely that many beneficiary banks will agree to cancel.

**2.** A concern often expressed by banks during the process of drafting Article 4A was that a beneficiary bank might need protection against the insolvency of prior banks in the chain. If the payment order is sent through Fedwire, the beneficiary's bank is fully protected because "the message is the money," and the beneficiary's bank is paid as soon as it receives the Fedwire payment order. 4A–209(b)(2) and 4A–403(a)(1). But in most other cases, the beneficiary's bank will not receive settlement on the payment order until after it has received the order. If it turns the money over to the beneficiary as soon as it receives the credit, it faces the risk that a prior bank in the chain may suspend payments before it settles with the beneficiary bank. Some banks wanted to solve this problem by being allowed to make provisional payments to their customers that would allow the beneficiary's bank to grab back the money paid out to the beneficiary if a prior bank failed before settlement. Strong arguments were made against this view by both users of the wire transfer system and the Fed; they contended that once the beneficiary's bank had made the money available to the beneficiary, it should be able to keep it. Receiver finality should be the goal of Article 4A. The users won this argument. Section 4A–405(c) invalidates provisional payments to beneficiaries, except in case of ACH transfers (4A–405(d), Comment 3) or, with respect to CHIPS transfers, in case of a meltdown of the entire American banking system (4A–405(e)), an event that Comment 4 cheerfully assures us "should never occur."

**3.** If a beneficiary bank cannot protect itself against up-stream insolvencies by making provisional payments to its customers, what can it do to guard against this risk? Patrikis et al., Wire Transfers, Chapter 10. First, it can reject the payment order if it doubts the solvency of the sending bank. 4A–210. Second, it can notify the beneficiary that it will not be allowed to withdraw the funds until the bank receives settlement from the sender of the order. 4A–209(b)(1). Third, it can withhold the funds until an hour after the opening of business on the day after receipt, by which time, if it has not already received settlement, it must reject to avoid acceptance. 4A–209(b)(3). But the competitive pressure on beneficiary's banks to afford their customers prompt payment upon receipt of payment orders is great. This is particularly true with respect to CHIPS banks, which are in direct competition with the Fedwire system that offers beneficiaries of Fedwire payments immediate access to the incoming funds. By adoption of new rules after the completion of Article 4A, CHIPS has created a loss-sharing system that requires CHIPS banks to contribute funds to allow the system to settle for payment orders sent over the system during a given day in the event that one or more banks are unable to meet their settlement obligations. Patrikis et al., Wire Transfers, Chapter 18. The level playing field between CHIPS and Fedwire has been achieved with respect to the early release of funds to beneficiaries.

## 5. The "Money-Back Guarantee"

The general rule is that an originator owes the originator's bank the amount of the payment order when the bank accepts the payment order.

4A–402(c) (second sentence). But what if payment never reaches the beneficiary intended by the originator? That is, the "funds transfer" (4A–104(a)) is not completed. For example, the payment is made to the wrong beneficiary or not made at all. As between the originator and its bank, which should bear the risk of loss? The originator still owes the beneficiary, and, if it is liable to its bank as well, it may have to pay twice. We see that under the "money-back guarantee" rule of 4A–402(c) (last sentence), the policy decision is made that the originator is not liable to its bank, and, if it has already paid, it may recover the payment. 4A–402(d). But what if the originator designated that the transfer be made by the originator's bank through a specified intermediary bank, and it is that bank that is at fault or doesn't send the payment because it has suspended payments? The originator's bank is required by 4A–302 to follow the originator's instructions with respect to intermediary banks. See 4A–402(e). The following case is the first authoritative holding on these matters.

# Grain Traders, Inc. v. Citibank, N.A.

United States Court of Appeals, Second Circuit, 1998.
160 F.3d 97.

■ JOHN M. WALKER, JR., CIRCUIT JUDGE.

Plaintiff Grain Traders, Inc., ("Grain Traders") appeals from the April 16, 1997, judgment granting summary judgment for defendant Citibank, N.A., ("Citibank") and dismissing Grain Traders's diversity action brought under Article 4A of New York's Uniform Commercial Code ("Article 4A") and principles of common law seeking a refund from Citibank for an alleged uncompleted electronic funds transfer.

## BACKGROUND

Grain Traders, in order to make a payment of $310,000 to Claudio Goidanich Kraemer ("Kraemer"), initiated a funds transfer on December 22, 1994, by issuing a payment order to its bank, Banco de Credito Nacional ("BCN"), that stated

WE HEREBY AUTHORIZE YOU DEBIT OUR ACCOUNT NR. 509364 FOR THE AMOUNT OF US $310,000.00 AND TRANSFER TO:

BANQUE DU CREDIT ET INVESTISSEMENT LTD. ACCOUNT 36013997 AT CITIBANK NEW YORK IN FAVOUR OF BANCO EXTRADER S.A. ACCOUNT NR. 30114—BENEFICIARY CLAUDIO GOIDANICH KRAEMER—UNDER FAX ADVISE TO BANCO EXTRADER NR. 00541– 318 0057/318–0184 AT. DISTEFANO/M. FLIGUEIRA.

Thus the transfer, as instructed by Grain Traders, required BCN to debit Grain Traders's account at BCN in the amount of $310,000, and then to issue a payment order to Citibank. That payment order, in turn, was to require Citibank to debit $310,000 from BCN's account at Citibank and to credit that amount to the account that Banque du Credit et Investissement Ltd. ("BCIL") maintained at Citibank. Citibank, in turn, was to issue a payment order to BCIL instructing it to transfer, by unspecified means, $310,000 to Banco Extrader, S.A. ("Extrader"). Extrader was then to credit the $310,000 to the account maintained at Extrader by Kraemer.

BCN duly carried out Grain Traders's instructions. Citibank, in turn, executed BCN's payment order by debiting $310,000 from BCN's account at Citibank, crediting that amount to BCIL's account at Citibank, and issuing a payment order to BCIL concerning the further transfers.

Both BCIL and Extrader suspended payments at some point after Citibank executed the payment order. BCIL apparently began closing its offices on December 31, 1994, and its banking license was revoked in July of 1995. Similarly, Extrader became insolvent sometime in late December of 1994 or early January of 1995. On December 28, 1994, apparently at Grain Traders's request, BCN contacted Citibank and requested cancellation of its payment order and return of the amount of the payment order. The message sent by BCN stated:

REGARDING OUR PAYMENT ORDER FROM 12/22/94 FOR USD 310,000 TO BANCO EXTRADER S.A. ACCT. NO. 30114 F/O BANQUE DE CREDIT ET INVESTISSEMENT LTD. ACCT NO. 36013997 F/C TO CLAUDIO GOLDANICH [SIC] KRAEMER. PLEASE NOTE THAT WE ARE REQUESTING FUNDS BACK AS SOON AS POSSIBLE.

YOUR IMMEDIATE ATTENTION TO THIS MATTER IS APPRECIATED.

Citibank sought authorization from BCIL to debit the amount that had been credited to its account on December 22, 1994, and, after several unsuccessful attempts to contact BCIL, received a message on January 3, 1995, from BCIL that purportedly authorized the debit. Citibank asserts that it was at this juncture that it determined that BCIL had exceeded its credit limitations and placed the account on a "debit no-post" status, meaning no further debits would be posted to the account. Citibank refused BCN's request to cancel the payment order, stating:

RE: YOUR PAYMENT [ORDER] . . . WE ARE UNABLE TO RETURN FUNDS AS BNF [SIC] BANK HAS AN INSUFFICIENT BALANCE IN THEIR ACCOUNT. FOR FURTHER INFORMATION WE SUGGEST THAT YOU CONTACT THEM DIRECTLY. WE CLOSE OUR FILE.

In November of 1995, Grain Traders filed this action seeking a refund from Citibank pursuant to U.C.C. §§ 4A–402(d), 4A–209, 4A–301, 4A–305, and 1–203, as well as common law theories of conversion and money had and received. Grain Traders alleges that the transfer was never completed—i.e., Extrader never credited Kraemer's account for the $310,000. Grain Traders further claims that the reason the transfer was not completed was because Citibank had already placed BCIL's account on a "hold for funds" status before it credited the $310,000 intended for Kraemer to BCIL's account. By making the credit to BCIL's allegedly frozen account, Grain Traders contends, Citibank improperly used the funds to offset BCIL's indebtedness to it and prevented BCIL from withdrawing the funds to complete the transfer.

Grain Traders moved for summary judgment on its Article 4A claim. Citibank cross-moved for summary judgment on the grounds that Grain Traders had failed to state a claim under Article 4A, could not establish its common law claims, and that its common law claims were, in any event, pre-empted by Article 4A. The district court denied summary judgment to Grain Traders and granted summary judgment in favor of Citibank. Grain Traders now appeals.

## DISCUSSION

In its opinion, the district court held that (1) Section 402 of Article 4A established a cause of action only by a sender against its receiving bank, thus Grain Traders, who was a sender only with respect to BCN, had sued the wrong bank; (2) Sections 4A–209, 4A–301, 4A–305, and 1–203 of the U.C.C. did not create causes of action; and (3) Grain Traders could not establish elements necessary to its common law claims of conversion and money had and received. See Grain Traders, Inc. v. Citibank, N.A., 960 F.Supp. 784, 789, 792–93 (S.D.N.Y.1997). The district court did not reach Citibank's argument that the common law claims were pre-empted by Article 4A. Id. at 793 n. 8. On appeal, Grain Traders argues that the district court erred in dismissing its claim under § 4–A–402 and its common law claims. * * * Grain Traders does not appeal the dismissal of its claims under Sections 4A–209, 4A–301, 4A–305, and 1–203 of the U.C.C., and thus these claims are not a subject of this opinion. For the following reasons, we affirm the district court's judgment.

* * *

## II.  Article 4A Claims

Article 4A of the U.C.C. governs the procedures, rights, and liabilities arising out of commercial electronic funds transfers. A funds transfer is defined as a

> series of transactions, beginning with the originator's payment order [and] includes any payment order issued by the originator's bank or an intermediary bank intended to carry out the originator's payment order.

§ 4A–104(a). A "payment order" is defined as

> an instruction of a sender to a receiving bank . . . to pay, or to cause another bank to pay, a fixed or determinable amount of money [where] the receiving bank is to be reimbursed by debiting an account of, or otherwise receiving payment from, the sender, and . . . the instruction is transmitted by the sender directly to the receiving bank.

§ 4A–103(a)(1). Thus, as noted by the district court, "funds are 'transferred' through a series of debits and credits to a series of bank accounts." Grain Traders, 960 F.Supp. at 788. A "sender" is defined as "the person giving the instruction [directly] to the receiving bank," and a "receiving bank" is defined as "the bank to which the sender's instruction is addressed." There are other defined roles in a given funds transfer for the senders, receiving banks, or other participants, including the "originator" of the funds transfer (here Grain Traders), the "originator's bank" (here BCN), the "beneficiary" (here Kraemer) and the "beneficiary's bank" (here Extrader). For any given funds transfer, there can be only one originator, originator's bank, beneficiary, and beneficiary's bank, but there can be several senders and receiving banks, one of each for every payment order required to complete the funds transfer. See § 4A–103.

### A.   Grain traders's refund claim under § 4A–402

Section 4A–402 ("Section 402") covers the obligation of a sender of a payment order to make payment to the receiving bank after the order has been accepted as well as the obligation of a receiving bank to refund payment in the event the transfer is not completed. It provides, in relevant part,

> (c) . . . With respect to a payment order issued to a receiving bank other than the beneficiary's bank, acceptance of the order by the receiving bank obliges the sender to pay the bank the amount of the sender's order. . . . The obligation of that sender to pay its payment order is excused if the funds transfer is not completed. . . .

> (d) If the sender of a payment order pays the order and was not obliged to pay all or part of the amount paid [because the funds transfer was not completed], the bank receiving payment is obliged to refund payment to the extent the sender was not obliged to pay.

§ 4A–402(c), (d). Thus, under Section 402(c), the sender's obligation to pay the receiving bank is excused in the event that the transfer is not completed. If payment has already been made, a sender can seek a refund from the bank it paid under Section 402(d). It was this so-called "money-back guarantee" provision that Grain Traders invoked to obtain a refund from Citibank.

The district court held that Grain Traders's refund action against Citibank, an intermediary bank for the purposes of Grain Traders's funds transfer, was barred because a Section 402 refund action could only be maintained by a "sender" against the receiving bank to whom the sender had issued a payment order and whom the sender had paid. Thus, because Grain Traders was a "sender" only with respect to the payment order it issued to BCN, Grain Traders could look only to BCN, the receiving bank, for a refund.

In reaching its conclusion, the district court relied on the plain language of Section 402(d) as well as other provisions of Article 4A. It found that the language of Section 402(d) establishes a right of refund only between a sender and the receiving bank it paid. BCN, not Grain Traders, was the sender that issued the payment order to Citibank and paid Citibank by having its account debited in the amount of $310,000. Grain Traders argues that the fact that Section 402(d) does not use the words "receiving bank" but instead refers to "the bank receiving payment" means that the sender can sue any bank in the chain that received payment. We agree with Citibank that because the words "receiving bank" are defined as the bank that receives a payment order, Section 402(d)'s use of the words "bank receiving payment" simply clarifies that the right to a refund arises only after the sender has satisfied its obligation to pay the receiving bank.

The Official Comment to § 4A–402 supports this interpretation. It states, in relevant part:

> [t]he money-back guarantee [of § 4A–402(d)] is particularly important to Originator if noncompletion of the funds transfer is due to the fault of an intermediary bank rather than Bank A [the Originator's bank]. *In that case Bank A must refund payment to Originator, and Bank A has the burden of obtaining refund from the intermediary bank that it paid.*

§ 4A–402, cmt. 2 (emphasis added). We think this comment makes plain the intent of the Article 4A drafters to effect an orderly unraveling of a funds transfer in the event that the transfer was not completed, and accomplished this by incorporating a "privity" requirement into the "money back guarantee" provision so that it applies only between the parties to a particular payment order and not to the parties to the funds transfer as a whole.

The district court also relied on the express right of subrogation created by Section 402(5), which applies when one of the receiving banks is unable to issue a refund because it has suspended payments. Section 402(5) provides that:

> If a funds transfer is not completed as stated in subsection (3) and an intermediary bank is obliged to refund payment as stated in subsection (4) but is unable to do so because not permitted by applicable law or because the bank suspends payments, a sender in the funds transfer that executed a payment order in compliance with an instruction, as stated in [§ 4–A–302(1)(a)] to route the funds transfer through that intermediary bank is entitled to receive or retain payment from the sender of the payment order that it accepted. The first sender in the funds transfer that issued an instruction requiring routing through that intermediary bank is subrogated to the right of the bank that paid the intermediary bank to refund as stated in subsection (4).

Where a right to refund has been triggered because a transfer was not completed, but one of the banks that received payment is unable to issue a refund because it has suspended payments, the orderly unraveling of the transfer is prevented and the risk of loss will be borne by some party to the transfer. Article 4–A allocates that risk of loss to the party that first designated the failed bank to be used in the transfer. *See* N.Y.U.C.C. § 4–A–402, cmt. 2 (where "Bank A [the sender] was required to issue its payment order to Bank C [the insolvent bank] because Bank C was designated as an intermediary bank by Originator[,] . . . . Originator takes the risk of insolvency of Bank C"). Under Section 402(5), all intervening senders are entitled to receive and retain payment and the party that designated the failed bank bears the burden of recovery by being subrogated to the right of the sender that paid the failed bank. We agree with the district court that

> the subrogation language of § 4–A–402(5) demonstrates that the originator does not, as a general matter, have a right to sue all the parties to a funds transfer.... [and] makes clear ... that under § 4–A–402(4) no right to a refund otherwise exists between the originator and an intermediary bank. This is evident because there would be no need for the subrogation language of subsection (5) if the originator (as the first sender) already had a right to assert a refund claim directly against all intermediary banks.

960 F.Supp. at 790.

In sum, we agree with the district court's thoughtful analysis and conclude that § 4A–402 allows each sender of a payment order to seek refund only from the receiving bank it paid. Not only do the provisions of Article 4A support the district court's interpretation, there are sound policy reasons for limiting the right to seek a refund to the sender who directly paid the receiving bank. One of Article 4A's primary goals is to promote certainty and finality so that "the various parties to funds transfers [will] be able to predict risk with certainty, to insure against risk, to adjust operational and security procedures, and to price funds transfer services appropriately." § 4A–102, cmt. To allow a party to, in effect, skip over the bank with which it dealt directly, and go to the next bank in the chain would result in uncertainty as to rights and liabilities, would create a risk of multiple or inconsistent liabilities, and would require intermediary banks to investigate the financial circumstances and various legal relations of the other parties to the transfer. These are matters as to which an intermediary bank ordinarily should not have to be concerned and, if it were otherwise, would impede the use of rapid electronic funds transfers in commerce by causing delays and driving up costs. Accordingly, we affirm the district court's dismissal of Grain Traders's refund claim under Section 402(4).

### B. Common Law Claims

The district court also granted summary judgment to Citibank on Grain Traders's common law claims for conversion and money had and received, finding that Grain Traders could not establish essential elements of those claims. We do not address the district court's holding, however, because we agree with Citibank's argument, raised below but not reached by the district court, that even assuming Grain Traders could establish its claims, they are precluded by Article 4A.

Whether and to what extent Article 4A precludes common law actions is a matter of first impression for this court. Article 4A was enacted to correct the perceived inadequacy of " 'attempt[ing] to define rights and obligations in funds transfers by general principles [of common law] or by analogy to rights and obligations in negotiable instruments law or the law of check collection.' " Banque Worms v. BankAmerica Int'l, 77 N.Y.2d 362,

369, 568 N.Y.S.2d 541, 570 N.E.2d 189 (1991) (quoting Official Comment to § 4A–102). The Official Comment to Section 4A–102 states that the provisions of Article 4A represent a careful and delicate balancing of [competing] interests and are intended to be the exclusive means of determining the rights, duties, and liabilities of the affected parties in any situation covered by particular provisions of the Article. Consequently, resort to principles of law or equity outside of Article 4A is not appropriate to create rights, duties and liabilities inconsistent with those stated in this Article.

Similarly, Section 4A–212 states, in relevant part,

[l]iability based on acceptance arises only when acceptance occurs as stated in Section 4A–209, and liability is limited to that provided in this Article. A receiving bank is not the agent of the sender or beneficiary of the payment order it accepts, or of any other party to the funds transfer, and the bank owes no duty to any party to the funds transfer except as provided in this article or by express agreement.

We agree with those courts that have interpreted the above language to preclude common law claims when such claims would impose liability inconsistent with the rights and liabilities expressly created by Article 4 A. See, e.g., Banco de la Provincia de Buenos Aires v. BayBank Boston N.A., 985 F.Supp. 364, 369–70 (S.D.N.Y.1997) (for conversion claim to stand, it cannot be inconsistent with Article 4A); Centre–Point Merchant Bank Ltd. v. American Express Bank Ltd., 913 F.Supp. 202, 206 (S.D.N.Y.1996) (exclusivity of Article 4A is restricted to any situation covered by particular provisions of the Article and resort to common law must not be inconsistent); Sheerbonnet, Ltd. v. American Express Bank, Ltd., 951 F.Supp. 403, 407–08 (S.D.N.Y.1995) (same); see also Cumis Ins. Soc., Inc. v. Citibank, N.A., 921 F.Supp. 1100, 1110 (S.D.N.Y.1996) (claim for conversion failed because bank's actions expressly authorized by Article 4A); Aleo International, Ltd. v. Citibank, N.A., 160 Misc.2d 950, 612 N.Y.S.2d 540, 541 (Sup. Ct. 1994) (no claim for negligence unless conduct complained of was not in conformity with Article 4A). Because we determine that the liability sought to be imposed by Grain Traders's common law claims would be inconsistent with the provisions of Article 4A, we do not reach the issue of whether common law claims that concern matters expressly addressed by Article 4A would be precluded as duplicative even if consistent. See, e.g., Centre–Point, 913 F.Supp. at 208 (dismissing common law claims because "specific Article 4A provisions" applied to the transactions at issue).

\* \* \*

## CONCLUSION

We hold that Section 402 of Article 4A imposes a privity requirement such that a sender seeking a refund for an uncompleted funds transfer may look only to the receiving bank to whom it issued a payment order and payment. As a result, Grain Traders may look only to BCN for a refund. We also hold that Grain Traders's common law claims are precluded because they seek to impose liability on Citibank that would be inconsistent with the provisions of Article 4A.

The judgment of the district court is affirmed.

## NOTES

**1.**  The court refers to 4A–402(e) but does not discuss whether it applies to this case. That provision would deprive Grain Traders of its right to recover from BCN and grant Grain Traders, by subrogation, Citibank's right to recover from BCIL. See the last paragraph of Comment 2. Perhaps the court viewed 4A–402(e) as irrelevant to the issue before the court, Grain Traders' right to recover from Citibank. The district court addressed the question of the applicability of 4A–402(e) and concluded that it could not decide the matter because the record was unclear on whether BCIL had suspended payments. 960 F.Supp. at 791.

**2.**  The issue of the degree to which Article 4A displaces common law principles has perhaps been the most widely litigated issue in funds transfer cases. Section 1–103(b) allows courts to invoke principles of law and equity to "supplement" the provisions of the Code, unless "displaced by the particular provisions of this [Act]." Anyone who has participated as a drafter of UCC provisions becomes familiar with the persistent gripe of advisors that something more specific than 1–103(b) should be drafted to deter courts from ignoring the Code provisions that the courts don't like in favor of judicial remedies such as restitution, negligence, money had and received, and the like, that empower courts to reach results more in keeping with their notions of justice. This is particularly true in cases involving consumers. But there are no consumers affected by Article 4A; funds transfers amount to more than a trillion dollars a day. Hence, the final draft was a series of compromises made among powerful, well represented interests (money center banks, Board of Governors of Federal Reserve System, the New York Federal Reserve Bank, and giant corporate users, e.g., Exxon, General Motors), and these behemoths wanted some assurance that the bargained-for advantages that Article 4A gave them would not be taken away from them by courts using common law principles to change the intended meaning of the statute.

The result was the inclusion of Comment to 4A–102, quoted in part in *Grain Traders*. The plea by the drafters made in this Comment is that Article 4A is the result of long years of hard bargaining, and the final draft is a good faith attempt to balance the various competing interests. It will come as no surprise to learn that the success of this Comment in taking the pen out of the judge's hand in order to expand Article 4A's displacement of the common law has been spotty. Some commentators see it as manifesting a touch of hubris on the part of the drafters. Some courts believe that common law principles can be applied in wire transfer cases so long as they are not "inconsistent" with specific Article 4A provisions. The case law is fully analyzed in 2 Clark & Clark, Law of Bank Deposits, Collections and Credit Cards & 17.02[3] (Rev. ed. 2005). The authors conclude a long discussion by observing rather generously, in our view: "In all of these cases, the courts appeared to hold that (1) Article 4A does not preempt common law causes of action in all cases, but that (2) preemption will be determined in each case by the extent to which the rules of Article 4A occupy the field covered by the particular common law cause of action." The drafters did not expect more.

## 6. ERRONEOUS EXECUTION OF PAYMENT ORDERS

### a. SENDING BANK'S ERRORS

A fertile field of litigation with respect to wire transfers is the case in which the receiving bank executes the sender's payment order by sending an erroneous payment order. In such cases the general principle adhered to by Article 4A is that the sender is liable for its own errors. The subject is discussed in Richard F. Dole, Jr., Receiving Bank Liability for Errors in Wholesale Wire Transfers, 69 Tul. L. Rev. 877 (1995).

For illustration, assume these facts. Originator (O) instructs its bank, Originator's Bank (OB), to send $100,000 to the account of Beneficiary (B) in Beneficiary's Bank (BB). OB executed O's payment order by instructing its correspondent bank, Intermediary Bank (IB) (4A–104(b)), to pay BB as indicated in the cases below. With respect to the payment order, O, OB and IB are senders and OB, IB and BB are receiving banks, and BB is also the beneficiary's bank. Thus, the funds transfer looks like this:

O———OB———IB———BB———B

Work through these elementary problems:

Case #1. OB executed the payment order by instructing IB to pay BB $100,000 for the account of B. IB mistakenly instructed BB to pay $100,000 for the account of X.

    a.   Did IB execute the payment order of OB? 4A–301(a).

    b.   Is OB entitled to payment from O? 4A–402(c).

    c.   Is IB entitled to payment from OB? 4A–402(c).

    d.   Is BB entitled to payment from IB? 4A–402(b).

    e.   Is IB entitled to recover from X? 4A–303(c).

Case #2. OB mistakenly instructed IB to pay BB $200,000 for B's account. IB executed OB's payment order by sending the same payment order to BB. BB deposited the funds in B's account and B withdrew the money. What are OB's rights against O and B under 4A–303(a)?

### b. DISCHARGE–FOR–VALUE RULE

Obligor instructed Bank A to pay $100,000 to Bank B for the account of X. Bank A mistakenly instructed Bank B to pay $100,000 for the account of Y. If Obligor owed a debt to Y in an amount in excess of $100,000, Y may claim that it is entitled to retain the funds under the discharge-for-value rule of the Restatement of Restitution § 14, under which a creditor is under no duty to make restitution even though the third party sent the money by mistake, so long as the creditor had no notice that the payment order was erroneously made. Some courts decline to follow the rule and hold that the money can be retained only if the recipient changed its position in reliance on the mistaken payment. The court in Banque Worms v. BankAmerica International, 568 N.Y.S.2d 541, 570 N.E.2d 189 (N.Y. Ct. App. 1991), adopted the discharge-for-value rule in a funds transfer transaction that went awry. Although the facts in that case occurred before enactment of Article 4A, the court viewed the rule as consistent with the policies of Article 4A. The court relied on Comment 2 to 4A–303 as showing that the drafters of Article 4A thought the discharge-for-value rule was appropriate in an analogous situation involving an erroneous payment order.

Finality of payment and the low cost of funds transfers are policy considerations that the *Banque Worms* court found support the discharge-for-value rule. Cf. Credit Lyonnais New York Branch v. Koval, 745 So.2d 837 (Miss.1999) (finality); General Electric Capital Corp. v. Central Bank, 49 F.3d 280 (7th Cir.1995) (finality and efficiency). Clearly, finality favors the rule. A beneficiary-creditor receiving funds can retain them as long as it received the funds without knowing or having notice that the payment was a mistake. Because detrimental reliance by the beneficiary is unnecessary, there are fewer occasions in which the transfer of funds will be disturbed than under a "mistake of fact" rule. In fact, finality favors allowing the recipient of a mistaken payment to keep it even if the recipient knew of the mistake.

Whether the discharge-for-value rule optimally lowers the cost of funds transfers compared to the "mistake of fact" rule is a closer question. A receiving bank issuing a payment order faces a risk that its sender will be unwilling or unable to reimburse it for the amount of the order. Both rules allocate this credit risk as between the receiving bank and the beneficiary, but they do so differently. The discharge-for-value rule increases the credit risk to the receiving bank as compared to the "mistake of fact" rule because there are fewer circumstances in which it can recover the funds from the beneficiary. Given this risk, the receiving bank can take precautions to avoid making mistaken payments or simply increase the price of executing a payment order. The "mistake of fact" rule shifts the receiving bank's credit risk to the beneficiary when the beneficiary does not detrimentally rely on the mistaken payment. This increases the cost to the beneficiary of dealing with the sender, and the increased cost presumably will be reflected in the price the beneficiary demands from it. The discharge-for-value rule optimally lowers the cost of funds transfers only if the marginal costs to the receiving bank associated with the rule are less than the marginal costs to the beneficiary associated with the "mistake of fact" rule. In estimating these costs, it is significant that the beneficiary in *Banque Worms* was a creditor who had entered into a revolving loan arrangement with the sender-debtor. Such arrangements almost always require the creditor to monitor its debtor. If so, the marginal costs to the beneficiary-creditor of detecting a mistaken payment might be slight.

The following case is a common fact situation and presents a detailed analysis of how courts apply the discharge-for-value doctrine.

# In re Calumet Farm, Inc.

United States Court of Appeals, Sixth Circuit, 2005.
398 F.3d 555.

■ GILMAN, CIRCUIT JUDGE.

This case arises out of a botched electronic wire transfer from Calumet Farm, Inc. to Peter M. Brant and White Birch Farm, Inc. (collectively, White Birch). On Friday, March 8, 1991, Calumet initiated the wire transfer of $77,301.58 by a payment order to its bank, First National Bank & Trust Company. This amount was calculated by Calumet as a payment of interest on its outstanding debt of over $1 million due to White Birch. When Calumet received written confirmation of the wire transfer from First National on the following Monday, March 11, 1991, it learned that $770,301.58, rather than $77,301.58, had mistakenly been transferred. White Birch refused to return the additional $693,000, and Calumet subsequently declared bankruptcy.

First National is now seeking restitution from White Birch for the excess payment. Both the bankruptcy court and district court ruled in favor of White Birch. The key issue on appeal is whether White Birch established the elements of the "discharge-for-value" defense to First National's restitution claim. For the reasons set forth below, we REVERSE the judgment of the district court and REMAND the case for the entry of judgment in favor of First National.

## I.  BACKGROUND

Most of the facts of this case were previously set forth by this court in *In re Calumet Farm, Inc.*, No. 95–5953, 1997 WL 253278, at *1–2 (6th Cir. May 14, 1997) (unpublished), as follows:

> White Birch is a thoroughbred horse farm in Connecticut owned by Peter Brant. In 1986, Calumet purchased a one-half interest in the thoroughbred stallion Mogambo from White Birch and executed a $6,500,000 promissory note ("the Mogambo note") evidencing the obligation. On October 31, 1990, Calumet defaulted in making its annual principal payment of [$1,300,000] on the debt. Brant and J.T. Lundy, president of Calumet, reached an agreement whereby Calumet would make the payment on or before March 15, 1991. Calumet also defaulted in making several intervening interest payments and, as of March 7, 1991, owed White Birch approximately $103,057.50 in interest and penalties.

> On March 8, 1991, Lundy instructed Calumet's bookkeeper, Angela Holleran [properly, "Hollearn"], to pay the interest due to White

Birch as of January 31, 1991, amounting to $77,301.58. Holleran thereupon called First National to arrange payment by wire transfer, and also called White Birch to inform it that a wire transfer payment was forthcoming; however, the substance of these conversations is disputed as to the amount that White Birch was to receive. The wire transfer, referenced as "MOGAMBO INT," was made to White Birch's account at Citibank in New York on March 8, 1991.

On March 11, 1991, Holleran received written confirmation of the wire transfer from First National and realized that $770,301.58, rather than $77,301.58, had been transferred. Holleran notified First National of the mistake and First National contacted Citibank to request reversal of the wire transfer. Because the money already had been credited to White Birch's account, Citibank refused to reverse the wire transfer. Thereafter, First National requested that Brant return the additional $693,000 erroneously transferred to him, but Brant refused to return the money unless First National acknowledged in writing that it had made the error in transferring the funds. * * *

In resolving cross-motions for summary judgment, the bankruptcy court determined on remand that there was insufficient evidence in the record to support a finding that White Birch had notice of the error in the amount transferred before the funds were credited to its account at Citibank. It therefore held that White Birch had satisfied the required elements of the discharge-for-value defense to First National's restitution claim. Accordingly, the bankruptcy court granted summary judgment in favor of White Birch and denied the cross-motion filed by First National. In March of 2003, the district court affirmed both determinations. First National now appeals, claiming that the lower courts failed to properly interpret and apply the discharge-for-value defense asserted by White Birch.

## II.  ANALYSIS

* * *

### B.  The discharge-for-value defense

In its earlier opinion, this court held that First National had standing to assert a claim for restitution under U.C.C. § 4A–303(a) (enacted as § 355.4A–303(1) of the Kentucky Revised Statutes and incorporated into Federal Reserve Regulation J, 12 C.F.R. §§ 210.25–31, which governs funds transfers). Section 4A–303(a) provides as follows:

> A receiving bank that (i) executes the payment order of the sender by issuing a payment order in an amount greater than the amount of the sender's order . . . is entitled to payment of the amount of the sender's order under Section 4A–402(c) if that subsection is otherwise satisfied. The bank is entitled to recover from the beneficiary of the erroneous order the excess payment received to the extent allowed by the law governing mistake and restitution.

This provision authorizes a bank to seek restitution from the beneficiary of the excess payment if the bank committed an error in executing the payment order. In the prior opinion, this court noted that § 4A–303(a) incorporates the discharge-for-value defense. 1997 WL 253278, at *4. The Restatement of Restitution defines the discharge-for-value defense as follows:

> A creditor of another or one having a lien on another's property who has received from a third person any benefit in discharge of the debt or lien, is under no duty to make restitution therefor, although the discharge was given by mistake of the transferor as to his interests or duties, *if the transferee* made no misrepresentation and *did not have notice of the transferor's mistake.*

Restatement of Restitution § 14(1) (emphasis added). Thus, when a creditor receives what appears to be a payment on a debt from someone other than the debtor, the creditor becomes a bona fide purchaser and may keep the mistaken payment if the creditor discharges the obligation of its debtor prior to becoming aware of the mistake.

Section 14(1) of the Restatement, however, does not specify the point in time by which notice of the mistake must be received. Nor did this court's prior opinion in the present case address the issue. And the two other appellate courts that have concluded that the discharge-for-value rule applies to wire transfers also failed to focus on the timing question. *See General Elec. Capital Corp. v. Central Bank*, 49 F.3d 280, 284 (7th Cir. 1995) (*GECC*); *Banque Worms v. BankAmerica Int'l*, 77 N.Y.2d 362, 568 N.Y.S.2d 541, 570 N.E.2d 189, 196 (1991).

Isolated language in both of the above cases, however, indicates that the notice must occur before the funds arrive. *See GECC*, 49 F.3d at 284 (holding that "a creditor should be able to treat funds credited in apparent payment of a debt as irrevocably his, unless news of the error precedes arrival of the funds"); *Banque Worms*, 568 N.Y.S.2d 541, 570 N.E.2d at 196 (explaining that "[w]hen a beneficiary receives money to which it is entitled and has no knowledge that the money was erroneously wired, the beneficiary should not have to wonder whether it may retain the funds; rather, such a beneficiary should be able to consider the transfer of funds as a final and complete transaction, not subject to revocation"). But the question in each case (as in this court's prior decision) was *whether* the discharge-for-value rule applies in this setting, not *how* it applies. Nor, at any rate, does the quoted language squarely address the point. In a wire transfer setting, is the relevant event when the beneficiary's bank receives the money, or when the beneficiary learns that the money is in its account, or when the beneficiary credits the money to the debtor's account? Neither this court's prior decision, *GECC*, nor *Banque Worms* purports to consider the question, much less answer it.

Traditionally, the U.C.C. provides that payment in discharge of an obligation occurs under the first option—"at the time a payment order for the benefit of the beneficiary is accepted by the beneficiary's bank in the funds transfer." U.C.C. § 4A–406(a). But this approach does not square with the notice exception to the discharge-for-value rule. Application of this U.C.C. definition of discharge would mean that the entity that must receive notice (here White Birch) is an entity other than the entity to whom the funds were wired (here Citibank). To divide the "receipt of payment" and "notice of error" elements between different entities makes little sense and at any rate is a recipe for reading the notice exception out of the rule.

Equally unpersuasive is the argument that the discharge-triggering event necessarily occurs only when the beneficiary has actual notice that funds have been placed in its account. Such notice may not connect the funds to a given debtor or to the size of the debtor's outstanding obligation. Furthermore, while actual notice of a mistake may of course be independently disclosed by the originator to the beneficiary, constructive notice of a mistake may also occur simply as a result of the size of the transfer when considered in connection with the name of the originator. In this case, for example, White Birch assuredly would have had constructive notice of the mistake if the transfer had been, say, for $7.7 million—if, in other words, First National had made a two-digit error rather than a one-digit error in transmitting Calumet's payment order. Any sensible application of the discharge-for-value rule in this unique setting must account for constructive as well as actual notice of a mistake.

That leaves what seems to us to be the most desirable option—that the discharge-for-value defense will apply unless the beneficiary receives notice of a mistake before the beneficiary of the transfer credits the debtor's account. In addition to aligning the entity that receives notice of any mistake with the entity that receives the payment, and permitting constructive notice to trigger the rule, this approach is consistent with one of the underlying principles of the discharge-for-value rule; namely, that the creditor has given value for the mistaken payment. Nor, despite White Birch's suggestion to the contrary, will this approach undermine the discharge-for-value rule on the theory that the rule will kick in only after the beneficiary on its own terms makes an accounting of how the transfer should be credited. The time value of money being what it is, most commercial recipients of such transfers can be counted on to promptly credit the debtor's account. As in most settings, at any rate, the rule applies only to commercially reasonable accountings. * * *

Both the bankruptcy court and the district court, in taking up the case on remand, erred in focusing on when White Birch *received the funds* rather than on when White Birch *credited Calumet's account*. In doing so, both courts effectively wrote out the element of "discharge" from the discharge-for-value defense. The undisputed record shows that White Birch did not credit the funds to Calumet's account until the afternoon of March 11, 1991. First National offered the testimony of Calumet employee Angela Hollearn to prove that White Birch was aware well before then that Calumet had intended to wire only $77,301.58 to White Birch for the payment of accrued interest. The bankruptcy court ruled against First National on the basis that Hollearn's testimony was equivocal on the issue of to whom she spoke and what was said on March 8, 1991 when she allegedly conveyed to White Birch the fact that a wire transfer had been sent, the amount of the transfer, and how that amount had been calculated.

The district court likewise dismissed Hollearn's testimony on this point as too speculative. It therefore determined that First National had not established that White Birch had notice of the error before receiving the funds. Without deciding whether the lower courts erred in excluding the disputed testimony as a matter of law, *see M.B.A.F.B. Federal Credit Union v. Cumis Ins. Soc'y, Inc.*, 681 F.2d 930, 932 (4th Cir.1982) (holding that a witness's testimony was admissible even though the witness admitted that it was only "possible" that he or his attorney had made certain statements), we note that there is no dispute that Hollearn notified White Birch of the error on the morning of March 11, 1991.

Furthermore, White Birch's behavior establishes that it was aware of the error as soon as it was informed of the wire transfer by its own bank. When White Birch discovered on the morning of March 11, 1991 that Citibank had credited its account for $770,301.58, it immediately transferred the additional $693,000 to Brant's personal account at Citibank, ostensibly so that "everything could be sorted out." It did not apply that amount to reduce Calumet's debt on the Mogambo note until later that day. If White Birch did not know or at least suspect that it had erroneously received the additional funds, it would have had no reason to segregate them into its owner's personal account. The fact that it segregated the precise amount of the overage, moreover, is strong evidence that White Birch knew exactly how much it was supposed to receive from Calumet. Even the wire transfer itself, after all, was referenced as "MOGAMBO INT." (Emphasis added.)

Thus, even if the bankruptcy court and district court correctly determined that White Birch did not have notice of the error before receiving the funds, White Birch certainly had notice before crediting Calumet's account. We therefore hold as a matter of law that White Birch had prior notice of the mistake in the funds transfer for purposes of the discharge-for-value rule and cannot avail itself of that defense. First National is therefore entitled to restitution from White Birch. * * *

### III.  CONCLUSION

For all of the reasons set forth above, we **REVERSE** the judgment of the district court and **REMAND** the case for the entry of judgment in favor of First National.

## 7.  FAILURE OF RECEIVING BANK TO EXECUTE PAYMENT ORDER

Since payments of obligations in very large transactions are made through the funds transfer system, the potential for large consequential damages to flow from a receiving bank's failure to execute a payment order is great. One of the major policy decisions to be resolved in the drafting of Article 4A was whether receiving banks should be liable for consequential damages for failure to execute payment orders. Banking advisors saw this decision as crucial for their industry: they contended that they could not continue to offer cheap and fast service all over the world if they bore the risk of unlimited liability for consequential damages; imposition of such liability would force them to recast their industry in a form very different from the robust and flourishing enterprise it was at the time Article 4A was drafted. They relied for support of their position on the decision in Evra Corp. v. Swiss Bank Corp., 673 F.2d 951 (7th Cir. 1982).

In *Evra* Hyman–Michaels chartered a ship, the Pandora, from the ship's Owner under an agreement to make semi-monthly payments for hire in advance. If a payment was late, Owner could cancel the charter. Payments were to be made by deposit in the Banque de Paris in Geneva for the account of Owner. With the intention of making a periodic payment, Hyman–Michaels (Originator) issued a payment order to Continental (Chicago) to pay $27,000 to Banque de Paris in Geneva for the account of Owner. Continental (Chicago) executed the order by issuing a payment order to Continental (London) and debited the account of Hyman–Michaels in the amount of the order. Continental (London) executed the payment order of Continental (Chicago) by issuing a payment order to Swiss Bank in Geneva. Swiss Bank was instructed to issue a payment order to Banque de Paris to complete the funds transfer, but, for unknown reasons, failed to do so. Market conditions changed after the ship was chartered, and the hire payments required by the ship charter were below market rates. Because the beneficiary did not receive timely payment, Originator lost a valuable ship charter. The lower court awarded the Originator $2.1 million for lost profits even though the amount of the payment order was only $27,000. The appellate court reversed, in part on the basis of the common law rule of *Hadley v. Baxendale* that consequential damages may not be awarded unless the defendant is put on notice of the special circumstances giving rise to them. Swiss Bank did not have enough information to infer that if it lost a $27,000 payment order it would face liability in excess of $2 million.

## PROBLEMS

**1.** How would this case be decided under Article 4A? Under Article 4A Hyman–Michaels is the originator of the funds transfer, Continental (Chicago) is the originator's bank, and Continental (London) and Swiss Bank are both "intermediary banks" (4A–104(b)). Each of the three banks is also a receiving bank with respect to the payment order it received. The duty of a receiving bank with respect to a payment order that it receives is stated in 4A–212. The duty of a receiving bank in executing a payment order is stated in 4A–302. The extent of liability of a receiving bank for late or improper execution or for failure to execute a payment order is stated in 4A–305. The right of the originator or other sender of a payment order to refund of amounts paid by them if the funds transfer is not completed is stated in 4A–402(c) and (d).

**2.** What is the policy basis of 4A–305's hard-hearted denial of consequential damages? Who is in the best position to evaluate the risk that a funds transfer will not be made on time and to manage that risk? See Comment 2 to 4A–305.

NOTE

*Evra* announces a default rule to the effect that a receiving bank is not liable for consequential damages resulting from its erroneous exclusion of a payment order, unless it has notice of the type or extent of damage at the time it executes the order. Thus, to avoid liability for consequential damages, receiving banks with such notice must contract around the rule. Section 4A–305(d) rejects that part of *Evra*'s default rule allowing recovery when the bank has the requisite notice. Under 4A–305(d) consequential damages are recoverable from the receiving bank only "to the extent provided in an express written agreement." Comment 2 to 4A–305 judges that, to effect low-cost and speedy funds transfers, most receiving banks are in a comparatively poor position against their senders to reduce the risk of issuing erroneous payment orders. This may remain true even when the receiving bank has notice of special circumstances bearing on the type or extent of loss resulting from its erroneous execution of a payment order. See Comment 2 (paragraph 3) to 4A–305. If so, parties to most funds transfers therefore prefer to contract around *Evra*'s default rule. Section 4A–305(d) saves them the cost of having to do so because under it consequential damages aren't recoverable from the receiving bank without an express written agreement allowing recovery. Section 4A–305(d)'s default rule denying recovery of consequential damages therefore may optimally reduce contracting costs associated with funds transfers. Presumably to reduce proof and other litigation costs incurred in showing an agreement to opt out of 4A–305's default rule against consequential damages, 4A–305(d) requires that opting out be by "express written agreement."

## 8.   FRAUDULENT PAYMENT ORDERS

A funds transfer is a very efficient method of payment. Large amounts can be transferred in a short time at low cost. But this great efficiency also provides a highly efficient method for the theft of money. The thief might steal funds in a bank account by fraudulently inducing either the bank or the owner of the account to make a wire transfer of the funds to an account controlled by the thief in some other bank. For example, the thief might electronically transmit to the bank a payment order purporting to be that of the owner of the account. If the bank is unaware that its customer did not send the order, the fraud can succeed. If the bank executes the fraudulent payment order, it has transferred funds on behalf of the customer without authority of the customer to do so. Who takes the loss? Has the thief stolen funds of the customer or funds of the bank? Under Article 4A a receiving bank that executes a payment order is not acting as the agent of the sender. 4A–212. But if the bank executes an order that it believes to be the order of its customer but which in fact was issued by a person not authorized to act for its customer, should the law of agency determine whether the customer is bound by the unauthorized payment order issued in its name? If agency law applies, the customer is not bound by the unauthorized order, the bank has no authority to debit the customer's account, and the bank takes the loss.

But the law of agency is not very useful in determining whether the risk of loss with respect to an unauthorized payment order transmitted electronically should fall upon the receiving bank's customer, the purported sender of the fraudulent payment order, or the receiving bank that accepted it. The agency doctrines of actual, implied, and apparent authority grew out of cases in which the person purporting to be the agent and the third party acting in reliance on the acts of the purported agent have some personal contact with each other. These doctrines do not work well in cases in which a commercial transaction normally is carried out in the name of a principal by a person who is anonymous and who has no direct contact with the third person. In the case of electronic transmission of a payment order, the receiving bank is acting on the basis of a message that appears on a computer screen. There is no way of determining the identity or authority of the person who caused the message to be sent. The receiving bank is not relying on the authority of any particular person to act for its customer. Instead, the receiving bank relies on a security procedure pursuant to which the authenticity of the message can be "tested" by various devices such as identification codes or other security information in the control of the customer designed to provide certainty that the message is that of the customer identified in the payment order as its sender.

In the funds transfer business, the concept of "authorized" is different from the concept found in agency law. A payment order is treated as the order of the person in whose name it is issued if it is properly tested pursuant to a security procedure and the order passes the test. Risk of loss rules regarding unauthorized payment orders with respect to which verification pursuant to a security procedure is in effect are stated in 4A–202 and 4A–203. The general rule is that a payment order is effective as the order of the customer, whether or not authorized, if the security procedure is commercially reasonable and the receiving bank proves that it accepted the order in good faith after verifying the order in compliance with the security procedure. There are certain exceptions and qualifications to this rule that are explained in the Comments to 4A–203. The general rule is based on the assumption that losses due to unauthorized payment orders can best be avoided by the use of commercially reasonable security procedures, and that the use of such procedures should be encouraged. If a commercially reasonable security procedure is not in effect or if the bank fails to comply with a commercially reasonable procedure, ordinary rules of agency apply with the effect that, if the payment order was not authorized by the customer, the receiving bank acts at its peril in accepting the order.

The Article 4A rules are designed to protect both the customer and the receiving bank. A receiving bank needs to be able to rely on objective criteria to determine whether it can safely act on a payment order. Employees of that bank can be trained to "test" a payment order according to the various steps specified in the security procedure. The bank is responsible for the acts of these employees. The interests of the customer are protected by providing an incentive to a receiving bank to make available to the customer a security procedure that is commercially reasonable. Prudent banking practice may require that security procedures be utilized with respect to virtually all payment orders, except for those in which personal contact between the customer and the bank eliminates the possibility of an unauthorized order. The burden of making available commercially reasonable security procedures is imposed on receiving banks because generally they determine what security procedures can be used and are in the best position to evaluate the efficacy of procedures offered to customers to combat fraud. The burden on the customer is to supervise its employees to assure compliance with the security procedure, to safeguard confidential security information, and to restrict access to transmitting facilities so that the security procedure cannot be breached.

Sections 4A–202 and 4A–203 were among the most contentious provisions in the drafting of Article 4A. Customers strongly believed that they should not be liable for unauthorized funds transfers: the banks control the security procedures and if a fraudulent payment order penetrates the security controls the bank should bear the loss. Bank representatives were just as firm in their belief that they could not transfer trillions of dollars a day all over the world at great speed in a highly automated process if they had to be concerned about whether the customer had actually authorized the payment order: if the payment order "tests," that is, meets their security procedures, they should be able to send the order without fear of liability. Sections 4A–202 and 4A–203 represent a compromise solution which satisfied neither side. Each time the authorization issue was discussed, customer representatives brought up the possibility that a brilliant hacker might crack even the most sophisticated security procedure and pull off the world's biggest bank robbery at the expense of the customer. Bankers said that it was tried every day and just couldn't be done.

## PROBLEMS

**1.** Bank One received a payment order to send $1 million to Account #567891234 in Bank Two for Boniface, a customer of Bank Two. The originator's name on the payment order was SoCorp, a customer of Bank One. The payment order complied with all security procedures agreed to by SoCorp and was accepted by Bank One and, subsequently, by Bank Two. Boniface disappeared after withdrawing the money from its account in Bank Two. When SoCorp learned of the transaction, it denied that it had authorized the payment order and demanded its money back from Bank One, which had deducted the amount of the transfer from SoCorp's account. An investigation showed that SoCorp did not authorize the payment order. As between SoCorp and Bank One, who should bear the loss of the funds that resulted from the fraud under 4A–202 and 4A–203? What additional information do you need before you can decide this case?

**2.** Under the heading "Cyber Caper," the Wall Street Journal reported that a 28–year–old Russian biochemistry grad student, "Vova," who worked for a trading company in St. Petersburg, broke into Citicorp's computers on Wall Street and, over a period of months, transferred about $12 million from customer's accounts to banks in Finland, Israel, Netherlands, San Francisco and Switzerland, where his confederates attempted to withdraw the funds. They succeeded in getting $400,000 out before the accounts were traced and frozen. Since, according to the Journal article, Citicorp moves about $500 billion a day in funds transfers, Vova seemed almost restrained in his thievery. Customers of Citicorp in Buenos Aires and Jakarta were shocked to learn that unauthorized transfers had been made from their accounts. In order to get into Citicorp's computers, Vova had to penetrate a security system so sophisticated that industry experts said what he did was "almost impossible." William M. Carley and Timothy L. O'Brien, Cyber Caper: How Citicorp System Was Raided and Funds Moved Around World, Wall St. J., Sept. 12, 1995, at A1. Assume that Vova was a brilliant hacker who penetrated the security system without the assistance of anyone associated with Citicorp or its customers whose accounts were debited, as between the customers whose accounts were charged and Citicorp, where would 4A–202 and 4A–203 throw the loss in the Cyber Caper case?

———————

By way of a postscript, when Vova was eventually extradited to this country, he pled guilty to charges of conspiracy to commit bank, wire and computer fraud. He admitted that he had used passwords acquired from "another Russian." Citibank doesn't know how the accomplice obtained the passwords, but there is no evidence that its employees were involved. Citibank has beefed up its security system. Dean Starkman, Russian Hacker Enters Fraud Plea in Citicorp Case, Wall St. J., Jan. 26, 1998, at B9A.

## 9.   INCORRECTLY IDENTIFIED BENEFICIARY

When 4A–207 was conceived, the drafters had in mind the type of fraud transaction involved in the following Problem in which the name identifies one person and the account number identifies a different person. The hypothetical case set out in Comment 2 to 4A–207 is similar to this Problem.

### PROBLEM

In the 1990s billions of dollars flowed into stock and bond mutual funds; new funds sprung up daily. These developments caught the attention of Thief who reasoned that these novice funds were unlikely to be as fraud-sensitive as his old prey, commercial banks. Thief developed a new MO for mutual funds and he employed it with success in the following case:

He impersonated Investor, who owned shares in a mutual fund (Fund) worth more than $1 million, by sending forged documents to Fund requesting redemption of $1 million of his shares and the wire transfer of these funds to Investor's account number 987654 in Dallas Bank. Thief preceded the redemption by agreeing to pay Coin Dealer $1 million for gold coins (impossible to trace) by wiring the funds to Coin Dealer's account in Dallas Bank. Fund was taken in by the impersonation and sent a payment order to Boston Bank requesting it to transfer $1 million to Investor as beneficiary to be credited to account number 987654 in Dallas Bank. Boston Bank carried out the instructions. When Dallas Bank received the payment order, designating the Investor as the beneficiary and the account number as 987654, it credited the designated account number which, of course, was the account of Coin Dealer, not Investor, who had no account in this bank. When Dallas Bank notified Coin Dealer of the credit, Coin Dealer released the gold coins to Thief who absconded. After Fund learned of the theft, it recredited Investor's account and sued Dallas Bank for return of the money, relying on 4A–207(b)(1), (c) and (d). Dallas Bank relied on a pre-Article 4A case, Bradford Trust Co. of Boston v. Texas American Bank–Houston, 790 F.2d 407 (5th Cir.1986), which held on similar facts that Fund should take the loss because it was the party in the best position to avoid the loss, it dealt directly with the impostor, and it sent the funds to the wrong account. What result under 4A–207? See Comments 2 and 3 to 4A–207.

---

Murphy's Law being what it is, virtually the first case arising under 4A–207 was *Corfan* in which the account number identified no one.

## Corfan Banco Asuncion Paraguay v. Ocean Bank

District Court of Appeal of Florida, 1998.
715 So.2d 967.

■ SORONDO, JUDGE.

Corfan Banco Asuncion Paraguay, a foreign banking corporation (Corfan Bank), appeals the lower court's entry of a Final Summary Judgment in favor of Ocean Bank, a Florida bank.

On March 22, 1995, Corfan Bank originated a wire transfer of $72,972.00 via its intermediary Swiss Bank to the account of its customer, Jorge Alberto Dos Santos Silva (Silva), in Ocean Bank. The transfer order bore Silva's name as the recipient and indicated that his account number was 010070210400 (in fact, this was a nonexistent account). Upon receipt of the wire transfer, Ocean Bank noticed a discrepancy in this number and before depositing the money, confirmed with Silva that his correct account number was 010076216406. Ocean Bank did not, however, inform Corfan Bank or Swiss Bank of the error. Once the correct number was confirmed by Silva, Ocean Bank accepted the wire transfer and credited Silva's account.

The next day, Corfan Bank became aware of the account number discrepancy and, without first checking with either Silva or Ocean Bank, sent a second wire transfer of $72,972.00 to Silva's correct account number at Ocean Bank. The second transfer order did not indicate that it was a correction, replacement or amendment of the March 22nd transfer. Because the information of the transfer was correct, it was automatically processed at Ocean Bank and was credited to Silva's account. Several days later, Corfan Bank inquired of Ocean Bank regarding the two transfers, maintaining that only one transfer was intended. By that time, Silva had withdrawn the proceeds of both wire transfers. When Ocean Bank refused to repay $72,972.00 to Corfan Bank, this litigation ensued. Corfan Bank proceeded on two claims, one based on the section 670.207, Florida Statutes (1995), which codifies as Florida law section 4A–207 of the Uniform Commercial Code (UCC), and one based on common law negligence. Ocean Bank answered denying liability under the statute and also contending that the negligence claim was precluded by the preemptive statutory scheme.

The trial court, emphasizing that Florida's adoption of the UCC sections concerning wire transfers did not abrogate the basic tenets of commercial law, found that Ocean Bank had not contravened § 4A–207 by crediting the erroneous March 22nd wire transfer to Silva's account. Finding that Corfan Bank was the party best situated to have avoided this loss, the court held that Corfan Bank must bear that loss and, therefore, the court granted Ocean Bank's motion for summary judgment as to count one (the UCC count). Additionally, the court dismissed count two (the negligence count).

We begin with a review of the exact language of § 4A–207(a):

> (a) Subject to subsection (b), if, in a payment order received by the beneficiary's bank, the name, bank account number, *or* other identification of the beneficiary refers to a nonexistent or unidentifiable person or account, no person has rights as a beneficiary of the order and acceptance of the order cannot occur.

Corfan Bank argues that this language is clear and unambiguous, where a name or bank account number, or other identification refers either to a nonexistent or unidentified person *or* a nonexistent account, the order *cannot* be accepted. Ocean Bank responds that such a "highly technical" reading of the statute is "contrary to commercial and practical considerations and common sense." It suggests that we look to the legislative intent and conclude that the "or" in the statute should be given conjunctive rather than disjunctive effect. We respectfully decline Ocean Bank's invitation to look behind the plain language of the statute and conclude that given its clarity it must be read as written.

In Capers v. State, 678 So.2d 330 (Fla. 1996), the Florida Supreme Court stated:

> [T]he plain meaning of statutory language is the first consideration of statutory construction. St. Petersburg Bank & Trust Co. v. Hamm, 414 So.2d 1071, 1073 (Fla. 1982). Only when a statute is of doubtful meaning should matters extrinsic to the statute be considered in construing the language employed by the legislature. Florida State Racing Comm'n v. McLaughlin, 102 So.2d 574, 576 (Fla. 1958).

Id. at 332. * * * These cases preclude the analysis urged by Ocean Bank. Although Ocean Bank's position has been noted in the legal literature,[4] "unambiguous language is not subject to judicial construction, however wise it may seem to alter the plain language." *Jett*, 626 So.2d at 693. * * *

* * *

The Supreme Court of Florida has fashioned only one exception to this general rule: "[t]his Court will not go behind the plain and ordinary meaning of the words used in the statute unless an unreasonable or ridiculous conclusion would result from failure to do so." Holly v. Auld, 450 So.2d 217, 219 (Fla. 1984). The plain and ordinary meaning of the words of the statute under review do not lead to either an unreasonable or ridiculous result. As discussed more thoroughly below, one of the critical considerations in the drafting of Article 4A was that parties to funds transfers should be able to "predict risk with certainty, to insure risk with certainty, to adjust operational and security procedures, and to price funds transfer services appropriately." See 19A Fla. Stat. Ann. 15 (U.C.C. cmt. 1995). All of these goals are reasonable and assured by the plain statutory language.

In the present case, although the payment order correctly identified the beneficiary, it referred to a nonexistent account number. Under the clear and unambiguous terms of the statute, acceptance of the order could not have occurred. As the Florida Supreme Court stated in *Jett*:

**4.** One respected treatise on the Uniform Commercial Code analyzes the code provision, 4A–207(a), which is identical to the statute in question, as follows:

> The requirements of subsection 4A–207(a) are stated in the disjunctive. Thus, apparently, if the payment order name and bank account number provide an identifiable or known person but "other identification of the beneficiary" refers to a nonexistent or unidentifiable person or account, subsection 4A–207(a) is literally applicable. The express deference in subsection 4A–207(a) to subsection 4A–207(b) does not appear to resolve this conundrum. Subsection 4A–207(b) provides rules only for payment orders in which the beneficiary is identified "by both name and an identifying or bank account number" in the instance in which the name and the number identify different persons.

> *It does not appear that this anomaly in subsection 4A–207(a) was intended; nonetheless, the subsection 4A–207(a) suggests only one preventive mechanism for avoiding this conundrum: the sender should include no "other identification of the beneficiary" which might "refer . . . to a nonexistent or unidentifiable person or account."* Then subsection 4A–207(a) would be harmonized with subsection 4A–207(b) as long as the name and account number refer to the same identifiable person or account. If they refer to different identifiable persons or accounts then subsection 4A–207(b) controls. If either the name or account number refers to a nonexistent or unidentifiable person then subsection 4A–207(a) is again applicable.

William D. Hawkland & Richard Moreno, Uniform Commercial Code Series, § 4A–207:01 (1993)(emphasis added).

We trust that if the legislature did not intend the result mandated by the statute's plain language, the legislature itself will amend the statute at the next opportunity.

*Jett*, 626 So.2d at 693.

As indicated above, the trial court dismissed count two of the complaint which sounded in negligence. The court concluded that the statutory scheme preempts the common law remedy of negligence. * * *

* * *

In addressing this issue we restrict our analysis to the pleadings and facts of this case. In pertinent part, count two reads as follows:

Ocean Bank owed Corfan Bank a duty of care to follow the accepted banking practice of the community, and to return the funds from the first transfer to Corfan Bank upon receipt due to the reference in the first transfer to a non-existent account number.

The duty claimed to have been breached by Ocean Bank in its negligence count is exactly the same duty established and now governed by the statute. Under such circumstances we agree with the trial judge that the statutory scheme preempts the negligence claim in this case and affirm the dismissal of count two.[5] We do not reach the issue of whether the adoption of Article 4A of the UCC preempts negligence claims in all cases.

We reverse the Final Summary Judgment entered by the trial court in favor of Ocean Bank as to count one of the complaint and affirm the dismissal of count two. We remand this case for further proceedings consistent with this opinion.

■ LEVY, J., concurs.

■ NESBITT, JUDGE, dissenting: [Opinion omitted.]


NOTE

In a case like *Corfan* in which the account number identifies no one, 4A–207 doesn't work as intended. Corfan Bank is responsible for the error and should bear the loss, but under the plain meaning of the statute, the court placed the loss on Ocean Bank. Section 4A–207(b) contains a drafting error and should be amended. One solution would be to amend subsection

---

**5.** We note that allowing a negligence claim in this case would "create rights, duties and liabilities inconsistent" with those set forth in § 4A–207. In a negligence cause of action, Ocean Bank would be entitled to defend on a theory of comparative negligence because Corfan Bank provided the erroneous account number which created the problem at issue and then initiated the second transfer without communicating with Ocean Bank. Section 670.207 does not contemplate such a defense. (Oddly enough, allowing Corfan Bank's negligence claim in this case might actually inure to Ocean Bank's benefit). As explained in the comment, one of the primary purposes of the section is to enable the parties to wire funds transfers to predict risk with certainty and to insure against risk. The uniformity and certainty sought by the statute for these transactions could not possibly exist if parties could opt to sue by way of pre-Code remedies where the statute has specifically defined the duties, rights and liabilities of the parties.

(b) by deleting the words in brackets and adding the underlined words as follows:

(b) If a payment order received by the beneficiary's bank identifies the beneficiary both by name and by an identifying or bank account number and the name and number [identify different persons] <u>do not refer to the same person</u>, the following rules apply:

(1) Except as otherwise provided in subsection (c), if the beneficiary's bank does not know that the name and number [refer to different persons] <u>do not refer to the same person</u>, it may rely on the number as the proper identification of the beneficiary of the order. The beneficiary's bank need not determine whether the name and number refer to the same person.

(2) If the beneficiary's bank pays the person identified by name or knows that the name and number [identify different persons] <u>do not refer to the same person</u>, no person has rights as beneficiary except the person paid by the beneficiary's bank if that person was entitled to receive payment from the originator of the funds transfer. If no person has rights as beneficiary, acceptance of the order cannot occur.

Since subsection (a) is subject to (b), if subsection (b) were amended as indicated, that subsection would apply to a case like *Corfan* because the name on the payment order referred to Silva and the account number did not refer to anyone. Thus, the name and number did not refer to the same person. Subsection (b)(2) would control.

## 10.   BANK–CUSTOMER AGREEMENT

The issue taken up by *Regatos* has been hotly debated by funds transfer participants. Although Article 4 is drafted almost entirely as a default statute, courts have placed limits on what statutory rights of customers can be limited by agreement, and there are many cases on the issue. Article 4A has taken a more restrictive approach: certain provisions designated in the statute may not be varied by agreement. 4A–501. The question before the court in *Regatos* is whether there are other provisions of the statute (4A–505 in this case) that are so basic to the operation of the statute that courts should not allow agreements to vary them. Provisions reducing the one-year period in 4A–505 to a much shorter time are presumably present in most funds transfer agreements; hence the clamor about the *Regatos* case as it has proceeded through the courts.

## Regatos v. North Fork Bank

Court of Appeals of New York, 2005.
838 N.E.2d 629.

■ ROSENBLATT, J.

The United States Court of Appeals for the Second Circuit, by certified questions, asks us whether a commercial bank customer can recover funds that the bank improperly transferred out of his account, even though he did not notify the bank of the unauthorized transfer until well after the time limit stated in his account agreement. This issue requires us to decide whether the one-year period of repose in our Uniform Commercial Code § 4–A–505 may be modified by agreement. We also resolve whether UCC 4–A–204 (1) requires the bank actually to send the customer notice of an unauthorized transfer in order to trigger the running of a "reasonable time" within the meaning of that section, or whether a private agreement to hold a customer's mail can allow constructive notice to start that period. These are questions of first impression in this Court, and apparently in every other court of last resort in states that have adopted the relevant statutes.

In accord with the United States District Court for the Southern District of New York, we hold for the customer on both questions. The one-year period of repose in UCC 4–A–505, governing the customer's time in which to notify the bank of the unauthorized transfer, may not be modified by contract. Furthermore, both the one-year statute of repose and the "reasonable time" referred to in section 4–A–204 (1), which determines the customer's ability to recover interest on the misallocated money, begin to run when the customer receives actual notice of the improper transfer.

## *I.*

Tomáz Mendes Regatos held a commercial account with Commercial Bank of New York, the predecessor to North Fork Bank. His agreement with the bank required him to notify the bank of any irregularity regarding his account within 15 days after the bank statement and items were first mailed or made available to him.[1] The agreement did not provide for notice to him of electronic funds transfers, except to the extent those transfers appeared on his monthly statements. The bank adopted a practice of holding Regatos's bank statements rather than mailing them to him, and expected him to request the statements when he wanted to see them.

On March 23, 2001, the bank received a funds transfer order from someone it believed to be Regatos, but failed to follow agreed security procedures[2] to confirm the order. Without authorization, the bank then

---

**1.** The relevant part of the account agreement stated that

> "[t]he depositor will exercise reasonable care and promptness in examining such statement and items to discover any irregularity including, but not limited to, any unauthorized signature or alteration and will notify the Bank promptly in writing of any such discovery, and in no event more than fifteen (15) calendar days subsequent to the time that such statement and items were first mailed or available to the depositor. In those situations in which the depositor has author-

ized the Bank to hold his correspondence, this section shall apply as if the depositor received such statement on the date shown on the statement."

**2.** The security procedures here involved nothing more than checking Regatos's signature against the signature on the faxed transfer order and calling him to confirm (*cf.* UCC 4–A–201 ["Comparison of a signature on a payment order or communication with an authorized specimen signature of the customer is not by itself a security procedure"]). Apparently, the bank did not require any password, even for large sums. Here, the transferred $450,000 out of his account. On April 6, 2001, the bank received another transfer order, again failed to follow its security procedures and without authorization transferred an additional $150,000 out of his account. Together, these transfers represented most of the value of the account.

Regatos did not learn of the unauthorized transfers until he checked his accumulated account statements on August 9, 2001. The transfers were reflected on statements issued on March 23, 2001 and April 25, 2001, but the bank held these statements until he asked for them, following its standard practice in relation to him. He informed the bank of the unauthorized transfers on the day he learned of them, August 9, 2001.

When the bank refused to reimburse Regatos for the lost funds, he sued in the United States District Court for the Southern District of New York. In a comprehensive, well-reasoned opinion, District Judge Shira Scheindlin denied the bank's motion for summary judgment and held that the one-year statute of repose may not be shortened by agreement. The court ruled that, in any event, the 15–day notice period set by the account agreement was unreasonable and invalid. The Federal District Court further held that the UCC 4–A–505 period to notify the bank began to run when Regatos received actual notice of the error on August 9, 2001 (*Regatos v. North Fork Bank*, 257 F.Supp.2d 632 [S.D.N.Y.2003]).

A federal jury found in favor of Regatos. Following UCC 4–A–204, the court awarded him both the principal ($600,000) and the interest from the date the bank improperly transferred the funds.

The bank appealed, and the United States Court of Appeals for the Second Circuit determined that the legal issues necessary to dispose of the case were novel, important questions of New York law. The Second Circuit certified to this Court, and we accepted, the following questions:

> "Can the one-year statute of repose established by New York U.C.C. [ ] 4–A–505 be varied by agreement? If so, are there any minimum limits on the variation thereof (such as 'reasonable time') that estop [the bank] from denying Regatos recovery in this case? . . .

> "In the absence of agreement, does New York U.C.C. Article 4–A require actual notice, rather than merely constructive notice? If so, can this requirement be altered by agreement of the parties and was such achieved here?" (*Regatos v. North Fork Bank*, 396 F.3d 493, 498–499 [Wesley, J.].)

We answer the first part of the first question "no," rendering the second part academic. We answer the first part of the second question "yes" and the second part of the second question "no."

---

bank compared the signature on the fax to its signature on file, but did not realize that the fax signature had been forged. The jury found that the bank did not telephone Regatos to confirm that the order was legitimate.

## II.

UCC 4–A–204 establishes a bank's basic obligation to make good on unauthorized and ineffective transfers and, with one exception, forbids any variation of that obligation by agreement. UCC 4–A–204 reads as follows:

"(1) If a receiving bank accepts a payment order issued in the name of its customer as sender which is (a) not authorized and not effective as the order of the customer under Section 4–A–202, . . . the bank shall refund any payment of the payment order received from the customer to the extent the bank is not entitled to enforce payment and shall pay interest on the refundable amount calculated from the date the bank received payment to the date of the refund. However, the customer is not entitled to interest from the bank on the amount to be refunded if the customer fails to exercise ordinary care to determine that the order was not authorized by the customer and to notify the bank of the relevant facts within a reasonable time not exceeding ninety days after the date the customer received notification from the bank that the order was accepted or that the customer's account was debited with respect to the order. The bank is not entitled to any recovery from the customer on account of a failure by the customer to give notification as stated in this section.

"(2) Reasonable time under subsection (1) may be fixed by agreement as stated in subsection (1) of Section 1–204, but the obligation of a receiving bank to refund payment as stated in subsection (1) may not otherwise be varied by agreement."

Furthermore, UCC 4–A–505 provides that

"[i]f a receiving bank has received payment from its customer with respect to a payment order issued in the name of the customer as sender and accepted by the bank, and the customer received notification reasonably identifying the order, the customer is precluded from asserting that the bank is not entitled to retain the payment unless the customer notifies the bank of the customer's objection to the payment within one year after the notification was received by the customer." (UCC 4–A–505.)

Regatos argues that the one-year statutory period is an integral part of the bank's "obligation . . . to refund payment" under UCC 4–A–204 (1) and so, pursuant to UCC 4–A–204 (2), "may not . . . be varied by agreement." The bank and its supporting amici point out that the notice provision is in section 4–A–505, not section 4–A–204 (1), and rely on UCC 4–A–501 (1), which declares that "[e]xcept as otherwise provided . . . the rights and obligations of a party to a funds transfer may be varied by agreement of the affected party."[5] The bank maintains that the customer's duty to notify the

---

**5.** In support of this position, the amici urge that article 4–A is not a consumer protection statute, especially considering that it applies solely to presumably sophisticated commercial parties. While this is true to some extent, the provision in section 4–A–204 refusing to allow parties to modify the bank's basic obligation to refund unauthorized transfer funds contradicts the amici's argument because the provision clearly protects

bank of the error before recovering misallocated funds is an "obligation" separate from that created by section 4–A–204 (1) and therefore modifiable.

We agree with Regatos's reading of the statutes. In context, the policy behind article 4–A encourages banks to adopt appropriate security procedures. Only when a commercially reasonable security procedure is in place (or has been offered to the customer) may the bank disclaim its liability for unauthorized transfers (UCC 4–A–202). Permitting banks to vary the notice period by agreement would reduce the effectiveness of the statute's one-year period of repose as an incentive for banks to create and follow security procedures.

While the issue is close, we cannot accept the bank's argument that the customer's responsibility to notify the bank of its error is modifiable. UCC 4–A–204 (1) states that "[t]he bank is not entitled to any recovery from the customer on account of a failure by the customer to give notification as stated in this section."[6] Accordingly, a bank has an obligation to refund the principal regardless of notice, provided such notice is given within one year in accordance with UCC 4–A–505 (*see* 3 James J. White and Robert S. Summers, Uniform Commercial Code § 22–4). Moreover, as the District Court pointed out, section 4–A–505 (the one-year notice period) appears in the "Miscellaneous Provisions" part of the article, not the parts touching upon substantive rights and obligations (*Regatos*, 257 F.Supp.2d 632, 644 n. 19). The period of repose in section 4–A–505 is essentially a jurisdictional attribute of the "rights and obligations" contained in UCC 4–A–204 (1). To vary the period of repose would, in effect, impair the customer's section 4–A–204 (1) right to a refund, a modification that section 4–A–204 (2) forbids.

Article 4–A was intended, in significant part, to promote finality of banking operations and to give the bank relief from unknown liabilities of potentially indefinite duration (*see Banque Worms v. BankAmerica Intl.*, 77 N.Y.2d 362, 371, 568 N.Y.S.2d 541, 570 N.E.2d 189). This legislative purpose does not suggest that those interests alter (or should alter) the statute's fine-tuned balance between the customer and the bank as to who should bear the burden of unauthorized transfers.

Therefore, we hold that the one-year repose period in section 4–A–505 cannot be modified by agreement. By notifying the bank on August 9, 2001, the day he received actual notice, and four or five months after the statements were available, Regatos acted either way within the year-long period of repose. This clearly satisfied the statutory requirement and he is entitled to recover at least his $600,000 principal.

consumers, even commercial consumers, from bearing the burden of this type of bank error.

**6.** "A customer that acts promptly is entitled to interest from the time the customer's account was debited or the customer otherwise made payment.... But the bank is not entitled to any recovery from the customer based on negligence for failure to inform the bank. Loss of interest is in the nature of a penalty on the customer designed to provide an incentive for the customer to police its account. There is no intention to impose a duty on the customer that might result in shifting loss from the unauthorized order to the customer" (UCC 4–A–204, Comment 2, reprinted in McKinney's Cons Laws of NY, Book 62 1/2, UCC 4–A–204, at 622).

*III.*

The Second Circuit next asks whether actual notice is required under article 4–A (or whether mere constructive notice will do) and, consequently, whether Regatos is also entitled to recover interest on the misdirected funds. * * *

Even where customers enter "hold mail" agreements with their banks, the actual notice rule still applies. Just as the one-year notice limitation is an inherent aspect of the customer's right to recover unauthorized payments, the actual notice requirement provides the bedrock for the exercise of that right. Permitting banks to enforce "agreements" to accept constructive notice would defeat article 4–A's guarantee of recovery for unauthorized payments.

In response to the second certified question, we answer that article 4–A requires actual notice, and that this requirement cannot be varied by a "hold mail" agreement, neither to begin the statute of repose, nor to begin "reasonable time" under the account agreement. Regatos notified the bank of his loss within an indisputably reasonable time after receiving actual notice, and is therefore entitled to recover the interest on his lost principal (UCC 4–A–204).

Accordingly, the first part of certified question 1 should be answered in the negative and the second part not answered as unnecessary, and the first part of certified question 2 should be answered in the affirmative and the second part in the negative.

CHIEF JUDGE KAYE and JUDGES G.B. SMITH, CIPARICK, GRAFFEO, READ and R.S. SMITH concur.

Following certification of questions by the United States Court of Appeals for the Second Circuit and acceptance of the questions by this Court pursuant to section 500.27 of the Rules of the Court of Appeals (22 NYCRR 500.27), and after hearing argument by counsel for the parties and consideration of the briefs and the record submitted, certified questions answered as follows: the first part of question 1 answered in the negative, and the second part of question 1 not answered as academic; and the first part of question 2 answered in the affirmative, and the second part of question 2 answered in the negative.

NOTE

As the *Regatos* court recognizes, the question whether 4A–505's one-year rule is mandatory is "close." A strong argument can be made that it is only a default rule. Article 4A carefully identifies the mandatory rules within its scope. Section 4A–501 state that Article 4A's rules may be varied by agreement, "[e]xcept as otherwise provided in this Article." Mandatory rules are expressly provided in 4A–202(f), 4A–204(b), 4A–402(f), and 4A–404(c). Article 4A does not designate 4A–505's one-year rule as mandatory. Given that the interests of both financial institutions and nonfinancial users of funds transfers were well represented in Article 4A's drafting

(Comment 2 to 4A–102), the failure to deem 4A–505's rule mandatory suggests that it is a default rule.

More general considerations reinforce this conclusion. Mandatory rules typically are justifiable on two grounds: paternalism or market failure. Paternalism has no role in Article 4A's rules, because parties to funds transfers covered by the Article are nonconsumers. Consumer funds transfers instead are covered by the EFTA and excluded from Article 4A's scope. 4A–108. Market failure can occur only when the contract governing a funds transfer produces negative externalities: costs created for nonparties to the funds transfer that are not internalized by either the sender of the payment order or the receiving bank. There is no reason to believe that a contractual provision reducing 4A–505's one-year period produces externalities. Instead, 4A–505 in effect functions as a sort of statutory limitation on the sender's recoverable damages. Under the section the sender cannot recover a payment made to the receiving bank if it fails to give notice of objection within a year after it received notice identifying the payment order. As such the provision allocates the costs and benefits of the limitation between the sender and the receiving bank. Because neither paternalistic concerns nor externalities plausibly are implicated by such allocations, 4A–505's one-year rule is best treated as a default rule only.

## B.   OTHER ELECTRONIC FUNDS TRANSFERS

### 1.   ELECTRONIC FUND TRANSFER ACT

Consumer electronic fund transfers are governed by the Electronic Fund Transfers Act, 15 U.S.C. § 1693 et seq., of 1978. Regulation E, 12 C.F.R. Part 205, issued by the Federal Reserve Board, prescribes regulations to carry out the purposes of the Act. Section 1693a(6) states that the "term 'electronic fund transfer' means any transfer of funds, other than a transaction originated by check, draft, or similar paper instrument, which is initiated through an electronic terminal, telephonic instrument, or computer or magnetic tape so as to order, instruct, or authorize a financial institution to debit or credit an account. Such term includes, but is not limited to, point-of-sale transfers, automated teller machine transactions, direct deposits or withdrawals of funds, and transfers initiated by telephone." "Account" is defined as meaning an account in a financial institution established for consumer purposes (§ 1693a(2)). "Financial institution" includes banks, credit unions, and savings and loan associations. In short, the EFTA applies to any electronic fund transfer that authorizes a bank to debit or credit a consumer's account. Section 4A–108 provides that Article 4A does not apply to a funds transfer any part of which is governed by the EFTA. The Comment to 4A–108 states that the intent of that section is to make Article 4A and the EFTA mutually exclusive. Thus, the EFTA preempts any application of Article 4A to consumer transactions.

The EFTA requires full disclosure of the terms and conditions of electronic funds transfers involving the consumer's account (§ 1693c), written documentation to the consumer for each transfer and periodic statements for each account of the consumer accessed by electronic funds transfers (§ 1693d). Periodic statements must be sent for each monthly cycle in which an electronic fund transfer has been made (§ 205.9(b)). The periodic statement must show the name of the person paid (§ 205.9(b)(1)(v)). As we will see in the next chapter, the absence of the names of payees on bank statements is a major gripe of drawers of checks. Written authorization is required for any preauthorized transfers with a copy provided to the consumer when made (1693e). Among the most important consumer protection provisions are those in § 1693f and § 205.11 for error resolution. The consumer has 60 days after receiving its periodic statement or other documentation to give the financial institution oral or written notice of error. A financial institution may require the consumer to give written confirmation of an error within 10 business days after oral notice of error (§ 205.11(b)(2)). Within 10 business days of receiving notice of error, the financial institution must determine if an error occurred and report the results of its investigation to the consumer within three days after completion of the investigation. The financial institution must correct any error discovered within one business day after discovery of the error. If the financial institution is unable to complete its investigation within 10 days, it may take up to 45 days from receipt of the notice of error to investigate further but only if it provisionally recredits the consumer's account in the amount of the alleged error. The 45–day period may be extended to 90 days in certain cases. § 205.11(c). Acts constituting error include unauthorized transfers and billing errors by the financial institution (§ 205.11(a)). For violation of the error resolution provisions, the financial institution may be subject to treble damages under § 1693f(e) and § 1693m. Consumer liability for unauthorized funds transfers is detailed in § 1693g and was discussed in detail earlier in our comparison of credit cards (covered by Truth in Lending) and debit cards (covered by ETFA) with respect to unauthorized use. We noted there that the lesser protection accorded holders of debit cards under § 1693g, has been largely offset, at least for the time being, by the voluntary pledges of Visa, MasterCard and other networks to observe ''zero liability'' on the part of cardholders. Section 1693m prescribes civil liability for financial institutions that fail to comply with the Act.

## 2.   AUTOMATED CLEARING HOUSE (ACH)

### a.   CONSUMER TRANSFERS

A lower cost, somewhat slower means of making electronic payments is through the automated clearing house (ACH) system, used to transfer money to or from consumer bank accounts through the ACH network, which links a large number of financial institutions, by ''batching'' numerous payments and sending them together. These transfers may be either credit or debit transfers. The difference between the two is discussed in Comment 4 to 4A–104. In a credit transfer the instruction to pay is given by the person making the payment, as is the case in Article 4A transfers. In a debit transfer the instruction to pay is made by the person receiving payment. An example of a credit transfer is one in which an employer pays its employees by direct deposit to their bank accounts. Suppose its employees have accounts in ten banks in the area. In such a case, the employer will prepare an electronic file with information concerning the bank accounts of each employee in which a deposit is to be made. This information will go to the employer's bank which forwards it to an ACH facility in the area. The ACH performs its clearing house function by repackaging this information for each bank in which the employees have accounts, which it forwards to these banks. ACH allows the party initiating the transfer to time the dates when the payments will be credited to the employees' accounts by their banks and when the debits will be made to the originator's account in its bank. After the ACH has determined the net balances between the employer's bank and the employees' banks, these banks will settle through the Federal Reserve System. Numerous government payments, such as social security and other benefits and pensions are made in this manner.

Equally common is the debit transaction. An example is one in which the debtor authorizes its creditor to draw each month on its bank account to make its monthly mortgage payments. The mortgage lender (mortgagee) will prepare an electronic file giving information on all mortgagors whose payments are due on a given date and send this file to its bank. The bank will forward this information to an ACH that will send the relevant information to each bank in which mortgagors have accounts. These banks will debit the mortgagors' accounts on the prescribed date. The mortgagee's bank will credit the mortgagee's account on that date and settlement between the banks will be made through the Federal Reserve System. Insurance premiums, and other recurring payments, are frequently made in this manner.

Since ACH transfer is a cheap, reliable method of moving credit from one bank account to another, it is used in many transactions in addition to those have we have mentioned above. Some of these are described in the following sections. The operational details of the ACH system are discussed in Donald I. Baker & Roland E. Brandel, The Law of Electronic Fund Transfer Systems, Chapter 3 (1988 & Cum. Supp. 1995); James V. Vergari & Virginia V. Shue, Fundamentals of Computer–High Technology Law 463–472 (1991), and 1 Clark & Clark, The Law of Bank Deposits, Check Collections and Credit Cards & 6.04 (Rev. ed. 2005). There are some 40 ACHs in the nation, most of which are operated by the Fed. According to Melanie L. Fein, Law of Electronic Banking § 5.02[A] (2003 Supp.), ACH networks are used by over 20,000 financial institutions, 500,000 businesses and 60% of all households. The ACH system processed trillions of dollars annually in transfers, including direct deposits of payrolls, pensions and annuities, as well as preauthorized bill payments and corporation-to-corporation payments. The ACH trade association is the National Automated Clearinghouse Association (NACHA), which prescribes operating rules for ACH transfers. See NACHA, 2006 ACH Rules (Corporate Edition). 3 White & Summers, Uniform Commercial Code § 22–2 (4th Prac. ed. 1995), discusses the intricacies of what law governs ACH payments and concludes that for all practical purposes the NACHA rules effectively do so. Clark & Clark, supra, concurs.

### b.   COMMERCIAL TRANSFERS

At the beginning of this chapter we noted how slow and costly it is for banks to manage the vast bulk of checks that must be cleared each day. The point made was that major businesses are moving to electronic payments to avoid having to use checks. The usual method employed by these businesses to pay their bills electronically to suppliers and governmental units is by ACH payments. One executive is quoted as saying: "We want computers talking to computers." Since ACH is a value-dated system, cash managers can plan the exact date payments will be credited to their payees' accounts and debited to their own accounts, and this knowledge allows them to utilize their funds more efficiently. However, usual estimates are that about 75% of business-to-business payments are still done by check. Robin Sidel, Banks, Customers Adapt to Paperless Check Processing, Wall St. J., Oct. 28, 2004, at B1.

The use of ACH to pay bills is similar in concept to Fedwire and Chips payments in that, for the most part, these business-to-business payments are credit transfers. But there are important differences. Fedwire and Chips are "big dollar" wholesale wire transfers that can often give same-day service. Although many more transfers are made by ACH, the amount of money sent is much less. Credit transfers over ACH between businesses are nominally covered by Article 4A, but 4A–501(b) effectively cedes governance to the NACHA rules.

### 3.   ELECTRONIC CHECK CONVERSION

Electronic check conversion has become a highly popular means of transferring funds from buyers' accounts to retail sellers. A merchant who receives a check in payment from a buyer scans the check to capture the MICR information from the check and keys-in the amount of the check. This information is sent through ACH to the buyer's bank and her account is debited for the amount of the check. The merchant can swiftly determine if an account has sufficient funds to cover the check amount. No checks are lost in the collection process and payment is fast; no float for buyers. This transaction amounts to a one-time electronic funds transfer from a buyer's account. The funds transfer is initiated by the buyer's delivery of a check to the merchant, either at the point of sale or by mailing the check to the merchant's address or dropbox, but the buyer's account is debited electronically through ACH. The check is voided by the merchant and may be returned to the buyer immediately after the merchant has gathered the information from it. There were 2.3 billion electronic check conversions through ACH in 2004. Clarks' Bank Deposits and Payments Monthly, Vol. 15, No. 4, September 2006, at 6.

Questions have arisen on whether a consumer buyer entering into such a transaction is entitled to the protections extended to consumers initiating electronic transfers by Regulation E. 12 CFR § 205(c) provides that "[A]ny transfer of funds originated by check" is excluded from coverage of Regulation E. The issue with respect to electronic check conversions is whether they are, in fact, check-originated transfers when the check functions only as a source of information to initiate an electronic fund transfer. In 2006 Regulation E was amended to specifically extend its coverage to electronic check conversion transactions. 12 CFR § 205(b)(2). This means that consumers must authorize an electronic funds transfer under Regulation E's procedure under which consumers are deemed to have authorized the transfer if they go through with the transaction after being given the required notice. The major operational change that Regulation E coverage requires is that even though merchants do not hold the account from which the electronic funds transfer is made, they are responsible for obtaining the consumer's authorization.

## 4.   INTERNET PAYMENTS

### a.   PAYMENTS THROUGH ONLINE PAYMENT SERVICES

The Internet has become a powerful global medium for the sale of goods, the providing of services, particularly financial services, and information of all kinds. The volume of goods sold on the Internet is huge and growing. Online stock transactions are vast. A growing percent of mortgage loans originate online. The examples of the commercial use of the Internet are endless. Not only the largest merchants have Web sites but tiny boutiques do so as well. The electronic catalog function of the Internet is inexpensive and unbounded in territory.

The use of the Internet for remote shopping of all kinds is well established, but making payments through the Internet is less common. For a remote payments system to develop on a large scale, there must be a means of moving credit through the banking system. Leaving aside the wholesale funds transfer systems of Fedwire and CHIPS, the two means commonly used for this task are the credit card clearing and settlement systems (e.g., the Visa and MasterCard networks) and the automated clearing house (ACH) system that connects nearly all banks. By far the most popular method of paying for consumer obligations incurred in Internet shopping is by credit cards, but in recent years interest has developed in offering individuals the convenience of making payments on the Internet merely by clicking a mouse.

Programs have been developed that allow payments to be made over the Internet. One successful example arose out of the great success of online auction selling. Many of the noncommercial auction sellers on eBay, some of whom may have just cleaned out their attics, cannot be expected to be authorized credit card merchants. This is also true for some small merchants who sell by auction over the Internet. Online payment services companies have been created to meet the needs of these sellers. The procedure is for online senders (buyers) and recipients (sellers) to set up accounts with an online payment service. A sender's account may be funded from the sender's bank account through ACH or by credit card; the transfer of funds by ACH is much cheaper. The sender can activate a transfer of funds from this account through the service company to another account holder of the company merely by sending an e-mail. After an online auction in which the sender makes a purchase, the payment, less a discount for the online payment service (usually about 2% of the amount of the transaction), is added to the recipient's account. If the recipient doesn't have an account with the online payments service at the time of the sale, the service may notify it that the sender's money has arrived and will be added to the seller's account when one is opened. Recipients may withdraw the money from their accounts by debit cards issued by the online-payment service, by credits to a credit card account, or by ACH transfers made to their bank accounts. PayPal, now owned by eBay, was the pioneer online payment service, and Google has recently entered the field. In 2005, users moved $27.5 billion through PayPal. PayPal Agrees to Better Detail Its Fraud Protection Policies, LATimes, Oct. 29, 2006, at C3.

Even merchants who are authorized to accept credit cards sometimes prefer to use an online payment service because the costs of Internet payments made through the ACH batching system are lower than the charges made by the credit card networks for the clearing and settlement of credit card payments. In the future, interbank agreements may reduce the need for an intermediary such as an online payment service entity. For a detailed treatment of Internet person-to-person payments, see Melanie L. Fein, Law of Electronic Banking § 6.05[B] (2003 Supp.), and Clarks' Bank Deposits and Payments Monthly, Vol. 9, No. 9, p. 4, March 2000.

### b. ONLINE BANKING AND BILL PAYING

Banks are pressing their customers to do their banking and bill paying online. They have strong incentives to do so: most charge their customers fees for online payment services; online payment users tend to stay with their banks longer and hold higher balances; and a banking transaction completed over the Internet costs the bank only a penny, compared with 27 cents for an ATM and $1.07 for a teller. Some banks give premiums to customers who convert to online bill paying. Estimates are that one-third of households, or about 35 million, use online banking. Jane J. Kim, Online Banking Gets More Sophisticated, Wall St. J., June 27, 2006, at D1. All the customer need do is to go to her bank's Web site, create a user name and password and indicate which account is to be accessed. At this point the customer can do just about anything online that can be done on a telephone: pay bills, transfer money between accounts, apply for credit cards, mortgages or other loans. The Kim article reports that major banks are adding personal finance tools to allow customers to manage their money online. Customers avoid the monthly chore of writing checks to pay their bills; no search for stamps and licking envelopes; busy customers save time and banks make money.

Customers can use online banking to make payments to anyone having a bank account, and the payments can be scheduled a year in advance. Thus, a customer can schedule at the beginning of the year all recurring payments to be made during the year; can keep her money in interest bearing savings accounts until the time of payment when the money can be transferred into a checking account; and can get a confirmation on the screen for every transaction. A problem is that a transfer can be made electronically only to a payee whose bank and account number are known either to the customer or the payor bank. To meet this problem, banks have signed up large numbers of businesses that are prepared to accept electronic payments to their accounts. Thus, in the usual case of a payment to a business, all the customer has to be sure about is the name and address of the payee, for the bank will know its account number. In cases in which the databank does not contain the payee's account number and the payee has not provided that number to the customer, payment may be made by the customer's bank's sending that person a paper check drawn on the customer's account. This must also be done when the payee is not equipped to receive electronic payments.

An alternative method of online bill paying is to accept the invitation of a growing number of companies that encourage debtors to pay their bills directly at the biller's Web site by authorizing the biller to charge the debtor's bank account or credit card. After giving the biller the information about the debtor's bank account or credit card to be charged the first time a payment is made, subsequently, all the debtor has to do is to click the "pay" button on the biller's Web site and the money is withdrawn from the bank account or charged to the credit card. Clearing can be done through the ACH system if a credit card is not used. The downside of direct billing is that the debtor must visit each Web site in order to pay. Customers can also arrange for automatic deductions to pay periodic bills.

There is wide-spread belief that online bill paying will not replace checks until the industry has incorporated electronic bill presentment or delivery as a feature of online bill paying. At present the customer usually receives bills by mail, but systems have been developed in which bills are received online. These systems turn paper bills into electronic bills if the customer arranges for her bills to be sent to a processing facility. This enables customers, having been alerted by a message "You have bills," to log onto a Web site and view any bills that had been presented; payment can be made by a click. Electronic bill presentment is regarded as likely to lead to much broader acceptance of computer banking.

## 5.   STORED VALUE OR PREPAID CARDS

The plastic cards that we call credit or debit cards are merely bearers of information, encoded in machine readable form on a magnetic strip on the back of a card. A stored value (or "prepaid" or "value-added") card uses a computer chip or magnetic strip to hold information that allows the cardholder to make purchases. More recent stored value cards ("smart" cards) use computer chips, which reliably retain information and allow encryption to avoid duplication or unauthorized use of the card. Long used in Europe and Asia, "smart" cards are less used in the United States. In Hong Kong, they are used in subways, movie theaters, parking meters, and even McDonald's, as well as for security purposes at schools and residential complexes. Stacy Forster, Smart Cards Escape the U.S. Mind, Wall St. J., July 16, 2002, at D2. Because they can store large quantities of information, their potential use is unlimited. "Smart" cards can serve as a health insurance card, containing the patient's medical records, or as electronic "dog tags" for soldiers. China is using these cards to allow their security authorities to store personal information about its citizens on ID cards with embedded microchips. Andrew Batson, China Orders Up To A Billion Smart Cards, Wall St. J., Aug. 12, 2003, at A10.

When used as a means of payment, the cards store a "value" of funds available for the cardholder's use. The balance of funds recorded on the card is debited at the merchant's terminal when the cardholder makes a purchase. Stored value cards therefore serve as substitutes for cash, although the information stored on the cards is not itself cash. Use of the card does not transfer funds to the merchant; it only transfers information telling it of its right to be paid by the card sponsor. Stored value cards are extensively treated in Donald I. Baker & Roland E. Brandel, The Law of Electronic Fund Transfer Systems, Chapter 9 (1988, Cum. Supp. 1995), and in 2 Clark & Clark, The Law of Bank Deposits, Collections and Credit Cards & 16.07 (Rev. ed. 2005).

Our interest in stored value cards is in their function as cash substitutes. Stored value card systems are of two basic sorts: "online" and "off line" systems. The stored value card systems differ as to whether transactions are made with or without communication with a central data facility operated by the system provider. "Online" systems process use of the card by communication from the facility giving authorization for a transaction. A record of the balance of funds available to the cardholder is maintained only at a central data facility. Off line systems involve card use without contact with a central data facility. These systems differ in turn according to where the primary record of the balance of funds on the card is maintained. If the primary record is maintained at a central data facility, the system is considered an off line "accountable" system. If the primary record is maintained on the card itself, the system is an off line "unaccountable" system. See Federal Reserve Board, Proposed Rules, 61 Fed. Reg. 19696 (1996). Almost all stored value card systems currently in use are off line unaccountable systems.

A simple example of card use in an off line unaccountable system is one in which the card is "loaded" with a sum of money, say $500, that the cardholder can use to purchase goods or services from participating merchants, telephone companies, transit systems and the like. The cardholder obtains the card by buying it from a bank teller, retailer, or by using a bank dispenser by inserting money or an ATM or credit card. It is disposable; when used up, it is worthless and may be thrown away. If the cardholder makes a purchase from a merchant, no identification is sought;

the card has its own verification and passwords. The merchant deducts the sale price by running the card through a terminal. The balance record contained in the card in turn is reduced by the amount of the sale price and is ascertainable by ATM or POS terminals. (In an off line accountable system, the primary balance record is reduced at the central data storage facility as well.) The merchant aggregates balances stored in its transaction records, usually on a daily basis, and transmits them electronically in a "batched" transmission to the system provider. Upon verifying the validity of the transmission, the provider transfers funds to the merchant equal to the aggregate amount of the transmissions minus a discount fee reflecting the system provider's expenses. At least with respect to the cardholder and participating merchant, the card is a complete substitute for cash.

More sophisticated cards may be "reloadable" by accessing the cardholder's bank account through an ATM machine or the Internet. They may be online through the use of ATM or POS terminals, and, like debit cards, the cardholder's bank account is debited upon use. However, until reloaded, these cards can transfer value only to the extent of the amount stored on the card. College students are familiar with these cards because a growing number of universities have combined them with the student's identification card, allowing the student to make on-campus purchases. Credit card companies have developed technologies that allow consumers to download dollar amounts from their bank accounts onto cards.

The question facing banks and merchants is whether the potential for stored value cards justifies the costs of converting from the present magnetic strip technology to one that will accommodate these cards. If sufficiently high volume can be obtained, banks may profit handsomely from stored value cards by the "float," that is, having cardholder's money until the card is used up, by charging fees from participating merchants and by keeping the few cents left on the card when the cardholder discards it. (In principle, competitive pressure could force card providers to pay interest on unused funds deposited with the provider, thus reducing profit from the "float.") As is true with the introduction of any new operational technology, the chicken-and-egg dilemma arises: banks and merchants would prefer not to convert to stored value cards until there are enough customers to promise ultimate profitability; customers would like not to go to the trouble of obtaining stored value cards until enough providers of goods and services are prepared to accept them.

Stored value cards have had a slow start in this country. Banks made a major promotional effort to popularize them in connection with the 1996 Olympic Games in Atlanta. They signed up merchants with some 1500 retail outlets, mostly fast food outlets and gas stations, and the Atlanta transit system. There results were encouraging but hardly a gold medal performance. Nikhil Deogun, The Smart Money is on "Smart Cards," but Electronic Cash Seems Dumb to Some, Wall St. J., Aug. 5, 1996, at B1. In 1997 VisaUSA, MasterCard International, Citibank and Chase Manhattan distributed 80,000 stored value cards to New Yorkers on Manhattan's Upper West Side; 700 merchants signed up to accept them. In 1998 they ended the program, citing little support from consumers and merchant complaints of slow processing. Brian Tracey, The Color of Money, Wall St. J., Nov. 16, 1998, at R28. Smart cards have been more successful in continental Europe, where governments along with some banks have ensured demand by installing pay telephones, bus-ticket machines and parking meters that accept (sometimes exclusively) smart cards. In America and Britain, where such decisions are more decentralized, guaranteeing demand for smart cards is harder. Keep the Change, The Economist, Nov. 21, 1998, at 73.

In the article, cited above, Stacy Forster concludes that so far stored value cards have been a failure in the U.S. in part because retailers have been reluctant to install the higher-end processing equipment necessary to read them. He refers to the Upper West Side flop and the view of Americans that the cards have to do more than serve as cash-substitutes before they will embrace them. Kathy Chu, Prepaid Cash Cards See Mixed Results, Wall St. J., September 10, 2003, at B4B, chronicles the lack of success of prepaid, reloadable cash cards aimed at teenagers and college students.

A related transaction is one in which employers issue "payroll cards" to their employees that allow them to access a bank account established for each employee by the employer into which the employee's salary is periodically deposited. An alternative is to pool all employees' salary accounts, with "subaccounts" for each employee. This allows employees who do not have bank accounts to avoid having to cash paychecks at check cashing agencies that charge hefty fees. These plastic cards have magnetic stripes that allow employees to obtain cash at ATMs or to make purchases from merchants with the cards in the same manner that they would with debit cards. Effective July 1, 2007, Fed regulations bring payroll card transactions within Regulation E. 71 FR 1437 (January 10, 2006). The regulation is discussed in 1 Barkley and Barbara Clark, The Law of Bank Deposits, Collections and Credit Cards, ¶ 16.06 [13][b] (Rev. ed. 2005).

# CHAPTER 15

# FRAUD, FORGERY, AND ALTERATION

## A. FORGERY

## 1. ALLOCATION OF LOSS BETWEEN CUSTOMER AND PAYOR BANK

### a. INTRODUCTION

Suppose Customer has a checking account in Payor Bank. Thief steals Customer's checkbook, writes a check payable to Payee, and signs Customer's name to the check as drawer. Because Thief was not authorized to sign Customer's name, the signature is ineffective as the signature of Customer unless some provision of Article 3 or Article 4 makes it effective. 3–403(a). Since Customer did not sign the check and did not authorize Thief to sign the check, Customer is not liable on the check. 3–401(a). The check, however, is not a nullity. Although it is not Customer's check, Article 3 treats it as Thief's check even though Thief signed it by using Customer's name. 3–403(a) and 3–401(b). Checks such as the check in this example, i.e., a check bearing a forged drawer's signature, are known as "forged checks." Such checks sometimes are transferred for value and paid by the drawee bank. Rights of a holder with respect to such checks can be acquired by persons who take them.

A more common type of forgery can be illustrated by the following example. Customer writes a check to the order of Payee, signs it as drawer, and mails it to Payee. Thief steals the check from Payee, indorses the check by signing Payee's name on the back of the check, and obtains payment of the check from Payor Bank. The check in this example is not a forged check because Customer's signature was not forged. Rather, the infirmity of the check is that it bears a "forged indorsement." Under 3–403(a) and 3–401 the signature by Thief is ineffective as the indorsement of Payee. Since Payee did not indorse the check, Thief cannot negotiate the check and no one can obtain rights as a holder unless some provision of Article 3 otherwise provides. 3–201(b) and 3–109(b).

What are the rights of Customer and Payor Bank toward each other if Payor Bank pays the forged check in the first example or the check bearing the forged indorsement in the second example? Under 4–401(a) a payor bank "may charge against the account of a customer an item that is properly payable from that account" and, to be properly payable, the check must be "authorized by the customer." Thus, in the case of the forged check, the Payor Bank may not debit Customer's account and is not entitled to reimbursement from Customer. The risk of loss falls on Payor Bank even though it may have had no way of discovering the forgery.

The result is the same in the case of the check bearing the forged indorsement. By the terms of the check Payor Bank was ordered by Customer to pay the check to the order of Payee. Since Payee did not receive payment and did not order payment to anybody else, Payor Bank did not comply with the terms of the check. Since Payor Bank did not pay a holder or other person entitled to receive payment, it has no right to reimbursement from Customer.

The general rule protecting Customer from loss from forgery is changed in some cases by other provisions of Article 3 or Article 4. Two of the most important provisions that may allow Payor Bank to shift the forgery loss to Customer are 3–406(a), discussed in *Thompson Maple Products*, and 4–406, discussed in *Espresso Roma*.

b.  NEGLIGENCE OF CUSTOMER CONTRIBUTING TO FORGERY

With respect to payment by a payor bank of a forged check or a check bearing a forged indorsement, if the bank can prove a failure by the customer to exercise ordinary care that substantially contributed to the making of the forged signature, the customer is precluded from asserting the forgery. 3–406(a). "Ordinary care" is defined in 3–103(a)(9). The leading case on the meaning of the words "substantially contributes to * * * the making of a forged signature" in 3–406(a) is *Thompson Maple Products*, the case that follows. Comment 2 to 3–406 discusses the meaning of the quoted words. In the absence of proof of negligence by the bank contributing to the loss, the effect of the preclusion is to give to the bank a right to reimbursement from the customer for the amount paid on the check. Under former 3–406, discussed in *Thompson Maple Products*, the preclusion against the customer did not occur if the bank was negligent in paying the check. This result is changed by Revised 3–406. Negligence by the bank does not prevent the preclusion from arising but, under subsection (b), the loss from the forgery can be apportioned between the negligent customer and the negligent bank.

## Thompson Maple Products, Inc. v. Citizens National Bank

Superior Court of Pennsylvania, 1967.
211 Pa.Super. 42, 234 A.2d 32.

■ HOFFMAN, JUDGE.

\* \* \*

The plaintiff [Thompson Maple Products] is a small, closely-held corporation, principally engaged in the manufacture of bowling pin "blanks" from maple logs. Some knowledge of its operations from 1959 to 1962 is essential to an understanding of this litigation.

The plaintiff purchased logs from timber owners in the vicinity of its mill. Since these timber owners rarely had facilities for hauling logs, such transportation was furnished by a few local truckers, including Emery Albers.

At the mill site, newly delivered logs were "scaled" by mill personnel, to determine their quantity and grade. The employee on duty noted this information, together with the name of the owner of the logs, as furnished by the hauler, on duplicate "scaling slips."

In theory, the copy of the scaling slip was to be given to the hauler, and the original was to be retained by the mill employee until transmitted by him directly to the company's bookkeeper. This ideal procedure, however, was rarely followed. Instead, in a great many instances, the mill employee simply gave both slips to the hauler for delivery to the company office. Office personnel then prepared checks in payment for the logs, naming as payee the owner indicated on the scaling slips. Blank sets of slips were readily accessible on the company premises.

Sometime prior to February, 1959, Emery Albers conceived the scheme which led to the forgeries at issue here. Albers was an independent log hauler who for many years had transported logs to the company mill. For a brief period in 1952, he had been employed by the plaintiff, and he was a trusted friend of the Thompson family. After procuring blank sets of scaling slips, Albers filled them in to show substantial, wholly fictitious deliveries of logs, together with the names of local timber owners as suppliers. He then delivered the slips to the company bookkeeper, who prepared checks payable to the purported owners. Finally, he volunteered to deliver the checks to the owners. The bookkeeper customarily entrusted the checks to him for that purpose.

Albers then forged the payee's signature and either cashed the checks or deposited them to his account at the defendant bank, where he was well known. * * *

In 1963, when the forgeries were uncovered, Albers confessed and was imprisoned. The plaintiff then instituted this suit against the drawee bank, asserting that the bank had breached its contract of deposit by paying the checks over forged endorsements. * * *

The trial court determined that the plaintiff's own negligent activities had materially contributed to the unauthorized endorsements, and it therefore dismissed the substantial part of plaintiff's claim. We affirm the action of the trial court.

Both parties agree that, as between the payor bank and its customer, ordinarily the bank must bear the loss occasioned by the forgery of a payee's endorsement.

* * *

The trial court concluded, however, that the plaintiff-drawer, by virtue of its conduct, could not avail itself of that rule, citing § 3–406 of the Code: "Any person who by his negligence substantially contributes to * * * the making of an unauthorized signature is precluded from asserting the * * * lack of authority against * * * a drawee or other payor who pays the instrument in good faith and in accordance with the reasonable commercial standards of the drawee's or payor's business." * * *

Before this Court, the plaintiff Company argues strenuously that this language is a mere restatement of pre-Code law in Pennsylvania. Under those earlier cases, it is argued, the term "precluded" is equivalent to "estopped," and negligence which will work an estoppel is only such as "directly and proximately affects the conduct of the bank in passing the forgery * * *." See, e.g., Coffin v. Fidelity–Philadelphia Trust Company, 374 Pa. 378, 393, 97 A.2d 857, 39 A.L.R.2d 625 (1953); Land Title Bank and Trust Company v. Cheltenham National Bank, 362 Pa. 30, 66 A.2d 768 (1949). The plaintiff further asserts that those decisions hold that "negligence in the conduct of the drawer's business," such as appears on this record, cannot serve to work an estoppel.

Even if that was the law in this Commonwealth prior to the passage of the Commercial Code, it is not the law today. The language of the new Act is determinative in all cases arising after its passage. This controversy must be decided, therefore, by construction of the statute and application of the negligence doctrine as it appears in § 3–406 of the Code. * * *

Had the legislature intended simply to continue the strict estoppel doctrine of the pre-Code cases, it could have employed the term "precluded," without qualification, as in § 23 of the old Negotiable Instruments Law, 56 P.S. § 28 (repealed). However, it chose to modify that doctrine in § 3–406, by specifying that negligence which *"substantially contributes to * * * the making of an unauthorized signature * * *."* will preclude the drawer from asserting a forgery. [emphasis supplied]. The Code has thus abandoned the language of the older cases (negligence which "directly and proximately affects the conduct of the bank in passing the forgery") and shortened the chain of causation which the defendant bank must establish. "[N]o attempt is made," according to the Official Comment to § 3–406, "to specify what is negligence, and the question is one for the court or jury on the facts of the particular case."

In the instant case, the trial court could readily have concluded that plaintiff's business affairs were conducted in so negligent a fashion as to have "substantially contributed" to the Albers forgeries, within the meaning of § 3–406.

Thus, the record shows that pads of plaintiff's blank logging slips were left in areas near the mill which were readily accessible to any of the haulers. Moreover, on at least two occasions, Albers was given whole pads of these blank logging slips to use as he chose. Mrs. Vinora Curtis, an employee of the plaintiff, testified:

"Q. Did you ever give any of these logging slips to Mr. Albers or any pads of these slips to Mr. Albers?

"A. Yes.

* * *

"Q. What was the reason for giving [a pad of the slips] to him, Mrs. Curtis?

"A. Well, he came up and said he needed it for [scaling] the logs, so I gave it to him."

Mrs. Amy Thompson, who also served as a bookkeeper for the plaintiff, testified:

"Q. As a matter of fact, you gave Mr. Albers the pack of your logging slips, did you not?

"A. Yes, I did once.

"Q. Do you remember what you gave them to him for?

"A. I don't right offhand, but it seems to me he said he was going out to look for some logs or timber or something and he needed them to mark some figures on * * *.

"Q. Well, if he was going to use them for scratch pads, why didn't you give him a scratch pad that you had in the office?

"A. That's what I should have done."

In addition, the plaintiff's printed scaling slips were not consecutively numbered. Unauthorized use of the slips, therefore, could easily go undetected. Thus, Mr. Nelson Thompson testified:

"Q. Mr. Thompson, were your slips you gave these haulers numbered?

"A. No, they were not.

"Q. They are now, aren't they?

"A. Yes.

"Q. Had you used numbered logging slips, this would have prevented anybody getting logging slips out of the ordinary channel of business and using it to defraud you?

"A. Yes."

Moreover, in 1960, when the company became concerned about the possible unauthorized use of its scaling slips, it required its own personnel to initial the slips when a new shipment of logs was scaled. However, this protective measure was largely ignored in practice. Mrs. Amy Thompson testified:

"Q. And later on in the course of your business, if you remember Mr. Thompson said he wanted the logging slips initialed by one of the so-called authorized people?

"A. Yes.

"Q. [D]idn't you really not pay too much attention to them at all?

"A. Well, I know we didn't send them back to be sure they were initialed. We might have noticed it but we didn't send them back to the mill.

"Q. In other words, if they came to you uninitialed, you might have noticed it but didn't do anything about it.

"A. Didn't do anything about it."

The principal default of the plaintiff, however, was its failure to use reasonable diligence in insuring honesty from its log haulers including Emery Albers. For many years, the haulers were permitted to deliver both the original and the duplicate of the scaling slip to the company office, and the company tolerated this practice. These slips supplied the bookkeeper with the payees' names for the checks she was to draw in payment for log deliveries. Only by having the company at all times retain possession of the original slip could the plaintiff have assured that no disbursements were made except for logs received, and that the proper amounts were paid to the proper persons. The practice tolerated by the plaintiff effectively removed the only immediate safeguard in the entire procedure against dishonesty on the part of the haulers.

Finally, of course, the company regularly entrusted the completed checks to the haulers for delivery to the named payees, without any explicit authorization from the latter to do so.

While none of these practices, in isolation, might be sufficient to charge the plaintiff with negligence within the meaning of § 3–406, the company's course of conduct, viewed in its entirety, is surely sufficient to support the trial judge's determination that it substantially contributed to the making of the unauthorized signatures.[6] In his words, that conduct was "no different than had the plaintiff simply given Albers a series of checks signed in blank for his unlimited, unrestricted use."

\* \* \*

Judgment affirmed.

■ WATKINS, J., dissents.

## NOTE

In Bank/First Citizens Bank v. Citizens & Associates, 82 S.W.3d 259 (Tenn. 2002), Drawer (D) was induced to invest in Payee by fraudulent representations made by Agent of Payee that she had the authority to grant franchise rights to investors. D entrusted checks payable to Payee to Agent for delivery to Payee. But Agent forged Payee's indorsement and deposited the checks in her account in Depositary Bank (DB), which obtained payment from Drawee Bank. In order to avoid liability on the presentment forged indorsement warranty it breached for collecting a check that contained a forged indorsement, DB sued D on ground that D's act of negligence in failing to inquire of Payee about Agent's authority

---

**6.** In this connection, the trial court also noted that the plaintiff at all times prior to the commencement of this litigation failed to keep an accurate inventory account. It could not therefore verify, at any given point in time, that it actually possessed the logs which it had paid for.

substantially contributed to the forgery. The court held that D was indeed negligent in giving Agent the checks without inquiring of Payee about Agent's authority but that this negligence did not substantially contribute to Agent's forgery of Payee's name in indorsing the checks for deposit in DB. Thus, the court reasoned, DB could not use the negligent drawer claim to relieve itself of liability. There was no causal connection between D's negligence and Agent's forgery. D's negligence did not increase the possibility that Agent would forge the indorsement. The court favorably cited a line of cases holding that only negligence that "proximately relates or contributes to the forgery, and not merely issuance of the checks, would relieve a collecting bank of liability for improper payment of a fraudulently endorsed check." Is this case contrary to *Thompson* on the "substantially contributes" issue? See Case #2 in Comment 3 to 3–406.

## PROBLEMS

**1.** In *Thompson Maple Products*, Albers either cashed or deposited the checks with his forged indorsement in the same bank on which they were drawn by the Thompson company. Banks call this an "on us" check, meaning the drawee bank is also the depositary bank. Note that 3–406(b) embraces a form of comparative negligence. If this case had been decided under Revised Article 3, could a case be made that Bank's conduct in *Thompson Maple Products* was not in exercise of ordinary care in paying the checks that were presented to it by Albers over a period of years that were payable to timber producers? Is there any legitimate reason why the payees would transfer the checks to Albers? Wouldn't the payees normally deposit these checks to their accounts?

**2.** Assume that the facts in *Thompson* were these: the checks made to the timber companies were made to corporate payees, and the indorsements of these companies would ordinarily be printed and "look official." Albers forged the indorsements of these companies by handwritten indorsements that were crudely done. Albers then wrote his own name under each of these indorsements. He deposited these checks in his account in Depositary Bank and withdrew the proceeds of the checks once they cleared. The checks were presented to the drawee, Citizens National Bank, which paid the checks. In subsequent litigation, the drawer, Thompson Maple Products, contended that the drawee bank is precluded from relying upon the drawer's negligence as a defense under 3–406 because of the drawee's failure to verify the indorsements. The drawee bank defended on the ground that a drawee has no duty to examine indorsements on checks that it has received from a depositary bank. Under the facts in this Problem, Albers had no deposit account in drawee bank and the drawee had no reason to be familiar with his signature. Is drawee bank correct in this case? See Guardian Life Ins. Co. of America v. Weisman, 223 F.3d 229 (3d Cir. 2000).

Do the comparative fault provisions of 3–406(b) create a new affirmative cause of action for negligence? The following case analyzes the issue.

# Halifax Corporation v. Wachovia Bank

Supreme Court of Virginia, 2004.
604 S.E.2d 403.

■ OPINION BY SENIOR JUSTICE HARRY L. CARRICO.

## *Introduction*

In the period from August 1995 to February 1999, Mary K. Adams embezzled approximately $15.4 million while serving as comptroller for companies that are now known as Halifax Corporation (Halifax). Adams accomplished the embezzlement by writing more than 300 checks on Halifax's account with Signet Bank and its successor, First Union National Bank (collectively, First Union). Adams used a stamp bearing the facsimile signature of Halifax's president and, in her own handwriting, made the checks payable to herself, to companies she had formed, or to cash. She deposited the checks in several accounts she maintained with Central Fidelity Bank and its successor, Wachovia Bank (collectively, Wachovia), receiving cash from some of the checks.

## *Procedural Background*

Upon discovery of the embezzlement, Halifax brought an action against First Union as the drawee bank and Wachovia as the depositary bank. (*Halifax I.*) The trial court granted summary judgment in favor of First Union. Halifax then took a nonsuit of the action against Wachovia and appealed to this Court from the order dismissing First Union. We affirmed the dismissal, holding that Halifax's claim was barred pursuant to Code § 8.4–406(f), part of the Uniform Commercial Code (hereinafter, UCC), for Halifax's failure to notify First Union of the unauthorized signatures within one year after the bank's statement covering the checks in question was made available to Halifax. *Halifax Corp. v. First Union Nat'l Bank*, 262 Va. 91, 104, 546 S.E.2d 696, 704 (2001).

While the appeal to this Court was pending, Halifax filed in the court below a three-count motion for judgment asserting that Wachovia and First Union were liable to Halifax for the amounts embezzled by Adams. (*Halifax II.*) Count I alleged negligence, gross negligence, and bad faith on the part of Wachovia in violation of Code §§ 8.3A–404,–405, and–406. Count II alleged common law conversion by Wachovia and First Union. Count III alleged that Wachovia and First Union aided and abetted Adams' breach of fiduciary duty.

The trial court dismissed the claims against First Union on the ground of res judicata. This Court refused Halifax's petition for appeal from that dismissal. *Halifax Corp. v. First Union Nat'l Bank*, March 5, 2002 (Record No. 012582).

Wachovia moved for summary judgment on Halifax's claims against it. The trial court granted the motion, holding, contrary to Halifax's contention, that Code § 8.3A–406 does not create an affirmative cause of action, that Halifax's common law claim for conversion had been displaced by Code § 8.3A–420(a), and that Halifax had failed to allege sufficient facts to state a cause of action for aiding and abetting Adams' breach of fiduciary duty, assuming such an action exists. From the final order embodying these holdings and granting final judgment in favor of Wachovia, we awarded Halifax this appeal.

### Factual Background

Since the trial court disposed of the case by granting Wachovia's motion for summary judgment, we will adopt those inferences from the facts that are most favorable to Halifax, the nonmoving party, unless the inferences are strained, forced, or contrary to reason. * * * The facts as alleged in Halifax's motion for judgment show that Mary Adams, also known as Mary Collins, became comptroller at Halifax's Richmond office in August 1995 and continued in that position until March 1999. She maintained four personal and two commercial accounts with Wachovia. One of the commercial accounts was styled "Collins Racing, Inc." and the other "Collins Ostrich Ranch."

When Adams first began embezzling money from Halifax in August 1995, she deposited in her personal accounts with Wachovia several checks each month for over $5,000.00. The amounts of the checks soon increased to between $10,000.00 and $15,000.00 each and before long to amounts ranging from $50,000.00 to $150,000.00 each, and deposits were made multiple times a day or week. For example, in July 1997, Adams deposited on July 9 a check for $95,550.00, on July 14, one check for $55,000.00 and another for $99,300.00, on July 16, a check for $93,500.00, on July 21, a check for $80,600.00, and, on July 30, a check for $149,305.00, totaling $573,255.00. In all, Adams drew 328 checks totaling $15,429,665.42 on Halifax's account with First Union.

Adams was "one of the best and largest individual customers" of Wachovia's branch where she did business. Managers and tellers saw Adams " 'a lot,' " and she stood out because of her large checks and banking activity." The entire branch was curious about her "because of her large checks," the likes of which "none of the tellers had ever seen . . . before." Some tellers claimed "to have believed or assumed that Adams 'was at least part owner' of the corporate drawer."

Wachovia "repeatedly accepted such huge handwritten checks drawn on the account of Adams' employer despite the gross disparity with Adams payroll amount [of about $1,000.00 per pay period] shown on each teller and manager screen." The tellers "had concerns about individual checks or the check activity, or both." Bank officials knew Adams was Halifax's comptroller and understood that "such transactions by a financial officer, or even a part owner, present[ed] a serious potential for fraud." Yet, branch "[m]anagers and supervisors told the tellers to do whatever Adams wanted."

### Discussion

#### Negligence, Gross Negligence, and Bad Faith

Halifax contends that Code § 8.3A–406, when read in light of Code §§ 8.3A–404 and–405, gives rise to an affirmative cause of action for the negligence of a depositary bank with respect to the alteration of an instrument or the making of a forged signature. These sections were part of the General Assembly's 1992 revision of the UCC.

It should be noted at this point, however, that the trial court stated in a footnote to its order granting Wachovia's motion for summary judgment that Halifax did "not contest Wachovia's motion as to Halifax's claims under Va.Code 8.3A–404 and 405," and Halifax does not now press those claims. * * *

Code § 8.3A–406 provides as follows:

**Negligence, contributing to forged signature or alteration of instrument.**—(a) A person whose failure to exercise ordinary care substantially contributes to an alteration of an instrument or to the making of a forged signature on an instrument is precluded from asserting the alteration or the forgery against a person who, in good faith, pays the instrument or takes it for value or for collection.

(b) Under subsection (a), if the person asserting the preclusion fails to exercise ordinary care in paying or taking the instrument and that failure substantially contributes to loss, the loss is allocated between the person precluded and the person asserting the preclusion according to the extent to which the failure of each to exercise ordinary care contributed to the loss.

(c) Under subsection (a), the burden of proving failure to exercise ordinary care is on the person asserting the preclusion. Under subsection (b), the burden of proving failure to exercise ordinary care is on the person precluded. * * *

Next, Halifax cites Official Comment 4 to Code § 8.3A–406, which reads as follows:

Subsection (b) ... adopts a concept of comparative negligence. If the person precluded under subsection (a) proves that the person asserting the preclusion failed to exercise ordinary care and that failure substantially contributed to the loss, the loss may be allocated between the two parties on a comparative negligence basis.

Halifax then says "[l]eading commentators recognize that the concept of comparative negligence, duty, and loss allocation provided in 3–406, like that in 3–404 and 3–405, creates a cause of action." Halifax quotes 2 James J. White & Robert S. Summers, *Uniform Commercial Code* § 19–3 (4th ed.1995) (hereinafter, White & Summers) to this effect:

"3–406 and the accompanying sections carry with them something that did not exist under the old Code, namely, a new cause of action." *Id.* at 247 "This mechanism is an affirmative cause of action for negligence under 3–406(b)(and similar causes of action under 3–404, 3–405, and 3–406) under which the depositor-employer recovers a part of its loss by affirmative proof that the negligent behavior of the defendant bank caused a portion of it." *Id.* "3–406(b) gives an affirmative cause of action." *Id.* at 248. "[T]he 1990 changes in 3–406, and the analogous changes having to do with comparative negligence in the other sections ... are likely to cause significant but subtle changes in the allocation of civil liability." *Id.* at 253.

According to Halifax, another White & Summers quotation explains the "significance of the subtle language changes in revised § 8.3A–406":

[The] allocation of liability based on comparative negligence is new, incorporated into the Code as part of the 1990 amendments to Article[s] 3 and 4. Before the 1990 amendments, "preclusion" cases were standard contributory negligence cases. A bank might first argue that the customer was negligent, and the customer would respond that the bank was contributorily negligent. If both claims were proven, negligence would disappear from the case and the bank would be barred from asserting the customer's negligence.

One consequence of adopting a comparative negligence standard is that there will have to be wider recognition of negligence as a basis not merely for defense (preclusion), but also as a basis for asserting an affirmative claim. For example, in section 3–406(a), a depositor may be precluded from asserting alteration if the depositor's failure to exercise ordinary care substantially contributed to the alteration. Under 3–406(b), the "loss is allocated" between the two parties if the bank also failed to exercise ordinary care. Although it does not say so in terms, the "loss allocated" language in 3–406(b) *must be interpreted* to grant an affirmative cause of action to the depositor in our hypothetical case as a means of recovering for that part of the loss which the bank should bear. As the statute is written, the bank's negligence no longer lifts the preclusion of 3–406(a), as it did before 1990. Rather, the bank's negligence gives other parties a cause of action to recover an appropriate share under 3–406(b). In that respect, the 1990 revisions state a subtle modification of the theories of recovery, and not merely a readjustment of the identity of those who bear losses.

White & Summers, § 19–1 at 239 (emphasis added) (footnotes omitted).

The views of White & Summers, however, are just not compatible with Virginia law. They say that Code § 3A–406(b) "must be interpreted" to create a cause of action. § 19–1 at 239. However, the rule in Virginia is that, unless the language of a legislative enactment is ambiguous, " 'there is no room for interpretation or construction; the plain meaning and intent of the [enactment] must be given it.' " *City of Emporia Bd. of Zoning Appeals v. Mangum*, 263 Va. 38, 41, 556 S.E.2d 779, 781 (2002) (quoting *Board of Zoning Appeals of the County of York v. 852 L.L.C.*, 257 Va. 485, 489, 514 S.E.2d 767, 769 (1999)).

" 'Language is ambiguous when it may be understood in more than one way, or simultaneously refers to two or more things.' " *Supinger v. Stakes*, 255 Va. 198, 205, 495 S.E.2d 813, 817 (1998) (quoting *Lee–Warren v. School Bd. of Cumberland County*, 241 Va. 442, 445, 403 S.E.2d 691, 692 (1991)). For Code § 8.3A–406 to be declared ambiguous, its language must lend itself to being understood in one way as creating a cause of action and in another way as not creating a cause of action. In our opinion, the statute cannot be understood as creating a cause of action for several reasons.

In the first place, the term "cause of action" or "may recover" or anything remotely resembling either term nowhere appears in Code § 8.3A–406. And this Court cannot supply the language that would have created an affirmative cause of action under the circumstances of this case. "[C]ourts are not permitted to rewrite statutes. This is a legislative function. The manifest intention of the legislature, clearly disclosed by its language, must be applied. There can be no departure from the words used where the intention is clear." *Supinger*, 255 Va. at 206, 495 S.E.2d at 817 (quoting *Anderson v. Commonwealth*, 182 Va. 560, 566, 29 S.E.2d 838, 841 (1944)).

Second, Official Comment 1 to Code § 8.3A–406 states that subsection (a) "adopts the doctrine" that a "*drawer* who so negligently draws an instrument as to facilitate its material alteration [or its forgery] is liable to a *drawee* who pays the altered [or forged] instrument in good faith." (Emphasis added.) But statutory language making a drawer liable to a drawee cannot possibly be taken as showing an intention to create a cause of action in favor of a drawer against a depositary bank.

Third, Official Comment 1 further states: "Section 3–406 does not make the negligent party liable in tort for damages resulting from the alteration. If the negligent party is estopped from asserting the alteration the person taking the instrument is fully protected because the taker can treat the instrument as having been issued in the altered form." We will assume Halifax is correct in saying the comment means "3–406 is not intended to make the negligent drawer subject to preclusion liable in tort." But Halifax is incorrect in saying "the comment shows the converse was intended, that 3–406 makes the bank liable in tort." This is not only a non sequitur but it is also contrary to the provision in the very next sentence of the Comment, which states that "the person taking the instrument is fully protected because the taker can treat the instrument as having been issued in the altered [or forged] form." It is difficult to imagine how something that is designed to protect the taker can logically be turned on its head and used to create a cause of action against the taker.

Finally, and of overriding importance, we follow the rule in Virginia that "when the General Assembly includes specific language in one section of a statute, but omits that language from another section of the statute, we must presume that the exclusion of the language was intentional." *Halifax I*, 262 Va. at 100, 546 S.E.2d at 702. Strikingly absent from Code § 8.3A–406 is the specific language contained in Code §§ 8.3A–404 and –405 that "the person bearing the loss may recover from the person failing to exercise ordinary care." The General Assembly knows how to create a cause of action when that is its intention, and the omission of the "may recover" or similar language from Code § 8.3A–406 represents an unambiguous manifestation of a contrary intention. * * *

Halifax cites several out-of-state decisions in support of its contention that "revised 3–406 provides a cause of action, in favor of a drawer against a depositary bank." * * * These are all trial court decisions; we find them unpersuasive. * * *

We conclude that the trial court did not err in its holding that Code § 8.3A–406 does not create an affirmative cause of action and in awarding summary judgment to Wachovia with respect to that claim. * * *

### *Conclusion*

Finding no error in the holdings of the trial court, we will affirm its judgment.

*Affirmed.*

c.   FAILURE OF CUSTOMER TO REPORT FORGERY

In cases involving forged checks, the malefactor often forges a series of checks on the same account over a period of time. Forgery with respect to a single check is much more likely to involve a forged indorsement rather than a forgery of the drawer's signature. Typically, repeated forged check cases involve a dishonest employee of the person whose signature is forged. Usually the employee has access to the employer's checkbook and often has duties related to bookkeeping. In the case of repeated forgeries the later forgeries could have been easily prevented if the person whose signature was forged had detected the earlier forgeries. Such detection is relatively easy because in most cases the payor bank, after paying a check, returns the cancelled check to the customer on whose account the check was drawn. The customer should be able to determine whether a check written on the its account is a forgery. On the other hand it may be very difficult for the payor bank to detect forgery. Since it is easy for the customer to detect a forgery, 4–406 imposes a duty on the customer to report forged checks to the bank. Failure of the customer to comply with this duty can, in some cases, result in a shifting of the loss from the bank to the customer. Although 3–406 applies to checks bearing a forged indorsement as well as forged checks, 4–406 does not apply to forged indorsements. Both sections also apply to altered checks which are discussed later in this chapter.

Given the rule that a payor bank bears the loss on a check it pays over a forged drawer's signature, banks had traditionally engaged in the labor intensive activity of sight review of all checks drawn on the bank. Bank employees compared the signature on each check with that on the signature specimen card on file. For a large bank, a typical setting was a big room, crammed with desks, with soft music, free softdrinks and aspirin, and other amenities designed to keep these unfortunate workers from losing their minds. As the volume of checks grew and automation became the norm, banks abandoned sight review except for checks that met certain risk criteria, the principal one being the amount of the check.

Now that forgers utilize desktop printers, sight review has become obsolete for the large volume of corporate and government checks on which signatures are printed. Even on personal checks in which a signature is written in ink, a sight reviewer, who can normally spend only a few seconds on each check, is no match for a skillful forger. Thus, banks came to the conclusion that sight review was not cost effective. Some banks purported to find no greater forgery losses without sight review than with it, and others contended that whatever losses they might suffer on the payment of forged checks of relatively small amounts did not justify the heavy labor costs involved. As we shall see, payor banks have better ways of fighting forgeries than sight review.

The legal problems raised by the abandonment of sight review occupied the courts for years. Julianna J. Zekan, Comparative Negligence Under the Code: Protecting Negligent Banks Against Negligent Customers, 26 U. Mich. J.L. Reform 125, 166–178 (1992). Under 4–406, the customer is obliged to examine its cancelled checks for forgeries and to notify the payor bank if any are found. If it fails to do so in a timely manner, the customer is precluded from raising the forgery *unless the bank fails to exercise ordinary care.* Before the 1990 revision of Articles 3 and 4 became effective, the case law was sharply divided on the issue whether a bank that did not conduct sight review of the checks in question was exercising ordinary care. In Medford Irrigation District v. Western Bank, 66 Or.App. 589, 676 P.2d 329 (Or.Ct.App.1984), the bank's automated system was programmed to pay all checks of $5,000 or less unless there was a hold or stop order on the check; checks for amounts in excess of that sum were selected out by the check sorting machine and individually reviewed. The court held that the bank was precluded from raising the customer's negligence on the ground that in order to exercise ordinary care a bank's system must be reasonably related to the detection of forged signatures. Since in this case the bank had no procedure for detecting forgeries in checks under $5,000 the bank was negligent *as a matter of law.*

The *Medford* view has been rejected in a number of cases. The Illinois Supreme Court held in Wilder Binding Co. v. Oak Park Trust & Savings Bank, 135 Ill.2d 121, 552 N.E.2d 783 (Ill. 1990), that whether a bank exercised ordinary care in paying a check is a question of fact. In Rhode Island Hospital Trust National Bank v. Zapata Corp., 848 F.2d 291 (1st Cir.1988) (Breyer, J.), the court approved the cost-benefit analysis rejected in *Medford.* Judge Breyer opined that there was no evidence that any increased forgery loss from the bank's automated system was unreasonable in light of the costs that the new practices would save. He relied on Learned Hand's view that duty should be defined by calculating the probability of injury times the gravity of harm to determine the burden of precaution that is warranted. United States v. Carroll Towing Co., 159 F.2d 169 (2d Cir.1947).

In the revision of Articles 3 and 4, the Drafting Committee was mindful of the need to make sure that Revised Article 4 would accommodate a system of electronic presentment, discussed in the preceding chapter, if such a system were developed. This tipped the scale in favor of adopting the line of authority rejecting *Medford.* This was implemented in the definition of "ordinary care" in 3–103(a)(9), discussed in Comment 5 to 3–103 and Comment 4 to 4–406. The following case discusses 3–103(a)(9) and is instructive in showing how banks attempt to prove ordinary care under that provision.

## Espresso Roma Corporation v. Bank Of America, N.A.

Court of Appeal, First District, California, 2002.
124 Cal.Rptr.2d 549.

■ Stein, Acting P.J.

Espresso Roma Corporation, Pacific Espresso Corporation, and David S. Boyd dba Hillside Residence Hall (appellants) appeal from a judgment dismissing their complaint alleging several causes of action against Bank of America, N.A. (Bank), based upon its payment of forged checks drawn on appellants' accounts by one of their former employees. The court entered judgment in favor of the Bank after it granted the Bank's motion for summary judgment on the ground that appellants were precluded by California Uniform Commercial Code section 4406, subdivisions (d) and (e) from asserting any claims against the Bank for unauthorized payment of checks drawn on their accounts. We shall affirm the judgment.

David S. Boyd is the president of Espresso Roma and Pacific Espresso Corporations and also runs Hillside Residence Hall. All three businesses had checking accounts with the Bank.

From late 1996 through April 1999, appellants employed Joseph Montanez, who eventually assumed certain bookkeeping responsibilities, learned how to generate company checks on the computer, and had access to blank checks. Starting in October 1997, Montanez downloaded company computer programs, stole blank checks, and printed company checks on his home computer which he used to pay his personal bills, and for personal purchases. He concealed his actions by removing the forged checks from the bank statements when he sorted the mail.

Boyd did not discover the forgeries, or report them to the Bank until May 1999. After Montanez left the company, a check was returned by a stereo company, bearing a signature that Boyd did not recognize. Boyd then reviewed the records and discovered that, from October 1997 through April 1999, Montanez had forged company checks in an amount totaling more than $330,000.

The Bank's motion for summary judgment was based upon section 4406, which limits a payor bank's liability to its customer for making payment upon checks with alterations or unauthorized signatures.

Pursuant to subdivision (f) of section 4406, the Bank asserted that appellants were absolutely precluded from asserting forgeries processed more than one year before the forgery was reported. By its terms subdivision (f) applies, "[w]ithout regard to care or lack of care of either the customer or the bank," (italics added) and precludes "a customer who does not within one year after the statement or items are made available to the customer . . . discover and report the customer's unauthorized signature" from asserting it against the Bank. The Bank also relied upon the conditional preclusion established by subdivisions (d) and (e) of section 4406. Subdivision (c) of section 4406 imposes a duty upon the customer promptly to review monthly statements or checks made available to the customer by the bank, to exercise reasonable care in discovering any unauthorized signature or alteration, and promptly to notify the bank of the discovery of such items. Pursuant to subdivision (d), if the customer fails to comply with these duties, when the same person has forged checks on the account, the customer is precluded from making a claim against the bank for the unauthorized payment unless the customer notified the bank no more than 30 days after the first forged item was included in the monthly statement or canceled checks, and should have been discovered. (§ 4406, subd. (d)(2).) This preclusion is conditional because the customer may avoid its application by establishing that the bank "failed to exercise ordinary care in paying the item and that the failure contributed to [the] loss." (§ 4406, subd. (e)) * * *.

In its order granting summary judgment, the court held that appellants were precluded by "sections 4406(d) and 4406(e) from asserting claims against the [B]ank for unauthorized payments of checks drawn on [appellants'] checking accounts." The court specifically ruled that appellants failed to create a triable issue of fact as to whether "the [B]ank's system of processing checks for [appellants' accounts] violated the [B]ank's . . . procedures" or varied unreasonably from general banking usage in the area. The court also ruled that the declaration of appellant's expert failed to create a triable issue of fact "as to whether the [B]ank failed to exercise ordinary care," and that the Bank had no duty to sight review the checks.[2]

Appellants argue that the burden never shifted to them to create a triable issue of fact because the Bank failed to meet its "burden of production to make a prima facie showing of the nonexistence of any triable issue of fact," that (1) despite the availability of monthly statements and canceled checks, appellants failed to discover and notify the Bank of the forgery within 30 days, and (2) it exercised ordinary care in paying the item. * * * Appellants further contend that, even if the burden did shift to them, the declaration of their own expert created a triable issue of fact on the issue whether the bank exercised ordinary care, precluding summary judgment in the Bank's favor.

## 1. APPELLANTS' FAILURE TO DISCOVER AND REPORT THE FORGERIES

Pursuant to section 4406, subdivision (d), the customer is precluded from making a claim against the bank for unauthorized payment unless the

---

**2.** The Bank contends that, even if triable issues of fact existed on the issue of exercise of ordinary care, the absolute preclusion set forth in section 4406, subdivision (f) applied, and was shortened by contract to a period of six months, thereby barring nearly half of appellants' claim without regard to exercise of ordinary care. We need not reach this contention because we shall uphold the summary judgment upon the ground that no triable issue of fact existed with respect to the application of the conditional preclusion set forth in section 4406, subdivisions (d) and (e).

customer notified the bank no more than 30 days after the *first* forged item was included in the monthly statement or canceled checks and should have been discovered. (§ 4406, subd. (d)(2); see also Official Comments on U. Com. Code, West's Ann. Cal. U. Com. Code, (2002 ed.) com. 2, § 4406, p. 190.)[3]

According to the complaint, the forged checks were presented for payment between October 1997 and May 1999, but appellants did not discover or report them until on or about May 15, 1999. To establish its prima facie case that the conditional issue preclusion created by section 4406, subdivision (d) applied, the Bank presented the deposition testimony of Boyd, that it made monthly account statements and canceled checks available to appellants shortly after the closing period of each statement. Boyd testified that he received statements on a monthly basis, and they included canceled checks. When Boyd began to suspect unauthorized checks were being written and reviewed the statements and checks in May 1999, he was able to identify, and reported, the forgery. This evidence supports the inference that the first monthly statement that would have reflected the forgery by Montanez would have been in November 1997 * * * Yet, despite having the means to discover the forgeries, more than a year and a half elapsed before appellants discovered and reported any of them, far beyond the 30 days specified in section 4406, subdivision (d). * * *

## 2. EVIDENCE THAT THE BANK EXERCISED ORDINARY CARE

Having established a prima facie case that the Bank made monthly statements and checks available, and that appellants failed to notify the Bank within 30 days, the issue preclusion pursuant to section 4406, subdivision (d) applies unless the customer can establish that the bank, "failed to exercise ordinary care in paying the item and that the failure contributed to [the] loss." (§ 4406, subd. (e).) "Ordinary care" is defined by section 3103, subdivision (a)(7) as follows: " 'Ordinary care' in the case of a person engaged in business means observance of reasonable commercial standards, prevailing in the area in which the person is located, with respect to the business in which the person is engaged. In the case of a bank that takes an instrument for processing for collection or payment by automated means, reasonable commercial standards do not require the bank to examine the instrument if the failure to examine does not violate the bank's prescribed procedures and the bank's procedures do not vary

---

**3.** The California Uniform Commercial Code comment 2 explains: "Subsection (d)(2) applies to cases in which the customer fails to report an unauthorized signature or alteration with respect to an item . . . and the bank subsequently pays other items of the customer with respect to which there is an alteration or unauthorized signature of the customer and the same wrongdoer is involved. If the payment of the subsequent items occurred after the customer has had a reasonable time, (not exceeding 30 days) to report *with respect to the first item*, and before the bank received notice of the unauthorized signature or alteration *of the first item*, the customer is precluded from asserting the alteration or unauthorized signature with respect to the subsequent items." (Official Comments on U.Com. Code, 23B West's Ann. Cal. U.Com. Code, *supra*, Com. 2, foll. § 4406 (2002 ed.) p. 190, italics added.)

unreasonably from general banking usage not disapproved by this [D]ivision or Division 4 (commencing with Section 4104.)''

As explained in *Story Road Flea Market, Inc. v. Wells Fargo Bank* (1996) 42 Cal.App.4th 1733, 1742, 50 Cal.Rptr.2d 524, a case in which the court upheld a motion for summary judgment in the Bank's favor based upon section 4406, subdivisions (d) and (e), ordinary care as used in section 4406 is a '' 'professional negligence' standard of care which looks at the procedures utilized in the banking industry rather than what a 'reasonable person' might have done under the circumstances.'' (*Id.* at p. 1741, 50 Cal.Rptr.2d 524.) '' '[R]easonable commercial standards do not require the bank to *examine the instrument* if the failure to examine does not violate the bank's prescribed procedures and the bank's procedures do not vary unreasonably from general banking usage.' '' (*Id.* at p. 1742, 50 Cal.Rptr.2d 524, italics added.)

The Bank, in support of its motion for summary judgment, presented a prima facie showing that it exercised ordinary care, through the declaration of its expert, Jack Thomas. In addition to stating his qualifications as an expert in the field, Thomas declared that he was ''familiar with the check processing strategies and procedures employed by banks similarly sized to Bank of America, including those within the San Francisco Bay area, which are 'bulk file bookkeeping' banks.'' He further explained that ''Bank of America is a 'bulk file bookkeeping' check processor,'' meaning that it processes checks automatically and does not visually examine individual checks or verify signatures. Thomas declared that Bank of America processes in excess of one million checks per day in California, and although it uses fraud filters, they are not designed to ''catch a crooked employee who forges his employer's checks, which only the employer would know are forged.'' Thomas declared that the Bank's ''practices and procedures are consistent with those of all other large 'bulk file bookkeeping' banks in California.'' Thomas also ''verified with the responsible [B]ank officer that [the Bank] followed its procedures with respect to the checks at issue in this litigation when it processed the checks.'' He concluded that the Bank ''exercised ordinary care in processing [appellants'] checks . . . in observance of reasonable commercial standards prevailing in the area in which Bank of America is located, and where [appellants] maintained their accounts.''

Appellants argue that this declaration was insufficient to define the reasonable commercial standard ''in the area,'' (§ 3103, subd. (a)(7)) and failed to demonstrate that the Bank's automated check processing did not vary unreasonably from general banking usage, because the expert stated that the Bank's practices conformed to commercial standards for ''bulk file bookkeeping'' in all of California and considered only the practices of similarly sized banks. Appellant, however, takes the reference to the entire State of California in isolation and out of context, because the expert specifically stated that he was also familiar with the practices of similarly sized banks in the ''San Francisco Bay area.'' Thus, read as a whole, the expert's declaration expressed the opinion that the Bank's practices conformed not only with those of similarly sized banks in the Bay Area, but also with similarly sized banks in the State of California. Nor are we persuaded by appellant's contention that it was necessary to offer expert opinion that the Bank's practices were consistent with those of *all* banks in the area, not just those of similarly sized banks. To the contrary, section 3103, subdivision (a)(7) defines ordinary care as "observance of reasonable commercial standards, prevailing in the area in which the person is located, with respect to the business in which the person is engaged," meaning the standard of reasonableness is set by comparable businesses. (See Official Comments on U.Com. Code 23B pt. 1 West's Ann. Cal. U.Com. Code, § 4406, p. 191 [ordinary care is established if the bank's "procedure is reasonable and is commonly followed by other comparable banks in the area" and was followed by the bank in processing the checks in issue.]) Size is a relevant factor in identifying comparable businesses because, in the banking context, a reasonable commercial standard for processing checks at a small bank with a relatively small volume of checks, and personal familiarity with its customers, would be quite different than what is reasonable for a large bank that processes upwards of a million checks per day. Thomas's declaration therefore established that the reasonable industry standard prevailing in the area for similarly sized banks was to bulk process checks through an automated system that employs fraud filters, but does not include sight review of individual checks for signature verification. The Bank's procedures conformed to this standard, which also was consistent with general bank usage as reflected by the practices of other bulk file bookkeeping banks in California, and it followed those procedures in this case. We conclude that Thomas's declaration was sufficient to establish a prima facie case that the Bank exercised ordinary care, thereby shifting the burden to appellant to create a triable issue of fact. (*Story Road Flea Market, Inc. v. Wells Fargo Bank, supra*, 42 Cal.App.4th 1733, 1738, 1743, 50 Cal.Rptr.2d 524 [expert declaration that bank processed checks, none of which were selected for sight review, in accordance with its own procedures, and consistent with reasonable commercial standards in the area, and general banking practices, shifted burden to plaintiff to create a triable issue of fact].)

Although appellants submitted the declaration of its own expert, John Moulton, in opposition, the trial court correctly concluded that it failed to create a triable issue of fact on the question whether the Bank "failed to exercise ordinary care in paying the item *and* that the failure contributed to [the] loss." (§ 4406, subd. (e), italics added.) Moulton declared that he called upon "large and small banks in Alameda County to inquire of their actual practices." These banks make decisions for payment of items at the branch where the account is kept and have the "means to check signatures for forgeries" present, whether it be by signature card or digital imaging. He also declared that these banks would manually examine checks which resulted in an overdraft, were unsigned, or exceeded a certain amount. He further declared that there were four instances of daily overdrafts occurring on days in which forged checks were processed, and one unsigned check that was processed and paid, all without selecting the checks for manual review.

The fundamental defect in Moulton's declaration is that, instead of defining the applicable reasonable commercial standard of care by looking at comparably sized banks using bulk file bookkeeping, he bases his opinion that the standard of care requires certain checks be selected for sight review, or other special handling, upon the practices of large and small banks. Without a showing that *comparable* banks in the area select individual checks for sight review, the fact that the Bank's system did not select individual checks for sight review, or signature verification, is insufficient to create a material issue of fact because section 3103, subdivision (a)(7) specifies that "reasonable commercial standards *do not require the bank to examine the instrument if the failure to examine does not violate the bank's prescribed procedures and the bank's procedures do not vary unreasonably from general banking usage.*" (Italics added.) Therefore, Moulton's declaration does not create a triable issue of fact with respect to the Bank's showing that its system of bulk processing of checks, which does not include sight review for signature verification, is commercially reasonable, and consistent with the practice of other comparably large banks in the area and in California.

Moreover, assuming arguendo that reasonable commercial standards did require that the Bank have established criteria for selecting some checks for sight review, Moulton's declaration still fails to create a triable issue of fact because it provides no basis to infer that the failure to have such a system *contributed to the loss.* (§ 4406, subd. (e) [the customer must show the Bank "failed to exercise ordinary care in paying the item *and* that the failure contributed to [the] loss" (italics added)].) Moulton does not specify what the criteria should be, in an automated check processing system that selects some checks for sight review, other than reviewing a check that causes an overdraft, or is in excess of some unspecified amount. Although Moulton declares that daily overdrafts occurred on four of the days forged items were processed, Moulton does not declare that it was forged checks which caused the overdrafts. Similarly, although Moulton identifies a check that was paid without a signature, he does not state whether this check is one of the items that appellants contend were paid without authorization, or how such a check would be identified and selected for sight review under the criteria he declares are commercially reasonable. Nor does he declare that any forged check was in an amount that, pursuant to the criteria he suggests, would have resulted in its selection for sight review. Therefore, even if such a system of selection for sight review had been used by the Bank, the declaration provides no basis for inferring that any of the unauthorized checks would have been selected for sight review, resulting in earlier discovery of the forgeries. Therefore, the declaration does not create a triable issue that the failure to have such a system contributed to the loss. (See *Story Road Flea Market, Inc. v. Wells Fargo Bank, supra*, 42 Cal.App.4th 1733, 1744, 50 Cal.Rptr.2d 524 [expert declaration that unauthorized checks were out of sequence failed to create an issue of fact, because under stated criteria for selecting checks for sight review, unauthorized checks would still not have been selected for sight review].) * * *

We conclude that the court properly granted the Bank's motion for summary judgment on the ground that section 4406, subdivisions (d) and (e) precluded appellants from asserting claims against the Bank for unauthorized payments of checks drawn on their checking accounts, and that appellants failed to create a triable issue of fact as to whether they failed to exercise ordinary care in paying the items and that the failure contributed to their loss.

The judgment is affirmed.

## NOTES

**1.** Should a bank be allowed to raise the 4–406(f) one-year bar if it was in bad faith when it paid the check? The subsection and the Comments are silent on the issue. Take this case: Drawer Company (D) employed Margaret Marvic in its accounts payable department. She fraudulently signed the name of D's treasurer, Travis, to a number of checks over a three-year period. These checks were all made payable to Margaret and drawn on D's account in Bank. Margaret's husband, Lazlo Marvic, an officer of Bank made certain that no questions were raised about the validity of the checks upon payment. When D finally began to raise questions about Margaret's honesty, she and Lazlo disappeared. When D demanded recredit of its account in Bank for the amount of the forged checks, Bank raised the one-year bar of 4–406(f). D countered by contending that Bank could not raise this barrier because it paid the checks in bad faith.

The authorities are divided on the bad faith issue. The thrust of 4–406 is to place on the drawer the burden of discovering a forged signature when the bank has returned the periodic bank statement and notifying the bank of the forgery. Under 4–406(f), without respect to the lack of due care of the bank, if the drawer has not reported the forgery within a year, the drawer is precluded from raising the forgery. But under the hypothetical facts given, the drawer has been hindered in performance of its duty to discover forgeries and give the requisite notice by the bad faith intervention of an officer of the bank. This is different from mere lack of care. Falk v. The Northern Trust Co., 763 N.E.2d 380 (Ill. App. 2001), held that the one-year limitation does not apply if the bank is in bad faith. But Halifax Corp. v. First Union Nat. Bank, 546 S.E.2d 696 (Va. 2001), noting that 4–406(f) says nothing about good faith while 4–406(d) and (e) do mention it, drew the negative implication and held the contrary. In neither case was there a clear case of bad faith. See 1–201(b)(20) "good faith." Unless the statute is amended, more judicial analysis will be required before we can be confident of the trend of the law in this area.

**2.** If the customer and payor bank enter into the increasingly common agreement that allows the bank to retain the cancelled checks and to send the customer a periodic statement of account, does the customer have enough information to detect forged checks drawn on its account? 4–406(a) and (b). Comment 1 to 4–406. The Federal Reserve Board has approved a plan to allow banks to send periodic statements and disclosure information to customers electronically if the customers consent. Banks can utilize e-mail or their Web site. Jonathan Nicholson, Fed Plan To Let Banks Send E–Mail Statements, Wall St. J., Aug. 19, 1999, at A2.

**3.** There has been disagreement in the courts on the question of what constitutes reasonable promptness by the customer in discovering an unauthorized signature and in notifying the bank when the wrongdoer is the person designated by the customer to check the monthly statement. Under 1–202(f), the customer would seem to be bound by the information supplied by the bank when that information reaches the customer's employee who is authorized to receive it and act on it. Under the law of agency, if that employee fails to notify the bank of the forgery, the customer should be bound by the employee's conduct regardless of whether the employee's failure to notify is due to negligence or is the deliberate act of the employee to cover up the employee's wrongdoing. The issue should not be whether the customer was negligent in the procedure chosen for reviewing the bank statements, if the employee receiving and acting on the statements was the designated agent of the customer for that purpose. See Warren Seavey, Notice Through An Agent, 65 U. Pa.L. Rev. 1, 7–8 (1916).

## PROBLEMS

The agreement between Bank and its corporate customer, Company, is that Bank is authorized to pay checks drawn on Company's account only if they are signed by the chief financial officer, Hardy, and her deputy, Olsen. Signature specimens of these two parties were on file with Bank.

**1.** Olsen signed his name to the check in dispute but Hardy did not. Bank paid the check. When Company demanded that Bank re-credit its account with the amount of the check, Bank contended that this should not be treated as an unauthorized signature on the part of Company because the signature on the check was not forged. Is Bank correct? See 3–403(b).

**2.** Olsen fraudulently wrote three checks on Company's account payable to the order of Olsen. Olsen signed his name to each check and forged the name of Hardy.

    a.   The first check, in the amount of $1,000, was paid by Bank on January 2 by automated equipment without any human examination of the check. The cancelled check was returned to Company on January 4.

    b.   The second check, in the amount of $2,000, was paid by Bank on February 20 by automated equipment without any human examination of the check. The cancelled check was returned to Company on March 3.

    c.   The third check, in the amount of $5,000, was paid by Bank on February 28. Before the check was paid, an employee of Bank examined the check but failed to detect the forgery of Hardy's signature. The cancelled check was returned to Company on March 3.

Under the established procedures of Bank, checks presented for payment in amounts less than $2,500 were not examined by anybody before payment. All checks paid by Bank were returned to Company each month along with the monthly statement of account.

The fraud by Olsen was discovered by Company in June. Olsen, who is insolvent, used the proceeds of the three checks to pay gambling debts. Company notified Bank of the forged checks on June 7, immediately after discovery of the fraud. Company demanded that Bank restore to Company account the $8,000 debited to the account as a result of payment of the checks.

With respect to each of the checks, state your opinion whether, under 4–406, Company is entitled to recover from Bank.

## NOTE: FRAUD PREVENTION MEASURES

Banks have attempted to reduce fraud losses by adopting fraud prevention measures. These are described in 1 Clark & Clark, ¶ 10.01 (Rev. ed. 2006). Traditional methods involving sight review or random examination are not very effective against professionals who have available desktop computers that can scan and alter documents to produce accurate reproductions, as well as color printers and copiers, unless precautions are taken by the customer or bank.

A common protection against alteration and counterfeiting (producing checks like those of the drawer) is the use of paper stock for checks with security features. Examination of checks will normally warn a potential forger that the check has safety features. Some of these are visible, like the legend "original document" which has a ghostly presence on the back of some checks and is difficult to copy. Others are warnings, such as the admonition that some awful things will happen to the check if photocopied. Still others are not revealed at all, leaving the would-be malefactor to worry about what he might be up against if he transgresses. Of course, security devices in the paper stock are not effective in the common insider case in which the forger has access to the genuine checks of the customer.

Some banks offer a service identified as "positive pay." In its most common form the bank's business customers notify the bank daily of the checks drawn by them. The information provided to the bank typically includes the MICR line, dollar amounts and payee identification. When checks drawn by that customer are presented for payment, the bank compares these checks with the list given by the customer. If the checks don't match, they are returned to the presenting bank. See ABA Subcommittee on Payments, Check Fraud: The Model Positive Pay Services Agreement and Commentary, 54 Bus. Law. 637 (1999). Banks have begun to offer imaging positive pay services, under which the bank posts online for the customer's benefit the entire image of suspect checks, not just their MICR line. When the returned checks reach the depositary bank, it will erase the provisional credit given its depositor. If the depositary bank has already allowed the depositor to withdraw the funds, it has the burden of pursuing this person to get the money back. Since banks under Regulation CC are making funds available for most checks either on the day of deposit or the next day, as we indicated in an earlier chapter, it is likely that the money has been withdrawn in cases in which the forger is the depositor.

After Regulation CC one of the favorite handiworks of skilled forgers has been cashier's checks, the proceeds of which must be available for withdrawal by the depositor the day after deposit. Some banks take thumb prints of persons cashing checks, which can then be compared with FBI files to identify a forger.

Software companies have developed programs that allow banks to scan accounts for possible forgeries without the assistance of customers. The program allows a bank to review the past activity of customers' accounts in order to construct an archive for each account that shows a profile of the customer's usage. Checks presented for payment on these accounts will be reviewed for aberrations from this profile that may point to suspect checks. Fraud detection factors may include whether the check is larger in amount than checks drawn on this account in the past, whether the check number duplicates other checks already paid, whether the check number is out of sequence with other checks the customer is currently drawing, whether the check lacks any check number, and whether the volume of activity in the customer's account exceeds past levels. 1 Clark & Clark, supra, & 10.01[6].

### d.   VALIDITY OF CONTRACTUAL "CUTDOWN" CLAUSES

Section 4–406 states two time limitations bearing on the customer's duty to discover and report unauthorized signatures or alterations. One appears in 4–406(d)(2) and bears on the repeat forgery issue. It provides that if there is a repeat forgery, the customer is precluded from asserting the forgery against the bank if payment was made before the bank received notice of the forgery "after the customer had been afforded a reasonable period of time, not exceeding 30 days, in which to examine the item or statement of account and notify the bank." The other is the overriding one-year notice preclusion in 4–406(f) that we discussed in Note 1 in the previous section. This is a strong statement of the policy of giving banks an outer time limit beyond which they no longer need to be concerned about forged checks even if the bank's negligence had led to the forgery. But 4–103(a) allows the parties to vary the effect of the terms of Article 4 by agreement, a subject that we will discuss in greater detail in the next chapter. Does this mean that the deposit agreement between the bank and its customer can cutdown this one-year period to six months, or 60 days, or 20 days? If so, the risk of forgery loss on the part of banks may be substantially reduced.

## National Title Insurance Corporation Agency v. First Union National Bank

Supreme Court of Virginia, 2002.
559 S.E.2d 668.

■ Opinion By JUSTICE CYNTHIA D. KISNER.

Pursuant to the provisions of Code § 8.4–406(f), a bank's customer is precluded from asserting against the bank an unauthorized signature or alteration on an item if the customer fails to report such fact to the bank within one year after a statement of account showing payment of the item is made available to the customer. The dispositive issue in this appeal is whether a bank and its customer may, by contractual agreement, shorten the one-year period provided in Code § 8.4–406(f). Because we conclude that Code § 8.4–103(a) permits the parties to vary that time period, we will affirm the judgment of the circuit court holding that an agreement reducing the period to 60 days is binding on the parties.

National Title Insurance Corporation Agency (National Title) opened an escrow checking account with First Union National Bank (First Union) in April 1996. At that time, the parties entered into a "DEPOSIT AGREE-MENT AND DISCLOSURES For Non–Personal Accounts" (Deposit Agreement) that defined and governed the relationship between them. The provisions of Paragraph 12 of that Deposit Agreement, which are at issue in this appeal, absolve First Union of any liability for paying an item containing an unauthorized signature, an unauthorized indorsement, or a material alteration if National Title does not report such fact to First Union within 60 days of the mailing of the account statement describing the questioned item. In pertinent part, Paragraph 12 states:

> You should carefully examine the statement and canceled checks when you receive them. If you feel there is an error on the statement, or that some unauthorized person has withdrawn funds from the account, notify us immediately. The statement is considered correct unless you notify us promptly after any error is discovered. Moreover, because you are in the best position to discover an unauthorized signature, an unauthorized [i]ndorsement or a material alteration, you agree that we will not be liable for paying such items if . . . (b) you have not reported an unauthorized signature, an unauthorized [i]ndorsement or material alterations to us within 60 days of the mailing date of the earliest statement describing these items. . . .

Subsequently, First Union paid two checks ostensibly drawn on National Title's account, both of which were counterfeit checks and were not executed by an authorized signatory to the account. The first check, paid in November 1998, was described in an account statement mailed on December 5, 1998, and the second check, paid in December 1998, was described in National Title's account statement mailed on January 5, 1999. National Title did not report either of the unauthorized signatures to First Union within 60 days of the mailing of the respective account statements describing the two checks.

After First Union refused to credit National Title's account in the amounts paid on the two checks bearing unauthorized signatures, National Title filed a motion for judgment seeking to recover its losses from First Union. In its answer, First Union asserted, among other things, that National Title was precluded from making this claim because it had failed to report the unauthorized signatures within the 60–day time period specified in Paragraph 12 of the Deposit Agreement between the parties.

Ruling on the parties' cross-motions for summary judgment, the trial court concluded that First Union and National Title could contractually reduce the one-year period for reporting unauthorized signatures set forth in Code § 8.4–406(f) and that the 60–day period agreed upon by the parties in this case is not "manifestly unreasonable" under the provisions of Code § 8.4–103. The court therefore denied National Title's motion for summary judgment and granted First Union's motion, entering judgment in favor of First Union. National Title now appeals from that final judgment.

Title 8.4 of Virginia's Uniform Commercial Code (UCC) establishes the rights and duties between banks and their customers with regard to deposits and collections. A bank may charge against the account of its customer only those items that are properly payable from that account. *See* Code § 8.4–401(a). Items bearing unauthorized signatures, such as the checks in this case, are not properly payable. *Id.*

However, a customer has certain duties with regard to discovering and reporting an unauthorized signature or alteration on an item. If a bank sends or makes available to its customer a statement of account showing payment of items for the account, "the customer must exercise reasonable promptness in examining the statement or the items to determine whether any payment was not authorized because of an alteration of an item or because a purported signature by or on behalf of the customer was not authorized." Code § 8.4–406(c). A customer must promptly report to the bank any unauthorized payment that the customer "should reasonably have discovered" based on the statement or items provided. *Id.*

If a customer fails to comply with these duties, the customer is precluded from asserting against the bank the unauthorized signature or alteration on the item. Code § 8.4–406(d)(1). However, if a customer establishes that the bank "failed to exercise ordinary care in paying the item and that the failure substantially contributed to loss, the loss is allocated between the customer precluded and the bank asserting the preclusion according to the extent" that the failure of each party contributed to the loss. Code § 8.4–406(e).[2] Finally, if a customer does not discover and report an unauthorized signature or alteration on an item within one year after the statement or items are made available to the customer, the customer is thereafter precluded from asserting against the bank the unauthorized signature or alteration. Code § 8.4–406(f). This preclusion applies irrespective of whether the bank paid the item containing the unauthorized signature or alteration in good faith. *Halifax Corp. v. First Union Nat'l Bank*, 262 Va. 91, 101, 546 S.E.2d 696, 703 (2001).

On appeal, National Title first argues that Code § 8.4–406(f) is a statute of repose, i.e., a rule of substantive law, and that the one-year period set forth in that section is, therefore, not subject to contractual

---

**2.** If a bank does not pay an item in good faith, the preclusion under Code § 8.4– 406(d) as to the customer does not apply. Code § 4.6–406(e).

modification by the parties. Next, National Title posits that Paragraph 12 of the Deposit Agreement imports the time bar established in Code § 8.4–406(f) into subsection (c), thereby rendering the preclusion in subsection (f) meaningless. National Title further asserts that Paragraph 12 impermissibly changes the comparative negligence provisions established in Code § 8.4–406(e) and reinstates the concept of contributory negligence into Code § 8.4–406(c). Finally, National Title contends that the 60–day time limit for reporting an unauthorized signature or alteration on an item is "manifestly unreasonable," but that, if Paragraph 12 is enforceable, the 60–day limit should be construed as the parties' definition of "reasonable promptness" in determining comparative negligence, rather than as an absolute bar to National Title's claim against First Union. We do not agree with National Title.

The issue in this appeal is whether a bank may, through a contractual agreement with its customer, shorten the one-year period provided in Code § 8.4–406(f) to a period of 60 days. In *Halifax Corp.*, 262 Va. at 101, 546 S.E.2d at 703, we characterized that one-year period as a statutorily prescribed notice that operates as "a condition precedent to the customer's right to file an action against the bank to recover losses caused by the unauthorized signature or alteration." * * * This condition precedent does not limit a customer's claim against a bank but requires that the customer first perform the duty to discover and report any unauthorized signature or alteration on an item before bringing suit against the bank. However, that characterization of subsection (f) as a condition precedent is not, as National Title suggests, determinative of the question whether a customer and a bank can, by agreement, shorten the one-year period. The provisions of Code § 8.4–103(a) provide the analytical framework for resolving that question.

Code § 8.4–103(a) states that

[t]he effect of the provisions of this title may be varied by agreement but the parties to the agreement cannot disclaim a bank's responsibility for its lack of good faith or failure to exercise ordinary care or limit the measure of damages for the lack or failure. However, the parties may determine by agreement the standards by which the bank's responsibility is to be measured if those standards are not manifestly unreasonable.

According to Official Comment 2 regarding § 4–103 of the UCC, "[s]ubsection (a) confers blanket power to vary all provisions of the Article by agreements of the ordinary kind." Thus, this statute allows a bank and its customer to vary by agreement the effect of the provisions of Title 8.4 as long as the agreement does not: (1) "disclaim a bank's responsibility for its lack of good faith," (2) "[disclaim a bank's responsibility for its] failure to exercise ordinary care," or (3) "limit the measure of damages for the lack or failure." Code § 8.4–103(a).

The clause in Paragraph 12 of the Deposit Agreement reducing the one-year period in Code § 8.4–406(f) to a period of 60 days does not run afoul of these limitations on the authority to vary the effect of the provisions of Title 8.4. The Deposit Agreement does not absolve First Union of its duty to exercise ordinary care or good faith, nor does it limit the measure of damages. Instead, Paragraph 12 merely varies the effect of Code § 8.4–406(f) in that the period of time in which National Title must report an unauthorized signature or alteration on an item, without having its claim for losses precluded by the bar in subsection (f), is shortened from one year to 60 days. * * * This reduction in the length of the statutory notice period is consistent with the concept embodied in Code § 8.4–406(f) that a bank can be held potentially liable for paying an item containing an unauthorized signature or alteration only for a limited period of time. Thus, we conclude that a bank and its customer may contractually shorten the one-year period contained in Code § 8.4–406(f) and that First Union and National Title did so in Paragraph 12 of the Deposit Agreement.

Notwithstanding this reduced time period, if National Title complies with its duty to exercise reasonable promptness in examining its account statement and reporting any unauthorized signature or altered item, First Union remains liable for paying an item bearing an unauthorized signature or alteration. Likewise, the comparative negligence provisions contained in Code § 8.4–406(e) remain in effect during the 60–day period after First Union makes available to National Title a statement showing payment of items from National Title's account. Thus, the provisions of Paragraph 12 at issue do not alter the scheme of liability between banks and their customers as set forth in Code § 8.4–406. * * *

Finally, National Title contends that the 60–day period for reporting unauthorized signatures or alterations is "manifestly unreasonable" under Code § 8.4–103(a). As used in subsection (a), this term is the test for determining the validity of an agreement that sets the standards by which a bank's responsibility for its lack of good faith or failure to exercise ordinary care is to be measured. While it is not necessary for us to decide in this case whether the test of manifest unreasonableness also applies to a determination regarding the validity of a reduction in the time period contained in Code § 8.4–406(f), we will utilize that standard in this appeal since it is the one advanced by National Title. In doing so, we conclude that the 60–day time limitation set forth in Paragraph 12 of the Deposit Agreement is not "manifestly unreasonable." Other jurisdictions have likewise upheld the validity of reductions in the one-year period provided in Code § 8.4–406(f) to periods similar to or shorter than 60 days.[4] * * *

A condition precedent such as the one set forth in Code § 8.4–406(f) recognizes that a customer is in a better position than a bank to know whether a signature is authorized or an item has been altered. * * * A reduction in the one-year period allowed in subsection (f) to a period of 60 days encourages diligence by a customer and is " 'in accord with public policy by limiting disputes in a society where millions of bank transactions

---

**4.** We do not decide today whether a period shorter than 60 days would be "manifestly unreasonable."

occur every day.' '' *Basse Truck Line, Inc. v. First State Bank*, 949 S.W.2d 17, 22 (Tex.App.1997) (quoting *Parent Teacher Ass'n*, 524 N.Y.S.2d at 340).

For these reasons, we will affirm the judgment of the circuit court.

NOTE

The validity of cut-down clauses has been much litigated. Clark & Clark, ¶ 10.05[1][c] (Rev. ed. 2006). If a 60–day limitation is permissible, what about a 20–day limit? See Stowell v. Cloquet Co-op Credit Union, 557 N.W.2d 567 (Minn. 1997).

## 2.   RIGHT OF PAYOR BANK TO RECOVER MISTAKEN PAYMENT OF CHECK

### a.   FORGED CHECKS

The law of mistake and restitution recognizes the general principle that a person who confers a benefit upon another person because of a mistake is entitled to restitution from the person receiving the benefit. For example, a shopkeeper receives a $10 bill from a customer in payment of goods purchased by the customer for a price of $8. The shopkeeper, who has an obligation to give the customer $2 change, gives the customer $12 because of a mistaken belief that the customer had paid with a $20 bill. The shopkeeper is entitled to get back the $10 paid by mistake. Restatement of Restitution § 19 (1937).

Mistake can also occur when money is paid for a negotiable instrument either by a person who buys the instrument or by a person such as a payor bank who pays the instrument. The law of mistake and restitution applies to negotiable instrument cases, but special rules apply in some cases. The mistake cases fall into various categories and most of the cases involve payment or acceptance of a check or other draft by the drawee. The principal categories involve forged checks, checks bearing a forged indorsement, altered checks, checks on which the drawer has stopped payment, and checks drawn on an account with insufficient funds to cover the check.

The seminal case in this area is *Price v. Neal*, 3 Burr. 1354, 97 Eng. Rep. 871 (K.B. 1762), which involved two forged bills of exchange drawn on Price and indorsed to Neal, a bona fide purchaser for value. Price paid Neal on the first bill and then accepted the second bill which was subsequently purchased by Neal. After Price paid the second bill he learned that the signature of the drawer of the bills had been forged. Price sued Neal to get his money back. Lord Mansfield, in deciding in favor of the defendant, stated:

> It is an action upon the case, for money had and received to the plaintiff's use. In which action, the plaintiff can not recover the money, unless it be against conscience in the defendant, to retain it: and great liberality is always allowed, in this sort of action.

But it can never be thought unconscientious in the defendant, to retain this money, when he has once received it upon a bill of exchange indorsed to him for a fair and valuable consideration, which he had bona fide paid, without the least priority or suspicion of any forgery.

Here was no fraud: no wrong. It was incumbent upon the plaintiff, to be satisfied "that the bill drawn upon him was the drawer's hand," before he accepted or paid it: but it was not incumbent upon the defendant, to inquire into it. Here was notice given by the defendant to the plaintiff of a bill drawn upon him: and he sends his servant to pay it and take it up. The other bill he actually accepts; after which acceptance, the defendant innocently and bona fide discounts it. The plaintiff lies by, for a considerable time after he has paid these bills; and then found out "that they were forged:" and the forger comes to be hanged. He made no objection to them, at the time of paying them. Whatever neglect there was, was on his side. The defendant had actual encouragement from the plaintiff himself, for negotiating the second bill, from the plaintiff's having without any scruple or hesitation paid the first: and he paid the whole value, bona fide. It is a misfortune which has happened without the defendant's fault or neglect. If there was no neglect in the plaintiff, yet there is no reason to throw off the loss from one innocent man upon another innocent man: but, in this case, if there was any fault or negligence in any one, it certainly was in the plaintiff, and not in the defendant.

Payment or acceptance by the drawee of a forged check or other draft is addressed in 3–418(a) and (c) and 3–417(a)(3). Under these provisions the rule of *Price v. Neal* is preserved. Section 4–208(a)(3) is identical in effect to 3–417(a)(3) and applies specifically to warranties made in the bank-collection process to a payor bank with respect to an Article 4 "draft" (4–104(a)(7)), which includes a check.

### PROBLEM

Taylor, an employee of Juliet, needed money to meet overdue bills. He broke into a storeroom and stole a pad of company checks. Taylor forged Juliet's name to a check for $307 drawn on Payor Bank which he made payable to him. He used the check to pay for groceries at Best Foods whose policy was to accept third-party checks only if they appeared to be paychecks, and this check clearly did. The name printed at the top of the check was Juliet's d/b/a, "Juliet Company," and Taylor typed on the signature line the company name, followed by a written signature of Juliet. The forgery was skillfully done and even a handwriting expert would have had difficulty in detecting it. Best Foods deposited the check in its account in Depositary Bank which presented the check to Payor Bank for payment. Payor Bank paid the check in ordinary course and Best Foods withdrew the amount from its account in Depositary Bank. Taylor shortly filed in bankruptcy.

(a) When Payor Bank learned of the forgery, it demanded that Depositary Bank reimburse it for the amount of the check. Is it entitled to recover on the basis of the Code provisions set out in the paragraph preceding the Problem?

(b) When Payor Bank learned of the forgery, it demanded that Best Foods, the party that dealt with the forger, reimburse it for the amount of the check. Is it entitled to recover? See the Code provisions set out above and, in addition, 3–416(a)(2) and its Article 4 counterpart, 4–207(a).

(c) Did Depositary Bank breach the warranty stated in 3–417(a)(1)?

---

During the redraft of Article 3 and 4, active consideration was given to rejecting the rule of *Price v. Neal*, but the doctrine has been retained. Does that doctrine allocate the loss resulting from forged checks in a fair manner in this Problem? For an article strongly supporting *Price v. Neal*, see James Steven Rogers, The Basic Principle of Loss Allocation for Unauthorized Checks, 39 Wake Forest L. Rev. 453 (2004). Professor Rogers believes that the fundamental principle of the check system and all other payment systems is that the burden of unpreventable losses should rest with the providers of the payment system rather than with the users of that system. *Price v. Neal* is entirely consistent with the basic principle of loss allocation for the check system.

b.  FORGED INDORSEMENT

PROBLEM

Drawer drew a check to the order of Payee. The check was stolen from Payee by Thief who signed Payee's name to the check as a blank indorsement. Thief then delivered the check to Jennifer, who purchased for value, in good faith and without notice that the indorsement was forged. Jennifer indorsed and deposited the check with Depositary Bank which presented the check and received payment from Payor Bank. Depositary Bank credited Jennifer's account and the credit was withdrawn. Payee then notified Drawer of the theft. Drawer notified Payor Bank, but was told that the check had already been paid. Is Payor Bank entitled to recover the amount of the check from either Depositary Bank or Jennifer? 3–417(a)(1), 4–208(a)(1), and Comments 2 and 3 to 3–417. If Depositary Bank has to pay, is Depositary Bank entitled to recover from Jennifer? 3–416(a)(1) and (2), 4–207(a)(1) and (2).

How can you reconcile this case with *Price v. Neal*? That case announced a finality policy for forged checks: it is better to end the transaction on an instrument when it is paid rather than reopen and upset a series of transactions at a later date when forgery is discovered. But the result reached in the Problem above with respect to forged indorsements is inconsistent with a finality policy. Is it justified because a transferee from a forger may achieve some protection against a forged indorsement by requiring identification while a drawee cannot? For a judicial discussion of these issues, see Perini Corp. v. First National Bank of Habersham County, 553 F.2d 398 (5th Cir. 1977).

### c.   REMOTELY CREATED CHECKS

Telemarketing has proved effective in selling goods and services. In the usual transaction the payment mechanism is a credit card; the buyer gives the credit card number to the telemarketer caller and is charged for the sale on its next statement. What if the buyer wants the article being offered but has no credit card or her credit cards are "maxed out"? No problem. If the buyer has a bank account, the telemarketer asks the buyer to read off the information on the MICR line (the payor bank's routing and transit number and the buyer's account number) of a check. If the buyer is willing to provide this information, the telemarketer prints a check drawn on buyer's account in the payor bank payable to itself, stamps on the signature line "customer authorized draft," or words to that effect, and deposits the check for collection in telemarketer's depositary bank. Unless the buyer stops payment, the check will be paid by the payor bank on the basis of the MICR information with no review of the signature.

If the buyer did not authorize the check, the rule of Price v. Neal places the loss of the unauthorized signature on the payor bank rather than the depositary bank. Interbank of New York v. Fleet Bank, 781 N.Y.S.2d 393 (N.Y. Sup. Ct. App. Div. 2004). This is a bad result because the depositary bank is in a better position to monitor the behavior of its customer, the telemarketer, than is the payor bank. The 2002 revisions of Article 3 impose the risk of an unauthorized signature on the depositary bank, following the lead of several states that had done so by amendments earlier. "Remotely-created consumer item" is defined in 3–103(a)(16) as meaning a check that "does not bear a handwritten signature purporting to be the signature of the drawer." Under 3–416(a)(6) the telemarketer warrants to the depositary bank that the check is authorized by the person on whom the check is drawn, and 3–417(a)(4) provides that the telemarketer and depositary bank warrant the same to the payor bank. These amendments are described in Comment 8 to 3–416 as implementing "a limited rejection of Price v. Neal." In 2006 the Fed preempted these provisions. 12 CFR § 229.2(fff) defines a remotely created check as one "that does not bear a signature applied, or purported to be applied, by the person on whom the check is drawn." 12 CFR § 229.34(d) provides that "[a] bank that transfers or presents a remotely created check and receives a settlement or other consideration warrants to the transferee bank, any subsequent collecting bank, and the paying bank that the person on whose account the remotely created check is drawn authorized the issuance of the check in the amount stated on the check and to the payee stated on the check." Unlike 3–416(a)(6) and 3–417(a)(4), the federally created warranty is not limited to remotely created consumer checks. It applies to remotely created checks drawn on the account of any person, including a business.

Neither the UCC amendments nor the Fed changes directly address the concern that the use of "remotely-created" checks by telemarketers is subject to abuse. Congress intervened to provide a degree of consumer protection by enacting the Telemarketing and Consumer Fraud and Abuse Prevention Act in 1994, which requires the Federal Trade Commission to issue rules "prohibiting deceptive telemarketing acts or practices." 15 U.S.C. § 6102(a)(1). Pursuant to this, the FTC rule provides that it is a deceptive telemarketing practice to submit for payment a draft drawn on a person's deposit account without that person's "express verifiable authorization." Authorization is deemed verifiable if the customer's authorization is obtained either in writing or on tape or if written confirmation of the transaction is sent to the customer prior to submission for payment of the customer's draft. 16 CFR § 310.3(a)(3). The burden of policing the activities of telemarketers or other users of remotely recreated checks falls ultimately on the bank closest to those persons, the bank of first deposit. The remotely created check issue is extensively discussed in 1 Clark & Clark, The Law of Bank Deposits, Collections and Credit Cards ¶ 10.02[2] (Rev. ed. 2005).

The FTC's Telemarketing Sales Rule, establishing the "Do–Not–Call" registry, 16 CFR § 310.4(b)(1)(iii), Mar. 31, 2003, should significantly reduce the volume of telemarketing sales, and, presumably, the abuses associated with telemarketing. Congress ratified the FTC Rule in HR 3161, Public Law No. 108–82, Sept. 25, 2003.

### d. OVERDRAFTS

If a payor bank pays a check that is forged or which bears a forged indorsement, it is clear that the bank paid the check by mistake. No bank would knowingly pay such a check because the check is not properly payable and the payor bank is not entitled to charge the account of the drawer. The payment of a check drawn on an account in which there are insufficient funds to cover the check is different. Under 4–401(a) such a check is properly payable and the drawer's account can be charged. Thus, it may not be clear at the time of payment whether the payor bank paid by mistake or intended to grant credit to the drawer. Intentional payment of checks that create overdrafts is very common. There is some authority denying a payor bank any right of restitution in overdraft cases, but most courts follow Restatement of Restitution § 29 (1937), which recognizes a limited right of restitution in such cases. In Article 3, overdraft cases are governed by 3–418(b) which gives to the payor bank a right to recover "to the extent permitted by the law governing mistake and restitution." But 3–418(b) is subject to 3–418(c). No right of restitution may be asserted against a person who took the check in good faith and for value or who in good faith changed position in reliance on payment of the check.

## 3. CONVERSION ACTIONS REGARDING CHECKS BEARING FORGED INDORSEMENT

### a. ACTION BY PAYEE

#### (1) INTRODUCTION

Section 3–420(a) restates the common law rule: "An instrument is * * * converted if it is taken by transfer, other than a negotiation, from a person not entitled to enforce the instrument or a bank makes or obtains payment with respect to the instrument for a person not entitled to enforce the instrument or receive payment." Thus, a person, including a depositary bank, taking after a forged indorsement is a converter, as is a drawee bank that pays such an instrument. A payee or other holder from whom the instrument has been taken has a choice of suing either the depositary bank (3–420(c)) or the drawee bank for the conversion even though neither knew that the indorsement was forged. Solve the following Problem on the basis of the text set out below and the statutes cited.

PROBLEM

Electronic Supply Co. (ESC) sells products by mail order and over the Internet as well as at its retail store, which also serves as its headquarters. Most of its sales are paid for by credit cards or cash but some are by checks drawn on banks throughout the nation. Thief, a former employee, broke into the retail store after the close of business and stole cash and unindorsed checks payable to ESC from buyers. He had prepared a stamp, bearing ESC's name, which he used to indorse the stolen checks. Beneath the stamped indorsement, Thief signed the name he used as an account holder at Depositary Bank (DB) and made an ATM deposit of the stolen checks in DB before dawn. The various payor banks on which the checks were drawn paid the checks when presented by DB though banking channels. DB allowed Thief to withdraw the proceeds of the checks before the forgeries were discovered. What are ESC's remedies with respect to (i) the drawers of the checks, (ii) the several payor banks on which the checks were drawn, and (iii) DB? Which remedy would you advise ESC to use? Why?

---

In a common type of forged indorsement case, the check is stolen by an employee of the payee. The check is an ordinary check mailed to the payee by the drawer in payment of an obligation owed to the payee. The check is received by the payee when the mail delivery is made and the payee becomes a holder of the check at that time. Suppose the check is stolen by an employee of the payee who works as a clerk in the payee's mailroom. The employee forges the payee's name as an indorsement of the check, and obtains payment from the drawee bank. How does the theft of the check and its collection affect the payee's rights with respect to the check and the obligation of the drawer to the payee that the check was intended to pay? Under 3–310(b), the obligation for which the check was received becomes "suspended" at the time the payee receives the check. In the hands of the payee, the check represents a right to receive money, which is a property right of the payee. This property right is provisionally substituted for the right of the payee to enforce the obligation for which the check was received. If the payee receives payment of the check, the obligation for which the check was received is discharged to the extent of the payment. 3–

310(b)(1). If the payee presents the check for payment and the check is dishonored, the payee has a cause of action against the drawer of the check either on the check (3–414(b)) or on the obligation for which the check was received. 3–310(b)(3).

What rights does the payee have if the check is stolen from the payee and the thief obtains payment from the drawee? Under 3–310(b)(1) "[p]ayment * * * of the check" results in discharge of the obligation for which a check was taken, but under 3–602(a), the check is not paid unless payment is made to a person entitled to enforce the check. Payment to the thief or a transferee of the thief does not result in payment of the check, and the obligation of the drawer on the check is not discharged. The payee of the check remains the owner of the check and the person entitled to enforce it. 3–301 and 3–309 (lost instruments). The drawee's payment to a person not entitled to enforce the check does not affect the payee's rights in the check. The payee, however, does not have a right to enforce the obligation for which the check was received. That obligation remains suspended under 3–310(b) because neither dishonor nor payment of the check has occurred. Under the last sentence of 3–310(b)(4), the payee of a stolen check who is not in possession of the check, has rights against the drawer only on the check. 3–309, 3–414, and Comment 4 to 3–310. Thus, the payee has the burden of asserting rights with respect to the stolen check, and there are several possible courses of action available to the payee against third parties as well as the drawer.

Although the payee from whom a check has been stolen has no right to obtain a substitute check from the drawer, sometimes the drawer will issue such a check. In the case in which payment with respect to the stolen check has not yet been made by the drawee, the drawee can be informed of the theft and payment to the thief may be avoided. If payment by the drawee has already been made, the drawer can insist that the drawee recredit the drawer's account because payment to the thief did not entitle the drawee to debit the drawer's account. 4–401. If the drawer refuses to issue a replacement check, the payee has a remedy against the drawer on the stolen check, but that remedy may not be convenient. 3–309. Often a forged indorsement case involves thefts of many checks from one payee by the same thief. Actions against the various drawers of the stolen checks may not be feasible. An action against the person who took the checks from the thief is usually a better remedy.

In the hands of the payee, a check is property and, if that property is stolen, the rules of conversion applying to personal property also apply to the check. Thus, the payee of the stolen check has an action in conversion against the thief for the amount of the check. But the law of conversion also allows an action to be brought against "innocent converters," i.e. persons who exercise dominion over stolen property without knowledge that it was stolen. Thus, if a thief sells stolen goods to a good faith purchaser for value, the owner has an action against the BFP as well. A stolen check bearing the forged indorsement of the payee can be turned into money by selling it to a depositary bank or other purchaser for cash, by depositing it to the thief's bank account for bank credit that can subsequently be withdrawn, or by presenting the check for payment to the drawee bank. Each of these takers of the check is a potential defendant. The common law was clear that a conversion action could be brought by the payee against the person who bought the check. The common law cases were divided on the issue of whether the drawee bank was liable in conversion if it paid a stolen check bearing a forged indorsement, but most courts held that a conversion action was available and that view was adopted by Article 3. Article 3 states the rules regarding conversion in 3–420.

### (2) DELIVERY OF CHECK TO PAYEE

Pre-revision authorities were divided on whether the payee of a check could sue a depositary bank for conversion when the check had been stolen before it was delivered to the payee. Section 3–420(a)(ii) states the view that a payee cannot bring conversion unless it has received delivery. Comment 1 explains that a payee has no interest in the check until it receives delivery. If a check has not been delivered to the payee, its rights against the drawer have not been affected by the theft; the drawer is still liable to the payee on the underlying obligation.

Article 3 does not define "delivery." It states that delivery may either be made directly to the payee or to an agent or co-payee. 3–420(a)(ii). Comment 1 to 3–420 says that a payee receives delivery when the check comes into the payee's possession. Words like "delivery," "agency," and "possession" are familiar but inexact terms, and Article 3 leaves their meaning to the body of common law that has grown around them. Clearly, delivery of a settlement check to the plaintiff's dishonest attorney is delivery to the plaintiff's agent. Leeds v. Chase Manhattan Bank, 752 A.2d 332 (N.J. Super. 2000). Comment 1 opines on a recurring issue when it observes that a payee has possession when a check is put into its mailbox. The court in Hancock Bank v. Ensenat, 819 So.2d 3 (Miss. App. 2001), relied on this Comment to hold that possession occurs when the check arrives at the payee's home mailing address.

### (3) LIABILITY OF DEPOSITARY BANK AS AGENT FOR COLLECTION

When a check is transferred to a depositary bank by its customer, the bank sometimes purchases the check from the customer by giving cash for it or by giving the customer a credit to the customer's account immediately available for withdrawal as of right. More commonly the depositary bank doesn't buy the check. Rather, it takes the check as agent of the customer to obtain payment of the check from the payor bank and pays the proceeds of the check to the customer after the check is paid. This distinction can have some importance in Article 3 because the status of the depositary bank as a holder in due course may depend upon whether it had given value for the check at the time the check was presented for payment. But in Article 4 the depositary bank is normally treated as an agent for collection whether or not the bank gave value to the customer for the check. 4–201(a).

Under former Article 3, the statute appeared to provide that a depositary bank, as well as subsequent collecting banks, was not liable for conversion if it acted merely as an agent for collection. This was a reversal of the common law rule, and some courts, by using creative statutory construction, refused to follow the literal wording of the statute. In justifying their deliberate misreading of the statute, courts pointed out that to do otherwise produced the ridiculous result that forced the payee to sue the payor bank in conversion and the payor bank to proceed against the depositary bank for breach of its presentment warranty. Two lawsuits instead of one. The issue is well discussed in Denn v. First State Bank, 316 N.W.2d 532 (Minn.1982), in which the court reluctantly read the statute literally but acknowledged that to do so produced a bad result.

Section 3–420(a) and (c) return to the pre-UCC rule that allowed the payee to sue the depositary bank directly in conversion. Not only is judicial economy served because the bank of first deposit is ultimately liable in forged indorsement cases owing to its presentment warranty to the payor bank under 3–417(a)(1), 4–208(a)(1), but also it is usually the most convenient defendant for the payee to sue in the common case of multiple forgeries in which an employee has forged the indorsement of the employer on checks drawn on many different payor banks, some in different states. Comment 3 to 3–420.

(4) UNAUTHORIZED INDORSEMENT

If a check is made payable to two persons, ambiguity sometimes arises whether both must indorse for the instrument to be negotiated or whether either may do so. Section 3–110(d) provides that if an instrument is payable to two or more persons alternatively, either may indorse, but if it is payable to them "not alternatively," all signatures are required. Section 3–403(b) states that the signature of an organization is unauthorized if one of the required signatures is lacking. How can we be sure when an instrument is payable to them alternatively so that one signature may constitute a negotiation?

## PROBLEM

In each of the following cases, the check was indorsed only by Michael Bijlani & Assoc. and was deposited in Bank. Under 3–110(d), in which case or cases should Bank have demanded Bay Village Inc.'s signature before taking the check?

Case #1. The check was payable to "Bay Village Inc. Michael Bijlani & Assoc." See Bijlani v. Nationsbank of Florida, 25 UCC Rep. Serv. 2d 1165, 1995 WL 264180 (Fla. Cir. Ct. 1995).

Case #2. How would Case #1 be decided if there were a slash (/) or virgule between "Inc." and "Michael"? See Purina Mills, Inc. v.

Security Bank & Trust, 547 N.W.2d 336 (Mich.App. 1996); Danco, Inc. v. Commerce Bank/Shore, N.A., 675 A.2d 663 (N.J.Sup.Ct. 1996).

Case #3. How would Case #1 be decided if there were a hyphen between "Inc." and "Michael"? See J.R. Simplot, Inc. v. Knight, 988 P.2d 955 (Wash. 1999).

### (5) FORGERY BY ENTRUSTED EMPLOYEE OF PAYEE

As we stated earlier, perhaps the most common cases of forged indorsements are the "inside jobs." An employee entrusted with the responsibility of dealing with checks payable to the employer forges the indorsement of the employer and covers up the forgery in the reconcilement process. Section 3–406(a) provides that if the payor bank can prove that the employer's failure to supervise the employee's activities and to monitor the financial records that the employee kept substantially contributed to the forgery, it can throw the forgery loss back on the employer. In the drafting of Revised Article 3, the contention was made that it was unfair to impose on the bank the burden of proving the employer's negligence. If the employer chose to entrust responsibility to an employee and the employee betrayed the trust, isn't it fair to put the risk of loss with respect to the employee's misconduct on the employer rather than the bank? The original Code recognized in Comment 4 to former 3–405 that in such cases the loss should fall on the employer as the risk of its business enterprise because it is normally in a better position to prevent forgeries by reasonable care in selecting or supervising employees "or if he is not, is at least in a better position to cover the loss by fidelity insurance." Section 3–405 implements this policy.

The following scenario is a summary of some of the facts, somewhat modified, of Cooper v. Union Bank, 9 Cal.3d 371, 107 Cal.Rptr. 1, 507 P.2d 609 (Cal. 1973). This fact situation is one of the templates the drafters had in mind in writing 3–405 and its analysis offers an informative journey through the statute. See Comment 3, Case #3.

Stell, a lawyer, was retained by Ruff to represent her in connection with her insolvency and litigation brought against her by several creditors. She informed Stell that her financial difficulties were primarily due to gambling losses she had sustained. A short time later Stell hired Ruff as a secretary and bookkeeper. Ruff's duties included posting the amounts of checks received by Stell to the proper accounts in Stell's accounting records and reconciling the monthly bank statement of deposits and withdrawals with respect to Stell's checking account with Stell's accounting records. Over a period of a year and a half, Ruff stole 29 checks payable to Stell that were received in the mail, and forged Stell's indorsement to these checks. Most of these checks were cashed over the counter at Depositary Bank at which both Stell and Ruff had checking accounts. A few of the checks were deposited to Ruff's account in Depositary Bank. Stell was well known to the tellers at the bank as a customer of the bank and Ruff was well known as Stell's secretary. It was the policy of Depositary Bank to allow checks payable to known customers to be cashed over the counter by the customer or the customer's secretary. The forgeries by Ruff were so well done that only a handwriting expert could have detected them.

Stell exercised almost no supervision over Ruff, never reviewed the books that she kept, and never checked the bank reconciliation of deposits to Stell's checking account. Stell brought an action in conversion against Depositary Bank with respect to the 29 checks that were transferred by Ruff to that bank.

Under the second sentence of 3–420(a), Depositary Bank is liable to Stell as a converter of the 29 checks that Ruff transferred to it if (1) Depositary Bank did not become the holder of the checks as a result of the transfer, i.e., the transfer was not a negotiation, and (2) Ruff was not a person entitled to enforce the checks when she transferred them to Depositary Bank, i.e., she was not a holder at the time of the transfer. Both of these elements depend upon whether the forgery by Ruff of Stell's signature was effective as Stell's indorsement in spite of the fact that it was a forgery. Section 3–405 addresses this issue.

Section 3–405 applies to this case if a "fraudulent indorsement" (3–405(a)(2)) was made by Ruff, and Ruff was entrusted by Stell, her employer, with "responsibility" (3–405(a)(3)) with respect to the checks that she transferred to Depositary Bank. Under the first sentence of 3–405(b), is the indorsement by Ruff effective as the indorsement of Stell? The first and last paragraphs of Comment 1 to 3–405 address this issue. The Ruff–Stell scenario should be compared with Case #1, Case #3, and Case #4 of Comment 3 to 3–405. If Stell is not entitled to recover from Depositary Bank as a converter of the 29 checks because of the first sentence of 3–405(b), is Stell entitled to any recovery against Depositary Bank based on the last sentence of 3–405(b)? Under that sentence is there any difference in result with respect to the checks cashed over the counter and the checks deposited to Ruff's account?

### b.   ACTION BY DRAWER

Forged indorsement cases usually involve a theft of the check from the payee, but sometimes the theft of the check occurs before the check is received by the payee. In *Stone & Webster*, which follows, an employee of the drawer of several checks stole the checks from the drawer before the checks could be mailed to the payee. The stolen checks were intended to pay debts of the drawer to the payee. In such a case the payee has no legal claim with respect to the checks because the payee never received them. The theft of the check and payment by the drawee to the thief do not change payee's rights with respect to the debt for which the check was written. The payee never became the owner of the check and the drawer's debt to the payee remains unpaid. 3–310(b) does not apply. The drawer of the stolen check has a continuing obligation to pay the debt for which the check was issued and thus is obliged to issue a replacement check to the payee.

The drawer normally will not suffer any loss with respect to a check bearing a forged indorsement if the drawer is free of negligence contributing to the theft and forgery. 3–406. The payor bank may not charge the drawer's account because a check bearing a forged indorsement is not properly payable according to Comment 1 to 4–401(a). Thus, the drawer is entitled to have the account in the payor bank credited for the amount of the payment. This remedy of the drawer is clear and convenient since in most cases the drawer's account will be in a local bank. Nevertheless, there have been a number of cases in which the drawer, instead of suing the payor bank, sued the depositary bank. Such a suit might be brought in the uncommon case in which the depositary bank is a local bank and the payor bank is out of state, or the drawer may simply be reluctant to sue the payor bank with which the drawer has a favorable business relationship. The issue in these cases is whether the drawer of a check stolen from it has a property right in the check that can be asserted in a conversion action. The authority on the issue was divided under original Article 3. The view expressed in the seminal case of *Stone & Webster* was adopted by 3–420(a)(i).

## Stone & Webster Engineering Corp. v. First National Bank & Trust Co.

Supreme Judicial Court of Massachusetts, 1962.
345 Mass. 1, 184 N.E.2d 358.

■ WILKINS, CHIEF JUSTICE.

In this action of contract or tort in four counts for the same cause of action a demurrer to the declaration was sustained, and the plaintiff, described in the writ as having a usual place of business in Boston, appealed. G.L. (Ter.Ed.) c. 231, § 96. The questions argued concern the rights of the drawer against a collecting bank which "cashed" checks for an individual who had forged the payee's indorsement on the checks, which were never delivered to the payee.

In the first count, which is in contract, the plaintiff alleges that between January 1, 1960, and May 15, 1960, it was indebted at various times to Westinghouse Electric Corporation (Westinghouse) for goods and services furnished to it by Westinghouse; that in order to pay the indebtedness the plaintiff drew three checks within that period on its checking account in The First National Bank of Boston (First National) payable to Westinghouse in the total amount of $64,755.44; that before delivery of the checks to Westinghouse an employee of the plaintiff in possession of the checks forged the indorsement of Westinghouse and presented the checks to the defendant; that the defendant "cashed" the checks and delivered the proceeds to the plaintiff's employee who devoted the proceeds to his own use; that the defendant forwarded the checks to First National and received from First National the full amounts thereof; and that First National charged the account of the plaintiff with the full amounts of the checks and has refused to recredit the plaintiff's checking account; wherefore the defendant owes the plaintiff $64,755.44 with interest.

Count 2, also in contract, is on an account annexed for money owed, namely $64,755.44, the proceeds of checks of the plaintiff "cashed" by the defendant on forged indorsements between January 1, 1960, and May 15, 1960.

Counts 3 and 4 in tort are respectively for conversion of the checks and for negligence in "cashing" the checks with forged indorsements.

By order, copies of the three checks were filed in court. The checks are respectively dated at Rowe in this Commonwealth on January 5, March 8, and May 9, 1960. Their respective amounts are $36,982.86, $10,416.58 and $17,355. They are payable to the order of "Westinghouse Electric Corporation, 10 High Street, Boston." The first two checks are indorsed in typewriting, "For Deposit Only: Westinghouse Electric Corporation By: Mr. O. D. Costine, Treasury Representative" followed by an ink signature "O. D. Costine." The Third check is indorsed in typewriting, "Westinghouse Electric Corporation By: [Sgd.] O. D. Costine Treasury Representative." All three checks also bear the indorsement by rubber stamp, "Pay to the order of any bank, banker or trust co. prior indorsements guaranteed * * * [date][1] The First National Bank & Trust Co. Greenfield, Mass."

The demurrer, in so far as it has been argued, is to each count for failure to state a cause of action.

\* \* \*

1.   Count 1, the plaintiff contends, is for money had and received. We shall so regard it. "An action for money had and received lies to recover money which should not in justice be retained by the defendant, and which in equity and good conscience should be paid to the plaintiff." Cobb v. Library Bureau, 268 Mass. 311, 316, 167 N.E. 765, 767; Adams v. First Nat. Bank, 321 Mass. 693, 694, 75 N.E.2d 502; Trafton v. Custeau, 338 Mass. 305, 308, 155 N.E.2d 159.

The defendant has no money in its hands which belongs to the plaintiff. The latter had no right in the proceeds of its own check payable to Westinghouse. Not being a holder or an agent for a holder, it could not have presented the check to the drawee for payment. * * * See Uniform Commercial Code § 3–419, comment 2: "A negotiable instrument is the property of the holder." See also Restatement 2d: Torts, Tent. draft no. 3, 1958, § 241A. The plaintiff contends that "First National paid or credited the proceeds of the checks to the defendant and charged the account of the plaintiff, and consequently, the plaintiff was deprived of a credit, and the defendant received funds or a credit which 'in equity and good conscience' belonged to the plaintiff."

---

**1.**  The respective dates are January 13, March 9, and May 11, 1960. Each check bears the stamped indorsement of the Federal Reserve Bank of Boston and on its face the paid stamp of The First National Bank of Boston.

In our opinion this argument is a non sequitur. The plaintiff as a depositor in First National was merely in a contractual relationship of creditor and debtor. * * * The amounts the defendant received from First National to cover the checks "cashed" were the bank's funds and not the plaintiff's. The Uniform Commercial Code does not purport to change the relationship. * * * Section 3–409(1) provides: "A check or other draft does not of itself operate as an assignment of any funds in the hands of the drawee available for its payment, and the drawee is not liable on the instrument until he accepts it." * * * Whether the plaintiff was rightfully deprived of a credit is a matter between it and the drawee, First National.

If we treat the first count as seeking to base a cause of action for money had and received upon a waiver of the tort of conversion—a matter which it is not clear is argued—the result will be the same. In this aspect the question presented is whether a drawer has a right of action for conversion against a collecting bank which handles its checks in the bank collection process. Unless there be such a right, there is no tort which can be waived.

The plaintiff relies upon the Uniform Commercial Code § 3–419, which provides, "(1) An instrument is converted when * * * (c) it is paid on a forged indorsement." This, however, could not apply to the defendant, which is not a "payor bank," defined in the Code, § 4–105(b), as "a bank by which an item is payable as drawn or accepted." * * *

A conversion provision of the Uniform Commercial Code which might have some bearing on this case is § 3–419(3). This section implicitly recognizes that, subject to defences, including the one stated in it, a collecting bank, defined in the Code, § 4–105(d), may be liable in conversion. In the case at bar the forged indorsements were "wholly inoperative" as the signatures of the payee, Code §§ 3–404(1), 1–201(43), and equally so both as to the restrictive indorsements for deposits, see § 3–205(c), and as to the indorsement in blank, see § 3–204(2). When the forger transferred the checks to the collecting bank, no negotiation under § 3–202(1) occurred, because there was lacking the necessary indorsement of the payee. For the same reason, the collecting bank could not become a "holder" as defined in § 1–201(20), and so could not become a holder in due course under § 3–302(1). Accordingly, we assume that the collecting bank may be liable in conversion to a proper party, subject to defences, including that in § 3–419(3). See A. Blum, Jr.'s, Sons v. Whipple, 194 Mass. 253, 255, 80 N.E. 501, 13 L.R.A.,N.S., 211. But there is no explicit provision in the Code purporting to determine to whom the collecting bank may be liable, and consequently, the drawer's right to enforce such a liability must be found elsewhere. Therefore, we conclude that the case must be decided on our own law, which, on the issue we are discussing, has been left untouched by the Uniform Commercial Code in any specific section. * * *

The authorities are hopelessly divided. We think that the preferable view is that there is no right of action. * * *

We state what appears to us to be the proper analysis. Had the checks been delivered to the payee Westinghouse, the defendant might have been liable for conversion to the payee. The checks, if delivered, in the hands of the payee would have been valuable property which could have been transferred for value or presented for payment; and, had a check been dishonored, the payee would have had a right of recourse against the drawer on the instrument under § 3–413(2). Here the plaintiff drawer of the checks, which were never delivered to the payee * * *, had no valuable rights in them. Since, as we have seen, it did not have the right of a payee or subsequent holder to present them to the drawee for payment, the value of its rights was limited to the physical paper on which they were written, and was not measured by their payable amounts. * * *

The enactment of the Uniform Commercial Code opens the road for the adoption of what seems the preferable view. An action by the drawer against the collecting bank might have some theoretical appeal as avoiding circuity of action. * * * It would have been in the interest of speedy and complete justice had the case been tried with the action by the drawer against the drawee and with an action by the drawee against the collecting bank. * * * So one might ask: If the drawee is liable to the drawer and the collecting bank is liable to the drawee, why not let the drawer sue the collecting bank direct? We believe that the answer lies in the applicable defences set up in the Code.

The drawer can insist that the drawee recredit his account with the amount of any unauthorized payment. Such was our common law. * * * This is, in effect, retained by the Code §§ 4–401(1), 4–406(4). But the drawee has defences based upon the drawer's substantial negligence, if "contributing," or upon his duty to discover and report unauthorized signatures and alterations. §§ 3–406, 4–406. As to unauthorized indorsements, see § 4–406(4). Then, if the drawee has a valid defence which it waives or fails upon request to assert, the drawee may not assert against the collecting bank or other prior party presenting or transferring the check a claim which is based on the forged indorsement. § 4–406(5). * * * If the drawee recredits the drawer's account and is not precluded by § 4–406(5), it may claim against the presenting bank on the relevant warranties in §§ 3–417 and 4–207, and each transferee has rights against his transferor under those sections.

If the drawer's rights are limited to requiring the drawee to recredit his account, the drawee will have the defences noted above and perhaps others; and the collecting bank or banks will have the defences in § 4–207(4) and § 4–406(5), and perhaps others. If the drawer is allowed in the present case to sue the collecting bank, the assertion of the defences, for all practical purposes, would be difficult. The possibilities of such a result would tend to compel resort to litigation in every case involving a forgery of commercial paper. It is a result to be avoided.

[The court sustained demurrers to all plaintiff's counts.]

## PROBLEM

Employee stole an unindorsed check from her employer, Payee, forged Payee's indorsement and deposited it in Depositary Bank (DB) for collection. Payor Bank (PB) paid the check upon presentment and debited Drawer's account for the amount of the check. When the forgery was discovered, PB erased the debit to Drawer's account and relied on DB's breach of presentment warranty in demanding the return of the amount that it paid DB in settlement for the check. DB defended on the ground that Drawer's lack of due care substantially contributed to the forgery and that PB should debit Drawer's account under 3–405 or 3–406 rather than proceeding against DB for breach of its warranty. If Drawer's conduct contributed to the forgery, should PB be allowed to shift the loss from the drawer to DB? See 3–417(c), Comment 6 to 3–417, and 4–208(c). DB's liability to PB is only to reimburse it for any loss resulting from the breach of warranty. 3–417(b), 4–208(b). If Drawer may not raise the forgery against PB because of 3–405 or 3–406, has PB been damaged by DB's breach of presentment warranty?

### 4.   IMPOSTORS AND FICTITIOUS PAYEES

We have seen that in forged indorsement cases, as a general rule, the loss falls on the bank of first deposit, the bank that dealt with the forger. But exceptions have been made to this rule in certain situations in which it seems unfair to allocate the loss in this manner. One of these exceptions is the impostor cases, covered by 3–404(a). Another is the fictitious payee cases, governed by 3–404(b). Still another is the payroll-padding cases to which 3–405 and other provisions apply. The drafting stratagem used to identify these cases in Article 3 is largely based on the intent of the issuer of the instrument with respect to the person to whom the instrument is payable. Hence, before looking at the exceptions, we examine the intent issue.

#### a.   INTENT OF ISSUER

In some cases in which a forged indorsement is alleged, it may not be clear whether there is a forged indorsement because it is not clear to whom the instrument is payable. In identifying the person to whom the instrument is payable, the starting point is 3–110.

Suppose Jane Doe writes a check to the order of Richard Roe. Under 3–110(a) the intent of Doe determines to whom the check is payable. There may be many people in the world named Richard Roe, but only the Richard Roe intended by Doe is the payee of the check. If the check gets into the hands of a different Richard Roe, an indorsement by that Richard Roe is ineffective as an indorsement of the payee of the check.

Change the facts. Suppose Doe made a mistake in writing the check. Intending to issue a check to a person that she thinks is Richard Roe, she writes that name as the payee of the check. In fact the name of the person to whom she intended to issue the check is Peter Poe and Poe has never used the name Richard Roe. If Doe delivers the check to Poe, Poe becomes the holder of the check even though the check states that it is payable to Richard Roe. An indorsement by Poe is effective because Poe is the payee of the check. Poe may indorse by signing either the name on the check or Poe's name. 3–110(a) and 3–204(d).

The rules stated in 3–110(a) apply to the issuer of a negotiable instrument in determining to whom the instrument is initially payable and the same rules apply in determining to whom an instrument is subsequently made payable by a holder making a special indorsement. 3–205(a). Thus, if Jane Doe is the payee of the check rather than the drawer and she indorses the check with the indorsement "Pay to Richard Roe," the person to whom the check becomes payable is determined by Doe's intent according to the rules in 3–110.

Section 3–110 is also important with respect to forged checks. Suppose Thief steals Jane Doe's checkbook and forges her name to a check on her bank account. The check is made payable to Richard Roe. Although Thief's act of signing Doe's name to the check is ineffective as the signature of Doe, the signature is effective as Thief's signature. 3–403(a). Under 3–110(a), it is the intention of Thief, the drawer of the check, that determines to whom the check is payable.

An organization such as a corporation must act through human agents in the drawing of checks, and the organization normally identifies officers who are authorized to sign checks in behalf of the organization. Often, the organization requires that its checks be signed by more than one authorized officer. Under 3–110(a) the intent of the authorized officer or officers signing in behalf of the organization determines to whom the check is payable. But in many cases, checks of organizations do not bear any manually-made signature in behalf of the organization. Rather, the check is produced by a check-writing machine and the signature of the drawer is a printed or facsimile signature. The terms of the check, including the name of the payee, are determined by information entered into the computer that controls the check-writing machine. The person providing the information usually is an authorized employee acting in good faith in behalf of the organization, but sometimes the person providing the information is acting fraudulently and might be either an employee authorized to operate the machine or a wholly unauthorized person. In all of these cases the intention of the person supplying the information determines to whom the check is payable. 3–110(b).

People engaged in fraud usually try to mask the fraud. For example, an employee authorized to operate a corporation's check-writing machine wishes to steal money by obtaining payment of checks produced by the machine. Instead of causing the machine to produce checks payable to the employee, the employee causes the machine to produce checks payable to a different payee. The payee named on the check may be an imaginary person, a so-called "fictitious payee," or the check may name as payee a real person who is not intended to have any interest in the check. In either case, the intent of the dishonest employee is to produce a check for the employee's benefit that the employee can turn into cash after indorsing it by signing the name of the payee indicated on the check. In either case, to whom is the check payable? Is the indorsement by the employee an effective indorsement or a forgery? These cases are governed by 3–404(b) which validates the indorsement and allows the check to be negotiated by the employee.

### b.  IMPOSTORS

Although 3–110(a) states that the intent of the person writing the check determines to whom the check is payable, in some cases it is not possible to clearly identify the payee that way. These cases involve issuance of checks to impostors. For example, if Rogers by impersonating Jacobs induces Drawer to issue to her an instrument payable to Jacobs, Drawer might well have dual intent: to make the check payable to the person to whom he issued the instrument (Rogers) and to the person he thought Rogers was (Jacobs). In this case the statute resolves the case by providing that if Rogers induced Drawer to issue the instrument to him by impersonating Jacobs, Roger's indorsement of Jacobs' name on the instrument is effective. 3–404(a). Since business organizations must operate through the acts of their agents, cases involving malefactors who impersonate agents are common. Unlike its predecessor, 3–404(a) applies to such impersonations.

### PROBLEMS

**1.** Pauley fraudulently induced Martini to write a check on Bank One for $5,000 payable to Herman by convincing Martini that Pauley was Herman, a person of high repute. Pauley took the check from Martini, indorsed Herman's name on the back of the check and deposited the check in Pauley's account in Bank Two. The check was presented by Bank Two to Bank One, Martini's bank, which paid the check. Pauley withdrew all the funds in his account in Bank Two and absconded. Martini claims that Bank One cannot debit his account for the amount of the check because Herman's indorsement was forged. Is Martini correct? See 3–404(a).

**2.** Pauley induced Martini to write a check on Bank One for $5,000 to the Red Cross of Cook County by leading Martini to believe that Pauley was chair of the local Red Cross chapter. Pauley wrote two indorsements on the check: first, "Cook County Red Cross", and second, "Pauley". Pauley deposited the check in his account in Bank Two, which presented it to Bank One, Martini's bank, which paid the check. Pauley withdrew the funds representing the check from his account and absconded. Martini claims that Bank One cannot debit his account for the amount of the check because Pauley forged the indorsement by writing "Cook County Red Cross" on the back of the check. Is Martini correct? See Comment 1 to 3–404.

———

The following case compares the former and the present impostor provisions with respect to agency impersonations. How does it help you solve the preceding problems?

# Title Insurance Company of Minnesota v. Comerica Bank–California

Court of Appeal, Sixth District, 1994.
27 Cal.App.4th 800, 32 Cal.Rptr.2d 735.

■ MIHARA, ASSOCIATE JUSTICE.

At issue in this appeal is the applicability and scope of the "impostor rule," which makes an indorsed check effective if the drawer was induced to issue the check by an impersonator of the payee. (Com.Code, § 3404, subd. (a); former Com.Code, § 3405, subd. (1)(a).) Plaintiff Title Insurance Company of Minnesota contends the trial court erroneously applied this rule in sustaining the demurrer of the drawee bank, respondent Comerica Bank–California ("Bank"), to plaintiff's complaint for negligence. We agree that the impostor rule is not applicable under the circumstances presented, and accordingly reverse the judgment of dismissal.

## ALLEGATIONS OF THE COMPLAINT

\* \* \*

Plaintiff is the assignee of the interests of First National Mortgage Company ("FNMC"), who made two equity loans to Helen Nastor ("Helen"), secured by deeds of trust. Plaintiff issued a policy of land title insurance for each of these loans.

On September 22, 1988, FNMC issued a check payable to Helen in the amount of $58,659.29, the proceeds of the first loan. FNMC gave the check to Helen's son, Rudy Nastor ("Rudy"), for delivery to Helen. That day, someone impersonating Helen indorsed the check and presented it to Bank, where FNMC held an account. Bank paid the impersonator the full amount of the check.

On December 29, 1988, FNMC made a second loan to Helen in the amount of $108,300. Part of the proceeds of this loan were used to pay off the first loan. The remainder was issued to Rudy in the form of a check made payable to him.

When FNMC failed to receive payment on the $108,300 loan, it initiated nonjudicial foreclosure proceedings against Helen's property. On October 17, 1989, Helen's attorney informed FNMC that its deed of trust on the property was invalid because it had been executed by Rudy using a forged power of attorney. Helen thereafter testified by deposition that she had not executed the power of attorney, nor had she indorsed or presented the check to Bank for payment.

FNMC made a claim for payment under the second title insurance policy, and plaintiff paid FNMC $108,300. Plaintiff, acting as subrogee and assignee with respect to FNMC's claim, then sued Bank for negligence, seeking recovery of the $108,000. According to the first amended complaint, Bank had a duty "to establish and practice such procedures and business practices as are or may be reasonably necessary and effective to avoid a breach of any of the duties of care owed by BANK . . . to the depositors and customers of BANK ... including therein a duty to immediately inform customers such as FNMC when impostors and/or forgers attempt to cash a check drawn on such customers' accounts with BANK." Bank breached this duty, plaintiff alleged, by failing to ensure "that only properly endorsed and presented checks of its depositors [were] paid." Had Bank "caught" the impostor trying to cash the check payable to Helen, it would have informed FNMC of the attempt, and FNMC would have discovered the forged power of attorney before it made the second loan.

## APPLICABILITY OF THE IMPOSTOR RULE

Bank's demurrer is based entirely on the asserted applicability of the impostor rule, which, according to Bank, interposes an "absolute defense" against plaintiff's allegations of negligence. Bank relies on the current provisions of section 3404, subdivision (a) (hereafter, "section 3404(a)"), which makes an indorsement by any person effective if an impostor had induced the issuance of the instrument to either the impostor or "a person acting in concert with the impostor."[1] In this case, argues Bank, Rudy was acting in concert with the impostor (the impersonator of Helen), who presented the check to Bank for payment.

Plaintiff responds that section 3404(a) is not applicable, because it was not enacted until 1992, after the events alleged in the complaint. Instead, plaintiff maintains, this case is controlled by former section 3405, subdivision (1)(a) (hereafter, "former section 3405(1)(a)"). The expression of the rule in the latter statute is substantially the same as that of the current provisions, but excluded from its reach are false representations of agency. Because Rudy obtained the check from FNMC by falsely representing that he was authorized to act as Helen's agent, plaintiff argues the transaction at issue is outside the scope of the impostor rule.

We agree with plaintiff that former section 3405(1)(a) governs the disposition of this case, since the events at issue took place in 1988, while that statute was still in effect. Former section 3405(1)(a) provided: "An indorsement by any person in the name of a named payee is effective if (a) An impostor by use of the mails or otherwise has induced the maker or drawer to issue the instrument to him or his confederate in the name of the payee...."

This section does not protect Bank from liability under the circumstances presented. As one California court explained prior to the enactment of former section 3405, the impostor rule is applicable only when the issuance of the check has been accomplished through *impersonation* of the payee: "[W]here a check is delivered to an impostor as payee and the drawer believes that the impostor is the person upon whose endorsement it

---

**1.** Section 3404(a) states: "If an impostor, by use of the mails or otherwise, induces the issuer of an instrument to issue the instrument to the impostor, or to a person acting in concert with the impostor, by impersonating the payee of the instrument or a person authorized to act for the payee, an indorsement of the instrument by any person in the name of the payee is effective as the indorsement of the payee in favor of a person who, in good faith, pays the instrument or takes it for value or for collection."

will be paid, the endorsement by such impostor in the name which he is using to impersonate another is not a forgery.... The soundness of the rule obtains in the fact that the money has actually been paid to the person for whom it was really intended. Because another person might bear the very name assumed by the impostor and might have some contractual relationships with the impostor does not subject to a loss the drawee bank when it has paid the check to the person intended as the payee." (Schweitzer v. Bank of America (1941) 42 Cal. App.2d 536, 540, 109 P.2d 441.) * * *

The reasoning of the *Schweitzer* court directs our analysis in the present case. If FNMC (the drawer) had been induced *by an impostor* of Helen to issue the check either to Rudy or to the impostor, then the indorsement would be considered effective as to FNMC under the impostor rule. The rationale for this result is that Bank has paid the person whom FNMC intended to receive the money. When viewed under principles of negligence or estoppel, the outcome of this scenario would be the same: the risk of loss would be shifted to the drawer of the instrument (FNMC), who was in a better position to detect the fraud. (See Fireman's Fund Ins. Co. v. Security Pacific Nat. Bank (1978) 85 Cal. App.3d 797, 830, 149 Cal. Rptr. 883 [burden of loss on party who deals with the forger]; Intelogic v. Merchants Nat. Bank (Ind.App. 2 Dist.1993) 626 N.E.2d 839, 842 [under UCC, loss resulting from forged indorsement should fall upon party best able to prevent it]; East Gadsden Bank v. First City Nat. Bank of Gadsden (1973) 50 Ala.App. 576, 281 So.2d 431, 433 [intended payee theory distinguished from negligence or estoppel theory].)

This case presents different facts, however. Here, FNMC made the check payable to the true Helen, not to an impostor representing herself as Helen. FNMC intended that Helen herself—not a person it believed to be Helen—indorse the check and receive the proceeds. There is no question that FNMC intended to deal solely with Helen. The rationale underlying the protection of the impostor rule thus does not apply here. * * *

A person's false representation that he or she is an agent of the payee is not sufficient. Uniform Commercial Code Comment 2 to former section 3405 notes: " 'Impostor' refers to impersonation, and does not extend to a false representation that the party is the authorized agent of the payee. The maker or drawer who takes the precaution of making the instrument payable to the principal is entitled to have his indorsement." (See Uniform Com.Code com., 23B to § 3405.) Here, Rudy obtained issuance of the check to Helen not by impersonating her, but by falsely representing that he was authorized to act on her behalf. Although clearly fraudulent, this conduct does not constitute impersonation and thus cannot be considered an inducement to issue the instrument within the meaning of former section 3405(1)(a). * * *

Bank's emphasis on the asserted fact that Rudy was acting in concert with Helen's impostor is of no consequence. To invoke the protection of former section 3405(1)(a) Bank would have to point to facts showing that *by impersonation* the impostor induced FNMC to issue the check either to her or to Rudy, her confederate. The complaint alleges no such facts, however. The only impersonation that took place was in the presentation of the check to Bank. * * *

The result is no different even under section 3404(a), the current version of the rule. The only significant change in this section is its recognition that the impostor may pretend to be either the payee or the payee's agent. As the Uniform Commercial Code Comment to the revised law notes, "Under former Section 3–405(1)(a), if Impostor impersonated Smith and induced the drawer to draw a check to the order of Smith, Impostor could negotiate the check. If Impostor impersonated Smith, the president of Smith Corporation, and the check was payable to the order of Smith Corporation, the section did not apply.... Section 3–404(a) gives Impostor the power to negotiate the check in both cases." (See Uniform Com.Code com., 23B to § 3404.) This comment makes it clear that impersonation is still required to invoke the impostor rule, whether the perpetrator of the deception pretends to be the principal or the agent. Misrepresentation of the perpetrator's agency status does not suffice. * * *

We must conclude, therefore, that the impostor rule is inapplicable under these circumstances. By correctly identifying himself as Rudy but falsely representing himself to be Helen's agent Rudy did not engage in the impersonation required by the impostor rule, as expressed both in former section 3405, which was applicable at the time of the transactions at issue, and in its contemporary form, section 3404(a). The impersonation by Helen's impostor cannot be said to have induced FNMC to issue the check, since it took place only afterward, when the impostor presented the check to Bank.

Bank does not challenge the legal sufficiency of the complaint in any respect other than the asserted bar of the impostor rule. Accordingly, we hold that the trial court incorrectly sustained Bank's demurrer based on the application of the impostor rule. * * *

### NOTE

Contrast these two cases: Case #1. Rudy induced Drawer to issue a check to Helen Corporation by falsely representing that he was the treasurer of that organization. Case #2. Rudy induced Drawer to issue a check to Helen Corporation by representing that he was Barnes, who actually was the treasurer of Helen Corporation. How would 3–404(a) apply to these cases? Which of these cases most resembles *Title Insurance Company*?

### c. FICTITIOUS PAYEES

The two basic fictitious payee cases are set out in Comment 2 to 3–404. In Case #1 Treasurer, authorized to draw checks in behalf of Corporation, fraudulently draws a corporate check to Supplier Co., a non-existent company. 3–404(b)(ii). In Case #2 the facts are the same except that Supplier Co. is an actual company that does business with Corporation, but Treasurer does not intend Supplier Co. to have any interest in the check. 3–404(b)(i). In both cases the Treasurer indorses the checks in the name of

Supplier Co and deposits them in Depositary Bank in an account controlled by Treasurer. Some cases had distinguished between Case #1 in which the payee is truly fictitious and Case #2 in which the payee is an actual person with which Corporation does business. Section 3–404(b) sweeps away this distinction and treats the indorsements as effective as the indorsement of the payee in both cases in favor of Corporation's Payor Bank and the Depositary Bank, if, in good faith, the Payor Bank paid the check or the Depositary Bank cashed the check over the counter or took it for collection.

The effect of the fictitious payee rule under 3–404(b) is to shift the loss to the Drawer instead of the Depositary Bank. Since the indorsement is effective as the indorsement of the payee, Payor Bank can charge Drawer's account because the check is properly payable under 4–401. The statement in Comment 1 to 4–401 that a check containing a forged indorsement is not properly payable does not apply because there is no forged indorsement. If Payor Bank does not charge Drawer's account and elects to proceed against Depositary Bank on breach of its presentment warranty under 4–208(a)(1), it cannot succeed because at the time of presentment Depositary Bank was a holder under 3–404(b)(1). Section 4–208(c) specifically empowers Depositary Bank to defend a breach of warranty suit by Payor Bank by proving that the indorsement is effective under 3–404(b).

Pre-revision 3–405(1) provided that "[a]n indorsement by any person in the name of a named payee is effective" if the drawer did not intend the payee to have an interest in the instrument. Some courts frustrated the manifest policy of this section by holding that even a slight variation between the indorsement and the name of the "named payee" precluded the section from applying, thereby making the indorsement a forgery, with the loss falling on the innocent depositary bank. Section 3–404(c)(i) addresses this problem by providing that an indorsement is made in the name of the person to whom the instrument is payable if it is made in a name substantially similar to the name of that person. Perhaps of greater importance is the provision in 3–404(c)(ii) that no indorsement at all is needed if the check is deposited in an account in a name substantially similar to the name of the person to whom the instrument is made payable.

The most important novelty in 3–404 is subsection (d) which allows "the person bearing the loss" in a fictitious payee case—usually the drawer—to recover from a person who fails to exercise due care in paying or taking an instrument for collection—usually the depositary bank—if that failure substantially contributes to the loss resulting from the payment of the instrument. See Comment 3 to 3–404. An example of the kind of case this provision is intended to deal with is set out in Comment 4 to 3–405: Malefactor works the fictitious payee scam and possesses a check for a large amount payable to the Ford Motor Company, a supplier of Malefactor's employer; Malefactor opens an account in Ford's name in Depositary Bank, asserting that he is the manager of a new Ford branch; he indorses the check in Ford's name, deposits the check and withdraws the proceeds by a wire transfer to a foreign country. Depositary Bank failed to require Malefactor to produce a corporate resolution or other evidence of authorization to act for the corporation when the account was opened. The premise of 3–404(d) is that in some cases the person taking the check might have detected the fraud and prevented the loss by exercise of ordinary care. If that person did not exercise ordinary care, it is reasonable to impose loss on that person to the extent its failure contributed to the loss. Comment 3. We see an application of this provision in *Gina Chin* in the next section.

## 5. THE DOUBLE FORGERY

We have seen that in cases of a forged drawer's signature the loss is generally borne by the payor bank and in cases of a forged indorsement the loss usually falls on the depositary bank, subject to the important exceptions discussed in this chapter. But what of the case—the all-time favorite negotiable instruments examination question—in which both the drawer's signature and the payee's indorsement are forged, the so-called double forgery? In the following case, Lehman, an employee of Chin, forged the signature of one of Chin's officers on checks payable to Chin's suppliers; Lehman then forged the indorsement of the payee of these checks and deposited them in his account in First Union. Before revision of Article 3, the courts had reached consensus that such cases should be treated as forged check cases, not as forged indorsement cases. The loss should fall on the drawee bank and not the depositary bank because the indorsement is not forged. In short, there is no double forgery; there is only one, the signature of the drawer. How would this case be decided under 3–404(b)? See Case #5 in Comment 2 to 3–404. How does 3–404(d) change this result? Comment 3 to 3–404. 1 Clark & Clark, The Law of Bank Deposits, Collections and Credit Cards & 12.07[3][b] (Rev. ed. 2006); White & Summers, Uniform Commercial Code §§ 15–6, 16–4e (4th ed. 1995).

## Gina Chin & Associates, Inc. v. First Union Bank

Supreme Court of Virginia, 1998.
500 S.E.2d 516.

■ LACY, JUSTICE.

Gina Chin & Associates, Inc. (Chin) filed a motion for judgment against First Union Bank alleging that First Union was negligent when it accepted checks drawn on Chin's accounts bearing both forged signatures of the drawer and forged indorsements of the payees. The trial court sustained First Union's demurrer and entered summary judgment. We awarded Chin an appeal, and we will reverse the judgment of the trial court because we conclude that Chin's motion for judgment pled a cause of action pursuant to §§ 3–404 and–405 of the Uniform Commercial Code.

In reviewing a case decided on a demurrer, we accept as true the facts alleged in the motion for judgment and all reasonable inferences to be drawn therefrom. * * * Chin, a food wholesaler, maintained checking accounts at Signet Bank and Citizens Bank of Washington, D.C. (the drawee banks). During 1994 and 1995, an employee of Chin, Amie Cheryl

Lehman, forged the signature of one of Chin's officers on a number of checks that were payable to Chin's suppliers. Lehman then forged the payees' indorsements and, with the assistance of a First Union teller, deposited the checks in an account which she held at First Union. The drawee banks then paid the checks and debited a total amount of $270,488.72 from Chin's accounts.

First Union asserts that, under the UCC, it is amenable to suit only by the drawee banks based on a breach of warranty of title theory. § 4–207. Chin's sole cause of action, according to First Union, is against the drawee banks for improperly charging Chin's accounts for the amount of the forged checks. See §§ 4–401–406. Under First Union's interpretation of §§ 3–404 and–405, Chin does not have a cause of action against it pursuant to those sections because they only apply to instances involving a forged indorsement of the payee and not to the circumstances where both the payee's indorsement and the signature of the drawer were forged.

While First Union correctly states that the UCC provides a drawer with a cause of action against a drawee bank that charges a drawer's account based on checks containing a forged signature of the drawer, its conclusion that §§ 3–404 and –405 cannot be utilized by a drawer against the depositary bank in a double forgery situation is erroneous.

Sections 3–404 and –405 were part of the 1992 revisions to the UCC. Revised § 3–404(b) provides that where the payee on a check is fictitious or not the person intended to have an interest in the check by the person determining to whom the check is payable, a forged payee's indorsement on the check is nevertheless effective for one who takes the check in good faith.[2] Similarly, where an employee vested with the responsibility for processing, signing, or indorsing the employer's check makes a fraudulent indorsement of such check, revised § 3–405 continues the prior provision's rule that the indorsement is effective if taken or paid in good faith. However, both revised sections provide that if the person taking the check fails to exercise ordinary care, "the person bearing the loss may recover from the person failing to exercise ordinary care to the extent the failure to exercise ordinary care contributed to the loss." §§ 3–404(d)–405(b).

The revisions to §§ 3–404 and–405 changed the previous law by allowing "the person bearing the loss" to seek recovery for a loss caused by the negligence of any person paying the instrument or taking it for value based on comparative negligence principles. The concept of comparative negligence introduced in the revised sections reflects a determination that all participants in the process have a duty to exercise ordinary care in the drawing and handling of instruments and that the failure to exercise that duty will result in liability to the person sustaining the loss. Nothing in the statutory language indicates that, where the signature of the drawer is forged, the drawer cannot qualify as a "person bearing the loss" or that the drawer is otherwise precluded from seeking recovery from a depositary

---

**2.** The person whose intent determines to whom an instrument is payable includes a person who forges the drawer's signature. See § 3–110(a).

bank under these sections. In the absence of any specific exclusion, we conclude that the sections are applicable in double forgery situations.

This conclusion is consistent with Comment 2 of the Official Comments to § 3–404, which states that subsection (b) "also applies to forged check cases." Another commentary also concludes that § 3–404 applies to double forgery situations. Remarking that under the previous law, double forgery cases were treated solely as forged drawer's signature cases, allowing the depositary bank to avoid liability, the commentary concludes that the result under the revised section "differs sharply."

> In fictitious payee double forgeries under the Revision, some of the ultimate loss will end up on the shoulders of the company that hired the dishonest bookkeeper and failed to supervise the miscreant. The rest will be shouldered by the depositary bank for [its] negligence....

Barkley Clark & Barbara Clark, The Law of Bank Deposits, Collections and Credit Cards & 12.07[3][b] (Rev. ed. 1995).

Accordingly, we hold that Chin was not precluded from asserting a cause of action against First Union pursuant to §§ 3–404 or–405. In light of this conclusion, we next examine Chin's motion for judgment to determine whether it is sufficient to state a cause of action under these sections.

Chin seeks recovery for a loss sustained as a result of the negligent actions of First Union. Chin alleged that its employee, Lehman, forged both its signature and the indorsement of the payees on a number of checks and, with the cooperation of an employee of First Union, deposited the checks into Lehman's account at First Union. The motion for judgment specifically alleged that the acceptance of the forged checks by First Union for payment "was negligent and was in contravention of established banking customs and standards" and "was due to the negligent failure of First Union Bank to supervise its employee." The pleading further asserts that this negligence caused Chin to suffer a loss of over $270,000.

These allegations are sufficient to state a cause of action against First Union pursuant to §§ 3–404 and–405. Accordingly, the trial court erred in sustaining First Union's demurrer. The judgment of the trial court is reversed and the case is remanded for further proceedings.

## NOTE

Since Chin's signature on the checks was forged, under 4–401(a) the drawee banks were not entitled to charge Chin's account, unless 3–406 or 4–406 applies, and these are not in issue in this case. If the drawee banks cannot charge Chin's account, how does Chin qualify as a "person bearing the loss" under 3–404(d)? In the last paragraph of Comment 3 to 3–404, the statement is made that in Case #5, which is a double forgery case in which the indorsement is effective under 3–404(b), the drawee bank has a cause of action under subsection (d).

## 6.   PAYROLL PADDING

We have seen examples of employee fraud that involve forgery of the employer's signature either as an indorsement of checks payable to the employer or as drawer of a check drawn on the employer's bank account. Another common type of employee fraud does not involve forgery of the employer's signature. This type of fraud is sometimes referred to as "payroll padding," and it can be illustrated by the following cases.

Case #1. Corporation pays its employees by check. Treasurer is authorized to sign checks on behalf of Corporation, but a signature by one other officer of Corporation is also necessary. Treasurer signed checks to pay employees on the April payroll. Intending to defraud Corporation, Treasurer included in the checks for that month three checks payable either to fictitious people or real people who sometimes work for Corporation but who did not work in April and therefore were not entitled to any pay. At the request of Treasurer, Vice President also signed the checks. Vice President did not know who was entitled to payment and did not raise any question about the checks. The checks were returned to Treasurer after they were signed. Treasurer took the three fraudulent checks and indorsed each of them by signing the name of the payee. She then deposited each of the checks in a bank in which she had an account. The checks were paid and Treasurer withdrew the proceeds of the checks. Assume Treasurer is judgment proof. If the indorsements by Treasurer are effective as indorsements of the payees of the three checks, Corporation takes the loss. If the indorsements are treated as forged indorsements, the depositary banks that collected the checks will take the loss. 3–417(a)(1), 4–208(a)(1). In this case the intent of Treasurer determines the person to whom each of the three checks is payable. 3–110(a) (last sentence). Under 3–404(b), Treasurer became the holder of each check and her indorsement in the name of the stated payee was effective as the indorsement of the payee of the check. Thus, Corporation takes the loss.

Case #2. Same as Case #1 except that Corporation's checks are produced by a check-writing or facsimile signature machine. Treasurer had access to the computer that operates the machine. She made entries in the computer that caused the machine to issue the three fraudulent checks. She obtained possession of the checks and then proceeded as in Case #1. Under 3–110(b) the intent of Treasurer determines the person to whom each of the three checks is payable. The analysis of Case #2 is identical to that of Case #1.

Case #3. Treasurer signs checks on behalf of Corporation to pay employees, but Clerk prepares the April payroll that tells Treasurer to whom to issue the checks and in what amount. This time the culprit is Clerk. Intending to defraud Corporation, Clerk includes in the payroll the names of three people who work part time for Corporation, but who performed no work during April. Clerk prepared checks of Corporation in accordance with the payroll and gave them to Treasurer for signature. Treasurer signed the checks and returned them to Clerk.

Clerk took the three fraudulent checks, indorsed each in the name of the payee named in the check, and dealt with the checks as Treasurer did in Case #1. This case is more complex. Assume Treasurer knew each of the three employees named in the three fraudulent checks, but she did not know that they did not work in April. Treasurer intended each check to be payable to the payee named in the check and, under 3–110(a), Treasurer's intent controls; hence 3–404(b) doesn't apply. Thus, Clerk's indorsements are forged indorsements and the normal result is that the loss is taken by the depositary bank that collected the check. In Case #1 and Case #2, Corporation took the loss because it was held responsible for the conduct of Treasurer, its faithless employee. In Case #3 the faithless employee is Clerk. Is there any good reason why Corporation should not also be responsible for the conduct of Clerk? In each case the faithless employee had duties with respect to the issuance of checks. The three cases are essentially similar. In Case #3, Treasurer performed the same function as Vice President did in Case #1 and the check writing machine did in Case #2. By preparing the payroll, Clerk as a practical matter determined to whom Corporation's checks were to be made payable. However, the result in Case #3 is not determined solely by 3–110(a) because 3–405 also applies. We previously examined cases covered by 3–405(a)(2)(i). This time the relevant provision is 3–405(a)(2)(ii).

## 7.   ALLOCATION OF LOSS BY CONTRACT

How far can banks go in protecting themselves from fraud or forgery losses by contracts with their customers? Section 4–103(a) gives broad authority to vary the effect of the statute by agreement, but there are limits beyond which banks cannot go in disclaiming their liability. We will discuss these limits in more detail in the next chapter. At this point we include a case on a bank's attempt to disclaim liability for paying counterfeit checks containing unauthorized facsimile signatures. We place the case here rather than in Chapter 16 so that you can assess the reasonableness of the bank's broad disclaimer provisions in the context of the material you have just studied on fraud and forgery.

## Jefferson Parish School Board v. First Commerce Corporation

Court of Appeal of Louisiana, Fourth Circuit, 1996.
669 So.2d 1298.

■ JONES, JUDGE.

Jefferson Parish School Board appeals a judgment of the trial court granting defendant First National Bank of Commerce's ("First NBC") Motion for Summary Judgment.

Appellant Jefferson Parish School Board maintained a checking account titled "general account," number 7003–42931, with appellee, First

NBC. Appellant desired to utilize a facsimile signature machine, and accordingly, adopted a facsimile signature resolution with First NBC.

In November of 1992, various instruments purporting to be checks made by appellant and drawn on the subject account were presented for payment and paid by First NBC. Upon receiving the monthly bank statement, appellant observed the instruments to be counterfeit. The checks were returned to First NBC each with an individual "Affidavit of Forgery, Alteration, Loss or Threat of Instrument." First NBC maintained that, pursuant to the resolution adopted by appellant, they were entitled to honor the instruments and appellant should bear the loss.

Appellant filed suit in the Civil District Court for the Parish of Orleans in October of 1993 seeking recovery of the amount paid on the checks. First NBC filed a motion for summary judgment alleging that the resolution adopted by appellant precludes such an action. The district court agreed and granted First NBC's Motion for Summary Judgment.

In their only assignment of error, appellant argues that the trial court erred in dismissing their case based on the adoption of the facsimile signature resolution. This assignment of error has no merit. The resolution contains the following provision:

> RESOLVED: That the First National Bank of Commerce, New Orleans, hereinafter referred to as "Bank", as a designated depository of this corporation, be and it is hereby requested, authorized and directed to honor, for the account and to the debit of the corporation, all checks, drafts, or other orders for the payment of money (inclusive of any such as may be payable to any of the officers of this Corporation or other persons hereinafter specified or whose names appear thereon as signor or signors thereof) drawn in the name of this Corporation on the account(s) of this Corporation with the Bank when bearing *or purporting to bear* the facsimile signatures as of any of the following: [facsimile signatures] and the Bank is and shall be entitled to honor and to charge this Corporation for all such checks, drafts, or other orders, *regardless of by whom or by what means the actual or purported facsimile signature or signatures thereon may have been affixed thereto, if such facsimile signature or signatures resemble the facsimile specimens* from time to time duly certified to or filed with the Bank by the Secretary or other officer of the Corporation. (emphasis added).

The resolution further provides:

> *That the said bank may rely on these resolutions until the receipt by the Bank of a certified copy of a resolution by the Board of Directors of this Corporation revoking the same, this Corporation expressly assuming all risks involved in any unauthorized use of such facsimile signature and agreeing that this Corporation shall be responsible for and chargeable with the amount of all checks, drafts, or other orders bearing such facsimile signature or signatures resembling the same, whether or not placed thereon by the authority of this Corporation.* (emphasis added).

The language of the facsimile agreement, a contract between the parties, is clear and unambiguous. The bank is authorized to honor *all checks* "purporting to bear" the facsimile signatures, "regardless of by what means" the actual or purported signature is affixed as long as the "signatures resemble the facsimile specimens." This is the only requirement imposed on the bank by the contract between the parties—to insure that any signatures "resemble" those provided by the Board on the signature card. This comports with the provision of § 4–103(1) in effect at the time of the agreement. The provision provides:

> The effect of the provisions of this chapter may be varied by agreement except that no agreement can disclaim a bank's responsibility for its own lack of good faith or failure to exercise ordinary care or can limit the measure of damages for such lack of failure; *but the parties may agree to determine the standards by which such responsibility is to be measured if those standards are not manifestly unreasonable.* (emphasis added).

Agreements confected pursuant to this statute are not unusual. See Springhill Bank and Trust Co. v. Citizens Bank and Trust Co., 505 So.2d 867 (La.App. 2d Cir.1987), and Perini Corp. v. First National Bank of Habersham County, 553 F.2d 398 (5th Cir.1977). In *Perini*, the court held that there was no cause of action for recovery of funds paid on forged checks where a resolution was adopted authorizing the drawee's payment of checks bearing signatures resembling the machine-endorsed facsimile signature.

The appellant erroneously argues that First NBC cannot prove any negligence on the part of the appellant's employees regarding the safeguarding of their checks on that account and of the facsimile signature plates of the employees used on that account. This argument incorrectly suggests that the appellant should not bear the burden of the loss if the facsimile plates were not used in the forgery. This position is clearly contrary to the resolution adopted by the appellants. As previously stated, the resolution provides that the bank is authorized to honor checks "regardless of by whom or by what means" the actual or purported signature is affixed as long as the "signatures resemble the facsimile specimens."

Additionally, appellants contend that the checks at issue contained errors that a diligent perusal of the documents would have revealed to experienced bank employees. Appellants base this argument on the fact that the checks in question were printed on different paper. This argument also lacks merit. First NBC is obligated to pay on any paper on which the signature of the drawer matches the signature on file. It is very common for customers to order their checks from different sources.

When reviewing trial court judgments on motions for summary judgment, appellate courts must use the same criteria applied by the trial courts. Thus, a summary judgment should be affirmed when "the pleadings, depositions, answers to interrogatories, and admissions on file, together with affidavits, if any, show that there is no genuine issue of material

fact, and that the mover is entitled to judgment as a matter of law." * * *
The only material fact in this case is the nature of the signatures and there
is no dispute that the signatures are nearly identical to the facsimile
signatures submitted by the appellants.

Therefore, for the reasons stated above, the judgment of the trial court
is affirmed.

### PROBLEM

A fundamental principle of banking law, established in Price v. Neal, is
that the drawee bank bears the loss in forged check cases. *Jefferson Parish*
allowed Bank to contract out of this basic liability by obtaining a resolution
from the Board exculpating Bank from liability for paying forged facsimile
checks bearing a drawer's signature that resembles the Board's signature
specimens. Would a resolution be valid that extends the bank's protection
from facsimile machine forgery losses to all cases in which the drawer's
signature, whether written by *hand* or by machine, resembles that of the
drawer's signature specimens?

### NOTE

The School Board was not negligent in this case and its facsimile
machine was not used by the counterfeiter; none of its employees had any
connection with the counterfeiter. The Board saw itself as an innocent
bystander. In this light, why isn't the disclaimer clause "manifestly unreasonable" as applied to this case? Compare Cumis Insurance Society, Inc. v.
Girard Bank, 522 F.Supp. 414 (E.D.Pa.1981), in which the court reached a
different result in a forged facsimile signature case. See 1 Clark & Clark,
The Law of Bank Deposits, Collections and Credit Cards & 10.02[1] (Rev.
ed. 2005). For a critique of *Jefferson Parish*, see James Steven Rogers, The
Basic Principles of Loss Allocation for Unauthorized Checks, 39 Wake
Forest L.Rev. 453, 484–496. (2004). Professor Rogers believes this case
poses the issue of whether the basic loss allocation scheme of the check
system should be variable by agreement. If so, are there any fundamental
principles of loss allocation in Article 4?

The limits of parties under 4–103(a) to vary their statutory rights and
obligations also has been tested with respect to stop payment orders,
discussed further in the next chapter. Section 4–403(a) obligates a bank to
stop payment on a check when ordered to do so by its customer or
authorized drawer if it has a reasonable opportunity to act. Banks' deposit
contracts with customers frequently specify the conditions under which
stop payment orders will be honored, and the litigated issue has been
whether the specified conditions are "manifestly unreasonable" under 4–
103(a). The results have been mixed. Compare Poullier v. Nacua Motors,
Inc., 439 N.Y.S.2d 85 (N.Y.Sup.Ct.1981) (bank's stipulation of information
needed for stop payment orders to be executed upheld), with FJS Electronics, Inc. v. Fidelity Bank, 431 A.2d 326 (Pa.Super.Ct. 1981) (refusing to give

effect to stipulation when inaccuracy in stop payment order insignificant). Some refusals to enforce contractually imposed restrictions are based on the extrastatutory requirement that the bank clearly disclose them to the customer; see, e.g., Staff Service Associates, Inc. v. Midlantic National Bank, 504 A.2d 148 (N.J.Super.Ct. 1985). Is there a problem of nondisclosure in *Jefferson Parish*, where the Parish School Board's resolution authorized honor of instruments containing signatures "purporting to bear" the facsimile signature? Cf. SOS Oil Corp. v. Norstar Bank of Long Island, 563 N.E.2d 258 (N.Y.Ct.App.1990). Or is the *Jefferson Parish* court simply refusing to regulate the substantive allocation of forgery risk between the customer and bank?

## B.   ALTERATION

### 1.   COMPLETE INSTRUMENTS

"Alteration," defined in 3–407(a), refers to a change that purports to modify the obligation of a party to an instrument if the change is unauthorized. Thus, if the payee raises the amount of a check without the consent of the drawer the check has been altered. But if the payee's act is authorized by the drawer before any other person becomes obligated on the check, the check has not been altered; the change is treated as a change made by the drawer.

The definition of alteration is very broad. It includes fraudulent changes as well as changes made in good faith. For example, the holder of a note changes the due date of the note because the holder believes in good faith that the original due date was erroneous. Even if the holder was mistaken, the alteration is not fraudulent. Under the second sentence of 3–407(b), the non-fraudulent alteration is ineffective to modify the obligation of the maker and the note is enforceable according to its original terms. Non-fraudulent alteration is described in the first paragraph of Comment 1 to 3–407.

The concept of alteration can apply to incomplete instruments described in 3–115 as well as complete instruments, but the effect of alteration is not the same in each case. A discussion of alteration of incomplete instruments follows in the next section.

Fraudulent alteration is the principal focus of 3–407 and can be illustrated by the following hypothetical case:

An authorized employee of Drawer, a large corporation, signed and delivered a typewritten check for $10 payable to the order of Payee. Without Drawer's consent Payee raised the amount of the check to $10,000 by adding a comma and three zeroes after the figure "10" and the word "thousand" after the word "ten." Payee deposited the check in Payee's account with Depositary Bank and the bank obtained $10,000 from Drawee in payment of the check. Drawee then debited Drawer's account in the same amount. Payee withdrew the $10,000 that had been credited to Payee's account in Depositary Bank with respect to the check. When Drawer learned that Drawee had debited $10,000 to Drawer's account with respect to the check, Drawer notified Drawee of the alteration.

Who takes the loss in the hypothetical case? The liability of the drawer with respect to a check is based on the terms of the order to pay made by the person against whom the drawer's liability is asserted. Liability on an altered check can be compared to liability on a forged check. In the absence of fault, the person whose signature as drawer is forged has no liability on the check because the order to pay on which liability is asserted was not made by that person. In the case of the check in the hypothetical case, Drawer can reasonably be held liable with respect to the order to pay $10 because that order was made by Drawer, but, in the absence of fault by Drawer, it is not reasonable to hold Drawer liable with respect to the raised amount because Drawer did not order payment of that amount.

How is this analysis reflected in 3–407? In the hypothetical case, to what extent is Drawee entitled to debit Drawer's account with respect to the check? 3–407(c). If Drawee had dishonored the check, to what extent would Depositary Bank have had a right to recover from Drawer? 3–414(b) and 3–407(c). What is the significance of the first sentence of 3–407(b), which states that "a party whose obligation is affected by the alteration" is discharged? See Comment 1 (second paragraph) to 3–407. If Drawee pays the check but is not entitled to full reimbursement from Drawer, what remedy does it have against Depositary Bank? 3–417(a)(2) and (b). If Depositary Bank is liable to Drawee, what recourse does Depositary Bank have against Payee? 3–416(a)(3) and (b).

Suppose, in the hypothetical case, that the employee who wrote the check in behalf of Drawer left blank spaces in the amount lines on the check, allowing Payee to raise the amount of the check without leaving any easily detectable evidence that the check had been altered. How does this additional fact affect your answers to the questions asked in the preceding paragraph? 3–406. See the following case.

## HSBC Bank USA v. F & M Bank Northern Virginia

United States Court of Appeals, Fourth Circuit, 2001.
246 F.3d 335.

■ HAMILTON, SENIOR CIRCUIT JUDGE:

On or about March 31, 1999, Donald Lynch purchased a check (the Check) from Allied Irish Bank (AIB) in Ireland. The Check was made payable to Advance Marketing and Investment Inc. (AMI) in the amount of US $250.00, which was hand written as "Two Hundred + Fifty" on the center line of the Check (with "US Dollars" hand written on the line below), (*i.e.*, the written portion of the Check), and "US$250.00" hand written on the upper right-hand side of the Check (*i.e.*, the numerical portion of the Check). The manner in which AIB made out the Check left just less than one-half inch of open space in the numerical portion and one inch of open space in the written portion.

The drawee/payor on the Check was Marine Midland Bank, now known as HSBC Bank USA (HSBC). Prior to the Check's deposit into AMI's account at F & M Bank Northern Virginia (F & M), the amount of the Check was altered from $250.00 to $250,000.00 by adding three zeros and changing the period to a comma in the numerical portion of the check and adding the letters "Thoud" in the written portion. The alteration was unauthorized, and the Check was endorsed "A.M.I., Inc."

F & M presented the Check for payment to HSBC. In so doing, F & M warranted, pursuant to Virginia Code § 8.4–207.2(a)(2), that the Check "had not been altered." Va.Code Ann. § 8.4–207.2(a)(2) (Cum.Supp.2000). HSBC honored the Check as presented and paid $250,000.00 to F & M, and debited AIB's account for that amount.

HSBC was subsequently advised by AIB of the Check's unauthorized alteration. HSBC then recredited AIB's account for the amount of the unauthorized alteration and brought the present diversity action against F & M in the United States District Court for the Eastern District of Virginia. Among other claims not relevant to the present appeal, [HSBC] alleged a claim for breach of presentment warranty pursuant to Uniform Commercial Code § 4–207(1)(c) and (2)(c).

Using the Virginia Commercial Code as the substantive law governing HSBC's breach of presentment warranty claim, on July 12, 2000, the district court conducted a bench trial on the claim.[1] F & M asserted as an affirmative defense that by leaving the open spaces as it did in the numerical and written portions of the Check, AIB failed to exercise ordinary care in preparing the Check, which failure substantially contributed to the unauthorized alteration of the Check.[2] The only evidence F & M

---

**1.** The parties agreed that Virginia's Commercial Code governed HSBC's breach of presentment warranty claim. The applicable provision of Virginia's Commercial Code provides as follows:

> (a) If an unaccepted draft is presented to the drawee for payment or acceptance and the drawee pays or accepts the draft, (i) the person obtaining payment or acceptance, at the time of presentment, and (ii) a previous transferor of the draft, at the time of transfer, warrant to the drawee that pays or accepts the draft in good faith that: . . . (2) the draft has not been altered. . . .

Va.Code Ann. § 8.4–207.2(a)(2) (Cum.Supp. 2000).

**2.** F & M asserted its affirmative defense pursuant to Virginia Commercial Code § 8.4–207.2(c), which provides, in relevant part, as follows:

If a drawee asserts a claim for breach of warranty under subsection (a) based on . . . an alteration of the draft, the warrantor may defend by proving that . . . the drawer is precluded under [Virginia Commercial Code] § 8.3A 406 . . . from asserting against the drawee the . . . alteration.

Va.Code Ann. § 8.4–207.2(c). To restate this section using the names of the actual parties in this case, the section provides that F & M, the warrantor, can defend against the warranty claim of HSBC, the drawee, by proving that AIB, the drawer, is precluded under Virginia Commercial Code § 8.3A–406 from asserting the unauthorized alteration of the Check against HSBC. Of relevance in this appeal, AIB is precluded from asserting the unauthorized alteration of the Check against HSBC under Virginia Commercial Code § 8.3A–406(a), if AIB failed to exercise ordinary care in preparing the check and such

actually submitted in support of its affirmative defense was the Check itself.

The district court found that HSBC had established all elements of its breach of presentment warranty claim under Virginia Commercial Code § 8.4–207.2(a)(2). The district court also found that AIB had exercised ordinary care in preparing the Check. In this last regard, the district court stated:

> I have examined this check. And, of course, there does have [sic] to be sufficient writing on a check that there is not an open space so someone can fill it in for additional amounts and alter the check.
>
> But regardless of what you do about writing in zero, zero over 100 and then put a line in, which is, I guess, the standard way to do it—I don't know that if I looked at all the checks in this country that I would know the standard. It is the way I have always done it. There is still some kind of an open space regardless of what you do.
>
> And so, the test has got to be is that line sufficiently filled so that someone cannot come along and add into that writing in a way that just alters the check so that it will go through unnoticed.
>
> That certainly wasn't done on this check. This check was substantially written across the line. As a matter of fact, it was written far enough along the line that you could not write the word "thousand" in. It had to be scrawled up in the manner in which it was.
>
> And I just[,] looking at this check[,] and the way it is made out, I can't find that the preparer was negligent or participated in the alteration of it.
>
> There was sufficient writing there that any alteration that was made was obvious. And I can't find negligence in that regard.

Subsequently, on July 31, 2000, the district court entered an order stating that for the reasons stated from the bench, judgment should be entered in favor of HSBC in the amount of $249,750.00, plus interest at the rate of 9% from April 13, 1999 to the date of the entry of judgment. The docket sheet reflects that such judgment was entered on July 31, 2000. F & M noted a timely appeal.[3]

On appeal, F & M contends the district court's factual finding that AIB exercised ordinary care in preparing the Check is clearly erroneous. F & M seeks reversal of the judgment in favor of HSBC solely upon this basis. For the reasons stated below, we affirm.

---

failure substantially contributed to the unauthorized alteration of the Check. Va.Code Ann. § 8.3A–406(a). Notably, the question of whether AIB failed to exercise ordinary care in preparing the Check is a question to be answered by the trier of fact. Va.Code Ann. § 8.3A–406 cmt. 1 (Cum.Supp.2000).

**3.** On September 13, 2000, a consent order was entered staying the effect of the judgment pending appeal upon F & M Bank's posting a supersedeas bond of $249,000, which it did.

F & M concedes that if the district court's factual finding that AIB exercised ordinary care in preparing the Check is not clearly erroneous, it cannot successfully rely upon its affirmative defense to HSBC's breach of presentment warranty claim and, therefore, the judgment in favor of HSBC should be affirmed. Fed.R.Civ.P. 52(a) (providing that a district court's finding of fact shall not be set aside unless clearly erroneous). We now turn to consider whether the district court's factual finding that AIB exercised ordinary care in preparing the Check is clearly erroneous. * * *

The only evidence submitted by F & M in support of its burden of proving that AIB failed to exercise ordinary care in making out the Check was the Check itself. The district court physically examined the Check, including the just less than one-half inch of open space in the numerical portion of the Check and the one inch of open space in the written portion of the Check. Based upon this physical examination, the district court found that AIB had filled in the open spaces in the numerical and written portions of the check sufficiently such that "any alteration that was made was obvious." Accordingly, the district court found that AIB had exercised ordinary care in making out the Check.

After reviewing a copy of the Check contained in the joint appendix (the sole evidence on this issue presented below), we are not left with a definite and firm conviction that the district court's finding that AIB exercised ordinary care in making out the Check is wrong, mistaken, or implausible. Indeed, we see sound logic in the district court's rationale that if the written portion of the Check contained enough writing such that the Check's alteration could only be accomplished with the "scrawled up," abbreviated form of the word "thousand," *i.e.* "Thoud," ordinary care was exercised in making out the Check. In short, we hold that the district court's factual finding that AIB exercised ordinary care in making out the check is not clearly erroneous.

We also note that F & M's reliance upon the following comment to Virginia Commercial Code § 8.3A–406 is misplaced:

> 3. The following cases illustrate the kind of conduct that can be the basis of a preclusion under Section 3–406(a): ... Case #3. A company writes a check for $10. The figure "10" and the word "ten" are typewritten in the appropriate spaces on the check form. A large blank space is left after the figure and the word. The payee of the check, using a typewriter with a type face similar to that used on the check, writes the word "thousand" after the word "ten" and a comma and three zeros after the figure "10." The drawee bank in good faith pays $10,000 when the check is presented for payment and debits the account of the drawer in that amount. The trier of fact *could* find that the drawer failed to exercise ordinary care in writing the check and that the failure substantially contributed to the alteration. In that case the drawer is precluded from asserting the alteration against the drawee if the check was paid in good faith.

Va.Code Ann. § 8.3A–406, cmt. 3 (Cum.Supp.2000) (emphasis added). This illustration is easily distinguishable from the facts of the present case.

First, the illustration involves typewritten preparation of a check. The small nature of typewritten characters obviously would take up much less space than the handwriting involved in the present case. Furthermore, the actual number of words and numbers typed on the check that is discussed in the commentary prior to alteration is significantly less than the number of words and numbers AIB hand wrote on the Check prior to its alteration.

Because the district court's finding that AIB exercised ordinary care in making out the Check is not clearly erroneous, we affirm the judgment in favor of HSBC.

NOTE

If the Drawer had left more open space on the check, would it have qualified as an incomplete instrument under 3–115(a)?

## 2.   INCOMPLETE INSTRUMENTS

Section 3–115(a). Incomplete Instrument.

(a) "Incomplete instrument" means a signed writing, whether or not issued by the signer, the contents of which show at the time of signing that it is incomplete but that the signer intended it to be completed by the addition of words or numbers.

Assume that A is indebted to B but is not sure of the precise amount of the debt. In payment of the debt A sends to B a check payable to B, leaving the amount of the check blank. A instructs B to complete the check by filling in the amount of the debt. If the amount of the debt is $10 and B fills in the check for that amount, there is no difficulty in enforcing the check against A. The intent of A has been carried out by B's completion of the check. The result is the same as if A had personally completed the check. When the check was received by B, the check was an "incomplete instrument," defined in 3–115(a). Because the amount of the check was not stated, the check was not a negotiable instrument under 3–104 and the last sentence of 3–115(b) applies. If B completes the check by writing in $10 as its amount, the check becomes an instrument under 3–104 and the last sentence of 3–115(b) states that the check can be enforced as completed. There is no alteration.

But if B fills in $10,000 rather than $10, the act of B is not authorized by A. Under 3–115(c) there is an alteration of the incomplete instrument and 3–407 applies. The case is analogous to the hypothetical case in the material in the previous section in which a check payable in the amount of $10 was altered by changing the amount to $10,000. In each case the drawer intended a check in the amount of $10 and in each case the payee raised the intended amount to $10,000.

Suppose B deposited the altered check to B's account in Depositary Bank and the bank obtained $10,000 from Drawee Bank in payment of the check. Drawee Bank then debited A's account in the same amount. B withdrew the $10,000 that had been credited to B's account in Depositary

Bank with respect to the check. When A learned that Drawee Bank had debited $10,000 to A's account with respect to the check, A notified Drawee Bank of the alteration. Who takes the loss in this case? To what extent is Drawee Bank entitled to debit A's account with respect to the check? 3–407(c). If Drawee Bank had dishonored the check, to what extent would Depositary Bank have had a right to recover from A? 3–414(b) and 3–407(c).

Compare the results in this case with the results in the hypothetical case in the previous section. Why are the results different? Is there any relationship between 3–406 and 3–407(c) as it applies to fraudulent completion of incomplete instruments?

## C.   RESTRICTIVE INDORSEMENTS

Indorsement of an instrument may serve several purposes, but most commonly an indorsement is made in order to negotiate the instrument. 3–204(a). The form of the indorsement can affect rights with respect to the instrument if it is stolen and collected or transferred to a third party. If a check indorsed in blank by the holder is stolen, the thief may negotiate the check to a transferee who may obtain rights as a holder in due course. If the stolen check was payable to an identified person and the payee made a special indorsement or did not indorse the check at all, the thief cannot negotiate the check and nobody taking through the thief can become a person entitled to enforce the check. Thus, the rights of a person taking a stolen check may depend upon whether an indorsement by the holder was made and whether the indorsement was special or in blank. The rights of the taker, however, can also depend upon whether the holder made a "restrictive indorsement," governed by 3–206.

The purpose of a restrictive indorsement is to restrict payment of the instrument. That restriction can be expressed as part of a special indorsement or an indorsement in blank. For example, an indorsement of a check consisting solely of the signature of the holder under the words "for deposit only" is a blank indorsement because it does not identify a person to whom it makes the check payable, and is a restrictive indorsement because it indicates that the check is to be deposited to an account. This restrictive indorsement is governed by 3–206(c). Comment 3 to 3–206. An indorsement "Pay to John Doe in trust for Jane Doe" is a special indorsement because it identifies John Doe as the person to whom the check is payable, and is a restrictive indorsement because it indicates that the proceeds of the check are to be paid for the benefit of Jane Doe. This restrictive indorsement is governed by 3–206(d). Comment 4 to 3–206.

Some attempts to restrict payment of an instrument by an indorser are nullified by 3–206. An indorsement "Pay to John Doe only" is ineffective to prohibit payment to any other holder. In spite of the indorsement, John Doe may indorse the instrument to another person and that person may become entitled to enforce the instrument. 3–206(a). An indorsement that attempts to prohibit payment unless a stated condition is satisfied is also ineffective to restrict payment. 3–206(b). Invalid restrictions are discussed in Comment 2 to 3–206.

PROBLEM

Banking by mail is a common practice. This problem considers the degree of protection the payee of a check gains by using a restrictive indorsement under 3–206. Peter, the payee of a check for $10,000 drawn on Payor Bank, indorsed and mailed the check to Bank One where he had an account. Before the check arrived at Bank One, Thief stole the check and wrote Thief's name under Peter's indorsement. Thief then deposited the check to Thief's account in Bank Two. Bank Two presented the check to Payor Bank and Payor Bank paid the check. Thief then withdrew the $10,000 that had been credited to Thief's account in Bank Two with respect to the check.

What are Peter's rights against Bank Two and Payor Bank if Peter's indorsement were as follows?

Case #1

For deposit only

Peter

Case #2

Pay to Bank One for Account No. 1234321

Peter

Case #3

Peter

For deposit only

---

When we are sending checks to our bank for deposit by mail, many of us use the kinds of restrictive indorsements set out in either Case #1 or Case #3. You may be surprised to learn that the court in Spencer v. Sterling Bank, 74 Cal.Rptr.2d 576 (Cal.Ct.App.1998), tells us that what we've been doing accomplishes nothing. The court held that under the plain meaning of 3–206(c)(2) a check indorsed "X, for deposit only" can be deposited in anyone's account in any bank; the depositary bank need not deposit the proceeds in the account of the person indorsing the check, usually the payee of the check, because the blank indorsement does not specify where or for whose benefit such a check is to be deposited. A few cases agree with *Spencer*, but the majority does not. The following case states the majority view. Which view do you believe is a correct interpretation of the statute?

# State of Qatar v. First American Bank

United States District Court, E.D. Virginia, 1995.
885 F.Supp. 849.

■ ELLIS, DISTRICT JUDGE.

At issue in this sequel to State of Qatar v. First American Bank of Virginia ("Qatar I")[1] is the meaning and legal significance of the phrase "for deposit only" following an indorsement on the back of a check. More specifically, the question presented is whether a depositary bank complies with the restrictive indorsement "for deposit only" when it deposits a check bearing that restriction into *any* person's account, or whether that restriction requires a depositary bank to deposit the check's proceeds only into the account of the named payee. For the reasons that follow, the Court holds that the unqualified language "for deposit only" following an indorsement on the back of a check requires a depositary bank to place the check's proceeds into the payee's[2] account, and the bank violates that restrictive indorsement when it credits the check to any other account.

The facts underlying this case are more fully set forth in *Qatar I* and are only briefly reiterated here. Plaintiffs are the State of Qatar and certain of its agencies (collectively, "Qatar"). From approximately 1986 to 1992, one of Qatar's employees, Bassam Salous, defrauded his employer by having checks drawn on Qatar's account in purported payment of false or duplicate invoices that he had created. Although all of the unauthorized checks were made payable to individuals and entities other than Salous, he nonetheless successfully deposited the checks into his own personal accounts with Defendant First American Bank of Virginia ("First American") and Central Fidelity Banks, Inc. (collectively, "the depositary banks").

After Qatar discovered this fraudulent scheme in 1992, it brought suit against the depositary banks for conversion. * * *

Only one category of checks remains in dispute. These checks all bear the forged indorsement of the payee named on the face of the check, followed by a stamped "for deposit only" restriction. In *Qatar I*, the Court denied the depositary banks' motion for summary judgment with respect to these checks on the ground that the depositary banks could be held liable for applying the proceeds of the checks in violation of the restrictive indorsements. *Qatar I*, 880 F.Supp. at 469, 470–71. Specifically, the Court stated:

> [W]hile the forged signature presented no barrier to payment given the effect of [U.C.C.] § 3–405, the accompanying restriction ("FOR DEPOSIT ONLY") provided a clear instruction to the depositary banks to deposit the funds only into the account of the last indorser—here, the named payee.

---

**1.** 880 F.Supp. 463 (E.D.Va.1995).

**2.** Throughout this Memorandum Opinion, "payee" is intended to refer to the last purported indorser.

The Court did not hold the depositary banks liable as a matter of law with respect to these checks, but decided to await the banks' presentation of defenses, if any, at trial. At trial, the depositary banks raised no defenses, but instead challenged for the first time the Court's assumption in *Qatar I* that the phrase "for deposit only", without further specification, directs a depositary bank to deposit the funds only into the account of the named payee. An indorsement in this form, they argued, is far less restrictive, as it merely directs that the check's proceeds be *deposited* in an account, not that they be deposited into a particular account. Thus, the depositary banks urged, they fully complied with the restrictive indorsements on these checks when they deposited the proceeds into Salous' account. Although this issue properly should have been raised at the summary judgment stage, the Court permitted the parties to research the matter and submit post-trial legal memoranda regarding this final, narrow issue. Qatar and First American did so, and the matter is now ripe for disposition.

It is now established that First American may be liable to Qatar for handling a check's proceeds in violation of a restrictive indorsement. *Qatar I*, 880 F.Supp. at 469, 470–71.[8] Under § 3–205(c) of the pre–1993 Uniform Commercial Code ("U.C.C." or "Code"),[9] restrictive indorsements are defined to "include the words 'for collection,' 'for deposit,' 'pay any bank,' or like terms signifying a purpose of deposit or collection." Thus, the U.C.C. makes clear that the phrase "for deposit only" is, in fact, a restrictive indorsement. But the Code does not define "for deposit only" or specify what bank conduct would be inconsistent with that restriction.[10] Nor does Virginia decisional law provide any guidance on this issue. As a result, reference to decisional law from other jurisdictions is appropriate.

Not surprisingly, most courts confronted with this issue have held that the restriction "for deposit only", without additional specification or directive, instructs depositary banks to deposit the funds only into the payee's account. In addition, commentators on commercial law uniformly agree that the function of such a restriction is to ensure that the checks' proceeds be deposited into the payee's account.[11]

---

**8.** It is important to note for the reader unfamiliar with *Qatar I* that First American is liable in conversion to Qatar, the drawer, for violating restrictive indorsements only because the forged indorsements are "effective" pursuant to former § 3–405(1)(c). Were this not a § 3–405(1)(c) case, the forged indorsements would be ineffective to negotiate the instrument, and any money paid to the depositary banks on the forged checks would be deemed to come from the drawee bank's own funds, not from Qatar's account. See *Qatar I*, 880 F.Supp. at 467–68.

**9.** Article three of the U.C.C. governs the law of negotiable instruments and was substantially amended effective January 1, 1993. Because all of the relevant events surrounding this case occurred prior to 1993, the former U.C.C. provisions apply here. All U.C.C. citations are to Va.Code, Title 8.3, amended by Va.Code, Title 8.3A (Supp.1994).

**10.** The amended Code provision on restrictive indorsements provides more guidance on the meaning of "for deposit only." § 3–206. Specifically, in describing particular types of restrictive indorsements, § 3–206(c)(ii) refers to indorsements "using the words 'for deposit,' 'for collection,' *or other words indicating a purpose of having the instrument collected by a bank for the indorser or for a particular account*" (emphasis added).

**11.** See, e.g., 1 William H. Lawrence, Commercial Paper and Payment Systems § 3.6[b][3], at 3–37 (1990) ("A payee who

This construction of "for deposit only" is commercially sensible and is adopted here. The clear purpose of the restriction is to avoid the hazards of indorsing a check in blank. Pursuant to former § 3–204(2), a check indorsed in blank "becomes payable to bearer." It is, essentially, cash. Thus, a payee who indorses her check in blank runs the risk of having the check stolen and freely negotiated before the check reaches its intended destination. To protect against this vulnerability, the payee can add the restriction "for deposit only" to the indorsement, and the depositary bank is required to handle the check in a manner consistent with that restriction. § 3–206(3). And in so adding the restriction, the payee's intent plainly is to direct that the funds be deposited into her own account, not simply that the funds be deposited into some account.[14] See 1 William H. Lawrence, Commercial Paper and Payment Systems § 3.6[b][3] (1990). Any other construction of the phrase "for deposit only" is illogical and without commercial justification or utility. Indeed, it is virtually impossible to imagine a scenario in which a payee cared that her check be deposited, but was indifferent with respect to the particular account to which the funds would be credited.

First American opposes this result, contending that the unqualified restriction "for deposit only" merely requires a depositary bank to deposit the check into an account, irrespective of which one. * * *

While it is true that the literal command of the bare words "for deposit only" is simply that the check be deposited, such rigid reliance on linguistics in disregard of practical considerations and plain common sense is both unwarranted and imprudent. This is especially so given that the individuals writing and relying upon these restrictive indorsements are not apt to be well versed in the subtleties of negotiable instruments law. As evidenced by numerous authorities, see supra note [11], and common experience, the unqualified phrase "for deposit only" is almost universally taken to mean

endorses a check 'for deposit only' provides notice to the depository [sic] bank that the check is to be credited to the payee's account.... The only way that a depository [sic] bank can apply value consistently with the endorsement is to credit the payee's account"); 4 William D. Hawkland & Lary Lawrence, U.C.C. Series § 3–206:05 (Art. 3), at 366 (1994) (rejecting proposition that "for deposit only" "would permit the proceeds to be credited to any account"); 2 Frederick M. Hart & William F. Willier, Bender's Uniform Commercial Code Service, Commercial Paper under the Uniform Commercial Code § 3A.02 (1994) ("When an instrument is indorsed 'For Deposit,' the indorsee, almost always a bank, is obligated to put any money received for the instrument in the indorser's account"); Julian B. McDonnell, Bank Liability for Fraudulent Checks: the Clash of the Utilitarian and Paternalist Creeds under the Uni-

form Commercial Code, 73 Geo.L.J. 1399, 1415 (1985) ("indorsers must deposit checks restrictively indorsed 'for deposit only' into the account of the indorser, rather than cash the check or deposit it into another's account"); James S. Rogers, Negotiability as a System of Title Recognition, 48 Ohio St.L.J. 197, 223 n. 94 (1987) ("the mechanism of restrictive indorsement 'for deposit only' enables a payee to [indorse a check in blank] without facing any of the risks that would otherwise flow from converting the instrument into bearer form"). See also 1 James J. White & Robert S. Summers, Uniform Commercial Code § 13–10 (3d ed. 1994 Supp.).

**14.** Of course, the payee can direct that the funds be delivered into someone else's account by including the particular account name or number in the restriction (e.g., "for deposit only into account of X" or "for deposit only into account #123456").

"for deposit only *into the payee's account.*" To disregard this common understanding in support of an illogical construction is to elevate form over substance. First American's argument to the contrary is a little like saying that a store sign reading "shirts and shoes required" does not restrict a trouserless man from entering the store.

Finally, it is worth noting that the new revisions to the negotiable instruments provisions of the U.C.C., see supra note 10, support the result reached here. Although these revisions are inapplicable to this case, the commentary following § 3–206 states that the new subdivision dealing with "for deposit only" and like restrictions "continues previous law." § 3–206 comment 3. Shortly thereafter, the commentary provides an example in which a check bears the words "for deposit only" above the indorsement. In those circumstances, the commentary states, the depositary bank acts inconsistently with the restrictive indorsement where it deposits the check into an account other than that of the payee. Id. Although the restriction in that example precedes the signature, whereas the restrictions on the checks at issue here follow the signature, this distinction is immaterial. The clear meaning of the restriction in both circumstances is that the funds should be placed into the payee's account.[17]

Therefore, First American violated the restrictive indorsements in depositing into Bassam Salous' account checks made payable to others and restrictively indorsed "for deposit only." Pursuant to the holding in *Qatar I*, then, First American is liable to Qatar for conversion in the amount of the total face values of these checks.

## PROBLEM

Peter, the payee of a check for $10,000 drawn on Payor Bank, gave the check to Faith, the legal guardian of Ward, her elderly father who had become legally incompetent. Peter told Faith that the check was a contribution to defray Ward's nursing home expenses. Before giving the check to Faith, Peter indorsed the check as follows:

> Pay to Faith as Guardian for Ward
>
> Peter

Faith indorsed the check by signing her name under Peter's indorsement and deposited the check to her personal account in Depositary Bank. Faith also had a fiduciary account as guardian for Ward in the same bank. Pursuant to her instructions, Depositary Bank credited Faith's personal

---

**17.** The facts of this case are unusual in that it was the forger, Bassam Salous, who added the restriction "for deposit only." While *his* intent clearly was not to direct that the funds be placed into the account of the named payee, the general purpose and meaning of the phrase "for deposit only" is unaltered. Cf. Society Nat'l Bank v. Security Fed. Sav. & Loan, 71 Ohio St.3d 321, 643 N.E.2d 1090 (1994). Although it is difficult to speculate regarding why Salous so indorsed the checks, Salous' idiosyncratic subjective intent is immaterial to First American's obligation to abide by the terms of the restrictive indorsement, an obligation which, if fulfilled, would have put an earlier stop to the ongoing fraud.

account $10,000 and obtained payment of the check from Payor Bank. Faith subsequently withdrew the $10,000 that had been credited to her personal account by writing checks on the account for her personal expenses.

Suit on behalf of Ward has been brought against Faith for breach of trust and against Depositary Bank and Payor Bank. Faith is insolvent and has no funds. What is the liability of Depositary Bank and Payor Bank? 3–206(d).

# CHAPTER 16

# THE BANK–CUSTOMER RELATIONSHIP

## A. INTRODUCTION

A customer with a deposit account in a bank has a contractual relationship with the bank that is governed by Part 4 of Article 4. If the bank pays a check written on the customer's account, 4–401(a) allows the bank to charge the customer's account only if the check is "properly payable." A check is properly payable if the customer has authorized the payment and it violates no agreement between the customer and the bank. Thus, a bank cannot charge a customer's account if the customer's signature is forged, but may charge the account even though the charge creates an overdraft. Of course, the bank does not have to pay an overdraft unless it has agreed to do so. 4–402(a). Agreements by banks to pay overdrafts up to specified limits are common. If a bank fails to pay a check that is properly payable and covered by funds in the customer's account, the bank has wrongfully dishonored the check under 4–402(a) and may be liable in damages under 4–402(b). A customer has the right for any reason or no reason to order a bank to stop payment of checks on the customer's account or to close the account, and if the bank fails to do so it may be liable for the loss caused by its failure. 4–403. However, a bank is not liable for dishonoring a "stale" check, one presented more than six months after its date. 4–404.

The provisions of Article 4 are only one source of rules on the bank-customer relationship. Federal statutes and Federal Reserve regulations are another source. The Truth-in-Savings Act, discussed later, became effective in 1992; it requires disclosure of the terms of consumer deposit accounts. The Expedited Funds Availability Act and Regulation CC expressly override the UCC. Regulation J does so as well. Still another source is provided by 4–103(a) under which the "effect of the provisions" of Article 4 may be varied by bank-customer agreements; it is customary for banks to have some form of deposit agreement with their customers. Section 4–103(a) restates and even enlarges upon the "freedom of contract" principle embodied in 1–302. Comment 1 to 4–103 says: "This section, therefore, permits within wide limits variation of the effect of provisions of the Article by agreement." Since deposit agreements have aspects of contracts of adhesion, a continuing matter of dispute between banks and their customers concerns the extent of the "wide limits" referred to in the Comment. We discuss this issue later in this chapter.

## B. STOP-PAYMENT ORDERS

Section 4–403(a) affords a customer an unrestricted right to stop payment on checks drawn on the customer's account or to close the account. Comment 1 to 4–403 is a ringing affirmation of this cherished right of bank customers, and Comment 7 adds that a payment in violation of a stop order is an improper payment even though made by inadvertence or mistake. The broad right given drawers by 4–403(a) to stop payment of checks is unique in payment systems, and it can be very valuable to drawers. Even if the check was given in payment of an obligation of the drawer on a valid contract, a stop payment order by the drawer deprives the payee of the coveted status of being a paid obligee, forcing the payee to proceed against the obligor by legal process for payment of the obligation. When a contract is breaking down, this is a huge tactical advantage for the drawer; facing the expense of enforcing its rights at law, the payee-obligee may give up and let the drawer out of the contract. But it must be noted that developments discussed in earlier chapters in which the check payments process has been greatly speeded up (Check 21, truncation, and electronic check conversion) have significantly limited the importance of stop orders.

Answer these elementary introductory questions about 4–403.

Question #1. Saxton is the remitter of a cashier's check issued by Bank. She learns that the payee of the check, who now has possession of the check, has possibly defrauded her. She orders Bank to stop payment of the check. Must Bank do so?

Question #2. Payee learns that his paycheck has been stolen from his wallet. He immediately notifies Bank on which the check was drawn to stop payment of the check. Must Bank do so?

Question #3. Baker and Able are partners but they don't trust each other. Their agreement with Bank is that both must sign any partnership check. Both signed a check for $10,000 payable to Payton. After the check had been delivered to Payton, Baker had second thoughts and ordered Bank to stop payment on the check. Must Bank do so?

Question #4. Husband and Wife have a joint account in Bank. Wife disapproved of some checks that Husband had been writing on the account and, without Husband's consent, ordered Bank to close the account even though this would result in the dishonor of several checks Husband had already written. Must Bank do so?

## 1. PROVING LOSS UNDER SECTION 4–403(C)

Subsection 4–403(a) grants a drawer an unlimited right to stop payment on checks and Comment 1 to 4–403 states that this right is a basic service that bank customers are entitled to receive whatever the inconvenience to the bank, but in a seeming contradiction subsection (c) imposes the burden of establishing any loss resulting from a bank's violation of a stop order on the customer. What justification is there for this provision? If the bank is the wrongdoer, shouldn't it bear the burden of proving absence of loss?

Although the meaning of 4–403(c) seems clear, courts have disagreed widely on its import. We use the facts of Hughes v. Marine Midland Bank, 127 Misc.2d 209, 484 N.Y.S.2d 1000 (City Ct. Rochester 1985), as the basis for discussing the divergence of views: Customer wrote a check payable to a real estate agent for advance rental on a vacation cottage in Florida. When Customer arrived at the cottage she found that it was not as advertised and stopped payment on the check in ample time for her Bank, located in New York, to act on the stop order. When Customer received her cancelled checks at the end of the month, she found to her surprise that Bank had mistakenly paid the check. She immediately demanded that Bank recredit her account for the amount of the check. Bank declined to recredit the account on the ground that Customer had not established her loss by merely showing that Bank had violated the stop order and had refused to recredit her account. The real estate agent was located in Florida, and Bank had no way of knowing about the transaction between Customer and the agent. For all Bank knew, Customer may have owed the money to the agent, and therefore Bank's payment might have paid a legitimate debt of Customer. Since only Customer knew these facts, Bank argued that she should have the burden of convincing Bank before it returned the money to her.

*Minority view.* Customer sued Bank for the amount of the check. Her proof of loss was her showing that Bank had paid the check over her valid stop order and had refused to recredit her account. A summary judgment for Customer was entered. The court held that Bank should have recredited Customer's account immediately and sought its remedy under 4–407. Under that provision, if Bank can show that its payment was made either to a holder in due course (4–407(1)) or to a holder of the check who was entitled to payment from Customer (4–407(2)), in order to prevent unjust enrichment, Bank is subrogated to the right of the holder to recover the amount of the check from Customer. If Bank finds that it has paid a holder who was not entitled to payment from Customer (e.g., this would be true if the agent had defrauded Customer), in order to prevent unjust enrichment, Bank is subrogated to Customer's right to get the money back from the holder (4–407(3)).

*Majority view.* Most courts believe that holdings like *Hughes* do not give adequate weight to the requirement of 4–403(c) that the customer must establish the loss. A statement of this view is found in the following quotation from Siegel v. New England Merchants National Bank, 386 Mass. 672, 437 N.E.2d 218, 222–223 (1982):

> The rule of § 4–403(3), that a depositor must prove his loss, may at first seem at odds with our earlier conclusion that § 4–401(1) provides the depositor with a claim against the bank in the amount of the check, leaving the bank with recourse through subrogation under § 4–407.

\* \* \* We believe, however, that § 4–403(3) was intended to operate within the process of credit and subrogation established by §§ 4–401(1) and 4–407. See § 4–403, Comment 8. When a bank pays an item improperly, the depositor loses his ability to exercise any right he had to withhold payment of the check. His "loss," in other words, is equivalent to his rights and defenses against the parties to whose rights the bank is subrogated—the other party to the initial transaction and other holders of the instrument. Section 4–403(3) simply protects the bank against the need to prove events familiar to the depositor, and far removed from the bank, before it can realize its subrogation rights. The depositor, who participated in the initial transaction, knows whether the payee was entitled to eventual payment and whether any defenses arose. Therefore, § 4–403(3) requires that he, rather than the bank, prove these matters. \* \* \*

This view of the three relevant sections of the code suggests a fair allocation of the burden of proof. The bank, which has departed from authorized bookkeeping, must acknowledge a credit to the depositor's account. It must then assert its subrogation rights, and in doing so must identify the status of the parties in whose place it claims. If the bank's subrogation claims are based on the check, this would entail proof that the third party subrogor was a holder, or perhaps a holder in due course. This responsibility falls reasonably upon the bank, because it has received the check from the most recent holder and is in at least as good a position as the depositor to trace its history.

The depositor must then prove any facts that might demonstrate a loss. He must establish defenses good against a holder or holder in due course, as the case may be. See UCC §§ 3–305, 3–306. If the initial transaction is at issue, he must prove either that he did not incur a liability to the other party, or that he has a defense to liability. Thus, the bank, if it asserts rights based on the transaction, need not make out a claim on the part of its subrogor against the depositor. Responsibility in this area rests entirely with the depositor, who participated in the transaction and is aware of its details. Further, the depositor must establish any consequential loss.

A few courts have adopted a variant of the majority rule, assigning shifting burdens of production. See, e.g., Mitchell v. Republic Bank & Trust Co., 239 S.E.2d 867 (N.C.Ct.App.1978); Thomas v. Marine Midland Tinkers National Bank, 381 N.Y.S.2d 797 (N.Y.Sup.Ct. 1976). These courts allocate the burden of proof as to loss to the customer. However, burdens of production of evidence of loss are allocated between the customer and the bank. The customer must present evidence that the bank paid a check against an effective stop-payment order. Thereafter the bank must present evidence that the customer did not suffer a loss when it paid against the order. The variant of the majority rule apparently does not read 4–403(c)'s requirement that customer bears "[t]he burden of establishing the fact and amount of loss" as including both burdens of production and proof.

Section 4–403(c) has long been a bone of contention between customers and banks. In violating a customer's stop-payment order, even if the payment is made to a holder on a valid debt of the customer, the bank has deprived the customer of the tactical advantage of forcing the holder to proceed against the customer for payment. Had the stop order in *Hughes* been honored by the bank, the agent might well have been unwilling to undertake the expense of suing the customer for the amount of the check, and might have given up on the transaction. But there is no basis in 4–403 or 4–407 for compensating a customer for this kind of loss.

A major difference between the majority and minority views is that under the majority view the bank usually keeps the money while the parties litigate; under the minority view the bank must recredit the customer's account upon learning that it has paid over a valid stop-payment order and then must proceed under 4–407 to get its money back from either the holder or the customer. The banks seek to shore up the policy of the majority view by claiming that many stop-payment orders are the result of "buyer's remorse" rather than valid defenses on the part of the customer; moreover, they strongly object to getting tied up in messy contract disputes between obligors and obligees. Customers find unfairness in a system that allows a bank that has wrongfully paid out over a stop-payment order to sit back and force the customer to proceed against it to get its money back.

A number of attempts were made to redraft 4–403(c) during the revision of Article 4, but no solution found consensus. The only substantive change made was the addition of the last sentence in 4–403(c), which clarified an issue on which there was some dispute in the case law. If a customer's checks presented subsequent to the violation of the stop order are dishonored because the check that should not have been paid depleted the customer's account balance, the customer can proceed against the bank under 4–402 to recover damages for wrongful dishonor. Since it costs money to attract customers and banks are reluctant to lose them, anecdotal evidence indicates that banks have worked out informal procedures to satisfy meritorious customer demands for a recredit after the bank violates a stop order. Under one plan, discussed by the Drafting Committee as a possible model for the redraft of Article 4, if the bank believes the customer's representations that it had paid out money the customer did not owe, it required the customer (1) to sign an affidavit stating facts indicating that the payment was made on a debt for which the customer was not liable, and (2) to enter into an agreement that it would cooperate in any litigation the bank might have to bring against the person who received the mistaken payment. Once this was done the bank would recredit the customer's account and initiate proceedings against the person who received payment.

A case applying the majority rule to interesting facts follows. Which has the better of the argument, the majority or the dissent?

# Dunnigan v. First Bank

Supreme Court of Connecticut, 1991.
217 Conn. 205, 585 A.2d 659.

■ BORDEN, ASSOCIATE JUSTICE.

In this appeal, we are called upon to define the meaning and scope of § 4–403(3) of the Uniform Commercial Code (Code) as applied to the facts of this case. The defendant bank appeals, after a court trial, from the judgment of the trial court in favor of the plaintiff, the trustee in bankruptcy of Cohn Precious Metals, Inc. (Cohn), a customer of the bank. We transferred the appeal to this court pursuant to Practice Book § 4023, and we now reverse the trial court's judgment.

The plaintiff brought this action against the bank for wrongfully paying a check issued by Cohn over Cohn's valid stop-payment order. The trial court determined that the plaintiff had established a loss within the meaning of § 4–403(3) as a result of the bank's payment of the check, and that the subrogation provisions of General Statutes § 4–407 did not defeat the rights of Cohn. The court accordingly rendered judgment for the amount of the check. This appeal followed.

The bank claims that judgment was improperly rendered for the plaintiff because (1) as a matter of law, Cohn did not suffer a loss within the meaning of § 4–403(3), and (2) the bank was subrogated to the rights of the payee of the check and of the collecting banks, pursuant to § 4–407. We agree with the bank's first claim and therefore need not reach its second claim. Furthermore, it is not necessary to define the relationship between §§ 4–403(3) and 4–407.

The parties stipulated to the following facts. On November 8, 1978, pursuant to purchase order 1142, Lamphere Coin, Inc. (Lamphere), a trader in coins and precious metals, delivered to Cohn certain silver dollars with a unit price of $1.71 and with a total value of $27,492.07. Cohn's bookkeeper incorrectly recorded the unit price of those coins, however, as $17.10, resulting in an erroneous total value of $47,098.93. On November 9, 1978, Cohn paid Lamphere $47,098.93 by wire transfer to Lamphere's bank account, resulting in an overpayment to Lamphere by Cohn of $19,606.86. On November 10, 1978, Lamphere delivered three and one-half bags of silver dollars to Cohn pursuant to Cohn's purchase order 1145. The value of the silver dollars was $21,175. On the same day, Cohn issued two checks drawn on its account at the bank to Lamphere, one in the amount of $12,175 and one in the amount of $9000, totaling $21,175.

Between November 10 and November 15, Cohn discovered its bookkeeper's error and, on November 14, 1978, directed the bank to stop-payment on the two checks totaling $21,175 that had been issued on November 10, 1978. The bank stopped payment on the $9000 check, but on or about November 20, 1978, the bank inadvertently honored the $12,175 check over the valid stop-payment order. Cohn retained the three and one-half bags of silver dollars, but never recovered its overpayment from Lamphere. As of November 20, 1978, the date of the improper payment of the check by the bank, and at all times thereafter Lamphere owed Cohn in excess of $13,000 as a result of these transactions.

The merits of this controversy revolve around the meaning of § 4–403(3), which provides that "[t]he burden of establishing the fact and amount of loss resulting from the payment of an item contrary to a binding stop order is on the customer." The bank argues that where there is good consideration for a particular check, or where the check was given as payment on a binding contract, the bank that paid the check over a valid stop payment order is not liable to its customer, because there was no "loss resulting from [its] payment...." Thus, in the bank's view a customer cannot establish a loss under this provision of the code by relying on the loss of credits due the customer from prior unrelated transactions between the customer and the payee of the check. The plaintiff argues, as the trial court concluded, that whether a customer has incurred a "loss" within the meaning of § 4–403(3) cannot be determined solely by focusing on the transaction underlying the particular check involved, but must be determined by focusing on the entire relationship between the customer and the payee of the check. The plaintiff contends that it is unreasonable to disregard the relative positions of the parties, especially where they have demonstrated a continuing course of business dealings, where there are likely to be such credits. Under such circumstances, the plaintiff claims that focusing on a single transaction is contrary to the intent of the Code. Thus, in the plaintiff's view, Cohn would have had a good "defense" to a claim by Lamphere on the check because of the overpayment, and by paying the check the bank caused Cohn a loss within the meaning of § 4–403(3).

The issue, therefore, is whether, on the facts of this case, the bank customer who sought to establish "the fact and amount of loss resulting from the payment of an item contrary to a binding stop payment order" pursuant to § 4–403(3) was entitled to do so by resorting to credits from prior transactions unrelated to that for which the check was issued, or whether the customer was limited to the facts of the particular transaction for which the check was issued. We conclude that the customer was limited to the facts of the particular transaction for which the check was issued, and that § 4–403(3) does not contemplate taking into account a loss by the customer of credits that arose from prior unrelated transactions. * * *

Under § 4–403(1), a bank customer has the right to order his bank to stop-payment on a check, so long as he does so in a timely and reasonable manner, and, under § 4–403(2), an oral stop-payment order is binding on the bank for a limited period of time. The fact that the bank has paid the check over the customer's valid stop-payment order does not mean, however, that the customer is automatically entitled to repayment of the amount of the check. Under § 4–403(3), the customer must also establish "the fact and amount of loss resulting from" the bank's improper payment.

The case law makes clear that "[t]he loss ... must be more than the mere debiting of his account." * * * Siegel v. New England Merchants National Bank, 386 Mass. 672, 437 N.E.2d 218 (1982) * * *. The commentators agree. See W. Hillman, Basic UCC Skills 1989, Article 3 and Article 4, p. 302; E. Peters, A Negotiable Instruments Primer (1974) p. 79; 1 J. White & R. Summers, Uniform Commercial Code (3d Ed. 1988) § 18–6, pp. 909–10. Otherwise, § 4–403(3) would be superfluous. Furthermore, whether the customer has suffered such a loss is in the first instance a question of fact. * * *

The cases and commentators also agree that where the check in question was supported by good consideration, or where the payee has enforceable rights against the maker based on the transaction underlying the check, the customer has suffered no loss within the meaning of § 4–403(3). Siegel v. New England Merchants National Bank, supra 386 Mass. at 678–79, 437 N.E.2d 218; * * * W. Hillman, supra, 302 E. Peters, supra; J. White & R. Summers, supra. As then Professor Peters explained, it "is implicit in § 4–403(3) that if a check was issued for good consideration . . . failure to observe a stop-payment order does no more than to accelerate the drawer's inevitable liability, and is therefore a defense to the payor bank." E. Peters, supra.

Applying these principles to the facts of this case, we conclude that as a matter of law Cohn suffered no "loss" within the meaning of § 4–403(3). The check was supported by good consideration because it was issued in payment for the silver coins that Lamphere delivered to Cohn. Furthermore, on the basis of that underlying transaction Lamphere had enforceable rights to payment by Cohn for those coins.

The plaintiff argues, however, that, although the particular check was supported by valid consideration and although there were no defenses available to it arising out of that particular transaction, the previous transaction between Cohn and Lamphere had supplied Cohn with a defense to payment of the check based on Cohn's overpayment to Lamphere. We disagree.

First, the language of § 4–403(3) suggests a narrower reading than would be required by the plaintiff's position. Section 4–403(3) places on the bank's customer the "burden of establishing the *fact and amount of loss resulting from the payment* of an item contrary to a binding stop-payment order . . . ." (Emphasis added.) By contrast, § 4–402, which deals with a bank's liability to its customer for a wrongful *dishonor*, as opposed to a wrongful payment, provides as follows: "A payor bank is liable to its customer for *damages proximately caused by the wrongful dishonor* of an item. When the dishonor occurs through mistake liability is limited to actual damages proved. If so proximately caused and proved damages may include damages for an arrest or prosecution of the customer or other consequential damages. Whether any consequential damages are proximately caused by the wrongful dishonor is a question of fact to be determined in each case." (Emphasis added.) Thus, pursuant to § 4–402 the wrongfully dishonoring bank may be liable for all consequential damages proximately caused by its wrongful conduct, including damages resulting from arrest or prosecution of the customer, whereas there is a conspicuous absence from § 4–403(3) of language indicating such a broad scope of liability for wrongful payment.

This difference in the scope of the language used in § 4–403(3), as compared to that used in § 4–402, is consistent with the notion that § 4–403(3) is intended to impose a limited, rather than broad, form of liability on banks. "The trade-off for requiring banks to accept stop orders under § 4–403(1) was the limitation of their liability under §§ 4–403(3) and 4–407." E. Peters, supra.

The case law and commentary support this more restrictive view of the scope of § 4–403(3). In determining whether a customer has established a "loss" under this section of the code, they focus on the check itself and on the transaction underlying it, and not on whether there were other prior, unrelated transactions between the maker and payee of the check. "In order to prove a loss under [§ 4–403(3) of] the Code, a customer must prove he was not liable to the payee *on the check.* White & Summers, Uniform Commercial Code 560 (2d ed. 1980); Brady, Brady on Bank Checks § 20.20 p. 20–45 (5th ed. 1979); 6 Reitman & Weisblatt, Banking Law § 133.B07(2) (Bender's Banking Law Service 1981)." (Emphasis added.) Bryan v. Citizens National Bank In Abilene, 628 S.W.2d 761, 763 (Tex. 1982) * * *. Although Cohn had an offset or counterclaim available to it with respect to Lamphere, it did not have a defense to payment of the check itself. * * *

In this case, the plaintiff seeks more than to establish a loss caused by the bank's failure to honor Cohn's stop-payment order. That "loss" occurred in fact on November 9, 1978, when Cohn overpaid for the coins it had received. Rather, the plaintiff seeks to recoup a loss resulting from a prior transaction separate from and independent of the stopped check. Thus, the plaintiff's position would permit the customer to establish a "loss" based on offsets or counterclaims against the payee based on prior unrelated transactions, no matter how remote from the check in question or from the transaction underlying it. We do not believe that the intent of § 4–403(3) ranges that far. * * *

The judgment is reversed, and the case is remanded with direction to render judgment for the defendant.

In this opinion CALLAHAN and HULL, JJ., concurred.

■ SHEA, ASSOCIATE JUSTICE, with whom GLASS, ASSOCIATE JUSTICE, joins, dissenting.

In this case it is undisputed that the drawer, Cohn Precious Metals, Inc. (Cohn), complied fully with General Statutes § 4–403(1) in stopping payment on the checks it had delivered to Lamphere Coin, Inc. (Lamphere), on November 10, 1978, while unaware of the overpayment of $19,606.86 on November 9, 1978. It is also clear that, but for the negligence of the bank in paying the $12,175 check contrary to the stop-payment order, Cohn could have offset its overpayment of the previous day against the value of the coins received from Lamphere on November 10, 1978. Thus, as the trial court concluded, the plaintiff trustee, on behalf of Cohn, sustained his "burden of establishing the fact and amount of loss resulting from payment of an item contrary to a binding stop-payment order" by the defendant bank, as § 4–403(3) requires.[1]

The majority opinion does not challenge, as unsupported by the evidence, the trial court's factual finding that Cohn suffered a loss resulting from the bank's negligent payment of the $12,175 check to Lamphere, but rejects this straightforward "but for" causation analysis in favor of a narrower view of the "resulting from payment" provision of § 4–403(3). The majority would restrict a bank's liability for paying a check contrary to a stop order to losses arising from the transaction in which the check was issued, such as a failure of consideration. I disagree, because there is nothing in the text of § 4–403(3) or its history to support such an unjustifiable curtailment of the right of the drawer recognized by § 4–403(3) to stop-payment on a check for any reason, so long as the order is given to the bank in a timely and reasonable manner, as in this case. The right, of course, would be illusory without recourse against the negligent bank. * * *

The majority stresses the difference between the "resulting from" causation language of § 4–403(3) and the more elaborate provision of § 4–402 that expressly makes the bank liable for consequential damages for wrongfully dishonoring a check, including such damages as may result from the arrest or prosecution of the customer. Such a provision in § 4–402 is probably necessary if liability for such damages is to be imposed because of the contract law limitation of damages to those that are reasonably foreseeable at the time of the contract. 3 Restatement (Second), Contracts § 351(1). Such a provision in § 4–403(3) is unnecessary to make a bank liable for the amount of a check it has paid after a stop-payment order, however, because it is obvious that such a loss to the drawer from the bank's oversight is readily foreseeable.

* * * The view of the majority that a drawer should be made to bear a loss that would have been avoided but for the bank's neglect, because it did not arise from the transaction in which the check was issued, places a substantial restriction on the right to stop-payment that § 4–403(1) purports to give.

With respect to § 4–407 and the defendant's claim to be a holder in due course, there is nothing in the record to indicate that the collecting bank ever allowed the payee to draw on the check after it was deposited. Since there is no proof that the collecting bank gave value, the defendant's

---

**1.** On the basis of the facts before us, the trial court's award of $12,175 damages may have been excessive. The amount of the overpayment of November 9, 1978, was $19,606.86. The value of the silver dollars received by Cohn on November 10, 1978 was $21,175. Before the two checks totaling $21,175 were issued for this purchase, Cohn owed Lamphere $1568.14. That debt was discharged by the bank's erroneous payment of the $12,175 check. Thus, Cohn received good consideration of $1568.14 as a result of the bank's payment and its loss is limited to the balance of the amount paid on the $12,175 check, $10,606.86.

claim to be subrogated to the status of a holder in due course is without foundation.

Accordingly, I dissent.

## 2.   OPERATIONAL ISSUES

If the customer gives an oral order to stop-payment, 4–403(b) provides that the order lapses after 14 calendar days unless confirmed in writing within that period. Usually the check will be presented and dishonored within the 14–day period after the oral order was given, but if the check is not presented during that period and the customer fails to confirm the order in writing, the bank may have a customer relations problem. Although 4–403(b) allows the bank to treat an unconfirmed oral stop-payment order as having no effect after the 14–day period, if the bank later pays the check, the customer may contend that it had not understood that it had to confirm in writing within a short period of time. Playing back the tape recording of the conversation regarding the stop-payment order to the customer is not likely to placate the customer; the directions to the customer may have been couched in banker's talk that customers (and sympathetic juries) find difficult to understand. On the other hand, if the bank suspects that the customer wants the stop-payment order to continue even though not confirmed and dishonors the subsequently presented check, the bank risks being held for wrongful dishonor. Banks customarily try to prevent misunderstandings in these cases by sending a written confirmation form to the customer as quickly as possible after the oral order is received with an exhortation to the customer to return the form immediately. The matter is discussed in 1 Clark & Clark, The Law of Bank Deposits, Collections and Credit Cards & 3.06[1][b] (Rev. ed. 2006).

## PROBLEMS

**1.**   Customers ordered Bank to stop-payment on check number 292 drawn on their account number 315–726 for $1000. The stop order was communicated to Bank in plenty of time to act on it. However, since the correct number of the check in question was 280 and not 292, Bank's computer, which was directed to identify only checks on a customer's account which bore the correct check number, did not identify the check, and it was paid. Bank denied liability for violating the stop order because under 4–403(a) banks must stop-payment on a check only if the check is described by the customer "with reasonable certainty." Bank conceded that its computer could have been directed to stop-payment by (1) check number alone, (2) by check number and amount of check, or (3) by amount of check alone. Did Customers identify the check with reasonable certainty? See Comment 5 to 4–403.

**2.**   Would the decision in Problem 1 be affected by a clause in the bank's stop order form stating: "In order to stop-payment on a check, you must inform the bank of the exact amount of the item, the number of the check, and your account number; otherwise our computer may not catch the stop order. Unless this is done the bank will not be responsible for any loss resulting from its failure to stop-payment"? 1 Clark & Clark, The Law of Bank Deposits, Collections and Credit Cards & 3.06[1][b] and [d] (Rev. ed. 2006). Is this clause valid under 4–103(a) as determining "the standards by which the bank's responsibility is to be measured" or is it invalid as an attempt to disclaim the bank's responsibility for its "failure to exercise ordinary care"? Comment 1 to 4–403.

**3.** Suppose Bank induces its customer to sign a stop-payment form containing the following clause: "In requesting you to stop-payment of this or any other item, the undersigned agrees to hold you harmless for all expenses and costs incurred by you on account of refusing payment of said item, and further agrees not to hold you liable on account of payment contrary to this request if same occurs through inadvertence, accident or oversight, or if by reason of such payment other items drawn by the undersigned are returned insufficient." Is this clause, or any part of it, enforceable? 4–103(a) and 4–403. See Opinion of Attorney General of Connecticut, 25 U.C.C. Rep. Serv. 238, 1978 WL 23495 (1978).

**4.** Given that the customer has an absolute right to stop-payment by complying with 4–403, is the drawee bank entitled to impose a charge for processing a stop-payment order? See Opinion of Attorney General of Michigan, 30 U.C.C. Rep. Serv. 1626, 1981 WL 137970 (1981); 33 U.C.C. Rep. Serv. 1445, 1981 WL 138014 (1981). 1 Clark & Clark, supra, ¶ 3.06[1][b]. If a typical charge for a stop order is $20, could a bank legally impose a $200 charge?

## NOTE: POSTDATED CHECKS

A luxury that manual processing of checks allowed customers was the postdated check. The customer could hold off an impatient creditor by writing a check for the debt and could control the time of payment by postdating the check. The customer could be confident that the check would not be paid before its date because a bank clerk would examine the check for date before payment by the bank. Under original Article 3 and pre–1990 Article 4, the check was not properly payable until the date of the check, and the bank could not charge the customer's account until that time. But when automated processing of checks became universal in the 1960s, there was no visual examination of the vast majority of checks. Checks were paid or dishonored on the basis of the balance in the account and the machine-readable information on the MICR line. Since there is no space on that line for the date of the check, the usual result is that the check is paid or dishonored without regard to its date. A bank prematurely paying a postdated check that depleted the customer's account balance could be liable for wrongfully dishonoring subsequent checks that would have been paid had the postdated check not been paid. A bank might seek protection against this liability by a clause in the bank-customer agreement allowing payment of any check at the time of presentment regardless of the date of the check. To the extent such a clause was enforceable, it deprived the customer of the ability to rely on postdating.

Section 4–401(c) offers a compromise that enables customers to post-date checks while protecting banks from potential liability for failure to examine each check for its date. Under this provision the bank can pay all checks at the time of presentment unless it has received a notice of postdating from the customer. This allows the bank time to order its computer to identify the described check when it is presented so that its date may be examined before a decision to pay is made. Banks charge a fee for processing notices of postdating just as they charge for stop-payment orders.

## C.  SECTION 4–303 AND THE "FOUR LEGALS"

### 1.  CLAIMS AFFECTING THE CUSTOMER'S ACCOUNT

In Chapter 13 we considered when a check is paid in order to determine how long a payor bank has to decide whether to dishonor. A related issue concerns the priority of parties who assert rights that affect the customer's bank account as against a check that is presented for payment from that account. Whether a payor bank will pay a check depends on whether the balance in the customer's account is large enough to cover the check. A number of events may occur after a check has been presented for payment that give rise to claims that affect the size of the customer's balance. The priority between these claims, often referred to as the "four legals," and the right of the holder of the check to be paid is governed by 4–303(a). The events enumerated in 4–303(a), are (1) knowledge or notice by the bank of the customer's death, incompetence or bankruptcy; (2) a customer's order received by the bank to stop payment; (3) legal process (e.g., garnishment) served on the bank by a creditor of the customer; and (4) setoff against the customer's account exercised by the payor bank. The "four legals" are discussed in 1 Clark & Clark, The Law of Bank Deposits, Collections and Credit Cards ¶ 6.03 (Rev. ed. 2006); 2 White & Summers, Uniform Commercial Code § 18–7 (5th Prac. ed. 2002).

We have seen in the previous section that a customer has an absolute right to stop payment on a check under 4–403(a), and the payor bank must honor a stop order received at a time that gives the bank "a reasonable opportunity" to act on it. Just as a bank's authority to pay a check of a customer may be revoked by the express direction of the customer, as in the case of a stop-payment order, it may also be revoked by operation of law as in the case of the death, adjudication of incompetence or bankruptcy of the customer. The risk to the bank in making unauthorized payment in these cases is similar to that involved in the case of stop-payment orders. Section 4–405(a) deals specifically with the bank's authority in the case of death or incapacity and 4–405(b) gives to the bank additional authority in the case of death. On the latter point see Comments 2 and 3 to 4–405.

The authority of the bank to act in the case of the bankruptcy of the customer is not dealt with by the UCC because the question is governed by federal rather than state law. Under Bankruptcy Code 541(a) the property of the bankrupt (including bank accounts) passes to the estate in bankruptcy when the bankruptcy case is commenced. Thus, after bankruptcy, payment by the bank of a check drawn on the account would be a payment of funds owned by the bankruptcy estate rather than by the bankrupt customer. Authority to dispose of property of the bankruptcy estate rests with the trustee in bankruptcy, and in the case of a Chapter 7 bankruptcy, this means that the bankrupt has no right to dispose of assets of the estate. But, under Bankruptcy Code 542(c) a bank, until it has "actual notice [or] actual knowledge" of the bankruptcy of its customer, may continue to pay checks of the customer. The latter provision codifies the result of Bank of Marin v. England, 385 U.S. 99 (1966), which recognized the same right of the bank under the previous statute, the Bankruptcy Act of 1898.

Attaching and judgment creditors of the customer are given the right under conditions set out in state statutes to reach the customer's bank accounts by legal process. The asset reached is the debt the payor bank owes the customer for the amount of the account. The process used is generally described as garnishment, under which a writ is served on the payor bank notifying it to pay over to a judicial officer for the benefit of the creditor the amount in the account up to the unpaid balance of the claim.

If the payor bank itself is a creditor of the customer, the bank may collect its debt extrajudicially by exercise of its traditional right of setoff. The bank may offset debts the customer owes the bank (loans the bank has made to the customer) against the debt the bank owes the customer (the balance of the customer's bank account). No legal process is involved in the bank's exercise of its right of setoff; bookkeeping entries indicating that the money has been withdrawn from the account suffice to effectuate the setoff.

## 2.   PRIORITY RULES OF SECTION 4–303

The problem that must be solved is at what point a check has reached the stage in the payor bank's payment process that the amount of that check can no longer be considered part of the customer's account balance and subject to the "legals." Section 4–303(a) addresses this issue. Under 4–303(a)(1), when a bank certifies a check, the amount of that check is no longer considered to be in the customer's account for purpose of the legals. The same is true when the check is presented over the counter for immediate payment and the presenter receives cash (4–303(a)(2)) or a cashier's or teller's check (4–303(a)(3)). See Comment 3 to 4–303. If the check has been effectively paid by expiration of the midnight deadline, any subsequent claim under one of the legals comes too late to be prior to the check (4–303(a)(4)).

A special rule is set out in 4–303(a)(5) for checks that will apply to the great bulk of checks that are presented to payor banks through banking channels. This provides that if a check is presented to a payor bank on Day 1, the amount of that check is no longer considered to be included in the customer's account for purposes of the legals after the close of the banking day on Day 2. However, the bank can shorten that period by setting a cutoff hour on Day 2 no earlier than one hour after the opening of business. This means that if a garnishment order is served on the payor bank after that cutoff hour, the balance of the account subject to the garnishment does not include the amount of the check in question, and the bank is protected if it pays the check. By the same token, the balance of the account subject to the payor's bank's right of setoff is similarly reduced after this point. Nor can a customer stop payment on the check after the cutoff hour. However, if a bankruptcy proceeding has been commenced involving the customer, Bankruptcy Code 362(a)(7) prevents the bank from exercising its setoff right, even if the bank does not know that the proceeding has been commenced. In this case the bank must obtain the permission of the bankruptcy court to do so.

## W & D Acquisition, LLC v. First Union National Bank

Supreme Court of Connecticut, 2003.
817 A.2d 91.

■ Borden, J.

The dispositive issue in this appeal is whether, as a matter of law, a banking institution has until the "midnight deadline" described in General Statutes § 42a–4–104 (a)(10) to comply with garnishment process under General Statutes § 42a–4–303 (a). The plaintiff, W & D Acquisition, LLC, claims that the duration of the "reasonable time" period in which to comply with garnishment process pursuant to § 42a–4–303 (a) is not defined by the midnight deadline, but is to be measured by a "reasonable time," considering the facts of the case. We agree with the plaintiff and, accordingly, we reverse the judgment of the trial court to the contrary.

The plaintiff brought this writ of scire facias alleging that the defendant, First Union National Bank, had failed to secure garnished funds held in the accounts of one of its customers, R.K.E. Associates (R.K.E.), which was a defendant in the underlying action. The defendant moved for summary judgment, arguing that it was not obligated to secure the garnished funds until its midnight deadline,[5] at which time only a nominal sum remained in the accounts subject to garnishment. The trial court ruled that, as a matter of law, a banking institution has until that time to secure garnished funds. Accordingly, the court granted the defendant's motion for summary judgment, except as to the nominal sum that remained in the accounts at the midnight deadline, as to which the court rendered judgment for the plaintiff. This appeal followed.

The parties presented the following undisputed facts on the motion for summary judgment. The plaintiff is a construction materials supplier that brought an action against R.K.E., a building contractor, for breach of a provisional credit contract. In that action, the plaintiff alleged that it had

**5.** In this case, the midnight deadline would be midnight of the banking day following service of the garnishment process.

supplied R.K.E. with $45,436.40 worth of construction materials on credit and that R.K.E. had failed to pay any of that balance. After demonstrating to the trial court that there was probable cause to believe that a judgment would enter in its favor, the plaintiff obtained an ex parte prejudgment garnishment order for up to $70,000 of the goods or estate of R.K.E. to secure the potential judgment. The defendant was one of four named garnishees, all of which were banking institutions where R.K.E. allegedly had deposited funds. At approximately noon on October 27, 1997, the plaintiff served a copy of the writ of garnishment and a copy of the complaint on the defendant at one of the defendant's branch locations in Danbury. At that time, R.K.E. held two accounts with the defendant, which are known here as account 1 and account 2. The balance in account 1 was $34,163.79, and it fluctuated with debits and credits throughout the ensuing hours. The balance in account 2 was $30.54, and it remained at that level throughout the entire relevant time period.

The defendant did not secure the money in either account when the garnishment papers were served. At 3:26 p.m. on that same day, an agent of R.K.E. entered the same Danbury branch location of the defendant and, by means of a counter withdrawal,[7] withdrew $32,318.26 in cash from account 1, leaving a balance of approximately $1845. Additional credits and debits reduced the balance of account 1 to $200.39 at the close of business on October 27, and $30.43 at the close of business on October 28. At midnight on October 28, 1997, the midnight deadline following the garnishment, the balance of account 1 remained at $30.43.

The plaintiff then brought this writ of scire facias to recover funds that it alleged the defendant should have secured in response to the garnishment. The defendant moved for summary judgment on the basis that it was not obligated to secure the garnished funds until the midnight deadline. The trial court granted the motion, and rendered judgment for the plaintiff in the amount of $60.97, the sum that remained in R.K.E.'s accounts at the midnight deadline.

On appeal, the plaintiff claims that the trial court improperly determined that, as a matter of law, a banking institution has until the midnight deadline described in § 42a–4–104 (a)(10) to comply with garnishment process pursuant to § 42a–4–303 (a). Specifically, the plaintiff claims that General Statutes §§ 42a–4–303 (a) and 52–329[9] require a bank to comply

---

**7.** The term "counter withdrawal" refers to the common practice of withdrawing funds from a bank account in person by filling out, signing and presenting a withdrawal slip to a bank teller. The withdrawal slip used in the transaction at issue in this case was a nonnegotiable encoded document, with fields for the account number, name of the account holder, authorized signature, date and dollar amount.

**9.** General Statutes § 52–329 provides in relevant part that "*from the time of leav-*

*ing [a] copy* [of the necessary garnishment process on a garnishee] all the effects of the defendant in the hands of any such garnishee, and any debt due from any such garnishee to the defendant ... shall be secured in the hands of such garnishee to pay such judgment as the plaintiff may recover...." (Emphasis added.) Nonetheless, the parties agree, as do we, that this provision cannot feasibly or fairly be applied literally, because a bank necessarily requires some period of time from the moment the process is left with it to take

with garnishment process within a "reasonable time" period, the precise duration of which will vary from case to case, depending upon the factual circumstances. We agree with the plaintiff. * * *

The statutory provision primarily at issue in this appeal is § 42a–4–303 (a). We first turn to its language. The language of § 42a–4–303 (a) strongly suggests that the relevant time period is a reasonable time depending upon all of the relevant facts and circumstances, rather than a fixed period terminating on the bank's midnight deadline.

Section 42a–4–303 (a) provides that "[a]ny ... legal process served upon ... a payor bank comes too late to terminate, suspend, or modify the bank's right or duty to pay an item or to charge its customer's account for the item if the ... legal process is received or served and *a reasonable time for the bank to act* thereon expires ... after the earliest of the following: (1) [t]he bank accepts ... the item; (2) the bank pays the item in cash...." (Emphasis added.) In other words, under § 42a–4–303 (a), a banking institution is obligated to secure funds within a "reasonable time" after receiving garnishment process, a form of "legal process," to prevent distribution of those funds in response to an "item." The "item[s]" at issue in this case include a withdrawal slip[10] tendered in exchange for $32,318.26 in cash as well as several checks drawn against account 1 in the hours that followed.[11]

Section 42a–4–303 (a) expressly provides that a banking institution must act within a "reasonable time"; it does not expressly provide that a banking institution must act before its midnight deadline. We do not decide the meaning of "reasonable time," as used in § 42a–4–303 (a), in a vacuum. General Statutes § 42a–1–204[12] further defines "reasonable time"

the practical steps necessary to secure the funds in its depositor's account.

Thus, both sides agree that this provision means that a bank has a reasonable time in which to act. They differ, however, regarding how to measure that reasonable time. The plaintiff contends that the reasonable time must be determined on a case-by-case basis, depending on all of the facts and circumstances. The defendant contends that, as a matter of law, its midnight deadline is the appropriate measurement of what is a reasonable time.

**10.** See footnote 7 of this opinion.

**11.** * * * [T]he withdrawal slip that R.K.E. handed to the defendant's teller was an "item" within the meaning of § 42a–4–303 (a). General Statutes § 42a–4–104 (a)(9) defines an " 'item' " as, inter alia, "an ... order to pay money handled by a bank for collection or payment...." An " '[o]rder' " is defined in General Statutes § 42a–3–103 (a)(6) as "a written instruction to pay money

signed by the person giving the instruction...." The withdrawal slip at issue in this appeal was a written instruction to pay out $32,318.26 in cash, handled by a bank, namely, the defendant, for payment, and signed by the agent of R.K.E., who gave the bank the instruction to pay. See footnote 7 of this opinion.

**12.** General Statutes § 42a–1–204 provides: "(1) Whenever this title requires any action to be taken within a reasonable time, any time which is not manifestly unreasonable may be fixed by agreement.

"(2) What is a reasonable time for taking any action depends on the nature, purpose and circumstances of such action.

"(3) An action is taken 'seasonably' when it is taken at or within the time agreed or if no time is agreed at or within a reasonable time."

as used in § 42a–4–303 (a). Section 42a–1–204 (1) specifically provides that the standards that it contains apply to conduct governed by "this title. . . ." "[T]his title" is title 42a of the General Statutes, the Uniform Commercial Code. The requirement in § 42a–4–303 (a) that a bank act within a "reasonable time," is a provision of the Uniform Commercial Code. Thus, the standards set forth in § 42a–1–204, which define the phrase "reasonable time," apply to § 42a–4–303 (a). Section 42a–1–204 (2) specifically provides: "What is a reasonable time for taking any action depends on the nature, purpose and circumstances of such action." Thus, textually, § 42a–4–303 (a) strongly indicates, by its open-textured language and by virtue of § 42a–1–204 (2), that its meaning is what is normally meant by the statutory use of the phrase "reasonable time," namely, a fact-specific inquiry depending on all of the circumstances of the case.

The conclusion that the phrase "reasonable time" as used in § 42a–4–303 (a) requires a fact-specific inquiry and is not synonymous with the midnight deadline is also consistent with the official commentary of the Uniform Commercial Code dealing with the very same "reasonable time" provision. Section 42a–4–303 is our state's version of § 4–303 of the Uniform Commercial Code. The official commentary to § 4–303 is a part of the circumstances surrounding the enactment of § 42a–4–303 (a), and, as such, is relevant to the legislature's intent. * * * Official comment 6 to § 4–303 of the Uniform Commercial Code provides in relevant part: "In the case of . . . legal process the effective time for determining whether [it was] received too late to affect the payment of an item and a charge to the customer's account by reason of such payment, is receipt plus a reasonable time for the bank to act on [the service of process] . . . . Usually, a relatively short time is required to communicate to the accounting department advice of one of these events but certainly some time is necessary. . . ." Thus, the official commentary unequivocally states that the time period is variable and depends upon the factual circumstances. It makes no mention of the bright-line rule created by the midnight deadline.

This conclusion is consistent with what we perceive to be the purpose of § 42a–4–303 (a), namely, to balance the interests of the garnishor in securing its potential debtor's funds against the need for the bank to have the necessary time in which to take the steps necessary to effectuate that security. Although, as the defendant suggests, a midnight deadline would give a bank more certainty and, in all likelihood, more time to take those steps, we see nothing in either the language or the purpose of the statute to justify that bright-line rule. * * *

The judgment is reversed and the case is remanded for further proceedings according to law.

PROBLEM

Payee deposited a check for $25,000 in Depositary Bank (DB) for collection. The check was drawn by Drawer on her account in Payor Bank (PB) and was presented through banking channels to PB at 10 a.m. on Day

1. At the time the check was presented, Drawer had $30,000 in collected funds in her account. At noon on Day 2, PB examined the check and noted that paying the check would leave only $5,000 in Drawer's account. This was of concern to PB because Drawer owed PB $20,000 on an overdue loan. At 2 p.m. on Day 2, PB made the bookkeeping entries that were required to setoff its $20,000 claim against Drawer's account. Since this act reduced Drawer's account to $10,000, PB returned the check, marked "not sufficient funds," to the presenting bank at 6 p.m. on Day 2. The close of PB's banking day was 5 p.m., and it had not opted for an earlier cutoff hour. Payee challenged PB's right to setoff against the check 26 hours after it had been presented to PB. Is Payee correct? See 4–303(a)(5) and Comment 4.

## D.   "HIGH-TO-LOW" BASIS OF POSTING

Bank receives five checks drawn on Customer's account that are presented on the same day: $1500 mortgage payment, $500 car payment, $100 credit card payment, $65 florist payment, and $60 gift shop payment. But Customer's account contained only $1525 on that date. Bank paid the $1500 check and returned the four others, charging the customer a $25 NSF (not sufficient funds) fee for each returned check. When Customer learned that Bank could have paid the four smaller checks and assessed only a single $25 NSF fee, he complained loudly. Bank explained that it followed the "high-to-low" posting basis, which meant that its policy was to pay the largest check first; moreover, the law clearly gives it the option of choosing this payment basis. Section 4–303(b) states: " * * * items may be accepted, paid, certified, or charged to the indicated account of its customer in any order."

Different banks use different posting rules. According to Rick Brooks, How Banks Make the Most of Bounced Checks, Wall St. J., Feb. 25, 1999, at B1, among the nation's five largest banks, three pay the largest checks first and two pay the smallest checks first. Other banks pay checks on the basis of check number; others say that they will sometimes deviate from their policy to give a customer a break when they see that a number of checks are likely to bounce. Some high-to-low banks justify their policy by maintaining that their customers tell them they want the largest checks paid first; they would rather owe the florist than have their mortgage check bounce. Before Revised Article 4, banks usually had clauses in their deposit agreements with their customers saying about what 4–303(b) now says. At the time Revised Article 4 was being drafted, the codification of these agreements was not controversial. But, during the enactment process, consumer groups in California and Texas were sufficiently concerned about the potential for abuse in 4–303(b) to persuade their legislatures to append the following to the Official Comments:

> The only restraint on the discretion given to the payor bank under subsection (b) is that the bank act in good faith. For example, the bank could not properly follow an established practice of maximizing the

number of returned checks for the sole purpose of increasing the amount of returned check fees charged to the customer.

Over time, enough customers have become sufficiently aggrieved by high-to-low posting that lawsuits have challenged the practice as merely a device for increasing banks' income from NSF fees. At the time of the Brooks' article, out of the 173 million checks processed daily, 1.3 million were NSF, and, with fees running up as high as $30 per check, the stakes are high. When pre-trial discovery in some of these suits turned up damaging intra-bank communications proposing that the high-to-low formula be adopted in order to increase revenue, the fat was in the fire. So far the banks have been winning these cases. See, e.g, Hill v. St. Paul Federal Bank for Savings, 768 N.E.2d 322 (Ill. App. 2002), which held that even if the motive of the bank in adopting the high-to-low posting order was to maximize profits, the motive was irrelevant because 4–303(b) authorizes high-to-low posting. Since issue in 2001 by the Comptroller of the Currency of Interpretative Letter #916 that is favorable to high-to-low posting, litigation appears to have diminished. See Clarks' Bank Deposits and Payments Monthly, Vol. 10, No. 6, Nov. 2001, at p.1, and Vol. 11, No. 8, Jan. 2003, at p.3.

## E.   WRONGFUL DISHONOR

Most business lawyers at some time receive a call from an irate client whose check has been bounced by a bank. Sometimes the bank has not been sufficiently contrite about its error, and your client wants to "teach that bank a lesson." What can you do for this client? As we will see, the answer to this in most cases is very little, other than to extract an apology from the chastened bank. Nonetheless, the lawyer would do well to ask the client some detailed questions about the facts surrounding the wrongful dishonor, for, under certain circumstances, 4–402(b) not only offers the wronged customer direct damages but is one of the few provisions in the UCC that offers consequential damages.

Section 4–402(b) is only the latest step in a long series of judicial and legislative efforts to strike a balance between the erring bank and the wronged customer. In nineteenth century rural America, in which everyone knew everyone else's business, wrongful dishonor of checks was treated as slander against the character of a business person ("trader"). 1 Clark & Clark, supra, ¶ 3.05[9][c] (Rev. ed. 2005). Being a "no account" was a serious accusation. The so-called "trader rule" was stated in 2 Morse, Banks and Banking 1007–1008 (6th ed., Voorhees, 1928):

[T]he better authority seems to be, that, even if * * * actual loss or injury is not shown, yet more than nominal damages shall be given. It can hardly be possible that a customer's check can be wrongfully refused payment without some impeachment of his credit, which must in fact be an actual injury, though he cannot from the nature of the case furnish independent distinct proof thereof. It is as in cases of libel and slander, which description of suit, indeed, it closely resembles, inasmuch as it is a practical slur upon the plaintiff's credit and repute in the business world. Special damage may be shown, if the plaintiff be able; but, if he be not able, the jury may nevertheless give such [temperate] damages as they conceive to be a reasonable compensation for that indefinite mischief which such an act must be assumed to have inflicted, according to the ordinary course of human events.

This was a plaintiff's lawyer's dream: if a bank wrongfully dishonored the check of a business customer, the customer got to the jury without showing any actual damage, and juries weren't any more fond of banks then than now. The banks fought back in the legislatures. At the behest of the American Bankers Association, a number of states enacted a version of the following: "No bank shall be liable to a depositor because of the nonpayment through mistake or error, and without malice, of a check which should have been paid unless the depositor shall allege and prove actual damage by reason of such nonpayment and in such event the liability shall not exceed the amount of damage so proved." Cal. Civ. Code § 3320 (repealed).

The original version of what is now 4–402(b) read: "A payor bank is liable to its customer for damages proximately caused by the wrongful dishonor of an item. When the dishonor occurs through mistake liability is limited to actual damages proved. If so proximately caused and proved damages may include damages for an arrest or prosecution of the customer or other consequential damages. Whether any consequential damages are proximately caused by the wrongful dishonor is a question of fact to be determined in each case." Comment 1 to Revised 4–402 contains a critique of this language and discusses the changes made in the revision.

## Loucks v. Albuquerque National Bank

Supreme Court of New Mexico, 1966.
76 N.M. 735, 418 P.2d 191.

■ LA FEL E. OMAN, JUDGE, Court of Appeals.

The plaintiffs-appellants, Richard A. Loucks and Del Martinez, hereinafter referred to as plaintiffs, Mr. Loucks and Mr. Martinez, respectively, were partners engaged in a business at Albuquerque, New Mexico, under the partnership name of L & M Paint and Body Shop.

By their complaint they sought both compensatory and punitive damages on behalf of the partnership, on behalf of Mr. Loucks, and on behalf of Mr. Martinez against the defendants-appellees, Albuquerque National Bank and W. J. Kopp, hereinafter referred to as defendants, the bank, and Mr. Kopp, respectively.

Prior to March 15, 1962 Mr. Martinez had operated a business at Albuquerque, New Mexico, under the name of Del's Paint and Body Shop. He did his banking with defendant bank and he dealt with Mr. Kopp, a vice-president of the bank.

On February 8, 1962 Mr. Martinez borrowed $500 from the bank, which he deposited with the bank in the account of Del's Paint and Body Shop. He executed an installment note payable to the bank evidencing this indebtedness.

On March 15, 1962 the plaintiffs formed a partnership in the name of L & M Paint and Body Shop. On that date they opened a checking account with the bank in the name of L & M Paint and Body Shop and deposited $620 therein. The signatures of both Mr. Loucks and Mr. Martinez were required to draw money from this account. The balance in the account of Del's Paint and Body Shop as of this time was $2.67. This was drawn from this account by a cashier's check and deposited in the account of L & M Paint & Body Shop on April 18, 1962.

Two payments of $50.00 each were made on Mr. Martinez' note of February 8, 1962, or on notes given as a renewal thereof. These payments were made by checks drawn by plaintiffs on the account of L & M Paint and Body Shop. The checks were payable to the order of the bank and were dated June 29, 1962 and August 28, 1962. A subsequent installment note was executed by Mr. Martinez on October 17, 1962 in the principal amount of $462 payable to the order of the bank. This was given as a replacement or renewal of the prior notes which started with the note of February 8, 1962.

Mr. Martinez became delinquent in his payments on this note of October 17, 1962 and the bank sued him in a Justice of the Peace court to recover the delinquency.

As of March 14, 1963 Mr. Martinez was still indebted to the bank on this note in the amount of $402, and on that date, Mr. Kopp, on behalf of the bank, wrote L & M Paint and Body Shop advising that its account had been charged with $402 representing the balance due ''on Del Martinez installment note,'' and the indebtedness was referred to in the letter as the ''indebtedness of Mr. Del Martinez.''

The charge of $402 against the account of L & M Paint and Body Shop was actually made on March 15, 1963, which was a Friday.

Although Mr. Martinez at one time testified he telephoned Mr. Kopp on either Friday or the following Monday about this charge, when he was questioned more closely he admitted he discussed the matter with Mr. Kopp by telephone on Friday. Mr. Loucks testified that as he recalled, it was on Monday. Both plaintiffs went to the bank on Monday, March 18, and talked with Mr. Kopp. They both told Mr. Kopp that the indebtedness represented by the note was the personal indebtedness of Mr. Martinez and was not a partnership obligation. Mr. Loucks explained that they had some outstanding checks against the partnership account. Mr. Kopp refused to return the money to the partnership account. There was evidence of some unpleasantness in the conversation. The partnership account, in which there was then a balance of only $3.66, was thereupon closed by the plaintiffs.

The bank refused to honor nine, and possibly ten, checks drawn on the account and dated between the dates of March 8 and 16, inclusive.

The checks dated prior to March 15 total $89.14, and those dated March 15 and 16 total $121.68. These figures do not include the tenth check to which some reference was made, but which was not offered into evidence and the amount of which does not appear in the record.

The case came on for trial before the court and a jury. The court submitted the case to the jury upon the question of whether or not the defendants wrongfully made the charge in the amount of $402 against the account of L & M Paint and Body Shop. The allegations of the complaint concerning punitive damages and compensatory damages, other than the amount of $402 allegedly wrongfully charged by the defendants against the partnership account, were dismissed by the court before the case was submitted to the jury. The jury returned a verdict for the plaintiffs in the amount of $402.

The plaintiffs have appealed and assert error on the part of the trial court in taking from the jury the questions of (1) punitive damages, (2) damages to business reputation and credit, (3) damages for personal injuries allegedly sustained by Mr. Loucks, and (4) in disallowing certain costs claimed by plaintiffs.

* * *

The plaintiffs, as partners, sought recovery on behalf of the partnership of $402 allegedly wrongfully charged against the partnership account. This question was submitted to the jury, was decided in favor of the partnership, and against the defendants, and no appeal has been taken from the judgment entered on the verdict. They also sought recovery on behalf of the partnership of $5,000 for alleged damages to its credit, good reputation, and business standing in the community, $1,800 for its alleged loss of income, and $14,404 as punitive damages.

Each partner also sought recovery of $5,000 for alleged damages to his personal credit, good reputation and business standing. Mr. Martinez sought punitive damages individually in the amount of $10,000, and Mr. Loucks sought punitive damages individually in the amount of $60,000. Mr. Loucks also sought $25,000 by way of damages he allegedly sustained by reason of an ulcer which resulted from the wrongful acts of the defendants.

The parties have argued the case in their respective briefs and in their oral arguments upon the theory that the questions here involved, except for Point IV, which deals with the disallowance by the trial court of some claimed costs, are questions of the damages which can properly be claimed as a result of a wrongful dishonor by a bank of checks drawn by a customer or depositor on the bank, and of the sufficiency of the evidence offered by plaintiffs to support their claims for damages.

Both sides quote UCC § 4–402. * * *

It would appear that the first question to be resolved is that of the person, or persons, to whom a bank must respond in damages for a wrongful dishonor. Here, the account was a partnership account, and if there was in fact a wrongful dishonor of any checks, such were partnership checks.

We have adopted the Uniform Commercial Code in New Mexico. In UCC § 4–402 it is clearly stated that a bank "is liable to its customer." In UCC § 4–104(1)(e), entitled "Definitions and index of definitions" it is stated that:

"(1) In this article unless the context otherwise requires

"(e) 'Customer' means any person having an account with a bank or for whom a bank has agreed to collect items and includes a bank carrying an account with another bank; * * * "

This requires us to determine who is a "person" within the contemplation of this definition. Under part II, article I of the Uniform Commercial Code, entitled "General Definitions and Principles of Interpretation," we find the term "person" defined in § 1–201(30) as follows: " 'Person' includes an individual or an organization * * *."

Subsection (28) of the same section expressly includes a "partnership" as one of the legal or commercial entities embraced by the term "organization."

It would seem that logically the "customer" in this case to whom the bank was required to respond in damages for any wrongful dishonor was the partnership. The Uniform Commercial Code expressly regards a partnership as a legal entity. This is consistent with the ordinary mercantile conception of a partnership. * * *

The Uniform Partnership Act, which has been adopted in New Mexico and appears as chapter 66, article I, N.M.S.A.1953, recognizes that a partnership has a separate legal entity for at least some purposes. * * *

Suits may be brought in New Mexico by or against the partnership as such. * * * A partnership is a distinct legal entity to the extent that it may sue or be sued in the partnership name. National Surety Co. v. George E. Breece Lumber Co., 60 F.2d 847 (10th Cir. 1932).

\* \* \*

The relationship, in connection with which the wrongful conduct of the bank arose, was the relationship between the bank and the partnership. The partnership was the customer, and any damages arising from the dishonor belonged to the partnership and not to the partners individually.

The damages claimed by Mr. Loucks as a result of the ulcer, which allegedly resulted from the wrongful acts of the defendants, are not consequential damages proximately caused by the wrongful dishonor as contemplated by § 4–402. In support of his right to recover for such claimed damages he relies upon the cases of Jones v. Citizens Bank of Clovis, 58 N.M. 48, 265 P.2d 366 and Weaver v. Bank of America Nat. Trust & Sav. Ass'n., 59 Cal.2d 428, 30 Cal. Rptr. 4, 380 P.2d 644. The California and New Mexico courts construed identical statutes in these cases. The New Mexico statute appeared as § 48–10–5, N.M.S.A.1953. This statute was repealed when the Uniform Commercial Code was adopted in 1961.

Assuming we were to hold that the decisions in those cases have not been affected by the repeal of the particular statutory provisions involved and the adoption of the Uniform Commercial Code, we are still compelled by our reasoning to reach the same result, because the plaintiffs in those cases were the depositor in the California case and the administratrix of the estate of the deceased depositor in the New Mexico case. In the present case, Mr. Loucks was not a depositor, as provided in the prior statute, nor a customer, as provided in our present statute. No duty was owed to him personally by reason of the debtor-creditor relationship between the bank and the partnership.

It is fundamental that compensatory damages are not recoverable unless they proximately result from some violation of a legally-recognized right of the person seeking the damages, whether such be a right in contract or tort. * * *

Insofar as the damage questions are concerned, we must still consider the claims for damages to the partnership. As above stated, the claim on behalf of the partnership for the recovery of the $402 was concluded by judgment for plaintiffs in this amount. This leaves (1) the claim of $5,000 for alleged damage to credit, reputation and business standing, (2) the claim of $1,800 for alleged loss of income, and (3) the claim of $14,404 as punitive damages.

The question with which we are first confronted is that of whether or not the customer, whose checks are wrongfully dishonored, may recover damages merely because of the wrongful dishonor. We understand the provisions of UCC § 4–402 to limit the damages to those proximately caused by the wrongful dishonor, and such includes any consequential damages so proximately caused. If the dishonor occurs through mistake, the damages are limited to actual damages proved.

It is pointed out in the comments to this section of the Uniform Commercial Code that:

" * * *

"This section rejects decisions which have held that where the dishonored item has been drawn by a merchant, trader or fiduciary he is defamed in his business, trade or profession by a reflection on his credit and hence that substantial damages may be awarded on the basis of defamation 'per se' without proof that damage has occurred. * * * " Uniform Commercial Code, § 4–402, Comment 3.

If we can say as a matter of law that the dishonor here occurred through mistake, then the damages would be limited to the "actual damages proved." Even if we are able to agree, as contended by defendants in their answer brief, that the defendants acted under a mistake of fact in " * * * that Mr. Kopp acting on behalf of the bank thought that the money was invested in the partnership and could be traced directly from Mr.

Martinez to the L & M Paint and Body Shop," still defendants cannot rely on such mistake after both Mr. Martinez and Mr. Loucks informed them on March 15 and 18 that this was a personal obligation of Mr. Martinez and that the partnership had outstanding checks. At least it then became a question for the jury to decide whether or not defendants had wrongfully dishonored the checks through mistake.

The problem then resolves itself into whether or not the evidence offered and received, together with any evidence properly offered and improperly excluded, was sufficient to establish a question as to whether the partnership credit and reputation were proximately damaged by the wrongful dishonors. There was evidence that ten checks were dishonored, that one parts dealer thereafter refused to accept a partnership check and Mr. Loucks was required to go to the bank, cash the check, and then take the cash to the parts dealer in order to get the parts; that some persons who had previously accepted the partnership checks now refused to accept them; that other places of business denied the partnership credit after the dishonors; and that a salesman, who had sold the partnership a map and for which he was paid by one of the dishonored checks, came to the partnership's place of business, and ripped the map off the wall because he had been given "a bad check for it."

This evidence was sufficient to raise a question of fact to be determined by the jury as to whether or not the partnership's credit had been damaged as a proximate result of the dishonors. This question should have been submitted to the jury.

Damages recoverable for injuries to credit as a result of a wrongful dishonor are more than mere nominal damages and are referred to as " * * * compensatory, general, substantial, moderate, or temperate, damages as would be fair and reasonable compensation for the injury which he [the depositor] must have sustained, but not harsh or inordinate damages. * * * " 5A Michie, Banks and Banking, § 243 at 576.

What are reasonable and temperate damages varies according to the circumstances of each case and the general extent to which it may be presumed the credit of the depositor would be injured. * * * The amount of such damages is to be determined by the sound discretion and dispassionate judgment of the jury. * * *

The next item of damages claimed on behalf of the partnership, which was taken from the jury, was the claim for loss of income in the amount of $1,800 allegedly sustained by the partnership as a result of the illness and disability of Mr. Loucks by reason of his ulcer. We are of the opinion that the trial court properly dismissed this claim for the announced reason that no substantial evidence was offered to support the claim, and for the further reason that the partnership had no legally-enforceable right to recover for personal injuries inflicted upon a partner.

Even if we were to assume that a tortuous act had been committed by defendants which proximately resulted in the ulcer and the consequent personal injuries and disabilities of Mr. Loucks, the right to recover for such would be in him. An action for damages resulting from a tort can only be sustained by the person directly injured thereby, and not by one claiming to have suffered collateral or resulting injuries. * * *

As was stated by Mr. Justice Holmes in Robins Dry Dock & Repair Co. v. Flint, 275 U.S. 303, 48 S.Ct. 134, 72 L.Ed. 290:

> " * * * no authority need be cited to show that, as a general rule, at least, a tort to the person or property of one man does not make the tort-feasor liable to another merely because the injured person was under a contract with that other, unknown to the doer of the wrong. * * * The law does not spread its protection so far."

The last question of damages concerns the claim for punitive damages. The trial court dismissed this claim for the reason that he was convinced there was no evidence of willful or wanton conduct on the part of defendants. Punitive or exemplary damages may be awarded only when the conduct of the wrongdoer may be said to be maliciously intentional, fraudulent, oppressive, or committed recklessly or with a wanton disregard of the plaintiffs' rights. * * *

Malice as a basis for punitive damages means the intentional doing of a wrongful act without just cause or excuse. This means that the defendant not only intended to do the act which is ascertained to be wrongful, but that he knew it was wrong when he did it. * * *

Although, as expressed above, we are of the opinion that there was a jury question as to whether defendants acted under a mistake of fact in dishonoring the checks, we do not feel that the unpleasant or intemperate remark or two claimed to have been made by Mr. Kopp, and his conduct, described by Mr. Martinez as having "run us out of the bank more or less," are sufficient upon which an award of punitive damages could properly have been made. Thus, the trial court was correct in taking this claim from the jury. * * *

It follows from what has been said that this cause must be reversed and remanded for a new trial solely upon the questions of whether or not the partnership credit was damaged as a proximate result of the dishonors, and, if so, the amount of such damages.


## NOTES

**1.** *"Liable to its customer."* Since *Loucks*, interesting developments have taken place on the issue of who can recover for damages incurred from a wrongful dishonor of the check of a corporate customer. Obviously a corporation cannot suffer emotional distress or acquire ulcers resulting from the bank's mistake, much less the personal embarrassment and social ostracism stemming from being jailed for writing a check that was wrongfully dishonored. But in a closely held corporation these damages may well be sustained by the individuals who own and operate the business. In an era in which plaintiffs are successfully seeking more adequate awards for their injuries, it comes as no surprise that courts are finding ways of reading the term "customer" more flexibly or finding alternative bases for liability. In Kendall Yacht Corp. v. United California Bank, 50 Cal.App.3d 949, 123 Cal.Rptr. 848 (Cal.Ct.App.1975), Corporation was the depositor and Laurence and Linda Kendall were officers and prospective shareholders who personally guaranteed Corporation's debts to Bank. Corporation never issued stock, and "it was, in effect, nothing but a transparent shell, having no viability as a separate and distinct legal entity." 123 Cal.Rptr. at 853. The court held that the Kendalls were "customers" within the meaning of 4–402: "Thus it was entirely foreseeable that the dishonoring of the Corporation's check would reflect directly on the personal credit and reputation of the Kendalls and that they would suffer the adverse personal consequences which resulted when the Bank reneged on its commitments." 123 Cal.Rptr. at 853. The court allowed recovery by the Kendalls of damages for emotional distress under 4–402.

Parrett v. Platte Valley State Bank & Trust Co., 236 Neb. 139, 459 N.W.2d 371 (1990), goes beyond *Kendall Yacht*. Parrett was the principal shareholder and president of the corporate customer. He personally participated in the business relationship between the corporate customer and the bank and entered into a personal guaranty for the corporation's obligations to the bank. When the bank wrongfully dishonored the corporate customer's check, Parrett was charged with felony theft and went to trial on the charge; at trial the charge was dismissed. Parrett sued for wrongful dishonor under 4–402. The lower court sustained the bank's demurrer on the ground that Parrett was not the customer. The Supreme Court of Nebraska, relying on *Kendall Yacht*, reversed and said:

> As reflected by Parrett's petition, the parties' business relationship, which included Parrett's personal guaranty for P & P Machinery's obligations to the bank, was such that it was foreseeable that dishonoring the corporation's check would reflect directly on Parrett. This is borne out by the fact that a criminal charge based on the dishonored check was brought against Parrett, but was dismissed during Parrett's trial. Since the consequences of the wrongful dishonor fell upon Parrett, it would elevate form over substance to say that he was not the bank's "customer" within the meaning of § 4–402. This is not to say that in every case a corporate officer has a wrongful dishonor action against the depository bank on which the corporation's check has been drawn and later dishonored. However, in view of the facts of this case alleged in Parrett's petition, Parrett has a cause of action against the bank.

459 N.W.2d at 378. Although the majority opinion in *Parrett* purported to rely on *Kendall Yacht*, the dissent pointed out that the key factor in that case was that the corporation was not a separate legal entity; the decision was based on veil-piercing. But in *Parrett* the corporate customer was clearly a separate legal entity and had always been treated as such by the bank.

Another line of decisions has held fast to the view expressed in *Loucks* that only the corporate customer can proceed under 4–402. See, e.g.,

Farmers Bank v. Sinwellan Corp., 367 A.2d 180 (Del.1976) (president of corporate customer denied right to sue under 4–402 for damages resulting from a criminal action brought against him because of the dishonor). An approach to allowing insiders to recover in cases in which corporate checks have been dishonored, even in jurisdictions taking the *Sinwellan* point of view, is to contend that 4–402 does not displace any cause of action that such an insider may have had against the bank at common law. See 1–103(b) and Comment 5 to 4–402.

**2.** *Damages*. Section 4–402(b) provides very broadly that a bank is liable for any damages proximately caused by a wrongful dishonor. Comment 1 to 4–402 describes a customer's right to sue as a "statutory cause of action." In most cases no damages can be proved, but if economic loss can be shown consequential damages will be awarded. Skov v. Chase Manhattan Bank, 407 F.2d 1318 (3d Cir.1969). The principal damages issue has been whether aggrieved customers can recover for emotional distress. Certainly a wrongful dishonor can proximately cause emotional distress, and this type of damage is within the limitation in the second sentence of 4–402(b) that the damages must be "actual." Although courts show their concern about the potential for abuse present in allowing damages for emotional distress, a number of courts have awarded customers damages for emotional distress in wrongful dishonor cases. The precedents are collected and discussed in Buckley v. Trenton Saving Fund Society, 111 N.J. 355, 544 A.2d 857 (1988). In that case the court held that the facts did not justify recovery for mental anguish and said:

> To some extent, slight emotional distress arising from the occasional dishonor of a check is one of the regrettable aggravations of living in today's society. See *Restatement*, [(Second) of Torts], § 436A comment b. Accordingly, we are reluctant to allow compensation for the intentional infliction of emotional distress when a bank wrongfully dishonors a check unless the bank's conduct is intentional, as well as reckless or outrageous, and the distress is severe or results in bodily injury. See *Hume*, 178 N.J.Super. 310, 428 A.2d 966; *Restatement*, [(Second) of Torts], § 46. When those conditions are met, a customer should be compensated for the emotional distress that is caused by the wrongful dishonor of a check.

544 A.2d at 864. Other courts are similarly restrictive on allowing damages for emotional distress in wrongful dishonor cases. See, e.g., Maryott v. First National Bank of Eden, 624 N.W.2d 96 (S.D. 2001).

Comment 1 to 4–402 points out in its last sentence that whether punitive damages are appropriate depends, under 1–305(a), on non–UCC state law. The matter is discussed in *Buckley*.

**3.** *Consequential damages*. Two further questions arise in connection with 4–402(b). First, why is the bank liable for consequential damages under 4–402(b) while a receiving bank that improperly executes or fails to execute a wire transfer is not liable for consequential damages under 4A–305(c)–(d), unless it expressly agrees to assume liability? Both 4–402(b) and 4A–305(c) set default rules; the question is why the default rules are set differently. The precaution-taking abilities of banks and customers, and the array of possible loss from wrongful dishonor of a check and improper execution of a wire transfer, seem to be the same. The costs of contracting around a default rule also do not appear to differ as between 4–402(b) and 4A–305(c). What, then, justifies setting different default rules? There might be a political explanation. Banks might have conceded an expanded potential liability under 4A–402(c)'s "money-back guarantee" and 4A–202 and 4A–203's unauthorized payment order provisions in exchange for limitations on recoverable damages under 4A–402(c). A similar sort of trade-off possibly was infeasible in the case of Article 4.

Second, does 4–402(b) set the default rule correctly with respect to consequential damages? There is room for doubt. Where contracting parties have asymmetric information and the less well informed party is the superior risk bearer, an important purpose of default rules can be to induce the party with the better information to disclose it to the less well informed party. See Ian Ayres & Robert Gertner, Filling Gaps in Incomplete Contracts: An Economic Theory of Default Rules, 99 Yale L. J. 87 (1989). This seems warranted in the context of wrongful dishonor of checks because customers typically are better informed than banks about the impact of wrongful dishonor on them. In order for banks to take the appropriate precautions, they need this information. However, allowing customers to recover consequential damages, including for emotional distress, under some plausible assumptions gives them a disincentive to disclose information to banks. As a result, banks might take inefficient precautions against wrongful dishonor. To see this, assume that customers are of two sorts, "low injury" and "high injury," and that banks cannot identify in advance a customer as being of one sort or another. "Low injury" customers suffer few consequential damages from wrongful dishonor, and no loss from emotional distress; "high injury" customers suffer significant consequential damages, including emotional distress. Banks will charge each customer a rate reflecting its expected liability to a mixed population of low and high injury customers. Thus, each customer pays this blended charge. Low injury customers pay a higher rate, and high injury customers a lower rate, than if banks could identify each customer's risk profile. Here high injury customers are subsidized by low risk customers. Banks in turn take inefficient levels of precaution because they overinvest in preventative measures for low injury customers and underinvest in them for high injury customers. An efficient default rule gives high and low injury customers incentives to reveal information about their respective types to banks.

Section 4–402(b) doesn't induce customers to do so. By allowing recovery of consequential damages, including damages for emotional distress, 4–402(b) gives all customers an enhanced level of protection. High injury customers therefore have no incentive to disclose information about their likely emotional distress resulting from banks' wrongful dishonor. They are protected by 4–402(b) and already benefit from the cross-subsidy provided by low injury customers. Low injury customers, who don't need 4–402(b)'s enhanced protection, also might not have an incentive to disclose their type to banks. For instance, if the population of customers contains a significant number of high injury customers and relatively few low injury customers, the subsidy provided to high injury customers might be slight. Disclosure therefore would produce a modest reduction in rates charged to low injury customers. If so, the costs of contracting around 4–402(b), to reduce the banks potential liability, might exceed the benefits of doing so for low risk customers. On the other hand, if the default rule excluded particular sorts of consequential damages, such as damages for emotional distress, high injury customers would be unprotected. Low injury customers would not need to incur contracting costs because the default rule already protects them. High injury customers would have to contract with banks, thus disclosing information about their type, but they receive a benefit in the form of enhanced protection (for an enhanced charge). Thus, 4–402(b) might be an inferior default rule.

This conclusion obviously is sensitive to the assumptions made. A realistic estimate of the population of customers would not divide it into two simplified sorts of customer: low and high injury. The more accurate assumption is that customers come in a continuum of risk profiles, from businesses suffering no emotional distress from wrongful dishonor, to the thick-skinned customer, to the socially sensitive or financially precarious customer. The extent of other sorts of consequential damage also realistically varies among customers, as does the size of contracting costs for customers of bargaining around a default rule. Section 4–402(b)'s default rule might be superior to other candidates, given the limited information available to lawmakers in designing or applying default rules. For the important effect of such details on the choice of default rule, see Barry E. Adler, The Questionable Ascent of Hadley v. Baxendale, 51 Stan. L. Rev. 1547 (1999); Alan Schwartz, The Default Rule Paradigm and the Limits of Contract Law, 3 S. Cal. Interdisc. L. J. 389 (1993); Lucian Ayre Bebchuk & Steven Shavell, Information and the Scope of Liability for Breach of Contract: The Rule of Hadley v. Baxendale, 7 J. L. Econ. & Org. 284 (1991).

## F.   THE BANK-CUSTOMER AGREEMENT

## 1.   DISCLOSURE: THE TRUTH-IN-SAVINGS ACT

Among the demands that consumer groups have made of deposit-holding institutions, one of the most persistent has been the call for improved disclosure of the terms of deposit accounts so that customers may better understand the agreements they are entering into with banks. The drive for improved disclosure has been at the core of the consumer movement in the second half of the last century. At the earliest stage of this movement, Senator Paul Douglas of Illinois, a former economics professor, noted that financial institutions quoted their finance charges to consumers in several different ways: annual percentage rate, monthly percentage rate, annual dollar amount, and so forth. These practices made it difficult for consumers to do effective credit shopping because they could not be sure which creditor was offering the lowest rates. He proposed what sounded like a modest solution: require all creditors to state their finance charges as an annual percentage rate or "simple annual interest," as he liked to put it. Creditors, seeing the head of the federal camel under the tent, tried to head off the legislation by asserting that the variety and complexity of consumer credit transactions were so great that such a law would be operationally impossible for creditors to comply with. After many years of heated discussions about the subject, Congress passed the Truth-in-Lending Act in 1968, which required disclosure of finance charges in terms of an annual percentage rate. 15 U.S.C. § 1601 et seq. Congress passed on to a reluctant Federal Reserve Board the task of solving by regulations the innumerable operational problems encountered. Regulation Z, 12 C.F.R. Part 226, resulted. There now is a considerable body of legislative, administrative and case law on the subject of the disclosure of consumer finance charges. The Truth-in-Lending Act served as a model for the deposit account disclosure legislation that came along more than two decades later.

Consumers had the same problems in attempting to compare the terms offered by banks and other depository institutions with respect to deposit accounts. These terms are usually contained either in the bank-customer agreement or in a separate brochure and are selectively publicized in advertisements designed to attract more depositors. Consumers complained that although most deposit institutions disclosed the interest rates they were paying on deposit accounts as an annual percentage rate based on the full amount of the principal in the account, others used methods that made it appear that the interest rate offered was higher than it actually was. As was the case with Truth in Lending, negotiations leading to Truth in Savings went on for years in Congress before the Act was finally passed in 1991 as part of the Federal Deposit Insurance Act, 12 U.S.C. § 4301 et seq. Again Congress fobbed off on the Fed the task of making the law workable, and Regulation DD, 12 C.F.R. Part 230, was completed in 1992 for this purpose. The Act and the Regulation are extensively discussed in 2 Clark & Clark, Bank Deposits, Collections and Credit Cards, Chapter 19 (Rev. ed. 2006).

(1) *Initial disclosure.* In brief, the Truth-in-Savings Act (TISA) requires federal and state deposit-holding institutions, e.g., banks, savings and loan associations, and credit unions, to disclose in a uniform manner the terms of their consumer deposit accounts at the time of entering into the deposit relationship with the customer. This initial disclosure must include interest rate information, the amounts of any service charges or other fees that may be imposed in connection with the account, and other salient features of the deposit account like minimum balance requirements, time account features (e.g., the effect of early withdrawal), and transaction limitations (e.g., limitations on the number of withdrawals or deposits). Regulation DD § 230.4. Although TISA applies to credit union accounts, Regulation DD does not; credit unions have parallel regulations. Regulation DD § 230.1(c).

The key items disclosed are the interest rate and the "annual percentage yield" (APY), which is the yield the interest rate produces with compounding. Regulation DD § 230.2(c). It is this figure that should be most useful to consumers in interest rate shopping. The model clause suggested by the Appendix to Regulation DD is:

The interest rate on your account is _____% with an annual percentage yield of _____%.

(2) *Periodic statement disclosures.* Additional disclosures must be made in the periodic, usually monthly, statements that depository institutions send to their customers. Regulation DD § 230.6. These disclosures must include the "annual percentage yield earned" during the statement period, the dollar amount of the interest earned during that period, the dollar amounts and kinds of fees imposed and the number of days in the statement period or the beginning and ending dates of the period.

(3) *Advertising.* The third level of disclosure regulation relates to advertising. As is true with any law attempting to regulate advertising, Regulation DD § 230.8 is very complex. In an attempt to force the depository institution to be fair in its advertising, Regulation DD calls for so much explanatory language that it will probably result in either less advertising or an information overload in the ads that are published. If the printed ad states a rate of return, it must state the rate as an APY, but if it does so it must include a host of additional disclosures if they relate to the kind of deposit being advertised, e.g., explanations concerning variable rates, the period of time the APY is offered, any minimum balance required to obtain the APY advertised, any minimum opening balance, a statement that the fees charged could reduce the earnings, a number of features of time accounts, and on and on. However, if the advertising is being done on radio, TV or billboards, the disclosure requirements are much reduced.

(4) *Changes in the terms of the deposit account.* Advance notice, usually 30 days, is required for changes "if the change may reduce the annual percentage yield or adversely affect the consumer." Regulation DD § 230.5(a)(1). Normally the bank-customer agreement will give the bank the right to change unilaterally certain terms of the account so long as some prior notice is given. Among the most common changes made are those in the service charges and fee amounts. Despite the specific reference in the quotation above to changes in annual percentage yield, 2 Clark & Clark, supra, ¶ 19.02[2][t] and ¶ 19.07[1][e][iv], points out that in the original version of Regulation DD the broad definition of "variable-rate account," Regulation DD § 230.2(v), as "an account in which the interest rate may change after the account is opened," means that most interest rate changes need not be disclosed in a change-in-terms notice unless the bank specifically commits to give advance notice of rate decreases. This result flows from Regulation DD § 230.5(a)(2)(i), which provides that no notice of change need be given for changes in interest rates in variable rate accounts. Since all deposit accounts in which the bank has the power to change rates were arbitrarily considered to be variable rate accounts under the broad definition of the term in former Regulation DD § 230.2(v), which

bears no relation to the common meaning of the term, the most important information that a customer needs to know, that the bank is lowering its interest rate, need be disclosed to the customer only if the bank has specifically agreed to make the disclosure. This wacky result was subsequently changed by adding to the definition of "variable-rate account," quoted above, the following: "unless the institution contracts to give at least 30 calendar days advance written notice of rate decreases." Under this amendment, a bank cannot lower rates unless it gives a 30–day notice.

(5) *Overdraft disclosures.* Bank customers may be offered overdraft protection as a feature of their deposit accounts, usually with a dollar limit stated. Although banks usually provide that overdraft protection is discretionary, the common practice is to allow qualified customers automatic protection. A flat fee is charged when an overdraft occurs; the usual assumption is that this fee is not a finance charge under Truth-in-Lending. Abuses have been alleged with respect to advertisements promoting overdraft programs as a reliable source of additional credit even though the fees may make it expensive to draw on them and the bank may have discretion whether to allow the overdraft. In 2006 Regulation DD was amended to add provisions prohibiting the advertising of an account as "free" or "no cost" if an activity fee is imposed. § 230.8(a)(2). Institutions promoting overdraft availability in advertisements must comply with the provisions of § 230.11, which prescribe that (i) periodic statements must disclose on each statement the total of fees imposed for overdrafts as well as the total of all fees paid for dishonoring items for the statement period and the calendar year to date (§ 230.11(a)(1)), and (ii) advertising disclosures for overdrafts must include the fees for the payment of each overdraft, the time period within which the customer must repay or cover any overdraft, and the circumstances under which the institution will not pay an overdraft (230.11(b)(1)).

## 2. "F<small>REEDOM OF</small> C<small>ONTRACT</small>" U<small>NDER</small> S<small>ECTION</small> 4–103(1)

The UCC adopts the principle of freedom of contract in 1–302(a), which provides that: "Except as otherwise provided in subsection (b) or elsewhere in [the Uniform Commercial Code], the effect of provisions of [the Uniform Commercial Code] may be varied by agreement." How far can the parties go in contracting away the provisions of the Code? Section 1–302(b) states that: "The obligations of good faith, diligence, reasonableness, and care prescribed by [the Uniform Commercial Code] may not be disclaimed by agreement. The parties, by agreement, may determine the standards by which the performance of those obligations is to be measured if those standards are not manifestly unreasonable." Comment 1 to 1–302 cautions that it is only the "effect" of the provisions of the UCC that may be varied by agreement, but "[t]he meaning of the statute itself must be found in its text, including its definitions, and in appropriate extrinsic aids; it cannot be varied by agreement."

Section 4–103(a) reiterates the freedom-of-contract principle for Article 4: "The effect of the provisions of this Article may be varied by agreement * * *." At bottom, almost all of Article 4's provisions are default rules only.

Comment 1 to 4–103 seems to go even further to say that constant technological changes affecting banking warrant giving parties even greater latitude than with respect to 1–302 to make changes by agreement. This seems to suggest that the provisions of Article 4 are even more subject to variation than other parts of the UCC. The Comment asserts that it would be unwise to interpret Article 4 as freezing the law in this dynamic area by mandatory rules. It concludes: "This section, therefore, permits within wide limits variation of the effect of provisions of the Article by agreement." This Comment impliedly recognizes two short-comings of the UCC. First, amending the provisions of the Code is a cumbersome procedure that usually takes a minimum of ten years before the changes are adopted in all states; thus the Code is not good at keeping up with technological change. Second, there is no state administrative agency devoted to keeping the Code up to date by issuance of regulations in the Article 4 area. To an extent, the Federal Reserve Board serves as such an administrative agency. Section 4–103(b) recognizes the Fed's power to make regulations varying the provisions of Article 4, and the Fed has frequently acted to modernize the law of bank collections. But the Fed is not particularly interested in bank-customer relations; its focus is on inter-bank relations.

Article 4's drafters concluded that private ordering is preferable to statutory regulation as a means of keeping the Code responsive to the needs of modern banking collection operations. Is this a defensible conclusion? The question raises the familiar problem of the comparative benefits and costs of setting contract terms by regulation or contract. The problem is a basic one of institutional design. Certainly there must be some limits on the degree to which terms in a deposit agreement can vary Article 4's provisions. It is difficult, however, to specify exactly those limits. True, deposit agreements have all the earmarks of contracts of adhesion: contracts drafted by the bank and offered to the prospective customer on a take-it-or-leave-it basis. If a customer does not like particular terms in the agreement, its only choice is to go to another bank. The recent trend in bank consolidations means that fewer competing banks are available and therefore possibly less variation in the terms of deposit agreements being offered. But it can't be concluded that the terms in deposit agreements, even if adhesion contracts, are adverse to the interests of customers. Adhesion contracts can be transaction cost saving devices and therefore consistent with either monopoly power or convergence of contract terms produced by competitive market competition.

The prominent terms of deposit agreements, such as conditions placed on stop-payment orders, authorized signatures, and waiver provisions, implicate issues of fairness and efficiency. They affect the incentives of customers and banks, and alter the costs of banking services for classes of customers. The central issue of statutory drafting is whether fairness and efficiency is better pursued by the terms being set by private ordering or substantive regulation. Given the fast pace of technological change in banking services and their price impact on all depositors, the political and judicial barriers to updating statutes, and the demanding informational requirements for effective substantive regulation in the area, Article 4's drafters presumably favored private ordering announced by 4–103(a). It is perhaps significant that the Federal Reserve Board to date has taken the same view with respect to many of the terms governing electronic payments systems; see Chapter 14 supra.

The only limitations stated in 4–103(a) are that "[t]he parties to the agreement cannot disclaim a bank's responsibility for its lack of good faith or failure to exercise ordinary care or limit the measure of damages for the lack or failure. However, the parties may determine by agreement the standards by which the bank's responsibility is to be measured if those standards are not manifestly unreasonable." Hostility to 4–103(a)'s freedom-of-contract principle is well expressed by Grant Gilmore, who described agreements that alter Article 4's default rules as "carrying a good joke too far." Grant Gilmore, The Uniform Commercial Code: A Reply to Professor Beutel, 61 Yale L. J. 364, 375 (1952). How should a court apply 4–103(a) to the following Problems? The issues raised by these Problems are discussed in detail in 1 Clark & Clark, The Law of Bank Deposits, Collections and Credit Cards § 3.01[3] (Rev. ed. 2005), and White & Summers, Uniform Commercial Code § 18–2 (5th ed. 2000).

## PROBLEMS

**1.** Husband (H) and Wife (W) have a joint checking account in Bank. Their deposit agreement with Bank provides, among other matters: (1) that either party may write checks on the account, may stop-payment of any check drawn on the account, or may close the account, and (2) that Bank may pay an overdraft drawn by either party, the account may be debited for the overdraft, and either party is liable for the amount of the overdraft without respect to whether that party signed the check or benefited from the overdraft. H wrote a check which Bank paid that overdrew the account. W did not know of the overdraft and she did not benefit in any way from the proceeds of the overdraft. H is insolvent and Bank seeks to hold W liable for the amount of the overdraft. May it do so? 4–401(b).

**2.** Corporate depositor (D) opens a demand deposit account in Bank from which D intends to pay its bills. The deposit agreement that D entered into with Bank contains the following clause: "You [D] may authorize the use of a facsimile signature device by a corporate resolution communicated to Bank. If you have authorized the use of a facsimile signature device, Bank may honor any check that bears or appears to bear your facsimile signature even if it was made by an unauthorized person or with a counterfeit facsimile device." Use of a facsimile device was duly authorized. Burglar breaks into D's premises and uses the facsimile machine to write a check to himself that Bank pays on presentment. May Bank debit D's account? Is the quoted clause enforceable in the face of 3–403(a), which provides that an unauthorized signature is ineffective, and 4–401(a), which provides that a bank may charge a customer's account only for checks that are properly payable? Comment 1 to 4–401 states "[a]n item containing a forged drawer's signature * * * is not properly payable." 1

Clark & Clark, supra, ¶ 3.01[3][c][iii], cites cases on both sides of the question, and, like White & Summers, supra, § 18–2 a., favors upholding the exculpatory clause. The quoted clause is based on one that appears in a model deposit account set out in 1 Clark & Clark, supra, ¶ 3.13[1].

**3.** Corporate depositor (D) opens a demand deposit account in Bank from which D intends to pay its bills. The deposit agreement that D entered into with Bank contains the following clause: "Unless you [D] shall notify Bank within fifteen calendar days of the delivery or mailing to you of any statement of account and cancelled checks of any objection to any check or item on the account, all objections for any cause or reason whatsoever, whether known or unknown, shall be absolutely barred and waived." A forged check was returned by Bank to D on June 1; D's reconciliation process did not turn up the forgery until July 15, at which time D gave Bank prompt notice of the forgery. Bank claimed that because D had failed to give the notice within the 15–day period prescribed in the agreement, D had no right to challenge its payment of the check. D noted that under 4–406(f), it had a year in which to object. Is Bank protected by the quoted clause? National Title Insurance Corporation Agency v. First Union National Bank, reprinted in the previous Chapter 15, upheld a 60–day contract cutdown clause; Stowell v. Cloquet Co-op Credit Union, 557 N.W.2d 567 (Minn. 1997), upheld a 20–day contract cutdown clause. 1 Clark & Clark, supra, ¶ 3.01[3][c][ii], cites some cases tending to uphold similar clauses. White & Summers, Uniform Commercial Code § 18–2 (4th ed. 1995), questions whether a clause with a 15–day cutoff date should be upheld. Herzog, Engstrom & Koplovitz P.C. v. Union National Bank, 640 N.Y.S.2d 703 (N.Y.App.Div.1996), refused to enforce a 14–day cutoff period.

## 3.   SERVICE CHARGES AND FEES

### a.   INTRODUCTION

Most banks impose charges on depositors for services performed by the bank in processing stop-payment orders, overdrafts, and checks deposited in the customer's account that have been returned because they were not paid by the bank on which they were drawn (NSF items), and many other services. Until the early '80s, regulations prohibited commercial banks from paying competitive interest rates on deposits; they lured customers by giving them gifts. But they also provided many free services: no per-check charges or the like. After deregulation, banks started paying market interest rates on deposits, but in order to cover their increased costs, banks began to impose charges for various services performed. The process was called "unbundling." Bankers believe that customers have never gotten used to service charges; they still view banks as quasi-public utilities that should be giving them toasters rather than charging them service fees. The story is told in Karen Hube & Matt Murray, New Charges Make Banking More Confusing, Wall St. J., Nov. 11, 1997, at C1. Bear in mind that since 1992, TISA has required that banks make an initial disclosure of the types and amounts of these fees, Regulation DD § 230.4(b)(4); that periodic statements must disclose the types and amounts of fees imposed during the statement period, Regulation DD § 230.6(a)(3); and that a 30–day advance notice must be given of any new fees or any increase in the amounts of fees, Regulation DD § 230.5(a).

The emergence of class actions to vindicate consumer rights allowed consumers to challenge banks on the validity of the terms of that classic example of a contract of adhesion, the bank-customer deposit agreement. The rules of the game were well known: if the class was certified and the plaintiff could get by a demurrer, the case could go to the jury. The plaintiffs had won the case because at this point the bank would usually settle. It would be difficult to find a juror who does not believe that bank service charges are excessive. An early example of the ensuing blizzard of class action litigation against banks is the following oft-cited case.

## Perdue v. Crocker National Bank

Supreme Court of California, 1985.
38 Cal.3d 913, 216 Cal.Rptr. 345, 702 P.2d 503.

■ BROUSSARD, JUSTICE.

Plaintiff filed this class action to challenge the validity of charges imposed by defendant Crocker National Bank for the processing of checks drawn on accounts without sufficient funds. (The parties refer to such checks as NSF checks and to the handling charge as an NSF charge.) He appeals from a judgment of the trial court entered after that court sustained defendant's general demurrer without leave to amend.

On July 3, 1978, plaintiff filed suit on behalf of all persons with checking accounts at defendant bank and a subclass of customers who have paid NSF charges to the bank. The complaint first alleges a contract under which the bank furnishes checking service in return for a maintenance charge. It then asserts that "It is the practice of defendants to impose and collect a unilaterally set charge for processing checks presented against plaintiffs' accounts when such accounts do not contain sufficient funds to cover the amount of the check." "Defendants have at various times unilaterally increased the NSF charge to an amount the defendants deemed appropriate, without reference to any criteria, and defendants imposed and collected the said increased amount without any explanation or justification by defendants to plaintiffs." At the time of filing of the suit, the charge was $6 for each NSF check, whether the check was honored or returned unpaid, even though "the actual cost incurred by the defendants in processing an NSF check is approximately $0.30."

The bank requires each depositor to sign a signature card which it uses "to determine and verify the authenticity of endorsements on checks". In extremely small (6 point) type, the signature card states that the undersigned depositors "agree with Crocker National Bank and with each other that ... this account and all deposits therein shall be ... subject to all applicable laws, to the Bank's present and future rules, regulations, practices and charges, and to its right of setoff for the obligations of any of us."

The card does not identify the amount of the charge for NSF checks, and the bank does not furnish the depositor with a copy of the applicable bank rules and regulations.

On the basis of these allegations, plaintiff asserts * * * causes of action: (1) for a judicial declaration that the bank's signature card is not a contract authorizing NSF charges; [and] (2) for a judicial declaration that such charges are oppressive and unconscionable * * *.

## I.  PLAINTIFF'S FIRST CAUSE OF ACTION: WHETHER THE SIGNATURE CARD IS A CONTRACT AUTHORIZING NSF CHARGES.

* * *

We conclude that plaintiff here is not entitled to a judicial declaration that the bank's signature card is not a contract authorizing NSF charges. To the contrary, we hold as a matter of law that the card is a contract authorizing the bank to impose such charges, subject to the bank's duty of good faith and fair dealing in setting or varying such charges. Plaintiff may, upon remand of this case, amend his complaint to seek a judicial declaration determining whether the charges actually set by the bank are consonant with that duty. * * *

## II.  PLAINTIFF'S SECOND CAUSE OF ACTION: WHETHER THE BANK'S NSF CHARGES ARE OPPRESSIVE, UNREASONABLE, OR UNCONSCIONABLE.

Plaintiff's second cause of action alleges that the signature card is drafted by defendant bank which enjoys a superior bargaining position by reason of its greater economic power, knowledge, experience and resources. Depositors have no alternative but to acquiesce in the relationship as offered by defendant or to accept a similar arrangement with another bank. The complaint alleges that the card is vague and uncertain, that it is unclear whether it is intended as an identification card or a contract, that it imposes no obligation upon the bank, and permits the bank to alter or terminate the relationship at any time,[8] then asserts that "The disparity between the actual cost to defendants and the amount charged by defendants for processing an NSF check unreasonably and oppressively imposes excessive and unfair liability upon plaintiffs." Plaintiff seeks a declaratory judgment to determine the rights and duties of the parties.

Plaintiff's allegations point to the conclusion that the signature card, if it is a contract, is one of adhesion. The term contract of adhesion "signifies a standardized contract, which, imposed and drafted by the party of superior bargaining strength, relegates to the subscribing party only the opportunity to adhere to the contract or reject it." (Neal v. State Farm Ins. Co. (1961) 188 Cal. App.2d 690, 694, 10 Cal. Rptr. 781) * * * The signature

---

**8.** The depositor also has the right to terminate the relationship at any time, but lacks the right asserted by the bank to alter the relationship without terminating it.

card, drafted by the bank and offered to the customer without negotiation, is a classic example of a contract of adhesion; the bank concedes as much.

In Graham v. Scissor–Tail, Inc., 28 Cal.3d 807, 171 Cal. Rptr. 604, 623 P.2d 165, we observed that "To describe a contract as adhesive in character is not to indicate its legal effect.... [A] contract of adhesion is fully enforceable according to its terms [citations] unless certain other factors are present which, under established legal rules—legislative or judicial—operate to render it otherwise." (Pp. 819–820, 171 Cal. Rptr. 604, 623 P.2d 165, fn. omitted.) "Generally speaking," we explained, "there are two judicially imposed limitations on the enforcement of adhesion contracts or provisions thereof. The first is that such a contract or provision which does not fall within the reasonable expectations of the weaker or 'adhering' party will not be enforced against him. [Citations.] The second—a principle of equity applicable to all contracts generally—is that a contract or provision, even if consistent with the reasonable expectations of the parties, will be denied enforcement if, considered in its context, it is unduly oppressive or 'unconscionable.' O" (P. 820, 171 Cal. Rptr. 604, 623 P.2d 165, fns. omitted.)

In 1979, the Legislature enacted Civil Code section 1670.5, which codified the established doctrine that a court can refuse to enforce an unconscionable provision in a contract. Section 1670.5 reads as follows: "(a) If the court as a matter of law finds the contract or any clause of the contract to have been unconscionable at the time it was made the court may refuse to enforce the contract, or it may enforce the remainder of the contract without the unconscionable clause, or it may so limit the application of any unconscionable clause as to avoid any unconscionable result. [&] (b) When it is claimed or appears to the court that the contract or any clause thereof may be unconscionable the parties shall be afforded a reasonable opportunity to present evidence as to its commercial setting, purpose, and effect to aid the court in making the determination."

In construing this section, we cannot go so far as plaintiff, who contends that even a conclusory allegation of unconscionability requires an evidentiary hearing. We do view the section, however, as legislative recognition that a claim of unconscionability often cannot be determined merely by examining the face of the contract, but will require inquiry into its setting, purpose, and effect.

Plaintiff bases his claim of unconscionability on the alleged 2,000 percent differential between the NSF charge of $6 and the alleged cost to the bank of $0.30.[11] The parties have cited numerous cases on whether the price of an item can be so excessive as to be unconscionable. The cited cases

---

**11.** The bank's briefs claim the alleged $0.30 cost is too low and plaintiff's briefs admit that a higher figure, but still $1 or less, might be more accurate. We do not, however, find in plaintiff's briefs a sufficiently clear concession to enable us to depart from the general principle that, in reviewing a judgment after the sustaining of a general demurrer without leave to amend, we must assume the truth of all material factual allegations in the complaint. (Alcorn v. Anbro Engineering, Inc., supra, 2 Cal. 3d 493, 496, 86 Cal. Rptr. 88, 468 P.2d 216.)

are from other jurisdictions, often from trial courts or intermediate appellate courts, and none is truly authoritative on the issue. Taken together, however, they provide a useful guide to analysis of the claim that a price is so excessive as to be unconscionable.

To begin with, it is clear that the price term, like any other term in a contract, may be unconscionable. * * * Allegations that the price exceeds cost or fair value, standing alone, do not state a cause of action. * * * Instead, plaintiff's case will turn upon further allegations and proof setting forth the circumstances of the transaction.

The courts look to the basis and justification for the price (cf. A & M Produce Co. v. FMC Corp., supra, 135 Cal. App.3d 473, 487, 186 Cal. Rptr. 114), including "the price actually being paid by ... other similarly situated consumers in a similar transaction." (Bennett v. Behring Corp., supra, 466 F.Supp. 689, 697, italics omitted.) The cases, however, do not support defendant's contention that a price equal to the market price cannot be held unconscionable. While it is unlikely that a court would find a price set by a freely competitive market to be unconscionable (see Bradford v. Plains Cotton Cooperative Assn. (10th Cir.1976) 539 F.2d 1249, 1255 [cotton futures]), the market price set by an oligopoly should not be immune from scrutiny. Thus, courts consider not only the market price, but also the cost of the goods or services to the seller (Frostifresh Corporation v. Reynoso (N.Y.Dist.Ct.1966) 52 Misc.2d 26, 274 N.Y.S.2d 757; Toker v. Westerman (1970) 113 N.J. Super. 452, 274 A.2d 78), the inconvenience imposed on the seller (see Merrel v. Research & Data, Inc., supra, 589 P.2d 120, 123), and the true value of the product or service (American Home Improvements, Inc. v. MacIver (1964) 105 N.H. 435, 201 A.2d 886, 889).

In addition to the price justification, decisions examine what Justice Weiner in *A & M Produce* called the "procedural aspects" of unconscionability. (See *A & M Produce Co.*, supra, 135 Cal. App.3d at p. 489, 186 Cal. Rptr. 114.) Cases may turn on the absence of meaningful choice (Patterson v. Walker–Thomas Furniture Co., supra, 277 A.2d 111, 113 and cases there cited), the lack of sophistication of the buyer (compare Geldermann & Co., Inc. v. Lane Processing, Inc. (8th Cir.1975) 527 F.2d 571, 576 [relief denied to sophisticated investor] with Frostifresh Corporation v. Reynoso, supra, 274 N.Y.S.2d 757 [relief granted to unsophisticated buyers]) and the presence of deceptive practices by the seller (ibid.; Vom Lehn v. Astor Art Galleries, Ltd., supra, 380 N.Y.S.2d 532).

Applying this analysis to our review of the complaint at hand, we cannot endorse defendant's argument that the $6 charge is so obviously reasonable that no inquiry into its basis or justification is necessary. In 1978 $6 for processing NSF checks may not seem exorbitant,[13] but price

**13.** Defendant cites Merrel v. Research & Data, Inc., supra, 589 P.2d 120, which held a $5 fee imposed by merchants for NSF checks was a "modest" amount (p. 123) and not unconscionable. NSF checks pose a sub-stantial inconvenience to a seller, who has been deceived into an involuntary extension of credit to a customer whose credit standing may not be very good. A bank, however, is not deceived. It checks the balance of the

alone is not a reliable guide. Small charges applied to a large volume of transactions may yield a sizeable sum. The complaint asserts that the cost of processing NSF checks is only $0.30 per check, which means that a $6 charge would produce a 2,000 percent profit; even at the higher cost estimate of $1 a check mentioned in plaintiff's petition for hearing, the profit is 600 percent.[14] Such profit percentages may not be automatically unconscionable, but they indicate the need for further inquiry.

Other aspects of the transaction confirm plaintiff's right to a factual hearing. Defendant presents the depositor with a document which serves at least in part as a handwriting exemplar, and whose contractual character is not obvious. The contractual language appears in print so small that many could not read it. State law may impose obligations on the bank (e.g., the duty to honor a check when the account has sufficient funds (Allen v. Bank of America, supra, 58 Cal. App.2d 124, 127, 136 P.2d 345)), but so far as the signature card drafted by the bank is concerned, the bank has all the rights and the depositor all the duties. The signature card provides that the depositor will be bound by the bank's rules, regulations, practices and charges, but the bank does not furnish the depositor with a copy of the relevant documents. The bank reserves the power to change its practices and fees at any time, subject only to the notice requirements of state law.

In short, the bank structured a totally one-sided transaction. The absence of equality of bargaining power, open negotiation, full disclosure, and a contract which fairly sets out the rights and duties of each party demonstrates that the transaction lacks those checks and balances which would inhibit the charging of unconscionable fees. In such a setting, plaintiff's charge that the bank's NSF fee is exorbitant, yielding a profit far in excess of cost, cannot be dismissed on demurrer. Under Civil Code section 1670.5, the parties should be afforded a reasonable opportunity to present evidence as to the commercial setting, purpose, and effect of the signature card and the NSF charge in order to determine whether that charge is unconscionable.

\* \* \*

## NOTES

**1.** *Perdue* was trouble for California banks. See Attorney Warns Perdue Case Only First of Upcoming Challenges to Bank Fees, 46 Wash. Fin. Rep. (BNA) No. 15, at 594 (April 14, 1986). Now every deposit account fee charged was open to challenge on whether it was unconscionable. Anecdotal evidence suggests that virtually every bank in California was

account, and may reject any overdraft. A fee reasonable to compensate the merchant for the cost, inconvenience, and risk of an NSF check may be excessive if exacted by a bank.

**14.** The complaint does not state the market price for the service of processing NSF checks, although one might infer it is similar to defendant's price since plaintiff alleges that if he did not contract with defendant, he would be "forced to accept a similar arrangement with other banks." The complaint does not set a figure for the "fair" or "true" value or worth of the service.

subjected to class actions on their service fees. Most of the cases were settled, after presumably enriching counsel on both sides of the suits. The Comptroller of the Currency found this situation intolerable.

**2.**   Since *Perdue*, class actions have burgeoned in consumer cases, and financial institutions have joined with other potential defendants in demanding legislative reform. In 2005 Congress enacted the Class Action Fairness Act of 2005, PL 109–2 (S 5), 119 Stat 4, aimed at curtailing abuses in consumer class actions. Congressional findings were that class members often receive little or no benefit from class actions, as in cases in which counsel are awarded large fees while leaving class members with awards of little or no value. The principal reform offered is to grant federal jurisdiction in class action cases in which the matter in controversy exceeds $5 million and any member of a class of plaintiffs is a citizen of a state different from that of any defendant. The district court may decline jurisdiction in certain cases in which more than one-third but less than two-thirds of the plaintiffs and the primary defendants are citizens of the state where the action was originally filed. The district court must decline jurisdiction if greater than two-thirds of the members of the proposed plaintiff class are citizens of the state where the action was originally filed. The objective is to curtail forum-shopping for courts and jury pools that are known to be overly hospitable to class actions.

## b.   FEDERAL PREEMPTION

In a reaction to *Perdue* and the numerous class actions against banks that it spawned, the Office of the Comptroller of the Currency (OCC) intervened decisively to preempt the area of deposit-related charges. The effect has been to make national banks virtually immune to attacks on the validity of the deposit service charges.

The following provision concerning deposit account service charges for national banks is found in 12 C.F.R. § 7.4002.

(a) *Authority to impose charges and fees.* A national bank may charge its customers non-interest charges and fees, including deposit account service charges.

(b) *Considerations.* (1) All charges and fees should be arrived at by each bank on a competitive basis and not on the basis of any agreement, arrangement, undertaking, understanding, or discussion with other banks or their officers. (2) The establishment of non-interest charges and fees, their amounts, and the method of calculating them are business decisions to be made by each bank, in its discretion, according to sound banking judgment and safe and sound banking principles. A national bank establishes non-interest charges and fees in accordance with safe and sound banking principles if the bank employs a decision-making process through which it considers the following factors, among others:

(1) The cost incurred by the bank in providing the service;

(2) The deterrence of misuse by customers of banking services;

(3) The enhancement of the competitive position of the bank in accordance with the bank's business plan and marketing strategy; and

(4) The maintenance of the safety and soundness of the institution.

(c) *Interest.* Charges and fees that are "interest" within the meaning of 12 U.S.C. 85 are governed by § 7.4001 and not by this section.

(d) *State law.* The OCC applies preemption principles derived from the United States Constitution, as interpreted through judicial precedent, when determining whether State laws apply that purport to limit or prohibit charges and fees described in this section. * * *

PROBLEM

The practice of banks in State A is to impose an additional charge for the use of their ATM machines by non-customers. Two cities in State A passed ordinances prohibiting this practice. National banks in these cities sought to have these ordinances permanently enjoined on the authority of § 7.4002. What result? See Bank of America v. City and County of San Francisco, 309 F.3d 551 (9th Cir. 2002).

In 2004 the OCC issued its boldest and most controversial preemption of state law in 12 C.F.R. § 7.4007 (deposit taking) and § 7.4008 (lending). The latter is set out in part below:

(a) *Authority of national banks.* A national bank may make, sell, purchase, participate in, or otherwise deal in loans that are not secured by liens on, or interest in, real estate, subject to such terms, conditions, and limitations prescribed by the Comptroller of the Currency and other applicable Federal law. * * *

(c) *Unfair and deceptive practices.* A national bank shall not engage in unfair or deceptive practices within the meaning of section 5 of the Federal Trade Commission Act, 15 U.S.C. 45(a)(1), and regulations promulgated thereunder in connection with loans made under this § 7.4008.

(d) *Applicability of state law.* (1) Except where made applicable by Federal law, state laws that obstruct, impair, or condition a national bank's ability to fully exercise its Federally authorized non-real estate lending powers are not applicable to national banks. (2) A national bank may make non-real estate loans without regard to state law limitations concerning:

* * *

(iv) The terms of credit, including the schedule for repayment of principal and interest, amortization of loans, balance, payments due, minimum payments, or term of maturity of the loan, including the circumstances under which a loan may be called due and payable upon the passage of time or a specified event external to the loan;

\* \* \*

(e) *State laws that are not preempted.* State laws on the following subjects are not inconsistent with the deposit-taking powers of national banks and apply to national banks to the extent that they only incidentally affect the exercise of national banks' deposit-taking powers:

(1) Contracts;

(2) Torts;

(3) Criminal law;

(4) Rights to collect debts;

(5) Acquisition and transfer of property;

(6) Taxation;

(7) Zoning; and

(8) Any other law the effect of which the OCC determines to be incidental to the non-real estate lending operations of national banks or otherwise consistent with the powers set out in paragraph (a) of this section.

The difficulties facing courts in interpreting preemption regulations are illustrated by two cases from the same judicial district concerning the same bank and involving identical issues. In Abel v. KeyBank USA, N.A., 313 F. Supp. 2d 720 (N.D. Ohio 2004), a student signed a note payable to a school to evidence his educational loan; the note was assigned to KeyBank; the school closed before the student completed his education. In Blanco v. KeyBank USA, N.A. (2005 WL 4135013) (slip opinion), the school was different but otherwise the facts were the same. In both cases the students relied on the Ohio Retail Installment Sales Act (RISA), which was interpreted to allow the students to raise their defenses under RISA against the bank. In both cases, the bank contended that § 7.4008 preempted RISA. In *Abel* the court held that the regulation preempted RISA because the state law significantly interfered with a national bank's ability to negotiate promissory notes and lend money. The value of such notes in Ohio will likely be worth less than notes issued in states not having RISA and the bank's ability to collect on notes will be impaired. In *Blanco* the court held that RISA had only an incidental effect on the operation of the bank; consumer protection law is traditionally regulated by the states. Section 7.4008 was in effect in both cases and referred to by both courts. Go figure.

Section 7.4007(c) is comparable to § 7.4008(e) in setting out state laws that are not preempted by the two regulations. Do UCC Articles 3 and 4 come within the state laws that are exempt from preemption?

## 4.   ARBITRATION

In *Perdue* bankers saw what they considered to be the perfect storm: a class action with the potential for a jury trial that might result in a large judgment even though members of the plaintiff class suffered what were, at best, only nominal damages. We have seen in this chapter the measures the banking industry has taken to prevent cases like this from occurring in the future. The 2005 federal class action legislation made it possible for banks in large dollar class actions to move such actions out of plaintiff-friendly state jurisdictions into the federal courts. The OCC has been moving to preempt state law with respect to bank fees and, after the amendments of 2004, a whole lot more. But the most effective weapon the banks have deployed is mandatory arbitration with a waiver of class actions and class arbitrations. Arbitration clauses with these waivers are rapidly finding their way into bank-customer agreements with respect to deposit accounts, loans and credit cards. The enforceability and meaning of these clauses are the primary issues today in bank-customer disputes.

*The basics.* The Federal Arbitration Act (FAA), 9 U.S.C. § 1 et seq., applies to both federal and state courts if the contract evidences a transaction involving interstate or foreign commerce and contains an arbitration clause. Southland Corporation v. Keating, 465 U.S. 1 (1984). Hence, the FAA may apply even to cases involving state law claims brought in state courts if the transaction falls within the capacious scope of interstate commerce. Almost all states have enacted arbitration acts that apply to the extent that the FAA is inapplicable, and about half the states have modeled their arbitration acts on the FAA. Section 2 of the FAA states:

> A written provision in any maritime transaction or a contract evidencing a transaction involving commerce to settle by arbitration a controversy thereafter arising out of such contract or transaction, or the refusal to perform the whole or any part thereof, or an agreement in writing to submit to arbitration an existing controversy arising out of such a contract, transaction, or refusal, shall be valid, irrevocable, and enforceable, save upon such grounds as exist at law or in equity for the revocation of any contract.

Thus, in order to deal with the traditional hostility of courts toward arbitration as a method of dispute resolution, Congress saw fit to federalize arbitration procedure and availability by enacting the FAA, which applies to cases in which there is an agreement in writing to arbitrate controversies arising out of contracts involving interstate commerce. Arbitration clauses commonly expressly state that they are governed by the FAA. Under sections 3 and 4, a court may stay a proceeding on any issue referable to arbitration until the arbitration has been had; a party aggrieved by the failure of another party to arbitrate may seek an order directing that arbitration proceed. Congress saw many benefits in arbitration. In H.R.Rep. No. 97–542, p. 13 (1982) it said: "The advantages of arbitration are many: it is usually cheaper and faster than litigation; it can have simpler procedural and evidentiary rules; it normally minimizes hostility and is less disruptive of ongoing and future business dealings among the parties; it is often more flexible in regard to scheduling of times and places of hearings and discovery devices * * *."

The Supreme Court has strongly supported arbitration. In Green Tree Financial Corp. v. Randolph, 531 U.S. 79 (2000), the contract provided that all disputes arising from or relating to the contract would be resolved by binding arbitration. In enlarged type the contract said: "The parties voluntarily and knowingly waive any right they have to a jury trial either pursuant to arbitration under this clause or pursuant to a court action by assignee (as provided herein)." 531 U.S. at 83, fn 1. The Court upheld Green Tree's motion to compel arbitration and said: "[W]e are mindful of the Federal Arbitration Act's purpose 'to reverse the longstanding judicial hostility to arbitration agreements . . . and to place arbitration agreements upon the same footing as other contracts.' In the light of that purpose, we have recognized that federal statutory claims can be appropriately resolved through arbitration, and we have enforced agreements to arbitrate that involved such claims. * * * We have likewise rejected generalized attacks on arbitration that rest on 'suspicion of arbitration as a method of weakening the protection afforded in the substantive law to would-be complainants.' * * * In determining whether statutory claims may be arbitrated, we first ask whether the parties agreed to submit their claims to arbitration, and then ask whether Congress has evinced an intention to preclude a waiver of judicial remedies for the statutory rights at issue." 531 U.S. at 89–90. Courts agree that disputes may be arbitrated "so long as the prospective litigant effectively may vindicate [his or her] statutory cause of action in the arbitral forum." 531 U.S. 90.

*Defenses to Arbitration.* Section 2 of the Act provides that an agreement to arbitrate made pursuant to that section "shall be valid, irrevocable, and enforceable, save upon such grounds as exist at law or in equity for the revocation of any contract." Generally applicable contract defenses such as fraud, duress or undue influence may be raised to invalidate an arbitration clause under this language. The accepted view is that this language also includes unconscionability. See Doctor's Associates, Inc. v. Casarotto, 517 U.S. 681, 682 (1996) ("[g]enerally applicable contract defenses, such as fraud, duress or unconscionability, may be applied to invalidate arbitration agreements without contravening § 2.") Proof of unconscionability focuses on the existence of both procedural and substantive unconscionability. Procedural unconscionability examines the manner in which the contract was negotiated and the circumstances of the parties: inequality of bargaining power, lack of disclosure, such as a clause hidden in boiler-plate contract, coercion on part of stronger party. Substantive unconscionability centers on whether the terms of the agreement are so one-sided as to shock the conscience.

Courts have divided over the unconscionability of arbitration clauses and there is no overriding trend in the recent case law. Cases finding arbitration clauses not unconscionable generally follow the reasoning at work in Hutcherson v. Sears Roebuck & Company, 342 Ill.App.3d 109 (Ill. App. 2003). In that case the court held that there was no procedural unconscionability because there was a clearly stated, conspicuous arbitration clause that gave the debtor the right to opt out if it did not agree to arbitration. Substantive unconscionability was absent because the court found no unfairness in the agreement and, moreover, federal policy strongly favors enforcement of arbitration provisions, even at the cost of the debtor's waiving her right to a class action.

Other courts have refused to enforce arbitration agreements on unconscionability grounds, citing the inequality of bargaining power and the take-it-or-leave-it basis on which arbitration clauses are offered as proof of procedural unconscionability. The wholly one-sided terms of arbitration agreements are relied on as showing substantive unconscionability. Ingle v. Circuit City Stores, Inc., 328 F.3d 1165 (9th Cir. 2003), forcefully presents this view.

*Waiver of Class Actions and Arbitrations.* In recent years, bank-customer arbitration agreements typically include waivers of class actions. Since under a valid arbitration agreement no action can be sustained, these clauses also include a bar against class arbitrations. A currently used clause provides:

> If either party elects to resolve a Claim by arbitration, that Claim shall be arbitrated on an individual basis. There shall be no right or authority for any Claims to be arbitrated on a class action basis or on bases involving Claims brought in a purported representative capacity on behalf of the general public, other Cardmembers or other persons similarly situated.

Customers who object to these waiver clauses usually do so on two grounds: (i) the inability to bring claims in a class action makes it infeasible to raise these claims because lawyers will not represent customers on an individual basis for small claims; and (ii) such a waiver is unconscionable under applicable state law. According to Alan S. Kaplinsky and Mark J. Levin, Consensus or Conflict? Most (But Not All) Courts Enforce Express Class Action Waivers in Consumer Arbitration Agreements, 60 Bus. Law. 775 (2005), a majority of courts have enforced clauses waiving class actions and arbitrations. The Supreme Court has not passed on the issue. The following opinion is a strong holding that a waiver of class arbitrations may be unenforceable as unconscionable.

## Muhammad v. County Bank of Rehoboth Beach, Delaware

Supreme Court of New Jersey, 2006.
2006 WL 2273448.

■ JUSTICE LaVECCHIA delivered the opinion of the Court.

In this appeal we must determine whether a provision in an arbitration agreement that is part of a consumer contract of adhesion is unconscionable and therefore unenforceable because it forbids class-wide arbitration. Plaintiff entered into a short-term loan agreement, the terms of which she claims violate the State's consumer-fraud statutes. Her complaint includes allegations that the State's civil usury limits are being evaded in loan transactions such as hers by means of a conspiracy involving complex financial dealings among out-of-state financial entities. The damages allegedly caused by such transactions are small on an individual-by-individual basis, but are substantial when aggregated into a class claim. Plaintiff seeks, therefore, to pursue a class action and is willing to pursue her class-wide claim in the arbitral forum but for the arbitration agreement's class-arbitration bar. Both the trial court and the Appellate Division found the class-arbitration bar enforceable.

Applying the controlling test for determining unconscionability for contracts of adhesion set forth in *Rudbart v. North Jersey District Water Supply Commission*,127 N.J.344, 605 A.2d 681 (N.J. 1992), we hold that the class-arbitration waiver in this consumer contract is unenforceable. Such a waiver would be unconscionable whether applied in a lawsuit or in arbitration. We further conclude that the appropriate remedy in these circumstances is to sever the unconscionable provision and enforce the otherwise valid arbitration agreement.

## I.

Defendant County Bank of Rehoboth Beach, Delaware (County Bank) is a federally-insured depository institution chartered under Delaware law. Defendant Main Street Service Corp. (Main Street) is a loan servicer for County Bank. Main Street operates a telephone service center in Pennsylvania. Defendants Easy Cash and Telecash are registered trade names of County Bank.

On May 23, 2003, plaintiff Jaliyah Muhammad, a part-time student at Berkeley College in Paramus, received a short-term, single advance, unsecured loan of $200 from County Bank. According to the terms of the LOAN NOTE AND DISCLOSURE form that Muhammad signed, the principal, along with a finance charge of sixty dollars, was due on June 13, 2003. The annual percentage rate listed on the loan note was 608.33%. According to Muhammad, she twice extended the loan (with a sixty dollar finance charge each time) because she could not repay it, resulting in a total of $180 in finance charges. Those facts are unchallenged by defendants. Muhammad also obtained two similar loans from County Bank, dated April 28, 2003 and June 6, 2003.

Muhammad had to complete and return three pages of standard form contracts in order to receive a loan. The first two pages, entitled "LOAN APPLICATION," were signed by Muhammad on April 28, 2003. Muhammad did not have to complete that form again in connection with the loans made on May 23, 2003 and June 6, 2003. The first page of the LOAN APPLICATION requested general personal information. The second page contained the relevant provisions concerning arbitration:

> AGREEMENT TO ARBITRATE ALL DISPUTES: By signing below and to induce us, County Bank of Rehoboth Beach, Delaware, to process your application for a loan, you and we agree that any and all claims, disputes or controversies that we or our servicers or agents have against you or that you have against us, our servicers, agents, directors, officers and employees, that arise out of your application for

a loan, the Loan Note or Agreement that you must sign to obtain the loan, this agreement to arbitrate all disputes, collection of the loan, or alleging fraud or misrepresentation, whether under the common law or pursuant to federal or state statute or regulation, including the matters subject to arbitration, *or otherwise, shall be resolved by binding individual (and not class) arbitration* by and under the Code of Procedures of the National Arbitration Forum ("NAF") in effect at the time the claim is filed. This agreement to arbitrate all disputes shall apply no matter by whom or against whom the claim is filed. . . .

NOTICE: YOU AND WE WOULD HAVE HAD A RIGHT OR OPPORTUNITY TO LITIGATE DISPUTES THROUGH A COURT AND HAVE A JUDGE OR JURY DECIDE THE DISPUTES BUT HAVE AGREED INSTEAD TO RESOLVE DISPUTES THROUGH BINDING ARBITRATION.

AGREEMENT NOT TO BRING, JOIN OR PARTICIPATE IN CLASS ACTIONS: To the extent permitted by law, by signing below you agree that you will not bring, join or participate in any class action as to any claim, dispute or controversy you may have against us or our agents, servicers, directors, officers and employees. You agree to the entry of injunctive relief to stop such a lawsuit or to remove you as a participant in the suit. You agree to pay the costs we incur, including our court costs and attorney's fees, in seeking such relief. This agreement is not a waiver of any of your rights and remedies to pursue a claim individually and not as a class action in binding arbitration as provided above. This agreement not to bring or participate in class action suits is an independent agreement and shall survive the closing and repayment of the loan for which you are applying. (Emphasis added).

Above the signature line, the LOAN APPLICATION also stated that "[b]y signing below you also agree to the Agreement to Arbitrate All Disputes and the Agreement Not To Bring, Join or Participate In Class Actions. . . ."

In respect of the May 23, 2003 loan, Muhammad also executed a LOAN NOTE AND DISCLOSURE form that included the following language.

*AGREEMENT TO ARBITRATE ALL DISPUTES:* You and we agree that any and all claims, disputes or controversies between you and us and/or the Company, any claim by either of us against the other or the Company (or the employees, officers, directors, agents or assigns of the other or the Company) and any claim arising from or relating to your application for this loan or any other loan you previously, now or may later obtain from us, this Loan Note, this agreement to arbitrate all disputes, your agreement not to bring, join or participate in class actions, regarding collection of the loan, alleging fraud or misrepresentation, whether under the common law or pursuant to federal, state or local statutes, regulation or ordinance, including disputes as to the matters subject to arbitration, or otherwise, *shall be resolved by binding individual (and not joint) arbitration* by and under the Code of Procedure of the National Arbitration Forum ("NAF") in effect at the time the claim is filed. This agreement to arbitrate all disputes shall apply no matter by whom or against whom the claim is filed.... This arbitration agreement is made pursuant to a transaction involving interstate commerce. It shall be governed by the Federal Arbitration Act, 9 U.S.C. Sections 1–16....

NOTICE: YOU AND WE WOULD HAVE HAD A RIGHT OR OPPORTUNITY TO LITIGATE DISPUTES THROUGH A COURT AND HAVE A JUDGE OR JURY DECIDE THE DISPUTES BUT HAVE AGREED INSTEAD TO RESOLVE DISPUTES THROUGH BINDING ARBITRATION.

*AGREEMENT NOT TO BRING, JOIN OR PARTICIPATE IN CLASS ACTIONS:* To the extent permitted by law, you agree that you will not bring, join or participate in any class action as to any claim, dispute or controversy you may have against us, our employees, officers, directors, servicers and assigns. You agree to the entry of injunctive relief to stop such a lawsuit or to remove you as a participant in the suit. You agree to pay the attorney's fees and court costs we incur in seeking such relief. This Agreement does not constitute a waiver of any of your rights and remedies to pursue a claim individually and not as a class action in binding arbitration as provided above. (Emphasis added).

If that were not clear enough, directly above the signature line, the LOAN NOTE AND DISCLOSURE form also stated, that "BY SIGNING BELOW, YOU AGREE TO ALL OF THE TERMS OF THIS NOTE, INCLUDING THE AGREEMENT TO ARBITRATE ALL DISPUTES AND THE AGREEMENT NOT TO BRING, JOIN OR PARTICIPATE IN CLASS ACTIONS."

Thus, the contracts signed by Muhammad contain two types of class-action prohibitions. The first, referred to herein as the "class-arbitration waivers," are found within the text of the arbitration clauses and highlighted above. They specifically bar class claims in arbitration. The second, referred to herein as the "broad class-action waivers," are separate from the arbitration clauses and prohibit Muhammad from bringing or participating in class-action suits brought in court as well as class claims brought in arbitration.

In February 2004, Muhammad filed a putative class-action suit in New Jersey Superior Court against County Bank, Easy Cash, Telecash, Main Street, John Doe, and John Roe. The complaint alleged that Easy Cash, Telecash, and Main Street violated the Consumer Fraud Act (CFA), N.J.S.A. 56:8–2, the civil usury statute, N.J.S.A. 31:1–1, and the New Jersey RICO statute, N.J.S.A. 2C:41–1, by charging, and conspiring to charge, illegal rates of interest. The complaint further alleged that County Bank aided and abetted the unlawful conduct of the other defendants by renting out its name and status without actually funding or meaningfully participating in the loans. Muhammad requested injunctive relief, restitution, damages, penalties, and costs.

Defendants removed the action to federal district court, but because Muhammad's claims were determined by that court not to be preempted by the Depository Institutions Deregulation and Monetary Control Act of 1980, 12 *U.S.C.* § 1831d, the case was remanded to state court. Defendants thereupon filed a motion to compel arbitration and to stay the action pending arbitration. They also filed a motion requesting a protective order in respect of discovery. Muhammad opposed defendants' motions and filed a cross-motion concerning discovery. Muhammad argued that the arbitration agreement was unconscionable based on the class-action waiver, discovery limitations in NAF's rules, the costs of the arbitration, and the bias inherent in NAF as an arbitration forum.[1] In response, defendants offered to arbitrate Muhammad's claims in the American Arbitration Association rather than the NAF—an offer that Muhammad rejected.

The trial court granted defendants' motion to compel arbitration pursuant to the Federal Arbitration Act (FAA), 9 *U.S.C.* § 4, and stayed the case pending arbitration. Muhammad filed a motion for leave to appeal, which was granted. In a published decision, the Appellate Division affirmed the trial court. *Muhammad v. County Bank of Rehoboth Beach*, 379 N.J.Super. 222, 877 A.2d 340 (App.Div.2005). Applying *Rudbart, supra*, 605 A.2d 681, the panel concluded that the arbitration agreement was not unconscionable. *Muhammad, supra*, 379 N.J.Super. at 237–48, 877 A.2d 340. In upholding the class-arbitration bar specifically, the Appellate Division relied on its earlier decision in *Gras v. Associates First Capital Corp.*, 786 A.2d 886 (2001), *certif. denied*, 171 N.J. 445, 794 A.2d 184 (2002), which, the panel believed, "directly address[ed]" the class-action waiver issue. *Muhammad, supra*, 379 N.J.Super. at 244–48, 877 A.2d 340. Judge Kestin filed a separate concurring opinion. *Id.* at 249, 877 A.2d 340.

Plaintiff filed a motion for leave to appeal, which we granted. 185 N.J. 254 (2005). Legal Services of New Jersey filed a brief as amicus curiae in support of Muhammad. AARP, the Consumers League of New Jersey, and the National Association of Consumer Advocates filed a joint brief in support of Muhammad. Also, the Attorney General on behalf of the New Jersey Division of Consumer Affairs filed a brief in Muhammad's support. The Chamber of Commerce of the United States of America and the New Jersey Business and Industry Association filed amicus briefs in support of defendants.

## II.

### A.

\* \* \*

---

**1.** If the parties fail to agree on discovery matters, *NAF Rule* 29C allows mandatory discovery where the "cost [of discovery] is commensurate with the amount of the Claim." Muhammad contends that because her damages are only $180, limiting discovery to that amount, in the context of a complex claim, precludes her from obtaining relief.

Because federal arbitration law does not prevent us from examining the validity of the class-arbitration waiver, we turn then to our own state law requirements in respect of contract unconscionability.[2]

## B.

It is well settled that courts "may refuse to enforce contracts that are unconscionable." *Saxon Constr. & Management Corp. v. Masterclean of N.C., Inc.*, 273 N.J.Super. 231, 236, 641 A.2d 1056 (App.Div.1994); *see also N.J.S.A.* 12A:2–302 (adopting Uniform Commercial Code provision recognizing unconscionability as basis for voiding contract or clause therein). The seminal case of *Rudbart, supra*, set out factors for courts to consider when determining whether a specific term in a contract of adhesion is unconscionable and unenforceable. 127 N.J. at 356, 605 A.2d 681. In *Rudbart, supra*, this Court recognized that adhesion agreements necessarily involve indicia of procedural unconscionability. *Ibid.; see generally Sitogum Holdings, Inc. v. Ropes*, 352 N.J.Super. 555, 564–66, 800 A.2d 915 (Ch.Div. 2002) (observing that unconscionability traditionally entails discussion of two factors: procedural unconscionability, which "can include a variety of inadequacies, such as age, literacy, lack of sophistication, hidden or unduly complex contract terms, bargaining tactics, and the particular setting existing during the contract formation process," and substantive unconscionability, which generally involves harsh or unfair one-sided terms). *Rudbart, supra*, notes that "the essential nature of a contract of adhesion is that it is presented on a take-it-or-leave-it basis, commonly in a standardized printed form, without opportunity for the 'adhering' party to negotiate except perhaps on a few particulars." 127 N.J. at 353, 605 A.2d 681.

The determination that a contract is one of adhesion, however, "is the beginning, not the end, of the inquiry" into whether a contract, or any specific term therein, should be deemed unenforceable based on policy considerations. *Id.* at 354, 605 A.2d 681. A sharpened inquiry concerning unconscionability is necessary when a contract of adhesion is involved.

> [I]n determining whether to enforce the terms of a contract of adhesion, courts have looked not only to the take-it-or-leave-it nature or the standardized form of the document but also to [(1)] the subject matter of the contract, [(2)] the parties' relative bargaining positions, [(3)] the degree of economic compulsion motivating the "adhering" party, and [(4)] the public interests affected by the contract.

[*Id.* at 356, 605 A.2d 681.]

Because adhesion contracts invariably evidence some characteristics of procedural unconscionability, the Court required a careful fact-sensitive

---

**2.** The Appellate Division concluded that defendants had waived any argument that Delaware law should be applied (based on a choice of law clause in the contract). The panel found the issue to have been waived because it was not raised before the trial court and was raised only in a footnote in defendants' Appellate Division brief. *Muhammad, supra*, 379 N.J.Super. at 234 n. 3, 877 A.2d 340. Defendants did not seek review of the Appellate Division's determination of that issue.

examination into substantive unconscionability.[3] *Ibid. Rudbart's* multi-factor analysis generally conforms to the case-by-case approach widely used for evaluating claims of unconscionability. . . .

### C.

The unconscionability issue in this matter centers on access to a class-wide proceeding in the arbitral setting. Although class arbitration specifically has never before been examined by this Court, the merits of the class-action procedure have been acknowledged many times in the context of court litigation. "By permitting claimants to band together, class actions equalize adversaries and provide a procedure to remedy a wrong that might other-wise go unredressed." *In re Cadillac V8–6–4 Class Action*, 93 N.J. 412, 424, 461 A.2d 736 (1983). "If each victim were remitted to an individual suit, the remedy could be illusory, for the individual loss may be too small to warrant a suit. . . . Thus the wrongs would go without redress, and there would be no deterrence to further aggressions." *Riley v. New Rapids Carpet Ctr.*, 61 N.J. 218, 225, 294 A.2d 7 (1972). Other courts have referred to such small damage cases as "negative value" suits recognizing that they "would be uneconomical to litigate individually." *In re Monumental Life Ins. Co.*, 365 F.3d 408, 411 n. 1 (5th Cir.2004).

The class-action vehicle remedies the incentive problem facing litigants who seek only a small recovery. "[A] class action can produce a substantial fund to compensate . . . [the class members'] attorney for his services." *In re Cadillac, supra*, 93 N.J. at 424, 461 A.2d 736. A "substantial fund" not only covers the attorney's actual fees, but also provides incentive in the form of possible contingency fees for attorneys to risk the prospect of receiving no recovery for their efforts. *See Amchem Products, Inc. v. Windsor*, 521 U.S. 591, 617 (1997) (stating that "[a] class action solves [the incentive problem created by small damages] by aggregating the relatively paltry potential recoveries into something worth someone's (usually an attorney's) labor."); *Eisen v. Carlisle & Jacquelin*, 417 U.S. 156, 161 (1974) (stating that "[n]o competent attorney would undertake this complex antitrust action to recover so inconsequential an amount [as $70]."). The class-action mechanism also overcomes the problem that small individual recoveries may fail to provide an adequate incentive for a litigant to investigate a claim or bring suit even if the litigant could secure representation. *See Varacallo v. Mass. Mutual Life Ins. Co.*, 226 F.R.D. 207, 234 (D.N.J.2005) (stating that "[a]bsent class certification, very few individuals would have the incentive . . . to bring individual claims"). And, not least of all, there is the additional justification that a class-action proceeding "can

---

**3.** This is not to say that when a contract of adhesion involves overwhelming procedural unconscionability, that those procedural factors are not included and weighed in the overall analysis for unconscionability. *See, e.g., Discover Bank, supra*, 36 Cal.4th 148, 30 Cal.Rptr.3d 76, 113 P.3d 1100 (finding gross unfairness in contract formation when bill stuffer contained adhesion con-tract's terms). In that circumstance a "sliding scale" analysis may be appropriate. *See Sitogum Holdings Inc., supra*, 352 N.J.Super. at 565–66, 800 A.2d 915 (noting that courts have employed a "sliding scale" analysis when considering, in tandem, the two factors of procedural and substantive unconscionability).

aid the efficient administration of justice by avoiding the expense, in both time and money, of relitigating similar claims." *In re Cadillac, supra*, 93 N.J. at 435, 461 A.2d 736.

In sum, the class-action mechanism is recognized to be valuable to litigants, to the courts, and to the public interest. Class actions fulfill the policies of this State even when only a small amount of damages is at stake. Not surprisingly, in light of the importance of its role generally, and specifically in recognition of its usefulness in connection with small-damages actions such as are often the case in consumer suits, this Court has instructed that "the class action rule should be construed liberally in a case involving allegations of consumer fraud." *Ibid.; see also Strawn v. Canuso*, 140 N.J. 43, 68, 657 A.2d 420 (1995) (stating that "a class action is the superior method for adjudication of consumer-fraud claims"); *Riley, supra*, 61 N.J. at 228, 294 A.2d 7 (stating that "a court should be slow to hold that a suit [under the CFA] may not proceed as a class action."). With those justifications for the class-action vehicle in mind we turn to consider the unconscionability of the contractual waiver of class-wide arbitration before us.

### III.

#### A.

The arbitration agreement signed by Muhammad is clearly a contract of adhesion. We, therefore, must apply *Rudbart's* four factors, as did the Appellate Division, in order to determine whether New Jersey contract law principles permit enforcement of the class-arbitration prohibitions found in the instant arbitration agreements.

The first three factors of the *Rudbart* analysis require only brief attention. In respect of subject matter, the circumstantial backdrop to our *Rudbart* inquiry is the payday loan agreement executed between the parties. The focus of our analysis, however, is on the agreement's mandatory arbitration provision that contains limits on discovery and bars class-wide arbitration. In respect of *Rudbart's* second factor, the gross disparity in the relative bargaining positions of the parties is self-evident from the nature of the payday loan contract between a consumer and a financial entity.[4] We add only that the contract Muhammad entered into is, in its most general sense, a consumer contract. Although those facts, in addition to our finding that the contract is one of adhesion, indicate a degree of procedural unconscionability in Muhammad's contract, they are insufficient to render the contract unenforceable. That said, adhesive consumer contracts, which are ordinarily enforceable, nonetheless may rise to the level of unconscionability when substantive contractual terms and conditions impact "public interests" adversely.

---

**4.** The third *Rudbart* factor addresses the degree of economic compulsion motivating the "adhering" party. In respect of that factor we note only that payday loans may be necessities for persons who need access to cash and who may have credit difficulty, compelling their acquiescence to loans bearing exorbitant interest rates. Muhammad seeks to represent a class of people who, like herself, are under an allegedly high degree of economic compulsion to enter into such loan contracts.

*Rudbart's* fourth factor, the most important to the present analysis, considers "the public interests affected by the contract." That factor requires us to determine whether the effect of the class-arbitration bar is to prevent plaintiff from pursuing her statutory consumer protection rights and thus to shield defendants from compliance with the laws of this State. Those "public interest" considerations ultimately determine whether we can permit enforcement of the provision in plaintiff's contract that allegedly precludes any realistic challenge to the substance of her loan-contract's terms.

In New Jersey, exculpatory waivers that seek a release from a statutorily imposed duty are void as against public policy. *McCarthy v. NASCAR, Inc.*, 48 N.J. 539, 542, 226 A.2d 713 (1967). Muhammad's claims are statutory; however, the class-arbitration waiver at issue, and class-action waivers in general, are not, in the strictest sense of the term, exculpatory clauses. *See Discover Bank, supra*, 30 Cal.Rptr.3d 76, 113 P.3d at 1108. The class-arbitration waiver does not preclude Muhammad from filing an individual claim in arbitration. The difficulty lies in the fact that her individual consumer-fraud case involves a small amount of damages, rendering individual enforcement of her rights, and the rights of her fellow consumers, difficult if not impossible. In such circumstances a class-action waiver can act effectively as an exculpatory clause.

> To permit the defendants to contest liability with each claimant in a single, separate suit, would, in many cases give defendants an advantage which would be almost equivalent to closing the door of justice to all small claimants. This is what we think the class suit practice was to prevent.
>
> [*Delgazzo v. Kenny*, 266 N.J.Super. 169, 193, 628 A.2d 1080 (App.Div.1993) (quoting *Hohmann v. Packard Instrument Co.*, 399 F.2d 711, 715 (7th Cir.1968)).]

Such waivers are problematic "when the waiver is found in a consumer contract of adhesion in a setting in which disputes between the contracting parties *predictably* involve small amounts of damages," as the California Supreme Court also recognized. *Discover Bank, supra*, 30 Cal.Rptr.3d 76, 113 P.3d at 1110 (emphasis added).

In most cases that involve a small amount of damages, "rational" consumers may decline to pursue individual consumer-fraud lawsuits because it may not be worth the time spent prosecuting the suit, even if competent counsel was willing to take the case. *See Kinkel v. Cingular Wireless, LLC*, 357 Ill.App.3d 556, 564, 293 Ill.Dec. 502 (Ill.App.Ct.) (observing that in context of individually pursued small damage claims, any potential recovery would be offset "by any costs incurred in presenting the claim and any lost wages for taking time from work to do so."), *appeal granted*, 216 Ill.2d 690, 298 Ill.Dec. 378, 839 N.E.2d 1025 (Ill.2005); *see also Carnegie v. Household Int'l, Inc.*, 376 F.3d 656, 661 (7th Cir.2004) (commenting that "only a lunatic or a fanatic sues for $30." ). Moreover, without the availability of a class-action mechanism, many consumer-fraud victims may never realize that they may have been wronged. As commentators have noted, often consumers do not know that a potential defendant's conduct is illegal. When they are being charged an excessive interest rate or a penalty for check bouncing, for example, few know or even sense that their rights are being violated. Nor, given the relatively small amounts at stake, would most consumers find it worthwhile to seek legal advice to determine whether this is the case.

[Jean R. Sternlight and Elizabeth J. Jensen, *Mandatory Arbitration: Using Arbitration to Eliminate Consumer Class Actions: Efficient Business Practice or Unconscionable Abuse*, 67 *Law & Contemp. Prob.* 75, 88 (2004).]

In addition to their impact on individual litigants, class-action waivers can functionally exculpate wrongful conduct by reducing the possibility of attracting competent counsel to advance the cause of action. Class-action waivers prevent an aggregate recovery that can serve as a source of contingency fees for potential attorneys. Although defendants have no obligation to provide counsel to plaintiff, they cannot take action that impedes ordinary citizens' access to representation to vindicate their rights. Defendants emphasize the availability of attorney's fees under the CFA; however, that fact is not dispositive in the instant case because the damages sought by Muhammad and those she seeks to represent are small. The availability of attorney's fees is illusory if it is unlikely that counsel would be willing to undertake the representation. The finance charge for the loan in this matter was $60. The class of people whom plaintiff seeks to represent may have similar claims about that size. In fact, plaintiff had to roll-over her loan two times, bringing her compensatory claims to $180 that, with the possibility of treble damages available under CFA, may add up to a maximum of less than $600. One may be hard-pressed to find an attorney willing to work on a consumer-fraud complaint involving complex arrangements between financial institutions of other jurisdictions when the recovery is so small. It cannot be that class-action waivers are less objectionable when a plaintiff is suing under a statute that *fails* to provide for attorney's fees (and damages multipliers). Such a perverse result would encourage under-enforcement of the very statutes that the Legislature has signaled as warranting strenuous enforcement.

We hold, therefore, that the presence of the class-arbitration waiver in Muhammad's consumer arbitration agreement renders that agreement unconscionable. As a matter of generally applicable state contract law, it was unconscionable for defendants to deprive Muhammad of the mechanism of a class-wide action, whether in arbitration or in court litigation. The public interest at stake in her ability and the ability of her fellow consumers effectively to pursue their statutory rights under this State's consumer protection laws overrides the defendants' right to seek enforcement of the class-arbitration bar in their agreement . . .

\* \* \*

## C.

Finally, although we find that the class-arbitration waivers in Muhammad's arbitration agreements are unconscionable and unenforceable, we find that the waivers are severable. Once the waivers are removed, the remainder of the arbitration agreement is enforceable . . .

### IV.

The judgment of the Appellate Division is reversed and the matter is remanded to the Law Division for further proceedings consistent with this opinion.

CHIEF JUSTICE PORITZ and JUSTICES LONG, ZAZZALI, and WALLACE join in JUSTICE LAVECCHIA's opinion. JUSTICE RIVERA-SOTO filed a separate opinion concurring in part and dissenting in part. JUSTICE ALBIN did not participate.

[JUSTICE RIVERA-SOTO's opinion is omitted.]

### NOTE

In California, the history of Discover Bank v. Superior Court, 113 P.3d 1100 (Cal. 2005), shows the way for creditors to avoid having their waiver clauses rejected even in those states holding such clauses unconscionable. In that case, the supreme court, in a 4 to 3 decision, reversed the appellate court and held the clause forbidding class-wide arbitration to be unconscionable, but, since the agreement had a Delaware choice-of-law provision, remanded the case to the appellate court to decide the choice-of-law issue. That court rapidly decided that enforceability of the waiver clause must be governed by Delaware law, under which such waiver clauses are upheld. Discover Bank v. Superior Court, 36 Cal.Rptr.3d 456 (Cal. App. 2005). In footnote 2 of *Muhammad*, the court states that there was a Delaware choice-of-law provision but that the Appellate Division concluded that Defendants had waived the issue because it was not raised before the trial court; Defendants did not seek review of issue.

*Separability*. Assume Lender moved to compel arbitration of a dispute arising out of a loan agreement with Debtor that contained an arbitration clause. Debtor opposed the motion by contending that she had been fraudulently induced to enter into the loan agreement by Lender's false representations, and, since the arbitration clause was a part of the fraudulently induced loan agreement, it should be unenforceable along with the remainder of the agreement; thus, the enforceability of the contract should be determined by a court rather than by an arbitrator. Or, suppose, as in the following case, the agreement containing the arbitration clause was void under state law; how could an arbitration clause in the agreement be enforceable if the agreement were void?

## Buckeye Check Cashing, Inc. v. Cardegna

Supreme Court of the United States, 2006.
126 S.Ct. 1204.

■ SCALIA, J., delivered the opinion of the Court, in which ROBERTS, C. J., and STEVENS, KENNEDY, SOUTER, GINSBURG, and BREYER, JJ., joined. THOMAS, J., filed a dissenting opinion. ALITO, J., took no part in the consideration or decision of the case.

■ JUSTICE SCALIA delivered the opinion of the Court.

We decide whether a court or an arbitrator should consider the claim that a contract containing an arbitration provision is void for illegality.

I

Respondents John Cardegna and Donna Reuter entered into various deferred-payment transactions with petitioner Buckeye Check Cashing (Buckeye), in which they received cash in exchange for a personal check in the amount of the cash plus a finance charge. For each separate transaction they signed a "Deferred Deposit and Disclosure Agreement" (Agreement), which included the following arbitration provisions:

> "1. *Arbitration Disclosure.* By signing this Agreement, you agree that i[f] a dispute of any kind arises out of this Agreement or your application therefore or any instrument relating thereto, th[e]n either you or we or third-parties involved can choose to have that dispute resolved by binding arbitration as set forth in Paragraph 2 below....
>
> 2. *Arbitration Provisions.* Any claim, dispute, or controversy ... arising from or relating to this Agreement ... or the validity, enforceability, or scope of this Arbitration Provision or the entire Agreement (collectively 'Claim'), shall be resolved, upon the election of you or us or said third-parties, by binding arbitration.... This arbitration Agreement is made pursuant to a transaction involving interstate commerce, and shall be governed by the Federal Arbitration Act ('FAA'), 9 U.S.C. Sections 1–16. The arbitrator shall apply applicable substantive law constraint *[sic]* with the FAA and applicable statu[t]es of limitations and shall honor claims of privilege recognized by law...."

Respondents brought this putative class action in Florida state court, alleging that Buckeye charged usurious interest rates and that the Agreement violated various Florida lending and consumer-protection laws, rendering it criminal on its face. Buckeye moved to compel arbitration. The trial court denied the motion, holding that a court rather than an arbitrator should resolve a claim that a contract is illegal and void *ab initio*. The District Court of Appeal of Florida for the Fourth District reversed, holding that because respondents did not challenge the arbitration provision itself, but instead claimed that the entire contract was void, the agreement to arbitrate was enforceable, and the question of the contract's legality should go to the arbitrator.

Respondents appealed, and the Florida Supreme Court reversed, reasoning that to enforce an agreement to arbitrate in a contract challenged as unlawful " 'could breathe life into a contract that not only violates state law, but also is criminal in nature....' " 894 So.2d 860, 862 (2005) (quoting *Party Yards, Inc. v. Templeton,* 751 So.2d 121, 123 (Fla.App. 2000)). We granted certiorari. 545 U.S. 1127, 125 S.Ct. 2937, 162 L.Ed.2d 864 (2005).

## II

### A

To overcome judicial resistance to arbitration, Congress enacted the Federal Arbitration Act (FAA), 9 U.S.C. §§ 1–16. Section 2 embodies the national policy favoring arbitration and places arbitration agreements on equal footing with all other contracts:

"A written provision in ... a contract ... to settle by arbitration a controversy thereafter arising out of such contract ... or an agreement in writing to submit to arbitration an existing controversy arising out of such a contract ... shall be valid, irrevocable, and enforceable, save upon such grounds as exist at law or in equity for the revocation of any contract."

Challenges to the validity of arbitration agreements "upon such grounds as exist at law or in equity for the revocation of any contract" can be divided into two types. One type challenges specifically the validity of the agreement to arbitrate. See, *e.g., Southland Corp. v. Keating*, 465 U.S. 1, 4–5, 104 S.Ct. 852, 79 L.Ed.2d 1 (1984) (challenging the agreement to arbitrate as void under California law insofar as it purported to cover claims brought under the state Franchise Investment Law). The other challenges the contract as a whole, either on a ground that directly affects the entire agreement (*e.g.*, the agreement was fraudulently induced), or on the ground that the illegality of one of the contract's provisions renders the whole contract invalid.[1] Respondents' claim is of this second type. The crux of the complaint is that the contract as a whole (including its arbitration provision) is rendered invalid by the usurious finance charge.

In *Prima Paint Corp. v. Flood & Conklin Mfg. Co.*, 388 U.S. 395, 87 S.Ct. 1801, 18 L.Ed.2d 1270 (1967), we addressed the question of who-court or arbitrator-decides these two types of challenges. The issue in the case was "whether a claim of fraud in the inducement of the entire contract is to be resolved by the federal court, or whether the matter is to be referred to the arbitrators." *Id.*, at 402, 87 S.Ct. 1801. Guided by § 4 of the FAA,[2] we held that "if the claim is fraud in the inducement of the arbitration

---

**1.** The issue of the contract's validity is different from the issue of whether any agreement between the alleged obligor and obligee was ever concluded. Our opinion today addresses only the former, and does not speak to the issue decided in the cases cited by respondents (and by the Florida Supreme Court), which hold that it is for courts to decide whether the alleged obligor ever signed the contract, *Chastain v. Robinson–Humphrey Co.*, 957 F.2d 851 (C.A.11 1992), whether the signor lacked authority to commit the alleged principal, *Sandvik AB v. Advent Int'l Corp.*, 220 F.3d 99 (C.A.3 2000); *Sphere Drake Ins. Ltd. v. All American Ins. Co.*, 256 F.3d 587 (C.A.7 2001), and whether the signor lacked the mental capacity to as-

sent, *Spahr v. Secco*, 330 F.3d 1266 (C.A.10 2003).

**2.** In pertinent part, § 4 reads:

"A party aggrieved by the alleged failure, neglect, or refusal of another to arbitrate under a written agreement for arbitration may petition any United States district court [with jurisdiction] ... for an order directing that such arbitration proceed in a manner provided for in such agreement.... [U]pon being satisfied that the making of the agreement for arbitration or the failure to comply therewith is not in issue, the court shall make an order directing the parties to proceed to arbitration in accordance with the terms of the agreement...."

clause itself-an issue which goes to the making of the agreement to arbitrate-the federal court may proceed to adjudicate it. But the statutory language does not permit the federal court to consider claims of fraud in the inducement of the contract generally." *Id.*, at 403–404, 87 S.Ct. 1801 (internal quotation marks and footnote omitted). We rejected the view that the question of "severability" was one of state law, so that if state law held the arbitration provision not to be severable a challenge to the contract as a whole would be decided by the court. See *id.*, at 400, 402–403, 87 S.Ct. 1801.

Subsequently, in *Southland Corp.*, we held that the FAA "create[d] a body of federal substantive law," which was "applicable in state and federal court." 465 U.S., at 12, 104 S.Ct. 852 (internal quotation marks omitted). We rejected the view that state law could bar enforcement of § 2, even in the context of state-law claims brought in state court. See *id.*, at 10–14, 104 S.Ct. 852; see also *Allied–Bruce Terminix Cos. v. Dobson*, 513 U.S. 265, 270–273, 115 S.Ct. 834, 130 L.Ed.2d 753 (1995).

B

*Prima Paint* and *Southland* answer the question presented here by establishing three propositions. First, as a matter of substantive federal arbitration law, an arbitration provision is severable from the remainder of the contract. Second, unless the challenge is to the arbitration clause itself, the issue of the contract's validity is considered by the arbitrator in the first instance. Third, this arbitration law applies in state as well as federal courts. The parties have not requested, and we do not undertake, reconsideration of those holdings. Applying them to this case, we conclude that because respondents challenge the Agreement, but not specifically its arbitration provisions, those provisions are enforceable apart from the remainder of the contract. The challenge should therefore be considered by an arbitrator, not a court.

In declining to apply *Prima Paint's* rule of severability, the Florida Supreme Court relied on the distinction between void and voidable contracts. "Florida public policy and contract law," it concluded, permit "no severable, or salvageable, parts of a contract found illegal and void under Florida law." 894 So.2d, at 864. *Prima Paint* makes this conclusion irrelevant. That case rejected application of state severability rules to the arbitration agreement *without discussing* whether the challenge at issue would have rendered the contract void or voidable. See 388 U.S., at 400–404, 87 S.Ct. 1801. Indeed, the opinion expressly disclaimed any need to decide what state-law remedy was available, *id.*, at 400, n. 3, 87 S.Ct. 1801, (though Justice Black's dissent *asserted* that state law rendered the contract void, *id.*, at 407, 87 S.Ct. 1801). Likewise in *Southland*, which arose in state court, we did not ask whether the several challenges made there— fraud, misrepresentation, breach of contract, breach of fiduciary duty, and violation of the California Franchise Investment Law—would render the contract void or voidable. We simply rejected the proposition that the enforceability of the arbitration agreement turned on the state legislature's judgment concerning the forum for enforcement of the state-law cause of action. See 465 U.S., at 10, 104 S.Ct. 852. So also here, we cannot accept the Florida Supreme Court's conclusion that enforceability of the arbitration agreement should turn on "Florida public policy and contract law," 894 So.2d, at 864.

C

Respondents assert that *Prima Paint's* rule of severability does not apply in state court. They argue that *Prima Paint* interpreted only §§ 3 and 4—two of the FAA's procedural provisions, which appear to apply by their terms only in federal court—but not § 2, the only provision that we have applied in state court. This does not accurately describe *Prima Paint*. Although § 4, in particular, had much to do with *Prima Paint's* understanding of the rule of severability, see 388 U.S., at 403–404, 87 S.Ct. 1801, this rule ultimately arises out of § 2, the FAA's substantive command that arbitration agreements be treated like all other contracts. The rule of severability establishes how this equal-footing guarantee for "a written [arbitration] provision" is to be implemented. Respondents' reading of *Prima Paint* as establishing nothing more than a federal-court rule of procedure also runs contrary to *Southland's* understanding of that case. One of the bases for *Southland's* application of § 2 in state court was precisely *Prima Paint's* "reli[ance] for [its] holding on Congress' broad power to fashion substantive rules under the Commerce Clause." 465 U.S., at 11, 104 S.Ct. 852; see also *Prima Paint, supra*, at 407, 87 S.Ct. 1801 (Black, J., dissenting) ("[t]he Court here holds that the [FAA], as a matter of *federal substantive law* ..." (emphasis added)). *Southland* itself refused to "believe Congress intended to limit the Arbitration Act to disputes subject only to *federal*-court jurisdiction." 465 U.S., at 15, 104 S.Ct. 852.

Respondents point to the language of § 2, which renders "valid, irrevocable, and enforceable" "a written provision in" or "an agreement in writing to submit to arbitration an existing controversy arising out of" a "contract." Since, respondents argue, the only arbitration agreements to which § 2 applies are those involving a "contract," and since an agreement void *ab initio* under state law is not a "contract," there is no "written provision" in or "controversy arising out of" a "contract," to which § 2 can apply. This argument echoes Justice Black's dissent in *Prima Paint*: "Sections 2 and 3 of the Act assume the existence of a valid contract. They merely provide for enforcement where such a valid contract exists." 388 U.S., at 412–413, 87 S.Ct. 1801. We do not read "contract" so narrowly. The word appears four times in § 2. Its last appearance is in the final clause, which allows a challenge to an arbitration provision "upon such grounds as exist at law or in equity for the revocation of any *contract*." (Emphasis added.) There can be no doubt that "contract" as used this last time must include contracts that later prove to be void. Otherwise, the grounds for revocation would be limited to those that rendered a contract voidable—which would mean (implausibly) that an arbitration agreement could be challenged as voidable but not as void. Because the sentence's final use of "contract" so obviously includes putative contracts, we will not read the same word earlier in the same sentence to have a more narrow meaning.[3] We note that neither *Prima Paint* nor *Southland* lends support to respondents' reading; as we have discussed, neither case turned on whether the challenge at issue would render the contract voidable or void.

\* \* \*

It is true, as respondents assert, that the *Prima Paint* rule permits a court to enforce an arbitration agreement in a contract that the arbitrator later finds to be void. But it is equally true that respondents' approach permits a court to deny effect to an arbitration provision in a contract that the court later finds to be perfectly enforceable. *Prima Paint* resolved this conundrum—and resolved it in favor of the separate enforceability of arbitration provisions. We reaffirm today that, regardless of whether the challenge is brought in federal or state court, a challenge to the validity of the contract as a whole, and not specifically to the arbitration clause, must go to the arbitrator.

The judgment of the Florida Supreme Court is reversed, and the case is remanded for further proceedings not inconsistent with this opinion.

*It is so ordered.*

NOTES

**1**.   An amicus brief of 13 law professors, supporting Professor Richard M. Alderman on behalf of the respondents, contended that the Act does not apply to validate an arbitration clause in this case unless there is a "contract," a threshold question for a court. Under Florida law a bargain that is void ab initio owing to illegality is not a contract. A state court cannot compel arbitration until it decides the illegality issue. How did the Court deal with this argument in its opinion? If a court had to determine the legality of a contract in order to determine the enforceability of an arbitration clause in it, what role would there be for the arbitrator? Could there even be an arbitration in which the arbitrator could find that a contract a court judged unenforceable under applicable state law in fact was valid and therefore enforceable?

**2**.   We omitted the extended discussion in the preceding case, *Muhammad*, of the separability issue. In that case, only the arbitration clause was attacked as unconscionable, unlike *Buckeye* in which the whole agreement was challenged as void under state law. Even though the court in *Muhammad* found the arbitration clause to be unenforceable because the waiver provision was unconscionable, the clause was found to be separable and the remainder of the contract was enforceable. This holding allowed the court, rather than an arbitrator, to decide the issue of unconscionability.

**3**.  Our more natural reading is confirmed by the use of the word "contract" elsewhere in the United States Code to refer to putative agreements, regardless of whether they are legal. For instance, the Sherman Act, 26 Stat. 209, as amended, states that "[e]very contract, combination . . ., or conspiracy in restraint of trade . . . is hereby declared to be illegal." 15 U.S.C. § 1. Under respondents' reading of "contract," a bewildering circularity would result: A contract illegal because it was in restraint of trade would not be a "contract" at all, and thus the statutory prohibition would not apply.

\*

# ACCOUNTS RECEIVABLE/INVENTORY LOAN AGREEMENT

This Accounts Receivable and Inventory Loan Agreement ("Agreement") is entered into as of October 30, 2003, by and between **XYZ. Inc.,** a California corporation **("Borrower")**, and **City National Bank,** a national banking association **("CNB")**.

1. **DEFINITIONS**. As used in this Agreement, these terms have the following meanings:

1.1 **"Account"** or **"Accounts"** has the meaning given in the Code, and includes, but is not limited to, any right to payment for goods sold or leased or for services rendered which is not evidenced by an instrument or chattel paper from any Person, whether now existing or hereafter arising or acquired, whether or not it has been earned by performance.

1.2 **"Account Debtor"** means the Person obligated on an Account.

1.3 **"Affiliate"** means any Person directly or indirectly controlling, controlled by, or under common control with Borrower, and includes any employee stock ownership plan of Borrower or an Affiliate. "Control" (including with correlative meaning, the terms "controlling," "controlled by" and "under common control with"), as applied to any Person, means the possession, directly or indirectly, of the power to direct or cause the direction of the management and policies of that Person, whether through the ownership of voting securities, by contract or otherwise.

1.4 **"Audit Fee"** is $500.00 per day for each field examination and audit of Borrower's operations, books and records and the Collateral.

1.5 **"Banker's Acceptance Commitment"** is $1,000,000.00.

1.6 **"Borrower's Loan Account"** means the statement of daily balances on the books of CNB in which will be recorded Revolving Credit Loans made by CNB to Borrower, payments made on such loans, and other appropriate debits and credits as provided by this Agreement. CNB will provide a statement of account for Borrower's Loan Account at least once each month on a date established by CNB, which statement will be accepted by and conclusively binding upon Borrower unless it notifies CNB in writing to the contrary, within five (5) days of receipt of such statement, or ten (10) days after sending of such statement if Borrower does not notify CNB of its non-receipt of the statement. Statements regarding other credit extended to Borrower will be provided separately.

1.7 **"Borrowing Base"** will be in an amount, determined by CNB, equal to the sum of:

1.7.1 Eighty percent (80%) of the Eligible Accounts ("Accounts Borrowing Base"); and

1.7.2 Twenty five percent (25%) of the Eligible Inventory ("Inventory Borrowing Base");

In no event will (a) the Inventory Borrowing Base exceed the lesser of (i) $2,000,000.00 or (ii) the Accounts Borrowing Base or (b) the Borrowing Base exceed the Revolving Credit Commitment.

1.8 **"Borrowing Base Certificate"** means the certificate, in form and satisfactory to CNB, executed by Borrower to evidence the Borrowing Base.

1.9 **"Business Day"** means a day that CNB's Head Office is open and conducts a substantial portion of its business.

1.10 **"Cash Flow from Operations"** will be determined on a consolidated basis for Borrower and the Subsidiaries and means the sum of (a) net income after taxes and before extraordinary items in accordance with GAAP, plus (b) amortization of intangible assets, plus (c) interest expense, plus (d) depreciation, each of such items computed on an annualized basis.

1.11 **"Code"** means the Uniform Commercial Code of California, as currently in effect and as amended and replaced from time to time, except where the Uniform Commercial Code of another state governs the perfection of a security interest in Collateral located in that state.

1.12 **"Collateral"** means all property securing the Obligations, as described in Section 8.

1.13 **"Commercial Letters of Credit"** means letters of credit issued pursuant to this Agreement and in response to Borrower's submission of an Irrevocable Letter of Credit Application and Security Agreement.

1.14 **"Commitment"** means CNB's commitment to make the Loans, issue Letters of Credit and create Banker's Acceptances in the aggregate principal amount outstanding at any one time of up to Twelve Million Dollars ($12,000,000.00).

1.15 **"Current Assets"** will be determined on a consolidated basis for Borrower and the Subsidiaries in accordance with GAAP excluding, however, loans to stockholders, management or employees, amounts due from Subsidiaries or Affiliates, deferred costs and other intangible assets.

1.16 **"Current Liabilities"** will be determined on a consolidated basis for Borrower and the Subsidiaries in accordance with GAAP and will include, without limitation: (a) all payments on Subordinated Debt required to be made within one (1) year after the date on which the determination is made, and (b) all indebtedness payable to stockholders, Affiliates, Subsidiaries or officers regardless of maturity, unless such indebtedness has been subordinated, on terms satisfactory to CNB, to the Obligations.

1.17 **"Debt"** means, at any date, the aggregate amount of, without duplication, (a) all obligations of Borrower or any Subsidiary for borrowed money, or reimbursement for open letters of credit and banker's acceptances, (b) all obligations of Borrower or any Subsidiary evidenced by bonds, debentures, notes or other similar instruments, (c) all obligations of Borrower or any Subsidiary to pay the deferred purchase price of property or services, (d) all capitalized lease obligations of Borrower or any Subsidiary, (e) all obligations or liabilities of others secured by a lien on any asset of Borrower or any Subsidiary, whether or not such obligation or liability is assumed, (f) all obligations guaranteed by Borrower or any Subsidiary, (g) all obligations, direct or indirect, for letters of credit, and (h) any other obligations or liabilities which are required by GAAP to be shown as liabilities on the balance sheet of Borrower or any Subsidiary.

1.18  **"Debt Service"** means (a) the aggregate amount of Current Maturity of Long–Term Debt plus (b) all interest incurred on borrowed money, computed on an annualized basis. "Current Maturity of Long–Term Debt" means that portion of Borrower's consolidated long-term liabilities, determined in accordance with GAAP, which will, by the terms thereof, become due and payable within one (1) year following the date of the balance sheet upon which such calculations are based.

1.19  **"Demand Deposit Account"** means Borrower's demand deposit account no. 001 895 037 maintained with CNB.

1.20  **"Dilution"** will be determined at the end of each month by CNB for the preceding three-month period by dividing total reductions, excluding cash collections of Accounts, by gross sales which gave rise to the Accounts for such three-month period.

1.21  **"Documentation Fee"** is $1,000.00.

1.22  **"Eligible Account"** means an Account of Borrower:

1.22.1  Upon which Borrower's right to receive payment is absolute and not contingent upon the fulfillment of any condition;

1.22.2  Against which is asserted no defense, counterclaim, discount or set-off, whether well-founded or otherwise;

1.22.3  That is a true and correct statement of a bona fide indebtedness incurred in the amount of the Account with respect to a money obligation owed by the Account Debtor, including but not limited to obligations arising, for goods sold or leased and delivered to, or for services rendered to and accepted by, the Account Debtor;

1.22.4  That is owned by Borrower free and clear of all liens, encumbrances, charges, interests and rights of others, except the security interests granted to CNB;

1.22.5  That does not arise from a sale or lease to or for services rendered to an employee, stockholder, director, Subsidiary or Affiliate of Borrower or any entity in which any employee, stockholder, director, Subsidiary or Affiliate of Borrower has any interest;

1.22.6  That is not the obligation of an Account Debtor that is the federal government unless perfected under the Federal Assignment of Claims Act of 1940, as amended;

1.22.7  That is not the obligation of an Account Debtor located in a foreign country, except Canada, unless the obligation is insured by foreign credit insurance satisfactory to CNB or through a letter of credit negotiated through CNB with drawing documents in order;

1.22.8 That is due and payable not more than thirty (30) days from the original invoice date unless otherwise agreed to in writing by CNB;

1.22.9 As to which not more than ninety (90) days has elapsed since the original invoice date;

1.22.10 As to which the Account Debtor has not:

(a) died, suspended business, made a general assignment for the benefit of creditors, become the subject of a petition under the Bankruptcy Code or consented to or applied for the appointment of a receiver, trustee, custodian or liquidator for itself or any of its property;

(b) become more than sixty (60) days past due, under the original terms of sale, with respect to 20% or more of the amounts owed by such Account Debtor to Borrower;

(c) had its check in payment of an Account returned unpaid; or

(d) become or appear to have become unable, in the opinion of CNB, to pay the Account in accord with its terms;

1.22.11 That does not, when added to all other Accounts that are obligations of the Account Debtor to Borrower, result in a total sum that exceeds twenty percent (20%) of the total balance then due on all Accounts; and

.22.12 That is not an obligation owed by the Account Debtor which is evidenced by chattel paper or an instrument as those terms are defined in the Code.

1.23 "**Eligible Inventory**" means Inventory, excluding work-in-process, raw materials, packing materials and supplies which (a) is owned by Borrower free and clear of all liens, encumbrances and rights of others, except the security interests granted to CNB; (b) is permanently located in the United States of America and in the physical possession of Borrower; (c) if not in the physical possession of Borrower, is in transit and covered by negotiable documents of title or air bills which have been presented for a drawing under a Letter of Credit issued pursuant to this Agreement; (d) if not in the physical possession of Borrower or in transit, is referred to in an open and unexpired Letter of Credit which has been issued pursuant to this Agreement; and (e) is not, in CNB's opinion, obsolete, unsalable, damaged, unfit for further processing or otherwise unacceptable to CNB. Eligible Inventory will be valued, in the case of finished goods, at the lower of cost or market in accordance with GAAP and, in the case of raw materials, at the lower of Borrower's cost, market or CNB's independent determination of the resale value of raw materials in such quantities and on such terms as CNB deems appropriate.

1.24 "**Equipment Acquisition Commitment**" is $500,000.00.

1.25  "**Eurocurrency Reserve Requirement**" means the aggregate (without duplication) of the rates (expressed as a decimal) of reserves (including, without limitation, any basic, marginal, supplemental, or emergency reserves) that are required to be maintained by banks during the Interest Period under any regulations of the Board of Governors of the Federal Reserve System, or any other governmental authority having jurisdiction with respect thereto, applicable to funding based on so-called "Eurocurrency Liabilities", including Regulation D (12 CFR 224).

1.26  "**Facility Fee**" is $20,000.00.

1.27  "**GAAP**" means generally accepted accounting principles, consistently applied.

1.28  "**Guarantors**" are Joe XYZ and Mabel XYZ.

1.29  "**Inventory**" means goods held for sale or lease in the ordinary course of business, work in process and any and all raw materials used in connection with the foregoing.

1.30  "**Interest Period**" means the period commencing on the date the LIBOR Loan is made (including the date a Prime Loan is converted to a LIBOR Loan, or a LIBOR Loan is renewed as a LIBOR Loan, which, in the latter case, will be the last day of the expiring Interest Period) and ending on the last day of the month occurring prior to or on the date which is one (1), two (2), three (3), six (6), nine (9) or twelve (12)] months thereafter, as selected by the Borrower; provided, however, no Interest Period may extend beyond the Termination Date.

1.31  "**Letters of Credit**" means Commercial Letters of Credit and Standby Letters of Credit.

1.32  "**Letters of Credit Commitment**" is $2,500,000.00.

1.33  "**LIBOR Base Rate**" means the British Banker's Association definition of the London InterBank Offered Rates as made available by Bloomberg LP, or such other information service available to CNB, for the applicable monthly period upon which the Interest Period is based for the LIBOR Loan selected by Borrower and as quoted by CNB on the Business Day Borrower requests a LIBOR Loan or on the last Business Day of an expiring Interest Period.

1.34  "**LIBOR Interest Rate**" means the rate per year (rounded upward to the next one-sixteenth (1/16th) of one percent (0.0625%), if necessary) determined by CNB to be the quotient of (a) the LIBOR Base Rate divided by (b) one minus the Eurocurrency Reserve Requirement for the Interest Period; which is expressed by the following formula:

$$\frac{\text{LIBOR Base Rate}}{1-\text{Eurocurrency Reserve Requirement}}$$

1.35  "**LIBOR Loan**" means any Loan tied to the LIBOR Interest Rate.

1.36  "**Loan**" or "**Loans**" means the loans extended by CNB to Borrower pursuant to Section 2.

1.37 "**Loan Documents**" means, individually and collectively, this Agreement, any note, guaranty, security or pledge agreement, financing statement and all other contracts, instruments, addenda and documents executed in connection with or related to extensions of credit under this Agreement.

1.38 "**Obligations**" means all present and future liabilities and obligations of Borrower to CNB hereunder and all other liabilities and obligations of Borrower to CNB of every kind, now existing or hereafter owing, matured or unmatured, direct or indirect, absolute or contingent, joint or several, including any extensions and renewals thereof and substitutions therefor.

1.39 "**Person**" means any individual or entity.

1.40 "**Potential Event of Default**" means any condition that with the giving of notice or passage of time or both would, unless cured or waived, become an Event of Default.

1.41 "**Prime Rate**" means the rate most recently announced by CNB at its principal office in Beverly Hills, California as its "Prime Rate." Any change in the interest rate resulting from a change in the Prime Rate will become effective on the day on which each change in the Prime Rate is announced by CNB.

1.42 "**Quick Assets**" means the sum of cash, plus cash equivalents, plus Accounts, plus securities classified as short-term marketable securities according to GAAP, as such items appear on Borrower's consolidated balance sheet, determined in accordance with GAAP.

1.43 "**Revolving Credit Commitment**" means CNB's commitment to make the Revolving Credit Loans, issue Letters of Credit and create Banker's Acceptances in the aggregate principal amount at any one time of up to Ten Million Dollars ($10,000,000.00).

1.44 "**Standby Letters of Credit**" means standby letters of credit issued pursuant to this Agreement and in response to Borrower's submission of an Irrevocable Standby Letter of Credit Application and Letter of Credit Agreement.

1.45 "**Subordinated Debt**" means Debt of Borrower or any Subsidiary, the repayment of which is subordinated, on terms satisfactory to CNB, to the Obligations. The holders of Subordinated Debt, as of the date of this Agreement, are: Joe XYZ.

1.46 "**Subsidiary**" means any corporation, the majority of whose voting shares are at any time owned, directly or indirectly, by Borrower and/or by one or more Subsidiaries.

1.47 "**Tangible Net Worth**" means the total of all assets appearing on a balance sheet prepared in accordance with GAAP for Borrower and the Subsidiaries on a consolidated basis, minus (a) all intangible assets, including, without limitation, unamortized debt discount, Affiliate, employee, officer and stockholder receivables or advances, goodwill, research and development costs, patents, trademarks, the excess of purchase price over underlying values of acquired companies, any covenants not to compete, deferred charges, copyrights, franchises and appraisal surplus; minus (b) the amount, if any, at which shares of stock of a non-wholly owned Subsidiary appear on the asset side of Borrower's consolidated balance sheet, as determined in accordance with GAAP; minus (c) all obligations which are required by GAAP to be classified as a liability on the consolidated balance sheet of Borrower and the Subsidiaries; minus (d) minority interests; and minus (e) deferred income and reserves not otherwise classified as a liability on the consolidated balance sheet of Borrower and the Subsidiaries.

1.48   **"Term Loan Commitment"** is $1,500,000.00.

1.49   **"Termination Date"** means December 31, 2004, unless the term of this Agreement is renewed by CNB for an additional period under Section 3, or such earlier termination date under Section 9.3 upon the occurrence of an Event of Default. Upon any renewal, the Termination Date will be the renewed maturity date determined by CNB.

1.50   **"Total Senior Liabilities"** means, as of any date of determination, the amount of all liabilities that should be reflected as a liability on a consolidated balance sheet of Borrower and the Subsidiaries prepared in accordance with GAAP, less Subordinated Debt.

1.51   **"Unused Facility Fee"** will be equal to one quarter of one percent (¼%) of the average daily difference between the Borrowing Base and the Revolving Credit Loans, Letters of Credit and Banker's Acceptances outstanding.

2.   **THE CREDIT**.

2.1   **Revolving Credit Loan**. Subject to the terms of this Agreement, CNB agrees to make loans ("Revolving Credit Loans") to Borrower, from the date of this Agreement up to but not including the Termination Date, at such times as Borrower may request, up to the amount of the Borrowing Base, less the amount of outstanding Letters of Credit and Banker's Acceptances. The Revolving Credit Loans may be repaid and reborrowed at any time up to the Termination Date; provided, however, that the aggregate unpaid principal amount of outstanding Revolving Credit Loans will at no time exceed the Borrowing Base less the amount of outstanding Letters of Credit and Banker's Acceptances.

2.1.1   **Interest**. The Revolving Credit Loans will bear interest from disbursement until due (whether at stated maturity, by acceleration on otherwise) at a rate equal to, at Borrower's option, either (a) for a LIBOR Revolving Loan, the LIBOR Interest Rate plus three percent (3%) per year, or (b) for a Prime Revolving Loan, the fluctuating Prime Rate plus one half of one percent (½%) per year. Interest on the Revolving Credit Loans and other charges incurred under this Agreement will accrue daily and be payable (a) monthly in arrears, on the last day of each month, commencing on the first such date following disbursement; (b) if a LIBOR Revolving Loan, upon any prepayment of any LIBOR Revolving Loan (to the extent accrued on the amount prepaid); and (c) at the Termination

Date. A Revolving Credit Loan tied to the LIBOR Interest Rate is called a "LIBOR Revolving Loan," and a Revolving Credit Loan tied to the Prime Rate is called a "Prime Revolving Loan." A Revolving Credit Loan will be a Prime Revolving Loan any time it is not a LIBOR Revolving Loan.

2.1.2  **Minimum Monthly Payments**. Borrower will pay CNB a monthly fee from the date hereof until the next Termination Date, whether or not the Obligations have been repaid, equal to $1,000.00 less the amount of interest paid by Borrower for Revolving Credit Loans for such month.

2.1.3  **Payment for Amounts Exceeding Borrowing Base**. Borrower will, immediately upon demand, repay the amount by which the unpaid principal amount of Borrower's Loan Account exceeds the amount CNB has agreed to lend under Section 2.1. The portion of the Revolving Credit Loans exceeding the Borrowing Base will bear additional interest of three percent (3.0%) per year over the rate set forth in Section 2.1.1 for Prime Loans.

2.1.4  **Application to Borrower's Loan Account**. Borrower agrees that CNB may make a charge equal to two (2) days' collection time at the interest rate set forth in Section 2.1.1 for Prime Loans, payable monthly in arrears on the first day of each month for the previous month for all uncollected funds as to which immediate credit is given by application to Borrower's Loan Account.

2.2  **Letter of Credit and Banker's Acceptance Facility**. CNB will, at the request of Borrower any time up to the Termination Date, issue Letters of Credit and create Banker's Acceptances, in connection with drawings thereunder, for the account of Borrower. The aggregate face amount of outstanding Letters of Credit at any time will not exceed the lesser of (a) the Letter of Credit Commitment or (b) the Borrowing Base less outstanding Revolving Credit Loans and Banker's Acceptances. The aggregate face amount of outstanding Banker's Acceptances at any time will not exceed the lesser of (a) the Banker's Acceptance Commitment or (b) the Borrowing Base less Revolving Credit Loans and Letters of Credit outstanding.

2.2.1  **Issuance of Letters of Credit**. Commercial Letters of Credit will be issued to finance the import of merchandise in accordance with an Irrevocable Letter of Credit Application and Security Agreement submitted by Borrower and incorporated herein by this reference, subject to the terms of this Agreement in the event of any conflict herewith. Standby Letters of Credit will be issued in accordance with an Irrevocable Standby Letter of Credit Application and Letter of Credit Agreement submitted by Borrower and incorporated herein by this reference, subject to the terms of this Agreement in the event of any conflict herewith. Letters of Credit will be issued on the normal documentation used by CNB from time to time in accord with the Uniform Customs and Practices for Documentary Credits (1993 Revision) International Chamber of Commerce Publication No. 500, or the International Standby Practices 1998, whichever is applicable. Commercial Letters of Credit will expire no more than 90 days after issuance. Unless CNB otherwise agrees in writing, no Standby

Letter of Credit may expire after the Termination Date. Standard CNB fees and charges will apply to the issuance of Letters of Credit.

2.2.2 **Creation of Banker's Acceptances**. Banker's Acceptances will be created in response to Borrower's request or the acceptance by CNB of a draft drawn against a Letter of Credit not payable at sight, on the normal documentation used by CNB, and will mature within 60 days. Creation of Banker's Acceptances will be subject to standard CNB fees and charges plus, if applicable, a payment equal to the CNB Banker's Acceptance Discount Rate plus two percent. There will be no obligation to accept drafts which would:

(a) not be eligible for discount by a Federal Reserve Bank;

(b) become a liability subject to reserve requirements under any regulation of the Board of Governors of the Federal Reserve System; or

(c) cause CNB to violate any lending limit imposed upon CNB by any law, regulation or administrative order.

2.2.3 **Reimbursement for Funding Letter of Credit**. Any sight drawing under a Letter of Credit will be deemed to be an irrevocable request for a Revolving Credit Loan under this Agreement. Borrower's obligation to reimburse CNB may also be satisfied by charging Borrower's Demand Deposit Account if requested by Borrower. All drawings under Letters of Credit which are not payable at sight will be deemed to be requests for the creation of Banker's Acceptances hereunder. CNB's obligation under this Subsection to make a Revolving Credit Loan or create a Banker's Acceptance will exist irrespective of the existence of any Potential Event of Default or Event of Default.

2.2.4 **Reimbursement for Payment of Banker's Acceptances**. The creation of a Banker's Acceptance will be deemed to be an irrevocable request for a Revolving Credit Loan made at the maturity date of the Banker's Acceptance. Borrower's obligation to pay such accepted draft may, at Borrower's request, be satisfied by charging Borrower's Demand Deposit Account. CNB's obligation under this Subsection to make a Revolving Credit Loan will exist irrespective of the existence of any Potential Event of Default or Event of Default.

2.3 **Term Loan Facility**. CNB agrees to make a term loan ("Term Loan") to Borrower, on or before November 30, 2003, in the amount of the Term Loan Commitment. The Term Loan will be evidenced by a promissory note ("Term Note") consistent with the terms of this Agreement.

2.3.1 **Interest on Term Loan**. The Term Loan will bear interest on the unpaid principal amount thereof at a fluctuating annual rate equal to the Prime Rate of CNB plus one half of one percent (½%). Interest on the Term Loan will be payable monthly on the first day of each month, commencing on the first such date after the date hereof and on the date the Term Loan is paid in full.

2.3.2 **Payment of Term Loan**. The principal amount of the Term Loan will be repaid by Borrower to CNB in forty eight (48) equal consecutive monthly installments, payable on the first day of each month commencing on January 1, 2004. All unpaid principal and interest will be due and payable forty eight (48) months after the funding of the Term Loan, or on the Termination Date, whichever first occurs.

2.4 **Equipment Acquisition Facility**. Prior to June 30, 2004, and provided that no Event of Default or Potential Event of Default exists at the time of Borrower's request, CNB agrees to make loans ("Equipment Acquisition Loans") to Borrower up to the amount of the Equipment Acquisition Commitment, for the acquisition of new fixed assets consisting of machinery and equipment. Each Equipment Acquisition Loan will be made (a) in an amount equal to eighty percent (80%) of the invoice purchase price for such assets, excluding sales taxes, delivery and set-up charges, and (b) when Borrower submits an appropriate purchase invoice and executes and delivers to CNB its promissory note, in form and substance satisfactory to CNB (the "Equipment Acquisition Note"). The Equipment Acquisition Note will provide for interest payable monthly at a fluctuating annual rate equal to the Prime Rate plus one half of one percent (½%), and principal payable at the same time as interest in sixty (60) equal monthly payments. Borrower will submit such further documents as are required to perfect a first lien in the purchased assets in favor of CNB. All unpaid principal and interest will be due and payable sixty (60) months after the funding of the Equipment Acquisition Loan or on the Termination Date, whichever first occurs. The Equipment Acquisition Loans may be repaid and reborrowed at any time up to the Termination Date; provided, however, that the aggregate unpaid principal amount of outstanding Equipment Acquisition Loans will at no time exceed the Equipment Acquisition Commitment.

2.5 **LIBOR Loan Terms and Conditions**

2.5.1 **Procedure for LIBOR Loans**. Borrower may request that a Revolving Credit Loan be a LIBOR Loan (including conversion of a Prime Revolving Loan to a LIBOR Revolving Loan, or continuation of a LIBOR Revolving Loan as a LIBOR Revolving Loan upon the expiration of the Interest Period). Borrower's request will be irrevocable, will be made to CNB using the "Notice of Borrowing" form attached hereto as Exhibit "A," no earlier than two (2) Business Days before and no later than 1:00 p.m. Pacific Time on the day the LIBOR Loan is to be made. If Borrower fails to select a LIBOR Loan in accordance herewith, the Loan will be a Prime Loan, and any outstanding LIBOR Loan will be deemed a Prime Loan upon expiration of the Interest Period.

2.5.2 **Availability of LIBOR Loans**. Notwithstanding anything herein to the contrary, each LIBOR Loan must be in the minimum amount of $500,000.00 and increments of $100,000.00. Borrower may not have more than five (5) LIBOR Loans outstanding at any one time under this Agreement. Borrower may have Prime Loans and LIBOR Loans outstanding simultaneously.

2.5.3 **Prepayment of Principal**. Borrower may not make a partial principal prepayment on a LIBOR Loan. Borrower may prepay the full outstanding principal balance on a LIBOR Loan prior to the end of the Interest Period, provided, however, that such prepayment is accompanied by a fee ("LIBOR Prepayment Fee") equal to the amount, if any, by which (a) the additional interest which would have been earned by CNB had the LIBOR Loan not been prepaid exceeds (b) the interest which would have been recoverable by CNB by placing the amount of the LIBOR Loan on deposit in the LIBOR market for a period starting on the date on which it was prepaid and ending on the last day of the applicable Interest Period. CNB's calculation of the LIBOR Prepayment Fee will be deemed conclusive absent manifest error.

2.5.4 **Suspension of LIBOR Loans**. If CNB, on any Business Day, is unable to determine the LIBOR Base Rate applicable for a new, continued, or converted LIBOR Loan for any reason, or any law, regulation, or governmental order, rule or determination, makes it unlawful for CNB to make a LIBOR Loan, Borrower's right to select LIBOR Loans will be suspended until CNB is again able to determine the LIBOR Base Rate or make LIBOR Loans, as the case may be. During such suspension, new Loans, outstanding Prime Loans, and LIBOR Loans whose Interest Periods terminate may only be Prime Loans.

2.6 **Optional Prepayments**. Subject to the provisions of Section 2.5.3, Borrower will have the right to prepay any Term Loan or Equipment Acquisition Loan provided that (a) each partial payment will be in an amount equal to the amount of the normal monthly payment or an integral multiple thereof, (b) on each prepayment, Borrower will pay the accrued interest on the prepaid principal, to the date of such prepayment, and (c) all prepayments will be applied to principal installments in the inverse order of their maturities.

2.7 **Default Interest Rate**. From and after written notice by CNB to Borrower of the occurrence of an Event of Default (and without constituting a waiver of such Event of Default), the Loans and any other amounts due CNB hereunder (and interest to the extent permitted by law) will bear additional interest at a fluctuating rate equal to five percent (5.0%) per year higher than the interest rate as determined in Sections 2.1.1 and 2.1.3, until the Event of Default has been cured; provided, however, for purposes of this Section, a LIBOR Loan will be treated as a Prime Loan upon the termination of the Interest Period. All interest provided for in this Section will be compounded monthly and payable on demand.

2.8 **Payments**. All payments will be in United States Dollars and in immediately available funds. Interest will accrue daily and will be computed on the basis of a 360–day year, actual days elapsed. All payments of principal, interest, fees and other charges incurred under this Agreement will be made by charging, and Borrower hereby authorizes CNB to charge, Borrower's Demand Deposit Account or Borrower's Loan Account. All loan disbursements made pursuant to this Agreement shall be made by direct deposit to Borrower's Demand Deposit Account. Borrower also authorizes CNB to charge to Borrower's Demand Deposit Account or Borrower's Loan

Account any payment credited against the Obligations which is dishonored by the drawee or maker thereof.

2.9   **Audit Fee and Unused Facility Fee**. Borrower will pay the Unused Facility Fee on the last day of each calendar quarter; such fee will be non-refundable and fully earned when paid. Further, Borrower will pay the Audit Fee annually. Borrower hereby authorizes CNB to charge Borrower's Demand Deposit Account or Borrower's Loan Account for the amount of each such fee.

3.   **TERM AND TERMINATION**.

3.1   **Establishment of Termination Date**. The term of this Agreement will begin as of the date hereof and continue until the Termination Date, unless the term is renewed for an additional period by CNB giving Borrower prior written notice, in which event the Termination Date will mean the renewed maturity date set forth in such notice. Notwithstanding the foregoing, CNB may, at its option, terminate this Agreement pursuant to Section 9.3; the date of any such termination will become the Termination Date as that term is used in this Agreement. Upon renewal, Borrower authorizes CNB to charge Borrower's Loan Account with the amount of the Facility Fee and any applicable Audit Fee.

3.2   **Obligations Upon the Termination Date**. Borrower will, upon the Termination Date:

3.2.1   Repay the amount of the balance due as set forth in Borrower's Loan Account plus any accrued interest, fees and charges; and

3.2.2   Pay CNB cash in the aggregate face amount of the Letters of Credit outstanding to be held as cash collateral for Borrower's obligation to reimburse CNB upon the funding of such Letters of Credit; and

3.2.3   Pay CNB cash in the aggregate face amount of the Banker's Acceptances outstanding to be held by CNB to make payment under the drafts which have been accepted; and

3.2.4   Pay the amounts due on all other Obligations owing to CNB. In this connection and notwithstanding anything to the contrary contained in the instruments evidencing such Obligations, the Termination Date hereunder will constitute the maturity date of such other Obligations.

3.3   **Survival of Rights**. Any termination of this Agreement will not affect the rights, liabilities and obligations of the parties with respect to any Obligations outstanding on the date of such termination. Until all Obligations have been fully repaid, CNB will retain its security interest in all existing Collateral and Collateral arising thereafter, and Borrower will continue to assign all Accounts to CNB and to immediately turn over to CNB, in kind, all collections received on the Accounts.

4.   **CONDITIONS PRECEDENT**.

4.1   **Extension of Credit**. The obligation of CNB to make any Loan or other extension of credit hereunder is subject to CNB's receipt of each of the following, in form and substance satisfactory to CNB, and duly executed as required by CNB:

4.1.1  All Loan Documents required by CNB, including but not limited to this Agreement and any guaranties required hereunder;

4.1.2  A subordination agreement ("Subordination Agreement") duly executed and delivered by Joe XYZ in the form customarily used by CNB;

4.1.3  (a) a copy of Borrower's Articles of Incorporation; (b) a Resolution of Borrower's Board of Directors approving and authorizing the execution, delivery and performance of this Agreement and any other documents required pursuant to this Agreement, certified by Borrower's corporate secretary; and, (c) a copy of the last certificate filed on behalf of Borrower containing the information required by California Corporations Code Section 1502(a) or Section 2117(a), as applicable;

4.1.4  (a) copies (and acknowledgement copies to the extent reasonably available) of financing statements (Form UCC–1) duly filed under the Code in all such jurisdictions as may be necessary or, in CNB's opinion, desirable to perfect CNB's security interests created under this Agreement; and (b) evidence that all filings, recordings and other actions that are necessary or advisable, in CNB's opinion, to establish, preserve and perfect CNB's security interests and liens as legal, valid and enforceable first security interests and liens in the Collateral have been effected;

4.1.5  Evidence that the insurance required by Section 6.6 hereof is in effect;

4.1.6  A complete list of claims made against Borrower together with an opinion of Borrower's counsel with respect to such claims, that the representations contained in Section 5.5 are true and correct as of the date of this Agreement;

4.1.7  Borrower's detailed and comprehensive statement of projected cash flows ("Cash Flow Statement"), a projected balance sheet ("Balance Sheet") and a projected income statement ("Income Statement") (collectively, the "Budget") for the period from January 1, 2004, through December 31, 2004. The Budget will be prepared in accordance with FASB 95, will be realistic and conservative, will be based upon considered analysis and diligent investigation of Borrower, and will disclose all material liabilities or expenses which Borrower expects to incur during said period;

4.1.8  The Documentation Fee and the pro-rated portion of the first Facility Fee through the initial Termination Date equal to $12,000.00; and

4.1.9  An assignment issued by an insurance company acceptable to CNB, of a key-man life insurance policy upon the life of Joe XYZ with the cash surrender value and with death benefits in the minimum amount of Five Million Dollars ($5,000,000.00).

4.2  **Conditions to Each Extension of Credit**. The obligation of CNB to make any Loan or other extension of credit hereunder will be subject to the fulfillment of each of the following conditions to CNB's satisfaction:

4.2.1  The representations and warranties of Borrower set forth in Section 5 will be true and correct on the date of the making of each Loan or other extension of credit with the same effect as though such representations and warranties had been made on and as of such date;

4.2.2  No Guarantor will have revoked his, her or its guaranty and no such guaranty will have become otherwise unenforceable with respect to future advances;

4.2.3  No holder of Subordinated Debt will be in violation of his, her or its Subordination Agreement executed in favor of CNB, and such Subordination Agreement is enforceable with respect to future advances;

4.2.4  There will be in full force and effect in favor of CNB a legal, valid and enforceable first security interest in, and a valid and binding first lien on the Collateral; and CNB will have received evidence, in form and substance acceptable to CNB, that all filings, recordings and other actions that are necessary or advisable, in the opinion of CNB, in order to establish, protect, preserve and perfect CNB's security interests and liens as legal, valid and enforceable first security interests and liens in the Collateral have been effected;

4.2.5  There will have occurred no Event of Default or Potential Event of Default; and

4.2.6  All other documents and legal matters in connection with the transactions described in this Agreement will be satisfactory in form and substance to CNB.

5.  **REPRESENTATIONS AND WARRANTIES**. Borrower makes the following representations and warranties, which will survive the making and repayment of the Loans and other extensions of credit:

5.1  **Corporate Existence, Power and Authorization**. Borrower and each Subsidiary is duly organized, validly existing and in good standing under the laws of the state of its organization, and is duly qualified to conduct business in each jurisdiction in which its business is conducted. The execution, delivery and performance of all Loan Documents executed by Borrower are within Borrower's powers and have been duly authorized by the Board of Directors of Borrower and do not require any consent or approval of the stockholders of Borrower.

5.2  **Binding Agreement**. The Loan Documents constitute the valid and legally binding obligations of Borrower, enforceable against Borrower in accordance with their terms.

5.3  **Ancillary Documents**. To the extent that any security agreement, subordination agreement or guaranty is required to be executed by a Subsidiary or Affiliate, the representations and warranties set forth in Sections 5.1 and 5.2 are also true and correct with respect to such Subsidiary and Affiliate and such document.

5.4  **Other Agreements**. The execution and performance of the Loan Documents will not violate any provision of law or regulation (including, without limitation, Regulations X and U of the Federal Reserve Board) or any order of any governmental authority, court or arbitration board or the Articles of Incorporation or Bylaws of Borrower, or result in the breach of or a default under any provisions of any agreement to which Borrower is a party.

5.5 **Litigation**. There is no litigation, tax claim, investigation or proceeding pending, threatened against or affecting Borrower, any Subsidiary or Guarantor, or any of their respective properties which, if adversely determined, would have a material adverse effect on the business, operation or condition, financial or otherwise, of Borrower or any Subsidiary or Guarantor.

5.6 **Financial Condition**. The most recent financial statements of Borrower and each Guarantor, if any, copies of which have been delivered to CNB, have been prepared in accordance with GAAP and are true, complete and correct and fairly present the financial condition of Borrower, its Subsidiaries and each Guarantor, including operating results, as of the accounting period referenced therein. There has been no material adverse change in the financial condition or business of Borrower or any Subsidiary or Guarantor since the date of such financial statements. Neither Borrower nor any Subsidiary or Guarantor has any material liabilities for taxes or long-term leases or commitments, except as disclosed in the financial statements.

5.7 **No Violations**. Borrower is not, nor is any Subsidiary, in violation of any law, ordinance, rule or regulation to which it or any of its properties is subject.

5.8 **Collateral**. Borrower owns and has possession of and has the right and power to grant a security interest in the Collateral, and the Collateral is genuine and free from liens, adverse claims, set-offs, defaults, prepayments, defenses and encumbrances except those in favor of CNB. No bills of lading, warehouse receipts or other documents or instruments of title are outstanding with respect to the Collateral or any portion of the Collateral, in favor of a Person other than Borrower. The office where Borrower keeps its records concerning all Accounts and where it keeps the bulk of its Inventory is 606 South Olive St. Suite 4800, Los Angeles, CA and all of its other places of business are as follows: 9701 Wilshire Blvd., 20th Floor, Beverly Hills, CA.

5.9 **ERISA**. Borrower is in compliance in all material respects with all applicable provisions of the Employee Retirement Income Security Act of 1974 ("ERISA"). No "Reportable Event" (as defined in ERISA and the regulations issued thereunder [other than a "Reportable Event" not subject to the provision for thirty (30) day notice to the Pension Benefit Guaranty Corporation ("PBGC") under such regulations]) has occurred with respect to any benefit plan of Borrower nor are there any unfunded vested liabilities under any benefit plan of Borrower. Borrower has met its minimum funding requirements under ERISA with respect to each of its plans and has not incurred any material liability to the PBGC in connection with any such plan.

5.10 **Consents**. No consent, license, permit, or authorization of, exemption by, notice or report to, or registration, filing or declaration with, any governmental authority or agency is required in connection with the execution, delivery and performance by Borrower of this Agreement or the transactions contemplated hereby.

5.11 **Use of Proceeds**. The proceeds of the Revolving Credit Loans will be used by Borrower solely for working capital purposes in the normal course of business. The proceeds of the Term Loan will be used by Borrower solely for a trip to Tahiti.

5.12 **Regulation U**. Borrower is not engaged principally, or as one of its principal activities, in the business of extending credit for the purpose of purchasing or carrying margin stock (within the meaning of Regulations U or X of the Federal Reserve Board). No part of the proceeds of the Loans will be used by Borrower to purchase or carry any such margin stock or to extend credit to others for the purpose of purchasing or carrying such margin stock.

5.13 **Environmental Matters**.

5.13.1 The operations of Borrower and each Subsidiary comply in all material respects with all applicable federal, state and local environmental, health and safety statutes, regulations and ordinances and fully comply with all terms of all required permits and licenses.

5.13.2 Borrower and each Subsidiary have received no notices of threatened or pending governmental or private civil, criminal or administrative proceeding regarding any environmental or health and safety statute, regulation or ordinance and have not been subject to any federal, state or local investigations, inspections or orders regarding any environmental or health and safety statute, regulation or ordinance.

5.13.3 Neither Borrower nor any Subsidiary knows of any facts or conditions which may exist which may subject Borrower or any Subsidiary to liability or contingent liability and neither Borrower nor any Subsidiary is presently liable or contingently liable for any removal, remedial, response or other costs or damages in connection with any release into the environment of toxic or hazardous substances or waste included on any federal, state or local hazardous chemical or substance lists under any federal, state or local statute, regulation or ordinance.

5.13.4 Borrower will, at all times, indemnify and hold CNB (which for purposes of this Section and Section 10.8 includes CNB's parent company and subsidiaries and all of their respective shareholders, directors, officers, employees, agents, representatives, successors, attorneys and assigns) harmless from and against any liabilities, claims, demands, causes of action, losses, damages, expenses (including without limitation reasonable attorneys' fees [which attorneys may be employees of CNB, or may be outside counsel]), costs, settlements, judgments or recoveries directly or indirectly arising out of or attributable to the use, generation, manufacture, production, storage, release, threatened release, discharge, disposal or presence of a hazardous substance on, under, or about Borrower's property or operations or property leased to or used by Borrower. For these purposes, the term "hazardous substances" means any substance which is or becomes designated as "hazardous" or "toxic" under any Federal, state, or local law. This indemnity will survive the Termination Date and the repayment of all Obligations of Borrower to CNB.

6.   **AFFIRMATIVE COVENANTS**. Borrower agrees that until payment in full of all Obligations, Borrower will comply with the following covenants:

6.1   **Collateral**.

6.1.1   Borrower will, on demand of CNB, make available to CNB, shipping and delivery receipts evidencing the shipment of the goods which gave rise to an Account; completion certificates or other proof of the satisfactory performance of services which gave rise to an Account; a copy of the invoice for each Account; and Borrower's copy of any written contract or order from which an Account arose. Unless previously requested by Borrower in writing to return such documents, CNB will be authorized to destroy any such documentation six (6) months after its receipt by CNB;

6.1.2   Borrower will advise CNB within ten (10) days whenever an Account Debtor refuses to retain, or returns, any goods from the sale of which an Account arose, when the sale exceeds $10,000.00, and will comply with any instructions which CNB may give regarding the sale or other disposition of such returns;

6.1.3   Borrower will give CNB, upon request, specific assignments of Accounts after they come into existence, and schedules of Accounts, the form and content of such assignments and schedules to be satisfactory to CNB; but, despite this provision for express assignments to CNB, CNB will have a continuing security interest in all Accounts irrespective of whether some Accounts are omitted from such assignments or whether any assignments are ever given; and Borrower will execute and deliver to CNB any instrument, document, financing statement, assignment or other writing which CNB may deem necessary or desirable to carry out on the terms of this Agreement, to perfect CNB's security interest in the Accounts, and any other Collateral for the Obligations, or to enable CNB to enforce its security interest in any of the foregoing;

6.1.4   Borrower will maintain, in accord with sound accounting practices, accurate records and books of account showing, among other things, all Inventory and Accounts, the proceeds of the sale or other disposition thereof and the collections therefrom. Borrower will not change the accounting method used to determine Borrower's Inventory cost without CNB's prior written approval. Borrower will permit representative(s) of CNB, at any reasonable time, to inspect, audit, examine and make extracts or copies from all books, records and other data relating to the Collateral, to inspect any of Borrower's properties and to confirm balances due on Accounts by direct inquiry to Account Debtors, and will give CNB, promptly upon request, all information regarding the business or finances of Borrower;

6.1.5 Borrower will, if requested by CNB, mark its records concerning its Inventory and Accounts in a manner satisfactory to CNB to show CNB's security interest therein;

6.1.6 Borrower will, if requested by CNB, provide CNB with a current physical count of its Inventory in the manner specified by CNB;

6.1.7 Borrower will endorse to the order of and deliver to CNB any negotiable instrument accepted by Borrower in lieu of payment in accord with the original terms of sale;

6.1.8 Borrower will pay CNB, upon demand, the cost, including, but not limited to reasonable attorneys' fees and expenses (which counsel may be CNB employees) expended or incurred by CNB (or allocable to CNB's in-house counsel) in the collection or enforcement of any Accounts or other Collateral if CNB itself undertakes such collection or enforcement, together with all taxes, charges and expenses of every kind or description paid or incurred by CNB under or with respect to loans hereunder or any Collateral therefor and Borrower authorizes CNB to charge the same to any deposit account of Borrower or Borrower's Loan Account maintained with CNB;

6.1.9 Borrower will promptly notify CNB of any occurrence or discovery of any event which would cause or has caused a previously Eligible Account to become ineligible;

6.1.10 Borrower will maintain the tangible Collateral in good condition and promptly notify CNB of any event causing loss or reduction of value of Collateral and the amount of such loss or reduction; and

6.1.11 Borrower will, upon request by CNB, but in no event less than once every six (6) months, supply CNB with a current list of the names and addresses of all Account Debtors.

6.2 **Financial Statements**. Borrower will furnish to CNB on a continuing basis:

6.2.1 Within thirty (30) days after the end of each month, or sooner if available, a financial statement consisting of not less than a balance sheet, income statement, reconciliation of net worth and statement of cash flows, with notes thereto, prepared in accordance with GAAP, which financial statement may be internally prepared;

6.2.2 Within forty-five (45) days after the end of each quarterly accounting period of each fiscal year, a financial statement consisting of not less than a balance sheet, income statement, reconciliation of net worth and statement of cash flows, with notes thereto, prepared in accordance with GAAP and accompanied by the following: (a) supporting schedules of costs of goods sold, operating expenses and other income and expense items, and (b) Borrower's certification as to whether any event has occurred which constitutes an Event of Default or Potential Event of Default, and if so, stating the facts with respect thereto, which financial statement may be internally prepared;

6.2.3  Within ninety (90) days after the close of Borrower's fiscal year, a copy of the annual audit report for Borrower and the Subsidiaries, including therein a balance sheet, income statement, reconciliation of net worth and statement of cash flows, with notes thereto, the balance sheet, income statement and statement of cash flows to be audited by a certified public accountant acceptable to CNB, certified by such accountant to have been prepared in accordance with GAAP and accompanied by the following: (a) supporting schedules of costs of goods sold, operating expenses and other income and expense items, and (b) Borrower's certification as to whether any event has occurred which constitutes an Event of Default or Potential Event of Default, and if so, stating the facts with respect thereto;

6.2.4  Contemporaneously with each annual review report required by Section 6.2.3 above, a copy of the representation letter from Borrower to its independent certified public accountant, in form and substance satisfactory to CNB, confirming in writing the oral representations made by Borrower to the accountant during the review process;

6.2.5  As soon as available, any written report pertaining to material items involving Borrower's internal controls submitted to Borrower by Borrower's independent public accountants in connection with each annual or interim special audit of the financial condition of Borrower and the Subsidiaries made by such accountants;

6.2.6  As soon as available, a copy of the letter to Borrower from its independent public accountants, in form and substance satisfactory to CNB, setting forth the scope of such accountants' engagement;

6.2.7  A proforma Budget as described in Section 4.1.7 prior to the end of each of Borrower's fiscal years for the next fiscal year;

6.2.8  Upon request by CNB, a copy of the Federal Income Tax Return of Borrower; and

6.2.9  Within ten (10) days of filing, a copy of the Federal Income Tax Return of each Guarantor, if any.

6.3  **Collateral Reports**. Borrower will supply the following collateral reports, together with such additional information, reports and/or statements as CNB may reasonably request, within fifteen (15) days after the end of each month:

6.3.1  A listing and aging by invoice date of all accounts receivable and accounts payable (together with sales and payment terms, and detail of outstanding balances due by invoice date from all Account Debtors);

6.3.2  A reconciliation of such aging with the previous aging delivered to CNB and CNB account records;

6.3.3  A listing of all Inventory, setting out types, locations and dollar value, which dollar value is in conformity with GAAP, in form acceptable to CNB; and

6.3.4   A Borrowing Base Certificate.

6.4   **Financial Statements of Guarantors**. No later than ninety (90) days after Borrower's fiscal year end of each year, Borrower will provide CNB with the financial statement, in form and substance satisfactory to CNB, of each Guarantor certified by such Guarantor to be true and correct.

6.5   **Taxes and Premiums**. Borrower will, and will cause each Subsidiary to, pay and discharge all taxes, assessments, governmental charges, and real and personal taxes including, but not limited to, federal and state income taxes, employee withholding taxes and payroll taxes, and all premiums for insurance required hereunder, prior to the date upon which penalties are attached thereto. CNB may pay, for the account of Borrower, any of the foregoing which Borrower fails to pay; any such amounts will be debited to Borrower's Loan Account and will be paid by Borrower to CNB, with interest thereon at the rate stated in Section 2.1.1 (exclusive of LIBOR Loans), upon demand.

6.6   **Insurance.**

6.6.1   Borrower will, and will cause each Subsidiary to, (a) keep its Inventory, equipment and any other tangible personal property which is Collateral insured for the benefit of CNB under a standard mortgagee protection clause (to whom any loss will be payable) in such amounts, by such companies and against such risks as may be satisfactory to CNB; (b) pay the cost of all such insurance; and (c) deliver certificates evidencing such insurance to CNB (and copies of policies if requested); and Borrower hereby assigns to CNB all right to receive proceeds of such insurance, and agrees to direct any insurer to pay all proceeds directly to CNB, and authorizes CNB to endorse Borrower's name to any draft or check for such proceeds;

6.6.2   In addition to the insurance required above, Borrower will, and will cause each Subsidiary to, maintain insurance of the types and in amounts customarily carried in its lines of business, including, but not limited to, fire, public liability, property damage, business interruption and worker's compensation, such insurance to be carried with companies and in amounts satisfactory to CNB, and deliver to CNB, upon request, schedules setting forth all insurance then in effect; and

6.6.3   If Borrower fails to provide and maintain the policies of insurance required hereunder, CNB may, but is not obligated to, procure such insurance, and Borrower will pay all premiums thereon promptly upon demand by CNB, together with interest thereon at the rate set forth in Section 2.1.1 hereof (exclusive of LIBOR Loans) from the date of expenditure until reimbursement by Borrower; and

6.6.4   Within sixty (60) days of the date hereof, Borrower will cause all issuers of key-man life insurance policies, to acknowledge the assignment to CNB of such policies, and monies payable thereunder, and furnish evidence thereof to CNB.

6.7   **Notice**. Borrower will promptly advise CNB in writing of (a) the opening of any new, or the closing of any existing, places of business, each location at which Inventory or equipment is or will be kept, and any change of Borrower's name, trade name or other name under which it does business or of any such new or additional name; (b) the occurrence of any Event of Default or Potential Event of Default; (c) any litigation pending or threatened where the amount or amounts in controversy exceed $50,000.00; (d) any unpaid taxes which are more than fifteen (15) days delinquent; and (e) any other matter which might materially or adversely affect Borrower's or any Subsidiary's or Guarantor's financial condition, property or business.

6.8   **Fair Labor Standards Act**. Borrower will, and will cause each Subsidiary to, comply with the requirements of, and all regulations promulgated under, the Fair Labor Standards Act.

6.9   **Corporate Existence**. Borrower will, and will cause each Subsidiary to, maintain its corporate existence and all of its rights, privileges and franchises necessary or desirable in the normal course of its business.

6.10   **Compliance with Law**. Borrower will, and will cause each Subsidiary to, comply with all requirements of all applicable laws, rules, regulations (including, but not limited to, ERISA with respect to each of their benefit plans, and all environmental and hazardous materials laws), orders of any governmental agency and all material agreements to which they are a party.

6.11   **Financial Tests**. Borrower will maintain at all times:

6.11.1   Tangible Net Worth plus Subordinated Debt of not less than $5,000,000.00

6.11.2   A ratio of Total Senior Liabilities to Tangible Net Worth plus Subordinated Debt of not more than 5.0 to 1;

6.11.3   A ratio of Cash Flow from Operations to Debt Service of not less than 2.0 to 1;

6.11.4   Current Assets less Current Liabilities of not less than $1,000,000.00;

6.11.5   A ratio of Current Assets to Current Liabilities of not less than 2.5 to 1; and

6.11.6   A ratio of Quick Assets to Current Liabilities of not less than 1.5 to 1.

6.12   **Proforma Budget**. Borrower will maintain the actual financial results measured on a cumulative basis, monthly, equal to no greater than 20% variation from the corresponding item of the proforma Budget (as defined in Section 4.1.7), unless otherwise agreed to by CNB.

7.   **NEGATIVE COVENANTS**. Borrower agrees that until payment in full of all the Obligations, Borrower will not, nor will it permit any Subsidiary to, do any of the following, without CNB's prior written consent:

7.1 **Borrowing**. Create, incur, assume or permit to exist any Debt except (a) Debt to CNB, (b) Subordinated Debt, and (c) trade Debt in the ordinary course of Borrower's business and (d) purchase money debt in an aggregate amount not to exceed $200,000.00 per Borrower's fiscal year incurred in connection with the acquisition of capital assets (including capitalized lease expenditures).

7.2 **Sale of Assets**. Sell, lease or otherwise dispose of any of Borrower's or any Subsidiary's assets, other than merchandise Inventory in the ordinary course of business.

7.3 **Loans**. Make loans or advances to any Person, except credit extended to employees or to customers in the ordinary course of business.

7.4 **Contingent Liabilities**. Assume, guarantee, endorse, contingently agree to purchase or otherwise become liable for the obligation of any Person, including Borrower, a Subsidiary or Affiliate, except (a) by the endorsement of negotiable instruments for deposit or collection or similar transactions in the ordinary course of business, and (b) contingent liabilities in favor of CNB.

7.5 **Investments**. Purchase or acquire the obligations or stock of, or any other interest in, any partnership, joint venture, limited liability company or corporation, except (a) direct obligations of the United States of America; or (b) investments in certificates of deposit issued by, and other deposits with, commercial banks organized under the United States or a State thereof having capital of at least One Hundred Million Dollars ($100,000,000.00).

7.6 **Mortgages, Liens, etc**. Mortgage, pledge, hypothecate, grant or contract to grant any security interest of any kind in any property or assets, to anyone except CNB.

7.7 **Involuntary Liens**. Permit any involuntary liens to arise with respect to any property or assets including but not limited to those arising from the levy of a writ of attachment or execution, or the levy of any state or federal tax lien which lien will not be removed within a period of thirty (30) days.

7.8 **Sale and Leaseback**. Enter into any sale-leaseback transaction.

7.9 **Mergers and Acquisitions**. Enter into any merger or consolidation, or acquire all or substantially all the assets of any Person, except a Subsidiary may be merged into or consolidated with another Subsidiary or with Borrower.

7.10 **Executive Compensation**. (a) Make any loan or advance to any shareholder of Borrower or any Subsidiary; or (b) pay salary, wages, bonus or other remuneration directly or indirectly to the shareholders in the aggregate of more than 60% of Borrower's pre-tax and pre-compensation profits for any fiscal year. Provided, however, that any amounts paid to or as compensation which are reloaned to Borrower as Subordinate Debt will not be governed by this limitation. Provided, however, if Borrower for any tax year elects to file as a Sub–Chapter S corporation under the federal and state income tax laws, distributions may be made to Borrower's shareholders in proportion to their holdings, in an aggregate amount equal to that payable by an individual in the highest tax bracket upon Borrower's taxable income computed as if Borrower were a tax-paying entity.

7.11  **Capital Expenditures**. Make or commit to make expenditures for capital assets (including capitalized lease expenditures) amounting, in the aggregate for Borrower and all Subsidiaries in any fiscal year of Borrower, to more than $100,000.00.

7.12  **Dividends and Purchase of Stock**. Redeem or repurchase stock or partnership interests, declare or pay any dividends or make any distribution, whether of capital, income or otherwise, and whether in cash or other property, except that any Subsidiary may declare distributions to Borrower; provided, however, if Borrower for any tax year elects to file as a Sub–Chapter S corporation under the federal or state income tax laws, distributions may be made to Borrower's shareholders during any current or subsequent tax year in proportion to their holdings, in an aggregate amount equal to that payable by an individual in the highest tax bracket upon Borrower's taxable income computed as if Borrower were a taxpaying entity.

7.13  **Obligations as Lessee**. Enter into any arrangement as owner or lessee of real or personal property if the aggregate of all debt service secured by Borrower's real or personal property and rental payments, with respect to real or personal property leased by Borrower, will exceed $200,000.00 in each fiscal year.

7.14  **Event of Default**. Permit a default to occur under any document or instrument evidencing Debt incurred under any indenture, agreement or other instrument under which such Debt may be issued, or any event to occur under any of the foregoing which would permit any holder of the Debt outstanding thereunder to declare the same due and payable before its stated maturity, whether or not such acceleration occurs or such default be waived.

8.  **SECURITY AGREEMENT**.

8.1  **Grant of Security Interest**. To secure all Obligations hereunder as well as all other Obligations to CNB, Borrower hereby grants and transfers to CNB a continuing security interest in the following property whether now owned or hereafter acquired:

8.1.1  All of Borrower's Inventory;

8.1.2  All of Borrower's Accounts;

8.1.3  All of Borrower's general intangibles as that term is defined in the Code;

8.1.4  All of Borrower's equipment, as that term is defined in the Code;

8.1.5  All of Borrower's interest in any patents (now existing or pending), copyrights, trade names, trademarks and service marks useful to the operation of Borrower's business;

8.1.6 All notes, drafts, acceptances, instruments, documents of title, policies and certificates of insurance, chattel paper, guaranties and securities now or hereafter received by Borrower or in which Borrower has or acquires an interest;

8.1.7 All cash and noncash proceeds of the foregoing property, including, without limitation, proceeds of policies of fire, credit or other insurance;

8.1.8 All of Borrower's books and records pertaining to any of the Collateral described in this Section 8.1; and

8.1.9 Any other Collateral which CNB and Borrower may designate as additional security from time to time by separate instruments including but not limited to the key-man life insurance policies on the lives of Joe XYZ.

8.2 **Notification of Account Debtors**. CNB will have the right to notify any Account Debtor to make payments directly to CNB, take control of the cash and noncash proceeds of any Account, and settle any Account, which right CNB may exercise at any time whether or not an Event of Default has occurred or whether Borrower was theretofore making collections thereon. Until CNB elects to exercise such right, Borrower is authorized on behalf of CNB to collect and enforce the Accounts. Immediately upon CNB's request, Borrower will deliver to CNB for application in accord with this Agreement, all checks, drafts, cash and other remittances in payment or on account of payment of its Accounts on the banking day following the receipt thereof, and in precisely the form received, except for the endorsement of Borrower where necessary to permit collection of the items, which endorsement Borrower hereby agrees to make. Pending such delivery, Borrower will not commingle any such checks, cash, drafts and other remittances with any of its other funds or property, but will hold them separate and apart therefrom expressly in trust for CNB. All such remittances will be accompanied by such statements and reports of collections and adjustments as CNB may specify.

8.3 **Attorney-In–Fact**. CNB or any of its officers is hereby irrevocably made the true and lawful attorney for Borrower with full power of substitution to do the following: (a) endorse the name of Borrower upon any and all checks, drafts, money orders and other instruments for the payment of moneys which are payable to Borrower and constitute collections on Accounts; (b) execute in the name of Borrower any schedules, assignments, instruments, documents and statements which Borrower is obligated to give CNB hereunder; (c) receive, open and dispose of all mail addressed to Borrower; (d) notify the Post Office authorities to change the address for delivery of mail addressed to Borrower to such address as CNB will designate; and (e) do such other acts in the name of Borrower which CNB may deem necessary or desirable to enforce any Account or other Collateral. The powers granted CNB hereunder are solely to protect its interests in the Collateral and will not impose any duty upon CNB to exercise any such powers.

## 9. EVENTS OF DEFAULT AND PROCEEDINGS UPON DEFAULT.

9.1   **Events of Default**. After expiration of any applicable cure period set forth in Section 9.2, the following will constitute Events of Default under this Agreement:

9.1.1   Borrower fails to pay when due any installment of principal or interest or any other amount payable under this Agreement, including but not limited to amounts payable under Section 2.1.3;

9.1.2   Any Person, or any Subsidiary of any Person, which is a party to any Loan Document fails to perform or observe any of the terms, provisions, covenants, agreements or obligations;

9.1.3   Any financial statement, representation or warranty made or furnished by Borrower or any Subsidiary or Guarantor in connection with the Loan Documents proves to be in any material respect incorrect;

9.1.4   The entry of an order for relief or the filing of an involuntary petition with respect to Borrower or any Subsidiary or Guarantor under the United States Bankruptcy Code; the appointment of a receiver, trustee, custodian or liquidator of or for any part of the assets or property of Borrower or any Subsidiary or Guarantor; or Borrower or any Subsidiary or Guarantor makes a general assignment for the benefit of creditors;

9.1.5   CNB's security interest in or lien on any portion of the Collateral becomes impaired or otherwise unenforceable;

9.1.6   Any Person obtains an order or decree in any court of competent jurisdiction enjoining or prohibiting Borrower or CNB from performing this Agreement, and such proceedings are not dismissed or such decree is not vacated within ten (10) days after the granting thereof;

9.1.7   Borrower or any Subsidiary neglects, fails or refuses to keep in full force and effect any governmental permit, license or approval which is necessary to the operation of its business;

9.1.8   All or substantially all of the property of Borrower or any Guarantor or Subsidiary is condemned, seized or otherwise appropriated;

9.1.9   The occurrence of (a) a Reportable Event (as defined in ERISA) which CNB determines in good faith constitutes grounds for the institution of proceedings to terminate any pension plan by the PBGC, (b) an appointment of a trustee to administer any pension plan of Borrower, or (c) any other event or condition which might constitute grounds under ERISA for the involuntary termination of any pension plan of Borrower, where such event set forth in (a), (b) or (c) results in a significant monetary liability to Borrower;

9.1.10   Dilution exceeds five percent (5%); or

9.1.11   Joe XYZ and Mabel XYZ no longer control at least eighty percent (%) of the stock of Borrower; or

9.1.12   Any obligee of Subordinated Debt fails to comply with the provisions of the documents evidencing such Subordinated Debt or any Subordination Agreement; or

9.1.13   Any Guarantor dies, becomes incapacitated, or revokes his or its Guaranty, or such Guaranty becomes otherwise unenforceable with respect to future advances; or

9.1.14   The Termination Date is not extended.

9.2   **Notice of Default and Cure of Potential Events of Default**. Except with respect to the Events of Default specified in Sections 9.1.1, 9.1.4, or 9.1.5 above, and subject to the provisions of Section 9.4, CNB will give Borrower at least ten (10) days' written notice of any event which constitutes, or with the lapse of time would become, an Event of Default, during which time Borrower will be entitled to cure same.

9.3   **CNB's Remedies**. Upon the occurrence of an Event of Default, at the sole and exclusive option of CNB, and upon written notice to Borrower, CNB may (a) declare the principal of and accrued interest on the Loans immediately due and payable in full, whereupon the same will immediately become due and payable; (b) terminate this Agreement as to any future liability or obligation of CNB, but without affecting CNB's rights and security interest in the Collateral and without affecting the Obligations owing by Borrower to CNB; and/or (c) exercise its rights and remedies under the Loan Documents and all rights and remedies of a secured party under the Code and other applicable laws with respect to the Collateral.

9.4   **Additional Remedies**. Notwithstanding any other provision of this Agreement, upon the occurrence of any event, action or inaction by Borrower, or if any action or inaction is threatened which CNB reasonably believes will materially affect the value of the Collateral, CNB may take such legal actions as it deems necessary to protect the Collateral, including, but not limited to, seeking injunctive relief and the appointment of a receiver, whether an Event of Default or Potential Event of Default has occurred under this Agreement.

10.   **MISCELLANEOUS**.

10.1   **Reimbursement of Costs and Expenses**. Borrower will reimburse CNB for all costs and expenses relating to this Agreement including, but not limited to, filing, recording or search fees, audit or verification fees, appraisals of the Collateral and other out-of-pocket expenses, and reasonable attorneys' fees and expenses expended or incurred by CNB (or allocable to CNB's in-house counsel) in documenting or administering the Loan Documents or collecting any sum which becomes due CNB under the Loan Documents, irrespective of whether suit is filed, or in the protection, perfection, preservation or enforcement of any and all rights of CNB in connection with the Loan Documents, including, without limitation, the fees and costs incurred in any out-of-court workout or a bankruptcy or reorganization proceeding.

10.2   **Dispute Resolution**.

10.2.1 **Mandatory Arbitration**. At the request of CNB or Borrower, any dispute, claim or controversy of any kind (whether in contract or tort, statutory or common law, legal or equitable) now existing or hereafter arising between CNB and Borrower and in any way arising out of, pertaining to or in connection with: (1) this Agreement, and/or any renewals, extensions, or amendments thereto; (2) any of the Loan Documents; (3) any violation of this Agreement or the Loan Documents; (4) all past, present and future loans; (5) any incidents, omissions, acts, practices or occurrences arising out of or related to this Agreement or the Loan Documents causing injury to either party whereby the other party or its agents, employees or representatives may be liable, in whole or in part, or (6) any aspect of the present or future relationships of the parties, will be resolved through final and binding arbitration conducted at a location determined by the arbitrator in Los Angeles County, California, and administered by the American Arbitration Association ("AAA") in accordance with the California Arbitration Act (Title 9, California Code of Civil Procedure Section 1280 et. seq.) and the then existing Commercial Rules of the AAA. Judgment upon any award rendered by the arbitrator(s) may be entered in any state or federal court having jurisdiction thereof.

10.2.2 **Real Property Collateral**. Notwithstanding the provisions of Section 10.2.1, no controversy or claim will be submitted to arbitration without the consent of all the parties if, at the time of the proposed submission, such controversy or claim arises from or relates to an obligation owed to CNB which is secured in whole or in part by real property collateral. If all parties do not consent to submission of such a controversy or claim to arbitration, the controversy or claim will be determined as provided in Section 10.2.3.

10.2.3 **Judicial Reference**. At the request of any party, a controversy or claim which is not submitted to arbitration as provided and limited in Sections 10.2.1 and 10.2.2 will be determined by a reference in accordance with California Code of Civil Procedure Sections 638 et. seq. If such an election is made, the parties will designate to the court a referee or referees selected under the auspices of the AAA in the same manner as arbitrators are selected in AAA-sponsored proceedings. The presiding referee of the panel, or the referee if there is a single referee, will be an active attorney or retired judge. Judgment upon the award rendered by such referee or referees will be entered in the court in which such proceeding was commenced in accordance with California Code of Civil Procedure Sections 644 and 645.

10.2.4 **Provisional Remedies, Self Help and Foreclosure**. No provision of this Agreement will limit the right of any party to: (1) foreclose against any real property collateral by the exercise of a power of sale under a deed of trust, mortgage or other security agreement or instrument, or applicable law, (2) exercise any rights or remedies as a secured party against any personal property collateral pursuant to the terms of a security agreement or pledge agreement, or applicable law, (3) exercise self help remedies such as setoff, or (4) obtain provisional or ancillary remedies such as injunctive relief or the appointment of a receiver from a court having jurisdiction before, during or after the pendency of any arbitration or referral. The institution and maintenance of an action for judicial relief or pursuit of provisional or ancillary remedies, or exercise of self help remedies will not constitute a waiver of the right of any party, including the plaintiff, to submit any dispute to arbitration or judicial reference.

10.2.5 **Powers and Qualifications of Arbitrators**. The arbitrator(s) will give effect to statutes of limitation, waiver and estoppel and other affirmative defenses in determining any claim. Any controversy concerning whether an issue is arbitratable will be determined by the arbitrator(s). The laws of the State of California will govern. The arbitration award may include equitable and declaratory relief. All arbitrator(s) selected will be required to be a practicing attorney or retired judge licensed to practice law in the State of California and will be required to be experienced and knowledgeable in the substantive laws applicable to the subject matter of the controversy or claim at issue.

10.2.6 **Discovery**. The provisions of California Code of Civil Procedure Section 1283.05 or its successor section(s) are incorporated herein and made a part of this Agreement. Depositions may be taken and discovery may be obtained in any arbitration under this Agreement in accordance with said section(s).

10.2.7 **Miscellaneous**. The arbitrator(s) will determine which is the prevailing party and will include in the award that party's reasonable attorneys' fees and costs (including allocated costs of in-house legal counsel). Each party agrees to keep all controversies and claims and the arbitration proceedings strictly confidential, except for disclosures of information required in the ordinary course of business of the parties or by applicable law or regulation.

10.3 **Cumulative Rights and No Waiver**. All rights and remedies granted to CNB under the Loan Documents are cumulative and no one such right or remedy is exclusive of any other. No failure or delay on the part of CNB in exercising any right or remedy will operate as a waiver thereof, and no single or partial exercise or waiver by CNB of any such right or remedy will preclude any further exercise thereof or the exercise of any other right or remedy.

10.4 **Applicable Law**. This Agreement will be governed by California law.

10.5 **Lien and Right of Set-off**. Borrower grants to CNB a continuing lien for all Obligations of Borrower to CNB upon any and all moneys, securities and other property of Borrower and the proceeds thereof, now or hereafter held or received by or in transit to CNB from or for Borrower, whether for safekeeping, custody, pledge, transmission, collection or otherwise, and also upon any and all deposits (general or special) and credits of Borrower with, and any and all claims of Borrower against, CNB at any time existing. Upon the occurrence of any Event of Default, CNB is hereby authorized at any time and from time to time, without notice to Borrower or any other Person to setoff, appropriate and apply any or all items hereinabove referred to against all Obligations of Borrower whether under this Agreement or otherwise, and whether now existing or hereafter arising.

10.6 **Notices.** Any notice required or permitted under any Loan Document will be given in writing and will be deemed to have been given when personally delivered or when sent by the U.S. mail, postage prepaid, certified, return receipt requested, properly addressed. For the purposes hereof, the addresses of the parties will, until further notice given as herein provided, be as follows:

| | |
|---|---|
| CNB: | City National Bank |
| | Special Assets Department |
| | 606 South Olive Street, Suite 2000, |
| | Los Angeles, CA 90014 |
| | Attention: Greg Meis, SVP |
| with copy to: | City National Bank, Legal Department |
| | 400 North Roxbury Drive |
| | Beverly Hills, California 90210–5021 |
| | Attention: Managing Counsel, Credit Unit |
| Borrower: | XYZ Corp. |
| | 1900 Olympic Blvd., |
| | Los Angeles, CA 90001 |
| | Attention: Joe XYZ |

10.7 **Assignments**. The provisions of this Agreement are hereby made applicable to and will inure to the benefit of CNB's successors and assigns and Borrower's successors and assigns; provided, however, that Borrower may not assign or transfer its rights or obligations under this Agreement without the prior written consent of CNB. CNB may assign this Agreement and its rights and duties hereunder. CNB reserves the right to sell, assign, transfer, negotiate, or grant participations in all or any part of, or any interest in CNB's rights and benefits hereunder. In connection therewith, CNB may disclose all documents and information which CNB now or hereafter may have relating to Borrower or Borrower's business.

10.8 **Indemnification**. Borrower will, at all times, defend and indemnify and hold CNB harmless from and against any and all liabilities, claims, demands, causes of action, losses, damages, expenses (including without limitation reasonable attorneys' fees [Which attorneys may be employees of CNB, or may be outside counsel]), costs, settlements, judgements or recoveries arising out of or resulting from (a) any breach of the representations, warranties, agreements or covenants made by Borrower herein; (b) any suit or proceeding of any kind or nature whatsoever against CNB arising from or connected with the transactions contemplated by this Agreement, the Loan Documents or any of the rights and properties assigned to CNB hereunder; and/or (c) any suit or proceeding that CNB may deem necessary or advisable to institute, in the name of CNB, Borrower or both, against any other Person, for any reason whatsoever to protect the rights of CNB hereunder or under any of the documents, instruments or agreements executed or to be executed pursuant hereto, including attorneys' fees and court costs and all other costs and expenses incurred by CNB (or allocable to CNB's in-house counsel), all of which will be charged to and paid by Borrower and will be secured by the Collateral. Any obligation or liability of Borrower to CNB under this Section will survive the Termination Date and the repayment of all Loans and other extensions of credit and the payment or performance of all other Obligations of Borrower to CNB.

10.9  **Complete Agreement**. This Agreement, together with other Loan Documents, constitutes the entire agreement of the parties and supersedes any prior or contemporaneous oral or written agreements or understandings, if any, which are merged into this Agreement. This Agreement may be amended only in a writing signed by Borrower and CNB.

10.10  **Headings.** Section headings in this Agreement are included for convenience of reference only and do not constitute a part of the Agreement for any purpose.

10.11  **Accounting Terms**. Except as otherwise stated in this Agreement, all accounting terms and financial covenants and information will be construed in conformity with, and all financial data required to be submitted will be prepared in conformity with, GAAP as in effect on the date hereof.

10.12  **Severability**. Any provision of the Loan Documents which is prohibited or unenforceable in any jurisdiction, will be, only as to such jurisdiction, ineffective to the extent of such prohibition or unenforceability, but all the remaining provisions of the Loan Documents will remain valid.

10.13  **Counterparts**. This Agreement may be signed in any number of counterparts which, when taken together, will constitute but one agreement.

10.14  **Joint and Several**. Should more than one Person sign this Agreement, the obligations of each signer will be joint and several.

IN WITNESS WHEREOF, CNB and Borrower have caused this Agreement to be executed as of the date first specified at the beginning of this Agreement.

**Borrower**           XYZ Corp.
                       A California corporation
                       By: _____
                               Joe XYZ, President

**CNB**                **City National Bank**, a
                       national banking association
                       By: _____
                               Sarah Davies, Chief Communicator

# LOCKBOX AGREEMENT

**◤**ᴿ City National Bank

This LOCKBOX AGREEMENT (the "Agreement") is between CITY NATIONAL BANK, a national banking association ("BANK"), and ("SUBSCRIBER"), with reference to the following lockbox services (the "Service") to be provided by BANK to SUBSCRIBER:

1. **SERVICE COMMENCEMENT.**

   (a) The Service shall commence on the Commencement Date shown on Schedule A. The Commencement Date may be extended by BANK by reason of delay caused by SUBSCRIBER or a cause beyond BANK'S reasonable control. BANK shall incur no liability for a delay in the Projected Commencement Date

   (b) On or before the date requested by BANK, SUBSCRIBER shall furnish BANK with copies of SUBSCRIBER'S invoice and envelope forms and such other forms and information as BANK may require to perform the Service.

   (c) On or before the date requested by BANK, SUBSCRIBER will open in the name of SUBSCRIBER a Post Office Box with the United States Postal Service or a private box for the receipt of mail with a private box provider (either such box is referred to herein as "Box") at the location set forth in Schedule A. The location shall be acceptable to BANK. SUBSCRIBER will grant BANK exclusive and unrestricted access to the Box on such form as shall be acceptable to the Box provider. At its option SUBSCRIBER may authorize BANK to open a Box in the name of SUBSCRIBER to which BANK shall have exclusive and unrestricted access. Such authorization shall be in such form as shall be acceptable to the Box provider. SUBSCRIBER shall be responsible to pay the Box rental fee. Upon termination of the Service, at the direction of SUBSCRIBER BANK will either close the Box or transfer it to SUBSCRIBER. and BANK shall have no further responsibility hereunder.

   (d) On or before the Commencement Date, SUBSCRIBER will open a demand deposit account with BANK as identified in Schedule A (the "Collection Account") and will maintain the Collection Account in good standing throughout the period of the Service.

   (e) SUBSCRIBER will direct its customers or debtors to mail invoices and remittances to be processed by the Service to the Box.

2. **REMITTANCE PROCESSING.**

(a) BANK will collect all mail received at the Box which is properly addressed to the Box on business days, which are days other than Saturdays, Sundays and holidays when either BANK or the Box provider is closed, according to a schedule established by BANK, which may be changed from time to time. BANK will return to the Box provider mail incorrectly delivered to the Box.

(b) BANK will open all correctly addressed mail and examine it for invoices, cash, checks and other remittances, correspondence and other materials. All cash will be removed, held in double custody and a memorandum of the amount thereof made on the invoice and Collection Report (if any—see Schedule A). The contents of mail not containing an invoice, remittance or cash will be delivered to SUBSCRIBER without further processing.

(c) Remittances, including checks, drafts, money orders and other instruments (collectively ''checks''), will be processed according to the following, unless otherwise specified in Schedule A. Checks will be reviewed for date, payee, signature, amount (written and numerical) and endorsements, if any. Unless otherwise specified in Schedule A, checks will not be reconciled to accompanying invoices. The following items will be delivered to SUBSCRIBER without further, processing:

 (i) Any check not drawn to the order of SUBSCRIBER, any others authorized payee designated on Schedule A or any recognizable variation thereof in BANK'S sole discretion.

 (ii) Any check bearing a restrictive notation or endorsement, or accompanied by correspondence stating ''paid in full,'' reserving rights or remedies, or containing any other restrictive language.

 (iii) Any stale-dated check or post-dated check unless in BANK's sole discretion the post-dated check would not reach the drawee bank through normal clearing channels until after the date thereof.

 (iv) Any check the endorsement and deposit of which by BANK might, in BANK'S sole judgment, subject BANK to unacceptable claim or liability.

Unless otherwise specified in Schedule A, the following extraordinary items will be processed as described below:

 (v) Unsigned checks may, in BANK's sole discretion, be delivered to SUBSCRIBER without further processing or deposited with a request to the drawee bank to obtain the payor's signature or other authority to pay. If returned, the Collection Account will be charged and the check will be delivered to SUBSCRIBER.

 (vi) Undated checks will be deposited.

(vii) Checks without accompanying invoices will be deposited.

(viii) Checks with a discrepancy between the written and numerical amounts will be deposited at the written amount.

(ix) Checks returned for insufficient funds may, in BANK's sole discretion, be presented to the drawee bank for payment a second time. If unpaid, the Collection Account will be charged and the check will be delivered to SUBSCRIBER.

(x) Checks returned for special endorsement will be endorsed "Pay to the Order of City National Bank" and BANK is hereby authorized to insert such endorsement. Checks returned for any other reason will be charged to the Collection Account and delivered to SUBSCRIBER.

(xi) Checks which are payable in foreign currency or are drawn on a bank outside the United States will not be credited to the Collection Account unless and until payment is received by BANK.

All checks in proper form will be endorsed "Credit the Account of the Within Named Payee, Absence of Endorsement Guaranteed by City National Bank" and, together with all cash, will be deposited to the Collection Account of the day processed and, unless otherwise specified in Schedule A, written advice of the credit will be delivered to SUBSCRIBER daily. Except as otherwise specified in this Agreement and the Schedules hereto, the processing of checks and the availability of funds will be subject to the terms and conditions of the deposit agreement applicable to the Collection Account and BANK'S normal procedures and regulations for deposits.

(d) Unless otherwise specified in Schedule A, SUBSCRIBER will furnish, at its expense, all invoices, envelopes and other forms requiring any special logo or imprint, and BANK will furnish, at its expense, all internal BANK forms, Collection Reports, advices of credit and similar forms.

3. **FEES AND CHARGES.**

SUBSCRIBER shall compensate BANK for the Service hereunder as provided in Schedule B and reimburse BANK for its out-of-pocket expenses.

4. **MISCELLANEOUS.**

(a) SUBSCRIBER agrees that this Agreement, including without limitation the fees in Schedule B, may be amended by BANK effective upon the earlier of the written acknowledgment thereof by SUBSCRIBER or 30 calendar days after written notice to SUBSCRIBER by BANK of the amendment.

(b) When performing the Service BANK shall exercise at least the same degree of care commonly exercised by banks and other service providers of similar size when providing similar services to

customers in California. BANK MAKES NO WARRANTY, EX-
PRESS OR IMPLIED, CONCERNING THE SERVICE INCLUD-
ING BUT NOT LIMITED TO THE IMPLIED WARRANTIES OF
MERCHANTABILITY AND FITNESS FOR A PARTICULAR
PURPOSE. BANK will not be liable for any loss, expense, error or
delay, including but not limited to any delay or inability to provide
access to the Service, caused by accidents, strikes, flood, fire,
electrical or mechanical failures, software defects, computer failure, acts or omissions by you, the Box provider or any third party
(including but not limited to acts or omissions of any telephone or
telecommunications carrier, legal constraints, acts of God or any
other causes or conditions which are beyond BANK's reasonable
control). BANK will not be liable to SUBSCRIBER for any damage
arising out of or related to BANK's performance of the Service
other than damage actually incurred resulting directly form
BANK's failure to exercise reasonable care. As a condition precedent to BANK's liability hereunder, SUBSCRIBER must notify
BANK in writing of any alleged negligence or breach by BANK as
promptly as reasonably possible, but in no event later than five (5)
business days following the day on which such alleged negligence
or breach was, or could reasonably have been, discovered by
SUBSCRIBER. BANK's entire liability and SUBSCRIBER's sole
remedy, including but not limited to liability for negligence, will
not exceed the fees actually paid to BANK by SUBSCRIBER for
the Service during the six (6) month period preceding the date of
the alleged negligence or breach. IN NO EVENT WILL BANK BE
LIABLE FOR SPECIAL, GENERAL, CONSEQUENTIAL, INCI-
DENTAL, EXEMPLARY OR SIMILAR DAMAGES, INCLUDING
BUT NOT LIMITED TO LOST PROFITS, EVEN IF BANK HAS
BEEN ADVISED OF THE POSSIBILITY THEREOF. This provi-
sion also limits the liability of BANK's agents, employees, affiliates
and vendors and will survive termination of the Service.

(b) SUBSCRIBER will at all times, defend, indemnify and hold
BANK (which includes BANK's shareholders, officers, directors,
other employees, agents, affiliates and vendors) harmless from and
against any and all liabilities, claims, demands, causes of action,
losses, damages, costs, expenses and attorneys' fees (including
those fees allocable to in-house counsel), settlements, judgments or
recoveries of third parties, other than SUBSCRIBER or BANK,
arising out of or relating, directly or indirectly, to SUBSCRIBER's
use of the Service or BANK's performance of BANK's obligations
hereunder provided that BANK exercised reasonable care, as stated herein, and acted in good faith. This provision will survive the
termination of the Service.

(c) Nothing in this Agreement shall be deemed to constitute either
party the agent or partner of the other, and the relationship
between the parties shall be that of independent contractors.

(d) All specifications, records, software, forms, systems and programs utilized or developed by BANK in connection with the Service are and will remain the sole property of BANK, unless supplied to BANK by SUBSCRIBER.

(e) Subject to any minimum term set forth in Schedule B, this Agreement will remain in effect until terminated by either party upon 30 calendar days' written notice to the other party, provided that SUBSCRIBER may terminate this Agreement on shorter notice (but not less than 10 days) at any time within 30 days after notice from BANK of any amendment to this Agreement or any Schedules hereto. If BANK terminates this Agreement, it will allow SUBSCRIBER a reasonable period of time beyond said 30 days, if necessary to make other arrangements, not to exceed 60 calendar days after such written notice of termination. SUBSCRIBER will reimburse BANK for any out-of-pocket costs incurred by reason of any termination hereunder.

(f) This Agreement supersedes any and all agreements entered into between BANK and SUBSCRIBER prior to the date of this Agreement relating to the Service. This Agreement is intended as a final expression of the parties' agreement with respect to the Service and such other terms are included herein, and as a complete and exclusive statement of such terms. This Agreement may not be amended or waived, in whole or in part, except as provided in Section 4(a) above or in a writing executed by both of the parties hereto.

(g) This Agreement is governed by the laws of the State of California.

(h) Any dispute arising out of or relating to this Agreement and the Service which the parties are unable to resolve informally shall be submitted for resolution in accordance with the terms of the City National Bank Standard Dispute Resolution Clause for Cash Management, a copy of which is attached hereto and which is incorporated herein by this reference. BY THIS AGREEMENT EACH PARTY WAIVES THE CONSTITUTIONAL RIGHT TO A JURY TRIAL TO RESOLVE CERTAIN DISPUTES ARISING UNDER THIS AGREEMENT.

(i) SUBSCRIBER represents and warrants to BANK that the signers of this Agreement have the corporate power and authority to execute, deliver and perform this Agreement and that when executed this Agreement is binding on SUBSCRIBER.

(j) Any notice required or permitted to be given under this Agreement will be in writing and will be deemed effective if to BANK, upon receipt, and if to SUBSCRIBER when placed in the United States mail postage prepaid to the address set forth in records of BANK, or such other address subsequently provided to BANK by written notice.

(k) This Agreement will inure to the benefit of and be binding upon both parties, their successors and assigns. No assignment may be made by SUBSCRIBER without the prior written consent of BANK. Nothing in this Agreement restricts the right of BANK to effect an assignment by merger, reorganization, sale of corporate assets or other corporate change.

(*l*) If any provision of this Agreement, or part of a provision, is held to be invalid, illegal, void or unenforceable, the remainder of the Agreement, or other parts or application of such provision, will not affected thereby.

**CITY NATIONAL BANK, a national banking association**

Date:_____     By:_____

Its: _____

_____

("SUBSCRIBER")

_____

_____

_____

(Address)

Date: _____     BY: _____

Its: _____

# APPENDIX III

# PROMISSORY NOTES

 CITY NATIONAL BANK

**REVOLVING NOTE**
(INTEREST TIED TO PRIME)

On *, *, the undersigned, * ("Borrower"), promises to pay to the order of **City National Bank**, a national banking association ("CNB"), at its office in this city, in lawful money of the United States of America and in immediately available funds, the principal sum of * **Dollars ($*)**, or so much thereof as may be advanced and be outstanding, with interest thereon to be computed on each advance from the date of its disbursement at a rate computed on the basis of a 360–day year, actual days elapsed, equal to the Prime Rate of CNB, as it exists from time to time, plus * percent (*%) per year. "Prime Rate" shall mean the rate most recently announced by CNB at its principal office in Beverly Hills, California, as its "Prime Rate." Any change in the Prime Rate shall become effective on the same business day on which the Prime Rate shall change, without prior notice to Borrower.

All or any portion of the principal of this Note may be borrowed, repaid and reborrowed from time to time prior to maturity, provided at the time of any borrowing no Event of Default (as herein defined) exists, and provided further that the total borrowings outstanding at any one time shall not exceed the principal amount stated above. Each borrowing and repayment hereunder shall be noted in the books and records of CNB. The excess of borrowings over repayments shall evidence the principal balance due hereon from time to time and at any time. Borrowings hereunder shall be conclusively presumed to have been made to or for the benefit of Borrower when made as noted in such books and records.

Interest accrued on this Note shall be payable on the * day of each *, commencing *, *.

The occurrence of any of the following with respect to any Borrower or any guarantor of this Note or any general partner of such Borrower or guarantor, shall constitute an "Event of Default" hereunder:

1. The failure to make any payment of principal or interest when due under this Note;

2. The filing of a petition by or against any of such parties under any provisions of the Bankruptcy Code;

3. The appointment of a receiver or an assignee for the benefit of creditors;

4. The commencement of dissolution or liquidation proceedings or the disqualification of any such parties which is a corporation, partnership, joint venture or any other type of entity;

5. The death or incapacity of any of such parties who is an individual;

6. The revocation of any guaranty of this Note, or any guaranty becomes unenforceable as to any future advances under this Note;

7. Any financial statement provided by any of such parties to CNB is false or misleading;

8. Any material default in the payment or performance of any obligation, or any default under any provisions of any contract or instrument pursuant to which any of such parties has incurred any obligation for borrowed money, any purchase obligation or any other liability of any kind to any person or entity, including CNB;

9. Any sale or transfer of all or a substantial or material part of the assets of any of such parties other than in the ordinary course of business; or

10. Any violation, breach or default under any letter agreement, guaranty, security agreement, deed of trust or any other contract or instrument executed in connection with this Note or securing this Note.

Upon the occurrence of any Event of Default, CNB, at its option, may declare all sums of principal and interest outstanding hereunder to be immediately due and payable without presentment, demand, protest or notice of dishonor all of which are expressly waived by each Borrower, and CNB shall have no obligation to make any further advances hereunder. Each Borrower agrees to pay all costs and expenses, including reasonable attorneys' fees, expended or incurred by CNB (or allocable to CNB's in-house counsel) in connection with the enforcement of this Note or the collection of any sums due hereunder and irrespective of whether suit is filed. Any principal or interest not paid when due hereunder shall thereafter bear additional interest from its due date at a rate of five percent (5.0%) per year higher than the interest rate as determined and computed above, and continuing thereafter until paid.

Should more than one person or entity execute this Note as a Borrower, the obligations of each Borrower shall be joint and several.

This Note and all matters relating thereto, shall be governed by the laws of the State of California.

### REVOLVING NOTE (With Accounts Receivable Borrowing Base)

On *, *, a * ("Borrower"), promises to pay to the order of City National Bank, a national banking association ("CNB"), at its office in this city, in United States Dollars and in immediately available funds, the principal sum of * Dollars ($*) ("Revolving Credit Commitment"), or so much thereof as may be advanced and be outstanding, with interest thereon to be computed on each advance from the date of its disbursement at a rate computed on a basis of a 360–day year, actual days elapsed, equal to the "Prime Rate" of CNB, as it exists from time to time, plus * percent (*%) per year. "Prime Rate" shall mean the rate most recently announced by CNB at its principal office in Beverly Hills, California, as its "Prime Rate." Any change in the Prime Rate shall become effective on the same business day on which the Prime Rate shall change, without prior notice to Borrower.

As provided herein, the principal of this Note may be borrowed, repaid and reborrowed from time to time prior to maturity, provided at the time of any borrowing no Event of Default (as hereinafter defined) exists, and provided further that the total borrowings outstanding at any one time shall not exceed the lesser of (i) the Revolving Credit Commitment or (ii) * percent (*%) of the total Eligible Accounts Receivable owing to Borrower from time to time. Each borrowing and repayment hereunder shall be noted in the books and records of CNB. The excess of borrowings over repayments shall evidence the principal balance due hereon from time to time and at any time. Borrowings hereunder shall be presumed to have been made to or for the benefit of Borrower when made as noted in such books and records.

Interest accruing on this Note shall be payable on the * day of each month, commencing *, *.

Eligible Accounts Receivable shall mean those accounts receivable owed to Borrower:

A.  Upon which Borrower's right to receive payment is absolute and not contingent upon the fulfillment of any condition whatsoever;

B.  Against which is asserted no defense, counterclaim, discount or setoff, whether well-founded or otherwise;

C.  That is a true and correct statement of a bona fide indebtedness incurred in the amount of the account receivable for goods sold or leased and delivered to, or for services rendered to and accepted by, the account debtor;

D.  That is owned by Borrower free and clear of all liens, encumbrances, charges, interests and rights of others, except security interests granted to CNB;

E.  That does not arise from a sale or lease to or for services rendered to any employee, stockholder, director, *[S]ubsidiary or affiliate of Borrower or any entity in which any employee, stockholder, director, *[S]ubsidiary or affiliate of Borrower has any interest;

F.  That is not the obligation of an account debtor that is the federal government unless perfected under the Assignment of Claims Act;

G.  That is not the obligation of an account debtor located in a foreign country;

H.  That is due and payable not more than thirty (30) days from the date of the billing therefor unless otherwise agreed to in writing by CNB;

I.   As to which not more than ninety (90) days have elapsed since the original invoice date;

J.   As to which the account debtor has not:

(i) died, suspended business, made a general assignment for the benefit of creditors, become the subject of a petition under the *Bankruptcy Code* or consented to or applied for the appointment of a receiver, trustee, custodian or liquidator for itself or any of its property;

(ii) become more than sixty (60) days past due, under the original terms of sale, with respect to 20% or more of the amounts owed by such account debtor to Borrower;

(iii) had its check in payment of an account receivable returned unpaid; or

(iv) become or appear to have become unable, in the opinion of CNB, to pay the account receivable in accordance with its terms; and

K.   That does not, when added to all other accounts receivable that are obligations of the account debtor to Borrower, at any time result in a total sum that exceeds twenty percent (20%) of the total balance then due on all accounts receivable.

The occurrence of any of the following with respect to any Borrower or guarantor of this Note or any general partner of such Borrower or guarantor, shall constitute an "Event of Default" hereunder:

1.   Failure to make any payment of principal or interest when due under this Note;

2.   Filing of a petition by or against any of such parties under any provision of the *Bankruptcy Code*;

3.   Appointment of a receiver or an assignee for the benefit of creditors;

4.   Commencement of dissolution or liquidation proceedings or the disqualification (under any applicable law or regulation) of any of such parties which is a corporation, partnership, joint venture or any other type of entity;

5.   Death or incapacity of any of such parties which is an individual;

6.   Revocation of any guaranty of this Note, or any guaranty of this Note becomes unenforceable as to any future advances under this Note;

7.   Any financial statement provided by any of such parties to CNB is false or materially misleading;

8.   Any material default in the payment or performance of any obligation, or any default under any provision of any contract or instrument pursuant to which any of such parties has incurred any

obligation for borrowed money, any purchase obligation or any other liability of any kind to any person or entity, including CNB;

9. Any sale or transfer of all or a substantial part of the assets of any of such parties other than in the ordinary course of business;

10. Any violation, breach or default under this Note, any letter agreement, guaranty, security agreement, deed of trust, subordination agreement or any other contract or instrument executed in connection with this Note or securing this Note;

11. Failure of Borrower, after twenty (20) days' written notice from CNB to Borrower, to reduce the principal balance hereunder to * percent (*%) of the total Eligible Accounts Receivable owing to Borrower;

12. Any obligee of [S]ubordinated [D]ebt shall fail to comply with the subordination provisions of the documents or instruments, including, without limitation, any subordination agreement, evidencing or relating to such [S]ubordinated [D]ebt;

13. Failure of Borrower to furnish CNB, within the times specified, the following statements:

13.1. Within [forty-five (45)/sixty (60)] days after the end of each quarterly accounting period of each fiscal year, a financial statement consisting of not less than a balance sheet, [and income statement, reconciliation of net worth and statement of cash flows,] with notes thereto, prepared in accordance with generally accepted accounting principles consistently applied, which financial statement may be internally prepared;

13.2. Within [ninety (90)/one hundred twenty (120)] days after the close of each fiscal year, a copy of the annual [audit report/review report/compilation report] for such year for Borrower and the Subsidiaries including therein a balance sheet, income statement, reconciliation of net worth and statement of cash flows, with notes thereto, the balance sheet, income statement and statement of cash flows to be [audited/reviewed/ compiled] by a certified public accountant acceptable to CNB, and [certified by such accountants to have been] prepared in accordance with generally accepted accounting principles consistently applied and accompanied by Borrower's certification as to whether any event has occurred which constitutes an Event of Default, and if so, stating the facts with respect thereto;

13.3. [Monthly/quarterly] reports of agings of Borrower's accounts payable and accounts receivable, together with a current list of names and addresses of all account debtors, as soon as available, but in no event later than thirty (30) days after the end of each *[month/fiscal quarter]*;

13.4. The Federal Income Tax Return for Borrower and each guarantor of this Note, *[and each general partner of Borrower or guarantor,]* within ten (10) days after its filing of each Return, respectively; and

13.5. Such additional information, reports and/or statements as CNB may, from time to time, reasonably request.

14. Failure of Borrower to furnish current financial statements of each guarantor of this Note *[and each general partner of Borrower or such guarantor]* on CNB's form or in such other form acceptable to CNB, certified by such guarantor *[or general partner]* to be true and correct, delivered within ninety (90) days after Borrower's fiscal year end of each year;

15. Failure of Borrower to maintain the following:

15.1. Tangible Net Worth *[plus Subordinated Debt]* of not less than $* at all times;

15.2. A ratio of Total Senior Liabilities to Tangible Net Worth *[plus Subordinated Debt]* of not more than * to 1 at all times;

15.3. A ratio of Current Assets to Current Liabilities of not less than * to 1 at all times;

15.4. A ratio of Quick Assets to Current Liabilities of not less than * to 1 at all times; and

15.5. Working Capital of not less than $* at all times.

For purposes of this Note, the following terms have the following meanings:

"**Current Assets**" shall be determined on a consolidated basis for Borrower and the Subsidiaries in accordance with generally accepted accounting principles, consistently applied, excluding, however, from the determination of Current Assets, loans to shareholders, management or employees, amounts due from Subsidiaries or affiliates, deferred costs, and other intangible assets.

"**Current Liabilities**" shall be determined on a consolidated basis for Borrower and the Subsidiaries in accordance with generally accepted accounting principles, consistently applied, and shall include without limitation (a) all payments on Subordinated Debt required to be made within one (1) year after the date on which the determination is made; and (b) all indebtedness payable to stockholders, affiliates, Subsidiaries or officers regardless of maturity, unless such indebtedness shall have been subordinated to CNB, on terms satisfactory to CNB.

"**Quick Assets**" shall mean the sum of cash, plus cash equivalents, plus accounts receivable, plus securities classified as short-term marketable securities according to generally accepted accounting principles, consistently applied, as such items appear on Borrower's consolidated balance sheet, determined in accordance with generally accepted accounting principles consistently applied.

"**Subordinated Debt**" shall mean indebtedness of Borrower or any Subsidiary the repayment of principal and interest of which is subordinated to CNB, on terms satisfactory to CNB.

"**Subsidiary**" shall mean any corporation, the majority of whose voting shares are at any time owned, directly or indirectly by Borrower and/or by one or more Subsidiaries.

"**Tangible Net Worth**" shall mean the total of all assets appearing on a balance sheet prepared in accordance with generally accepted accounting principles consistently applied for Borrower and the Subsidiaries on a consolidated basis, minus (a) all intangible assets, including, without limitation, unamortized debt discount, affiliate, employee and officer receivables or advances, goodwill, research and development costs, patents, trademarks, the excess of purchase price over underlying values of acquired companies, any covenants not to compete, deferred charges, copyrights, franchises and appraisal surplus; minus (b) all obligations which are required by generally accepted accounting principles consistently applied to be reflected as a liability on the consolidated balance sheet of Borrower and the Subsidiaries; minus, (c) the amount, if any, at which shares of stock of a non-wholly owned Subsidiary appear on the asset side of Borrower's consolidated balance sheet, as determined in accordance with generally accepted accounting principles consistently applied; minus (d) minority interests; and minus (e) deferred income and reserves not otherwise reflected as a liability on the consolidated balance sheet of Borrower and the Subsidiaries.

"**Total Senior Liabilities**" shall mean, as of any date of determination, the amount of all obligations that should be reflected as a liability on a consolidated balance sheet of Borrower and the Subsidiaries prepared in accordance with generally accepted accounting principles, consistently applied, less Subordinated Debt.

"**Working Capital**" shall mean Current Assets minus Current Liabilities.

Upon the occurrence of any Event of Default, CNB, at its option, may declare all sums of principal and interest outstanding hereunder to be immediately due and payable without presentment, demand, protest or notice of dishonor all of which are expressly waived by Borrower, and CNB shall have no obligation to make any further advances hereunder. Borrower agrees to pay all costs and expenses, including reasonable attorneys' fees (which counsel may be CNB employees), expended or incurred by CNB (or allocable to CNB's in-house counsel) in connection with the enforcement of this Note or the collection of any sums due hereunder and irrespective of whether suit is filed. Any principal or interest not paid when due hereunder shall thereafter bear additional interest from its due date at a rate of five percent (5.0%) per year higher than the interest rate as determined and computed above, and continuing thereafter until paid.

Should more than one person or entity execute this Note as Borrower, the liability and obligations of each Borrower shall be joint and several.

This Note and all matters relating thereto, shall be governed by the laws of the State of California.

# INDEX

References are to pages.

†